# Street by Street

# GREATER MANCHESTER

## Enlarged areas BOLTON, BURY, OLDHAM, ROCHDALE, STOCKPORT, WIGAN

Plus Altrincham, Ashton-under-Lyne, Glossop, Hazel Grove, Leigh, Middleton, Sale, Salford, Stalybridge, Stretford, Wilmslow

**3rd edition October 2007**
© Automobile Association Developments Limited 2007

Original edition printed May 2001

Enabled by [Ordnance Survey] This product includes map data licensed from Ordnance Survey® with the permission of the Controller of Her Majesty's Stationery Office. © Crown copyright 2007. All rights reserved. Licence number: 100021153.

The copyright in all PAF is owned by Royal Mail Group plc.

Published by AA Publishing (a trading name of Automobile Association Developments Limited, whose registered office is Fanum House, Basing View, Basingstoke, Hampshire RG21 4EA. Registered number 1878835).

Produced by the Mapping Services Department of The Automobile Association. (A03490)

A CIP Catalogue record for this book is available from the British Library.

Printed by Oriental Press in Dubai

Ref: MX044y

| Key to map pages | ii-iii |
|---|---|
| Key to map symbols | iv–1 |
| Enlarged map pages | 2-15 |
| Main map pages | 16-131 |
| Index – towns & villages | 132-133 |
| Index – streets | 133-196 |
| Index – featured places | 196-204 |
| Acknowledgements | 204 |

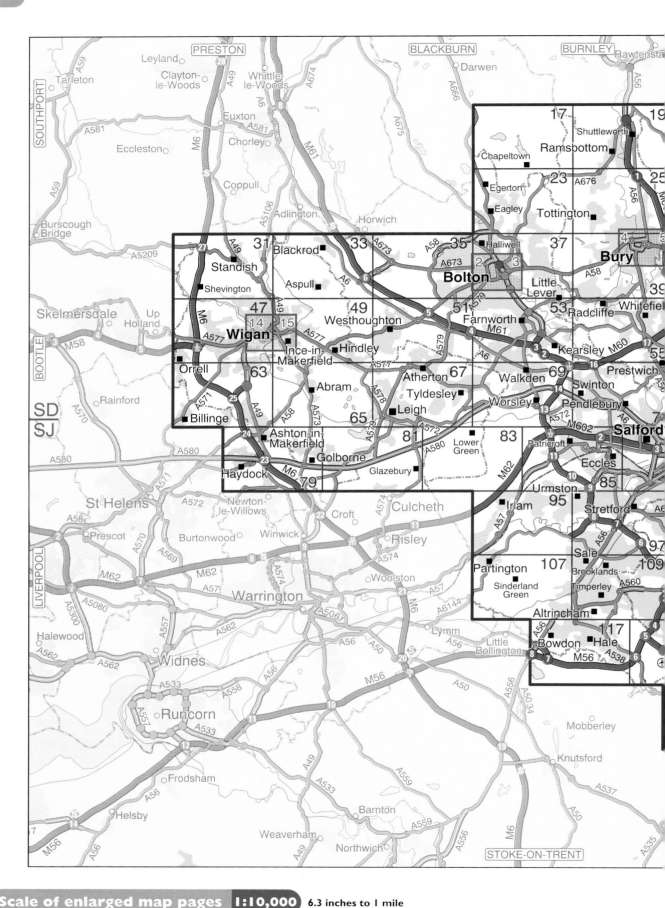

**Scale of enlarged map pages** 1:10,000 6.3 inches to 1 mile

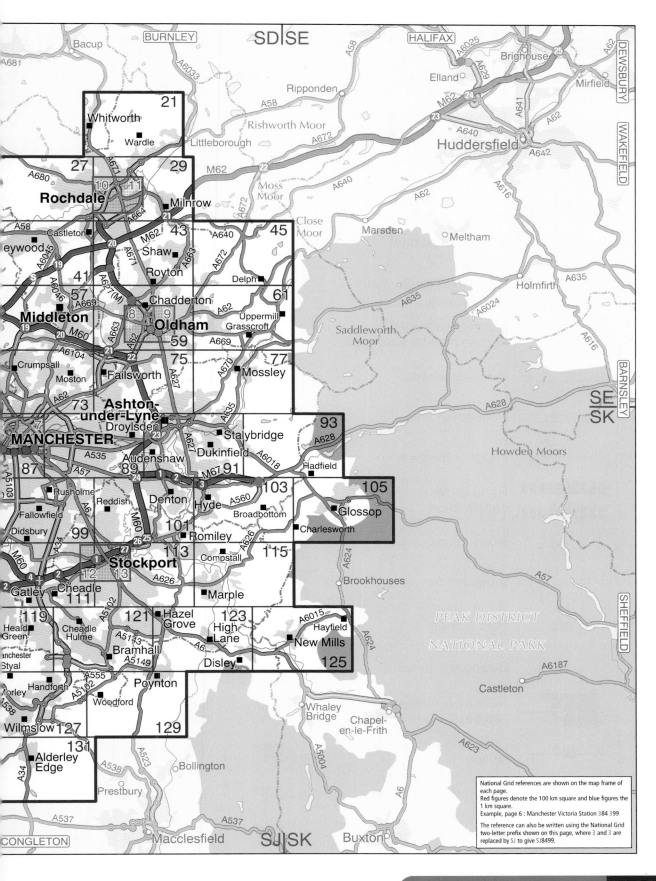

National Grid references are shown on the map frame of each page.
Red figures denote the 100 km square and blue figures the 1 km square.
Example, page 6 : Manchester Victoria Station 384 399

The reference can also be written using the National Grid two-letter prefix shown on this page, where 3 and 3 are replaced by SJ to give SJ8499.

**3.6 inches to 1 mile**  **Scale of main map pages 1:17,500**

0 ─── 1/2 ─── miles ─── 1

0 ─── 1/2 ─── 1 ─── kilometres ─── 1 1/2 ─── 2

| | |
|---|---|
| Junction 9 | Motorway & junction |
| Services | Motorway service area |
| | Primary road single/dual carriageway |
| Services | Primary road service area |
| | A road single/dual carriageway |
| | B road single/dual carriageway |
| | Other road single/dual carriageway |
| | Minor/private road, access may be restricted |
| ← ← | One-way street |
| | Pedestrian area |
| | Track or footpath |
| | Road under construction |
| | Road tunnel |
| P | Parking |
| P+ | Park & Ride |
| | Bus/coach station |
| | Railway & main railway station |
| | Railway & minor railway station |
| ⊖ | Underground station |
| ⊖ | Light railway & station |
| +++++++++ | Preserved private railway |

| | |
|---|---|
| LC | Level crossing |
| • • • • | Tramway |
| - - - - - - | Ferry route |
| .............. | Airport runway |
| - · - · - · - | County, administrative boundary |
| ⋎⋎⋎⋎⋎⋎⋎ | Mounds |
| 93 | Page continuation 1:17,500 |
| 7 | Page continuation to enlarged scale 1:10,000 |
| | River/canal, lake |
| | Aqueduct, lock, weir |
| 465 ▲ Winter Hill | Peak (with height in metres) |
| | Beach |
| | Woodland |
| | Park |
| | Cemetery |
| | Built-up area |
| | Industrial/business building |
| | Leisure building |
| | Retail building |
| | Other building |
| IKEA | IKEA store |

| | | | |
|---|---|---|---|
| ⊓⊔⊓⊔⊓⊔ | City wall | ✗ | Castle |
| A&E | Hospital with 24-hour A&E department | ⌂ | Historic house or building |
| PO | Post Office | Wakehurst Place (NT) | National Trust property |
| 📖 | Public library | M | Museum or art gallery |
| i | Tourist Information Centre | 🦅 | Roman antiquity |
| i | Seasonal Tourist Information Centre | ⊥ | Ancient site, battlefield or monument |
| ⬛ | Petrol station, 24 hour Major suppliers only | 🏭 | Industrial interest |
| † | Church/chapel | ❋ | Garden |
| 🚻 | Public toilets | ◉ | Garden Centre Garden Centre Association Member |
| ♿ | Toilet with disabled facilities | 🌷 | Garden Centre Wyevale Garden Centre |
| PH | Public house AA recommended | 🌳 | Arboretum |
| ⊕ | Restaurant AA inspected | 🐂 | Farm or animal centre |
| Madeira Hotel ▄ | Hotel AA inspected | 🦌 | Zoological or wildlife collection |
| 🎭 | Theatre or performing arts centre | 🦜 | Bird collection |
| 📽 | Cinema | ⊃ | Nature reserve |
| ⚑ | Golf course | 🐟 | Aquarium |
| ▲ | Camping AA inspected | V | Visitor or heritage centre |
| 🚐 | Caravan site AA inspected | ⚘ | Country park |
| ▲🚐 | Camping & caravan site AA inspected | ⌒ | Cave |
| 🎡 | Theme park | ✗ | Windmill |
| ⛪ | Abbey, cathedral or priory | 🛢 | Distillery, brewery or vineyard |

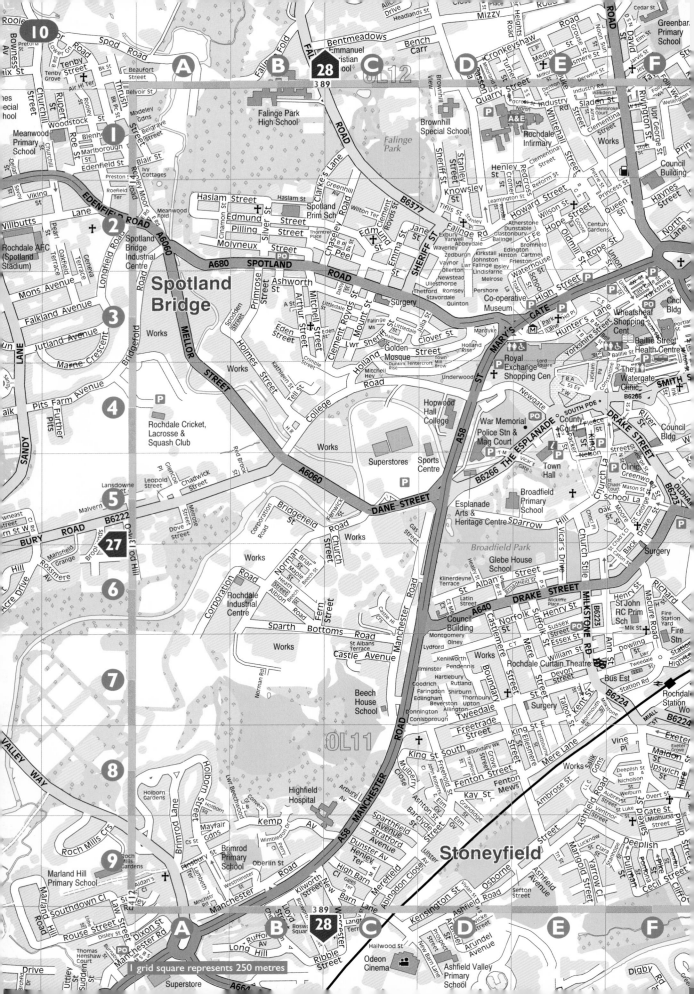

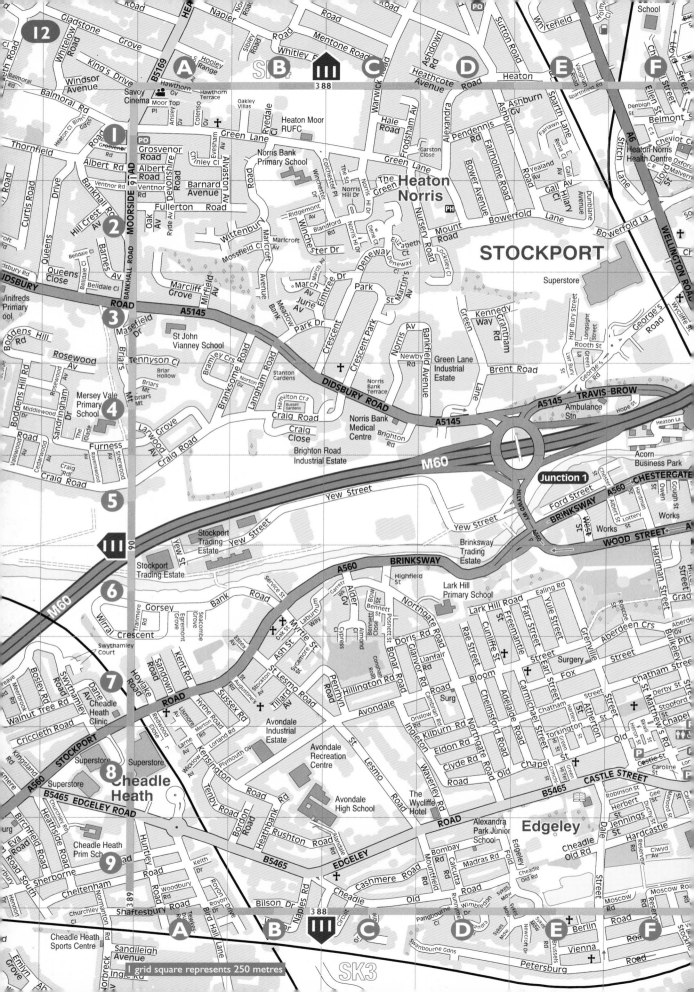

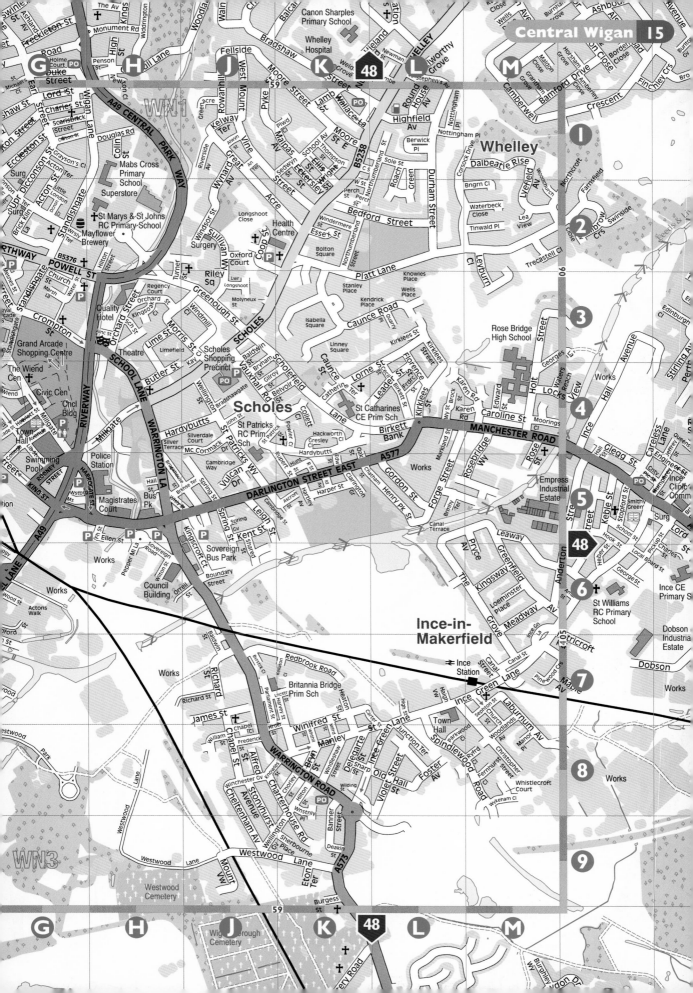

Whelley

Scholes

Ince-in-Makerfield

WN1

WN3

Broadheadow Farm

Knowsley Lane

G H J K L M

74 75 76

19

Wet Moss

1

Lancashire County
Blackburn

2

Orrell Cote Farm

3

Edgworth Moor

Moorside Road

Crowthorn Road

Crowthorn Road Works

18

Broadhead Road

Hill Top

Broadhead Rd

School Lane

4

Blackburn
Bury

18

5

Broadhead Road

Plantation Road

17

Ainsdale Av

Foxdale Close

Greenway

Green Lea

**Edgworth**

Hawkshaw Lane

6

Holcombe Hey
Fold Farm

Blackburn Road

Horrocks Road

Moorfield

Crow Tree Road

Middle Barn

Weatherfield

PO

Edgworth
Vale

Red Earth
Farm

Bury Road

Meadow Way

Bolton Road

Edgworth
CC

Harpour La

7

Turton & Edgworth
CE/Methodist
Primary School

Witton Weavers
Way

Beech St

Surgery

**Turton
Bottoms**

Wellington
Mews

Bury Road

Higher House
Farm

8

PO

Bolton Rd

Wellington Road

Vale Street

Knotts Brow

The Gardens

Hawkshaw Lane

Birches

Spenleach Lane

**Chapeltown**

74

75

23

76

G H J K L M

Bottom o' th
Knotts Brow

Walves

**Hawkshaw**

Blackburn
Bolton

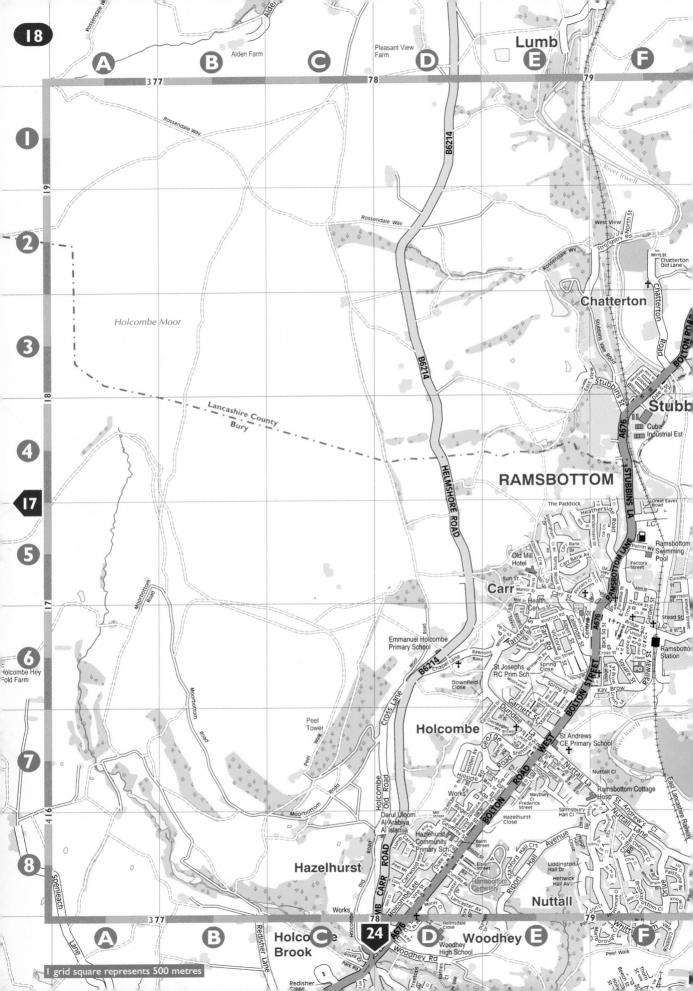

18

A    B    C    D    E    Lumb    F

3 77    78    79

1

19

Rossendale Way

2

Holcombe Moor

Rossendale Way

Pleasant View Farm

Alden Farm

River Irwell

West View

Strongstry Road

Mint St
Chatterton Old Lane

Chatterton

Lancashire County
Bury

3

18

B6214

Stubb

Cuba
Industrial Est

4

RAMSBOTTOM

17

The Paddock

Heatherside

5

17

Moorbottom Road

Old Mill Hotel

Carr

HELMSHORE ROAD

Ramsbottom Swimming Pool

Factory Street

Ramsbottom Station

6

Holcombe Hey Fold Farm

Emmanuel Holcombe Primary School

B6214    Chapel Lane

St Josephs RC Prim Sch

Downfield Close

PO

Ramsbotto Station

7

Peel Tower

Peel Walk

Cross Lane

Holcombe

St Andrews CE Primary School

BOLTON ROAD WEST    BOLTON STREET

Nuttall La

Ramsbottom Cottage Hosp

East Lancashire Railway

8

416

Spenleach

Moorbottom Road

Holcombe Old Road

Darul Uloom Al-Arabiya Al Islamia

Hazelhurst Community Primary Sch

Works

Hazelhurst

MB CARR ROAD

Holcombe Lee

Works

Ramsbottom Cemetery

Frederick Street

Salmsbury Hall Cl

Nuttall

3 77    78    79

A    B    Holco    Brook    C e    24    A676    D    Woodhey    E    F

Woodhey Rd    Woodhey High School

1 grid square represents 500 metres

Bolton

Chapeltown

G H J 17 K L M

74 75 76

Higher House Farm

Hawkshaw

Blackburn Bolton

Walves Reservoir

Bottom o' th' Knotts Brow

RAMSBOTTOM ROAD

BOLTON

Quarlton Dr

St Marys CE Primary School

Troutbeck Close

B6213 TOTTINGTON ROAD

Two Brooks Lane

Hawkshaw Lane

Greenhalgh Close

Moor Way Cl

I

2

3

Walsh Fold

Jumbles Country Park

Brown Barn Farm

Watling Street

A676

BURY ROAD

BRADSHAW ROAD

Affetside

Harry Fold

Bury Bolton

4

24

5

Slack Lane

Top o' th' Knotts

Watling Street

Side of the Moor

Tottington Road

Bowstone Hill Road

Bradshaw Road

Harwood Road

6

Four Lane

7

Bradshaw Meadows

New Heys Way

Brookside

Seaford Road

Catterall Crs

Birch Av

Reddish

Riding Gate

Old Green Gate

Hulme Road

Broadstone Road

Tottington Road

Heaton Av

Hillside

Astley Rd

Lea Gate

The Coppice

St Maxentius CE Primary School

Cottage Croft

LEE GATE

Church St

King St

Back King St

Back Lee St

Duxbury

Hope Av

Back Longsight N

Longsight

PO

Harwood Health Centre

Mayfield

Thorn Lea

Ashdene Crs

Normwood

Linfield

Acre Fld

Oakdale

Vinwood Cl

Harwood Lane

Hough Fold Way

Longsight Lane

Rose Lea

Ruins Lane

B6196

Methodist Cem

Brook Gdns

Bramdean Av

Westcott

Shaftcot Cl

St Brendan RC Primary School

Brookfold Lane

Milford Rd

The Crescent

Greenwoods La

Lincoln Gro

HARDY MILL ROAD

Hardy Mill Primary School

Prospect Hl

Bramhall

Links Road

Harwood Golf Club (Bolton)

Harwood Road

Reading Road

Brook Road

Bentley Hall

8

Bentley Hall

Bolton Open Golf Club

Golf Course

Harwood Rd

Devon Cl

South Av

Ferndown Rd

Green Bank

Castle Croft

Christ Church La

Hough Fold

Heathfield

Belmont

Spillingstone

Sandown View

Spinningstone

37

HILL ROAD

Links Road

Golf Course

B6196

G H J 37 K L M

74 75 76

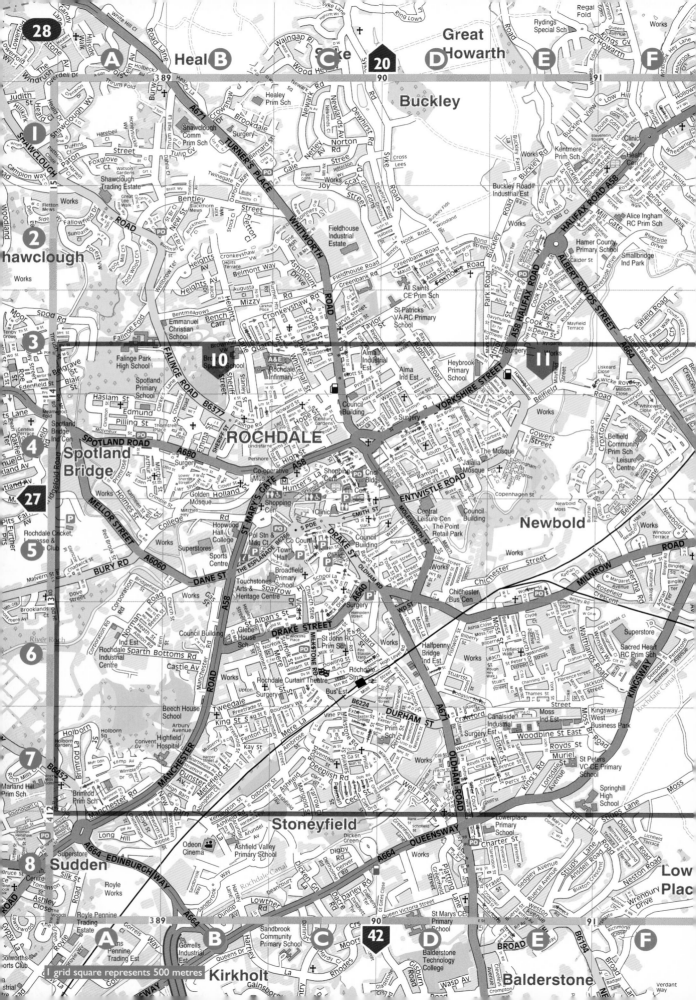

A  B  C  D  E  F

353  54  55

I

Dangerous Corner

Hunger Hill

St Josephs Catholic Primary School

Moss House

Moss Lane

Mossy Lea Fold

MOSSY LEA ROAD

Wrightington Hotel & Country Club

Pepper Lane

Hyatt Crs

Robin Hill Lane

Robin Hill Drive

Shevington Moor

Standish Community High School

2  LANE  A5209  CROW ORCHARD RD

M6

Boundary Lane

Whiteacre

Marple

Broadacre

Brookfield Road

Pepper Lane

Old

Dobson Cl

Cripple Ga

Shevington Moor

Cressett

Junction 27  CROW ORCHARD ROAD

SHEVINGTON LANE

Premier Travel Inn

ALMOND BROOK

Wrightington Hospital

3  B5375  Works  North Quarry Business Park  Stonecrop

Back Lane

WN6

Aspinall Rd

Arbour Lane

Beacon Vw  Skull House Mews  Apple Hey  SKULL HOUSE LA  Apple Lane  Appley La

4  Appley Lane  Dawber Delph  Ruecroft Close  MILES LANE  Glen Dr  Back Lane  Whitehall Av  Rookery  Moor Av  Park  Vale Cl  Woodnook Rd  Greaves  Runshaw  Shevington Vale

Shevington Vale Primary School  Newgate  Avenue

Paradise Farm  Shevington High School

5  Farrier Wy  Appley Bridge Station  MILL Lane  Mill Bank  The Dell  Shellingford Close  Chisacre Drive  Finch Mill Av  Grovewood Dr  Hermitage Close  Highgate  PO  The Nook  MILES LANE  Kilburn Dr  SHEVINGTON LANE  Willowbrook Dr  B5206  Park Av  Longbrook  Millbrook Prim Sch

6  Speakmans Drive  Knightscliffe Crs  Boardman Road  Staynum  MILES LANE  Shevington Community Primary School  Clnc  B5375  Calico Wood Avenue  Surgery  Miles Lane  Manor Rd  Tower Lyndon  GATHURST LA  St Bernadettes Catholic Prim Sch  B5375  CHURCH LANE  Coach  Elmfield  Redwood  The Glade  Foxfield

7  Wigan  Lancashire County  Forest Fold Farm  Gathurst Golf Club  NEW MILES LANE  Highfield Av  B5206  Martland Av  Inward Drive  Dixon Rd  Churchfield  Shevington  WIGAN ROAD  Works

8  Bank Top  Leeds & Liverpool Canal  Golf Course  The Oval  GATHURST LANE  St Anne's Dr  Naylorfarm Av  Beechwood Avenue  Douglas Dr  Woodlands Dr  Queensway  Prince's Park  Greenvale  Vicarage Lane  Works  B5375  WIGAN  Linley Cl  Margaret Av  Princes Av

353  54  55

A  B  C  46  D  E  F  Crooke

Gathurst

Crooke Road

Ackhurst Lane

Gathurst

I grid square represents 500 metres

1 grid square represents 500 metres

A    B    C    D    E    F

Rooden Reservoir

1

ROCHDALE

La Pergola Hotel

2

Oldham Way

Crompton Circuit

Slences

Crompton Fold

3
BUCKSTONES ROAD B6197

Jordan Av

Works

Crompton Moor

Old Tame

A672

4

Buckstones Prim Sch

Hillside

Brushes Clough Reservoir

43

East Crompton St Georges CE Primary School

Mantley Lane

Slackcote Lane
Works

Slackcote

5

Dog Hill

B6197

Grains Road

OLDHAM

6

Clough

BUCKSTONES          ROAD

Besom Hill Reservoir

Grains Bar

SHIP    LANE

7

Fullwood

Council Building

RIPPONDEN ROAD

King Lane

Bishop Park

Ship Lane

Medlock Valley Way

Besom Hill

GRAINS ROAD

B6197

St. Thomas Moorside CE (VA) Primary School

Hill Top Community Special School

8

Sholver

Sholver Lane

Medlock Valley Way

A    B    C    D    E    F

Strine Dale

1 grid square represents 500 metres

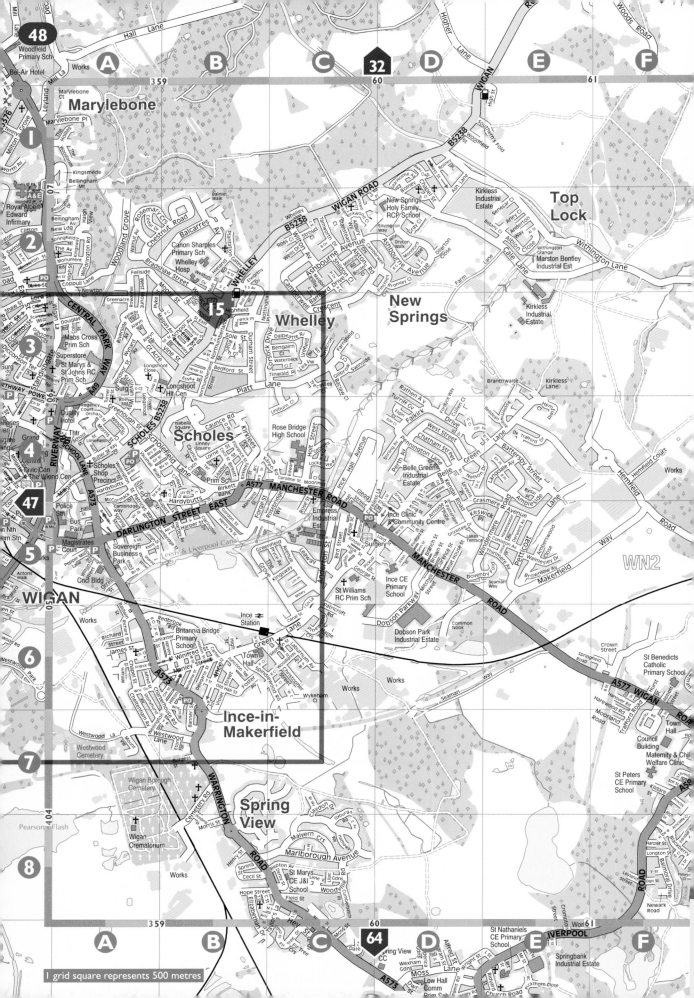

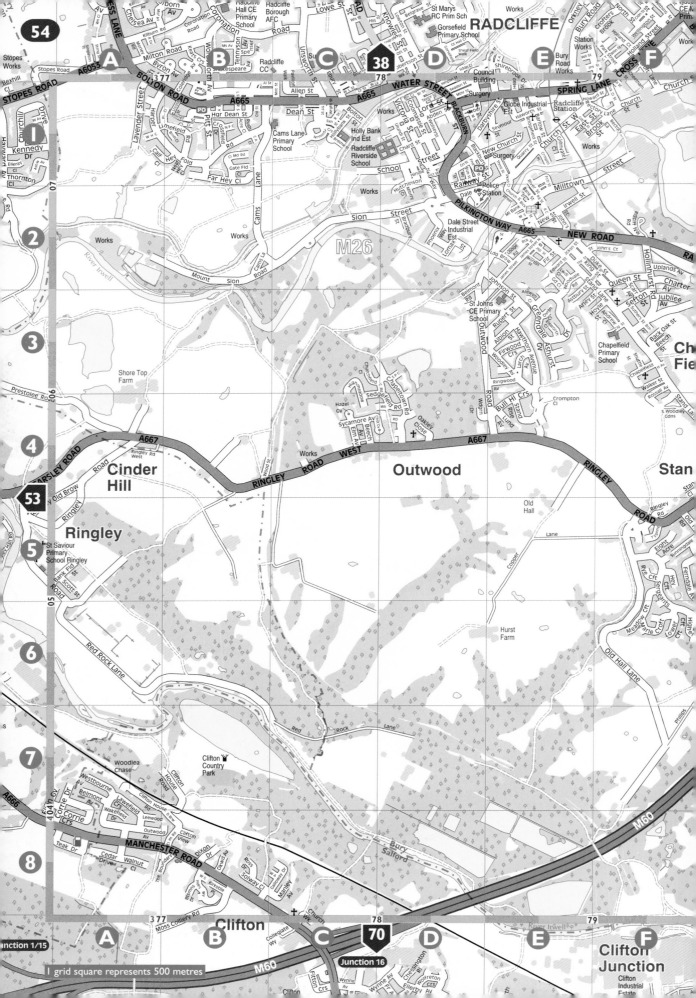

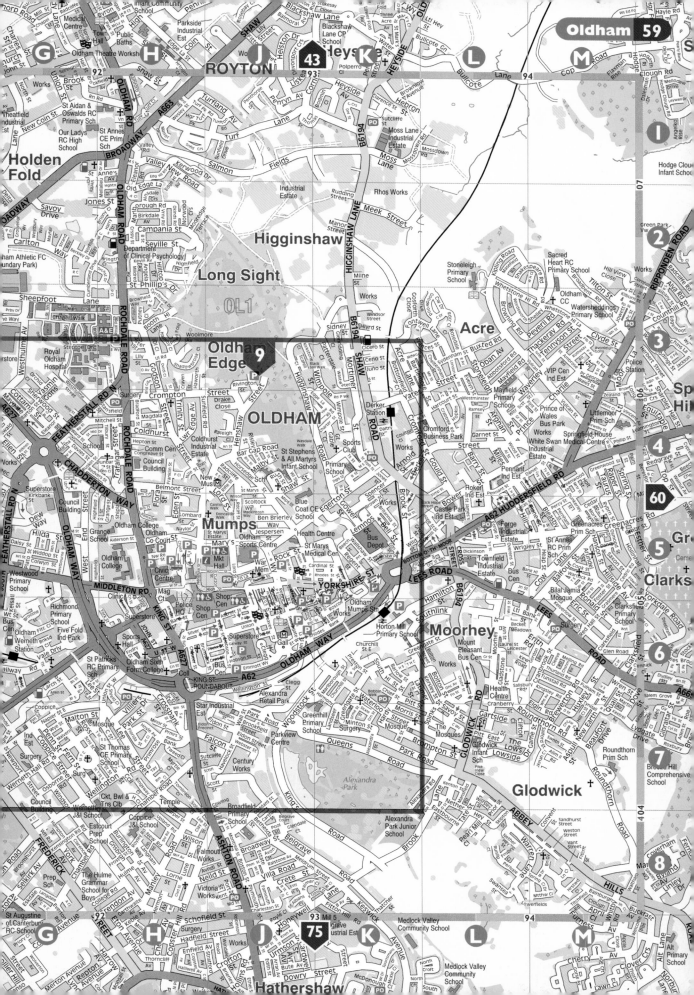

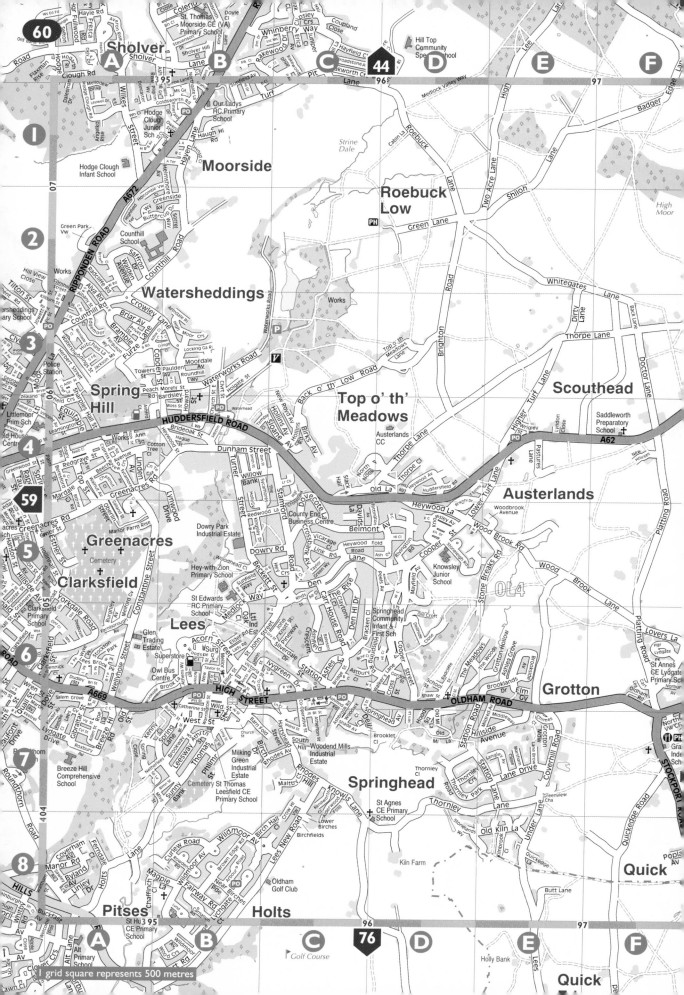

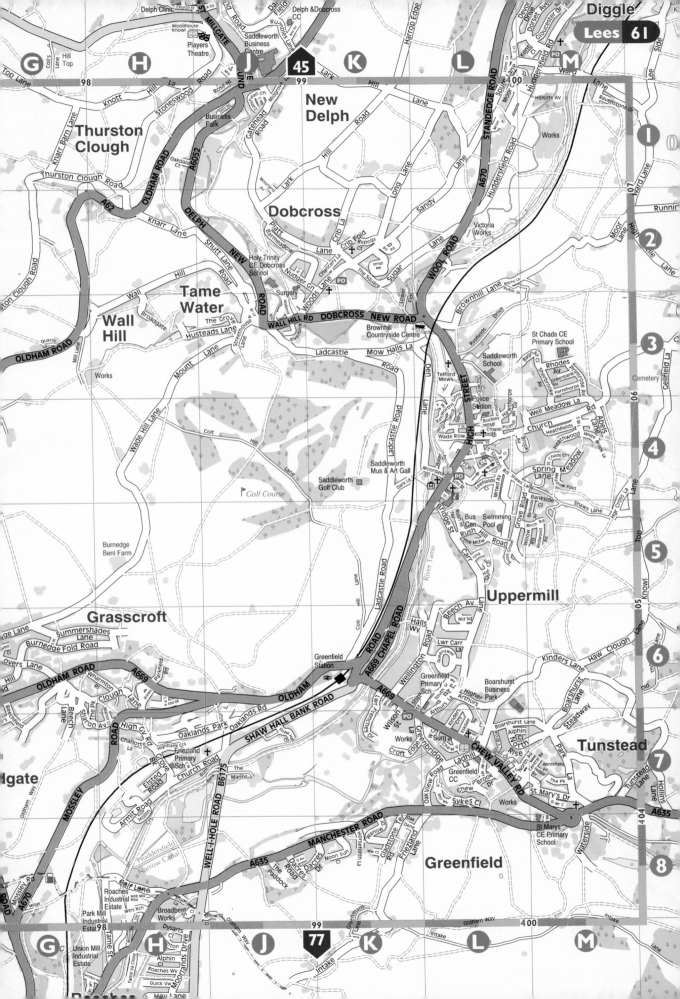

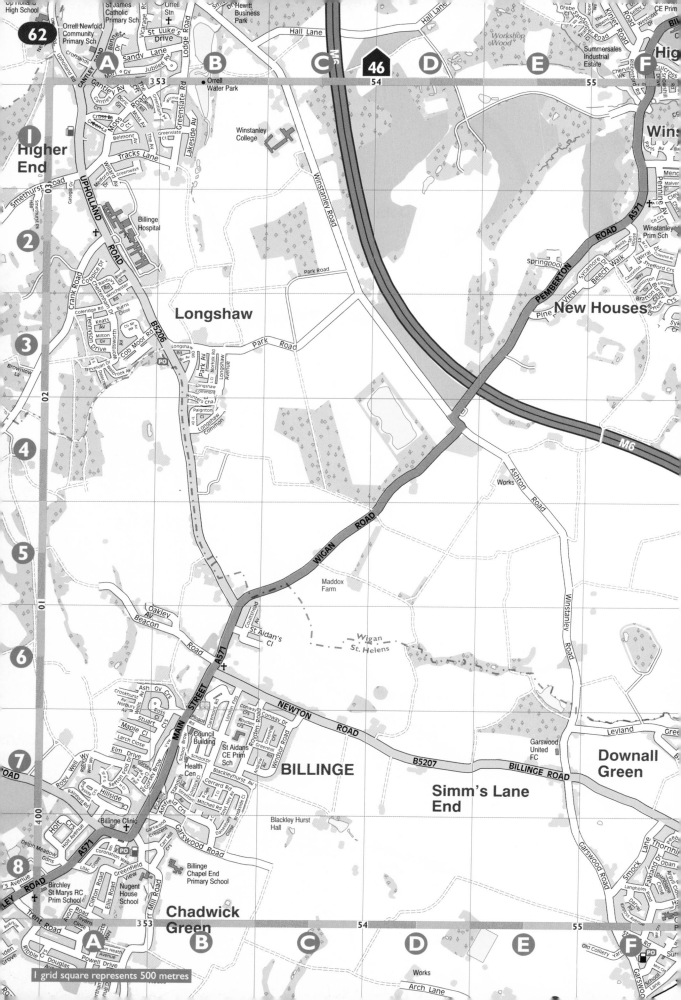

**64**

**63**

**48**

**79**

A   B   C   D   E   F

**Platt Bridge**

**ABRAM**

**Bamfurlong**

**Bryn Gates**

**Dover**

**Stubshaw Cross**

**Town Green**

**Edge Green**

1 grid square represents 500 metres

359   03   02   01   400   359   60   61

LIVERPOOL

Leeds & Liverpool Canal

A573

A58

WARRINGTON RD

LILY LANE

BOLTON ROAD

AYE BRIDGE ROAD

A573

B5237

BICKERSHAW

COLBORNE

B5207

Crematorium

Marlborough Avenue

Works

Police Station

Spring View CC

St Marys CE J&I School

St Nathaniels CE Primary School

Springbank Industrial Estate

Works

Low Hall Comm Prim Sch

Church Road

Health Centre

Oakbank

Medical Centre

Platt Bridge Clinic

Holy Family RC Prim Sch

Abram CE Prim Sch

Council Building

Miller's Lane

Victoria Road

New Street

Wigan Street

Warrington Rd

Winstanley Rd

Bryn Gates Lane

Abram Bryn Gates Primary School

Beech Tree Houses

Maypole Industrial Estate

Riding Lane

Willow Grove School

Ashton Town AFC

St Wilfrids Cath Prim Sch

Jameson's Farm

Chadwick's Farm

Aye Bridge Farm

Lightshaw Hall Farm

Locker La

Greenbank Park

Parkfields

Crankwood Road

Lightshaw Lane

Leeds & Liverpool Canal

ASHTON-IN-MAKERFIELD

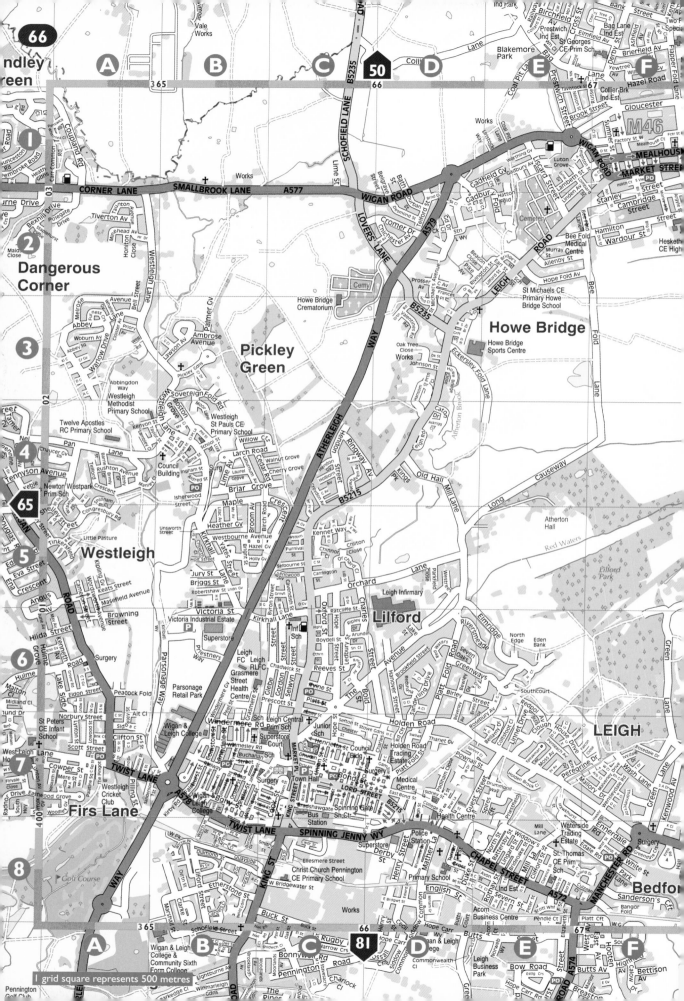

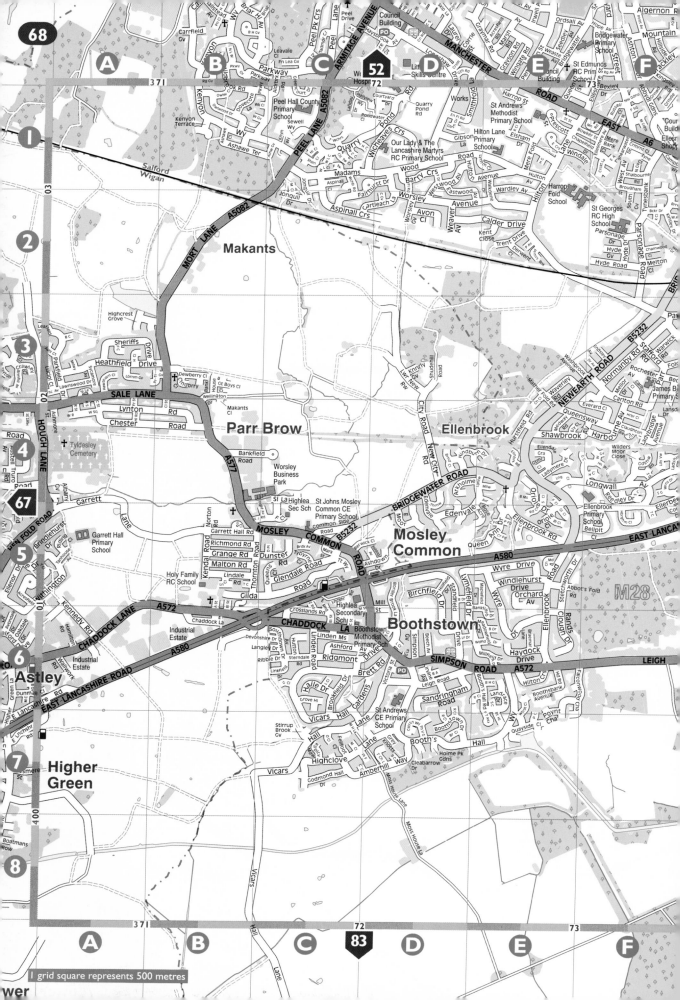

Greenfield

G H J 61 K L M

Roaches

Woodend

White Gate

Alphin

469
Alphin
Pike

Abraham's
Chair

Buckton
Moor

MOSSLEY

Micklehurst
CC

Mossley Hollins
High School

Micklehurst

Micklehurst All Saints
Primary School

Heyheads

Stamford
Golf Club

Carrbrook

Buckton Vale
Primary
School

Golf Course

Carrbrook
Industrial
Estate

Slatepit
Moor

Buckton
Vale

Millbrook
Primary School

Turf
Pits

St Raphaels
Catholic
Primary School

Stalybridge Millbrook
CC

Sun Green

Hydegreen

Millbrook

SK15

G H J 92 K L M

Brushes

Brushes Road

**82**
**Bedford**

ARLFC

Surgery
erson's

Bettis
Av

Council
Building

MANCHESTER
Lodge
La

Bedford High School
York Street

Kent
Street

Warwick st

Rutland
Street

**A**  **B**

3 68

Marsland Green La

Debdale
La

Green Avenue

Manc
Rd

Sandy
La

Peel   Lane

Lingards Rd

School

A572

Manchester Rd

ROAD

A580

**Town Lane**

Cleworth
Cl

Boatmans
Row

Higher Gre

First Av

**Astley
Green**

**67**
69

A5E

**C**  **D**  **E**  **F**

70

Leeds and Liverpool Canal

Morley's La

Morley's Lane

Morley's
Lane

**I**

Dun

Hope

Lower
Green
Lane

**Lower
Green**

**2**

Grove   Dunham
Gv

EAST LANCASHIRE ROAD   A580

Hope
Lane

Moss Brook

Moss Lane

Moss Side

Great
Moss Rd

Allwood
Farm

Sandy La

**3**

Lane

98

Netherbarrow Farm

Turf Nest
Farm

Rindle Road

**4**

Hesnall
Close

Warrington   Wigan

**81**

Warri
Acre

Sandfield
Crescent

Windy Bank
Farm

Bedford
Moss

**5**

Queen's Av

Duke Av

97

LC

**6**

Light Oaks
Road

Old   Moss   Lane

Light Oaks
Moss Farm

**7**

RINGTON ROAD

Millbrook C

Hawthorne
Av

Hey St/Rd

3 96

Moss   Lane

Wigan
Salford

Olive Mount
Farm

Astley Road

**8**

Works

Moss House
Farm

Holm Leigh
Farm

Little
Woolden
Moss

Twelve Yards Road

**A**  **B**  **C**  **D**  **E**  **F**

3 68   69   70

**I grid square represents 500 metres**

G H J **68** K L M

I

2

3

Nook Lane

The Avenue

Malkins Wood Farm

Rock Road

Botany Bay Wood

Moss Bank Farm

Salford Wigan

Birch Farm

84

Barton Moss Rd

M62

5

Barton

6

Bartonmoss Farm

Twelve Yards Road

Chat Moss

Twelve Yards Road

Raspberry Lane

M62

7

LIVERPOOL Road

Barton Grange

Moss Farm

Cutnook Lane

Raspberry Lane

Fiddlers Lane

8

Crossfield Rd

Addison Road

Mond Rd

Boundary Rd

Boundary Trading Estate

Merlin Road

Morrion Road

Martin Dr

McLean Dr

Neville Dr

Keal Dr

Curlew Dr

Leyland Av

Hartley Grove

Silver Street

Silverdale Av

Lyndhurst Av

The Crescent

Marlborough Av

Princes Av

Mayfield Industrial Park

G Larkhill H J **94** K L M

St Josephs The Workers RC Prim Sch

Fiddlers Lane, Primary School

Flixton FC

Woodsend Primary School

Manchester Ship Canal

ASTLEY

M62

Cutnook Lane

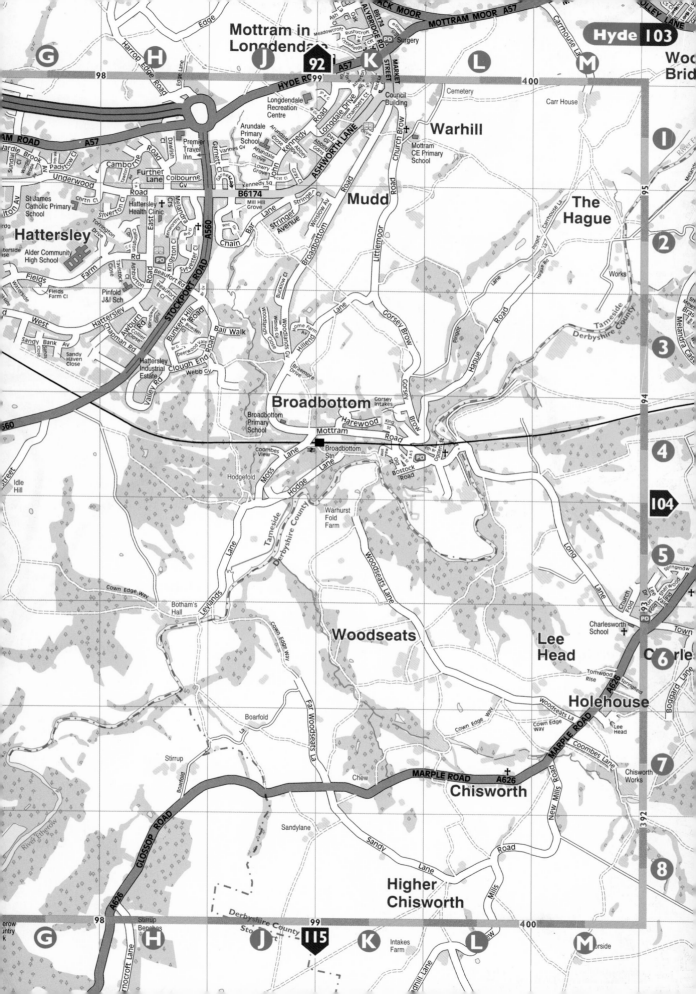

G H J **92** K L M

Mottram in Longdendale

MOTTRAM MOOR A57

Woo Brid

BLACK MOOR

98 HYDE RD 99 A57 400 95

Longdendale Recreation Centre

Arundale Primary School

Premier Travel Inn

Further Lane

Colbourne Gv

Camborne Road

Underwood

RAM ROAD A57

Padstow Av

Wardle Brook Av

St James Catholic Primary School

Hattersley Health Clinic

Hattersley

Alder Community High School

Fields Farm

Fields Farm Cl

Sandy Bank Av

West

Pinfold J&I Sch

Hattersley Chapman Rd

Bunker's Hill

Ball Walk

Clough End Road

Hattersley Industrial Estate

Webb Gv

Valley Rd

B6174

Mill Hill Grove

Stringer Avenue

Broadbottom

Bar Lane

Chain

Woodlands Cl

Home Farm

Hillend

Braemore Drive

ASHWORTH LANE

STOCKPORT ROAD

A560

Council Building

Church Brow

Mottram CE Primary School

**Warhill**

Carr House

Cemetery

**Mudd**

Littlemoor Road

**The Hague**

Works

Tameside Derbyshire County

400

94

**Broadbottom**

Gorsey Brow

Gorsey Intakes

Harewood

Mottram Road

King St

Old Bostock Road

Broadbottom Primary School

Coombes View

Moss Lane

Hodge Lane

Hodgefold

Warhurst Fold Farm

Tameside Derbyshire County

Woodseats Lane

Broadbottom Stn

Hague Road

Pingot

Pingot Rd

Melandra Cast

93

**I**

**2**

**3**

**4**

**104**

**5**

Idle Hill

Cown Edge Way

Botham's Hall

Leylands

Cown Edge Way

**Woodseats**

Long Lane

**Lee Head**

Charlesworth School

Springmdw

Sherwood

Church Fold

Holehouse

Tomwood Rise

A626 Springfield

**C** rle

**6**

A626

Boarfold

Boarfold

Far Woodseats La

Stirrup

Chew

**Chisworth**

MARPLE ROAD A626

Woodseats La

Cown Edge Way

Cown Edge Way

MARPLE ROAD

Coombes Lane

New Mills Road

Lee Head

Chisworth Works

**7**

GLOSSOP ROAD

A626

River Etherow

Sandylane

Sandy Lane

**Higher Chisworth**

Mills Road

**8**

392

98 G H J **115** 99 K L 400 M

Stirrup Benches

Derbyshire County Sto

Intakes Farm

Knarr Lane

G H J K L M

Swineshaw
Reservoir

WOODHEAD

04 05 06

**I**

Yellow
Sl

95

Shire Hill
Hospital.

Kilmory
Fold

Hawkshead
Fold

Moorside

Blackshaw Clough

Charles Lane

Shire Wy

Hkd Rd

Charles St

Hope St

Water St

**2**

All Saints
Cath Primary
School

Well Gate

Church St

Church Dn La Church St

Wesley St

Shepley Street

Mossy Lea
Farm

B6105

Kingsmoor
Fla

Hall Meadow Rd

Kingsmoor
Park Close

Old
Hall

Old Hall

PO

**Old
Glossop**

Works

Duke of Norfolk
CE Prim Sch

Riverside

Manor Park Road

Corn St

York
Street

Jordan
Street

Sunningdale
Dr

Sunningdale
Dr

Pyegrove

Woodcock
Grove

Queen's
Drive

Pyegrove

Woodcock
Farm

WOODCOCK ROAD A57

**3**

King Edward AV

Kt Rd

RV Cl

Thomas St

Birch
Gn

Cowbrook
Avenue

Hurstbrook

Hurst Rd

Hurst Mills
Industrial
Est

Golf Course

Snake Pass

94

Smithy
St

Quay

Surg

A57 **SHEFFIELD ROAD**

Mill St

35 Hills

MGn

Cl

Frw's

SNAKE PASS A57

**STREET EAST**

Milltown
St

**GLOSSOP**

Croft Manor

Pl Ct

Pl Ct

Mattersage

Hurst Cl

Hurst Crs

Cl

Hampshire

Wind in the
Willows Hotel

Derbyshire Level

Glossop
& District
Golf Club

Hurst
Reservoir

**4**

The Bank

Siant

Cross

Cross

Shirebrook Drive

Horns Bank

Carr B Bk

Hurst Drive

Kg Cup

Plover Cl

Myflwr Cl

Lh Wy

Shirebrook

Hillwood Dr

Appleton

Winnats

Hebden
Dr

Gloucester
Wv

St Marys
RC Prim Sch

Gladstone
Cl

Road

Morley
Street

Cliffe

Shirebrook Drive

Heron Cl

Wiltshire Brs

Yorkshire
Way

Warwick
Cl

93

Highfield Road

Uplands

Whitfield
Cross
Avenue

Rd

Cliffe

Padfield Ga

Carr Farm

Hghll
MGn

King
Charles
Court

Linacre

Leicester Drive

Bracken
Way

Southview
Road

Riverbank
Wy

Wingfield
Gr

Highbank Rd

Hurstnook
Farm

Span
Clough

Hurst Brook

**5**

Jumble

Level

**6**

Hague

Street

Derbyshire

**Moorfield**

Span
Moor

Works

Kidd Road

Gnat Hole

Wood's
Cabin

**7**

Bray
Clough

Black
Moor

392

**8**

04 05 06

Whitethorn
Clough
Moor

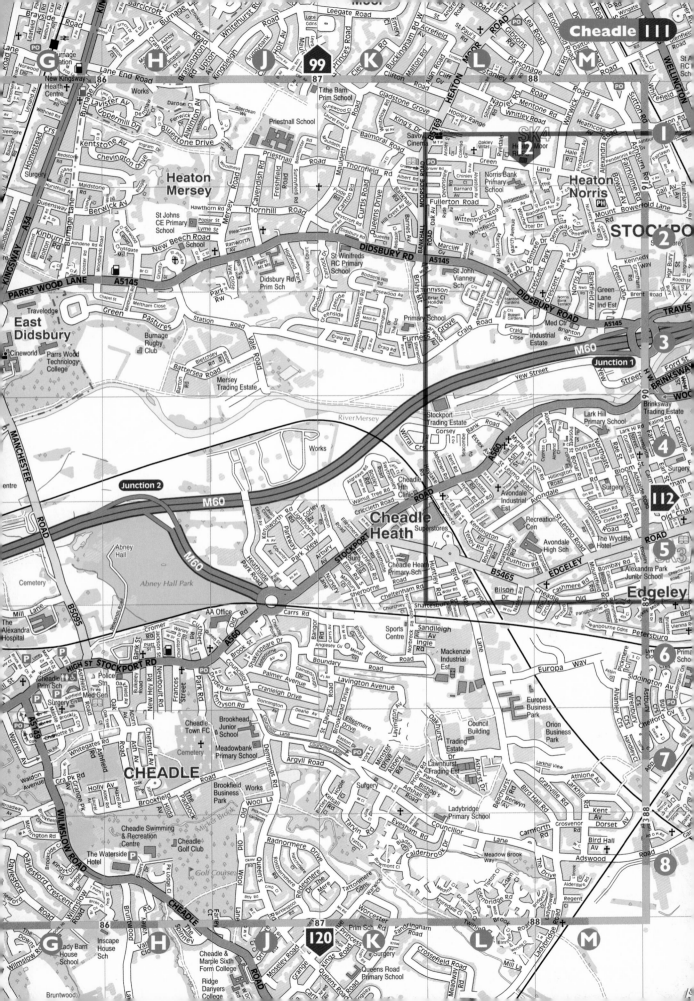

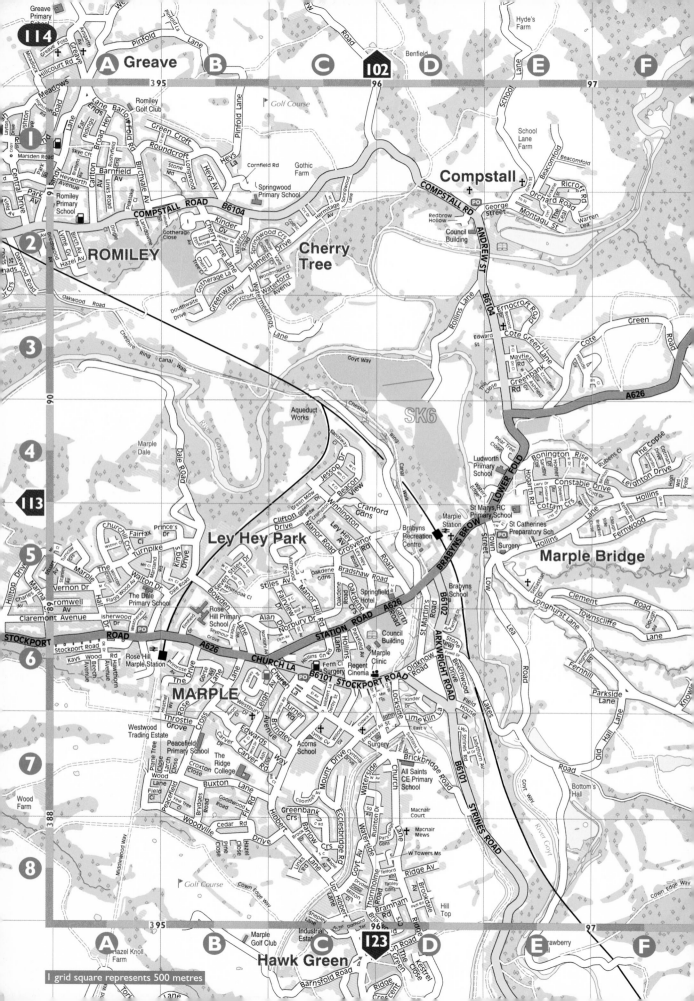

Golf Course

**G** **H** **J** 114 **K** **L** **M** The Banks

Marple Golf Club

**Hawk Green**

Barnsfold Road

Windlehurst School

**Marpleridge**

Strawberry Hill

Doodfield
Doodfield Works

Pucksbridge Rd

Works

Ridge Fold

Ridge-End

**Windlehurst**

Cown Edge Way

Turf Lea Farm

**Strines**

Strines Station

River Goyt

Lomber Hey House

Wybersley Road

Turf Lea Road

**Woodend**

Andrew Lane

Dove House Farm

Peak Forest Canal

Hague Bar Primary School

Stockport Cheshire Council

**HIGH LANE**

High Lane Medical Centre

Wybersley Hall

124

Golf Course

Stanley Hall

Disley Golf Club

Meadow Close

Carr Brow

Alders Road

Lyme Road

Jacksons

Hilton Road

Stanley Hall

The Ridgeway

Hollinwood

**6**

Brookside Primary School

Manifold Drive

Park Road

Light Alders Lane

Edge Road

Amalgamated Sports Club

Lymewood Drive

Homestead Road

Leafield Rd

Market Street

Surgery

Primary School

Chantry Road

Brookside Farm

Legh Road

Farm La

Coppice Lane

**DISLEY**

Disley Station

Buxton Old Road

Heysbank Road

**Da**

Shearhall Avenue

Pool House Farm

Red Lane

Green Lane

Royal Elizabeth Avenue

Govt Road

**Higher Disley**

Middlecale Farm

Parkgate

Cockhead

**8** Lane Ends

**G** **H** **J** **K** **L** **M**

Platt Wood Farm

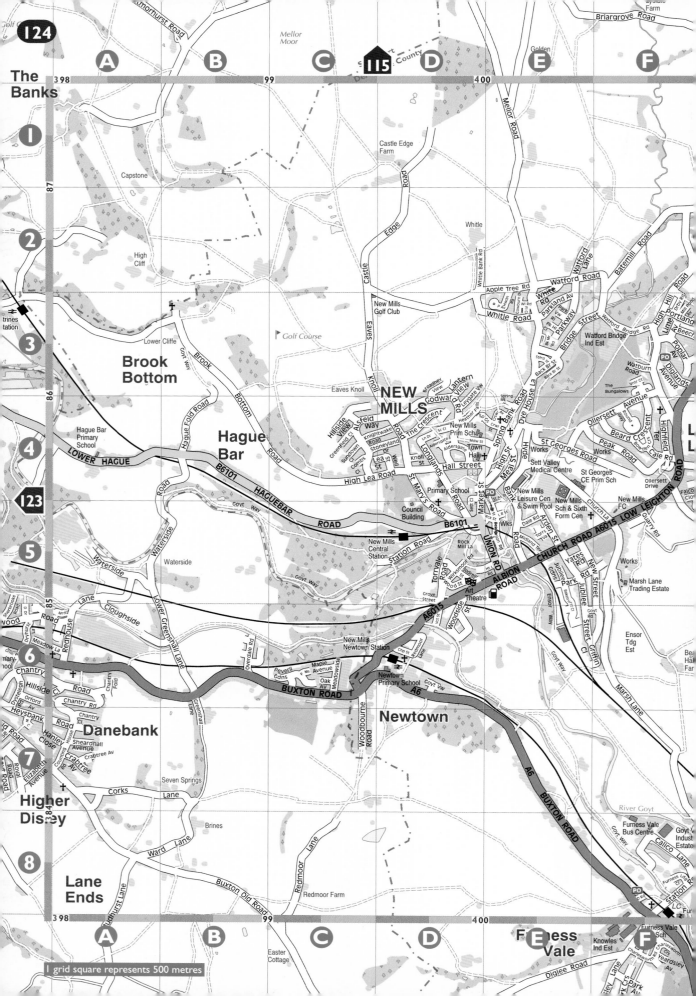

G H J K L M

02 03 04

Aspenshaw
Hall

Wethercotes

Cliff

Swallow
House
Lane

Pike Cl

Bank Vale Road

Lea Rd

Fairy Bank CS

Road

Birch Lane

Hayfield
Primary School

Market Street

Fairy Bank
Rd

Cote Lane

I

Thornsett
Primary School

River Sett

Chendre

Birch Cl

Wood

Council Building

Bowden Cl

PO

Bank

PH

Vicarage

Quarry Road

PH

MILLS

PO

Wood La

Surg

Hayfield
Site

Sycamore Road

Spinnerbottom

Birch Vale
Industrial
Estate

Works

NEW

ROAD

Church St

Thornsett
Trading Estate

Works

Station Rd

Birch Hall Cl

The

A6015

Station
Rd

2

Thornsett

Works

Lantern Pike
View

Sett Valley Trail

Hayfield
Road

Birches

St John
Street

Valley
Road

Hayfield

Morland Road

Ridge Top Lane

Highgate Road

HAYFIELD ROAD

Ridge Top

87

3

A6 CHAPEL

Over Lee Farm

Barnsfold Farm

86

Cold Harbour
Farm

Over Hill Road

Ollersett

Far Phoside

4

New
ghton

Moor Lodge

5

Piece Farm

85

Hills Farm

Laneside Road

6

Shedyard
Farm

New
Allotments

7

Over Hill Road

Beardwood Farm

84

Ladypit Road

8

Gowhole

Vale Station

The Haugh

Cloughhead

Throstle B

Cracken Edge

G H J K L M

02 03 04

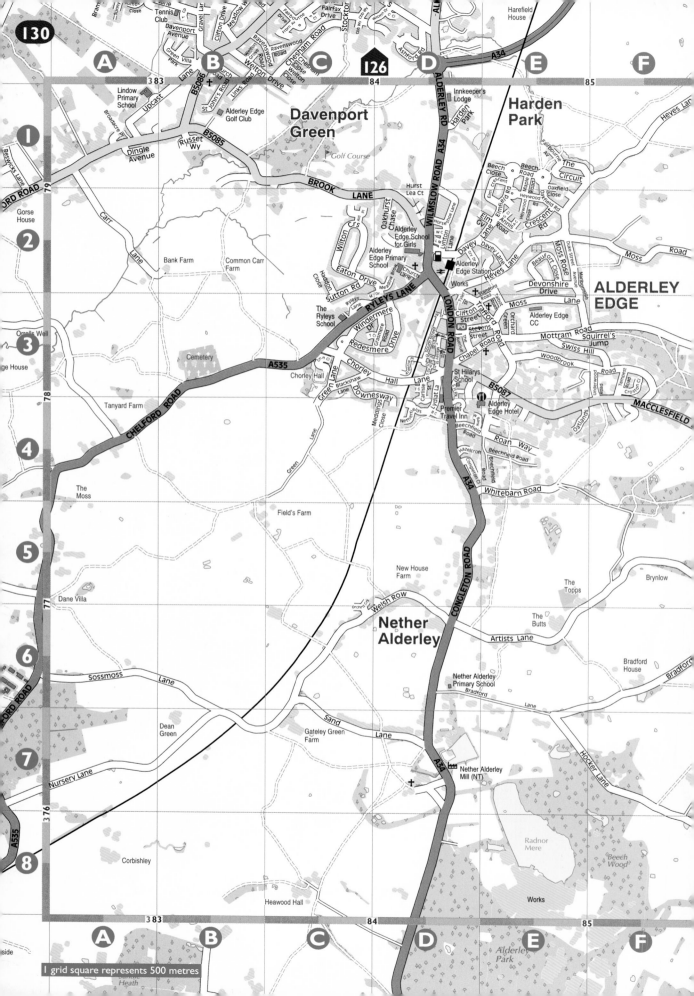

G H J 127 K L M

Farm

Brook House Farm

Wilms Road

A538

River

De Vere Mottram Hall Golf Club

De Vere Mottram Hall Hotel

86 87 88

Golf Course

79

I

1

r Farm

Hough Green Farm

Brook Farm

Higher House Farm

Lower House

Alderley Road

Mottram Road

The Crescent

Rushton Fold

PO

Hough

Findlow Farm

Mottram St Andrew

Clock House Farm

Danielhill

Hill Top

Old Wilmslow Road

Moss Lane

Mottram St Andrew Primary School

Priest Lane

Lane

Mottram Cross

Smithy

Legh Hall

Wilmslow Road

Oak Road

Allen's Farm

Hunter's Pool Farm

Greendale

Lane

2

3

78

4

Hough Lane

Alderley Edge

The Wizard

Artists Lane

Edge House Farm

Adder's Moss

Mount Farm

Hunters Pool

Withinlee Farm

Withinlee Road

Holm Way

Road

77

5

6

Macclesfield Road

Finlow Hill

Lane

Finlow Hill Farm

Prestbury Road

School Lane

Ashbrook Road

Festival

Prestbury Road

Hare Hill (NT)

Oak Road

Chelford Road

Harebarrow Farm

376

7

Hayman's Farm

Slade Lane

B5087

Greendale Road

Vardentown

Birtles Lane

Fittontown Farm

Macclesfield Road

8

Higher House Farm

Hocker Lane

Hocker Lane

Acton Farm

Shawcross

Yewtree

Wrigley Lane

G H J K L M

86 87 88

Abbey Hey ..... 89 J7
Abram ..... 64 F4
Acre ..... 59 L3
Adlington ..... 128 F7
Adswood ..... 112 A7
Affetside ..... 23 L4
Ainsworth ..... 38 A5
Alder Forest ..... 69 J8
Alderley Edge ..... 130 F2
Alkrington Garden Village ..... 57 K6
Alt ..... 76 A1
Alt Hill ..... 75 M4
Altrincham ..... 108 C7
Ancoats ..... 7 L4
Arden Park ..... 101 G8
Ardwick ..... 7 M9
Ashley ..... 117 G7
Ashley Heath ..... 116 F4
Ashton-in-Makerfield ..... 79 G1
Ashton-under-Lyne ..... 90 B1
Ashton Upon Mersey ..... 96 C6
Aspull ..... 33 G7
Aspull Common ..... 80 E3
Astley ..... 67 M6
Astley Bridge ..... 22 E8
Astley Green ..... 67 M1
Atherton ..... 66 F1
Audenshaw ..... 90 B5
Austerlands ..... 60 E4
Backbower ..... 102 B4
Bagslate Moor ..... 27 J4
Balderstone ..... 42 E1
Baldingstone ..... 25 H3
Bamford ..... 27 G5
Bamfurlong ..... 64 B4
Bank Lane ..... 19 G5
Bank Top ..... 22 D7
Bardsley ..... 75 K3
Barton Upon Irwell ..... 85 G4
Bedford ..... 66 F8
Beech Hill ..... 47 J2
Belfield ..... 29 G5
Belle Vue ..... 88 E7
Benchill ..... 110 A7
Bentgate ..... 43 J1
Besses o' th' Barn ..... 55 J5
Beswick ..... 88 C3
Bickershaw ..... 65 H4
Billinge ..... 62 C7
Birch ..... 40 F8
Birtle ..... 26 B5
Blackford Bridge ..... 39 J8
Black Lane ..... 38 C6
Blackley ..... 73 H3
Blackmoor ..... 67 K7
Blackrod ..... 32 F1
Bleak Hey Nook ..... 45 M5
Boar's Head ..... 31 K6
Bolholt ..... 24 D8
Bolton ..... 3 G5
Booth Green ..... 129 J5
Boothstown ..... 68 D6
Bottom o' th' Moor ..... 34 B1
Bowdon ..... 116 B3
Bowgreen ..... 116 C3
Bowlee ..... 56 D3
Bradford ..... 88 C2
Bradley Fold ..... 37 L5
Bradshaw ..... 22 F6
Bramhall ..... 120 F7
Bramhall Moor ..... 121 K2
Bramhall Park ..... 120 E3
Bredbury ..... 113 H1
Bredbury Green ..... 113 K2
Breightmet ..... 37 K4
Brinnington ..... 100 E7
Broadbottom ..... 103 J4
Broadfield ..... 40 E3
Broadhalgh ..... 27 J5
Broadheath ..... 107 M5
Broadley ..... 20 A7
Broadoak Park ..... 69 M7
Bromley Cross ..... 22 D6
Brook Bottom ..... 76 D2
Brook Bottom ..... 124 A3
Brookfield ..... 104 A2
Brooklands ..... 108 E2
Brooksbottoms ..... 24 F1
Broughton Park ..... 72 A3
Brownlow Fold ..... 35 M3
Brunswick ..... 87 L6
Brushes ..... 92 B1
Bryn ..... 63 J6
Bryn Gates ..... 64 C5
Buckley ..... 28 D1
Buckton Vale ..... 77 H7
Buersil Head ..... 42 F3
Burnage ..... 99 H7
Burnden ..... 36 D8
Burnedge ..... 43 H3
Bury ..... 4 D3
Busk ..... 8 C3
Calderbrook ..... 21 M3
Caldermoor ..... 21 K6
Cale Green ..... 112 C6
Captain Fold ..... 41 H1
Carr ..... 18 E5
Carrbrook ..... 77 K5
Carr Green ..... 106 C6
Carrington ..... 95 H6
Carrington Moss ..... 107 J1
Castlefield ..... 6 B7
Castle Hill ..... 101 H5
Castleton ..... 41 M2
Chadderton ..... 58 B5
Chadderton Fold ..... 58 C2
Chadkirk ..... 113 L4
Chadwick Green ..... 62 B8
Chapel Field ..... 54 F3
Chapeltown ..... 23 G1
Charlestown ..... 71 L8
Charlestown ..... 73 K1
Charlestown ..... 104 E6
Charlesworth ..... 104 A6
Chatterton ..... 18 E3
Cheadle ..... 111 H7
Cheadle Heath ..... 111 K5
Cheadle Hulme ..... 120 C4
Cheetham Hill ..... 72 E6
Chequerbent ..... 50 F3
Cherry Tree ..... 114 C2
Chesham ..... 25 K7
Chew Moor ..... 34 F8
Chisworth ..... 103 L7
Chorlton-cum-Hardy ..... 98 A5
Chunal ..... 104 F8
Cinder Hill ..... 54 A4
Clarksfield ..... 60 A5
Clayton ..... 88 F1
Cliff ..... 125 K1

Clifton ..... 70 B1
Clifton Green ..... 70 E2
Clifton Junction ..... 70 F1
Clough ..... 21 L5
Clough ..... 44 A6
Collyhurst ..... 73 G6
Compstall ..... 114 D1
Cooper Turning ..... 33 L7
Copley ..... 91 M2
Copster Hill ..... 75 G8
Cox Green ..... 22 C3
Crankwood ..... 64 F7
Crimble ..... 27 J8
Crofts Bank ..... 84 F8
Crompton Fold ..... 43 M3
Crooke ..... 46 F1
Crowhill ..... 75 J4
Crumpsall ..... 72 C3
Cutgate ..... 27 K4
Daisy Hill ..... 50 D6
Daisy Nook ..... 74 F7
Dale ..... 45 J7
Dales Brow ..... 70 A6
Dane Bank ..... 100 E3
Danebank ..... 124 A7
Dangerous Corner ..... 65 M2
Darcy Lever ..... 37 G7
Darn Hill ..... 40 C3
Daubhill ..... 35 M8
Davenport ..... 112 B8
Davenport Green ..... 118 B2
Davenport Green ..... 130 C1
Davyhulme ..... 84 E8
Deane ..... 51 L1
Dean Row ..... 127 K4
Dearnley ..... 21 K8
Debdale ..... 89 J8
Delph ..... 45 H8
Denshaw ..... 45 G2
Denton ..... 101 J1
Didsbury ..... 110 E1
Diggle ..... 45 M8
Dimple ..... 16 A8
Disley ..... 123 K6
Dobcross ..... 61 J2
Doffcocker ..... 35 K2
Dog Hill ..... 44 B5
Dover ..... 64 E6
Downall Green ..... 62 F7
Droylsden ..... 89 H3
Dukinfield ..... 90 F5
Dumplington ..... 84 F5
Dunham Town ..... 107 G8
Dunham Woodhouses ..... 106 E8
Dunscar ..... 22 A3
Eagley ..... 22 B5
East Didsbury ..... 111 G3
Eccles ..... 85 K3
Edenfield ..... 19 H1
Edge Fold ..... 16 D3
Edge Fold ..... 51 M3
Edge Green ..... 79 J1
Edgeley ..... 12 E9
Edgworth ..... 17 H6
Egerton ..... 22 B2
Ellenbrook ..... 68 D4
Ellesmere Park ..... 70 B8
Elton ..... 38 E2
Facit ..... 20 C1
Failsworth ..... 74 B5
Fairfield ..... 40 A1
Fairfield ..... 89 K5
Fallowfield ..... 98 E4
Far Moor ..... 46 B7
Farnworth ..... 52 E4
Fern Bank ..... 91 L3
Fernhill ..... 4 E1
Fernhill Gate ..... 35 J8
Finney Green ..... 127 G2
Firgrove ..... 29 H6
Firs Lane ..... 66 A7
Firswood ..... 97 L1
Firwood Fold ..... 36 F1
Fishpool ..... 4 E1
Fitton Hill ..... 75 K2
Flixton ..... 95 K3
Flowery Field ..... 91 G8
Foggbrook ..... 113 J5
Four Gates ..... 33 M8
Four Lane Ends ..... 24 A7
Fowley Common ..... 81 L7
Free Town ..... 5 L1
Fullwood ..... 44 A7
Fulshaw Park ..... 126 E7
Gamesley ..... 104 B2
Gathurst ..... 46 C1
Gatley ..... 110 D8
Gee Cross ..... 102 B5
Gigg ..... 39 K5
Gillbent ..... 120 B6
Gilnow ..... 2 B6
Gin Pit ..... 67 J5
Glazebury ..... 81 L6
Glodwick ..... 59 L7
Glossop ..... 105 H3
Godley ..... 102 B1
Godley Hill ..... 102 E2
Golborne ..... 79 L5
Goose Green ..... 47 H8
Gorse Hill ..... 97 H1
Gorton ..... 88 F8
Gowhole ..... 125 C8
Grains Bar ..... 44 D6
Grasscroft ..... 61 G6
Gravel Hole ..... 43 C5
Great Howarth ..... 20 E8
Great Lever ..... 52 D1
Great Moor ..... 112 F6
Greave ..... 102 A8
Greenacres ..... 60 A5
Greendale ..... 131 M5
Greenfield ..... 61 L8
Greengate ..... 29 G1
Greenheys ..... 52 A7
Greenmount ..... 24 D7
Greenside ..... 89 L1
Grotton ..... 60 E6
Guide Bridge ..... 90 B3
Hadfield ..... 93 K8
Hag Fold ..... 50 E8
Haggate ..... 58 F1
Hague Bar ..... 124 A3
Haigh ..... 32 D2
Hale ..... 117 H2
Halebarns ..... 117 M4
Halfway Houses ..... 37 M6
Hall i' th' Wood ..... 22 D8
Halliwell ..... 36 B1
Handforth ..... 119 L8
Harden Park ..... 130 E1

Hargate Hill ..... 104 B4
Harper Green ..... 52 E3
Harpurhey ..... 73 H5
Hart Common ..... 49 L5
Hartshead Green ..... 76 D4
Hartshead Pike ..... 76 C3
Harwood ..... 37 K1
Harwood Lee ..... 23 H7
Hathershaw ..... 75 J1
Hattersley ..... 103 G2
Haugh ..... 43 M1
Haughton Green ..... 101 K4
Hawk Green ..... 123 C1
Hawkley ..... 63 K1
Hawkshaw ..... 23 M1
Haydock ..... 78 A6
Hayfield ..... 125 L2
Hazel Grove ..... 122 C3
Hazelhurst ..... 18 C8
Hazelhurst ..... 69 L6
Hazelhurst ..... 76 D7
Heady Hill ..... 40 D2
Heald Green ..... 119 J3
Healds Green ..... 58 C1
Healey ..... 20 C8
Heap Bridge ..... 39 M3
Heatley ..... 106 A7
Heaton ..... 35 K4
Heaton Chapel ..... 99 M6
Heaton Mersey ..... 111 H1
Heaton Moor ..... 99 K8
Heaton Norris ..... 12 C2
Heaviley ..... 13 M9
Heights ..... 45 G6
Heyheads ..... 77 G5
Heyrod ..... 76 E8
Heyside ..... 43 K8
Heywood ..... 40 F1
Higginshaw ..... 59 J2
High Crompton ..... 43 K4
Higher Blackley ..... 56 F8
Higher Boarshaw ..... 57 M1
Higher Broughton ..... 72 A6
Higher Chisworth ..... 103 K8
Higher Dinting ..... 104 D2
Higher Disley ..... 123 M7
Higher Folds ..... 67 H6
Higher Green ..... 68 A7
Higher Poynton ..... 129 M2
Higher Woodhill ..... 25 G7
Highfield ..... 46 F8
Highfield ..... 52 C5
High Lane ..... 123 G5
Hill Top ..... 53 G8
Hilton House ..... 33 K6
Hilton Park ..... 71 K2
Hindley ..... 49 H8
Hindley Green ..... 49 M8
Hindsford ..... 67 G2
Hobroyd ..... 104 E5
Hockley ..... 129 L1
Holcombe ..... 18 D7
Holcombe Brook ..... 24 C1
Holden Fold ..... 59 G1
Holehouse ..... 103 M6
Hollingworth ..... 92 F6
Hollins ..... 35 L7
Hollins ..... 52 A4
Hollins ..... 57 J1
Hollinwood ..... 74 D3
Holts ..... 60 B8
Hooley Bridge ..... 26 F7
Hooley Brow ..... 27 G8
Hooley Hill ..... 90 B5
Hope Green ..... 129 H3
Hough ..... 131 G3
Howe Bridge ..... 66 E3
Hulme ..... 87 H6
Hunger Hill ..... 30 C1
Hunger Hill ..... 51 H5
Hurst ..... 76 A7
Hurstead ..... 21 G8
Hyde ..... 102 A1
Ince-in-Makerfield ..... 15 L6
Irlam ..... 94 C3
Irlams o' th' Height ..... 70 F7
Jericho ..... 26 B8
Johnson Fold ..... 35 G1
Jubilee ..... 43 L2
Kearsley ..... 53 L6
Kenyon ..... 80 D8
Kersal ..... 71 L3
Kingston ..... 101 L1
Kirkhams ..... 55 L6
Kirkholt ..... 42 B1
Kirklees ..... 24 E5
Kitt Green ..... 47 H5
Kitt's Moss ..... 120 F6
Knott Lanes ..... 75 J5
Lacey Green ..... 126 F3
Lady House ..... 29 H8
Lamberhead Green ..... 46 D7
Land Gate ..... 63 K5
Landslow Green ..... 92 E5
Lane Ends ..... 115 G3
Lane Ends ..... 124 A8
Lane Head ..... 80 C6
Langley ..... 57 L8
Lark Hill ..... 67 K7
Lately Common ..... 81 M3
Lee Head ..... 103 M6
Lees ..... 60 B6
Leigh ..... 66 F7
Levenshulme ..... 99 M4
Lever-Edge ..... 52 A2
Ley Hey Park ..... 114 B5
Lilford ..... 66 D6
Limefield ..... 25 J6
Limehurst ..... 75 K6
Lime Side ..... 75 G3
Linfitts ..... 45 G7
Linnyshaw ..... 69 H1
Little Bolton ..... 85 L2
Littleborough ..... 21 M7
Little Clegg ..... 29 H2
Little Hulton ..... 52 C8
Little Lever ..... 37 L8
Little Moor ..... 113 G4
Littlemoss ..... 74 F8
Little Scotland ..... 32 D2
Longshaw ..... 62 B3
Long Sight ..... 59 H2
Longsight ..... 88 C7
Lostock ..... 34 B6
Lostock Junction ..... 35 C7
Low Compton ..... 43 H6
Lower Bredbury ..... 112 F2
Lower Broughton ..... 71 M8
Lower Green ..... 82 F1
Lower Kersal ..... 71 K6

Lower Place ..... 28 F8
Low Leighton ..... 124 F4
Lowton ..... 80 A4
Lowton Common ..... 80 D4
Lowton Heath ..... 79 M6
Lowton St Mary's ..... 80 D5
Luzley ..... 76 E5
Luzley Brook ..... 43 J7
Lydgate ..... 60 F7
Makants ..... 68 B2
Manchester ..... 6 A5
Markland Hill ..... 35 H4
Marland ..... 27 L7
Marple ..... 114 B6
Marple Bridge ..... 114 E5
Marpleridge ..... 123 H2
Marsh Green ..... 46 F3
Marylebone ..... 48 A1
Matley ..... 92 C6
Mellor ..... 115 H6
Micklehurst ..... 77 H3
Middlebrook ..... 33 L4
Middleton ..... 57 G3
Middlewood ..... 122 D7
Midway ..... 129 H2
Miles Platting ..... 88 A1
Millbrook ..... 77 G8
Mill Brow ..... 115 H4
Mill Hill ..... 3 H5
Milnrow ..... 29 K6
Monton ..... 85 C1
Moorclose ..... 57 M4
Moorend ..... 115 K6
Moorfield ..... 105 J6
Moorhey ..... 59 L6
Moorside ..... 60 B1
Moorside ..... 70 A5
Morley ..... 126 A3
Moses Gate ..... 52 F2
Mosley Common ..... 68 D5
Mossbrow ..... 106 A5
Mossley ..... 77 G2
Mossley Brow ..... 76 F3
Moss Nook ..... 119 H4
Moss Side ..... 87 K8
Moston ..... 73 L5
Mottram in Longdendale ..... 92 C8
Mottram Rise ..... 92 B5
Mottram St Andrew ..... 131 K3
Mudd ..... 103 K2
Mumps ..... 9 K4
Nangreaves ..... 25 H1
Nether Alderley ..... 130 D6
Newall Green ..... 109 K8
Newbold ..... 11 M4
New Boston ..... 78 C6
New Bury ..... 52 D5
New Delph ..... 61 K1
Newhey ..... 29 K8
New Houses ..... 62 E3
New Mills ..... 124 D4
New Moston ..... 73 M4
New Springs ..... 48 D3
Newton ..... 91 H7
Newton Heath ..... 73 K7
Newton-le-Willows ..... 79 G7
Newton Wood ..... 90 D6
Newtown ..... 47 H6
Newtown ..... 70 B3
Newtown ..... 124 D7
Nimble Nook ..... 58 D8
Nob End ..... 53 K2
Norbury Moor ..... 122 A3
Norden ..... 27 G3
Northenden ..... 110 A4
Northern Moor ..... 109 J3
North Reddish ..... 100 B3
Nuttall ..... 18 E8
Oak Bank ..... 55 K5
Offerton ..... 113 H5
Offerton Green ..... 113 K6
Old Boston ..... 78 E5
Oldfield Brow ..... 107 L7
Old Glossop ..... 105 H2
Oldham ..... 9 H2
Oldham Edge ..... 9 J1
Old Tame ..... 44 E4
Old Trafford ..... 86 E7
Openshaw ..... 88 F4
Ordsall ..... 86 E5
Orrell ..... 46 D5
Orrell Post ..... 46 B5
Outwood ..... 54 D4
Over Hulton ..... 51 K5
Padfield ..... 93 M7
Park Bridge ..... 75 M2
Parr Brow ..... 68 B4
Partington ..... 106 C2
Patricroft ..... 84 F2
Peel Green ..... 84 C4
Peel Hall ..... 119 H2
Pemberton ..... 46 F7
Pendlebury ..... 70 F5
Pendleton ..... 86 D1
Pennington ..... 81 G1
Pennington Green ..... 49 H2
Pickley Green ..... 66 B3
Pimhole ..... 5 K5
Pitses ..... 60 A8
Plank Lane ..... 65 L7
Platt Bridge ..... 64 E2
Pocket Nook ..... 52 B8
Poolstock ..... 14 C8
Portwood ..... 112 D1
Pownall Park ..... 126 D4
Poynton ..... 122 B8
Prestolee ..... 53 L4
Prestwich ..... 55 J8
Quick ..... 60 F8
Quick Edge ..... 76 E1
Radcliffe ..... 38 D8
Rainsough ..... 71 K3
Rakewood ..... 29 M3
Ramsbottom ..... 18 E4
Reddish ..... 100 A4
Red Rock ..... 32 A4
Redvales ..... 39 H6
Rhodes ..... 56 E5
Ridge Hill ..... 76 C8
Ringley ..... 54 A3
Roaches ..... 77 G1
Rochdale ..... 11 H4
Roebuck Low ..... 60 D2
Roe Cross ..... 92 C7
Roe Green ..... 69 J4
Romiley ..... 114 A2
Rose Hill ..... 3 H9
Rosehill ..... 116 E3
Roundthorn ..... 109 H7
Royton ..... 43 J8

Rusholme ..... 99 G1
St George's ..... 86 F6
Sale ..... 96 G6
Salford ..... 86 B5
Salford Quays ..... 86 B5
Scholes ..... 15 J4
Scot Lane End ..... 33 H5
Southead ..... 60 C3
Sedgley Park ..... 71 M2
Seedley ..... 86 B1
Shakerley ..... 67 K2
Sharples ..... 22 A8
Sharston ..... 110 C7
Shaw ..... 43 K6
Shawclough ..... 27 M2
Shawfield ..... 27 J2
Shaw Heath ..... 13 G8
Shaw Side ..... 43 L7
Shevington ..... 30 D7
Shevington Moor ..... 30 D3
Shevington Vale ..... 30 C4
Sholver ..... 44 A8
Shore ..... 21 K6
Shuttleworth ..... 19 H5
Side of the Moor ..... 23 H4
Simister ..... 56 B4
Simmondley ..... 104 C5
Simm's Lane End ..... 62 D7
Sinderland Green ..... 107 G3
Skellorn Green ..... 129 H4
Slackcote ..... 44 F5
Slattocks ..... 41 M6
Smallbridge ..... 29 G1
Smallshaw ..... 75 L6
Smithy Bridge ..... 29 K1
Smithy Green ..... 120 D4
South Reddish ..... 100 B7
Spotland Bridge ..... 10 A3
Springfield ..... 47 H2
Springhead ..... 60 C7
Spring Hill ..... 60 A4
Spring View ..... 48 A7
Stake Hill ..... 42 B7
Stalybridge ..... 91 J3
Stand ..... 54 F4
Standish ..... 31 J3
Standish Lower Ground ..... 46 F1
Stanley Green ..... 120 A4
Stancyliffe ..... 57 L1
Starling ..... 38 D2
Stepping Hill ..... 113 G8
Stockport ..... 12 D2
Stoneclough ..... 53 L5
Stonefield ..... 10 D9
Stoneyfield ..... 28 E3
Strangeways ..... 6 C2
Stretford ..... 96 E3
Strines ..... 123 L3
Stubbins ..... 18 F4
Stubshaw Cross ..... 64 A7
Styal ..... 119 H8
Sudden ..... 27 M8
Summerseat ..... 24 E3
Summit ..... 40 C2
Summit ..... 21 M5
Sun Green ..... 77 H8
Sunny Bank ..... 39 K8
Swinton ..... 70 A4
Swinton Park ..... 70 E6
Syke ..... 20 D8
Tamer Lane End ..... 65 L4
Tame Water ..... 61 H3
Taunton ..... 75 H7
The Banks ..... 115 G8
The Hague ..... 103 M2
Thornham Fold ..... 42 D5
Thornsett ..... 125 G2
Thorns Green ..... 117 L7
Thurston Clough ..... 61 G7
Timperley ..... 108 D5
Tintwistle ..... 93 L5
Tonge Fold ..... 3 M3
Tonge Moor ..... 37 G2
Tontine ..... 46 A6
Top Lock ..... 48 D2
Top of Hebers ..... 41 H8
Top o' th' Meadows ..... 60 C4
Toppings ..... 22 E5
Torkington ..... 122 D2
Tottington ..... 24 B6
Town Green ..... 64 A8
Town Lane ..... 67 L8
Town of Lowton ..... 79 K7
Trafford Park ..... 85 K7
Trub ..... 41 M5
Tunshill ..... 30 A1
Tunstead ..... 61 M7
Turf Hill ..... 29 G8
Turn ..... 19 K3
Turton Bottoms ..... 17 H7
Twiss Green ..... 81 H7
Tyldesley ..... 67 L3
Unsworth ..... 55 K2
Uppermill ..... 61 L5
Urmston ..... 85 H8
Walkden ..... 53 G8
Wall Hill ..... 61 H3
Walmersley ..... 25 H5
Walshaw ..... 24 B8
Warburton Green ..... 117 L6
Wardle ..... 21 H6
Wardley ..... 69 M3
Wardsend ..... 129 L3
Warhill ..... 103 L1
Waterloo ..... 75 J7
Watersheddings ..... 60 A3
Water's Nook ..... 50 E4
Weaste ..... 86 B3
Well Green ..... 117 M1
Werneth ..... 8 B7
Werneth Low ..... 102 C7
West Didsbury ..... 98 B7
Westhoughton ..... 50 A3
Westleigh ..... 66 A5
Westwood Park ..... 69 K8
Whalley Range ..... 98 B2
Wheatley ..... 15 M1
Whitefield ..... 55 H5
White Gate ..... 74 C1
Whitley ..... 31 K8
Whitworth ..... 20 B5
Wigan ..... 14 D2
Willows ..... 35 M7
Wilmslow ..... 126 F6
Wilmslow Park ..... 127 G5
Windlehurst ..... 123 G3
Wingates ..... 50 A1
Winstanley ..... 62 F1
Winstanleys ..... 31 M5

| | | | | | |
|---|---|---|---|---|---|
| Winton | 84 F1 | Woodford | 128 B2 | Woodhouses | 107 L2 | Woodseats | 103 K6 | Worsley | 69 J5 |
| Withington | 98 F6 | Woodgate Hill | 26 A8 | Woodlands | 91 L5 | Woods End | 95 H1 | Worsley Hall | 46 F6 |
| Wolstenholme | 26 F1 | Woodhey | 24 D1 | Wood Lanes | 129 L4 | Woodsmoor | 121 K1 | Worsley Mesnes | 47 J8 |
| Woodend | 77 H2 | Woodhouse Park | 118 E3 | Woodley | 101 M7 | Woolfold | 24 D8 | Wythenshawe | 118 D1 |
| Woodend | 123 L4 | Woodhouses | 74 D6 | Wood Road | 24 F3 | Woolley Bridge | 93 G8 | Yew Tree | 91 H5 |

## USING THE STREET INDEX

Street names are listed alphabetically. Each street name is followed by its postal town or area locality, the Postcode District, the page number, and the reference to the square in which the name is found.

Standard index entries are shown as follows:

**Abberley Dr** *NEWH/MOS* M40 ....**74** A2

Street names and selected addresses not shown on the map due to scale restrictions are shown in the index with an asterisk:

**Abbeyfield Sq** *OP/CLY* M11* ... **88** E4

## GENERAL ABBREVIATIONS

| | | | | | | | | |
|---|---|---|---|---|---|---|---|---|
| ACC | ACCESS | CUTT | CUTTINGS | HOL | HOLLOW | NW | NORTH WEST | SKWY | SKYWAY |
| ALY | ALLEY | CV | COVE | HOSP | HOSPITAL | O/P | OVERPASS | SMT | SUMMIT |
| AP | APPROACH | CYN | CANYON | HRB | HARBOUR | OFF | OFFICE | SOC | SOCIETY |
| AR | ARCADE | DEPT | DEPARTMENT | HTH | HEATH | ORCH | ORCHARD | SP | SPUR |
| ASS | ASSOCIATION | DL | DALE | HTS | HEIGHTS | OV | OVAL | SPR | SPRING |
| AV | AVENUE | DM | DAM | HVN | HAVEN | PAL | PALACE | SQ | SQUARE |
| BCH | BEACH | DR | DRIVE | HWY | HIGHWAY | PAS | PASSAGE | ST | STREET |
| BLDS | BUILDINGS | DRO | DROVE | IMP | IMPERIAL | PAV | PAVILION | STN | STATION |
| BND | BEND | DRY | DRIVEWAY | IN | INLET | PDE | PARADE | STR | STREAM |
| BNK | BANK | DWGS | DWELLINGS | IND EST | INDUSTRIAL ESTATE | PH | PUBLIC HOUSE | STRD | STRAND |
| BR | BRIDGE | E | EAST | INF | INFIRMARY | PK | PARK | SW | SOUTH WEST |
| BRK | BROOK | EMB | EMBANKMENT | INFO | INFORMATION | PKWY | PARKWAY | TDG | TRADING |
| BTM | BOTTOM | EMBY | EMBASSY | INT | INTERCHANGE | PL | PLACE | TER | TERRACE |
| BUS | BUSINESS | ESP | ESPLANADE | IS | ISLAND | PLN | PLAIN | THWY | THROUGHWAY |
| BVD | BOULEVARD | EST | ESTATE | JCT | JUNCTION | PLNS | PLAINS | TNL | TUNNEL |
| BY | BYPASS | EX | EXCHANGE | JTY | JETTY | PLZ | PLAZA | TOLL | TOLLWAY |
| CATH | CATHEDRAL | EXPY | EXPRESSWAY | KG | KING | POL | POLICE STATION | TPK | TURNPIKE |
| CEM | CEMETERY | EXT | EXTENSION | KNL | KNOLL | PR | PRINCE | TR | TRACK |
| CEN | CENTRE | F/O | FLYOVER | L | LAKE | PREC | PRECINCT | TRL | TRAIL |
| CFT | CROFT | FC | FOOTBALL CLUB | LA | LANE | PREP | PREPARATORY | TWR | TOWER |
| CH | CHURCH | FK | FORK | LDG | LODGE | PRIM | PRIMARY | U/P | UNDERPASS |
| CHA | CHASE | FLD | FIELD | LGT | LIGHT | PROM | PROMENADE | UNI | UNIVERSITY |
| CHYD | CHURCHYARD | FLDS | FIELDS | LK | LOCK | PRS | PRINCESS | UPR | UPPER |
| CIR | CIRCLE | FLS | FALLS | LKS | LAKES | PRT | PORT | V | VALE |
| CIRC | CIRCUS | FM | FARM | LNDG | LANDING | PT | POINT | VA | VALLEY |
| CL | CLOSE | FT | FORT | LTL | LITTLE | PTH | PATH | VIAD | VIADUCT |
| CLFS | CLIFFS | FTS | FLATS | LWR | LOWER | PZ | PIAZZA | VIL | VILLA |
| CMP | CAMP | FWY | FREEWAY | MAG | MAGISTRATE | QD | QUADRANT | VIS | VISTA |
| CNR | CORNER | FY | FERRY | MAN | MANSIONS | QU | QUEEN | VLG | VILLAGE |
| CO | COUNTY | GA | GATE | MD | MEAD | QY | QUAY | VLS | VILLAS |
| COLL | COLLEGE | GAL | GALLERY | MDW | MEADOWS | R | RIVER | VW | VIEW |
| COM | COMMON | GDN | GARDEN | MEM | MEMORIAL | RBT | ROUNDABOUT | W | WEST |
| COMM | COMMISSION | GDNS | GARDENS | MI | MILL | RD | ROAD | WD | WOOD |
| CON | CONVENT | GLD | GLADE | MKT | MARKET | RDG | RIDGE | WHF | WHARF |
| COT | COTTAGE | GLN | GLEN | MKTS | MARKETS | REP | REPUBLIC | WK | WALK |
| COTS | COTTAGES | GN | GREEN | ML | MALL | RES | RESERVOIR | WKS | WALKS |
| CP | CAPE | GND | GROUND | MNR | MANOR | RFC | RUGBY FOOTBALL CLUB | WLS | WELLS |
| CPS | COPSE | GRA | GRANGE | MS | MEWS | RI | RISE | WY | WAY |
| CR | CREEK | GRG | GARAGE | MSN | MISSION | RP | RAMP | YD | YARD |
| CREM | CREMATORIUM | GT | GREAT | MT | MOUNT | RW | ROW | YHA | YOUTH HOSTEL |
| CRS | CRESCENT | GTWY | GATEWAY | MTN | MOUNTAIN | S | SOUTH | | |
| CSWY | CAUSEWAY | GV | GROVE | MTS | MOUNTAINS | SCH | SCHOOL | | |
| CT | COURT | HGR | HIGHER | MUS | MUSEUM | SE | SOUTH EAST | | |
| CTRL | CENTRAL | HL | HILL | MWY | MOTORWAY | SER | SERVICE AREA | | |
| CTS | COURTS | HLS | HILLS | N | NORTH | SH | SHORE | | |
| CTYD | COURTYARD | HO | HOUSE | NE | NORTH EAST | SHOP | SHOPPING | | |

## POSTCODE TOWNS AND AREA ABBREVIATIONS

| | | | | | | | | |
|---|---|---|---|---|---|---|---|---|
| ALT | Altrincham | CCHDY | Chorlton-cum-Hardy | LIT | Littleborough | PWCH | Prestwich | WALK | Walkden |
| ANC | Ancoats | DTN/ASHW | Denton/Audenshaw | LYMM | Lymm | RAD | Radcliffe | WARRN/WOL | Warrington north/ Woolston |
| AIMK | Ashton-in-Makerfield | DID/WITH | Didsbury/Withington | MCFLDN | Macclesfield north | RNFD/HAY | Rainford/Haydock | WGTN/LGST | West Gorton/ Longsight |
| AUL | Ashton-under-Lyne | DROY | Droylsden | MCFLDS | Macclesfield south | RAMS | Ramsbottom | | |
| AULW | Ashton-under-Lyne west | DUK | Dukinfield | MANAIR | Manchester Airport | RAW/HAS | Rawtenstall/Haslingden | WHTN | Westhoughton |
| ATH | Atherton | ECC | Eccles | MPL/ROM | Marple/Romiley | RDSH | Reddish | WHTF | Whitefield |
| BKLY | Blackley | EDGY/DAV | Edgeley/Davenport | MDTN | Middleton (Gtr. Man) | ROCH | Rochdale | WHIT | Whitworth |
| BOL | Bolton | EDGW/EG | Edgeworth/Egerton | MILN | Milnrow | ROY/SHW | Royton/Shaw | WGN | Wigan |
| BOLE | Bolton east | FAIL | Failsworth | MOSL | Mossley | RUSH/FAL | Rusholme/Fallowfield | WGNE/HIN | Wigan east/Hindley |
| BOLS/LL | Bolton south/Little Lever | FWTH | Farnworth | NM/HAY | New Mills/Hayfield | SALE | Sale | WGNNW/ST | Wigan northwest/ Standish |
| BRAM/HZG | Bramhall/Hazel Grove | GLSP | Glossop | NEWH/MOS | Newton Heath/ Moston | SLFD | Salford | | |
| BRO | Broughton | GOL/RIS/CUL | Golborne/ Risley/Culcheth | NEWLW | Newton-le-Willows | SALQ | Salford Quays | WGNS/IIMK | Wigan south/ Ince-in-Makerfield |
| BRUN/LGST | Brunswick/Longsight | | | NTHM/RTH | Northern Moor/Roundthorn | SKEL | Skelmersdale | | |
| BNG/LEV | Burnage/Levenshulme | GTN | Gorton | | | STLY | Stalybridge | WGNW/BIL/OR | Wigan west/ Billinge/Orrell |
| BURY | Bury | HALE/TIMP | Hale/Timperley | OFTN | Offerton | STKP | Stockport | | |
| CMANE | Central Manchester east | HTNM | Heaton Moor | OLDTF/WHR | Old Trafford/ Whalley Range | STRET | Stretford | WILM/AE | Wilmslow/ Alderley Edge |
| CMANW | Central Manchester west | HEY | Heywood | OLD | Oldham | SWIN | Swinton | | |
| CSLFD | Central Salford | HOR/BR | Horwich/Blackrod | OLDE | Oldham east | TOD | Todmorden | WYTH/NTH | Wythenshawe/ Northenden |
| CHAD | Chadderton | HULME | Hulme | OLDS | Oldham south | TOT/BURYW | Tottington/ Bury west | | |
| CHF/WBR | Chapel-en-le- Frith/ Whalley Bridge | HYDE | Hyde | OP/CLY | Openshaw/Clayton | TRPK | Trafford Park | | |
| CHD/CHDH | Cheadle (Gtr. Man)/ Cheadle Hulme | IRL | Irlam | ORD | Ordsall | TRPK | Trafford Park | | |
| CHH | Cheetham Hill | KNUT | Knutsford | PART | Partington | TYLD | Tyldesley | | |
| CHLY/EC | Chorley/Eccleston | LEIGH | Leigh | POY/DIS | Poynton/Disley | UPML | Uppermill | | |
| | | LHULT | Little Hulton | | | URM | Urmston | | |

## Index – Streets

### 1

| | |
|---|---|
| **3rd St** *WGNE/HIN* WN2 | **64** B5 |
| **4th St** *WGNE/HIN* WN2 | **64** C5 |

### A

| | |
|---|---|
| **Abberley Dr** *NEWH/MOS* M40 | **74** A2 |
| **Abberley Wy** *WGNS/IIMK* WN3 | **46** E8 |
| **Abberton Rd** *DID/WITH* M20 | **98** D6 |
| **Abbey Cl** *ALT* WA14 | **116** C3 |
| *BOLS/LL* BL3 | **51** L2 |
| *RAD* M26 | **38** B7 |
| *STRET* M32 | **96** C1 |
| **Abbey Ct** *POY/DIS* SK12 | **129** H1 |
| *RAD* M26 | **38** B8 |
| *WGNNW/ST* WN6 | **47** H2 |
| **Abbey Crs** *HEY* OL10 | **26** E8 |
| **Abbeycroft Cl** *TYLD* M29 | **67** M6 |
| **Abbey Dl** *WGNNW/ST* WN6 | **30** A5 |

| | |
|---|---|
| **Abbeydale** *WHIT* OL12 | **10** D2 |
| **Abbeydale Cl** *AUL* OL6 | **76** C6 |
| **Abbeydale Gdns** *WALK* M28 | **52** F8 |
| **Abbeydale Rd** *NEWH/MOS* M40 | **73** M4 |
| **Abbey Dr** *LIT* OL15 | **29** J1 |
| *SWIN* M27 | **70** B4 |
| *TOT/BURYW* BL8 | **38** D3 |
| *WGNW/BIL/OR* WN5 | **46** B6 |
| **Abbeyfields** *WGNNW/ST* WN6 | **47** J2 |
| **Abbeyfield Sq** *OP/CLY* M11* | **88** E4 |
| **Abbey Gdns** *HYDE* SK14 | **103** J1 |
| **Abbey Gv** *CHAD* OL9 | **58** D8 |
| *ECC* M30 | **85** H2 |
| *HYDE* SK14 | **103** J1 |
| *STKP* SK1 | **112** E4 |
| **Abbey Hey La** *GTN* M18 | **89** H6 |
| **Abbey Hills Rd** *OLDS* OL8 | **59** M8 |
| **Abbey La** *LEIGH* WN7 | **66** A3 |
| **Abbey Lawn** *OLDTF/WHR* M16 | **97** L1 |
| **Abbeylea Dr** *WHTN* BL5 | **50** D2 |
| **Abbey Rd** *CHD/CHDH* SK8 | **111** K7 |
| *DROY* M43 | **89** J1 |
| *FAIL* M35 | **74** E4 |
| *GOL/RIS/CUL* WA3 | **80** F4 |

| | |
|---|---|
| *MDTN* M24 | **41** J8 |
| *RNFD/HAY* WA11 | **78** B5 |
| *SALE* M33 | **96** D6 |
| *TYLD* M29 | **67** M5 |
| *UPML* OL3 | **45** H7 |
| **Abbey Sq** *LEIGH* WN7 | **66** A3 |
| **Abbey St** *LEIGH* WN7 | **66** C6 |
| **Abbeyville Wk** *HULME* M15 * | **87** H7 |
| **Abbeyway North** *RNFD/HAY* WA11 | **78** D5 |
| **Abbeyway South** *RNFD/HAY* WA11 | **78** D6 |
| **Abbeywood Av** *GTN* M18 * | **89** H8 |
| **Abbingdon Wy** *LEIGH* WN7 | **66** A3 |
| **Abbots Cft** *WHTN* BL5 | **50** C6 |
| **Abbotsbury Cl** *POY/DIS* SK12 | **121** M7 |
| **Abbots Cl** *SALE* M33 | **97** G7 |
| **Abbotsfield Cl** *URM* M41 * | **95** G1 |
| **Abbot's Fold Rd** *WALK* M28 | **68** E5 |
| **Abbotsford Cl** *GOL/RIS/CUL* WA3 | **80** A3 |
| **Abbotsford Dr** *MDTN* M24 | **41** G8 |
| **Abbotsford Gv** *ALT* WA14 | **108** B4 |
| **Abbotsford Rd** *BOL* BL1 | **35** K3 |
| *CCHDY* M21 | **97** L3 |

| | |
|---|---|
| *CHAD* OL9 * | **58** B4 |
| *OLD* OL1 | **59** L3 |
| **Abbotside Cl** *OLDTF/WHR* M16 | **98** A1 |
| **Abbotsleigh Dr** *BRAM/HZG* SK7 | **121** H2 |
| **Abbotts Gn** *TYLD* M29 | **67** K8 |
| **Abbott St** *BOLS/LL* BL3 | **2** C9 |
| *ROCH* OL11 | **41** L1 |
| *WGNE/HIN* WN2 | **48** F6 |
| **Abden St** *RAD* M26 | **54** D1 |
| **Abels La** *UPML* OL3 | **61** M4 |
| **Aber Av** *OFTN* SK2 | **112** F8 |
| **Abercarn Cl** *CHH* M8 | **72** D5 |
| **Abercorn Rd** *BOL* BL1 | **35** L1 |
| **Abercorn St** *OLDE* OL4 * | **60** A6 |
| **Abercrombie Ct** *SALE* M33 | **97** G7 |
| **Aberdeen Crs** *EDGY/DAV* SK3 | **12** E7 |
| **Aberdeen Gdns** *WHIT* OL12 | **20** D5 |
| **Aberdeen St** *BRUN/LGST* M13 | **87** L7 |
| **Aberford Rd** *NTHM/RTH* M23 | **109** K7 |
| **Abergele Gv** *EDGY/DAV* SK3 | **12** F6 |
| **Abergele Rd** *RUSH/FAL* M14 | **99** H4 |
| **Abergele St** *OFTN* SK2 | **112** C6 |
| **Aberley Fold** *LIT* OL15 | **21** K5 |

### 1 – Abs

| | |
|---|---|
| **Abernant Cl** *OP/CLY* M11 | **88** C3 |
| **Abernethy St** *HOR/BR* BL6 | **34** A2 |
| **Aber Rd** *CHD/CHDH* SK8 | **111** K6 |
| **Abersoch Av** *RUSH/FAL* M14 | **99** H4 |
| **Abingdon Av** *WHTF* M45 | **55** J3 |
| **Abingdon Cl** *CHAD* OL9 * | **58** E8 |
| *ROCH* OL11 | **28** B8 |
| *WHTF* M45 | **55** J3 |
| **Abingdon Rd** *BOLE* BL2 | **3** L2 |
| *BRAM/HZG* SK7 | **121** G2 |
| *RDSH* SK5 | **100** C5 |
| *URM* M41 | **96** B1 |
| **Abingdon St** *AUL* OL6 | **91** G2 |
| *CMANE* M1 | **7** G6 |
| **Abinger Rd** *AIMK* WN4 | **63** G8 |
| **Abington Dr** *WGNE/HIN* WN2 | **64** C3 |
| **Abington Rd** *SALE* M33 | **108** F1 |
| **Abney Gra** *MOSL* OL5 | **77** H4 |
| **Abney Rd** *HTNM* SK4 | **99** M7 |
| *MOSL* OL5 | **76** F4 |
| **Aboukir St** *MILN* OL16 | **11** H3 |
| **Abram Cl** *RUSH/FAL* M14 | **98** D3 |
| **Abram St** *SLFD* M6 | **71** J6 |
| **Absalom Dr** *CHH* M8 | **72** C5 |

Abson St OLD OL1 .............8 D1
Acacia Av CHD/CHDH SK8 ...120 C2
  DTN/ASHW M34 .............101 K1
  HALE/TIMP WA15 ...........117 H1
  SWIN M27 ..................70 B6
  WILM/AE SK9 ...............126 D7
Acacia Crs WGNNW/ST WN6 ...47 J1
Acacia Dr HALE/TIMP WA15 ..117 H1
  SLFD M6 ...................85 L1
Acacia Rd RDSH SK5 ........100 C4
Acacia St NEWLW M12 ........78 C8
The Acacias URM M41 ........96 B2
Academy Wk HULME M15 * ....87 H7
Ace MI CHAD OL9 * ..........58 C8
Acer Cl HYDE SK14 .........102 D2
  ROCH OL11 .................41 J7
Acer Gv BRO M7 .............72 A5
Acheson St GTN M18 .........89 G7
Ackers La PART M31 .........95 H6
Ackers St BRUN/LGST M13 ....87 L7
Acker St MILN OL16 * .......10 F3
Ackhurst Dr
  NTHM/RTH M23 ............109 K6
Ack La East BRAM/HZG SK7 ..120 E5
Ack La West CHD/CHDH SK8 ..120 D5
Ackroyd Av GTN M18 .........89 K6
Ackroyd St OP/CLY M11 ......89 H5
Ackworth Dr
  NTHM/RTH M23 ............109 K6
Ackworth Rd SWIN M27 .......70 B3
Acme Dr SWIN M27 ...........70 E4
Acomb St HULME M15 .........87 L7
  RUSH/FAL M14 ..............98 E1
Acorn Av CHD/CHDH SK8 .....111 H7
  HYDE SK14 ................102 B4
Acorn Cl BNG/LEV M19 .......99 J4
  LEIGH WN7 .................81 J1
  WHTF M45 ..................55 J6
Acorn Ct LEIGH WN7 .........81 L1
Acorn St OLDE OL4 ..........60 B6
Acorn Wy OLD OL1 ............9 H4
A Ct AIMK WN4 ..............78 E2
Acre Barn ROY/SHW OL2 ......43 H4
Acre Cl RAMS BL0 ...........18 C3
Acre Fld BOLE BL2 ..........23 G8
Acrefield SALE M33 ........108 D1
Acrefield Av HTNM SK4 ......99 K8
  URM M41 ...................96 C3
Acre La CHD/CHDH SK8 ......120 D6
  OLD OL1 ....................9 M1
Acresbrook STLY SK15 .......91 M5
Acres Ct WYTH/NTH M22 .....110 A8
Acresdale HOR/BR BL6 .......34 F6
Acresfield TYLD M29 ........67 M5
Acresfield Av DTN/ASHW M34 .89 L3
Acresfield Cl HOR/BR BL6 * .32 F1
  SWIN M27 ..................70 D6
Acresfield Rd
  HALE/TIMP WA15 ..........108 D4
  HYDE SK14 .................91 J7
  LHULT M38 .................52 E8
  MDTN M24 ..................57 M1
  SLFD M6 ...................71 G7
Acres Fold Av WYTH/NTH M22 110 B8
Acres La STLY SK15 .........91 L3
Acres Rd CCHDY M21 .........97 K4
  CHD/CHDH SK8 * ...........110 D7
Acres St TOT/BURYW BL8 .....24 C7
Acre St CHAD OL9 ...........74 E2
  DTN/ASHW M34 ............101 H1
  GLSP SK13 ................104 F5
  RAD M26 ...................54 B1
  WHIT OL12 .................20 B3
Acreswood Av WGNE/HIN WN2 ..49 K8
Acre Top Rd BKLY M9 ........56 E7
Acreville Gv GOL/RIS/CUL WA3 81 M5
Acton Av OP/CLY M11 .........9 M2
  WGN WN1 ...................15 G2
  WHIT OL12 .................15 G6
Acton St BOL BL1 ...........35 M2
  MILN OL16 .................11 G7
Adair St CMANE M1 ..........7 M6
  ROCH OL11 .................41 L7
Adam Cl CHD/CHDH SK8 ......111 H8
Adams Cl CCHDY M21 ........97 L6
Adams Cl POY/DIS SK12 .....129 J2
Adams Dr WGNS/IIMK WN3 ....47 J7
Adamson Gdns
  DID/WITH M20 ............110 C1
Adamson Rd ECC M30 ........84 F4
Adamson St AIMK WN4 ........78 D1
Adamson Wk RUSH/FAL M14 * ..98 E1
Adam St AUL OL6 ............90 F1
  BOLS/LL BL3 ...............2 F9
  OLDS OL8 ..................75 J2
Ada St BKLY M9 .............73 G3
  OLDE OL4 ...................9 M7
  RAMS BL0 ..................18 D7
  WHIT OL12 .................28 D2
Adbaston Rd STRET M32 ......85 K7
Adcroft St STKP SK1 ........13 L8
Addenbrook Rd CHH M8 .......72 B7
Adderley Rd GLSP SK13 .....104 C3
Addingham Cl BKLY M9 .......56 F8
Addington Cl WGNE/HIN WN2 ..49 G8
Addington Rd BOLS/LL BL3 ...51 J1
Addington St ANC M4 ........7 J2
Addison Av AUL OL6 .........91 G1
Addison Cl BRUN/LGST M13 ...87 M6
Addison Crs OLDTF/WHR M16 ..97 L1
Addison Dr MDTN M24 ........57 M2
Addison Rd HALE/TIMP WA15 .117 G2
  IRL M44 ...................83 M8
  PART M31 ..................95 G6
  STRET M32 .................96 E2
  URM M41 ...................96 A3
Adelaide Rd BRAM/HZG SK7 ..121 G6
  EDGY/DAV SK3 ..............12 D7
Adelaide St BOLS/LL BL3 ....36 A8
  CHH M8 ....................72 C7
  ECC M30 ...................85 G3
  HEY OL10 ..................41 G2
  MDTN M24 ..................57 K4
  RAMS BL0 ..................18 D8
  SWIN M27 ..................70 A5
Adelaide St East HEY OL10 ..41 H2
Adelphi Dr LHULT M38 .......52 E7
Adelphi Gv LHULT M38 .......52 E7
Adelphi St CSLFD M3 .........6 A3
  RAD M26 ...................38 C7
  WGNNW/ST WN6 ..............31 H3
Aden Cl WGTN/LGST M12 ......88 A4
Aden St OLDE OL4 ...........60 A7
Adisham Dr BOL BL1 .........36 C5
Adlington Cl HALE/TIMP WA15 109 G6
  POY/DIS SK12 .............129 K2
  TOT/BURYW BL8 .............38 D3
Adlington Dr STRET M32 .....86 C8
Adlington Pk MCFLDN SK10 ..129 G3
Adlington Rd WILM/AE SK9 ..127 J5

Adlington St BOLS/LL BL3 ...52 A1
  OLDE OL4 ..................60 A3
  WGTN/LGST M12 .............88 A4
Adrian Rd BOL BL1 ..........35 M2
Adrian St NEWH/MOS M40 .....73 K5
Adrian Ter MILN OL16 .......11 M6
Adscombe St OLDTF/WHR M16 ..87 H8
Adshall Rd CHD/CHDH SK8 ...111 K7
Adshead Cl WYTH/NTH M22 ...118 D1
Adstock Wk NEWH/MOS M40 .....7 L1
Adstone Cl ANC M4 ..........88 A3
Adswood Cl OLDE OL4 ........60 A3
Adswood La East OFTN SK2 ..112 C6
Adswood La West
  EDGY/DAV SK3 .............112 B6
Adswood Old Hall Rd
  CHD/CHDH SK8 .............112 A8
Adswood Rd CHD/CHDH SK8 ...111 M8
  EDGY/DAV SK3 .............112 A7
Adswood St NEWH/MOS M40 ....88 B2
Adswood Ter EDGY/DAV SK3 ..112 B6
Adwell Cl GOL/RIS/CUL WA3 ..80 D4
Aegean Dr BRO M7 ...........71 M7
Aegean Rd ALT WA14 ........107 M6
Affetside Dr TOT/BURYW BL8 .38 B2
Affleck Av RAD M26 .........53 K4
Afflick Cl OLD OL1 .........59 L4
Age Cft OLDS OL8 ...........75 M1
Agecroft Enterprise Pk
  SWIN M27 * ................71 H5
Agecroft Rd MPL/ROM SK6 ...113 K3
  SWIN M27 ..................71 H4
  WHTF M45 ..................55 G6
Agecroft Rd East
  HALE/TIMP WA15 ..........117 G1
Agecroft Rd West PWCH M25 ..71 K2
Agincourt St HEY OL10 * ....40 E2
Agnes Cl CHAD OL9 ..........58 F8
Agnes St BNG/LEV M19 .......99 K2
  BRO M7 ....................72 C5
  CHAD OL9 ...................8 B8
Agnew Pl SLFD M6 ...........71 H8
Agnew Rd GTN M18 ...........88 F7
Aigburth Gv RDSH SK5 ......100 B2
Ailsa Cl NEWH/MOS M40 ......73 G7
Aimson Rd East
  HALE/TIMP WA15 ..........108 F6
Aimson Rd West
  HALE/TIMP WA15 ..........108 F6
Ainley Rd WYTH/NTH M22 ....118 F1
Ainley Wd DUK SK16 .........91 G5
  UPML OL3 ..................45 H7
Ainsbrook Av BKLY M9 .......73 L1
  UPML OL3 ..................45 J8
Ainscoughs Ct LEIGH WN7 ...66 B8
Ainscow Av HOR/BR BL6 ......34 C4
Ainsdale Av ATH M46 ........50 F8
  BRO M7 ....................72 A3
  EDGW/EG BL7 ...............17 G1
  TOT/BURYW BL8 .............38 C2
Ainsdale Cl BRAM/HZG SK7 ..121 J5
  OLDS OL8 ..................59 G8
Ainsdale Crs ROY/SHW OL2 ...59 H2
Ainsdale Dr CHD/CHDH SK8 ..119 K3
  SALE M33 ................108 B2
  WHIT OL12 .................20 B5
Ainsdale Rd BOLS/LL BL3 ....52 B3
Ainsdale St WGTN/LGST M12 ..88 C6
Ainsford Rd DID/WITH M20 ..99 G7
Ainsley Gv WALK M28 ........69 G2
Ainslie Rd BOL BL1 .........35 K3
Ainsty Rd RUSH/FAL M14 .....87 K8
Ainsworth Av HOR/BR BL6 ....34 B3
Ainsworth Cl DTN/ASHW M34 100 E1
Ainsworth Ct BOLE BL2 ......2 A1
Ainsworth Hall Rd BOLE BL2 .37 L5
Ainsworth La BOLE BL2 ......3 L1
Ainsworth Rd BOLS/LL BL3 ...53 K1
  RAD M26 ...................38 C7
  TOT/BURYW BL8 .............38 D2
Ainsworth St BOL BL1 .......35 M2
  MILN OL16 .................11 G7
Aintree Av SALE M33 .......107 M1
Aintree Dr BRAM/HZG SK7 ...122 B2
Aintree Dr ROCH OL11 .......27 H4
Aintree Gv EDGY/DAV SK3 ...112 B7
Aintree Rd BOLS/LL BL3 .....53 K2
Aintree St OP/CLY M11 ......88 E3
Aintree Wk CHAD OL9 .........8 C4
Airedale Cl CHD/CHDH SK8 ..110 F6
Airedale Ct ALT WA14 ......108 B3
Aire Dr BOLE BL2 ...........22 F7
Airewoorth St WHTN BL5 ......50 B1
Air Hill Ter WHIT OL12 * ...27 M3
Airton Cl NEWH/MOS M40 .....87 M1
Airton Pl WGNS/IIMK WN3 ....63 L1
Aitken Cl RAMS BL0 .........18 E7
Aitken St BNG/LEV M19 * ....99 M3
Ajax Dr BURY BL9 ...........55 J1
Ajax St RAMS BL0 ...........18 E7
  ROCH OL11 .................41 L1
Aked Cl WGTN/LGST M12 ......88 A6
Akesmoor Dr OFTN SK2 ......112 E6
Alan Av FAIL M35 ...........74 C7
Alanbrooke Wk HULME M15 * ..87 H7
Alandale Av DTN/ASHW M34 ...90 B5
Alandale Rd EDGY/DAV SK3 ...12 C9
Alan Dr HALE/TIMP WA15 ....117 M1
  MPL/ROM SK6 .............114 B6
Alan Rd DID/WITH M20 .......98 F6
  HTNM SK4 .................111 L1
Alan St BOL BL1 ............36 A1
Alan Turing Wy
  NEWH/MOS M40 .............88 B1
Alasdair Cl OLDS OL8 .......58 C4
Alba Cl ECC M30 ............85 G3
Alban St BRO M7 ............72 A7
Albany Av OP/CLY M11 .......89 J3
Albany Cl LHULT M38 ........52 E7
Albany Dr BURY BL9 .........39 J3
Albany Rd URM M41 ..........95 H3
Albany St BRAM/HZG SK7 ....121 G8
  CCHDY M21 .................97 L3
  ECC M30 ...................84 C1
  WILM/AE SK9 ..............126 D7
Albany St MDTN M24 .........57 L5
  OLDE OL4 ..................60 A5
  ROCH OL11 .................11 H9
Alba Wy STRET M32 ..........85 K7
Albemarle Av DID/WITH M20 ..98 D6
Albemarle Rd CCHDY M21 .....97 K4
  SWIN M27 ..................70 B5
Albemarle St AUL OL6 .......90 F1
  RUSH/FAL M14 ..............87 K6
Albemarle Ter AUL OL6 * ....90 F1
Alberbury Av
  HALE/TIMP WA15 ..........109 G5
Albermare Rd SWIN M27 ......70 B5

Alberta St BOLS/LL BL3 .....35 M7
  HTNM SK4 ..................99 H2
  MPL/ROM SK6 .............123 G5
Alberta Gv WILM/AE SK9 ....126 C7
Alberdale Rd
  CHD/CHDH SK8 ............111 M8
Albert Av DUK SK16 .........90 F6
  GTN M18 ...................89 H8
  PWCH M25 ..................71 M3
  ROY/SHW OL2 ...............43 K7
  URM M41 ...................96 B2
  WALK M28 ..................53 C7
Albert Cl CHD/CHDH SK8 ....120 C2
  WHTF M45 ..................55 K4
Albert Colliery Est
  WGNE/HIN WN2 * ............71 K5
Albert Ct ALT WA14 ........108 A8
Albert Dr WHTF M45 .........55 C4
Albert Gdns
  NEWH/MOS M40 .............74 A7
Albert Gv FWTH BL4 .........53 C4
  WGTN/LGST M12 .............88 D8
Albert Hill St DID/WITH M20 * 110 E1
Alberton Cl WGNE/HIN WN2 ...32 F6
Albert Park Rd BRO M7 ......71 M7
Albert Pl ALT WA14 ........108 A7
  BRUN/LGST M13 .............99 J1
Albert Rd CHD/CHDH SK8 ....120 C2
  ECC M30 ...................85 J2
  FWTH BL4 ..................53 G4
  HALE/TIMP WA15 ...........117 G1
  HTNM SK4 ..................12 A1
  HYDE SK14 ................102 C2
  SALE M33 ..................96 F8
Albert Rd East
  HALE/TIMP WA15 ..........117 G1
Albert Rd West BOL BL1 .....35 K4
Albert Royds St MILN OL16 ..11 L1
Albert Sq ALT WA14 ........116 F1
  CMANW M2 ...................6 F5
  STLY SK15 .................91 J3
Albert St ALT WA14 .........78 E1
  BOLS/LL BL3 * .............53 L1
  BRAM/HZG SK7 .............121 H1
  BURY BL9 ...................5 J4
  CHAD OL9 ..................74 E1
  DROY M43 ..................89 L3
  DTN/ASHW M34 * ...........101 J1
  EDGY/DAV SK3 ..............12 F5
  FWTH BL4 ..................53 G4
  GLSP SK13 .................93 K7
  HEY OL10 ..................40 E2
  HYDE SK14 ................102 C1
  IRL M44 ...................94 B6
  LIT OL15 ..................21 L6
  MDTN M24 ..................57 M2
  MILN OL16 .................29 J7
  OLDE OL4 ..................60 A4
  OLDTF/WHR M16 .............88 C3
  PWCH M25 * ................55 M7
  RAMS BL0 ..................18 E6
  ROY/SHW OL2 ...............43 K5
  ROY/SHW OL2 ...............43 K5
  WGN WN1 ...................15 G2
  WGNW/BIL/OR WN5 ...........14 A6
  WHIT OL12 .................20 A4
Albert St West FAIL M35 ....74 A6
Albert Ter STKP SK1 ........13 J4
Albine Cl HTNM SK4 ........112 B1
Albion Cl HTNM SK4 ........112 B1
  ECC M30 ...................69 K8
  SLFD M6 ...................86 C2
Albion Dr DROY M43 .........89 K2
Albion Fold DROY M43 .......89 K2
Albion Gdns STLY SK15 ......91 L2
Albion Gardens Cl
  ROY/SHW OL2 ...............43 J8
Albion Gv ON SALE M33 .....96 D8
Albion Pk
  GOL/RIS/CUL WA3 * .........81 M6
Albion Pl BRAM/HZG SK7 * ..121 M1
  BRO M7 ....................71 M7
  ORD M5 ....................86 D2
  PWCH M25 ..................55 K8
  ROCH OL11 .................10 B6
  RUSH/FAL M14 ..............98 F3
Albion St AUL OL6 ..........90 F1
  BOLS/LL BL3 * .............51 L1
  CHAD OL9 ..................58 D6
  CMANE M1 ...................7 K8
  FAIL M35 ..................74 B5
  FWTH BL4 ..................53 K6
  LEIGH WN7 .................66 B4
  ORD M5 ....................86 E2
  WGNE/HIN WN2 ..............49 G8
Albion Wy ORD M5 ...........86 E3
Albury Dr BNG/LEV M19 .....111 G2
Albury Wy WGNE/HIN WN2 .....27 J2
Albyns Av CHH M8 ...........72 D5
Alcester Av EDGY/DAV SK3 ..111 J5
Alcester Cl MDTN M24 .......57 L6
  TOT/BURYW BL8 .............38 E1
Alcester Rd CHD/CHDH SK8 ..110 E8
  SALE M33 .................108 E2
Alcester St CHAD OL9 .......74 D1
Aldborough Cl
  DID/WITH M20 ..............98 E6
Aldbourne Cl
  NEWH/MOS M40 .............73 G7
Aldbury Ter BOL BL1 * ......36 A3
Aldcliffe GOL/RIS/CUL WA3 ..80 C5
Aldcroft St GTN M18 ........89 K6
Alden Cl WGN WN1 ...........31 L3
  WHTF M45 ..................55 K4
Alder Av AIMK WN4 ..........63 J7
  BURY BL9 ...................5 M3
  POY/DIS SK12 .............129 K1
  WGNW/BIL/OR WN5 ...........47 G6
Alderbank HOR/BR BL6 .......33 J1
  WHIT OL12 .................21 G5
Alderbank Cl FWTH BL4 .....52 E5
Aldercroft Av BOLE BL2 .....37 G3
  WYTH/NTH M22 .............118 E2

Alder Cl AUL OL6 ...........75 L5
  CHD/CHDH SK8 ............119 M4
  GLSP SK13 .................93 J8
  LEIGH WN7 .................81 J2
Alder Ct CHH M8 * ..........72 C3
Aldercroft Av BOLE BL2 .....37 G3
  WYTH/NTH M22 .............118 E2

Alderdale Dr DROY M43 ......89 G2
  HTNM SK4 ..................99 H2
  MPL/ROM SK6 .............123 G5
Alderdale Gv WILM/AE SK9 ..126 C7
Alderdale Rd
  CHD/CHDH SK8 ............111 M8
Alder Dr HALE/TIMP WA15 ...109 H8
  STLY SK15 .................91 M1
  SWIN M27 ..................69 M3
Alderfield Rd STRET M32 ....97 J3
Alderfold St ATH M46 .......67 G1
Alder Forest Av ECC M30 ....69 K8
Aldergate Gv AUL OL6 .......76 C7
Alderglen Rd CHH M8 ........72 C6
Alder Gv DTN/ASHW M34 .....101 K1
  EDGW/EG BL7 ...............22 F6
  EDGY/DAV SK3 ..............12 C6
  STRET M32 .................97 H2
Alder La OLDS OL8 ..........75 G2
  WGNE/HIN WN2 ..............49 L7
Alder Lee Cl WGNS/IIMK WN3 .63 L2
  GOL/RIS/CUL WA3 ...........80 A5
Alderley Cl BRAM/HZG SK7 ..122 B6
  POY/DIS SK12 .............129 K2
Alderley La LEIGH WN7 ......81 L2
Alderley Ldg WILM/AE SK9 ..126 E2
Alderley Rd MCFLDN SK10 ...131 J2
  RDSH SK5 .................100 C7
  SALE M33 .................109 H2
  URM M41 ...................95 K2
  WILM/AE SK9 ..............126 A7
Alderley St AUL OL6 ........76 A7
Alderley Wy EDGY/DAV SK3 ..112 B8
Alderman Foley Dr
  WHIT OL12 .................27 K2
Alderman Sq
  WGTN/LGST M12 .............88 B2
Aldermary Rd CCHDY M21 ....98 A7
Aldermaston Gv BKLY M9 .....56 E6
Alder Meadow Cl WHIT OL12 ..27 K3
Aldermere Crs URM M41 ......95 H2
Alderminster Av LHULT M38 ..52 D7
Aldermoor Cl OP/CLY M11 ....88 F4
Alderney Rd WGNS/IIMK WN3 ..63 K1
Alder Rd CHD/CHDH SK8 ....111 L7
  FAIL M35 ..................74 D6
  GOL/RIS/CUL WA3 ...........80 C4
  MDTN M24 ..................57 M2
  ROCH OL11 .................42 A2
Alders Av WYTH/NTH M22 ...109 M7
Alders Ct OLDS OL8 .........75 M4
Aldersgate NM/HAY SK22 ....124 D3
Aldersgate Rd
  CHD/CHDH SK8 ............120 E7
  OFTN SK2 .................112 E6
Aldersgreen Av
  MPL/ROM SK6 .............123 H5
Alders Green Rd
  WGNE/HIN WN2 ..............49 K7
Alderside Rd BKLY M9 .......73 G4
Aldersley Av BKLY M9 .......56 E8
Alderson St CHAD OL9 .......9 G4
  SLFD M6 ...................71 K8
Alders Rd POY/DIS SK12 ....123 J5
  WYTH/NTH M22 .............109 M7
The Alders WGNNW/ST WN6 ...31 G8
Alder St ATH M46 ...........67 G1
  BOLS/LL BL3 ...............52 C1
  ECC M30 ...................69 K8
  SLFD M6 ...................86 C2
Aldersyde St BOLS/LL BL3 ...52 A1
  WHTN BL5 ..................50 B6
Alderton Dr AIMK WN4 .......78 C1
  WHTN BL5 ..................50 B6
Alderue Av WYTH/NTH M22 ..110 A6
Alderwood Folde OLDE OL4 ...60 C8
Aldfield Rd NTHM/RTH M23 ..109 J3
Aldford Cl DID/WITH M20 ...110 F1
Aldford Gv BOLE BL2 ........37 L7
Aldford Pl WILM/AE SK9 ....130 C2
Aldford Wy WGNNW/ST WN6 ...31 H4
Aldham Av NEWH/MOS M40 .....73 M4
Aldon St AUL OL6 ...........75 M8
Aldred Cl CHH M8 ...........72 E6
Aldred St BOLS/LL BL3 ......51 L1
  ECC M30 ...................84 F3
  FAIL M35 ..................74 B5
  LEIGH WN7 .................66 B4
  ORD M5 ....................86 E2
  WGNE/HIN WN2 ..............49 G8
Aldridge Cl
  WGNS/IIMK WN3 .............63 L1
Aldsworth Dr BOLS/LL BL3 ...36 B8
  NEWH/MOS M40 .............73 H7
Aldwick Av DID/WITH M20 ...110 F1
Aldwinians Cl
  DTN/ASHW M34 .............90 B7
Aldworth Gv SALE M33 ......96 A8
Aldwych ROCH OL11 ..........42 C1
Aldwych Av RUSH/FAL M14 ...98 E1
Aldwyn Cl DTN/ASHW M34 .....90 B7
  RAD M26 ...................54 E3
Aldwyn Crs BRAM/HZG SK7 ..121 L2
Aldwyn Park Rd
  DTN/ASHW M34 .............89 M5
Alexander Av FAIL M35 ......74 D4
Alexander Briant Ct
  FWTH BL4 * ................52 F5
Alexander Dr BURY BL9 .....55 K3
  HALE/TIMP WA15 ..........108 K3
  MILN OL16 .................29 J6
Alexander Gdns BRO M7 .....72 A8
Alexander Rd BOLE BL2 .......3 M1
Alexander St ROCH OL11 .....41 L2
  SLFD M6 ...................86 B2
  TYLD M29 ..................67 K4
Alexandra Av HYDE SK14 ....101 M2
  RUSH/FAL M14 ..............98 C2
  WHTF M45 ..................55 K4
Alexandra Cl EDGY/DAV SK3 111 M6
Alexandra Ct URM M41 .......95 H3
Alexandra Crs OLD OL1 ......59 L4
  WGNW/BIL/OR WN5 ...........47 H5
Alexandra Dr BNG/LEV M19 ..99 J5
Alexandra Gv IRL M44 .......94 C4
Alexandra Ms OLDS OL8 * ....9 M9
Alexandra Rd
  AIMK WN4 ..................63 J6
  AUL OL6 ...................75 M8
  DTN/ASHW M34 .............90 D8
  ECC M30 ...................84 E4
  FWTH BL4 ..................53 K6
  HOR/BR BL6 ................34 B4
  HTNM SK4 ..................12 D1
  OLDTF/WHR M16 .............87 K8
  RAD M26 ...................53 K4
  SALE M33 .................109 G1
  WALK M28 ..................52 F7
Alexandra Rd South
  OLDTF/WHR M16 .............98 B1

Alexandra St AUL OL6 .......76 A8
  BOLS/LL BL3 * .............36 A8
  BRO M7 ....................87 C1
  FWTH BL4 ..................53 C5
  HEY OL10 ..................41 H4
  HYDE SK14 ................101 M3
  IRL M44 ...................94 B6
  LIT OL15 ..................21 L6
  RAMS BL0 ..................18 E7
  ROY/SHW OL2 ...............43 K5
  TYLD M29 ..................67 J3
  WALK M28 ..................69 G1
  WGN WN1 ...................47 L2
  WGNE/HIN WN2 ..............64 D7
  WGNS/IIMK WN3 .............15 J8
  WHIT OL12 .................20 B2
Alfreton Av DTN/ASHW M34 ..101 K4
Alfreton Rd OFTN SK2 ......113 G6
Alfriston Dr NTHM/RTH M23 ..109 K2
Alger Ms AUL OL6 ...........76 A8
Algernon Rd WALK M28 .......52 F8
Algernon St ECC M30 ........85 G1
  SWIN M27 ..................70 A4
  WGNE/HIN WN2 ..............49 C7
  WGNS/IIMK WN3 .............47 K8
Alger St AUL OL6 ...........76 A8
Algreave Rd EDGY/DAV SK3 ..111 K4
Alice Ingham Ct ROCH OL11 ..27 L3
Alice St BOLS/LL BL3 .......35 M7
  HYDE SK14 ................102 B5
  SALE M33 ..................97 C8
  SWIN M27 ..................70 E4
  WHIT OL12 .................28 D3
Alicia Dr WHIT OL12 ........28 B2
Alison Kelly Cl BKLY M9 ....73 H4
Alison St ROY/SHW OL2 ......43 K4
  RUSH/FAL M14 ..............98 C1
Alker Rd NEWH/MOS M40 * ....88 A1
Alker St WGNW/BIL/OR WN5 ...47 J6
Alkrington Cl BURY BL9 .....55 K2
Alkrington Gn MDTN M24 .....57 J6
Alkrington Hall Rd North
  MDTN M24 .................57 J5
Alkrington Hall Rd South
  MDTN M24 .................57 H6
Alkrington Park Rd MDTN M24 57 H5
Allama Iqbal Rd OLDE OL4 ...59 M7
Allandale ALT WA14 ........107 L8
Allandale Dr ROY/SHW OL2 ..42 F7
Allandale Rd BNG/LEV M19 ...99 J3
Allan Roberts Cl BKLY M9 ...73 G3
Allanson Rd WYTH/NTH M22 ..110 B3
Allan St TYLD M29 ..........67 J4
Alldis Cl WGTN/LGST M12 ....88 B7
Alldis St OFTN SK2 ........112 E7
  HYDE SK14 ................102 B5
  SALE M33 ..................97 C8
  SWIN M27 ..................70 E4
  WHIT OL12 .................28 E3
Allenby Gv WHTN BL5 ........50 B5
Allenby Rd IRL M44 .........94 A8
  SWIN M27 ..................69 M6
Allen Av GOL/RIS/CUL WA3 ...81 M8
  ROY/SHW OL2 ...............43 L5
Allen Cl ROY/SHW OL2 .......43 K6
Allendale Dr BURY BL9 ......55 K1
Allendale Gdns BOL BL1 .....36 B2
Allen Dale Wk CSLFD M3 ......6 A2
Allen Rd URM M41 ...........96 C3
Allen St BOLS/LL BL3 .......53 K1
  MILN OL16 .................11 H8
  OLDS OL8 ...................9 C7
  RAD M26 ...................54 C1
  TOT/BURYW BL8 .............4 A3
Allerby Wy GOL/RIS/CUL WA3 .80 B4
Allerdean Wk HTNM SK4 .....111 J4
Allerford St OLDTF/WHR M16 .87 H8
Allerton Cl WHTN BL5 .......50 D3
Allerton Wk BRUN/LGST M13 * 87 L6
Allesley Cl WHTN BL5 .......50 D3
Allesley Dr BRO M7 .........72 C2
Allgreave Cl SALE M33 .....109 H3
Alliance St WGN WN1 ........15 H3
Alligin Cl CHAD OL9 ........58 D4
Allingham St BRUN/LGST M13 88 B3
Allington ROCH OL11 ........10 D7
Allington Dr ECC M30 .......70 B8
Alliott Wk HULME M15 * .....87 H7
Allison Gv ECC M30 .........84 E3
Allison St CHH M8 ..........72 E7
Allotment Rd IRL M44 .......94 A6
All Saint's Cl ROY/SHW OL2 .43 C7
All Saints Ct STRET M32 * ..96 E2
All Saints Gv WGNE/HIN WN2 49 H7
All Saints Pl TOT/BURYW BL8 .4 A2
All Saints' Rd HTNM SK4 ...112 A1
All Saints' St BOL BL1 .....36 A1
  NEWH/MOS M40 .............73 M7
All Saints Ter WHIT OL12 ...28 E2
Allscott Wy AIMK WN4 .......78 F1
Allsopp St BOLS/LL BL3 * ....2 E7
Alma La WILM/AE SK9 .......126 C6
Alma Rd BNG/LEV M19 .......99 K4
  BRAM/HZG SK7 ............122 C4
  HTNM SK4 ..................99 L7
  SALE M33 .................108 B2
Alma St ATH M46 ...........66 F1
  BOLS/LL BL3 ...............53 L1
  ECC M30 ...................85 G3
  FWTH BL4 * ................53 L7
  LEIGH WN7 .................66 C4
  RAD M26 ...................38 C2
  STLY SK15 .................91 M5
  TYLD M29 ..................67 J4
  WHIT OL12 .................20 C2
Alminstone Cl
  NEWH/MOS M40 .............74 A8

Almond Av BURY BL9 5 M3
Almond Brook Rd
WGNNW/ST WN6 30 F3
Almond Cl EDGY/DAV SK3 12 C6
FAIL M35 74 C6
LIT OL15 21 K6
SLFD M6 86 D2
Almond Crs WGNNW/ST WN6 31 J5
Almond Dr SALE M33 96 C6
Almond Gv BOL BL1 * 36 C1
WGNW/BIL/OR WN5 47 H6
Almond Rd OLDE OL4 60 A3
Almond St BOL BL1 22 C8
FWTH BL4 52 F4
NEWH/MOS M40 * 72 E8
Almond Tree Rd
CHD/CHDH SK8 120 C3
Almond Wy HYDE SK14 102 E2
Alms Hill Rd CHH M8 72 D5
Alness Rd OLDTF/WHR M16 98 B2
Alnwick Cl WGNE/HIN WN2 33 G7
Alnwick Dr BURY BL9 39 K7
Alnwick Rd BKLY M9 57 G7
Alpha Ct DTN/ASHW M34 100 F1
Alphagate Dr DTN/ASHW M34 100 F1
Alpha Pl HULME M15 * 6 D8
Alpha Rd STRET M32 96 F2
Alpha St OP/CLY M11 89 H5
SLFD M6 86 C1
Alpha St West SLFD M6 86 B1
Alphin Cl MOSL OL5 77 H1
UPML OL3 61 L7
Alphingate Cl STLY SK15 77 G8
Alphin Sq MOSL OL5 77 G3
Alphonsus St OLDTF/WHR M16 86 F8
Alpine Dr LEIGH WN7 65 M4
MILN OL16 29 K5
ROY/SHW OL2 58 F1
WHIT OL12 21 G6
Alpine Rd STKP SK1 13 M4
Alpine St OP/CLY M11 88 E2
Alport Av OLDTF/WHR M16 * 97 M2
Alresford Rd MDTN M24 57 J7
SLFD M6 71 G7
Alsager Cl CCHDY M21 97 L6
Alsfeld Wy NM/HAY SK22 124 C4
Alsop Av BRO M7 * 71 L5
Alstead Av HALE/TIMP WA15 117 J1
Alston Av ROY/SHW OL2 43 L5
SALE M33 108 C1
STRET M32 96 E1
Alston Cl BRAM/HZG SK7 * 121 J3
Alstone Dr ALT WA14 107 K6
Alstone Rd HTNM SK4 99 M6
Alston Gdns BNG/LEV M19 99 J7
Alston Lea ATH M46 51 H8
Alston Rd GTN M18 89 H7
WGNE/HIN WN2 48 C2
Alston St BOLS/LL BL3 * 52 B1
TOT/BURYW BL8 * 24 F8
Altair Av WYTH/NTH M22 118 F4
Altair Pl BRO M7 71 M8
Altcar Gv RDSH SK5 100 B2
Altcar Wk WYTH/NTH M22 118 E2
Alt Cl LEIGH WN7 66 A7
Alt Fold Dr OLDS OL8 75 M1
Alt Gv AUL OL6 75 M1
Altham Cl BURY BL9 39 G5
Alt Hill La AUL OL6 75 M2
Alt La OLDS OL8 75 M4
Alton Av URM M41 95 G2
Alton Cl AIMK WN4 63 K8
AUL OL6 75 M5
BURY BL9 39 K7
Alton Rd WILM/AE SK9 126 D4
Alton Sq OP/CLY M11 89 H5
Alton St OLDS OL8 75 J1
Altrincham Rd
NTHM/RTH M23 109 G5
WILM/AE SK9 119 G8
WYTH/NTH M22 109 M5
Altrincham St CMANE M1 7 J7
Alum Crs BURY BL9 55 K1
Alvanley Cl SALE M33 108 E3
WGNW/BIL/OR WN5 46 F3
Alvanley Crs EDGY/DAV SK3 111 M6
Alvan Sq OP/CLY M11 * 89 H5
Alva Rd OLDE OL4 60 A2
Alvaston Av HTNM SK4 12 A1
Alvaston Rd GTN M18 89 H8
Alveley Av DID/WITH M20 98 F7
Alverstone Rd DID/WITH M20 98 F6
Alveston Dr WILM/AE SK9 127 G4
Alvington Gv BRAM/HZG SK7 121 J3
Alwin Rd ROY/SHW OL2 43 K4
Alwinton Av HTNM SK4 111 H1
Alworth Rd BKLY M9 57 G7
Alwyn Cl LEIGH WN7 81 J3
Alwyn Dr BRUN/LGST M13 88 B8
Alwyn St WGN WN1 15 J1
Alwyn Ter WGN WN1 15 J1
Amar St WGNE/HIN WN2 * 48 C5
Amathyst Cl WGNE/HIN WN2 48 D2
Ambassador Pl
HALE/TIMP WA15 * 108 B7
Amber Gdns DUK SK16 * 90 E4
WGNE/HIN WN2 49 H8
Ambergate ATH M46 67 G2
Amber Gv WHTN BL5 50 C4
Amberhill Wy WALK M28 68 D7
Amberley Cl BOLS/LL BL3 35 J7
WGNE/HIN WN2 48 C2
Amberley Dr HALE/TIMP WA15 117 K4
IRL M44 94 D3
NTHM/RTH M23 109 K8
Amberley Rd SALE M33 96 B7
Amberley Wk CHAD OL9 8 C4
Amberswood Cl
WGNE/HIN WN2 48 E5
Amberwood CHAD OL9 58 B4
Amberwood Dr
NTHM/RTH M23 109 G6
Amblecote Dr East LHULT M38 52 D6
Amblecote Dr West LHULT M38 52 D6
Ambleside STLY SK15 91 K1
WGNE/HIN WN2 48 E4
WGNW/BIL/OR WN5 46 F5
Ambleside Av AULW OL7 75 J8
HALE/TIMP WA15 108 F7
Ambleside Cl BOLE BL2 23 J8
MDTN M24 57 H3
Ambleside Rd RDSH SK5 100 C6
URM M41 95 H3
Ambrose Av LEIGH WN7 66 B3
Ambrose Ct WYTH/NTH M22 * 110 A3
Ambrose Dr DID/WITH M20 98 B8
Ambrose St ROCH OL11 10 E8
WGTN/LGST M12 88 D5
Ambush St OP/CLY M11 89 J5
Amelia St DTN/ASHW M34 90 C8
HYDE SK14 102 B2
Amersham Cl URM M41 84 E7
Amersham Pl BNG/LEV M19 99 K6
Amersham St ORD M5 86 C3
Amesbury Dr WGNS/IIMK WN3 62 F2
Amesbury Gv RDSH SK5 100 C7
Amesbury Rd BKLY M9 57 H8
Amherst Rd DID/WITH M20 98 F5
Amis Gv GOL/RIS/CUL WA3 80 B4
Amlwch Av OFTN SK2 113 G6
Ammons Wy UPML OL3 45 J7
Ammon Wrigley Cl OLD OL1 9 J4
Amory St WGTN/LGST M12 7 L7
Amos Av NEWH/MOS M40 73 M8
Amos St BKLY M9 73 J5
SLFD M6 86 B2
Ampney Cl ECC M30 84 E1
Amwell St CHH M8 72 E5
Amy St MDTN M24 57 L3
WHIT OL12 27 L3
Anaconda Dr CSLFD M3 6 C1
Anchorage Quay SALQ M50 86 D4
Anchorage Rd URM M41 96 D3
Anchor Cl BNG/LEV M19 99 M3
Anchor Ct CHH M8 * 72 C3
Anchor La FWTH BL4 52 C5
Anchorside Cl CCHDY M21 97 L5
Anchor St OLD OL1 9 J3
Ancoats Gv ANC M4 88 A3
Ancoats Gv North ANC M4 88 A3
Ancoats St OLDE OL4 60 B6
Ancroft Dr WGNE/HIN WN2 65 H1
Ancroft St HULME M15 87 H6
Anderby Wk WHTN BL5 50 B2
Anderton Cl TOT/BURYW BL8 38 C3
Anderton Gv AUL OL6 76 B7
Anderton La HOR/BR BL6 33 H1
Anderton St WGNE/HIN WN2 48 C5
Anderton Wy WGNE/HIN WN2 48 C5
WILM/AE SK9 127 H1
Andoc Av ECC M30 85 J3
Andover Av MDTN M24 57 L7
Andover Crs WGNS/IIMK WN3 62 F2
Andover Rd RNFD/HAY WA11 78 B4
Andover St ECC M30 84 F3
Andre St OP/CLY M11 * 88 F3
Andrew Av
WGNW/BIL/OR WN5 62 C7
Andrew Cl RAD M26 54 F3
TOT/BURYW BL8 24 C3
Andrew La BOL BL1 22 C6
MPL/ROM SK6 123 G3
Andrew Rd BKLY M9 73 G3
Andrews Av URM M41 95 H1
Andrew St AUL OL6 * 76 A7
BURY BL9 5 H5
CHAD OL9 58 D4
DROY M43 74 F8
FAIL M35 74 B4
HTNM SK4 13 G3
HYDE SK14 102 C1
MDTN M24 57 M5
MOSL OL5 76 F4
MPL/ROM SK6 114 D2
Anerley Rd DID/WITH M20 98 E8
Anfield Cl BURY BL9 55 L1
Anfield Rd BOLS/LL BL3 52 B2
CHD/CHDH SK8 120 B2
NEWH/MOS M40 74 A3
SALE M33 96 F7
Angela Av ROY/SHW OL2 59 H2
Angela St HULME M15 6 B9
Angel Cl DUK SK16 90 E5
Angelko Ri OLD OL1 60 A1
Angelo St BOL BL1 36 A1
Angel St ANC M4 7 H1
BRAM/HZG SK7 121 M1
DTN/ASHW M34 90 D8
Anglers Rest IRL M44 94 B7
Anglesea Av OFTN SK2 112 C6
Anglesey Cl AULW OL7 75 J6
Anglesey Dr POY/DIS SK12 122 A6
Anglesey Gv CHD/CHDH SK8 111 J6
Anglesey Rd AULW OL7 75 J6
Anglesey Water
POY/DIS SK12 122 A6
Angleside Av BNG/LEV M19 99 H8
Angle St BOLE BL2 3 K1
Anglia Gv BOLS/LL BL3 35 M8
Angora Dr CSLFD M3 6 A1
Angouleme Wy BURY BL9 4 E4
Angus Av HEY OL10 40 D3
LEIGH WN7 65 M6
Anita St ANC M4 7 K2
Anjou Bvd WGNW/BIL/OR WN5 47 H4
Annable Rd DROY M43 89 L3
GTN M18 89 H6
IRL M44 94 C4
MPL/ROM SK6 113 G1
Annald Sq DROY M43 89 K4
Annan Gv AIMK WN4 64 B7
Annan St DTN/ASHW M34 * 90 C8
Anne Cl AULW OL7 75 K6
Annecy Cl TOT/BURYW BL8 24 E8
Anne Line Cl ROCH OL11 * 11 G9
Anne Nuttall Rd HULME M15 6 B9
Annersley Av ROY/SHW OL2 43 K6
Annesley Crs WGNS/IIMK WN3 63 J1
Annesley Rd NEWH/MOS M40 74 B3
Anne St DUK SK16 91 G4
Annette Av NEWLW WA12 78 D7
Annie St ORD M5 86 B2
RAMS BL0 18 D8
Annis Cl WILM/AE SK9 130 E2
Annisdale Cl ECC M30 84 E2
Annisfield Av UPML OL3 61 M7
Annis Rd BOLS/LL BL3 35 L8
WILM/AE SK9 130 E2
Annis St BKLY M9 73 H5
Ann La TYLD M29 67 M7
Ann Sq OLDE OL4 60 A4
Ann St AULW OL7 90 C4
DTN/ASHW M34 101 H1
FWTH BL4 53 H5
HEY OL10 41 G1
HYDE SK14 101 M1
LEIGH WN7 66 B4
RDSH SK5 100 B8
ROCH OL11 10 E7
Anscombe Cl NEWH/MOS M40 88 A1
Ansdell Av CCHDY M21 97 L5
Ansdell Dr DROY M43 89 H2
Ansdell Rd MILN OL16 28 E8
RDSH SK5 100 D3
WGNW/BIL/OR WN5 47 G7
Ansdell St CHH M8 72 D5
Ansell Cl GTN M18 89 G6
Anselms Ct OLDS OL8 58 F8
Ansford Av WGNE/HIN WN2 64 E4
Ansleigh Av CHH M8 72 D3
Ansley Gv HTNM SK4 12 A1
Anslow Cl NEWH/MOS M40 73 G7
Anson Av SWIN M27 70 B6
Anson Cl BRAM/HZG SK7 121 H7
Anson Pl WGNW/BIL/OR WN5 46 F4
Anson Rd DTN/ASHW M34 100 D2
POY/DIS SK12 129 M1
RUSH/FAL M14 88 A8
SWIN M27 70 B6
WILM/AE SK9 127 J3
Anson St BOL BL1 36 C1
ECC M30 84 E1
WGNW/BIL/OR WN5 47 J5
Answell Av CHH M8 72 D2
Antares Av BRO M7 87 G1
Anthony Cl WGTN/LGST M12 88 B5
Anthony St MOSL OL5 76 E3
Anthorn Rd WGNS/IIMK WN3 63 H1
Antilles Cl WGTN/LGST M12 88 D8
Antler Ct AIMK WN4 63 L6
Antrim Cl BNG/LEV M19 111 G2
WGNS/IIMK WN3 62 F2
Anvil Cl WGNW/BIL/OR WN5 46 A7
Anvil Wy OLD OL1 9 H4
Apethorn La HYDE SK14 101 M4
Apfel La CHAD OL9 8 A4
Apollo Av BURY BL9 55 J1
Apperley Gra ECC M30 70 B8
Appian Wy BRO M7 72 B7
Appleby Av HALE/TIMP WA15 108 F7
HYDE SK14 90 F7
Appleby Cl EDGY/DAV SK3 112 A7
TOT/BURYW BL8 38 C2
Appleby Gdns BOLE BL2 * 3 H1
Appleby Rd CHD/CHDH SK8 110 E8
Apple Cl OLDS OL8 75 M1
Apple Dell Av
GOL/RIS/CUL WA3 79 M3
Appledore Dr BOLE BL2 37 J2
NTHM/RTH M23 109 G5
Appledore Wk CHAD OL9 8 A7
Appleford Av
NTHM/RTH M23 109 K8
Appleford Dr CHH M8 72 E6
Apple Hey WGNNW/ST WN6 30 A4
Apple La WGNNW/ST WN6 30 A4
Apple St HYDE SK14 102 F5
Applethwaite
WGNE/HIN WN2 48 E4
Appleton Dr GLSP SK13 105 J4
Appleton Gv SALE M33 108 B2
Appleton La WHTN BL5 50 C3
Appleton Rd
HALE/TIMP WA15 117 G3
HTNM SK4 100 A6
Appleton St
WGNS/IIMK WN3 14 E4
Apple Tree Ct ORD M5 86 D2
Apple Tree Rd NM/HAY SK22 124 E3
Apple Wy MDTN M24 57 L6
Applewood CHAD OL9 58 A5
Appleyard Cl SWIN M27 71 G4
Appley La North
WGNNW/ST WN6 30 A4
Apprentice La WILM/AE SK9 126 D1
April Cl OLDS OL8 59 M8
Apsley Cl ALT WA14 116 D3
Apsley Gv ALT WA14 116 D3
WGTN/LGST M12 87 M6
Apsley Rd DTN/ASHW M34 90 C8
Apsley St STKP SK1 13 K4
Aquarius La SLFD M6 * 71 M8
Aquarius St HULME M15 87 K7
Aqueduct Rd BOLS/LL BL3 3 M9
Aragon Dr HEY OL10 40 F2
Aragon Wy MPL/ROM SK6 114 B6
Arbor Av BNG/LEV M19 99 K5
Arbor Dr BNG/LEV M19 99 J5
Arbor Gv DROY M43 89 J1
LHULT M38 52 B8
Arbory Av NEWH/MOS M40 73 L4
Arbory Cl LEIGH WN7 66 F7
Arbour Cl BURY BL9 25 H6
SLFD M6 86 C1
Arbour La WGNNW/ST WN6 30 E3
Arbour Rd OLDE OL4 60 B8
Arbroath St DROY M43 89 H3
Arbury Av EDGY/DAV SK3 111 J5
ROCH OL11 10 C8
The Arcades AUL OL6 * 90 E1
Arcade St WGN WN1 15 G4
Arcadia Av SALE M33 108 D3
Archer Av BOLE BL2 3 L2
Archer Gv BOLE BL2 3 M2
Archer Pk MDTN M24 57 H4
Archer Pl STRET M32 96 C2
Archer St LEIGH WN7 81 L2
MOSL OL5 76 F2
OFTN SK2 112 F7
OP/CLY M11 88 D2
WALK M28 68 B6
Archie St ORD M5 86 D5
Arch St BOL BL1 2 A2
Archway HULME M15 87 J7
Arclid Cl WILM/AE SK9 127 J2
Arcon Cl MILN OL16 29 H6
Arcon Dr OLDTF/WHR M16 98 B1
Arcon Pl ALT WA14 107 K6
Ardale Av NEWH/MOS M40 73 M2
Ardcombe Av BKLY M9 56 F7
Ardeen Wk BRUN/LGST M13 * 87 M6
Arden Av MDTN M24 57 L7
Arden Cl AUL OL6 76 C6
BURY BL9 4 D8
GLSP SK13 104 D5
Arden Ct BRAM/HZG SK7 120 F3
Ardenfield DTN/ASHW M34 101 K5
Ardenfield Dr
WYTH/NTH M22 119 H1
Arden Gv NEWH/MOS M40 73 M3
Arden Lodge Rd
NTHM/RTH M23 109 H5
Arden Rd MPL/ROM SK6 101 H5
Ardens Cl SWIN M27 70 A2
Arden St CHAD OL9 74 D1
NM/HAY SK22 124 E5
Ardent Wy PWCH M25 71 L3
Arderne Pl WILM/AE SK9 130 D3
Arderne Rd
HALE/TIMP WA15 108 D4
Ardern Gv STKP SK1 13 K7
Ardern Rd CHH M8 72 C3
Ardwick Gn North
WGTN/LGST M12 7 M9
Ardwick Gn South
BRUN/LGST M13 7 L8
Ardwick Ter WGTN/LGST M12 88 A6
Arena Ap HOR/BR BL6 33 M5
Argo St BOLS/LL BL3 36 A8
Argosy Dr ECC M30 84 C5
MANAIR M90 118 B5
Argus St OLDS OL8 74 F2
Argyle Av RUSH/FAL M14 88 B8
WALK M28 52 F7
WHTF M45 55 K4
Argyle Crs HEY OL10 40 E3
Argyle St ATH M46 66 F2
BRAM/HZG SK7 121 M2
BURY BL9 25 J8
DROY M43 89 K3
GTN M18 89 G7
HEY OL10 40 C3
MILN OL16 28 D8
MOSL OL5 76 F3
OLD OL1 59 L4
SWIN M27 70 B5
WGNE/HIN WN2 49 H7
WGNW/BIL/OR WN5 47 J6
Argyll Av STRET M32 96 E2
Argyll Cl AIMK WN4 62 F8
FAIL M35 74 E5
Argyll Park Rd FAIL M35 74 E5
Argyll Rd CHAD OL9 74 C1
CHD/CHDH SK8 111 J7
Argyll St AUL OL6 91 H1
Arkendale Cl FAIL M35 * 74 F5
Arkholme WALK M28 68 D4
Arkle Av WILM/AE SK9 120 A8
Arkle Dr CHAD OL9 58 C4
Arkley Wk BRUN/LGST M13 87 L6
Ark St BNG/LEV M19 99 K2
Arkwright Cl BOL BL1 35 M3
Arkwright Dr MPL/ROM SK6 114 D6
Arkwright Rd MPL/ROM SK6 114 D6
Arkwright St CHAD OL9 8 C6
HOR/BR BL6 33 M2
Arlen Ct BOLE BL2 3 J8
Arlen Rd BOLE BL2 3 J8
Arlen Wy HEY OL10 * 40 E2
Arley Av BURY BL9 25 H7
DID/WITH M20 98 C7
Arley Cl ALT WA14 108 A4
DUK SK16 91 G6
WGNE/HIN WN2 48 E2
Arley Dr ROY/SHW OL2 43 M4
SALE M33 108 D2
Arley Gv EDGY/DAV SK3 112 A8
Arley La WGN WN1 32 A3
Arley Mere Cl CHD/CHDH SK8 120 B1
Arley Moss Wk
BRUN/LGST M13 * 7 K9
Arley St RAD M26 54 E3
WGNS/IIMK WN3 48 B8
Arley Wy ATH M46 67 H2
Arlies Cl STLY SK15 76 D8
Arlies La STLY SK15 76 E7
Arlies St AUL OL6 76 A8
Arlington Av DTN/ASHW M34 101 K2
PWCH M25 71 L2
SWIN M27 70 A6
Arlington Cl BURY BL9 24 F2
ROY/SHW OL2 59 H2
Arlington Crs WILM/AE SK9 126 C7
Arlington Dr LEIGH WN7 80 F4
OFTN SK2 121 J1
POY/DIS SK12 129 H1
Arlington Rd CHD/CHDH SK8 110 F8
STRET M32 96 E3
Arlington St AUL OL6 90 F1
BOLS/LL BL3 52 C1
CHH M8 72 C6
CSLFD M3 6 B1
Arlington Wy WILM/AE SK9 126 C7
Arliss Av BNG/LEV M19 99 K4
Armadale Av BKLY M9 57 K8
Armadale Cl EDGY/DAV SK3 112 B8
Armadale Rd BOLS/LL BL3 35 H8
DUK SK16 90 F4
Armdale Ri OLDE OL4 60 B3
Armentieres STLY SK15 91 K3
Armitage Av LHULT M38 52 C8
Armitage Cl HYDE SK14 102 B4
MDTN M24 57 G5
OLDS OL8 74 F1
Armitage Gv LHULT M38 52 C8
Armitage Rd ALT WA14 116 F1
Armitage St ECC M30 84 F3
Armit Rd UPML OL3 61 H8
Armitstead St WGNE/HIN WN2 49 G8
Armour Pl BKLY M9 72 F2
Armoury Bank AIMK WN4 78 E1
Armoury St EDGY/DAV SK3 13 H7
Arm Rd LIT OL15 21 J7
Armstrong Hurst Cl WHIT OL12 28 E2
Armstrong St HOR/BR BL6 33 M2
WGNE/HIN WN2 * 48 D1
Arncliffe Cl WGNE/HIN WN2 48 F8
Arncliffe Dr NTHM/RTH M23 118 C1
Arncliffe Ri OLDE OL4 44 D8
Arncot Rd BOL BL1 22 C7
Arncott Cl ROY/SHW OL2 43 K8
Arne Cl OFTN SK2 113 K7
Arnesby Av SALE M33 97 H6
Arnesby Gv BOLE BL2 3 K2
Arne St CHAD OL9 * 58 D7
Arnfield Dr WALK M28 68 E6
Arnfield La GLSP SK13 93 J4
Arnfield Rd DID/WITH M20 98 F6
EDGY/DAV SK3 112 A7
Arnold Av HEY OL10 41 H5
HYDE SK14 102 C5
Arnold Cl DUK SK16 91 H5
Arnold Dr DROY M43 89 K3
MDTN M24 57 M1
Arnold Rd EDGW/EG BL7 22 C4
HYDE SK14 102 C5
OLDTF/WHR M16 98 B3
Arnold St BOL BL1 36 A2
EDGY/DAV SK3 13 G8
OLD OL1 9 M3
Arnott Crs HULME M15 87 J7
Arnside Av BRAM/HZG SK7 121 L2
CHAD OL9 58 D7
HTNM SK4 100 A6
WGNE/HIN WN2 48 D5
Arnside Cl CHD/CHDH SK8 110 E8
MPL/ROM SK6 123 G4
ROY/SHW OL2 44 A5
Arnside Dr HYDE SK14 90 F8
ROCH OL11 27 H7
SLFD M6 85 L1
Arnside Gv BOLE BL2 37 H4
SALE M33 96 E7
Arnside Rd WGNE/HIN WN2 49 K7
WGNW/BIL/OR WN5 46 E5
Arnside St RUSH/FAL M14 98 E2
Arran Av OLDS OL8 75 J1
SALE M33 108 F1
STRET M32 96 D2
Arran Cl BOLS/LL BL3 35 H7
Arrandale Ct URM M41 * 96 A1
Arran Gdns URM M41 84 F7
Arran Gv RAD M26 38 B7
Arran Rd DUK SK16 90 F5
Arran St BRO M7 72 A6
NEWH/MOS M40 73 J4
Arras Gv RDSH SK5 100 C1
Arreton Sq RUSH/FAL M14 99 G1
Arrowfield Rd CCHDY M21 98 A6
Arrowhill Rd RAD M26 38 C4
Arrowsmith Rd
RNFD/HAY WA11 78 C5
Arrow St BOL BL1 2 C2
BRO M7 72 A7
LEIGH WN7 81 L1
Arthington St MILN OL16 11 J3
Arthog Dr HALE/TIMP WA15 117 H4
Arthog Rd DID/WITH M20 110 F2
HALE/TIMP WA15 117 H4
Arthur Av WALK M28 52 F7
Arthur La BOLE BL2 37 L2
Arthur Rd OLDTF/WHR M16 97 M1
Arthurs La UPML OL3 61 L7
Arthur St BOLS/LL BL3 53 K1
ECC M30 84 F3
FWTH BL4 53 G4
HEY OL10 * 41 G2
HYDE SK14 101 M3
LEIGH WN7 66 B8
PWCH M25 55 J8
RDSH SK5 100 B5
ROY/SHW OL2 43 K5
SWIN M27 70 A5
TOT/BURYW BL8 4 A5
WALK M28 69 G3
WALK M28 69 J2
WGNE/HIN WN2 49 H7
WHIT OL12 10 B3
Artillery Pl WYTH/NTH M22 * 110 C8
Artillery St BOLS/LL BL3 2 F8
CSLFD M3 6 D6
Artists La MCFLDN SK10 130 E6
Arundale WHTN BL5 50 C2
Arundale Av OLDTF/WHR M16 98 B3
Arundale Cl HYDE SK14 103 J1
Arundale Gv HYDE SK14 103 J1
Arundel Av BRAM/HZG SK7 121 M4
ROCH OL11 28 B8
URM M41 94 F3
WHTF M45 55 L5
Arundel Cl HALE/TIMP WA15 117 L3
STLY SK15 77 J6
TOT/BURYW BL8 24 F6
Arundel Dr LEIGH WN7 66 C6
Arundel Gra GLSP SK13 104 D4
Arundel Gv OFTN SK2 112 E8
Arundel Rd CHD/CHDH SK8 120 C6
Arundel St AUL OL6 91 H1
BOL BL1 22 B7
GLSP SK13 104 F3
HULME M15 6 B8
MOSL OL5 76 F3
OLDE OL4 59 M5
ROCH OL11 28 B8
SWIN M27 69 M3
WGNE/HIN WN2 49 H7
WGNW/BIL/OR WN5 47 J6
Asby Cl MDTN M24 57 G2
Ascension Rd BRO M7 72 A8
Ascot Av SALE M33 107 M1
STRET M32 97 J1
Ascot Cl CHAD OL9 8 C4
ROCH OL11 27 H4
Ascot Dr ATH M46 51 H8
BRAM/HZG SK7 122 C2
URM M41 94 F2
Ascot Mdw BURY BL9 4 D8
Ascot Pde BNG/LEV M19 99 J6
Ascot Rd BOLS/LL BL3 53 J1
NEWH/MOS M40 73 L8
Ascroft St OLD OL1 9 J6
WGN WN1 15 K5
Asgard Dr ORD M5 86 F4
Asgard Gv ORD M5 86 F4
Ash Av ALT WA14 107 K7
CHD/CHDH SK8 111 H7
IRL M44 94 A7
Ashawe Cl LHULT M38 68 B1
Ashawe Gv LHULT M38 68 C1
Ashawe Ter LHULT M38 68 B1
Ashbank Av BOLS/LL BL3 35 H6
Ashbee St BOL BL1 36 B1
Ashberry Cl WILM/AE SK9 127 H4
Ashborne Dr BURY BL9 25 G2
Ashbourne Av BOLE BL2 3 K7
CHD/CHDH SK8 111 J6
MDTN M24 57 M1
URM M41 95 H2
WGNE/HIN WN2 48 D2
WGNE/HIN WN2 49 J7
Ashbourne Cl LEIGH WN7 66 A3
WHIT OL12 21 H6
Ashbourne Ct GLSP SK13 105 J4
Ashbourne Crs SALE M33 109 G2
Ashbourne Dr AUL OL6 76 D6
MPL/ROM SK6 123 G6
Ashbourne Gv BRO M7 72 B5
WALK M28 69 H4
WHTF M45 55 H4
Ashbourne Rd BRAM/HZG SK7 122 B4
DTN/ASHW M34 101 H2
ECC M30 85 H3
SLFD M6 70 F7
STRET M32 85 K8
Ashbourne Sq OLDS OL8 9 H9
Ashbourne St ROCH OL11 27 H3
Ashbridge TRPK M17 85 L6
Ashbridge Rd FAIL M35 74 E6
Ashbrook Av DTN/ASHW M34 100 E1
Ashbrook Cl CHD/CHDH SK8 119 K3
DTN/ASHW M34 100 E1
Ashbrook Crs WHIT OL12 21 G8
Ashbrook Farm Cl RDSH SK5 100 C2
Ashbrook Hey La WHIT OL12 21 G8
Ashbrook La RDSH SK5 100 C2
Ashbrook Rd MCFLDN SK10 131 J6
OLDE OL4 60 C7
Ashbrook St OP/CLY M11 89 K5
Ashburn Av BNG/LEV M19 99 J7
Ashburn Cl HOR/BR BL6 34 A4
Ashburner St BOL BL1 2 D6
Ashburn Gv HTNM SK4 12 D1
Ashburn Rd HTNM SK4 12 D1
Ashburton Cl HYDE SK14 103 H2
Ashburton Rd EDGY/DAV SK3 112 B8
Ashburton Rd West
TRPK M17 85 H5
Ashbury Cl BOLS/LL BL3 2 C8
Ashbury Dr RNFD/HAY WA11 78 A5
Ashbury Pl NEWH/MOS M40 * 73 H8
Ashby Av BNG/LEV M19 99 H8
Ashby Cl FWTH BL4 52 E1
Ashby Gv LEIGH WN7 65 M4
WHTF M45 55 K5
Ashby Rd WGNS/IIMK WN3 63 L1
Ash Cl AUL OL6 76 A7
HYDE SK14 92 D8
OFTN SK2 112 F7
WGNNW/ST WN6 30 A5
WHIT OL12 21 G8

Ashcombe Dr *BOLE* BL2 ... 37 K6
  *RAD* M26 ... 38 A7
Ashcott Av *WYTH/NTH* M22 ... 110 A8
Ashcroft *WILM/AE* SK9 ... 126 D7
Ashcroft Av *BOLE* BL2 ... 71 H8
  *WGNNW/ST* WN6 ... 47 J1
Ashcroft St *CHAD* OL9 ... 58 D7
  *WGNE/HIN* WN2 ... 49 H8
Ashdale Av *BOLS/LL* BL3 ... 35 H7
Ashdale Cl *RDSH* SK5 ... 100 C7
Ashdale Crs *DROY* M43 ... 89 J3
Ashdale Dr *CHD/CHDH* SK8 ... 119 K2
  *DID/WITH* M20 ... 99 G7
  *WGNS/IIMK* WN3 ... 63 J7
Ashdene *AUL* OL6 ... 90 F2
Ashdene Av *OLD* OL1 ... 8 C1
  *OLDE* OL4 ... 60 C5
Ashdene Crs *BOLE* BL2 ... 23 G8
Ashdene Ri *OLD* OL1 ... 44 A8
Ashdene Rd *BNG/LEV* M19 ... 111 G2
  *DID/WITH* M20 ... 99 G6
  *WILM/AE* SK9 ... 126 D7
Ashdown Av *BKLY* M9 ... 57 G8
  *MPL/ROM* SK6 ... 101 M7
Ashdown Dr *BOLE* BL2 ... 70 D6
  *SWIN* M27 ... 70 D6
  *WALK* M28 ... 68 C5
Ashdowne Lawns *STLY* SK15 ... 92 A1
Ashdown Gv *BKLY* M9 ... 57 G8
Ashdown Rd *HTNM* SK4 ... 111 M1
Ashdown Ter *BKLY* M9 ... 57 G8
Ashdown Wy *ROY/SHW* OL2 ... 43 H4
Ash Dr *SWIN* M27 ... 70 D6
Asher St *BOLS/LL* BL3 ... 51 M1
Ashes Cl *STLY* SK15 ... 91 M4
Ashes Dr *BOLE* BL2 ... 37 J4
Ashes La *GLSP* SK13 ... 104 E2
  *MILN* OL16 ... 29 H5
  *OLDE* OL4 ... 60 C5
  *STLY* SK15 ... 91 M4
Ashfield *DTN/ASHW* M34 ... 90 D7
Ashfield Av *ATH* M46 ... 50 F8
  *ROCH* OL11 ... 10 E9
  *WGNE/HIN* WN2 ... 49 J8
Ashfield Cl *SLFD* M6 ... 86 B1
Ashfield Crs *CHD/CHDH* SK8 ... 111 C6
  *OLDE* OL4 ... 60 C5
  *WGNW/BIL/OR* WN5 ... 46 B3
Ashfield Dr *NEWH/MOS* M40 ... 74 A8
  *WGNE/HIN* WN2 ... 32 F7
Ashfield Gv *BOL* BL1 ... 22 D6
  *EDGY/DAV* SK3 ... 112 C6
  *GTN* M18 * ... 89 J8
  *IRL* M44 ... 94 B6
  *MPL/ROM* SK6 ... 114 E3
Ashfield House Gdns
  *WGNNW/ST* WN6 ... 31 J5
Ashfield La *MILN* OL16 ... 29 J5
Ashfield Park Dr
  *WGNNW/ST* WN6 ... 31 J4
Ashfield Rd *BRUN/LGST* M13 ... 99 H1
  *CHD/CHDH* SK8 ... 111 D8
  *EDGY/DAV* SK3 ... 112 C6
  *GLSP* SK13 ... 104 B1
  *HALE/TIMP* WA15 ... 117 G3
  *ROCH* OL11 ... 10 E9
  *SALE* M33 ... 96 E1
  *URM* M41 ... 96 A2
Ashfield Sq *DROY* M43 ... 89 J3
Ashford *SALE* M33 ... 95 M8
Ashford Av *ECC* M30 ... 84 F4
  *RDSH* SK5 ... 100 C2
  *SWIN* M27 ... 69 M6
  *WALK* M28 ... 68 C6
Ashford Cl *BOLE* BL2 ... 23 H8
  *TOT/BURYW* BL8 ... 38 E3
  *WILM/AE* SK9 ... 119 L8
Ashford Ct *OLDE* OL4 ... 60 A4
Ashford Gv *WALK* M28 ... 69 G4
Ashford Ms *STLY* SK15 ... 104 A3
Ashford Ri *WGN* WN1 ... 31 L8
Ashford Rd *DID/WITH* M20 ... 98 D5
  *HTNM* SK4 ... 100 A6
  *WILM/AE* SK9 ... 126 E8
Ashford St *HEY* OL10 ... 40 C2
Ashford Wk *BOL* BL1 * ... 2 C1
  *CHAD* OL9 * ... 58 D6
Ashgate Av *WYTH/NTH* M22 ... 110 B8
Ash Gv *WA14* ... 116 E3
  *BOL* BL1 ... 35 L4
  *BOLE* BL2 ... 37 J1
  *CHD/CHDH* SK8 ... 119 K4
  *DROY* M43 ... 89 K4
  *GOL/RIS/CUL* WA3 ... 79 M4
  *HALE/TIMP* WA15 ... 108 C5
  *HTNM* SK4 ... 100 A7
  *LIT* OL15 ... 21 K7
  *MILN* OL16 ... 43 K1
  *MPL/ROM* SK6 ... 114 B7
  *OLDE* OL4 ... 60 D5
  *PWCH* M25 ... 55 K6
  *RAMS* BL0 ... 24 C1
  *ROY/SHW* OL2 ... 43 G6
  *RUSH/FAL* M14 ... 88 B8
  *STLY* SK15 ... 91 J2
  *STRET* M32 ... 96 F4
  *TOT/BURYW* BL8 ... 24 D7
  *WALK* M28 ... 69 H3
  *WGNNW/ST* WN6 ... 31 J4
  *WGNW/BIL/OR* WN5 ... 46 C6
  *WHTN* BL5 ... 50 B5
Ashgrove *MILN* OL16 ... 42 E3
Ash Grove Crs
  *WGNW/BIL/OR* WN5 ... 62 B6
Ash Hill Dr *MOSL* OL5 ... 77 H4
Ashia Cl *MILN* OL16 ... 11 H6
Ashill Wk *CSLFD* M3 ... 6 D1
Ashington Cl *BOL* BL1 ... 35 L1
Ashington Dr *TOT/BURYW* BL8 ... 38 B3
Ashkirk St *GTN* M18 ... 89 G7
Ashland Av *AIMK* WN4 ... 63 K8
  *WGN* WN1 ... 47 M2
Ashlands *SALE* M33 ... 96 D7
Ashlands Av *NEWH/MOS* M40 ... 73 M3
  *WALK* M28 ... 69 M6
Ashlands Rd *DTN/ASHW* M34 ... 90 B6
Ashlands Rd *HALE/TIMP* WA15 ... 108 C4
Ash La *HALE/TIMP* WA15 ... 117 J3
  *WGNE/HIN* WN2 ... 48 D2
Ashlar Dr *WGTN/LGST* M12 ... 88 A4
Ash Lawns *BOL* BL1 ... 35 L5
Ashlea Gv *OLDE* OL4 ... 60 C6
Ashleigh Av *GLSP* SK13 ... 104 E2
Ashleigh Cl *ROY/SHW* OL2 ... 59 H2
Ash Leigh Dr *BOL* BL1 ... 35 H4
Ashleigh Rd *HALE/TIMP* WA15 ... 108 E4

Ashley Av *BOLE* BL2 ... 37 G4
  *OLDTF/WHR* M16 ... 87 G8
  *SWIN* M27 ... 70 A6
  *URM* M41 ... 95 H2
Ashley Cl *ROCH* OL11 ... 27 M8
Ashley Court Dr
  *NEWH/MOS* M40 ... 74 C3
Ashley Crs *SWIN* M27 ... 70 A5
Ashley Dr *BRAM/HZG* SK7 ... 120 E6
  *LEIGH* WN7 ... 65 M4
  *SALE* M33 ... 108 B2
  *SWIN* M27 ... 70 A6
Ashley Gdns *HYDE* SK14 ... 102 B3
  *MPL/ROM* SK6 ... 122 F4
Ashley La *BKLY* M9 ... 73 J4
Ashley Ms *HYDE* SK14 ... 102 B3
  *WHTF* M45 ... 55 L5
Ashleymill La *ALT* WA14 ... 116 F4
Ashley Mill La North
  *ALT* WA14 ... 116 F4
Ashley Rd *ALT* WA14 ... 116 F1
  *ALT* WA14 ... 116 F7
  *DROY* M43 ... 89 H2
  *OFTN* SK2 ... 112 F4
  *WGNE/HIN* WN2 ... 65 L1
  *WILM/AE* SK9 ... 126 E3
Ashley St *ANC* M4 ... 7 J1
  *CHAD* OL9 ... 8 D3
  *HEY* OL10 ... 91 H8
  *SLFD* M6 ... 86 B2
Ashlor St *BURY* BL9 ... 4 D7
Ashlyn Gv *RUSH/FAL* M14 ... 99 G4
Ashlynne *AUL* OL6 ... 90 F1
Ashmeade *HALE/TIMP* WA15 ... 117 K3
Ashmond Rd *OLDE* OL4 ... 60 C6
Ashmoor Rd *WYTH/NTH* M22 ... 118 F3
Ashmore Av *EDGY/DAV* SK3 ... 111 J5
Ashmore St *TYLD* M29 ... 68 A4
Ashmount Dr *WHIT* OL12 ... 28 C2
Ashness Cl *HOR/BR* BL6 ... 33 J1
Ashness Dr *BOLE* BL2 ... 37 H5
  *BRAM/HZG* SK7 ... 121 H4
  *MDTN* M24 ... 57 C1
Ashover Av *WGTN/LGST* M12 ... 88 C6
Ashover Cl *BOL* BL1 ... 22 C6
Ashover St *STRET* M32 ... 97 H1
Ashridge Cl *HOR/BR* BL6 ... 34 F6
Ashridge Dr *DUK* SK16 ... 90 E3
  *ECC* M30 ... 84 F4
Ashridge Wy
  *WGNNW/ST* WN6 ... 46 E3
Ash Rd *DROY* M43 ... 89 J2
  *DTN/ASHW* M34 ... 89 K8
  *FWTH* BL4 ... 53 J7
  *PART* M31 ... 106 A1
  *POY/DIS* SK12 ... 129 K1
  *RNFD/HAY* WA11 ... 78 B3
Ash Sq *OLDE* OL4 ... 60 A4
Ashstead Rd *SALE* M33 ... 108 F3
Ash St *BKLY* M9 ... 73 C5
  *BOLE* BL2 ... 3 G6
  *BRAM/HZG* SK7 ... 121 M1
  *BURY* BL9 ... 5 J4
  *DTN/ASHW* M34 ... 90 A5
  *EDGY/DAV* SK3 ... 12 B7
  *FAIL* M35 ... 74 B4
  *GOL/RIS/CUL* WA3 ... 79 L2
  *HEY* OL10 ... 40 E1
  *MDTN* M24 ... 57 M3
  *OLDE* OL4 ... 59 L6
  *ROCH* OL11 ... 41 M2
  *SLFD* M6 ... 86 C2
  *TYLD* M29 ... 67 K3
Ashton Av *ALT* WA14 ... 108 B6
Ashton Crs *CHAD* OL9 ... 74 D1
Ashton Field Dr *WALK* M28 ... 52 F8
Ashton Gallery *WGN* WN1 * ... 14 F3
Ashton Gdns *GLSP* SK13 ... 104 F5
Ashton Heath *AIMK* WN4 ... 78 F2
Ashton Hill La *DROY* M43 ... 89 K4
Ashton La *MDTN* M24 ... 57 K4
  *SALE* M33 ... 96 C7
Ashton New Rd *OP/CLY* M11 ... 88 C3
Ashton Old Rd *OP/CLY* M11 ... 88 B4
Ashton Pl *BRAM/HZG* SK7 ... 122 C5
Ashton Rd *BKLY* M9 ... 57 G7
  *DROY* M43 ... 89 K3
  *DTN/ASHW* M34 ... 90 B7
  *FAIL* M35 ... 74 F6
  *GOL/RIS/CUL* WA3 ... 79 J2
  *HYDE* SK14 ... 91 H7
  *MPL/ROM* SK6 ... 101 M6
  *NEWLW* WA12 ... 78 F6
  *OLDS* OL8 ... 9 H8
  *PART* M31 ... 106 F1
  *SALE* M33 ... 95 M8
  *WGNW/BIL/OR* WN5 ... 62 E4
Ashton Rd East *FAIL* M35 ... 74 D5
Ashton Rd West *FAIL* M35 ... 74 B5
Ashton St *BOLS/LL* BL3 ... 35 L8
  *BOLS/LL* BL3 ... 53 L1
  *CHAD* OL9 ... 74 C1
  *DUK* SK16 ... 90 D6
  *GLSP* SK13 ... 104 F5
  *HEY* OL10 ... 40 F2
  *MPL/ROM* SK6 ... 101 M6
  *ROCH* OL11 ... 10 C8
Ash Tree Av *DROY* M43 ... 89 J2
Ash Tree Dr *DUK* SK16 ... 91 J5
Ash Tree Gv *CHH* M8 ... 72 D7
  *HYDE* SK14 ... 91 L7
Ash Tree Rd *CHH* M8 ... 72 D7
Ashurst *BOLE* BL2 ... 23 H8
Ashurst Av *AIMK* WN4 ... 78 D2
Ashurst Cl *BOLE* BL2 ... 37 J1
  *HYDE* SK14 ... 102 D3
Ashurst Dr *EDGY/DAV* SK3 ... 111 L7
Ashurst Gv *RAD* M26 ... 54 E3
Ashurst Rd *WGNNW/ST* WN6 ... 30 D2
  *WYTH/NTH* M22 ... 119 H1
Ashville Ter *NEWH/MOS* M40 ... 73 J3
Ash Wk *CHAD* OL9 ... 8 A3
  *MDTN* M24 ... 57 J6
Ashway *AUL* OL6 ... 90 D1
Ashway Clough North
  *OFTN* SK2 ... 113 G7
Ashway Clough South
  *OFTN* SK2 ... 113 G7
Ashwell Av *GOL/RIS/CUL* WA3 ... 80 A3
Ashwell Rd *NTHM/RTH* M23 ... 109 L5
Ashwell St *BOLE* BL2 ... 36 E1

Ashwood Crs *MPL/ROM* SK6 ... 114 C5
Ashwood Dr *LIT* OL15 ... 21 K7
  *ROY/SHW* OL2 ... 42 F7
  *TOT/BURYW* BL8 ... 24 E6
Ashwood Rd *POY/DIS* SK12 * ... 123 M6
Ashworth Av *BOLS/LL* BL3 ... 53 M1
  *CHAD* OL9 ... 58 E8
  *LIT* OL15 ... 21 J7
Ashworth Gdns *UPML* OL3 ... 61 L7
  *HYDE* SK14 ... 103 J1
Ashworth Ms *HEY* OL10 ... 40 D2
Ashworth Rd *ROCH* OL11 ... 26 E3
Ashworth St *CHH* M8 ... 72 B7
  *DTN/ASHW* M34 ... 90 B8
  *FAIL* M35 ... 74 A6
  *FWTH* BL4 ... 52 F4
  *HEY* OL10 ... 41 G4
  *RAD* M26 ... 38 F8
  *TOT/BURYW* BL8 ... 4 B3
  *WGNE/HIN* WN2 ... 49 H1
Asia St *BOLS/LL* BL3 ... 52 D1
Askern Av *WYTH/NTH* M22 ... 118 F1
Askett Cl *NEWH/MOS* M40 ... 74 C8
Askrigg Cl *ATH* M46 ... 66 C4
Askwith Rd *WGNE/HIN* WN2 ... 65 J1
Aspell Cl *MDTN* M24 ... 57 J4
Aspen Cl *HALE/TIMP* WA15 ... 109 H7
  *WHTN* BL5 ... 50 C2
Aspen Gdns *WHIT* OL12 * ... 27 K3
Aspen Gn *DTN/ASHW* M34 ... 101 K2
Aspenshaw Rd *NM/HAY* SK22 ... 125 G1
Aspen Wk *WGNNW/ST* WN6 * ... 47 K1
Aspen Wy *MPL/ROM* SK6 ... 123 J5
Aspenwood *AIMK* WN4 ... 78 D2
Aspen Wd *HYDE* SK14 ... 102 C1
Aspenwood Dr *BKLY* M9 ... 72 F5
Aspen Wood Dr *CHAD* OL9 ... 58 B5
Aspenwood Dr *SALE* M33 ... 95 M8
Aspinall Cl *HOR/BR* BL6 ... 33 K3
  *WALK* M28 ... 68 C1
Aspinall Crs *WALK* M28 ... 68 C2
Aspinall Rd *WGNNW/ST* WN6 ... 30 C2
Aspinall St *HEY* OL10 ... 41 H2
  *HOR/BR* BL6 ... 34 A3
  *MDTN* M24 ... 57 M5
  *RUSH/FAL* M14 ... 98 F1
  *WGNE/HIN* WN2 ... 64 D2
Aspinall Wy *HOR/BR* BL6 ... 33 M4
Aspin La *ANC* M4 ... 7 H1
Aspland Rd *HYDE* SK14 ... 102 C5
Aspull Common *LEIGH* WN7 ... 80 F3
Aspull Ct *LEIGH* WN7 ... 80 F3
Aspull St *OLDE* OL4 ... 59 M7
Asquith Av *DUK* SK16 ... 90 F6
Asquith Rd *RDSH* SK5 ... 100 C3
Assheton Av *DTN/ASHW* M34 ... 89 M3
Assheton Cl *AUL* OL6 ... 90 F1
  *NEWLW* WA12 * ... 78 D8
Assheton Crs *NEWH/MOS* M40 ... 74 A8
Assheton Rd *NEWH/MOS* M40 ... 74 A8
  *ROY/SHW* OL2 ... 43 J5
Assheton St *MDTN* M24 ... 57 K2
Assheton Wy *MDTN* M24 ... 57 K4
Assisi Gdns *WGTN/LGST* M12 ... 88 B5
Assumption Rd *MDTN* M24 ... 57 C1
Astan Av *DROY* M43 ... 89 C1
Astbury Av *DTN/ASHW* M34 ... 90 A3
Astbury Cl *BURY* BL9 ... 5 J9
  *GOL/RIS/CUL* WA3 ... 80 E4
  *HALE/TIMP* WA15 * ... 108 B6
  *OLDE* OL4 ... 60 C6
Astbury Crs *EDGY/DAV* SK3 ... 112 A6
Astbury St *RAD* M26 ... 38 A6
Aster Av *FWTH* BL4 ... 52 D3
Aster Rd *RNFD/HAY* WA11 ... 78 C6
Aster St *OLD* OL1 ... 9 G1
Astley Cl *ROY/SHW* OL2 ... 43 J5
Astley Ct *IRL* M44 ... 94 B4
Astley Gdns *DUK* SK16 ... 90 E4
Astley Gv *STLY* SK15 ... 91 J1
Astley Hall Dr *RAMS* BL0 ... 18 F8
  *TYLD* M29 ... 67 L2
Astley La *BOL* BL1 ... 36 A1
Astley Rd *BOLE* BL2 ... 23 H7
  *IRL* M44 ... 82 F7
  *STLY* SK15 ... 91 J2
Astley St *BOL* BL1 ... 36 B2
  *DUK* SK16 ... 90 E4
  *HTNM* SK4 ... 13 G4
  *LEIGH* WN7 ... 66 E8
  *OP/CLY* M11 ... 88 F3
  *STLY* SK15 ... 91 K4
  *TYLD* M29 ... 67 K5
Aston Av *RUSH/FAL* M14 ... 98 D3
Aston Cl *EDGY/DAV* SK3 ... 111 M6
Aston Gv *TYLD* M29 ... 67 M3
Astor Rd *BNG/LEV* M19 ... 99 H5
  *SALQ* M50 ... 85 M3
Atcham Gv *BKLY* M9 ... 56 F8
Athenian Gdns *BRO* M7 ... 71 M7
Athens Dr *WALK* M28 ... 68 F3
Athens St *STKP* SK1 ... 13 M5
Athens Wy *STKP* SK1 ... 13 M5
Atherfield *BOLE* BL2 ... 23 H8
Atherleigh Gv *LEIGH* WN7 ... 66 C5
Atherleigh Wy *LEIGH* WN7 ... 66 C4
  *LEIGH* WN7 ... 81 C1
Atherley Gv *NEWH/MOS* M40 ... 74 C2
Atherstone *WHIT* OL12 ... 10 D2
Atherstone Av *CHH* M8 ... 72 D2
Atherstone Cl *TOT/BURYW* BL8 ... 24 F8
Atherton Av *HYDE* SK14 ... 103 K1
Atherton Cl *FAIL* M35 ... 74 D4
Atherton La *IRL* M44 ... 94 B7
Atherton Rd *WGNE/HIN* WN2 ... 49 C7
Atherton Sq *WGN* WN1 * ... 14 F3
Atherton St *CSLFD* M3 ... 6 C6
  *ECC* M30 ... 84 F3
  *EDGY/DAV* SK3 ... 111 M7
  *OLDE* OL4 ... 60 C7
  *WGNE/HIN* WN2 ... 65 H4
  *WGNW/BIL/OR* WN5 ... 14 A7
Athertons Yd *WGN* WN1 * ... 31 M8
Atherton Wy *ECC* M30 ... 84 E3
Athlone Av *BOL* BL1 ... 22 D4
  *BURY* BL9 ... 25 H4
  *CHD/CHDH* SK8 ... 111 M7
  *NEWH/MOS* M40 ... 73 K4
Athol Cl *NEWLW* WA12 ... 78 D6
Athol Crs *WGNE/HIN* WN2 ... 49 L8
Athole St *ORD* M5 ... 86 C5
Atholl Av *STRET* M32 ... 86 B8
Atholl Cl *BOLS/LL* BL3 ... 35 J6
Atholl Dr *HEY* OL10 ... 40 D4

Atholl Gv *WGNS/IIMK* WN3 ... 63 K1
Athol Rd *BRAM/HZG* SK7 ... 120 F7
  *OLDTF/WHR* M16 ... 98 B3
Athol St *AUL* OL6 ... 90 F1
  *ECC* M30 ... 84 F3
  *GTN* M18 ... 100 B1
  *HTNM* SK4 ... 12 F1
  *RAMS* BL0 ... 18 F5
Atkinson Av *BOLS/LL* BL3 ... 52 E1
Atkinson Rd *SALE* M33 ... 96 B6
  *URM* M41 ... 96 A2
Atkinson St *CHAD* OL9 ... 6 D5
  *ROCH* OL11 ... 41 M2
  *STKP* SK1 ... 13 M8
Atkin St *WALK* M28 ... 68 C4
Atlanta Av *MANAIR* M90 ... 118 C4
Atlantic St *ALT* WA14 ... 107 K6
Atlas Pk *WYTH/NTH* M22 * ... 119 H3
Atlas St *AULW* OL7 ... 75 K8
  *DUK* SK16 ... 91 K8
  *OLDS* OL8 ... 9 H7
Atlow Dr *NTHM/RTH* M23 ... 109 L7
Attenbury's La *ALT* WA14 ... 108 B4
Attercliffe Rd *CCHDY* M21 ... 97 K5
Attewell St *OP/CLY* M11 * ... 88 D7
Attingham Wk
  *WGNS/IIMK* WN3 ... 47 K7
Attleboro Rd
  *NEWH/MOS* M40 ... 73 K5
Attlee Av *GOL/RIS/CUL* WA3 ... 81 L8
Attlee Wy *WGTN/LGST* M12 ... 88 B3
Attock Cl *CHAD* OL9 ... 8 A4
Attwood Rd *HALE/TIMP* WA15 ... 108 E7
Attwood St *WGTN/LGST* M12 ... 99 L1
Atwood Rd *DID/WITH* M20 ... 110 F1
Atwood St *CMANE* M1 ... 7 G7
Auberson Rd *BOLS/LL* BL3 ... 52 A1
Aubrey Rd *RUSH/FAL* M14 ... 99 H1
Aubrey St *ROCH* OL11 ... 10 E8
  *SALQ* M50 ... 86 D5
Auburn Av *HYDE* SK14 ... 102 B4
  *MPL/ROM* SK6 ... 101 J8
Auburn Dr *URM* M41 ... 96 B3
Auburn Rd *DTN/ASHW* M34 ... 101 G2
  *OLDTF/WHR* M16 ... 86 E8
Auburn St *BOLS/LL* BL3 ... 36 A8
  *CMANE* M1 ... 7 J6
Auckland Dr *SLFD* M6 ... 71 K7
Auckland Rd *BNG/LEV* M19 ... 99 L4
Audax Wk *NEWH/MOS* M40 ... 73 L8
Auden Cl *OP/CLY* M11 ... 89 G3
Audenshaw Hall Gv
  *DTN/ASHW* M34 ... 89 L5
Audenshaw Rd
  *DTN/ASHW* M34 ... 89 M5
Audlem Cl *NEWH/MOS* M40 ... 88 D1
Audley Av *STRET* M32 ... 85 J8
Audley Rd *BNG/LEV* M19 ... 99 L2
Audley St *AUL* OL6 ... 91 H2
  *MOSL* OL5 ... 77 G4
Audlum Ct *BURY* BL9 ... 5 J4
Audrey Av *GTN* M18 ... 89 H7
Audrey St *BKLY* M9 ... 73 J4
Aughton Cl
  *WGNW/BIL/OR* WN5 ... 62 B8
Aughton St *WGNE/HIN* WN2 ... 48 F8
Augusta Cl *WHIT* OL12 ... 28 B3
Augusta St *WHIT* OL12 ... 28 B3
Augustine Webster Cl *BKLY* M9 ... 73 H4
  *BOLS/LL* BL3 ... 36 D8
Augustus St *ANC* M4 ... 7 H1
  *BOLS/LL* BL3 ... 36 D8
Auriga Wk *BRO* M7 ... 86 F1
Austell Rd *WYTH/NTH* M22 ... 118 F3
Austen Av *BURY* BL9 ... 39 J6
Austen Rd *ECC* M30 ... 85 G3
Austin Dr *AIMK* WN4 ... 63 H8
  *DID/WITH* M20 ... 98 F8
Austin Gv *BNG/LEV* M19 ... 99 H4
Austin's La *HOR/BR* BL6 ... 34 C5
Austin St *LEIGH* WN7 ... 66 A7
Autumn St *BRUN/LGST* M13 ... 87 M8
Avallon Cl *TOT/BURYW* BL8 ... 24 D5
Avalon Dr *DID/WITH* M20 ... 110 F4
Avebury Cl *BRO* M7 ... 72 C6
  *GOL/RIS/CUL* WA3 ... 80 B4
  *HOR/BR* BL6 ... 34 C3
Avebury Rd *NTHM/RTH* M23 ... 109 K7
Avens Rd *PART* M31 ... 106 C1
Avenue St *BOL* BL1 ... 2 C1
  *STKP* SK1 ... 13 K2
The Avenue *BOLE* BL2 ... 3 J5
  *BRO* M7 ... 71 M7
  *BURY* BL9 ... 25 J7
  *CHD/CHDH* SK8 ... 119 J3
  *ECC* M30 ... 85 G2
  *GLSP* SK13 ... 93 K8
  *HALE/TIMP* WA15 ... 117 H4
  *LEIGH* WN7 ... 66 C6
  *MPL/ROM* SK6 ... 113 G1
  *NEWLW* WA12 ... 78 E4
  *ROY/SHW* OL2 ... 43 K6
  *SALE* M33 ... 108 A3
  *URM* M41 ... 95 H2
  *WALK* M28 ... 69 G8
  *WALK* M28 ... 69 G5
  *WALK* M28 ... 69 H5
  *WGN* WN1 ... 48 A3
  *WGNNW/ST* WN6 ... 31 H8
  *WGNW/BIL/OR* WN5 ... 62 A1
  *WHTN* BL5 ... 50 A5
  *WILM/AE* SK9 ... 130 D3
Averham Cl *AIMK* WN4 ... 78 E3
Averhill *WALK* M28 ... 68 E4
Averill St *NEWH/MOS* M40 ... 74 A1
Averon Ri *OLD* OL1 ... 44 A8
Avian Dr *RUSH/FAL* M14 ... 98 E4
Aviary Rd *WALK* M28 ... 69 H6
Aviator Wy *WYTH/NTH* M22 ... 118 F4
Aviemore Cl *AIMK* WN4 ... 63 G8
  *RAMS* BL0 ... 24 D2
Avis St *ROY/SHW* OL2 ... 43 K6
Avocet Cl *LEIGH* WN7 ... 66 D6
  *NEWLW* WA12 ... 78 E4
Avocet Dr *ALT* WA14 ... 107 L4
  *IRL* M44 ... 94 D1
Avonbrook Dr *NEWH/MOS* M40 ... 74 A1
Avoncliff Cl *BOL* BL1 ... 36 A1
Avon Cl *MILN* OL16 ... 43 K1
  *MPL/ROM* SK6 ... 114 B7
  *WALK* M28 ... 68 D2
Avoncourt Dr *DID/WITH* M20 ... 98 D8
Avondale *SWIN* M27 ... 70 D2
Avondale Av *BRAM/HZG* SK7 ... 122 B2
  *BURY* BL9 ... 25 H8
Avondale Crs *URM* M41 ... 95 M1

Avondale Dr *RAMS* BL0 ... 24 C1
  *SLFD* M6 ... 70 F2
  *TYLD* M29 ... 67 H8
Avondale Ri *WILM/AE* SK9 ... 127 H6
Avondale Rd *BRAM/HZG* SK7 ... 122 B2
  *EDGY/DAV* SK3 ... 12 C7
  *FWTH* BL4 ... 52 C4
  *STRET* M32 ... 86 B8
  *WGN* WN1 ... 47 M2
  *WHTF* M45 ... 55 H3
Avondale St *BOL* BL1 ... 35 M3
  *CHH* M8 ... 72 C6
  *OLDS* OL8 ... 59 H6
  *WGNNW/ST* WN6 ... 31 H2
Avon Dr *BURY* BL9 ... 25 J4
Avon Gdns *BNG/LEV* M19 ... 99 K6
Avonhead Cl *HOR/BR* BL6 ... 33 K2
Avonlea Dr *BNG/LEV* M19 ... 99 H6
Avonlea Rd *DROY* M43 ... 89 J3
  *SALE* M33 ... 108 A3
Avonleigh Gdns *OLD* OL1 ... 59 M3
Avon Rd *AIMK* WN4 ... 64 B7
  *BNG/LEV* M19 ... 99 G5
  *CHAD* OL9 ... 58 C4
  *CHD/CHDH* SK8 ... 119 K5
  *FWTH* BL4 ... 53 L7
  *HALE/TIMP* WA15 ... 117 G4
  *HEY* OL10 ... 40 D2
  *ROY/SHW* OL2 ... 43 L4
  *TYLD* M29 ... 67 M5
Avon St *BOL* BL1 ... 35 L3
  *EDGY/DAV* SK3 ... 13 H9
  *LEIGH* WN7 ... 66 E8
  *OLDS* OL8 ... 9 K5
Avril Cl *RDSH* SK5 ... 100 C4
Avro Cl *RUSH/FAL* M14 ... 98 E3
Avroe Rd *ECC* M30 ... 84 C5
Avro Wy *MANAIR* M90 ... 118 D4
Awburn Rd *HYDE* SK14 ... 103 H3
Axbridge Wk *NEWH/MOS* M40 ... 88 D1
Axeholme Ct *HOR/BR* BL6 ... 33 J1
Axford Cl *BRO* M7 ... 72 C6
Axon Sq *OLDTF/WHR* M16 ... 87 J8
Aycliffe Gv *BRUN/LGST* M13 ... 99 H1
Aycliffe Rd *CCHDY* M21 ... 98 A5
Aye Bridge Rd
  *WGNE/HIN* WN2 ... 64 E7
Aylesbury Av *DTN/ASHW* M34 ... 101 J3
  *URM* M41 ... 85 H8
Aylesbury Cl *ORD* M5 ... 86 D3
Aylesbury Crs *WGNE/HIN* WN2 ... 65 M2
Aylesbury Gv *MDTN* M24 ... 57 M2
Aylesby Av *GTN* M18 ... 88 E8
Aylesford Rd *RUSH/FAL* M14 ... 99 G1
Aylesford Wk *BOL* BL1 * ... 2 C1
Aylsham Cl *MPL/ROM* SK6 ... 101 J7
Aylsham Ms *SWIN* M27 ... 70 A4
Aylwin Dr *SALE* M33 ... 108 C1
Ayr Av *OLDS* OL8 ... 75 J1
Ayr Cl *BRAM/HZG* SK7 ... 122 C2
Ayrefield Gv *WGNNW/ST* WN6 ... 30 A8
Ayres Rd *OLDTF/WHR* M16 ... 86 F8
Ayr Gv *HEY* OL10 ... 40 D4
Ayrshire Rd *BRO* M7 ... 71 K6
Ayr St *BOLE* BL2 ... 22 E8
Ayrton Gv *LHULT* M38 ... 52 D7
Aysgarth Av *WGN* ... *CHD/CHDH* SK8 ... 110 F6
  *GTN* M18 ... 89 H6
  *MPL/ROM* SK6 ... 102 A8
Aysgarth Cl *SALE* M33 ... 108 A1
Ayshford Cl *ALT* WA14 ... 107 L6
Ayton Gv *RUSH/FAL* M14 ... 88 B3
Aytoun St *CMANE* M1 ... 7 J5
Azalea Av *GTN* M18 ... 89 G6

## B

Babbacombe Gv *BKLY* M9 ... 56 E7
Babbacombe Rd *OFTN* SK2 ... 112 F6
Back Abingdon Rd *BOL* BL3 * ... 3 L2
Back Acton St *CMANE* M1 * ... 7 J6
Back Adcroft St *STKP* SK1 ... 13 K8
Back Adrian Rd *BOL* BL1 * ... 35 M2
Back Adrian Rd East *BOL* BL1 * ... 35 M2
Back Ainscow St *BOL* BL1 * ... 3 L2
Back Ainsworth La *BOLE* BL2 ... 3 L2
Back Ainsworth Rd North
  *TOT/BURYW* BL8 ... 38 F2
Back Ainsworth Rd South
  *TOT/BURYW* BL8 ... 38 F2
Back Ainsworth St *BOL* BL1 ... 36 A2
Back Albert St *BURY* BL9 ... 5 J4
Back Albion Pl *BURY* BL9 ... 25 J8
Back Alder St *BOLS/LL* BL3 ... 52 C1
Back Alexander St *BOLS/LL* BL3 ... 35 M8
Back Alfred St *BOLS/LL* BL3 ... 36 E8
Back Alice St *BOLS/LL* BL3 * ... 53 L1
  *BOLS/LL* BL3 ... 53 L1
Back Alicia St *BOLS/LL* BL3 ... 37 G8
Back All Saints' St *BOL* BL1 ... 2 F5
Back Alston St *BOLS/LL* BL3 ... 52 B1
Back Andrew St *BURY* BL9 ... 5 H5
Back Andrew St North
  *BURY* BL9 ... 5 J5
Back Anglia Gv *BOLS/LL* BL3 ... 35 M8
Back Annis Rd *BOLS/LL* BL3 * ... 35 L8
Back Anson St *BOL* BL1 ... 36 A1
Back Apple Ter *BOL* BL1 * ... 36 A2
Back Argo St *BOLS/LL* BL3 ... 36 A8
Back Argyle St *BURY* BL9 ... 25 J7
Back Arlington St *BOLS/LL* BL3 ... 52 C1
Back Arnold St *BOL* BL1 * ... 35 M2
Back Arnold Ter *BOL* BL1 * ... 35 M2
Back Ashbee St *BOL* BL1 ... 36 B1
Back Ashford Wk *BOL* BL1 * ... 35 M2
Back Ashley St *ANC* M4 ... 7 J1
Back Ash St *BOLE* BL2 ... 3 G6
  *BURY* BL9 ... 5 J4
Back Ashton St *BOLS/LL* BL3 * ... 35 L8
Back Ashworth La *BOL* BL1 ... 22 C7
Back Ashworth St
  *TOT/BURYW* BL8 ... 4 A3
Back Astley St *BOL* BL1 ... 36 B2
Back Augustus St
  *BOLS/LL* BL3 ... 36 D8
Back Augustus St West
  *BOLS/LL* BL3 ... 36 D8
Back Avenue St *BOL* BL1 * ... 2 A2
Back Avondale St *BOL* BL1 * ... 35 M3
Back Baldwin St *BOLS/LL* BL3 * ... 2 C8
Back Baldwin St North
  *BOLS/LL* BL3 ... 2 C8
Back Balloon St *ANC* M4 * ... 7 G2
Back Banbury St *BOLE* BL2 * ... 36 F3
Back Bankfield St *BOLS/LL* BL3 ... 35 M7
Back Bank St *CHH* M8 ... 72 D8

Back Bantry St BOLS/LL BL3 2 C9
Back Barbara St BOLS/LL BL3 36 A8
Back Bark St BOL BL1 2 D4
Back Bashall St BOL BL1 35 M4
Back Battenberg Rd BOL BL1 35 M4
Back Baxendale St BOL BL1 22 B8
Back Bayley St BOL BL1 2 A2
Back Baythorpe St BOL BL1 * 36 C2
Back Baytorpe St North
BOL BL1 * 36 C1
Back Beaconsfield St
BOLS/LL BL3 2 A7
Back Beaconsfield Ter BOLE BL2 3 J1
Back Bedford St BOL BL1 2 A3
Back Beech St BOL BL1 36 C2
Back Beechwood St
BOLS/LL BL3 52 C1
Back Belbeck St
TOT/BURYW BL8 38 F2
Back Bell La BURY BL9 5 H3
Back Belmont Rd BOL BL1 22 B7
Back Belmont Rd East BOL BL1 22 B7
Back Bennett's La BOL BL1 35 M2
Back Bennett's La East BOL BL1 35 M2
Back Benson St BURY BL9 5 H6
Back Bentinck St BOL BL1 35 L3
Back Bentley St BOLE BL2 3 L8
Back Bertrand Rd BOL BL1 35 M6
Back Beverley Rd BOL BL1 35 M4
Back Birch St BURY BL9 5 G2
Back Blackbank St BOL BL1 36 C3
Back Blackburn Rd BOL BL1 36 C2
Back Blackburn Rd East
EDGW/EG BL7 22 A1
Back Blackburn Rd West
BOL BL1 36 B1
EDGW/EG BL7 * 22 B4
Back Blackburn St BOL BL1 36 C1
Back Blackwood St
BOLS/LL BL3 36 D8
Back Bolton Rd North
TOT/BURYW BL8 38 F3
Back Bolton Rd South
TOT/BURYW BL8 4 A5
Back Bolton St BOL BL1 36 C2
Back Bolton St South BURY BL9 4 D4
Back Bond St West BURY BL9 5 J4
Back Boundary St BOL BL1 36 A2
Back Bowen St BOL BL1 * 35 L3
Backbower La HYDE SK14 102 C4
Back Bowness Rd BOLS/LL BL3 36 A8
Back Bradford Rd BOLS/LL BL3 52 D1
Back Bradford Rd West
BOLS/LL BL3 52 D1
Back Bradford St BOLE BL2 3 K5
Back Bradford St East BOLE BL2 3 J5
Back Bradford St South
BOLE BL2 3 H6
Back Bradford St West
BOLE BL2 3 J5
Back Bradshaw BOLE BL2 22 F8
Back Bradshaw Brow West
BOLE BL2 * 22 F8
Back Bradshawgate BOL BL1 2 F5
Back Bradshaw Rd East
BOLE BL2 23 G7
Back Bradshaw St MILN OL16 11 H2
Back Brandon St BOLS/LL BL3 36 A8
Back Brandon St North
BOLS/LL BL3 36 A8
Back Brandwood St
BOLS/LL BL3 35 M8
Back Bridgeman St
BOLS/LL BL3 36 B8
Back Bridge St BOL BL1 2 E3
CSLFD M3 6 E4
NM/HAY SK22 124 E3
RAMS BL0 18 F6
Back Brierley St BURY BL9 4 E9
Back Brierley St South
BURY BL9 4 E9
Back Brigade St BOL BL1 35 M5
Back Brindley St BOL BL1 22 C8
Back Brink's Pl BOL BL1 * 2 C4
Back Bristol Av BOLE BL2 3 L1
Back Bristol St BOLS/LL BL3 2 B8
Back Broach St BOLS/LL BL3 36 B8
Back Broad o' th' La BOL BL1 * 22 B8
Back Broad St BURY BL9 4 E5
Back Bromwich St BOLE BL2 3 J6
Back Brookfield St BOLE BL2 3 J4
Back Brook St North BURY BL9 5 H1
Back Broom St BOLE BL2 3 H4
MILN OL16 29 L8
Back Burnaby St BOLS/LL BL3 2 A9
Back Burnham Av BOL BL1 35 K3
Back Bury New Rd BOLE BL2 3 H5
Back Bury New Rd East
BOLE BL2 3 J5
Back Bury Old Rd BOLE BL2 3 H4
Back Bury Rd BOLE BL2 37 G5
Back Bury Rd East BOLE BL2 3 M4
Back Bury Rd South BOLE BL2 3 L4
BOLE BL2 37 G5
Back Bushell St BOLS/LL BL3 * 35 L8
Back Byrom St
TOT/BURYW BL8 24 E8
Back Byrom St South
TOT/BURYW BL8 24 E8
Back Calder Rd BOLS/LL BL3 52 B1
Back Caledonia St BOLS/LL BL3 35 M7
Back Calvert Rd BOLS/LL BL3 52 C1
Back Cambridge St AULW OL7 90 C3
Back Camp St BRO M7 * 72 A7
Back Canada St BOL BL1 36 A2
HOR/BR BL6 33 L1
Back Canning St BURY BL9 4 F1
Back Carl St BOL BL1 36 A2
Back Carter St BOLS/LL BL3 36 D8
Back Castle St BOLE BL2 3 J5
Back Cateaton St BURY BL9 4 F2
Back Cecilia St BOLS/LL BL3 36 D8
Back Cecil St BOLE BL2 3 J5
MOSL OL5 * 76 F4
Back Cedar St BURY BL9 5 K3
Back Cedar St North BURY BL9 5 K3
Back Cemetery Rd East
BOLE BL2 3 K4
Back Cestrian St BOLS/LL BL3 * 52 C1
Back Chalfont St BOL BL1 36 C2
Back Chapel St BNG/LEV M19 99 K3
BRAM/HZG SK7 * 122 A1
HOR/BR BL6 * 33 M1
TOT/BURYW BL8 24 C5
WHIT OL12 * 21 G5
Back Chapman St BOL BL1 35 L3
Back Charles Holden St
BOL BL1 2 A6
Back Chaucer St BOL BL1 36 A3
Back Cheapside BOL BL1 2 E5
Back Chesham Rd North
BURY BL9 * 25 K8
Back Chesham Rd South
BURY BL9 25 K8
Back Chester St BURY BL9 25 K8
Back China La CMANE M1 7 J5
Back Chorley New Rd BOL BL1 2 A3
Back Chorley New Rd North
BOL BL1 35 L5
Back Chorley Old Rd BOL BL1 35 K3
Back Chorley Old Rd North
BOL BL1 35 L3
Back Chorley Old Rd South
BOL BL1 35 K3
Back Chorley St BOL BL1 2 C4
Back Chorley St East BOL BL1 * 2 C3
Back Church Av BOLS/LL BL3 35 M8
Back Church Rd BOL BL1 35 K2
BOL BL1 35 M2
Back Church Rd North BOL BL1 35 M2
Back Church St BOL BL1 2 F3
BOLS/LL BL3 53 K1
Back Clarendon Rd BOLE BL2 3 M4
Back Clarke St BOL BL1 * 35 M4
Back Clay St East
EDGW/EG BL7 * 22 D5
Back Clay St West
EDGW/EG BL7 * 22 D5
Back Clegg's Buildings
BOL BL1 * 2 C3
Back Clegg St BOLE BL2 3 M5
Back Clifton St BURY BL9 25 J8
Back Cloister St BOL BL1 * 35 M2
Back Clyde St BOL BL1 36 B2
Back Cobden St BOL BL1 36 A1
Back Colenso Rd BOLE BL2 * 37 G5
Back College Land CSLFD M3 * 6 E4
Back College Wy BOLS/LL BL3 2 B6
Back Columbia Rd BOL BL1 * 35 M4
Back Common St WHTN BL5 49 L5
Back Coniston St BOL BL1 * 36 C1
Back Coop St BOL BL1 22 B8
Back Cornall St
TOT/BURYW BL8 38 F1
Back Corson St BOLS/LL BL3 53 G2
Back Cottam St
TOT/BURYW BL8 4 A2
Back Cotton St BOL BL1 36 A2
Back Cowm La WHIT OL12 20 A1
Back Cox Green Rd North
EDGW/EG BL7 22 C4
Back Crawford Av BOLE BL2 3 J6
Back Crawford St BOLE BL2 * 3 J6
Back Crescent Av BOL BL1 2 B3
Back Crescent Rd BOLS/LL BL3 36 D8
Back Crescent Rd West
BOLS/LL BL3 52 D1
Back Croft La BOLS/LL BL3 3 J9
Back Cromer Av BOLE BL2 3 L1
Back Cross La NEWLW WA12 78 E8
Back Crostons Rd
TOT/BURYW BL8 4 B3
Back Croston St BOLS/LL BL3 35 M8
Back Crumpsall St North
BOL BL1 36 B1
Back Cundey St BOL BL1 * 35 M3
Back Curzon Rd BOL BL1 35 M5
Back Cyril St BOLS/LL BL3 3 H9
Back Daisy St BOLS/LL BL3 35 M8
Back Darley St FWTH BL4 53 H4
Back Darwen Rd North
EDGW/EG BL7 22 C4
Back Darwen Rd South
EDGW/EG BL7 22 D5
Back Darwin St BOL BL1 * 36 A2
Back Deal St BOLS/LL BL3 * 52 C1
BURY BL9 5 K5
Back Deane Church La
BOLS/LL BL3 * 35 L8
Back Deane Church La West
BOLS/LL BL3 * 35 L8
Back Deane Rd BOLS/LL BL3 35 M7
Back Deane Rd North
BOLS/LL BL3 2 B7
Back Delamere St South
BURY BL9 * 25 K7
Back Denton St BURY BL9 25 J8
Back Derby St BOLS/LL BL3 2 C8
BURY BL9 5 G4
Back Design St BOLS/LL BL3 * 35 L8
Back Devonshire Rd BOL BL1 35 K3
Back Devon St North BURY BL9 4 E8
Back Devon St South BURY BL9 4 F9
Back Dijon St BOLS/LL BL3 35 M8
Back Dijon St North
BOLS/LL BL3 35 M8
Back Dobie St BOLS/LL BL3 * 36 D8
Back Doffcocker Brow
BOL BL1 35 J3
Back Dorset St BOLE BL2 3 H5
Back Dougill St BOL BL1 35 L3
Back Dougill St South BOL BL1 35 L3
Back Drake St MILN OL16 10 F6
Back Drummond St BOL BL1 * 22 B8
Back Ducie Av BOL BL1 35 M5
Back Duckworth St BURY BL9 25 K8
Back Duncan St BRO M7 71 M5
HOR/BR BL6 * 33 M1
Back Dunstan St BOLE BL2 3 L4
Back Durham St ROCH OL11 11 G8
Back Duxbury St BOL BL1 * 36 A2
Back Earnshaw St
BOLS/LL BL3 * 51 M1
Back Eastbank St BOL BL1 36 C1
Back East St BURY BL9 5 G6
Back Eckersley Rd BOL BL1 36 B1
Back Edditch Gv BOLE BL2 3 M5
Back Edditch Gv North
BOLE BL2 3 M5
Back Eden St BOL BL1 36 B1
Back Edgmont Av
BOLS/LL BL3 * 36 A8
Back Eldon St BURY BL9 4 F1
Back Ellesmere Rd
BOLS/LL BL3 51 M1
Back Ellesmere St BOLS/LL BL3 2 A7
Back Elm St BURY BL9 5 K5
Back Elmwood Gv BOL BL1 * 35 M4
Back Elmwood Gv West
BOL BL1 * 35 M4
Back Elsworth St CSLFD M3 87 K1
Back Emmett St HOR/BR BL6 33 L1
Back Empire Rd BOLE BL2 37 G4
Back Empress St BOL BL1 35 L3
Back Ena St BOLS/LL BL3 * 52 D1
Back Ernest St BOL BL1 2 A6
Back Eskrick St BOL BL1 * 36 A2
Back Eskrick St East BOL BL1 * 36 A2
Back Eskrick St South BOL BL1 36 A2
Back Eskrick St West BOL BL1 36 A2
Back Essingdon St BOLS/LL BL3 36 A8
Back Essingdon St South
BOLS/LL BL3 36 A8
Back Eustace St BOLS/LL BL3 52 D1
Back Euxton St BOLS/LL BL3 36 A8
Back Everton St North
BOL BL1 * 36 C2
Back Ewart St BOL BL1 * 36 B2
Back Fairhaven Rd BOL BL1 36 C1
Back Fair St BOLS/LL BL3 51 M2
Back Fenton St
TOT/BURYW BL8 38 F1
Back Fern St East
BOLS/LL BL3 35 M6
Back Fir St BURY BL9 5 K4
Back Fletcher St BURY BL9 5 H4
RAD M26 * 53 L5
Back Fletcher St South
BOLS/LL BL3 2 E9
Back Flora St BOLS/LL BL3 * 36 B8
Back Florence Av BOL BL1 22 C8
Back Fortune St BOLS/LL BL3 3 J9
Back Foundry St BURY BL9 5 G5
Back Frances St BOL BL1 36 A2
Back Frank St BOL BL1 * 36 A3
BURY BL9 5 G6
Back Fylde St BOLS/LL BL3 53 G2
Back Gainsborough Av
BOLS/LL BL3 51 M1
Back Garside Gv BOL BL1 * 35 M2
Back Garston St BURY BL9 25 K8
Back Gaskell St BOL BL1 2 B3
Back Gaskell St East BOL BL1 * 2 B3
Back Gaythorne St BOL BL1 * 36 C1
Back George Barton St
BOLE BL2 3 K1
Back George St BOLS/LL BL3 36 D8
CMANE M1 7 G5
HOR/BR BL6 33 M1
Back Gibraltar St BOLS/LL BL3 2 B7
Back Gibraltar St South
BOLS/LL BL3 * 2 A7
Back Gigg La BURY BL9 4 F9
Back Gilmour St MDTN M24 57 K4
Back Gilnow Gv BOL BL1 2 A6
Back Gilnow La West
BOLS/LL BL3 35 M6
Back Gilnow Rd BOL BL1 35 M6
Back Glen Av BOLS/LL BL3 * 35 L7
Back Glenboro Av
TOT/BURYW BL8 38 E2
Back Glen Bott St BOL BL1 * 36 A2
Back Gloster St BOLE BL2 3 H5
Back Goldsmith St BOLS/LL BL3 36 A8
Back Goodlad St
TOT/BURYW BL8 24 E8
Back Gordon Av BOLS/LL BL3 35 M7
Back Gorses Mt BOLE BL2 3 M8
Back Grafton St ALT WA14 108 A8
BOL BL1 2 A3
Back Grantham Cl BOL BL1 * 36 B3
Back Grasmere St BOL BL1 36 C2
Back Greaves St OLD OL1 * 9 K6
Back Greenhalgh St
BOLS/LL BL3 * 53 K1
Back Greenland Rd
BOLS/LL BL3 52 C1
Back Green La BOLS/LL BL3 52 E2
Back Green La South
BOLS/LL BL3 52 C1
Back Green St MDTN M24 57 L3
Back Gregory Av BOLE BL2 37 H4
Back Grendon St BOLS/LL BL3 51 M1
Back Gresham St BOL BL1 * 36 C1
Back Grosvenor St STLY SK15 91 K3
Back Grove St BOL BL1 36 A2
Back Hadwin St BOL BL1 2 E1
Back Halliwell La CHH M8 * 72 C5
Back Halliwell Rd BOL BL1 36 B2
Back Halliwell Rd South
BOL BL1 36 A2
Back Halstead St BOLE BL2 3 H5
BURY BL9 25 K8
Back Hamilton St BRO M7 * 72 A6
BURY BL9 25 J8
Back Hampson St
NEWH/MOS M40 73 G8
Back Hanson St BURY BL9 25 J8
Back Hargreaves St BOL BL1 36 B2
Back Harper's La South
BOL BL1 * 35 L2
Back Hartington Rd BOL BL1 * 35 M4
Back Hart St WHTN BL5 49 L5
Back Harvey St
TOT/BURYW BL8 38 F1
Back Haslam St BURY BL9 * 25 K8
Back Haslam Ter BOLE BL2 3 L4
Back Hatfield Rd BOL BL1 35 M3
Back Hawthorne Rd
BOLS/LL BL3 * 35 L8
Back Hawthorne Rd East
BOLS/LL BL3 * 35 L7
Back Hawthorn Rd West
BOLS/LL BL3 * 35 L7
Back Haydn St BOL BL1 36 A2
Back Haydock St BOL BL1 2 E2
Back Hayward St
TOT/BURYW BL8 4 A2
Back Hengist St BOLE BL2 * 3 M4
Back Hennon St BOL BL1 36 A3
Back Henrietta St
BOLS/LL BL3 * 35 L8
Back Henry Lee St BOLS/LL BL3 51 M1
Back Heywood St East
BURY BL9 5 H5
Back Heywood St West
BURY BL9 5 H6
Back High Bank St BOLE BL2 3 M5
Back Higher Darcy St BOLE BL2 3 L9
Back Higher Shady La West
EDGW/EG BL7 22 E5
Back Higher Swan La
BOLS/LL BL3 52 A1
Back Higher Swan La West
BOLS/LL BL3 52 A1
Back High St BOLS/LL BL3 36 B8
EDGW/EG BL7 16 F8
Back High St South
BOLS/LL BL3 36 B8
Back High St West
BOLS/LL BL3 * 36 B8
Back Hilden St BOLE BL2 3 H6
Back Hilden St West BOLE BL2 3 H6
Back Hilton St BOLE BL2 3 M4
BRO M7 72 A5
BURY BL9 5 G1
Back Hind St BOLE BL2 3 M4
Back Holland St BOL BL1 22 C8
Back Holland St East BOL BL1 * 22 C8
Back Holly Pl BOL BL1 22 B8
Back Holly St BOL BL1 22 C8
BURY BL9 5 J4
Back Holly St South BURY BL9 5 J4
Back Hopefield St BOLS/LL BL3 36 A8
Back Hope St BRO M7 72 A5
OLD OL1 59 L5
Back Horbury St
TOT/BURYW BL8 38 F2
Back Horeb St East
BOLS/LL BL3 * 2 A9
Back Hornby St BURY BL9 25 J7
Back Hornby St East
BURY BL9 4 F2
Back Hornby St West
BURY BL9 * 4 F2
Back Horne St North BURY BL9 4 E8
Back Horne St South BURY BL9 4 E9
Back Horsa St BOLE BL2 3 J1
Back Horsa St North BOLE BL2 * 3 J1
Back Hotel St BOL BL1 * 2 E4
Back Hough La East
EDGW/EG BL7 22 D5
Back Howarden St BOL BL1 * 22 B7
Back Howcroft St
BOLS/LL BL3 * 36 A8
Back Howe St BRO M7 71 M5
Back Hughes St BOL BL1 36 A2
Back Hulbert St
TOT/BURYW BL8 * 38 F3
Back Hulme St ORD M5 86 F3
TOT/BURYW BL8 4 B2
Back Hulton La BOLS/LL BL3 51 K2
Back Hulton La South
BOLS/LL BL3 * 51 K2
Back Hulton La West
BOLS/LL BL3 * 35 K8
Back Huntley Mount Rd
BURY BL9 5 K2
Back Hurst St BOLS/LL BL3 51 M1
BURY BL9 5 H6
Back Huxley St BOL BL1 35 M2
Back Ingham St BURY BL9 5 H6
Back Ingham St East
BURY BL9 5 H6
Back Irlam St BOL BL1 36 B1
Back Irlam St North BOL BL1 * 36 B1
Back Ivy Bank Rd BOL BL1 22 B7
Back Ivy Rd BOL BL1 35 M3
Back Ivy Rd West BOL BL1 * 35 M2
Back James St BOLS/LL BL3 53 L1
Back Jauncey St BOLS/LL BL3 35 M7
Back John Brown St BOL BL1 * 2 B3
Back John Cross St
BOLS/LL BL3 * 36 B8
Back Johnson St BOL BL1 * 2 F6
Back Junction St CMANE M1 7 K4
Back Keighley St BOL BL1 35 M2
Back Kendal Rd BOL BL1 35 M4
Back Kershaw St BURY BL9 5 J5
Back Kingholm Gdns BOL BL1 * 36 A3
Back Kingsley St BOL BL1 36 A2
Back King St BOL BL1 2 D4
OLDS OL8 9 H6
Back King St North
EDGW/EG BL7 22 C4
Back King St South BOLE BL2 23 G7
Back Knight St
TOT/BURYW BL8 38 F2
Back Knowl St STLY SK15 91 L2
Back Knowsley Rd BOL BL1 * 35 L2
Back Knowsley St BOL BL1 2 E4
BURY BL9 4 E5
Back Kylemore Av
BOLS/LL BL3 * 35 L7
Back La ALT WA14 106 E7
AULW OL7 75 H8
BOL BL1 2 C3
GLSP SK13 104 B6
HALE/TIMP WA15 117 H7
HYDE SK14 92 D8
MOSL OL5 76 D2
OLDE OL4 60 F3
WGNNW/ST WN6 30 C3
WHIT OL12 20 B3
WHTN BL5 51 L6
Back Lark St BOL BL1 2 C1
Back Latham St BOL BL1 36 C2
Back Lathom St BURY BL9 25 K8
Back Laurel St BURY BL9 5 K4
Back Lawn St BOL BL1 35 M3
Back Leachfield St BOL BL1 36 A1
Back Leach St BOLS/LL BL3 2 C9
Back Lee Av BOLS/LL BL3 52 B1
Back Lee St UPML OL3 61 L4
Back Lena St BOL BL1 36 C2
Back Lenora St BOLS/LL BL3 * 35 L7
Back Lever Edge La
BOLS/LL BL3 51 M2
BOLS/LL BL3 52 C1
Back Lever Edge La South
BOLS/LL BL3 52 B1
Back Lever St BOLS/LL BL3 2 E9
Back Lever St North
BOLS/LL BL3 37 K8
Back Lever St South
BOLS/LL BL3 * 36 B8
Back Lightburne Av BOL BL1 35 L5
Back Lilly St BOL BL1 2 A2
Back Lincoln Rd BOL BL1 * 35 M4
Back Lindley St BOLS/LL BL3 * 53 L1
Back Linton Av BURY BL9 25 J7
Back Longden St BOL BL1 35 M4
Back Longfield Rd
BOLS/LL BL3 * 51 L1
Back Long La BOLE BL2 37 H5
Back Longsight North
BOLE BL2 23 H7
Back Longsight South
BOLE BL2 23 G7
Back Longworth Rd
EDGW/EG BL7 22 A1
Back Lonsdale St
TOT/BURYW BL8 4 A4
Back Lord St BOLS/LL BL3 53 L1
BURY BL9 5 G6
Back Loxham St BOLS/LL BL3 53 G2
Back Lumsden St BOLS/LL BL3 2 C9
Back Luton St BOLS/LL BL3 36 D8
Back Lytton St BOL BL1 36 A3
Back Mackenzie St BOL BL1 22 A8
Back Malvern Av BOL BL1 35 K3
BURY BL9 25 J7
Back Manchester Old Rd
BURY BL9 4 D7
Back Manchester Rd BOLE BL2 3 G7
BOLS/LL BL3 52 F2
BURY BL9 4 D5
Back Manchester Rd East
BOLE BL2 * 3 G8
Back Manchester Rd South
BOLS/LL BL3 3 H9
Back Manchester Rd West
BOLS/LL BL3 36 E8
Back Manchester St HEY OL10 * 41 H3
Back Manor St BURY BL9 5 H4
Back Maple St BOLS/LL BL3 * 2 B8
Back Marion St South
BOLS/LL BL3 * 52 F2
Back Market St BOLS/LL BL3 53 L1
BURY BL9 4 E5
LEIGH WN7 66 C7
NEWLW WA12 78 D8
RAD M26 53 L5
WGNE/HIN WN2 * 49 G7
Back Market St West BURY BL9 4 E4
Back Markland Hill La BOL BL1 35 J3
Back Markland Hill La East
BOL BL1 * 35 J3
Back Markland Hill La West
BOL BL1 * 35 J3
Back Marlborough St BOL BL1 2 A3
Back Marsh Fold La BOL BL1 * 35 M4
Back Mary St BOLS/LL BL3 * 2 B8
Back Mason St BURY BL9 5 H5
Back Massie St
CHD/CHDH SK8 * 111 G6
Back Mawdsley St BOL BL1 2 E5
Back Maxwell St BOL BL1 * 22 B8
Back Maybank St BOLS/LL BL3 2 B9
Back Mayfield Av BOLS/LL BL3 52 E1
Back Mayor St BOL BL1 2 A6
TOT/BURYW BL8 4 A2
Back Maze St BOLS/LL BL3 3 M9
Back McDonna St BOL BL1 35 M1
Back McKean St BOLS/LL BL3 36 D8
Back McKean St North
BOLS/LL BL3 * 36 D8
Back Melbourne Rd
BOLS/LL BL3 35 M7
Back Melbourne St STLY SK15 91 K2
Back Mellor Gv BOL BL1 * 35 L3
Back Mellor Gv West BOL BL1 * 35 L3
Back Mellor Rd NM/HAY SK22 124 E3
Back Melrose Av BOL BL1 35 K3
Back Melville St BOLS/LL BL3 52 D1
Back Mercia St BOLS/LL BL3 35 M7
Back Meredith St BOLS/LL BL3 52 C1
Back Mere Gdns BOL BL1 2 C2
Back Merlin Gv BOL BL1 * 35 L3
Back Merton St
TOT/BURYW BL8 4 B2
Back Mesnes St WGN WN1 15 G2
Back Methwold St
BOLS/LL BL3 * 35 M8
Back Milford Rd BOLS/LL BL3 52 B1
Back Miller St BOL BL1 * 22 B8
Back Millet St BURY BL9 4 C5
Back Mill St North
EDGW/EG BL7 * 22 C4
Back Mill St South
EDGW/EG BL7 * 22 C4
Back Milner Av BURY BL9 25 J7
Back Minorca St BOLS/LL BL3 * 36 B8
Back Monmouth Av BURY BL9 25 J7
Back Moor HYDE SK14 92 D8
Back Moorfield Gv BOLE BL2 36 E3
Back Moorgate West BURY BL9 5 H3
Back Mornington Rd East
BOL BL1 35 M4
Back Morris Green La
BOLS/LL BL3 51 M2
Back Morris Green La East
BOLS/LL BL3 51 M2
Back Moss Ter BOL BL1 2 E3
Back Mostyn Av BURY BL9 25 J7
Back Mowbray St BOL BL1 * 35 L3
Back Murton Ter BOL BL1 22 C8
Back Musgrave Rd BOL BL1 35 M4
Back Musgrave Rd North
BOL BL1 35 M4
Back Myrtle St BURY BL9 5 K4
Back Myrtle St South BURY BL9 5 K5
Back Nebo St BOLS/LL BL3 36 A8
Back Nelson St HOR/BR BL6 * 34 A1
Back Nelson St North BURY BL9 4 F8
Back Nelson St South BURY BL9 4 F9
Back Nevada St BOL BL1 36 B3
Back Newbold St
TOT/BURYW BL8 38 F2
Back New George St
TOT/BURYW BL8 4 A3
Back Newhall La BOL BL1 35 K3
Back Newport Rd
BOLS/LL BL3 * 36 D8
Back Newport St BOL BL1 2 E6
Back Newton St BOL BL1 36 B2
Back Nixon Rd BOLS/LL BL3 51 M1
Back Normanby St
BOLS/LL BL3 51 M2
Back Norris St BOLS/LL BL3 * 53 K1
Back Northern Gv BOL BL1 35 M3
Back Nunnery Rd
BOLS/LL BL3 * 35 L8
Back Nut St BOL BL1 36 A2
Back Oak St RAD M26 54 F3
Back Olaf St BOLE BL2 3 J1
Back Oldham Rd MILN OL16 11 G6
Back Olga St BOL BL1 36 A2
Back Olga St North BOL BL1 * 36 A2
Back Olive Bank
TOT/BURYW BL8 24 E8
Back Oram St BURY BL9 25 K8
Back Oriel St BOLS/LL BL3 35 M7
Back Ormrod St BURY BL9 5 J5
Back Osborne Gv BOL BL1 35 M3
Back o' th' Low Rd OLDE OL4 60 C4
Back Owen's Rw HOR/BR BL6 33 M1
Back Oxford Gv North BOL BL1 35 M3
Back Oxford St BURY BL9 5 H6
Back Packer St BOL BL1 35 M2
Back Palace St BOL BL1 2 E3
Back Palm St BOL BL1 36 C1
Back Parkdale Rd BOLE BL2 3 L1
Back Parkfield Rd BOLS/LL BL3 52 D1
Back Parkhills Rd North
BURY BL9 4 E8
Back Parkhills Rd South
BURY BL9 4 F9
Back Parkinson St
BOLS/LL BL3 * 35 M7
Back Park Rd BOL BL1 2 A5
Back Park St BOL BL1 2 A3
Back Park Vw BOL BL1 22 C6
Back Park View Rd
BOLS/LL BL3 * 35 M8
Back Parsonage St BURY BL9 5 J3
Backparsons La BURY BL9 4 F4
Back Partington St
BOLS/LL BL3 51 M2
Back Patience St WHIT OL12 * 27 M3
Back Patterson St
BOLS/LL BL3 * 35 K8
Back Peabody St BOLS/LL BL3 * 36 B8
Back Peace St BOLS/LL BL3 * 2 A9
Back Pedder St BOL BL1 35 M3
Back Peers St TOT/BURYW BL8 4 A5
Back Penarth Rd BOLS/LL BL3 * 35 L8
Back Pennington Rd
BOLS/LL BL3 52 C1
Back Percy St BURY BL9 5 K2

Back Peter St BURY BL9 .....5 H3
Back Peveril St BOLS/LL BL3 .....51 L1
Back Phoenix St BURY BL9 .....4 D3
Back Piccadilly CMANE M1 .....7 J5
Back Pikes La West
  BOLS/LL BL3 .....35 M7
Back Pine St BOL BL1 .....36 C2
  BURY BL9 .....5 K4
Back Pleasant St BOL BL1 .....36 F3
Back Pool Fold CMANW M2 * .....6 F4
Back Poplar Av BOL BL1 .....22 C8
Back Porter St BURY BL9 .....5 K4
Back Portland St AUL OL6 .....90 D2
Back Portugal St BOL BL2 .....3 J5
Back Primrose Gv BOL BL1 .....22 C8
Back Primula St BOL BL1 .....22 C8
Back Proctor St
  TOT/BURYW BL8 * .....38 F3
Back Progress St BOL BL1 * .....36 C3
Back Quay St CSLFD M3 .....6 C5
Back Quebec St BOLS/LL BL3 .....2 A4
Back Queensgate BOL BL1 .....35 M4
Back Queen St BOL BL1 .....2 D5
Back Radcliffe Rd East
  BOL BL2 * .....3 J4
Back Raimond St BOL BL1 .....35 M1
Back Rainshaw St BOL BL1 .....22 C8
Back Rake St BURY BL9 .....5 J8
Back Randal St BOLS/LL BL3 * .....35 M7
Back Range St BOLS/LL BL3 .....36 A8
Back Raphael St BOL BL1 .....36 A5
Back Raven St BURY BL9 .....5 C1
Back Rawson St BOL BL1 .....35 M5
Back Rawson Rd North
  BOL BL1 .....35 M3
Back Raymond Av BURY BL9 .....25 J8
Back Red Bank ANC M4 .....87 K1
Back Redhill Gv BOL BL1 .....2 C2
Back Regent St BURY BL9 .....4 F1
Back Ribblesdale Rd
  BOLS/LL BL3 .....36 A8
Back Richard Burch St
  BURY BL9 .....5 G2
Back Richelieu St BOLS/LL BL3 .....36 D8
Back Rigby La North
  BOLE BL2 * .....22 F6
Back Rigby La South BOLE BL2 .....22 F6
Back Rishton La East
  BOLS/LL BL3 .....52 C1
Back Rishton La East
  BOLS/LL BL3 .....52 C1
Back Rochdale Old Rd North
  BURY BL9 .....5 M2
Back Rochdale Old Rd South
  BURY BL9 .....5 M2
Back Rochdale Old South Rd
  BURY BL9 .....39 M1
Back Rochdale Rd BURY BL9 .....5 H4
Back Rochdale Rd South
  BURY BL9 .....5 H5
Back Rock Av BOL BL1 .....35 M1
Back Roland St BOL BL1 .....35 M7
Back Romer St BOLE BL2 .....3 M4
Back Rosamond St
  BOLS/LL BL3 .....35 M8
Back Roscow Av BOLE BL2 .....37 H4
Back Rose Bank BURY BL9 .....25 J8
Back Roseberry St BOLS/LL BL3 .....35 M8
Back Rossini St BOL BL1 * .....36 A1
Back Rowena St BOLS/LL BL3 * .....52 F2
Back Rowland St BOLS/LL BL3 * .....51 L1
Back Roxalina St BOLS/LL BL3 .....36 B8
Back Royal Av BURY BL9 .....25 J7
Back Royds St MILN OL16 .....11 H9
Back Rudolph St BOLS/LL BL3 .....52 C1
Back Rumworth St
  BOLS/LL BL3 .....36 A8
Back Rushton Rd BOL BL1 * .....35 L3
Back Russell St BOL BL1 * .....35 M4
Back Russell St BOL BL1 .....35 M3
Back Rutland Gv BOL BL1 .....35 M3
Back Ryefield St BOL BL1 .....3 L1
Back St Anne's St BURY BL9 .....25 J8
Back St Ann St BOL BL1 .....2 B2
Back St Augustine St BOL BL1 .....36 A2
Back St George's Rd ANC M4 * .....7 J1
  BOL BL1 .....2 D3
Back St George's Rd North
  BOL BL1 .....2 B3
Back St Helens Rd
  BOLS/LL BL3 .....36 A8
Back St Helens Rd South
  BOLS/LL BL3 .....51 L2
Back St James's St OLD OL1 * .....59 L5
Back St Mark's La CHH M8 * .....72 C4
Back St Mary's Pl BOLS/LL BL3 .....4 D5
Back St Philip's Av BOLS/LL BL3 .....36 A8
Back St Thomas St East
  BOL BL1 * .....36 A2
Back Salford LEIGH WN7 .....66 C7
Back Salford St BURY BL9 .....25 K8
Back Salisbury St BOLS/LL BL3 .....2 B6
Back Salisbury Ter BOLE BL2 .....37 G3
Back Sandon St West
  BOLS/LL BL3 .....36 A8
Back Sandy Bank Rd
  EDGW/EG BL7 .....17 G7
Back Sankey St BURY BL9 .....4 C4
Back Sapling Rd BOLS/LL BL3 .....51 L2
Back Sapling Rd South
  BOLS/LL BL3 .....51 L2
Back Scholes St TOT/BURYW BL8 * .....4 A3
Back Scott St OLDS OL8 * .....9 H9
Back Scowcroft St BOLE BL2 .....3 J1
Back Settle St BOLS/LL BL3 .....52 A1
Back Settle St North
  BOLS/LL BL3 .....52 B1
Back Seymour Rd BOL BL1 * .....35 L3
Back Shakerley Rd TYLD M29 * .....67 J3
Back Sharman St BOLS/LL BL3 .....3 J9
Back Shaw-street BURY BL9 .....5 K3
Back Shepherd St BURY BL9 .....5 K3
Back Sherwood St BOL BL1 .....36 C1
Back Shipton St BOL BL1 .....36 C1
Back Short St ATH M46 .....67 H3
Back Silverdale St BOL BL1 .....35 M1
Back Silver St BURY BL9 .....4 E5
Back Skipton St BOLE BL2 .....3 K1
Back Smethurst La
  BOLS/LL BL3 .....51 L2
Back Smethurst La West
  BOLS/LL BL3 .....51 L2
Back Sofa St BOL BL1 .....35 L3
Back Soho St BOL BL1 .....2 E6
Back Somerset Rd BOL BL1 .....35 M1
Back Somerville St BOL BL1 * .....35 M1
Back South Cross East
  BURY BL9 .....5 G5
Back South Pde CSLFD M3 .....6 E4
Back South St BOLS/LL BL3 .....52 B1
Back South View St BOLE BL2 .....3 M5
Back Spa Rd BOL BL1 .....2 A6
Back Spa Rd North BOL BL1 .....2 A6

Back Spa Rd West BOL BL1 * .....2 A6
Back Spear St ANC M4 * .....7 J3
Back Springfield St
  BOLS/LL BL3 .....36 E8
Back Spring Gdns BOL BL1 * .....2 E6
  MDTN M24 .....57 K2
Back Spring St East BURY BL9 .....5 C6
Back Spring St West BURY BL9 .....5 K4
Back Square St RAMS BL0 .....18 F6
Back Stainsbury St
  BOLS/LL BL3 .....35 M8
Back Stanley St RAMS BL0 * .....18 E7
Back Stephen St
  TOT/BURYW BL8 .....38 F2
Back Stewart St BOL BL1 .....36 B3
Backstone St BOL BL1 .....3 J1
Back Sunlight Rd BOL BL1 .....35 M5
Back Sunning Hill St
  BOLS/LL BL3 .....36 A8
Back Sunnyside Rd BOL BL1 .....35 M2
Back Swan La BOLS/LL BL3 .....36 A8
Back Tavistock Rd BOL BL1 .....2 A6
Back Teak St BURY BL9 .....5 K5
Back Tenterden St BURY BL9 .....4 D5
Back Thicketford Rd
  BOLE BL2 * .....36 F3
Back Thicketford Rd West
  BOLE BL2 .....36 E3
Back Thomasson Cl BOL BL1 .....36 B3
Back Thomas St ANC M4 * .....7 H3
Back Thorns Rd BOL BL1 .....36 B1
Back Thorn St BOL BL1 .....36 C2
Back Thorpe St BOL BL1 .....36 C2
Back Thurnham St
  BOLS/LL BL3 .....51 M1
Back Tinline St BOL BL1 .....5 J5
Back Tonge Moor Rd BOLE BL2 .....36 E2
Back Tonge Moor Rd East
  BOLE BL2 * .....3 J1
Back Tonge Old Rd BOLE BL2 .....3 M4
Back Tong St BOLS/LL BL3 .....37 K8
Back Tottington Rd
  TOT/BURYW BL8 * .....24 E8
Back Tottington Rd East
  BOLE BL2 .....23 H7
Back Tottington Rd North
  TOT/BURYW BL8 .....4 A2
Back Tottington Rd South
  TOT/BURYW BL8 .....4 A2
Back Tudor St BOLS/LL BL3 .....35 M8
Back Turner St ANC M4 * .....7 H3
Back Turton Rd East BOLE BL2 .....22 F7
Back Turton Rd West BOLE BL2 .....22 F8
Back Uganda St BOLS/LL BL3 .....51 M1
Back Ulleswater St BOLE BL2 .....36 C2
Back Union Rd BOLE BL2 .....3 H1
  NM/HAY SK22 .....124 E5
Back Unsworth St South
  BOLS/LL BL3 .....2 B9
Back Uttley St BOL BL1 .....36 A2
Back Venice St BOLS/LL BL3 .....35 M8
Back Vernon St BOL BL1 * .....2 C3
  BURY BL9 .....4 F1
Back Vernon St South BOL BL1 * .....2 C3
Back Vickerman St BOL BL1 .....36 A2
Back Victoria Gv BOL BL1 .....35 M3
Back Victoria Gv North
  BOL BL1 .....35 M3
Back Victory St East BOL BL1 .....35 M4
Back View St BOL BL1 .....2 A3
Back Vincent St BOL BL1 .....2 A6
Back Vine St BOLS/LL BL3 .....35 M6
Back Viola St BOL BL1 .....36 B1
Back Waldeck St BOL BL1 .....35 M4
Back Walmersley Rd East
  BURY BL9 .....5 H4
Back Walmersley Rd West
  BURY BL9 .....5 G1
Back Walnut St BOL BL1 .....36 C1
Back Walshaw Rd North
  TOT/BURYW BL8 .....4 A2
Back Walshaw Rd South
  TOT/BURYW BL8 .....38 F1
Back Wapping St BOL BL1 * .....36 A2
Back Wardle St BOLE BL2 .....3 M3
Back Wash La BURY BL9 .....5 K4
Back Wash La South BURY BL9 .....5 L4
Back Water St EDGW/EG BL7 .....22 A2
  STKP SK1 .....13 K2
Back Waverley Rd BOL BL1 .....36 B1
Back Webster St BOLS/LL BL3 .....4 E8
Back Wellington Rd South
  BURY BL9 .....5 G1
Back Wells St BURY BL9 .....4 D7
Back Westbank St BOL BL1 .....2 A6
Back Westbourne Av
  BOLS/LL BL3 .....52 D1
Back Weston St North
  BOLS/LL BL3 .....36 D8
Back Weston St South
  BOLS/LL BL3 .....36 C8
Back Westwood Rd BOL BL1 * .....35 M4
Back Wheatfield St BOLE BL2 * .....3 L8
Back Whittle Gv BOL BL1 .....35 M4
Back Whittle St
  TOT/BURYW BL8 .....4 A2
Back Wigan Rd BOLS/LL BL3 .....35 L7
Back Wigan Rd North
  BOLS/LL BL3 .....35 K8
Back Wigan Rd South
  BOLS/LL BL3 .....35 L7
Back Willows BOLS/LL BL3 .....35 L8
Back Willows La BOLS/LL BL3 .....36 A8
Back Willows La North
  BOLS/LL BL3 .....35 L8
Back Willows La South
  BOLS/LL BL3 .....35 M8
Back Wilmot St BOL BL1 .....35 M1
Back Wilton St BOL BL1 .....36 C1
Back Windermere St BOL BL1 .....36 C1
Back Windsor Gv BOL BL1 .....35 M3
Back Wolfenden St BOL BL1 * .....36 B2
Back Woodbine Rd
  BOLS/LL BL3 .....51 M1
Back Woodfield St
  BOLS/LL BL3 .....52 D1
Back Woodgate St
  TOT/BURYW BL8 * .....4 A3
Back Wood St HOR/BR BL6 .....33 M1
Back Worcester St BOL BL1 .....36 B3
Back Wordsworth St BOL BL1 .....36 A2
Back Worsel St BOLS/LL BL3 .....35 M8
Back Worsel St North
  BOLS/LL BL3 .....35 M8
Back Wynne St BOL BL1 .....36 B2
Back Yates St BOLE BL2 .....3 H1
Baclaw St WGN WN1 .....48 C3
Bacon Av DTN/ASHW M34 .....101 K5
Bacup St NEWH/MOS M40 .....73 K4
Badbury St RNFD/HAY WA11 .....78 A3
Badby St ANC M4 .....88 A3

Baddeley Cl EDGY/DAV SK3 .....112 A7
Bader Dr HEY OL10 .....41 G5
Bader Dr HEY OL10 .....2 E5
Badger Cl HYDE SK14 .....91 H8
  MILN OL16 .....42 F1
  MPL/ROM SK6 .....123 H1
Badger Edge La OLDE OL4 .....60 F1
Badger La MILN OL16 .....42 F1
Badger Rd ALT WA14 .....107 M4
Badgers Wk
  WYTH/NTH M22 .....119 G3
Badgers Wy GLSP SK13 .....104 E5
Bag La ATH M46 .....50 E8
Bagnall Cl UPML OL3 .....61 M3
  WHIT OL12 .....27 J2
Bagshaw La WGNE/HIN WN2 .....69 H2
Bagshaw St HYDE SK14 .....91 G7
Bagslate Moor La ROCH OL11 .....27 J4
Bagstock Av POY/DIS SK12 .....129 J3
Baguley Crs EDGY/DAV SK3 .....112 A6
  MDTN M24 .....56 D6
Baguley Dr BURY BL9 .....55 K2
Baguley La SALE M33 .....109 H2
Baguley Rd SALE M33 .....97 H8
Baguley St DROY M43 .....89 G3
Bahama Cl BOLS/LL BL3 .....35 M7
Bahama Rd RNFD/HAY WA11 .....78 A4
Baildon Rd ROCH OL11 .....27 L3
Baildon St NEWH/MOS M40 .....73 K5
Bailey Fold WHTN BL5 .....50 A3
Bailey La BOLE BL2 .....37 H3
  MANAIR M90 .....118 D3
  PART M31 .....94 C8
Bailey Rd TRPK M17 .....85 K5
Bailey St OP/CLY M11 .....89 G3
  PWCH M25 .....55 M7
Bailey Wk ALT WA14 .....116 E4
Baillie St MILN OL16 .....10 F3
  RAD M26 .....39 H7
Baillie St East MILN OL16 .....11 G3
The Bails BRO M7 .....71 M6
Bainbridge Av
  GOL/RIS/CUL WA3 .....80 C4
Bainbridge Cl
  WGTN/LGST M12 * .....88 A6
Bainbridge Rd OLDE OL4 .....60 A3
Bainburgh Clough OLDS OL8 .....59 M8
Baines Av IRL M44 .....94 C3
Baines St BOL BL1 .....35 L4
Bain St SWIN M27 .....70 C5
Baird St CMANE M1 .....7 K6
Baitings Cl WHIT OL12 .....26 F2
Bakehurst Cl NM/HAY SK22 .....124 E5
Baker St FWTH BL4 .....53 L6
  HEY OL10 .....41 H4
  HTNM SK4 .....13 G1
  MDTN M24 .....57 L4
  RAMS BL0 .....18 E7
  STLY SK15 .....91 L3
  WGNS/IIMK WN3 .....14 D8
Bakewell Av AUL OL6 .....76 C6
  DTN/ASHW M34 .....101 K4
Bakewell Dr
  WGNNW/ST WN6 .....31 K8
Bakewell Ms GLSP SK13 .....104 A3
Bakewell St BRAM/HZG SK7 .....122 A4
  DROY M43 .....89 H2
  ECC M30 .....84 E4
  STRET M32 .....96 F1
Bakewell Wk EDGY/DAV SK3 .....12 F7
  GTN M18 .....88 F3
Bala Cl ORD M5 .....86 D2
Balcarres Av WGN WN1 .....48 B2
Balcarres Rd WGNE/HIN WN2 .....32 E8
Balcary Gv BOL BL1 .....35 L4
Balcombe Cl TOT/BURYW BL8 .....24 E5
Balderstone Rd ROCH OL11 .....42 D2
Baldock Rd DID/WITH M20 .....111 G1
Baldrine Dr WGNE/HIN WN2 .....49 L7
Baldwin Rd BNG/LEV M19 .....99 J6
Baldwin St BOLS/LL BL3 .....2 C8
  WGN WN1 .....15 J3
  WGNE/HIN WN2 .....65 L1
  WGNS/IIMK WN3 .....15 J7
  WGNW/BIL/OR WN5 .....46 E7
Bale St CMANW M2 .....6 F6
Balfern Cl WHTN BL5 .....50 B3
Balfern Fold WHTN BL5 .....50 B3
Balfour Gv RDSH SK5 .....100 C4
Balfour Rd ALT WA14 .....108 A5
  URM M41 .....95 L2
Balfour St BOLS/LL BL3 .....2 A7
  CHH M8 .....72 D4
  OLDE OL4 .....59 M5
  ROY/SHW OL2 .....43 L4
  SLFD M6 .....71 J6
Balham Wk WGTN/LGST M12 .....88 C6
Balharry Av RNFD/HAY WA11 .....78 C5
Balinge WHIT OL12 .....10 D2
Ballantine St NEWH/MOS M40 .....73 M8
Ballantyne Wy
  GOL/RIS/CUL WA3 .....80 B4
Ballard Cl LIT OL15 .....21 M5
Ballard Wy ROY/SHW OL2 .....43 M5
Ballater Av URM M41 .....95 K3
Ballbrook Av DID/WITH M20 .....98 D7
Balleratt St BNG/LEV M19 .....99 K3
Balliol Cl MPL/ROM SK6 .....101 M8
Balliol St CHH M8 .....72 D4
  SWIN M27 .....70 B4
Balliol Wy AIMK WN4 .....63 J8
Balloon St ANC M4 .....7 G2
Ball St MILN OL16 .....11 L3
  WGNNW/ST WN6 .....47 H2
Ball Wk HYDE SK14 .....103 J3
Balmain Av GTN M18 .....99 M1
Balmain Rd URM M41 .....95 J3
Balmer Rd NTHM/RTH M23 .....109 K7
Balmfield St CHH M8 .....72 D7
Balmoral Av BOLS/LL BL3 .....53 K1
  CHD/CHDH SK8 .....120 C1
  DTN/ASHW M34 .....90 A5
  GOL/RIS/CUL WA3 .....80 A3
  HYDE SK14 .....102 A1
  ROCH OL11 .....27 L4
  ROY/SHW OL2 .....43 H3
  URM M41 .....95 J3
  WHTF M45 .....55 H3

Balmoral Dr ALT WA14 .....108 C4
  DTN/ASHW M34 .....89 K8
  HEY OL10 .....40 D3
  LEIGH WN7 .....67 G6
  MPL/ROM SK6 .....123 G5
  POY/DIS SK12 .....129 H1
  STLY SK15 .....91 K1
  WGNE/HIN WN2 .....48 F1
Balmoral Gra PWCH M25 .....72 B1
Balmoral Gv
  BRAM/HZG SK7 .....122 B1
Balmoral Rd AIMK WN4 .....63 K8
  FWTH BL4 .....52 F5
  HALE/TIMP WA15 .....108 B8
  HTNM SK4 .....111 K1
  RUSH/FAL M14 .....99 G4
  SWIN M27 .....70 D2
  WGNW/BIL/OR WN5 .....47 H6
Balmoral St GTN M18 .....88 F6
Balmoral Wy WILM/AE SK9 .....126 E6
Balmore Cl BOLS/LL BL3 .....51 K1
Balm St RAMS BL0 .....18 D8
Balniel Wk WGN WN1 .....48 B2
Balsam Cl BRUN/LGST M13 * .....7 K9
Balshaw Av IRL M44 .....94 C3
Balshaw Cl BOLS/LL BL3 .....35 M7
Balshaw Ct IRL M44 .....94 C3
Baltic Rd ALT WA14 .....107 K6
Baltic St ORD M5 .....86 B2
Bamber Av SALE M33 .....109 H1
Bamber Cft WHTN BL5 .....50 B1
Bamber St BKLY M9 .....57 G7
Bamber Wk BOLS/LL BL3 * .....2 B9
Bamburgh Cl RAD M26 .....37 H7
Bamburgh Dr AULW OL7 .....75 H7
Bamburgh Pl AIMK WN4 .....63 K7
Bambury St BURY BL9 .....5 L2
  MDTN M24 .....57 K2
Bamford Av DTN/ASHW M34 .....101 J4
  MDTN M24 .....57 L4
Bamford Cl BRUN/LGST M13 * .....7 K9
  CHD/CHDH SK8 .....119 M4
Bamford Cl ROCH OL11 .....27 L6
Bamford Dr WGNE/HIN WN2 .....15 M1
Bamford Fold GLSP SK13 .....104 B3
Bamford Gdns
  HALE/TIMP WA15 .....109 G7
Bamford Gv GLSP SK13 .....104 B3
  DID/WITH M20 .....110 D1
Bamford Ms GLSP SK13 .....104 B3
  ROCH OL11 .....27 H5
Bamford Prec DID/WITH M20 .....110 D1
Bamford Rd BKLY M9 .....56 D3
  RAMS BL0 .....19 H4
  RAMS BL0 .....19 H4
Bamford St CHAD OL9 .....8 C2
  LIT OL15 .....21 K7
  OP/CLY M11 .....88 D2
  ROY/SHW OL2 .....43 H8
  STKP SK1 .....13 J6
Bamford Wy ROCH OL11 .....27 J6
Bampton Av OFTN SK2 .....112 E5
  WHTN BL5 .....50 B3
Bampton Rd WYTH/NTH M22 .....118 E5
Banbury Cl LEIGH WN7 .....81 H3
Banbury Dr ALT WA14 .....108 E4
Banbury Ms SWIN M27 .....70 A3
Banbury Rd FAIL M35 .....74 D8
  MDTN M24 .....57 J7
  NTHM/RTH M23 .....109 J7
  WGNW/BIL/OR WN5 .....62 A2
Banbury St BOLE BL2 .....36 F3
  STKP SK1 .....13 J5
Bancroft Cl MPL/ROM SK6 .....113 H1
Bancroft Fold HYDE SK14 .....91 L7
Bancroft Rd HALE/TIMP WA15 .....117 J1
  SWIN M27 .....70 B3
Banff Gv HEY OL10 .....40 D3
Banff Rd RUSH/FAL M14 .....87 M8
Bangor Fold LEIGH WN7 .....66 F8
Bangor Rd CHD/CHDH SK8 .....111 K6
Bangor St AUL OL6 .....91 H2
  BOL BL1 .....2 D2
  HULME M15 .....87 G7
  MILN OL16 .....11 J7
  RDSH SK5 .....100 C8
Banham Av WGNS/IIMK WN3 .....62 F1
Bank Av WGNW/BIL/OR WN5 .....46 A7
Bank Barn La WHIT OL12 .....21 H6
Bankbottom GLSP SK13 .....93 K7
Bank Bridge Rd OP/CLY M11 .....88 D7
Bankbrook WGNNW/ST WN6 .....31 G8
Bank Buildings
  WGNE/HIN WN2 * .....64 D7
Bank Cl LIT OL15 .....29 K1
Banker St BOLS/LL BL3 .....3 M9
Bankes Av WGNW/BIL/OR WN5 .....46 D6
Bankfield Av BRUN/LGST M13 .....99 H1
  DROY M43 .....89 K2
  HTNM SK4 .....12 D1
  IRL M44 .....94 A7
Bankfield Cl BKLY M9 .....73 G3
  BOLS/LL BL3 .....35 M8
  HTNM SK4 .....112 B1
Bankfield Dr OLDS OL8 .....75 L2
  WALK M28 .....68 D6
Bankfield La ROCH OL11 .....27 H4
Bankfield Rd CHD/CHDH SK8 .....120 B3
  FWTH BL4 .....53 G6
  MPL/ROM SK6 .....101 L6
  SALE M33 .....96 B6
  TYLD M29 .....68 B4
Bankfield St BKLY M9 .....73 G3
  BOLS/LL BL3 .....35 M8
  HTNM SK4 .....112 B1
Bank Field St RAD M26 .....54 A5
Bank Hall TOT/BURYW BL8 .....38 D2
Bankhall Cl WGNE/HIN WN2 .....65 L3
Bankhall Rd HTNM SK4 .....111 K2
Bank Hey WHTN BL5 * .....50 B1
Bank Hill St OLDE OL4 .....59 L5
Bank House Cl TYLD M29 .....68 B3
Bank House Rd BKLY M9 .....72 F1
Bankhouse Rd
  TOT/BURYW BL8 .....24 F8
Banklands Cl IRL M44 .....94 A7
Bank La GLSP SK13 .....93 K5
  LHULT M38 .....52 C6
  SLFD M6 .....71 J2
  WHIT OL12 .....21 G5
Bankley St BNG/LEV M19 .....99 K3
Bank Mellor Rd NM/HAY SK22 .....124 E3
Bankmill Cl BRUN/LGST M13 * .....7 J9
Bank Pas GOL/RIS/CUL WA3 * .....79 K3
Bank Pl CSLFD M3 .....6 A3

Bank Rd CHH M8 .....72 C2
  MPL/ROM SK6 .....113 K1
  SKEL WN8 .....30 A7
  STLY SK15 .....77 H7
Banks Ct LEIGH WN7 .....66 A7
Banks Cft HEY OL10 .....41 G5
Bankside HALE/TIMP WA15 .....117 M6
  HYDE SK14 .....103 G3
Bank Side WHTN BL5 .....50 C4
Bankside Av AIMK WN4 .....63 K4
  RAD M26 .....39 G8
  UPML OL3 .....61 M5
Bankside Cl CHAD OL9 .....8 A3
  MPL/ROM SK6 .....114 E3
  UPML OL3 .....61 M4
  WILM/AE SK9 .....127 K3
Bankside Ct HTNM SK4 * .....111 K1
Bankside Rd DID/WITH M20 .....110 E5
Banks La STKP SK1 .....112 E4
Bank Stanway Av BOLS/LL BL3 .....2 B7
  BOL BL1 .....2 C4
  BRO M7 .....72 C4
  BURY BL9 .....4 D5
  CHD/CHDH SK8 .....111 H6
  CSLFD M3 .....6 A3
  DROY M43 .....89 J4
  DTN/ASHW M34 .....90 D4
  DTN/ASHW M34 .....101 L4
  EDGW/EG BL7 .....16 B3
  FWTH BL4 .....53 G4
  GLSP SK13 .....93 J7
  GOL/RIS/CUL WA3 .....79 K3
  HEY OL10 .....40 E2
  HYDE SK14 .....102 A1
  MPL/ROM SK6 .....101 L7
  NEWH/MOS M40 .....73 M2
  NM/HAY SK22 .....125 M2
  OLDE OL4 .....60 A6
  OP/CLY M11 .....88 D2
  RAD M26 .....54 E2
  RAMS BL0 .....19 H5
  ROCH OL11 .....28 D8
  ROY/SHW OL2 .....43 K5
  SALE M33 .....96 F7
  TOT/BURYW BL8 .....24 C8
  WGNE/HIN WN2 .....64 D1
  WGNW/BIL/OR WN5 .....47 H5
  WHTF M45 .....55 H3
Bankswood Cl GLSP SK13 .....93 K8
The Bank GLSP SK13 .....105 G4
Bank Top AUL OL6 .....90 F2
  HEY OL10 .....40 E1
Bank Top Gv BOL BL1 .....35 K4
Bank Top Pk OLDE OL4 .....60 A6
Bank Top St HEY OL10 .....40 E1
Bank Vale Rd NM/HAY SK22 .....125 M4
Bankwell St HULME M15 .....87 H7
Bankwood WGNNW/ST WN6 .....30 B6
Banky La SALE M33 .....95 M6
Bannach Dr CHD/CHDH SK8 .....58 D4
Bannatyne Cl NEWH/MOS M40 .....74 D1
Banner Dale Cl
  BRUN/LGST M13 .....88 C3
Bannerman Rd PWCH M25 .....71 L1
Bannerman Rd DROY M43 .....89 L3
Banner St WGNE/HIN WN2 .....49 H7
  WGNS/IIMK WN3 .....15 K9
Banner Wk OP/CLY M11 .....88 D2
Bannister Dr CHD/CHDH SK8 .....120 B2
Bannister St BOLE BL2 .....37 H4
  OFTN SK2 .....13 K8
Bannister Wy WGNS/IIMK WN3 .....63 K7
Bann St EDGY/DAV SK3 .....13 G6
Banstead Av WYTH/NTH M22 .....110 A5
Bantry Av BKLY M9 .....72 E1
Bantry St BOLS/LL BL3 .....3 J1
Baptist St ANC M4 .....7 J1
Barathea Cl ROCH OL11 .....41 L1
Barbara Rd BOLS/LL BL3 .....51 K2
Barbeck Cl NEWH/MOS M40 .....88 B1
Barberry Bank EDGW/EG BL7 .....22 A2
Barberry Cl ALT WA14 .....107 L5
Barber St GLSP SK13 .....93 L7
  OP/CLY M11 * .....89 K2
Barbican St DID/WITH M20 .....98 E5
Barbirolli Sq CMANW M2 .....6 F7
Barbon Wk ANC M4 * .....7 L3
Barbrook Cl WGNNW/ST WN6 .....30 F6
Barbury Cl LEIGH WN7 .....66 C5
Barchester Av BOLE BL2 .....37 H3
Barchester Rd
  CHD/CHDH SK8 .....110 F8
Barcicroft Rd BNG/LEV M19 .....99 H8
Barclay Rd POY/DIS SK12 .....129 J2
Barclays Av SLFD M6 .....71 G6
Barcliffe Av NEWH/MOS M40 .....73 M4
Barclyde St ROCH OL11 .....10 C8
Barcombe Cl OLDE OL4 .....60 A2
  STRET M32 .....96 C1
Barcroft Rd BOL BL1 .....35 L2
Barcroft St BURY BL9 .....4 A4
Bardale Gv AIMK WN4 .....78 D1
Bardell Cl POY/DIS SK12 * .....129 H2
Bardney Av WGNS/IIMK WN3 .....79 J2
Bardon Cl BOL BL1 * .....36 A3
Bardon Rd NTHM/RTH M23 .....109 J6
Bardsea Av WYTH/NTH M22 .....118 F3
Bardsley Av FAIL M35 .....74 C5
Bardsley Cl BOLE BL2 .....23 G7
  HYDE SK14 .....103 H2
Bardsley Gate Av STLY SK15 .....92 B4
Bardsley St CHAD OL9 .....74 C1
  HTNM SK4 .....112 A1
  MDTN M24 .....57 K3
  NEWH/MOS M40 .....74 A7
  OLDE OL4 .....60 B4
  OLDE OL4 .....60 B4
Bardwell Av WHTN BL5 .....50 A4
Barehill St LIT OL15 .....21 M6
Bare St BOL BL1 .....3 H3
Barff Rd ORD M5 .....85 M2
Barfold Cl OFTN SK2 .....113 K7
Barford Dr WGNW/BIL/OR WN5 .....46 A7
  WILM/AE SK9 .....127 G3
Barford Gv HOR/BR BL6 .....34 C3
Bar Gap Rd OLDE OL1 .....9 J3
Baring St CMANE M1 .....7 K7
Barkan Wy SWIN M27 .....70 E4
Barker Rd MPL/ROM SK6 .....113 J1
Barker's La SALE M33 .....96 C7
Barker St BURY BL9 .....4 C2
  CSLFD M3 .....72 C8
  LEIGH WN7 .....66 B5
  OLD OL1 .....9 H1
  WGN WN1 * .....65 M7
Barke St LIT OL15 .....21 J1
Barking St NEWH/MOS M40 .....88 J1

Bark St BOL BL1 2 D4
FWTH BL4 53 L7
Bark St East BOL BL1 2 E3
Bark Wk HULME M15 87 J6
Barkway Rd STRET M32 96 D3
Barkwell La MOSL OL5 76 E3
Bar La BOL BL1 22 B7
Barlborough Rd
WGNW/BIL/OR WN5 47 G7
Barlea Av NEWH/MOS M40 74 A3
Barley Brook Meadow BOL BL1 22 C6
Barley Brook St
WGNNW/ST WN6 14 D1
Barleycorn Cl SALE M33 109 K1
Barley Cft CHD/CHDH SK8 120 B4
Barleycroft GLSP SK13 93 J8
Barley Croft Rd HYDE SK14 91 H7
Barleycroft St
OLDTF/WHR M16 87 J8
Barley Dr BRAM/HZG SK7 121 G5
Barleyfield Wk MDTN M24 57 H3
Barley Hall St HEY OL10 41 H1
Barlow Cl BURY BL9 25 J7
Barlow Ct WALK M28 * 69 H1
Barlow Crs MPL/ROM SK6 114 C8
Barlow Fold BURY BL9 39 J7
Barlow Fold Cl BURY BL9 39 H7
Barlow Fold Rd MPL/ROM SK6 114 A1
RDSH SK5 100 C4
Barlow Hall Rd CCHDY M21 97 M7
Barlow La ECC M30 84 F2
Barlow La North RDSH SK5 100 C4
Barlow Moor Cl WHIT OL12 27 H2
Barlow Moor Ct DID/WITH M20 98 C8
Barlow Moor Rd CCHDY M21 97 L5
DID/WITH M20 98 B8
Barlow Park Av BOL BL1 22 A7
Barlow Pl BRUN/LGST M13 7 L9
Barlow Rd ALT WA14 107 L4
BNG/LEV M19 99 M3
DUK SK16 91 G4
ORD M5 86 F3
STRET M32 86 C8
WILM/AE SK9 126 F3
Barlow's Cft CSLFD M3 6 D3
Barlow's La South
BRAM/HZG SK7 121 L1
Barlow St BURY BL9 5 G3
ECC M30 85 G3
HEY OL10 41 H4
HOR/BR BL6 33 M2
MILN OL16 11 G4
OLDE OL4 9 M7
RAD M26 54 E1
WALK M28 53 G8
Barlow Wood Dr
MPL/ROM SK6 123 K1
Barmeadow UPML OL3 61 J2
Barmhouse Cl HYDE SK14 102 D1
Barmhouse La HYDE SK14 102 D1
Barmhouse Ms HYDE SK14 102 D1
Barmouth St OP/CLY M11 88 C4
Barmouth Wk OLDS OL8 74 E2
Barnaby Rd POY/DIS SK12 129 H2
Barnabys Rd WHTN BL5 50 A1
Barn Acre HOR/BR BL6 33 H3
Barnacre Av BOLE BL2 37 J5
NTHM/RTH M23 118 B1
Barnard Av HTNM SK4 12 A2
WHTF M45 55 L5
Barnard Cl AULW OL7 75 J7
Barnard Rd GTN M18 99 L1
Barnard St BOLE BL2 * 3 L3
Barnbrook St BURY BL9 5 H3
Barnby St WGTN/LGST M12 99 K1
Barn Cl GLSP SK13 105 G5
URM M41 94 F2
Barnclose Rd WYTH/NTH M22 118 F3
Barn Ct BOLE BL2 * 36 F2
Barncroft Dr HOR/BR BL6 34 C1
Barncroft Gdns
WYTH/NTH M22 * 109 M7
Barncroft Rd FWTH BL4 53 G4
Barnes Av HTNM SK4 111 K2
Barnes Cl FWTH BL4 53 G4
RAMS BL0 24 D1
Barnes Dr FWTH BL4 52 C3
Barnes St FWTH BL4 52 E3
Barnes Ter FWTH BL4 53 K5
Barneswell St NEWH/MOS M40 73 M7
Barnet Rd BOL BL1 35 L2
Barnett Av DID/WITH M20 98 E6
Barnett Dr CSLFD M3 6 B2
Barnfield URM M41 95 L4
Barnfield Av MPL/ROM SK6 114 A1
Barnfield Cl EDGW/EG BL7 22 B2
ORD M5 86 C3
RAD M26 54 B1
TYLD M29 67 J3
Barnfield Crs SALE M33 96 C7
Barnfield Dr WALK M28 68 E6
WHTN BL5 50 D3
Barn Field La WHIT OL12 20 E5
Barnfield Ri ROY/SHW OL2 43 K3
Barnfield Rd BNG/LEV M19 99 H8
HYDE SK14 91 L7
SWIN M27 70 A2
Barnfield Rd East
EDGY/DAV SK3 112 C8
Barnfield Rd West
EDGY/DAV SK3 112 A8
Barnfield St DTN/ASHW M34 90 A8
HEY OL10 41 H2
WHIT OL12 28 C2
Barn Fold OLDE OL4 60 B7
Barngate Dr MOSL OL5 76 F4
Barngate Rd CHD/CHDH SK8 110 D6
Barngill Gv WGNS/IIMK WN3 63 H1
Barn Gv DTN/ASHW M34 90 A5
Barnham Cl GOL/RIS/CUL WA3 79 K4
Barn Hl WHTN BL5 50 B3
Barnhill Av PWCH M25 71 L2
Barnhill Dr PWCH M25 71 L2
Barnhill Rd PWCH M25 71 K1
Barnhill St RUSH/FAL M14 87 J8
Barn Hill Ter WHTN BL5 50 B3
Barn La GOL/RIS/CUL WA3 79 J5
Barnley Cl IRL M44 94 E1
Barn Meadow EDGW/EG BL7 17 G7
Barnsdale Cl BOLE BL2 37 M3
Barnsdale Dr CHH M8 72 D7
Barnsfold Av RUSH/FAL M14 98 F4
Barnsfold Rd MPL/ROM SK6 123 H1
Barnside Av WALK M28 69 H2
Barnside Cl BURY BL9 25 H4
Barnside Wy FAIL M35 74 F5
Barns La ALT WA14 106 D7
Barnsley St STKP SK1 13 M6
WGNNW/ST WN6 47 K1
Barns Pl HALE/TIMP WA15 117 L4
Barnstable Dr NEWH/MOS M40 72 F6
Barnstead Av DID/WITH M20 99 G7
Barnston Av RUSH/FAL M14 98 E2
Barnston Cl BOL BL1 22 C8
Barn St BOL BL1 2 D5
OLDS OL8 9 H6
WHTF M45 55 J5
Barnton Cl GOL/RIS/CUL WA3 80 A5
Barnview Dr IRL M44 94 D3
Barnwell Av GOL/RIS/CUL WA3 81 G8
Barnwell Cl DTN/ASHW M34 90 B7
Barnwood Cl BOL BL1 * 36 B3
Barnwood Dr BOL BL1 36 B3
Barnwood Rd NTHM/RTH M23 118 C1
Barnwood Ter BOL BL1 36 B3
Baroness Gv BRO M7 71 M8
Baron Fold Crs LHULT M38 52 C7
Baron Fold Gv LHULT M38 52 C7
Baron Fold Rd LHULT M38 * 52 C7
Baron Gn CHD/CHDH SK8 119 M5
Baron Rd HYDE SK14 102 C5
Barons Ct FAIL M35 74 A6
Baron St BURY BL9 4 C6
MILN OL16 10 F5
Baron Wk BOLS/LL BL3 53 M1
Barrack Hl MPL/ROM SK6 113 K2
Barrack Hill Cl MPL/ROM SK6 113 K1
Barrack Sq WGN WN1 * 15 G4
Barracks Rd WGNE/HIN WN2 65 G3
Barrack St HULME M15 6 A9
Barracks Yd WGN WN1 14 F4
Barra Dr URM M41 85 G7
Barrass St OP/CLY M11 89 G5
Barratt Gdns MDTN M24 57 G1
Barrett Av FWTH BL4 53 J5
Barrett Ct BURY BL9 5 J4
Barrfield Rd SLFD M6 71 H8
Barr Hill Av SLFD M6 71 H7
Barrhill Cl HULME M15 87 G6
Barrie St LEIGH WN7 66 A4
Barrie Wy BOL BL1 22 E8
Barrington Av CHD/CHDH SK8 120 C3
DROY M43 89 J3
Barrington Cl ALT WA14 108 A6
WGNS/IIMK WN3 63 G2
Barrington Rd ALT WA14 108 A6
Barrington St OP/CLY M11 88 F2
Barrisdale Cl BOLS/LL BL3 35 J7
Barron Meadow LEIGH WN7 66 A5
Barrow Bridge Rd BOL BL1 35 K1
Barrowcroft Cl WGN WN1 31 L3
Barrowdale Rd
GOL/RIS/CUL WA3 79 L4
Barrowfield Rd
WYTH/NTH M22 118 C2
Barrowfields MDTN M24 57 K2
Barrow Hill Rd CHH M8 72 C7
Barrow La HALE/TIMP WA15 117 K5
Barrow Meadow
CHD/CHDH SK8 120 B4
Barrows Ct BOL BL1 2 E6
Barrowshaw Cl WALK M28 68 F2
Barrow St AIMK WN4 64 A8
ORD M5 6 A4
Barrs Fold Cl WHTN BL5 50 A1
Barrs Fold Rd WHTN BL5 50 A2
Barrule Av BRAM/HZG SK7 122 A3
Barry Crs WALK M28 68 D1
Barry Lawson Cl CHH M8 * 72 C5
Barry Ri ALT WA14 116 C2
Barry Rd NTHM/RTH M23 109 L2
RDSH SK5 100 C7
Barry St OLD OL1 59 L4
Barsham Dr BOLS/LL BL3 2 B8
Bar St WGNE/HIN WN2 64 D3
Bar Ter WHIT OL12 20 A5
Bartlam Pl OLD OL1 9 K5
Bartlemore St OLD OL1 9 M1
Bartlett Rd ROY/SHW OL2 43 L6
Bartlett St OP/CLY M11 88 E5
Bartley Rd WYTH/NTH M22 109 M4
Barton Av URM M41 95 L2
WGN WN1 47 L2
Barton Cl WILM/AE SK9 127 H2
Barton Clough
WGNW/BIL/OR WN5 62 B7
Barton Dock Rd STRET M32 85 K8
URM M41 85 H6
Barton Fold HYDE SK14 102 A3
Barton Hall Av ECC M30 84 D3
Barton Highlevel Br TRPK M17 84 E5
Barton La ECC M30 85 G4
Barton Moss Rd ECC M30 83 M5
Barton Rd ECC M30 84 F4
FWTH BL4 52 E5
HTNM SK4 111 H3
HYDE SK14 90 F7
MDTN M24 57 J4
STRET M32 96 D1
SWIN M27 70 D5
URM M41 84 F8
WALK M28 69 J7
Barton St CHAD OL9 8 E2
CSLFD M3 6 D7
FWTH BL4 53 H5
GOL/RIS/CUL WA3 79 K4
WGNE/HIN WN2 64 E1
WGNW/BIL/OR WN5 46 E7
Barway Rd CCHDY M21 97 J3
Barwell Cl GOL/RIS/CUL WA3 79 M3
Barwell Rd SALE M33 96 B7
Barwell Sq FWTH BL4 52 E2
Barwick Pl SALE M33 96 D8
Basechurch Wk
WGTN/LGST M12 * 88 C6
Basford Rd OLDTF/WHR M16 97 L1
Bashall St BOL BL1 35 M4
Basil Ct MILN OL16 11 K6
Basildon Cl BRUN/LGST M13 88 A7
Basil St BOLS/LL BL3 2 C8
HTNM SK4 12 F1
MILN OL16 11 K6
RUSH/FAL M14 * 98 F1
Basle Cl BRAM/HZG SK7 121 G1
Baslow Av BNG/LEV M19 99 L2
WGNE/HIN WN2 65 J1
Baslow Dr BRAM/HZG SK7 122 B4
CHD/CHDH SK8 119 L4
Baslow Gv RDSH SK5 100 C7
Baslow Ms GLSP SK13 104 B3
Baslow Rd DROY M43 89 H1
DTN/ASHW M34 101 J4
STRET M32 96 D1
Baslow St OP/CLY M11 88 B3
Bassenthwaite Cl MDTN M24 57 G1
Basset Av SLFD M6 71 M7
Bassett Gv WGNS/IIMK WN3 62 F3
Bassett Wy WHIT OL12 28 B2
Bass La BURY BL9 25 H1
Bass St BOLE BL2 3 L4
DUK SK16 90 E4
Basswood Gn WGNE/HIN WN2 65 K1
Basten Dr BRO M7 72 A6
Batchelor Cl CCHDY M21 98 B5
Bateman St HOR/BR BL6 34 A2
Batemill Rd NM/HAY SK22 124 F2
Bates Cl ROCH OL11 42 A3
Bateson Dr OLDE OL4 60 C6
Bateson St STKP SK1 13 L3
Bateson Wy OLDS OL8 * 9 J8
Bates St BRUN/LGST M13 88 C8
DUK SK16 90 F4
Bath Cl BRAM/HZG SK7 122 C2
Bath Crs CHD/CHDH SK8 120 D6
OLDTF/WHR M16 86 F7
Batheaston Gv LEIGH WN7 66 A5
Bath St ALT WA14 116 F2
ATH M46 66 D1
BOL BL1 2 E3
CHAD OL9 8 D8
WGNE/HIN WN2 48 C2
WHIT OL12 11 H1
Batley St BKLY M9 73 H4
MOSL OL5 76 E3
Batridge Rd EDGW/EG BL7 16 D5
Batsmans Dr SWIN M27 54 B8
Battenberg Rd BOL BL1 35 M4
Battersbay Gv
BRAM/HZG SK7 122 A2
Battersby Ct OFTN SK2 * 113 H6
Battersby St BURY BL9 26 A8
LEIGH WN7 66 E8
OP/CLY M11 * 89 H5
ROCH OL11 27 L6
WGNE/HIN WN2 48 E4
Battersea Rd HTNM SK4 111 H3
Battery La WILM/AE SK9 126 B6
Batty St CHH M8 72 F7
Baucher Rd WGNS/IIMK WN3 47 J7
The Baum MILN OL16 10 E3
Baverstock Cl WGNS/IIMK WN3 15 J7
Baxendale St BOL BL1 22 B8
Baxter Gdns NTHM/RTH M23 109 K5
Baxter Rd SALE M33 96 E8
Baxter's Rw WGNE/HIN WN2 65 L2
Baxter St OLDS OL8 74 E2
WGNNW/ST WN6 31 J3
Baybutt St RAD M26 * 54 F1
Baycliff Cl WGNE/HIN WN2 65 J1
Baycroft Gv NTHM/RTH M23 109 K3
Baydon Av BRO M7 72 C6
Bayfield Gv NEWH/MOS M40 * 73 K3
Bayle Cl HYDE SK14 91 H7
Bayley Ct BOL BL1 2 A2
Bayley St STLY SK15 91 H2
Baysdale Av BOLS/LL BL3 35 J8
Bayston Wk WGTN/LGST M12 88 C6
Bay St CHAD OL9 8 E5
HEY OL10 40 E1
WHIT OL12 11 H1
Bayswater Av NEWH/MOS M40 73 M8
Bayswater St BOLS/LL BL3 51 M2
Baythorpe St BOL BL1 36 C1
Baytree Av CHAD OL9 58 B4
DTN/ASHW M34 90 D8
Bay Tree Av WALK M28 69 K7
Baytree Dr MPL/ROM SK6 101 J8
Baytree Gv RAMS BL0 24 E2
Baytree La MDTN M24 58 A4
Baytree Rd WGNNW/ST WN6 47 J2
Baytree Wk WHIT OL12 20 A3
Baywood St BKLY M9 73 G4
Bazaar St SLFD M6 71 K8
Bazley Rd WYTH/NTH M22 110 A3
Bazley St BOL BL1 35 J1
Beacomfold MPL/ROM SK6 114 E1
Beacon Cl ATH M46 66 D2
Beacon Dr NTHM/RTH M23 118 C2
Beacon Gv OLDS OL8 59 M8
Beacon Hl
WGNW/BIL/OR WN5 * 62 A5
Beacon Rd MPL/ROM SK6 113 K3
TRPK M17 85 H5
WGNE/HIN WN2 65 K4
WGNNW/ST WN6 30 E2
WGNW/BIL/OR WN5 62 A6
Beaconsfield RUSH/FAL M14 * 98 F5
Beaconsfield Rd ALT WA14 108 A5
Beaconsfield St BOLS/LL BL3 2 A7
Beaconsfield Ter STLY SK15 77 J5
The Beacons WGNNW/ST WN6 30 A5
Beacon Vw MPL/ROM SK6 114 C4
Beadham Dr BKLY M9 56 D7
Beadle Av WHIT OL12 21 H7
Beaford Cl WGNW/BIL/OR WN5 46 E7
Bealbank Cl MILN OL16 43 K1
Beal Cl HTNM SK4 111 G1
Beal Crs MILN OL16 11 M1
Bealcroft Cl MILN OL16 29 H5
Beal Dr WGNE/HIN WN2 64 D2
Beale Gv CCHDY M21 97 L4
Bealey Av RAD M26 39 H7
Bealey Cl GTN M18 88 E6
RAD M26 39 G8
Bealey Dr BURY BL9 39 G5
Beal La ROY/SHW OL2 43 M6
Beaminster Rd HTNM SK4 111 J1
Beaminster Wk
BRUN/LGST M13 * 87 M7
Beamish Cl BRUN/LGST M13 87 M6
Beamsley Dr WYTH/NTH M22 118 D2
Beanfields WALK M28 69 J7
Bean Leach Av OFTN SK2 113 J6
Bean Leach Dr OFTN SK2 113 J6
Bean Leach Rd BRAM/HZG SK7 113 H8
Beard Crs NM/HAY SK22 124 F4
Beard Rd GTN M18 * 88 F8
Beardsmore Dr
GOL/RIS/CUL WA3 80 B4
Beard St DROY M43 89 J3
ROY/SHW OL2 59 H1
Beardwood Rd BKLY M9 57 G8
Bearswood Cl HYDE SK14 102 C3
Beathwaite Dr
BRAM/HZG SK7 120 E3
Beatrice Av CHD/CHDH SK8 120 B2
GTN M18 89 J8
Beatrice Rd BOL BL1 35 M4
WALK M28 69 L5
Beatrice St DTN/ASHW M34 101 H1
FWTH BL4 52 E4
ROCH OL11 * 10 A5
SWIN M27 70 B3
Beatrice Wignall St
DROY M43 * 89 K4
Beatrix Dr GLSP SK13 104 B1
Beatson Wk ANC M4 7 L4
Beattock Cl HULME M15 * 6 B9
Beattock St HULME M15 6 B9
Beatty Dr WHTN BL5 50 B3
Beauchamp St AUL OL6 90 F1
Beaufont Dr OLDE OL4 59 M7
Beaufort Av DID/WITH M20 98 D7
SALE M33 108 F2
SWIN M27 70 A5
Beaufort Cha WILM/AE SK9 127 K3
Beaufort Cl HYDE SK14 103 H3
WILM/AE SK9 130 E2
Beaufort Rd AUL OL6 91 G1
HYDE SK14 103 H2
OFTN SK2 113 G8
SALE M33 108 F1
Beaufort St CSLFD M3 6 C7
ECC M30 84 E1
PWCH M25 55 M8
WGNE/HIN WN2 * 49 G7
WGNW/BIL/OR WN5 47 H6
WHIT OL12 28 A3
Beauly Cl RAMS BL0 24 D2
Beaumaris Cl LEIGH WN7 65 M7
Beaumaris Crs BRAM/HZG SK7 121 L4
Beaumaris Rd WGNE/HIN WN2 65 K1
Beaumonds Wy ROCH OL11 27 J6
Beaumont Cha BOLS/LL BL3 51 J1
Beaumont Cl LIT OL15 21 K7
Beaumont Dr BOLS/LL BL3 35 H7
Beaumont Gv
WGNW/BIL/OR WN5 46 E4
Beaumont Rd CCHDY M21 97 L5
HOR/BR BL6 35 H6
Beaumont St AUL OL6 90 F1
Beauvale Av OFTN SK2 112 F5
Beaverbrook Av
GOL/RIS/CUL WA3 81 L8
Beaver Ct AIMK WN4 63 M6
Beaver Dr BURY BL9 39 L8
Beaver Rd DID/WITH M20 110 E1
Beaver St CMANE M1 7 G7
Bebbington Cl SALE M33 109 J2
Bebbington St OP/CLY M11 * 88 F3
Beccles Rd SALE M33 108 E3
Beckenham Cl
TOT/BURYW BL8 38 E3
Beckenham Rd CHH M8 72 D5
Becket Av BRO M7 72 B6
Becket Mdw OLDE OL4 59 L6
Beckett St GTN M18 88 F8
OLDE OL4 60 B5
Beckfield Rd NTHM/RTH M23 109 K7
Beckfoot Dr BRUN/LGST M13 99 H1
Beckford St NEWH/MOS M40 73 H7
Beck Gv ROY/SHW OL2 44 A4
WALK M28 69 J3
Beckhampton Cl
BRUN/LGST M13 87 M7
Beckley Av PWCH M25 71 K2
Beckley Cl ROY/SHW OL2 43 K8
Beckside RDSH SK5 100 D3
TYLD M29 67 H4
Beck St CSLFD M3 6 C3
OP/CLY M11 * 89 H5
Beckton Gdns WYTH/NTH M22 118 E1
Beckwith WGNE/HIN WN2 64 E1
Becontree Av DTN/ASHW M34 90 D8
Becontree Dr NTHM/RTH M23 109 G6
Bedells La WILM/AE SK9 126 E6
Bede St BOL BL1 35 M2
Bedford Av HYDE SK14 102 B1
OLDTF/WHR M16 98 A2
ROY/SHW OL2 43 J5
SALE M33 109 G2
SWIN M27 * 70 B5
WALK M28 68 F3
Bedford Dr ATH M46 66 D3
HALE/TIMP WA15 108 F6
Bedford Pl AIMK WN4 63 K7
Bedford Rd ECC M30 85 H1
OLDTF/WHR M16 97 K2
URM M41 84 F8
Bedford St BOL BL1 2 A3
BURY BL9 25 K8
EDGW/EG BL7 22 A2
HEY OL10 41 H2
LEIGH WN7 * 66 D7
PWCH M25 55 M7
RDSH SK5 100 B5
WGN WN1 15 K2
WGNW/BIL/OR WN5 * 46 F7
Bedlam Gn BURY BL9 4 F4
Bednal Av NEWH/MOS M40 73 H8
Bedwell St OLDTF/WHR M16 98 C1
Bedworth Cl BOLE BL2 3 J8
Beechacre RAMS BL0 19 G7
Beech Av ATH M46 67 H1
BOLS/LL BL3 53 L2
BRAM/HZG SK7 122 A2
CHD/CHDH SK8 110 E7
DROY M43 89 J3
DTN/ASHW M34 90 A8
EDGY/DAV SK3 112 C6
FWTH BL4 52 D4
FWTH BL4 53 L7
GLSP SK13 104 D4
GOL/RIS/CUL WA3 80 C5
HOR/BR BL6 34 B3
IRL M44 94 F1
MPL/ROM SK6 114 A6
NM/HAY SK22 124 F3
OLD OL1 58 D2
OLDE OL4 60 A4
RAD M26 54 C4
RNFD/HAY WA11 78 C5
SLFD M6 71 H8
UPML OL3 61 L6
URM M41 95 M3
WALK M28 68 D6
WHTF M45 55 J5
WYTH/NTH M22 110 A4
Beech Cl BOLE BL2 22 F6
PWCH M25 71 M1
WHIT OL12 20 A3
WILM/AE SK9 130 E1
Beech Cottages WILM/AE SK9 130 D4
Beech Ct WILM/AE SK9 * 127 H6
Beech Crs LEIGH WN7 81 H1
POY/DIS SK12 122 A8
WGNNW/ST WN6 31 H4
Beechcroft PWCH M25 71 M2
Beechcroft Av BOLE BL2 37 G6
Beechcroft Gv BOLE BL2 37 H6
Beechdale Cl NEWH/MOS M40 73 M4
Beech Dr LEIGH WN7 81 J2
Beeches Ms DID/WITH M20 98 B8
The Beeches ATH M46 * 67 G1
BOL BL1 22 A6
DID/WITH M20 98 C8
MOSL OL5 77 H2
Beechey Sq OLD OL1 9 L4
Beechfield ALT WA14 116 E1
OLDE OL4 61 G6
SALE M33 108 C2
Beechfield Av LHULT M38 52 D7
RAD M26 54 F3
URM M41 95 K1
WGNE/HIN WN2 49 K8
WILM/AE SK9 126 C7
Beechfield Cl OLDE OL4 60 C6
ROCH OL11 27 H6
Beechfield Dr BURY BL9 39 J5
LEIGH WN7 81 J1
Beechfield Ms HYDE SK14 * 102 D1
Beechfield Rd BOL BL1 35 L2
CHD/CHDH SK8 120 D4
EDGY/DAV SK3 112 C8
GLSP SK13 104 B1
MILN OL16 29 H7
SWIN M27 70 B7
WILM/AE SK9 130 D4
Beechfield St CHH M8 72 D6
Beech Gv AULW OL7 90 C3
LEIGH WN7 81 H2
LHULT M38 52 B7
RUSH/FAL M14 99 G4
SALE M33 96 C8
SLFD M6 71 H8
STLY SK15 91 J4
TOT/BURYW BL8 24 D3
WGNE/HIN WN2 64 F5
WGNNW/ST WN6 47 H1
WILM/AE SK9 126 E6
Beech Grove Cl BURY BL9 25 L8
Beech Hall St WGNNW/ST WN6 47 K2
Beech Hill Av WGNNW/ST WN6 47 H1
Beech Hill La WGNNW/ST WN6 47 H1
Beech Hill Rd OLDE OL4 60 F6
Beech Holme Gv STKP SK1 112 F4
Beech Hurst Cl
OLDTF/WHR M16 * 98 A2
Beech La MPL/ROM SK6 113 M2
OLDE OL4 61 G6
WILM/AE SK9 126 E6
Beech Ms CCHDY M21 97 K4
OFTN SK2 112 D7
Beech Mt AULW OL7 75 K6
BKLY M9 73 G4
Beechpark Av WYTH/NTH M22 109 M5
Beech Rd CCHDY M21 97 L4
CHD/CHDH SK8 120 D3
EDGY/DAV SK3 112 B6
GOL/RIS/CUL WA3 79 K3
HALE/TIMP WA15 117 G1
MPL/ROM SK6 123 H5
SALE M33 97 G8
WILM/AE SK9 130 E1
Beech St AIMK WN4 63 K6
ATH M46 67 H1
BOL BL1 36 C2
BURY BL9 5 K4
BURY BL9 24 F1
ECC M30 84 E3
EDGW/EG BL7 17 G7
FAIL M35 74 B4
MDTN M24 * 57 J4
MILN OL16 29 K8
OLD OL1 9 L5
RAD M26 54 F3
ROCH OL11 10 B6
SWIN M27 70 C5
Beech Tree Av
WGNNW/ST WN6 30 A4
Beech Tree Houses
WGNE/HIN WN2 64 B6
Beechurst Rd CHD/CHDH SK8 111 L7
Beech Vw HYDE SK14 102 D2
Beech Wk LEIGH WN7 81 H2
MDTN M24 57 J6
STRET M32 96 F4
WGNNW/ST WN6 31 G4
WGNS/IIMK WN3 62 F2
Beechway MPL/ROM SK6 123 H5
WILM/AE SK9 126 D7
Beechwood ALT WA14 116 D3
GLSP SK13 104 C5
ROY/SHW OL2 44 A4
Beechwood Av AIMK WN4 78 D2
CCHDY M21 97 M5
LIT OL15 29 K1
MPL/ROM SK6 113 M2
NEWLW WA12 79 G8
RAMS BL0 19 G6
STLY SK15 76 F8
URM M41 95 H1
WGNNW/ST WN6 30 C7
Beechwood Ct
TOT/BURYW BL8 24 E7
Beechwood Crs TYLD M29 67 K6
WGNW/BIL/OR WN5 46 B6
Beechwood Dr HYDE SK14 102 C3
MOSL OL5 76 F2
MPL/ROM SK6 114 D6
ROY/SHW OL2 42 F6
SALE M33 95 M8
WALK M28 69 L6
WILM/AE SK9 * 127 J4
Beechwood Gv
CHD/CHDH SK8 120 C4
Beechwood La
GOL/RIS/CUL WA3 81 G8
Beechwood Rd OLDS OL8 75 J2
PWCH M25 72 A1
Beechwood St BOLS/LL BL3 52 C1
Beede St OP/CLY M11 88 E4
Beedon Av BOLS/LL BL3 37 K8
Bee Fold La ATH M46 66 E2
Beeford Dr WGNW/
BIL/OR WN5 46 B7
Beehive Gn WHTN BL5 50 E3
Beehive St OLDS OL8 75 J1
Beeley St HYDE SK14 102 B2
SLFD M6 71 L7
Beenham Cl SALE M33 107 M1
Beeston Av BRO M7 71 L6
HALE/TIMP WA15 108 C6
Beeston Cl BOL BL1 22 D6
Beeston Gv EDGY/DAV SK3 112 B7
LEIGH WN7 67 G5
WHTF M45 55 L5
Beeston Rd SALE M33 96 B8
WILM/AE SK9 119 M7
Beeston St BKLY M9 73 H5
Beeth St OP/CLY M11 89 H6
Beeton Gv BRUN/LGST M13 88 B8
Beever St OLD OL1 9 L4
OLDTF/WHR M16 86 F7
Begley Cl MPL/ROM SK6 113 J3
Begonia Av FWTH BL4 52 D3
Beilby Rd RNFD/HAY WA11 78 C5
Belayse Cl BOL BL1 35 L2
Belbeck St TOT/BURYW BL8 38 F2
Belbeck St South
TOT/BURYW BL8 4 A5
Belcroft Cl WYTH/NTH M22 110 B4
Belcroft Dr LHULT M38 52 B6
Belcroft Gv LHULT M38 * 52 B7
Belding Av NEWH/MOS M40 74 C3
Beldon Rd BKLY M9 56 E8
Belfairs Cl AULW OL7 75 L6
Belfield Cl MILN OL16 11 M2
Belfield La MILN OL16 11 L4
Belfield Mill La MILN OL16 11 M2

Belfield Old Rd MILN OL16 11 L2
Belfield Rd DID/WITH M20 110 E1
MILN OL16 11 K2
PWCH M25 72 B1
Belford Av DTN/ASHW M34 100 D1
Belford Dr BOLS/LL BL3 52 B1
Belford Rd STRET M32 97 G1
Belfort Dr ORD M5 86 E4
Belfry Cl WILM/AE SK9 127 H4
Belfry Crs WGNNW/ST WN6 31 J2
Belgate Cl WGTN/LGST M12 88 D8
Belgium St ROCH OL11 27 H5
Belgrave Av FAIL M35 74 E4
MPL/ROM SK6 114 C6
OLDS OL8 59 K8
URM M41 95 H1
Belgrave Cl LEIGH WN7 80 F4
WGNS/IIMK WN3 63 G1
Belgrave Ct OLDS OL8 59 J8
Belgrave Crs ECC M30 85 J1
HOR/BR BL6 34 A1
OFTN SK2 112 E8
Belgrave Dr RAD M26 38 D8
Belgrave Gdns BOL BL1 36 B2
Belgrave Rd ALT WA14 116 E1
IRL M44 94 A7
NEWH/MOS M40 74 B3
OLDS OL8 59 J8
SALE M33 96 D8
Belgrave St ATH M46 66 D1
BOL BL1 36 B2
HEY OL10 40 F3
RAD M26 38 D8
WHIT OL12 10 A1
Belgrave St South BOL BL1 2 C1
Belgravia Gdns CCHDY M21 97 K4
HALE/TIMP WA15 117 G4
Belgravia Ms ROY/SHW OL2 43 M5
Belhaven Rd CHH M8 72 C2
Bellairs St BOLS/LL BL3 51 M1
Bellamy Dr LEIGH WN7 66 E7
Bella St BOLS/LL BL3 35 M8
Bell Clough Rd DROY M43 89 L1
Bell Crs OP/CLY M11 88 C4
Belldale Cl HTNM SK4 111 K2
Belldean WGNE/HIN WN2 48 D4
Belle Green La WGNE/HIN WN2 48 D4
Belle Isle Av WHIT OL12 20 B6
Bellerby Cl WHTF M45 55 H4
Belleville Av WYTH/NTH M22 119 G4
Belle Vue Av WGTN/LGST M12 88 C7
Belle Vue St
WGNW/BIL/OR WN5 47 G7
WGTN/LGST M12 88 D6
Belle Vue Ter BURY BL9 4 D6
Bellfield Av CHD/CHDH SK8 120 D3
OLDS OL8 75 J2
Bellfield Cl BKLY M9 72 F2
Bellfield Vw BOL BL1 36 D1
Bellhill Gdns SLFD M6 86 C1
Bellingham Av WGN WN1 47 M2
Bellingham Cl ROY/SHW OL2 43 L4
TOT/BURYW BL8 38 C2
Bellingham Dr WGN WN1 47 M2
Bellingham Mt WGN WN1 48 A1
Bellis Cl WGTN/LGST M12 88 B3
Bell La BURY BL9 5 H3
MILN OL16 29 L5
WGNW/BIL/OR WN5 46 E4
Bellott St CHH M8 72 D6
Bellott Wk OLD OL1 * 9 H2
Bellpit Cl WALK M28 68 F5
Bells Croft Av
NEWH/MOS M40 * 73 L5
Bellshill Crs MILN OL16 11 M1
Bell St DROY M43 89 L2
LEIGH WN7 66 A3
MILN OL16 10 E3
OLD OL1 9 M4
WGNE/HIN WN2 49 H6
Bell Ter ECC M30 84 F4
Bellwood WHTN BL5 49 M5
Belmont Av ATH M46 51 J8
DTN/ASHW M34 90 A8
GOL/RIS/CUL WA3 79 M3
OLDE OL4 60 D5
SLFD M6 85 K1
SWIN M27 54 A7
WGNE/HIN WN2 65 J3
WGNW/BIL/OR WN5 62 A1
Belmont Cl HTNM SK4 13 G1
Belmont Dr MPL/ROM SK6 114 E3
TOT/BURYW BL8 38 D3
WGNE/HIN WN2 32 F7
Belmont Rd BOL BL1 22 A6
BRAM/HZG SK7 121 H7
CHD/CHDH SK8 110 E6
HALE/TIMP WA15 117 G2
RAD M26 54 D3
SALE M33 96 D6
WGNE/HIN WN2 49 J7
Belmont St ECC M30 85 G1
HTNM SK4 12 F1
OLD OL1 9 G3
OLDE OL4 60 B7
SALQ M50 86 A3
Belmont Ter PART M31 * 95 G6
Belmont Vw BOLE BL2 23 J8
Belmont Wk BRUN/LGST M13 * 87 M6
Belmont Wy CHAD OL9 8 D2
HTNM SK4 13 G1
WHIT OL12 28 B2
Belmore Rd SALE M33 108 E3
Belper Rd ECC M30 84 E4
HTNM SK4 111 J3
Belroy Ct PWCH M25 * 71 L1
Belsay Cl AULW OL7 75 H7
Belsay Dr NTHM/RTH M23 109 K8
Belsfield Ter AUL OL6 * 75 M4
Belstone Av NTHM/RTH M23 118 C1
Belstone Cl BRAM/HZG SK7 121 H2
Belthorne Av BKLY M9 73 K2
Belton Av MILN OL16 11 M1
Belton Cl GOL/RIS/CUL WA3 79 K5
Beltone Cl STRET M32 96 E3
Belton Wk CHAD OL9 8 E6
Belvedere Av ATH M46 51 J8
RDSH SK5 100 C2
TOT/BURYW BL8 24 D3
Belvedere Cl LEIGH WN7 67 G5
Belvedere Ct PWCH M25 * 71 K1
Belvedere Dr DUK SK16 91 H4
MPL/ROM SK6 112 F1
Belvedere Pl WGNS/IIMK WN3 47 J7
Belvedere Ri OLD OL1 60 A1
Belvedere Rd AIMK WN4 78 F1
NEWLW WA12 78 E8
RUSH/FAL M14 99 H4
SLFD M6 86 D1
Belvedere St SLFD M6 * 86 E1
Belvoir Av BNG/LEV M19 * 99 K2
BRAM/HZG SK7 122 A4
Belvoir Mdw MILN OL16 21 J8
Belvoir St BOLE BL2 3 L4
WGN WN1 15 J4
Belvor Av DTN/ASHW M34 90 B5
Belwood Rd CCHDY M21 97 K5
Bembridge Cl RUSH/FAL M14 98 F1
Bembridge Ct WGNS/IIMK WN3 63 H2
Bembridge Dr BOLS/LL BL3 37 G7
Bembridge Rd
DTN/ASHW M34 101 L4
Bempton Cl OFTN SK2 113 K7
Bemrose Av ALT WA14 107 M6
Bemsley Pl ORD M5 * 86 D4
Benbecula Wy URM M41 84 F7
Benbow Av WGTN/LGST M12 88 C7
Benbow St SALE M33 96 E7
Ben Brierley Wy OLD OL1 9 K4
Bench Carr WHIT OL12 28 B3
Benchill Court Rd
WYTH/NTH M22 110 B8
Benchill Dr WYTH/NTH M22 110 A7
Benchill Rd WYTH/NTH M22 109 M6
Bendall St OP/CLY M11 89 H4
Ben Davies Ct MPL/ROM SK6 * 113 M2
Bendemeer URM M41 95 M1
Bendix St ANC M4 7 J2
Benedict Ct BRO M7 71 M7
Benedict Dr DUK SK16 90 F6
Benfield Av NEWH/MOS M40 73 M2
Benfield St HEY OL10 41 G2
Benfleet Cl WGTN/LGST M12 * 88 D6
Bengairn Cl WGN WN1 15 M2
Bengal La AUL OL6 75 M8
Bengal St ANC M4 7 K2
EDGY/DAV SK3 13 G7
LEIGH WN7 66 C7
Benjamin Fold AIMK WN4 63 L7
Benjamin St AULW OL7 90 D3
Benmore Cl HEY OL10 40 D2
Benmore Rd BKLY M9 73 J1
Bennet St RAD M26 38 A8
Bennett Cl EDGY/DAV SK3 12 C6
Bennett Dr BRO M7 72 B6
WGNW/BIL/OR WN5 46 A8
Bennett Rd CHH M8 72 C3
Bennett's La BOL BL1 35 M2
Bennett St AULW OL7 90 C3
EDGY/DAV SK3 12 C6
HYDE SK14 90 F7
HYDE SK14 93 G7
STLY SK15 * 91 K3
STRET M32 * 96 F3
WGTN/LGST M12 88 B6
Benny La DROY M43 90 A1
Benson Cl BRO M7 72 B7
Benson St BURY BL9 5 H6
EDGW/EG BL7 17 G7
Ben St OP/CLY M11 88 E2
Bentcliffe Wy ECC M30 85 K3
Bentfield Crs MILN OL16 29 K8
Bent Fold Dr BURY BL9 * 55 K3
Bentgate Cl MILN OL16 29 K8
Bentgate St MILN OL16 43 K1
Bentham Cl TOT/BURYW BL8 38 B1
Bentham Pl WGNNW/ST WN6 31 J2
Bentham Rd WGNNW/ST WN6 31 H3
Bent Hill St BOLS/LL BL3 * 35 K8
Bentinck Cl ALT WA14 * 107 M8
Bentinck Rd ALT WA14 107 M8
Bentinck St AUL OL6 90 D2
BOL BL1 35 L3
FWTH BL4 52 F3
HULME M15 6 A9
WGNS/IIMK WN3 47 J8
WHIT OL12 27 M3
Bent La CHH M8 72 C5
PWCH M25 55 M8
Bent Lanes URM M41 84 D7
Bentley Av MDTN M24 42 A7
Bentley Cl RAD M26 39 G8
Bentley Ct FWTH BL4 53 G3
Bentley Fold TOT/BURYW BL8 24 C8
Bentley Fold Cottages
TOT/BURYW BL8 * 24 C8
Bentley Hall Rd
TOT/BURYW BL8 23 M8
Bentley La BURY BL9 25 K3
Bentley Ms WHIT OL12 * 28 B2
Bentley Rd BRO M7 72 B4
CCHDY M21 97 K3
DTN/ASHW M34 101 J1
Bentley St BOLE BL2 3 L8
CHAD OL9 8 B4
FWTH BL4 53 G3
OLD OL1 59 L4
WHIT OL12 28 B2
Bentmeadows WHIT OL12 28 B3
Benton Dr MPL/ROM SK6 114 F4
Benton St BKLY M9 73 J5
Bents Av MPL/ROM SK6 113 K1
URM M41 95 H3
Bents Farm Cl LIT OL15 * 21 K7
Bentside Rd POY/DIS SK12 123 M7
Bent Spur Rd FWTH BL4 53 K7
Bent St CHH M8 72 D7
FWTH BL4 53 H5
Bentworth Cl WHTN BL5 50 C6
Bentworth Wk BKLY M9 73 H5
Beresford Av BOLS/LL BL3 35 M7
Beresford Crs OLDE OL4 60 A4
RDSH SK5 100 B1
Beresford Rd BRUN/LGST M13 99 J1
STRET M32 86 B8
Beresford St FAIL M35 74 B5
MILN OL16 29 L8
OLDE OL4 59 M4
RUSH/FAL M14 98 C1
WGNNW/ST WN6 14 B2
Berigan Cl WGTN/LGST M12 88 B7
Berisford Cl HALE/TIMP WA15 108 B5
Berkeley Av CHAD OL9 74 C1
RUSH/FAL M14 88 B8
STRET M32 85 K8
WGNS/IIMK WN3 63 G2
Berkeley Cl HYDE SK14 102 A3
LEIGH WN7 80 F4
OFTN SK2 112 F4
Berkeley Ct NEWLW WA12 78 C8
Berkeley Crs HYDE SK14 102 A3
RAD M26 37 M7
Berkeley Dr MILN OL16 28 E8
Berkeley Rd BOL BL1 22 B8
BRAM/HZG SK7 122 B1
Berkeley St AUL OL6 90 D1
Berkley Av BNG/LEV M19 99 K2
Berkley Dr ROY/SHW OL2 59 G2
Berkley St ROY/SHW OL2 43 G7
Berkley Wk LIT OL15 21 K7
Berkshire Cl CHAD OL9 8 B9
Berkshire Ct BURY BL9 39 J5
Berkshire Pl CHAD OL9 8 C8
Berkshire Rd NEWH/MOS M40 88 A1
Berlin Rd EDGY/DAV SK3 112 A6
Berlin St BOLS/LL BL3 35 M6
Bermondsay St ORD M5 86 E4
Bernard Gv BOL BL1 35 M2
Bernard St BKLY M9 73 G4
GLSP SK13 104 F3
WHIT OL12 28 B1
Berne Av HOR/BR BL6 33 K1
Berne Cl BRAM/HZG SK7 112 B8
CHAD OL9 8 C7
Bernice Av CHAD OL9 8 A7
Bernice St BOL BL1 35 M2
Berriedale Cl
OLDTF/WHR M16 * 98 A2
Berrie Gv BNG/LEV M19 99 K4
Berrington Gv AIMK WN4 78 D1
Berry Brow NEWH/MOS M40 74 B8
UPML OL3 61 L7
Berry Cl WILM/AE SK9 126 E7
Berrycroft La MPL/ROM SK6 113 K1
Berryfold Wy TYLD M29 67 K4
Berry St CMANE M1 7 K7
ECC M30 84 E4
STLY SK15 91 M4
SWIN M27 70 C2
UPML OL3 61 L7
Bertha Rd MILN OL16 11 L5
Bertha St BOL BL1 36 A2
OP/CLY M11 88 E5
ROY/SHW OL2 43 L7
Bertie St ROCH OL11 28 A8
Bertram St SALE M33 97 H8
WGTN/LGST M12 * 88 D6
Bertrand Rd BOL BL1 35 M5
Bert St BOLS/LL BL3 51 L1
Berwick Av HTNM SK4 111 G2
URM M41 96 D2
WHTF M45 55 K5
Berwick Cl HEY OL10 40 D3
WALK M28 68 C5
Berwick Pl WGN WN1 15 L1
Berwick St MILN OL16 11 J6
Berwyn Av BKLY M9 56 F7
CHD/CHDH SK8 111 L7
MDTN M24 57 M4
Berwyn Cl OLDS OL8 75 H1
Beryl Av TOT/BURYW BL8 24 C5
Beryl St BOL BL1 36 C1
Besom La STLY SK15 92 B1
Bessemer Rd IRL M44 94 C6
Bessemer St OP/CLY M11 88 F5
Bessemer Wy OLD OL1 9 H4
Bessie's Well Pl
WGNNW/ST WN6 * 31 J4
Bessybrook Cl HOR/BR BL6 34 F6
Beswick Dr FAIL M35 74 D6
Beswicke Royds St MILN OL16 11 L1
Beswicke St WHIT OL12 10 C2
Beswick Rw ANC M4 7 G2
Beswick St ANC M4 88 A2
DROY M43 89 L3
Beta Av STRET M32 96 F3
Beta St BOL BL1 2 D2
Bethany La MILN OL16 29 M8
Bethany Ms WGNE/HIN WN2 49 L8
Bethel Av FAIL M35 74 B5
Bethel St HEY OL10 40 F2
Bethersden Rd WGN WN1 31 L8
Bethesda St OLDS OL8 59 J8
Bethnall Dr RUSH/FAL M14 98 D4
Betjeman Pl ROY/SHW OL2 44 A5
Betleymere Rd
CHD/CHDH SK8 111 J8
Betley Rd RDSH SK5 100 C3
Betley St CMANE M1 7 L6
HEY OL10 * 40 F3
RAD M26 38 F8
Betnor Av STKP SK1 112 E3
Betony Cl WHIT OL12 28 A1
Betsham St HULME M15 87 J7
Bettison Av LEIGH WN7 81 M1
Bettwood Dr CHH M8 72 C2
Betula Gv BRO M7 72 A5
Betula Ms ROCH OL11 27 G3
Beulah Av WGNW/BIL/OR WN5 62 A8
Bevan Cl WGTN/LGST M12 88 B3
Bevendon Sq BRO M7 72 B6
Beveridge St RUSH/FAL M14 98 D1
Beverley Av DTN/ASHW M34 101 K2
LEIGH WN7 66 D7
URM M41 85 H8
WGNW/BIL/OR WN5 62 B3
Beverley Cl WHTF M45 55 L3
Beverley Pl MILN OL16 * 11 G3
Beverley Rd BOL BL1 35 M4
BOLS/LL BL3 53 J1
OFTN SK2 112 F4
SWIN M27 70 F5
WGNW/BIL/OR WN5 46 E4
Beverley St BKLY M9 73 H3
Beverley Wk OLDS OL8 * 9 H9
Beverly Cl AUL OL6 75 L6
Beverly Rd RUSH/FAL M14 99 G5
Beverston ROCH OL11 10 D7
Beverston Dr BRO M7 72 B6
Bevill Sq CSLFD M3 6 C2
Bevin Av GOL/RIS/CUL WA3 81 L8
Bevington St AIMK WN4 63 J7
Bevis Gn BURY BL9 25 J4
Bewerley Cl WGNS/IIMK WN3 14 D8
Bewick St BOLE BL2 36 E1
Bewley Gv LEIGH WN7 66 D6
Bewley St OLDS OL8 75 G2
Bexhill Av HALE/TIMP WA15 108 C6
Bexhill Cl BOLS/LL BL3 53 M1
Bexhill Dr BRUN/LGST M13 99 H1
LEIGH WN7 65 M2
Bexhill Rd EDGY/DAV SK3 112 B8
Bexhill Wk CHAD OL9 8 A6
Bexington Rd OLDTF/WHR M16 * 98 A1
Bexley Cl GLSP SK13 104 F1
URM M41 84 E8
Bexley Dr LHULT M38 68 F1
TOT/BURYW BL8 38 E3
Bexley Sq CSLFD M3 6 B3
Bexley St CHAD OL9 8 D8
WGNE/HIN WN2 65 L1
Beyer Cl GTN M18 88 F7
Bibby La BNG/LEV M19 99 J6
Bibby St BURY BL9 39 J7
HYDE SK14 * 91 G7
Bibury Av WYTH/NTH M22 118 D1
Bickerdike Av WGTN/LGST M12 99 L1
Bickershaw Dr WALK M28 68 F2
Bickershaw La WGNE/HIN WN2 64 F3
Bickerstaffe Cl ROY/SHW OL2 43 K7
Bickerton Dr BRAM/HZG SK7 121 K3
Bickerton Rd ALT WA14 107 L7
Bickley Gv TYLD M29 67 M6
Biddall Dr NTHM/RTH M23 109 L6
Biddisham Wk
NEWH/MOS M40 * 73 G8
Biddulph Av OFTN SK2 112 F7
Bideford Dr BOLE BL2 37 K6
NTHM/RTH M23 109 J5
Bideford Rd OFTN SK2 112 F3
ROCH OL11 41 L1
Bidford Cl TYLD M29 67 M3
Bidston Av RUSH/FAL M14 98 E2
Bidston Cl ROY/SHW OL2 44 A6
TOT/BURYW BL8 38 C2
Bidston Dr WILM/AE SK9 127 J2
Big Fold HOR/BR BL6 * 33 G2
Biggin Gdns HEY OL10 41 H5
Bignor St CHH M8 72 D6
Bilbao St BOL BL1 35 M4
Bilberry St MILN OL16 11 J6
Bilbrook St ANC M4 87 L1
Billberry Cl WHTF M45 55 L4
Billing Av WGTN/LGST M12 7 L8
Billinge Ar WGN WN1 * 14 F3
Billinge Cl BOL BL1 2 E2
Billinge Rd AIMK WN4 62 E7
WGNS/IIMK WN3 46 F8
WGNW/BIL/OR WN5 47 H6
Billington Av NEWLW WA12 78 F7
Billington Rd SWIN M27 71 H4
Bill Williams Cl OP/CLY M11 88 F4
Billy La SWIN M27 70 C2
Billy's La CHD/CHDH SK8 120 C3
Bilson Dr EDGY/DAV SK3 12 B9
Binbrook Wk BOLS/LL BL3 36 B8
Bindloss Av ECC M30 85 K1
Bingham Dr
NTHM/RTH M23 109 J6
Bingham St SWIN M27 70 C4
Bingley Cl OP/CLY M11 88 C4
Bingley Dr URM M41 84 C8
Bingley Rd MILN OL16 11 M5
Bingley Sq MILN OL16 11 M5
Bingley Ter MILN OL16 11 M5
Bingley Wk BRO M7 71 J4
FWTH BL4 53 G5
Binns Nook Rd WHIT OL12 28 D2
Binns Pl ANC M4 7 K4
Binns St STLY SK15 91 H3
Binsley Cl IRL M44 94 D3
Binstead Cl RUSH/FAL M14 99 H1
Birbeck St MOSL OL5 * 76 F2
Birchacre Gv RUSH/FAL M14 99 G5
Birchall Av
GOL/RIS/CUL WA3 81 G8
Birchall Cl DUK SK16 91 G6
Birchall Gn MPL/ROM SK6 101 K7
Birchall Wy HULME M15 87 J6
Birch Av FAIL M35 74 C7
HTNM SK4 99 L8
IRL M44 94 A7
MDTN M24 57 K5
MPL/ROM SK6 114 A2
OLD OL1 58 D2
OLDS OL8 75 G2
OLDTF/WHR M16 86 D8
SALE M33 108 E1
SLFD M6 71 H8
TOT/BURYW BL8 24 D7
WGNNW/ST WN6 31 J4
WHIT OL12 21 H8
WHTF M45 55 J6
WHTN BL5 50 C5
WILM/AE SK9 126 D6
Birch Cl WHIT OL12 20 A7
Birch Crs MILN OL16 43 K1
NEWLW WA12 78 C8
Birchdale ALT WA14 116 E2
Birchdale Av CHD/CHDH SK8 119 K2
Birch Dr BRAM/HZG SK7 121 L2
OLDE OL4 60 B7
SWIN M27 70 E4
Birchenall St
NEWH/MOS M40 73 J4
Birchenlea St CHAD OL9 74 D1
Birches Rd EDGW/EG BL7 17 G8
The Birches MOSL OL5 76 E3
NM/HAY SK22 125 L2
SALE M33 96 B7
Birchfield BOLE BL2 23 H6
Birchfield Av ATH M46 50 E8
BURY BL9 40 B3
Birchfield Dr ROCH OL11 27 M7
WALK M28 68 D5
Birchfield Gv BOLS/LL BL3 35 H8
Birchfield Ms HYDE SK14 * 102 A2
Birchfield Rd EDGY/DAV SK3 111 K5
Birchfields HALE/TIMP WA15 117 H3
OLDE OL4 60 C8
Birchfields Av BRUN/LGST M13 99 H2
Birchfields Rd BRUN/LGST M13 99 H1
Birchfold Cl LHULT M38 52 E8
Birchgate Wk BOLS/LL BL3 2 D9
Birch Gn GLSP SK13 105 H3
Birch Gv AIMK WN4 62 F7
DTN/ASHW M34 90 C6
DTN/ASHW M34 101 H1
HALE/TIMP WA15 109 H7
PWCH M25 55 K6
RAMS BL0 24 D1
RUSH/FAL M14 99 G1
Birch Hall Cl NM/HAY SK22 125 J2
OLDE OL4 60 B8
Birch Hall La
BRUN/LGST M13 99 H2
Birch Hey Cl WHIT OL12 21 G8
Birch Hill Crs WHIT OL12 21 J8
Birch Hill La WHIT OL12 21 H6
Birchington Rd
DID/WITH M20 98 D4
Birchinlee Av ROY/SHW OL2 58 E1
Birchin Pl ANC M4 * 7 H4
Birch La BRUN/LGST M13 88 B8
DUK SK16 91 G5
Birchlea HALE/TIMP WA15 108 C8
Birch-lea Cl BURY BL9 39 J5
Birchleaf Gv ORD M5 85 M2
Birch Mt WHIT OL12 21 J8
Birch Polygon
RUSH/FAL M14 99 G1
Birch Rd ALT WA14 107 J3
ATH M46 67 H1
CHD/CHDH SK8 110 D7
CHH M8 72 E3
FWTH BL4 53 J6
LEIGH WN7 66 C5
MDTN M24 57 M2
PART M31 95 J8
PART M31 106 A1
POY/DIS SK12 129 K2
RNFD/HAY WA11 78 B5
SWIN M27 70 A7
UPML OL3 61 M5
WALK M28 69 H3
WGNE/HIN WN2 64 E5
WHIT OL12 21 H7
Birchside Av GLSP SK13 104 E2
Birch St AULW OL7 90 C3
BOLE BL2 3 J7
BURY BL9 5 G2
DROY M43 * 89 L4
HEY OL10 41 G3
RAD M26 39 H7
STLY SK15 76 F7
TYLD M29 * 67 K3
WGNE/HIN WN2 49 G7
WGNNW/ST WN6 14 C1
WGTN/LGST M12 88 D6
WHIT OL12 21 G6
Birch Ter HYDE SK14 * 101 M2
Birch Tree Av BRAM/HZG SK7 122 C3
Birch Tree Cl ALT WA14 116 E3
Birch Tree Dr WYTH/NTH M22 118 F1
Birch Tree Rd
GOL/RIS/CUL WA3 80 C4
Birch Tree Wy HOR/BR BL6 34 B3
Birchvale Av MPL/ROM SK6 114 A1
Birchvale Cl HULME M15 6 C9
Birchway BRAM/HZG SK7 120 F5
MPL/ROM SK6 123 H5
Birchwood CHAD OL9 58 B5
DROY M43 89 L1
Birchwood Cl LEIGH WN7 81 J1
WGNS/IIMK WN3 62 F3
Birchwood Crs HYDE SK14 91 K6
Birchwood Dr NEWH/MOS M40 73 G6
WILM/AE SK9 127 H5
Birchwood Rd MDTN M24 57 M4
Birchwood Wy DUK SK16 * 91 G6
Bird Hall Av CHD/CHDH SK8 111 M8
Birdhall Gv BNG/LEV M19 99 K4
Bird Hall Rd CHD/CHDH SK8 111 L7
Birdlip Dr NTHM/RTH M23 118 C1
Bird St WGNE/HIN WN2 48 C5
Birkby Dr MDTN M24 57 H2
Birkdale Av ATH M46 50 F7
ROY/SHW OL2 59 H2
WHTF M45 55 G6
Birkdale Cl BRAM/HZG SK7 121 H5
HEY OL10 41 G4
HYDE SK14 91 J7
Birkdale Dr SALE M33 108 B2
TOT/BURYW BL8 38 E2
Birkdale Gdns BOLS/LL BL3 2 B9
Birkdale Gv ECC M30 85 J2
RDSH SK5 100 C7
Birkdale Pl SALE M33 * 96 C6
Birkdale Rd MILN OL16 28 F8
RDSH SK5 100 C7
Birkdale St CHH M8 72 D5
Birkenhills Dr BOLS/LL BL3 35 H7
Birkett Bank WGN WN1 15 L4
Birkett Cl BOL BL1 22 A6
Birkett Dr BOL BL1 22 A6
Birkett St WGN WN1 15 L4
Birkinbrook Cl WHTF M45 55 K3
Birkinheath La ALT WA14 116 D8
Birks Av OLDE OL4 60 C4
Birks Dr TOT/BURYW BL8 24 E6
Birkside Cl WGNS/IIMK WN3 63 K3
Birkworth Ct OFTN SK2 113 G6
Birley Cl HALE/TIMP WA15 108 C5
WGNNW/ST WN6 30 C4
Birley Pk DID/WITH M20 110 C1
Birley St BOL BL1 22 B8
BURY BL9 25 J7
LEIGH WN7 66 D6
NEWLW WA12 79 G8
WHIT OL12 28 D3
Birling Dr NTHM/RTH M23 109 L8
Birnham Gv HEY OL10 40 D3
Birshaw Cl ROY/SHW OL2 43 L7
Birtenshaw Crs EDGW/EG BL7 22 E5
Birtle Dr TYLD M29 67 M5
Birtle Rd BURY BL9 26 B5
Birtles Av RDSH SK5 100 C1
Birtles Cl CHD/CHDH SK8 111 K8
DUK SK16 91 G6
Birtles La MCFLDN SK10 131 K8
Birtlespool Rd CHD/CHDH SK8 111 J8
Birtley Wk NEWH/MOS M40 * 7 M1
Birt St NEWH/MOS M40 73 G8
Birwood Rd CHH M8 72 E2
Biscay Cl OP/CLY M11 88 C3
Bishopbridge Cl BOLS/LL BL3 36 C8
Bishop Cl OLDTF/WHR M16 87 H8
Bishopdale Cl ROY/SHW OL2 43 G7
Bishopgate St CHAD OL9 58 D7
Bishop Marshall Cl
NEWH/MOS M40 * 73 G7
Bishop Marshall Wy MDTN M24 41 G8
Bishop Reeves Rd
RNFD/HAY WA11 78 B5
Bishop Rd SLFD M6 70 E8
URM M41 95 H2
Bishops Cl ALT WA14 116 D3
AULW OL7 75 K7
BOLS/LL BL3 52 D2
CHD/CHDH SK8 111 K7
Bishopsgate CMANW M2 6 F6
Bishopsgate Wk MILN OL16 28 F8
Bishops Meadow MDTN M24 57 G1
Bishops Ms SALE M33 96 B6
Bishop's Rd BOLS/LL BL3 52 D2
PWCH M25 71 M1
Bishop St MDTN M24 58 A5
MILN OL16 28 E3
STKP SK1 13 L4
Bishopton Cl BNG/LEV M19 99 M3
Bisley Av NTHM/RTH M23 109 J6
Bisley St OLDS OL8 8 F7
Bismarck St OLDE OL4 9 M8
Bispham Av BOLE BL2 37 J5
Bispham Cl TOT/BURYW BL8 38 C3
Bispham Ct
WGNW/BIL/OR WN5 62 A2
Bispham Dr AIMK WN4 63 J7
Bispham Gv BRO M7 72 B5
Bispham St BOLE BL2 * 3 L2
Bittern Cl POY/DIS SK12 128 E1
ROCH OL11 27 J5
Bittern Dr DROY M43 89 M1
Blackbank St BOL BL1 36 C2
Blackberry Cl ALT WA14 107 L4
Blackberry Dr WGNE/HIN WN2 48 F8
Blackberry La RDSH SK5 100 E5
Black Brook Rd HTNM SK4 100 A5
Blackburn Cl GOL/RIS/CUL WA3 80 C4
Blackburne Dr NEWLW WA12 78 D8
Blackburn Gdns DID/WITH M20 98 D8
Blackburn Pl ORD M5 86 F3
Blackburn Rd EDGW/EG BL7 16 F3
EDGW/EG BL7 22 A1
Blackburn St CSLFD M3 6 A1
OLDTF/WHR M16 86 F7
PWCH M25 55 M8
RAD M26 54 E2
Blackcap Cl WALK M28 68 E5
Blackcarr Rd NTHM/RTH M23 109 L7

Blackchapel Dr MILN OL16 .....42 E1
Blackcroft ST SWIN M27 .....70 B4
Blackdown Gv OLDS OL8 .....75 H1
Blackfield La BRO M7 .....71 M4
Blackford Av BURY BL9 .....39 J8
Blackford Rd BNG/LEV M19 .....99 L5
Blackford Wk
  NEWH/MOS M40 .....88 A1
Blackfriars Rd CSLFD M3 .....6 C1
Blackfriars St CSLFD M3 .....6 E3
Blackhill Cl BRUN/LGST M13 .....7 K9
Blackhorse Av HOR/BR BL6 * .....32 F2
Blackhorse Cl HOR/BR BL6 .....32 F1
Black Horse St BOL BL1 .....2 E6
Blackhurst Brow
  MCFLDN SK10 .....131 L1
Black La RAMS BL0 .....19 L5
Blackleach Dr WALK M28 .....53 C8
Blackledge Cl
  WGNW/BIL/OR WN5 .....46 B7
Blackledge St BOLS/LL BL3 .....35 M8
Blackley Cl BURY BL9 .....55 K2
Blackleyhurst Av
  WGNW/BIL/OR WN5 .....62 B7
Blackley New Rd BKLY M9 .....72 C1
Blackley Park Rd BKLY M9 .....73 C3
Blackleigh St MDTN M24 .....56 E5
  OLDTF/WHR M16 .....86 F7
Blacklock St CSLFD M3 .....72 C8
Blackmoor Av TYLD M29 .....67 L1
Blackmore Rd STRET M32 .....96 C3
Black Moss Cl RAD M26 .....54 A1
Black Moss Rd ALT WA14 .....107 H5
Blackpits Rd ROCH OL11 .....27 C5
Blackpool St OP/CLY M11 .....88 F2
Blackrock MOSL OL5 .....76 F6
Blackrock St OP/CLY M11 .....88 C3
Blackrod By-Pass Rd
  HOR/BR BL6 .....33 J4
Blackrod Dr TOT/BURYW BL8 .....38 D3
Black Sail Wk OLD OL1 .....9 K1
Blackshaw Clough
  GLSP SK13 .....105 H1
Blackshaw La BOLS/LL BL3 .....35 M6
  ROY/SHW OL2 .....43 J8
  WILM/AE SK9 .....150 C3
Blackshaw Rd GLSP SK13 .....105 H2
Blackshaw St EDGY/DAV SK3 .....13 H6
Blacksmith La ROCH OL11 .....27 L8
Blacksmiths Fold ATH M46 .....67 H1
Blackstock La MILN OL16 .....11 M2
Blackstone Av MILN OL16 .....11 M2
Blackstone Rd OFTN SK2 .....113 G2
Blackthorn Av BNG/LEV M19 .....99 K5
  WGNW/ST WN6 .....47 J1
Blackthorn Cl WGTN/LGST M12 .....28 B2
Blackthorne Cl BOL BL1 .....35 K3
Blackthorne Rd SALE M33 .....108 A2
Blackthorn Rd HYDE SK14 .....102 B6
Blackthorn Ms WHIT OL12 .....28 B2
Blackthorn Rd OLDS OL8 .....74 F4
Blackwin St WGTN/LGST M12 .....88 D6
Blackwood Dr
  NTHM/RTH M23 .....109 G4
Blackwood St BOLS/LL BL3 .....36 D8
Bladen Cl CHD/CHDH SK8 .....111 K8
Bladon St CMANE M1 * .....7 J6
Blair Av LHULT M38 .....52 E8
  URM M41 .....95 H2
  WGNE/HIN WN2 .....65 L1
Blair Cl BRAM/HZG SK7 .....121 L4
  ROY/SHW OL2 .....43 L5
  SALE M33 .....107 M3
Blairhall Av NEWH/MOS M40 .....73 K4
Blair La BOLE BL2 .....37 G3
Blairmore Dr BOLS/LL BL3 .....35 H8
Blair Rd OLDTF/WHR M16 .....98 B3
Blair St EDGY/DAV SK3 .....13 G7
  FWTH BL4 .....53 K6
  OLDTF/WHR M16 .....87 G7
  WHIT OL12 .....10 A1
Blake Cl WGNS/IIMK WN3 .....47 K7
Blakedown Wk
  WGTN/LGST M12 .....88 B7
Blake Dr OFTN SK2 .....113 H5
Blakefield Dr WALK M28 .....69 H3
Blake Gdns BOL BL1 .....36 A3
Blakelock St ROY/SHW OL2 .....43 K5
Blakemere Av SALE M33 .....109 H1
Blakemore Pk ATH M46 .....50 E8
Blakemore Wk
  WGTN/LGST M12 .....88 B7
Blake St BOL BL1 .....36 A2
  EDGW/EG BL7 .....22 D5
  MILN OL16 .....11 H3
Blakeswell Cl URM M41 .....95 C1
Blakey Cl BOLS/LL BL3 .....35 J8
Blakey St WGTN/LGST M12 .....88 D8
Blanchard St HULME M15 .....87 H7
Blanche St WHIT OL12 .....28 D7
Blanche Wk OLD OL1 .....9 L3
Bland Cl FAIL M35 .....74 B5
Blandford Av WALK M28 .....69 K4
  TYLD M29 .....67 K3
Blandford Cl TOT/BURYW BL8 .....25 J7
Blandford Ct STLY SK15 .....91 K2
Blandford Dr NEWH/MOS M40 .....73 M2
  HOR/BR BL6 .....34 D3
Blandford Rd ECC M30 .....84 E2
  HTNM SK4 .....12 C2
  SLFD M6 .....71 L7
Blandford St AUL OL6 .....90 D1
  STLY SK15 .....91 K2
Bland St PWCH M25 .....71 L2
Bland St OLDTF/WHR M16 * .....87 H8
Blanefield Cl CCHDY M21 .....98 B5
Blantyre Av WALK M28 .....69 L2
Blantyre Rd SWIN M27 .....70 E6
Blantyre St ECC M30 .....84 D1
  HULME M15 .....6 B8
  SWIN M27 .....70 A4
  WGNE/HIN WN2 .....49 H6
Blanwood Dr CHH M8 .....72 E5
Blaven Cl EDGY/DAV SK3 .....112 C1
Blaydon Cl WGNE/HIN WN2 .....33 G7
Blazemoss Bank OFTN SK2 .....113 G7
Bleach St WGNE/HIN WN2 .....48 C1
Bleackley St TOT/BURYW BL8 .....24 F8
Bleadale Cl WILM/AE SK9 .....127 H3
Bleak Hey Nook La UPML OL3 .....45 M5
Bleak Hey Rd WYTH/NTH M22 .....119 H1
Bleakholt Rd RAMS BL0 .....19 J3
Bleakledge Gn WGNE/HIN WN2 .....49 H6
Bleaklow St WHIT OL12 .....28 D7
Bleaklow Cl WGNS/IIMK WN3 .....63 L2
Bleak St BOLE BL2 .....36 E2
Bleasby St OLDE OL4 .....59 M5
Bleasdale Cl HOR/BR BL6 .....34 C4

Bleasdale Rd BOL BL1 .....35 J2
  NEWLW WA12 .....78 E8
  WYTH/NTH M22 .....118 C2
Bleasdale St ROY/SHW OL2 .....43 G7
Bleasefell Cha WALK M28 .....68 D7
Bleatarn Rd STKP SK1 .....112 E5
Bledlow Cl ECC M30 .....85 H1
Blenheim Av OLDTF/WHR M16 .....98 A2
Blenheim Cl ALT WA14 .....116 F3
  BURY BL9 .....39 J7
  GLSP SK13 .....93 K7
  HEY OL10 .....41 H2
  POY/DIS SK12 .....122 B8
  WILM/AE SK9 .....127 H5
Blenheim Dr LEIGH WN7 .....67 H5
Blenheim Rd AIMK WN4 .....79 C2
  BOLE BL2 .....37 H5
  CHD/CHDH SK8 .....120 D2
  OLDTF/WHR M16 .....97 K1
  WGNW/BIL/OR WN5 .....46 H4
Blenheim St OLDE OL4 .....60 A3
  TYLD M29 .....67 J4
  WHIT OL12 * .....27 M3
Blenheim Wy AUL OL6 .....76 B8
Blenheim Wy OLD OL1 .....60 A3
Blenmar Cl RAD M26 .....38 F7
Bleriot St BOLS/LL BL3 .....52 A1
Bletchley Cl BRUN/LGST M13 .....88 A7
Bletchley Rd HTNM SK4 .....111 H5
Blethyn St BOLS/LL BL3 .....51 L2
Blewberry Cl LEIGH WN7 .....66 C5
Bligh Rd WHTN BL5 .....50 B3
Blinco Rd URM M41 .....96 C3
Blind La WGTN/LGST M12 .....88 A5
Blindsill Rd FWTH BL4 .....52 A3
Blissford Cl WGNE/HIN WN2 .....49 G8
Blisworth Av ECC M30 .....85 H4
Blisworth Cl ANC M4 .....88 A3
Block La CHAD OL9 .....8 B6
Blodwell St SLFD M6 .....86 C2
Blomley St ROCH OL11 .....43 M2
Bloomfield Dr BURY BL9 .....55 L1
Bloomfield Rd FWTH BL4 .....53 M1
Bloomfield St BOL BL1 .....36 B1
  WALK M28 .....68 D5
Bloomsbury Gv
  HALE/TIMP WA15 .....108 D6
Bloomsbury La
  HALE/TIMP WA15 .....108 D6
Bloom St CMANE M1 .....7 H6
  CSLFD M3 .....6 D3
  EDGY/DAV SK3 .....12 D7
  RAMS BL0 .....18 D1
Blossom Pl MILN OL16 * .....10 E3
Blossom Rd PART M31 .....106 B8
Blossoms Hey CHD/CHDH SK8 .....120 A3
Blossoms La BRAM/HZG SK7 .....127 L2
Blossoms St OFTN SK2 * .....13 K9
Blossom St ANC M4 * .....7 K3
  CSLFD M3 .....6 D2
  TYLD M29 .....67 K3
Blucher St AULW OL7 .....90 C5
  ORD M5 .....86 F5
  WGTN/LGST M12 .....88 D6
Blueball La PWCH M25 .....56 D3
Blue Bell Av NEWH/MOS M40 .....73 K3
  WGNNW/ST WN6 .....31 J8
Bluebell Av RNFD/HAY WA11 .....78 D5
Bluebell Cl HYDE SK14 .....91 J7
  NM/HAY SK22 .....125 L1
Bluebell Dr ROCH OL11 .....41 L1
Bluebell Gv CHD/CHDH SK8 .....111 G8
Bluebell Wy WILM/AE SK9 .....127 C3
Blueberry Dr ROY/SHW OL2 .....44 A5
Blueberry Rd ALT WA14 .....116 C2
Bluefields ROY/SHW OL2 .....44 A4
Blue Ribbon Wk SWIN M27 .....70 D3
Bluestone Dr HTNM SK4 .....111 H1
Bluestone Rd NEWH/MOS M40 .....73 K4
  RDSH SK5 .....100 C4
Blundell Cl BURY BL9 .....55 L1
Blundell La HOR/BR BL6 .....32 D2
Blundell Ms WGNS/IIMK WN3 .....47 G8
Blundells Rd WGNS/IIMK WN3 .....47 G8
Blundell St BOL BL1 .....2 E6
Blundering La STLY SK15 .....92 A6
Blunn St OLDS OL8 .....59 J8
Blyborough Cl SLFD M6 .....71 H8
Blyth Av LIT OL15 * .....29 J1
  HALE/TIMP WA15 .....109 G6
Blythe Av BRAM/HZG SK7 .....120 E6
Blyton St HULME M15 .....87 L7
Boad St CMANE M1 .....7 K6
Boardale Dr MDTN M24 .....57 H5
Boardman Cl BOL BL1 .....36 B2
  RDSH SK5 .....100 B8
Boardman Fold Cl MDTN M24 .....57 K7
Boardman Fold Rd MDTN M24 .....57 K7
Boardman La MDTN M24 .....56 E4
Boardman Rd CHH M8 .....72 E5
Boardman St BOL BL1 .....36 B2
  ECC M30 .....85 H3
  HOR/BR BL6 .....33 C2
  HYDE SK14 .....102 A2
Board St AUL OL6 .....76 A8
  BOL BL1 .....2 E4
Boarfold La GLSP SK13 .....103 J7
Boar Green Cl NEWH/MOS M40 .....73 M5
Boarshaw Clough MDTN M24 .....57 L2
Boarshaw Clough Wy
  MDTN M24 .....57 M2
Boarshaw Crs MDTN M24 .....57 M2
Boarshaw La MDTN M24 .....58 A1
Boarshaw Rd MDTN M24 .....57 M1
Boars Head Av
  WGNNW/ST WN6 .....31 K5
Boarshurst La UPML OL3 .....61 M7
Boat La IRL M44 .....94 E2
Boatmans Rw TYLD M29 .....67 M8
Bobbin Wk ANC M4 * .....7 L4
  OLDE OL4 .....9 M7
Bob Brook Cl NEWH/MOS M40 .....73 M4
Bob Massey Cl OP/CLY M11 .....88 F4
Bob's La IRL M44 .....94 A8
Boddens Hill Rd HTNM SK4 .....111 H3
Bodden St GOL/RIS/CUL WA3 .....80 D3
Boddington Rd ECC M30 .....84 C3
Bodiam Rd TOT/BURYW BL8 .....24 C8
Bodley St OP/CLY M11 .....88 F2
Bodmin Cl ROY/SHW OL2 .....59 K1
Bodmin Crs RDSH SK5 .....100 E7
Bodmin Dr BRAM/HZG SK7 .....121 H5
  WGNE/HIN WN2 .....64 D3
Bodmin Rd SALE M33 .....96 A7
  TYLD M29 .....67 L4
Bodney Wk BKLY M9 * .....87 H1
Bogburn La WGNNW/ST WN6 .....30 D1
Boggard La GLSP SK13 .....104 A3
Boggart Hill Dr BKLY M9 .....73 H1
Bognor Rd CHD/CHDH SK8 .....111 J6
Bolam Cl NTHM/RTH M23 .....109 J3
Boland Dr RUSH/FAL M14 .....99 G4

Bolbury Crs SWIN M27 .....71 C4
Bolderod Pl OLD OL1 * .....9 L3
Boiderstone Pl OFTN SK2 .....113 H8
Bolderwood Dr
  WGNE/HIN WN2 .....49 G8
Bold Av ALT WA14 .....116 F1
  BOL BL1 .....2 E6
  BURY BL9 .....5 H2
  HULME M15 .....87 H7
  LEIGH WN7 .....66 C7
  SWIN M27 .....70 D2
  WGNW/BIL/OR WN5 .....47 H7
Bolesworth Cl CCHDY M21 .....97 J4
Boleyn Ct HEY OL10 .....40 F3
Bolholt Ter TOT/BURYW BL8 .....24 E8
Bolivia St ORD M5 .....85 M2
Bollin Av WILM/AE SK9 .....116 D4
Bollin Cl FWTH BL4 .....53 K6
Bollin Ct HULME M15 .....87 G6
Bollin Dr ALT WA14 .....108 B4
  SALE M33 .....108 C2
Bollings Yd BOL BL1 .....2 F6
Bollington Rd HTNM SK4 .....100 F4
  NEWH/MOS M40 .....88 A3
Bollington St AULW OL7 .....90 D3
Bollin Hl WILM/AE SK9 .....126 E4
Bollin Sq ALT WA14 .....116 D3
Bollin Wk WHTF M45 .....55 M2
  WILM/AE SK9 .....126 F5
Bollinway
  HALE/TIMP WA15 .....117 J4
Bollinwood Cha
  WILM/AE SK9 .....127 H5
Bolney St WGNE/HIN WN2 .....48 D2
Bolshaw Rd
  CHD/CHDH SK8 .....119 K6
Bolton Av BNG/LEV M19 .....111 C4
  CHD/CHDH SK8 .....120 D6
Bolton Cl GOL/RIS/CUL WA3 .....80 E4
  POY/DIS SK12 .....121 M8
  PWCH M25 .....71 J2
Bolton House Rd
  WGNE/HIN WN2 .....65 J5
Bolton Old Rd ATH M46 .....67 C1
Bolton Rd AIMK WN4 .....64 B7
  AIMK WN4 .....78 E1
  ATH M46 .....51 H8
  BOLE BL2 .....22 F7
  EDGW/EC BL7 .....17 G8
  FWTH BL4 .....53 C2
  FWTH BL4 .....53 H5
  RAD M26 .....38 A8
  ROCH OL11 .....27 K8
  SLFD M6 .....70 F4
  SWIN M27 .....70 F4
  TOT/BURYW BL8 .....4 A5
  TOT/BURYW BL8 .....23 M2
  TOT/BURYW BL8 .....38 D4
  WALK M28 .....53 G8
  WGNE/HIN WN2 .....32 F7
  WHTN BL5 .....51 H8
Bolton Rd North RAMS BL0 .....18 F3
Bolton Rd West RAMS BL0 .....18 B8
Bolton Sq WGN WN1 .....15 K2
Bolton St AIMK WN4 .....63 C7
  CSLFD M3 .....6 C3
  OLDE OL4 .....9 M6
  RAD M26 .....54 C1
  RAMS BL0 .....18 E1
  RDSH SK5 .....100 B5
  TOT/BURYW BL8 .....4 B4
Bombay Rd EDGY/DAV SK3 .....12 D9
  WGNW/BIL/OR WN5 .....46 F4
Bombay St AUL OL6 .....76 A8
  CMANE M1 .....7 H7
Bonar Cl EDGY/DAV SK3 * .....12 C6
Bonar Rd EDGY/DAV SK3 .....12 C7
Boncarn Dr NTHM/RTH M23 .....109 K8
Bonchurch Wk
  WGTN/LGST M12 .....88 E6
Bond Cl HYDE SK14 .....103 H1
Bondmark Rd GTN M18 .....88 D6
Bond Sq BRO M7 * .....72 B6
Bond St ATH M46 .....67 J3
  BURY BL9 .....5 J4
  DTN/ASHW M34 .....101 J4
  LEIGH WN7 .....66 C7
  RAMS BL0 .....19 H2
  STLY SK15 .....91 K1
  WGTN/LGST M12 .....7 L1
  WHIT OL12 .....28 D2
Bongs Rd OFTN SK2 .....113 J6
Bonhill Wk OP/CLY M11 .....88 E2
Bonington Ri
  MPL/ROM SK6 .....114 E4
Bonis Crs OFTN SK2 .....112 F8
Bonny Brow St MDTN M24 .....56 E5
Bonnywell Rd LEIGH WN7 .....81 J1
Bonsall St HULME M15 .....87 K6
Bonscale Crs MDTN M24 .....57 H1
Bonville Cha ALT WA14 .....107 K3
Bonville Rd ALT WA14 .....107 L7
Boodle St ANC M4 .....88 A3
Boond St ANC M4 * .....88 A3
  CSLFD M3 .....6 F2
Boonfields EDGW/EG BL7 .....22 D4
Booth Av RUSH/FAL M14 .....99 C5
Booth Bridge Cl
  MDTN M24 * .....56 F5
Boothby Rd SWIN M27 .....70 B3
Boothby St OFTN SK2 .....112 F8
Booth Cl STLY SK15 .....91 J3
  TOT/BURYW BL8 .....24 C7
Boothcote
  DTN/ASHW M34 .....90 A6
Booth Dr URM M41 .....84 C1
Boothfield ECC M30 .....84 D1
Boothfield Rd
  WYTH/NTH M22 .....109 H6
Boothfields
  TOT/BURYW BL8 .....4 A3
Booth Hall Dr
  TOT/BURYW BL8 .....24 C7
Booth Hall Rd BKLY M9 .....73 K1
Booth Hill La OLD OL1 .....59 H3
Booth Rd ALT WA14 .....107 M8
  BOLS/LL BL3 .....53 L2
  DTN/ASHW M34 .....89 K5
  OLDTF/WHR M16 .....97 M1
  SALE M33 .....96 E6
  WALK M28 .....68 E6
Booth's Brow Rd AIMK WN4 .....63 C6
Booth's Hall Gv WALK M28 .....68 E6
Booth's Hall Rd WALK M28 .....68 E6
Booth's Hall Wy WALK M28 .....68 E6
Boothstown Dr WALK M28 .....68 D6

Booth St AUL OL6 * .....90 E2
  BOL BL1 .....35 M1
  CHAD OL9 .....8 C6
  CMANW M2 .....6 F5
  CSLFD M3 .....6 F5
  DTN/ASHW M34 .....90 C7
  EDGY/DAV SK3 .....13 H8
  HYDE SK14 .....92 F8
  HYDE SK14 .....102 B3
  MDTN M24 .....57 H4
  OLDE OL4 .....60 B6
  STLY SK15 .....91 J4
  TOT/BURYW BL8 .....24 C7
Booth St East BRUN/LGST M13 .....87 L6
Booth St West HULME M15 .....87 K6
Booth Wy TOT/BURYW BL8 .....24 C7
Boot La BOL BL1 .....35 C3
Bootle St CMANW M2 .....6 E5
Bor Av WGNS/IIMK WN3 .....47 L8
Bordale Av BKLY M9 .....73 J5
Bordan St OP/CLY M11 .....88 D2
Borden Cl WGNE/HIN WN2 .....48 C2
Border Brook La WALK M28 .....68 D7
Border Wy BURY BL9 .....39 K6
Bordley Wk NTHM/RTH M23 .....109 H3
Bordon Cl EDGY/DAV SK3 .....12 D9
Boringdon Cl
  NEWH/MOS M40 .....73 L3
Borland Av NEWH/MOS M40 .....74 A3
Borough Av RAD M26 .....39 C7
Borough Av WGNE/HIN WN2 .....65 L1
Borough Av HALE/TIMP WA15 .....108 B8
  SALQ M50 .....86 A3
Borough St STLY SK15 .....91 K3
The Borrans WALK M28 * .....68 C7
Borron St NEWLW WA12 .....78 E7
Borron St OP/CLY M11 .....88 D2
Borrowdale Av BOL BL1 .....35 C6
  CHD/CHDH SK8 .....110 E8
Borrowdale Cl ROY/SHW OL2 .....43 C6
Borrowdale Crs AULW OL7 .....75 J8
  DID/WITH M20 .....98 B8
Borrowdale Dr BURY BL9 .....55 K1
  ROCH OL11 .....27 L8
Borrowdale Rd MDTN M24 .....57 H2
  OFTN SK2 .....112 E6
  WGNW/BIL/OR WN5 * .....46 E5
Borsdane Av WGNE/HIN WN2 .....49 H8
Borsden St SWIN M27 .....70 A3
Borth Av OFTN SK2 .....112 F5
Borwell St NEWH/MOS M40 .....88 D7
Boscobel Rd BOLS/LL BL3 .....52 E2
Boscombe Av ECC M30 .....84 F4
Boscombe Dr BRAM/HZG SK7 .....121 L2
Boscombe Pl WGNE/HIN WN2 .....49 H8
Boscombe St RDSH SK5 .....100 C3
  RUSH/FAL M14 .....98 E2
Boscow Rd BOLS/LL BL3 .....53 K2
Bosden Av WILM/AE SK9 .....119 M7
Bosden Cl WILM/AE SK9 .....119 M7
Bosden Fold STKP SK1 .....13 K6
Bosdenfold Rd BRAM/HZG SK7 .....122 A1
Bosden Hall Rd
  BRAM/HZG SK7 .....122 A1
Bosdin Rd East URM M41 * .....95 H3
Bosdin Rd West URM M41 .....95 H3
Bosley Av DID/WITH M20 .....98 D4
Bosley Cl WILM/AE SK9 .....127 H2
Bosley Dr POY/DIS SK12 .....129 L1
Bosley Rd EDGY/DAV SK3 .....111 K4
Bossall Av BKLY M9 .....57 H8
Bossington Cl OFTN SK2 .....112 F4
Bostock Wk BRUN/LGST M13 * .....7 L7
Boston Cl BRAM/HZG SK7 .....120 F5
  FAIL M35 .....74 C4
  GOL/RIS/CUL WA3 .....81 J8
Boston Ct SALQ M50 .....86 B4
Boston Gv LEIGH WN7 .....66 B3
Boston St BOL BL1 * .....36 B2
  HULME M15 .....87 J7
  HYDE SK14 .....102 B2
  OLDS OL8 .....59 J8
Boswell Av DTN/ASHW M34 .....90 A3
Boswell Pl WGNS/IIMK WN3 .....47 J8
Boswell Wy MDTN M24 .....42 A4
Bosworth Sq ROCH OL11 * .....28 A8
Bosworth St OP/CLY M11 .....88 D4
  ROCH OL11 .....10 D9
Botanical Av OLDTF/WHR M16 .....86 D7
Botany Cl HEY OL10 .....40 F2
Botany La AUL OL6 .....75 M8
Botany Rd ECC M30 .....69 K8
  MPL/ROM SK6 .....101 K6
Botesworth Cl WGNE/HIN WN2 .....49 L1
Botha Cl OP/CLY M11 .....88 F4
Botham Cl HULME M15 .....87 K7
Bothwell Rd NEWH/MOS M40 .....7 M1
Bottesford Av DID/WITH M20 .....98 C7
Bottomfield Cl OLD OL1 .....9 M1
Bottomley Side BKLY M9 .....72 F2
Bottom o' th' Knotts Brow
  EDGW/EG BL7 .....23 J1
Bottom o' th' Moor BOLE BL2 .....37 G2
  HOR/BR BL6 .....34 C1
  OLD OL1 .....9 M5
Bottom St HYDE SK14 .....102 C4
Boughey St LEIGH WN7 .....66 B7
Boulden Dr TOT/BURYW BL8 .....24 F7
Boulder Dr NTHM/RTH M23 .....118 C2
Boulderstone Rd STLY SK15 .....76 D8
The Boulevard
  BRAM/HZG SK7 .....122 A2
  DID/WITH M20 .....98 B6
  HYDE SK14 .....93 C7
Boundary Cl MOSL OL5 .....76 F6
  MPL/ROM SK6 .....101 M7
Boundary Dr BOLE BL2 .....37 K7
Boundary Edge RAMS BL0 .....19 L1
Boundary Gdns BOL BL1 * .....36 A2
  OLD OL1 .....9 C2
Boundary Gv NTHM/RTH M23 .....109 J2
Boundary La HULME M15 .....87 K6
  WGNNW/ST WN6 .....30 D1
Boundary Park Rd OLD OL1 .....58 F3
Boundary Rd CHD/CHDH SK8 .....111 J6
  IRL M44 .....94 H1
  SWIN M27 .....70 B2
Boundary St BOL BL1 .....36 A2
  BOLE BL2 .....37 L7
  LEIGH WN7 .....66 B6
  LIT OL15 .....21 M6
  ROCH OL11 .....10 D7
  TYLD M29 .....67 K3
  WGN WN1 .....15 J3
  WHIT OL12 * .....28 D2
Boundary St East CMANE M1 * .....7 H9
Boundary St West HULME M15 * .....87 K6
Boundary Ter
  WYTH/NTH M22 * .....119 H6

The Boundary SWIN M27 .....54 A8
Boundary Wk ROCH OL11 .....10 D8
Boundry Gn DTN/ASHW M34 .....90 B7
Bourdon St NEWH/MOS M40 .....88 A1
Bourget St BRO M7 .....72 C4
Bournbrook Av LHULT M38 .....52 D6
Bourne Av GOL/RIS/CUL WA3 .....80 A4
  SWIN M27 .....70 C5
Bourne Dr NEWH/MOS M40 .....73 L3
Bournelea Av BNG/LEV M19 .....99 H6
Bourne Rd ROY/SHW OL2 .....43 K4
Bourne St CHAD OL9 .....74 E2
  HTNM SK4 .....100 B8
  WILM/AE SK9 .....126 D6
Bourneville Dr
  TOT/BURYW BL8 .....38 D2
Bournville Av HTNM SK4 .....100 B8
Bournville Gv BNG/LEV M19 .....99 L3
Bourton Cl TOT/BURYW BL8 .....38 E1
Bourton Ct TYLD M29 .....68 A3
Bourton Dr GTN M18 .....88 E8
Bowden Cl GOL/RIS/CUL WA3 .....81 J8
  HYDE SK14 .....103 H3
  LEIGH WN7 .....81 M2
  NM/HAY SK22 .....125 L1
  ROCH OL11 .....42 A4
Bowden Crs NM/HAY SK22 .....124 F4
Bowden House La
  WILM/AE SK9 .....127 K4
Bowden La MPL/ROM SK6 .....114 B5
Bowden Rd GLSP SK13 .....104 F1
  SWIN M27 .....70 D5
Bowden St BRAM/HZG SK7 .....122 A1
  DTN/ASHW M34 .....101 H4
Bowdon Av RUSH/FAL M14 .....98 C3
Bowdon Ri ALT WA14 .....116 F2
Bowdon St EDGY/DAV SK3 .....13 G7
Bowen Cl BRAM/HZG SK7 .....121 H4
Bowen St BOL BL1 .....35 L3
Bower Av BRAM/HZG SK7 .....121 M3
  HTNM SK4 .....12 D1
  WHIT OL12 .....27 M3
Bower Ct CHYDE SK14 .....91 K7
Bower Cup Fold STLY SK15 * .....77 H8
Bowerfield Av BRAM/HZG SK7 .....121 M4
Bowerfield Crs BRAM/HZG SK7 .....121 M4
Bowerfold La HTNM SK4 .....12 A2
Bower Gdns STLY SK15 .....92 A4
Bower Rd HALE/TIMP WA15 .....117 C3
Bowers Av URM M41 .....84 E8
Bowers St RUSH/FAL M14 .....99 G5
Bower St BRO M7 * .....72 B6
  BURY BL9 .....5 M2
  NEWH/MOS M40 .....73 J7
  OLD OL1 .....9 M4
  RDSH SK5 .....100 C4
Bower Ter DROY M43 .....89 M1
Bowery Av CHD/CHDH SK8 .....120 B6
Bowes Cl TOT/BURYW BL8 .....24 E7
Bowes St RUSH/FAL M14 .....99 G5
Bowfell Dr MPL/ROM SK6 .....123 G4
Bowfell Gv BKLY M9 .....72 E2
Bowfell Rd URM M41 .....95 L2
Bowgreave Av BOLE BL2 .....37 J5
Bow Green Rd ALT WA14 .....116 C3
Bowgreen Wk HULME M15 .....87 G6
Bowker Av DTN/ASHW M34 .....101 L4
Bowker Bank Av CHH M8 .....72 C2
Bowker Cl ROCH OL11 .....27 H3
Bowkers Rw BOL BL1 * .....2 F5
Bowker St BRO M7 .....72 A6
  HYDE SK14 .....102 B1
  WALK M28 .....68 E1
Bowlacre Rd HYDE SK14 .....102 A6
Bowland Av AIMK WN4 .....63 L8
  GOL/RIS/CUL WA3 .....79 M3
  GTN M18 .....89 K8
Bowland Cl AUL OL6 .....75 M5
  OFTN SK2 .....113 H7
  ROY/SHW OL2 .....43 H5
  TOT/BURYW BL8 .....38 B1
Bowland Dr BOL BL1 .....35 H2
Bowland Rd DTN/ASHW M34 .....100 E1
  GLSP SK13 .....104 D4
  MPL/ROM SK6 .....101 L7
  NTHM/RTH M23 .....109 C4
Bow La ALT WA14 .....116 C4
  CMANW M2 .....6 F5
Bowlee Cl WHTF M45 .....55 K3
Bowler St BNG/LEV M19 .....99 L3
  ROY/SHW OL2 .....43 L5
Bowlers Wk WHIT OL12 .....28 D2
Bowley Av WYTH/NTH M22 .....118 C2
Bowling Green Cl CHAD OL9 .....58 D8
Bowling Green St HEY OL10 .....41 C2
  HYDE SK14 .....101 M2
The Bowling Gn RAMS BL0 .....19 J6
Bowling Green Wy ROCH OL11 .....27 J6
Bowling Rd GTN M18 .....100 A8
The Bowlings WGNNW/ST WN6 .....47 K2
Bowling St CHAD OL9 .....74 E2
Bowman Crs AUL OL6 .....91 G1
Bow Meadow Gra
  WGTN/LGST M12 .....88 C8
Bowmont Cl CHD/CHDH SK8 .....111 H8
Bowness Av CHD/CHDH SK8 .....120 D3
  HTNM SK4 .....100 B6
  IRL M44 .....94 A8
  WHIT OL12 .....27 M3
Bowness Dr SALE M33 .....96 C7
Bowness Pl WGNE/HIN WN2 .....48 E4
Bowness Rd AULW OL7 .....75 J8
  BOLS/LL BL3 .....36 A8
  BOLS/LL BL3 .....57 C3
  MDTN M24 .....57 C3
Bowness St OP/CLY M11 .....89 J5
  STRET M32 .....97 G3
Bowring St BRO M7 * .....71 M7
Bow Rd LEIGH WN7 .....81 L1
Bowscale Cl BRUN/LGST M13 .....88 C8
Bowstone Hill Rd BOLE BL2 .....23 L7
Bow St BOL BL1 .....2 E4
  CMANW M2 .....6 E5
  DUK SK16 .....90 F2
  EDGY/DAV SK3 .....12 C6
  OLD OL1 .....9 K5
  ROCH OL11 .....42 A1
Bowyer Gdns BOLS/LL BL3 .....51 J1
Boxgrove Rd SALE M33 .....96 B7
Boxhill Dr NTHM/RTH M23 .....109 K3
Box St LIT OL15 .....21 L7
  RAMS BL0 .....19 G6
Boxtree Av GTN M18 .....100 A1
Boyd St WGNNW/ST WN6 .....31 J4
Boydell St LEIGH WN7 .....66 C6
Boyd St WGTN/LGST M12 .....88 E7
Boyd's Wk DUK SK16 .....90 F5

Boyer St *OLDTF/WHR* M16 ........ 86 E7
Boyle St *BOL* BL1 ........ 35 K3
   *CHH* M8 ........ 72 E6
Boysnope Whf *ECC* M30 ........ 84 A8
Brabant Rd *CHD/CHDH* SK8 ........ 120 D2
Brabazon Pl
   *WGNW/BIL/OR* WN5 ........ 46 F4
Brabham Cl *CCHDY* M21 ........ 97 L4
Brabham Ms *SWIN* M27 ........ 69 M5
Brabyns Av *MPL/ROM* SK6 ........ 114 F5
Brabyns Brow *MPL/ROM* SK6 ........ 114 D5
Brabyns Rd *HYDE* SK14 ........ 102 B5
Bracadale Dr *EDGY/DAV* SK3 ........ 112 B8
Bracewell Cl *WGTN/LGST* M12 ........ 88 D7
Bracken Av *WALK* M28 ........ 69 H1
Bracken Cl *BOL* BL1 ........ 22 A6
   *DROY* M43 ........ 89 M2
   *HEY* OL10 ........ 41 G4
   *HYDE* SK14 ........ 93 G6
   *MPL/ROM* SK6 ........ 114 F5
   *OLDE* OL4 ........ 60 C6
   *SALE* M33 ........ 95 M7
Bracken Dr *NTHM/RTH* M23 ........ 109 L7
Brackenhurst Av *MOSL* OL5 ........ 77 H4
Bracken Lea *WHTN* BL5 ........ 50 C7
Bracken Lea Fold *WHIT* OL12 ........ 27 L2
Bracken Pl *EDGY/DAV* SK3 ........ 112 A7
Bracken Rd *ATH* M46 ........ 65 G2
   *LEIGH* WN7 ........ 65 L1
Brackenside *RDSH* SK5 ........ 100 D4
Bracken Wy *GLSP* SK13 ........ 105 J5
Brackenwood Cl *ROY/SHW* OL2 ........ 58 F2
Brackenwood Dr
   *CHD/CHDH* SK8 ........ 111 C8
Brackenwood Ms
   *WILM/AE* SK9 ........ 127 J3
Brackley Av *HULME* M15 ........ 6 A9
   *IRL* M44 ........ 94 A6
   *TYLD* M29 ........ 67 L3
Brackley Dr *MDTN* M24 ........ 57 K7
Brackley Ldg *ECC* M30 * ........ 85 J1
Brackley Rd *ECC* M30 ........ 70 A8
   *HTNM* SK4 ........ 100 A7
   *WHTN* BL5 ........ 51 K4
Brackley Sq *OLD* OL1 * ........ 9 M3
Brackleys St *FWTH* BL4 ........ 53 G4
   *OLD* OL1 * ........ 9 L3
   *WALK* M28 ........ 52 F8
Bracondale Av *BOL* BL1 ........ 35 L2
Bradbourne Cl *BOLS/LL* BL3 ........ 2 D9
Bradburn Cl *ECC* M30 ........ 85 G3
Bradburn Rd *IRL* M44 ........ 94 B5
Bradburn St *ECC* M30 ........ 85 G3
Bradburn Wk *CHH* M8 ........ 72 E6
Bradbury Av *ALT* WA14 ........ 107 K7
Bradbury St *AULW* OL7 * ........ 75 K8
   *HYDE* SK14 ........ 102 B3
   *RAD* M26 ........ 54 D3
Bradda Mt *BRAM/HZG* SK7 ........ 121 H2
Braddan Av *SALE* M33 ........ 108 F1
Bradden Cl *ORD* M5 ........ 86 D3
Braddocks Cl *WHIT* OL12 ........ 21 H8
Braddon Av *URM* M41 ........ 96 A1
Braddon Rd *MPL/ROM* SK6 ........ 101 K7
Braddon St *OP/CLY* M11 ........ 88 F3
Braddyll Rd *WHTN* BL5 ........ 51 J4
Brade Cl *OP/CLY* M11 ........ 88 F4
Bradfield Av *AULW* OL7 ........ 75 K8
Bradfield Cl *BOLS/LL* BL3 ........ 52 L1
Bradfield Crs *BOLS/LL* BL3 * ........ 36 D8
Bradfield La *MCFLDN* SK10 ........ 130 D6
Bradfield Park Dr *BOLE* BL2 ........ 3 K6
Bradford Rd *BOLS/LL* BL3 ........ 52 D2
   *ECC* M30 ........ 70 B8
   *NEWH/MOS* M40 ........ 88 A2
Bradford St *BOLE* BL2 ........ 3 H5
   *FWTH* BL4 ........ 53 C5
   *OLD* OL1 ........ 9 G2
   *WGNS/IIMK* WN3 ........ 14 F6
Bradford Ter *BURY* BL9 * ........ 4 C7
Bradgate Av *CHD/CHDH* SK8 ........ 119 M3
Bradgate Cl *WYTH/NTH* M22 ........ 110 B4
Bradgate Rd *ALT* WA14 ........ 107 K3
   *SALE* M33 ........ 108 E2
Bradgreen Rd *ECC* M30 ........ 84 F1
Bradley Av *BRO* M7 * ........ 71 L5
Bradley Cl *HALE/TIMP* WA15 ........ 108 B5
Bradley Dr *BURY* BL9 ........ 55 L2
Bradley Fold Rd *BOLE* BL2 ........ 37 L6
Bradley Green Rd *HYDE* SK14 ........ 91 J6
Bradley La *MILN* OL16 ........ 29 L8
   *RAD* M26 ........ 37 L7
   *STRET* M32 ........ 96 D5
   *WGNW/ST* WN6 ........ 31 J8
Bradleys Count *CMANE* M1 * ........ 7 J4
Bradley Smithy Cl *WHIT* OL12 ........ 28 B2
Bradley St *CMANE* M1 ........ 7 J3
   *MILN* OL16 ........ 29 L8
Bradney Cl *BKLY* M9 ........ 56 E8
Bradnor Rd *WYTH/NTH* M22 ........ 110 A5
   *FAIL* M35 ........ 74 B7
   *WHTF* M45 ........ 55 H2
Bradshaw Av *DID/WITH* M20 ........ 98 E5
Bradshaw Brow *BOLE* BL2 ........ 22 F8
Bradshaw Cl *WGNNW/ST* WN6 ........ 31 G3
Bradshaw Crs *MPL/ROM* SK6 ........ 114 D5
Bradshaw Fold Av
   *NEWH/MOS* M40 ........ 74 A1
Bradshawgate *BOL* BL1 ........ 2 F5
   *LEIGH* WN7 ........ 66 C7
   *WGN* WN1 ........ 15 J4
Bradshaw Hall Dr *BOLE* BL2 ........ 22 F6
Bradshaw Hall Fold *BOLE* BL2 * ........ 23 G6
Bradshaw Hall La
   *CHD/CHDH* SK8 ........ 119 M4
Bradshaw La *STRET* M32 ........ 97 H4
Bradshaw Mdw *BOLE* BL2 ........ 23 G6
Bradshaw Rd *BOLE* BL2 ........ 23 G5
   *MPL/ROM* SK6 ........ 114 C5
   *TOT/BURYW* BL8 ........ 23 M6
Bradshaw St *ANC* M4 * ........ 67 G1
   *ATH* M46 ........ 67 G1
   *BRO* M7 ........ 72 B6
   *FWTH* BL4 ........ 53 H3
   *HEY* OL10 ........ 41 H2
   *OLD* OL1 ........ 9 K5
   *RAD* M26 ........ 54 C1
   *WGN* WN1 ........ 48 A2
   *WGNW/BIL/OR* WN5 ........ 46 D6
Bradshaw St North *BRO* M7 ........ 72 A4
Bradstock Rd *OLDTF/WHR* M16 ........ 98 B1
Bradstone Rd *CHH* M8 ........ 72 C7
Bradwell Av *DID/WITH* M20 ........ 98 C6
   *STRET* M32 ........ 96 D1
Bradwell Dr *CHD/CHDH* SK8 ........ 119 L5
Bradwell Pl *BOLE* BL2 ........ 36 E3

Bradwell Rd *BRAM/HZG* SK7 ........ 122 A4
   *GOL/RIS/CUL* WA3 ........ 80 B5
Bradwen Av *CHH* M8 ........ 72 D3
Bradwen Cl *DTN/ASHW* M34 ........ 101 K3
Brady St *STKP* SK1 ........ 13 L1
Braeburn La *LEIGH* WN7 ........ 66 A7
   *URM* M41 ........ 95 K3
Braemar Av *STRET* M32 ........ 96 D2
   *URM* M41 ........ 95 K3
Braemar Dr *BURY* BL9 ........ 40 A2
Braemar Gv *HEY* OL10 ........ 40 D3
Braemar La *WALK* M28 ........ 68 E6
Braemar Rd *BRAM/HZG* SK7 ........ 122 B1
   *RUSH/FAL* M14 ........ 99 H4
   *SALE* M33 ........ 107 M2
Braemore Rd *ROY/SHW* OL2 ........ 43 H4
   *WGNS/IIMK* WN3 ........ 62 F2
Braemore Dr *HYDE* SK14 ........ 103 J3
Brae Side *OLDS* OL8 ........ 75 H2
Braeside *STRET* M32 * ........ 96 D3
Braeside Cl *OFTN* SK2 ........ 113 J7
Braeside Crs
   *WGNW/BIL/OR* WN5 ........ 62 A7
Braeside Gv *BOLS/LL* BL3 ........ 35 H7
Braewood Cl *BURY* BL9 ........ 39 M1
Bragenham St *GTN* M18 ........ 88 F7
Brailsford Rd *BOLE* BL2 ........ 36 F1
   *RUSH/FAL* M14 ........ 99 H4
Braintree Rd *WGN/NTH* M22 ........ 119 G4
Braithwaite *WGNNW/ST* WN6 ........ 30 D6
Braithwaite Rd
   *GOL/RIS/CUL* WA3 ........ 80 A3
   *MDTN* M24 ........ 41 G8
Brakehouse Cl *MILN* OL16 ........ 29 H6
Brakenhurst Dr *BRO* M7 ........ 72 C6
Brakesmere Gv *WALK* M28 ........ 52 C8
Braley St *WGTN/LGST* M12 * ........ 7 H9
Bramah Edge Ct *GLSP* SK13 ........ 93 J6
Bramall Cl *BURY* BL9 ........ 55 L2
Bramall St *HYDE* SK14 ........ 91 G8
Bramble Av *OLDE* OL4 ........ 60 A3
   *ORD* M5 ........ 86 F5
Bramble Bank *GLSP* SK13 ........ 105 H4
Bramble Cl *LIT* OL15 ........ 21 K7
Bramble Cft *HOR/BR* BL6 ........ 50 D1
Bramble Gv
   *WGNW/BIL/OR* WN5 ........ 47 H5
The Brambles *AIMK* WN4 ........ 63 G7
Bramblewood *WHTN* BL5 ........ 50 B5
Brambling Cl *DTN/ASHW* M34 ........ 89 M2
   *OFTN* SK2 ........ 113 K8
Brambling Dr *WHTN* BL5 ........ 50 M5
Brambling Wy
   *GOL/RIS/CUL* WA3 ........ 80 B3
Bramcote Av *BOLE* BL2 ........ 3 J8
   *NTHM/RTH* M23 ........ 109 L1
Bramdean Av *BOLE* BL2 ........ 23 H7
Bramfield Wk *HULME* M15 * ........ 6 A9
Bramford Cl *WHTN* BL5 ........ 50 B6
Bramhall Av *BOLE* BL2 ........ 23 K8
Bramhall Cl *DUK* SK16 ........ 91 G6
   *HALE/TIMP* WA15 ........ 108 C8
   *MILN* OL16 ........ 29 H7
   *SALE* M33 ........ 109 H1
Bramhall La *EDGY/DAV* SK3 ........ 112 C8
Bramhall La South
   *BRAM/HZG* SK7 ........ 121 D6
Bramhall Moor La
   *BRAM/HZG* SK7 ........ 121 K3
Bramhall Park Rd
   *BRAM/HZG* SK7 ........ 120 F3
Bramhall St *BOLS/LL* BL3 ........ 52 L1
   *GTN* M18 ........ 89 H7
Bramham Rd *MPL/ROM* SK6 ........ 114 D8
Bramley Av *BNG/LEV* M19 ........ 99 K4
   *STRET* M32 ........ 96 D1
Bramley Cl *BRAM/HZG* SK7 ........ 121 G6
   *SWIN* M27 ........ 69 M6
   *WILM/AE* SK9 ........ 126 B8
Bramley Crs *HTNM* SK4 ........ 12 A4
Bramley Dr *BRAM/HZG* SK7 ........ 121 G6
   *TOT/BURYW* BL8 ........ 24 F5
Bramley Meade *BRO* M7 ........ 72 B5
Bramley Rd *BOL* BL1 ........ 22 C6
   *BRAM/HZG* SK7 ........ 121 G6
   *ROCH* OL11 ........ 27 H4
Bramley St *BRO* M7 ........ 72 B7
Brammay Dr *TOT/BURYW* BL8 ........ 24 B7
Brampton Cl *WGNE/HIN* WN2 ........ 64 C3
Brampton Rd *BOLS/LL* BL3 ........ 51 K1
   *BRAM/HZG* SK7 ........ 121 H2
Brampton St *ATH* M46 * ........ 67 G1
Bramway *BRAM/HZG* SK7 ........ 120 E5
   *MPL/ROM* SK6 ........ 123 H5
Bramwell Dr *BRUN/LGST* M13 ........ 87 M6
Bramwell St *STKP* SK1 ........ 112 L4
Bramworth Av *RAMS* BL0 ........ 18 E6
Brancaster Dr
   *GOL/RIS/CUL* WA3 ........ 80 A3
Brancaster Rd *CMANE* M1 * ........ 7 H8
Branch Cl *TOT/BURYW* BL8 ........ 4 C2
Branch Rd *LIT* OL15 ........ 29 H3
Branch St *WGNE/HIN* WN2 ........ 48 D5
Branch Wy *RNFD/HAY* WA11 ........ 78 A4
Brancker St *WHTN* BL5 ........ 50 F4
Brandish Cl *BRUN/LGST* M13 ........ 88 A8
Brandle Av *TOT/BURYW* BL8 ........ 24 F8
Brandlehow Dr *MDTN* M24 ........ 56 F2
Brandlesholme Rd
   *TOT/BURYW* BL8 ........ 24 F6
Brandon Av *CHD/CHDH* SK8 ........ 119 K3
   *DTN/ASHW* M34 ........ 100 C1
   *ECC* M30 ........ 70 D8
   *WYTH/NTH* M22 ........ 109 M4
Brandon Brow *OLD* OL1 * ........ 9 H2
Brandon Cl *TOT/BURYW* BL8 ........ 25 C7
   *WILM/AE* SK9 ........ 127 H2
Brandon Crs *ROY/SHW* OL2 ........ 43 K4
Brandon Rd *SLFD* M6 ........ 70 E7
Brandon St *BOLS/LL* BL3 ........ 36 M8
   *MILN* OL16 ........ 29 H6
Brandram Rd *PWCH* M25 ........ 55 L8
Brandreth Pl *WGNNW/ST* WN6 ........ 31 J3
Brandsby Gdns *ORD* M5 * ........ 86 D4
Brandwood *OLD* OL1 ........ 58 B3
Brandwood Av *CCHDY* M21 ........ 98 A8
Brandwood Cl *WALK* M28 ........ 68 D4
Brandwood St *BOLS/LL* BL3 ........ 35 M8
Branfield Av *CHD/CHDH* SK8 ........ 119 M3
Branksome Av *PWCH* M25 ........ 55 K8
Branksome Dr *BKLY* M9 ........ 56 E6
   *CHD/CHDH* SK8 ........ 119 M3
   *SLFD* M6 ........ 70 D7
Branksome Rd *HTNM* SK4 ........ 12 A4
Brannach Dr *CHAD* OL9 ........ 58 D4
Bransby Av *BKLY* M9 ........ 57 H8
Branscombe Dr *SALE* M33 ........ 95 M7
Branscombe Gdns
   *BOLS/LL* BL3 * ........ 37 G7
Bransdale Av *ROY/SHW* OL2 ........ 42 F8
Bransdale Cl *BOLS/LL* BL3 ........ 35 J8
Bransdale Dr *AIMK* WN4 ........ 79 G1

Bransfield Cl *WGNS/IIMK* WN3 ........ 63 K1
Brewer St *CMANE* M1 ........ 7 J4
Brewerton Rd *OLDE* OL4 ........ 59 M7
Brewery La *LEIGH* WN7 ........ 66 D7
Brewery St *ALT* WA14 ........ 108 A8
   *STKP* SK1 ........ 13 K2
Brewster St *BKLY* M9 ........ 73 G4
   *MDTN* M24 ........ 57 K2
Brian Av *DROY* M43 * ........ 89 M1
Brian Redhead Ct
   *HULME* M15 ........ 6 C9
Brian Rd *FWTH* BL4 ........ 52 D2
Brian St *ROCH* OL11 ........ 41 L2
Briaracre Ter *AUL* OL6 * ........ 75 M4
Briar Av *BRAM/HZG* SK7 ........ 122 B2
   *OLDE* OL4 ........ 60 A3
Briar Cl *AIMK* WN4 ........ 63 K8
   *SALE* M33 ........ 95 M8
   *URM* M41 ........ 95 K1
   *WGNE/HIN* WN2 ........ 49 L8
   *WHIT* OL12 ........ 27 K3
Briar Crs *WYTH/NTH* M22 ........ 110 B7
Briarcroft Dr *ATH* M46 ........ 66 D3
Briardene
   *DTN/ASHW* M34 * ........ 90 D8
Briardene Gdns
   *WYTH/NTH* M22 ........ 110 B8
Briarfield *EDGW/EG* BL7 ........ 22 A2
Briarfield Rd
   *CHD/CHDH* SK8 ........ 120 D1
   *DID/WITH* M20 ........ 99 G6
   *FWTH* BL4 ........ 52 D3
   *HALE/TIMP* WA15 ........ 108 F6
   *HTNM* SK4 ........ 100 B6
   *UPML* OL3 ........ 61 K2
   *WALK* M28 ........ 69 J5
Briar Gv *CHAD* OL9 ........ 58 E3
   *LEIGH* WN7 ........ 66 B4
   *MPL/ROM* SK6 ........ 101 K7
Briar Hill Av *LHULT* M38 ........ 52 B8
Briar Hill Cl *LHULT* M38 ........ 52 B8
Briar Hill Gv *LHULT* M38 ........ 52 B8
Briar Hill Wy *SLFD* M6 * ........ 86 D1
Briar Hollow *HTNM* SK4 ........ 12 A4
Briarlands Av
   *BRAM/HZG* SK7 ........ 120 F6
   *SALE* M33 ........ 108 C2
Briarlea Gdns *BNG/LEV* M19 ........ 99 H7
Briarley Gdns *MPL/ROM* SK6 ........ 101 M6
Briarly *WGNNW/ST* WN6 ........ 31 K5
Briarmere Wk *CHAD* OL9 ........ 8 C4
Briar Rd *GOL/RIS/CUL* WA3 ........ 79 L4
   *WGNW/BIL/OR* WN5 ........ 47 C5
Briars Mt *HTNM* SK4 ........ 12 A4
Briars Pk *BRAM/HZG* SK7 ........ 120 E3
Briarstead Cl *BRAM/HZG* SK7 ........ 120 F5
Briar St *BOLE* BL2 ........ 37 G5
   *ROCH* OL11 ........ 10 B6
Briarwood *CHD/CHDH* SK8 ........ 120 D3
Briarwood Av *DROY* M43 ........ 89 H1
   *NTHM/RTH* M23 ........ 109 G4
Briarwood Cha
   *CHD/CHDH* SK8 ........ 120 D3
Briarwood Crs *MPL/ROM* SK6 ........ 114 C8
Briary Dr *TYLD* M29 ........ 67 L4
Brice St *DUK* SK16 ........ 90 E4
Brickbridge Rd *MPL/ROM* SK6 ........ 114 D7
   *MILN* OL16 ........ 28 D2
Brickfield St *GLSP* SK13 ........ 93 L7
Brickhill La *HALE/TIMP* WA15 ........ 117 K8
Brickhouses *GLSP* SK13 * ........ 103 J7
Brickkiln La *ATH* WA14 ........ 106 F8
Brickkiln Rw *ALT* WA14 ........ 116 E5
Brickley St *CSLFD* M3 ........ 87 K1
Brick St *ANC* M4 * ........ 7 H3
   *BURY* BL9 ........ 5 J3
Bridcrest Ct
   *CHD/CHDH* SK8 * ........ 120 C2
Bridge Dr *CHD/CHDH* SK8 ........ 111 C8
   *WILM/AE* SK9 ........ 127 H1
Bridge End *NEWH/MOS* M40 ........ 73 K5
Bridge Bank Rd *LIT* OL15 ........ 29 H4
Bridge Cl *PART* M31 ........ 106 D1
   *RAD* M26 ........ 54 D7
Bridgecrest Ct
   *CHD/CHDH* SK8 * ........ 120 C2
Bridge Dr *HALE/TIMP* WA15 ........ 108 C5
   *WILM/AE* SK9 ........ 127 H1
Bridge End *NEWH/MOS* M40 ........ 14 D4
Bridge End Rd *WILM/AE* SK9 ........ 127 G3
Bridgefield Crs *OLDE* OL4 ........ 60 C6
Bridgefield Dr *BURY* BL9 ........ 39 M2
Bridgefield St *RAD* M26 ........ 54 E1
   *ROCH* OL11 ........ 10 B5
   *STKP* SK1 ........ 13 H4
Bridgefold Rd *ROCH* OL11 ........ 27 M5
Bridgefoot Cl *WALK* M28 ........ 68 D7
Bridge Gv *HALE/TIMP* WA15 ........ 108 C5
Bridge Hall Dr *BURY* BL9 ........ 39 M2
Bridge Hall Fold *BURY* BL9 ........ 39 M2
Bridge Hall La *BURY* BL9 ........ 40 A2
Bridge La *BRAM/HZG* SK7 ........ 121 J3
Bridgelea Ms *DID/WITH* M20 ........ 98 E6
Bridgelea Rd *DID/WITH* M20 ........ 98 E6
Bridgeman Pl *BOLE* BL2 ........ 3 J3
Bridgeman St *BOLS/LL* BL3 ........ 2 E1
   *FWTH* BL4 ........ 53 G3
Bridgeman Ter *WGN* WN1 ........ 14 F1
Bridgemere Cl *RAD* M26 ........ 38 C7
Bridgend Cl *CHD/CHDH* SK8 ........ 111 M8
   *WGTN/LGST* M12 ........ 88 D6
Bridgenorth Av *URM* M41 ........ 96 C2
Bridgenorth Dr *LIT* OL15 ........ 29 J1
Bridge Rd *BURY* BL9 ........ 4 D3
   *HALE/TIMP* WA15 ........ 108 F5
Bridges Av *BURY* BL9 ........ 39 G6
Bridges Ct *BOL* BL1 * ........ 2 E6
Bridge's St *ATH* M46 ........ 66 E2
Bridge St *BOL* BL1 ........ 2 E4
   *BURY* BL9 ........ 5 H1
   *CSLFD* M3 ........ 6 D4
   *DROY* M43 ........ 89 M1
   *DTN/ASHW* M34 ........ 90 C5
   *FWTH* BL4 ........ 53 H3
   *GOL/RIS/CUL* WA3 ........ 79 K5
   *HEY* OL10 ........ 40 F2
   *MDTN* M24 ........ 57 K4
   *MILN* OL16 ........ 29 J1
   *NM/HAY* SK22 ........ 124 C3
   *OLD* OL1 ........ 59 C3
   *OLDE* OL4 ........ 60 C6
   *RAD* M26 ........ 53 L4
   *RAMS* BL0 ........ 18 F6
   *ROCH* OL11 ........ 41 H6
   *ROY/SHW* OL2 * ........ 43 M4
   *STKP* SK1 ........ 13 J3
   *STLY* SK15 ........ 91 J3

SWIN M27 ........ 70 D4
   *UPML* OL3 ........ 61 L5
   *WGNE/HIN* WN2 ........ 49 L6
   *WGNS/IIMK* WN3 ........ 14 F6
   *WHIT* OL12 ........ 20 A5
   *WHIT* OL12 ........ 28 F1
Bridge St Brow *STKP* SK1 ........ 13 J3
Bridgewater Pl *MANE* M17 ........ 84 F6
Bridgewater Pl *CMANE* M1 ........ 7 G2
Bridgewater Rd *ALT* WA14 ........ 108 A5
   *SWIN* M27 ........ 70 E5
   *WALK* M28 ........ 68 F2
Bridgewater St *BOL* BL1 ........ 2 A6
   *CSLFD* M3 ........ 84 E2
   *ECC* M30 ........ 84 F2
   *FWTH* BL4 ........ 53 G4
   *LHULT* M38 ........ 52 E8
   *OLD* OL1 ........ 9 L3
   *SALE* M33 ........ 96 F7
   *STRET* M32 ........ 97 H2
   *WGNE/HIN* WN2 ........ 49 H6
   *WGNS/IIMK* WN3 ........ 14 E5
   *WGNW/BIL/OR* WN5 ........ 14 A7
Bridgewater Viad *CSLFD* M3 ........ 6 D7
Bridgewater Wy
   *OLDTF/WHR* M16 ........ 86 F6
Bridgfield Cl *MPL/ROM* SK6 ........ 123 G5
Bridgnorth Rd *BKLY* M9 ........ 72 D1
Bridle Cl *DROY* M43 ........ 89 M1
   *URM* M41 ........ 95 H3
Bridle Fold *RAD* M26 ........ 38 D8
Bridle Rd *BRAM/HZG* SK7 ........ 128 D3
   *PWCH* M25 ........ 56 B5
Bridle Wy *BRAM/HZG* SK7 ........ 128 D3
Bridleway *NM/HAY* SK22 ........ 124 F3
Bridlington Av *SLFD* M6 * ........ 85 M1
Bridlington Cl
   *NEWH/MOS* M40 ........ 73 M6
Bridport Av *NEWH/MOS* M40 ........ 74 A4
Bridson La *BOLE* BL2 ........ 37 G3
Bridson St *OLDE* OL4 ........ 59 M5
   *ORD* M5 ........ 86 B3
Brief St *BOLE* BL2 ........ 36 F3
Brien Av *ALT* WA14 ........ 108 A6
Briercliffe Cl *GTN* M18 ........ 88 F8
Brierfield Av *ATH* M46 ........ 50 F8
Brierfield Dr *BURY* BL9 ........ 25 H4
Brierholme Av *EDGW/EG* BL7 ........ 22 B3
Brierley Av *FAIL* M35 ........ 74 D5
   *WHTF* M45 ........ 55 H2
Brierley Cl *AUL* OL6 ........ 76 D6
   *DTN/ASHW* M34 ........ 101 H2
Brierley Dr *MDTN* M24 ........ 57 K5
Brierley Rd East *SWIN* M27 ........ 70 B3
Brierley Rd West *SWIN* M27 ........ 70 B3
Brierley St *BURY* BL9 ........ 4 E3
   *CHAD* OL9 ........ 8 D2
   *DUK* SK16 ........ 91 G3
   *HEY* OL10 ........ 41 G2
   *OLDS* OL8 ........ 75 J1
Brierley Wk *CHAD* OL9 ........ 8 D2
Brierton Dr *WYTH/NTH* M22 ........ 118 D3
Brierwood *BOLE* BL2 ........ 3 J8
Brierwood Cl *ROY/SHW* OL2 ........ 59 H3
Briery Av *BOLE* BL2 ........ 23 G6
Brigade Dr *STRET* M32 ........ 96 F1
Brigade St *BOL* BL1 ........ 35 M5
Brigadier Cl *DID/WITH* M20 ........ 98 E6
Brigantine Cl *ORD* M5 ........ 86 D4
Briggs Cl *SALE* M33 ........ 107 M3
Briggs Fold Cl *EDGW/EG* BL7 ........ 22 B2
Briggs Fold Rd *EDGW/EG* BL7 ........ 22 B2
Briggs Rd *STRET* M32 ........ 86 C8
Briggs St *CSLFD* M3 ........ 6 B1
   *LEIGH* WN7 ........ 66 B5
Brigham St *OP/CLY* M11 ........ 88 F4
Bright Cir *URM* M41 ........ 85 H6
Brightgate Wy *STRET* M32 ........ 85 G6
Brighton St *GTN* M18 ........ 89 G6
Brighton Av *BNG/LEV* M19 ........ 99 H3
   *BOL* BL1 ........ 35 K3
   *BRO* M7 ........ 72 B6
   *RDSH* SK5 ........ 100 C2
   *URM* M41 ........ 95 H2
Brighton Gv *HYDE* SK14 ........ 102 B3
   *RUSH/FAL* M14 ........ 99 G2
   *SALE* M33 ........ 96 D7
   *URM* M41 ........ 95 H2
Brighton Range *GTN* M18 ........ 89 J8
Brighton Rd *HTNM* SK4 ........ 12 D3
   *OLDE* OL4 ........ 60 D3
Brighton St *ANC* M4 ........ 87 K1
   *BURY* BL9 ........ 5 K2
Bright Rd *ECC* M30 ........ 85 H2
Brightstone Wk
   *RUSH/FAL* M14 ........ 88 B8
Bright St *AUL* OL6 ........ 91 G2
   *BURY* BL9 ........ 5 J2
   *CHAD* OL9 ........ 74 D1
   *DROY* M43 ........ 89 L3
   *LEIGH* WN7 ........ 66 B5
   *MILN* OL16 ........ 11 H8
   *OLDS* OL8 ........ 9 H8
   *RAD* M26 ........ 38 F8
Brightwater Cl *WHTF* M45 ........ 55 K4
Brignall Gv *GOL/RIS/CUL* WA3 ........ 80 A3
Brigstock Av *GTN* M18 ........ 88 F8
Briksdal Wy *HOR/BR* BL6 ........ 34 F5
Brimelow St *MPL/ROM* SK6 ........ 112 F1
Brimfield Av *TYLD* M29 ........ 67 M3
Brimmy Croft La *UPML* OL3 ........ 44 F1
Brimrod La *ROCH* OL11 ........ 10 A9
Brimscombe Av
   *WYTH/NTH* M22 ........ 118 C3
Brindale Rd *RDSH* SK5 ........ 100 F8
Brindle Cl *SLFD* M6 ........ 71 J8
Brindle Heath Rd *SLFD* M6 ........ 71 J8
Brindlehurst Dr *TYLD* M29 ........ 68 A5
Brindle St *TYLD* M29 ........ 67 K3
   *WGNE/HIN* WN2 ........ 49 J5
Brindley Av *BKLY* M9 ........ 56 E7
   *MPL/ROM* SK6 ........ 114 C7
   *SALE* M33 ........ 108 D6
   *WALK* M28 ........ 68 D6
Brindley Cl *ATH* M46 ........ 66 D2
   *FWTH* BL4 ........ 52 E4
Brindley Rd *OLDTF/WHR* M16 ........ 86 E7
Brindley St *ECC* M30 ........ 84 E1
   *HOR/BR* BL6 ........ 33 M2
   *SWIN* M27 ........ 70 C3
   *WALK* M28 ........ 68 C6
   *WGNW/BIL/OR* WN5 ........ 46 F7
Brinell Dr *IRL* M44 ........ 94 C7
Brinkburn Rd *BRAM/HZG* SK7 ........ 122 L1
Brinklow Cl *OP/CLY* M11 ........ 89 G5
Brinksway Av *WYTH/NTH* M22 ........ 119 C2
Brinks La *BOLE* BL2 ........ 37 K5

Brinksway *BOL* BL1 .................................34 F5
  *EDGY/DAV* SK3 ...............................12 C6
Brinksworth Cl *BOLE* BL2 ....................37 K4
Brinnington Crs *RDSH* SK5 .............100 E3
Brinnington Rd *RDSH* SK5 ..............100 F8
  *STKP* SK1 ..........................................13 M1
Brinsop Hall La *WHTN* BL5 ...............33 K7
Brinsop Sq *WGTN/LGST* M12 ...........88 E6
Brinsworth Dr *CHH* M8 ......................72 D6
Briony Av *HALE/TIMP* WA15 .........117 L2
Briony Cl *ROY/SHW* OL2 ....................59 H9
Brisbane Av *BRAM/HZG* SK7 .........121 H7
Brisbane St *BRUN/LGST* M13 ...........87 L7
Briscoe La *NEWH/MOS* M40 ............73 K8
Briscoe Ms *BOLS/LL* BL3 ..................36 D8
Briscoe St *OLD* OL1 ..............................9 J3
Bristle Hall Wy *WHTN* BL5 ...............50 C2
Bristle St *HULME* M15 .......................87 K6
Bristol Av *AUL* OL6 ..............................75 L5
  *BNG/LEV* M19 ..................................99 L4
  *BOLE* BL2 ............................................3 L1
Bristol St *BRO* M7 ..............................72 B5
Bristowe St *OP/CLY* M11 ..................89 C1
Britain St *BURY* BL9 ...........................39 H6
Britannia Av *ROY/SHW* OL2 ............43 M6
Britannia Cl *RAD* M26 .......................54 D1
Britannia Rd *SALE* M33 ......................96 E7
  *WGNW/BIL/OR* WN5 ......................46 F4
Britannia St *AULW* OL7 ......................90 C4
  *HEY* OL10 ..........................................40 E2
  *OLD* OL1 ..............................................9 M4
  *SLFD* M6 ...........................................71 K6
Britannia Wy *BOLE* BL2 ....................36 D2
Britnall Av *WGTN/LGST* M12 ...........88 B7
Briton St *MILN* OL16 .........................11 J2
  *ROY/SHW* OL2 ................................43 J7
Brixham Av *DID/WITH* M20 ...........120 B5
Brixham Dr *SALE* M33 ........................96 A6
Brixham Rd
  *OLDTF/WHR* M16 ...........................86 B8
Brixham Wk *BRAM/HZG* SK7 .........121 J3
  *BRUN/LGST* M13 ............................87 M7
Brixton Av *DID/WITH* M20 ...............98 D6
Broach St *BOLS/LL* BL3 ......................36 B8
Broad Acre *WHIT* OL12 ......................27 H2
Broadacre Pl *WILM/AE* SK9 ...........130 A1
Broadbent Av *AUL* OL6 ......................75 M6
  *DUK* SK16 ..........................................91 G4
Broadbent Cl *ROY/SHW* OL2 ...........43 J7
  *STLY* SK15 .........................................77 H6
Broadbent Dr *BURY* BL9 ...................26 B8
Broadbent Gv *HYDE* SK14 ...............103 H3
Broadbent Rd *OLD* OL1 .....................59 M2
Broadbent St *HYDE* SK14 .................91 G8
  *SWIN* M27 ........................................70 A5
Broadbottom Rd *HYDE* SK14 .........103 J2
Broadcarr La *MOSL* OL5 ....................76 D3
Broadfield Cl *DTN/ASHW* M34 ......101 L4
Broadfield Dr *LIT* OL15 ......................29 J1
Broadfield Gv *RDSH* SK5 .................100 B1
Broadfield Rd *BOLS/LL* BL3 ..............50 D3
  *RUSH/FAL* M14 ................................98 D1
Broadfields Stile *MILN* OL16 ...........10 D6
Broadfield St *HEY* OL10 ....................40 E4
  *MILN* OL16 ........................................11 G5
Bradford Rd *BOLS/LL* BL3 .................35 J7
Broadgate *CHAD* OL9 .........................58 A6
  *MDTN* M24 .......................................58 A6
  *UPML* OL3 .........................................61 H3
Broadgate Meadow
  *SWIN* M27 * .......................................70 C5
Broadgreen Gdns *FWTH* BL4 * ........53 G2
Broadhalgh Av *ROCH* OL11 ..............27 K5
Broadhalgh Rd *ROCH* OL11 ..............27 K6
Broadhead Rd *EDGW/EG* BL7 ...........17 J5
Broadheath *BRAM/HZG* SK7 ............50 D3
Broad Hey *MPL/ROM* SK6 ...............114 A1
Broadhey Vw *NM/HAY* SK22 .........124 D3
Broad Hill *BRAM/HZG* SK7 .............121 J5
Broadhill Rd *BNG/LEV* M19 .............99 H6
  *STLY* SK15 ........................................77 K6
Broadhurst *DTN/ASHW* M34 ...........90 D7
Broadhurst Av *OLD* OL1 ......................8 C1
  *SWIN* M27 ........................................70 C1
Broadhurst Ct *BOLS/LL* BL3 .............36 A8
Broadhurst Gv *AUL* OL6 .....................75 M6
Broadhurst St *BOLS/LL* BL3 * ..........36 A8
  *EDGY/DAV* SK3 .................................13 H9
Broad Ing *ROCH* OL11 * .....................27 L3
Broadlands *WGNNW/ST* WN6 ..........30 E6
Broadlands Rd *WALK* M28 .................69 M6
Broad La *HALE/TIMP* WA15 ............117 K4
  *MILN* OL16 .........................................42 F1
  *UPML* OL3 .........................................45 H5
Broad Lea *URM* M41 ..........................95 M1
Broadlea Gv *WHIT* OL12 .....................27 M2
Broadlea Rd *BNG/LEV* M19 ...............99 H7
Broadley Av *GOL/RIS/CUL* WA3 ......79 M5
  *WYTH/NTH* M22 ............................110 A8
Broadmeadow *EDGW/EG* BL7 ..........22 E4
Broadmeadow Av
  *OLDTF/WHR* M16 ...........................98 C3
Broadmoss Dr *BKLY* M9 .....................73 K1
Broadmoss Rd *BKLY* M9 ....................73 K1
Broadmount Ter *CHAD* OL9 * ...........58 E8
Broadoak Av *WALK* M28 ....................68 C5
  *WYTH/NTH* M22 ............................109 M7
Broadoak Crs *AUL* OL6 .......................75 L7
Broadoak Crs *OLDS* OL8 .....................75 K2
Broadoak Dr *WYTH/NTH* M22 ........110 A7
Broad Oak La *BURY* BL9 .....................39 M1
  *DID/WITH* M20 ..............................110 F4
Broad Oak Pk *ECC* M30 .......................70 A8
  *WALK* M28 ........................................69 L6
Broad Oak Rd *BOLS/LL* BL3 ..............52 D2
Broadoak Rd *AUL* OL6 .......................75 M6
  *BRAM/HZG* SK7 .............................121 H6
  *ROCH* OL11 .......................................27 H6
  *WYTH/NTH* M22 ............................109 M8
Broadoaks *BURY* BL9 .........................40 A1
Broadoaks Rd *SALE* M33 ....................96 D8
  *URM* M41 ..........................................95 L3
Broad Oak Ter *BURY* BL9 ...................40 B1
Broad o' th' La *BOL* BL1 ......................22 B8
Broadriding Rd
  *WGNNW/ST* WN6 ..........................30 B6
Broad Rd *SALE* M33 ............................96 F7
Broad Shaw La *MILN* OL16 ................43 G3
Broadstone Av *OLDE* OL4 ..................44 C8
Broadstone Cl *PWCH* M25 .................71 K2
  *WHIT* OL12 .......................................27 K3
Broadstone Hall Rd North
  *HTNM* SK4 ......................................100 A6
Broadstone Hall Rd South
  *HTNM* SK4 ......................................100 B6
Broadstone Rd *BOLE* BL2 ...................23 G7
  *HTNM* SK4 ......................................100 A6
Broad St *BURY* BL9 ...............................4 E5
  *MDTN* M24 .......................................56 F5
  *SLFD* M6 ...........................................71 H7

Broad Wk *WHTN* BL5 ..........................50 B5
  *WILM/AE* SK9 .................................126 D4
Broadway *ATH* M46 .............................51 J7
  *BRAM/HZG* SK7 .............................121 H2
  *CHAD* OL9 ...........................................8 A1
  *CHAD* OL9 .........................................74 C1
  *CHD/CHDH* SK8 .............................110 F8
  *DROY* M43 .........................................74 A4
  *FAIL* M35 ...........................................74 A4
  *FWTH* BL4 .........................................52 D2
  *HALE/TIMP* WA15 ..........................117 J3
  *HOR/BR* BL6 .....................................34 A1
  *HYDE* SK14 ........................................90 E7
  *IRL* M44 .............................................94 D3
  *OFTN* SK2 ........................................112 F5
  *PART* M31 ..........................................94 D8
  *ROY/SHW* OL2 ................................59 H1
  *SALE* M33 ..........................................96 D7
  *SALO* M50 .........................................86 B4
  *URM* M41 ..........................................84 B8
  *WALK* M28 ........................................69 G3
  *WGNE/HIN* WN2 ............................49 K7
Broadway Av *CHD/CHDH* SK8 .......111 G8
Broadway Cl *URM* M41 .......................84 B8
Broadway North *DROY* M43 .............89 K4
Broadway St *OLDS* OL8 ......................74 B3
  *LEIGH* WN7 .......................................81 H3
Broadwood *RO:/BR* BL6 ....................34 F5
Broadwood Cl *POY/DIS* SK12 .........123 H5
Brocade Cl *CSLFD* M3 ...........................6 A1
Broche Cl *ROCH* OL11 .........................41 L1
Brock Av *BOLE* BL2 ..............................37 J5
Brock Cl *OP/CLY* M11 .........................89 C5
Brock Dr *CHD/CHDH* SK8 .................120 C4
Brockenhurst Dr *BOLE* BL2 ..............23 J7
Brockford Dr *BKLY* M9 ........................57 H7
Brockholes *GLSP* SK13 .....................104 C4
Brockhurst Wk
  *BRAM/HZG* SK7 ............................121 J3
Brocklebank Rd *MILN* OL16 .............29 G5
  *RUSH/FAL* M14 ...............................98 E2
Brocklehurst Av *BURY* BL9 .................5 G7
Brocklehurst St *BKLY* M9 ..................73 K4
Brock Mill La *WGN* WN1 ...................31 M8
Brock Pl *WGNE/HIN* WN2 .................64 C2
Brockstedes Av *AIMK* WN4 ...............63 H6
Brock St *CMANE* M1 * ...........................7 J6
  *WGN* WN1 ........................................15 L4
The Brock *ROY/SHW* OL2 ..................43 J8
Brockway *MILN* OL16 .........................42 F1
Brocstedes Rd *AIMK* WN4 ................63 G5
Brodick Dr *BOLE* BL2 ...........................37 J6
Brodick St *NEWH/MOS* M40 * ..........73 J4
Brogan St *GTN* M18 ............................89 G1
Brogden Av *GOL/RIS/CUL* WA3 ........81 H8
Brogden Dr *CHD/CHDH* SK8 ..........110 E7
Brogden Gv *SALE* M33 ......................108 D1
Brogden Ter *SALE* M33 .......................96 D8
Bromborough Av
  *DID/WITH* M20 ...............................98 D4
Bromfield *WHIT* OL12 * .......................10 E2
Bromfield Av *BKLY* M9 ........................73 G3
Bromleigh Av *CHD/CHDH* SK8 ......110 E6
Bromley Av *GOL/RIS/CUL* WA3 ......80 A5
  *ROY/SHW* OL2 ................................60 A1
  *URM* M41 ..........................................95 H3
Bromley Cl *WGNE/HIN* WN2 ............48 D2
Bromley Crs *AUL* OL6 ..........................75 L6
Bromley Cross Rd
  *EDGW/EG* BL7 .................................22 E5
Bromley Dr *LEIGH* WN7 .....................66 A4
Bromley Rd *SALE* M33 ......................108 F2
Bromley St *ANC* M4 .............................87 L1
  *CHAD* OL9 ........................................74 D2
  *DTN/ASHW* M34 * ...........................101 J1
Bromlow St *OP/CLY* M11 ...................88 F3
Brompton Av *FAIL* M35 .......................74 E4
Brompton Rd *HTNM* SK4 ..................111 K2
  *RUSH/FAL* M14 ...............................98 E2
  *STRET* M32 .......................................96 C1
Brompton Rd *OLDE* OL4 .......................9 M8
Brompton Wy *WILM/AE* SK9 ..........119 L4
Bromsgrove Av *ECC* M30 ...................84 C2
Bromshill Dr *BRO* M7 .........................72 B6
Bromwich St *BOLE* BL2 .........................3 J7
Bronington Cl *WYTH/NTH* M22 ....110 B5
Bronte Av *BURY* BL9 ...........................39 H6
Bronte Cl *BOL* BL1 ...............................36 A3
  *OLD* OL1 ...........................................44 A8
  *WGNS/IIMK* WN3 ............................47 K7
  *WHIT* OL12 .......................................27 K3
Bronte St *HULME* M15 ........................87 K7
Bronville Cl *OLD* OL1 ..........................58 E3
Brook Av *WYTH/NTH* M22 ................110 B7
  *DROY* M43 * ......................................89 J3
  *HALE/TIMP* WA15 ..........................108 B6
  *HTNM* SK4 ......................................100 A7
  *ROY/SHW* OL2 ................................43 L4
  *SWIN* M27 ........................................70 C5
  *UPML* OL3 .........................................61 J3
  *WILM/AE* SK9 .................................130 C1
Brook Bank *BOLE* BL2 * ......................37 G1
Brookbank Cl *MDTN* M24 ...................57 L5
Brook Bottom Rd
  *NM/HAY* SK22 ................................124 B3
Brookbottom Rd *RAD* M26 ................38 C6
Brookburn Rd *CCHDY* M21 ...............97 K5
Brook Cl *HALE/TIMP* WA15 ............108 B6
  *TYLD* M29 .........................................67 K2
  *WHTF* M45 .......................................55 L4
Brookcot Rd *NTHM/RTH* M23 ........109 J3
Brookcroft Av
  *WYTH/NTH* M22 ............................110 A7
Brookcroft Rd
  *WYTH/NTH* M22 ............................110 A7
Brookdale *ATH* M46 .............................51 J4
  *WHIT* OL12 .......................................28 B1
Brookdale Av *DTN/ASHW* M34 ........90 B5
  *MPL/ROM* SK6 ................................114 D8
  *NEWH/MOS* M40 ............................74 A8
Brookdale Cl *BOL* BL1 .........................36 C2
  *MPL/ROM* SK6 ................................113 J1
Brookdale Pk *LHULT* M38 * ..............52 E6
Brookdale Ri *BRAM/HZG* SK7 ........121 H1
Brookdale Rd *BRAM/HZG* SK7 ........110 C7
  *CHD/CHDH* SK8 .............................110 C7
  *WGNE/HIN* WN2 ............................49 J7
Brookdale St *FAIL* M35 .......................74 B5
Brookdean Cl *BOL* BL1 .......................35 M1
Brookdene Rd *BNG/LEV* M19 ...........99 H6
  *BURY* BL9 ..........................................55 L3
Brook Dr *MPL/ROM* SK6 ...................114 C8
  *TYLD* M29 .........................................67 H6
  *WHTF* M45 .......................................55 K4
Brooke Dr *WILM/AE* SK9 ..................119 M8
Brookes St *MDTN* M24 ........................57 L2

Brooke Wy *WILM/AE* SK9 * ...............119 M8
Brook Farm La *PART* M31 .................106 C3
Brookfield *PWCH* M25 .........................55 L8
  *ROY/SHW* OL2 ................................43 K3
Brookfield Av *BOLE* BL2 .....................37 M3
  *CCHDY* M21 .....................................97 M5
  *HALE/TIMP* WA15 ..........................108 C4
  *MPL/ROM* SK6 ................................101 K8
  *POY/DIS* SK12 ................................129 G1
  *ROY/SHW* OL2 ................................59 H1
  *SLFD* M6 ...........................................85 M1
  *STKP* SK1 ...........................................13 M8
  *URM* M41 ..........................................95 K2
Brookfield Cl *STKP* SK1 .......................13 M8
Brookfield Crs *CHD/CHDH* SK8 .......111 G8
Brookfield Dr
  *HALE/TIMP* WA15 ............................108 D5
  *LIT* OL15 ............................................21 K6
  *SWIN* M27 ........................................70 B3
  *WALK* M28 ........................................68 C6
Brookfield Gdns
  *WYTH/NTH* M22 ............................109 M6
Brookfield Gv *AUL* OL6 ........................91 G2
  *CHD/CHDH* SK8 ..............................111 H7
  *CHH* M8 ............................................72 D3
  *ECC* M30 ...........................................69 L8
  *GOL/RIS/CUL* WA3 .........................80 F8
  *WGNNW/ST* WN6 ...........................30 C2
Brooksmouth *TOT/BURYW* BL8 ........4 B5
Brook Green La *GTN* M18 .................100 C1
Brookhead Av *DID/WITH* M20 * .......98 C5
Brookhead Dr *CHD/CHDH* SK8 ......111 K7
Brookhey *HYDE* SK14 ..........................101 L1
Brookhey Av *BOLS/LL* BL3 ................52 C1
Brookhey Rd *ALT* WA14 ...................107 H2
  *PART* M31 * .......................................95 H8
Brookhill Cl *UPML* OL3 .......................45 M7
Brookhill St *NEWH/MOS* M40 ...........88 B1
Brookhouse Av *ECC* M30 ...................84 D3
  *FWTH* BL4 .........................................52 F6
Brook House Cl *BOLE* BL2 ..................37 H1
  *TOT/BURYW* BL8 .............................24 B4
Brookhouse Mill La
  *TOT/BURYW* BL8 .............................24 C4
Brookhouse St *WGN* WN1 .................15 H5
Brookhurst La *LHULT* M38 ................52 B6
Brookhurst Rd *GTN* M18 ....................89 G8
Brookland Av *DTN/ASHW* M34 .......101 G2
  *FWTH* BL4 .........................................52 F5
  *WGNE/HIN* WN2 ............................49 G7
Brookland Gv *BOL* BL1 ........................35 K2
Brookland Rd *WGN* WN1 ...................47 L1
Brooklands *HOR/BR* BL6 .....................33 M1
Brooklands Av *AIMK* WN4 .................79 G2
  *ATH* M46 ...........................................51 G8
  *CHAD* OL9 ...........................................8 A8
  *DID/WITH* M20 ................................98 D6
  *LEIGH* WN7 .......................................81 H1
Brooklands Cl *DTN/ASHW* M34 ........90 A8
  *HTNM* SK4 ......................................100 A7
  *IRL* M44 .............................................94 C2
  *MOSL* OL5 ........................................59 H6
Brooklands Ct *ROCH* OL11 ................27 M6
Brooklands Crs *SALE* M33 ................108 E1
Brooklands Dr *DROY* M43 ..................89 M1
  *GLSP* SK13 ......................................104 E3
  *OLDE* OL4 ..........................................60 E6
  *WGNW/BIL/OR* WN5 ......................46 A7
Brooklands Pde *OLDE* OL4 * ............60 E6
Brooklands Rd *BRAM/HZG* SK7 .....122 A3
  *NTHM/RTH* M23 ...........................108 F4
  *PWCH* M25 .......................................72 B2
  *RAMS* BL0 ........................................24 C2
  *RDSH* SK5 ......................................100 B2
  *SALE* M33 ........................................108 E1
  *SWIN* M27 ........................................70 A6
Brooklands Station Ap
  *SALE* M33 ........................................108 D1
Brooklands St *ROY/SHW* OL2 ...........43 G7
The Brooklands *HEY* OL10 * ..............40 F2
Brookland St *MILN* OL16 * ..................42 E1
Brook La *BURY* BL9 ...............................39 K7
  *HALE/TIMP* WA15 ..........................108 B6
  *MILN* OL16 ........................................42 E1
  *OLDE* OL4 ..........................................60 B6
  *OLDS* OL8 ..........................................59 K8
  *UPML* OL3 .........................................61 J3
  *WGNW/BIL/OR* WN5 ......................46 F3
  *WILM/AE* SK9 .................................130 C1
Brooklawn Dr *DID/WITH* M20 ..........98 D6
  *PWCH* M25 .......................................55 M6
Brookledge La *MCFLDN* SK10 ........129 G6
Brookleigh Rd *DID/WITH* M20 .........99 G6
Brooklet Cl *OLDE* OL4 .........................60 D7
Brooklyn Av *LIT* OL15 .........................21 L5
  *OLDTF/WHR* M16 ............................97 H2
  *URM* M41 ..........................................95 H2
Brooklyn Crs *CHD/CHDH* SK8 ........111 G7
Brooklyn Rd *CHD/CHDH* SK8 ..........111 G7
  *OFTN* SK2 ........................................112 F6
Brooklyn St *BOL* BL1 ...........................36 B3
  *OLD* OL1 ...........................................59 M3
Brook Meadow *GLSP* SK13 .............105 H3
  *WHTN* BL5 .......................................50 D4
Brook Rd *CHD/CHDH* SK8 .................111 G6
  *HTNM* SK4 .......................................99 M7
  *RUSH/FAL* M14 ...............................98 F5
  *URM* M41 ..........................................95 M1
Brooks Av *BRAM/HZG* SK7 ..............121 M1
  *HYDE* SK14 ......................................102 B3
  *RAD* M26 ...........................................38 C6
Brooksbottom Cl *RAMS* BL0 ............18 B1
Brooks Dr *CHD/CHDH* SK8 ...............119 L2
  *FAIL* M35 ...........................................74 B6
  *HALE/TIMP* WA15 ..........................109 G8
  *HALE/TIMP* WA15 ..........................108 F4
  *HALE/TIMP* WA15 ..........................117 M4
Brooks End *ROCH* OL11 ......................27 H5
Brookshaw St *BURY* BL9 ......................5 H1
  *OP/CLY* M11 .....................................88 D3
Brooks Houses *LEIGH* WN7 ..............66 B4
Brookside *GLSP* SK13 .........................104 E4
  *OLDE* OL4 ..........................................60 A6
  *WGNS/IIMK* WN3 * ...........................47 J4

Brookside Av *AIMK* WN4 ....................63 J5
  *DROY* M43 .........................................89 M1
  *FWTH* BL4 .........................................52 F5
  *OFTN* SK2 ........................................113 H6
  *OLDE* OL4 ..........................................60 E6
  *POY/DIS* SK12 ................................129 J1
Brookside Cl *ATH* M46 .........................51 H8
  *BOLE* BL2 ..........................................23 G7
  *CHD/CHDH* SK8 ..............................111 G8
  *GLSP* SK13 ........................................93 J8
  *HYDE* SK14 ......................................102 D1
  *RAMS* BL0 ........................................16 A5
  *WGNW/BIL/OR* WN5 ......................62 B8
Brookside Crs *MDTN* M24 ..................57 M6
  *TOT/BURYW* BL8 .............................24 C4
  *WALK* M28 ........................................69 H1
Brookside Dr *HYDE* SK14 .................102 D1
  *PWCH* M25 .......................................72 A3
Brookside La *MPL/ROM* SK6 ...........123 C5
Brookside Rd *BOLE* BL2 ......................37 G4
  *CHD/CHDH* SK8 .............................110 D6
  *NEWH/MOS* M40 ............................73 K3
  *SALE* M33 ........................................108 D2
  *WGN* WN1 ........................................31 J3
Brook St *AIMK* WN4 .............................78 F2
  *ATH* M46 ...........................................66 F1
  *BOL* BL1 ...............................................2 E4
  *BRAM/HZG* SK7 .............................122 A2
  *BURY* BL9 .............................................5 H1
  *CHAD* OL9 ...........................................8 B3
  *CHD/CHDH* SK8 ..............................111 G6
  *CMANE* M1 ..........................................7 H8
  *FAIL* M35 ...........................................74 A6
  *FWTH* BL4 .........................................53 H3
  *GLSP* SK13 .......................................104 F3
  *GOL/RIS/CUL* WA3 .........................79 K5
  *GOL/RIS/CUL* WA3 .........................80 D3
  *HYDE* SK14 ......................................102 B3
  *OLD* OL1 ..............................................9 M3
  *RAD* M26 ...........................................53 K5
  *RAD* M26 ...........................................54 F1
  *ROY/SHW* OL2 ................................59 G1
  *SALE* M33 ..........................................96 F7
  *SLFD* M6 ...........................................71 L8
  *SWIN* M27 ........................................70 A4
  *WGNE/HIN* WN2 ............................48 D5
  *WHIT* OL12 .......................................21 G6
  *WHTN* BL5 .......................................50 C3
Brook St East *AUL* OL6 .......................90 D2
Brook St West *AUL* OL6 ......................90 D2
Brookthorn Cl *OFTN* SK2 ..................113 J7
Brookthorpe Av *BNG/LEV* M19 ........99 H6
Brookthorpe Rd
  *TOT/BURYW* BL8 .............................38 D1
Brookvale *WGNNW/ST* WN6 ............14 A1
Brookview *WGNE/HIN* WN2 ..............49 G8
Brookwater Cl *TOT/BURYW* BL8 .......24 F5
Brookway *HALE/TIMP* WA15 ...........108 C6
  *LIT* OL15 ............................................21 L8
  *OLDE* OL4 ..........................................60 B7
  *OLDE* OL4 ..........................................61 H6
Brookway *BNG/LEV* M19 .....................99 H8
Brookwood Av *CHH* M8 ......................72 F4
  *SALE* M33 ........................................108 B1
Brookwood Cl
  *DTN/ASHW* M34 ...........................101 K5
Brooky Moor *EDGW/EG* BL7 * ..........17 H6
Broom Av *BNG/LEV* M19 .....................99 H6
  *BRO* M7 ............................................72 B4
  *RDSH* SK5 ......................................100 C6
Broome Gv *FAIL* M35 ..........................74 C6
Broomehouse Av *IRL* M44 .................94 B4
Broome St *CHAD* OL9 * .........................8 E6
Broomfield *SWIN* M27 .........................71 G6
Broomfield Cl *BOLE* BL2 .....................37 M4
  *RDSH* SK5 ......................................100 C6
  *WILM/AE* SK9 * ................................127 J4
Broomfield Crs *MDTN* M24 ................57 M6
  *OFTN* SK2 ........................................112 D8
Broomfield Dr *CHH* M8 .......................72 D8
  *RDSH* SK5 ......................................100 C6
Broomfield La
  *HALE/TIMP* WA15 ...........................117 G2
Broomfield Pl
  *WGNNW/ST* WN6 ...........................31 H3
Broomfield Rd *BOLS/LL* BL3 ..............35 M7
  *HTNM* SK4 .......................................99 M8
Broomfields *DTN/ASHW* M34 ...........90 D7
Broomflat Cl *WGNNW/ST* WN6 ........31 H3
Broomgrove La
  *DTN/ASHW* M34 .............................90 D8
  *SWIN* M27 ........................................71 G6
Broomhall Rd *BKLY* M9 .......................56 D7
  *SWIN* M27 ........................................70 C5
Broomhey Av *WGN* WN1 ....................31 M9
Broomhey Ter *WGN* WN1 ...................15 L5
Broomhill Dr *BRAM/HZG* SK7 ........120 F3
Broomholme *WGNNW/ST* WN6 ........30 A5
Broomhurst Av *OLDS* OL8 ..................59 G8
Broom La *BNG/LEV* M19 .....................99 L4
  *BRO* M7 ............................................72 A4
Broom Rd *HALE/TIMP* WA15 ............117 G1
  *PART* M31 ........................................106 C2
Broomstair Rd *DTN/ASHW* M34 .......90 C6
Broom Wy *WHTN* BL5 ..........................50 D4
Broomwood Rd
  *HALE/TIMP* WA15 ..........................108 F2
Broomwood Wk *HULME* M15 * ..........87 J6
Broseley Av *DID/WITH* M20 ..............111 G1
  *GOL/RIS/CUL* WA3 .........................81 G8
Broseley La *GOL/RIS/CUL* WA3 ......81 G7
Broseley Rd *OLDTF/WHR* M16 ..........97 K2
Brosscroft *GLSP* SK13 ........................93 K6
Brosscroft *GLSP* SK13 ........................93 K6
Brosscroft Village *GLSP* SK13 .........93 K6
Brotherdale Cl *ROY/SHW* OL2 ..........43 K3
Brotherod Hall Rd *WHIT* OL12 ..........27 M2
Brotherton Cl *HULME* M15 ..................6 A7
Brotherton Dr *CSLFD* M3 ......................6 B1
Brotherton Wy *NEWLW* WA12 .........78 D3
Brougham St *WALK* M28 .....................68 F2
Brough St *WGNE/HIN* WN2 ...............65 H1
Broughton Av
  *GOL/RIS/CUL* WA3 .........................80 A3
  *LHULT* M38 .......................................52 D8
Broughton Cl *MDTN* M24 ...................57 G2
Broughton La *BRO* M7 .........................72 A7

Broughton Rd *MCFLDN* SK10 ..........129 G7
  *RDSH* SK5 ......................................100 C8
  *SLFD* M6 ...........................................86 D1
Broughton Rd East *SLFD* M6 .............71 L8
Broughton St *BOL* BL1 .........................36 A2
  *CHH* M8 ............................................72 C7
Broughville Dr *DID/WITH* M20 ........110 F4
Brow Av *MDTN* M24 ............................57 L6
Browfield Av *ORD* M5 ..........................85 M8
Browfield Wy *OLD* OL1 .......................59 H3
Browmere Dr *DID/WITH* M20 ............98 C8
Brownacre St *DID/WITH* M20 ............98 E6
Brown Bank Rd *LIT* OL15 ...................29 J1
Browncross St *CSLFD* M3 .....................6 C4
Brown Edge Rd *OLDE* OL4 .................60 B8
Brownhill La *UPML* OL3 .......................61 L5
Brownhills Cl *TOT/BURYW* BL8 ........24 A4
Brownhills Rd *CCHDY* M21 .................97 L4
Brownhill St *OP/CLY* M11 * ................88 D4
Browning Av *ATH* M46 .........................51 H7
  *DROY* M43 .........................................89 K3
  *WGNS/IIMK* WN3 ............................47 J8
Browning Cl *BOL* BL1 ...........................36 B3
Browning Gv *WGNNW/ST* WN6 ........47 H1
Browning Rd *MDTN* M24 .....................57 L2
  *OLD* OL1 ...........................................59 L3
  *RDSH* SK5 ......................................100 A3
  *SWIN* M27 ........................................70 B4
Browning St *CSLFD* M3 .........................6 B3
  *HULME* M15 .....................................87 G6
  *LEIGH* WN7 .......................................66 A6
Brown La *CHD/CHDH* SK8 ................119 J3
Brownlea Av *DUK* SK16 ........................90 F5
Brownley Court Rd
  *WYTH/NTH* M22 ...........................110 B7
Brownley Rd *WYTH/NTH* M22 .........110 B7
Brown Lodge St *LIT* OL15 ...................29 J1
Brownlow Av *ROY/SHW* OL2 .............59 K1
  *WGNE/HIN* WN2 ............................48 E5
Brownlow Cl *POY/DIS* SK12 .............129 J2
Brownlow Wy *BOL* BL1 ..........................2 C1
Brownmere *WGNNW/ST* WN6 ..........47 J2
Brownrigg Cl *MDTN* M24 ....................56 F3
Brownside Cl *MILN* OL16 ....................28 F1
Brown's La *WILM/AE* SK9 ..................127 J4
Brownslow Wk
  *BRUN/LGST* M13 * ............................7 K9
Browns Rd *BOLE* BL2 ...........................37 G6
Brown St *ALT* WA14 ...........................116 F1
  *BOL* BL1 ...............................................2 F4
  *CHAD* OL9 .........................................58 D5
  *CSLFD* M3 ...........................................6 D4
  *FAIL* M35 ...........................................74 B5
  *HEY* OL10 ..........................................40 F1
  *HOR/BR* BL6 .....................................33 G2
  *LIT* OL15 ............................................21 L7
  *MDTN* M24 .......................................57 K2
  *OLD* OL1 ..............................................9 M4
  *RAD* M26 ...........................................18 C6
  *RAMS* BL0 ........................................86 C3
  *SLFD* M6 ...........................................86 C3
  *STKP* SK1 ...........................................13 H3
  *TYLD* M29 .........................................67 J5
  *WGNE/HIN* WN2 ............................48 D5
  *WGNE/HIN* WN2 ............................65 H3
  *WGNS/IIMK* WN3 ............................14 E5
  *WILM/AE* SK9 .................................130 D3
Brown St North *LEIGH* WN7 ..............66 D7
Brown St South *LEIGH* WN7 .............66 D8
Brownsville Rd *HTNM* SK4 ................99 L7
Brownville Gv *DUK* SK16 ....................91 H5
Brownwood Av *STKP* SK1 .................112 E3
Brownwood Cl *SALE* M33 ..................108 F3
Brows Av *NTHM/RTH* M23 ...............109 K2
Brow St *ROCH* OL11 .............................10 B5
Broxton Av *BOLS/LL* BL3 .....................51 L1
  *WGNW/BIL/OR* WN5 ......................47 H5
Broxton St *NEWH/MOS* M40 ..............88 C1
Broxwood Cl *GTN* M18 * .....................89 G7
Bruce St *ROCH* OL11 ............................27 M8
Brundage Rd *WYTH/NTH* M22 .........118 F2
Brundretts Rd *CCHDY* M21 ................97 L4
Brundrett St *STKP* SK1 ........................13 M7
Brunel Av *ORD* M5 ...............................86 E3
Brunel Cl *STRET* M32 ...........................97 H2
Brunel St *BOL* BL1 ................................36 A1
  *HOR/BR* BL6 .....................................33 M2
Brunet Wk *WGTN/LGST* M12 * .........88 C6
Brunstead Ct *NTHM/RTH* M23 ........109 G6
Brunswick Av *HOR/BR* BL6 ................34 A2
  *DID/WITH* M20 ................................99 H4
  *NEWLW* WA12 .................................78 C8
Brunswick Rd *ALT* WA14 ..................108 A5
  *DID/WITH* M20 ................................98 F6
Brunswick Sq *OLD* OL1 * .......................9 J6
Brunswick St *BRUN/LGST* M13 * .......87 M6
  *BURY* BL9 .............................................4 F3
  *DUK* SK16 ..........................................90 F4
  *HEY* OL10 ..........................................40 F2
  *LEIGH* WN7 .......................................66 D8
  *MILN* OL16 ........................................11 H2
  *MOSL* OL5 .........................................76 C3
  *OLD* OL1 ..............................................9 H6
  *ROY/SHW* OL2 ................................43 L5
  *STRET* M32 .......................................96 F4
Brunton Rd *RDSH* SK5 .......................100 C6
Brunt St *RUSH/FAL* M14 .....................98 F3
Bruntwood Av *CHD/CHDH* SK8 ......119 J3
Bruntwood La *CHD/CHDH* SK8 ......110 F8
Brushes Av *STLY* SK15 ........................92 A1
Brushes Rd *STLY* SK15 ........................92 A1
Brussels Rd *EDGY/DAV* SK3 .............112 A6
Bruton Av *STRET* M32 .........................96 B3
Bryan Rd *CCHDY* M21 ..........................97 L2
Bryan St *OLDE* OL4 ..............................59 M3
Bryant Cl *BRUN/LGST* M13 ................87 M7
Bryantsfield *BOL* BL1 ..........................35 G6
Bryce St *HYDE* SK14 ............................91 G8
Brydges Rd *MPL/ROM* SK6 ...............114 B7
Brydon Av *WGTN/LGST* M12 * ...........7 M8
Brydon Cl *SLFD* M6 ..............................86 D2
Bryham St *WGN* WN1 ..........................15 J4
Bryndale Gv *SALE* M33 ......................108 C3
Brynden Av *DID/WITH* M20 ...............98 F7
Bryn Dr *RDSH* SK5 .............................100 C7
Brynford Av *BKLY* M9 ..........................56 D7
Bryn Gates La
  *WGNE/HIN* WN2 ............................63 M4
Bryngs Dr *BOLE* BL2 ............................23 J8
Brynhall Cl *RAD* M26 ...........................38 B7
Brynheys Cl *LHULT* M38 ......................52 D7
Bryn La *WGNE/HIN* WN2 ...................47 H9
Brynorme Rd *CHH* M8 ..........................72 D2
Bryn Rd *AIMK* WN4 ..............................63 M8
Bryn Rd South *AIMK* WN4 .................63 M8
  *AIMK* WN4 .......................................78 E1
  *WGNS/IIMK* WN3 ............................15 K8
Brynton Rd *BRUN/LGST* M13 ...........99 H2
Bryn Wk *BOL* BL1 * ................................2 E2
Bryone Dr *OFTN* SK2 .........................112 E7

Bryony Cl WGNW/BIL/OR WN5....46 A7
  WYTH/NTH M22....118 E3
Buchanan Dr WGNE/HIN WN2....65 L1
Buchanan Rd
  WGNW/BIL/OR WN5....47 H5
Buchanan St LEIGH WN7....66 B7
  RAMS BL0....18 E6
  SWIN M27....70 C3
Buchan St OP/CLY M11....88 E2
Buckden Rd HTNM SK4....100 A5
Buckfast Av OLDS....59 M8
  RNFD/HAY WA11....78 C5
Buckfast Cl CCHDY M21....97 J3
  CHD/CHDH SK8....120 D5
  HALE/TIMP WA15....117 K2
  POY/DIS SK12....121 M7
Buckfast St MDTN M24....57 J4
  SALE M33....96 A6
Buckfield Av ORD M5....86 E5
Buckhurst Rd BNG/LEV M19....99 K3
  BURY BL9....25 L1
Buckingham Av HOR/BR BL6....34 A3
  SLFD M6....86 A2
  WHTF M45....55 K5
Buckingham Cl
  WGNW/BIL/OR WN5....47 H7
Buckingham Dr DUK SK16....91 J8
  TOT/BURYW BL8....38 E4
Buckingham Park Cl
  ROY/SHW OL2....43 L4
Buckingham Rd ALT WA14....108 C3
  CCHDY M21....97 L3
  CHD/CHDH SK8....120 B2
  DROY M43....89 M7
  HTNM SK4....99 M7
  POY/DIS SK12....129 H1
  PWCH M25 *....71 J2
  STLY SK15....91 K1
  STRET M32....86 C3
  SWIN M27....70 D2
  WILM/AE SK9....126 D6
Buckingham Rd West
  HTNM SK4....99 K8
Buckingham St MILN OL16....11 H2
  OFTN SK2....112 C6
  ORD M5....86 C3
Buckingham Wy
  HALE/TIMP WA15....108 D6
Buckland Av BKLY M9....72 D1
Buckland Dr
  WGNW/BIL/OR WN5....46 E3
Buckland Gv HYDE SK14....102 A4
Buckland Rd SLFD M6....71 G8
Buck La SALE M33....96 B6
Buckley Av OP/CLY M11....88 F8
Buckley Brook St WHIT OL12....28 E2
Buckley Cha MILN OL16....29 H7
Buckley Cl HYDE SK14....102 B5
Buckley Dr MPL/ROM SK6....113 K3
  UPML OL3....44 F3
Buckley Farm La WHIT OL12....28 C2
Buckley Flds WHIT OL12....28 D2
Buckley Hill La MILN OL16....29 H7
Buckley La FWTH BL4....52 F5
  WHIT OL12....28 E1
  WHTF M45....55 H7
Buckley Rd GTN M18....88 E8
  WHIT OL12....28 E1
Buckley Sq FWTH BL4....52 F6
Buckley St BURY BL9....5 G2
  CHAD OL9....58 D5
  DROY M43....89 K4
  DTN/ASHW M34....90 A5
  HEY OL10....41 G1
  MILN OL16....11 G2
  OLDE OL4....60 B7
  OP/CLY M11....89 H5
  RDSH SK5....100 B2
  ROY/SHW OL2....43 M5
  STLY SK15....91 J4
  UPML OL3....61 L4
  WGNW/ST WN6....47 L2
Buckley St West
  WGNW/ST WN6....47 K2
Buckley Vw WHIT OL12....28 E1
Bucklow Av PART M31....94 D8
  RUSH/FAL M14....98 E3
Bucklow Cl HYDE SK14....103 J3
  OLDE OL4....60 B1
Bucklow Dr WYTH/NTH M22....110 B4
Bucklow Vw ALT WA14....116 C1
Buckstones Rd OLD OL1....44 B6
  ROY/SHW OL2....43 M3
Buck St LEIGH WN7....66 C8
Buckthorn Cl CCHDY M21....98 A6
  HALE/TIMP WA15....109 H7
  WHTN BL5....50 C2
Buckthorn La ECC M30....84 C3
Buckton Cl UPML OL3....45 M7
Buckton Dr STLY SK15....77 H7
Buckton Vale Ms STLY SK15....77 J5
Buckton Vale Rd STLY SK15....77 H4
Buckwood Cl BRAM/HZG SK7....122 C1
Buddleia Gv BRO M7 *....72 A6
Bude Av RDSH SK5....100 E7
  TYLD M29....67 M4
  URM M41....95 L4
Bude Cl BRAM/HZG SK7....121 H5
Budworth Av DID/WITH M20....98 E3
Budworth Rd SALE M33....109 H1
Buerden Av WGNS/IIMK WN3....48 E8
Buersil Av MILN OL16....28 E8
Buersil St MILN OL16....42 E1
Buerton Av BKLY M9....56 D7
Bugle St CMANE M1 *....6 D7
Buile Dr BKLY M9....57 J8
Buile Hill Av LHULT M38....52 C1
Buile Hill Dr ORD M5....86 A1
Buile Hill Gv LHULT M38....52 C1
Buile St BRO M7....72 B5
Bulford Av WYTH/NTH M22....118 D2
Bulkeley Rd CHD/CHDH SK8....111 H6
  POY/DIS SK12....129 J1
  WILM/AE SK9....127 G1
Bulkeley St EDGY/DAV SK3....12 C6
Bullcote Gn ROY/SHW OL2....43 L8
Bullcote La ROY/SHW OL2....43 L8
Bullcroft Dr TYLD M29....67 M6
Buller Ms TOT/BURYW BL8....38 E3
Buller Rd BRUN/LGST M13....93 J2
Buller St BOLS/LL BL3....52 F2
  DROY M43....89 K5
  TOT/BURYW BL8....38 F3
Bullfinch Dr BURY BL9....25 L1
Bull Hill Crs RAD M26....54 E4
Bullock St STKP SK1....13 K9
Bullough St ATH M46....66 F2
Bullows Rd LHULT M38....52 A4
Bulteel St BOLS/LL BL3....51 M2
  ECC M30....84 E1
  WALK M28....68 B6
  WGNW/BIL/OR WN5....47 G6

Bulwer St MILN OL16....11 H2
The Bungalows
  BRAM/HZG SK7 *....113 J8
  NM/HAY SK22....124 F3
Bunkers HI MPL/ROM SK6....113 L3
  WHTF M45....71 H1
Bunkers Hill Rd HYDE SK14....103 H3
Bunkershill Rd
  MPL/ROM SK6....113 L4
Bunsen St CMANE M1 *....7 J4
Bunting Cl COL/RIS/CUL WA3....80 B4
Bunting Ms WALK M28....68 E4
Bunyan Cl OLD OL1....44 A8
Bunyan St WHIT OL12....10 F1
Bunyard St CHH M8....72 E6
Burbage Rd NEWH/MOS M40....118 C2
Burbridge Cl OP/CLY M11....88 B4
Burchall Fld MILN OL16....11 K4
Burdale Dr SLFD M6....70 F8
Burder St SLFD M6....70 F2
Burdett Av WHIT OL12....27 J3
Burdett Wy WGTN/LGST M12....88 B7
Burdith Av RUSH/FAL M14....98 D2
Burdon Av WYTH/NTH M22....110 B8
Burford Av BRAM/HZG SK7....120 E7
  OLDTF/WHR M16....98 A2
  URM M41....96 B1
Burford Crs WILM/AE SK9....126 C6
Burford Dr BOLS/LL BL3....2 C1
  OLDTF/WHR M16....98 A2
  SWIN M27....70 B2
Burford Gv SALE M33....108 B3
Burford Rd OLDTF/WHR M16....98 A2
  RUSH/FAL M14....75 M7
Burgess Av AUL OL6....76 A5
Burgess Dr FAIL M35....74 C5
Burgess St WGNS/IIMK WN3....15 K9
Burghley Av OLDS....60 A6
Burghley Cl RAD M26....37 L7
  STLY SK15....91 K2
Burghley Dr RAD M26....37 L7
Burghley Wy WGNS/IIMK WN3....48 C3
Burgin Wk NEWH/MOS M40....72 F8
Burgundy Dr TOT/BURYW BL8....24 C5
Burke St BOL BL1....36 A2
Burkitt St HYDE SK14....102 B2
Burland Cl BRO M7....72 A7
Burland St WGNW/BIL/OR WN5....47 J5
Burleigh Cl BRAM/HZG SK7....121 J3
Burleigh Ms CCHDY M21....97 L6
Burleigh Rd STRET M32....86 B8
Burleigh St HULME M15....87 L7
Burlescombe Cl ALT WA14....107 L6
Burley Av GOL/RIS/CUL WA3....80 A3
Burley Crs WGNS/IIMK WN3....62 F2
Burley St HTNM SK4 *....12 C2
Burlington Av OLDS....59 H6
Burlington Cl HTNM SK4....111 H2
Burlington Dr EDGY/DAV SK3....112 C8
Burlington Gdns
  EDGY/DAV SK3....112 C8
Burlington Ms EDGY/DAV SK3....112 C8
Burlington Rd ALT WA14....108 A7
  DID/WITH M20....98 F5
  ECC M30....70 B8
Burlington St AULW OL7....90 C2
  BRUN/LGST M13....87 L7
  ROCH OL11....28 D8
  WGNE/HIN WN2....49 H7
Burlton Gv WGNE/HIN WN2....48 C3
Burman St OP/CLY M11....89 J5
Burnaby St BOLS/LL BL3....2 A1
  OLDS OL8....8 D9
Burnage Av BNG/LEV M19....99 J4
Burnage Hall Rd BNG/LEV M19....99 H5
Burnage La BNG/LEV M19....111 G2
Burnage Range BNG/LEV M19....99 K3
Burnaston Gv
  WGNW/BIL/OR WN5....47 G7
Burn Bank UPML OL3....61 H7
Burnbray Av BNG/LEV M19....99 H6
Burndale Dr BURY BL9....25 L5
Burnden Rd BOLS/LL BL3....3 K9
Burnden Wy HOR/BR BL6....33 M4
Burnedge Cl WHIT OL12....20 B1
Burnedge Fold Rd OLDE OL4....61 G6
Burnedge La OLDE OL4....60 F6
Burnell Cl NEWH/MOS M40....7 M1
Burnet Cl MILN OL16....28 F8
  TYLD M29....67 L5
Burnett Av ORD M5....86 E4
Burnett Cl NEWH/MOS M40....73 G7
Burnfell GOL/RIS/CUL WA3....80 B5
Burnfield Rd GTN M18....100 A1
Burnham Av BOL BL1....35 K3
  RDSH SK5....100 C3
Burnham Cl CHD/CHDH SK8....120 B2
  GOL/RIS/CUL WA3....81 H8
Burnham Dr BNG/LEV M19....99 J5
  URM M41....95 M1
Burnham Gv WGNE/HIN WN2....48 C2
Burnham Rd DTN/ASHW M34....100 D1
Burnhill Ct WGNNW/ST WN6....31 H4
Burnley La CHAD OL9....8 C1
Burnley Rd BURY BL9....25 H4
Burnley St CHAD OL9....8 A3
  FAIL M35....74 D5
Burnmoor Rd BOLE BL2....37 J4
Burnsall Av GOL/RIS/CUL WA3....80 C4
  WHTF M45....55 G4
Burnsall Gv ROY/SHW OL2....43 G8
Burns Av ATH M46....51 G1
  BURY BL9....39 J6
  CHD/CHDH SK8....111 J6
  LEIGH WN7....65 M4
  SWIN M27....70 A3
Burns Cl AIMK WN4....63 J2
  OLD OL1....44 B7
  OP/CLY M11....88 C3
  WCNS/IIMK WN3....47 K8
  WGNW/BIL/OR WN5....62 A3
Burns Crs OFTN SK2....113 H5
Burns Fold DUK SK16....91 K5
Burns Gdns PWCH M25 *....71 J1
Burnside GLSP SK13....93 J8
  HALE/TIMP WA15....117 M5
  RAMS BL0....19 G2
  ROY/SHW OL2....44 A4
  STLY SK15....92 A5
Burnside Av HTNM SK4....100 B6
  SLFD M6....70 F2
Burnside Cl HEY OL10....41 G3
  MPL/ROM SK6....113 J1
  RAD M26....38 C6
  STLY SK15....92 A5
  TYLD M29....67 L5
  WILM/AE SK9....127 G1
Burnside Crs MDTN M24....57 H1
Burnside Dr BNG/LEV M19....99 H5
Burnside Rd BOL BL1....35 L2
  CHD/CHDH SK8....110 D7
  MILN OL16....11 M7

Burns Rd DTN/ASHW M34....101 K5
  LHULT M38....52 E7
  WGNE/HIN WN2....64 D1
Burns St BOLS/LL BL3....2 E7
  HEY OL10....41 G3
Burnthorp Av BKLY M9....72 E1
Burnthorpe Cl ROCH OL11....27 H6
Burnvale WGNS/IIMK WN3....63 G2
Burran Rd WYTH/NTH M22....118 F4
Burrington Dr LEIGH WN7....65 J6
Burrows Av CCHDY M21....97 L6
Burrs Cl TOT/BURYW BL8....24 F6
Burrswood Av BURY BL9....25 H6
Burrswood Dr BURY BL9....25 H6
Bursar Cl NEWLW WA12....79 G8
Burslem Av DID/WITH M20....98 D4
Burstead St GTN M18....89 H6
Burstock St ANC M4....87 L1
Burston St GTN M18....88 F6
Burton Av DID/WITH M20....98 E6
  HALE/TIMP WA15....108 D3
  TOT/BURYW BL8....24 C8
Burton Dr POY/DIS SK12....121 M8
Burton Gv WALK M28....69 M4
Burton Rd DID/WITH M20....98 D8
  OLDE OL4....60 B8
Burton St HTNM SK4....112 B1
  MDTN M24....57 J4
  OLDE OL4....60 B6
Burton Wk CSLFD M3....6 B2
  WALK M28....100 B8
Burtonwood Ct MDTN M24....57 J3
Burtree St WGTN/LGST M12 *....88 D6
Burwell Cl BOLS/LL BL3....36 A8
  GLSP SK13....104 D4
  LEIGH WN7....66 D8
  WHIT OL12....28 A1
Burwell Gv NTHM/RTH M23....109 J5
Bury & Bolton Rd RAD M26....38 A5
Bury & Rochdale Old Rd
  HEY OL10....26 F7
Bury Av OLDTF/WHR M16....97 M2
Bury New Rd BOL BL1....3 G3
  BOLE BL2....37 L5
  BRO M7....72 B3
  BURY BL9....40 B3
  PWCH M25....55 K7
  RAMS BL0....19 G6
  WGNE/HIN WN2....49 G7
  WHTF M45....55 J3
Bury Old Rd BOLE BL2....37 J4
  BRO M7....72 B3
  BURY BL9....19 J8
  BURY BL9....40 B3
  RAMS BL0....19 J3
  WHTF M45....55 K6
Bury Pl OP/CLY M11....88 F7
Bury Rd BOLE BL2....3 L4
  EDGW/EG BL7....17 H6
  EDGW/EG BL7....24 E8
  RAD M26....38 E8
  RAMS BL0....19 J3
  ROCH OL11....27 J6
  TOT/BURYW BL8....24 E8
Bury St CSLFD M3....6 D2
  HEY OL10....40 C2
  MOSL OL5....76 F4
  RAD M26....38 F8
  WHTF M45....55 J4

Butts St LEIGH WN7....81 K1
Buxted Rd OLD OL1....59 L3
Buxton Av AUL OL6....76 C6
  DID/WITH M20....98 C6
Buxton Crs MILN OL16....28 E8
  SALE M33....109 G3
Buxton La DROY M43....89 H4
  MPL/ROM SK6....114 D7
Buxton Ms GLSP SK13....104 B3
Buxton Rd CHD/CHDH SK8....120 B8
  OFTN SK2....112 F8
  POY/DIS SK12....124 C6
  STRET M32....96 D1
Buxton St BRAM/HZG SK7....121 M1
  CHD/CHDH SK8....110 D7
  CMANE M1....7 J7
  HEY OL10....41 G3
  TOT/BURYW BL8....24 C8
  WHIT OL12....20 B1
Buxton Ter HYDE SK14....93 C6
Bye Rd RAMS BL0....19 H5
Byfield Rd WYTH/NTH M22....109 M8
Byfleet Cl WGNS/IIMK WN3....62 F3
Byland Av CHD/CHDH SK8....120 D6
  OLDE OL4....60 A8
Byland Cl BOL BL1....36 B2
Bylands Cl POY/DIS SK12 *....121 M8
Bylands Fold DUK SK16....91 G6
Byley Ri WGNNW/ST WN6....31 H4
Byng St FWTH BL4....53 G4
  HEY OL10....41 H4
Byrcland Cl WGTN/LGST M12....88 D4
Byre Cl SALE M33....109 K1
Byrness Cl ATH M46....51 H1
Byrom Av BNG/LEV M19....99 H3
Byrom La COL/RIS/CUL WA3....80 C2
Byrom St ALT WA14....116 F1
  CSLFD M3....6 D6
  OLDTF/WHR M16....87 G8
  ORD M5....86 D4
Byron Av BNG/LEV M19....99 G4
  PWCH M25....71 J7
  RAD M26....38 A8
  SWIN M27....70 B4
  WGNE/HIN WN2....49 G7
  WHTF M45....55 J3
Byron Cl WGNE/HIN WN2....64 E4
Byron Dr CHD/CHDH SK8....111 J6
Byron Gv LEIGH WN7....66 B5
  RDSH SK5....100 B3
Byron Rd DTN/ASHW M34....101 J4
  MDTN M24....57 L2
  STRET M32....97 H1
  TOT/BURYW BL8....24 C2
Byron's Dr HALE/TIMP WA15....108 D6
Byron St ECC M30....85 G3
  LEIGH WN7....66 C6
  OLDS OL8....74 E2
  ROY/SHW OL2....43 H8
Byron Wk FWTH BL4....52 E6
Byrth Rd OLDS OL8....75 J4

## C

Cabin La OLDE OL4....60 D1
Cablestead Wk OP/CLY M11....88 C4
Cable St ANC M4....7 H2
  BOL BL1....2 F2
  CSLFD M3....6 D2
Cabot Pl RDSH SK5....100 C8
Cabot St BRUN/LGST M13 *....87 L6
Caddington Rd CCHDY M21....97 M4
Cadishead Wy IRL M44....94 D7
Cadman Gv WGNE/HIN WN2....49 G8
Cadman's Yd
  WGNW/BIL/OR WN5....47 G7
Cadnam Dr WYTH/NTH M22....119 H1
Cadogan Dr WGNS/IIMK WN3....63 G2
Cadogan Pl BRO M7 *....72 B3
Cadogan St RUSH/FAL M14....87 K8
Cadum Wk BRUN/LGST M13....87 M6
Caen Av NEWH/MOS M40....73 M1
Caernarvon Cl TOT/BURYW BL8....24 C3
Caernarvon Rd BRAM/HZG SK7....121 J3
Caernarvon Rd WGNE/HIN WN2....65 K1
Caesar St ROCH OL11....42 D7
Cairn Brae NEWLW WA12....78 F8
Cairn Dr ROCH OL11....27 H7
  SLFD M6....71 M8
Cairngorm Dr BOLS/LL BL3....35 K5
Cairns Pl AUL OL6....76 A7
Cairn Wk OP/CLY M11 *....88 C3
Cairnwell Rd CHAD OL9....58 D4
Caister Av WHTF M45....55 K5
Caister Cl OLDTF/WHR M16....98 B4
Caistor St STKP SK1....112 E1
Caistor Wk OLD OL1....9 J4
Caithness Cl NTHM/RTH M23....109 K8
Caithness Dr BOLS/LL BL3....35 H7
Caithness Rd HEY OL10....27 H7
Cakebread St WGTN/LGST M12 *....7 M8
Calbourne Crs WGTN/LGST M12....99 L1
Calcutta Rd EDGY/DAV SK3....12 D9
Caldbeck Av BOL BL1....35 J3
  SALE M33....97 H7
Caldbeck Cl AIMK WN4....63 J2
Caldbeck Dr FWTH BL4....52 B5
  MDTN M24....57 H3
Caldecott Rd BKLY M9....56 D7
Calder Av IRL M44....94 D8
  LIT OL15....21 L5
  WGNE/HIN WN2....65 M1
  WYTH/NTH M22....110 A4
Calderbank St
  WGNW/BIL/OR WN5....47 H7
Calderbeck Wy
  WYTH/NTH M22....110 B8
Calderbrook Dr
  CHD/CHDH SK8....111 K8
Calderbrook Rd LIT OL15....21 M4
Calderbrook Wy OLDE OL4....59 L7
Calderburn Cl HOR/BR BL6....34 A3
Calder Cl BURY BL9....25 K4
  POY/DIS SK12....129 K4
  RDSH SK5....100 D3
Calder Ct URM M41....84 B8
Calder Crs WHTF M45....55 L2
Calder Dr FWTH BL4....52 A6
  SWIN M27....70 B3
  WALK M28....68 D2
  WGNE/HIN WN2....64 D2
Calder Gv ROY/SHW OL2....43 K4
Calder Pl WGNW/BIL/OR WN5....46 F5
Calder Rd BOLS/LL BL3....52 B1

Caldershaw La WHIT OL12....27 K2
Caldershaw Rd WHIT OL12....27 K3
Calder St MILN OL16....28 E2
  ORD M5....6 A7
Caldervale Av CCHDY M21....97 M3
Calderwood Cl
  TOT/BURYW BL8....24 C5
Caldew Cl NTHM/RTH M23....109 J8
Caldey Rd NTHM/RTH M23....109 G8
Caldford Cl WGNE/HIN WN2....32 F6
Caldon Cl ECC M30....85 G4
Caldwell Av TYLD M29....67 L8
Caldwell Cl RDSH SK5....100 C3
  WHTN BL5....50 C7
Caldy Dr RAMS BL0....24 D1
Caldy Rd SLFD M6....71 G8
  WILM/AE SK9....127 H1
Caleb Cl TYLD M29....67 M6
Caledon Av NEWH/MOS M40....73 K4
Caledonian Dr ECC M30....85 H4
Caledonia St BOLS/LL BL3....35 M8
  RAD M26....38 F8
Caledonia Wy STRET M32....85 K7
Cale Gn OFTN SK2....112 C6
Cale La WGNE/HIN WN2....48 E2
Cale Rd NM/HAY SK22....124 F4
Cale St BRO M7....35 J2
  CMANE M1....7 J9
Caley St CMANE M1....35 J2
Calf Hey LIT OL15....21 K6
Calf Hey Cl RAD M26....54 B1
Calf Hey North ROCH OL11....28 D8
Calf Hey Rd ROY/SHW OL2....44 A4
Calf Hey South ROCH OL11....28 D8
Calf La MOSL OL5....61 L5
Calgarth Dr MDTN M24....57 J1
Calgary St GTN M18....88 F7
Calico Cl CSLFD M3....6 A1
Calico Crs STLY SK15....77 K6
Calico La CHF/WBR SK23....124 F8
Calico Wood Av
  WGNNW/ST WN6....30 C6
Callaghan Wk HEY OL10....40 F3
Calland Av HYDE SK14....102 F2
Callander Ct
  WGNW/BIL/OR WN5....47 H5
Callender St RAMS BL0....18 E6
Calliards Rd MILN OL16....21 J8
Callingdon Rd CCHDY M21....98 A7
Callington Cl HYDE SK14....103 H2
Callington Dr HYDE SK14....103 H2
Callis Rd BOLS/LL BL3....35 M6
Callum Wk BRUN/LGST M13 *....87 M6
Calluna Ms DID/WITH M20....98 D8
Calow Dr LEIGH WN7....81 M1
Caltha St RAMS BL0....18 E6
Calthorpe Av BKLY M9....72 F5
Calton Av BRO M7....71 K5
Calton Cl WGNS/IIMK WN3....47 J8
Calve Croft Rd
  WYTH/NTH M22....119 H3
Calveley Wk WGNNW/ST WN6....31 H4
Calver Av ECC M30....84 F4
Calver Cl URM M41....95 G1
Calverhall Wy AIMK WN4....78 D1
Calver Hey Cl WHTN BL5....50 F2
Calverleigh Cl BOLS/LL BL3....51 K2
Calverley Av BNG/LEV M19....99 J5
Calverley Cl WILM/AE SK9....127 C4
Calverley Wy WHIT OL12....20 C8
Calverly Rd CHD/CHDH SK8....111 K7
Calver Ms GLSP SK13....104 C2
Calverton Dr NEWH/MOS M40....73 M5
Calvert Rd BOLS/LL BL3....52 C1
Calvert St ORD M5....86 A2
Calver Wk NEWH/MOS M40 *....7 M1
Calvine Wk NEWH/MOS M40 *....87 M1
Calvin St BOL BL1....2 F1
Cambeck Cl WHTF M45....55 L3
Cambell Rd ECC M30....84 E2
Camberley Cl BRAM/HZG SK7....121 J8
Camberley Dr ROCH OL11....27 J6
Cambert La GTN M18....88 F7
Camberwell Crs
  WGNE/HIN WN2....48 C2
Camberwell Dr AULW OL7....75 K5
Camberwell St CHH M8....72 D8
  OLDS OL8....59 H8
Camberwell Wy ROY/SHW OL2....42 F8
Camborne Rd HYDE SK14....103 H1
Cambourne Dr BOLS/LL BL3....35 K7
Cambo Wk HTNM SK4....111 G1
Cambrai Crs ECC M30....69 K8
Cambrian Dr MILN OL16....21 K6
Cambrian Rd EDGY/DAV SK3....12 F9
Cambrian St NEWH/MOS M40....88 B2
Cambria Sq BOLS/LL BL3....35 M7
Cambria St BOLS/LL BL3....35 M7
  OLDE OL4....59 M5
Cambridge Av OLDTF/WHR M16....97 M2
  ROCH OL11....27 K6
  WILM/AE SK9....126 C6
  SALE M33....108 C3
Cambridge Dr BOLS/LL BL3....37 L8
  DTN/ASHW M34....100 C1
  MPL/ROM SK6....101 M7
Cambridge Gv ECC M30....85 J2
  WHTF M45....55 K3
Cambridge Rd BKLY M9....73 G3
  CHD/CHDH SK8....110 E6
  DROY M43....89 J1
  FAIL M35....74 C2
  HALE/TIMP WA15....117 G2
  HOR/BR BL6....34 C4
  HTNM SK4....99 M7
  URM M41....95 L3
Cambridge St ATH M46....66 F2
  AULW OL7....90 C3
  BRO M7....72 B8
  CHAD OL9....8 B9
  CMANE M1....6 F8
  DUK SK16....91 J2
  OFTN SK2....112 D6
  STLY SK15....91 K2
  WGN WN1....15 J5
Camdale Wk CHH M8 *....72 D8
Camden Av NEWH/MOS M40....73 M8
Camden Cl BOLE BL2....37 J2
Camden St MOSL OL5....77 G3
Camelford Cl HULME M15....87 K6
Camellia Rd BOL BL1....35 L5
Camelot Cl NEWLW WA12....78 C4

Cameron Ct ROY/SHW OL2 43 G6
Cameron Pl
WGNW/BIL/OR WN5 47 H4
Cameron St BOL BL1 22 A7
CMANE M1 * 6 E7
LEIGH WN7 66 A5
TOT/BURYW BL8 4 A4
Camm St WGNE/HIN WN2 64 D4
Campania St ROY/SHW OL2 59 H2
Campbell Cl TOT/BURYW BL8 24 B8
Campbell Ct FWTH BL4 52 F2
Campbell Rd BOLS/LL BL3 51 K2
BRUN/LGST M13 99 J2
SALE M33 108 D1
SWIN M27 70 B6
Campbell St FWTH BL4 52 E3
RDSH SK5 100 C3
WGNW/BIL/OR WN5 47 G7
WHIT OL12 * 28 B2
Campbell Wy WALK M28 68 F1
Campden Wy WILM/AE SK9 119 M8
Campion Gv AIMK WN4 63 J8
Campion Wy WHIT OL12 27 M1
Camp Rd AIMK WN4 78 B1
Camp St AUL OL6 90 E1
BRO M7 71 M8
CSLFD M3 6 D6
TOT/BURYW BL8 38 F1
Camrose Gdns BOL BL1 36 B3
Camrose Wk BRUN/LGST M13 * 88 A7
Cams Acre Cl RAD M26 54 B1
Cams La RAD M26 54 B2
Canaan GOL/RIS/CUL WA3 80 F4
Canada St BOL BL1 35 M2
HOR/BR BL6 33 L1
NEWH/MOS M40 73 H8
OFTN SK2 112 D6
Canal Bank ECC M30 84 F1
Canal Bridge La DROY M43 89 G3
Canal Cottages Yd ANC M4 * 7 M5
Canal Rd ALT WA14 108 B5
Canal Side ECC M30 84 F1
Canal St CHAD OL9 74 E1
CMANE M1 7 H6
DROY M43 89 K4
HEY OL10 41 H4
HYDE SK14 101 M1
LIT OL15 21 M7
MPL/ROM SK6 114 D6
ORD M5 * 86 F3
ROCH OL11 11 H9
STKP SK1 13 K6
STLY SK15 * 91 K3
WGNE/HIN WN2 15 M7
WGNNW/ST WN6 47 J3
Canal Ter WGN WN1 15 L5
Canary Wy SWIN M27 71 H5
Canberra Rd BRAM/HZG SK7 121 H7
WGNW/BIL/OR WN5 46 F3
Canberra St OP/CLY M11 88 F2
Canberra Wy ROCH OL11 42 D1
Candahar St BOLS/LL BL3 52 D1
Candleford Pl OFTN SK2 113 H8
Candleford Rd DID/WITH M20 * 98 E6
Candlestick Ct BURY BL9 26 A8
Candy La MCFLDN SK10 129 G4
Canisp Cl CHAD OL9 58 D4
Canley Cl STKP SK1 13 K7
Canmore Cl BOLS/LL BL3 51 K1
Cannel Fold WALK M28 68 E5
Canning Cl WGNE/HIN WN2 48 F8
Canning Dr BOL BL1 36 B2
Canning St BOL BL1 * 36 B2
BURY BL9 4 F1
HTNM SK4 13 H2
Cannock Dr HTNM SK4 111 K2
Cannon Ct CSLFD M3 6 F3
Cannon Gv BOLS/LL BL3 2 A8
Cannon St ATH M46 67 G1
BOLS/LL BL3 2 B8
CHAD OL9 9 G5
CSLFD M3 6 A2
ECC M30 85 H3
HYDE SK14 92 F7
RAD M26 38 C7
RAMS BL0 18 D8
Cannon St North BOLS/LL BL3 * 2 B7
Cann St TOT/BURYW BL8 24 A5
Canon Cl WGNNW/ST WN6 31 J2
Canon Dr ALT WA14 116 D3
Canon Flynn Ct MILN OL16 11 M4
Canon Green Dr CSLFD M3 6 C2
Canons Cl BOL BL1 35 L2
Canons Gv NEWH/MOS M40 73 H7
Canonsleigh Cl CHH M8 72 B7
Canon St BURY BL9 5 H1
MILN OL16 28 E2
Canonsway SWIN M27 70 B5
Canon Tighe Ct CHAD OL9 * 58 D5
Canon Wilson Cl
RNFD/HAY WA11 78 A6
Cansfield Ct FWTH BL4 53 K6
Cansfield Gv AIMK WN4 63 K8
Canterbury Av
GOL/RIS/CUL WA3 80 A3
Canterbury Cl ATH M46 51 H8
DUK SK16 91 G6
ROCH OL11 27 K5
Canterbury Crs MDTN M24 58 A2
Canterbury Dr PWCH M25 71 M2
TOT/BURYW BL8 25 G8
Canterbury Gdns ORD M5 85 K2
Canterbury Gv BOLS/LL BL3 52 A1
Canterbury Pk DID/WITH M20 110 C1
Canterbury Rd
HALE/TIMP WA15 117 L1
STKP SK1 112 E3
URM M41 95 M1
Canterbury St AUL OL6 75 M8
Canterfield Cl DROY M43 90 A2
Cantrell St OP/CLY M11 88 E3
Canute Rd STRET M32 97 H1
Canute St BOLE BL2 36 F3
ORD M5 * 86 E2
RAD M26 54 B1
Cape Gdns ROY/SHW OL2 43 L6
Capella Wk BRO M7 71 M8
Capenhurst Cl
NTHM/RTH M23 109 J8
POY/DIS SK12 122 B8
Capesthorne Cl
BRAM/HZG SK7 122 B4
Capesthorne Dr ROY/SHW OL2 43 J5
Capesthorne Rd
BRAM/HZG SK7 122 B4
DUK SK16 91 G6
HALE/TIMP WA15 109 G6
MPL/ROM SK6 123 G5
WILM/AE SK9 126 F7
Cape St DID/WITH M20 98 F5
Capital Rd OP/CLY M11 89 J5
Capitol Cl BOL BL1 35 K1
Cappadocia Wy WHTN BL5 50 A5
Capps St WGNE/HIN WN2 64 E1
Capricorn Rd BKLY M9 73 L1
Capricorn Wy SLFD M6 * 71 M8
Capstan St BKLY M9 73 H4
Captain Clarke Rd HYDE SK14 90 D8
Captain Fold HEY OL10 * 41 H2
Captain Fold Rd LHULT M38 52 C7
Captain Lees Gdns WHTN BL5 50 D4
Captain Lees Rd WHTN BL5 50 D4
Captain's Clough Rd BOL BL1 35 L2
Captain's La AIMK WN4 78 F1
Capton Cl BRAM/HZG SK7 121 J2
Carawood Cl
WGNNW/ST WN6 30 A5
Car Bank Av ATH M46 51 G8
Car Bank Sq ATH M46 51 G8
Car Bank St ATH M46 50 E8
Carberry Rd GTN M18 89 H7
Carden Av SWIN M27 70 A5
URM M41 95 H2
Carder Cl SWIN M27 70 C5
Carders Cl LEIGH WN7 66 B8
Cardew Av WYTH/NTH M22 110 B8
Cardiff Cl OLDS OL8 74 E3
Cardiff St BRO M7 72 B5
Cardigan Dr BURY BL9 39 H5
Cardigan Rd OLDS OL8 74 E2
Cardigan St ROY/SHW OL2 43 H8
SLFD M6 * 86 B3
WHIT OL12 28 B1
Cardinal Ms MDTN M24 57 G2
Cardinal St CHH M8 72 E6
OLD OL1 9 L5
Carding Gv CSLFD M3 6 C1
Cardroom Rd ANC M4 7 L4
Cardus St BNG/LEV M19 99 K3
Cardwell Gdns BOL BL1 * 36 B2
Cardwell Rd ECC M30 84 D3
Cardwell St OLDS OL8 75 J1
Careless La WGNE/HIN WN2 48 C5
Caremine Av BNG/LEV M19 99 L2
Carey Cl BRO M7 * 72 A8
WGNS/IIMK WN3 63 G2
Carey Wk HULME M15 87 J7
Carfax Fold WHIT OL12 27 L2
Carfax St GTN M18 89 G7
Carill Av NEWH/MOS M40 73 K3
Carill Dr RUSH/FAL M14 99 G4
Carina Pl BRO M7 71 M8
Carisbrook Av URM M41 95 M3
WHTF M45 55 K6
Carisbrook Dr SWIN M27 70 D6
Carisbrooke Av
BRAM/HZG SK7 121 M3
Carisbrooke Dr BOL BL1 36 C1
Carisbrooke Rd LEIGH WN7 67 G6
Carisbrook St BKLY M9 73 G5
Carlburn St OP/CLY M11 89 G2
Carleton Rd POY/DIS SK12 122 E8
Carley Gv BKLY M9 56 F8
Carlford Gv PWCH M25 71 J1
Carlile St EDGY/DAV SK3 13 G7
Carlin Ga HALE/TIMP WA15 108 D6
Carling Dr WYTH/NTH M22 119 G2
Carlingford Cl EDGY/DAV SK3 112 B7
Carlisle Cl BOLS/LL BL3 53 K2
MPL/ROM SK6 113 K3
WHTF M45 55 L5
Carlisle Crs AUL OL6 75 M5
Carlisle Dr ALT WA14 108 B4
IRL M44 94 D2
Carlisle St CHAD OL9 8 D9
EDGW/EG BL7 22 D4
SWIN M27 70 C2
WGNE/HIN WN2 * 49 H6
WGNW/BIL/OR WN5 47 G6
WHIT OL12 28 B1
WILM/AE SK9 130 D4
Carloon Rd NTHM/RTH M23 109 L3
Carlow Dr WYTH/NTH M22 119 G2
Carl St BOL BL1 * 36 A2
Carlton Av BOLS/LL BL3 35 K8
BRAM/HZG SK7 120 F7
CHD/CHDH SK8 120 B1
MPL/ROM SK6 114 A1
OLDE OL4 60 A3
PWCH M25 72 B2
WHTF M45 55 G3
WILM/AE SK9 127 G2
Carlton Cl BOLE BL2 37 H1
HOR/BR BL6 33 G2
WALK M28 68 F3
Carlton Ct HALE/TIMP WA15 117 K3
Carlton Crs STKP SK1 13 M3
URM M41 96 A3
Carlton Dr CHD/CHDH SK8 110 D6
PWCH M25 72 B2
Carlton Gv HOR/BR BL6 34 A3
WGNE/HIN WN2 * 65 J1
Carlton Pl BRAM/HZG SK7 122 C3
FWTH BL4 * 53 G3
Carlton Range GTN M18 * 89 J8
Carlton Rd AUL OL6 75 M7
BOL BL1 35 J3
GOL/RIS/CUL WA3 80 A3
HALE/TIMP WA15 117 K2
HTNM SK4 111 K2
HYDE SK14 102 D1
OLDTF/WHR M16 98 A1
SALE M33 96 D6
SLFD M6 71 H8
URM M41 95 J2
WALK M28 68 F3
Carlton St BOLE BL2 3 G6
BURY BL9 4 F9
ECC M30 85 G1
FWTH BL4 53 G3
OLDTF/WHR M16 86 F8
WGNS/IIMK WN3 14 E8
Carlton Wy ROY/SHW OL2 59 G2
Carlyle Cl CHH M8 72 D6
Carlyle Gv LEIGH WN7 65 M4
Carlyle St BURY BL9 4 C4
Carlyn Av SALE M33 97 G8
Carmel Av ORD M5 86 F5
Carmel Cl ORD M5 86 F4
Carmel Ct BKLY M9 73 G3
Carmenna Dr BRAM/HZG SK7 121 H5
Carmichael Cl PART M31 106 B1
Carmichael St EDGY/DAV SK3 12 E8
Car Mill Ms WILM/AE SK9 126 F2
Carmine Fold MDTN M24 57 J2
Carmona Dr PWCH M25 55 K8
Carmona Gdns BRO M7 71 M3
Carmoor Rd BRUN/LGST M13 87 M7
Carnaby St BKLY M9 73 J3
Carna Rd RDSH SK5 100 B2
Carnarvon St BRO M7 * 72 B5
CSLFD M3 87 J1
OLDS OL8 74 E2
STKP SK1 13 M6
Carnation Rd FWTH BL4 52 D3
OLDE OL4 60 B8
Carnegie Av BNG/LEV M19 99 L3
Carnegie Cl SALE M33 108 A1
Carnegie Dr AIMK WN4 63 K7
Carnforth Av CHAD OL9 58 D6
ROCH OL11 42 A5
WGNE/HIN WN2 49 K8
Carnforth Dr SALE M33 108 D1
TOT/BURYW BL8 24 D2
Carnforth Rd CHD/CHDH SK8 111 M8
HTNM SK4 99 M6
Carnforth Sq MDTN M24 42 A5
Carnforth St RUSH/FAL M14 98 E1
Carnoustie BOLS/LL BL3 51 K1
Carnoustie Cl
NEWH/MOS M40 73 M5
WILM/AE SK9 127 H4
Carnoustie Dr
CHD/CHDH SK8 119 L3
RAMS BL0 18 E6
Carnwood Cl
NEWH/MOS M40 74 A4
Carolina Wy SALQ M50 86 B3
Caroline St AUL OL6 90 F1
BOLS/LL BL3 36 A8
BRO M7 72 B8
EDGY/DAV SK3 12 F8
IRL M44 94 B4
STLY SK15 91 K3
WGN WN1 15 M4
WGNS/IIMK WN3 14 E5
Carpenters La ANC M4 7 H3
Carpenters Wk DROY M43 89 J3
Carpenters Wy MILN OL16 28 E8
Carradale Dr SALE M33 95 M7
Carradon Dr
WGNNW/ST WN6 31 H3
Carr Av PWCH M25 71 J2
Carr Bank GLSP SK13 105 H4
Carr Bank Av BKLY M9 72 C1
RAMS BL0 18 E5
Carr Bank Dr RAMS BL0 18 E5
Carr Bank Rd RAMS BL0 18 E5
Carrbrook Cl STLY SK15 77 J6
Carrbrook Crs STLY SK15 77 J6
Carr Brook Dr ATH M46 51 H8
Carrbrook Dr ROY/SHW OL2 59 H3
Carrbrook Rd STLY SK15 77 J5
Carrbrook Ter RAD M26 38 F8
Carr Brow MPL/ROM SK6 123 J5
Carr Cl STKP SK1 112 E4
Carr Common Rd
WGNE/HIN WN2 66 A1
Carr Dr FWTH BL4 52 C3
Carrfield Av EDGY/DAV SK3 112 D8
HALE/TIMP WA15 109 G7
LHULT M38 52 B8
Carrfield Gv LHULT M38 52 B8
Carr Fold RAMS BL0 18 E5
Carrgate Rd DTN/ASHW M34 101 L3
Carrgreen Cl BNG/LEV M19 99 J7
Carrgreen La LYMM WA13 106 C6
Carrhill Quarry Cl MOSL OL5 76 F2
Carrhill Rd MOSL OL5 76 F2
Carrhill Ter MOSL OL5 * 76 F2
Carrhouse La HYDE SK14 92 F8
Carr House Rd OLDE OL4 60 C5
Carriage Dr LIT OL15 21 M5
NEWH/MOS M40 73 G7
The Carriage Dr GLSP SK13 93 H8
The Carriages ALT WA14 * 107 M8
Carriage St OLDTF/WHR M16 87 G7
Carrick Gdns MDTN M24 41 J8
Carrie St BOL BL1 35 L4
Carrigart PWCH M25 71 K1
Carrill Gv East BNG/LEV M19 99 K3
Carrington Cl MILN OL16 29 G1
Carrington Dr BOLS/LL BL3 36 C8
Carrington Field St STKP SK1 13 L9
Carrington Gv LEIGH WN7 * 66 C5
Carrington La PART M31 95 K5
SALE M33 96 B7
Carrington Rd RUSH/FAL M14 98 F4
STKP SK1 112 E2
URM M41 95 H4
Carrington St CHAD OL9 74 E1
LEIGH WN7 66 C5
SWIN M27 70 E3
Carrington Ter SWIN M27 * 70 D3
Carr La GOL/RIS/CUL WA3 80 D5
LEIGH WN7 81 H4
STLY SK15 77 J5
UPML OL3 45 M7
UPML OL3 61 L5
WGNS/IIMK WN3 63 K1
WILM/AE SK9 130 A2
Carr Lea OLDE OL4 60 F6
Carr Mill Crs
WGNW/BIL/OR WN5 62 B8
Carr Mill Ms WILM/AE SK9 * 126 F3
Carr Mill Rd
WGNW/BIL/OR WN5 62 B8
Carron Av BKLY M9 73 H3
Carron Gv BOLE BL2 37 J5
Carr Ri STLY SK15 77 J5
Carr Rd HALE/TIMP WA15 117 K2
IRL M44 94 E2
Carrs Av CHD/CHDH SK8 111 K6
Carrsdale Dr BKLY M9 72 F2
Carrsfield Rd
WYTH/NTH M22 110 B6
Carrslea Cl RAD M26 38 B7
Carrs Rd CHD/CHDH SK8 111 J6
Carr St AUL OL6 76 A7
LEIGH WN7 65 M7
RAMS BL0 18 E5
SWIN M27 70 A5
WGNE/HIN WN2 49 G6
Carrsvale Av URM M41 95 L2
Carrswood Rd
NTHM/RTH M23 108 F4
Carruthers Cl HEY OL10 41 J1
Carruthers St ANC M4 88 A3
Carr Vw NM/HAY SK22 * 124 F7
Carrwood HALE/TIMP WA15 117 K6
Carrwood Av BRAM/HZG SK7 121 G4
Carrwood Hey RAMS BL0 18 D8
Carrwood Rd
BRAM/HZG SK7 120 F3
WILM/AE SK9 126 D4
Carsdale Rd WYTH/NTH M22 119 G5
Carslake Av BOL BL1 35 M4
Carslake Rd
NEWH/MOS M40 73 G7
Carson Rd BNG/LEV M19 99 K4
Carstairs Av OFTN SK2 112 D8
Carstairs Cl CHH M8 72 C5
Car St WGNE/HIN WN2 64 D3
Carswell Cl TYLD M29 67 M3
Carter Cl DTN/ASHW M34 * 101 J2
Carter Pl HYDE SK14 * 91 G7
Carter St BOLS/LL BL3 36 D8
BRO M7 * 72 A7
FWTH BL4 * 53 H5
HYDE SK14 91 G7
MOSL OL5 76 F4
SALQ M50 85 M3
STLY SK15 91 L2
WGNS/IIMK WN3 15 K7
Carthage St OLDS OL8 59 J8
Cartleach Gv WALK M28 68 D2
Cartleach La WALK M28 68 C2
Cartmel WHIT OL12 10 E2
Cartmel Av HTNM SK4 100 A6
MILN OL16 29 J8
WGN WN1 47 L1
Cartmel Cl BOLS/LL BL3 51 G2
BRAM/HZG SK7 121 L1
BURY BL9 55 K1
CHD/CHDH SK8 119 L1
OLDS OL8 75 G1
Cartmel Crs BOLE BL2 36 F2
CHAD OL9 74 C2
Cartmel Dr HALE/TIMP WA15 109 G6
Cartmel Gv WALK M28 69 L5
Cartridge Cl WYTH/NTH M22 119 H1
Cartridge St HEY OL10 40 F2
Cartwright Gv LEIGH WN7 66 A3
Cartwright Rd CCHDY M21 97 K4
Cartwright St
DTN/ASHW M34 90 C6
HYDE SK14 91 K7
Carver Av PWCH M25 55 M7
Carver Cl OLDTF/WHR M16 86 E7
Carver Dr MPL/ROM SK6 114 B7
Carver Rd HALE/TIMP WA15 117 G2
MPL/ROM SK6 114 B7
Carver St OLDTF/WHR M16 86 E7
Carver Wk HULME M15 * 87 J7
Carville Gv WGNE/HIN WN2 49 L8
Carville Rd BKLY M9 73 M1
Carwood Gv HOR/BR BL6 34 A3
Cascade Dr BRO M7 72 B7
Case Rd RNFD/HAY WA11 78 A6
Cashgate Ct OLDS OL8 74 F1
Cashmere Rd EDGY/DAV SK3 12 C9
Cashmoor Wk WGTN/LGST M12 88 B6
Cashmore Dr WGNE/HIN WN2 49 G8
Caspian Rd ALT WA14 107 K6
BKLY M9 73 L1
Cass Av ORD M5 86 D4
Cassidy Cl ANC M4 7 K2
Cassidy Gdns MDTN M24 41 G8
Casson Ga WHIT OL12 28 B3
Casson St FAIL M35 74 C5
Casterton Wy WALK M28 68 D7
Castle Av DTN/ASHW M34 101 H2
ROCH OL11 10 C7
Castlebrook Cl BURY BL9 39 L8
Castle Cl DROY M43 89 L2
Castle Ct AUL OL6 75 L5
Castle Cft BOLE BL2 37 G1
Castlecroft Av HOR/BR BL6 33 G2
Castlecroft Rd BURY BL9 4 D4
Castledene Av SLFD M6 86 B1
Castle Edge Rd NM/HAY SK22 124 D2
Castle Farm Dr OFTN SK2 112 E6
Castle Farm La OFTN SK2 * 112 F7
Castlefield Av BRO M7 72 B4
Castlefield Br ORD M5 6 A6
Castleford Cl BOL BL1 * 2 B2
Castleford St OLD OL1 8 D1
Castle Gv LEIGH WN7 67 G6
RAMS BL0 24 D2
Castle Hall Cl STLY SK15 91 L3
Castle Hall Ct STLY SK15 * 91 K3
Castle Hall Vw STLY SK15 91 K3
Castle Hey Cl BURY BL9 55 M1
Castle Hl GLSP SK13 105 H1
NEWLW WA12 79 H8
Castle Hill Crs ROCH OL11 10 C6
Castle Hill Dr BKLY M9 72 F3
Castle Hill Pk MPL/ROM SK6 * 101 J6
WGNE/HIN WN2 49 J6
Castle Hill Rd BURY BL9 25 M6
PWCH M25 72 A2
WGNE/HIN WN2 49 H6
Castle Hill St BOLE BL2 36 E2
Castle La STLY SK15 77 J4
Castlemere Cl WGNS/IIMK WN3 63 G3
Castlemere Dr ROY/SHW OL2 44 A4
Castlemere Rd BKLY M9 72 F1
Castlemere St ROCH OL11 10 D6
Castlemere Ter ROCH OL11 10 D7
Castle Mill La
HALE/TIMP WA15 117 J7
Castlemoor Av BRO M7 71 L4
Castle Quay HULME M15 6 C8
Castlerea Cl ECC M30 85 G4
Castlerigg Cl HTNM SK4 100 A5
Castlerigg Dr MDTN M24 56 F2
ROY/SHW OL2 42 F6
Castle Ri WGNE/HIN WN2 49 H7
Castle Rd BURY BL9 39 M8
Castle Shaw Rd OFTN SK2 113 H7
Castle St ATH M46 67 J3
BOLE BL2 3 J6
BURY BL9 4 E4
BURY BL9 24 F2
CSLFD M3 6 C7
ECC M30 85 J2
EDGY/DAV SK3 12 E8
FWTH BL4 * 53 G5
GLSP SK13 93 K8
HYDE SK14 102 C1
MDTN M24 58 A5
STLY SK15 91 K3
WGNE/HIN WN2 49 H6
Castleton Av STRET M32 96 E1
Castleton Crs GLSP SK13 104 B3
Castleton Dr MPL/ROM SK6 123 H6
Castleton Gv AUL OL6 76 C6
Castleton Rd BRAM/HZG SK7 122 A3
BRO M7 72 B4
ROY/SHW OL2 42 F4
STRET M32 85 K8
Castleton Rd South ROCH OL11 42 A2
Castleton St ALT WA14 107 M5
BOLE BL2 36 E2
CHAD OL9 8 C7
Castleton Wk OP/CLY M11 * 88 C3
Castleton Wy WGNS/IIMK WN3 62 F2
Castle Wy SWIN M27 70 D2
Castleway HALE/TIMP WA15 117 L5
ROCH OL11 41 L2
SLFD M6 71 H8
WGNE/HIN WN2 49 J7
Castlewood Gdns OFTN SK2 112 F7
Castlewood Rd BRO M7 71 J4
Castlewood Sq BOLE BL2 36 F3
Catchdale Cl BKLY M9 56 F7
Catches Cl ROCH OL11 27 L4
Catches La ROCH OL11 27 L3
Cateaton St BURY BL9 4 F2
CSLFD M3 6 F3
Caterham Av BOLS/LL BL3 51 J2
Caterham St ANC M4 88 A3
Catfield Wk HULME M15 * 6 B9
Catford Rd NTHM/RTH M23 109 J7
Cathedral Ap CSLFD M3 6 F2
Cathedral Cl DUK SK16 91 G6
Cathedral Gdns ANC M4 * 6 F2
Cathedral Gates CSLFD M3 * 6 F3
Cathedral Rd CHAD OL9 58 D3
Cathedral St CSLFD M3 6 F3
Catherine Houses HTNM SK4 * 111 J2
Catherine Rd ALT WA14 116 E1
CHH M8 72 B3
MPL/ROM SK6 113 J3
SWIN M27 69 M5
Catherine St BOLS/LL BL3 51 L2
BRAM/HZG SK7 113 H8
BURY BL9 39 H6
ECC M30 84 D1
HYDE SK14 102 A1
LEIGH WN7 66 C6
OLDE OL4 60 B6
OP/CLY M11 89 H5
Catherine Ter WGN WN1 15 K4
Catherston Cl OLDTF/WHR M16 98 B1
Cathrine St East
DTN/ASHW M34 101 G1
Cathrine St West
DTN/ASHW M34 101 G1
Catlow La ANC M4 * 7 H3
Catlow St BRO M7 72 B8
Caton Cl BURY BL9 4 D9
Caton Dr ATH M46 66 D4
Caton St MILN OL16 10 F6
Cato St RAMS BL0 18 D8
Catterall Crs BOLE BL2 23 G6
Catterick Av DID/WITH M20 110 F1
SALE M33 107 M2
Catterick Dr BOLS/LL BL3 53 K1
Catterick Rd DID/WITH M20 110 F1
Catterwood Dr MPL/ROM SK6 114 E2
Cattlin Wy OLDS OL8 74 F2
Caunce Av GOL/RIS/CUL WA3 79 K5
Caunce Rd WGN WN1 15 K3
Caunce St WGN WN1 15 K4
The Causeway ALT WA14 108 A8
CHAD OL9 58 A7
Causewood Cl OLDE OL4 44 B8
Causey Dr MDTN M24 57 G1
Cavanagh Cl BRUN/LGST M13 88 A6
Cavan Cl EDGY/DAV SK3 111 J5
Cavan Dr RNFD/HAY WA11 78 A5
Cavell St CMANE M1 * 7 J4
Cavell Wy ORD M5 86 D3
Cavendish Av DID/WITH M20 98 C6
SWIN M27 70 F1
Cavendish Dr WGNS/IIMK WN3 63 G2
Cavendish Gdns BOLS/LL BL3 51 M1
Cavendish Gv ECC M30 85 H1
Cavendish Ms WILM/AE SK9 126 E7
Cavendish Pl AUL OL6 * 90 D1
Cavendish Rd ALT WA14 116 E1
BRAM/HZG SK7 121 M3
BRO M7 72 A3
DID/WITH M20 98 C6
ECC M30 85 H1
HTNM SK4 111 J2
ROCH OL11 42 B1
STRET M32 86 B8
URM M41 96 B2
WALK M28 69 L6
Cavendish St AUL OL6 90 E2
HULME M15 7 H9
LEIGH WN7 66 C5
OLDS OL8 9 H7
Cavendish Wy ROY/SHW OL2 58 F2
Caversham Gv BOL BL1 35 M4
Caversham Dr BKLY M9 73 H4
Cawdor Ct FWTH BL4 52 F2
Cawdor Pl HALE/TIMP WA15 108 F6
Cawdor Rd RUSH/FAL M14 98 F3
Cawdor St ECC M30 84 F3
FWTH BL4 52 E2
HULME M15 6 A9
LEIGH WN7 66 C8
SWIN M27 70 A4
WALK M28 69 H2
WGNE/HIN WN2 49 H7
WGNW/BIL/OR WN5 47 J6
Cawley Av GOL/RIS/CUL WA3 81 H8
PWCH M25 71 J2
Cawley La MCFLDN SK10 129 J5
Cawley Ter BKLY M9 * 56 D7
Cawood Sq RDSH SK5 100 F6
Cawston Wk CHH M8 72 D6
Caxton Cl WGNS/IIMK WN3 63 J2
Caxton Rd RUSH/FAL M14 98 E3
Caxton St CSLFD M3 * 6 D3
HEY OL10 41 G2
ROCH OL11 41 M2
Caxton Wy ORD M5 86 E3
Caygill St CSLFD M3 6 D2
Cayley St MILN OL16 11 J5
Caythorpe St RUSH/FAL M14 98 D1
Cayton St WGTN/LGST M12 99 K1
C' Ct AIMK WN4 78 E2
The Ceal MPL/ROM SK6 114 E2
Cecil Av SALE M33 108 B1
WGNNW/ST WN6 47 K2
Cecil Dr URM M41 95 H2
Cecil Gv GTN M18 89 G8
Cecilia St BOLS/LL BL3 36 D8
Cecil Rd BKLY M9 57 G8
ECC M30 85 H3
HALE/TIMP WA15 117 G2
STRET M32 96 F3
Cecil St BOLE BL2 3 J5
BURY BL9 4 F6
DUK SK16 90 E4
EDGY/DAV SK3 * 13 G8
HULME M15 87 L7
LEIGH WN7 66 D8
LIT OL15 21 K7
MOSL OL5 76 F4
OLDS OL8 9 G9
ROCH OL11 10 F9
ROY/SHW OL2 42 F8
STLY SK15 91 L3
WALK M28 69 G1
WGN WN1 15 L4
WGNS/IIMK WN3 48 B8
Cedar Av ALT WA14 107 M8
ATH M46 50 E8
AUL OL6 76 A7
BOLS/LL BL3 53 L2
BRAM/HZG SK7 122 A2
GOL/RIS/CUL WA3 80 C5
HEY OL10 40 F1
HOR/BR BL6 34 B3
STLY SK15 91 M1

WGNE/HIN WN2.....65 J1
WGNNW/ST WN6.....31 J4
WHTF M45.....55 J6
Cedar Bank CI MILN OL16.....29 G5
Cedar CI GLSP SK13.....104 E2
POY/DIS SK12.....129 J1
Cedar Ct HALE/TIMP WA15.....108 E7
Cedar Crs CHAD OL9.....8 B3
RAMS BL0.....18 F5
Cedar Dr DROY M43.....89 L2
SWIN M27.....54 A8
URM M41.....95 M3
WGN WN1.....48 A2
Cedar Gv AIMK WN4.....63 G7
DTN/ASHW M34.....101 H1
DUK SK16.....91 J4
FWTH BL4.....52 E4
HTNM SK4.....99 M7
PWCH M25.....55 K6
RNFD/HAY WA11.....78 B5
ROY/SHW OL2.....43 G6
ROY/SHW OL2.....43 L6
RUSH/FAL M14.....99 C4
WGNW/BIL/OR WN5.....46 C6
WHTN BL5.....50 B5
Cedar La MILN OL16.....43 L1
OLDE OL4.....61 G6
Cedar Lawn
CHD/CHDH SK8 *.....120 C2
Cedar Ms AULW OL7.....75 K7
Cedar PI BRO M7.....71 M8
Cedar Rd CHD/CHDH SK8.....110 D7
FAIL M35.....74 C6
HALE/TIMP WA15.....117 G1
LEIGH WN7.....66 B4
MDTN M24.....57 M4
MPL/ROM SK6.....114 B8
OFTN SK2.....112 E8
PART M31.....106 B1
SALE M33.....96 A6
Cedars Rd WYTH/NTH M22.....118 F1
Cedar St OL6.....76 A8
BURY BL9.....5 J3
HYDE SK14.....91 G7
OLDE OL4.....59 M5
WHIT OL12.....28 C5
Cedar Vw AUL OL6.....76 B7
Cedarwood Av HTNM SK4.....111 K3
Cedarwood CI WYTH/NTH M22.....110 E4
Cedar Wood Ct BOL BL1 *.....35 J4
Cedric Rd CHH M8.....72 E4
OLDE OL4.....59 M5
Cedric St STKP SK1.....86 A2
Celandine CI LIT OL15.....21 K7
Celandine Wk WGNS/IIMK WN3.....46 E8
Celia St CHH M8.....72 F4
Cellini Sq BOL BL1.....36 A3
Celtic St STKP SK1.....13 M6
Cemetery La BOLE BL2.....3 K4
DROY M43.....89 G3
DTN/ASHW M34.....90 C6
DTN/ASHW M34.....101 J3
FAIL M35.....74 C6
FWTH BL4.....53 J3
GLSP SK13.....93 M8
MOSL OL5.....77 G5
ORD M5.....86 B3
RAD M26.....38 D7
RAMS BL0.....18 D8
ROY/SHW OL2.....42 F7
SWIN M27.....70 A4
WGNS/IIMK WN3.....48 B8
Cemetery Rd North SWIN M27.....70 B2
Cemetery Rd MDTN M24.....57 K3
WHTN BL5.....50 B3
Cennick CI OLDE OL4.....59 M6
Ceno St OLD OL1.....9 L1
Centaur CI SWIN M27.....70 C2
Centenary Ct BOLS/LL BL3.....36 C8
Centenary Wy SALQ M50.....85 K3
Central Av AMK M46.....51 H8
BNG/LEV M19.....99 K2
BURY BL9.....6 C6
FWTH BL4.....52 D4
LEIGH WN7 *.....81 M1
LIT OL15.....21 M6
RAMS BL0.....19 G2
SALE M33.....108 A3
SLFD M6.....71 H7
SWIN M27.....71 G2
UPML OL3.....61 M7
URM M41.....85 H6
WALK M28.....52 F7
Central Dr BRAM/HZG SK7.....25 J4
BURY BL9.....119 M4
CHD/CHDH SK8.....119 M4
CHH M8.....72 E3
MPL/ROM SK6.....113 M1
RDSH SK5.....100 D7
SWIN M27.....70 E5
URM M41.....96 A2
WGNNW/ST M27.....30 E6
WHTN BL5.....50 B3
Central Flats WGNE/HIN WN2 *.....48 C5
Central Park Est TRPK M17 *.....85 M6
Central Park Wy WGN WN1.....15 H1
Central St DID/WITH M20.....98 D7
MANAIR M90.....118 E6
PART M31.....106 C1
Central St BOL BL1 *.....2 D4
CMANW M2.....6 E6
RAMS BL0.....18 F6
Central Wy ALT WA14.....108 A8
Centre Ct LEIGH WN7.....80 E3
Centre Gdns BOL BL1.....36 A3
Centre Park Rd BOL BL1.....2 A1
Centurion Gv BRO M7.....72 B7
Century Gdns WHIT OL12.....10 C1
Century Ldg FWTH BL4.....52 F4
Cestrian St BOLS/LL BL3.....52 C1
Ceylon St NEWH/MOS M40.....73 K6
OLDE OL4.....60 A7
Chadbury PI HOR/BR BL6.....50 F1
Chadderton Dr BURY BL9.....55 K3
Chadderton Fold OLDS OL8.....58 C2
Chadderton Hall Rd CHAD OL9.....58 C3
Chadderton Park Rd CHAD OL9.....58 C3
Chadderton Prec CHAD OL9 *.....8 B4
Chadderton St ANC M4.....7 J2
Chadderton Wy CHAD OL9.....8 F3
OLD OL1.....58 F3
Chaddesley Wk OP/CLY M11 *.....88 A6
Chaddock La TYLD M29.....68 A6
The Chaddock Level WALK M28.....68 F7
Chadkirk Rd MPL/ROM SK6.....113 M3
Chadvil Rd CHD/CHDH SK8.....110 F7
Chadwell Rd OFTN SK2.....113 H5
Chadwick CI MILN OL16.....29 K7
RUSH/FAL M14 *.....98 E1
WILM/AE SK9.....127 G3
Chadwick Fold BURY BL9.....25 J5
Chadwick Hall Rd ROCH OL11.....27 L6

Chadwick La MILN OL16.....42 F2
ROCH OL11.....41 K2
Chadwick Rd ECC M30.....85 H2
URM M41.....96 C2
Chadwick St AUL OL6.....91 H2
BOLE BL2.....3 H6
BOLS/LL BL3.....53 L1
BURY BL9.....26 B8
GLSP SK13.....104 E4
LEIGH WN7.....66 C6
MILN OL16.....29 H5
MPL/ROM SK6.....114 C7
ROCH OL11.....10 A5
STKP SK1.....13 J7
SWIN M27.....70 C4
WGNE/HIN WN2.....49 H6
WGNS/IIMK WN3.....14 D7
Chaffinch CI DROY M43.....89 M1
OLDE OL4.....60 B8
WYTH/NTH M22.....110 C7
Chaffinch Dr BURY BL9.....5 M1
Chaffinch Gv STLY SK15 *.....77 H5
Chain Bar La HYDE SK14.....103 J2
Chain Rd BKLY M9.....57 G7
Chain St CMANE M1.....7 G5
Chalbury CI WGNE/HIN WN2 *.....49 G8
Chalcombe Gra
WGTN/LGST M12 *.....88 C8
Chale CI NEWH/MOS M40.....88 A1
Chale Dr MDTN M24.....57 M6
Chalfont Av URM M41 *.....96 B2
Chalfont CI OLDS OL8 *.....59 L8
Chalfont Dr CHH M8.....72 D5
TYLD M29.....67 K5
WALK M28.....69 H4
Chalfont St BOL BL1.....36 C2
Chalford Rd NTHM/RTH M23.....118 C1
Challenge Wy
WGNW/BIL/OR WN5.....46 F3
Challenor Sq WGTN/LGST M12 *.....88 D6
Challum Dr CHAD OL9.....58 D4
Chamber Hall CI OLDS OL8.....59 G8
Chamberhall St BURY BL9.....4 E2
Chamber House Dr ROCH OL11.....41 L1
Chamberlain Dr WILM/AE SK9.....127 H3
Chamberlain Rd STLY SK15.....76 F7
Chamberlain St BOLS/LL BL3.....2 B7
Chamber Rd OLDS OL8.....74 F1
ROY/SHW OL2.....43 K5
Chambers Ct WILM/AE SK9.....103 K1
Chambers Field Ct ORD M5.....86 D3
Champness Hall MILN OL16 *.....10 F5
Chancel Av ORD M5.....86 F4
Chancel CI DUK SK16.....90 F6
Chancel La WILM/AE SK9.....126 F4
Chancellor La WGTN/LGST M12.....88 A4
Chancel Ms STKP SK1.....13 L4
Chancel PI CMANE M1 *.....7 L5
MILN OL16.....10 E5
Chancery CI TYLD M29.....67 L4
Chancery La BOL BL1.....2 F5
CMANW M2.....6 F5
ROY/SHW OL2 *.....43 K5
UPML OL3.....61 K2
Chancery St CHAD OL9.....8 D2
OLDE OL4.....59 M6
Chancery Wk CHAD OL9 *.....8 D2
Chandler Wy GOL/RIS/CUL WA3.....80 B4
Chandley St CHD/CHDH SK8 *.....111 G6
Chandos Gv ORD M5.....86 A2
Chandos Rd CCHDY M21.....97 M3
HTNM SK4.....99 L6
PWCH M25.....71 L2
Chandos Rd South CCHDY M21.....97 M3
Chandos St ROY/SHW OL2.....43 M5
Change Wy CSLFD M3.....6 C1
Changing Ct MILN OL16.....11 K7
Channing St MILN OL16.....11 J7
Channing St MILN OL16.....11 J7
Chanters ATH M46.....67 H1
The Chanters WALK M28.....68 F5
Chantlers Av TOT/BURYW BL8.....38 D3
Chantry CI POY/DIS SK12.....124 A7
RDSH SK5.....100 B5
WHTN BL5.....50 C7
Chantry Fold POY/DIS SK12.....124 A6
Chantry Rd POY/DIS SK12.....123 M6
Chantry Wk AIMK WN4.....63 J7
Chapel Aly BOL BL1 *.....2 E4
Chapel Brow GLSP SK13.....93 K5
GLSP SK13.....104 B6
Chapel CI BURY BL9.....39 L8
DUK SK16.....90 F4
WGNS/IIMK WN3.....15 J8
Chapel CI ALT WA14.....108 A8
Chapel Cft ROY/SHW OL2.....43 G8
Chapel Dr AUL OL6.....76 B7
HALE/TIMP WA15.....117 G1
Chapelfield RAD M26.....54 F3
Chapelfield CI STLY SK15.....77 G8
Chapelfield Dr WALK M28.....68 E1
Chapel Field Rd
DTN/ASHW M34.....101 J1
Chapelfield Rd WGTN/LGST M12.....7 M7
Chapel Flds EDGW/EG BL7.....16 F8
Chapel Fields La
WGNE/HIN WN2.....49 H1
Chapelfield St BOL BL1.....36 B1
Chapel Gdns TOT/BURYW BL8.....24 B3
Chapel Ga MILN OL16.....29 J6
Chapel Gra EDGW/EG BL7.....16 F8
Chapel Gn DTN/ASHW M34.....101 J1
Chapel Green Rd
WGNE/HIN WN2.....49 H6
Chapel Gv URM M41.....96 B2
Chapel HI LIT OL15.....21 M6
Chapelhill Dr BKLY M9.....72 F1
Chapel La BKLY M9.....72 E1
GLSP SK13.....93 J7
HALE/TIMP WA15.....117 G5
PART M31.....106 C1
ROCH OL11.....26 E4
ROY/SHW OL2.....43 G8
SALE M33.....96 B6
TOT/BURYW BL8.....18 D6
WGNS/IIMK WN3.....14 F7
WILM/AE SK9.....126 D6
Chapel Meadow WALK M28.....68 E1
Chapel PI AIMK WN4 *.....78 E1
BOLS/LL BL3.....3 L8
URM M41.....85 G4
Chapel Rd IRL M44.....94 D2
OLDS OL8.....74 F1
PWCH M25.....71 J3
SALE M33.....96 F1
SWIN M27.....69 M5
UPML OL3.....61 K6
WILM/AE SK9.....126 D6
Chapel Sq DTN/ASHW M34.....47 C8
Chapelstead WHTN BL5.....50 C7

Chapel St AIMK WN4.....78 E1
ATH M46.....67 G1
AUL OL6.....90 F1
BNG/LEV M19.....99 K3
BOL BL1.....3 G3
BOLS/LL BL3.....53 K1
BRAM/HZG SK7.....122 A1
BURY BL9.....4 F3
CHD/CHDH SK8.....111 G6
CSLFD M3.....6 C3
DROY M43.....89 L3
DTN/ASHW M34.....90 C6
DUK SK16.....90 F4
ECC M30.....84 F3
EDGW/EG BL7.....22 A1
FWTH BL4.....53 H4
GLSP SK13.....104 F3
HEY OL10.....41 G2
HOR/BR BL6.....33 C2
HOR/BR BL6.....33 H1
HTNM SK4.....111 J3
HYDE SK14.....102 A3
LEIGH WN7.....66 D8
MDTN M24.....56 F5
MDTN M24.....57 J4
MOSL OL5.....76 E3
MPL/ROM SK6.....101 L7
NM/HAY SK22.....124 D6
OLDE OL4.....60 B6
PWCH M25.....55 K8
RNFD/HAY WA11.....78 A4
ROCH OL11.....28 D8
ROY/SHW OL2.....43 C8
ROY/SHW OL2 *.....43 L5
STLY SK15.....91 K2
SWIN M27.....70 D3
TOT/BURYW BL8.....24 C5
TYLD M29.....67 K3
UPML OL3.....61 L4
WALK M28.....68 F2
WGNE/HIN WN2.....48 D1
WGNE/HIN WN2.....49 G7
WGNE/HIN WN2.....64 D2
WGNE/HIN WN2.....65 H3
WGNS/IIMK WN3.....14 C5
WGNS/IIMK WN3.....48 E7
WGNW/BIL/OR WN5.....46 E7
WHIT OL12.....20 A4
WHIT OL12.....21 G5
WILM/AE SK9.....130 D5
Chapeltown Rd EDGW/EG BL7.....22 E4
RAD M26.....54 D3
Chapeltown St CMANE M1.....7 L6
Chapel Vw DUK SK16.....90 F4
Chapel View CI HYDE SK14.....102 B5
Chapel Wk OLD OL1.....59 G3
Chapel Wks CHD/CHDH SK8.....120 D6
CMANW M2.....6 F4
Chapelway Gdns ROY/SHW OL2.....43 G6
Chaple Wy GLSP SK13.....93 J7
Chaplin CI SLFD M6.....71 H8
Chapman Ms GTN M18 *.....89 G7
Chapman Rd HYDE SK14.....103 H3
Chapman St BOL BL1.....35 L3
GTN M18.....89 G6
Chappell Rd DROY M43.....89 K2
Chappeltown Rd RAD M26.....54 C3
Chapter St NEWH/MOS M40.....73 J8
Charcoal Rd ALT WA14.....116 B1
Charcoal Woods ALT WA14.....116 C1
Chard Dr WYTH/NTH M22.....118 F3
Chardin Av MPL/ROM SK6.....114 F4
Chard St RAD M26.....54 D1
Charges St AULW OL7.....90 C3
Chariot St OP/CLY M11.....89 G4
Charity St LEIGH WN7.....66 C6
Charlbury Av PWCH M25.....72 A1
Charlbury Wy ROY/SHW OL2.....43 K7
Charlecote Rd POY/DIS SK12.....122 B8
Charles Av DTN/ASHW M34.....90 K5
MPL/ROM SK6.....113 M6
Charles Ct BOL BL1 *.....2 F3
Charles Halle Rd
RUSH/FAL M14.....87 K7
Charles Holden St BOL BL1.....2 A6
Charles La GLSP SK13.....105 J2
MILN OL16.....29 K7
Charles Ms HYDE SK14 *.....29 K7
BURY BL9.....39 K7
DROY M43.....89 G7
HALE/TIMP WA15.....108 F7
ROY/SHW OL2.....43 M4
URM M41.....96 B2
Charles Morris CI FAIL M35.....74 E4
Charles Shaw CI OLDE OL4.....60 B3
Charles St AULW OL7.....90 C2
BOL BL1.....3 G3
BRAM/HZG SK7.....121 M1
BURY BL9.....4 E5
CHAD OL9.....8 D7
CMANE M1.....7 H7
DROY M43 *.....89 H3
DTN/ASHW M34.....90 C7
DUK SK16.....90 F4
EDGW/EG BL7.....22 A2
FWTH BL4.....53 H3
GLSP SK13.....104 F3
GOL/RIS/CUL WA3.....79 K3
HEY OL10.....41 H4
IRL M44.....94 B6
LEIGH WN7.....66 C5
LIT OL15.....21 J7
ROY/SHW OL2.....43 G8
SLFD M6.....71 J8
STKP SK1.....13 L8
SWIN M27.....70 A3
TYLD M29.....67 J3
WGN WN1.....15 G1
WGNE/HIN WN2.....49 H5
WHTF M45.....55 J5
Charleston CI SALE M33.....108 A2
Charleston Sq URM M41.....95 L1
Charleston St OLDS OL8.....59 J8
Charlestown Rd BKLY M9.....73 G2
GLSP SK13.....104 F4
Charlestown Rd East
OFTN SK2.....121 J1
Charlestown Rd West
EDGY/DAV SK3.....121 H1
Charlestown Wy AUL OL6.....90 D1
Charles Whittaker St
WHIT OL12.....27 J3
Charlesworth Av
BOLS/LL BL3.....52 E2
DTN/ASHW M34.....101 J4
WGNE/HIN WN2.....49 J8
Charlesworth St
OP/CLY M11.....88 C4
STKP SK1.....13 J8
Charlock CI WHTN BL5.....50 A6
Charlock Sq ALT WA14.....107 L4
Charlotte Dr
FWTH BL4.....53 J7
Charlotte La OLDE OL4.....61 H7
Charlotte PI HALE/TIMP WA15.....117 H1

Charlotte St BOL BL1.....36 B2
CHD/CHDH SK8.....111 H7
CMANW M2.....7 G5
EDGW/EG BL7.....16 F8
MILN OL16.....28 D8
RAMS BL0.....18 E7
STKP SK1.....112 E1
Charlton Av ECC M30.....85 G3
HYDE SK14.....91 K8
PWCH M25.....71 L1
Charlton CI AIMK WN4.....63 K8
Charlton Dr SALE M33.....96 F8
SWIN M27.....70 A2
Charlton Fold WALK M28.....52 F7
Charlton PI CMANE M1.....7 K8
Charlton Rd BNG/LEV M19.....99 L2
Charminster Dr CHH M8.....72 E4
Charmouth CI NEWLW WA12.....78 E8
Charmouth Wk
WYTH/NTH M22.....119 H1
Charnley CI NEWH/MOS M40.....88 B1
Charnley St WHTF M45.....55 J4
Charnock Dr BOL BL1.....2 D1
Charnock St WGNE/HIN WN2.....64 D1
Charnville Rd CHD/CHDH SK8.....110 C8
Charnwood MPL/ROM SK6.....123 H5
Charnwood Av
DTN/ASHW M34.....100 E1
Charnwood CI AUL OL6.....75 M5
ROY/SHW OL2.....43 H4
TYLD M29.....67 L4
WALK M28.....68 F2
Charnwood Crs
BRAM/HZG SK7.....121 M4
Charnwood Rd BKLY M9.....57 G2
MPL/ROM SK6.....101 M7
Charter Av RAD M26.....54 F3
Charter CI SALE M33.....108 A1
Charterhouse Rd
WGNS/IIMK WN3.....15 J8
Charter Rd HALE/TIMP WA15.....108 B8
Charter St CSLFD M3.....87 J1
MILN OL16.....28 D8
OLD OL1.....9 L2
Chartwell CI SLFD M6.....86 C2
Chartwell Dr NTHM/RTH M23.....109 C5
Chase Briar Wd
CHD/CHDH SK8 *.....120 D3
Chasefield ALT WA14.....116 C2
Chaseley Rd SLFD M6.....71 H8
The Chase WALK M28.....69 K7
Chasewood BNG/LEV M19 *.....99 K3
Chassen Av URM M41.....95 L3
Chassen Ct URM M41.....95 L3
Chassen Rd BOL BL1.....35 L5
URM M41.....95 L3
Chataway Rd CHH M8.....72 E4
Chatburn Av GOL/RIS/CUL WA3.....79 M3
ROCH OL11.....10 C2
Chatburn Gdns HEY OL10.....40 C2
Chatburn Rd BOL BL1.....35 J1
CCHDY M21.....97 M4
Chatburn Sq ROCH OL11.....42 A4
Chatcombe Rd
WYTH/NTH M22.....118 C2
Chatfield Rd CCHDY M21.....97 L4
Chatford CI BRO M7.....72 B8
Chatham Ct DID/WITH M20 *.....98 D6
Chatham Gdns BOLS/LL BL3.....2 B8
Chatham Gv DID/WITH M20.....98 D6
Chatham PI BOLS/LL BL3 *.....2 B8
Chatham Rd GTN M18 *.....100 B1
OLDTF/WHR M16.....97 M1
Chatham St CMANE M1.....7 J5
EDGY/DAV SK3.....12 E7
HYDE SK14.....102 A3
LEIGH WN7.....66 C5
WGN WN1.....15 K5
WGNE/HIN WN2.....48 D4
Chatley Rd ECC M30.....84 C3
Chatley St CSLFD M3.....72 C8
Chatswood Av OFTN SK2.....112 C6
Chatsworth Av
GOL/RIS/CUL WA3.....81 J8
PWCH M25.....55 L8
WGNS/IIMK WN3.....48 C8
Chatsworth CI AIMK WN4.....63 J8
BURY BL9.....39 K7
DROY M43.....89 G5
HALE/TIMP WA15.....108 F7
ROY/SHW OL2.....43 M4
URM M41.....96 B2
Chatsworth Dr LEIGH WN7.....67 G5
Chatsworth Gv
OLDTF/WHR M16.....98 A3
Chatsworth Ms
BRAM/HZG SK7.....120 D6
Chatsworth Rd
BRAM/HZG SK7.....122 B3
DROY M43.....89 H2
ECC M30.....70 D8
GTN M18.....88 F7
MPL/ROM SK6.....123 H6
RAD M26.....38 D7
STRET M32.....96 C1
WALK M28.....69 J7
WILM/AE SK9.....126 C8
Chatsworth St OLDE OL4.....59 M6
WGNW/BIL/OR WN5.....46 F7
WHIT OL12.....28 B1
Chatterls CI WGNE/HIN WN2.....49 H8
Chatterton CI DID/WITH M20.....98 F6
Chatterton La MPL/ROM SK6.....115 K4
Chatterton Old La RAMS BL0.....18 F2
Chatterton Rd RAMS BL0.....18 F2
Chattock St OLDTF/WHR M16.....98 B1
Chatton CI TOT/BURYW BL8.....38 C3
Chatwood Rd NEWH/MOS M40.....74 A2
Chaucer Av DROY M43.....89 K3
DTN/ASHW M34.....101 K6
RDSH SK5.....100 A4
Chaucer Gv LEIGH WN7.....65 H4
Chaucer Ms STKP SK1.....112 E1
Chaucer PI WGN WN1.....47 M1
WGNE/HIN WN2.....64 D3
Chaucer Ri DUK SK16.....91 K5
Chaucer Rd MDTN M24.....57 J2
Chaucer St BOL BL1.....36 A3
OLDS OL8.....9 H6
ROCH OL11.....41 M2
ROY/SHW OL2.....43 M7
Chauncy Rd NEWH/MOS M40.....74 B1
Chaytor Av NEWH/MOS M40.....73 L5
Cheadle Av BRO M7.....72 C5
Cheadle Old Rd EDGY/DAV SK3.....12 C9
Cheadle PI CHD/CHDH SK8 *.....111 L7
Cheadle Point CHD/CHDH SK8.....111 H8
Cheadle Sq BOL BL1.....2 D5
Cheadle St OP/CLY M11.....89 G4

Cheadle Wd CHD/CHDH SK8.....120 A4
Cheam Rd HALE/TIMP WA15.....108 C4
Cheapside CMANW M2.....6 F4
HYDE SK14.....102 B3
Cheap Side MDTN M24.....57 K2
Cheapside OLD OL1.....9 H5
Cheapside Sq BOL BL1 *.....2 E4
Cheddar St GTN M18.....89 G7
Cheddington CI
CHD/CHDH SK8.....120 C5
Chedlee Dr CHD/CHDH SK8.....120 A3
Chedlin Dr NTHM/RTH M23.....109 K8
Chedworth Crs LHULT M38.....52 B1
Chedworth Dr
NTHM/RTH M23.....109 L6
Chedworth Gv BOLS/LL BL3 *.....2 C8
Cheeryble St DROY M43.....89 J4
Cheetham Fold Rd HYDE SK14.....102 A4
Cheetham Hi ROY/SHW OL2.....43 L6
Cheetham Hill Rd ANC M4.....7 H1
CHH M8.....72 D5
DUK SK16.....91 G6
Cheetham PI MPL/ROM SK6.....101 L8
Cheetham Rd SWIN M27.....70 D5
The Cheethams HOR/BR BL6.....33 H5
Cheetham St FAIL M35.....74 D4
MDTN M24.....57 J4
MILN OL16.....10 E3
NEWH/MOS M40.....73 H7
OLD OL1 *.....59 L5
RAD M26.....38 F8
ROY/SHW OL2.....43 M4
Cheetwood Rd CHH M8.....72 C7
Cheetwood St BRO M7.....72 B8
Chelbourne Dr OLDS OL8 *.....74 E2
Chelburn CI OFTN SK2.....113 C7
WGNE/HIN WN2.....65 H3
Chelford Av BOL BL1.....22 B7
GOL/RIS/CUL WA3.....80 A5
Chelford CI HALE/TIMP WA15.....108 B6
MDTN M24.....57 M2
WGNS/IIMK WN3.....63 J2
Chelford Dr SWIN M27.....70 B2
TYLD M29.....67 M6
Chelford Gv EDGY/DAV SK3.....111 K4
Chelford Rd MCFLDN SK10.....131 L7
OLDTF/WHR M16.....97 M1
SALE M33.....109 H2
WILM/AE SK9.....119 M7
Chellow Dene MOSL OL5.....76 E3
Chell St BRUN/LGST M13.....88 C8
Chelmarsh Av AIMK WN4.....78 F1
Chelmer Gv HEY OL10.....40 D1
Chelmorton Gv
WGNS/IIMK WN3.....62 F2
Chelmsford Av
NEWH/MOS M40.....73 L8
Chelmsford Dr
WGNS/IIMK WN3.....47 K8
Chelmsford Ms WGN WN1.....47 M1
Chelmsford Rd EDGY/DAV SK3.....12 D7
Chelmsford St OLDS OL8.....9 C7
Chelsea Av RAD M26.....38 A8
Chelsea CI ROY/SHW OL2.....43 L5
WHTN BL5.....50 B5
Chelsea Ct WHTN BL5 *.....50 B5
Chelsea Rd BOLS/LL BL3.....51 M1
NEWH/MOS M40.....73 M7
URM M41.....93 J7
Chelsea St BURY BL9.....99 J7
ROCH OL11.....10 A9
Chelsfield Gv CCHDY M21.....98 A4
Chelston Dr CHD/CHDH SK8.....119 L6
Cheltenham Av
WGNS/IIMK WN3.....15 J3
Cheltenham Crs BRO M7.....72 B5
Cheltenham Dr NEWLW WA12.....78 F7
SALE M33.....96 F8
WGNW/BIL/OR WN5.....62 A2
Cheltenham Gn MDTN M24.....57 K6
Cheltenham Rd CCHDY M21.....97 L2
EDGY/DAV SK3.....12 B9
MDTN M24.....57 K6
Cheltenham St OLD OL1.....59 L5
ROCH OL11.....28 A8
SLFD M6.....71 K8
WGNE/HIN WN2.....48 D2
Chelwood CI BOL BL1.....22 A5
Chelwood Dr DROY M43.....89 J2
Chelwood Ms HOR/BR BL6 *.....34 E5
Chelwood Pk AIMK WN4.....78 E3
Chendre CI NM/HAY SK22.....125 L1
Chendre Rd BKLY M9.....73 J1
Cheney CI OP/CLY M11 *.....89 G5
Chepstow Av SALE M33.....107 K4
Chepstow CI ROCH OL11.....27 J4
Chepstow Dr BRAM/HZG SK7.....122 C2
OLD OL1.....59 L3
Chepstow Gv LEIGH WN7.....67 H5
Chepstow Rd CCHDY M21.....97 K5
SWIN M27.....70 D2
Chepstow St CMANE M1.....6 F7
Chepstow St South
CMANE M1 *.....6 F7
Chequers Rd CCHDY M21.....97 L4
Chequers St WGN WN1.....14 E4
Cherington CI NTHM/RTH M23.....109 L2
WILM/AE SK9.....127 K1
Cherington Dr TYLD M29.....67 M3
Cherington Rd CHD/CHDH SK8.....110 F8
Cheriton Av SALE M33.....96 F7
Cheriton CI HYDE SK14.....103 G2
Cheriton Dr BOLE BL2.....37 H6
Cheriton Ri OFTN SK2.....113 K6
Cheriton Rd URM M41.....95 G2
Cherrington Dr ROCH OL11.....42 A4
Cherry Av AUL OL6.....75 L6
BURY BL9.....5 M5
OLDS OL8.....75 H1
Cherrybrook Dr
WGNS/IIMK WN3.....63 G3
Cherry CI BURY BL9.....39 K5
NEWLW WA12.....78 C8
WHTF M45.....113 H5
Cherrycroft MPL/ROM SK6.....114 B3
Cherry Dr SWIN M27.....69 C4
Cherry Gv LEIGH WN7.....66 C4
ROCH OL11.....27 K4
ROY/SHW OL2.....42 F6
STLY SK15.....91 J1
WGNNW/ST WN6.....47 J1
Cherry Hall Dr ROY/SHW OL2.....43 H5
Cherry Hinton OLD OL1 *.....8 E2
Cherry Holt Av HTNM SK4.....99 J8
Cherry La MILN OL16.....44 E1
SALE M33.....107 M2
Cherry Orchard CI
BRAM/HZG SK7.....120 F3
Cherry St PWCH M25.....55 M7

Cherryton Wk BRUN/LGST M13....87 M6
Cherry Tree Av FWTH BL4....52 C4
  POY/DIS SK12....129 K1
Cherry Tree Cl
  HALE/TIMP WA15....108 E7
  MPL/ROM SK6....114 B2
  WILM/AE SK9....127 J4
Cherry Tree Ct OFTN SK2....112 F8
Cherry Tree Dr BRAM/HZG SK7....122 C4
Cherry Tree Gv LEIGH WN7....66 A6
  ATH M46....50 E8
Cherry Tree La ALT WA14....116 C7
  MPL/ROM SK6....114 B2
  OFTN SK2....112 F7
  TOT/BURYW BL8....4 A6
Cherry Tree Rd
  CHD/CHDH SK8....120 B3
  GOL/RIS/CUL WA3....80 C4
  NTHM/RTH M23....109 J4
Cherry Tree Wk STRET M32....96 E3
Cherry Tree Wy BOLE BL2....22 F7
  HOR/BR BL6....34 B3
Cherry Wk CHD/CHDH SK8....120 E4
Cherrywood CHAD OL9....58 A5
Cherrywood Av WHTN BL5....51 K5
Cherrywood Cl WALK M28....68 E4
Chertsey Cl GTN M18....89 H7
  ROY/SHW OL2....43 L4
Chervil Cl RUSH/FAL M14....98 E3
Chervil Wk WGNS/IIMK WN3....46 F8
Chervil Cl RUSH/FAL M14....98 E4
Cherwell Av HEY OL10....40 D1
Cherwell Cl CHD/CHDH SK8....120 C5
  OLDS OL8....74 F3
  WGNE/HIN WN2....55 M6
  WHTF M45....55 K5
Cherwell Rd WHTN BL5....50 C2
Chesham Av BOL BL1....36 B2
  ROCH OL11....42 A5
  URM M41....95 H1
  WYTH/NTH M22....109 M8
Chesham Cl GLSP SK13....93 L7
  WILM/AE SK9....126 D8
Chesham Crs BURY BL9....5 L1
Chesham Fold Rd BURY BL9....5 L2
Chesham Pl ALT WA14....116 E2
Chesham Rd BURY BL9....25 L7
  ECC M30 *....84 F4
  OLDE OL4....59 M6
  WILM/AE SK9....126 D8
Cheshire Cl STRET M32....96 E3
Cheshire Ct RAMS BL0....19 G6
Cheshire Ring Canal Wk
  ALT WA14....107 H7
  MCFLDN SK10....129 L6
  MPL/ROM SK6....101 L6
  MPL/ROM SK6....123 C6
  POY/DIS SK12....122 F8
Cheshire Rd PART M31....106 A2
  STLY SK15....77 G7
Cheshire Sq STLY SK15....77 H7
Cheshire St MOSL OL5....77 G4
Chesney Av CHAD OL9....74 B2
Chesshyre Av ANC M4 *....88 A3
Chessington Ri SWIN M27....70 D8
Chester Av BOLS/LL BL3....37 L8
  DUK SK16....91 H5
  GOL/RIS/CUL WA3....80 A4
  HALE/TIMP WA15....117 H7
  ROCH OL11....27 K6
  SALE M33....107 L3
  STLY SK15....92 A1
  URM M41....96 B1
  WHTF M45....55 K5
Chester Cl BOLS/LL BL3....37 L8
  IRL M44....94 A7
  WILM/AE SK9....127 J3
Chester Dr AIMK WN4....79 G2
  RAMS BL0....18 D8
Chesterfield Gv AUL OL6....91 G1
Chesterfield St OLDE OL4....59 L6
Chestergate EDGY/DAV SK3....12 E1
Chester Rd BRAM/HZG SK7....121 M4
  BRAM/HZG SK7....128 B2
  HULME M15....6 A9
  OLDTF/WHR M16....86 F7
  POY/DIS SK12....121 K8
  POY/DIS SK12....121 M5
  STRET M32....96 F4
  TYLD M29....68 A4
Chester St ATH M46....67 H2
  BURY BL9....25 K8
  CHAD OL9....8 C9
  DTN/ASHW M34....101 J2
  EDGY/DAV SK3....12 E5
  HULME M15....6 F9
  LEIGH WN7....66 C7
  PWCH M25....72 K7
  SWIN M27....70 B5
Chesterton Cl WGNS/IIMK WN3....14 C9
Chesterton Dr BOLS/LL BL3....35 H7
Chesterton Gv DROY M43....89 K2
Chesterton Rd
  NTHM/RTH M23....109 G4
Chester Wk BOL BL1 *....36 B2
Chesterwood CHAD OL9....58 C8
Chestnut Av ATH M46 *....5 K4
  BURY BL9....5 K4
  CCHDY M21....97 L4
  CHD/CHDH SK8....111 H7
  DROY M43....89 H1
  IRL M44....94 A7
  LEIGH WN7....81 H1
  TOT/BURYW BL8....24 D7
  WALK M28....69 G2
  WHTF M45....55 L8
Chestnut Cl BOLS/LL BL3....125 C8
  NM/HAY SK22....124 E4
  OLDE OL4....60 A4
  STLY SK15....91 K4
  WILM/AE SK9....127 J4
Chestnut Crs OLDS OL8....75 K2
Chestnut Dr BURY BL9....25 J5
  LEIGH WN7....81 J1
  POY/DIS SK12....129 K1
  SALE M33....108 A3
  WHTN BL5....50 C5
Chestnut Gdns
  DTN/ASHW M34....101 H2
  HEY OL10....40 F5
Chestnut Gv AIMK WN4....64 A6
  FAIL M35....74 C6
  GOL/RIS/CUL WA3....54 C4
  RAD M26....54 C4
  WHTN BL5....49 G8
Chestnut La LEIGH WN7....81 J2
Chestnut Rd ECC M30....69 K8
  WGN WN1....48 B2
Chestnut St CHAD OL9....74 D1

Chesworth Cl STKP SK1....13 J6
Chesworth Fold STKP SK1....13 J7
Chetham Ct WHTF M45 *....86 E5
Chetwode Av AIMK WN4....78 B3
Chetwyn Av EDGW/EG BL7....22 D5
Chetwynd Av URM M41....95 M3
Chetwynd Cl SALE M33....96 B6
Chevassut St HULME M15....87 H6
Chevington Dr BKLY M9....73 G6
  HTNM SK4....111 G1
Cheviot Av CHD/CHDH SK8....120 B2
  OLDS OL8....75 H1
  ROY/SHW OL2....58 F1
Cheviot Cl BOL BL1....22 A7
  CHAD OL9....58 D7
  HTNM SK4....12 F1
  MDTN M24....57 J8
  MILN OL16....29 K6
  RAMS BL0....18 F8
  SLFD M6....86 B1
  TOT/BURYW BL8....38 D1
  WGNS/IIMK WN3....62 F2
Cheviot Rd BRAM/HZG SK7....121 K3
  ROY/SHW OL2....43 K4
Cheviot St CSLFD M3....87 J1
Chevithorne Cl ALT WA14....107 L7
Chevril Cl HULME M15....87 K6
  SLFD M6....86 E2
Chevron Pl ALT WA14....108 A5
Chew Brook Dr UPML OL3....61 J7
Chew Moor La WHTN BL5....50 D2
Chew V DUK SK16....91 J5
  UPML OL3....61 L7
Chew Valley Rd UPML OL3....61 J7
Chicago Av MANAIR M90....118 D5
Chichester Av ATH M46....66 D2
Chichester Cl LIT OL15....29 J1
  SALE M33....108 A1
Chichester Crs CHAD OL9....58 D3
Chichester Rd HULME M15....87 H1
  MPL/ROM SK6....113 M2
Chichester Rd South
  HULME M15 *....87 H1
Chichester St MILN OL16....11 J5
Chidlow Av DID/WITH M20....98 D5
Chidwall Rd WYTH/NTH M22....118 D2
Chief St OLDE OL4 *....9 M7
Chiffon Wy CSLFD M3....6 A1
Chigwell Cl WYTH/NTH M22....110 B7
Chilcote Av SALE M33....96 B8
Childwall Cl BOLS/LL BL3....52 B2
Chilgrove Av HOR/BR BL6....33 C3
Chilham Rd ECC M30....70 A7
  WALK M28....69 H2
Chilham St BOLS/LL BL3....51 L2
  SWIN M27....70 B6
  WGNW/BIL/OR WN5....46 B4
Chillingham Dr LEIGH WN7....66 E8
Chilmark Dr NTHM/RTH M23....109 K6
Chiltern Av ATH M46....51 J7
  URM M41....95 J1
Chiltern Cl AIMK WN4....78 F2
  BRAM/HZG SK7....121 K3
  RAMS BL0....18 E4
  ROY/SHW OL2....43 J4
  WALK M28....69 H4
Chiltern Dr BOLE BL2....3 L4
  HALE/TIMP WA15....117 H1
  OFTN SK2....112 D8
  ROY/SHW OL2....42 F8
  SWIN M27....70 C6
  TOT/BURYW BL8....24 E8
  WGNS/IIMK WN3....62 F1
Chiltern Gdns SALE M33....108 A1
Chiltern Rd GOL/RIS/CUL WA3....81 H8
  RAMS BL0....18 F8
Chiltern Wy TYLD M29....67 L4
Chilton Av CHAD OL9....58 D6
Chilton Cl LEIGH WN7....66 C5
Chilton Dr MDTN M24....57 M5
Chilworth St RUSH/FAL M14....98 E1
Chime Bank CHH M8....72 F5
Chimes Ct OLDE OL4....60 E7
Chimes Rd AIMK WN4....63 J6
China La BOL BL1....2 C3
  CMANE M1....7 J5
Chingford Wk
  BRUN/LGST M13 *....88 C8
  STRET M32....85 K8
Chinley Av NEWH/MOS M40....73 M4
  HTNM SK4....12 A1
  SALE M33....109 G1
Chinley Cl BRAM/HZG SK7....121 G1
  HTNM SK4....12 A1
  SALE M33....109 G1
Chinley St SLFD M6....71 L7
Chinnor Cl LEIGH WN7....66 C5
Chinwell Vw BNG/LEV M19....99 K3
Chip Hill Rd BOLS/LL BL3....35 K8
Chippendale Pl AUL OL6....76 B7
Chippenham Av OFTN SK2....112 F5
Chippenham Ct ANC M4....88 A2
Chippenham Rd ANC M4....7 M3
Chipping Fold MILN OL16....29 J7
Chipping Rd BOL BL1....35 J2
Chipstead Av WGTN/LGST M12....88 B7
Chirmside St TOT/BURYW BL8....38 E3
Chirton Rd RNFD/HAY WA11....78 A5
Chisacre Dr WGNNW/ST WN6....30 A5
Chiselden Av WYTH/NTH M22....119 J3
Chiselhurst St CHH M8....72 D5
Chisholm Cl WGNNW/ST WN6....30 E2
Chisholme Cl TOT/BURYW BL8....24 C2
Chisholm St OP/CLY M11....89 G5
Chisledon Av BRO M7 *....72 C8
Chisledon Cl RNFD/HAY WA11....78 A5
Chislehurst Av URM M41....95 M1
Chislehurst Cl TOT/BURYW BL8....39 M1
Chiswell St WGNW/BIL/OR WN5....46 A5
Chiswick Dr RAD M26....37 L7
Chiswick Rd DID/WITH M20....110 F1
Chisworth Cl BRAM/HZG SK7....121 G1
  LEIGH WN7....66 B5
Chisworth St BOLE BL2....36 E1
Choir St BRO M7....72 B8
Chokeberry Cl ALT WA14....107 L4
Cholmondeley Av ALT WA14....108 B4
Cholmondeley Rd SLFD M6....70 E8
Chomlea Mnr SLFD M6 *....70 F7
Choral Gv BRO M7....72 A7
Chorley Cl TOT/BURYW BL8....38 C3
Chorley Hall Cl WILM/AE SK9....130 C3
Chorley Hall La WILM/AE SK9....130 D5
Chorley New Rd BOL BL1....35 H5
  HOR/BR BL6....34 A1
Chorley Old Rd BOL BL1....2 A1
  HOR/BR BL6....34 B1
Chorley Rd SALE M33....109 H2
  SWIN M27....70 A3
  WGNNW/ST WN6....31 L6
  WHTN BL5....33 M3

Chorley St BOL BL1....2 C3
  STRET M32....86 C7
  WGNS/IIMK WN3....15 K8
Chorley Wood Av
  BNG/LEV M19....99 J6
Chorlton Dr CHD/CHDH SK8....111 H6
Chorlton Fold ECC M30....70 A7
Chorlton Gv STKP SK1....112 C5
Chorlton Pl CCHDY M21....97 L3
Chorlton Rd HULME M15....6 B9
Chorlton St CMANE M1....7 H5
  OLDTF/WHR M16....86 F7
Chorlton Ter
  BRUN/LGST M13 *....87 L6
Chowbent Cl ATH M46....67 H1
Chretien Rd WYTH/NTH M22....110 B2
Christchurch Av ORD M5....86 B2
Christchurch Cl BOLE BL2....37 J2
Christ Church Ct BOLE BL2....37 J1
Christchurch Rd SALE M33....95 M7
Christie Rd STRET M32....97 H2
Christie St ROY/SHW OL2....43 L5
Christleton
  ROCH OL11....27 H3
Christleton Av HTNM SK4....100 F1
Christopher Acre
  ROCH OL11....27 H3
Christopher St
  NEWH/MOS M40....74 A8
  ORD M5....86 D3
  WGNS/IIMK WN3....15 M8
Chronnell Dr BOLE BL2....37 H4
Chudleigh Cl ALT WA14....107 L8
  BRAM/HZG SK7....121 J1
Chudleigh Rd CHH M8....72 D2
Chulsey Gate La HOR/BR BL6....34 D8
Chulsey St BOLS/LL BL3....51 L1
Chunal La GLSP SK13....104 F6
Church Av DTN/ASHW M34....101 K4
  HYDE SK14....102 C4
  MDTN M24....42 A6
  NEWH/MOS M40....73 M7
  SLFD M6....86 A2
  WGNE/HIN WN2....65 J4
Church Bank BOL BL1....2 F4
Churchbank STLY SK15....92 A2
Church Brow ALT WA14....108 A3
  HYDE SK14....102 A3
  HYDE SK14....103 K1
Church Cl GLSP SK13....105 H2
  RAD M26....38 E4
  RAMS BL0....18 E4
  WILM/AE SK9....127 H1
Church Ct BURY BL9 *....5 H3
  DUK SK16....90 E3
Church Cft BURY BL9....39 L8
Churchdale Rd BKLY M9....56 F8
Church Dr PWCH M25....55 J8
Churchfield WGNNW/ST WN6....30 D6
Churchfield Cl RAD M26....54 C3
Churchfield Rd SLFD M6....71 G6
Churchfields ALT WA14....116 D3
  DTN/ASHW M34....90 B5
  SALE M33....96 A6
Churchfield Wk OP/CLY M11 *....88 F4
Churchgate BOL BL1....2 F5
  STKP SK1....13 J4
  WILM/AE SK9....119 M8
Churchgate Buildings
  CMANE M1 *....7 L6
Church Gates WGN WN1....14 F4
Church Gn RAD M26....38 G8
  SLFD M6 *....86 C1
Church Green Gdns
  GOL/RIS/CUL WA3....79 K3
Church Gv HEY OL10....41 H4
  WGN WN1 *....15 K4
Churchill Av BOLE BL2....38 A3
  GOL/RIS/CUL WA3....81 L8
Churchill Cl HEY OL10....41 H4
Churchill Crs MPL/ROM SK6....114 A5
  RDSH SK5....100 B3
Churchill Dr BOLS/LL BL3....53 M1
  FWTH BL4....52 C2
Churchill Rd ALT WA14....108 A5
Churchill St BOLE BL2 *....3 M4
  HTNM SK4....112 A1
  OLDE OL4....9 L7
  OLDE OL4....9 M8
  ROCH OL11....27 M3
Churchill St East OLDE OL4....9 M7
Churchill Wy SLFD M6....86 D2
  TRPK M17....85 M5
Churchlands La
  WGNNW/ST WN6....31 J3
Church La BKLY M9....73 H5
  BNG/LEV M19....99 J6
  BRAM/HZG SK7....128 A2
  BRO M7....71 J3
  GOL/RIS/CUL WA3....80 A5
  MILN OL16....10 E5
  MOSL OL5....77 G3
  MPL/ROM SK6....113 M2
  MPL/ROM SK6....114 B6
  MPL/ROM SK6....114 D7
  NM/HAY SK22....124 E4
  OLD OL1....9 J5
  PWCH M25....55 K8
  SALE M33....96 D6
  WGNNW/ST WN6....30 D6
  WHTF M45....55 H4
  WILM/AE SK9....130 D2
Church Mdw BOLE BL2....37 J7
Church Ms DTN/ASHW M34....101 H1
Church Rd BOL BL1....35 L2
  CHD/CHDH SK8....110 D7
  CHD/CHDH SK8....120 D5
  ECC M30....85 J5
  FWTH BL4....53 H4
  HTNM SK4....12 F3
  HYDE SK14....92 G8
  MDTN M24....58 A5
  MILN OL16....11 J6
  MPL/ROM SK6....115 H6
  NM/HAY SK22....124 E5
  RAD M26....53 K4
  RAMS BL0....19 H4
  RNFD/HAY WA11....78 B6
  ROY/SHW OL2....43 L4
  SALE M33....97 G8
  TYLD M29....67 H7
  UPML OL3....61 H7
  UPML OL3....61 M4

URM M41....95 K4
  URM M41....96 A3
  WALK M28....69 G1
  WGNE/HIN WN2....64 E1
  WILM/AE SK9....126 C8
  WILM/AE SK9....127 H1
  WYTH/NTH M22....110 B3
Church Rd East SALE M33....97 G8
Churchside Cl BKLY M9....73 G2
Church Stile MILN OL16....10 E5
Churchston Av BRAM/HZG SK7....121 J1
Church St ALT WA14....108 A7
  ANC M4....7 H3
  AUL OL6....90 F2
  BOLE BL2....23 C7
  BOLE BL2....38 A5
  BOLS/LL BL3....3 J1
  BURY BL9....5 J1
  CHD/CHDH SK8....111 G6
  DROY M43....89 L3
  DTN/ASHW M34 *....90 C5
  DUK SK16....90 E4
  ECC M30....85 H2
  FAIL M35....74 C4
  FWTH BL4....53 H5
  GLSP SK13....93 J5
  GLSP SK13....93 K8
  GLSP SK13....105 G2
  GOL/RIS/CUL WA3....79 L3
  HEY OL10....41 G2
  HOR/BR BL6....34 F3
  HOR/BR BL6....33 M1
  HTNM SK4....13 G1
  HYDE SK14....102 A3
  LEIGH WN7....66 C7
  LIT OL15....21 M7
  MDTN M24....57 K2
  MILN OL16....29 G1
  MILN OL16....29 L8
  MPL/ROM SK6....101 K7
  MPL/ROM SK6....114 C7
  NEWLW WA12....79 H8
  NM/HAY SK22....125 M2
  OLDE OL4....60 B7
  RAMS BL0....18 F6
  ROY/SHW OL2....43 G8
  STLY SK15....91 K2
  STRET M32....96 F3
  SWIN M27....70 B4
  SWIN M27....70 E4
  TOT/BURYW BL8....24 C7
  UPML OL3....45 H8
  WGN WN1....15 G3
  WGNE/HIN WN2....32 E6
  WGNE/HIN WN2....49 G7
  WGNNW/ST WN6....31 H3
  WGNS/IIMK WN3....15 M7
  WGNW/BIL/OR WN5....46 A7
  WGNW/BIL/OR WN5....46 E6
  WHIT OL12....10 C5
  WHIT OL12....12 C4
  WHTN BL5....50 B3
  WILM/AE SK9....126 F5
Church St East OLDE OL4....60 B4
  RAD M26....38 F8
Church St South GLSP SK13....105 H2
Church St West RAD M26....54 E1
Church Ter MILN OL16....29 K7
  OLD OL1....9 J5
  SALE M33....96 D6
Church Vw HYDE SK14....102 A3
  IRL M44....94 D2
  WHIT OL12....27 H2
Church Wk ALT WA14....108 A7
  FWTH BL4....53 H5
  STLY SK15....91 K1
  SWIN M27....54 C8
  TOT/BURYW BL8 *....24 A3
Churchward Sq HOR/BR BL6....33 M2
Churchwood Rd
  DID/WITH M20....110 E1
Churnet St NEWH/MOS M40....73 G7
Churnett Cl WHTN BL5....50 C2
Churning Ter IRL M44....94 E1
Churston Av BKLY M9....57 H8
Churton Av SALE M33....108 B1
Churton Gv WGNNW/ST WN6....30 E2
Churton Rd GTN M18....99 H1
Churwell Av HTNM SK4....99 J8
Cicero St BKLY M9....73 H4
  OLD OL1....9 L1
Cinnamon St WHIT OL12....10 A2
Cinder Hl BURY BL9 *....25 L8
Cinder Hill La OLD OL1....58 D1
Cinder St ANC M4 *....7 L1
Cinnabar Dr MDTN M24....57 J2
Cinnamon Av WGNE/HIN WN2....49 K8
Cinnamon Cl WYTH/NTH M22....110 B4
Cipher St ANC M4....7 L1
Circle St TRPK M17....86 B6
The Circuit CHD/CHDH SK8....120 D5
  DID/WITH M20....98 E7
  EDGY/DAV SK3....111 M4
  WILM/AE SK9....126 B7
  WILM/AE SK9....130 E1
Circular Rd DID/WITH M20....98 F7
  DTN/ASHW M34....101 H3
  PWCH M25....71 L3
Circus St CMANE M1 *....7 J5
Cirencester Cl LHULT M38....52 D6
Ciss La URM M41....96 B2
Citrus Wy SLFD M6....86 D2
City Av DTN/ASHW M34....101 H2
City Gdns DTN/ASHW M34 *....101 H2
  WALK M28....68 D4
  WGNW/BIL/OR WN5....46 E5
City Rd East HULME M15....6 E6
City Wk SWIN M27....70 E4
Clacton Wk BRUN/LGST M13 *....87 L6
Clague St OP/CLY M11....88 D2
Claife Av NEWH/MOS M40....73 J4
Clammerclough Rd FWTH BL4....53 J4
Clandon Av ECC M30....84 E2
Clanwood Cl WGNS/IIMK WN3....63 H2
Clapgate MPL/ROM SK6....114 B5
Clap Gate La WGNS/IIMK WN3....63 H1
Clapgate Rd ROCH OL11....27 H3
Clapham St NEWH/MOS M40....73 M4
Clara Gorton Ct MILN OL16....11 K6
Clara St CHAD OL9....58 F8
  ROCH OL11....10 E9
  WHIT OL12....20 B3
Clare Av WILM/AE SK9....127 G1
Clarebank BOL BL1....35 J5
Clare Cl TOT/BURYW BL8....25 G1

Claremont Av ALT WA14....108 A4
  DID/WITH M20....98 C7
  HTNM SK4....99 M7
  MPL/ROM SK6....113 M6
  WGNE/HIN WN2....49 J1
Claremont Ct BOL BL1 *....36 B3
Claremont Dr ALT WA14....108 B4
  LHULT M38....52 E7
Claremont Gdns AUL OL6....76 B8
Claremont Gv DID/WITH M20....110 D1
  HALE/TIMP WA15....117 G1
Claremont Range GTN M18 *....89 J7
Claremont Rd CHD/CHDH SK8....120 C4
  GOL/RIS/CUL WA3....81 G8
  MILN OL16....29 J7
  OLDTF/WHR M16....98 C1
  ROCH OL11....27 M5
  SALE M33....96 E7
  SLFD M6....70 E8
  WGNW/BIL/OR WN5....62 B7
Claremont St AUL OL6....76 B8
  CHAD OL9....8 C1
  FAIL M35....74 C4
  OLDS OL8....75 J2
  SLFD M6....70 F6
Clarence Ar AUL OL6 *....90 F2
Clarence Av OLDS OL8....59 G8
  TRPK M17....85 J6
  WHTF M45....55 K5
Clarence Ct BOL BL1 *....2 C3
Clarence Rd AUL OL6....126 E6
  BRUN/LGST M13....99 H1
  HALE/TIMP WA15....117 H1
  HTNM SK4....99 L7
  SWIN M27....69 M5
Clarence St AIMK WN4....63 J8
  ATH M46....67 H3
  BOL BL1....2 E3
  BRO M7....72 A4
  CMANW M2 *....6 F5
  FWTH BL4....53 H3
  GOL/RIS/CUL WA3....79 K3
  HYDE SK14....91 H8
  LEIGH WN7....66 E8
  NEWLW WA12....78 E8
  ROY/SHW OL2....59 K1
  STLY SK15....91 H3
  WGNE/HIN WN2....48 D5
  WHIT OL12....28 A2
Clarence Yd WGN WN1....14 F4
Clarendon Av
  HALE/TIMP WA15....108 B7
  HTNM SK4....111 L1
Clarendon Cottages
  WILM/AE SK9....126 E1
Clarendon Crs ECC M30....85 J1
  SALE M33....97 G7
Clarendon Gv BOLE BL2....3 J7
Clarendon Pl HYDE SK14....102 B2
Clarendon Rd BOLE BL2....3 M5
  BRAM/HZG SK7....122 B1
  DTN/ASHW M34....89 L5
  DTN/ASHW M34....101 L2
  ECC M30....85 J1
  HYDE SK14....102 A1
  IRL M44....94 B5
  OLDTF/WHR M16....97 M2
  SALE M33....97 G8
  SWIN M27....70 C4
  URM M41....95 H1
Clarendon Rd West CCHDY M21....97 L2
Clarendon St BOLS/LL BL3....2 E5
  BURY BL9....5 H1
  DUK SK16....90 E4
  HULME M15....87 H6
  HYDE SK14....102 A1
  MILN OL16....28 E8
  MOSL OL5....77 G4
  RDSH SK5....112 C1
  WHTF M45....55 J4
Clare Rd BNG/LEV M19....99 K4
  RDSH SK5....100 C3
Clare St CMANE M1....7 K8
  DTN/ASHW M34....90 B3
  ORD M5....86 B7
Claribel St OP/CLY M11....88 B4
Claridge Rd CCHDY M21....97 K3
Clarington Gv WGN WN1....15 K5
Clarion St ANC M4....7 L1
Clark Av GTN M18....89 H7
Clarke Av GOL/RIS/CUL WA3....81 J8
  ORD M5....86 B5
Clarke Brow MDTN M24....57 K2
Clarke Crs HALE/TIMP WA15....117 K1
  LHULT M38....52 E7
Clarkes Cft BURY BL9....39 M1
Clarke's La WHIT OL12....10 B2
Clarke St AULW OL7 *....90 C4
  BOL BL1....35 M4
  HEY OL10....41 G2
  LEIGH WN7....66 B8
  WHIT OL12....28 E2
Clarksfield Rd OLDE OL4....59 M6
Clarksfield St OLDE OL4....59 M6
Clarkson Cl DTN/ASHW M34....101 G2
  MDTN M24....57 H2
Clark Wy HYDE SK14....102 A1
Clarkwell Cl OLD OL1....9 G5
Claude Rd CCHDY M21....97 J3
Claude St CHH M8....72 D5
  ECC M30....69 G8
  SWIN M27....70 A4
  WGNW/BIL/OR WN5....47 G6
Claudia Sq STLY SK15....77 H7
Claughton Av BOLE BL2....37 J5
  WALK M28....68 F4
Claughton Rd
  TOT/BURYW BL8....24 C7
Claverton Rd
  NTHM/RTH M23....109 H3
Claxton Av BKLY M9....73 G3
Clay Bank DROY M43....89 H3
Claybank Dr
  TOT/BURYW BL8....24 B5
Clay Bank St HEY OL10....40 F1
Claybar Dr ECC M30....85 H1
Claybridge Cl
  WGNW/BIL/OR WN5....46 E3
Claybrook Cl ATH M46....66 D2
Claybrook Wk OP/CLY M11 *....88 D3
Clayburn Rd HULME M15....87 H6
Claycourt Av ECC M30....69 L8
Claydon Dr RAD M26....37 L7
  WGNS/IIMK WN3....48 C3
Clayfield Dr ROCH OL11....27 J4
Claygate Dr BKLY M9....57 G7
Clayhill Gv
  GOL/RIS/CUL WA3....80 E4
Claylands Cl HYDE SK14....93 G8

Clay La HALE/TIMP WA15 .......108 F8
NTHM/RTH M23 .......109 J8
ROCH OL11 .......27 H4
WILM/AE SK9 .......119 J2
WILM/AE SK9 .......126 A8
Claymere Av ROCH OL11 .......27 H4
Claymore St BOLS/LL BL3 .......52 C1
GTN M18 .......89 H6
Claypool Rd HOR/BR BL6 .......34 B3
Clay St EDGW/EG BL7 .......22 D5
LIT OL15 .......21 K7
OLDS OL8 .......59 H8
Claythorpe Wk PWCH M25 .......72 B2
Clayton Av BOLE BL2 .......3 J9
DID/WITH M20 .......110 E1
GOL/RIS/CUL WA3 .......80 B4
Claytonbrook Rd
OP/CLY M11 .......88 F3
Clayton Cl HULME M15 .......87 H7
Clayton Hall Rd OP/CLY M11 .......88 E4
TOT/BURYW BL8 .......38 C3
Clayton House Rd SWIN M27 .......54 B8
Clayton La OP/CLY M11 .......88 E4
Clayton La South
WGTN/LGST M12 .......88 D5
Claytons Cl OLDE OL4 .......60 C5
Clayton St BOLE BL2 .......3 K9
CHAD OL9 .......74 D1
DTN/ASHW M34 .......101 J2
DUK SK16 .......91 H1
FAIL M35 .......74 B5
OP/CLY M11 .......88 E1
WGNS/IIMK WN3 .......14 D4
WHIT OL12 .......28 E2
Cleabarrow Dr
WALK M28 .......68 D7
Cleadon Av GTN M18 .......88 F8
Cleadon Dr South
TOT/BURYW BL8 .......24 F7
Clearwater Dr
DID/WITH M20 .......98 C7
Cleavley St ECC M30 .......84 E2
Clee Av BRUN/LGST M13 .......99 J2
Cleethorpes Av BKLY M9 .......72 E1
Cleeve Rd NTHM/RTH M23 .......109 K2
OLDE OL4 .......59 M6
Cleeve Wy CHD/CHDH SK8 .......120 D6
Clegg Hall Rd MILN OL16 .......29 G2
Clegg Pl AUL OL6 .......76 A8
Clegg's Buildings BOL BL1 * .......2 C3
Clegg's La LHULT M38 .......52 D7
Clegg St BOLE BL2 .......3 M5
DROY M43 * .......89 J3
LIT OL15 .......21 K5
MILN OL16 .......29 K7
MPL/ROM SK6 .......113 J1
OLD OL1 .......9 K6
OLDE OL4 .......60 D6
TYLD M29 .......67 K6
WHIT OL12 .......20 A2
WHTF M45 .......55 J5
Cleggswood Av LIT OL15 .......29 K1
Clelland St FWTH BL4 .......53 H5
Clement Av ATH M46 .......50 E8
Clement Ct MILN OL16 .......11 K6
Clementina St WHIT OL12 .......10 E1
Clementine Cl SLFD M6 .......86 E2
Clement Rd MPL/ROM SK6 .......114 C5
Clement Royds St WHIT OL12 .......10 C3
Clement Stott Cl BKLY M9 .......57 J8
Clement St HTNM SK4 .......12 F1
Cleminson St CSLFD M3 .......6 B3
Clemshaw Cl HEY OL10 .......40 F3
Clerewood Av CHD/CHDH SK8 .......119 K5
Clerke St BURY BL9 .......4 F4
Clevedon Av GTN M18 .......88 F8
Clevedon Dr WGNS/IIMK WN3 .......46 F8
Clevedon Rd CHAD OL9 .......58 D3
Clevedon St BKLY M9 .......73 H5
Cleveland Av BNG/LEV M19 .......99 L2
HYDE SK14 * .......101 M2
SLFD M6 .......85 M1
WGNS/IIMK WN3 .......14 A3
Cleveland Cl RAMS BL0 .......24 F1
Cleveland Dr WHN4 .......63 M8
GOL/RIS/CUL WA3 .......80 A8
MILN OL16 .......29 K6
Cleveland Gdns BOLS/LL BL3 .......35 L8
Cleveland Gv ROY/SHW OL2 .......58 F2
Cleveland Rd CHH M8 .......72 E2
HALE/TIMP WA15 .......117 H1
HTNM SK4 .......99 K8
Cleveland St BOLS/LL BL3 * .......35 L8
Cleveleys Av BOLE BL2 .......4 D9
BURY BL9 .......4 D9
CCHDY M21 .......97 M5
CHD/CHDH SK8 .......119 K3
MILN OL16 .......42 E1
Cleveleys Gv BRO M7 .......72 B5
Cleves Ct HEY OL10 .......40 F3
Clevlands Cl TYLD M29 .......67 M8
Cleworth Cl MDTN M24 .......57 J2
Cleworth St HULME M15 * .......6 A9
Cleworth Wk HULME M15 .......6 A9
Clibran St CHH M8 .......72 E6
Clifden Dr WYTH/NTH M22 .......119 G2
Cliff Av BRO M7 .......71 M6
BURY BL9 .......25 G2
TOT/BURYW BL8 .......24 B5
Cliff Crs BRO M7 .......71 M6
Cliff Dl STLY SK15 .......91 J4
Cliffdale Dr CHH M8 .......72 D3
Cliffe Rd GLSP SK13 .......105 G5
Cliff Gv HTNM SK4 .......99 L8
Cliff Hill Rd ROY/SHW OL2 .......43 M3
Cliffmere Cl CHD/CHDH SK8 .......120 B1
Clifford Av DTN/ASHW M34 .......90 B7
HALE/TIMP WA15 .......108 D6
Clifford Rd BOLS/LL BL3 * .......51 K2
POY/DIS SK12 .......121 L8
WILM/AE SK9 .......126 D6
Clifford St ECC M30 .......84 E4
LEIGH WN7 .......66 E8
ROCH OL11 .......10 F9
SWIN M27 .......70 E4
Cliff Rd WILM/AE SK9 .......126 F4
Cliff Side WILM/AE SK9 .......126 F4
Clifton Av CHD/CHDH SK8 .......119 J2
ECC M30 .......85 G1
HALE/TIMP WA15 .......108 B7
OLDE OL4 .......59 L7
RUSH/FAL M14 .......99 G4
TYLD M29 .......67 K3
Clifton Cl HEY OL10 .......40 F3
OLDE OL4 .......59 L7
OLDTF/WHR M16 .......87 G1
Clifton Ct FWTH BL4 .......52 E1
Clifton Crs ROY/SHW OL2 .......59 K1
WGN WN1 .......47 M2
Clifton Dr CHD/CHDH SK8 .......110 C7
CHD/CHDH SK8 .......119 J2

HOR/BR BL6 .......32 E1
MPL/ROM SK6 .......114 C5
SWIN M27 .......70 A2
WILM/AE SK9 .......126 C8
Clifton Gv
OLDTF/WHR M16 .......87 G7
SWIN M27 .......70 A2
Clifton Holmes UPML OL3 .......45 H7
Clifton House Rd SWIN M27 .......54 B8
Cliftonmill Mdw
GOL/RIS/CUL WA3 .......79 J4
Clifton Park Rd OFTN SK2 .......112 D7
Clifton Pl PWCH M25 * .......55 K7
Clifton Rd WN4 .......63 J6
CCHDY M21 .......97 M4
ECC M30 .......85 G1
HTNM SK4 .......99 K8
LEIGH WN7 .......81 H3
MDTN M24 .......42 A6
PWCH M25 .......55 H8
SALE M33 .......108 L1
URM M41 .......95 K2
WCNW/BIL/OR WN5 .......62 A8
Clifton St AUL OL6 .......90 D1
BOL BL1 .......2 C3
BURY BL9 .......25 J8
FAIL M35 .......74 D3
FWTH BL4 .......52 E2
FWTH BL4 .......53 J5
LEIGH WN7 .......66 A7
MILN OL16 .......29 J6
NEWH/MOS M40 .......73 J8
OLDTF/WHR M16 .......87 G7
ROCH OL11 * .......11 G9
TYLD M29 .......68 B4
UPML OL3 .......61 L7
WGN WN1 .......15 G1
WGNS/IIMK WN3 .......47 K8
WILM/AE SK9 .......130 D3
Clifton Vw SWIN M27 .......54 B8
Cliftonville Dr SWIN M27 .......70 E6
Cliftonville Rd MILN OL16 .......42 F4
Clinton Av RUSH/FAL M14 .......98 D2
Clinton Gdns RUSH/FAL M14 .......98 D2
Clinton St AUL OL6 * .......76 A8
Clinton Wk OLDE OL4 * .......9 L7
Clippers Quay SALQ M50 .......86 D6
Clipsley Crs OLDE OL4 .......44 C8
Clitson Wk BRAM/HZG SK7 .......121 J2
Clitheroe Cl HEY OL10 .......41 G1
Clitheroe Dr TOT/BURYW BL8 .......38 C2
Clitheroe Rd BRUN/LGST M13 .......99 J1
Clito St BKLY M9 .......73 J4
Clive Av WHTF M45 .......55 H3
Clivedale Pl BOL BL1 .......2 F5
Clively Av SWIN M27 .......70 E3
Clive Rd FAIL M35 .......74 B5
WHTN BL5 .......50 B6
Clive St ANC M4 .......7 J1
AULW OL7 .......75 K7
BOL BL1 .......35 L5
OLDS OL8 .......75 G2
Clivia Gv BRO M7 * .......72 A6
Cloak St CMANE M1 .......7 H8
Clock House Av DROY M43 .......89 H1
Clockhouse Ms DROY M43 * .......89 H1
Clock St CHAD OL9 .......74 E2
Clock Tower Cl HYDE SK14 .......102 B3
WALK M28 .......68 C1
Cloister Cl DUK SK16 .......90 F6
Cloister Rd HTNM SK4 .......111 L2
The Cloisters CHD/CHDH SK8 .......111 K7
MILN OL16 .......28 E3
SALE M33 .......97 G8
WHTN BL5 .......50 B7
Cloister St BKLY M9 .......73 J4
BOL BL1 .......35 M2
Clondberry Cl TYLD M29 .......68 B3
Clopton Wk HULME M15 .......87 H6
Closebrook Rd
WGNW/BIL/OR WN5 .......47 G6
Close La WGNE/HIN WN2 .......65 J1
WGNE/HIN WN2 .......65 L3
Closes Farm BOLS/LL BL3 .......51 L2
Close St WGNE/HIN WN2 .......49 J8
The Close ALT WA14 .......107 M7
ATH M46 .......51 J7
BOLE BL2 .......36 E1
DTN/ASHW M34 .......90 A8
MDTN M24 .......57 L1
MPL/ROM SK6 .......114 E2
STLY SK15 .......76 C8
TOT/BURYW BL8 .......38 A3
Clothorn Rd DID/WITH M20 .......98 E8
Cloudstock Gv LHULT M38 .......52 B7
Clough Av LEIGH WN7 .......66 E7
WILM/AE SK9 .......127 H3
Clough Bank BKLY M9 * .......73 G2
Cloughbank RAD M26 .......53 M5
Clough Dr PWCH M25 .......55 J8
Clough End Rd HYDE SK14 .......103 J3
Cloughfield Av ORD M5 .......86 E4
Cloughfold RAD M26 .......53 L5
Clough Fold Rd HYDE SK14 .......101 M3
Clough Ga HYDE SK14 * .......102 C4
OLDS OL8 .......75 G2
Clough Gv AIMK WN4 .......63 J7
WHTF M45 .......55 G2
Clough House Dr LEIGH WN7 .......66 E7
Clough House La WHIT OL12 .......20 F6
Clough La HEY OL10 .......26 F8
OLDE OL4 .......61 H6
PWCH M25 .......55 J8
Clough Meadow BOL BL1 .......35 G6
MPL/ROM SK6 .......101 M7
Clough Meadow Rd RAD M26 .......54 B1
Clough Park Av OLDE OL4 .......61 H6
Clough Rd BKLY M9 .......73 J4
DROY M43 .......89 L2
FAIL M35 .......74 D5
LIT OL15 .......21 L4
MDTN M24 .......57 K2
ROY/SHW OL2 .......44 A6
Cloughs Av OLDE OL4 .......58 A4
Clough Side MPL/ROM SK6 .......114 C5
Cloughside POY/DIS SK12 .......124 A6
Clough St FWTH BL4 .......53 J5
MDTN M24 .......57 L2
NEWH/MOS M40 .......73 M8
RAD M26 .......54 F3
WHIT OL12 .......21 G6
Clough Ter LIT OL15 .......21 L5
The Clough AIMK WN4 .......63 G8
AULW OL7 .......75 K6
BOL BL1 * .......35 H4
RDSH SK5 .......100 E6
Clough Top Rd BKLY M9 .......73 K2
Cloughwood Crs
WGNNW/ST WN6 .......30 A5

Clovelly Av LEIGH WN7 .......66 C4
OLDS OL8 .......74 F2
Clovelly Rd CCHDY M21 .......97 M4
OFTN SK2 .......112 F4
SWIN M27 .......69 M5
Clovelly St NEWH/MOS M40 .......74 A7
ROCH OL11 .......41 L1
Clover Av EDGY/DAV SK3 .......112 A8
Cloverbank Av BNG/LEV M19 .......99 G3
Clover Crs OLDS OL8 .......75 M1
Clover Cft SALE M33 .......109 G3
Cloverdale Dr AIMK WN4 .......78 F2
Cloverdale Sq BOL BL1 .......35 K3
Clover Hall Crs MILN OL16 .......11 M1
Cloverley Dr HALE/TIMP WA15 .......108 D8
Clover Rd HALE/TIMP WA15 .......108 B1
MPL/ROM SK6 .......114 B1
Clover St WGNNW/ST WN6 .......47 K2
WHIT OL12 .......10 D3
Clover Vw MILN OL16 .......11 K3
Clowes St CHAD OL9 .......74 D2
CSLFD M3 .......6 D7
WGTN/LGST M12 .......88 D6
Club St OP/CLY M11 .......89 K5
Clumber Cl POY/DIS SK12 .......129 J1
Clumber Rd GTN M18 .......89 J8
POY/DIS SK12 .......129 J1
Clunton Av BOLS/LL BL3 .......35 L8
Clutha Rd EDGY/DAV SK3 .......112 C8
Clwyd Av EDGY/DAV SK3 .......12 F9
Clyde Av WHTF M45 .......55 J4
Clyde Ct MILN OL16 .......11 J6
Clyde Rd DID/WITH M20 .......98 C8
EDGY/DAV SK3 .......12 D8
RAD M26 .......38 C7
TYLD M29 .......67 M5
Clydesdale St OLDS OL8 .......59 H8
Clyde St AULW OL7 .......90 C3
BOL BL1 * .......36 B2
LEIGH WN7 .......66 E8
OLD OL1 .......59 M3
Clyde Ter RAD M26 * .......38 C7
Clyne St STRET M32 .......86 C7
Coach House Dr
WGNNW/ST WN6 .......30 E6
Coach La ROCH OL11 .......27 H7
Coach Rd HYDE SK14 .......92 F7
TYLD M29 .......67 M6
Coach St ATH M46 .......67 G1
Coalbrook Wk WGTN/LGST M12 .......88 A4
Coalburn St WGTN/LGST M12 .......88 D7
Coal Pit La ATH M46 .......66 E1
LEIGH WN7 .......66 B4
OLDS OL8 .......75 G5
Coal Rd RAMS BL0 .......19 K4
Coalshaw Green Rd CHAD OL9 .......74 D1
Coatbridge St OP/CLY M11 .......88 F3
Cobalt Av URM M41 .......85 J6
Cobb Cl CHH M8 .......72 B1
Cobbett's Wy WILM/AE SK9 .......126 D8
Cobble Bank BKLY M9 .......72 F1
Cobden St AUL OL6 * .......91 G2
BKLY M9 .......73 H3
BOL BL1 .......36 A1
BURY BL9 .......5 H2
CHAD OL9 .......8 B5
EDGW/EG BL7 * .......22 A2
HEY OL10 .......41 G3
NEWLW WA12 .......79 G8
OLDE OL4 .......60 A3
RAD M26 .......38 C6
SLFD M6 .......71 J8
TYLD M29 .......67 K5
Coberley Av URM M41 .......84 C8
Cob Hall Rd STRET M32 .......96 F3
Cobham Av BOLS/LL BL3 .......52 A1
NEWH/MOS M40 .......73 M2
Coblers Hl UPML OL3 .......45 J7
Cob Moor Av
WGNW/BIL/OR WN5 .......62 A3
Cob Moor Rd
WGNW/BIL/OR WN5 .......62 A3
Cobourg St CMANE M1 .......7 J7
Coburg Av BRO M7 .......72 A8
Cochrane Av WGTN/LGST M12 .......88 B7
Cochrane St BOLS/LL BL3 .......2 F5
Cock Brow HYDE SK14 .......102 F5
Cock Clod St RAD M26 .......54 F1
Cockcroft St BKLY M9 .......73 G3
Cockerell Springs BOLE BL2 * .......3 G6
Cocker Hl STLY SK15 .......91 L2
Cocker Mill La ROY/SHW OL2 .......43 J7
Cockers La STLY SK15 .......92 B4
Cocker St LHULT M38 .......52 D8
Cockey Moor Rd BOLE BL2 .......38 A3
Cockhall La WHIT OL12 .......20 A3
Coconut Gv SLFD M6 .......86 D2
Codale Dr BOLE BL2 .......37 J4
Coddington Av OP/CLY M11 .......89 H4
Code La WHTN BL5 .......33 L8
Coe St BOLS/LL BL3 .......2 E8
Coghlan Cl OP/CLY M11 * .......88 F2
Coin St ROY/SHW OL2 .......43 H8
Colborne Av ECC M30 .......84 E2
MPL/ROM SK6 .......113 L2
RDSH SK5 .......100 C1
Colbourne Av HYDE SK14 .......103 H2
Colbourne Gv HYDE SK14 .......103 H2
Colburn Rd WGNS/IIMK WN3 .......63 K2
Colby Rd WGNS/IIMK WN3 .......63 K2
Colchester Av BOLE BL2 .......37 H4
Colchester Cl NTHM/RTH M23 .......109 K3
Colchester Dr FWTH BL4 .......52 C3
Colchester Pl HTNM SK4 .......12 B1
Colchester Wk OLD OL1 * .......9 J4
Colclough Cl NEWH/MOS M40 .......73 L6
Colclough La TYLD M29 .......67 L7
Coldfield Dr NTHM/RTH M23 .......109 J6
Cold Greave Cl MILN OL16 .......29 M8
Coldhurst St OLD OL1 .......9 G2
Coldstone Dr AIMK WN4 .......63 G8
Coldstream Av BKLY M9 .......57 G8
Cole Av NEWLW WA12 .......78 F8
Colebrook Dr NEWH/MOS M40 .......73 K6
Colebrook Rd
HALE/TIMP WA15 .......108 D6
Coleby Av OLDTF/WHR M16 .......86 F8
NTHM/RTH M22 .......119 H3
Colclough Pl
GOL/RIS/CUL WA3 .......81 J8
Coldale Dr MDTN M24 .......56 F2
Coleford Gv BOL BL1 .......2 C6
Colemore Av DID/WITH M20 .......111 G3
Colenso Ct BOLE BL2 .......3 M4
Colenso Gv HTNM SK4 .......12 A1
Colenso St OLDS OL8 .......75 G1
Coleport Cl CHD/CHDH SK8 .......120 C3
Coleridge Av MDTN M24 .......57 M1
RAD M26 .......54 B1
WGNW/BIL/OR WN5 .......46 D6

Coleridge Cl RDSH SK5 .......100 B3
Coleridge Rd LIT OL15 .......29 J2
OLD OL1 .......44 B8
OLDTF/WHR M16 .......97 M1
RDSH SK5 .......100 B3
TOT/BURYW BL8 .......24 C2
WGNW/BIL/OR WN5 .......62 A3
Colerne Wy
WGNS/IIMK WN3 .......63 G2
Colesbourne Cl LHULT M38 .......52 D6
Coleshill Ri WGNS/IIMK WN3 .......62 F7
Coleshill St NEWH/MOS M40 .......88 B1
Cole St NEWH/MOS M40 .......73 J4
Colgate Crs RUSH/FAL M14 .......98 E4
Colgate La ORD M5 .......86 D6
Colgrove Av NEWH/MOS M40 .......73 M2
Colina Dr BRO M7 .......72 B7
Colindale Av BKLY M9 .......57 H8
Colindale Cl BOLS/LL BL3 * .......35 M7
Colin Brd HTNM SK4 .......100 B8
Colin St WGN WN1 .......15 J3
Colinton Cl BOL BL1 .......36 A3
Colinwood Cl BURY BL9 .......55 J1
Collard St ATH M46 .......50 E8
Coll Dr URM M41 .......85 G7
College Av OLDS OL8 .......75 G1
WGN WN1 .......15 G5
College Cl BOLS/LL BL3 .......2 D7
OFTN SK2 .......112 E6
WILM/AE SK9 .......126 C4
College Dr OLDTF/WHR M16 .......97 M2
College Rd ECC M30 .......85 K2
OLDS OL8 .......59 G8
OLDTF/WHR M16 .......97 M2
WHIT OL12 .......10 B4
College St LEIGH WN7 .......66 D7
College Wy BOLS/LL BL3 .......2 C7
Collegiate Wy SWIN M27 .......70 C1
Collen Crs TOT/BURYW BL8 .......24 E6
Collett Cl WGN WN1 .......15 K4
Collett St OLD OL1 .......59 M4
Colley St MILN OL16 .......11 H1
STRET M32 .......86 C7
Collie Av SLFD M6 .......71 M7
Collier Av MILN OL16 .......29 J5
Collier Cl HYDE SK14 .......103 H3
Collier Hl OLDS OL8 .......75 G1
Collier Hill Av OLDS OL8 .......74 F1
Colliers Ct LEIGH WN7 .......81 H1
Collier's Ct ROCH OL11 .......42 E3
Collier St CSLFD M3 .......6 D7
GLSP SK13 .......104 F4
SWIN M27 .......70 B5
WGNE/HIN WN2 .......49 G6
Colliery La ATH M46 .......50 D8
Colliery St OP/CLY M11 .......88 D3
Collin Av GTN M18 .......88 F8
Collingburn Av ORD M5 .......86 E5
Colling Cl IRL M44 .......94 D3
Collinge Av MDTN M24 .......57 M4
Collinge St HEY OL10 .......40 F2
MDTN M24 .......58 A5
ROY/SHW OL2 * .......43 L5
TOT/BURYW BL8 .......24 E8
WGNE/HIN WN2 .......64 D2
Collingham St CHH M8 .......72 B8
Colling St RAMS BL0 .......18 E7
Collington Cl WGTN/LGST M12 .......88 D7
Collingwood Av DROY M43 .......89 H1
Collingwood Cl POY/DIS SK12 .......129 L1
Collingwood Dr SWIN M27 .......70 D5
Collingwood Rd BNG/LEV M19 .......99 G3
Collingwood St ROCH OL11 .......41 M4
WGNNW/ST WN6 .......31 H3
Collingwood Wy OLD OL1 * .......9 J2
WHTN BL5 .......50 B7
Collins La WHTN BL5 .......50 C6
Collins St TOT/BURYW BL8 .......24 C8
Collins Wy CHAD OL9 .......74 F1
Collisdene Rd
WGNW/BIL/OR WN5 .......46 A6
Collop Dr HEY OL10 .......41 H5
Coll's La UPML OL3 .......45 G8
Collyhurst Av WALK M28 .......69 H2
Collyhurst Rd
NEWH/MOS M40 .......72 E8
Collyhurst St NEWH/MOS M40 .......72 E8
Colman Gdns ORD M5 .......86 E5
Colmore Dr BKLY M9 .......57 K8
Colmore Gv BOLE BL2 .......22 E8
Colmore St BOLE BL2 .......36 E1
Colnbrook WGNNW/ST WN6 .......30 E3
Colne Rd ROCH OL11 .......42 A3
Colonial Rd OFTN SK2 .......112 D6
Colshaw Dr WILM/AE SK9 .......127 H3
Colshaw Rd NTHM/RTH M23 .......109 K7
Colson Dr MDTN M24 .......57 L5
Colt Hill La UPML OL3 .......61 J4
Coltsfoot Cl LEIGH WN7 .......66 E7
Coltsfoot Dr ALT WA14 .......107 L4
Columbia Av GTN M18 .......89 J8
Columbia Rd BOL BL1 .......35 M4
Columbia St OLDS OL8 .......59 J8
Columbine Cl WHIT OL12 .......27 M1
Columbine St OP/CLY M11 .......89 G5
Colville Dr TOT/BURYW BL8 .......38 E3
Colville Gv HALE/TIMP WA15 .......108 D6
SALE M33 .......108 B3
Colville Rd OLD OL1 .......59 G3
Colwell Av STRET M32 .......96 E3
Colwick Av ALT WA14 .......108 B6
Colwith Av BOLE BL2 .......37 H3
Colwyn Av MDTN M24 .......57 K6
RUSH/FAL M14 .......99 H4
Colwyn Crs RDSH SK5 .......100 C7
Colwyn Dr WGNE/HIN WN2 .......65 M2
Colwyn Gv ATH M46 .......50 F7
Colwyn Rd BRAM/HZG SK7 .......121 H4
CHD/CHDH SK8 .......120 A3
SWIN M27 .......69 M6
Colwyn St CHAD OL9 .......8 B1
ROCH OL11 .......41 L2
SLFD M6 .......86 C1
Combe Cl OP/CLY M11 .......88 C1
Combermere Av
DID/WITH M20 .......98 D5
Combermere Cl
CHD/CHDH SK8 .......111 J8
TYLD M29 .......67 L2
Combermere St DUK SK16 .......90 F3
Combs Cl NM/HAY SK22 .......124 C4
Combs Ms GLSP SK13 .......104 A3
Comer Ter SALE M33 .......96 D8
Comet Rd
WGNW/BIL/OR WN5 .......46 F4
Comet St CMANE M1 .......7 K5
Commercial Av
CHD/CHDH SK8 .......120 A7
Commercial Brow HYDE SK14 .......91 H3
Commercial Rd
BRAM/HZG SK7 .......121 M1

Commercial St CHAD OL9 .......8 D7
CSLFD M3 .......6 D8
HYDE SK14 .......102 B3
Commodore Pl
WGNW/BIL/OR WN5 .......47 H3
Common La GOL/RIS/CUL WA3 .......81 G8
LEIGH WN7 .......65 H3
PART M31 .......94 F8
TYLD M29 .......67 K3
Common Nook WGNE/HIN WN2 .......48 D6
Common Side Rd WALK M28 .......68 C5
Common St WHTN BL5 .......49 L5
Commonwealth Cl LEIGH WN7 .......81 K1
Community St AULW OL7 .......90 C3
Como St BOLS/LL BL3 * .......35 M8
Como Wk GTN M18 .......88 E6
Compass St OP/CLY M11 .......88 F5
Compstall Av RUSH/FAL M14 .......98 E3
Compstall Gv GTN M18 .......89 H6
Compstall Mills Est
MPL/ROM SK6 * .......114 C2
Compton Cl URM M41 * .......94 F3
Compton Dr NTHM/RTH M23 * .......118 C3
Compton Fold ROY/SHW OL2 .......43 M3
Compton Wy MDTN M24 .......57 M5
Comus St ORD M5 .......86 F4
Concert La CMANW M2 .......7 G5
Concord Av WGNS/IIMK WN3 .......63 L1
Concord Pl SLFD M6 .......71 K7
Condor Cl DROY M43 * .......89 M1
Condor Pl SLFD M6 .......71 K7
Conduit Wk BRUN/LGST M13 * .......87 L6
Conduit St AUL OL6 .......90 F2
GLSP SK13 .......93 J5
OLD OL1 .......60 A1
Conewood Wk
BRUN/LGST M13 .......87 M6
Coney Gv NTHM/RTH M23 .......109 K5
Coneymead STLY SK15 .......76 D8
Congham Rd EDGY/DAV SK3 .......12 C7
Congleton Av RUSH/FAL M14 .......98 D2
Congleton Cl WILM/AE SK9 .......130 E6
Congleton Rd MCFLDN SK10 .......130 D6
Congou St CMANE M1 .......7 L5
Congreave St OLD OL1 * .......9 G3
Congresbury Rd LEIGH WN7 .......66 A5
Coningsby Dr BKLY M9 .......73 G4
Coningsby Gdns
GOL/RIS/CUL WA3 .......80 B4
Conisber Cl EDGW/EG BL7 .......22 B3
Conisborough ROCH OL11 .......10 C7
Conisborough Pl WHTF M45 .......55 L5
Coniston Av AIMK WN4 .......63 H6
ATH M46 .......51 G7
BKLY M9 .......73 G4
FWTH BL4 .......52 B5
HYDE SK14 .......90 F8
LHULT M38 .......52 D8
OLDS OL8 .......75 G1
SALE M33 .......108 F2
WGN WN1 .......47 L1
WGNE/HIN WN2 .......48 S3
WGNW/BIL/OR WN5 .......46 C5
WHTF M45 .......55 J4
Coniston Cl BOLS/LL BL3 .......37 K8
CHAD OL9 .......58 D5
DTN/ASHW M34 .......90 E2
RAMS BL0 .......18 F5
Coniston Dr BURY BL9 .......39 H3
MDTN M24 .......57 H2
STLY SK15 .......91 K1
WGNE/HIN WN2 .......64 E4
WILM/AE SK9 .......119 L8
Coniston Park Dr
WGNNW/ST WN6 .......31 K5
Coniston Rd CHD/CHDH SK8 .......110 E6
HOR/BR BL6 .......33 C1
MPL/ROM SK6 .......114 B8
PART M31 .......94 F8
RDSH SK5 .......100 C6
STRET M32 .......96 F1
SWIN M27 .......70 C6
TYLD M29 .......67 K5
URM M41 .......95 H4
WGNE/HIN WN2 .......49 H8
Coniston St LEIGH WN7 .......66 B5
NEWH/MOS M40 .......73 M7
SLFD M6 .......71 L8
Coniston Wk
HALE/TIMP WA15 .......109 G7
Conival Wy CHAD OL9 .......58 D3
Conmere Sq HULME M15 .......6 F9
Connaught Av BNG/LEV M19 .......99 J5
MILN OL16 .......11 L5
WHTF M45 .......55 K5
Connaught Cl WILM/AE SK9 .......127 G4
Connaught Sq BOLE BL2 .......36 E3
Connaught St OLDS OL8 .......9 H7
TOT/BURYW BL8 .......38 E3
Connel Cl BOLE BL2 .......37 J6
Connell Rd NTHM/RTH M23 .......109 K6
Connell Wy HEY OL10 * .......41 J1
Connery Crs AUL OL6 .......76 A6
Connie St OP/CLY M11 .......88 F4
Conningsby Cl EDGW/EG BL7 .......22 C3
Connington Av BKLY M9 .......73 G3
Connington Cl ROY/SHW OL2 .......42 F3
Connor Wy CHD/CHDH SK8 .......110 C8
Conrad Cl ROCH OL11 .......44 B8
WGNS/IIMK WN3 .......14 C9
Conran St BKLY M9 .......73 G5
Consort Av ROY/SHW OL2 .......42 F6
Consort Cl DUK SK16 .......90 F6
Consort Pl ALT WA14 .......116 C1
Constable Cl BOL BL1 .......36 A3
Constable Dr MPL/ROM SK6 .......114 E4
WILM/AE SK9 .......127 J4
Constable St GTN M18 .......89 H6
Constance Gdns ORD M5 .......86 C3
Constance Rd BOLS/LL BL3 .......35 M7
PART M31 .......106 C1
Constance St HULME M15 * .......6 D8
Constantia St WGNS/IIMK WN3 .......64 C1
Constantine La MILN OL16 .......10 F4
Constantine St OLDE OL4 .......60 A6
Consul St WYTH/NTH M22 .......110 B3
Convamore Rd
BRAM/HZG SK7 .......120 F6
Convent St OLDE OL4 .......59 M8
Convent St ROCH OL11 .......42 D4
Conway Av BOL BL1 .......35 K3
IRL M44 .......94 C4
SWIN M27 .......70 E2
WHTF M45 .......55 J3

Conway Cl HEY OL10 ....40 D1
 WN7 ....67 H5
 MDTN M24 ....57 K5
 OLDTF/WHR M16 * ....97 K1
 RAMS BL0 ....18 E6
Conway Crs
 TOT/BURYW BL8 ....24 C2
 WGNW/BIL/OR WN5 ....62 B6
Conway Dr
 BRAM/HZG SK7 ....121 L3
 BURY BL9 ....40 A2
 HALE/TIMP WA15 ....108 F6
 STLY SK15 ....91 K1
 WGNE/HIN WN2 ....33 G8
 WGNW/BIL/OR WN5 ....62 C7
Conway Gv CHAD OL9 ....58 C4
 CHD/CHDH SK8 ....120 G1
 SALE M33 ....109 G1
 URM M41 ....85 G8
 WGNE/HIN WN2 ....49 J8
Conway Rd AIMK WN4 ....64 B7
 CHD/CHDH SK8 ....120 C5
 LEIGH WN7 ....66 B3
 MILN OL16 ....28 E3
 OLDE OL4 ....59 M5
 WGNE/HIN WN2 ....64 D3
Conway St FWTH BL4 ....53 G5
 RDSH SK5 ....100 B8
 WGNW/BIL/OR WN5 ....46 F7
Conyngham Rd RUSH/FAL M14 ....88 A8
Cook Av RNFD/HAY WA11 ....78 B5
Cooke Cl AIMK WN4 ....63 J6
 BRAM/HZG SK7 ....121 M1
 DTN/ASHW M34 ....101 J1
 FAIL M35 ....74 C4
 FWTH BL4 ....53 H5
 HYDE SK14 ....91 J7
Cook St BURY BL9 ....5 G5
 CSLFD M3 ....6 C3
 DTN/ASHW M34 ....90 C6
 ECC M30 ....84 F2
 EDGY/DAV SK3 ....12 F5
 LEIGH WN7 ....66 C7
 MILN OL16 ....28 E3
 OLDE OL4 ....59 M5
 WGNE/HIN WN2 ....64 D3
Cook Ter MILN OL16 ....28 E3
Cooling La TYLD M29 ....67 G4
Coomassie St HEY OL10 ....40 F2
 RAD M26 ....54 D1
 SLFD M6 ....86 C1
Coombe Cl TYLD M29 ....67 L4
Coombes Av HYDE SK14 ....102 C3
 MPL/ROM SK6 ....114 C7
Coombes La GLSP SK13 ....103 M7
Coombes St OFTN SK2 ....112 E7
Coombes Vw HYDE SK14 ....103 H4
Co-operation St FAIL M35 ....74 C3
Co-operative St
 BRAM/HZG SK7 ....122 A1
 LEIGH WN7 ....66 A7
 LHULT M38 ....52 B7
 OLDE OL4 ....60 C6
 ROY/SHW OL2 * ....43 L5
 SLFD M6 ....86 C2
 UPML OL3 * ....61 L4
Cooper Fold MDTN M24 ....41 K8
Cooper La BKLY M9 ....57 J1
 MDTN M24 ....57 J1
Coopers Gln WGNE/HIN WN2 ....48 D4
Cooper St BRAM/HZG SK7 ....122 B1
 BRO M7 ....6 F5
 CMANW M2 ....6 F5
 DROY M43 ....89 H3
 DUK SK16 ....90 E3
 GLSP SK13 ....104 E4
 OFTN SK2 ....13 K8
 OLDE OL4 ....60 D5
 STRET M32 ....97 G3
 WHIT OL12 ....21 H8
Coopers Wk MILN OL16 ....28 F2
Cooper Ter MILN OL16 ....11 J2
Coop St ANC M4 ....7 J2
 BOL BL1 ....22 B8
 WGN WN1 ....
Copage Dr MPL/ROM SK6 ....101 K8
Cope Bank BOL BL1 ....35 M3
Cope Bank West BOL BL1 * ....35 L2
Cope Cl OP/CLY M11 ....89 H5
Copeland Av SWIN M27 ....70 D3
Copeland Cl MDTN M24 ....56 F3
Copeland Dr
 WGNNW/ST WN6 ....31 J4
Copeland Ms BOL BL1 * ....35 K5
Copeland Cl HYDE SK14 ....91 G7
Copeman Cl
 BRUN/LGST M13 ....87 M6
Copenhagen Sq
 MILN OL16 ....11 H3
Copenhagen St MILN OL16 ....11 H3
 NEWH/MOS M40 ....73 K6
Copesthorne Cl
 WGNE/HIN WN2 ....32 F6
Cope St BOL BL1 ....35 M3
Copgrove Rd CCHDY M21 ....97 L5
Copley Av STLY SK15 ....91 M2
Copley Park Ms STLY SK15 ....91 M2
Copley Rd CCHDY M21 ....97 K2
Copley St ROY/SHW OL2 * ....43 L2
Coplow Dl WGNE/HIN WN2 ....65 H1
Copperas Cl
 WGNNW/ST WN6 ....30 D5
Copperas La DROY M43 ....89 H4
 WGNE/HIN WN2 ....32 D6
Copperas St ANC M4 ....7 H3
Copperbeech Cl
 WYTH/NTH M22 ....110 B3
Copper Beech Dr
 GLSP SK13 ....104 B3
 STLY SK15 ....92 A1
Copperbeech Dr
 WGNNW/ST WN6 ....31 L5
Copper Beech Mnr
 GLSP SK13 ....104 B3
Copperfield Ct WA14 * ....116 E1
Copperfield Rd
 CHD/CHDH SK8 ....120 D7
 POY/DIS SK12 ....129 H2
Copperfields HOR/BR BL6 ....50 E1
 WILM/AE SK9 ....127 G4
Copper La WHTF M45 ....54 E5
Coppice Av POY/DIS SK12 ....123 J6
 SALE M33 ....108 A2
Coppice Cl HOR/BR BL6 ....50 D1
 MPL/ROM SK6 ....101 L8
Coppice Ct CHD/CHDH SK8 ....119 K4

The Coppice BKLY M9 ....73 K2
 BOLE BL2 ....23 G7
 HALE/TIMP WA15 ....117 K4
 PWCH M25 ....55 K8
 RAMS BL0 ....18 D8
 WALK M28 ....69 J4
 WALK M28 ....69 M7
Coppice Wk DTN/ASHW M34 ....101 G2
Coppice Wy WILM/AE SK9 ....127 J1
Coppingford Cl WHIT OL12 ....27 K2
Copping St WGTN/LGST M12 ....88 C6
The Coppins WILM/AE SK9 ....126 C8
Coppleridge Dr CHH M8 ....72 D2
Copplestone Dr SALE M33 ....95 M4
Coppull La WGN WN1 ....48 A2
Copse Av WYTH/NTH M22 ....119 G1
Copse Dr BURY BL9 ....25 J6
The Copse EDGW/EG BL7 ....22 F2
 HALE/TIMP WA15 ....117 M5
 MPL/ROM SK6 ....114 F4
 NEWLW WA12 ....78 D8
 WGNW/BIL/OR WN5 ....46 D6
Copson St DID/WITH M20 ....98 E5
Copster Av OLDS OL8 ....75 H1
Copster Hill Rd OLDS OL8 ....75 H1
Copster Pl OLDS OL8 ....75 H1
Copthall La CHH M8 ....72 C4
Copthorne Cl HEY OL10 ....41 G4
Copthorne Crs BRUN/LGST M13 ....99 H2
Copthorne Dr BOLE BL2 ....37 H6
Copthorn Wk TOT/BURYW BL8 ....24 C7
Copwood Head Cl WHIT OL12 ....20 C8
Coral Av CHD/CHDH SK8 ....120 C5
Coral Gv LEIGH WN7 ....66 B8
Coralin Wy AIMK WN4 ....63 J6
Coral Rd CHD/CHDH SK8 ....120 C5
Coral St BRUN/LGST M13 ....7 L9
 WGNNW/ST WN6 ....47 K1
Coram St GTN M18 ....89 J1
Corbar Rd OFTN SK2 ....112 E7
Corbel Wy ECC M30 ....85 G1
Corbett St MILN OL16 ....11 H2
 OP/CLY M11 ....88 D3
Corbett Wy UPML OL3 ....44 F3
Corbrook Rd CHAD OL9 ....58 B3
Corby St WGTN/LGST M12 ....88 D6
Corcoran Dr MPL/ROM SK6 ....114 C2
Corda Av WYTH/NTH M22 ....110 A4
Cordingley Av DROY M43 ....89 J4
Cordova Av DTN/ASHW M34 ....100 C1
Corelli St NEWH/MOS M40 ....73 J8
Corfe Cl URM M41 ....94 F3
 WGNE/HIN WN2 ....33 G7
Corfe Crs BRAM/HZG SK7 ....121 M3
Corhampton Crs ATH M46 ....51 H7
Corinthian Av BRO M7 ....71 M7
Corkland Cl AUL OL6 ....91 G2
Corkland Rd CCHDY M21 ....97 L4
Corkland St AUL OL6 ....91 H2
Corks La POY/DIS SK12 ....124 D3
Cork St BURY BL9 ....5 J4
 WGTN/LGST M12 ....88 A4
Corley Av EDGY/DAV SK3 ....111 J5
Corley Wk OP/CLY M11 * ....88 C5
Cormallen Gv FAIL M35 ....74 D5
Cormorant Cl LHULT M38 ....68 F1
Cornall St TOT/BURYW BL8 ....38 F1
Cornbrook Arches HULME M15 ....86 F5
Cornbrook Cl WHIT OL12 ....21 G6
 WHTN BL5 ....51 K6
Cornbrook Gv OLDTF/WHR M16 * ....87 G7
Cornbrook Park Rd
 HULME M15 ....86 F6
Cornbrook Rd OLDTF/WHR M16 ....87 G7
Cornbrook Wy
 OLDTF/WHR M16 ....87 G7
Corn Cl BRUN/LGST M13 ....87 M7
Cornelian Gv AIMK WN4 ....63 J7
Cornell St ANC M4 ....7 K2
Corner Brook HOR/BR BL6 ....50 D1
Corner Cft WILM/AE SK9 ....126 E8
Corner La LEIGH WN7 ....66 A2
Cornergate WHTN BL5 ....50 B7
Corner St AUL OL6 ....90 F7
Cornet St BRO M7 ....72 A7
Cornfield STLY SK15 ....92 B5
Cornfield Cl BURY BL9 ....25 J5
 SALE M33 ....109 J1
Cornfield Dr WYTH/NTH M22 ....118 E1
Cornfield Rd MPL/ROM SK6 ....114 F4
Cornfield St MILN OL16 ....29 K7
Cornford Av GTN M18 ....99 L1
Corn Hey Rd SALE M33 ....107 M2
Cornhill Av URM M41 ....95 H8
Corn Hill La DTN/ASHW M34 ....89 K7
Cornhill Rd URM M41 ....95 H1
Cornhill St OLDE OL4 ....59 J1
Cornishway WYTH/NTH M22 ....118 F4
Cornish Wy ROY/SHW OL2 ....59 J1
Cornlea Dr WALK M28 ....68 F5
Corn Mill Cl WHIT OL12 ....21 H3
Corn Mill La STLY SK15 ....91 L3
Corn St FAIL M35 ....73 M6
 GLSP SK13 ....105 G3
 LEIGH WN7 ....66 A7
 OLDE OL4 ....9 M5
Cornwall Av BNG/LEV M19 ....99 J3
 TYLD M29 ....67 K1
 WHTN BL5 ....51 J4
Cornwall Crs RDSH SK5 ....100 F6
 UPML OL3 ....45 L8
 WGN WN1 ....31 L3
Cornwall Dr BURY BL9 ....49 J6
 WGNE/HIN WN2 ....
Cornwallis Rd WGNS/IIMK WN3 ....14 A7
Cornwall Pl WGNW/BIL/OR WN5 ....46 F6
Cornwall Rd CHD/CHDH SK8 ....119 K4
 DROY M43 ....89 K1
 IRL M44 ....94 A7
Cornwell Cl WILM/AE SK9 ....127 H4
Corona Av HYDE SK14 ....102 B3
 OLDS OL8 ....75 G1
Coronation Av ATH M46 ....50 F7
 DUK SK16 ....91 J5
 GOL/RIS/CUL WA3 ....81 M5
 HEY OL10 ....41 G7
 HYDE SK14 ....102 B3
Coronation Dr
 RNFD/HAY WA11 ....67 G6
Coronation Gdns RAD M26 ....38 B8
Coronation Rd AUL OL6 ....75 M6
 DROY M43 ....89 J1
 FAIL M35 ....74 B6
 RAD M26 ....38 B8
 WGNNW/ST WN6 ....47 L7

Coronation Sq CMANE M1 ....7 M7
Coronation St AIMK WN4 ....63 H6
 BOL BL1 ....2 E5
 DTN/ASHW M34 ....100 F1
 OP/CLY M11 * ....88 F2
 ORD M5 ....86 E4
 RDSH SK5 ....100 B8
 SWIN M27 ....70 D3
 WGNS/IIMK WN3 ....14 E7
Coronation Wk
 WGNW/BIL/OR WN5 ....62 A8
Corporation Rd DTN/ASHW M34 ....90 A7
 ROCH OL11 ....10 B5
Corporation St ANC M4 ....7 G3
 HYDE SK14 * ....102 A2
 MDTN M24 ....57 K4
 STKP SK1 ....13 K3
 STLY SK15 ....91 K3
 WGN WN1 ....14 E7
Corran Cl ECC M30 ....84 E2
Corranstone Cl HOR/BR BL6 ....33 L1
Correction Brow
 POY/DIS SK12 ....122 E6
Corrie Cl DTN/ASHW M34 ....101 J3
Corrie Crs FWTH BL4 ....54 A8
Corrie Dr FWTH BL4 ....54 A8
Corrie Rd SWIN M27 ....70 D1
Corrie Wy MPL/ROM SK6 ....101 H7
Corrigan St GTN M18 ....89 H6
Corringham Rd BNG/LEV M19 ....99 M5
Corring Wy BOL BL1 ....22 E8
Corrin Rd BOL BL1 ....3 K8
Corris Av BKLY M9 ....56 F8
Corry Rd WGNE/HIN WN2 ....49 H8
Corsey Rd WGNE/HIN WN2 ....49 H8
Corsock Dr WGN WN1 ....15 L1
Corston Gv HOR/BR BL6 ....33 G3
Corwen Av BKLY M9 ....73 H4
Corwen Cl OLDS OL8 ....74 F7
Cosgate Cl WGNW/BIL/OR WN5 ....46 B7
Cosgrove Crs FAIL M35 ....74 B7
Cosgrove Rd FAIL M35 ....74 B7
Cosham Rd WYTH/NTH M22 ....119 H1
Cossack Wy WGNS/IIMK WN3 ....62 F1
Costessey Wy WGNS/IIMK WN3 ....62 F1
Costobadie Cl HYDE SK14 ....103 J1
Cosworth Cl LEIGH WN7 ....66 E8
Cotaline Cl ROCH OL11 ....41 L1
Cotefield Av BOLS/LL BL3 ....52 C1
Cotefield Cl MPL/ROM SK6 ....114 C7
Cotefield Rd WYTH/NTH M22 ....118 D2
Cote Green La MPL/ROM SK6 ....114 F3
Cote Green Rd MPL/ROM SK6 ....114 F3
Cote La LIT OL15 ....21 K6
 MOSL OL5 ....77 H1
 NM/HAY SK22 ....125 M1
 UPML OL3 ....45 L5
Cotford Rd BOL BL1 ....22 C7
Cotham St CSLFD M3 ....87 C7
Cotman Dr MPL/ROM SK6 ....114 F4
Cotswold Av BRAM/HZG SK7 ....121 K3
 CHAD OL9 ....58 D7
 GOL/RIS/CUL WA3 ....80 A6
 ROY/SHW OL2 ....43 J4
 URM M41 ....95 J1
 WGNW/BIL/OR WN5 ....46 F7
Cotswold Crs MILN OL16 ....29 K5
 TOT/BURYW BL8 ....38 E1
Cotswold Dr ROY/SHW OL2 ....58 E1
 SLFD M6 ....86 C1
Cotswold Rd HTNM SK4 ....12 F1
Cottage Cft BOLE BL2 ....23 G7
Cottage Gdns MPL/ROM SK6 ....113 G1
Cottage Gn WILM/AE SK9 ....126 C7
Cottage La GLSP SK13 ....104 B2
Cottam Crs MPL/ROM SK6 ....114 E5
Cottam Gv SWIN M27 ....70 D5
Cottam St OLD OL1 ....8 E2
 TOT/BURYW BL8 ....4 A2
Cottenham La BRO M7 ....72 B8
Cottenham St BRUN/LGST M13 ....87 L6
Cotterdale Cl OLDTF/WHR M16 ....98 A2
Cotteril Cl SALE M33 ....108 F3
Cotterill St SLFD M6 ....86 D2
Cotter St WGTN/LGST M12 ....7 L8
Cottesmore Cl WHIT OL12 ....20 A6
Cottesmore Dr CHH M8 ....72 F4
Cottesmore Gdns
 HALE/TIMP WA15 ....117 L4
Cottesmore Wy
 GOL/RIS/CUL WA3 ....79 L3
Cottingham Dr AUL OL6 ....75 M8
Cottingham Rd
 WGTN/LGST M12 ....88 B6
Cottingley Cl BOL BL1 ....22 A7
Cotton Cl HYDE SK14 ....102 B3
Cottonfields EDGW/EG BL7 ....22 C5
Cotton Fold MILN OL16 ....11 L7
Cotton Hl DID/WITH M20 ....98 F7
Cotton La DID/WITH M20 ....98 F6
Cotton Mill Crs CHAD OL9 ....58 E8
Cotton St ANC M4 ....7 K3
 BOL BL1 ....36 A2
 LEIGH WN7 ....66 A7
Cotton St East AUL OL6 ....90 F7
Cotton St West AUL OL6 ....90 D2
Cotton Tree Cl OLDE OL4 ....60 A4
Cotton Tree St HTNM SK4 ....13 C4
Cottonwood Dr SALE M33 ....95 M7
Cottrell Rd HALE/TIMP WA15 ....117 M5
Coucill Sq FWTH BL4 ....53 H4
Coulsden Dr BKLY M9 ....73 C1
Coulthart St AUL OL6 ....90 E1
Coulthurst St RAMS BL0 ....18 E6
Coulton Cl OLD OL1 ....9 M3
Coultshead Av
 WGNW/BIL/OR WN5 ....62 B6
Council Av AIMK WN4 ....78 E1
Councillor La CHD/CHDH SK8 ....111 J7
Councillor St WGTN/LGST M12 ....88 B3
Countess Av CHD/CHDH SK8 ....120 A7
Countess Gv BRO M7 ....72 A7
Countess La RAD M26 ....38 A7
Countess Pl PWCH M25 ....55 M8
Countess Rd DID/WITH M20 ....110 E1
Countess St AUL OL6 ....91 G2
 OFTN SK2 ....112 D7
Counthill Dr CHH M8 ....72 B2
Counthill Rd OLDE OL4 ....60 A3
Counting House Rd
 POY/DIS SK12 ....124 A7
Count St MILN OL16 ....11 H9
County Av AUL OL6 ....76 B8
County Rd LHULT M38 ....52 D8

County St CMANW M2 ....6 F5
 OLDS OL8 ....74 F2
Coupes Gn WHTN BL5 ....50 B6
Coupland Cl OLDE OL4 ....44 C8
 WHIT OL12 ....20 A4
Coupland Rd WGNE/HIN WN2 ....49 L8
 WGNE/HIN WN2 ....66 A1
Coupland St HULME M15 ....87 K7
 WHIT OL12 ....20 A4
Courier Pl
 WGNW/BIL/OR WN5 ....47 H3
Courier St GTN M18 ....89 H6
Course Vw OLDE OL4 ....76 B1
Court Dr NEWH/MOS M40 ....74 B8
Courtfield Av BKLY M9 ....57 C8
Courthill St STKP SK1 ....13 M6
Courtney Gn WILM/AE SK9 ....127 H2
Courtney Pl ALT WA14 ....116 C3
Court St BOLE BL2 ....3 H5
 UPML OL3 ....61 L4
Courts Vw SALE M33 ....96 F7
The Courtyard BOL BL1 * ....36 C3
 HEY OL10 ....41 J3
 HYDE SK14 * ....93 D7
Cousin Flds EDGW/EG BL7 ....22 F5
Covell Rd POY/DIS SK12 ....121 M7
Covent Gdn STKP SK1 ....13 J5
Coventry Av EDGY/DAV SK3 ....111 J5
Coventry Gv CHAD OL9 ....58 D3
Coventry Rd RAD M26 ....38 C7
Coventry St ROCH OL11 * ....10 F7
Coverdale Av BOL BL1 ....35 K4
 ROY/SHW OL2 ....43 L4
Coverdale Cl HEY OL10 ....40 F3
 WGNE/HIN WN2 ....64 C2
Coverdale Crs WGTN/LGST M12 ....88 A6
Coverdale Rd WHTN BL5 ....50 A4
Coverham Av OLDE OL4 ....60 B2
Coverhill Rd OLDE OL4 ....60 E7
Covert Rd OLDE OL4 ....76 B1
 WYTH/NTH M22 ....110 B7
The Coverts WGNNW/ST WN6 ....47 J3
The Cove HALE/TIMP WA15 ....117 H1
Covington Pl WILM/AE SK9 ....126 F6
Cowan St NEWH/MOS M40 ....88 A2
Cowbrook Av GLSP SK13 ....105 H3
Cowburn Dr NM/HAY SK22 ....124 E3
Cowburn St CSLFD M3 ....87 K1
 HEY OL10 ....41 H3
 LEIGH WN7 ....66 A7
 WGNE/HIN WN2 ....49 J8
Cowdals Rd HOR/BR BL6 ....34 E8
Cowesby St RUSH/FAL M14 ....98 D1
Cowhill La AUL OL6 ....90 F1
Cowie St ROY/SHW OL2 ....43 L4
Cow La BOLS/LL BL3 ....51 L2
 BRAM/HZG SK7 ....113 G8
 FAIL M35 ....74 B5
 HALE/TIMP WA15 ....117 H7
 HYDE SK14 ....93 C6
 OLDE OL4 ....59 M5
 SALE M33 ....97 H6
 WILM/AE SK9 ....127 G6
Cow Lees WHTN BL5 ....50 D3
Cowley Gv BOL BL1 ....22 A7
Cowley St NEWH/MOS M40 ....73 M6
Cowling St BRO M7 ....71 J4
 WGNS/IIMK WN3 ....14 E7
Cowlishaw ROY/SHW OL2 ....43 K7
Cowlishaw La ROY/SHW OL2 ....43 L7
Cowlishaw Rd HYDE SK14 ....102 C7
Cowm Park Wy North
 WHIT OL12 ....20 A2
Cowm Park Wy South
 WHIT OL12 ....20 A4
Cowper St LEIGH WN7 ....66 A7
 MDTN M24 ....58 A5
Coxfield WGNNW/ST WN6 ....30 A5
Cox Green Cl EDGW/EG BL7 ....22 A1
Cox Green Rd EDGW/EG BL7 ....16 A3
Coxton Rd WYTH/NTH M22 ....119 C3
Cox Wy ATH M46 ....67 C1
Crabbe St ANC M4 ....87 K1
Crab La BKLY M9 ....56 E9
Crabtree Av HALE/TIMP WA15 ....117 M5
 POY/DIS SK12 ....124 A7
Crab Tree La ATH M46 ....67 C2
Crabtree La OP/CLY M11 ....89 C4
Crabtree Rd OLD OL1 ....59 L4
 WGNW/BIL/OR WN5 ....47 C5
Craddock Rd SALE M33 ....108 F3
Craddock St MOSL OL5 ....76 F3
Cradley Av OP/CLY M11 ....89 C4
Crag Av BURY BL9 ....25 G2
Cragg Rd OLD OL1 ....58 D2
Cragie St CHH M8 ....72 C7
Crag La BURY BL9 ....25 G2
Cragside Wy WILM/AE SK9 ....127 C6
Craig Av TOT/BURYW BL8 ....38 E3
 URM M41 ....95 J4
Craig Cl HTNM SK4 ....12 B4
Craighall Av BNG/LEV M19 ....99 J4
Craighall Rd BOL BL1 ....22 B6
Craiglands MILN OL16 ....42 E2
Craigmore Av DID/WITH M20 ....98 A3
Craignair Ct SWIN M27 ....70 F4
Craig Rd GTN M18 ....88 F8
 HTNM SK4 ....12 A3
Craigslands Av NEWH/MOS M40 ....73 K6
Craig Wk OLDS OL8 ....9 J9
Craigweil Av DID/WITH M20 ....110 F1
Craigwell Rd PWCH M25 ....72 A2
Cramer St NEWH/MOS M40 ....7 J7
Crammond Cl NEWH/MOS M40 ....74 A4
Cramond Cl BOL BL1 ....36 A3
 WGNS/IIMK WN3 ....47 C3
Cramond Wk BOL BL1 ....36 A3
Crampton Dr HALE/TIMP WA15 ....117 L4
Crampton La PART M31 ....95 C6
Cranage Rd BNG/LEV M19 ....99 L4
Cranark Cl BOL BL1 ....35 K5
Cranberry Av WGNE/HIN WN2 ....47 J1
Cranberry Cl ALT WA14 ....107 L4
Cranberry Dr BOLS/LL BL3 ....35 J8
 DTN/ASHW M34 ....100 F1
Cranberry Rd PART M31 ....106 C3
Cranberry St OLDE OL4 ....59 L7
Cranborne Cl HOR/BR BL6 ....34 E5
Cranbourne Av
 CHD/CHDH SK8 ....120 D2

Cranbourne Cl
 HALE/TIMP WA15 ....108 D6
Cranbourne Rd AULW OL7 ....75 L7
 CCHDY M21 ....97 L4
 HTNM SK4 ....99 L8
 OLDTF/WHR M16 ....86 F8
 ROCH OL11 ....27 H6
Cranbourne St ORD M5 ....86 F3
Cranbourne Ter AUL OL6 ....75 L7
Cranbrook Av AIMK WN4 ....63 K8
Cranbrook Gdns AULW OL7 * ....75 L8
 GTN M18 ....100 B1
Cranbrook Rd ECC M30 ....69 K8
 OLDE OL4 ....59 M6
 RAD M26 ....38 F7
Cranbrook St AULW OL7 ....75 L8
 CHAD OL9 ....8 A7
Cranbrook Wk CHAD OL9 ....8 A7
Cranby St WGNE/HIN WN2 ....49 G7
Crandon Dr DID/WITH M20 ....110 F4
Cranesbill Cl WYTH/NTH M22 ....118 E3
Crane St BOLS/LL BL3 ....51 L1
 WGTN/LGST M12 ....7 M9
Cranfield Cl NEWH/MOS M40 ....88 A2
Cranfield Rd HOR/BR BL6 ....34 A5
 WGNS/IIMK WN3 ....63 K1
Cranford Av DID/WITH M20 ....99 G8
 SALE M33 ....96 F6
 STRET M32 ....97 J1
 WHTF M45 ....55 H2
Cranford Cl SWIN M27 ....70 E6
 WHTF M45 ....55 H2
Cranford Dr IRL M44 ....94 C1
Cranford Gdns MPL/ROM SK6 ....114 C1
 URM M41 ....95 H1
Cranford Rd URM M41 ....95 H1
 WILM/AE SK9 ....126 E3
Cranford St BOLS/LL BL3 ....51 L1
Cranham Av GOL/RIS/CUL WA3 ....80 B5
Cranham Cl TOT/BURYW BL8 ....38 E1
Cranham Close Crs
 LHULT M38 ....52 D6
Cranham Rd WYTH/NTH M22 ....118 C2
Crank Rd WGNW/BIL/OR WN5 ....62 A3
Crankwood Rd LEIGH WN7 ....64 E6
 WGNE/HIN WN2 ....64 E6
Cranleigh WGNNW/ST WN6 ....31 J4
Cranleigh Av HTNM SK4 ....99 J8
Cranleigh Cl HOR/BR BL6 ....33 C3
 OLDE OL4 ....60 B3
Cranleigh Dr BRAM/HZG SK7 ....122 C4
 CHD/CHDH SK8 ....111 J6
 SALE M33 ....96 D7
 SALE M33 ....108 F3
 TYLD M29 ....67 L4
 WALK M28 ....69 H4
Cranlington Dr CHH M8 ....72 C6
Cranmer Ct HEY OL10 ....40 F3
Cranmere Av BNG/LEV M19 ....99 M2
Cranmer Dr SALE M33 ....108 A2
Cranmer Rd DID/WITH M20 ....98 E8
Cranshaw St TYLD M29 ....68 A4
Cranstal Dr WGNE/HIN WN2 ....49 K7
Cranston Dr DID/WITH M20 ....110 E4
 SALE M33 ....109 H1
Cranston Gv CHD/CHDH SK8 ....110 C7
Cranswick St RUSH/FAL M14 ....98 D1
Crantock Dr CHD/CHDH SK8 ....119 L4
 STLY SK15 ....92 A1
Crantock St WGTN/LGST M12 ....99 L1
Cranwell Av GOL/RIS/CUL WA3 ....81 J3
Cranwell Dr BNG/LEV M19 ....99 H8
Cranworth Av TYLD M29 ....67 K6
Cranworth St STLY SK15 ....91 L2
Craston Rd BRUN/LGST M13 ....99 H1
Crathie Ct BOL BL1 ....35 L3
Craven Av GOL/RIS/CUL WA3 ....80 B5
 ORD M5 ....86 E4
Craven Ct ALT WA14 * ....107 M5
 ORD M5 ....86 D6
Craven Gdns ROCH OL11 * ....10 D8
Cravenhurst Av
 NEWH/MOS M40 ....73 L8
Craven Pl BOL BL1 ....35 H2
 OP/CLY M11 ....88 F2
Craven Rd ALT WA14 ....107 M5
 RDSH SK5 ....100 C6
Craven St AUL OL6 ....76 A7
 BURY BL9 ....5 L2
 OLD OL1 ....8 E5
 ORD M5 ....86 F3
Craven St East HOR/BR BL6 ....34 A2
Craven Ter SALE M33 ....96 F8
Cravenwood Rd CHH M8 ....72 D4
Crawford Av BOLE BL2 ....3 J6
 TYLD M29 ....67 J2
 WALK M28 ....69 J4
 WGNE/HIN WN2 ....32 F7
Crawford Pl WGN WN1 * ....48 A1
Crawford St AUL OL6 ....91 G2
 BOLE BL2 ....3 H5
 ECC M30 ....85 C1
 MILN OL16 ....11 H8
 NEWH/MOS M40 ....73 M7
 WGN WN1 ....14 F4
 WGNE/HIN WN2 ....32 F7
Crawley Av ECC M30 ....85 K1
 WYTH/NTH M22 ....118 F1
Crawley Cl TYLD M29 ....67 M3
Crawley Gv OFTN SK2 ....112 E6
Craydon St BNG/LEV M19 ....99 L4
Crayfield Rd BNG/LEV M19 ....99 L4
Crayford Rd NEWH/MOS M40 ....73 L8
The Cray MILN OL16 ....29 H6
Cray Wk BRUN/LGST M13 ....7 J9
Creaton Wy MDTN M24 ....41 G8
Creden Av WYTH/NTH M22 ....119 H1
Crediton Cl ALT WA14 ....107 L6
 HULME M15 ....87 J7
Crediton Dr BOLE BL2 ....37 K5
 WGNE/HIN WN2 ....64 D3
Cresbury St WGTN/LGST M12 * ....88 A3
Crescent ORD M5 ....6 A3
Crescent Av AIMK WN4 ....63 K8
 BOL BL1 ....22 D4
 CHH M8 ....72 D4
 FWTH BL4 ....52 F6
 PWCH M25 ....71 L2
 SWIN M27 ....70 D4
 WHTN BL5 ....51 K4
Crescent Cl DUK SK16 ....90 F3
 EDGY/DAV SK3 ....112 D7
Crescent Dr CHH M8 ....72 E3
 LHULT M38 ....52 E7
Crescent Fold HYDE SK14 * ....103 J4
Crescent Gv BNG/LEV M19 * ....99 K3
 PWCH M25 ....71 L2
Crescent Pk HTNM SK4 ....12 C4

**Crescent Range**
RUSH/FAL M14.................98 F1
**Crescent Rd** ALT WA14......107 K6
BOLS/LL BL3....................52 E1
CHAD OL9.......................74 B2
CHD/CHDH SK8................110 F6
CHH M8.........................72 D4
DUK SK16.......................90 F3
FWTH BL4.......................53 J6
HALE/TIMP WA15..............117 G2
HOR/BR BL6.....................34 B4
ROCH OL11......................27 L8
STKP SK1......................112 E1
WILM/AE SK9..................130 E2
**Crescent St** CHH M8..........72 D4
**The Crescent** ALT WA14.....107 K7
BNG/LEV M19...................99 K3
BOLE BL2........................23 J8
BOLS/LL BL3....................53 L2
BURY BL9........................5 H3
CHD/CHDH SK8................110 F6
DROY M43.......................89 J3
EDGW/EG BL7....................22 D4
EDGY/DAV SK3.................112 D8
HALE/TIMP WA15..............108 C5
HOR/BR BL6.....................34 A5
IRL M44.........................94 E1
MCFLDN SK10..................131 K2
MDTN M24.......................57 H4
MOSL OL5........................75 K3
MPL/ROM SK6..................101 G8
NM/HAY SK22..................124 D4
PWCH M25.......................55 L8
RAD M26.........................38 A7
ROY/SHW OL2....................43 K6
STLY SK15.......................92 A6
URM M41.........................95 J1
WGNE/HIN WN2..................48 E5
WGNW/BIL/OR WN5..............47 G6
WHIT OL12.......................20 A4
WHTN BL5........................50 B5
**Crescent Wy** EDGY/DAV SK3..112 D7
**Cressfold** LHULT M38..........52 B8
**Cressfield Gv**
WGNW/ST WN6...................47 J2
**Cressingham Rd** BOLS/LL BL3..51 K1
STRET M32......................96 E3
**Cressington Cl** ORD M5 *......86 B2
**Cresswell Av** NM/HAY SK22...124 E4
**Cresswell Gv** DID/WITH M20...98 D7
**Cresswell St** NM/HAY SK22...124 E4
**Crestfield Gv**
WGNNW/ST WN6..................47 J2
**The Crest** DROY M43...........89 K5
**Crestwood Av** WGNS/IIMK WN3..63 H1
**Creswick Cl** WGNE/HIN WN2....48 F8
**Crete** OLDS OL8................59 J8
**Crewe Rd** NTHM/RTH M23.....109 H4
**Crib Fold** UPML OL3............61 K2
**Crib La** UPML OL3..............61 K2
**Criccieth Rd** EDGY/DAV SK3...111 K5
**Criccieth St** OLDTF/WHR M16...87 J8
**Cricketers Wy** WHTN BL5.......50 B8
**Cricketfield La** WALK M28......68 F1
**Cricket's La** AUL OL6...........90 F1
**Cricket's La North** AUL OL6.....90 F1
**Cricket St** BOLS/LL BL3.........2 E4
DTN/ASHW M34 *................90 D8
WGNNW/ST WN6.................14 B3
**Cricket Vw** MILN OL16..........29 J7
**Cricklewood Rd**
WYTH/NTH M22.................118 E2
**Crimble La** ROCH OL11..........27 H7
**Crimble St** WHIT OL12...........10 D1
**Crime La** OLDS OL8..............75 G5
**Crimsworth Av**
OLDTF/WHR M16.................97 L2
**Crinan Wk** NEWH/MOS M40......88 A1
**Cringlebarrow Cl** WALK M28.....68 C7
**Cringle Cl** BOLS/LL BL3..........35 H8
**Cringle Dr** CHD/CHDH SK8.....110 F8
**Cringleford Wk**
WGTN/LGST M12................88 C7
**Cringle Hall Rd** BNG/LEV M19...99 J4
**Cringle Rd** BNG/LEV M19........99 L5
**Crippen St** ATH M46.............66 D3
**Cripple Ga** WGNNW/ST WN6....30 D3
**Cripple Gate La** ROCH OL11....42 B3
**Crispin Rd** WYTH/NTH M22.....119 G4
**Critchley Cl** HYDE SK14.......102 C3
**Criterion St** RDSH SK5.........100 C2
**Croal Av** WGNE/HIN WN2........64 D2
**Croal St** BOL BL1................A6
**Croasdale Av** RUSH/FAL M14....98 E3
**Croasdale Cl** ROY/SHW OL2.....43 H7
**Croasdale St** BOL BL1............2 F1
**Crocus Dr** ROY/SHW OL2.........43 K7
**Crocus St** BOL BL1...............22 C8
**Croft Acres** RAMS BL0..........19 G2
**Croft Av** ATH M46...............67 G2
GOL/RIS/CUL WA3................79 J2
PWCH M25.......................56 C4
WGNW/BIL/OR WN5...............46 A7
**Croft Bank** BRO M7 *............71 M7
GTN M18.........................89 H7
**Croft Brow** OLDS OL8...........75 H2
**Croft Cl** HALE/TIMP WA15.....117 L6
**Croft Ct** LEIGH WN7.............80 F3
**Croft Dr** TOT/BURYW BL8.......24 B6
**Croft Edge** UPML OL3............61 K7
**Crofters Brook** RAD M26.........38 F3
**Crofters Gn** WILM/AE SK9.....126 D6
**The Crofters** SALE M33.........109 J1
**Crofters Wk** BOLE BL2...........22 F6
**Croft Ga** BOLE BL2..............23 H8
**Croft Gates Rd** MDTN M24.......57 G5
**Croft Gv** LHULT M38.............52 C7
**Croft Head** ROY/SHW OL2........43 G8
**Croft Head Dr** MILN OL16........29 J5
**Croft Hill Rd** NEWH/MOS M40...73 K3
**Croftlands** RAMS BL0............24 D1
WGNW/BIL/OR WN5...............46 A8
**Croftlands Rd** WYTH/NTH M22..110 B8
**Croft La** BOLS/LL BL3.............3 J9
BURY BL9........................39 K7
RAD M26.........................38 F8
**Croftleigh Cl** WHTF M45.........55 H2
**Croft Mnr** GLSP SK13...........105 H3
**Crofton Av** HALE/TIMP WA15..108 C4
**Crofton St** OLDS OL8.............75 H1
OLDTF/WHR M16..................87 G8
RUSH/FAL M14....................98 E1
**Croft Pl** TYLD M29...............67 J4
**Croft Rd** CHD/CHDH SK8........120 C1
SALE M33.......................109 H2
WILM/AE SK9...................126 C8
**Crofts Bank Rd** URM M41........84 F8
**Croftside Av** WALK M28..........69 H1
**Croftside Cl** WALK M28..........69 H1
**Croftside Gv** WALK M28.........69 H1
**Croftside Wy** WILM/AE SK9....127 G6

**Croft St** BOLS/LL BL3............36 E8
BRO M7..........................71 M7
BURY BL9..........................5 H4
FAIL M35........................74 D3
GOL/RIS/CUL WA3 *..............79 K4
HYDE SK14......................102 A2
LHULT M38.......................52 C7
OP/CLY M11......................88 E3
STLY SK15.......................91 J2
WHIT OL12.......................28 F1
WHTN BL5........................50 B1
**The Croft** BURY BL9.............39 K6
GLSP SK13......................93 K6
HYDE SK14........................92 D8
OLDS OL8........................75 H2
PART M31.........................95 G6
WGNW/BIL/OR WN5...............46 A8
**Croftwood Sq**
WGNW/BIL/OR WN5...............46 C2
**Croichbank** TOT/BURYW BL8....23 L2
**Cromar Rd** BRAM/HZG SK7.....122 B1
**Cromarty Av** CHAD OL9..........74 C1
**Cromarty Wk** OP/CLY M11.......88 C3
**Crombie Av** WYTH/NTH M22....110 A4
**Crombouke Dr** LEIGH WN7.......66 B3
**Crombouke Fold** WALK M28......68 C3
**Cromdale Av** BOL BL1............35 L4
BRAM/HZG SK7..................122 B1
**Cromedale Crs**
WGNNW/ST WN6..................31 K5
**Cromer Av** BOLE BL2..............3 L1
DID/WITH M20...................98 E6
DTN/ASHW M34..................100 D1
**Cromer Dr** ATH M46..............66 D2
SALE M33.......................108 F1
TOT/BURYW BL8..................25 G7
WGNS/IIMK WN3..................63 H1
**Cromer St** MDTN M24.............57 K3
OP/CLY M11 *...................89 G3
ROY/SHW OL2....................43 L5
STKP SK1........................13 M3
WHIT OL12.......................10 D1
**Cromford Av** STRET M32.........96 F1
**Cromford Dr**
WGNW/BIL/OR WN5...............46 E7
**Cromford Gdns** BOL BL1..........36 C2
**Cromford St** OLD OL1.............9 M2
**Cromhurst St** CHH M8............72 D4
**Cromley Rd** MPL/ROM SK6.....123 G5
OFTN SK2.......................121 J1
**Crompton Av** BOLE BL2...........37 H4
MILN OL16........................42 E1
**Crompton Circuit**
ROY/SHW OL2....................44 B3
UPML OL3.......................44 C2
**Crompton Cl** BOL BL1............22 D8
MPL/ROM SK6..................114 C5
RAD M26.........................54 E4
**Crompton Pl** BOL BL1.............2 F5
**Crompton Rd** BNG/LEV M19.....99 K5
HOR/BR BL6......................34 C4
RAD M26.........................53 K4
**Crompton St** AUL OL6............76 B8
BOL BL1...........................3 G3
BURY BL9..........................4 E4
CHAD OL9.........................8 C5
FWTH BL4........................53 H5
OLD OL1...........................9 H2
ROY/SHW OL2....................43 L5
ROY/SHW OL2 *..................59 H1
SWIN M27.........................70 B4
WALK M28........................69 J2
WGN WN1.........................15 G3
WGNE/HIN WN2..................48 E8
WGNS/IIMK WN3..................14 C6
**Crompton V** BOLE BL2............37 C4
GOL/RIS/CUL WA3................80 E4
ROY/SHW OL2....................43 L6
**Cromwell Av** CHD/CHDH SK8...110 D6
MPL/ROM SK6..................113 M5
OLDTF/WHR M16..................97 M2
RDSH SK5.......................100 D3
**Cromwell Cl** NEWLW WA12.......78 D8
**Cromwell Gv** BNG/LEV M19......99 K3
BRO M7..........................71 M7
**Cromwell Range**
RUSH/FAL M14....................99 G2
**Cromwell Rd** BRAM/HZG SK7...120 F6
ECC M30.........................84 F2
IRL M44..........................94 B5
MPL/ROM SK6..................101 G6
PWCH M25.......................55 M8
ROY/SHW OL2....................42 F6
SLFD M6.........................71 K8
STRET M32........................97 H3
SWIN M27........................70 B3
WHTF M45........................55 G2
**Cromwell St** BOL BL1..............2 C6
HEY OL10........................41 G3
HTNM SK4.........................12 F1
OLD OL1...........................9 J7

**Crossby Cl** MDTN M24............57 J7
**Crow Hl South** MDTN M24.......57 J6
**Crosscliffe St** OLDTF/WHR M16..87 J8
BOLE BL2.........................37 J4
WGNE/HIN WN2..................49 L1
**Crossefield Rd** CHD/CHDH SK8.120 C1
**Crossen St** BOLS/LL BL3...........3 M9
**Cross Field Cl** ROY/SHW OL2....43 M3
**Crossfield Cl** DTN/ASHW M34..101 K2
STLY SK15.......................91 K3
WHIT OL12........................21 G5
**Crossfield Dr** RAD M26...........54 B1
**Crossfield Gv** MPL/ROM SK6..114 E3
OFTN SK2.......................112 E8
**Crossfield Pl** ROCH OL11.........11 G9
**Crossfield Rd** ECC M30...........83 M8
HALE/TIMP WA15................117 K2
WHIT OL12........................21 G6
WILM/AE SK9....................119 M8
**Crossfields** EDGW/EG BL7.......22 E4
**Crossford Dr** SALE M33..........96 A6
**Cross Gates Rd** MILN OL16.......29 J5
**Crossgill** TYLD M29...............67 J7
**Cross Glebe St** AUL OL6..........90 F1
**Cross Gv** HALE/TIMP WA15.....108 B7
**Crosshill St** OLDTF/WHR M16...87 J8
**Cross Keys St** ANC M4.............7 H1
**Cross Knowle Vw** URM M41......84 D8
**Crossland Rd** CCHDY M21........97 L5
DROY M43........................89 K2
**Crosslands** PWCH M25...........71 K1
**Crosslands Cl** WALK M28.........68 C6
**Cross La** DROY M43...............89 G2
GTN M18..........................89 G7
MPL/ROM SK6..................114 B7
ORD M5...........................86 D3
RAD M26.........................38 F8
TOT/BURYW BL8..................18 D1
WGNW/BIL/OR WN5................62 A1
WILM/AE SK9....................127 K4
**Cross La East** PART M31.........106 D1
**Cross La West** PART M31.........106 D4
**Crosslee Rd** BKLY M9.............57 J8
**Cross Lees** WHIT OL12............28 D1
**Crossley Ct** ANC M4..............88 A3
**Crossley Crs** AUL OL6.............90 F1
**Crossley Rd** BNG/LEV M19......99 K5
SALE M33.......................108 F1
**Crossley St** BOLS/LL BL3..........37 K8
GTN M18..........................88 E6
MILN OL16........................29 H6
ROY/SHW OL2....................43 M5
STLY SK15.......................91 J2
**Crossmead** DR BKLY M9..........57 H7
**Crossmeadow Cl** ROCH OL11....27 K4
**Crossmoor Crs** MPL/ROM SK6.113 M2
**Crossmoor Dr** BOLE BL2..........3 K2
**Crossmoor Gv** MPL/ROM SK6.113 M2
**Cross Ormrod St** BOLS/LL BL3....2 B7
**Cross Ri** GLSP SK13.............105 H4
**Cross Rd** CCHDY M21.............97 L5
CHD/CHDH SK8.................119 K5
**Cross St** ALT WA14.............108 A8
ATH M46.........................50 E8
AUL OL6..........................76 A7
AUL OL6..........................90 D2
BOL BL1..........................53 L1
BOLS/LL BL3......................53 L1
BURY BL9..........................4 F4
CMANW M2........................6 F4
CSLFD M3..........................6 D5
DTN/ASHW M34..................90 B7
EDGW/EG BL7....................22 C5
FWTH BL4........................53 C3
FWTH BL4........................53 L7
GLSP SK13........................93 K7
GLSP SK13......................104 F3
GOL/RIS/CUL WA3................79 K5
HEY OL10........................41 H3
HYDE SK14........................93 G8
HYDE SK14......................102 A2
LEIGH WN7.......................66 D8
MDTN M24........................57 J4
MOSL OL5........................76 F2
NM/HAY SK22 *.................124 E4
OLDE OL4.........................59 L5
OLDE OL4.........................60 D6
OLDTF/WHR M16..................87 G7
RAMS BL0........................18 F6
ROCH OL11........................41 M2
SALE M33.........................96 E7
STLY SK15........................77 G8
STRET M32........................97 G2
SWIN M27.........................71 G2
TYLD M29........................67 J2
URM M41.........................95 M3
WALK M28........................69 G7
WGNE/HIN WN2..................49 G7
WGNNW/ST WN6.................31 H5
WGNS/IIMK WN3..................14 F6
WGNS/IIMK WN3..................48 B8
WGNW/BIL/OR WN5 *............55 H3
WHTF M45........................55 H3
**The Cross** GLSP SK13.............93 K7
TOT/BURYW BL8...................24 C6
**Crosswaite Rd** OFTN SK2........113 G6
**Crossway** BRAM/HZG SK7......121 G7
DID/WITH M20...................110 L1
DROY M43........................89 K3
OFTN SK2.......................112 D8
**Crossway Cl** AIMK WN4..........64 B7
**Crossways** OLDS OL8..............75 K3
**Croston Cl** WILM/AE SK9........130 F3
**Croston Close Rd** BURY BL9......25 L2
**Crostons Rd** TOT/BURYW BL8....4 B3
**Croston St** BOLS/LL BL3..........35 M8
WGNE/HIN WN2..................49 K1
**Croston Wk** OP/CLY M11 *......88 B3
**Croton St** HTNM SK4.............12 H1
**Croughton Cl** OP/CLY M11 *.....89 G5
**Crowborough Cl** HOR/BR BL6....34 C3
**Crowborough Wk** HULME M15...87 J7
**Crowcroft Rd** BRUN/LGST M13...99 J2
**Crowden Dr** GLSP SK13...........93 K7
**Crowden Rd** NEWH/MOS M40....73 H2
**Crow Hl** STLY SK15................77 H7
**Crow Hl North** MDTN M24........57 J6

**Crowhill Rd** AULW OL7...........75 J8
**Crow Hl South** MDTN M24.......57 J6
**Crowhurst Dr** WGN WN1..........47 L1
**Crowland Gdns**
CHD/CHDH SK8.................120 D6
**Crowland Rd** BOLE BL2...........36 F2
NTHM/RTH M23.................118 B1
**Crow La** RAMS BL0................18 F6
**Crow La East** NEWLW WA12.....78 F8
**Crow La West** NEWLW WA12....78 D8
**Crowley La** OLDE OL4.............60 A3
**Crowley Rd** BKLY M9.............73 J4
HALE/TIMP WA15................108 E6
**Crown Ct** BRAM/HZG SK7......121 M1
**Crowndale** EDGW/EG BL7........17 G5
**Crowneast St** ROCH OL11.......27 M5
**Crown Fields Cl** NEWLW WA12..78 E7
**Crown Gdns** EDGW/EG BL7.......17 G6
MILN OL16........................11 H9
NEWLW WA12.....................78 E8
**Crowngreen Rd** ECC M30.........85 H3
**Crown Gv** WGNE/HIN WN7........67 G6
**Crown Hl** MOSL OL5...............77 G4
**Crownhill Dr** DROY M43..........89 K2
**Crown La** ANC M4..................7 H1
HOR/BR BL6.......................33 J1
**Crown Park Dr**
NEWLW WA12.....................78 E8
**Crown Passages**
HALE/TIMP WA15................117 G2
**Crown Point Av**
NEWH/MOS M40 *................73 M7
**Crown Rd** HEY OL10..............40 E2
**Crown Sq** CSLFD M3.................6 D5
**Crown St** ATH M46................66 F1
AUL OL6..........................90 E2
BOL BL1...........................2 F4
CSLFD M3..........................6 D6
DTN/ASHW M34..................90 B8
FAIL M35........................74 C4
HULME M15.......................6 C8
MILN OL16........................11 J9
MPL/ROM SK6..................101 J8
MPL/ROM SK6..................123 H1
NEWH/MOS M40 *................73 M7
ROY/SHW OL2....................43 L5
WGNE/HIN WN2..................48 F6
WGNS/IIMK WN3..................14 E7
**Crow Orchard Rd**
WGNNW/ST WN6.................30 D2
**Crowsdale Pl** OFTN SK2.........113 H8
**Crowshaw Dr** WHIT OL12........28 B1
**Crow's Nest** BOLS/LL BL3........37 J7
**Crowswood Dr** STLY SK15.......77 G8
**Crowther Av** ORD M5.............86 D4
**Crowther Dr** WGNS/IIMK WN3...63 H3
**Crowther St** GTN M18............89 G7
LIT OL15.........................21 J8
MILN OL16........................28 E8
**Crowthorn Dr** NTHM/RTH M23.118 C2
**Crowthorn Rd** AULW OL7.........90 C3
EDGW/EG BL7....................17 J3
HTNM SK4........................100 A5
ON SALE M33...................108 A2
**Crow Trees La** EDGW/EG BL7....16 F5
**Crow Wood Rd**
GOL/RIS/CUL WA3................80 A3
**Croxdale Cl** AULW OL7...........75 J7
**Croxton Av** MILN OL16...........11 L3
**Croxton Cl** MPL/ROM SK6......114 B7
SALE M33.......................108 A2
**Croyde Cl** BOLE BL2..............37 J2
WYTH/NTH M22.................119 H5
**Croydon Av** LEIGH WN7..........66 C5
ROCH OL11........................42 A5
ROY/SHW OL2....................42 F6
**Croydon Dr** NEWH/MOS M40....73 M8
**Croydon Sq** ROCH OL11..........42 A4
**Crummock Cl** BOLS/LL BL3.......53 J1
**Crummock Dr** MDTN M24.........57 H1
WGNS/IIMK WN3..................63 J1
**Crummock Rd**
CHD/CHDH SK8.................119 K1
FWTH BL4........................52 B5
**Crumpsall La** CHH M8............72 C3
**Crumpsall St** BOL BL1............36 B2
**Crumpsall V** CHH M8.............72 F2
**Crumpsall Wy** CHH M8...........72 E3
**Crundale Rd** BL2.................22 C6
**Cruttenden Rd** OFTN SK2.......112 F8
**Cryer St** DROY M43...............74 F8
**Crystal Cl** WGNE/HIN WN2......64 D1
**Cubley Rd** BRO M7................72 B4
**Cuckoo Gv** PWCH M25...........55 L6
**Cuckoo La** BURY BL9.............39 M2
PWCH M25.......................55 L6
**Cuddington Av**
DID/WITH M20...................98 D4
**Cuddington Crs**
EDGY/DAV SK3..................112 A6
**Cudworth Rd** BKLY M9...........56 D7
**Culand St** WGTN/LGST M12......88 B6
**Culbert Av** DID/WITH M20......110 F1
**Culcheth Av** MPL/ROM SK6.....114 C6
**Culcheth La** WGNE/HIN WN2...64 E3
**Culcheth Hall Dr**
GOL/RIS/CUL WA3................81 J8
**Culcheth La**
NEWH/MOS M40..................73 M8
**Culcheth Rd** ALT WA14..........116 F1
**Culcross Av** WGNS/IIMK WN3...46 F8
**Culford Cl** WGTN/LGST M12.....88 B7
**Culham Cl** BOL BL1 *.............36 A2
**Cullen Cl** WGNE/HIN WN2.......48 D3
**Cullen Gv** BKLY M9...............73 H1
**Cullercoats Wk**
WGTN/LGST M12.................99 L1
**Culmere Rd** WYTH/NTH M22...118 F3
**Culraven Av** WGNE/HIN WN2.....32 K5
**Culross Av** BOLS/LL BL3..........35 H6
NEWH/MOS M40..................74 B3
**Culvercliff Wk** CSLFD M3..........6 D6
**Culver Rd** EDGY/DAV SK3.......112 A4
**Culvert St** MILN OL16.............42 C2
OLDE OL4.........................60 B5
WGNNW/ST WN6.................47 K2
**Culverwell Dr** ORD M5...........86 C6
**Culzean Cl** LEIGH WN7...........66 E6
**Cumberbatch Pl**
WGNS/IIMK WN3..................48 C8
**Cumber Cl** WILM/AE SK9.......126 B8
**Cumber Dr** WILM/AE SK9.......126 B8
**Cumberland Av** DUK SK16.......91 M4
HEY OL10........................40 C2
RDSH SK5.......................100 F8
SWIN M27........................70 C2
TYLD M29........................67 J2
**Cumberland Cl** BURY BL9........39 M5
**Cumberland Dr** ALT WA14.....116 C4
OLD OL1..........................59 L3
**Cumberland Gv** AULW OL7......75 L8

**Cumberland Rd** ATH M46........51 H8
BKLY M9.........................73 G3
PART M31.......................106 A2
ROCH OL11........................44 B3
SALE M33.......................108 F2
URM M41.........................95 M3
**Cumberland St** BRO M7..........72 A4
STLY SK15........................91 J2
WGN WN1.........................15 K1
**Cumberland Wy** WILM/AE SK9..126 B8
ROY/SHW OL2....................43 J4
WGNE/HIN WN2..................64 D2
**Cumbrae Gdns** ORD M5..........86 B3
**Cumbrae Rd** BNG/LEV M19.....99 M3
**Cumbrian Cl** BRUN/LGST M13 *..87 M6
ROY/SHW OL2....................43 J4
WGNE/HIN WN2..................64 C2
**Cummings St** OLDS OL8...........74 F2
**Cummins Wk** SLFD M6............71 L8
**Cunard Cl** BRUN/LGST M13......87 M6
**Cundiffe Dr** ROY/SHW OL2......44 A5
**Cundey St** BOL BL1 *..............35 M3
**Cundiff Rd** CCHDY M21............97 L6
**Cundy St** HYDE SK14..............91 M8
**Cunliffe Av** NEWLW WA12.......78 E7
RAMS BL0........................18 D8
**Cunliffe Brow** BOL BL1............35 L3
**Cunliffe Ct** LEIGH WN7............65 K8
**Cunliffe Dr** LEIGH WN7..........108 F1
**Cunliffe St** EDGY/DAV SK3.......12 D6
HYDE SK14........................90 F8
LEIGH WN7........................65 M7
RAMS BL0........................18 F5
**Cunningham Dr** BURY BL9........55 L3
WYTH/NTH M22.................119 J4
**Cunningham Rd** WHTN BL5.....49 M5
**Curate St** STKP SK1................13 M5
**Curlew Cl** GOL/RIS/CUL WA3....80 A4
ROCH OL11........................27 J5
**Curlew Dr** IRL M44................83 K8
**Curlew Rd** OLDE OL4..............60 C5
**Curlew Wy** GLSP SK13...........104 C3
**Currier La** AUL OL6...............90 C4
**Curteis Cl** WALK M28.............69 M5
**Curtis Gv** GLSP SK13.............93 K4
**Curtis Rd** BNG/LEV M19..........99 M3
HTNM SK4..........................9 H9
**Curtis St** BOLS/LL BL3............51 M2
ROY/SHW OL2....................47 G6
**Curzon Av** RUSH/FAL M14........88 B8
**Curzon Cl** ROCH OL11.............42 C2
**Curzon Dr** HALE/TIMP WA15...108 E6
**Curzon Gn** OFTN SK2............113 C4
**Curzon Ms** WILM/AE SK9........126 E6
**Curzon Rd** AUL OL6................75 M8
BOL BL1..........................35 M5
BRO M7...........................72 A5
CHD/CHDH SK8.................119 G5
OFTN SK2........................113 G5
POY/DIS SK12..................129 J2
ROCH OL11........................42 C2
SALE M33.........................96 E1
STRET M32........................97 G3
**Curzon St** MOSL OL5..............76 F3
OLD OL1...........................9 J3
**Cutacre Cl** TYLD M29.............52 L3
**Cutacre La** WHTN BL5............52 A6
**Cutgate Cl** NTHM/RTH M23....109 H3
**Cutgate Rd** WHIT OL12............27 L3
**Cuthbert Av** BNG/LEV M19.......99 L2
**Cuthbert Mayne Ct** MILN OL16..10 D6
**Cuthbert Rd** CHD/CHDH SK8...111 H6
**Cuthbert St** BOLS/LL BL3.........51 K2
WGNW/BIL/OR WN5...............47 G6
**Cutland St** NEWH/MOS M40......73 K6
**Cutland Wy** LIT OL15.............21 L8
**Cut La** WHIT OL12..................27 J3
**Cutler Hill Rd** FAIL M35...........74 F5
**Cutnook La** IRL M44...............83 J4
**Cutter Cl** ORD M5..................86 D4
**Cycle St** OP/CLY M11..............88 C4
**Cyclone St** OP/CLY M11...........88 C4
**Cygnet St** WGNS/IIMK WN3......14 B1
**Cygnus Av** BRO M7................86 F1
**Cymbal Ct** RDSH SK5............112 B1
**Cynthia Dr** MPL/ROM SK6.....114 C7
**Cypress Av** CHAD OL9..............8 A3
**Cypress Cl** EDGY/DAV SK3........12 C6
**Cypress Gdns** MILN OL16.........29 C5
**Cypress Gv** DTN/ASHW M34...101 K1
FWTH BL4........................53 J5
**Cypress Oaks** STLY SK15.........92 A1
**Cypress Rd** DROY M43............89 K1
ECC M30.........................85 K3
OLDE OL4.........................60 A4
WGNW/BIL/OR WN5...............47 M6
**Cypress St** MDTN M24............57 M4
**Cypress Wy** MPL/ROM SK6.....123 J5
**Cyprus Cl** OLDE OL4..............60 A7
ORD M5...........................86 C3
**Cyprus St** STRET M32.............97 G2
**Cyril St** ROY/SHW OL2.............43 M5
RUSH/FAL M14....................98 E1
**Cyrus St** NEWH/MOS M40........88 B2

**D**

**Daccamill Dr** SWIN M27...........70 C6
**Dacre Av** OLDTF/WHR M16.......97 L2
**Dacre Cl** MDTN M24...............56 E3
**Dacre Rd** ROCH OL11.............28 C8
**Dacres Av** UPML OL3.............61 K8
**Dacres Dr** UPML OL3.............61 K8
**Dacres Rd** UPML OL3.............61 K8
**Daffodil Cl** WHIT OL12.............28 B1
**Daffodil Rd** FWTH BL4............52 D3
**Daffodil St** BOL BL1...............22 C2
**Dagenham Rd** RUSH/FAL M14 *..98 F1
**Dagmar St** WALK M28.............52 F8
**Dagnall Av** CCHDY M21...........97 L6
**Dahlia Cl** BNG/LEV M19...........99 J6
WHIT OL12........................28 A1
**Daimler St** CHH M8................72 D6
**Dain Cl** DUK SK16.................91 G4
**Daine Av** NTHM/RTH M23......109 L3
**Dainton St** WGTN/LGST M12.....88 A5
**Daintry Cl** HULME M15...........87 J6
**Daintry Rd** CHAD OL9.............8 C8
**Dairydale Cl** IRL M44.............94 E1
**Dairyground Rd**
BRAM/HZG SK7..................121 G5
**Dairyhouse La** ALT WA14......107 L5
**Dairy House La**
BRAM/HZG SK7..................127 M1
**Dairy House Rd**
BRAM/HZG SK7..................120 D7
**Dairy St** CHAD OL9..................8 A5
**Daisy Av** BRUN/LGST M13........88 B8
FWTH BL4........................53 J5
**Daisy Bank** NEWH/MOS M40....73 M7
**Daisy Bank Av** SWIN M27........70 F6

Daisybank Cl WGNE/HIN WN2 49 G7
Daisy Bank La CHD/CHDH SK8 119 J3
Daisy Bank Rd RUSH/FAL M14 88 B8
Daisyfield HOR/BR BL6 * 34 A3
Daisyfield Cl WYTH/NTH M22 118 E3
Daisyfield Ct TOT/BURYW BL8 38 F3
Daisy Hall Dr WHTN BL5 50 B7
Daisyhill Cl SALE M33 97 H8
Daisyhill Ct WHTN BL5 50 C7
Daisy Hill Rd MOSL OL5 77 G3
Daisy Ms EDGY/DAV SK3 112 A8
Daisy Rd WGNW/BIL/OR WN5 47 H6
Daisy St BOLS/LL BL3 35 M8
CHAD OL9 8 E4
CHAD OL9 58 D4
OFTN SK2 13 K9
TOT/BURYW BL8 38 E2
WHIT OL12 10 C3
Daisy Wy MPL/ROM SK6 123 H5
Dakerwood Cl
NEWH/MOS M40 73 M7
Dakins Rd LEIGH WN7 81 L2
Dakley St OP/CLY M11 88 F5
Dakota Av SALQ M50 86 B4
Dakota South SALQ M50 86 C4
Dalbeattie Ri WGN WN1 15 H1
Dalbeattie St BKLY M9 73 H4
Dalberg St WGTN/LGST M12 88 A5
Dalbury Dr NEWH/MOS M40 72 F7
Dalby Av SWIN M27 70 B5
Dalby Gv STKP SK1 13 M4
Dalby Rd WGNE/HIN WN2 49 L7
Dale Av BRAM/HZG SK7 121 H4
ECC M30 84 F1
MOSL OL5 77 H1
Dalebank ATH M46 50 F7
Dalebank Ms SWIN M27 * 54 A7
Dalebeck Cl WHTF M45 55 L4
Dale Brook Av DUK SK16 91 G6
Dalebrook Ct HTNM SK4 * 12 D4
Dalebrook Rd SALE M33 108 F3
Dalecrest WGNW/BIL/OR WN5 62 A3
Dale Flds UPML OL3 45 J8
Daleford Sq BRUN/LGST M13 * 7 K9
Dalegarth Av BOL BL1 34 F5
Dale Gv AULW OL7 75 K7
HALE/TIMP WA15 108 C5
IRL M44 94 B6
LEIGH WN7 65 M8
Dalehead Dr ROY/SHW OL2 44 A5
Dalehead Gv LEIGH WN7 65 M8
Dale La UPML OL3 45 J7
Dale Lee WHTN BL5 50 D4
Dale Rd GOL/RIS/CUL WA3 79 K5
MDTN M24 57 L2
MPL/ROM SK6 114 B5
NM/HAY SK22 124 E5
Dales Av CHH M8 72 C2
WHTF M45 55 G3
Dalesbrook Cl BOLS/LL BL3 37 K8
Dales Brow BOL BL1 21 A1
SWIN M27 * 70 A6
Dales Brow Av AULW OL7 75 L7
Dalesfield Crs MOSL OL5 77 H3
Dalesford Cl LEIGH WN7 80 F4
Dales Gv WALK M28 69 J3
Daleside Av AIMK WN4 63 K4
Dales La WHTF M45 55 H3
Dalesman Cl BKLY M9 73 J4
Dalesman Dr OLD OL1 60 A1
Dalesman Wk HULME M15 * 87 J6
Dales Park Dr SWIN M27 * 70 A6
Dale St AUL OL6 76 D6
CMANE M1 7 J4
EDGY/DAV SK3 12 E9
FWTH BL4 * 53 H3
LEIGH WN7 65 M7
MDTN M24 57 L5
MILN OL16 11 L4
MILN OL16 29 J6
RAD M26 54 D2
RAMS BL0 18 F4
ROY/SHW OL2 43 L6
STLY SK15 91 J3
SWIN M27 70 B6
TOT/BURYW BL8 24 F8
WGNS/IIMK WN3 64 C1
WHTF M45 55 H3
WHTN BL5 50 C7
Dale St East AUL OL6 90 D2
HOR/BR BL6 34 A3
Dale St West AUL OL6 90 D2
HOR/BR BL6 34 A2
Daleswood Av WHTF M45 55 G3
Dale Vw DTN/ASHW M34 101 K5
HYDE SK14 102 A4
LIT OL15 29 J2
NEWLW WA12 79 H8
Dalham Av BKLY M9 73 K2
Dalkeith Gv BOLS/LL BL3 35 J7
Dalkeith Rd RDSH SK5 100 C5
WGNE/HIN WN2 49 K7
Dalkeith St GTN M18 88 E6
Dallas Ct SALQ M50 86 B4
Dalley Av BRO M7 72 A8
Dallimore Rd NTHM/RTH M23 109 H6
Dalmahoy Cl NEWH/MOS M40 73 M4
Dalmain Cl CHH M8 72 C6
Dalmeny Ter ROCH OL11 28 C8
Dalmorton Rd CCHDY M21 98 A4
Dalny St BNG/LEV M19 99 L3
Dalston Av FAIL M35 74 E4
Dalston Dr BRAM/HZG SK7 120 E7
DID/WITH M20 110 F2
Dalston Gv WGNS/IIMK WN3 63 G1
Dalton Av MILN OL16 29 G5
RUSH/FAL M14 98 D2
STRET M32 85 J8
WHTF M45 55 K5
Dalton Cl MILN OL16 29 H5
RAMS BL0 18 D8
WGNW/BIL/OR WN5 46 E5
Dalton Dr SWIN M27 71 G5
WGNS/IIMK WN3 63 H1
Dalton Fold WHTN BL5 50 C4
Dalton Gdns URM M41 95 L1
Dalton Gv AIMK WN4 63 K8
HTNM SK4 99 M8
Dalton Rd BKLY M9 57 G7
MDTN M24 56 E5
Dalton St ANC M4 87 L1
CHAD OL9 8 A4
ECC M30 85 G1
FAIL M35 74 B4
OLD OL1 * 59 L5
SALE M33 96 F6
TOT/BURYW BL8 38 E2
Daltry St OLD OL1 9 M2
Dalveen Av URM M41 84 F8
Dalveen Dr HALE/TIMP WA15 108 C5
Dalwood Cl WGNE/HIN WN2 49 J8
Dalymount Cl BOLE BL2 36 E2
Damask Av CSLFD M3 6 A2
Dame Hollow CHD/CHDH SK8 119 M5
Dameral Cl CHH M8 * 72 D6
Damery Ct BRAM/HZG SK7 121 G4
Damery Rd BRAM/HZG SK7 121 G4
Dame St CHAD OL9 8 E2
Dam Head Dr BKLY M9 73 H1
Damian Dr NEWLW WA12 78 D7
Damien St BNG/LEV M19 99 L2
Dam La AIMK WN4 79 J1
Dams Head Fold WHTN BL5 50 C3
Damson Gn MDTN M24 57 M4
Dan Bank MPL/ROM SK6 113 M6
Danby Cl HYDE SK14 91 J8
Danby Ct OLD OL1 58 G2
Danby Pl HYDE SK14 91 J8
Danby Rd BOLS/LL BL3 52 B1
HYDE SK14 91 J8
Dane Av EDGY/DAV SK3 * 111 K4
PART M31 94 C8
Dane Bank MDTN M24 57 L5
Dane Bank Dr POY/DIS SK12 123 M6
Danebank Ms DTN/ASHW M34 100 E2
Danebank Wk BRUN/LGST M13 * 7 K9
Danebridge Cl FWTH BL4 * 53 H4
Danebury Cl WGNE/HIN WN2 * 49 G8
Dane Cl BRAM/HZG SK7 120 F2
Danecroft Cl BRUN/LGST M13 87 A7
Dane Dr WILM/AE SK9 127 H6
Danefield Ct CHD/CHDH SK8 119 M4
Danefield Rd SALE M33 96 F6
Dane Hill Cl POY/DIS SK12 123 M7
Daneholme Rd BNG/LEV M19 99 H7
Dane Ms SALE M33 * 96 E6
Dane Rd DTN/ASHW M34 100 D2
SALE M33 96 F6
Danes Av WGNE/HIN WN2 49 H6
Danes Brook Cl
WGNE/HIN WN2 49 H6
Danesbury Cl
WGNW/BIL/OR WN5 62 B8
Danesbury Ri CHD/CHDH SK8 111 G7
Danesbury Rd BOLE BL2 22 E8
Danes Gn WGNE/HIN WN2 49 H5
Daneshill PWCH M25 55 L6
Danesmoor Dr BURY BL9 25 K8
Danesmoor Rd DID/WITH M20 98 D7
Danes Rd RUSH/FAL M14 99 G2
Dane St BOLS/LL BL3 * 35 M8
OLDE OL4 59 M5
OP/CLY M11 89 H5
WHIT OL12 10 C5
Danesway PWCH M25 72 A2
SWIN M27 70 F6
WGN WN1 47 L1
Danesway Ct BOL BL1 36 A2
Daneswood Av BKLY M9 * 57 J8
WHIT OL12 20 A5
Danett Cl WGTN/LGST M12 88 D6
Danforth Gv BNG/LEV M19 99 L4
Daniel Adamson Av PART M31 106 A1
Daniel Adamson Rd SALQ M50 86 A4
Daniel Fold WHIT OL12 27 L2
Daniel's La STKP SK1 * 13 J3
Daniel St BRAM/HZG SK7 122 A2
HEY OL10 * 40 E2
OLD OL1 59 M4
ROY/SHW OL2 59 K1
WHIT OL12 20 B3
Danisher La OLDS OL8 75 J4
Dannywood Cl HYDE SK14 101 M4
Danson St NEWH/MOS M40 88 B1
Dantall Av BKLY M9 73 K2
Dante Cl ECC M30 70 D8
Danty St DUK SK16 * 90 E3
Dantzic St ANC M4 7 G3
ANC M4 87 L1
Danwood Cl DTN/ASHW M34 101 L3
Darbishire St BOL BL1 3 G1
Darby La WGNE/HIN WN2 49 G6
Darby Rd IRL M44 94 D6
Darbyshire Cl BOL BL1 35 M4
Darbyshire St RAD M26 54 D1
Darcy St BOLE BL2 3 L8
Darden Cl HTNM SK4 111 H1
Darell Wk CHH M8 72 E6
Daresbury Av URM M41 84 A8
Daresbury Cl EDGY/DAV SK3 112 A7
SALE M33 109 J1
Daresbury Rd CCHDY M21 97 J3
Daresbury St CHH M8 72 D5
Dargai St OP/CLY M11 89 G3
Dargle Rd SALE M33 96 E6
Darian Av WYTH/NTH M22 118 F4
Daric Cl LEIGH WN7 80 F3
Dark La HOR/BR BL6 32 E1
MOSL OL5 77 G3
MPL/ROM SK6 113 G1
UPML OL3 45 H6
UPML OL3 61 K4
WGTN/LGST M12 88 A4
Darley Av CCHDY M21 97 M6
CHD/CHDH SK8 110 E7
DID/WITH M20 98 E8
ECC M30 84 F4
FWTH BL4 53 H3
Darley Gv FWTH BL4 53 H3
Darley Rd BRAM/HZG SK7 122 B5
OLDTF/WHR M16 97 M1
ROCH OL11 28 C8
WGNS/IIMK WN3 63 L1
Darley St BOL BL1 36 A3
FWTH BL4 53 H4
OP/CLY M11 88 B3
SALE M33 96 E8
STRET M32 86 B8
Darley Ter BOL BL1 * 36 A3
Darlington Cl TOT/BURYW BL8 24 E8
Darlington Rd DID/WITH M20 98 D6
ROCH OL11 42 C1
Darlington St TYLD M29 67 K3
WGNE/HIN WN2 48 D5
Darlington St East TYLD M29 67 L3
WGN WN1 15 J5
Darliston Av BKLY M9 56 D7
Darnall Av DID/WITH M20 98 E4
Darnbrook Dr WYTH/NTH M22 118 D3
Darncombe Cl OLDTF/WHR M16 87 J8
Darnhall St WGNS/IIMK WN3 * 48 C8
Darnley Av WALK M28 68 F3
Darnley St OLDTF/WHR M16 87 G8
Darnton Gdns AUL OL6 91 H1
Darnton Rd AUL OL6 91 H1
Darran Av WGNS/IIMK WN3 63 J1
Darras Rd GTN M18 89 M8
Dart Cl CHAD OL9 58 C4
Dartford Av ECC M30 84 E2
RDSH SK5 100 E6
Dartford Cl WGTN/LGST M12 88 A6
Dartford Rd URM M41 95 M3
Dartington Cl BRAM/HZG SK7 121 H1
NTHM/RTH M23 109 G6
Dartington Rd WGNE/HIN WN2 64 C2
Dartmouth Cl OLDS OL8 59 J8
Dartmouth Crs RDSH SK5 100 F7
Dartmouth Rd CCHDY M21 97 M4
WHTF M45 55 K5
Dartnall Cl POY/DIS SK12 123 J6
Darton Av NEWH/MOS M40 88 B1
Darvel Av AIMK WN4 62 F8
Darvel Cl BOLE BL2 37 J6
Darwell Av ECC M30 84 F4
Darwen Rd EDGW/EG BL7 22 C4
Darwen St OLDTF/WHR M16 86 F7
Darwin Gv BRAM/HZG SK7 121 G6
Darwin St AULW OL7 90 D2
BOL BL1 36 A2
HYDE SK14 91 K6
OLDE OL4 59 M7
Dashwood Rd PWCH M25 55 J7
Datchett Ter ROCH OL11 28 C8
Dauntesy Av SWIN M27 * 70 C5
Davehall Av WILM/AE SK9 126 E5
Davenfield Gv DID/WITH M20 110 E1
Davenfield Rd DID/WITH M20 110 E1
Davenham Rd RDSH SK5 100 C2
SALE M33 96 B6
WILM/AE SK9 119 M8
Davenhill Rd BNG/LEV M19 99 K4
Davenport Av DID/WITH M20 98 E5
WILM/AE SK9 126 C8
Davenport Dr MPL/ROM SK6 101 L6
Davenport Fold Rd BOLE BL2 * 23 K8
Davenport Gdns BOL BL1 2 D3
Davenport Park Rd OFTN SK2 112 D7
Davenport Rd BRAM/HZG SK7 121 M1
Davenport St BOL BL1 2 C3
DROY M43 * 89 H3
DTN/ASHW M34 90 B4
Daventry Rd CCHDY M21 98 A4
ROCH OL11 42 C1
Daveylands URM M41 84 C7
WILM/AE SK9 127 H6
Davey La WILM/AE SK9 130 D2
David Brow BOLS/LL BL3 51 K2
David Cl DTN/ASHW M34 * 101 K3
David Lewis Cl MILN OL16 11 L6
David's Farm Cl MDTN M24 57 M5
Davids La OLDE OL4 60 C5
Davidson Dr MDTN M24 57 M6
David's Rd DROY M43 89 H2
David St DTN/ASHW M34 101 K3
RDSH SK5 100 B5
TOT/BURYW BL8 38 F1
WHIT OL12 28 C3
David St North WHIT OL12 * 28 C3
Davies Av CHD/CHDH SK8 119 K6
NEWLW WA12 78 F8
Davies Rd MPL/ROM SK6 113 G1
PART M31 106 D1
Davies Sq RUSH/FAL M14 87 K8
Davies St AULW OL7 90 C3
FWTH BL4 53 K5
OLD OL1 8 F3
WGNE/HIN WN2 64 D2
Davis St ECC M30 85 H3
Davy Av SWIN M27 71 G2
Davyhulme Rd STRET M32 96 F1
URM M41 84 B8
Davyhulme Rd East STRET M32 97 G1
Davyhulme St WHIT OL12 28 D3
Davy St NEWH/MOS M40 * 72 E8
Dawber Delph
WGNNW/ST WN6 30 A4
Dawber St AIMK WN4 64 A8
Dawley Cl AIMK WN4 78 D1
Dawlish Av CHAD OL9 58 C3
CHD/CHDH SK8 120 B4
DROY M43 89 H2
RDSH SK5 100 F7
Dawlish Cl BRAM/HZG SK7 121 G5
HYDE SK14 103 H1
Dawlish Rd CCHDY M21 97 M6
SALE M33 96 B7
Dawlish Wy GOL/RIS/CUL WA3 79 J3
Dawnay St OP/CLY M11 * 88 E5
Dawn St ROY/SHW OL2 * 43 L6
Dawnwood Sq
WGNW/BIL/OR WN5 46 F2
Dawson Av WGNNW/ST WN6 47 K1
Dawson La BOL BL1 2 C4
Dawson Rd ALT WA14 108 A5
CHD/CHDH SK8 119 M4
Dawson St ATH M46 * 66 F1
BURY BL9 4 F5
CSLFD M3 6 B7
CSLFD M3 * 6 E2
HEY OL10 40 F2
HYDE SK14 102 B3
OLDE OL4 60 B7
STKP SK1 112 E1
SWIN M27 70 D4
Day Dr FAIL M35 74 C6
Day Gv HYDE SK14 103 K1
Daylesford Cl CHD/CHDH SK8 110 F8
Daylesford Crs CHD/CHDH SK8 111 G8
Daylesford Rd CHD/CHDH SK8 111 G8
Deacon Cl ALT WA14 116 D3
Deacons Cl STKP SK1 13 L4
Deacons Crs TOT/BURYW BL8 24 D7
Deacons Dr SLFD M6 71 G6
Deacon St MILN OL16 28 E3
Deakin St WGNS/IIMK WN3 15 K9
Deal Av RDSH SK5 100 E6
Deal Cl NEWH/MOS M40 74 A7
Dealey Rd BOLS/LL BL3 35 K8
Deal St BOLS/LL BL3 52 C1
BURY BL9 5 K3
CSLFD M3 * 6 D3
HYDE SK14 102 B2
Deal Wk CHAD OL9 58 D6
Dean Av NEWH/MOS M40 73 L6
OLDTF/WHR M16 97 L1
Deanbank Av BNG/LEV M19 99 J4
Dean Bank Dr MILN OL16 42 E3
Dean Brook Cl NEWH/MOS M40 73 M5
Dean Cl FWTH BL4 52 C4
PART M31 94 C8
RAMS BL0 19 G1
WHTF M45 55 G5
WILM/AE SK9 127 G3
Dean Ct BOL BL1 2 F2
GOL/RIS/CUL WA3 79 K5
HULME M15 * 87 G6
Deancourt ROCH OL11 28 B8
Dean Crs WGNW/BIL/OR WN5 46 E4
Dean Dr ALT WA14 116 D3
WILM/AE SK9 127 G3
Deane Av BOLS/LL BL3 35 L7
CHD/CHDH SK8 111 J7
HALE/TIMP WA15 108 D7
Deane Church La BOLS/LL BL3 35 L8
Deane Rd BOLS/LL BL3 35 M7
Deanery Wy STKP SK1 13 J3
Deane Wk BOLS/LL BL3 2 C7
Dean La BRAM/HZG SK7 122 A4
NEWH/MOS M40 73 L6
Dean Meadow NEWLW WA12 78 F8
Dean Moor Rd BRAM/HZG SK7 121 J2
Dean Rd CSLFD M3 6 D1
GOL/RIS/CUL WA3 79 K5
GTN M18 89 H8
IRL M44 94 B6
WILM/AE SK9 127 J1
Dean Row Rd WILM/AE SK9 127 G3
Deanscourt Av SWIN M27 70 B5
Deansgate BOL BL1 2 E4
HULME M15 6 D8
WGNE/HIN WN2 49 H6
Deansgate La
HALE/TIMP WA15 108 B5
Deanshut Rd OLDS OL8 75 K2
Deans Rd SWIN M27 70 B5
Dean St AUL OL6 90 D1
CMANE M1 7 K4
FAIL M35 74 B5
MILN OL16 28 E3
MOSL OL5 76 E3
RAD M26 54 C1
STLY SK15 91 K3
Deansway SWIN M27 70 B5
Deanswood Dr BKLY M9 56 D7
Dean Ter AUL OL6 75 L3
Deanwater Cl BRUN/LGST M13 7 K9
Deanwater Ct
CHD/CHDH SK8 * 119 M5
STRET M32 * 96 F4
Deanway NEWH/MOS M40 73 K4
URM M41 95 G2
WILM/AE SK9 127 G4
Dean Wood Av
WGNW/BIL/OR WN5 46 B3
Dearden Av LHULT M38 52 D7
Dearden Clough RAMS BL0 19 H2
Dearden Fold RAMS BL0 19 H2
TOT/BURYW BL8 * 38 F3
Deardens St TOT/BURYW BL8 38 F3
Dearden St BOLS/LL BL3 37 K8
HULME M15 87 H6
LIT OL15 21 M6
STLY SK15 * 91 K2
Dearmans Pl CSLFD M3 6 D3
Dearne Dr STRET M32 97 H2
Dearnley Cl LIT OL15 21 K8
Debdale Av GTN M18 89 J8
Debdale La GTN M18 89 J8
TYLD M29 67 J8
Deben Cl WGNNW/ST WN6 31 G3
Debenham Av NEWH/MOS M40 73 M8
Debenham Ct FWTH BL4 * 53 G5
Debenham Rd STRET M32 96 D3
De Brook Cl URM M41 95 H3
Dee Av HALE/TIMP WA15 109 G7
Dee Dr FWTH BL4 53 K7
Deepcar St BNG/LEV M19 99 K2
Deepdale LEIGH WN7 81 M1
OLDE OL4 60 A6
Deepdale Av DID/WITH M20 98 D4
MILN OL16 11 M7
ROY/SHW OL2 42 F4
Deepdale Cl RDSH SK5 100 C3
Deepdale Dr SWIN M27 71 G5
Deepdale Rd BOLE BL2 37 J3
Deeping Av OLDTF/WHR M16 98 A2
Deep La LIT OL15 29 M3
Deeplish Rd ROCH OL11 10 F9
Deeplish St ROCH OL11 10 F8
Deeply Vale La BURY BL9 25 M2
Deeracre Av OFTN SK2 112 F6
Deerfold Cl GTN M18 * 89 G7
Deerhurst Dr CHH M8 72 C6
Dee Rd TYLD M29 67 M5
Deeroak Cl GTN M18 88 E6
Deerpark Rd OLDTF/WHR M16 98 B1
Deerwood V HYDE SK14 103 H3
Defence St BOLS/LL BL3 2 B7
Defiance St ATH M46 66 F1
Deganwy Gv RDSH SK5 100 C7
Degas Cl BRO M7 71 L4
Delacourt Rd RUSH/FAL M14 98 D4
Delafield Av WGTN/LGST M12 99 K2
Delaford Av WALK M28 69 H5
Delaford Cl EDGY/DAV SK3 112 B8
Delahays Dr HALE/TIMP WA15 117 J2
Delahays Range GTN M18 89 J8
Delahays Rd HALE/TIMP WA15 117 K2
Delaine Rd DID/WITH M20 98 F6
Delamere Av GOL/RIS/CUL WA3 80 B6
ROY/SHW OL2 44 A4
SALE M33 109 H1
SLFD M6 70 F6
STRET M32 97 G2
SWIN M27 70 E2
WHTF M45 55 H4
Delamere Cl BRAM/HZG SK7 122 C1
MPL/ROM SK6 101 M7
STLY SK15 77 H6
Delamere Rd BNG/LEV M19 99 K4
BRAM/HZG SK7 122 C1
CHD/CHDH SK8 110 E7
DTN/ASHW M34 100 E2
MILN OL16 28 F8
OFTN SK2 112 E8
URM M41 95 J2
WILM/AE SK9 119 M8
Delamere St AUL OL6 90 E2
BURY BL9 25 K7
OLDS OL8 59 L8
OP/CLY M11 89 J5
Delamer Rd ALT WA14 116 E1
Delaunays Rd CHH M8 72 E2
SALE M33 96 C8
Delbooth Av URM M41 84 B8
Delegarte St WGNS/IIMK WN3 15 K8
Delfhaven Ct WGNNW/ST WN6 31 K5
Delfur Rd BRAM/HZG SK7 121 H5
Delhi Rd IRL M44 94 C4
Dellar St WHIT OL12 27 M3
Dell Av SWIN M27 71 G5
WGNNW/ST WN6 47 H1
Dell Cl OLDE OL4 60 C7
Dellcot Cl PWCH M25 72 A2
SLFD M6 70 E7
Dellcot La WALK M28 69 J7
Dell Gdns WHIT OL12 27 L2
Dellhide Cl OLDE OL4 60 D6
Dell Meadow WHIT OL12 20 A7
Dell Rd WHIT OL12 27 M1
Dell Side MPL/ROM SK6 113 H1
Dellside Cl AIMK WN4 63 G6
Dellside Gv WALK M28 69 H1
Dell Side Wy WHIT OL12 27 M2
The Dell BOLE BL2 22 F7
WGNNW/ST WN6 30 A5
Delph Av EDGW/EG BL7 22 A1
Delph Brook Wy EDGW/EG BL7 22 A2
Delph Gv LEIGH WN7 66 A3
Delph Hl BOL BL1 35 H2
Delph Hill Cl BOL BL1 35 H2
Delphi Av WALK M28 69 G2
Delph La BOLE BL2 37 M3
UPML OL3 45 J7
Delph New Rd UPML OL3 61 J2
Delph Rd UPML OL3 44 F5
Delphside Cl
WGNW/BIL/OR WN5 46 A7
Delph St BOLS/LL BL3 2 B9
MILN OL16 29 J6
WGNNW/ST WN6 14 D1
The Delph WALK M28 * 69 J6
Delside Av NEWH/MOS M40 73 K4
Delta Cl ROY/SHW OL2 59 G2
Delta Rd DTN/ASHW M34 90 B5
Delves Rd ALT WA14 108 A4
Delvino Wk RUSH/FAL M14 87 K8
Delwood Gdns
WYTH/NTH M22 110 A8
De-massey Cl MPL/ROM SK6 * 101 L6
Demesne Cl STLY SK15 91 M3
Demesne Crs STLY SK15 91 M3
Demesne Dr STLY SK15 91 M3
Demesne Rd OLDTF/WHR M16 98 B2
Demmings Rd CHD/CHDH SK8 111 J7
Dempsey Dr BURY BL9 55 L2
Denbigh Cl BRAM/HZG SK7 121 L4
Denbigh Dr ROY/SHW OL2 43 J6
Denbigh Gv ATH M46 50 F7
Denbigh Pl ORD M5 86 D3
Denbigh Rd BOLE BL2 3 J8
DTN/ASHW M34 101 J3
SWIN M27 70 D2
Denbigh St HTNM SK4 12 F1
OLDS OL8 * 75 J1
Denbigh Wk HULME M15 87 H7
Denbury Dr ALT WA14 107 L7
Denbury Gn BRAM/HZG SK7 121 J3
Denbydale Wy ROY/SHW OL2 42 F8
Denby La HTNM SK4 100 A8
Denby Rd DUK SK16 90 F5
Dencombe St BRUN/LGST M13 88 C8
Dene Av NEWLW WA12 78 C8
Dene Bank BOLE BL2 22 F7
Dene Brow DTN/ASHW M34 101 L4
Dene Ct HTNM SK4 12 C2
Dene Dr MDTN M24 57 J5
Denefield Cl MPL/ROM SK6 114 E3
Deneford Rd DID/WITH M20 110 D2
Dene Gv LEIGH WN7 65 L8
Dene Hollow RDSH SK5 100 D3
Denehurst Rd ROCH OL11 27 M4
Denehurst St
WGTN/LGST M12 * 88 C6
Dene Pk DID/WITH M20 110 D2
Dene Rd DID/WITH M20 110 D1
Dene Rd West DID/WITH M20 110 C1
Deneside Crs BRAM/HZG SK7 122 B1
Dene St BOLE BL2 22 F7
LEIGH WN7 65 L8
Denesway SALE M33 108 B1
Deneway BRAM/HZG SK7 120 E5
HTNM SK4 12 C2
MPL/ROM SK6 123 H5
Deneway Cl HTNM SK4 12 C3
Deneway Ms HTNM SK4 * 12 C2
Denewell Cl BRUN/LGST M13 88 A7
Denford Cl WGNS/IIMK WN3 63 J1
Denham Cl BOL BL1 22 D7
Denham Dr BRAM/HZG SK7 120 F5
IRL M44 94 D3
WGNS/IIMK WN3 63 K1
Denham St BRUN/LGST M13 88 A8
Den Hill Dr OLDE OL4 60 C6
Denhill Rd HULME M15 87 J8
Denholme Rd ROCH OL11 28 C8
Denholm Rd DID/WITH M20 110 F4
Denhurst Rd LIT OL15 21 L6
Denis Av OLDTF/WHR M16 98 B2
Denison Rd BRAM/HZG SK7 122 A4
RUSH/FAL M14 98 F1
Denison St RUSH/FAL M14 98 F1
Deniston Rd HTNM SK4 99 L7
Den La OLDE OL4 60 C5
UPML OL3 61 L4
Denmark Rd HULME M15 87 K8
SALE M33 96 E6
Denmark St ALT WA14 108 A8
CHAD OL9 8 D2
MILN OL16 11 H2
OLDE OL4 * 59 L5
Denmark Wy CHAD OL9 8 D3
Denmore Rd NEWH/MOS M40 73 M2
Dennington Dr URM M41 84 F8
Dennison Av DID/WITH M20 98 E5
Dennison Rd CHD/CHDH SK8 120 C4
Denshaw Av DTN/ASHW M34 90 A7
Denshaw Cl BNG/LEV M19 111 H1
Denshaw Rd UPML OL3 44 F7
Densmead Wk NEWH/MOS M40 7 M1
Densmore St FAIL M35 * 74 B5
Denson Rd HALE/TIMP WA15 108 E4
Denstone Av ECC M30 85 H1
SALE M33 108 B1
URM M41 95 M1
Denstone Crs BOLE BL2 37 G2
Denstone Rd RDSH SK5 100 C3
SLFD M6 71 G7
URM M41 95 M1
Dentdale Cl BOL BL1 35 G6
Denton Gv WGNW/BIL/OR WN5 46 E4
Denton Hall Farm Rd
DTN/ASHW M34 100 F2
Denton La CHAD OL9 8 A7
Denton Rd BOLE BL2 37 L6
DTN/ASHW M34 90 B7
Denton St BURY BL9 4 F1
HEY OL10 40 F3
WHIT OL12 10 E1
Denver Av NEWH/MOS M40 88 A1
Denver Dr HALE/TIMP WA15 108 D6
Denver Rd ROCH OL11 28 C8
Denville Crs WYTH/NTH M22 119 G1
Denzell Gdns ALT WA14 * 116 C1
Depleach Rd CHD/CHDH SK8 111 G7
Deptford Av NTHM/RTH M23 118 C1
De Quincey Rd ALT WA14 108 A3
Deramore Cl AUL OL6 91 H1
Deramore St RUSH/FAL M14 98 E1
Derby Av SLFD M6 86 B2
Derby Ct CHAD OL9 8 C9
SALE M33 108 F1
Derby Gv BNG/LEV M19 99 L3
Derby Range HTNM SK4 99 L8
Derby Rd AUL OL6 91 G1
GOL/RIS/CUL WA3 79 M3
HTNM SK4 99 M8
NM/HAY SK22 124 F3
ORD M5 86 B2
RAD M26 53 K4

RUSH/FAL M14 ... 98 F5
SALE M33 ... 96 K8
URM M41 ... 96 A1
WHTF M45 ... 55 K6
Derbyshire Av STRET M32 ... 96 E1
Derbyshire Crs STRET M32 ... 96 E1
Derbyshire Gv STRET M32 ... 96 D1
Derbyshire La STRET M32 ... 96 E1
Derbyshire La West STRET M32 ... 96 D1
Derbyshire Level GLSP SK13 ... 105 J6
Derbyshire Rd NEWH/MOS M40 ... 74 A8
PART M31 ... 106 A2
POY/DIS SK12 ... 122 F7
SALE M33 ... 96 F8
WGNS/IIMK WN3 ... 63 G3
Derbyshire Rd South
SALE M33 ... 109 G2
Derbyshire Rw BOL BL1 * ... 36 B1
Derbyshire St OP/CLY M11 ... 88 F5
Derby St ALT ... 108 B7
ATH M46 ... 50 F8
AULW OL7 ... 75 K7
BOLS/LL BL3 ... 2 C8
BURY BL9 ... 5 G4
CHAD OL9 ... 8 C9
CHH M8 ... 72 B7
DTN/ASHW M34 ... 90 A8
EDGY/DAV SK3 ... 12 F7
FAIL M35 ... 74 D3
GLSP SK13 ... 104 F4
HEY OL10 ... 40 E2
HOR/BR BL6 ... 34 A3
LEIGH WN7 ... 66 D8
MOSL OL5 ... 77 G4
MPL/ROM SK6 ... 114 C5
PWCH M25 ... 55 K8
RAMS BL0 ... 19 G6
ROCH OL11 ... 11 G8
WGNS/IIMK WN3 ... 48 C8
WHTN BL5 ... 50 C3
Dereham CI TOT/BURYW BL8 ... 25 G7
Dereham Wy WGNS/IIMK WN3 ... 63 J2
Derg St SLFD M6 ... 86 C2
Derker St OLD ... 9 M3
Dermot Murphy CI
DID/WITH M20 ... 98 C6
Dernford Av BNG/LEV M19 ... 99 J4
Derngate Dr WGNNW/ST WN6 ... 31 K5
Derry Av WYTH/NTH M22 ... 110 B8
Derwent Av AULW OL7 ... 75 K8
CCHDY M21 ... 98 A7
DROY M43 ... 89 H3
GOL/RIS/CUL WA3 ... 79 M3
HALE/TIMP WA15 * ... 109 G1
HEY OL10 ... 41 G4
MILN OL16 ... 29 L6
WGNE/HIN WN2 ... 48 E5
WHTF M45 ... 55 L4
Derwent CI BOLS/LL BL3 ... 53 J1
DTN/ASHW M34 ... 100 E2
GLSP SK13 ... 105 J4
LEIGH WN7 ... 81 H1
PART M31 ... 106 E2
WALK M28 ... 68 E2
WHTF M45 ... 55 L5
Derwent Dr BRAM/HZG SK7 ... 120 E7
BURY BL9 ... 39 G5
CHAD OL9 ... 58 D5
FWTH BL4 ... 53 L7
LIT OL15 ... 29 J2
ROY/SHW OL2 ... 43 K4
SALE M33 ... 108 D2
WILM/AE SK9 ... 126 D2
Derwent PI WGNW/BIL/OR WN5 ... 46 F5
Derwent Rd AIMK WN4 ... 64 B7
FWTH BL4 ... 52 C5
MDTN M24 ... 57 H1
MPL/ROM SK6 ... 123 C4
STRET M32 ... 97 G1
URM M41 ... 95 H2
WGNE/HIN WN2 ... 49 H7
WGNW/BIL/OR WN5 ... 46 C4
Derwent St CHH M8 ... 72 F6
DROY M43 * ... 89 G3
LEIGH WN7 ... 81 H1
ORD M5 ... 86 F4
TYLD M29 ... 67 K5
WHIT OL12 ... 28 C3
Derwent Ter STLY SK15 ... 91 H4
Derwent Wy LEIGH WN7 ... 80 E3
Design St BOLS/LL BL3 ... 51 L1
Desmond Av WYTH/NTH M22 ... 110 B8
Desmond St ATH M46 ... 66 D2
De Trafford Dr WGNE/HIN WN2 ... 48 E4
The De Traffords IRL M44 ... 94 D1
Dettingen St SLFD M6 ... 71 H6
Deva CI BRAM/HZG SK7 ... 121 M3
POY/DIS SK12 ... 121 K8
Deva Sq CHAD OL9 ... 8 C9
Devas St HULME M15 ... 87 L7
Deverill Av GTN M18 ... 89 J8
Devine CI CSLFD M3 ... 6 A2
ROY/SHW OL2 ... 43 C6
Devisdale Gra ALT WA14 * ... 116 D1
Devisdale Rd ALT WA14 ... 107 L8
Devoke Av WALK M28 ... 69 H2
Devoke Gv FWTH BL4 ... 52 B4
Devoke Rd WYTH/NTH M22 ... 118 D2
Devon Av BNG/LEV M19 ... 99 J4
WHTF M45 ... 55 K4
Devon CI BOLS/LL BL3 ... 37 L8
RDSH SK5 ... 100 F8
ROY/SHW OL2 ... 43 J5
SLFD M6 ... 85 K1
WGNE/HIN WN2 ... 33 G7
WGNW/BIL/OR WN5 ... 46 F6
Devon Dr BOLE BL2 ... 37 M3
UPML OL3 ... 45 M8
WGN WN1 ... 31 L3
Devonport Crs ROY/SHW OL2 ... 43 J8
Devon Rd DROY M43 ... 89 K1
FAIL M35 ... 74 B6
IRL M44 ... 94 A7
PART M31 ... 106 B2
TYLD M29 ... 67 J2
URM M41 ... 95 H3
Devonshire CI HEY OL10 ... 40 D3
URM M41 ... 96 B2
Devonshire Dr WALK M28 ... 68 B6
WILM/AE SK9 ... 130 A2
Devonshire PI PWCH M25 ... 72 A7
Devonshire Rd ALT WA14 ... 107 M6
ATH M46 ... 50 F7
BOL BL1 ... 35 L4
BRAM/HZG SK7 ... 122 B4
CCHDY M21 ... 97 M4
ECC M30 ... 85 H2
HTNM SK4 ... 12 A2
ROCH OL11 ... 42 C2
SLFD M6 ... 85 K1

WALK M28 ... 52 F6
Devonshire St BRO M7 ... 72 B6
BRUN/LGST M13 ... 88 A6
Devonshire St East FAIL M35 * ... 74 A7
Devonshire St North
WGTN/LGST M12 ... 88 A5
Devonshire St South
BRUN/LGST M13 ... 88 A7
Devon St BOLE BL2 ... 3 H5
BURY BL9 ... 4 E8
CHAD OL9 ... 58 E8
FWTH BL4 ... 53 G2
LEIGH WN7 ... 67 H8
ROCH OL11 ... 10 E7
SWIN M27 ... 70 C2
WGNE/HIN WN2 ... 49 H7
Devon Wy OLDS OL8 ... 74 F2
Dewar CI OP/CLY M11 ... 88 D3
Dewberry CI TYLD M29 ... 68 B3
Dewes Av SWIN M27 ... 70 E2
Dewey St OP/CLY M11 ... 89 G5
Dewham CI WHTN BL5 ... 50 C3
Dewhirst Rd WHIT OL12 ... 20 D7
Dewhirst Wy WHIT OL12 ... 20 D8
Dewhurst Clough Rd
EDGW/EG BL7 ... 22 C3
Dewhurst Ct EDGW/EG BL7 ... 22 A1
Dewhurst Rd BOLE BL2 ... 37 H1
Dewhurst St CHH M8 ... 72 C8
HEY OL10 * ... 41 H2
Dewint Av MPL/ROM SK6 ... 114 E4
Dew Meadow CI WHIT OL12 ... 28 C2
Dewsnap CI DUK SK16 * ... 90 F6
Dewsnap La DUK SK16 ... 90 F6
HYDE SK14 ... 92 D6
Dew Wy OLDS OL8 ... 8 E4
Dexter Av BKLY M9 ... 56 D7
Deyne Av PWCH M25 ... 55 L8
RUSH/FAL M14 ... 87 M8
Deyne St ORD M5 ... 86 B2
Dial Ct FWTH BL4 * ... 53 G4
Dial Park Rd OFTN SK2 ... 113 G8
Dial St HALE/TIMP WA15 ... 117 L4
OFTN SK2 ... 112 F7
Dialstone La OFTN SK2 ... 112 F5
Diamond St LEIGH WN7 ... 66 B8
OFTN SK2 ... 112 D6
WGNNW/ST WN6 ... 47 K1
Diamond Ter MPL/ROM SK6 ... 123 H1
Diane Rd AIMK WN4 ... 64 B8
Dicconson Crs WGN WN1 ... 15 G2
Dicconson La WHTN BL5 ... 33 K8
Dicconson St WGN WN1 ... 14 F1
Dicconson Ter WGN WN1 ... 14 F1
Dicken Gn ROCH OL11 ... 28 C8
Dicken Green La ROCH OL11 ... 28 C8
Dickens CI CHD/CHDH SK8 ... 120 D7
Dickens Dr WGNE/HIN WN2 ... 64 E4
Dickens La POY/DIS SK12 ... 129 J1
Dickenson Rd RUSH/FAL M14 ... 99 J1
Dickens PI WGNS/IIMK WN3 ... 47 J3
Dickens Rd ECC M30 ... 85 G3
Dickens St HEY OL10 * ... 40 E2
OLD OL1 ... 24 B8
Dickinson CI BOL BL1 * ... 36 B3
Dickinson St BOL BL1 ... 36 B3
CMANE M1 ... 7 G6
OLDE OL4 ... 59 L5
Didcot Rd WYTH/NTH M22 ... 118 E3
Didley Sq WGTN/LGST M12 * ... 88 B2
Didsbury Gv WGNE/HIN WN2 ... 49 G7
Didsbury Pk DID/WITH M20 ... 110 F3
Didsbury Rd HTNM SK4 ... 12 B4
Digby Rd ROCH OL11 ... 28 C8
Dig Gate La MILN OL16 ... 43 H1
Diggles La ROCH OL11 ... 27 H6
Diggle St ROY/SHW OL2 ... 43 L6
WGNNW/ST WN6 ... 14 C2
Diglands Av NM/HAY SK22 ... 124 F3
Dijon St BOLS/LL BL3 ... 35 M8
Dilham Ct BOL BL1 ... 35 M4
Dillmoss Wk HULME M15 * ... 87 G6
Dillon Dr WGTN/LGST M12 ... 88 B7
Dilworth CI HEY OL10 ... 40 C2
Dilworth St OFTN SK2 ... 113 H1
Dilworth St HULME M15 ... 87 L7
Dimple Pk EDGW/EG BL7 ... 22 A1
Dingle Av ROY/SHW OL2 ... 43 M3
WILM/AE SK9 ... 130 A1
Dingle Bank Rd
BRAM/HZG SK7 ... 120 F3
Dingle CI GLSP SK13 ... 104 D4
MPL/ROM SK6 ... 114 A2
Dingle Dr DROY M43 ... 89 L1
Dingle Gv CHD/CHDH SK8 ... 110 C6
Dingle Rd MDTN M24 ... 57 H6
Dingle Ter AUL OL6 ... 75 L2
The Dingle BRAM/HZG SK7 ... 120 E3
HYDE SK14 ... 102 B6
Dingle Wk BOL BL1 ... 2 E2
WGNNW/ST WN6 ... 31 G8
Dinmor Rd WYTH/NTH M22 ... 118 F4
Dinnington Dr CHH M8 ... 72 C6
Dinorwic CI CHH M8 ... 72 B7
Dinsdale Dr BOLS/LL BL3 ... 2 A8
Dinting Av DID/WITH M20 ... 98 D5
Dinting La GLSP SK13 ... 104 D3
Dinting Rd GLSP SK13 ... 104 E2
Dinton St HULME M15 ... 86 F5
Dirty La OLDE OL4 ... 60 E3
UPML OL3 ... 45 L4
Dirty Leech WHIT OL12 ... 20 D6
Discovery Pk HTNM SK4 * ... 99 M7
Disley Av DID/WITH M20 ... 98 C6
Disley St ROCH OL11 ... 28 A4
Distaff Rd POY/DIS SK12 ... 121 K8
Ditton Brook WHTN BL5 ... 50 C3
Ditton Mead CI WHIT OL12 ... 28 C2
Division St BOLS/LL BL3 ... 52 C1
OLDE OL4 ... 28 E2
Dixey St HOR/BR BL6 ... 33 K1
Dixon Av BRO M7 ... 72 A6
NEWLW WA12 ... 78 F7
Dixon CI RNFD/HAY WA11 ... 78 D4
SALE M33 ... 109 G2
Dixon Closes ROCH OL11 ... 27 H5
Dixon Dr SWIN M27 ... 54 B8
WGNNW/ST WN6 ... 30 D7
Dixon Green Dr FWTH BL4 ... 52 F4
Dixon Rd DTN/ASHW M34 ... 101 L3
Dixon St AUL OL6 ... 76 A8
HOR/BR BL6 ... 33 L1
IRL M44 ... 94 B4
MDTN M24 ... 57 K2
NEWH/MOS M40 ... 73 L6
OLD OL1 ... 9 H3
OLDE OL4 ... 60 A8
ROCH OL11 ... 28 A8
SLFD M6 ... 71 J4
WHTN BL5 ... 50 B1

Dobb Brow Rd WHTN BL5 ... 50 A5
Dobb Hedge CI
HALE/TIMP WA15 ... 117 L6
Dobbin Dr ROCH OL11 ... 42 C1
Dobbinets La
HALE/TIMP WA15 ... 117 M1
Dobcross CI BRUN/LGST M13 ... 99 K2
Dobcross New Rd UPML OL3 ... 61 K3
Dobhill St FWTH BL4 ... 53 C4
Dobroyd St CHH M8 ... 72 D4
Dobson CI BRUN/LGST M13 ... 88 A6
Dobson Pkwy
WGNE/HIN WN2 ... 48 D6
Dobson Rd BOL BL1 ... 35 M5
Dobson St BOL BL1 ... 36 A2
Doctor Fold La HEY OL10 ... 40 F7
Doctor La OLDE OL4 ... 60 F3
Doctors La BURY BL9 ... 4 C4
Doctor's Nook LEIGH WN7 ... 66 C7
Dodd Cft MILN OL16 ... 43 C2
Doddington La ORD M5 ... 86 D4
DTN/ASHW M34 * ... 101 H3
Dodd St WHTN BL5 ... 49 L1
Dodd's Farm La
WGNE/HIN WN2 ... 49 H1
Dodd St ORD M5 ... 86 A2
Dodge Fold OFTN SK2 ... 113 H6
Dodge HI HTNM SK4 ... 13 H1
Dodgson La OLDE OL4 ... 60 F3
Dodgson St MILN OL16 ... 11 H7
Dodhurst Rd
WGNE/HIN WN2 ... 49 J6
Dodworth CI
HULME M15 ... 87 J6
Doe Brow SWIN M27 ... 54 B8
Doefield Av WALK M28 ... 69 C4
Doeford CI
GOL/RIS/CUL WA3 ... 81 H7
Doe Hey Gv FWTH BL4 ... 52 E2
Doe Hey Rd BOLS/LL BL3 ... 52 E2
Doffcocker Brow BOL BL1 ... 35 J3
Doffcocker La
BOL BL1 ... 35 J3
Dogford Rd ROY/SHW OL2 ... 43 G7
Dog Hill Lne ROY/SHW OL2 ... 44 B5
Dolbey St ORD M5 ... 86 B3
Dolefield CSLFD M3 ... 6 D5
D'Olivera Ct MDTN M24 ... 57 H2
Dollond St BKLY M9 ... 73 H3
Dolphin PI
WGTN/LGST M12 ... 7 M9
Dolphin St WGTN/LGST M12 ... 7 M9
Doman St BOLS/LL BL3 ... 2 E9
Dombey Rd POY/DIS SK12 ... 129 H2
Domestic Ap MANAIR M90 ... 118 E6
The Dome ALT WA14 * ... 108 A8
Domett St BKLY M9 ... 72 F2
Dominic CI NTHM/RTH M23 ... 109 H3
Donald Av HYDE SK14 ... 102 C3
Donald St CMANE M1 * ... 7 H7
Dona St STKP SK1 ... 13 M6
Don Av SLFD M6 ... 85 M2
Doncaster Av DID/WITH M20 ... 98 D5
Doncaster CI BOLS/LL BL3 ... 53 J1
OLD OL1 ... 44 A8
Doncaster Wk OLD OL1 * ... 9 J4
Donhead Wk BRUN/LGST M13 * ... 87 M6
Donkey La WILM/AE SK9 ... 126 C5
Donleigh St NEWH/MOS M40 ... 74 A7
Donnington Av
CHD/CHDH SK8 ... 111 J7
Donnington CI LEIGH WN7 ... 81 G3
Donnington Gdns WALK M28 * ... 69 G3
Donnington Rd GTN M18 ... 89 H7
RAD M26 ... 37 M7
Denison St WGTN/LGST M12 ... 88 B2
Donovan Av NEWH/MOS M40 ... 72 F8
Don St BOLS/LL BL3 ... 52 A1
MDTN M24 ... 57 M3
Doodson Av IRL M44 ... 94 C4
Doodson Sq FWTH BL4 ... 53 G4
Dooley La MPL/ROM SK6 ... 113 L5
Dootson St WGNE/HIN WN2 ... 49 K6
WGNE/HIN WN2 ... 64 D3
Dorac Av CHD/CHDH SK8 ... 119 L6
Dora St RAMS BL0 ... 18 D8
Dorchester Av BOLE BL2 ... 37 H3
DTN/ASHW M34 ... 101 J3
PWCH M25 ... 71 M2
URM M41 ... 96 C1
Dorchester CI
HALE/TIMP WA15 ... 117 L1
WILM/AE SK9 ... 127 H4
Dorchester Ct
CHD/CHDH SK8 ... 120 D3
SALE M33 ... 108 E2
Dorchester Dr
NTHM/RTH M23 ... 109 H3
ROY/SHW OL2 ... 59 C2
Dorchester Gv HEY OL10 ... 40 F7
Dorchester Rd
BRAM/HZG SK7 ... 121 K3
SWIN M27 ... 70 C6
Dorclyn Av URM M41 ... 96 A2
Dorfield CI MPL/ROM SK6 ... 113 H1
Doric Av MPL/ROM SK6 ... 113 G2
Doric CI OP/CLY M11 ... 88 C3
Doris Av BOLE BL2 ... 37 G5
Doris Rd EDGY/DAV SK3 ... 12 C7
Doris St MDTN M24 ... 57 K2
Dorket Gv WHTN BL5 ... 50 A6
Dorking Av NEWH/MOS M40 ... 73 K8
Dorking CI BOL BL1 ... 36 C1
STKP SK1 ... 112 E5
Dorlan Av GTN M18 ... 89 J8
Dorland Gv OFTN SK2 ... 112 E5
Dorman St OP/CLY M11 ... 89 G5
Dormer St BOL BL1 ... 36 C1
Dorney St GTN M18 ... 89 C1
Dorning Rd SWIN M27 ... 70 D5
Dorning St ATH M46 ... 67 J3
ECC M30 ... 85 J1
FWTH BL4 ... 53 J4
HOR/BR BL6 ... 33 H5
LEIGH WN7 ... 66 B7
TOT/BURYW BL8 ... 24 E3
WGN WN1 ... 14 E3
Dorothy Gv LEIGH WN7 ... 66 B8
Dorothy Rd BRAM/HZG SK7 ... 122 B8
Dorothy St BRO M7 ... 72 C5
RAMS BL0 ... 18 E7
Dorrington Rd
EDGY/DAV SK3 ... 111 K5
SALE M33 ... 96 A3
Dorris St BNG/LEV M19 ... 99 L4
BOLS/LL BL3 * ... 51 M1
Dorrit CI POY/DIS SK12 ... 129 J2

Dorset Av BRAM/HZG SK7 ... 120 F3
CHD/CHDH SK8 ... 111 H8
DTN/ASHW M34 ... 89 M4
FWTH BL4 ... 52 F4
RDSH SK5 ... 100 F7
ROY/SHW OL2 ... 43 J5
RUSH/FAL M14 ... 98 D2
TYLD M29 ... 67 J1
UPML OL3 ... 45 M8
Dorset CI FWTH BL4 ... 52 F4
HEY OL10 ... 40 D3
WGNW/BIL/OR WN5 ... 46 F6
Dorset Dr BURY BL9 ... 5 H8
Dorset Rd ALT WA14 ... 107 L8
ATH M46 ... 50 F8
BNG/LEV M19 ... 99 M3
DROY M43 ... 89 J1
FAIL M35 ... 74 C7
IRL M44 ... 94 A7
WGN WN1 ... 31 L3
Dorset St AUL OL6 ... 91 G2
BOLE BL2 ... 3 H5
CHAD OL9 ... 8 C9
LEIGH WN7 ... 67 J8
ROCH OL11 ... 10 E7
STRET M32 ... 97 G3
SWIN M27 ... 70 C2
WGNE/HIN WN2 ... 49 H6
Dorsey St ANC M4 * ... 7 J3
Dorstone CI
NEWH/MOS M40 ... 73 M8
WGNE/HIN WN2 ... 49 L7
Drapers Ct GOL/RIS/CUL WA3 ... 80 C5
Draycott CI WGNE/HIN WN2 ... 65 J3
Draycott St BOL BL1 ... 36 C2
Draycott St East BOL BL1 ... 36 C2
Drayfields DROY M43 ... 90 A2
Drayford CI NTHM/RTH M23 ... 109 J2
Drayton CI BOL BL1 ... 36 A2
SALE M33 ... 108 A2
WILM/AE SK9 ... 127 H3
Drayton Dr CHD/CHDH SK8 ... 119 K5
Drayton Gv HALE/TIMP WA15 ... 108 D3
Drayton St HULME M15 ... 87 H7
Drayton Wk OLDTF/WHR M16 ... 86 F7
Dresden St NEWH/MOS M40 ... 73 M4
Drewett St NEWH/MOS M40 ... 73 M8
Dreyfus Av OP/CLY M11 ... 88 F2
Driffield St ECC M30 ... 84 F4
RUSH/FAL M14 ... 98 D3
Drill Wk ANC M4 ... 7 M4
Drinkwater Rd PWCH M25 ... 71 J3
Driscoll St BRUN/LGST M13 ... 99 J1
The Drive ATH M46 * ... 50 F6
BRO M7 ... 71 M4
BURY BL9 ... 25 J4
CHD/CHDH SK8 ... 111 M8
DID/WITH M20 ... 110 F1
HALE/TIMP WA15 ... 117 M4
LEIGH WN7 ... 81 J1
MPL/ROM SK6 ... 113 G1
MPL/ROM SK6 ... 114 B6
PWCH M25 ... 55 L8
RAMS BL0 ... 19 G2
RDSH SK5 ... 100 B3
SALE M33 ... 108 B3
Droitwich Rd NEWH/MOS M40 ... 73 G8
WYTH/NTH M22 ... 110 A4
Dronfield Rd SLFD M6 ... 71 G8
Droughts La PWCH M25 ... 56 A4
Droxford Gv ATH M46 ... 51 H7
Droylsden Rd DTN/ASHW M34 ... 89 L3
NEWH/MOS M40 ... 74 A7
Druids CI EDGW/EG BL7 ... 22 A1
Druid St AIMK WN4 ... 78 F2
Drummer's La AIMK WN4 ... 63 H5
Drummond Sq
WGNW/BIL/OR WN5 ... 47 H5
Drummond St BOL BL1 ... 22 B8
Drummond Wy LEIGH WN7 ... 66 E7
Drury La CHAD OL9 ... 74 D1
Drury St BNG/LEV M19 ... 99 K3
Drybrook CI BRUN/LGST M13 ... 88 B7
Dryburgh Av BOL BL1 ... 36 A1
Dryden Av BOL BL1 ... 63 J5
CHD/CHDH SK8 ... 111 H6
SWIN M27 ... 69 L5
Dryden CI DUK SK16 ... 91 L5
MPL/ROM SK6 ... 114 C8
WGNS/IIMK WN3 ... 47 K7
Dryden Rd OLDTF/WHR M16 ... 97 M1
Dryden St BRUN/LGST M13 ... 88 A6
Dryden Wk ROY/SHW OL2 ... 43 K8
Dryhurst Dr POY/DIS SK12 ... 123 M6
Dryhurst La POY/DIS SK12 ... 123 M6
Dryhurst Wk HULME M15 ... 87 K6
Drymoss OLDS OL8 ... 75 J3
Drysdale Vw BOL BL1 ... 22 B8
Dryton Wk WGNE/HIN WN2 ... 48 D2
Drywood Av WALK M28 ... 69 C4
Ducal St ANC M4 ... 72 E6
Duchess Park CI ROY/SHW OL2 ... 43 L4
Duchess Rd CHH M8 ... 72 D2
Duchess St ROY/SHW OL2 ... 43 K4
Duchess Wk BOLS/LL BL3 ... 35 L8
Duchy Av WALK M28 ... 69 G4
WHTN BL5 ... 51 K4
Duchy Bank SLFD M6 ... 71 G6
Duchy Rd SLFD M6 ... 71 H7
Duchy St EDGY/DAV SK3 ... 12 E8
SLFD M6 ... 86 C2
Ducie Av BOL BL1 ... 35 M5
Ducie St CMANE M1 ... 7 K5
OLDS OL8 ... 75 J2
RAD M26 ... 38 C7
WHTF M45 ... 55 K5
Duckshaw La FWTH BL4 ... 52 F4
Duckworth Rd PWCH M25 ... 71 J3
Duckworth St BURY BL9 ... 25 K8
ROY/SHW OL2 ... 43 K5
Duddon Av BOLE BL2 ... 37 J3
Duddon CI WHTF M45 ... 55 J3
Duddon Dr WGNNW/ST WN6 ... 31 J3
Dudley Av BOLE BL2 ... 3 M1
Dudley CI HULME M15 ... 87 H7
Dudley Rd HALE/TIMP WA15 ... 108 D3
IRL M44 ... 94 A8
OLDTF/WHR M16 ... 98 A1
SALE M33 ... 96 F6
SWIN M27 ... 70 C3
Dudley St AIMK WN4 ... 63 K7
BRO M7 ... 72 B5
ECC M30 ... 84 F3
OLDE OL4 ... 60 C7
Dudlow Wk HULME M15 * ... 87 G6
Dudwell CI BOL BL1 ... 36 B1
Duerden St BOLS/LL BL3 * ... 51 K2
Duffield Ct MDTN M24 ... 57 J7
Duffield Gdns MDTN M24 ... 57 J7
Duffield Rd MDTN M24 ... 57 J7
OLD OL1 ... 9 G7
Duffins CI WHIT OL12 ... 28 A1
Dugdale Av BKLY M9 ... 57 H8

Dugie St *RAMS* BL0 .....................18 E5
Duke Av *CHD/CHDH* SK8 ...........120 B6
Duke Ct *OLDTF/WHR* M16 ..............81 M5
Dukefield St *WYTH/NTH* M22 .......110 B4
Duke PI *CSLFD* M3 ..........................6 C7
Duke Rd *BOLE* BL2 .........................37 M3
   *HYDE* SK14 .............................91 J7
Dukes Fold *GLSP* SK13 ................104 B5
Dukes Platting *AUL* OL6 ................76 C7
Duke St *GLSP* SK13 ......................104 B5
   *AIMK* WN4 ..............................78 F1
   *AUL* OL6 .................................90 E2
   *BOL* BL1 ...................................2 D3
   *BRO* M7 ...................................72 A4
   *CSLFD* M3 .................................6 C7
   *CSLFD* M3 .................................7 G7
   *DTN/ASHW* M34 .....................101 H1
   *ECC* M30 ................................74 D4
   *FAIL* M35 ................................74 D4
   *GOL/RIS/CUL* WA3 ..................79 K3
   *HEY* OL10 ..............................40 D2
   *LEIGH* WN7 ............................66 D8
   *LHULT* M38 .............................52 D7
   *LIT* OL15 .................................21 L7
   *MOSL* OL5 ..............................77 H3
   *RAD* M26 ................................54 E2
   *RAMS* BL0 ...............................18 D8
   *ROY/SHW* OL2 .........................43 M6
   *STKP* SK1 ................................13 J5
   *STLY* SK15 ..............................91 J3
   *TYLD* M29 ...............................67 M6
   *WALK* M28 ...............................69 L2
   *WCN* WN1 ...............................47 M2
   *WGNE/HIN* WN2 ......................64 D1
   *WGNS/IIMK* WN3 .....................47 J8
   *WHIT* OL12 ..............................28 C5
   *WILM/AE* SK9 ........................130 C2
Duke St North *BOL* BL1 ..................2 D2
Dukes Wk *HALE/TIMP* WA15 .......117 H1
Dukinfield Rd *HYDE* SK14 ..............90 F7
Dukinfield St *LEIGH* WN7 * .............66 D7
Dulford Wk *BRUN/LGST* M13 * .......87 H7
Dulgar St *OP/CLY* M11 * ..................88 E4
Dulverton Gdns *BOLS/LL* BL3 * .....53 L3
Dulverton St *NEWH/MOS* M40 .......73 L6
Dulwich Cl *SALE* M33 ...................108 A1
Dulwich St *ANC* M4 .........................87 L1
Dumbarton Cl *RDSH* SK5 .............100 C5
Dumbarton Dr *HEY* OL10 ................40 D3
Dumbarton Gn
   *WGNNW/ST* WN6 ....................47 H2
Dumbarton Rd *RDSH* SK5 .............100 C5
Dumbell St *SWIN* M27 .....................70 C2
Dumber La *SALE* M33 ......................96 C6
Dumers Cl *RAD* M26 ........................39 G8
Dumers La *RAD* M26 .......................39 H7
Dumfries Av *UPML* OL3 ...................44 F2
Dumfries Dr *UPML* OL3 ...................44 F2
Dumfries Hollow *HEY* OL10 ............41 J1
Dunbar Dr *BOLS/LL* BL3 ..................36 B8
Dunbar Gv *HEY* OL10 ......................40 C4
Dunbar St *OLD* OL1 ...........................9 G3
Dunblane Av *BOLS/LL* BL3 ..............35 H7
   *HTNM* SK4 ..............................12 E2
Dunblane Cl *AIMK* WN4 ...................78 F8
Dunblane Gv *HEY* OL10 ...................40 D4
Duncan Av *NEWLW* WA12 ...............78 F7
Duncan Dr *WGNNW/BIL/OR* WN5 ...47 H5
Duncan Rd *BRUN/LGST* M13 ...........99 J1
Duncan St *BRO* M7 ..........................71 M6
   *DUK* SK16 ...............................90 E6
   *HOR/BR* BL6 .............................33 M1
   *ORD* M5 ...................................86 F4
Dunchurch Cl *HOR/BR* BL6 .............35 G6
Dunchurch Rd *SALE* M33 .................96 B8
Dun *CSLFD* M3 ..................................6 B3
Duncombe Cl *BRAM/HZG* SK7 .......121 L3
Duncombe Dr *NEWH/MOS* M40 .......73 L5
Duncombe Rd *BOLS/LL* BL3 .............52 B2
Duncombe St *BRO* M7 .....................72 B6
Duncote Gv *ROY/SHW* OL2 ...............43 J7
Dundee *HEY* OL10 ...........................40 D4
Dundee Cl *HEY* OL10 .......................40 D4
Dundee La *RAMS* BL0 ......................18 E6
Dundonald Rd *CHD/CHDH* SK8 .....120 C5
   *DID/WITH* M20 ......................110 F1
Dundonald St *OFTN* SK2 ...............112 C6
Dundraw Cl *MDTN* M24 ...................56 E3
Dundrennan Cl *POY/DIS* SK12 ......121 M7
Dunecroft *DTN/ASHW* M34 * ............90 D8
Dunedin Dr *SLFD* M6 .......................71 J7
Dunedin Rd *TOT/BURYW* BL8 ..........24 C2
Dunelm Dr *SALE* M33 .....................109 L3
Dunham Cl *WHTN* BL5 .....................50 A7
Dunham Gv *LEIGH* WN7 ...................81 M2
Dunham Lawn *ALT* WA14 ...............107 L8
Dunham Ms *ALT* WA14 * ................116 B3
Dunham Ri *ALT* WA14 ....................107 M8
Dunham Rd *ALT* WA14 ...................116 B2
   *ALT* WA14 ...............................116 B2
   *DUK* SK16 ...............................91 G6
   *LYMM* WA13 ...........................106 B5
   *PART* M31 ................................95 G3
Dunham St *HULME* M15 ...................87 H6
   *OLDE* OL4 ...............................60 B4
Dunkeld Rd *NTHM/RTH* M23 .........109 J6
Dunkerley Av *FAIL* M35 ...................74 C5
Dunkerley Ct *AULW* OL7 * ...............75 K7
   *OLDE* OL4 ...............................59 M5
   *ROY/SHW* OL2 * ......................43 G2
Dunkery Rd *WYTH/NTH* M22 .........118 F3
Dunkirk La *HYDE* SK14 .....................90 F6
Dunkirk Ri *WHIT* OL12 .....................10 C4
Dunkirk St *DROY* M43 ......................89 L3
Dunley Cl *WGTN/LGST* M12 ............88 D7
Dunlin Av *NEWLW* WA12 ..................78 F8
Dunlin Cl *BOLE* BL2 .........................23 K7
   *OFTN* SK2 ..............................113 K7
   *POY/DIS* SK12 .......................128 E1
   *ROCH* OL11 ..............................27 L1
Dunlin Dr *IRL* M44 ...........................94 D1
Dunlin Gv *LEIGH* WN7 ......................66 F1
Dunlop Av *ROCH* OL11 .....................42 B1
Dunlop St *CSLFD* M3 * ......................6 E5
Dunmail Cl *TYLD* M29 .......................67 M6
Dunmail Dr *MDTN* M24 .....................57 H1
Dunmaston Av
   *HALE/TIMP* WA15 .................109 G5
Dunmere Rd *CHD/CHDH* SK8 ........110 D4
Dunmow Ct *OFTN* SK2 ...................113 H7
Dunne La *GLSP* SK13 .....................105 H2
Dunnisher Rd *NTHM/RTH* M23 .......109 L8
Dunnock Cl *OFTN* SK2 ...................113 J7
Dunollie Rd *SALE* M33 ....................109 H1
Dunoon Dr *BOL* BL1 .........................22 A7
Dunoon Rd *RDSH* SK5 ....................100 C5
   *WGNE/HIN* WN2 ......................33 G7

Dunrobin Cl *HEY* OL10 ......................40 D4
Dunscar Dr *WHTF* M45 .....................55 G5
Dunscore Rd
   *NTHM/RTH* M23 ....................109 G4
Dunsdale Dr *AIMK* WN4 ....................78 H1
Dunsfold Dr
   *NTHM/RTH* M23 ....................109 G4
Dunsley Av
   *NEWH/MOS* M40 .....................74 A2
Dunsmore Cl
   *OLDTF/WHR* M16 .....................87 G8
Dunsop Dr *BOL* BL1 ..........................35 J1
Dunstable *WHIT* OL12 .......................10 D2
Dunstable St *BNG/LEV* M19 .............99 L3
Dunstall Rd
   *WYTH/NTH* M22 ....................110 B7
Dunstan St *BOLE* BL2 .........................3 L4
Dunster Av
   *DTN/ASHW* M34 .......................90 B5
   *BKLY* M9 ..................................57 H8
   *RDSH* SK5 ................................99 M8
   *SWIN* M27 ...............................70 E2
Dunster Cl *BRAM/HZG* SK7 ...........121 L3
   *WGNE/HIN* WN2 ......................64 D3
Dunster Dr *URM* M41 ........................94 F3
Dunster PI *WALK* M28 ........................68 C5
Dunster Rd *WALK* M28 ......................68 C5
Dunsters Av
   *TOT/BURYW* BL8 .....................24 F7
Dunsterville Ter *ROCH* OL11 * ...........10 E7
Dunston St *OP/CLY* M11 ....................88 F4
Dunton Gn *RDSH* SK5 .....................100 E6
Dunvegan Rd
   *BRAM/HZG* SK7 ....................122 B3
Dunwood Av *ROY/SHW* OL2 .............43 M4
Dunwoods Park Cts
   *ROY/SHW* OL2 .........................43 M3
Dunworth St
   *RUSH/FAL* M14 ........................98 E1
Durant St *ANC* M4 * ............................7 J1
Durban Cl *ROY/SHW* OL2 ..................43 K6
Durban Rd *BOL* BL1 ...........................22 B7
Durban St *ATH* M46 ...........................66 F7
   *AULW* OL7 ...............................90 B3
   *OLDS* OL8 ................................74 F1
   *ROCH* OL11 ..............................41 M2
Durden Ms
   *ROY/SHW* OL2 .........................43 L6
Durham Av *URM* M41 ........................96 B1
Durham Cl *BOLS/LL* BL3 ...................35 M8
   *DUK* SK16 ...............................91 G6
   *MPL/ROM* SK6 .......................113 K3
   *TYLD* M29 ...............................67 K1
Durham Crs *FAIL* M35 ........................75 G8
Durham Dr *AUL* OL6 ..........................76 A4
   *BURY* BL9 ...................................5 J8
   *RAMS* BL0 ...............................24 D1
Durham Rd *SLFD* M6 .........................70 D6
   *WGNE/HIN* WN2 ......................49 H7
Durham St *BKLY* M9 * .........................73 H5
   *BOL* BL1 ..................................36 C2
   *CHAD* OL9 ...............................58 F8
   *DROY* M43 ...............................89 J3
   *RAD* M26 .................................39 F7
   *ROCH* OL11 ..............................10 B2
   *WGN* WN1 ................................15 L1
Durley Av *CHH* M8 ............................72 E5
   *HALE/TIMP* WA15 .................108 E5
Durling Av *WGTN/LGST* M12 .............7 M9
Durnford Av *URM* M41 .......................96 D2
Durnford Cl *WHIT* OL12 .....................27 G2
Durnford St *MDTN* M24 .....................57 K1
Durrell Wy *GOL/RIS/CUL* WA3 ...........80 B4
Durrington PI *WHTN* BL5 ...................50 B6
Dutton Gv *LEIGH* WN7 .......................81 M2
Dutton St *CSLFD* M3 ...........................87 J1
Duty St *BOL* BL1 .................................36 B1
Duxbury Av *BOLE* BL2 ........................23 H7
   *BOLS/LL* BL3 ............................52 E3
Duxbury Dr *BURY* BL9 .........................5 M4
Duxbury St *BOL* BL1 ...........................36 A2
Dyche St *ANC* M4 * ...............................7 J2
Dye House La *MILN* OL16 ...................28 F1
Dye La *MPL/ROM* SK6 ......................113 L2
Dyers Ct *LIT* OL15 * ...........................21 L6
Dyer St *GOL/RIS/CUL* WA3 .................79 J4
   *OP/CLY* M11 .............................88 D5
   *ORD* M5 ...................................86 F5
Dymchurch Av *RAD* M26 ....................53 M5
Dymchurch St *NEWH/MOS* M40 .......73 M8
Dysarts Cl *MOSL* OL5 .........................77 H1
Dysart St *AUL* OL6 ..............................91 G2
   *WGN* SK2 ...............................112 E7
Dyserth Gv *RDSH* SK5 ......................100 C1
Dyson Cl *FWTH* BL4 ...........................53 G4
Dyson Gv *OLDE* OL4 ...........................60 C4
Dyson St *FWTH* BL4 * .........................53 G5
   *MOSL* OL5 ...............................76 E2
Dystelegh Rd *POY/DIS* SK12 ...........123 M7

## E

Eades St *SLFD* M6 ..............................86 D1
Eadington St *CHH* M8 ........................72 D3
Eafield Av *MILN* OL16 .........................29 J5
Eafield Cl *MILN* OL16 ..........................29 J5
Eafield Rd *LIT* OL15 ...........................29 H1
   *MILN* OL16 ..............................28 F3
Eagar St *NEWH/MOS* M40 .................73 M6
Eagle Dr *SLFD* M6 ..............................71 K7
Eagle Mill Ct *UPML* OL3 * ..................45 J7
Eagle St *ANC* M4 ..................................7 J2
   *BOLE* BL2 ...................................3 H4
   *CHAD* OL9 .................................9 G5
   *ROCH* OL11 ..............................11 G5
Eagley Brook Wy *BOL* BL1 .................36 C1
Eagley Brow *BOL* BL1 .........................22 C5
Eagley Dr *TOT/BURYW* BL8 ...............38 D3
Eagley Vw *TOT/BURYW* BL8 ..............38 D3
Eagley Wy *BOL* BL1 ............................22 C6
Ealand Cha *HOR/BR* BL6 ...................33 H1
Ealing Av *RUSH/FAL* M14 ...................98 E2
Ealing PI *BNG/LEV* M19 * ...................99 K6
Ealing Rd *EDGY/DAV* SK3 .................12 C6
Eames Av *RAD* M26 ............................55 L1
Earby Gv *BKLY* M9 ..............................57 J3
Earle Rd *BRAM/HZG* SK7 .................121 G2
Earlesdon Crs *LHULT* M38 .................52 D7
Earlesfield Cl *SALE* M33 ...................108 A2
Earl St *AULW* OL7 ...............................90 C3
   *CHD/CHDH* SK8 ....................120 A7
   *HTNM* SK4 ...............................99 M8
   *RAMS* BL0 ...............................18 E6
Earlston Av *DTN/ASHW* M34 ...........100 D1

Earl St *ATH* M46 .................................66 E2
   *BRO* M7 .....................................5 G4
   *BURY* BL9 ...................................5 G4
   *DTN/ASHW* M34 .......................89 K8
   *EDGY/DAV* SK3 ........................12 C5
   *HEY* OL10 .................................40 F2
   *MOSL* OL5 ................................76 D3
   *PWCH* M25 ...............................55 M8
   *RAMS* BL0 ...............................19 G6
   *ROCH* OL11 ..............................41 M4
   *SALE* M33 .................................96 F7
   *WGN* WN1 ...............................47 M2
   *WGNE/HIN* WN2 ......................48 D5
Earls Wy *FAIL* M35 ..............................74 A6
Earl Sway *GLSP* SK13 .......................104 E4
Earlswood Wk *BOLS/LL* BL3 ..............36 C8
Earl Wk *WGTN/LGST* M12 * ................88 C8
Early Bank *STLY* SK15 ........................91 M5
Early Bank Rd *HYDE* SK14 ..................91 L6
Earnshaw Av *STKP* SK1 ....................112 E3
   *WHIT* OL12 ..............................28 B1
Earnshaw Cl *AULW* OL7 * ...................75 J7
Earnshaw St *BOLS/LL* BL3 * ..............51 M1
   *HYDE* SK14 ..............................93 G8
Easby Cl *CHD/CHDH* SK8 .................120 D6
   *POY/DIS* SK12 .......................121 M7
Easby Rd *MDTN* M24 ..........................57 J1
   *WILM/AE* SK9 .........................130 C2
Easedale Av *BOL* BL1 .........................35 K4
Easedale Rd *BOL* BL1 .........................35 M8
   *NEWH/MOS* M40 .....................73 M4
East Aisle Rd *TRPK* M17 .....................85 M8
East Av *BNG/LEV* M19 .........................99 J5
   *CHD/CHDH* SK8 ....................119 M4
   *GOL/RIS/CUL* WA3 ..................79 M3
   *LEIGH* WN7 ..............................81 M1
   *STLY* SK15 ...............................91 K1
   *WHTF* M45 ...............................55 J8
East Bank *BOL* BL1 .............................36 C2
East Bond St *LEIGH* WN7 ...................66 D7
Eastbourne Gv *BOL* BL1 .....................35 K4
Eastbourne St *OLDS* OL8 ...................59 L8
   *ROCH* OL11 ..............................10 E8
East Bridgewater St
   *LEIGH* WN7 ..............................66 D8
Eastbrook Av *RAD* M26 * .....................38 F8
Eastburn Av *NEWH/MOS* M40 ...........87 M1
East Central Dr *SWIN* M27 .................70 E5
Eastchurch Cl *FWTH* BL4 ....................53 G5
Eastcombe Av *BRO* M7 .......................71 L5
Eastcote Rd *RDSH* SK5 .....................100 C7
East Crs *MDTN* M24 ............................57 J5
Eastdale PI *ALT* WA14 .......................108 A5
East Downs Rd *CHD/CHDH* SK8 ......116 E2
   *CHD/CHDH* SK8 ....................120 B2
East Dr *BURY* BL9 ................................39 L8
   *MPL/ROM* SK6 .......................123 H1
   *SLFD* M6 ..................................71 H7
   *SWIN* M27 ...............................70 E5
Easterdale *OLDE* OL4 .........................59 M6
Eastern Av *SWIN* M27 .........................71 G2
Eastern By-Pass *OP/CLY* M11 ............88 F2
   *OP/CLY* M11 ............................89 G4
Eastern Cir *BNG/LEV* M19 ..................99 K6
Eastfield *SLFD* M6 ...............................85 M1
Eastfield Av *MDTN* M24 ......................57 K5
   *NEWH/MOS* M40 .....................88 B1
Eastford Sq *NEWH/MOS* M40 ............72 E8
Eastgate *WGNE/HIN* WN2 ..................64 C5
Eastgate *WHIT* OL12 ...........................20 A5
East Gate St *MILN* OL16 .....................10 F5
East Gra *OP/CLY* M11 .........................88 F1
East Gv *BRUN/LGST* M13 ...................87 M7
Eastgrove Av *BOL* BL1 ........................22 B6
Eastham Av *BURY* BL9 ........................25 H6
   *RUSH/FAL* M14 ........................98 E3
Eastham Wy *LHULT* M38 .....................52 F7
Easthaven Av *OP/CLY* M11 .................89 L5
East Hill St *OLDE* OL4 * ........................9 M7
Eastholme Dr *BNG/LEV* M19 ..............99 L5
Easthope Cl *DID/WITH* M20 ................98 L5
East Lancashire Rd
   *GOL/RIS/CUL* WA3 ..................80 B3
   *GOL/RIS/CUL* WA3 ..................82 A2
   *NEWLW* WA12 ..........................79 G5
   *RNFD/HAY* WA11 .....................78 C5
   *SWIN* M27 ...............................70 B6
   *TYLD* M29 ...............................67 M7
   *WALK* M28 ...............................68 F5
Eastlands *BKLY* M9 .............................57 G7
East Lea *DTN/ASHW* M34 ..................101 K1
Eastleigh Av *BRO* M7 ..........................72 B4
Eastleigh Crs *LEIGH* WN7 ...................81 M1
Eastleigh Dr *NEWH/MOS* M40 ............88 B1
Eastleigh Rd *CHD/CHDH* SK8 ...........119 K3
   *PWCH* M25 ...............................72 B1
East Lynn Dr *WALK* M28 ......................69 K2
East Meade *BOLS/LL* BL3 ....................52 B2
   *CCHDY* M21 ..............................97 L5
   *PWCH* M25 ...............................72 A2
   *SWIN* M27 ...............................70 B6
East Moor *WALK* M28 ..........................68 D5
Eastmoor Dr *NEWH/MOS* M40 ...........74 A8
Eastmoor Gv *BOLS/LL* BL3 ................51 L2
East Mt *WGNNW/BIL/OR* WN5 ............46 C6
East Newton St *ANC* M4 * ....................7 M1
Easton Cl *MDTN* M24 ..........................57 M5
   *WGNS/IIMK* WN3 .....................63 K7
Easton Dr *CHD/CHDH* SK8 ...............111 K7
Easton Rd *DROY* M43 ..........................89 H2
East Ordsall La *CSLFD* M3 ....................6 B4
Eastover *MPL/ROM* SK6 ....................113 L4
Eastpark Cl *BRUN/LGST* M13 * ...........87 M6
East Park Cl *BRUN/LGST* M13 * ...........87 H1
East Philip St *CSLFD* M3 .......................6 D1
East Rd *BOL* BL1 ..................................22 B8
   *CTN* M18 ..................................99 L1
   *MANAIR* M90 ..........................118 E6
   *STLY* SK15 ...............................77 H6
   *STRET* M32 ...............................85 L8
   *URM* M41 .................................85 J7
   *WGTN/LGST* M12 ....................99 K1
Eastry Av *RDSH* SK5 .........................100 D5
East St *AIMK* WN4 ..............................64 A8
   *ATH* M46 ..................................67 J3
   *AUL* OL6 ..................................76 A8
   *BURY* BL9 ...................................5 G6
   *DTN/ASHW* M34 .......................90 C6
   *MILN* OL16 ...............................11 G2
   *MILN* OL16 ...............................11 G5
   *RAD* M26 .................................54 D1
   *RAMS* BL0 ...............................18 E6
   *WHIT* OL12 ..............................11 G2
East Union St *OLDTF/WHR* M16 .........86 F6
East Vw *BURY* BL9 ..............................24 D7
   *MDTN* M24 ...............................57 K2
   *RAMS* BL0 ...............................18 E3
Eastville Gdns *BNG/LEV* M19 .............99 J3
East Wk *EDGW/EG* BL7 .......................22 H2
Eastward Av *WILM/AE* SK9 ...............126 A5

East Wy *BOL* BL1 .................................36 E1
   *OLD* OL1 ....................................9 G1
Eastway *MDTN* M24 ............................57 J3
   *ROY/SHW* OL2 .........................43 L6
   *SALE* M33 ...............................108 A3
   *URM* M41 .................................95 H1
Eastwell Rd *AIMK* WN4 ......................78 H1
Eastwood Av *DROY* M43 .....................89 H3
   *NEWH/MOS* M40 .....................74 C3
   *URM* M41 .................................96 A2
   *WALK* M28 ...............................68 D1
Eastwood Gv *LEIGH* WN7 ...................65 M7
Eastwood Cl *NEWH/MOS* M40 ...........74 C3
Eastwood Cl *DTN/ASHW* M34 ............90 A5
Eastwood Ter *BOL* BL1 ........................35 J4
Eatock St *WGNE/HIN* WN2 .................64 E1
Eatock Wy *WHTN* BL5 .........................50 A6
Eaton Cl *CHD/CHDH* SK8 ..................120 F6
   *POY/DIS* SK12 .......................129 J1
   *SWIN* M27 ...............................70 A5
Eaton Dr *AULW* OL7 ...........................75 J8
   *HALE/TIMP* WA15 ..................108 D4
   *WILM/AE* SK9 .........................130 C2
Eaton Rd *ALT* WA14 ..........................116 A3
   *CHH* M8 ...................................72 C5
   *SALE* M33 ...............................96 D8
East St *WGNE/HIN* WN2 .....................49 H6
Eaves Knoll Rd *NM/HAY* SK22 ..........124 D4
Eaves La *CHAD* OL9 ............................58 D7
Ebbdale Cl *STKP* SK1 .........................13 L2
Ebberstone St *RUSH/FAL* M14 ...........98 D3
Ebden St *CMANE* M1 * ..........................7 J7
Ebenezer St *GLSP* SK13 ....................104 F5
   *HULME* M15 ..............................6 F8
Ebor Cl *ROY/SHW* OL2 ........................43 K4
Ebor Rd *WYTH/NTH* M22 * ................110 B8
Ebor St *LIT* OL15 ................................21 M7
Ebsworth St *NEWH/MOS* M40 ............73 J4
Ebury St *RAD* M26 ..............................54 C1
Ecclesbridge Rd
   *MPL/ROM* SK6 .......................114 C7
Eccles Cl *OP/CLY* M11 .........................88 F3
Eccleshall St *OP/CLY* M11 * ................88 F3
Eccles New Rd *SALQ* M50 ...................85 L2
Eccles Old Rd *SLFD* M6 .......................85 M1
Eccles St *RAMS* BL0 ............................18 E6
   *WGNNW/BIL/OR* WN5 .............46 E4
Eccleston Av *BOLE* BL2 ......................36 E3
   *RUSH/FAL* M14 ........................98 D3
   *SWIN* M27 ...............................70 A5
Eccleston Cl *TOT/BURYW* BL8 ............38 D3
Eccleston Rd *EDGY/DAV* SK3 ...........112 B8
   *WGN* WN1 ...............................15 G1
Eccleston St *FAIL* M35 * .......................74 D4
Eccup La *WILM/AE* SK9 .....................126 A5
Echo St *CMANE* M1 * .............................7 J7
Eckersley Av *NTHM/RTH* M23 ...........109 J6
Eckersley Fold La *ATH* M46 .................66 D3
Eckersley Rd *BOL* BL1 .........................36 A1
Eckersley St *BOLS/LL* BL3 ..................35 M8
   *WGN* WN1 ...............................15 G2
Eckford St *CHH* M8 ..............................72 E6
Eclipse Cl *MILN* OL16 ..........................11 L4
Edale Av *DTN/ASHW* M34 ..................101 K4
   *NEWH/MOS* M40 .....................74 B8
   *RDSH* SK5 ..............................100 D3
   *URM* M41 .................................95 L3
Edale Cl *ALT* WA14 ............................116 E5
   *ATH* M46 ..................................66 F1
   *BRAM/HZG* SK7 ....................122 A4
   *CHD/CHDH* SK8 ....................119 M5
   *IRL* M44 ...................................94 D3
Edale Crs *GLSP* SK13 ........................104 F3
Edale Dr *WGNNW/ST* WN6 ..................31 H7
Edale Gv *AUL* OL6 ...............................76 D6
   *SALE* M33 .............................108 B2
Edale Rd *BOLS/LL* BL3 * ......................35 K8
   *FWTH* BL4 ................................52 F5
   *LEIGH* WN7 ..............................66 B8
   *STRET* M32 ...............................96 F1
Edale St *SLFD* M6 ................................71 J7
Edbrook Wk *BRUN/LGST* M13 * ...........88 A7
Eddie Colman Cl
   *NEWH/MOS* M40 * ...................73 J7
Eddisbury Av *DID/WITH* M20 ...............98 C4
   *URM* M41 .................................84 A8
Eddisford Dr *GOL/RIS/CUL* WA3 .........81 C7
Edditch Gv *BOLE* BL2 ............................3 M5
Eddleston St *AIMK* WN4 ......................63 K8
Eddystone Cl *ORD* M5 .........................86 D3
Eden Av *BOL* BL1 .................................36 B1
   *GOL/RIS/CUL* WA3 ..................81 M8
   *MPL/ROM* SK6 .......................123 G5
   *RAMS* BL0 ...............................19 G4
Eden Bank *LEIGH* WN7 .......................66 B6
Edenbridge Dr *RAD* M26 .....................53 L5
Edenbridge Rd
   *CHD/CHDH* SK8 ....................111 L8
   *NEWH/MOS* M40 .....................74 B8
Eden Cl *HEY* OL10 ...............................40 D4
   *HULME* M15 .............................87 K7
   *STKP* SK1 ................................13 G6
   *WILM/AE* SK9 .........................126 C7
Eden Ct *RAMS* BL0 ..............................19 G2
Edendale Dr *WYTH/NTH* M22 ............110 F8
Edenfield La *WALK* M28 .......................69 J8
Edenfield Rd *PWCH* M25 .....................72 B1
   *ROCH* OL11 ..............................10 A2
   *WHIT* OL12 ..............................26 C1
Edenfield St *ROCH* OL11 .....................27 M3
Eden Gv *BOL* BL1 .................................36 B1
   *LEIGH* WN7 ..............................65 M7
Edenhall Av *BNG/LEV* M19 ..................99 J4
Edenhall Gv *WGNE/HIN* WN2 ..............65 J1
Edenhurst Dr
   *HALE/TIMP* WA15 ..................108 E7
Edenhurst Rd *OFTN* SK2 ...................112 E6
Eden Park Rd *CHD/CHDH* SK8 ..........120 A4
Eden PI *CHD/CHDH* SK8 ....................111 L8
Edensor Dr *HALE/TIMP* WA15 ...........111 K8
Eden St *BOL* BL1 ..................................36 B1
   *OLD* OL1 ....................................9 L5
   *RAMS* BL0 ...............................19 G2
   *WHIT* OL12 ..............................10 B3
Edenvale *WALK* M28 ...........................68 D4
Eden Wy *ROY/SHW* OL2 .......................43 K4
Edgar St *BOLS/LL* BL3 ...........................2 D5
   *MILN* OL16 ...............................28 F2
   *RAMS* BL0 ...............................18 E6
Edgar St West *RAMS* BL0 ...................18 E6
Edgbaston Dr *OLDTF/WHR* M16 .........97 K3
Edgecote Cl *WYTH/NTH* M22 ............110 C6
Edgedale Av *BNG/LEV* M19 .................99 H4
Edgefield Av *BKLY* M9 .........................57 H8

Edge Fold *FWTH* BL4 * .........................51 M3
Edge Fold Crs *WALK* M28 ....................69 G4
Edge Fold Rd *WALK* M28 .....................69 G3
Edge Gn *WALK* M28 * ..........................68 F3
Edge Green La
   *GOL/RIS/CUL* WA3 ..................79 J2
Edge Green Rd *AIMK* WN4 ..................64 C8
Edge Green St *AIMK* WN4 ...................64 A8
Edge Hall Rd
   *WGNW/BIL/OR* WN5 .................46 B8
Edge Hill Av *ROY/SHW* OL2 ................59 H2
Edgehill Cha *WILM/AE* SK9 ...............127 J5
Edgehill Cl *ORD* M5 .............................86 C2
Edge Hill Rd *BOLS/LL* BL3 ...................51 L1
   *ROY/SHW* OL2 .........................59 H1
Edgehill St *SLFD* M6 ............................85 M1
Edgehill St *ANC* M4 * .............................7 J3
Edge La *DROY* M43 ..............................89 H3
   *EDGW/EG* BL7 .........................16 D4
   *HYDE* SK14 ..............................92 B8
   *STRET* M32 ...............................97 H3
Edge Lane Rd *OLD* OL1 .........................9 K2
Edge Lane St *ROY/SHW* OL2 ..............43 H8
Edgeley Fold *EDGY/DAV* SK3 .............12 E9
Edgeley Rd *EDGY/DAV* SK3 ................12 C9
   *URM* M41 .................................95 K4
Edgemoor *ALT* WA14 .........................116 C2
Edgemoor Cl *OLDE* OL4 ......................60 A3
   *RAD* M26 .................................38 D7
Edgemoor Dr *ROCH* OL11 ...................27 J7
Edgerley PI *AIMK* WN4 ........................78 D1
Edgerton Rd *GOL/RIS/CUL* WA3 .........80 B4
Edge St *ANC* M4 ....................................7 H3
Edge Vw *OLD* OL1 ................................58 B3
Edgeware Av *PWCH* M25 .....................56 C8
Edge Ware Gv *WGNS/IIMK* WN3 ..........63 K3
Edgeware Rd *CHAD* OL9 ......................74 B1
   *ECC* M30 ..................................69 K8
Edgewater *ORD* M5 ..............................86 A2
Edgeway *WILM/AE* SK9 .....................126 F7
Edgeway Rd *WGNS/IIMK* WN3 .............63 K3
Edgewood *WGNNW/ST* WN6 ...............30 D7
Edgeworth Av *BOLE* BL2 ......................38 A3
Edgeworth Dr *RUSH/FAL* M14 ............98 H5
   *GOL/RIS/CUL* WA3 ..................79 J3
   *WGNE/HIN* WN2 ......................65 K1
Edgeworth V *EDGW/EG* BL7 * .............17 H6
Edgmont Av *BOLS/LL* BL3 ...................35 L8
Edgware Rd *NEWH/MOS* M40 .............73 L8
Edgworth Cl *HEY* OL10 ........................40 B4
Edgworth Dr *TOT/BURYW* BL8 ............38 D3
Edilom Rd *CHH* M8 ...............................72 B2
Edinburgh Cl *CHD/CHDH* SK8 ...........111 J6
   *WGNE/HIN* WN2 ......................48 D3
Edinburgh Dr *MPL/ROM* SK6 .............101 M8
   *WGN* WN1 ...............................65 L1
   *WGNW/BIL/OR* WN5 .................47 G7
Edinburgh Rd *BOLS/LL* BL3 ...............53 K2
   *NEWH/MOS* M40 .....................73 G8
Edinburgh Wy *ROCH* OL11 ..................28 A8
Edington *WHIT* OL12 ............................10 D2
Edison Rd *ECC* M30 .............................84 F4
Edison St *OP/CLY* M11 .........................89 H5
Edith Av *RUSH/FAL* M14 ......................98 D3
Edith Cavell Cl *OP/CLY* M11 * ..............88 F3
Edith St *BOL* BL1 .................................35 M6
   *FWTH* BL4 ................................53 C5
   *OLDS* OL8 ................................75 J1
   *WGNS/IIMK* WN3 .....................14 D5
Edlin Cl *WGTN/LGST* M12 ...................88 B7
Edlingham *ROCH* OL11 * ......................10 C7
Edmonds St *MDTN* M24 ......................57 L3
Edmonton Rd *EDGY/DAV* SK3 ...........112 D8
   *NEWH/MOS* M40 .....................73 K8
Edmund Cl *HTNM* SK4 ........................112 B1
Edmund Dr *LEIGH* WN7 .......................65 M7
Edmunds Ct *BOLS/LL* BL3 ....................2 B7
Edmund St *CSLFD* M3 * .........................6 A3
   *DROY* M43 ...............................89 K4
   *FAIL* M35 .................................74 E8
   *RAD* M26 .................................38 F8
   *ROY/SHW* OL2 .........................43 M5
   *SLFD* M6 ..................................86 B1
   *WHIT* OL12 ..............................10 A2
Edna Rd *LEIGH* WN7 ...........................65 M5
Edna St *HYDE* SK14 ...........................102 A2
Edridge Wy *WGNE/HIN* WN2 ..............48 F8
Edson Rd *CHH* M8 ................................56 C8
Edstone Cl *BOLS/LL* BL3 .....................37 J5
Edward Av *CCHDY* M21 ........................29 J1
   *LIT* OL15 .................................21 H8
   *MPL/ROM* SK6 .......................113 H1
   *SLFD* M6 ..................................85 M1
Edward Charlton Rd
   *OLDTF/WHR* M16 .....................97 K2
Edward Ct *ALT* WA14 .........................107 K5
Edward Rd *CHAD* OL9 ............................8 C6
Edward Ms *CHAD* OL9 * .........................8 D8
Edward Rd *BKLY* M9 .............................57 H7
   *ROY/SHW* OL2 .........................43 K6
Edwards Cl *MPL/ROM* SK6 ................114 D7
Edwards Dr *WHTF* M45 ........................55 L4
Edward St *AUL* OL6 ..............................91 H2
   *BKLY* M9 ..................................73 H4
   *BOLS/LL* BL3 ..............................2 B8
   *BRO* M7 ...................................72 B8
   *BURY* BL9 ...................................4 F6
   *CHAD* OL9 .................................8 D5
   *DROY* M43 * ..............................89 K4
   *DTN/ASHW* M34 .......................90 A5
   *DTN/ASHW* M34 .......................90 D6
   *DUK* SK16 ................................90 F6
   *FWTH* BL4 ................................53 G5
   *GLSP* SK13 .............................104 F3
   *HOR/BR* BL6 .............................33 K1
   *HYDE* SK14 .............................101 M1
   *LEIGH* WN7 ..............................66 A7
   *MDTN* M24 ...............................57 K2
   *MILN* OL16 ...............................11 H2
   *MPL/ROM* SK6 .......................114 D7
   *PWCH* M25 ...............................55 K7
   *RAD* M26 .................................54 E2
   *SALE* M33 ...............................96 F7
   *STKP* SK1 ................................13 J6
   *WGN* WN1 ...............................15 M4
   *WGN* WN1 ...............................15 K5
Edward Wy *MPL/ROM* SK6 ................114 B7
Edwin Rd *STKP* SK1 * ..........................88 D3
Edwin St *BURY* BL9 ...............................4 E5
   *STKP* SK1 ...............................112 E4
   *WGN* WN1 ...............................15 K5
Eeasbrook *URM* M41 ............................96 A3
Egbert St *NEWH/MOS* M40 .................73 L5
Egerton Ct *WALK* M28 * .......................69 K4

Egerton Crs *DID/WITH* M20 * ........98 E5
Egerton Dr *SALE* M33 * ........96 E7
Egerton Ldg *EDGW/EG* BL7 ........22 B3
Egerton Ms *DROY* M43 ........89 K4
   *RUSH* M14 ........99 G4
Egerton Moss
   *HALE/TIMP* WA15 ........117 G7
Egerton Pk *WALK* M28 ........69 L5
Egerton Pl *ROY/SHW* OL2 ........43 K6
Egerton Rd *ECC* M30 ........70 A8
   *EDGY/DAV* SK3 ........112 D8
   *HALE/TIMP* WA15 ........117 J2
   *RUSH/FAL* M14 ........99 G4
   *WALK* M28 ........69 G1
   *WHTF* M45 ........55 J5
   *WILM/AE* SK9 ........126 F4
Egerton Rd North
   *CCHDY* M21 ........97 M3
   *HTNM* SK4 ........99 M7
Egerton Rd South *CCHDY* M21 ........97 M4
   *HTNM* SK4 ........99 M8
Egerton St *AUL* OL6 ........90 F1
   *CSLFD* M3 ........6 B4
   *DROY* M43 ........89 L3
   *DTN/ASHW* M34 ........90 A7
   *ECC* M30 ........84 E2
   *FWTH* BL4 ........52 F3
   *HEY* OL10 ........40 F3
   *HULME* M15 ........6 D7
   *MDTN* M24 * ........56 F5
   *MOSL* OL5 ........76 F2
   *OLD* OL1 ........9 K4
   *PWCH* M25 ........55 M8
   *WGNE/HIN* WN2 ........64 G5
Egerton Ter *RUSH/FAL* M14 ........99 G4
Egerton V *EDGW/EG* BL7 ........22 A2
Eggar Cl *TYLD* M29 ........67 L5
Eggington St
   *NEWH/MOS* M40 ........72 F7
Egham Ct *BOLE* BL2 * ........3 J1
Egmont St *CHH* M8 ........72 D4
   *MOSL* OL5 ........77 G4
   *SLFD* M6 ........71 H6
Egremont Av *DID/WITH* M20 ........98 D5
Egremont Cl *WHTF* M45 ........55 K5
Egremont Ct *BRO* M7 * ........71 M4
Egremont Gv *EDGY/DAV* SK3 ........12 A6
Egremont Rd *MILN* OL16 ........29 H8
Egret Dr *IRL* M44 ........94 D1
Egyptian St *BOL* BL1 ........2 E1
Egypt La *PWCH* M25 ........56 B2
Ehlinger Av *GLSP* SK13 ........93 K7
Eida Wy *TRPK* M17 ........85 M4
Eight Acre *WHTF* M45 ........54 F5
Eighth Av *OLDS* OL8 ........75 G3
Eighth St *TRPK* M17 ........85 M6
Eileen Gv *RUSH/FAL* M14 ........98 F2
Eileen Gv West *RUSH/FAL* M14 ........98 F2
Elaine Av *BKLY* M9 ........73 L2
Elaine Cl *AIMK* WN4 ........64 A7
Elbe St *WGTN/LGST* M12 * ........7 M7
Elbow La *ROCH* OL11 ........11 G6
Elbow St *BNG/LEV* M19 ........99 K3
Elbut La *BURY* BL9 ........26 C7
Elcho Ct *ALT* WA14 ........116 D2
Elcho Rd *ALT* WA14 ........116 D1
Elcombe Av *GOL/RIS/CUL* WA3 ........80 B5
Elcot Cl *NEWH/MOS* M40 * ........72 F7
   *WGN* WN1 ........31 L8
Elderberry Wy *WILM/AE* SK9 ........127 J4
Elder Cl *OFTN* SK2 ........113 G4
   *TOT/BURYW* BL8 ........24 C7
Eldercot Cl *BOLS/LL* BL3 ........35 K8
Eldercot Rd *BOLS/LL* BL3 ........35 K8
Eldercroft Rd
   *HALE/TIMP* WA15 ........108 F7
Elder Dr *BOLS/LL* BL3 ........37 H7
Elderfield Dr *MPL/ROM* SK6 ........101 J8
Elder Gv *NEWH/MOS* M40 ........74 C2
Eldermount Rd *BKLY* M9 ........73 C2
Elder Rd *OLDE* OL4 ........60 B6
Elder St *MILN* OL16 ........11 J8
Elderwood *CHAD* OL9 ........58 B5
Eldon Cl *DTN/ASHW* M34 ........90 B5
Eldon Gdns *AIMK* WN4 ........63 K6
Eldon Pl *ECC* M30 ........84 F3
Eldon Prec *OLB..* ........9 H8
Eldon Rd *EDGY/DAV* SK3 ........12 D8
   *IRL* M44 ........94 D2
Eldon St *BOLE* BL2 ........36 E3
   *BURY* BL9..* ........4 F1
   *LEIGH* WN7 ........66 A6
   *OLDS* OL8 ........9 J8
Eldon Street East *OLDS* OL8..* ........9 J8
Eldridge Dr *NEWH/MOS* M40 ........73 K7
Eldroth Av *WYTH/NTH* M22 ........118 F1
Eleanor Rd *CCHDY* M21 ........97 J4
   *ROY/SHW* OL2 ........59 H2
Eleanor St *BOL* BL1 ........22 D7
   *OLD* OL1 ........9 J1
   *WGNS/IIMK* WN3 ........14 C6
Electo St *OP/CLY* M11 ........89 H5
Elevator Rd *TRPK* M17 ........86 B6
Eleventh St *TRPK* M17 ........86 A6
Elf Mill Cl *EDGY/DAV* SK3 ........112 B6
Elford Gv *GTN* M18 ........89 K8
Elgar St *WGTN/LGST* M12 ........99 K1
Elgin Av *AIMK* WN4 ........63 G8
   *DID/WITH* M20 * ........98 C5
Elgin Cl *WGNE/HIN* WN2 ........48 D4
Elgin Dr *SALE* M33 ........109 H1
Elgin Rd *DUK* SK16 ........90 F6
   *OLDE* OL4 ........59 L6
Elgin St *AULW* OL7 ........75 G8
   *BOL* BL1 ........35 M2
   *STLY* SK15 ........91 L3
Elgol Cl *EDGY/DAV* SK3 ........112 C7
Elgol Dr *BOLS/LL* BL3 ........35 H7
Elham Cl *RAD* M26 ........53 M5
Eliot Dr *WGNS/IIMK* WN3 ........47 G5
Eliot Rd *ECC* M30 ........85 G3
Eli St *CHAD* OL9 ........74 D1
Eliza Ann St *NEWH/MOS* M40 ........84 F3
   *NEWH/MOS* M40 ........72 F8
Elizabethan Dr
   *WGNS/IIMK* WN3 ........48 B8
Elizabeth Av *MILN* OL16 ........29 H6
Elizabeth Ct *ATH* M46 ........66 E8
   *DTN/ASHW* M34 ........90 D7
   *POY/DIS* SK12 ........123 M7
   *ROY/SHW* OL2 ........58 F1
   *STKP* SK1 ........13 K7
   *WGNE/HIN* WN2 ........65 H3
Elizabeth Slinger Rd
   *DID/WITH* M20 ........98 B8

Elizabeth St *ATH* M46 ........67 G1
   *AUL* OL6 ........75 L8
   *CHH* M8 ........72 D7
   *DTN/ASHW* M34 ........101 G1
   *HEY* OL10 ........40 F2
   *HYDE* SK14 ........102 A1
   *LEIGH* WN7 ........81 L1
   *RAD* M26 ........54 D1
   *RAMS* BL0 ........19 G1
   *ROCH* OL11 ........41 M1
   *SWIN* M27 ........70 D3
   *WGNE/HIN* WN2 ........48 D4
   *WHTF* M45 ........55 J5
Eliza St *HULME* M15 ........87 H6
   *RAMS* BL0 ........19 G6
Elkanagh Gdns *SLFD* M6 ........86 C1
Elkstone Av *LHULT* M38 ........52 D6
Elkstone Cl *WGNS/IIMK* WN3 ........62 F2
Elkwood Cl *WGN* WN1 ........31 L8
Elladene Pk *CCHDY* M21 ........97 M4
Ellanby Cl *RUSH/FAL* M14 ........98 E1
Elland Cl *BURY* BL9 ........55 L2
   *WHTN* BL5 ........50 A1
Ellaston Dr *URM* M41 ........96 A2
Ellastone Rd *SLFD* M6 ........70 F8
Ellbourne Rd *BKLY* M9 ........72 D1
Ellenbrook Cl *WHIT* OL12 ........88 E6
Ellenbrook Rd *WALK* M28 ........68 E4
Ellen Brook Rd
   *WYTH/NTH* M22 ........118 F4
Ellendale Gra *WALK* M28 ........68 E4
Ellen Gv *FWTH* BL4 ........54 A7
Ellenhall Cl *BKLY* M9 ........73 G4
Ellenor Dr *TYLD* M29 ........67 M5
Ellenroad Ap *MILN* OL16 ........29 K8
Ellenrod Dr *WHIT* OL12 ........27 K2
Ellenrod La *WHIT* OL12 ........27 K2
Ellenshaw Cl *WHIT* OL12 ........27 K2
Ellen St *BOL* BL1 ........35 M1
   *CHAD* OL9 ........8 E3
   *DROY* M43 ........89 L4
   *HTNM* SK4 ........112 A1
   *WGN* WN1 ........15 H5
Ellen Wilkinson Crs
   *WGTN/LGST* M12 ........88 D7
Elleray Cl *BOLS/LL* BL3 ........53 M1
Elleray Rd *MDTN* M24 ........57 J7
   *SLFD* M6 ........71 G7
Ellerbeck Cl *BOLE* BL2 ........22 F7
Ellerbeck Crs *WALK* M28 ........68 F5
Ellerby Av *SWIN* M27 ........70 D1
Ellerscroft *NM/HAY* SK22 * ........125 G3
   *ECC* M30 ........85 H2
   *MPL/ROM* SK6 ........114 C6
   *WALK* M28 ........68 F1
Ellesmere Cir *URM* M41 ........85 G5
Ellesmere Cl *DUK* SK16 ........91 H5
Ellesmere Dr *CHD/CHDH* SK8 ........111 J5
Ellesmere Gdns *BOLS/LL* BL3 ........52 A1
Ellesmere Rd *AIMK* WN4 ........63 J7
   *ALT* WA14 ........108 A6
   *BOLS/LL* BL3 ........51 M1
   *CCHDY* M21 ........97 M3
   *ECC* M30 ........70 B8
   *EDGY/DAV* SK3 ........111 K5
   *GOL/RIS/CUL* WA3 ........81 H8
   *WGNW/BIL/OR* WN5 ........47 G6
Ellesmere Rd North *HTNM* SK4 ........99 M7
Ellesmere Rd South
   *CCHDY* M21 ........97 M4
   *ECC* M30 ........85 G3
   *FAIL* M35 ........74 C4
   *FWTH* BL4 ........53 G4
   *LEIGH* WN7 ........66 C8
   *LHULT* M38 ........68 F1
   *ROCH* OL11 ........10 E8
   *SWIN* M27 ........70 A5
   *SWIN* M27 ........70 D3
   *TYLD* M29 ........67 K3
   *TYLD* M29 ........67 M7
Ellesmere Ter *RUSH/FAL* M14 ........99 G5
Ellingham Cl *OP/CLY* M11 ........88 C3
Elliot Sq *OLD* OL1 ........9 M3
Elliot St *BOL* BL1 ........35 M1
   *OLDE* OL4 ........60 B6
Elliott Av *GOL/RIS/CUL* WA3 ........79 L3
   *HYDE* SK14 ........91 G7
Elliott Dr *SALE* M33 ........96 B8
   *WGNE/HIN* WN2 ........49 G5
Elliott St *FWTH* BL4 ........52 F5
   *TYLD* M29 ........67 H4
   *WHIT* OL12 ........11 G2
Ellis Crs *WALK* M28 ........68 E1
Ellis Dr *CHH* M8 ........72 E3
Ellis Fold *WHIT* OL12 ........27 H2
Ellis La *MDTN* M24 ........56 F4
Ellison Cl *HYDE* SK14 ........93 G7
Ellison St *GLSP* SK13 ........105 G3
Ellis Rd *WGNW/BIL/OR* WN5 ........62 A8
Ellis St *BOLS/LL* BL3 ........2 B9
   *CHH* M8 ........72 D8
   *HULME* M15 ........87 H6
   *HYDE* SK14 ........102 C2
   *TOT/BURYW* BL8 * ........38 C2
   *WGN* WN1 ........15 L1
Elliston Sq *WGTN/LGST* M12 ........88 D6
Ellonby Ri *HOR/BR* BL6 ........34 F7
Elm Cl *BOL* BL1 ........86 C1
Ellwood Rd *STKP* SK1 ........112 E3
Elly Clough *ROY/SHW* OL2 * ........58 F1
Elm Av *AIMK* WN4 ........63 G7
   *GOL/RIS/CUL* WA3 ........93 H3
   *HOR/BR* BL6 ........34 B3
   *RAD* M26 ........54 C4
   *WGNNW/ST* WN6 ........31 J4
   *WGNW/BIL/OR* WN5 ........47 H6
Elmbank Av *DID/WITH* M20 ........98 A8
Elmbank Rd *MDTN* M24 ........57 M4
Elmbridge Wk *BOLS/LL* BL3 * ........2 A8
Elm Cl *HYDE* SK14 ........92 D8
   *POY/DIS* SK12 ........129 K1
Elm Crs *WALK* M28 ........68 E2
   *WILM/AE* SK9 ........130 E2
Elm Ct *WGN* WN1 ........31 L8
Elmdale Av *CHD/CHDH* SK8 ........119 K2
Elmdale Wk *HULME* M15 * ........87 K6
Elm Dr *STRET* M32 ........96 F4
   *WGNW/BIL/OR* WN5 ........32 E6
Elmfield *WGNNW/ST* WN6 ........30 E6
Elmfield Av *ATH* M46 ........66 E8
   *WYTH/NTH* M22 ........110 B4
Elmfield Dr *MPL/ROM* SK6 ........114 B6
Elmfield Rd *DTN/ASHW* M34 ........89 M4
   *EDGY/DAV* SK3 ........112 C7
   *WGN* WN1 ........31 L7
   *WILM/AE* SK9 ........130 E1
Elmfield St *BOL* BL1 ........36 C2
   *CHH* M8 ........72 D6
Elmgate Gv *BNG/LEV* M19 ........99 K3

Elm Gv *AUL* OL6 ........75 M7
   *DID/WITH* M20 ........110 E1
   *DROY* M43 ........89 G2
   *DTN/ASHW* M34 ........90 A8
   *EDGW/EG* BL7 ........22 A8
   *FWTH* BL4 ........52 E4
   *GLSP* SK13 ........104 E2
   *HYDE* SK14 ........102 C2
   *MILN* OL16 ........43 K1
   *OLDE* OL4 ........60 E6
   *PWCH* M25 ........55 K6
   *ROCH* OL11 ........10 D9
   *SALE* M33 ........96 E6
   *SWIN* M27 ........70 D3
   *URM* M41 ........96 B2
   *WHIT* OL12 ........21 C7
   *WILM/AE* SK9 ........130 D2
Elmham Wk
   *NEWH/MOS* M40 ........72 F8
Elmhow Gv *WGNS/IIMK* WN3 ........63 K2
Elmhurst Dr *BNG/LEV* M19 ........99 J3
Elmira Wy *ORD* M5 ........86 D6
Elmley Cl *OFTN* SK2 ........113 K7
Elmore Wd *LIT* OL15 ........21 K6
Elmpark Ga *WHIT* OL12 ........27 L1
Elmpark Gv *WHIT* OL12 ........27 L1
Elmpark V *WHIT* OL12 ........27 L1
Elmpark Vw *WHIT* OL12 ........27 L1
Elmpark Wy *WHIT* OL12 ........27 L1
Elm Rd *BOLS/LL* BL3 ........53 L2
   *CHD/CHDH* SK8 ........110 D7
   *DID/WITH* M20 ........98 D8
   *FWTH* BL4 ........53 J7
   *HALE/TIMP* WA15 ........117 G5
   *MPL/ROM* SK6 ........123 H5
   *OLDS* OL8 ........75 G3
   *RNFD/HAY* WA11 * ........78 B5
   *WGNE/HIN* WN2 ........64 F5
Elm Rd South *EDGY/DAV* SK3 ........111 K5
   *WHTN* BL5 ........50 A1
Elms Cl *WHTF* M45 ........55 J2
Elmscott Wk *BRUN/LGST* M13 ........88 A7
Elmsdale Av *BKLY* M9 ........56 F7
Elmsfield Av *ROCH* OL11 ........11 J3
Elmsleigh Rd *CHD/CHDH* SK8 ........119 J5
Elmsmere Rd *DID/WITH* M20 ........111 G1
   *STLY* SK15 ........92 A1
   *WHTF* M45 ........55 J3
Elms St *WHTF* M45 ........55 J3
Elmstead Av *DID/WITH* M20 ........98 D6
Elmsted Cl *CHD/CHDH* SK8 ........120 D7
The Elms *GOL/RIS/CUL* WA3 ........80 C5
   *LIT* OL15 ........21 J8
   *MOSL* OL5 ........76 E3
Elmstone Cl *BKLY* M9 ........72 F2
Elmstone Dr *ROY/SHW* OL2 ........43 C7
Elmstone Gv *BOL* BL1 ........2 E1
Elm St *BURY* BL9 ........5 K5
   *ECC* M30 ........85 G3
   *FAIL* M35 ........74 C4
   *FWTH* BL4 ........53 G4
   *HEY* OL10 ........41 G2
   *LEIGH* WN7 ........81 G2
   *MDTN* M24 ........57 M4
   *MPL/ROM* SK6 ........101 J8
   *RAMS* BL0 ........19 G6
   *SWIN* M27 ........70 B3
   *TYLD* M29 ........67 K3
   *WGNE/HIN* WN2 ........64 D2
   *WHIT* OL12 ........20 B2
   *WHIT* OL12 ........28 C3
Elmswood Av *RUSH/FAL* M14 ........98 C2
Elmswood Dr *HYDE* SK14 * ........102 D1
Elmsworth Av *BNG/LEV* M19 ........99 L3
Elmton Rd *BKLY* M9 ........73 H1
Elm Tree Cl *FAIL* M35 ........74 E5
   *STLY* SK15 ........91 J5
   *WYTH/NTH* M22 ........118 F1
Elmtree Dr *HTNM* SK4 ........12 B3
Elm Tree Rd *GOL/RIS/CUL* WA3 ........80 C5
   *MPL/ROM* SK6 ........112 F1
Elmwood *SALE* M33 ........95 M8
Elmwood Av *AIMK* WN4 ........78 D2
Elmwood Cl *WHTN* BL5 ........51 K6
Elmwood Dr *ROY/SHW* OL2 ........42 F7
Elmwood Gv *BKLY* M9 ........73 J5
   *BOL* BL1 * ........35 M4
   *FWTH* BL4 ........52 F6
Elmwood Pk *STLY* SK15 ........92 A1
Elnup Av *WGNNW/ST* WN6 ........30 E6
Elsa Rd *BNG/LEV* M19 ........99 K3
Elsdon Dr *ATH* M46 ........51 H8
   *GTN* M18 ........89 G6
Elsdon Gdns *BOLE* BL2 ........36 E3
Elsdon Rd *BRUN/LGST* M13 ........99 J2
Elsfield Cl *BOL* BL1 ........36 A2
Elsham Cl *BOL* BL1 ........36 C1
Elsham Dr *WALK* M28 ........68 E1
Elsham Gdns *GTN* M18 ........88 D8
Elsie St *BKLY* M9 ........73 H4
   *FWTH* BL4 ........52 F6
   *RAMS* BL0 ........18 D8
Elsinore Av *IRL* M44 ........94 D3
Elsinore Cl *FAIL* M35 ........74 E5
Elsinore Rd *OLDTF/WHR* M16 ........86 D6
Elsinore St *BOLE* BL2 ........36 E1
Elsma Rd *NEWH/MOS* M40 ........74 B8
Elsmore Rd *RUSH/FAL* M14 ........98 D3
Elson St *TOT/BURYW* BL8 ........24 E8
Elstead Gv *AIMK* WN4 ........63 G8
Elsted Rd *UPML* OL3 ........61 H7
Elston Av *NEWLW* WA12 ........78 F7
Elstree Av *NEWH/MOS* M40 ........73 L8
Elswick Av *BOLS/LL* BL3 ........35 L7
   *BRAM/HZG* SK7 ........121 L7
   *CCHDY* M21 ........98 A8
Elsworth Cl *RAD* M26 ........54 E3
Elsworth Dr *BOL* BL1 ........2 B3
Elsworth St *CSLFD* M3 ........87 K1
Elterwater Cl *TOT/BURYW* BL8 ........24 E8
Elterwater Rd *FWTH* BL4 ........52 B5
Eltham Av *OFTN* SK2 * ........112 F7
Eltham Cl *AIMK* WN4 ........79 G1
Eltham Dr *URM* M41 ........84 F8
Eltham St *BNG/LEV* M19 ........99 G4
Elton Av *BNG/LEV* M19 ........99 K4
   *FWTH* BL4 ........53 G6
Elton Brook Cl *TOT/BURYW* BL8 ........38 E1
Elton Cl *GOL/RIS/CUL* WA3 ........93 H3
   *WHTF* M45 ........55 K4
   *WILM/AE* SK9 ........127 J3
Elton Dr *BRAM/HZG* SK7 ........121 M4
Elton Rd *SALE* M33 ........108 A2

Elton St *BOLE* BL2 ........3 H4
   *BRO* M7 ........87 G1
   *ROCH* OL11 ........41 M5
   *STRET* M32 ........86 C7
Elton's Yd *BRO* M7 ........87 G1
Elton Vale Rd *TOT/BURYW* BL8 ........38 E2
Elvate Crs *CHH* M8 ........72 B7
Elverdon Cl *HULME* M15 ........87 H7
Everston Cl *WYTH/NTH* M22 ........110 B3
Elverston Wy *CHAD* OL9 ........8 C3
Elvey St *NEWH/MOS* M40 ........73 J7
Elvington Cl
   *WGNW/BIL/OR* WN5 ........46 E3
Elvington Crs *WALK* M28 ........68 F4
Elway Rd *AIMK* WN4 ........78 F1
Elwick Cl *OLDTF/WHR* M16 ........98 C1
Elworthy Gv *WGN* WN1 ........48 A5
Elwyn Av *WYTH/NTH* M22 ........110 A5
Ely Av *STRET* M32 ........96 C1
Ely Dr *WALK* M28 ........68 E4
Ely Crs *FAIL* M35 ........74 C7
Ely Dr *TOT/BURYW* BL8 ........4 C1
   *TYLD* M29 ........67 M5
Ely Gv *BOL* BL1 * ........2 B7
Elysian St *OP/CLY* M11 ........88 F4
Ely St *CHAD* OL9 ........8 B9
Emaline Gra *SLFD* M6 ........86 B2
Embankment Rd *EDGW/EG* BL7 ........16 F7
Ember St *OP/CLY* M11 * ........89 G2
Embla Wk *BOLS/LL* BL3 ........36 D8
Emblem St *BOLS/LL* BL3 ........2 B8
Embleton Cl *BOLE* BL2 ........23 H8
   *BOLE* BL2 ........37 H3
Embsay Cl *BOL* BL1 ........22 A7
Emerald Av *LEIGH* WN7 ........66 B8
Emerald Dr *OLD* OL1 ........60 B3
Emerald Rd *WYTH/NTH* M22 ........119 H5
Emerald St *BOL* BL1 ........36 C1
   *DTN/ASHW* M34 ........101 H1
   *WGNNW/ST* WN6 ........47 K1
Emerson Av *ECC* M30 ........85 K1
Emerson Dr *MDTN* M24 ........57 J3
Emerson St *ORD* M5 ........86 A3
Emery Av *CCHDY* M21 ........97 M6
Emery Cl *ALT* WA14 ........108 A5
   *HTNM* SK4 ........99 K8
Emily Beavan Cl *OP/CLY* M11 ........88 D1
Emily Cl *FAIL* M35 ........74 D7
Emily Pl *DROY* M43 ........89 J3
Emley St *BNG/LEV* M19 ........99 L3
Emlyn Gv *CHD/CHDH* SK8 ........111 K6
Emlyn St *FWTH* BL4 ........52 F5
   *SWIN* M27 ........70 A4
   *WALK* M28 ........69 G1
   *WGNE/HIN* WN2 ........48 F7
Emmanuel Cl *BOLS/LL* BL3 * ........2 B8
Emmanuel Pl *BOLS/LL* BL3 ........2 B8
Emma St *OLDS* OL8 ........75 J1
   *WHIT* OL12 ........10 C2
Emmerson St *SWIN* M27 ........70 C3
Emmett St *HOR/BR* BL6 ........33 L1
Emmett St East
   *NEWH/MOS* M40 ........73 H7
Emmott St *HEY* OL10 ........40 F7
Emmott Wy *OLD* OL1 ........9 K6
Empire Rd *BOLE* BL2 ........37 G4
   *HEY* OL10 ........41 G2
   *LEIGH* WN7 ........66 A6
   *MDTN* M24 ........57 M4
Empire St *CHH* M8 ........72 D5
Empress Av *MPL/ROM* SK6 ........114 C7
Empress Dr *HTNM* SK4 ........100 A8
   *LEIGH* WN7 ........67 H6
Empress St *BOL* BL1 * ........35 L3
   *CHH* M8 ........72 C4
   *OLDTF/WHR* M16 ........86 F6
Emsworth Dr *SALE* M33 ........108 F3
Ena Crs *LEIGH* WN7 ........65 M5
Ena St *BOLS/LL* BL3 ........52 D1
   *OLD* OL1 ........59 M3
Enbridge St *ORD* M5 * ........86 D4
Encombe Pl *CSLFD* M3 ........6 A3
Endcott Cl *GTN* M18 ........88 E1
Enderby Rd *NEWH/MOS* M40 ........73 M3
Ending Rake *WHIT* OL12 ........20 B8
Endon Dr *CCHDY* M21 ........98 C4
Endon St *BOL* BL1 ........35 L3
Endsleigh Dr *DID/WITH* M20 ........98 F6
Endsley Av *WALK* M28 ........68 E1
Energy St *NEWH/MOS* M40 * ........88 D1
Enfield Av *BNG/LEV* M19 ........99 K6
   *OLDS* OL8 ........75 H1
Enfield Cl *BOL* BL1 ........36 B3
   *BURY* BL9 ........39 J7
   *ECC* M30 ........85 G4
   *ROCH* OL11 ........27 H3
Enfield Dr *OP/CLY* M11 ........88 F2
Enfield Gv *LEIGH* WN7 ........66 D6
Enfield Rd *ECC* M30 ........70 A8
   *SWIN* M27 ........70 B6
Enfield St *HYDE* SK14 * ........102 D1
   *WALK* M28 ........53 G7
   *WGNW/BIL/OR* WN5 ........46 F6
Enford Av *WYTH/NTH* M22 ........118 C2
Engell Cl *GTN* M18 ........88 F7
Engine Fold Rd *WALK* M28 ........68 D1
Engine La *ATH* M46 ........51 K8
Engine St *CHAD* OL9 ........58 E8
Engledene *BOL* BL1 ........22 A6
English St *LEIGH* WN7 ........66 D6
Enid Cl *BRO* M7 ........72 B7
Enid Pl *WGNE/HIN* WN2 ........64 C4
Ennerdale Av *AIMK* WN4 ........63 L8
   *BOLE* BL2 ........37 J3
   *CCHDY* M21 ........98 A8
   *ROY/SHW* OL2 ........42 F5
   *SWIN* M27 ........70 C6
Ennerdale Dr *BURY* BL9 ........55 K2
   *CHD/CHDH* SK8 ........119 K1
   *HALE/TIMP* WA15 ........108 D5
   *SALE* M33 ........96 B7
Ennerdale Gv *AULW* OL7 ........75 J3
   *FWTH* BL4 ........52 B4
Ennerdale Pl *WGNE/HIN* WN2 ........48 E4
Ennerdale Rd *LEIGH* WN7 ........66 F8
   *MDTN* M24 ........57 J2
   *MPL/ROM* SK6 ........101 J8
   *PART* M31 ........106 B1
   *ROCH* OL11 ........27 L8
   *STKP* SK1 ........112 F1
   *STRET* M32 ........96 F1
   *TYLD* M29 ........67 L5
   *WGNE/HIN* WN2 ........64 B2
Ennerdale Ter *STLY* SK15 ........91 K1
Ennis Cl *NTHM/RTH* M23 ........109 H7
Ennismore Av *ECC* M30 ........85 K2
Ensor Wy *NM/HAY* SK22 ........124 E5
Enstone Dr *NEWH/MOS* M40 ........74 A3
Enstone Wy *TYLD* M29 ........67 M3
Enterprise Pk *HOR/BR* BL6 ........33 M7
Enterprise Wy
   *GOL/RIS/CUL* WA3 ........80 D5

Entwisle Av *URM* M41 ........84 E5
Entwisle Rd *MILN* OL16 ........11 G3
Entwisle Rw *FWTH* BL4 ........53 G4
Entwisle St *FWTH* BL4 ........53 G5
   *MILN* OL16 ........29 H6
   *SWIN* M27 ........70 A3
Entwistle Gv *LEIGH* WN7 ........81 M4
Entwistle Hall La *EDGW/EG* BL7 ........16 E5
Entwistle St *BOLE* BL2 ........3 K3
Enver Rd *CHH* M8 ........72 E4
Enville Rd *ALT* WA14 ........116 E1
   *NEWH/MOS* M40 ........73 L3
   *SLFD* M6 ........71 H6
Enville St *AUL* OL6 ........90 F1
   *BKLY* M9 ........73 C1
   *DTN/ASHW* M34 ........90 B5
Envoy Cl *WGNW/BIL/OR* WN5 ........47 H3
Ephraim's Fold *WGNE/HIN* WN2 ........33 G6
Epping Cl *AUL* OL6 ........75 M5
   *CHAD* OL9 ........8 C3
Epping Dr *SALE* M33 ........95 M7
Epping Rd *DTN/ASHW* M34 ........100 E2
Epping St *HULME* M15 ........87 J6
Eppleworth Ri *SWIN* M27 ........70 D1
Epsom Av *BNG/LEV* M19 ........99 J2
   *SALE* M33 ........107 M2
   *WILM/AE* SK9 ........120 A8
Epsom Cl *BRAM/HZG* SK7 ........122 B2
   *ROCH* OL11 ........27 H4
Epsom Dr *WGNE/HIN* WN2 ........64 C5
Epworth St *ANC* M4 ........7 M5
Equitable St *MILN* OL16 ........29 J7
   *OLDE* OL4 ........60 A4
Era St *BOLE* BL2 ........37 C5
   *SALE* M33 ........96 E3
Ercall Av *WGTN/LGST* M12 ........88 B6
Erica Av *OLDE* OL4 ........44 C8
Erica Cl *RDSH* SK5 ........100 C4
Erica Dr *BNG/LEV* M19 ........99 H4
Eric Brook Cl *RUSH/FAL* M14 ........98 D1
Eric Bullows Cl
   *WYTH/NTH* M22 ........118 C3
Eric St *LIT* OL15 ........21 L6
   *OLDE* OL4 ........59 M6
Erin St *OP/CLY* M11 * ........89 H5
Erith Cl *RDSH* SK5 ........100 E6
Erith Rd *OLDE* OL4 ........59 L6
Erlesmere Av *DTN/ASHW* M34 ........90 D8
Erlesmere Cl *OLDE* OL4 ........44 C8
Erlington Av *OLDTF/WHR* M16 ........97 L1
Ermen Rd *ECC* M30 ........84 F4
Ermington Dr *CHH* M8 ........72 C6
Erneley Cl *WGTN/LGST* M12 ........99 L1
Ernest St *BOL* BL1 ........2 A3
   *CHD/CHDH* SK8 ........110 F6
   *OFTN* SK2 ........112 D6
   *PWCH* M25 ........55 J8
Ernest Ter *WHIT* OL12 ........28 E3
Erniouen Av *BOL* BL1 ........35 K4
Ernocroft Gv *GTN* M18 * ........89 H6
Ernocroft La *MPL/ROM* SK6 ........115 H1
Ernocroft Rd *MPL/ROM* SK6 ........114 C3
Erradale Crs *WGNS/IIMK* WN3 ........63 G2
Errington Cl *OFTN* SK2 ........113 H6
Errington Dr *BRO* M7 ........72 A8
Errol Av *BKLY* M9 ........56 D7
   *WYTH/NTH* M22 ........109 M8
Erskine Cl *BOLS/LL* BL3 ........35 K8
Erskine Pl *WGNE/HIN* WN2 ........64 C3
Erskine Rd *BKLY* M9 ........57 H7
   *PART* M31 ........106 C1
   *HULME* M15 ........87 G6
   *MPL/ROM* SK6 ........114 C2
Erwin St *NEWH/MOS* M40 ........73 K6
Erwood Rd *BNG/LEV* M19 ........99 K4
Eryngo St *STKP* SK1 ........13 M5
Escott Cl *OLDTF/WHR* M16 ........98 C1
Esher Dr *SALE* M33 ........108 E4
Esk Cl *URM* M41 ........84 D8
Eskdale *CHD/CHDH* SK8 ........110 F8
Eskdale Av *BOLE* BL2 ........37 J2
   *BRAM/HZG* SK7 ........120 E7
   *DID/WITH* M20 ........98 D5
   *HOR/BR* BL6 ........33 H5
   *MPL/ROM* SK6 ........101 J7
   *OLDS* OL8 ........59 G8
   *ROCH* OL11 ........27 L8
   *ROY/SHW* OL2 ........43 G5
   *UPML* OL3 ........61 L7
   *WGN* WN1 ........47 L1
Eskdale Dr *HALE/TIMP* WA15 ........108 F5
   *MDTN* M24 ........57 J1
Eskdale Gv *FWTH* BL4 ........52 C4
Eskdale Ms *UPML* OL3 * ........61 L7
   *WGNE/HIN* WN2 ........49 H7
Eskrick St *BOL* BL1 ........36 A2
Eskrigge Cl *BRO* M7 ........72 C4
Esmond Rd *CHH* M8 ........72 D5
Esmont Dr *MDTN* M24 ........57 H1
The Esplanade *MILN* OL16 ........10 D5
Essex Av *BURY* BL9 ........40 B3
   *DID/WITH* M20 ........98 E8
   *DROY* M43 ........89 K1
   *EDGY/DAV* SK3 ........12 B7
Essex Cl *FAIL* M35 ........74 C7
   *ROY/SHW* OL2 ........43 J5
Essex Dr *BURY* BL9 ........5 G9
Essex Pl *TYLD* M29 ........67 M3
Essex Rd *GTN* M18 ........100 C1
   *RDSH* SK5 ........99 M5
   *WGN* WN1 ........31 L4
Essex St *CMANW* M2 ........6 F5
   *HOR/BR* BL6 ........34 A3
   *ROCH* OL11 ........10 E7
   *WGN* WN1 ........15 K2
Essex Wy *OLDTF/WHR* M16 ........87 G7
Essingdon St *BOLS/LL* BL3 ........36 A8
Essington Dr *NEWH/MOS* M40 ........73 G6
Estate St *OLDS* OL8 ........59 J8
Estate St South *OLDS* OL8 ........59 J8
Est Bank Rd *RAMS* BL0 ........24 B2
Esther St *OLDE* OL4 ........59 M5
Esthwaite Dr *TYLD* M29 ........67 K3
Estonfield Dr *URM* M41 ........96 C2
Eston St *BRUN/LGST* M13 ........88 A3
Eswick St *OP/CLY* M11 ........88 F3
Etchells Rd *CHD/CHDH* SK8 ........13 M1
Etchell St *NEWH/MOS* M40 * ........57 G8
Ethel Av *BKLY* M9 ........56 F8
Ethel Ct *MILN* OL16 ........11 K6
Ethel St *BOLS/LL* BL3 ........52 D2
   *OLDS* OL8 ........75 J1
   *WHIT* OL12 ........20 B2
Ethel Ter *BNG/LEV* M19 ........99 K5

Etherley Cl IRL M44 94 D2
Etherow Av MPL/ROM SK6 114 B2
NEWH/MOS M40 * 74 C2
Etherow Brow HYDE SK14 103 L4
Etherow Wy GLSP SK13 93 H7
Etherstone St CHH M8 72 F4
LEIGH WN7 66 B8
Eton Av OLDS OL8 75 H1
Eton Cl OLDTF/WHR M16 87 G7
ROCH OL11 27 L6
Eton Ct OLDTF/WHR M16 * 87 G7
Eton Dr CHD/CHDH SK8 119 L2
Eton Hill Rd RAD M26 38 F7
Eton St LEIGH WN7 81 J1
Eton Ter WGNS/IIMK WN3 15 K9
Eton Wy WGNW/BIL/OR WN5 46 C4
Eton Wy North RAD M26 38 F7
Eton Wy South RAD M26 38 F7
Etruria Cl BRUN/LGST M13 88 B7
Ettington Cl TOT/BURYW BL8 38 D1
Ettrick Cl OP/CLY M11 89 G5
Euclid Cl OP/CLY M11 88 B3
Europa Ga TRPK M17 86 A7
Europa Wy EDGY/DAV SK3 111 M6
RAD M26 53 K5
TRPK M17 86 A7
Eustace St BOLS/LL BL3 52 D1
CHAD OL9 8 B1
Euston Av BKLY M9 73 K1
Euxton Cl TOT/BURYW BL8 38 D4
Evan Cl DID/WITH M20 110 D1
Evans Cl DID/WITH M20 110 D1
RNFD/HAY WA11 78 C5
Evans Rd ECC M30 84 D3
Evans St AUL OL6 76 A8
CSLFD M3 6 D1
LEIGH WN7 66 C7
MDTN M24 57 L4
OLD OL1 9 J3
Evanstone Cl HOR/BR BL6 33 L1
Evan St NEWH/MOS M40 73 H7
Eva Rd EDGY/DAV SK3 111 K5
Eva St LEIGH WN7 65 M5
RUSH/FAL M14 98 F1
WHIT OL12 28 D2
Evelyn St OLD OL1 59 L3
RUSH/FAL M14 99 G4
Evening St FAIL M35 74 C4
Evenley Cl OP/CLY M11 * 89 H6
Everard Cl WALK M28 68 E4
Everard St ORD M5 86 F5
Everbrom Rd BOLS/LL BL3 51 K2
Everest Av AULW OL7 75 L7
Everest Cl HYDE SK14 91 K8
Everest Pl WGN WN1 47 M2
Everest Rd ATH M46 50 F7
HYDE SK14 91 K8
Everest St ROCH OL11 42 D2
Everett Rd DID/WITH M20 98 E6
Everglade OLDS OL8 75 K3
The Evergreens HOR/BR BL6 34 B3
Everleigh Cl BOLE BL2 23 H7
Everleigh Dr BRO M7 72 C6
Eversden Ct BRO M7 * 72 B8
Everside Dr CHH M8 72 B6
Eversley Rd DID/WITH M20 110 D1
Everton Rd OLDS OL8 75 G1
RDSH SK5 100 C2
Everton St AIMK WN4 63 G7
SWIN M27 70 B4
Every St ANC M4 88 A3
BURY BL9 4 F1
RAMS BL0 * 19 G6
Evesham Av GLSP SK13 93 K7
HTNM SK4 12 A1
NTHM/RTH M23 109 G5
Evesham Cl BOLS/LL BL3 2 B7
LEIGH WN7 81 G3
MDTN M24 57 L7
Evesham Dr FWTH BL4 * 52 E2
Evesham Drive WILM/AE SK9 127 G2
Evesham Gdns MDTN M24 * 57 K7
Evesham Gv AUL OL6 75 M5
SALE M33 97 H8
Evesham Rd BKLY M9 73 K2
CHD/CHDH SK8 111 K8
MDTN M24 57 K7
Evesham Wk BOLS/LL BL3 2 B8
MDTN M24 57 L7
OLDS OL8 9 H9
Eveside Cl CHD/CHDH SK8 * 111 L8
Eve St OLDS OL8 75 J2
Ewan St GTN M18 89 G6
Ewart Av ORD M5 86 D3
Ewart St BOL BL1 36 B2
Ewhurst Av SWIN M27 70 A6
Ewing Cl CHH M8 72 D3
Ewood OLDS OL8 75 K4
Ewood Dr TOT/BURYW BL8 38 D4
Exbourne Rd WYTH/NTH M22 118 E3
Exbury WHIT OL12 10 D2
Exbury St RUSH/FAL M14 99 G5
Excalibur Wy IRL M44 94 C5
Excelsior Gdns HEY OL10 41 J4
Excelsior Ter LIT OL15 29 J1
Exchange Quay ORD M5 86 D6
Exchange Sq CSLFD M3 6 F3
Exchange St BOL BL1 * 2 E5
CSLFD M3 * 6 F4
EDGY/DAV SK3 13 G5
RAMS BL0 19 G1
Exeter Av BOLE BL2 36 E2
DTN/ASHW M34 101 J3
ECC M30 70 D8
FWTH BL4 52 C3
RAD M26 38 A7
Exeter Cl CHD/CHDH SK8 120 B4
DUK SK16 90 F6
Exeter Dr AUL OL6 76 A5
IRL M44 94 E2
WGNE/HIN WN2 33 G7
Exeter Gv ROCH OL11 10 F8
Exeter Rd RDSH SK5 100 F7
URM M41 85 G8
WGNE/HIN WN2 49 H7
Exeter St ROCH OL11 10 E5
SLFD M6 86 B2
Exford Av WGNS/IIMK WN3 47 L8
Exford Cl NEWH/MOS M40 88 A1
RDSH SK5 100 C6
Exford Dr BOLE BL2 37 K6
Exit Rd West MANAIR M90 118 D5
Exmoor Cl AUL OL6 75 M5
Exmouth Av RDSH SK5 100 F7
Exmouth Pl MILN OL16 42 D1
Exmouth Rd SALE M33 96 A7
Exmouth Sq MILN OL16 * 28 D8
Exmouth St MILN OL16 42 D1
Exmouth Wk OLDTF/WHR M16 98 B1
Eyam Gv OFTN SK2 113 G8
Eyam Ms GLSP SK13 104 A2
Eyam Rd BRAM/HZG SK7 122 A4
Eycott Dr MDTN M24 57 G3
Eyebrook Rd ALT WA14 116 C3
Eyet St LEIGH WN7 66 B7
Eynford Av RDSH SK5 100 E7
Eyre St HULME M15 87 K7

## F

Faber St ANC M4 87 K1
Factory Brow HOR/BR BL6 33 G1
MDTN M24 56 F5
Factory Fold WGNE/HIN WN2 * 48 D5
Factory La BKLY M9 73 G3
CSLFD M3 * 6 A4
Factory St MDTN M24 57 J4
RAD M26 54 E1
RAMS BL0 18 E6
TYLD M29 67 J3
Factory St East ATH M46 66 F1
Factory St West ATH M46 66 F1
Faggy La WGNS/IIMK WN3 15 G6
Failsworth Rd FAIL M35 74 E5
Fair Acres BOLE BL2 37 H1
Fairacres WGNNW/ST WN6 30 E3
Fairacres Rd MPL/ROM SK6 123 G4
Fairbairn St HOR/BR BL6 33 L2
Fairbank Dr MDTN M24 57 G2
Fairbottom St OLD OL1 9 G5
Fairbourne Av WGNS/IIMK WN3 47 K8
WILM/AE SK9 126 D8
WILM/AE SK9 130 E1
Fairbourne Cl WILM/AE SK9 126 D8
Fairbourne Dr
HALE/TIMP WA15 108 E3
WILM/AE SK9 126 D8
Fairbourne Rd BNG/LEV M19 99 M3
DTN/ASHW M34 101 H2
Fairbrook Dr SLFD M6 86 B2
Fairbrother St ORD M5 86 F5
Fairburn Cl URM M41 84 D8
Fairclough St BOLS/LL BL3 36 C8
OP/CLY M11 88 D2
WGN WN1 15 H5
WGNE/HIN WN2 49 G6
Fairfax Av DID/WITH M20 98 E8
HALE/TIMP WA15 108 D6
Fairfax Cl MPL/ROM SK6 114 A5
Fairfax Dr LIT OL15 29 J1
WILM/AE SK9 126 D8
Fairfax Rd PWCH M25 55 K7
Fairfield Av CHD/CHDH SK8 120 B2
DROY M43 89 K3
MPL/ROM SK6 101 K8
WGNE/HIN WN2 64 D2
WGNW/BIL/OR WN5 47 G7
Fairfield Dr BURY BL9 40 A1
Fairfield Rd DROY M43 89 K4
FWTH BL4 52 F5
HALE/TIMP WA15 108 F7
MDTN M24 57 H3
OP/CLY M11 89 H5
Fairfields EDGW/EG BL7 22 C4
OLDS OL8 75 H2
Fairfield Sq DROY M43 89 K4
Fairfield St CMANE M1 7 K7
SLFD M6 71 G7
WGNW/BIL/OR WN5 46 F7
Fairford Cl RDSH SK5 100 C7
Fairford Dr BOLS/LL BL3 2 C9
Fairford Wy RDSH SK5 100 C7
WILM/AE SK9 127 H5
Fairhaven Av CCHDY M21 97 L5
WHTF M45 55 G5
WHTN BL5 50 E4
Fairhaven Cl BRAM/HZG SK7 121 H5
Fairhaven St WGTN/LGST M12 88 C6
Fairhills Rd IRL M44 94 D4
Fairholme Av AIMK WN4 63 L8
URM M41 95 M2
Fairholme Rd DID/WITH M20 98 F6
HTNM SK4 12 D1
Fairhope Av SLFD M6 70 E8
Fairhurst Av WGNNW/ST WN6 31 G1
Fairhurst Dr WALK M28 68 C2
Fairhurst St LEIGH WN7 66 B7
WGNS/IIMK WN3 14 D4
Fairisle Cl OP/CLY M11 88 C3
Fairlands Rd BURY BL9 25 J5
SALE M33 108 C2
Fairlands St ROCH OL11 42 E2
Fairlawn HTNM SK4 12 C2
Fairlawn Cl RUSH/FAL M14 87 K8
Fairlea DTN/ASHW M34 101 K2
Fairlea Av DID/WITH M20 110 F2
Fairlee Av DTN/ASHW M34 89 M3
Fairleigh Av SLFD M6 85 M1
Fairless Rd ECC M30 85 G3
Fairlie Av BOLS/LL BL3 35 J7
Fairlie Dr HALE/TIMP WA15 108 E4
Fairlyn Cl WHTN BL5 51 K5
Fairlyn Dr WHTN BL5 51 K5
Fairman Dr WGNE/HIN WN2 49 H5
Fairman St OLDTF/WHR M16 98 C1
Fairmead Rd NTHM/RTH M23 109 M3
Fairmile Dr DID/WITH M20 110 F4
Fairmount Av BOLE BL2 37 H4
Fairmount Rd SWIN M27 69 L6
Fairoak Ct BOLS/LL BL3 2 A8
Fair Oak Rd BNG/LEV M19 99 J7
Fairstead Cl WHTN BL5 50 A4
Fairstead Wk OP/CLY M11 89 J5
Fair St BOLS/LL BL3 * 51 M2
CMANE M1 7 L5
SWIN M27 70 D3
Fair Vw WGNW/BIL/OR WN5 62 A7
Fairview Av BNG/LEV M19 99 J2
DTN/ASHW M34 100 D3
Fair View Av
WGNW/BIL/OR WN5 62 A7
Fairview Cl AIMK WN4 63 L8
CHAD OL9 58 B4
MPL/ROM SK6 114 C5
WHIT OL12 26 F2
Fairview Dr MPL/ROM SK6 114 C5
Fairview Rd DTN/ASHW M34 100 D3
HALE/TIMP WA15 108 F7
Fairway BRAM/HZG SK7 120 F6
CHD/CHDH SK8 110 E8
DROY M43 89 K4
PWCH M25 72 A2
ROCH OL11 41 L3
SWIN M27 70 F5
WHIT OL12 20 A5
Fairway Av BOLE BL2 23 K8
NTHM/RTH M23 109 G5
Fairway Crs ROY/SHW OL2 43 G6
Fairway Dr SALE M33 108 B2
Fairway Rd BURY BL9 55 K1
OLDE OL4 60 B8
Fairways HOR/BR BL6 33 M1
Fairways Cl GLSP SK13 105 J3
The Fairways AIMK WN4 78 A2
WHTF M45 55 J6
WHTN BL5 50 B4
The Fairway NEWH/MOS M40 74 A4
OFTN SK2 113 G5
Fairwood Rd NTHM/RTH M23 109 G5
Fairy Bank Crs NM/HAY SK22 125 M1
Fairy Bank Rd NM/HAY SK22 125 M1
Fairy La CHH M8 72 B7
SALE M33 97 J8
SALE M33 109 L1
Fairy St TOT/BURYW BL8 4 A5
Fairywell Cl WILM/AE SK9 127 H3
Fairywell Dr SALE M33 108 D3
Fairywell Rd
HALE/TIMP WA15 108 E5
Faith St BOL BL1 35 K3
LEIGH WN7 65 M7
Falcon Av URM M41 96 B2
Falcon Cl BURY BL9 5 J1
LEIGH WN7 66 E7
NM/HAY SK22 124 F4
WHIT OL12 27 G2
Falcon Crs SWIN M27 70 E2
Falcon Dr CHAD OL9 8 C3
IRL M44 83 L8
LHULT M38 52 D7
MDTN M24 57 H1
Falconers Gn WGNS/IIMK WN3 47 L7
Falcon St OLDS OL8 9 H8
Falconwood Cha WALK M28 68 E6
Falconwood Cl
WGNNW/ST WN6 14 C2
Falfield Dr CHH M8 72 E7
Falinge Fold WHIT OL12 28 A3
Falinge Ms WHIT OL12 10 C3
Falinge Rd WHIT OL12 10 D2
Falkirk Dr BOLE BL2 37 J6
WGNE/HIN WN2 48 D4
Falkirk Gv WGNW/BIL/OR WN5 46 F4
Falkirk St OLDE OL4 59 M5
Falkland Av NEWH/MOS M40 73 G8
ROCH OL11 27 M4
Falkland Cl OLDE OL4 44 B8
Falkland Dr AIMK WN4 62 F8
Falkland Rd BOLE BL2 37 K5
Fall Birch Rd HOR/BR BL6 34 C4
Fallons Rd WALK M28 69 M3
Fallow Av GTN M18 100 A2
Fallow Cl WHTN BL5 50 B2
Fallowfield Av ORD M5 86 E4
Fallowfield Dr WHIT OL12 28 A2
Fallow Fields Dr RDSH SK5 100 D3
Fallowfield Wy ATH M46 67 H3
The Fallows CHAD OL9 58 D7
Falls Gv CHD/CHDH SK8 119 J1
Falmer Cl GTN M18 89 J6
TOT/BURYW BL8 24 F6
Falmer Dr WYTH/NTH M22 118 F3
Falmouth Av SALE M33 96 A7
URM M41 95 H1
Falmouth Crs RDSH SK5 100 F7
Falmouth Rd IRL M44 94 E2
Falmouth St NEWH/MOS M40 73 J8
OLDS OL8 59 J8
ROCH OL11 * 11 G7
Falsgrave Cl NEWH/MOS M40 73 K7
Falshaw Dr BURY BL9 25 H4
Falstaff Ms MPL/ROM SK6 113 K1
Falston Av NEWH/MOS M40 74 A2
Falstone Av RAMS BL0 18 F8
Falstone Cl WGNS/IIMK WN3 63 G2
Falterley Rd NTHM/RTH M23 109 H4
Fancroft Rd WYTH/NTH M22 109 M7
Faraday Av CHH M8 72 D6
SWIN M27 71 G2
Faraday Cl WGNNW/ST WN6 14 C4
Faraday Dr BOL BL1 36 B3
Faraday Ri WHIT OL12 27 L3
Faraday St CMANE M1 7 J4
Farcroft Av RAD M26 38 F7
Farcroft Cl NTHM/RTH M23 109 J4
OFTN SK2 113 H5
Far Cromwell Rd
MPL/ROM SK6 101 G6
Fardale ROY/SHW OL2 43 L6
Farden Dr NTHM/RTH M23 109 G4
Fardon Cl WGNS/IIMK WN3 63 J1
Farefield Av GOL/RIS/CUL WA3 79 J2
Farewell Cl ROCH OL11 41 M2
Far Hey Cl RAD M26 54 B1
Farholme ROY/SHW OL2 58 F2
Faringdon ROCH OL11 10 C7
Faringdon Wk BOLS/LL BL3 2 C8
Farland Pl BOLS/LL BL3 35 J7
Farlands Dr DID/WITH M20 110 E5
Farlands Ri MILN OL16 42 F1
Far La GTN M18 89 G8
Farley Av GTN M18 89 K8
Farley Ct CHD/CHDH SK8 111 J8
Farley Rd SALE M33 108 F2
Farley Wy RDSH SK5 100 B3
Farliegh Cl WHTN BL5 50 D2
Farman St BOLS/LL BL3 * 52 A1
Farm Av STRET M32 85 K8
Farm Cl HTNM SK4 99 M6
TOT/BURYW BL8 24 C6
Farmers Cl SALE M33 109 K2
Farmer St HTNM SK4 112 A1
Farmfield SALE M33 96 B6
Farm Hl PWCH M25 * 55 K7
Farmlands Wk OLD OL1 43 M8
Farm La HYDE SK14 102 A4
POY/DIS SK12 123 J6
PWCH M25 56 B4
WALK M28 69 J7
WGNE/HIN WN2 48 D2
Farm Meadow Rd
WGNW/BIL/OR WN5 46 B7
Farm Rd OLDS OL8 74 F4
Farmside Av IRL M44 94 D1
Farmstead Cl FAIL M35 74 F6
Farm St FAIL M35 74 A6
HEY OL10 41 H4
OLD OL1 58 E3
Farm Wk ALT WA14 116 A2
LIT OL15 21 K7
MILN OL16 28 F3
Farmway MDTN M24 57 J5
Farm Yd BNG/LEV M19 99 K3
Farn Av RDSH SK5 100 B2
Farnborough Av OLDE OL4 60 A6
Farnborough Rd BOL BL1 22 B6
NEWH/MOS M40 88 A1
Farndale Gv AIMK WN4 78 F2
Farndale Sq LHULT M38 68 F1
Farndon Av BRAM/HZG SK7 113 J8
Farndon Cl SALE M33 109 H1
Farndon Dr HALE/TIMP WA15 108 D6
Farndon Rd RDSH SK5 100 B2
Farnham Av BKLY M9 57 G7
Farnham Cl BOL BL1 * 2 C1
CHD/CHDH SK8 120 C5
LEIGH WN7 66 C6
Farnham Dr IRL M44 94 D3
Farnley Cl WHIT OL12 27 J2
Farnley St WGTN/LGST M12 * 88 D6
Farnsfield WGN WN1 48 C3
Farnsworth Cl AULW OL7 75 L7
Farnworth Dr RUSH/FAL M14 98 F2
Farnworth St BOLS/LL BL3 * 35 M8
HEY OL10 40 F2
LEIGH WN7 * 66 E8
Farrand Rd OLDS OL8 74 E2
Farrant Rd WGTN/LGST M12 99 K1
Farrar Rd DROY M43 89 J4
Farr Cl WGNS/IIMK WN3 47 J7
Farrell St BRO M7 87 H1
WGNW/BIL/OR WN5 46 F7
Farrer Rd BRUN/LGST M13 99 J2
Far Ridings MPL/ROM SK6 114 A1
Farrier Cl SALE M33 109 J1
Farrier's Cft WGNNW/ST WN6 47 H1
Farriers La ROCH OL11 27 L8
Farringdon St SLFD M6 * 86 B1
Farrowdale Av ROY/SHW OL2 43 L6
Farrow St ROY/SHW OL2 43 L6
Farrow St East ROY/SHW OL2 43 L6
Farr St EDGY/DAV SK3 12 E6
Farwood Cl OLDTF/WHR M16 86 F7
Far Woodseats La GLSP SK13 103 J7
Fastnet St OP/CLY M11 88 D4
Faulkenhurst Ms OLD OL1 8 C1
Faulkenhurst St OLD OL1 8 C1
Faulkner Dr HALE/TIMP WA15 108 E8
Faulkner Rd STRET M32 97 H3
Faulkner St BOLS/LL BL3 2 D9
CMANE M1 7 G6
MILN OL16 10 F4
Fauvel Rd GLSP SK13 104 F3
Faversham Brow OLD OL1 * 9 H2
Faversham St NEWH/MOS M40 73 L5
Fawborough Rd
NTHM/RTH M23 109 J3
Fawcetts Fold WHTN BL5 34 B8
Fawcett St BOLE BL2 3 K4
Fawley Av HYDE SK14 102 A3
Fawley Gv WYTH/NTH M22 110 A8
Fawns Keep STLY SK15 92 B6
WILM/AE SK9 127 H5
Fay Av BKLY M9 73 L2
Fay Gdns GLSP SK13 93 H8
Faywood Dr MPL/ROM SK6 114 D6
Fearney Side BOLS/LL BL3 53 J1
Fearnham Cl LEIGH WN7 81 H3
Fearnhead Cl FWTH BL4 53 H4
Fearnhead St BOLS/LL BL3 35 M8
Fearn St HEY OL10 40 F2
Featherstall Brook Vie LIT OL15 21 L7
Featherstall Rd LIT OL15 21 K7
Featherstall Rd North OLD OL1 8 F2
Featherstall Rd South CHAD OL9 8 E7
Fecit La RAMS BL0 19 L4
Federation St ANC M4 7 G2
PWCH M25 55 J7
Feldom Rd NTHM/RTH M23 109 J2
Fellbridge Cl WHTN BL5 50 D3
Fellbrigg Cl GTN M18 99 M1
Fellfoot Cl WALK M28 68 C7
Fellpark Rd NTHM/RTH M23 109 K2
Fells Gv WALK M28 69 J3
Fellside BOLE BL2 37 K1
WGN WN1 48 A2
Fellside Cl TOT/BURYW BL8 * 24 C3
Fellside Gdns LIT OL15 21 K5
Fellside Gn STLY SK15 91 K1
Fell St LEIGH WN7 65 M7
TOT/BURYW BL8 38 F2
Felltop Dr RDSH SK5 100 D4
Felskirk Rd WYTH/NTH M22 118 E4
Felsted BOL BL1 35 H4
Felt Ct DTN/ASHW M34 100 F2
Felthorpe Dr CHH M8 72 C6
Felton Av WYTH/NTH M22 118 E1
Felton Cl BURY BL9 39 K7
Felton Wk BOL BL1 36 B2
Fencegate Av HTNM SK4 100 A7
Fence St OFTN SK2 113 G8
Fenchurch Av NEWH/MOS M40 73 M8
Fencot Dr WGTN/LGST M12 88 D8
Fenella St BRUN/LGST M13 88 B8
Fenham Cl NEWH/MOS M40 * 72 F7
Fenmore Av GTN M18 99 L1
Fennel St ANC M4 6 F2
Fenners Cl BOLS/LL BL3 52 A1
Fenney St BRO M7 72 A7
Fenney St East BRO M7 72 B6
Fenn St HULME M15 87 H6
Fenside Rd WYTH/NTH M22 110 B7
Fenton Av OFTN SK2 112 F8
Fenton Ms ROCH OL11 10 D8
Fenton St OLDE OL4 59 L6
ROCH OL11 10 D8
ROY/SHW OL2 43 L7
TOT/BURYW BL8 38 F1
WGTN/LGST M12 88 D7
Fenton Wy WGNE/HIN WN2 49 J8
Fenwick Cl WHTN BL5 50 C6
Fenwick Dr HTNM SK4 111 H1
MDTN M24 57 G3
Fenwick St HULME M15 87 K6
ROCH OL11 10 C5
Ferdinand St NEWH/MOS M40 * 73 G8
Fereday St WALK M28 52 F8
Ferguson Gdns WHIT OL12 28 C1
Ferguson Ri
WGNW/BIL/OR WN5 47 H4
Ferguson Wy OLDE OL4 60 A3
Fernacre SALE M33 96 F7
Fernally St HYDE SK14 102 B2
Fern Av URM M41 95 K2
Fern Bank NEWH/MOS M40 * 73 M5
Fernbank RAD M26 * 54 D4
Fern Bank STLY SK15 91 M4
Fern Bank Cl STLY SK15 91 M4
Fern Bank Dr NTHM/RTH M23 109 H4
Fern Bank St HYDE SK14 102 B4
Fernbray Av BNG/LEV M19 99 G8
Fernbray Rd WGNE/HIN WN2 49 J7
Fernbrook Cl BRUN/LGST M13 88 A7
Fern Cl ATH M46 67 G2
MDTN M24 58 A4
MPL/ROM SK6 114 C6
OLDE OL4 60 C6
WGNNW/ST WN6 30 D6
Fern Clough BOL BL1 35 J5
Ferncough Rd BKLY M9 73 G6
Fern Crs STLY SK15 91 M4
Ferndale HYDE SK14 91 K7
Ferndale Av MILN OL16 42 F3
OFTN SK2 112 E8
WHTF M45 54 F5
Ferndale Cl OLDE OL4 60 A8
Ferndale Gdns BNG/LEV M19 99 H6
Ferndale Rd SALE M33 108 E2
Fern Dene WHIT OL12 27 L2
Ferndene Rd DID/WITH M20 98 E7
WHTF M45 55 M5
Ferndown Av BRAM/HZG SK7 121 L3
CHAD OL9 58 A5
Ferndown Dr IRL M44 94 D1
Ferndown Rd BOLE BL2 37 H1
NTHM/RTH M23 109 G4
Ferney Field Rd MDTN M24 58 B6
Ferngate Dr DID/WITH M20 98 E6
Ferngrove BURY BL9 5 M1
Fernhill MPL/ROM SK6 114 E6
Fernhill Av BOLS/LL BL3 35 K8
Fernhill Cl GLSP SK13 105 G1
Fernhill Dr GTN M18 88 E8
Fern Hill La WHIT OL12 27 K1
Fernhills EDGW/EG BL7 22 B2
Fernhill St BURY BL9 4 F2
Fernholme Ct OLDS OL8 58 F8
Fernhurst Cl WGNS/IIMK WN3 15 M8
Fernhurst Rd DID/WITH M20 98 F7
Fernhurst St OLD OL1 8 C1
Fernie St ANC M4 * 87 K1
Fernilee Cl NM/HAY SK22 124 E3
Fern Lea CHD/CHDH SK8 119 K3
Fernlea HALE/TIMP WA15 117 H3
Fernlea Av OLD OL1 8 C1
Fernlea Cl GLSP SK13 93 H8
WHIT OL12 27 L2
Fernlea Crs SWIN M27 70 B5
Fernlea Gv AIMK WN4 63 G7
Fern Lea Gv LHULT M38 52 C8
Fernleigh HOR/BR BL6 * 34 A3
Fernleigh Av BNG/LEV M19 99 M3
Fernleigh Dr OLDTF/WHR M16 * 86 F7
Fernley Av DTN/ASHW M34 101 K2
Fernley Rd OFTN SK2 112 E6
Fern Lodge Dr AUL OL6 76 A7
Fernone WILM/AE SK9 127 H1
Ferns Gv BOL BL1 35 L5
Fernside RAD M26 53 L6
Fernside Av DID/WITH M20 99 G7
Fernside Gv WALK M28 * 53 H8
WGNS/IIMK WN3 63 G3
Fernside Wy WHIT OL12 27 K3
Fernstead BOLS/LL BL3 35 M6
Fernstone Cl HOR/BR BL6 33 K1
Fern St BOLS/LL BL3 35 M6
BURY BL9 4 F2
CHAD OL9 58 D4
CHH M8 72 D8
FWTH BL4 53 H3
OLDS OL8 8 F8
RAMS BL0 19 G6
ROCH OL11 10 C6
WHIT OL12 21 G6
Fernthorpe Av UPML OL3 61 M3
Fern Vw HALE/TIMP WA15 109 H7
Fernview Dr RAMS BL0 24 E3
Fernwood MPL/ROM SK6 114 F5
Fernwood Av GTN M18 100 A1
Fernwood Gv WILM/AE SK9 127 G4
Ferrand Rd LIT OL15 21 M6
Ferrer St AIMK WN4 63 J6
Ferring Wk CHAD OL9 * 8 A7
Ferris St OP/CLY M11 89 G4
Ferrous Wy IRL M44 94 C6
Ferryhill Rd IRL M44 94 D2
Ferrymasters Wy IRL M44 94 D3
Ferry Rd IRL M44 94 E2
Ferry St OP/CLY M11 88 B4
Festival Dr MCFLDN SK10 131 J6
Fettler Cl SWIN M27 70 B6
Feversham Cl ECC M30 70 C8
Fewston Cl BOL BL1 22 B7
Fiddlers La IRL M44 83 L8
Field Bank Gv BNG/LEV M19 99 L3
Field Cl BRAM/HZG SK7 120 F8
MPL/ROM SK6 114 A7
Fieldcroft ROCH OL11 27 L5
Fielden Av CCHDY M21 97 L3
Fielden Ct CCHDY M21 98 A7
Fielden Rd DID/WITH M20 98 C7
Fielders Wy SWIN M27 54 B8
Fieldfare Av NEWH/MOS M40 73 L8
Fieldfare Cl GOL/RIS/CUL WA3 80 A4
Fieldfare Wy AULW OL7 75 K5
Fieldhead Av ROCH OL11 27 K5
TOT/BURYW BL8 38 D3
TYLD M29 67 L7
Fieldhead Ms WILM/AE SK9 127 J4
Fieldhead Rd WILM/AE SK9 127 J4
Field House La MPL/ROM SK6 114 D7
Fieldhouse Rd WHIT OL12 28 C2
Fielding Av POY/DIS SK12 129 J2
Fielding St ECC M30 84 F3
MDTN M24 57 K2
Field La AUL OL6 76 A7
Field Pl DID/WITH M20 110 E1
Field Rd MILN OL16 29 G5
SALE M33 96 B6
Fields Crs HYDE SK14 93 G6
Fieldsend Cl STLY SK15 92 A4
Fieldsend Dr LEIGH WN7 80 F4
Fields End Fold ECC M30 83 M8
Fields Farm Cl HYDE SK14 103 G3
Fields Farm Rd HYDE SK14 103 H2
Fields Gv HYDE SK14 93 G7
Fieldside Cl BRAM/HZG SK7 120 F8
Fields New Rd CHAD OL9 58 D7
The Fields WGNE/HIN WN2 32 F8
WGNNW/ST WN6 31 J4
Field St DROY M43 89 J4
FAIL M35 74 B5
GTN M18 89 H6
HYDE SK14 91 G7
MPL/ROM SK6 113 J1
ROCH OL11 28 D8
SLFD M6 86 C2
WGNE/HIN WN2 49 H8
WGNNW/ST WN6 14 D3
WGNS/IIMK WN3 48 C8
Fieldsway OLDS OL8 75 H2
Field Vale Dr RDSH SK5 100 D3
Fieldvale Rd SALE M33 108 B3
Field View Wk
OLDTF/WHR M16 98 C2
Field Wk HALE/TIMP WA15 * 117 K1
Fieldway MILN OL16 42 E1
WGNE/HIN WN2 64 E2
Fife Av CHAD OL9 58 C8
Fifield Cl OLDS OL8 75 K1
Fifth Av BOL BL1 35 L5
BOLS/LL BL3 37 J8
BURY BL9 26 A8
DUK SK16 90 E5
OLDS OL8 74 F2
OP/CLY M11 88 F2
TRPK M17 85 M7
Fifth St TRPK M17 85 M7

Fulwell Av TYLD M29 67 H4
Fulwood Av BKLY M9 57 J8
Fulwood Cl TOT/BURYW BL8 38 C3
Fulwood Rd
GOL/RIS/CUL WA3 80 B6
Furbarn La ROCH OL11 27 G4
Furbarn Rd ROCH OL11 27 G4
Furlong Cl WGNE/HIN WN2 64 C5
Furlong Rd WYTH/NTH M22 118 D2
Furnace St DUK SK16 90 E3
HYDE SK14 90 F8
Furness Av AULW OL7 75 J7
BOLE BL2 36 E2
HEY OL10 26 F8
LIT OL15 21 L6
OLDS OL8 59 M8
WHTF M45 55 K4
Furness Cl GLSP SK13 105 J4
MILN OL16 29 H6
POY/DIS SK12 121 L8
Furness Crs LEIGH WN7 66 A3
Furness Gv HTNM SK4 111 K3
Furness Lodge Cl
CHF/WBR SK23 124 F8
Furness Quay SALQ M50 86 D5
Furness Rd BOL BL1 35 L5
CHD/CHDH SK8 120 E6
MDTN M24 57 J1
RUSH/FAL M14 98 F3
URM M41 96 A1
Furness Sq BOLE BL2 36 E2
Furnival Rd GTN M18 88 F6
Furnival St LEIGH WN7 66 C5
RDSH SK5 100 B2
Furrow Dr ECC M30 69 L8
Further Fld ROCH OL11 27 G3
Further Heights Rd WHIT OL12 28 B2
Further Hey Cl OLDE OL4 60 B5
Further La HYDE SK14 103 H1
Further Pits ROCH OL11 27 M5
Furze Av WHTN BL5 50 C5
Furzegate MILN OL16 42 F1
Furze La OLDE OL4 60 A3
Fushia Gv BRO M7 * 72 A6
Futura Pk HOR/BR BL6 33 M3
Fylde Av BOLE BL2 37 H5
CHD/CHDH SK8 119 L4
Fylde Rd HTNM SK4 111 K2
Fylde St BOLS/LL BL3 53 G2
Fylde St East BOLS/LL BL3 53 G2


## G


Gable Av WILM/AE SK9 126 E5
Gable Dr MDTN M24 57 H3
The Gables SALE M33 * 108 E1
Gable St BOLE BL2 * 23 G7
OP/CLY M11 88 C4
Gabriel's Ter MDTN M24 57 M5
The Gabriels ROY/SHW OL2 43 J5
Gadbury Av ATH M46 66 E1
Gadbury Fold ATH M46 66 D2
Gaddum Rd ALT WA14 116 C3
DID/WITH M20 110 F1
Gadfield Gv ATH M46 66 D1
Gadwall Cl WALK M28 69 G4
Gail Av HTNM SK4 12 E2
Gail Cl FAIL M35 74 B7
WILM/AE SK9 130 E2
Gainford Av CHD/CHDH SK8 110 E8
Gainford Gdns NEWH/MOS M40 73 L3
Gainford Rd RDSH SK5 100 C3
Gainford Wk BOLS/LL BL3 * 36 B8
Gainsborough Av BOLS/LL BL3 51 M1
DID/WITH M20 * 98 F7
MPL/ROM SK6 114 E4
OLDS OL8 59 H8
STRET M32 * 97 J1
Gainsborough Cl
WGNS/IIMK WN3 63 G1
WILM/AE SK9 127 H4
Gainsborough Dr
CHD/CHDH SK8 111 J6
ROCH OL11 42 C1
Gainsborough Rd CHAD OL9 58 B4
DTN/ASHW M34 90 A3
RAMS BL0 24 D3
Gainsborough St BRO M7 72 B5
Gairloch Av STRET M32 96 E2
Gair Rd RDSH SK5 100 C8
Gair St HYDE SK14 91 G8
Gaitskell Cl WGTN/LGST M12 88 B3
Galbraith Rd DID/WITH M20 110 F1
Galbraith St CMANE M1 * 7 H7
Galbraith Wy ROCH OL11 27 H4
Gale Dr MDTN M24 57 G2
Gale Rd PWCH M25 71 J1
Gales Ter ROCH OL11 10 C9
Gale St HEY OL10 40 E2
WHIT OL12 28 C1
Galgate Cl HULME M15 6 C9
TOT/BURYW BL8 38 C3
Galindo St BOLE BL2 22 F8
Galland St OLDE OL4 60 A5
Galloway Cl BOLS/LL BL3 35 H7
HEY OL10 40 C3
Galloway Dr SWIN M27 54 C8
Galloway Rd SWIN M27 * 70 A6
Gallowsclough Rd STLY SK15 92 B6
Galston St OP/CLY M11 88 D4
Galsworthy Av CHH M8 72 D7
Galvin Rd BKLY M9 72 E1
Galway St OLD OL1 9 J6
Galwey Gv WGN WN1 31 M8
Gambleside Cl WALK M28 68 E4
Gamble St LEIGH WN7 66 D7
Gambrel Bank Rd AUL OL6 75 L6
Gambrel Gv AUL OL6 75 L6
Game St OLDE OL4 59 M7
Gamma Wk OP/CLY M11 88 E2
Gandy La WHIT OL12 20 A8
Gantley Av WGNW/BIL/OR WN5 46 A8
Gantley Crs
WGNW/BIL/OR WN5 62 A1
Gantley Rd WGNW/BIL/OR WN5 46 A8
Gantock Wk RUSH/FAL M14 98 F1
Ganton Av WHTF M45 55 G5
Garbrook Av BKLY M9 56 F7
Garden Av DROY M43 89 L2
STRET M32 97 G2
SWIN M27 70 A5
Garden City RAMS BL0 24 D2
Garden Cl LIT OL15 29 J2
Gardenfold Wy DROY M43 89 L2
Garden La ALT WA14 108 A7
CSLFD M3 6 D2
CSLFD M3 6 E4
MILN OL16 11 G3
WALK M28 68 D6
Garden Ms AUL OL6 * 91 G2
Garden Rw HEY OL10 26 E8
The Gardens BOL BL1 22 C6
EDGW/EG BL7 17 H8
Garden St DTN/ASHW M34 90 C6
ECC M30 85 H3
FWTH BL4 53 H4
HEY OL10 40 F1
HYDE SK14 91 H8
MILN OL16 29 L8
OFTN SK2 * 112 F7
OLD OL1 9 M4
RAMS BL0 18 F6
TOT/BURYW BL8 24 C5
TYLD M29 67 K4
Garden Ter ROY/SHW OL2 42 F5
Garden Wk AUL OL6 75 M8
Garden Wall Cl ORD M5 86 F4
Garden Wy LIT OL15 29 J2
Gardinar Cl WGN WN1 31 L3
Gardner Rd PWCH M25 55 J8
Gardner St SLFD M6 86 D1
WGTN/LGST M12 88 E6
Garfield Av BNG/LEV M19 99 L3
Garfield Cl ROCH OL11 27 H4
Garfield Gv BOLS/LL BL3 2 B7
Garfield St BOLS/LL BL3 51 M1
STKP SK1 * 13 L2
Garforth Av ANC M4 7 M2
Garforth Crs DROY M43 89 M1
Garforth Ri BOL BL1 35 K5
Garforth St CHAD OL9 8 C4
Gargrave Av BOL BL1 35 J2
Gargrave St BRO M7 71 J4
OLDE OL4 59 L6
Garland Rd WYTH/NTH M22 119 G1
Garlick St CHAD OL9 9 G6
GTN M18 89 G7
HYDE SK14 * 102 C1
Garnant Cl BKLY M9 73 J4
Garner Av
HALE/TIMP WA15 108 D3
Garner Cl ALT WA14 116 F2
Garner Dr ECC M30 * 84 F1
ORD M5 86 A1
TYLD M29 67 L7
Garner's La EDGY/DAV SK3 112 A8
EDGY/DAV SK3 112 C7
Garnet St OLD OL1 59 L4
Garnett Cl HYDE SK14 103 J1
Garnett Rd HYDE SK14 103 J1
Garnett St BOL BL1 36 B1
RAMS BL0 18 E7
STKP SK1 13 J5
Garratt Wy GTN M18 88 F7
Garret Gv ROY/SHW OL2 43 M5
Garrett Hall Rd WALK M28 68 B5
Garrett La TYLD M29 68 A5
Garrett Wk EDGY/DAV SK3 12 C6
Garrick Gdns WYTH/NTH M22 110 A8
Garsdale Cl BURY BL9 39 K5
Garsdale La BOL BL1 35 K3
Garside Av GOL/RIS/CUL WA3 80 A5
Garside Gv BOL BL1 35 M2
WGNS/IIMK WN3 63 H2
Garside Hey Rd
TOT/BURYW BL8 24 F6
Garside St BOL BL1 2 C5
DTN/ASHW M34 * 101 J2
HYDE SK14 102 B3
Garstang Av BOLE BL2 37 H6
Garstang Dr TOT/BURYW BL8 38 C3
Garston Av ATH M46 50 E7
Garston Cl HTNM SK4 12 D1
LEIGH WN7 66 B3
Garston St BURY BL9 25 K8
Garswood Crs
WGNW/BIL/OR WN5 62 B8
Garswood Dr TOT/BURYW BL8 24 E6
Garswood Rd AIMK WN4 62 E8
BOLS/LL BL3 52 B2
RUSH/FAL M14 98 D2
WGNW/BIL/OR WN5 62 B8
Garswood St AIMK WN4 78 E1
Garth Av HALE/TIMP WA15 108 B6
Garthland Rd BRAM/HZG SK7 122 B1
Garthmere Rd ATH M46 51 J7
Garthorne Cl OLDTF/WHR M16 87 H8
Garthorp Rd NTHM/RTH M23 109 H3
Garth Rd MPL/ROM SK6 114 D6
OFTN SK2 112 F5
WYTH/NTH M22 110 A8
The Garth ORD M5 86 A2
Garthwaite Av OLDS OL8 75 H1
Garton Dr GOL/RIS/CUL WA3 80 B3
Gartside St AULW OL7 * 90 B3
CSLFD M3 6 D5
OLDE OL4 59 L7
UPML OL3 * 45 H8
Garwick Rd BOL BL1 35 L1
Garwood St HULME M15 6 D9
Gascoyne St RUSH/FAL M14 98 E1
Gaskell Cl LIT OL15 * 21 L6
Gaskell Ri OLD OL1 44 B7
Gaskell Rd ALT WA14 108 A6
ECC M30 85 H3
Gaskell St BOL BL1 2 C2
DUK SK16 * 90 E3
NEWH/MOS M40 73 M7
SWIN M27 70 C2
WGNE/HIN WN2 49 H5
Gaskill St HEY OL10 40 D2
Gas St AUL OL6 90 E1
BOL BL1 2 C5
FWTH BL4 53 G3
HEY OL10 41 G2
HTNM SK4 13 G4
HYDE SK14 93 G7
ROCH OL11 10 E7
WGNE/HIN WN2 64 E2
Gatcombe Sq RUSH/FAL M14 98 F1
Gateacre Wk NTHM/RTH M23 109 H5
Gate Field Cl RAD M26 54 B1
Gategill Gv WGNW/BIL/OR WN5 62 A2
Gatehead Cft UPML OL3 61 J1
Gatehead Ms UPML OL3 61 J1
Gatehead Rd UPML OL3 61 J1
Gatehouse Rd WALK M28 52 D8
Gate Keeper Fold AULW OL7 75 K5
Gatemere Cl WALK M28 68 E4
Gatesgarth Rd MDTN M24 56 F2
Gateshead Cl RUSH/FAL M14 87 L8
Gate St DUK SK16 90 D6
OP/CLY M11 88 F4
ROCH OL11 10 F9
Gateway Crs CHAD OL9 58 B8
Gateway Rd GTN M18 * 88 F6
The Gateways SWIN M27 70 C3
The Gateway NEWH/MOS M40 73 J6
Gathill Cl CHD/CHDH SK8 120 B3
Gathurst Hall
WGNNW/ST WN6 * 46 C1
Gathurst La WGNNW/ST WN6 30 D7
Gathurst Rd
WGNW/BIL/OR WN5 46 B4
Gathurst St GTN M18 89 H6
Gatley Av RUSH/FAL M14 98 D3
Gatley Brow OLD OL1 * 9 H2
Gatley Cl TYLD M29 67 L3
Gatley Gn CHD/CHDH SK8 110 D7
Gatley Rd CHD/CHDH SK8 110 F7
SALE M33 109 H1
Gatling Av WGTN/LGST M12 99 K2
Gatwick Av NTHM/RTH M23 109 L6
Gavin Av ORD M5 86 D3
Gawsworth Av DID/WITH M20 110 F3
Gawsworth Cl BRAM/HZG SK7 121 G7
EDGY/DAV SK3 112 A7
GLSP SK13 93 K7
HALE/TIMP WA15 109 G6
POY/DIS SK12 129 K2
ROY/SHW OL2 43 J5
Gawsworth Ms
CHD/CHDH SK8 110 E7
Gawsworth Rd
GOL/RIS/CUL WA3 79 J3
SALE M33 109 H2
Gawthorne Cl BRAM/HZG SK7 121 L2
Gawthorpe Cl BURY BL9 39 K7
Gaydon Rd SALE M33 96 A8
Gaynor Av RNFD/HAY WA11 78 C5
Gaythorne St BOL BL1 36 C1
Gaythorn St ORD M5 86 F3
Gayton Cl WGNS/IIMK WN3 63 G1
Geddington Rd ALT WA14 107 M4
Gee Cross Fold HYDE SK14 102 B5
Gee La ECC M30 84 E1
Gee St EDGY/DAV SK3 12 F8
Gellert Pl WHTN BL5 50 B6
Gellert Rd WHTN BL5 50 B6
Gemini Rd SLFD M6 71 M8
Gencoyne Dr BOL BL1 22 A6
Gendre Rd EDGW/EG BL7 22 B4
Geneva Rd BRAM/HZG SK7 120 F1
Geneva Ter ROCH OL11 27 M4
Geneva Wk CHAD OL9 8 C6
Genista Gv BRO M7 * 72 A6
Geoffrey St BURY BL9 5 H1
RAMS BL0 18 D8
WHTN BL5 51 J4
George Barton St BOLE BL2 3 J1
George La MPL/ROM SK6 101 K8
George Leigh St ANC M4 7 J3
George Mann Cl
WYTH/NTH M22 118 E3
George Richards Wy
ALT WA14 107 L5
George Rd RAMS BL0 18 E7
George's Cl POY/DIS SK12 129 J1
Georges La WGN WN1 15 M4
George Sq OLD OL1 9 H6
George's Rd HTNM SK4 12 F3
SALE M33 108 E1
George's Rd West
POY/DIS SK12 129 J1
George's Ter
WGNW/BIL/OR WN5 46 A7
George St AIMK WN4 63 M8
ATH M46 67 G1
AUL OL6 90 F1
BURY BL9 5 G5
CHAD OL9 58 D5
CMANE M1 7 G6
DTN/ASHW M34 101 K1
ECC M30 84 F3
FAIL M35 74 C4
FWTH BL4 52 E5
GLSP SK13 104 F4
HEY OL10 40 E1
HOR/BR BL6 33 M1
IRL M44 94 E1
LIT OL15 * 21 M7
MILN OL16 11 G2
MILN OL16 29 G1
MILN OL16 29 H5
MOSL OL5 76 F3
MPL/ROM SK6 114 E2
NEWLW WA12 * 78 D8
OLD OL1 9 H6
PWCH M25 71 L3
RAD M26 54 C1
ROY/SHW OL2 43 M4
STKP SK1 13 L4
STLY SK15 91 K2
URM M41 96 B2
WGNE/HIN WN2 48 C5
WGNE/HIN WN2 49 H8
WHIT OL12 20 A4
WHTF M45 55 H3
WHTN BL5 50 C4
WILM/AE SK9 130 D3
George St East STKP SK1 112 E4
George St North BRO M7 72 C4
George St South BRO M7 72 B4
George St West STKP SK1 112 E4
Georgette Dr CSLFD M3 6 D1
Georgia Av DID/WITH M20 98 C6
Georgiana St FWTH BL4 52 E3
Georgina Ct BOLS/LL BL3 51 L2
Georgina St BOLS/LL BL3 51 L2
Gerald Av CHH M8 72 D4
Gerald Rd SLFD M6 71 K7
Gerard St AIMK WN4 78 E1
Germain Cl BKLY M9 56 F7
Gerrard Av HALE/TIMP WA15 108 D4
Gerrard Cl WGNE/HIN WN2 49 G2
Gerrard Rd WGNW/BIL/OR WN5 62 B7
Gerrards Cl IRL M44 94 D2
Gerrards Gdns HYDE SK14 102 B5
Gerrards Hollow HYDE SK14 102 A5
The Gerrards HYDE SK14 102 A5
Gerrard St FWTH BL4 53 H4
LEIGH WN7 * 66 C7
ROCH OL11 42 D3
SLFD M6 86 D1
STLY SK15 91 L3
WHTN BL5 50 B3
Gerrards Wd HYDE SK14 102 A5
Gertrude Cl ORD M5 86 D4
Gervis Cl NEWH/MOS M40 * 73 G7
Ghyll Gv WALK M28 69 H2
Giants Hall Rd WGNNW/ST WN6 47 H1
Giants Seat Gv SWIN M27 71 G4
Gibb La MPL/ROM SK6 115 H7
Gibbon Av WYTH/NTH M22 118 F2
Gibbon's Rd AIMK WN4 78 A2
Gibbon St BOLS/LL BL3 2 A9
OP/CLY M11 88 D2
Gibb Rd WALK M28 69 L5
Gibbs St ORD M5 6 A4
Gibfield Dr ATH M46 66 D2
Gib La NTHM/RTH M23 109 M4
Gibraltar La DTN/ASHW M34 101 L4
Gibraltar St BOLS/LL BL3 2 A7
OLDE OL4 60 A7
Gibsmere Cl HALE/TIMP WA15 109 G6
Gibson Av GTN M18 89 J5
Gibson Gv WALK M28 68 D1
Gibson La WALK M28 68 D1
Gibson Pl ANC M4 87 K1
Gibsons Rd HTNM SK4 99 L8
Gibson St BOLE BL2 36 F3
MILN OL16 11 M2
OLDE OL4 * 59 M6
WGNE/HIN WN2 65 G2
Gibson Wy ALT WA14 107 M4
Gibwood Rd WYTH/NTH M22 109 M4
Gidlow Av WGNNW/ST WN6 47 K2
Gidlow La WGNNW/ST WN6 14 C2
WGNNW/ST WN6 31 K8
Gidlow St GTN M18 89 H6
WGNE/HIN WN2 48 D4
WGNE/HIN WN2 49 G6
Gifford Av BKLY M9 57 J8
Gifford Pl WGNE/HIN WN2 49 J8
Gigg La BURY BL9 5 H9
Gilbertbank MPL/ROM SK6 101 K8
Gilbert Rd HALE/TIMP WA15 117 H3
Gilbert St ECC M30 84 E4
HULME M15 6 D8
RAMS BL0 18 F3
SLFD M6 * 86 C3
WALK M28 68 F3
WGNE/HIN WN2 48 F7
Gilbrook Wy MILN OL16 42 E2
Gilchrist Rd IRL M44 94 B6
Gilda Brook Rd ECC M30 85 K3
Gilda Crs ECC M30 85 K1
Gilda Rd WALK M28 68 B5
Gildenhall FAIL M35 74 D5
Gilderdale Cl ROY/SHW OL2 43 L4
Gildersdale Dr BKLY M9 56 E6
Gildridge Rd
OLDTF/WHR M16 98 B3
Gilesgate RUSH/FAL M14 98 E1
Giles St WGTN/LGST M12 88 D8
Gillan Rd WGNNW/ST WN6 47 L2
Gill Av WGNNW/ST WN6 30 E6
Gillbent Rd CHD/CHDH SK8 120 C6
Gillbrook Rd DID/WITH M20 110 E2
Gillbrow Crs WGN WN1 48 C3
Gillemere Gv ROY/SHW OL2 43 M5
Gillers Gn WALK M28 68 F2
Gillford Av BKLY M9 73 J4
Gillingham Rd ECC M30 84 E2
Gillingham Sq OP/CLY M11 88 C4
Gill St BKLY M9 73 J3
STKP SK1 112 E1
Gillwood Dr MPL/ROM SK6 113 J3
Gilman Cl BKLY M9 * 72 F2
Gilman St BKLY M9 72 F2
Gilmerton Dr
NEWH/MOS M40 * 73 M7
Gilmore Dr PWCH M25 55 L7
Gilmore St EDGY/DAV SK3 13 H8
Gilmour St MDTN M24 57 K4
Gilmour Ter BKLY M9 73 J3
Gilnow Gdns BOL BL1 35 M6
Gilnow Gv BOL BL1 2 A6
Gilnow La BOLS/LL BL3 35 M6
Gilnow Rd BOL BL1 35 M6
Gilpin Pl WGNE/HIN WN2 64 C2
Gilpin Rd URM M41 96 C3
Gilroy St WGN WN1 15 J4
Giltbrook Av NEWH/MOS M40 73 H8
Gilwell Dr NTHM/RTH M23 109 J8
Gilwood Gv MDTN M24 41 J8
Gin Croft La RAMS BL0 19 H1
Gingham Pk RAD M26 38 B7
Gipsy La OFTN SK2 112 F6
ROCH OL11 41 M1
Gird La MPL/ROM SK6 115 H3
Girton Av AIMK WN4 63 J8
Girton St BRO M7 72 B8
Girvan Av NEWH/MOS M40 74 A2
Girvan Cl BOLS/LL BL3 51 M1
Girvan Crs AIMK WN4 62 F8
Gisborn Dr SLFD M6 71 J7
Gisburn Av BOL BL1 35 K2
GOL/RIS/CUL WA3 79 J2
Gisburn Dr TOT/BURYW BL8 38 B1
Gisburne Av NEWH/MOS M40 74 A2
Gisburn Rd ROCH OL11 42 D1
Givendale Dr CHH M8 72 D2
Givvons Fold OLDE OL4 60 A3
Glabyn Av HOR/BR BL6 34 C4
Gladden Hey Dr
WGNS/IIMK WN3 63 G3
Glade Brow OLDE OL4 * 60 D6
Gladeside Rd WYTH/NTH M22 109 M8
Glade St BOL BL1 35 M5
The Glade BOL BL1 2 A1
HTNM SK4 111 K3
WGNNW/ST WN6 30 E6
Gladewood Cl WILM/AE SK9 127 G4
Gladstone Cl BOL BL1 * 36 B2
GLSP SK13 105 G4
Gladstone Ct HULME M15 87 H8
Gladstone Crs ROCH OL11 42 D1
Gladstone Gv HTNM SK4 111 K1
Gladstone Ms HTNM SK4 * 13 H1
Gladstone Pl FWTH BL4 52 F3
Gladstone Rd ALT WA14 108 A6
ECC M30 85 H2
FWTH BL4 52 F3
URM M41 96 B2
Gladstone St BOL BL1 36 B2
BURY BL9 5 K3
GLSP SK13 93 K8
GLSP SK13 104 F4
OFTN SK2 112 F8
OLDE OL4 59 L6
SWIN M27 70 D4
WHTN BL5 50 B3
Gladstone Terrace Rd
UPML OL3 61 K8
Gladstone Wy NEWLW WA12 78 E8
Gladwyn Av DID/WITH M20 98 B8
Gladys St BOLS/LL BL3 53 G2
Glaisdale OLDE OL4 60 A6
Glaisdale Cl AIMK WN4 78 F1
BOLE BL2 36 F2
Glaisdale St BOLE BL2 36 E2
Glaister La BOLE BL2 37 G3
Glamis Av HEY OL10 41 H5
OP/CLY M11 88 F1
STRET M32 96 D2
Glamis Cl LEIGH WN7 67 G6
Glamorgan Pl CHAD OL9 8 C8
Glandon Dr CHD/CHDH SK8 120 E5
Glanford Av BKLY M9 72 D1
Glanvor Rd EDGY/DAV SK3 12 C7
Glassbrook St WGNNW/ST WN6 14 C1
Glasshouse St ANC M4 7 L1
Glasson Wk CHAD OL9 58 D6
Glass St FWTH BL4 * 53 H5
Glastonbury WHIT OL12 10 D2
Glastonbury Av
CHD/CHDH SK8 120 E6
GOL/RIS/CUL WA3 80 E4
HALE/TIMP WA15 117 K2
Glastonbury Dr POY/DIS SK12 121 M7
Glastonbury Rd STRET M32 96 C1
TYLD M29 67 L5
Glaswen Gv RDSH SK5 100 C8
Glazebrook Cl HEY OL10 40 F3
Glazebury Dr NTHM/RTH M23 109 L7
WHTN BL5 50 C2
Glazedale Av ROY/SHW OL2 42 F8
Glaze Wk WHTF M45 55 M2
Gleaves Av BOLE BL2 23 K8
Gleaves Rd ECC M30 85 H3
Gleave St BOL BL1 * 2 F3
SALE M33 96 E6
Glebe Av AIMK WN4 78 E2
Glebe Cl WGNNW/ST WN6 31 H3
Glebe End St WGNNW/ST WN6 14 D3
Glebeland Rd BOLS/LL BL3 35 K7
Glebelands Rd
NTHM/RTH M23 109 J6
PWCH M25 55 K7
SALE M33 96 D6
Glebe La OLD OL1 60 B1
Glebe Rd URM M41 96 A2
WGNNW/ST WN6 31 J4
Glebe St BOLE BL2 3 G6
CHAD OL9 74 D1
LEIGH WN7 66 C6
RAD M26 54 E1
ROY/SHW OL2 43 L5
STKP SK1 13 M5
WGNE/HIN WN2 65 M2
WHTN BL5 50 B3
Gleden St NEWH/MOS M40 88 B2
Gledhall St STLY SK15 91 K2
Gledhill Av ORD M5 86 D5
Gledhill Cl ROY/SHW OL2 43 K3
Gledhill St DID/WITH M20 98 E5
Gledhill Wy EDGW/EG BL7 22 D4
Glegg St WGNE/HIN WN2 48 C4
Glemsford Cl NEWH/MOS M40 * 73 L6
WGNS/IIMK WN3 63 L1
Glenacre Gdns GTN M18 100 B1
Glenart ECC M30 85 H1
Glen Av BKLY M9 73 H3
BOLS/LL BL3 35 L7
FWTH BL4 53 L6
SALE M33 96 D6
SWIN M27 70 A4
WALK M28 69 K4
Glenavon Dr ROY/SHW OL2 43 J4
WHIT OL12 28 A1
Glenbarry Cl BRUN/LGST M13 87 L6
Glenbarry St WGTN/LGST M12 88 A4
Glenbeck Cl HOR/BR BL6 34 A3
Glenbeck Rd WHTF M45 55 H3
Glenboro Av TOT/BURYW BL8 38 E2
Glen Bott St BOL BL1 36 A2
Glenbourne Pk
BRAM/HZG SK7 120 F7
Glenbranter Av
WGNE/HIN WN2 48 D4
Glenbrook Gdns FWTH BL4 53 G2
Glenbrook Hl GLSP SK13 104 F2
Glenbrook Rd BKLY M9 56 D7
Glenburn St BOLS/LL BL3 52 A1
Glenby Av WYTH/NTH M22 119 H1
Glencar WHTN BL5 50 A5
Glencastle Rd GTN M18 88 F7
Glencoe Cl HEY OL10 40 B3
Glencoe Dr BOLE BL2 37 J6
SALE M33 107 M2
Glencoe Pl ROCH OL11 10 A5
Glencoe St OLDS OL8 * 74 F2
Glen Cottages BOL BL1 * 35 H2
Glencross Av OLDTF/WHR M16 97 K2
Glendale SWIN M27 70 E3
Glendale Av AIMK WN4 63 M8
BNG/LEV M19 99 J6
BURY BL9 55 J1
Glendale Ct OLDS OL8 59 J8
Glendale Dr BOLS/LL BL3 35 J6
Glendale Rd ECC M30 85 K1
GTN M18 88 F8
WALK M28 68 C5
Glendene Av BRAM/HZG SK7 120 F7
DROY M43 89 M1
Glenden Foot WHIT OL12 28 A2
Glendevon Cl BOLS/LL BL3 35 J8
WGNE/HIN WN2 48 D4
Glendevon Pl WHTF M45 55 L5
Glendinning St SLFD M6 86 B2
Glendon Ct OLD OL1 44 B8
Glendon Crs AUL OL6 75 L5
Glendore ORD M5 85 M2
Glendower Dr NEWH/MOS M40 72 F7
Glen Dr WGNNW/ST WN6 30 B4
Gleneagles BOLS/LL BL3 51 J1
Gleneagles Av HEY OL10 41 G4
Gleneagles Cl BRAM/HZG SK7 121 J5
GOL/RIS/CUL WA3 80 C5
WILM/AE SK9 127 H4
Gleneagles Rd CHD/CHDH SK8 119 L3
URM M41 84 B8
Gleneagles Wy RAMS BL0 18 E7
Glenfield ALT WA14 107 L8
Glenfield Cl OLDE OL4 60 A6
Glenfield Dr POY/DIS SK12 129 H1
Glenfield Rd HTNM SK4 100 A8
Glenfield Sq FWTH BL4 52 E2
Glenfyne Rd SLFD M6 71 G7
Glen Gdns WHIT OL12 28 C1
Glengarth UPML OL3 61 L5
Glengarth Dr HOR/BR BL6 34 F6
Glen Gv MDTN M24 57 M6
ROY/SHW OL2 43 G7
Glenhaven Av URM M41 95 M2
Glenholme Rd BRAM/HZG SK7 120 F5
Glenhurst Rd BNG/LEV M19 * 99 H7
Glenilla Av WALK M28 69 H5
Glenlea Dr DID/WITH M20 110 E4
Glenmaye Gv WGNE/HIN WN2 49 K7
Glenmere Cl PWCH M25 55 J6
Glenmere Rd DID/WITH M20 110 F4
Glenmoor Rd STKP SK1 13 L5
Glenmore Av DID/WITH M20 98 B8
FWTH BL4 52 D2
Glenmore Cl BOLS/LL BL3 35 H7
ROCH OL11 27 H7
Glenmore Dr CHH M8 72 E5
FAIL M35 74 E4
Glenmore Gv DUK SK16 90 F4
Glenmore Rd TOT/BURYW BL8 24 C2
Glenmore St BURY BL9 4 D6
Glenmuir Cl IRL M44 94 D2
Glenolden St OP/CLY M11 89 G2
Glenpark LEIGH WN7 66 D6
Glenridding Cl OLD OL1 59 K3
Glenridge Cl BOL BL1 36 C2

Glen Ri HALE/TIMP WA15 .............108 D7
Glen Rd OLDE OL4 .............59 N6
Glen Royd WHIT OL12 .............27 M3
Glensdale Dr NEWH/MOS M40 .............74 B3
Glenside Av GTN M18 .............100 A1
Glenside Dr BOLS/LL BL3 .............52 C2
  MPL/ROM SK6 .............101 L7
  WGNE/HIN WN2 .............127 G6
Glenside Gdns FAIL M35 .............74 D5
Glenside Gv WALK M28 .............69 H1
Glen St RAMS BL0 .............18 E5
  SALQ M50 .............86 C5
The Glen BOL BL1 .............35 H5
  MDTN M24 .............57 L6
Glenthorn Av BKLY M9 .............57 G6
Glenthorne St BOL BL1 .............36 B3
Glentrool Ms BOL BL1 .............35 K5
Glent Vw STLY SK15 .............76 D8
Glentwood ALT WA14 .............116 F3
Glenvale Cl RAD M26 .............54 E1
Glen Vw ROY/SHW OL2 .............43 G7
Glenview Rd TYLD M29 .............67 J2
Glenville Rd CHH M8 .............72 C7
Glenville Wk DTN/ASHW M34 .............101 K2
Glenwood Av HYDE SK14 .............91 G7
Glenwood Cl RAD M26 .............54 E2
Glenwood Dr BKLY M9 .............73 H5
  MDTN M24 .............57 M2
Glenwyn Av BKLY M9 .............57 H8
Globe Cl DUK SK16 .............90 E5
  EDGW/EG BL7 .............22 A1
Globe Sq DUK SK16 .............90 D5
Glodwick Rd OLDE OL4 .............59 L7
Glossop Brook Rd GLSP SK13 .............104 E3
Glossop Rd GLSP SK13 .............104 A4
  MPL/ROM SK6 .............105 H8
Glossop Wy WGNE/HIN WN2 .............49 H8
Gloster St BOLE BL2 .............3 L4
Gloucester Av BNG/LEV M19 .............99 L4
  GOL/RIS/CUL WA3 .............80 A3
  HEY OL10 .............40 F5
  HOR/BR BL6 .............34 A2
  MPL/ROM SK6 .............114 C6
  WHIT OL12 .............21 H8
  WHTF M45 .............55 J4
Gloucester Cl AUL OL6 .............76 A4
Gloucester Crs WGNE/HIN WN2 .............49 H6
Gloucester Dr SALE M33 .............96 A8
  UPML OL3 .............45 M8
Gloucester Pl ATH M46 .............51 G8
  SLFD M6 .............86 C1
Gloucester Ri DUK SK16 .............91 K5
Gloucester Rd CHD/CHDH SK8 .............119 L1
  DROY M43 .............89 K1
  DTN/ASHW M34 .............100 D2
  HYDE SK14 .............102 B4
  MDTN M24 .............56 F5
  POY/DIS SK12 .............129 H1
  SLFD M6 .............70 F8
  URM M41 .............96 A3
  WGNW/BIL/OR WN5 .............46 C6
Gloucester St ATH M46 .............66 F1
  CMANE M1 .............6 F8
  ORD M5 .............86 F4
  SLFD M6 .............71 K8
Gloucester St North CHAD OL9 .............8 C9
Gloucester Wy GLSP SK13 .............105 J4
Glover Dr HYDE SK14 .............102 H3
Glover St LEIGH WN7 .............65 M4
Glyn Av HALE/TIMP WA15 .............117 J2
Glynne St FWTH BL4 .............52 F4
Glynrene Dr SWIN M27 .............69 M2
Glynwood Pk FWTH BL4 .............52 F4
Goadsby St ANC M4 .............7 H2
Goats Gate Ter WHTF M45 * .............55 L2
Godbert Av CCHDY M21 .............97 M7
Goddard La GLSP SK13 .............93 K6
Goddard St OLDS OL8 .............59 J8
Godfrey Av DROY M43 .............89 G1
Godfrey Rd SLFD M6 .............70 F7
Godlee Dr SWIN M27 .............70 E5
Godley Cl OP/CLY M11 .............88 F5
Godley Hill Rd HYDE SK14 .............102 E1
Godley St HYDE SK14 .............91 J8
Godmond Hall Dr WALK M28 .............68 C7
Godolphin Cl ECC M30 .............85 G2
Godson St OLD OL1 .............9 G1
Godward Rd NM/HAY SK22 .............124 D4
Godwin St GTN M18 .............89 H6
Golborne Av DID/WITH M20 .............98 C5
Golborne Dale Rd
  NEWLW WA12 .............79 K8
Golborne Gallery WGN WN1 * .............14 F3
Golborne Pl WGN WN1 * .............15 K3
Golborne Rd AIMK WN4 .............64 A8
  GOL/RIS/CUL WA3 .............79 M4
Golborne St NEWLW WA12 .............79 H7
Goldbourne Dr ROY/SHW OL2 .............43 L4
Goldbrook Cl HEY OL10 .............41 H3
Goldcrest Cl WALK M28 .............68 C5
  WYTH/NTH M22 .............110 C2
Goldenhill Av OP/CLY M11 .............88 F1
Golden St ECC M30 .............85 G3
  ROY/SHW OL2 .............44 B4
Goldenways WGN WN1 .............47 M2
Goldfinch Dr BURY BL9 .............25 M7
Goldfinch Wy DROY M43 .............89 M1
Goldie Av WYTH/NTH M22 .............119 H3
Goldrill Av BOLE BL2 .............37 J4
Goldrill Gdns BOLE BL2 .............37 J4
Goldsmith Av OLD OL1 .............44 B8
  ORD M5 .............86 A2
Goldsmith Pl WGNS/IIMK WN3 .............47 K8
Goldsmith Rd RDSH SK5 .............100 A3
Goldsmith St BOLS/LL BL3 .............36 A8
Gold St CMANE M1 * .............7 H5
Goldswcrthy Rd URM M41 .............95 H2
Goldsworth Rd OLD OL1 .............60 A1
Goldsworthy Rd URM M41 .............95 H1
Golf Rd HALE/TIMP WA15 .............117 H1
  SALE M33 .............97 J8
Golfview Dr ECC M30 .............70 A8
Gooch St HOR/BR BL6 .............33 L2
Goodacre HYDE SK14 .............91 L6
Gooden St HEY OL10 .............41 H5
Goodiers Dr ORD M5 .............86 D4
Goodier St NEWH/MOS M40 .............73 H7
  SALE M33 .............96 D8
Goodier Vw HYDE SK14 .............91 J7
Goodison Cl BURY BL9 .............55 L1
Goodman St BKLY M9 .............73 H4
Goodrich ROCH OL11 .............41 H2
Goodridge Av WYTH/NTH M22 .............118 E2
Goodrington Rd WILM/AE SK9 .............127 J2
Goodshaw Rd WALK M28 .............68 F4

Good Shepherd Cl MILN OL16 .............11 H3
Goodwill Cl SWIN M27 .............70 C5
Goodwin Sq BKLY M9 * .............73 G5
Goodwin St BOL BL1 .............3 G3
Goodwood Av
  NTHM/RTH M23 .............109 C4
  SALE M33 .............95 M8
Goodwood Cl BOLS/LL BL3 .............53 J1
Goodwood Crs
  HALE/TIMP WA15 .............108 F6
Goodwood Dr EDGY/DAV SK3 .............112 B8
  OLD OL1 .............59 L3
  SWIN M27 .............70 E5
Goodwood Rd MPL/ROM SK6 .............114 B7
Goole St OP/CLY M11 .............88 D4
Goose Cote Hl EDGW/EG BL7 .............22 B3
Goose Gn ALT WA14 .............108 A8
Goose La WHIT OL12 .............10 C2
Goosetrey Cl WILM/AE SK9 .............127 J3
Goostrey Av DID/WITH M20 .............98 C4
Gordon Av AIMK WN4 .............63 H8
  BNG/LEV M19 .............99 L3
  BOLS/LL BL3 .............35 M7
  BRAM/HZG SK7 .............121 J5
  CHAD OL9 .............74 D1
  OLDE OL4 .............59 M6
  RNFD/HAY WA11 .............78 A7
Gordon Cl WGNW/BIL/OR WN5 .............47 H4
Gordon Ct LIT OL15 .............21 M6
Gordon Pl DID/WITH M20 .............98 E7
Gordon Rd ECC M30 .............85 G1
  SALE M33 .............96 E6
  SWIN M27 .............69 M6
Gordonstoun Crs
  WGNW/BIL/OR WN5 .............46 C5
Gordon St AUL OL6 * .............76 A8
  BRO M7 .............72 A8
  BURY BL9 .............4 D1
  CHAD OL9 .............58 C8
  GTN M18 .............89 H6
  HTNM SK4 .............13 H2
  HYDE SK14 .............102 B2
  LEIGH WN7 .............66 C6
  MILN OL16 .............43 L1
  OLDE OL4 .............60 D6
  OLDTF/WHR M16 .............87 G8
  ROCH OL11 * .............11 H9
  ROY/SHW OL2 .............43 M5
  STLY SK15 .............91 L3
  WGN WN1 .............15 L5
Gordon Ter BKLY M9 * .............73 H4
Gordon Wy HEY OL10 .............40 F3
Gore Av FAIL M35 .............74 E5
  ORD M5 .............86 A2
Gorebrook Ct WGTN/LGST M12 .............88 D3
Gore Cl BURY BL9 .............39 M3
Gore Crs ORD M5 .............86 A2
Goredale Av GTN M18 .............100 B1
Gore Dr ORD M5 .............86 A1
Gorelan Rd NEWH/MOS M40 * .............89 G7
Gore St CMANE M1 .............7 J4
  CSLFD M3 .............6 C4
  SLFD M6 .............86 D1
  WGNW/BIL/OR WN5 .............46 E6
Goring Av GTN M18 .............89 G6
Gorman St WGNNW/ST WN6 .............14 B3
Gorman Wk WGNS/IIMK WN3 .............14 A7
Corrells Wy ROCH OL11 .............42 A1
Correls Cl ROCH OL11 .............42 A1
Gorrel St ROCH OL11 .............11 H9
Gorse Av DROY M43 .............89 M2
  MOSL OL5 .............77 H3
  MPL/ROM SK6 .............114 B6
  OLDS OL8 .............75 M1
  STRET M32 .............97 J3
Gorse Bank BURY BL9 .............39 M1
Gorse Bank Rd
  HALE/TIMP WA15 .............117 L5
Gorse Crs STRET M32 .............97 J1
Gorse Dr LHULT M38 .............52 C6
  STRET M32 .............97 J1
Gorsefield Cl RAD M26 .............38 C8
Gorsefield Dr SWIN M27 .............70 C5
Gorsefield Hey WILM/AE SK9 .............127 L6
Gorse Hall Cl STLY SK15 .............91 J5
Gorse Hall Dr STLY SK15 .............91 K4
Gorse Hall Rd DUK SK16 .............91 K4
Gorselands CHD/CHDH SK8 .............120 D7
Gorse La STRET M32 .............97 J1
Gorse Rd MILN OL16 .............29 J6
  SWIN M27 .............70 B6
  WALK M28 .............69 H2
Gorses Dr WGNE/HIN WN2 .............32 F6
Gorses Mt BOLE BL2 .............3 M8
Gorse Sq PART M31 .............106 A1
Gorses Rd BOLE BL2 .............37 G7
  BOLS/LL BL3 .............37 G7
Gorse St CHAD OL9 .............58 C8
  STRET M32 .............97 H1
The Gorse ALT WA14 .............116 D4
Gorse Wy GLSP SK13 .............105 H5
Gorseway RDSH SK5 .............100 E8
Gorsey Av WYTH/NTH M22 .............109 M8
Gorsey Bank Rd EDGY/DAV SK3 .............12 B6
Gorsey Brow HYDE SK14 .............103 K3
Gorsey Brow Cl
  WGNW/BIL/OR WN5 .............62 A7
Gorsey Clough Wk
  TOT/BURYW BL8 .............24 C7
Gorsey Dr WYTH/NTH M22 .............109 M8
Gorseyfields DROY M43 .............89 K4
Gorsey Hey WHTN BL5 .............50 A5
Gorsey Hey WHTN BL5 .............50 B5
Gorsey Hill St HEY OL10 .............41 G5
Gorsey Intakes HYDE SK14 .............103 K4
Gorsey La ALT WA14 .............107 L7
  AUL OL6 .............76 C6
  LYMM WA13 .............106 D6
Gorsey Mount St STKP SK1 .............13 K5
Gorsey Rd WILM/AE SK9 .............126 E5
  WYTH/NTH M22 .............109 M8
Gorsey Wy AUL OL6 .............76 B6
Gorston Wk WYTH/NTH M22 .............118 E4
Gort Cl BURY BL9 .............26 C6
Gorton Crs DTN/ASHW M34 .............100 F4
Gorton Gv WALK M28 .............52 F7
Gorton La WGTN/LGST M12 .............88 C5
Gorton Rd OP/CLY M11 .............88 C5
  RDSH SK5 .............100 C4
Gorton St AULW OL7 .............90 C3
  BOLE BL2 .............3 H3
  CHAD OL9 .............8 D8
  CSLFD M3 * .............6 E1
  ECC M30 .............84 D3
  FWTH BL4 .............52 E5
  HEY OL10 .............41 H2
Gortonvilla Wk
  WGTN/LGST M12 .............88 C6
Gosforth Cl OLD OL1 .............59 K3
  TOT/BURYW BL8 .............24 F7

Goshen La BURY BL9 .............39 J6
Gosport Sq SLFD M6 * .............72 A7
Goss Hall St OLDE OL4 * .............59 M6
Gotha Wk BRUN/LGST M13 * .............87 M6
Gotherage Cl
  MPL/ROM SK6 .............114 B2
Gotherage La MPL/ROM SK6 .............114 B2
Gothic Cl MPL/ROM SK6 .............114 C2
Gough St EDGY/DAV SK3 .............12 F5
  HEY OL10 * .............41 H2
Goulden Rd DID/WITH M20 .............98 D7
Goulden St ANC M4 .............7 J2
  SLFD M6 .............86 B2
Goulder Rd GTN M18 .............100 B1
Gould St
  DTN/ASHW M34 .............101 H1
  OLD OL1 .............59 L4
Gourham Dr
  CHD/CHDH SK8 .............120 B2
Govan St WYTH/NTH M22 .............110 B3
Gowan Dr MDTN M24 .............57 J8
Gowanlock's St BOL BL1 .............36 B2
Gowan Rd OLDTF/WHR M16 .............98 B3
Gower Av BRAM/HZG SK7 .............121 L1
Gowerdale Rd RDSH SK5 .............100 F7
Gower Hey
  Gdns HYDE SK14 .............102 B3
Gower Rd HTNM SK4 .............100 A8
  HYDE SK14 .............102 A3
Gowers St MILN OL16 .............11 J2
Gower St OL6 * .............90 F1
  BOL BL1 .............2 F3
  FWTH BL4 .............52 F3
  LEIGH WN7 .............66 B8
  OLD OL1 .............9 L4
  SWIN M27 .............70 D3
  WGNW/BIL/OR WN5 .............14 A7
Gowran Pk OLDE OL4 .............60 A6
Gowy Cl WILM/AE SK9 .............127 J3
Goyt Av MPL/ROM SK6 .............114 C8
Goyt Crs MPL/ROM SK6 .............113 J1
  STKP SK1 .............112 E1
Goyt Hey Av
  WGNW/BIL/OR WN5 .............62 B8
Goyt Rd MPL/ROM SK6 .............114 C8
  NM/HAY SK22 .............124 B6
  POY/DIS SK12 .............123 M7
  STKP SK1 .............112 E1
Goyt Valley Rd
  MPL/ROM SK6 .............113 J2
Goyt Vw NM/HAY SK22 .............124 D6
Goyt Wy MPL/ROM SK6 .............114 C3
  NM/HAY SK22 .............124 E6
  NM/HAY SK22 .............124 E6
  POY/DIS SK12 .............124 C5
Grace St LEIGH WN7 .............65 M7
  WHIT OL12 .............28 D2
Grace Wk ANC M4 .............88 A3
Gracie Av OLD OL1 .............59 L3
Gradwell St EDGY/DAV SK3 .............12 F6
Grafton Av ECC M30 .............70 D8
Grafton Ct MILN OL16 .............11 K7
The Graftons ALT WA14 .............108 A3
Grafton St ALT WA14 .............108 B3
  ATH M46 .............66 D3
  AUL OL6 .............91 G2
  BOL BL1 .............2 A3
  BRUN/LGST M13 .............87 L7
  BURY BL9 .............4 F9
  FAIL M35 .............74 C4
  HTNM SK4 .............112 B1
  MILN OL16 .............11 K7
  OLD OL1 .............44 B8
  STLY SK15 .............92 A1
Graham Dr POY/DIS SK12 .............123 L6
Graham Rd SLFD M6 .............70 F8
  STKP SK1 .............13 M6
Graham St AULW OL7 .............90 C3
  BOL BL1 .............2 E2
  OP/CLY M11 .............88 D4
  WGNE/HIN WN2 .............64 D3
Grainger Av WGTN/LGST M12 .............99 K1
Grains Rd ROY/SHW OL2 .............43 M5
  UPML OL3 .............44 E7
Grain Vw ORD M5 .............86 D4
Gralam Cl SALE M33 .............109 H3
Gramer St RUSH/FAL M14 * .............98 E1
Grand Central Sq STKP SK1 * .............13 H6
Grandidge St ROCH OL11 .............10 D8
Grand Union Wy ECC M30 .............85 G4
Granford Cl ALT WA14 * .............108 A5
Grange Av BNG/LEV M19 .............99 J4
  BOLS/LL BL3 .............35 M1
  CHD/CHDH SK8 .............120 B1
  ECC M30 .............70 A8
  HALE/TIMP WA15 .............108 E5
  HALE/TIMP WA15 .............117 J2
  HTNM SK4 .............99 M7
  MILN OL16 .............29 J8
  OLDS OL8 .............58 F8
  STRET M32 .............97 G2
  SWIN M27 .............70 A6
  URM M41 .............95 H2
  WGNS/IIMK WN3 .............14 D9
  WGNW/BIL/OR WN5 .............46 E5
Grange Cl GOL/RIS/CUL WA3 .............79 M6
  HYDE SK14 .............102 C3
Grange Ct OLDS OL8 * .............58 F8
Grange Crs URM M41 .............95 M3
Grange Dr BKLY M9 .............73 J1
  ECC M30 .............70 A8
Grangeforth Rd CHH M8 .............72 C4
Grange Gv WHTF M45 .............55 J4
Grange La DID/WITH M20 .............110 E2
  UPML OL3 .............61 K7
Grange Park Av AUL OL6 .............76 C6
  CHD/CHDH SK8 .............111 G7
  WILM/AE SK9 .............126 E4
Grangepark Rd BKLY M9 .............73 J1
Grange Park Rd
  CHD/CHDH SK8 .............111 G7
  EDGW/EG BL7 .............22 F6
Grange Pl IRL M44 .............94 A7

Grange Rd AIMK WN4 .............63 J6
  ALT WA14 .............116 E3
  BOLS/LL BL3 .............35 L7
  BRAM/HZG SK7 .............121 J2
  CCHDY M21 .............97 K2
  ECC M30 .............69 J8
  EDGW/EG BL7 .............22 F5
  FWTH BL4 .............52 D3
  HALE/TIMP WA15 .............108 E5
  MDTN M24 .............42 A6
  RNFD/HAY WA11 .............78 A7
  RUSH/FAL M14 .............98 D2
  SALE M33 .............96 C8
  TOT/BURYW BL8 .............38 E2
  URM M41 .............95 M3
  WALK M28 .............68 E5
  WGNE/HIN WN2 .............65 H3
  WHIT OL12 .............20 B2
Grange Rd North HYDE SK14 .............102 C2
Grange Rd South HYDE SK14 .............102 C3
Grange St CHAD OL9 .............9 G4
  FAIL M35 .............74 A6
  LEIGH WN7 .............81 H1
  SLFD M6 .............86 B2
  WGNE/HIN WN2 .............49 G8
The Grange HYDE SK14 .............102 C3
  OLD OL1 * .............59 L4
  RUSH/FAL M14 .............98 F1
  WHTN BL5 .............49 M4
Grangethorpe Dr
  BNG/LEV M19 .............99 H5
Grangethorpe Rd
  RUSH/FAL M14 .............98 F2
  URM M41 .............95 M3
Grange Va RNFD/HAY WA11 .............78 A6
Grangeville WILM/AE SK9 .............119 M8
Grangewood EDGW/EG BL7 .............22 F5
Grangewood Dr BKLY M9 .............73 G5
Granite St OLD OL1 .............59 L4
Gransden Dr CHH M8 .............72 F6
Granshaw St NEWH/MOS M40 .............88 B1
Gransmoor Av OP/CLY M11 .............89 J5
Gransmoor Rd OP/CLY M11 .............89 J5
Grantchester Pl FWTH BL4 .............52 C3
Grantchester Wy BOLE BL2 .............37 H3
Grant Cl BKLY M9 .............73 G2
Grantham Cl BOL BL1 * .............36 B3
Grantham Dr TOT/BURYW BL8 .............25 C7
Grantham Gv WGNE/HIN WN2 .............49 J8
Grantham Rd HTNM SK4 .............12 D3
Grantham St OLDE OL4 .............9 M8
Grantley St AIMK WN4 .............63 K7
Grant Rd WGNS/IIMK WN3 .............63 K5
Grants La BL0 .............18 F6
Grant St FWTH BL4 .............52 E2
  ROCH OL11 .............42 A2
Grantwood AIMK WN4 .............63 K5
Granville Av BRO M7 .............72 B4
Granville Cl CHAD OL9 .............8 C4
Granville Ct MILN OL16 .............43 L1
Granville Gdns DID/WITH M20 .............110 D2
Granville Rd BOLS/LL BL3 .............51 M1
  CHD/CHDH SK8 .............111 M7
  DTN/ASHW M34 .............89 L3
  HALE/TIMP WA15 .............108 H6
  RUSH/FAL M14 .............98 F4
  URM M41 .............96 B1
  WILM/AE SK9 .............126 D7
Granville St AUL OL6 .............91 G2
  CHAD OL9 .............8 C3
  ECC M30 .............85 G1
  FWTH BL4 .............53 G3
  LEIGH WN7 .............66 C5
  OLD OL1 .............9 G5
  WALK M28 .............68 F1
  WGNE/HIN WN2 * .............49 H7
Granville Wk CHAD OL9 .............8 C3
Grapnel Wy GLSP SK13 .............93 H7
Graphite Wy GLSP SK13 .............93 K8
Grasmere Av AULW OL7 .............75 M8
  FWTH BL4 .............52 C5
  HEY OL10 .............41 G4
  HTNM SK4 .............100 B6
  SWIN M27 .............69 M2
  URM M41 .............95 H3
  WGNE/HIN WN2 .............48 D5
  WGNE/HIN WN2 .............49 H8
  WGNW/BIL/OR WN5 .............46 C5
  WHTF M45 .............54 F5
Grasmere Cl STLY SK15 .............76 F2
  OLD OL1 .............9 K6
  OLDE OL4 .............60 C6
  ROY/SHW OL2 .............43 M5
Grasmere Crs BRAM/HZG SK7 .............121 C4
  ECC M30 .............69 J8
  MPL/ROM SK6 .............123 G3
Grasmere Dr AIMK WN4 .............63 J7
  BURY BL9 .............39 K5
Grasmere Gv AULW OL7 .............75 M8
Grasmere Rd CHD/CHDH SK8 .............119 H1
  HALE/TIMP WA15 .............108 F6
  OLDE OL4 .............59 M6
  PART M31 .............106 B1
  ROY/SHW OL2 .............43 C1
  SALE M33 .............108 F2
  STRET M32 .............97 G1
  SWIN M27 .............70 C6
  WGNW/BIL/OR WN5 .............46 F5
  WILM/AE SK9 .............130 D3
Grasmere St BOL BL1 .............36 C2
  LEIGH WN7 .............66 B7
  WGTN/LGST M12 .............99 L1
  WHIT OL12 .............28 C3
Grasmere Ter WGNE/HIN WN2 .............64 E4
Grason Av WILM/AE SK9 .............127 G3
Grasscroft RDSH SK5 .............100 F6
Grasscroft Cl RUSH/FAL M14 .............98 C2
Grasscroft Rd STLY SK15 .............77 K3
  WGNE/HIN WN2 .............49 K8
Grassfield Av BRO M7 .............71 M6
Grassholme Dr OFTN SK2 .............113 L7
Grassington Av
  NEWH/MOS M40 .............73 K3
Grassington Ct
  TOT/BURYW BL8 .............24 B8
Grassington Dr BURY BL9 .............40 B3
Grassington Pl BOLE BL2 .............36 D3
Grass Md DTN/ASHW M34 .............101 K4
Grassmoor Crs GLSP SK13 .............104 C3
Gratrix Av ORD M5 .............86 C5
Gratrix La SALE M33 .............109 J3
Gratrix St GTN M18 .............89 H8
Gratten Cl WALK M28 .............52 F7
Gravel Bank Rd MPL/ROM SK6 .............101 L6
Gravel La CSLFD M3 .............6 E2
  WILM/AE SK9 .............126 E7
Gravenmoor Dr BRO M7 .............72 B6
Grave Oak La LEIGH WN7 .............81 L3
Graver La NEWH/MOS M40 .............74 A1
Gray Av RNFD/HAY WA11 .............78 A6
Gray Cl HYDE SK14 .............103 J1

Graysands Rd
  HALE/TIMP WA15 .............117 H1
Grayson Av WHTF M45 .............55 K5
Grayson Rd LHULT M38 .............52 E8
Grayson's Cl WGN WN1 .............15 C1
Grayson Wy UPML OL3 .............61 L6
Gray St BOL BL1 .............2 E3
Gray St North BOL BL1 .............2 E2
Graythorpe Wk ORD M5 * .............86 D3
Graythorp Wk RUSH/FAL M14 .............98 E1
Graythwaite Rd BOL BL1 .............35 J2
Grazing Dr IRL M44 .............94 F1
Greame St OLDTF/WHR M16 .............98 C1
Great Acre WGN WN1 .............15 J1
Great Ancoats St ANC M4 * .............7 J4
  CMANE M1 .............88 A4
Great Bank Rd WHTN BL5 .............50 A2
Great Bent Cl WHIT OL12 .............21 H4
Great Boys Cl TYLD M29 .............68 B3
Great Bridgewater St
  CMANE M1 .............6 E7
Great Cheetham St East
  BRO M7 .............72 B6
Great Cheetham St West
  BRO M7 .............71 M7
Great Clowes St BRO M7 .............72 A5
Great Delph RNFD/HAY WA11 .............78 A5
Great Ducie St CHH M8 .............72 C8
  CSLFD M3 .............6 F1
Great Eaves Rd RAMS BL0 .............6 F1
Great Egerton St STKP SK1 .............13 H3
Greatfield Rd WYTH/NTH M22 .............109 L8
Great Flatt WHIT OL12 .............27 L3
Great Fold LEIGH WN7 .............67 H8
Great Gable Cl OLD OL1 .............9 L2
Great Gates Cl ROCH OL11 .............28 D8
Great Gates Rd ROCH OL11 .............42 D2
Great George St CSLFD M3 .............6 A3
  MILN OL16 .............10 F5
  WGNS/IIMK WN3 .............14 E4
Great Hall Cl RAD M26 .............38 D8
Great Heaton Cl MDTN M24 * .............56 F5
Great Holme BOLS/LL BL3 .............52 C1
Great Howarth WHIT OL12 .............20 F8
Great Jackson St HULME M15 .............6 C6
Great John St CSLFD M3 .............6 C6
Great Jones St WGTN/LGST M12 .............88 D3
Great Lee WHIT OL12 .............28 A1
Great Lee Wk WHIT OL12 .............28 A2
Great Marlborough St
  CMANE M1 .............6 F7
Great Marld Cl BOL BL1 .............35 J2
Great Meadow ROY/SHW OL2 .............43 J3
Great Moor St BOL BL1 .............2 E6
  OFTN SK2 .............112 E7
Great Moss Rd TYLD M29 .............82 F2
Great Newton St
  NEWH/MOS M40 .............73 M7
Great Norbury St HYDE SK14 .............102 A2
Great Portwood St STKP SK1 .............13 K2
Great Southern St
  RUSH/FAL M14 .............98 E1
Great Stone Cl RAD M26 * .............54 A1
Great Stone Rd STRET M32 .............86 F8
Great Stones Cl EDGW/EG BL7 .............22 B2
Great St CMANE M1 .............7 M6
Great Underbank STKP SK1 .............13 J4
Great Western St
  OLDTF/WHR M16 .............87 H8
  MPL/ROM SK6 .............102 A3
Greave MPL/ROM SK6 .............102 A3
Greave Av ROCH OL11 .............27 L4
Greave Fold MPL/ROM SK6 .............101 M8
Greave Rd STKP SK1 .............112 F4
Greaves Av FAIL M35 .............74 B6
Greaves Cl WGNNW/ST WN6 .............30 C4
Greaves Rd WILM/AE SK9 .............126 C4
Greaves St MOSL OL5 .............76 F2
  OLD OL1 .............9 K6
  OLDE OL4 .............60 C6
  ROY/SHW OL2 .............43 M5
Greave St ROY/SHW OL2 .............43 M5
Grebe Cl POY/DIS SK12 .............123 K8
  WGNS/IIMK WN3 .............46 E8
Grecian Crs BOLS/LL BL3 .............36 C8
Grecian St BRO M7 .............71 M7
Grecian St North BRO M7 .............71 M7
Grecian Ter BRO M7 * .............71 M7
Gredle Cl URM M41 .............96 C2
Greeba Rd NTHM/RTH M23 .............109 H6
Greek St CMANE M1 .............7 J7
  EDGY/DAV SK3 .............13 H7
Greenacre WGN WN1 .............15 J1
Green Acre WHTN BL5 .............50 C5
Greenacre Cl RAMS BL0 .............19 H5
Greenacre La WALK M28 .............53 H8
Green Acre Pk BOL BL1 * .............36 C3
Greenacres EDGW/EG BL7 .............17 H6
Greenacres Cl LEIGH WN7 .............80 E4
Greenacres Dr BNG/LEV M19 .............99 H8
Greenacres Rd OLDE OL4 .............59 M5
Greenall St AIMK WN4 .............63 L7
Green Av BOLS/LL BL3 .............52 E1
  LHULT M38 .............52 E7
  SWIN M27 .............70 C5
  TYLD M29 .............67 K8
Green Bank BOLE BL2 .............37 H1
  GLSP SK13 .............104 C3
Greenbank FWTH BL4 .............52 F3
  WGNE/HIN WN2 .............65 K1
  WGNW/BIL/OR WN5 .............62 A1
Greenbank Av CHD/CHDH SK8 .............110 D7
  HTNM SK4 .............99 M7
  SWIN M27 * .............70 A6
  UPML OL3 .............61 K1
  WGNW/BIL/OR WN5 .............62 A1
Greenbank Crs MPL/ROM SK6 .............114 E3
Greenbank Dr LIT OL15 .............29 J1
Greenbank Rd BOLS/LL BL3 .............35 L3
  CHD/CHDH SK8 .............110 D6
  MPL/ROM SK6 .............114 E3
  RAD M26 .............38 C2
  SALE M33 .............96 B7
  SLFD M6 .............86 B1
  WHIT OL12 .............20 D2
Green Bank Ter HTNM SK4 .............13 H2
Greenbarn Wy HOR/BR BL6 .............33 C3
Greenbeech Cl MPL/ROM SK6 .............114 D5
Green Booth Cl DUK SK16 .............91 J5
Green Bridge Cl ROCH OL11 * .............28 B8
Green Brook St BURY BL9 .............25 K8
Greenbrow Rd
  NTHM/RTH M23 .............118 D1
Greenburn Dr BOLE BL2 .............37 H2
Green Cl ATH M46 .............66 F1
  CHD/CHDH SK8 .............110 D6
Green Common La
  WGNE/HIN WN2 .............48 D2
Green Ct GOL/RIS/CUL WA3 .............80 E3
Greencourt Dr LHULT M38 .............52 C8

Green Cts ALT WA14 ........................ 116 D1
Green Cft MPL/ROM SK6 ..................... 114 A1
Greencroft Meadow
　ROY/SHW OL2 .............................. 43 J7
Greencroft Rd ECC M30 ..................... 69 L8
Greencroft Wy MILN OL16 ................... 29 C1
Greendale ATH M46 ......................... 51 H8
Greendale Crs LEIGH WN7 ................... 66 F8
　RAD M26 .................................. 54 E3
Greendale Dr BKLY M9 ...................... 73 H1
Green Dr BNG/LEV M19 ...................... 99 J3
　HALE/TIMP WA15 .......................... 108 D5
　HOR/BR BL6 .............................. 34 F5
　WILM/AE SK9 ............................. 127 H2
Green End BNG/LEV M19 ..................... 99 H7
　DTN/ASHW M34 ............................ 101 L4
Green End Rd BNG/LEV M19 .................. 99 H7
Greenfield Av ECC M30 ..................... 84 D5
　URM M41 ................................. 96 A2
　WGNE/HIN WN2 ............................ 15 M6
Greenfield Cl EDGY/DAV SK3 ............... 112 B6
　HALE/TIMP WA15 .......................... 108 F6
　NM/HAY SK22 ............................. 124 C4
　TOT/BURYW BL8 ........................... 38 D3
　WHTN BL5 ................................ 50 D3
Greenfield Ct HEY OL10 .................... 41 C3
Greenfield La MILN OL16 ................... 29 C1
　ROCH OL11 ............................... 28 D8
　ROY/SHW OL2 ............................. 43 L6
Greenfield Rd AUL M46 ..................... 51 H7
Greenfields WGNNW/ST WN6 .................. 31 H4
Greenfields Cl NEWLW WA12 ................. 78 F8
　WGNE/HIN WN2 ............................ 15 M6
Greenfields Crs AIMK WN4 .................. 63 L8
Greenfield St DTN/ASHW M34 ............... 90 A5
　GLSP SK13 ............................... 93 K6
　HYDE SK14 ............................... 102 A2
　ROCH OL11 ............................... 28 D8
Greenfield Vw
　WGN/BIL/OR WN5 .......................... 62 A8
Green Fold GTN M18 ........................ 89 J6
Green Fold Av FWTH BL4 .................... 52 E5
Green Fold La WHTN BL5 .................... 50 B5
Greenfold Wy LEIGH WN7 .................... 81 L2
Greenford Cl CHD/CHDH SK8 ................ 111 L8
　WGNW/BIL/OR WN5 ......................... 46 A6
Greenford Rd CHH M8 ....................... 72 D5
Green Gables Cl
　CHD/CHDH SK8 ........................... 119 K3
Greengate CSLFD M3 ........................ 6 E3
　HALE/TIMP WA15 .......................... 117 M5
　HYDE SK14 ............................... 102 A4
　MDTN M24 ................................ 57 M7
　NEWH/MOS M40 ............................ 73 M1
Greengate Cl WHIT OL12 .................... 21 H8
Greengate East
　NEWH/MOS M40 ............................ 73 M1
Greengate La BOLE BL2 ..................... 37 J4
　PWCH M25 ................................ 55 K8
Greengate Rd DTN/ASHW M34 ................ 90 D8
Greengate St OLDE OL4 ..................... 9 L8
Greengate West CSLFD M3 ................... 6 C1
Greengrove Bank MILN OL16 ................ 28 F1
Greenhalgh Moss La
　TOT/BURYW BL8 ........................... 24 E7
Greenhalgh St FAIL M35 .................... 73 M6
　HEY OL10 ................................ 13 H2
Greenhalgh Wk ANC M4 ...................... 7 L3
Green Hall Ms WILM/AE SK9 ................ 126 F6
Greenham Rd NTHM/RTH M23 ................ 109 H6
Greenhaven Cl WALK M28 .................... 69 J1
Green Hayes Av WGN WN1 .................... 47 M1
Greenheys WGN/BIL/OR WN5 .................. 46 D5
Greenheys BOLE BL2 ........................ 37 H1
　DROY M43 ................................ 89 K2
Greenheys La HULME M15 .................... 87 J7
Greenheys La West
　HULME M15 ............................... 87 J7
Greenheys Rd LHULT M38 .................... 52 B6
Greenhill OLD OL1 ......................... 9 L6
　PWCH M25 ................................ 55 K8
Greenhill Av BOLS/LL BL3 ................. 35 L7
　FWTH BL4 ................................ 52 F6
　ROY/SHW OL2 ............................. 43 H3
　SALE M33 ................................ 96 D6
　WHIT OL12 ............................... 10 C2
Greenhill Crs
　WGN/BIL/OR WN5 .......................... 62 C7
Greenhill La BOLS/LL BL3 ................. 35 L8
Greenhill Pas OLD OL1 ..................... 9 L6
Green Hill Rd HYDE SK14 .................. 102 D5
Greenhill Rd CHH M8 ....................... 72 D5
　HALE/TIMP WA15 .......................... 108 F6
　MDTN M24 ................................ 57 M5
　TOT/BURYW BL8 ........................... 38 D3
　WGNW/BIL/OR WN5 ......................... 62 C7
Green Hill St EDGY/DAV SK3 ............... 12 E8
Green Hill Ter OLDE OL4 ................... 9 L8
Greenhill Ter OLDE OL4 .................... 9 L8
Green Hollow Fold STLY SK15 .............. 91 J5
Greenholm Cl NEWH/MOS M40 ................ 74 A3
Greenhow St DROY M43 ...................... 89 J4
Greenhurst Crs OLDS OL8 ................... 75 K2
Greenhurst La AUL OL6 ..................... 76 B6
Greenhurst Rd AUL OL6 ..................... 76 A5
Greenhythe Rd
　CHD/CHDH SK8 ........................... 119 L6
Greening Rd BNG/LEV M19 .................. 99 J3
Greenland Av WGNNW/ST WN6 ................ 31 H4
Greenland Cl TYLD M29 ..................... 67 L2
Greenland Rd BOLS/LL BL3 ................. 52 C2
　TYLD M29 ................................ 67 L6
Greenlands Cl CHD/CHDH SK8 .............. 120 A4
Greenland St CHH M8 ....................... 72 C5
　SLFD M6 ................................. 71 L7
Green La AUL OL6 .......................... 75 L7
　BOLS/LL BL3 ............................. 52 C1
　BRAM/HZG SK7 ........................... 121 M1
　ECC M30 ................................. 84 F2
　FAIL M35 ................................ 74 B8
　FWTH BL4 ................................ 53 K5
　GLSP SK13 ............................... 93 J8
　GLSP SK13 .............................. 104 C4
　GOL/RIS/CUL WA3 ......................... 80 D2
　GTN M18 ................................. 89 G6
　HALE/TIMP WA15 ......................... 108 E8
　HEY OL10 ................................ 41 H1
　HTNM SK4 ................................ 12 C1
　HTNM SK4 ................................ 12 C1
　HYDE SK14 ............................... 92 F6
　LIT M44 ................................. 94 A7
　LEIGH WN7 ............................... 66 F7
　HTNM SK4 ................................ 13 K1
　MDTN M24 ................................ 58 A5
　MPL/ROM SK6 ............................ 113 L3

OLDE OL4 .................................. 60 D2
OLDS OL8 .................................. 75 H2
POY/DIS SK12 ............................. 122 E8
POY/DIS SK12 ............................. 123 M7
SALE M33 .................................. 96 B6
WGNE/HIN WN2 .............................. 49 L7
WGNNW/ST WN6 .............................. 31 H4
WGNW/BIL/OR WN5 ........................... 62 A1
WHIT OL12 * ............................... 10 D2
WHTF M45 .................................. 55 J5
WILM/AE SK9 .............................. 126 F5
WGN WN1 .................................. 130 C4
Green La North
　HALE/TIMP WA15 ......................... 108 E8
Greenlea Av GTN M18 ...................... 100 A1
Greenleach La WALK M28 .................... 69 J4
Greenlea Cl
　WGNW/BIL/OR WN5 ......................... 46 A7
Greenleaf Cl WALK M28 ..................... 68 C6
Greenleas HOR/BR BL6 ...................... 34 F6
Greenlees St WHIT OL12 .................... 10 E2
Greenleigh Cl BOL BL1 ..................... 22 A7
Greenmans La UPML OL3 ..................... 77 K1
Green Meadow WHIT OL12 .................... 21 H8
Green Mdw
　GOL/RIS/CUL WA3 ......................... 80 B7
　MPL/ROM SK6 ............................ 114 C5
　WHTN BL5 ................................ 50 A5
Green Meadows Dr
　MPL/ROM SK6 ............................ 114 C5
Green Meadows Wk
　WYTH/NTH M22 ........................... 119 G3
Greenmount Cl
　TOT/BURYW BL8 ........................... 24 C2
Greenmount Ct BOL BL1 ..................... 35 K4
Greenmount Dr HEY OL10 .................... 41 J5
　TOT/BURYW BL8 ........................... 24 C1
Greenmount La BOL BL1 ..................... 35 J4
Greenmount Pk FWTH BL4 .................... 53 K6
Greenoak RAD M26 .......................... 53 M5
Green Oak Dr SALE M33 .................... 108 F3
　WALK M28 ................................ 52 F7
Greenoak Cl BOLS/LL BL3 .................. 35 K1
Greenough St ATH M46 ...................... 66 D3
　WGN WN1 ................................. 15 J3
Greenpark Cl
　TOT/BURYW BL8 ........................... 24 B3
Greenpark Rd
　WYTH/NTH M22 ........................... 110 A3
Green Park Vw OLD OL1 ..................... 60 A2
Green Pastures HTNM SK4 .................. 111 H3
Green Pine Rd HOR/BR BL6 ................. 34 A5
Greenrigg Cl
　WGNNW/ST WN6 ............................ 31 H3
Green Rd PART M31 ........................ 106 B1
Greenroyd Av BOLE BL2 ..................... 37 H2
Greenroyde ROCH OL11 * .................... 10 C9
Greens Arms Rd
　EDGW/EG BL7 ............................. 16 B5
Greensbridge Gdns WHTN BL5 ............... 50 C3
Greenshall La POY/DIS SK12 .............. 124 B6
Greenshank Cl LEIGH WN7 .................. 66 E7
　NEWLW WA12 .............................. 78 F8
　ROCH OL11 * ............................. 27 J5
Greenside BOLE BL2 ........................ 23 M5
　HTNM SK4 ............................... 111 K3
　WALK M28 ................................ 69 K7
　OLDE OL4 ................................ 60 A2
Greenside Cl DUK SK16 ..................... 91 K4
　TOT/BURYW BL8 ........................... 23 L1
Greenside Dr DROY M43 ..................... 89 J1
　IRL M44 ................................. 94 C3
　TOT/BURYW BL8 ........................... 24 C4
Greenside La DROY M43 ..................... 89 H1
Greenside Pl DTN/ASHW M34 ............... 101 K4
Greenside Vw HYDE SK14 .................... 91 J7
Green Side Wy MDTN M24 .................... 57 M7
Greenslate Ct
　WGNW/BIL/OR WN5 ......................... 62 B1
Green & Slater Homes
　HTNM SK4 * ............................. 111 K1
Greenslate Rd
　WGNW/BIL/OR WN5 ......................... 62 B1
Greensmith Wy WHTN BL5 .................... 50 B2
Greenson Dr MDTN M24 ...................... 57 H5
Greenstead Av CHH M8 ...................... 72 D4
The Greens WHIT OL12 ...................... 20 A3
Greenstone Av HOR/BR BL6 ................. 33 K1
Greenstone Dr SLFD M6 ..................... 71 J7
Green St ATH M46 .......................... 67 H5
　BOL BL1 ................................. 2 F4
　ECC M30 ................................. 84 E4
　EDGY/DAV SK3 ........................... 112 C6
　FWTH BL4 ................................ 53 J3
　HYDE SK14 ............................... 102 B3
　MDTN M24 ................................ 57 M5
　OLDS OL8 ................................ 8 F7
　RAD M26 ................................. 54 D1
　RAMS BL0 * .............................. 19 H1
　RUSH/FAL M14 ............................ 99 H5
　STRET M32 ............................... 96 F4
　TOT/BURYW BL8 ........................... 24 C4
　TYLD M29 ................................ 67 K3
　WGNE/HIN WN2 ............................ 64 E2
　WGNS/IIMK WN3 ........................... 14 F7
　WILM/AE SK9 ............................ 130 E3
Greensward Cl
　WGNNW/ST WN6 ............................ 30 E3
The Green CHD/CHDH SK8 ................... 120 B4
　GLSP SK13 .............................. 104 D5
　HTNM SK4 ................................ 12 C2
　MPL/ROM SK6 ............................ 123 J1
　OLDS OL8 ................................ 75 K1
　ROCH OL11 ............................... 41 M1
　SWIN M27 ................................ 70 E2
　TOT/BURYW BL8 ........................... 24 C3
　WALK M28 ................................ 69 J7
　WGNW/BIL/OR WN5 ......................... 46 E6
　WILM/AE SK9 ............................ 127 J1
Greenthorne Av HTNM SK4 ................. 100 A5
Greenthorne Cl EDGW/EG BL7 ............... 17 H5
Green Tree Gdns
　MPL/ROM SK6 ............................ 113 L2
Greenvale ROCH OL11 ....................... 27 G4
　WGNNW/ST WN6 ............................ 30 C8
Greenvale Dr CHD/CHDH SK8 ............... 110 F6
Greenview Cha OLDE OL4 .................... 60 B7
Greenview Dr DID/WITH M20 ............... 110 F4
　ROCH OL11 ............................... 27 J4
Green Villa Pk WILM/AE SK9 .............. 126 C6
Green Wk ALT WA14 ........................ 116 C1
　CHD/CHDH SK8 ........................... 110 D6
　HALE/TIMP WA15 ......................... 108 C5
　OLDTF/WHR M16 ........................... 97 M2
　STRET M32 ............................... 96 E1
Green Wks PWCH M25 ........................ 71 M1
Greenwatch Cl ECC M30 ..................... 84 F3
Green Wy BOL BL1 .......................... 36 E1
　ROCH OL11 ............................... 41 L3

Greenway AIMK WN4 ......................... 63 K8
　ALT WA14 ............................... 107 K7
　BRAM/HZG SK7 ........................... 120 F6
　HOR/BR BL6 .............................. 34 C1
　HYDE SK14 .............................. 102 A3
　MDTN M24 ................................ 57 H7
　MPL/ROM SK6 ............................ 114 B3
　ROY/SHW OL2 ............................. 43 J3
　WILM/AE SK9 ............................ 126 E6
　WYTH/NTH M22 ........................... 110 B4
Greenway Av BNG/LEV M19 .................. 99 L4
Greenway Cl SALE M33 ..................... 108 A1
　TOT/BURYW BL8 ........................... 38 E1
Greenway Dr MOSL OL5 ...................... 76 F2
Greenway Rd CHD/CHDH SK8 ................ 119 L6
　HALE/TIMP WA15 ......................... 108 D3
Greenways AULW OL7 ........................ 75 J6
　LEIGH WN7 ............................... 66 D6
　NEWH/MOS M40 ............................ 74 A3
　WGNNW/ST WN6 ............................ 31 K6
　WGNW/BIL/OR WN5 ......................... 62 A1
Greenwich Ct NEWH/MOS M40 ................ 74 A4
　ROCH OL11 ............................... 27 J6
Greenwood Av AUL OL6 ...................... 75 M7
　HOR/BR BL6 .............................. 34 A4
　OFTN SK2 ............................... 112 F6
　SWIN M27 ................................ 70 E3
　WALK M28 ................................ 68 F1
　WGNW/BIL/OR WN5 ......................... 47 H5
Greenwood Cl
　HALE/TIMP WA15 ......................... 109 G7
　WALK M28 ................................ 68 B5
Greenwood Dr WILM/AE SK9 ................ 127 H4
Greenwood La HOR/BR BL6 .................. 34 B3
Greenwood Rd
　WGNNW/ST WN6 ............................ 31 H2
　WYTH/NTH M22 ........................... 109 M7
Greenwoods La HTNM SK4 ................... 100 A5
Greenwood St ALT WA14 ................... 108 A8
　FWTH BL4 ................................ 53 G4
　LIT OL15 ................................ 21 M7
　MILN OL16 ............................... 10 F5
　OLDE OL4 ................................ 59 M4
　OLDS OL8 * .............................. 75 J3
　SLFD M6 ................................. 71 J8
Greenwood V BOL BL1 ....................... 36 B1
Greenwood V South
　BOL BL1 ................................. 36 C1
Greer St OP/CLY M11 ....................... 88 F4
Greetland Dr BKLY M9 ...................... 57 J8
Gregge St HEY OL10 ........................ 41 H8
Greg Ms WILM/AE SK9 ...................... 126 F2
Gregory Av ATH M46 ........................ 50 F7
　BOLE BL2 ................................ 37 H4
　MPL/ROM SK6 ............................ 113 J3
Gregory St HYDE SK14 ...................... 91 H7
　OLDS OL8 ................................ 74 F1
　WGNE/HIN WN2 * .......................... 48 F6
　WGTN/LGST M12 ........................... 88 C6
　WHTN BL5 ................................ 49 K5
Gregory Wy RDSH SK5 ...................... 100 C6
Gregson Fld BOLS/LL BL3 .................. 36 B8
Gregson Rd RDSH SK5 ...................... 100 B6
Gregson St OLD OL1 ........................ 9 H3
Greg St RDSH SK5 ......................... 100 B6
Grelley Wk RUSH/FAL M14 .................. 98 E1
Grenaby Av WGNE/HIN WN2 .................. 49 K7
Grendale Av BRAM/HZG SK7 ................ 122 A3
　STKP SK1 ............................... 112 E3
Grendon Av OLDS OL8 ....................... 75 H1
Grendon Cl BOLS/LL BL3 ................... 51 M1
Grendon Wk WGTN/LGST M12 ................. 88 C6
Grenfel Cl WGNS/IIMK WN3 ................. 14 B9
Grenfell Rd DID/WITH M20 ................ 110 D1
Grenham Av HULME M15 ...................... 87 G6
Grenville Rd BRAM/HZG SK7 ............... 121 L1
Grenville St DUK SK16 ..................... 90 F4
　EDGY/DAV SK3 ............................ 12 E6
　STLY SK15 ............................... 77 G8
Gresford Cl CCHDY M21 ..................... 97 K4
Gresham Ct WHTF M45 ....................... 55 C5
Gresham Dr CHAD OL9 ....................... 8 D5
Gresham St BOL BL1 ........................ 36 C1
　DTN/ASHW M34 ............................ 90 C8
Gresham Wk HTNM SK4 ...................... 112 B1
Gresley Av HOR/BR BL6 ..................... 33 L1
Gresley Cl WGN WN1 ........................ 15 K4
Gresty Av WYTH/NTH M22 ................... 119 H3
Greswell St DTN/ASHW M34 ................. 90 B8
Greta Av CHD/CHDH SK8 .................... 119 L6
Gretna Av ATH M46 ........................ 66 D3
Greton Cl BRUN/LGST M13 .................. 88 B8
Gretton Cl ROY/SHW OL2 ................... 43 J8
Greville St BRUN/LGST M13 ............... 99 H1
Grey Cl MPL/ROM SK6 ...................... 101 K8
Greyfriars AIMK WN4 ....................... 78 C1
Greyfriars Rd WYTH/NTH M22 .............. 118 C2
Greyhound Dr SLFD M6 ...................... 71 L7
Greyhound Rd MCFLDN SK10 ................ 131 L7
Grey Knotts WALK M28 ...................... 68 C7
Greylag Crs WALK M28 ...................... 69 G4
Greylands Cl SALE M33 ..................... 96 B8
Greylands Rd DID/WITH M20 ............... 110 F4
Grey Mare La OP/CLY M11 ................... 88 D4
Greymont Rd BURY BL9 ...................... 25 J6
Grey Rd AIMK WN4 .......................... 63 K8
　ALT WA14 ............................... 107 M7
Greystoke Av BNG/LEV M19 ................. 99 M3
　HALE/TIMP WA15 ......................... 109 G6
　SALE M33 ............................... 108 E1
Greystoke Crs WHTF M45 ................... 55 H2
Greystoke Dr BOL BL1 ...................... 36 A2
　MDTN M24 ................................ 57 G2
　WILM/AE SK9 ............................ 130 C2
Greystoke La FAIL M35 ..................... 74 A6
Greystoke St STKP SK1 .................... 101 K8
Greystone Av CCHDY M21 ................... 98 C4
Grey St AUL OL6 ........................... 90 F1
　DTN/ASHW M34 ........................... 101 G1
　MDTN M24 ................................ 57 J3
　PWCH M25 ................................ 55 L8
　STLY SK15 ............................... 91 M3
　WGTN/LGST M12 ........................... 88 B6
Greyswood Av CHH M8 ....................... 72 C6
Greytown Cl SLFD M6 ....................... 71 J7
Greywood Av BURY BL9 ...................... 5 L4
Grierson St BOL BL1 ....................... 36 B1
　OLDTF/WHR M16 ........................... 87 H8
Griffe La BURY BL9 ........................ 55 M1
Griffin Cl BURY BL9 ....................... 5 K1
Griffin Ct CSLFD M3 * ..................... 6 B4
Griffin Gv BNG/LEV M19 ................... 99 K4
Griffin La CHD/CHDH SK8 ................. 119 M5
Griffin Rd FAIL M35 ....................... 74 A5
Griffiths Cl BRO M7 * ..................... 72 A8
Griffiths St NEWH/MOS M40 ................ 73 M3
Grimes St WHIT OL12 ....................... 27 J3
Grime St RAMS BL0 ......................... 18 D8

Grimscott Cl BKLY M9 * .................... 73 J3
Grimshaw Av FAIL M35 ...................... 74 D4
Grimshaw Cl MPL/ROM SK6 ................. 101 K8
Grimshaw Ct GOL/RIS/CUL WA3 ............. 79 M8
　NEWH/MOS M40 ............................ 73 J7
Grimshaw St FAIL M35 * .................... 74 A4
　GOL/RIS/CUL WA3 ......................... 79 K5
　STKP SK1 ................................ 13 M4
Grimstead Cl NTHM/RTH M23 ............... 109 H6
Grindall Av NEWH/MOS M40 ................. 73 L2
Grindley Av CCHDY M21 ..................... 98 A7
Grindlow St BRUN/LGST M13 ............... 88 B7
Grindon Av BRO M7 ......................... 71 K5
Grindrod St RAD M26 ....................... 38 C5
Grindsbrook Rd RAD M26 ................... 38 C5
Grinton Av BRUN/LGST M13 ................. 99 H2
Grisdale Dr MDTN M24 ...................... 57 H2
Grisdale Rd BOLS/LL BL3 .................. 35 M7
Grisebeck Wy OLD OL1 ...................... 9 H4
Grisedale Av ROY/SHW OL2 ................. 42 F4
Grisedale Cl GTN M18 ...................... 88 F8
　MDTN M24 ................................ 57 G1
Grisedale Dr WGNE/HIN WN2 ................ 49 H2
Grisedale Rd MPL/ROM SK6 ................ 101 L8
Groby Pl ALT WA14 ........................ 107 M7
Groby Rd ALT WA14 ........................ 107 M8
　CCHDY M21 ............................... 97 L4
　DTN/ASHW M34 ............................ 90 B5
Groby Rd North
　DTN/ASHW M34 ............................ 90 A4
Groby St OLDS OL8 ......................... 75 K1
　STLY SK15 ............................... 91 M3
Groom St CMANE M1 * ....................... 7 J9
Grosvenor Av
　GOL/RIS/CUL WA3 ......................... 80 A4
　WHTF M45 ................................ 55 H4
　WILM/AE SK9 ............................ 126 E6
Grosvenor Cl WALK M28 ..................... 52 F7
Grosvenor Ct AULW OL7 ..................... 90 D3
　CHD/CHDH SK8 ........................... 111 G6
Grosvenor Crs HYDE SK14 ................. 105 M5
Grosvenor Dr POY/DIS SK12 ............... 129 G1
　WALK M28 ................................ 52 F7
Grosvenor Gdns BRO M7 ..................... 72 A8
　STLY SK15 ............................... 91 K3
　WYTH/NTH M22 ........................... 110 B6
Grosvenor House STLY SK15 ............... 91 K3
Grosvenor Pl AULW OL7 * ................... 90 D3
　CHD/CHDH SK8 ........................... 111 G6
Grosvenor Rd ALT WA14 ................... 108 B6
　CHD/CHDH SK8 ........................... 84 D1
　HTNM SK4 ................................ 12 A1
　HYDE SK14 .............................. 102 A3
　LEIGH WN7 ............................... 66 A6
　MPL/ROM SK6 ............................ 114 C5
　SALE M33 ................................ 96 C7
　SWIN M27 ................................ 70 C2
　URM M41 ................................. 95 M2
　WALK M28 ................................ 52 F7
　WHTF M45 ................................ 55 H4
Grosvenor Sq SALE M33 ..................... 96 B8
　AULW OL7 ................................ 90 D3
　BOLE BL2 ................................ 3 G7
　BOLS/LL BL3 ............................. 37 K8
　BRAM/HZG SK7 * ......................... 122 A1
　BRUN/LGST M13 ........................... 7 J9
　BURY BL9 ................................ 4 F8
　DTN/ASHW M34 ............................ 90 A8
　EDGY/DAV SK3 ............................ 13 J7
　FWTH BL4 ................................ 53 G3
　HEY OL10 ................................ 40 F3
　PWCH M25 ................................ 55 M8
　RAD M26 ................................. 54 C1
　ROCH OL11 ............................... 41 M3
　STLY SK15 ............................... 91 K3
　STRET M32 ............................... 97 G2
　SWIN M27 ................................ 70 C2
　WGNE/HIN WN2 ............................ 49 G7
　WGNW/BIL/OR WN5 ......................... 47 J6
Grosvenor Wy ROY/SHW OL2 ................. 59 C2
Grotton Hollow OLDE OL4 ................... 60 F7
Grotton Mdw OLDE OL4 ...................... 60 E7
Grouse St WHIT OL12 ....................... 28 C3
Grove Av FAIL M35 ......................... 74 B7
　WILM/AE SK9 ............................ 126 E6
Grove Bank OLDE OL4 ....................... 61 H7
Grove Ct RUSH/FAL M14 ..................... 98 F1
　BRAM/HZG SK7 * ......................... 122 A1
　SALE M33 ................................ 97 G8
Grove Ms WALK M28 ......................... 68 C6
Grovehurst SWIN M27 ....................... 69 L6
Grove La CHD/CHDH SK8 .................... 120 D7
　DID/WITH M20 ........................... 110 E2
　HALE/TIMP WA15 ......................... 108 D4
　HALE/TIMP WA15 ......................... 117 J1
　WGNNW/ST WN6 ............................ 31 J4
Grove Ms WALK M28 * ....................... 69 G1
Grove Pl WGNNW/ST WN6 ..................... 31 J4
Grove Rd HALE/TIMP WA15 ................. 117 G1
　MDTN M24 ................................ 57 J2
　STLY SK15 ............................... 77 G8
　UPML OL3 ................................ 61 L9
Grove St AIMK WN4 ......................... 63 K8
　AULW OL7 ................................ 75 H7
　BOL BL1 ................................. 2 D1
　BRAM/HZG SK7 * ......................... 122 A1
　BRO M7 .................................. 72 B7
　DROY M43 ................................ 89 J4
　DUK SK16 ................................ 91 G3
　FWTH BL4 ................................ 53 H4
　HEY OL10 ................................ 41 H7
　LEIGH WN7 ............................... 66 E8
　NM/HAY SK22 ............................ 124 D5
　OLD OL1 ................................. 9 M4
　ROCH OL11 ............................... 10 D8
　UPML OL3 ................................ 61 L7
　WILM/AE SK9 * .......................... 126 F5
Grove Wy WILM/AE SK9 ..................... 126 F5
Grovewood Cl AULW OL7 ..................... 75 H7
Grovewood Dr
　WGNNW/ST WN6 ............................ 30 B5

Grundey St BRAM/HZG SK7 ................. 122 A2
Grundy Av PWCH M25 ........................ 71 H2
Grundy Cl BURY BL9 ........................ 5 H7
Grundy Rd FWTH BL4 ........................ 53 H5
Grundy's TYLD M29 ......................... 67 M7
Grundy St BOLS/LL BL3 ..................... 36 A8
　HEY OL10 ................................ 41 H4
　HTNM SK4 ............................... 111 H2
　WALK M28 ................................ 69 J1
　WHTN BL5 ................................ 50 B5
Guardian Cl WHIT OL12 ..................... 21 H7
Guardian Ms NTHM/RTH M23 * .............. 108 F3
Guernsey Cl BNG/LEV M19 .................. 99 K6
Guest St LEIGH WN7 ........................ 66 D7
Guide La AULW OL7 ......................... 90 B4
Guide Post Sq
　BRUN/LGST M13 * ........................ 88 A6
Guide Post St BRUN/LGST M13 ............. 88 A6
Guide St SALO M50 ......................... 85 M3
Guido St BOL BL1 .......................... 36 A2
　FAIL M35 ................................ 74 B5
Guild Av WALK M28 ......................... 69 G2
Guildford Av CHD/CHDH SK8 ............... 120 C6
Guildford Cl NEWH/MOS M40 ............... 73 M5
Guildford Crs WGNNW/ST WN6 .............. 47 J1
Guildford Dr AUL OL6 ...................... 75 M5
Guildford Gv MDTN M24 ..................... 57 M1
Guildford Rd BNG/LEV M19 ................. 99 L2
　BOL BL1 ................................. 35 L2
　DUK SK16 ................................ 91 K5
　SLFD M6 ................................. 70 E8
　URM M41 ................................. 85 H8
Guildford St MILN OL16 * ................. 11 G5
Guildhall Cl HULME M15 .................... 87 K7
Guild St EDGW/EG BL7 ...................... 22 E6
Guilford Rd ECC M30 ....................... 84 E3
Guinness Rd TRPK M17 ...................... 85 K4
Guiseley Cl BURY BL9 ...................... 25 H4
Gullane Cl NEWH/MOS M40 ................... 73 M5
Gull Cl POY/DIS SK12 ..................... 128 C1
Gulvain Pl CHAD OL9 ....................... 58 C4
Gun Rd GLSP SK13 ......................... 115 L1
　MPL/ROM SK6 ............................ 115 M5
Gunson St NEWH/MOS M40 ................... 7 M1
Gun St ANC M4 ............................. 7 K3
Gunters Av WHTN BL5 ....................... 50 B6
Gurner Av ORD M5 .......................... 86 E5
Gurney St ANC M4 .......................... 88 A3
Gutter La RAMS BL0 ........................ 18 E5
Guy Fawkes St ORD M5 ...................... 86 E5
Guywood La MPL/ROM SK6 ................... 113 M1
Gwelo St OP/CLY M11 ....................... 88 D2
Gwenbury Av STKP SK1 ..................... 112 E3
Gwendor Av CHH M8 ......................... 72 C1
Gwladys St STLY SK15 ...................... 77 H6
Gylden Cl HYDE SK14 ....................... 92 F1
Gypsy La ROCH OL11 ........................ 41 M1

# H

Habergham Cl WALK M28 ..................... 68 F5
Hackberry Cl ALT WA14 .................... 107 L4
Hacken Bridge Rd BOLS/LL BL3 ............. 37 G8
Hacken La BOLS/LL BL3 ..................... 36 F8
Hackford Cl BOL BL1 ....................... 35 M4
　TOT/BURYW BL8 ........................... 25 G7
Hacking St BRO M7 ......................... 72 B6
　BURY BL9 ................................ 5 H5
　PWCH M25 ................................ 55 K8
Hackle St OP/CLY M11 ...................... 88 F2
Hackleton Cl ANC M4 ....................... 88 A3
Hackness Rd CCHDY M21 ..................... 97 K4
Hackney Av NEWH/MOS M40 .................. 73 M8
Hackney Cl RAD M26 ........................ 38 C5
Hackworth Cl WGN WN1 ...................... 15 K4
Hadbutt La TYLD M29 ....................... 67 J8
Haddington Dr BKLY M9 ..................... 73 H1
Haddon Av NEWH/MOS M40 .................... 73 M8
Haddon Cl BURY BL9 ........................ 39 K7
　MPL/ROM SK6 ............................ 123 G6
　WILM/AE SK9 ............................ 130 C2
Haddon Gv HALE/TIMP WA15 ................ 108 F2
　RDSH SK5 ............................... 100 B5
　SALE M33 ............................... 108 D1
Haddon Hall Rd DROY M43 .................. 89 H2
Haddon Ms GLSP SK13 ...................... 104 A2
Haddon Rd BRAM/HZG SK7 ................... 122 A3
　CCHDY M21 ............................... 97 H8
　CHD/CHDH SK8 ........................... 119 L5
　ECC M30 ................................. 84 F4
　GOL/RIS/CUL WA3 ......................... 80 A8
　WALK M28 ................................ 69 M7
　WGNS/IIMK WN3 ........................... 15 H7
Haddon St SLFD M6 ......................... 71 L7
　STRET M32 ............................... 86 A8
Haddon Wy ROY/SHW OL2 ..................... 43 M4
Hadfield Cl RUSH/FAL M14 ................. 99 G1
Hadfield Pl GLSP SK13 ..................... 93 J8
Hadfields Av HYDE SK14 ................... 105 M5
Hadfield Sq GLSP SK13 .................... 104 F4
Hadfield St BRO M7 ........................ 72 B6
　DUK SK16 ................................ 90 D5
　GLSP SK13 .............................. 104 F4
　OLDS OL8 ................................ 75 H1
　OLDTF/WHR M16 ........................... 86 F6
Hadleigh Cl BOL BL1 ....................... 22 D6
Hadley Av BRUN/LGST M13 ................... 99 H2
Hadley Cl CHD/CHDH SK8 ................... 120 B3
Hadley St SLFD M6 ......................... 71 J7
Hadlow Gn RDSH SK5 ....................... 100 E6
Hadlow Wk
　NEWH/MOS M40 * .......................... 88 B1
Hadwin St BOL BL1 ......................... 2 F1
Hafton Rd BRO M7 .......................... 71 L6
Hag Bank La POY/DIS SK12 ................ 123 M5
Haggate ROY/SHW OL2 ....................... 58 F1
Haggate Crs ROY/SHW OL2 .................. 58 F1
Hagley Rd ORD M5 .......................... 86 D6
The Hags BURY BL9 ......................... 39 K7
Haguebar Rd NM/HAY SK22 ................. 124 A6
Hague Bush Cl
　GOL/RIS/CUL WA3 ......................... 80 B3
Hague Fold Rd NM/HAY SK22 ............... 124 B8
Hague Rd DID/WITH M20 ..................... 98 D7
　HYDE SK14 .............................. 103 M2
Hague St AUL OL6 .......................... 75 M8
　GLSP SK13 .............................. 105 G5
　NEWH/MOS M40 ............................ 73 J7
　OLDE OL4 ................................ 60 B4
Haig Ct TOT/BURYW BL8 ..................... 38 D4
Haig Hall Cl RAMS BL0 ..................... 18 E8
Haigh Av HTNM SK4 ........................ 100 F7
Haigh Hall Cl RAMS BL0 ................... 18 E8
Haigh La CHAD OL9 ......................... 58 C4
Haigh Pk HTNM SK4 ........................ 100 B7
Haigh Rd WGNE/HIN WN2 ..................... 32 F1

Haigh St BOL BL1 ........................2 E2
  ROCH OL11 ..........................11 G7
Haigh Vw WGN WN1 ...............48 A2
  WGNS/IIMK WN3 ..............15 L7
Haig Rd STRET M32 ................97 G3
  TOT/BURYW BL8 .................38 E2
Haig St WGNS/IIMK WN3 ......14 D5
Haile Dr WALK M28 .................68 C6
Hailsham Cl TOT/BURYW BL8 .....24 F5
Hail St RAMS BL0 * ..................18 D8
Halbury Wk BOL BL1 * .............36 C2
Halcyon Cl WHIT OL12 ...........27 L2
Halcon Rd DID/WITH M20 ......99 G7
Hale Bank WHTN BL5 .............50 C2
Hale Cl LEIGH WN7 ..................81 L2
Hale Gv AIMK WN4 ..................63 J7
Hale La FAIL M35 .....................74 B4
Hale Low Rd HALE/TIMP WA15 ...117 H1
  HALE/TIMP WA15 .............117 J2
  HTNM SK4 .............................12 C1
Hales Cl DROY M43 .................89 J1
Halesden Rd HTNM SK4 .......100 A7
Halesfield Wk WGNE/HIN WN2 ...65 L2
Hale Vw ALT WA14 .................116 F2
Halewood Av COL/RIS/CUL WA3...79 J3
Haley Cl RDSH SK5 ................100 C4
Haley Rd CHH M8 ....................72 D5
Half Acre RAD M26 ..................38 C6
Half Acre Dr HALE/TIMP WA15 ...116 F2
Half Acre La HOR/BR BL6 .......32 F3
  ROCH OL11 ..........................27 L6
Half Acre Ms ROCH OL11 .......27 L6
Half Acre Rd ROCH OL11 ........27 L6
Halfacre Rd WYTH/NTH M22 ...109 M8
Half Edge La ECC M30 ...........85 J1
Half Moon La OFTN SK2 .......113 H6
Halford Dr OLDTF/WHR M16 ...87 L4
Half St CSLFD M3 * ....................6 D1
Halford Dr NEWH/MOS M40 ...73 L4
Halifax St MILN OL16 ..............28 E2
Halifax St AUL OL6 ...................75 L8
Hallacres La CHD/CHDH SK8 ...120 A4
Hallam Rd NEWH/MOS M40 ...73 L7
Hallam St OFTN SK2 ..............112 D6
  RAD M26 .................................38 G8
Hallas Gv NTHM/RTH M23 ...109 L3
  RUSH/FAL M14 .....................99 G1
  SALE M33 ...............................96 B6
  STLY SK15 ...............................76 F7
Hall Bank ECC M30 .................84 F2
Hallbottom St HYDE SK14 .....91 J7
Hallbridge Gdns BOL BL1 ......36 D1
Hall Cl HYDE SK14 ....................92 D7
  WGNNW/ST WN6 ...............30 E6
The Hall Coppice EDGW/EG BL7 ...22 A3
Hallcroft PART M31 ................94 C8
Hallcroft Gdns MILN OL16 ....29 H6
Hall Dr HYDE SK14 ...................92 D7
  MDTN M24 .............................57 J6
Hall Farm Av URM M41 ..........95 L1
Hall Farm Cl BRAM/HZG SK7 ...122 L1
Hall Fold WHIT OL12 ...............20 A4
Hall Gdns WHIT OL12 .............27 M2
Hallgate WGN WN1 ................14 F4
  WHTN BL5 ...............................50 B7
Hallgate Dr CHD/CHDH SK8 ...119 J2
Hallgate Rd STKP SK1 ............112 E4
Hall Green Cl DUK SK16 * .......90 F3
Hall Green Rd DUK SK16 ........90 F3
Hall Gv RUSH/FAL M14 ..........99 G1
Hall House La LEIGH WN7 .....66 F8
Halliday Rd NEWH/MOS M40 ...73 L8
Halliford Rd NEWH/MOS M40 ...73 K6
Hallington Cl BOLS/LL BL3 ....36 C8
Hall i' th' Wood La BOL BL1 ...22 D8
Halliwell Av OLDS OL8 ............75 H1
Halliwell La CHH M8 ................72 C5
Halliwell Rd BOL BL1 ...............36 A2
  PWCH M25 .............................71 J3
Halliwell St CHAD OL9 * .........74 D3
  MILN OL16 .............................29 H5
  WHIT OL12 .............................10 C3
Halliwell St West CHH M8 * ...72 C5
Hall La FWTH BL4 .....................53 H1
  HOR/BR BL6 ...........................34 B5
  MPL/ROM SK6 .....................101 L4
  NTHM/RTH M23 ..................109 L6
  PART M31 ...............................94 C8
  WGN WN1 ..............................32 A8
  WGNE/HIN WN2 ...................49 G3
  WGNNW/ST WN6 ...............30 A2
  WGNW/BIL/OR WN5 ...........46 C8
  WHIT OL12 .............................20 A4
Hall Lane Av WGNE/HIN WN2 ...49 G4
Hall Lee Dr WHTN BL5 ............50 D3
Hall Meadow CHD/CHDH SK8 ...120 A3
Hall Meadow Rd GLSP SK13 ...105 J4
Hall Moss La BRAM/HZG SK7 ...120 E8
Hall Moss Rd BKLY M9 ............73 K1
Hallows Av CCHDY M21 ..........97 M7
Hallows Farm Av WHIT OL12 ...28 A3
Hall Pool Dr OFTN SK2 ..........113 H5
Hall Rd ALT WA14 ...................116 E3
  AUL OL6 ..................................75 M7
  BRAM/HZG SK7 ...................120 F2
  RNFD/HAY WA11 ..................78 B5
  RUSH/FAL M14 .....................99 G1
  WILM/AE SK9 .......................126 E5
  WILM/AE SK9 .......................127 J1
Hallroyd Brow OLD OL1 * .........9 H2
Hallstead Av LHULT M38 ........52 B8
Hallstead Gv LHULT M38 ........52 B8
Hall St AUL OL6 ........................91 H2
  BOLS/LL BL3 ..........................53 L2
  BURY BL9 ................................24 F3
  CHD/CHDH SK8 ...................111 C6
  CMANW M2 ..............................6 F6
  FAIL M35 .................................74 A6
  HEY OL10 ................................41 G3
  HYDE SK14 ...........................101 L1
  MDTN M24 * ..........................57 K4
  NM/HAY SK22 ......................124 D4
  OLDE OL4 ...............................59 L5
  RAD M26 .................................38 C6
  ROY/SHW OL2 ......................43 G8
  STKP SK1 ................................112 E4
  SWIN M27 ...............................70 D3
  TOT/BURYW BL8 * ..................4 A1
  TOT/BURYW BL8 ...................24 F3
  WGN WN1 ..............................15 H5
  WGNE/HIN WN2 ...................48 C5
  WGNE/HIN WN2 ...................64 B5
  WHIT OL12 .............................20 A4
Hallsville Rd BNG/LEV M19 ...99 M3
Halls Wy UPML OL3 .................61 K6
Hallsworth Rd ECC M30 .........84 D3
Hallview Wy WALK M28 ..........68 C1
Hall Wood Av RNFD/HAY WA11...78 C4

Hallwood Av SLFD M6 .............70 F8
Hallwood Rd NTHM/RTH M23 ...109 M6
  WILM/AE SK9 .......................127 J1
Hall Wood Rd WILM/AE SK9 ...127 J2
Hallworth Av DTN/ASHW M34 ...89 L3
Hallworth Rd CHH M8 .............72 E4
Hallworthy Cl LEIGH WN7 .....80 E3
Halmore Rd NEWH/MOS M40 ...88 A2
Halsall Cl BURY BL9 .................25 J6
Halsall Dr BOLS/LL BL3 ...........52 B2
Halsbury Cl WGTN/LGST M12 ...88 B2
Halsey Cl CHAD OL9 .................74 B1
Halshaw La FWTH BL4 ............53 J5
Halsmere Dr BKLY M9 .............73 H1
Halstead Av CCHDY M21 .........97 K5
  SLFD M6 .................................71 H7
Halstead Dr IRL M44 ...............94 A2
  LEIGH WN7 .............................66 E7
Halstead St BOLE BL2 ...............3 H5
  BURY BL9 ................................25 K7
Halstead Wk BURY BL9 * ........25 K7
Halstock Rd NEWH/MOS M40 ...73 G7
Halstone Av WILM/AE SK9 ...126 C8
Halston St HULME M15 ...........87 H6
Halter Cl RAD M26 ...................38 D7
Halton Bank SLFD M6 .............71 J8
Halton Dr HALE/TIMP WA15 ...108 E3
Halton Rd OP/CLY M11 ............88 F2
Halton St BOLE BL2 ....................3 K5
  HYDE SK14 ...........................102 C1
  RNFD/HAY WA11 * ...............78 B6
Halvard Av BURY BL9 ..............25 J6
Halvard Ct BURY BL9 ..............25 J6
Halvis Gv OLDTF/WHR M16 ....97 L2
Hambledon Cl BOLS/LL BL3 ...35 J7
Hambledon Cl ATH M46 .........51 H4
Hambleton Cl TOT/BURYW BL8 ...38 C3
Hambleton Dr SALE M33 ........96 A4
Hambleton Rd CHD/CHDH SK8 ...119 L4
Hamblett St LEIGH WN7 .........65 L7
Hambridge Cl CHH M8 ............72 D5
  HYDE SK14 .............................91 J7
Hamer Dr OLDTF/WHR M16 ...87 G7
Hamer Hall Crs WHIT OL12 ....28 E3
Hamer HI BKLY M9 ...................72 F1
Hamer La MILN OL16 ...............11 J1
Hamer St BOLE BL2 ..................36 E3
  HEY OL10 ................................40 E2
  RAD M26 .................................38 F8
  RAMS BL0 ...............................24 E2
Hamerton Rd NEWH/MOS M40 ...72 F8
Hamilcar Av ECC M30 ..............85 H3
Hamilton Av ECC M30 .............85 H3
  IRL M44 ...................................94 A8
  ROY/SHW OL2 ......................58 E1
Hamilton Cl PWCH M25 .........71 K1
  TOT/BURYW BL8 ...................38 E1
Hamilton Ct WGNNW/ST WN5 * ...47 H4
Hamilton Crs HTNM SK4 .........12 B4
Hamilton Gv OLDTF/WHR M16 ...87 G7
Hamilton Ms ECC M30 * ..........84 E1
  PWCH M25 * ...........................71 K1
Hamilton Rd AIMK WN4 .........62 F8
  BRUN/LGST M13 ...................99 J1
  PWCH M25 .............................71 K1
  TYLD M29 ................................68 A6
  WGNE/HIN WN2 ...................49 J8
  WHTF M45 ..............................55 H4
Hamilton Sq HTNM SK4 .........13 C1
  WGNW/BIL/OR WN5 ...........47 H4
Hamilton St ATH M46 ..............66 F2
  AULW OL7 ..............................90 C3
  BOL BL1 ...................................22 B8
  BRO M7 * .................................72 A5
  BURY BL9 ................................25 J8
  CHAD OL9 ...............................58 D5
  ECC M30 ..................................84 E1
  LEIGH WN7 .............................66 A6
  OLDE OL4 .................................9 M6
  OLDTF/WHR M16 ..................87 G7
  STLY SK15 ...............................91 J2
  SWIN M27 ...............................70 A3
Hamilton Wy HEY OL10 ..........40 D3
Hamlet Dr SALE M33 ...............96 B6
The Hamlet HOR/BR BL6 ........34 E4
Hammerstone Rd GTN M18 ...88 F6
Hammett Rd CCHDY M21 .......97 K4
Hammond Av HTNM SK4 ......100 B7
Hamnet Cl BOL BL1 ...................2 D7
Hamnett St HYDE SK14 * ......102 D7
Hamon Rd HALE/TIMP WA15 ...108 B8
Hampden Crs GTN M18 ..........88 F7
Hampden Pl ECC M30 .............85 G2
Hampden Pl
  WGNW/BIL/OR WN5 * .........47 G3
Hampden Rd PWCH M25 .......55 L8
  ROY/SHW OL2 ......................44 A6
  SALE M33 ...............................108 D1
Hampden St HEY OL10 ............41 G3
  ROCH OL11 ............................10 F6
Hampshire Cl BURY BL9 ............5 J9
  GLSP SK13 .............................105 J4
Hampshire Rd CHAD OL9 ..........8 B8
  DROY M43 ..............................89 K1
  PART M31 .............................106 A2
  RDSH SK5 ..............................100 F7
Hampson Cl AIMK WN4 ..........78 E2
  ECC M30 * ...............................84 E1
Hampson Crs WILM/AE SK9 ...119 L8
Hampson Fold RAD M26 .........38 C8
Hampson Mill La BURY BL9 ...39 J7
Hampson Rd AUL OL6 .............76 B6
  STRET M32 .............................96 F2
Hampson St ATH M46 * ..........66 F1
  CSLFD M3 .................................6 B6
  DROY M43 ..............................89 K2
  ECC M30 * ...............................84 E3
  NEWH/MOS M40 * ...............73 G4
  RAD M26 .................................54 D1
  SALE M33 ...............................97 G8
  STKP SK1 * .............................112 E4
  SWIN M27 ...............................70 D3
Hampstead Av URM M41 ........95 H3
Hampstead Dr OFTN SK2 ......112 F7
  WHTF M45 ..............................55 H3
Hampstead La OFTN SK2 ......112 F7
Hampstead Rd
  WGNNW/ST WN6 ...............31 G3
Hampton Gv ALT WA14 .........108 B3
  BURY BL9 ................................25 J6
  CHD/CHDH SK8 ...................120 A2
  LEIGH WN7 .............................67 H5
Hampton Rd BOLS/LL BL3 ......52 D1
  CCHDY M21 ............................97 J3
  FAIL M35 .................................74 D4
  IRL M44 ...................................94 A3
  URM M41 ................................96 A3
Hampton St OLDS OL8 ............59 G8

Hamsell Rd BRUN/LGST M13 ....7 L9
Hanborough Cl TYLD M29 ......67 H4
Hancock St RUSH/FAL M14 ....98 E1
Hancock St STRET M32 ...........97 M2
Handel Av URM M41 ...............95 K2
Handel Ms SALE M33 ..............96 F8
Handel St BOL BL1 ...................36 A1
Handforth Gv BRUN/LGST M13 ...99 H2
Handforth Rd RDSH SK5 .......100 C7
  WILM/AE SK9 .......................127 J3
Hand La LEIGH WN7 .................81 H3
Handley Av RUSH/FAL M14 ....98 E3
Handley Cl EDGY/DAV SK3 ....111 M7
Handley Gdns BOL BL1 ...........35 L5
Handley Rd BRAM/HZG SK7 ...121 L5
Handley St BURY BL9 .................4 F9
  WHIT OL12 * ..........................10 B2
Hands La ROCH OL11 ..............27 K5
Handsworth St
  WGTN/LGST M12 ..................88 A5
Hanging Chadder La
  ROY/SHW OL2 ......................42 F5
Hankinson Cl PART M31 ........106 C2
Hankinson Wy SLFD M6 .........86 D1
Hanley Cl MDTN M24 ..............57 K7
  POY/DIS SK12 ......................123 M7
Hanlith Ms BNG/LEV M19 .....99 J4
Hanlon St CHH M8 ...................72 C3
Hanmer St WGNE/HIN WN2 ...49 G7
Hannah Baldwin Cl
  OP/CLY M11 ...........................88 C4
Hannah St WGTN/LGST M12 ...99 K2
Hannerton Rd ROY/SHW OL2 ...44 A4
Hannesburg Gdns
  NTHM/RTH M23 ..................109 J8
Hannet Rd WYTH/NTH M22 ...118 F3
Hanover Ct BRO M7 .................72 A5
  WALK M28 ..............................69 L6
Hanover Crs RUSH/FAL M14 ...88 A8
Hanover Gdns BRO M7 ...........72 B4
Hanover Rd ALT WA14 ...........107 L5
  WGNE/HIN WN2 ...................48 F6
Hanover St ANC M4 ...................7 G2
  BOL BL1 .....................................2 E5
  LEIGH WN7 .............................66 D6
  LIT OL15 ..................................21 L7
  MOSL OL5 ...............................76 F2
  STLY SK15 ...............................91 J2
Hanover St North
  DTN/ASHW M34 ...................90 B4
Hanover St South
  DTN/ASHW M34 * .................90 B4
Hansby Cl OLD OL1 ..................59 H3
Hansdon Cl CHH M8 ................72 C3
Hansom Dr ATH M46 ...............66 D4
Hanson Ms STKP SK1 .............112 E4
Hanson Pk MDTN M24 * .........57 L3
Hanson Rd NEWH/MOS M40 ...73 K5
Hanson St BURY BL9 ...............25 J8
  MDTN M24 .............................57 K4
  OLD OL1 ..................................59 L5
Hanworth Cl
  BRUN/LGST M13 .....................7 K9
Hapton Av STRET M32 .............97 G3
Hapton Pl HTNM SK4 ..............13 C1
Hapton St BNG/LEV M19 ........99 K3
Harbern Cl ECC M30 ................70 A8
Harbern Dr LEIGH WN7 ..........66 A2
Harbord St MDTN M24 * .........57 K4
Harboro Gv SALE M33 .............96 C8
Harboro Rd SALE M33 .............96 C8
Harboro Wy SALE M33 ............96 C8
Harbour Farm Rd HYDE SK14 ...91 H7
Harbour La MILN OL16 ............29 J7
Harbour La North MILN OL16...29 J6
Harbourne Av WALK M28 .......68 F4
Harbourne Cl WALK M28 ........68 F4
Harbury Cl BOLS/LL BL3 ..........51 K1
Harbury Crs WYTH/NTH M22 ...109 M7
Harcles Dr RAMS BL0 ..............18 F5
Harcombe Rd DID/WITH M20...98 F6
Harcourt Av URM M41 .............96 A3
Harcourt Cl URM M41 ..............96 C3
Harcourt Rd ALT WA14 ..........108 A6
  SALE M33 ...............................96 D6
Harcourt St OLD OL1 ...............59 L4
  RDSH SK5 ..............................100 C4
  STRET M32 .............................97 H1
  WALK M28 ..............................53 G7
Hardcastle Av WGNS/IIMK WN3 ...15 J8
Hardberry Pl OFTN SK2 .........113 H6
Hardcastle Gdns BOLE BL2 ....22 F6
Hardcastle Rd EDGY/DAV SK3 ...12 F9
Hardcastle St BOL BL1 ............36 C2
Harden Dr BOLE BL2 ................37 L2
Harden Hills ROY/SHW OL2 ...44 A4
Harden Pk WILM/AE SK9 .......130 D1
Hardfield Rd MDTN M24 ........57 K7
Hardfield St HEY OL10 ............41 G3
Hardicker St HTNM SK4 ..........99 L5
Hardie Av FWTH BL4 ...............52 E5
Harding St ANC M4 ..................88 A3
  CSLFD M3 .................................6 C3
  HYDE SK14 .............................91 G7
  SLFD M6 .................................71 K8
  STKP SK1 ................................112 E3
Hard La WHIT OL12 .................20 E4
Hardman Av MPL/ROM SK6 ...113 K1
  PWCH M25 .............................55 K8
Hardman Cl RAD M26 ..............38 C6
Hardman La FAIL M35 .............74 B4
Hardman Rd RDSH SK5 .........100 C4
Hardmans La EDGW/EG BL7 ...22 C5
Hardman's Ms WHTF M45 ......55 J6
Hardman St BURY BL9 ..............4 F1
  CHAD OL9 ...............................74 E1
  CSLFD M3 .................................6 D5
  EDGY/DAV SK3 ......................12 F6
  FAIL M35 .................................74 A5
  FWTH BL4 ...............................53 H5
  HEY OL10 ................................41 G2
  RAD M26 .................................38 C6
  WGNS/IIMK WN3 * ...............14 E8
Hardon Gv BRUN/LGST M13 ...99 J3
Hardrow Cl WGNS/IIMK WN3 ...63 J2
Hardrush Fold FAIL M35 ..........74 D6
Hardshaw Cl BRUN/LGST M13 * ...87 J2
Hardwick Cl MPL/ROM SK6 ...123 H6
Hardwicke Rd POY/DIS SK12 ...122 B8
Hardwick Rd AIMK WN4 .........63 K7
  PART M31 .............................106 C1

Harris Av DTN/ASHW M34 ....100 E1
  HEY OL10 ................................85 C2
Harris Cl DTN/ASHW M34 .....100 E1
  HEY OL10 ................................40 E3
Harris Dr BURY BL9 ..................55 L2
  HYDE SK14 .............................91 K8
Harrison Av BNG/LEV M19 .....99 L3
Harrison Cl WHIT OL12 ...........27 J3
Harrison Crs HOR/BR BL6 .......32 F1
Harrisons Dr MPL/ROM SK6 ...101 M7
Harrison St ANC M4 .................88 A3
  BRO M7 ...................................72 A8
  ECC M30 ..................................84 D4
  HYDE SK14 ...........................102 C4
  LHULT M38 .............................52 D8
  OFTN SK2 ...............................13 K9
  OLD OL1 * .................................9 J6
  RAMS BL0 ...............................18 F5
  STLY SK15 ...............................91 K2
  WGNE/HIN WN2 ...................65 L1
  WGNW/BIL/OR WN5 ...........14 A7
Harrison Wy NEWLW WA12 ....78 F8
Harris Rd WGNNW/ST WN6 ...30 E2
Harris St BOLS/LL BL3 ................2 C7
  BRO M7 ...................................72 B8
  DID/WITH M20 .....................110 D2
  HEY OL10 ................................41 J2
  WILM/AE SK9 .......................126 E1
Harrogate Av PWCH M25 .......72 A2
Harrogate Cl OP/CLY M11 .......89 H5
Harrogate Dr RDSH SK5 ........100 A4
Harrogate Rd RDSH SK5 .......100 B3
Harrogate St WGN WN1 ..........15 C5
Harrop Edge La UPML OL3 ......45 L7
Harrop Edge Rd HYDE SK14 ...92 B8
Harrop Fold OLDS OL8 ............75 K3
Harrop Green La UPML OL3 ....45 M7
Harrop La MCFLDN SK10 ......129 J3
Harrop Rd HALE/TIMP WA15 ...117 H2
Harrop St BOLS/LL BL3 ...........35 K8
  GTN M18 .................................89 J6
  STKP SK1 .................................13 L8
  STLY SK15 ...............................91 J2
  WALK M28 ..............................68 E1
Harrow Av BNG/LEV M19 .......99 K6
  OLDS OL8 ...............................75 C1
  ROCH OL11 ............................27 K6
Harrow Cl BURY BL9 ................39 J7
  WGNW/BIL/OR WN5 ...........46 C4
  WILM/AE SK9 .......................127 H4
Harrow Crs LEIGH WN7 ...........81 J1
Harrow Dr SALE M33 ..............108 D2
Harrow Ms ROY/SHW OL2 ......43 L9
Harrow Pl WGNS/IIMK WN3 ...48 C8
Harrow Rd BOL BL1 ..................35 L5
  SALE M33 ...............................108 D2
  WGNW/BIL/OR WN5 ...........47 C3
Harrow St CHH M8 ...................72 E3
  ROCH OL11 * .........................42 E2
Harrycroft Rd MPL/ROM SK6 ...101 L7
Harry Rd RDSH SK5 ................100 C4
Harry Rowley Cl
  WYTH/NTH M22 * ...............118 C2
Harry's Ct LEIGH WN7 .............66 A7
Harry St CHAD OL9 ...................8 D7
  ROCH OL11 ............................41 L1
  ROY/SHW OL2 ......................59 H2
Harry Thorneycroft Wk
  OP/CLY M11 ...........................88 C2
Harrytown MPL/ROM SK6 .....113 K2
Harswell Cl WGNW/BIL/OR WN5...46 B7
Hart Av DROY M43 ...................89 J3
  SALE M33 ...............................109 J1
Hart Ct MOSL OL5 ...................76 E2
Hart Dr BURY BL9 .....................39 L8
Harter St CMANE M1 .................7 G5
Hartfield Cl BRUN/LGST M13 ...87 M6
Hartfield Wk BOLE BL2 ..............3 L3
Hartford Av HEY OL10 .............40 E2
  HTNM SK4 ............................100 H6
  WILM/AE SK9 .......................126 D7
Hartford Cl HEY OL10 ..............40 E1
Hartford Gdns
  HALE/TIMP WA15 ...............109 J3
Hartford Rd SALE M33 ...........108 A3
  URM M41 ................................85 H8
Hartford Sq CHAD OL9 * ...........8 D7
Hartford St DTN/ASHW M34 * ...90 B7
Harthill St CHH M8 ...................86 B1
Hartington Cl URM M41 ..........96 B2
Hartington Ct ROY/SHW OL2 ...43 H8
Hartington Dr BRAM/HZG SK7 ...122 A4
  OP/CLY M11 ...........................88 E1
  WGNNW/ST WN6 ...............31 J5
Hartington Rd ALT WA14 ......108 A5
  BOL BL1 ...................................35 M4
  BRAM/HZG SK7 ...................121 G6
  CCHDY M21 ............................97 L4
  CHD/CHDH SK8 ...................119 M4
  ECC M30 ..................................85 J2
  MPL/ROM SK6 .....................123 G6
  OP/CLY M11 ...........................88 E1
  WGNNW/ST WN6 ...............31 J5
Hartington St RUSH/FAL M14 ...98 C1
Hartis Av BRO M7 .....................72 B4
Hartland Cl OFTN SK2 ............112 F4
  POY/DIS SK12 ......................123 M7
  TYLD M29 ................................67 L4
Hartland St HEY OL10 .............41 G2
Hartlebury ROCH OL11 ...........10 D7
Hartlepool Cl RUSH/FAL M14 ...98 E1
Hartley Av WYTH/NTH M25 ...71 M1
  WGN WN1 ..............................15 K5
Hartley Gv IRL M44 ..................83 G1
  WGNW/BIL/OR WN5 ...........46 E5
Hartley Hall Gdns
  OLDTF/WHR M16 ..................98 B3
Hartley La ROCH OL11 .............28 B8
Hartley Rd ALT WA14 .............107 M7
  CCHDY M21 ............................97 M1
Hartley St EDGY/DAV SK3 .......12 E7
  HEY OL10 ................................41 G2
  HOR/BR BL6 ...........................33 L2
  LIT OL15 ..................................29 C5
  MILN OL16 .............................29 C5
  NEWH/MOS M40 ..................92 A1
  STLY SK15 ...............................91 J3
  WGNW/BIL/OR WN5 ...........46 E5
  WHIT OL12 .............................21 G6
  WHIT OL12 .............................27 L2
Hartley Ter WCNS/IIMK WN3 ...14 F6
Hart Mill Cl MOSL OL5 ............76 E2
Harton Av GTN M18 .................89 G8
Harton Cl ROY/SHW OL2 .........43 K6
Hart Rd RUSH/FAL M14 ...........98 E3

Harts Farm Ms LEIGH WN7 66 C5
Hartshead Av AUL OL6 75 M6
STLY SK15 91 K1
Hartshead Cl AUL OL6 76 B8
OP/CLY M11 89 K5
Hartshead Crs FAIL M35 74 F6
Hartshead Rd AUL OL6 * 75 M6
Hartshead St OLDE OL4 60 C7
Hartshead Vw HYDE SK14 102 C3
Hartsop Dr MDTN M24 56 F2
Hartspring Av SWIN M27 70 D5
Hart St ALT WA14 108 B7
CMANE M1 7 H6
DROY M43 89 K2
TYLD M29 67 M4
WHTN BL5 49 L5
Hartswell Cl GOL/RIS/CUL WA3 79 K3
Hartswood Cl DTN/ASHW M34 90 D8
Hartswood Rd DID/WITH M20 99 G6
Hartwell Cl BOLE BL2 36 F3
OP/CLY M11 88 C4
Harvard Cl MPL/ROM SK6 101 M7
Harvard Gv SLFD M6 85 M1
Harvard Rd GTN M18 88 F7
Harvard St ROCH OL11 28 D8
Harvest Cl SALE M33 109 K1
SLFD M6 71 H7
Harvest Pk BOL BL1 35 M4
Harvey Ct LEIGH WN7 80 E3
Harvey La GOL/RIS/CUL WA3 79 J3
Harvey St BOL BL1 36 A1
STKP SK1 13 J4
TOT/BURYW BL8 38 F1
WGNS/IIMK WN3 15 J7
WHIT OL12 28 E3
Harvin Gv DTN/ASHW M34 101 K2
Harwich Cl BNG/LEV M19 * 99 K3
RDSH SK5 100 F6
Harwin Cl WHIT OL12 28 A1
Harwood Ct SLFD M6 71 L8
Harwood Crs TOT/BURYW BL8 24 B5
Harwood Dr TOT/BURYW BL8 38 D3
Harwood Gv BOLE BL2 * 36 E3
Harwood Meadow BOLE BL2 37 J1
Harwood Rd BNG/LEV M19 99 H6
BOLE BL2 23 L8
HTNM SK4 111 H2
Harwood St HTNM SK4 13 G1
LIT OL15 21 K7
Harwood V BOLE BL2 37 H1
Haseldine St AIMK WN4 63 J6
Haseley Cl POY/DIS SK12 122 A7
RAD M26 37 L7
TYLD M29 67 K4
Haselhurst Wk
NTHM/RTH M23 109 J2
Hasguard Cl BOL BL1 35 J5
Haskoll St HOR/BR BL6 34 A3
Haslam Brow BURY BL9 4 D8
Haslam Hall Ms BOL BL1 35 H5
Haslam Hey Cl BOLE BL2 * 37 M3
TOT/BURYW BL8 38 C2
Haslam Rd EDGY/DAV SK3 112 B6
Haslam St BOLS/LL BL3 2 B9
BURY BL9 25 K8
MDTN M24 * 57 M5
WHIT OL12 10 B2
Haslemere Av
HALE/TIMP WA15 117 L6
Haslemere Dr CHD/CHDH SK8 120 C3
Haslemere Rd DID/WITH M20 99 G6
URM M41 95 L3
Haslington Rd WYTH/NTH M22 119 G2
Hasper Av DID/WITH M20 98 D5
Hassall Av DID/WITH M20 98 C4
Hassall St RAD M26 39 H7
STLY SK15 * 91 L3
Hassnes Cl WGNS/IIMK WN3 63 L2
Hassop Av BRO M7 71 K5
Hassop Cl OP/CLY M11 88 B3
Hassop Rd RDSH SK5 100 D3
Hastings Av CCHDY M21 97 K4
WHTF M45 55 L5
Hastings Cl CHD/CHDH SK8 120 E2
STKP SK1 112 E5
WHTF M45 55 L5
Hastings Dr URM M41 95 H1
Hastings Rd BOL BL1 35 L4
ECC M30 69 K8
PWCH M25 55 M7
Hastings St ROCH OL11 10 F8
Haston Cl RDSH SK5 100 C8
Hasty La HALE/TIMP WA15 118 B5
Hatchett Rd WYTH/NTH M22 119 G3
Hatchmere Cl CHD/CHDH SK8 111 J8
HALE/TIMP WA15 109 G6
Hatfield Av BNG/LEV M19 99 J6
Hatfield Rd BOL BL1 35 M3
Hatford Cl TYLD M29 67 M3
Hathaway Ct LEIGH WN7 66 E6
Hathaway Dr BOL BL1 22 D7
Hathaway Gdns
MPL/ROM SK6 113 J1
Hathaway Rd BURY BL9 55 K1
Hathaway Wk WGNS/IIMK WN3 48 C8
Hatherley Rd DID/WITH M20 99 G6
Hatherlow MPL/ROM SK6 113 K2
Hatherlow La BRAM/HZG SK7 121 M2
Hatherop Cl ECC M30 84 E3
Hathersage Crs GLSP SK13 104 B2
Hathersage Dr GLSP SK13 105 J4
Hathersage Rd
BRUN/LGST M13 87 M8
Hathershaw St CHAD OL9 8 C7
Hathershaw La OLDS OL8 75 J1
Hatro Ct URM M41 96 D3
Hatters Ct STKP SK1 13 K7
Hattersley Rd East HYDE SK14 103 H2
Hattersley Rd West
HYDE SK14 102 F3
Hatter St ANC M4 7 J2
Hatton Av ATH M46 51 G7
Hatton Fold ATH M46 66 E2
Hatton Gv BOL BL1 22 D7
Hattons Ct STRET M32 96 F1
Hattons Rd TRPK M17 85 L6
Hatton St STKP SK1 13 H3
WGTN/LGST M12 99 K1
Haugh Hill Rd OLDE OL4 60 B1
Haugh La MILN OL16 29 M8
Haughton Cl MPL/ROM SK6 101 K6
Haughton Dr WYTH/NTH M22 110 A3
Haughton Green Rd
DTN/ASHW M34 101 L4
Haughton Hall Rd
DTN/ASHW M34 101 K1
Haughton St DTN/ASHW M34 90 C7
HYDE SK14 102 B3
Havana Cl OP/CLY M11 88 C3
Haveley Rd WYTH/NTH M22 109 M7
Havelock Dr BRO M7 72 A8
Havelock St OLDS OL8 9 J9
Havenbrook Gv RAMS BL0 * 24 D1
Haven Cl BRAM/HZG SK7 121 L3
OLDE OL4 61 G6
RAD M26 38 A7
Haven Dr DROY M43 89 H2
Haven La OLDE OL4 60 B1
Havenscroft Av ECC M30 85 G4
Havenside Cl OLDE OL4 60 B1
Haven St SLFD M6 86 B3
The Haven HALE/TIMP WA15 117 H1
Havenwood Rd WGN WN1 31 L8
Havercroft Cl
WGNS/IIMK WN3 63 H1
Haverfield Rd BKLY M9 73 H1
Haverford St WGTN/LGST M12 88 C6
Haverhill Gv BOLE BL2 36 E2
Haversham Rd CHH M8 72 B2
Havers Rd GTN M18 89 H7
Havisham Cl HOR/BR BL6 34 E8
Hawarde Cl NEWLW WA12 78 D8
Hawarden Av
OLDTF/WHR M16 97 M2
Hawarden Rd ALT WA14 108 A6
Hawarden St BOL BL1 22 B8
Haw Clough La UPML OL3 61 M6
Hawdraw Gn OFTN SK2 113 H6
Hawes Av FWTH BL4 52 B5
RUSH/FAL M14 99 H5
SWIN M27 * 70 C6
Hawes Cl OFTN SK2 112 D6
TOT/BURYW BL8 24 E7
Hawes Crs AIMK WN4 63 L7
Haweswater Av TYLD M29 67 L5
WGNE/HIN WN2 48 E5
Haweswater Cl
DTN/ASHW M34 100 D2
Haweswater Crs
BURY BL9 39 L7
Haweswater Dr
MDTN M24 57 H2
Hawfinch Gv
WALK M28 69 G4
Hawk Cl BURY BL9 5 K1
Hawker Av BOLS/LL BL3 52 A1
Hawkeshead Rd CHH M8 72 E6
Hawke St STLY SK15 91 M3
Hawk Green Rd
MPL/ROM SK6 123 H1
Hawkhurst Rd
BRUN/LGST M13 99 J1
Hawkhurst St LEIGH WN7 66 F8
Hawkins St RDSH SK5 100 B8
Hawkley Av
WGNS/IIMK WN3 63 J2
Hawkridge Cl WHTN BL5 50 C6
Hawkridge Dr
NTHM/RTH M23 109 J2
Hawkrigg Cl
WGNNW/ST WN6 31 J5
Hawk Rd IRL M44 94 D1
NM/HAY SK22 124 F4
Hawkshaw Cl TOT/BURYW BL8 23 L1
WGNE/HIN WN2 48 D1
Hawkshaw Ct ORD M5 86 D3
Hawkshaw La TOT/BURYW BL8 17 L6
Hawkshaw St HOR/BR BL6 33 L2
Hawkshead Dr BOLS/LL BL3 51 K1
MDTN M24 57 H3
ROY/SHW OL2 43 G6
Hawkshead Fold GLSP SK13 105 H1
Hawkshead Rd GLSP SK13 105 H2
ROY/SHW OL2 43 K4
Hawksheath Cl EDGW/EG BL7 22 C3
Hawksley St HOR/BR BL6 34 A2
OLDS OL8 74 F1
Hawksmoor Dr ROY/SHW OL2 43 L4
Hawkstone Av DROY M43 89 H1
WHTF M45 55 G5
Hawkstone Cl BOLE BL2 37 H1
Hawkswick Dr
NTHM/RTH M23 109 K2
Hawkworth TYLD M29 67 L7
Hawley Dr HALE/TIMP WA15 117 K4
Hawley Gn WHIT OL12 28 A2
Hawley La HALE/TIMP WA15 117 K4
Hawley St BNG/LEV M19 99 L4
Haworth Av RAMS BL0 24 E2
Haworth Cl BURY BL9 39 J6
Haworth Dr STRET M32 96 D1
Haworth Rd GTN M18 88 F8
Haworth St EDGW/EG BL7 17 G7
OLD OL1 9 H2
RAD M26 54 E1
TOT/BURYW BL8 24 C8
WGNE/HIN WN2 * 49 G6
Hawthorn Av AIMK WN4 62 F7
ECC M30 85 G1
HALE/TIMP WA15 108 C5
MPL/ROM SK6 114 A6
RAD M26 54 E3
RAMS BL0 19 H2
RAMS BL0 24 D2
TOT/BURYW BL8 24 F8
URM M41 96 C3
WALK M28 69 H3
WGN WN1 31 L6
WGNE/HIN WN2 65 K1
WGNW/BIL/OR WN5 46 C6
WGNW/BIL/OR WN5 47 G6
WILM/AE SK9 126 E5
Hawthorn Bank GLSP SK13 93 J8
Hawthorn Cl HALE/TIMP WA15 108 C5
TYLD M29 68 A3
WGNW/BIL/OR WN5 62 A7
Hawthorn Crs OLDS OL8 75 J2
ROY/SHW OL2 * 43 L6
TOT/BURYW BL8 24 C5
Hawthorn Dr BNG/LEV M19 99 J5
IRL M44 94 A7
SLFD M6 70 D8
STLY SK15 91 J4
SWIN M27 70 F5
Hawthorne Av FWTH BL4 52 E4
GOL/RIS/CUL WA3 81 M7
HOR/BR BL6 34 B3
Hawthorne Dr WALK M28 69 L5
Hawthorne Gv AULW OL7 90 C3
CHAD OL9 8 B3
LEIGH WN7 * 66 B5
MPL/ROM SK6 101 H8
POY/DIS SK12 122 E8
Hawthorne Rd BOLS/LL BL3 35 L8
Hawthorne St BOLS/LL BL3 35 L7
Hawthorn Gv BRAM/HZG SK7 120 E6
HTNM SK4 12 A1
HYDE SK14 93 G6
HYDE SK14 102 A3
WILM/AE SK9 126 F5
Hawthorn La CCHDY M21 * 97 J4
SALE M33 96 A6
WILM/AE SK9 126 E5
Hawthorn Pk WILM/AE SK9 126 E5
Hawthorn Rd CHD/CHDH SK8 110 D7
DROY M43 89 M2
DTN/ASHW M34 89 L8
FWTH BL4 53 L7
HALE/TIMP WA15 117 G1
HTNM SK4 111 H2
NEWH/MOS M40 74 B3
OLDS OL8 74 E3
ROCH OL11 27 H6
STRET M32 97 H4
WHTN BL5 50 C5
Hawthorn Rd South
DROY M43 89 M2
The Hawthorns
DTN/ASHW M34 90 A6
Hawthorn St DTN/ASHW M34 90 B6
GTN M18 89 G6
WILM/AE SK9 126 E6
Hawthorn Ter HTNM SK4 12 A1
Hawthorn Vw WILM/AE SK9 126 E5
Hawthorn Wk LIT OL15 21 K7
WILM/AE SK9 * 126 E5
Hawthorpe Gv UPML OL3 61 L4
Haxby Rd GTN M18 100 A1
Haxey Wk HOR/BR BL6 33 J1
Haybarn Rd NTHM/RTH M23 109 L5
Hayburn Rd OFTN SK2 112 F4
Haycock Cl STLY SK15 92 B5
Hay Cft CHD/CHDH SK8 120 A4
Haydn Av RUSH/FAL M14 87 L8
Haydn Fold GLSP SK13 104 A6
Haydock Av SALE M33 107 M2
Haydock Cl STRET M32 86 C8
Haydock Dr BRAM/HZG SK7 122 B2
HALE/TIMP WA15 108 E7
WALK M28 68 E6
Haydock La EDGW/EG BL7 22 E4
RNFD/HAY WA11 78 A4
Haydock Park Gdns
NEWLW WA12 78 E3
Haydock St AIMK WN4 78 E2
BOL BL1 2 E2
NEWLW WA12 78 D8
Haye's Rd IRL M44 94 B7
Hayes St LEIGH WN7 65 K8
LEIGH WN7 66 B5
Hayeswater Rd URM M41 84 F8
Hayfell Rd WGNS/IIMK WN3 63 K3
Hayfield Av MPL/ROM SK6 101 K8
TYLD M29 67 M6
Hayfield Cl MDTN M24 57 M1
OLDE OL4 44 C8
TOT/BURYW BL8 24 C3
WGTN/LGST M12 88 B6
Hayfield Rd MPL/ROM SK6 101 K8
NM/HAY SK22 125 G3
SLFD M6 70 E8
Hayfield St SALE M33 96 D8
Hayfield Wk HALE/TIMP WA15 108 F6
Hayle Rd OLD OL1 44 A8
Hayley St WGTN/LGST M12 * 88 B8
Hayling Cl TOT/BURYW BL8 24 F7
Hayling Rd SALE M33 96 B7
Haymaker Ri WHIT OL12 21 G6
Hayman Av LEIGH WN7 81 G2
Haymarket St BURY BL9 4 E5
The Haymarket BURY BL9 4 F4
Haymill Av LHULT M38 52 D6
Haymond Cl SLFD M6 71 K6
Haynes St BOLS/LL BL3 51 L1
WHIT OL12 10 F2
Haysbrook Av LHULT M38 52 C8
Haysbrook Cl AULW OL7 75 K5
Haythorp Av WYTH/NTH M22 119 G1
Hayward Av BOLS/LL BL3 53 M1
Hayward Gv WGNNW/ST WN6 31 G2
Haywards Cl GLSP SK13 104 F1
Hayward St TOT/BURYW BL8 4 A2
Haywood Cl GOL/RIS/CUL WA3 80 B3
Hazel Av AUL OL6 76 B6
BURY BL9 5 L4
CHD/CHDH SK8 111 H7
LHULT M38 52 B7
MILN OL16 43 K1
MPL/ROM SK6 114 A2
OLDTF/WHR M16 98 A2
RAD M26 53 K4
RAMS BL0 24 E3
SALE M33 108 E1
SWIN M27 70 D5
TOT/BURYW BL8 24 C7
WGNNW/ST WN6 31 K8
WHTN BL5 50 C5
Hazelbadge Cl POY/DIS SK12 121 L8
Hazelbadge Rd POY/DIS SK12 121 L8
Hazelbank Av DID/WITH M20 98 E5
Hazelbottom Rd CHH M8 72 E5
Hazel Cl DROY M43 89 M2
MPL/ROM SK6 114 B8
Hazelcroft WILM/AE SK9 130 D4
Hazeldene WHTN BL5 50 A7
Hazel-dene Cl BURY BL9 39 J5
Hazeldene Rd NEWH/MOS M40 74 B3
Hazel Dr OFTN SK2 113 G6
POY/DIS SK12 129 K1
WYTH/NTH M22 119 J4
Hazelfields WALK M28 69 L5
Hazel Gv CHAD OL9 8 B2
FWTH BL4 52 E4
GOL/RIS/CUL WA3 79 L4
LEIGH WN7 66 B5
ORD M5 85 M2
RAD M26 54 C4
URM M41 96 B2
Hazel Hall La TOT/BURYW BL8 24 E3
Hazelhurst Cl BOL BL1 36 B2
RAMS BL0 18 E8
Hazelhurst Dr MDTN M24 41 J8
Hazelhurst Fold WALK M28 69 M5
Hazelhurst Rd AUL OL6 76 C6
STLY SK15 76 D8
WALK M28 69 L5
Hazel La OLDS OL8 75 G2
Hazelmere Av ECC M30 69 L8
Hazelmere Gdns
WGNE/HIN WN2 49 H8
Hazel Mt EDGW/EG BL7 22 B2
Hazel Rd ALT WA14 108 A7
ATH M46 50 F8
CHD/CHDH SK8 120 D3
MDTN M24 57 L2
STLY SK15 91 M1
WHTF M45 55 L4
Hazel St BRAM/HZG SK7 * 122 A1
DTN/ASHW M34 90 B6
RAMS BL0 18 D8
Hazel Ter BKLY M9 * 57 G8
Hazelton Cl LEIGH WN7 81 H3
Hazelwell SALE M33 108 E1
Hazelwood CHAD OL9 58 B5
Hazelwood Av BOLE BL2 37 H1
Hazelwood Cl HYDE SK14 102 D2
Hazelwood Dr BURY BL9 25 J5
DTN/ASHW M34 90 B6
Hazelwood Rd BOL BL1 35 L2
BRAM/HZG SK7 122 A2
HALE/TIMP WA15 117 G2
OFTN SK2 112 D8
WGN WN1 31 L8
WILM/AE SK9 127 H4
WYTH/NTH M22 118 F4
Hazlehurst Gv AIMK WN4 78 F1
Hazlemere FWTH BL4 53 K5
Headen Av
WGNW/BIL/OR WN5 46 E7
Headingley Dr
OLDTF/WHR M16 97 K1
Headingley Rd RUSH/FAL M14 99 G5
Headingley Wy BOLS/LL BL3 52 A1
Headland Cl GOL/RIS/CUL WA3 80 B6
Headlands Dr PWCH M25 71 K2
Headlands Rd BRAM/HZG SK7 121 H3
Headlands St WHIT OL12 28 B3
Heady Hill Cl HEY OL10 40 D3
Heady Hill Rd HEY OL10 40 D2
Heald Av RUSH/FAL M14 98 E1
Heald Cl ALT WA14 116 E2
LIT OL15 29 K1
WHIT OL12 27 M1
Heald Dr ALT WA14 116 E2
WHIT OL12 27 M1
Heald Gv CHD/CHDH SK8 119 J3
RUSH/FAL M14 98 E1
Heald La LIT OL15 29 K1
Heald Pl RUSH/FAL M14 98 E1
Heald Rd ALT WA14 116 E2
Healds Gn OLD OL1 58 C1
Heald St STKP SK1 13 L2
Healdwood Rd MPL/ROM SK6 101 M8
Healey Av HEY OL10 41 H1
WHIT OL12 20 B8
Healey Cl BRO M7 71 M4
NTHM/RTH M23 109 J2
Healey Gv WHIT OL12 20 A7
Healey La WHIT OL12 20 C8
Healey St MILN OL16 10 D6
Healing St ROCH OL11 11 H9
Heanor Av DTN/ASHW M34 101 K4
Heap Br BURY BL9 39 M2
Heap Brow BURY BL9 40 A3
Heape St ROCH OL11 41 M3
Heaplands TOT/BURYW BL8 24 C3
Heap Rd WHIT OL12 27 G2
Heaps Farm Ct STLY SK15 92 A4
Heap St BOLS/LL BL3 36 B8
BURY BL9 40 A3
OLDE OL4 59 M5
RAD M26 54 E1
WHTF M45 * 55 J5
Heapworth Av RAMS BL0 18 E6
Heapy Cl TOT/BURYW BL8 38 C2
Heardman Av WGNNW/ST WN6 14 B1
Heath Av BRO M7 71 M8
RAMS BL0 24 E3
Heathbank Rd BKLY M9 56 F7
CHD/CHDH SK8 120 B4
EDGY/DAV SK3 12 B9
Heathcliffe Wk
BRUN/LGST M13 87 M7
Heath Cl BOLS/LL BL3 51 L2
Heathcote Av HTNM SK4 111 M1
Heathcote Rd GTN M18 88 F8
Heath Crs OFTN SK2 112 C7
Heather Av DROY M43 89 M2
IRL M44 94 A6
ROY/SHW OL2 44 A4
Heather Bank
TOT/BURYW BL8 * 24 B5
Heather Bank Cl GLSP SK13 104 D5
Heather Brae NEWLW WA12 78 D8
Heather Brow STLY SK15 92 B5
Heather Cl OLDE OL4 60 B3
Heatherdale Dr CHH M8 72 D6
Heather Falls NM/HAY SK22 124 D4
Heatherfield BOL BL1 22 A7
EDGW/EG BL7 17 H6
Heatherfield Ct WILM/AE SK9 127 J4
Heather Gv AIMK WN4 64 B8
DROY M43 89 L4
HYDE SK14 93 G6
LEIGH WN7 66 B5
WGNW/BIL/OR WN5 47 H5
Heather Lea DTN/ASHW M34 101 K2
Heather Rd ALT WA14 117 G3
Heatherside RDSH SK5 100 D3
STLY SK15 92 A2
Heatherside Av MOSL OL5 77 H3
Heatherside Rd RAMS BL0 18 E5
The Heathers OFTN SK2 112 E8
Heather St OP/CLY M11 88 E2
Heather Wy MPL/ROM SK6 114 B7
Heatherway SALE M33 96 A7
Heath Farm La PART M31 106 E1
Heathfield BOLE BL2 23 J8
FWTH BL4 53 H3
WALK M28 69 J7
WILM/AE SK9 126 E7
Heathfield Av CHD/CHDH SK8 110 E7
DTN/ASHW M34 101 G2
HTNM SK4 99 M7
Heathfield Cl SALE M33 109 J1
Heathfield Dr BOLS/LL BL3 51 L2
SWIN M27 70 D6
TYLD M29 68 A3
Heathfield Rd BURY BL9 55 J1
OFTN SK2 112 C6
Heathfields UPML OL3 61 M4
Heathfield St NEWH/MOS M40 73 M7
Heath Gdns WGNE/HIN WN2 65 M1
Heathland Rd BRO M7 71 L3
Heathlands Dr PWCH M25 71 K3
Heathland Ter EDGY/DAV SK3 13 H9
Heath La GOL/RIS/CUL WA3 80 A6
LEIGH WN7 65 L7
Heathlea WGNE/HIN WN2 65 M2
Heathlea Cl BOL BL1 22 B6
Heathmoor Av
GOL/RIS/CUL WA3 80 A6
Heath Pl BRO M7 71 M8
Heath Rd AIMK WN4 78 E2
ALT WA14 116 F2
GLSP SK13 104 F1
HALE/TIMP WA15 108 C4
OFTN SK2 112 C6
WHIT OL12 21 G6
Heathside Gv WALK M28 69 G1
Heathside Park Rd
EDGY/DAV SK3 111 J5
Heathside Rd DID/WITH M20 98 F7
EDGY/DAV SK3 111 K5
Heath St AIMK WN4 78 F2
CHH M8 72 C5
GOL/RIS/CUL WA3 79 K4
ROCH OL11 10 B6
The Heath AULW OL7 75 K5
GLSP SK13 104 F1
MDTN M24 57 L6
Heathwood UPML OL3 61 M4
Heathwood Rd BNG/LEV M19 99 H8
Heatley Rd MILN OL16 29 G6
Heaton Av BOL BL1 35 J3
BOLE BL2 23 H7
BOLS/LL BL3 37 K8
BRAM/HZG SK7 120 F1
FWTH BL4 52 F4
Heaton Cl BURY BL9 39 K7
HTNM SK4 111 K1
Heaton Ct BURY BL9 39 H5
Heaton Dr BURY BL9 39 K7
Heaton Fold BURY BL9 4 E9
Heaton Grange Dr BOL BL1 35 K5
Heaton Gv BURY BL9 39 H5
Heaton La HTNM SK4 12 F4
Heaton Moor Rd HTNM SK4 111 L1
Heaton Mt BOL BL1 35 J3
Heaton Park Rd BKLY M9 56 D7
Heaton Park Rd West BKLY M9 56 D7
Heaton Rd BOLE BL2 37 L7
DID/WITH M20 98 F5
HOR/BR BL6 35 G6
HTNM SK4 112 A1
Heatons Gv WHTN BL5 50 D2
Heaton St BRO M7 72 B5
DTN/ASHW M34 101 G1
MDTN M24 56 E5
MILN OL16 29 K7
PWCH M25 55 M8
WGN WN1 47 M2
WGNE/HIN WN2 33 G6
WGNNW/ST WN6 31 H3
WGNS/IIMK WN3 15 K7
Heaviley Gv OFTN SK2 112 D6
Hebble Butt Cl MILN OL16 * 29 H6
Hebble Cl BOLE BL2 22 E7
Hebburn Dr TOT/BURYW BL8 24 F7
Hebburn Wk RUSH/FAL M14 87 L8
Hebden Av GOL/RIS/CUL WA3 81 M8
MPL/ROM SK6 101 K8
SLFD M6 85 M1
Hebden Dr GLSP SK13 105 J4
Hebden Wk HULME M15 87 J7
Hebdon Cl AIMK WN4 63 K7
Heber Pl LIT OL15 21 M7
Heber St RAD M26 54 D1
WGNE/HIN WN2 48 C5
Hebron St ROY/SHW OL2 59 K1
Hector Av MILN OL16 11 J2
Hector Rd BRUN/LGST M13 99 J1
WGNW/BIL/OR WN5 47 G3
Heddles Ct LEIGH WN7 * 66 B8
Heddon Cl HTNM SK4 111 H1
Hedgemead WGNNW/ST WN6 14 B2
Hedge Rows WHIT OL12 20 A2
The Hedgerows HYDE SK14 102 D1
RNFD/HAY WA11 78 C5
Hedges St FAIL M35 74 D4
Hedley St BOL BL1 35 M2
Heeley St WGN WN1 47 L2
Heginbottom Crs AUL OL6 75 M7
Heights Av WHIT OL12 28 B3
Heights Cl WHIT OL12 28 B2
Heights La OLD OL1 58 C2
UPML OL3 45 G5
WHIT OL12 28 B3
The Heights HOR/BR BL6 34 A3
Helena St SLFD M6 70 F7
Helen St AIMK WN4 63 K8
BRO M7 71 M7
ECC M30 84 E4
FWTH BL4 53 G4
GOL/RIS/CUL WA3 79 J3
Helensville Av SLFD M6 71 J7
Helga St NEWH/MOS M40 73 G8
Helias Cl WALK M28 68 C1
Hell Nook GOL/RIS/CUL WA3 79 J3
Helmclough Wy WALK M28 68 F4
Helmet St CMANE M1 7 M7
Helmsdale WALK M28 68 F2
Helmsdale Av BOLS/LL BL3 35 J6
Helmsdale Cl RAMS BL0 24 D1
Helmshore Av OLDE OL4 60 A1
Helmshore Rd TOT/BURYW BL8 18 D4
Helmshore Wk BRUN/LGST M13 * 7 K9
Helmshore Wy ROY/SHW OL2 43 L4
Helmsman Wy
WGNS/IIMK WN3 14 D9
Helsby Cl OLDE OL4 60 D6
Helsby Gdns BOL BL1 22 C8
Helsby Rd SALE M33 109 H2
Helsby Wk WGTN/LGST M12 88 B4
Helsby Wy WGNS/IIMK WN3 62 F2
Helston Cl BRAM/HZG SK7 121 H5
IRL M44 94 E2
Helston Dr ROY/SHW OL2 43 J8
Helston Gv CHD/CHDH SK8 119 L4
Helston Wy TYLD M29 67 M4
Helvellyn Dr MDTN M24 57 G2
Helvellyn Rd
WGNW/BIL/OR WN5 46 E5
Helvellyn Wk OLD OL1 9 L1
Hembury Av BNG/LEV M19 99 J6
Hembury Cl MDTN M24 57 L2
Hemfield Cl WGNE/HIN WN2 48 E4
Hemfield Ct WGNE/HIN WN2 48 F4
Hemfield Rd WGNE/HIN WN2 48 F4
Hemley Cl WHTN BL5 50 A6
Hemlock Av OLDS OL8 75 H1
Hemming Dr ECC M30 85 H3
Hemmington Dr BKLY M9 73 G5
Hemmons Rd WGTN/LGST M12 99 L2
Hempcroft Rd
HALE/TIMP WA15 108 F7
Hempshaw La STKP SK1 13 K8
Hemsley St BKLY M9 73 H3
Hemsley St South BKLY M9 73 H4
Hemswell Cl SLFD M6 71 H8
Hemsworth Rd BOL BL1 2 B2
GTN M18 100 A1
Henbury Dr MPL/ROM SK6 101 L6
Henbury La CHD/CHDH SK8 120 B6
Henbury Rd WILM/AE SK9 * 119 M8
Henbury St OFTN SK2 112 F8
RUSH/FAL M14 98 D1
Henderson Av SWIN M27 70 C3
Henderson St BNG/LEV M19 99 L4
LIT OL15 21 L7
WHIT OL12 28 E2
Henderville St LIT OL15 21 L6
Hendham Cl BRAM/HZG SK7 121 J2
Hendham Dr ALT WA14 107 L7
Hendham V BKLY M9 72 F5
Hendon Dr BURY BL9 39 J7
EDGY/DAV SK3 111 K5
Hendon Gv LEIGH WN7 66 C4
Hendon Rd BKLY M9 56 F8
WGNW/BIL/OR WN5 47 G4

Hendon St *LEIGH* WN7 ... 66 C4
Hendriff Pl *WHIT* OL12 ... 28 C3
Hen Fold Rd *TYLD* M29 ... 67 M5
Hengist St *BOLE* BL2 ... 3 M4
  *GTN* M18 ... 89 G8
Henley Av *CHD/CHDH* SK8 ... 120 B2
  *IRL* M44 ... 94 B6
  *OLDTF/WHR* M16 ... 97 L1
Henley Cl *TOT/BURYW* BL8 ... 38 E4
Henley Dr *AULW* OL7 ... 75 J8
  *HALE/TIMP* WA15 ... 108 C5
Henley Gv *BOLS/LL* BL3 ... 51 M1
Henley Pl *BNG/LEV* M19 ... 99 K6
Henley St *CHAD* OL9 ... 74 D1
  *OLD* OL1 ... 8 F2
  *WGNE/HIN* WN2 ... 32 E6
  *WHIT* OL12 ... 10 D1
Henley Ter *ROCH* OL11 ... 10 C9
Henniker Rd *BOLS/LL* BL3 ... 51 K2
Henniker St *SWIN* M27 ... 70 B6
  *WALK* M28 ... 69 G3
Hennon St *BOL* BL1 ... 36 A3
Henrietta St *AUL* OL6 ... 75 L8
  *BOLS/LL* BL3 ... 35 L8
  *LEIGH* WN7 ... 66 C7
  *OLDTF/WHR* M16 ... 86 F7
Henry Herman St *BOLS/LL* BL3 ... 51 M1
Henry Lee St *BOLS/LL* BL3 ... 51 M1
Henry Park St *WGN* WN1 ... 15 L5
Henry St *ANC* M4 ... 3 G7
  *BOLE* BL2 ... 3 G7
  *DROY* M43 ... 89 K3
  *DTN/ASHW* M34 * ... 101 L4
  *ECC* M30 ... 84 F3
  *FAIL* M35 ... 74 C5
  *GLSP* SK13 ... 104 F3
  *HYDE* SK14 ... 102 A2
  *LEIGH* WN7 ... 81 K1
  *LIT* OL15 ... 29 J1
  *MDTN* M24 ... 57 J4
  *OLDTF/WHR* M16 ... 86 F7
  *PWCH* M25 ... 55 M7
  *RAMS* BL0 ... 19 G1
  *ROCH* OL11 ... 10 E6
  *STKP* SK1 ... 112 E4
  *TYLD* M29 ... 67 K3
  *WGNS/IIMK* WN3 ... 48 B8
  *WHIT* OL12 ... 21 G1
Henshall Av *ALT* WA14 ... 106 F1
Henshaw Ct *OLDTF/WHR* M16 ... 86 E8
Henshaw La *CHAD* OL9 ... 74 C2
Henshaw St *OLD* OL1 ... 9 H5
  *STRET* M32 ... 97 G2
Henshaw Wk *BOL* BL1 ... 36 B2
Henson Gv *HALE/TIMP* WA15 ... 108 D8
Henthorn St *ROY/SHW* OL2 ... 43 L6
Henton Wk *NEWH/MOS* M40 ... 72 F8
Henty Cl *ECC* M30 ... 84 E3
Henwick Hall Av *RAMS* BL0 ... 18 E8
Henwood Rd *DID/WITH* M20 ... 98 F7
Hepley Rd *POY/DIS* SK12 ... 129 J1
Hepple Cl *HTNM* SK4 ... 111 H5
Heppleton Rd *NEWH/MOS* M40 ... 74 A2
Hepple Wk *AULW* OL7 * ... 75 H7
Hepton St *OLD* OL1 ... 9 G3
Hepworth Cl *GOL/RIS/CUL* WA3 ... 79 J2
Hepworth St *HYDE* SK14 ... 102 B5
Herbert St *BOLS/LL* BL3 ... 53 L1
  *CHAD* OL9 ... 8 B5
  *CHH* M8 * ... 72 C7
  *DROY* M43 ... 89 J3
  *DTN/ASHW* M34 ... 90 D8
  *EDGY/DAV* SK3 ... 12 F8
  *OLDE* OL4 ... 60 A3
  *PWCH* M25 ... 55 J8
  *RAD* M26 ... 38 C7
  *STRET* M32 ... 97 G2
  *WGNS/IIMK* WN3 ... 14 D5
  *WHTN* BL5 ... 50 B3
Hereford Av
  *GOL/RIS/CUL* WA3 * ... 79 L4
  *AUL* OL6 ... 76 A5
  *ROY/SHW* OL2 ... 43 J5
Hereford Crs *BOLS/LL* BL3 ... 37 L8
Hereford Dr *BURY* BL9 ... 5 C8
  *PWCH* M25 ... 71 M2
  *SWIN* M27 ... 70 C3
  *WILM/AE* SK9 ... 127 J1
Hereford Gv *URM* M41 ... 95 M2
Hereford Rd *BOL* BL1 ... 35 L4
  *CHD/CHDH* SK8 ... 111 K8
  *ECC* M30 ... 70 D7
  *RDSH* SK5 ... 100 F7
  *WGNE/HIN* WN2 ... 49 J6
Hereford St *BOL* BL1 ... 36 C2
  *CHAD* OL9 ... 8 C8
  *ROCH* OL11 ... 11 G8
  *SALE* M33 ... 96 E8
  *STLY* SK15 ... 92 A5
Hereford Wy *MDTN* M24 ... 57 M3
Herevale Gra *WALK* M28 ... 68 E5
Herevale Hall Dr *RAMS* BL0 ... 18 E8
Heriston Av *DTN/ASHW* M34 ... 101 H1
Heritage Gdns *DID/WITH* M20 ... 110 C2
Herle Dr *WYTH/NTH* M22 ... 118 E3
Hermitage Av *MPL/ROM* SK6 ... 114 C2
Hermitage Cl *WGNNW/ST* WN6 ... 30 B5
Hermitage Gdns
  *MPL/ROM* SK6 ... 114 C2
  *HALE/TIMP* WA15 ... 117 J1
Hermon Av *OLDS* OL8 ... 75 H1
Herne St *OP/CLY* M11 ... 88 D4
Heron Av *DUK* SK16 ... 91 H5
Heron Cl *GLSP* SK13 ... 105 J4
Heron Ct *SLFD* M6 ... 85 L1
Herondale Cl *NEWH/MOS* M40 ... 73 L7
Heron Dr *DTN/ASHW* M34 ... 89 M3
  *IRL* M44 ... 94 D1
  *POY/DIS* SK12 ... 128 E1
  *WGNS/IIMK* WN3 ... 63 H2
Heron Ml *OLDS* OL8 * ... 75 G1
Heron Pl *WGNNW/BIL/OR* WN5 ... 46 F4
Heron St *EDGY/DAV* SK3 ... 12 A7
  *HULME* M15 ... 87 H7
  *OLDS* OL8 ... 74 F1
  *SWIN* M27 ... 70 D3
Heron's Wy *BOLE* BL2 ... 3 G8
Herons Whf *WGNNW/ST* WN6 ... 30 A5
Heron Vw *GLSP* SK13 ... 104 C3
Herries St *AUL* OL6 ... 76 A8
Herristone Av *CHH* M8 ... 72 D2
Herrod Av *HTNM* SK4 ... 100 B7
Herschel St *NEWH/MOS* M40 ... 73 K4
Hersey St *SLFD* M6 ... 86 B2
Hertford Dr *TYLD* M29 ... 67 M3
Hertford Rd *BKLY* M9 ... 73 J5
Hertfordshire Park Cl
  *ROY/SHW* OL2 ... 43 L4
Hertford St *AULW* OL7 ... 90 D3
Hesford Av *BKLY* M9 ... 73 J5

Hesketh Av *BOL* BL1 ... 22 C7
  *DID/WITH* M20 ... 110 D1
  *ROY/SHW* OL2 ... 43 K7
Hesketh Ct *ATH* M46 ... 66 F1
Hesketh Dr *WGNNW/ST* WN6 ... 30 D2
Hesketh Meadow La
  *GOL/RIS/CUL* WA3 ... 80 C3
Hesketh Rd *MILN* OL16 ... 11 L4
  *SALE* M33 ... 108 C1
Hesketh St *ATH* M46 ... 51 G8
  *HTNM* SK4 * ... 13 G1
  *LEIGH* WN7 ... 66 A7
  *WGNW/BIL/OR* WN5 ... 47 H5
Hesnall Cl *GOL/RIS/CUL* WA3 ... 81 M4
Hessel St *SALQ* M50 ... 86 A3
Hester Wk *HULME* M15 * ... 87 J6
Heston Av *BRUN/LGST* M13 ... 99 H2
Heston Dr *URM* M41 ... 95 M1
Heswall Av *DID/WITH* M20 ... 98 E5
Heswall Dr *TOT/BURYW* BL8 ... 24 B7
Heswall Rd *RDSH* SK5 ... 100 C3
Hetherington Wk
  *WGTN/LGST* M12 ... 88 C3
Hethorn St *NEWH/MOS* M40 ... 73 M7
Hetton Av *BRUN/LGST* M13 ... 99 H2
Heversham Av *ROY/SHW* OL2 ... 44 A5
Hewart Cl *NEWH/MOS* M40 ... 72 F8
Hewart Dr *BURY* BL9 ... 39 M2
Hewitt Av *DTN/ASHW* M34 ... 100 C1
Hewitt St *HULME* M15 ... 6 D8
Hewlett Rd *CCHDY* M21 ... 97 K3
Hewlett St *BOLE* BL2 ... 3 J8
  *WGN* WN1 ... 15 G4
  *WHTN* BL5 ... 49 L5
Hexham Av *BOL* BL1 ... 35 J3
  *WGNS/IIMK* WN3 ... 63 J1
Hexham Cl *ATH* M46 ... 51 H8
  *CHAD* OL9 ... 8 C4
  *OFTN* SK2 ... 113 H7
Hexham Rd *GTN* M18 ... 88 E8
Hexon Cl *SLFD* M6 ... 86 B1
Hey Bottom La *WHIT* OL12 ... 20 E6
Heybrook Cl *WHTF* M45 ... 55 M4
Heybrook Rd *NTHM/RTH* M23 ... 109 L7
Heybrook St *MILN* OL16 * ... 11 J1
Heybury Cl *OP/CLY* M11 ... 88 C4
Hey Crs *OLDE* OL4 ... 60 A6
Hey Cft *WHTF* M45 ... 54 F5
Heycrofts Vw *RAMS* BL0 ... 19 H1
Heyes Av *HALE/TIMP* WA15 ... 108 E5
  *RNFD/HAY* WA11 ... 78 A7
Heyes Dr *HALE/TIMP* WA15 ... 108 E5
Heyes La *HALE/TIMP* WA15 ... 108 E4
  *WILM/AE* SK9 ... 130 E2
Heyes Leigh
  *HALE/TIMP* WA15 * ... 108 E5
Heyes Rd *WGNW/BIL/OR* WN5 ... 46 B6
Heyes Ter *HALE/TIMP* WA15 * ... 108 E4
Heyford Av *NEWH/MOS* M40 ... 74 A2
Heyford Rd
  *WGNW/BIL/OR* WN5 ... 47 C4
Hey Head La *LIT* OL15 ... 21 M4
Heyheads New Rd *STLY* SK15 ... 77 H5
Hey Hill Cl *ROY/SHW* OL2 ... 43 K7
Heyland Rd *NTHM/RTH* M23 ... 109 K6
Heyridge Dr *WYTH/NTH* M22 ... 110 A3
Heyrod St *CMANE* M1 ... 7 L6
  *STLY* SK15 ... 77 G7
Heyrose Wk *HULME* M15 ... 87 G6
Heys Av *MPL/ROM* SK6 ... 114 B1
  *NTHM/RTH* M23 ... 109 K3
  *SWIN* M27 ... 70 A2
Heysbank Rd *POY/DIS* SK12 ... 123 M7
Heys Cl North *SWIN* M27 ... 69 M2
Heyscroft Rd *DID/WITH* M20 ... 98 F6
  *HTNM* SK4 ... 111 K2
Heysham Av *DID/WITH* M20 ... 98 C5
Heysham Rd
  *WGNW/BIL/OR* WN5 ... 46 E5
Hey Shoot La
  *GOL/RIS/CUL* WA3 ... 81 M7
Heyside Av *ROY/SHW* OL2 ... 43 K8
Heyside Cl *STLY* SK15 ... 77 H6
Heyside Wy *BURY* BL9 ... 5 G6
Heys La *HEY* OL10 ... 40 D2
  *MPL/ROM* SK6 ... 114 B1
Heys Rd *AUL* OL6 ... 91 G1
  *PWCH* M25 ... 55 L7
Heys St *TOT/BURYW* BL8 ... 4 B4
The Heys *AUL* OL6 ... 91 G1
  *PWCH* M25 ... 55 L7
  *RDSH* SK5 ... 100 D3
Hey St *MILN* OL16 ... 11 J3
  *WGNNW/ST* WN6 ... 14 D3
Heys Vw *PWCH* M25 ... 55 L8
The Hey *ROY/SHW* OL2 * ... 44 B3
Heythrop Cl *WHTF* M45 ... 55 H3
Heywood Av *GOL/RIS/CUL* WA3 ... 79 L3
  *OLDE* OL4 ... 60 D4
  *SWIN* M27 ... 70 E2
Heywood Cl *WILM/AE* SK9 ... 130 E2
Heywood Fold Rd *OLDE* OL4 ... 60 C5
Heywood Gdns *BOLS/LL* BL3 ... 36 B8
  *PWCH* M25 ... 55 L8
Heywood Gv *SALE* M33 ... 96 E6
Heywood Hall Rd *HEY* OL10 ... 41 G1
Heywood La *OLDE* OL4 ... 60 D5
Heywood Old Rd *HEY* OL10 ... 40 F8
  *MDTN* M24 ... 56 D4
Heywood Pk *PWCH* M25 ... 71 L1
  *ROCH* OL11 ... 41 L2
  *SALE* M33 ... 108 E1
  *WILM/AE* SK9 ... 130 E2
Heywoods Hollow *BOL* BL1 ... 36 C1
Heywood St *BOL* BL1 ... 2 E1
  *BOLS/LL* BL3 ... 53 L1
  *BURY* BL9 ... 5 H6
  *CHH* M8 ... 72 D6
  *FAIL* M35 ... 74 A5
  *OLDE* OL4 ... 60 B4
  *SWIN* M27 ... 70 B4
Heywood Wy *SLFD* M6 ... 86 C1
Heyworth Av *MPL/ROM* SK6 ... 114 A1
Heyworth St *ORD* M5 * ... 86 B3
  *HYDE* SK14 ... 102 B3
Hibbert Crs *FAIL* M35 ... 74 D5
Hibbert La *MPL/ROM* SK6 ... 114 C7
Hibbert St *BOL* BL1 ... 36 C2
  *HTNM* SK4 ... 100 B7
  *NM/HAY* SK22 * ... 124 D6
  *OLDE* OL4 ... 60 C5
  *RUSH/FAL* M14 ... 98 F1
Hibernia St *BOLS/LL* BL3 ... 35 M7
Hibernia Wy *STRET* M32 ... 85 K7
Hibson Av *WHIT* OL12 ... 27 H2
Hibson Cl *WHIT* OL12 ... 21 G6
Hickenfield Rd *HYDE* SK14 ... 91 J7
Hicken Pl *HYDE* SK14 ... 91 J7

Hickton Dr *ALT* WA14 ... 107 L7
Hieland Rd *WGN* WN1 ... 48 B2
Higginshaw La *OLD* OL1 ... 59 K2
Higginshaw Rd *OLD* OL1 ... 9 L1
Higginson Rd *RDSH* SK5 ... 100 B5
Higgs Cl *OLDE* OL4 ... 60 A5
Higham Cl *ROY/SHW* OL2 ... 43 K7
Higham La *HYDE* SK14 ... 102 C4
Higham St *CHD/CHDH* SK8 ... 120 C4
Higham Vw *SLFD* M6 ... 86 D1
High Ash Gv
  *DTN/ASHW* M34 ... 90 A5
High Av *BOLE* BL2 * ... 37 H5
High Bank *ALT* WA14 ... 108 A7
  *ATH* M46 ... 51 K6
  *EDGW/EG* BL7 ... 22 C5
  *GTN* M18 ... 89 H7
Highbank Dr
  *DID/WITH* M20 ... 110 E4
High Bank Av *STLY* SK15 ... 92 A5
High Bank Cl *IRL* M44 ... 94 A6
Highbank Crs *OLDE* OL4 ... 61 H7
High Bank Crs *PWCH* M25 ... 71 M1
Highbank Dr
  *DID/WITH* M20 ... 110 E4
High Bank Gv *PWCH* M25 ... 71 M1
High Bank La *WHIT* OL12 ... 20 A1
High Bank Rd *MDTN* M24 ... 57 K5
  *DROY* M43 ... 89 J4
  *ROY/SHW* OL2 ... 43 K5
High Bank Side *STKP* SK1 ... 13 J4
High Bank St *BOLE* BL2 * ... 3 M5
High Barn Cl *ROCH* OL11 ... 10 C2
High Barn La *WHIT* OL12 ... 20 A1
High Barn Rd *MDTN* M24 ... 57 K5
  *ROY/SHW* OL2 ... 43 K8
High Beeches *BOLE* BL2 ... 37 L7
High Beeches Crs *AIMK* WN4 ... 63 K6
High Bent Av
  *CHD/CHDH* SK8 ... 120 C6
Highbridge Cl *BOLE* BL2 ... 37 K6
Highbury Av *IRL* M44 ... 94 D3
  *URM* M41 ... 95 H2
Highbury Cl *WHTN* BL5 ... 50 A6
Highbury Rd *HTNM* SK4 ... 99 M6
  *OLDTF/WHR* M16 ... 98 B3
Highbury Wy *ROY/SHW* OL2 ... 43 G6
Highclere Av *CHH* M8 ... 72 C6
Highclere Rd *CHH* M8 ... 72 C6
Highcliffe Ct *WGNNW/ST* WN6 ... 31 J5
Highcliffe Rd *BKLY* M9 ... 72 E3
Highclove La *WALK* M28 ... 68 C7
High Crest Av *CHD/CHDH* SK8 ... 110 C7
Highcroft *BOLE* BL2 ... 36 D1
  *HYDE* SK14 ... 102 B5
Highcroft Av *DID/WITH* M20 ... 98 B8
High Croft Cl *DUK* SK16 ... 91 K4
Highcroft Rd *MPL/ROM* SK6 ... 113 J6
Highcroft Wy *WHIT* OL12 ... 20 D8
Highdales Rd *NTHM/RTH* M23 ... 109 L7
High Elm Dr *HALE/TIMP* WA15 ... 117 M5
High Elm Rd *HALE/TIMP* WA15 ... 117 M5
High Elms *OLDE* OL4 ... 120 D7
Higher Ainsworth Rd *RAD* M26 ... 38 D5
Higher Ardwick
  *WGTN/LGST* M12 ... 7 M9
Higher Arthurs *UPML* OL3 ... 61 L6
Higher Bank Rd *LIT* OL15 ... 29 K1
Higher Barlow Rw *STKP* SK1 ... 13 K6
Higher Barn *HOR/BR* BL6 ... 34 C1
Higher Barn Rd *GLSP* SK13 ... 93 H8
Higher Bents La
  *MPL/ROM* SK6 ... 113 J1
Higher Bridge St *BOL* BL1 * ... 2 E2
Higher Brook Cl *HOR/BR* BL6 ... 34 A3
Higher Bury St *HTNM* SK4 ... 12 E5
Higher Cambridge St
  *HULME* M15 ... 87 K7
Higher Carr La *UPML* OL3 ... 61 L5
Higher Chatham St
  *HULME* M15 * ... 87 K6
Higher Cleggswood Av
  *LIT* OL15 ... 29 K1
Higher Cft *ECC* M30 ... 84 F4
  *WHTF* M45 ... 54 F6
Higher Crossbank *OLDE* OL4 ... 60 F5
Higher Cross La *UPML* OL3 ... 61 M5
Higher Damshead *WHTN* BL5 ... 50 C4
Higher Darcy St *BOLE* BL2 ... 3 L8
Higher Dean St *RAD* M26 ... 54 B1
Higher Downs *ALT* WA14 ... 116 E1
Higher Drake Meadow
  *WHTN* BL5 ... 55 H4
Higher Dunscar *EDGW/EG* BL7 ... 22 B3
Higher Fold Farm
  *MPL/ROM* SK6 ... 123 G3
Higher Fold La *RAMS* BL0 ... 19 H5
Higher Fullwood *OLD* OL1 ... 44 A8
Higher Gn *AUL* OL6 ... 75 M8
Higher Green La *TYLD* M29 ... 67 M6
Higher Henry St *HYDE* SK14 ... 102 A3
Higher Highfield Ct
  *WGNE/HIN* WN2 * ... 32 E6
Higher Hillgate *STKP* SK1 ... 13 K6
Higher House Cl *CHAD* OL9 ... 58 D8
Higher Knowles *HOR/BR* BL6 ... 34 B2
Higher La *WGNE/HIN* WN2 ... 32 D8
High Meadow
  *CHD/CHDH* SK8 * ... 120 A4
Highmeadow *RAD* M26 ... 54 C3
Higher Lime Rd *OLDS* OL8 ... 74 F4
Higher Ldg *WHIT* OL12 ... 26 F2
Higher Lomax La *HEY* OL10 ... 40 E1
Higher Lydgate Pk *OLDE* OL4 ... 60 F6
Higher Market St *FWTH* BL4 ... 53 H4
Higher Mdw *BNG/LEV* M19 ... 99 H3
Higher Ormond St
  *HULME* M15 * ... 87 K6
Higher Oswald St *ANC* M4 ... 7 H2
Higher Pk *ROY/SHW* OL2 ... 43 M3
Higher Pit La *BOLE* BL2 ... 38 B4
Higher Ridings *EDGW/EG* BL7 ... 22 C5
Higher Ri *ROY/SHW* OL2 ... 43 K5
Higher Rd *URM* M41 ... 96 B2
Higher Rw *BURY* BL9 ... 5 K2
Higher Shady La *EDGW/EG* BL7 ... 22 F5
Higher Shore Rd *LIT* OL15 ... 21 J5
Higher Southfield *WHTN* BL5 ... 50 B5
Higher Summerseat *RAMS* BL0 ... 24 E3
Higher Swan La *BOLS/LL* BL3 ... 36 A8
Higher Tame St *STLY* SK15 ... 91 L2
Higher Turf La *OLDE* OL4 ... 60 E4
Higher Turf Pk *ROY/SHW* OL2 ... 59 H1
Higher Wharf St *AULW* OL7 ... 90 E2
Higher Wheat La *MILN* OL16 ... 11 L3
Higher Wood St *MDTN* M24 ... 57 J2
Highfield *CHD/CHDH* SK8 ... 119 L1
  *SALE* M33 ... 108 F1
  *WGNS/IIMK* WN3 ... 47 G8

Highfield Av *ATH* M46 ... 51 H7
  *BOLE* BL2 ... 37 K1
  *GOL/RIS/CUL* WA3 ... 79 J4
  *HEY* OL10 ... 40 D2
  *LEIGH* WN7 ... 81 M1
  *MPL/ROM* SK6 ... 113 J2
  *RAD* M26 ... 54 F3
  *WALK* M28 ... 68 B4
  *WGN* WN1 ... 15 L1
  *WGNNW/ST* WN6 ... 30 D6
Highfield Cl *EDGY/DAV* SK3 ... 112 C3
  *HYDE* SK14 ... 91 J6
  *STRET* M32 ... 96 F4
Highfield Crs *WILM/AE* SK9 ... 127 G3
Highfield Dr *ECC* M30 ... 85 G1
  *FWTH* BL4 ... 52 D5
  *MDTN* M24 ... 57 J5
  *MOSL* OL5 ... 76 F4
  *ROY/SHW* OL2 ... 59 H2
  *SWIN* M27 ... 70 F5
  *URM* M41 ... 95 M1
  *WGNNW/ST* WN6 ... 31 J5
Highfield Est
  *WILM/AE* SK9 ... 127 G3
Highfield Gdns *HYDE* SK9 ... 93 G7
  *HYDE* SK14 ... 102 C1
Highfield Gln *AUL* OL6 ... 76 C7
Highfield Grange Av
  *WGNS/IIMK* WN3 ... 63 G2
Highfield Gv
  *WGNE/HIN* WN2 ... 32 F1
Highfield La *BURY* BL9 ... 55 J7
  *GOL/RIS/CUL* WA3 ... 80 A5
Highfield Pk *HTNM* SK4 ... 111 J2
Highfield Park Rd
  *MPL/ROM* SK6 ... 101 H8
Highfield Pkwy
  *BRAM/HZG* SK7 ... 120 F8
Highfield Pl *GTN* M18 ... 89 H7
  *PWCH* M25 ... 55 K7
Highfield Range *GTN* M18 ... 89 G8
Highfield Rd
  *BNG/LEV* M19 ... 99 M3
  *BOL* BL1 ... 35 L2
  *BRAM/HZG* SK7 ... 121 H1
  *BRAM/HZG* SK7 ... 122 C2
  *CHD/CHDH* SK8 ... 120 B3
  *ECC* M30 ... 70 A8
  *FWTH* BL4 ... 52 B4
  *GLSP* SK13 ... 105 G4
  *HALE/TIMP* WA15 ... 108 E7
  *HALE/TIMP* WA15 ... 117 J2
  *HOR/BR* BL6 ... 33 H3
  *LHULT* M38 ... 52 C7
  *MILN* OL16 ... 29 K6
  *MPL/ROM* SK6 ... 114 C7
  *NM/HAY* SK22 ... 125 M1
  *POY/DIS* SK12 ... 121 J8
  *PWCH* M25 ... 55 K6
  *RAMS* BL0 ... 19 G1
  *ROCH* OL11 ... 27 H3
  *SLFD* M6 ... 86 C1
  *STRET* M32 ... 96 F4
Highfield St *BRO* M7 ... 72 C5
  *CHAD* OL9 ... 8 F5
  *DTN/ASHW* M34 ... 90 D8
  *DUK* SK16 ... 90 E3
  *EDGY/DAV* SK3 ... 12 C6
  *FWTH* BL4 ... 52 C4
  *MDTN* M24 ... 57 L4
Highfield Ter *BKLY* M9 ... 73 G4
  *NM/HAY* SK22 ... 124 F4
  *OLDE* OL4 ... 60 A2
Highgate *BOLS/LL* BL3 ... 50 F2
Highgate Av *URM* M41 ... 84 D8
Highgate Crs *GTN* M18 ... 89 G8
  *WGNNW/ST* WN6 ... 30 B5
Highgate Dr *LHULT* M38 ... 52 B7
  *ROY/SHW* OL2 ... 42 F5
Highgate La *LHULT* M38 ... 52 B7
  *WHIT* OL12 ... 20 A6
Highgate Rd *ALT* WA14 ... 107 L8
  *NM/HAY* SK22 ... 125 M2
High Gates *SALE* M33 ... 97 H7
Highgrove *HALE/TIMP* WA15 ... 108 D3
Highgrove Rd *BOL* BL1 ... 36 A1
High Grove Rd *CHD/CHDH* SK8 ... 110 F7
  *OLDE* OL4 ... 61 H7
The Highgrove *BOL* BL1 ... 35 G3
High Hill Rd *NM/HAY* SK22 ... 124 F3
High Houses *BOL* BL1 * ... 22 A6
High Hurst Cl *MDTN* M24 * ... 56 F5
Highland Rd *EDGW/EG* BL7 ... 22 F4
  *HOR/BR* BL6 ... 34 B3
Highlands *LIT* OL15 ... 29 K1
  *ROY/SHW* OL2 ... 58 F1
Highlands Dr *OFTN* SK2 ... 113 J6
Highlands Rd *OFTN* SK2 ... 113 J6
  *ROCH* OL11 ... 27 G7
  *ROY/SHW* OL2 ... 43 G2
  *ROY/SHW* OL2 ... 58 F1
The Highlands *MOSL* OL5 * ... 76 E3
High La *CCHDY* M21 ... 97 L4
  *GLSP* SK13 ... 104 B5
  *MPL/ROM* SK6 ... 101 L4
High Lea *CHD/CHDH* SK8 ... 110 F7
High Lea Rd *NM/HAY* SK22 ... 124 F4
High Lee La *OLDE* OL4 ... 44 E8
High Legh Rd *OP/CLY* M11 ... 89 G4
High Knowll *ROCH* OL11 ... 10 F7
Highmarsh Crs *NEWLW* WA12 ... 78 A3
High Meadow
  *CHD/CHDH* SK8 * ... 120 A4
Highmeadow *RAD* M26 ... 54 C3
High Moor Crs *OLDE* OL4 ... 60 B3
Highmore Dr *BKLY* M9 ... 73 H1
High Mt *BOLE* BL2 ... 37 H1
High Pk *BKLY* M9 ... 30 F6
High Peak Rd *AUL* OL6 ... 76 D6
  *WHIT* OL12 ... 20 A6
High Peak St *NEWH/MOS* M40 ... 73 L6
High Rid La *HOR/BR* BL6 ... 34 E3
Highshore Dr *CHH* M8 ... 72 C5
High Stile St *FWTH* BL4 ... 53 H5
Highstone Dr *CHH* M8 ... 72 F6
Highstones Gdns *GLSP* SK13 * ... 105 J2
High St *ALT* WA14 ... 108 A8
  *ANC* M4 ... 7 H4
  *ATH* M46 ... 67 G1
  *BOLS/LL* BL3 ... 36 B8
  *BOLS/LL* BL3 ... 51 L1
  *BRAM/HZG* SK7 ... 122 D2
  *CHD/CHDH* SK8 ... 111 G6
  *DROY* M43 ... 89 K3
  *EDGW/EG* BL7 ... 16 B8
  *GOL/RIS/CUL* WA3 ... 79 K4
  *HEY* OL10 ... 40 E2

  *HYDE* SK14 ... 102 C1
  *LEIGH* WN7 ... 66 D7
  *LIT* OL15 ... 21 K7
  *MDTN* M24 ... 57 G2
  *MOSL* OL5 ... 77 G2
  *NEWLW* WA12 ... 79 G8
  *OLD* OL1 ... 9 J5
  *OLDE* OL4 ... 60 B6
  *ROY/SHW* OL2 ... 43 G8
  *ROY/SHW* OL2 ... 43 L6
  *STKP* SK1 ... 13 J4
  *STLY* SK15 ... 91 K3
  *TOT/BURYW* BL8 ... 38 C1
  *TYLD* M29 ... 67 J3
  *TYLD* M29 ... 67 L7
  *UPML* OL3 ... 45 J8
  *WALK* M28 ... 68 F1
  *WGN* WN1 ... 48 A2
  *WGNE/HIN* WN2 ... 48 E1
  *WGNNW/ST* WN6 ... 31 J5
  *WGNS/IIMK* WN3 ... 15 L7
  *WHIT* OL12 ... 10 E1
High St East *GLSP* SK13 ... 105 G3
High St West *GLSP* SK13 ... 104 E3
Highthorne Gn *ROY/SHW* OL2 ... 42 F4
Highview *GLSP* SK13 ... 104 D5
High View St *BOL* BL1 ... 22 B7
  *BOLS/LL* BL3 * ... 35 M8
Highwood *ROCH* OL11 ... 27 H3
Highwood Cl *BOLE* BL2 * ... 37 J3
  *GLSP* SK13 ... 104 E5
High Wood Fold
  *BRAM/HZG* SK7 ... 114 C4
Highwoods Cl *AIMK* WN4 ... 63 L7
Highworth Cl *BOLS/LL* BL3 * ... 2 C9
Highworth Dr *NEWH/MOS* M40 ... 74 A2
Higson Av *CCHDY* M21 ... 97 L5
  *ECC* M30 ... 84 F4
  *MPL/ROM* SK6 ... 113 J2
Hilary Av *ATH* M46 ... 50 F7
  *CHD/CHDH* SK8 ... 119 M4
  *GOL/RIS/CUL* WA3 ... 80 A3
  *OLDS* OL8 ... 75 J3
Hilary Cl *HTNM* SK4 ... 12 E2
Hilary Gv *FWTH* BL4 ... 52 F5
Hilary Rd *WYTH/NTH* M22 ... 118 D3
Hilary St *ROCH* OL11 * ... 42 A3
Hilbre Av *ROY/SHW* OL2 ... 59 G2
Hilbre Rd *BNG/LEV* M19 ... 99 J3
Hilbre Wy *WILM/AE* SK9 ... 119 M8
Hilda Av *CHD/CHDH* SK8 ... 111 H7
  *TOT/BURYW* BL8 ... 24 C6
Hilda Gv *RDSH* SK5 ... 100 C8
Hilda Rd *HYDE* SK14 ... 102 A5
Hilda St *BOLS/LL* BL3 ... 36 D8
  *CHAD* OL9 ... 8 F4
  *HEY* OL10 ... 41 G2
  *LEIGH* WN7 ... 65 M6
Hilden Ct *OLDTF/WHR* M16 ... 87 G8
Hilden St *BOLE* BL2 ... 3 H6
Hilditch Cl *NTHM/RTH* M23 ... 109 L6
Hildyard St
  *WGNW/BIL/OR* WN5 ... 14 A8
Hiley Rd *ECC* M30 ... 84 C4
Hilgay Cl *WGNS/IIMK* WN3 ... 63 G1
Hillam Cl *URM* M41 ... 96 C3
Hillary Av *AULW* OL7 ... 75 L7
  *WGNW/BIL/OR* WN5 ... 47 G7
Hillary Rd *HYDE* SK14 ... 91 K7
Hillbank *WGNNW/ST* WN6 ... 31 K5
Hillbank Cl *BOL* BL1 ... 35 M1
Hill Bank Cl *STLY* SK15 ... 77 G7
Hillbank St *MDTN* M24 ... 42 A6
Hillbeck Crs *AIMK* WN4 ... 63 G8
Hillbre Wy *WILM/AE* SK9 ... 119 M8
Hillbrook Av *NEWH/MOS* M40 * ... 73 L2
Hillbrook Rd *BRAM/HZG* SK7 ... 120 F6
  *STKP* SK1 ... 112 F4
Hillbury Rd *BRAM/HZG* SK7 ... 121 H3
Hill Cl *OLDE* OL4 ... 59 M7
Hillcote Wk *GTN* M18 ... 88 E6
Hill Cot Rd *BOL* BL1 ... 22 B7
Hill Court Ms *MPL/ROM* SK6 ... 113 L2
  *MPL/ROM* SK6 ... 123 C5
Hillcourt St *CMANE* M1 ... 7 H9
Hill Crs *BKLY* M9 ... 72 F1
  *LEIGH* WN7 ... 65 M4
Hill Crest *ATH* M46 ... 51 J7
Hillcrest *HYDE* SK14 ... 102 C5
  *MDTN* M24 ... 57 J4
  *SLFD* M6 ... 85 K1
  *WGNE/HIN* WN2 ... 64 E2
Hillcrest Av *HEY* OL10 ... 40 D1
Hill Crest Av *HTNM* SK4 ... 111 K2
  *LEIGH* WN7 ... 65 M4
Hillcrest Crs *HEY* OL10 ... 40 D1
Hillcrest Dr *BNG/LEV* M19 ... 99 M5
  *DTN/ASHW* M34 ... 101 L3
Hillcrest Rd *BRAM/HZG* SK7 ... 121 H3
  *OFTN* SK2 ... 112 F6
  *PWCH* M25 ... 71 J2
  *ROCH* OL11 ... 41 M2
  *TYLD* M29 ... 68 A4
Hillcroft *OFTN* SK2 ... 113 H6
  *OLDS* OL8 ... 75 D4
Hillcroft Cl *CHH* M8 ... 72 D4
Hillcroft Rd *ALT* WA14 ... 107 K7
Hilldale Av *BKLY* M9 ... 57 G8
Hill Dr *WILM/AE* SK9 ... 127 G3
Hill End *MPL/ROM* SK6 ... 102 A8
Hillend La *HYDE* SK14 ... 103 J3
Hill End Rd *UPML* OL3 ... 45 J8
Hill Farm Cl *OLDS* OL8 ... 75 L1
Hillfield *SLFD* M6 ... 86 A2
Hillfield Cl *BRUN/LGST* M13 ... 88 A7
Hillfield Dr *BOLE* BL2 ... 3 K4
  *WALK* M28 ... 68 D5
Hillfoot Wk *HULME* M15 * ... 87 G6
Hillgate Av *ORD* M5 ... 86 A4
Hillgate St *AUL* OL6 ... 75 M8
Hillier St *BKLY* M9 ... 73 H4
Hillier St North *BKLY* M9 ... 73 H4
Hillingdon Dr *NEWH/MOS* M40 ... 73 L2
Hillingdon Rd *STRET* M32 ... 97 H3
  *WHTF* M45 ... 54 F5
Hillington Rd *EDGY/DAV* SK3 ... 12 C1
  *SALE* M33 ... 96 B8
Hillkirk Dr *WHIT* OL12 ... 27 H1
Hillkirk St *OP/CLY* M11 ... 88 B3
Hill La *BKLY* M9 ... 73 G1
  *BOLE* BL2 ... 37 H2
  *HOR/BR* BL6 ... 32 E1
Hillman Cl *NEWH/MOS* M40 ... 73 G7

Hill Mt DUK SK16 91 K4
Hillreed WGNNW/ST WN6 14 A1
Hill Ri ALT WA14 107 K7
MPL/ROM SK6 113 L2
RAMS BL0 18 D8
Hillsborough Dr BURY BL9 55 L2
Hill's Ct TOT/BURYW BL8 24 E8
Hillsdale Gv BOLE BL2 37 H1
Hill Side BOL BL1 35 J5
Hillside Av AIMK WN4 63 J4
ATH M46 51 H8
BRO M7 71 K4
EDGW/EG BL7 22 E5
FWTH BL4 52 F5
HOR/BR BL6 33 H3
HYDE SK14 102 C6
OLDE OL4 59 M5
OLDE OL4 60 E7
ROY/SHW OL2 43 H7
ROY/SHW OL2 44 A5
STLY SK15 77 J6
UPML OL3 61 M1
WALK M28 52 F8
WHTF M45 55 H2
Hillside Cl BOLE BL2 23 H7
BOLS/LL BL3 51 G2
BRAM/HZG SK7 121 J5
GLSP SK13 104 B1
NEWH/MOS M40 73 K3
POY/DIS SK12 123 M6
WGNS/IIMK WN3 63 G1
WGNW/BIL/OR WN5 62 A8
Hillside Crs AUL OL6 76 C7
BURY BL9 25 J6
Hillside Dr MDTN M24 57 L3
SWIN M27 71 G6
Hillside Gv MPL/ROM SK6 114 E3
Hillside Rd HALE/TIMP WA15 117 J1
MPL/ROM SK6 101 M7
OFTN SK2 113 G5
RAMS BL0 18 D7
Hillside St BOLS/LL BL3 2 A9
Hillside Vw DTN/ASHW M34 101 K5
NM/HAY SK22 124 C4
Hillside Wk WHIT OL12 20 B8
Hillside Wy WHIT OL12 20 A3
Hills La BURY BL9 55 M2
Hillspring Rd OLDE OL4 60 D6
Hillstone Av WHIT OL12 20 A8
Hillstone Cl TOT/BURYW BL8 24 C2
Hill St AULW OL7 90 D2
BRO M7 72 A6
BURY BL9 24 F1
DID/WITH M20 98 E5
HEY OL10 40 F2
LEIGH WN7 66 B7
MDTN M24 57 K1
MILN OL16 11 H4
MPL/ROM SK6 113 L2
OLDE OL4 59 L5
RAD M26 38 C8
ROY/SHW OL2 43 M6
TOT/BURYW BL8 24 C8
WGNE/HIN WN2 49 G6
WGNNW/ST WN6 14 D1
Hill Top ATH M46 51 J7
BOLS/LL BL3 37 K8
HALE/TIMP WA15 117 J3
MPL/ROM SK6 113 L1
Hill Top Av CHD/CHDH SK8 120 D4
PWCH M25 55 L8
WILM/AE SK9 126 F4
Hilltop Av BKLY M9 73 G1
WHTF M45 55 L4
Hill Top Ct CHD/CHDH SK8 120 D3
Hill Top Dr HALE/TIMP WA15 117 J2
ROCH OL11 42 D2
Hilltop Dr MPL/ROM SK6 113 M5
ROY/SHW OL2 59 H2
TOT/BURYW BL8 24 B6
Hilltop Gv WHTF M45 55 L4
Hill Top La UPML OL3 45 G8
Hilltop Rd GLSP SK13 104 E1
Hill Top Rd WALK M28 53 G8
Hill Vw STLY SK15 92 A6
Hill View Cl OLD OL1 59 M2
Hillview Rd BOL BL1 * 22 B8
DTN/ASHW M34 100 D3
Hillwood Av CHH M8 72 C1
Hillwood Dr GLSP SK13 105 J4
Hillyard St TOT/BURYW BL8 38 F1
Hilly Cft EDGW/EG BL7 22 C4
Hilmarton Cl BOLE BL2 23 H7
Hilrose Av URM M41 96 C2
Hilton Av HOR/BR BL6 33 K1
URM M41 96 A2
Hilton Cl LEIGH WN7 66 D7
Hilton Ct EDGY/DAV SK3 * 13 G6
Hilton Crs AUL OL6 75 M7
PWCH M25 71 L2
WALK M28 68 E6
Hilton Dr AULW OL7 75 J7
PWCH M25 71 L2
Hilton Fold La MDTN M24 57 L3
Hilton Gv POY/DIS SK12 121 M8
WALK M28 68 E1
Hilton La PWCH M25 71 K2
WALK M28 68 E2
Hilton Pl WGNE/HIN WN2 32 F6
Hilton Rd BRAM/HZG SK7 121 H2
BURY BL9 4 F5
POY/DIS SK12 122 E7
POY/DIS SK12 123 K5
WYTH/NTH M22 110 B7
Hiltons Cl OLDS OL8 9 G9
Hiltons Farm Cl
DTN/ASHW M34 90 B7
Hilton Sq SWIN M27 70 D3
Hilton St AIMK WN4 78 E1
ANC M4 7 H3
BOLE BL2 3 M4
BRO M7 72 B7
BURY BL9 5 G1
EDGY/DAV SK3 12 F6
HYDE SK14 * 91 J7
LHULT M38 52 D8
WGN WN1 15 H2
WGNS/IIMK WN3 15 K8
Hilton St North BRO M7 72 A6
Hilton Wk MDTN M24 56 F4
Himley Rd OP/CLY M11 88 F1
Hinchcombe Cl LHULT M38 * 52 D6
Hinchley Rd BKLY M9 73 L1
Hinchley Wy SWIN M27 70 C2
Hinckley St OP/CLY M11 88 C4
Hindburn Cl WHTF M45 55 L4
Hindburn Dr WALK M28 68 D4
Hinde St NEWH/MOS M40 73 K4
Hind Hill St HEY OL10 41 G3
Hindle Dr ROY/SHW OL2 58 F1
Hindles Cl ATH M46 66 D2
Hindle St RAD M26 54 D1
Hindley Av WYTH/NTH M22 118 D2
Hindley Mill La WGNE/HIN WN2 49 H5
Hindley Rd WHTN BL5 50 A7
Hindley St AULW OL7 90 C3
STKP SK1 13 K7
Hindley Wk WGN WN1 * 14 F3
Hind Rd WGNW/BIL/OR WN5 47 G4
Hindsford Cl NTHM/RTH M23 109 G3
Hindsford St ATH M46 67 J3
Hinds La BURY BL9 38 F5
TOT/BURYW BL8 4 A8
Hind St BOLE BL2 3 M4
Hinkler Av BOLS/LL BL3 52 B1
Hinton WHIT OL12 10 D2
Hinton Cl ROCH OL11 27 H6
Hinton Gv HYDE SK14 102 D4
Hinton St ANC M4 * 7 K1
OLDS OL8 9 K8
Hipley Cl MPL/ROM SK6 101 K7
Hirons La OLDE OL4 60 D7
Hirst Av WALK M28 53 G7
Hitchen Cl DUK SK16 91 J5
Hitchen Dr DUK SK16 91 J5
Hitchin Wk BRUN/LGST M13 87 M7
Hive St OLDS OL8 74 E2
Hoade St WGNE/HIN WN2 49 H5
Hobart Cl BRAM/HZG SK7 121 H8
Hobart St BOL BL1 36 A2
GTN M18 89 G7
Hobby Gv LEIGH WN7 66 E7
Hob Hey La GOL/RIS/CUL WA3 81 G8
Hob Hl STLY SK15 91 J3
Hobhill Mdw GLSP SK13 105 G5
Hob La EDGW/EG BL7 16 F5
Hob Mill Ri MOSL OL5 61 H8
Hobson Ct DTN/ASHW M34 90 B6
Hobson Crs DTN/ASHW M34 90 B6
Hobson Moor Rd HYDE SK14 92 C6
Hobson St FAIL M35 74 A6
OLD OL1 9 J7
OP/CLY M11 89 K5
RDSH SK5 100 C2
Hockenhull Cl WYTH/NTH M22 119 G2
Hocker La MCFLDN SK10 130 E7
Hockerley Cl SALE M33 96 A7
Hockery Vw WGNE/HIN WN2 48 F8
Hockley Cl POY/DIS SK12 129 K1
Hockley Paddock
POY/DIS SK12 129 K1
Hockley Rd NTHM/RTH M23 109 J7
POY/DIS SK12 129 K1
Hodder Av LIT OL15 21 K6
WGNE/HIN WN2 64 C2
Hodder Bank OFTN SK2 113 H7
Hodder Cl WGNW/BIL/OR WN5 47 G5
Hodder Wy WHTF M45 55 M4
Hoddesdon St CHH M8 72 E5
Hodge Clough Rd OLD OL1 43 M8
Hodge La HYDE SK14 103 J4
SLFD M6 86 C3
Hodge Rd OLD OL1 60 A1
WALK M28 69 G2
Hodges St WGNNW/ST WN6 47 K2
Hodge St BKLY M9 73 J3
Hodgson Dr HALE/TIMP WA15 108 D4
Hodgson St AUL OL6 90 D2
CHH M8 72 C7
Hodnet Dr AIMK WN4 78 F1
Hodnett Av URM M41 95 H3
Hodson Fold OLDS OL8 75 K3
Hodson Rd SWIN M27 70 B2
Hodson St WGNS/IIMK WN3 14 F6
Hogarth Ri OLD OL1 44 A8
Hogarth Rd MPL/ROM SK6 114 E4
ROCH OL11 42 C2
Holbeach Cl TOT/BURYW BL8 25 G7
WGNE/HIN WN2 49 H8
Holbeck TYLD M29 67 L7
Holbeck Av WHIT OL12 20 B8
Holbeck Cl HOR/BR BL6 34 A4
Holbeck Gv RUSH/FAL M14 88 B8
Holbeton Cl CHH M8 72 B7
Holborn Av FAIL M35 74 E5
LEIGH WN7 66 C4
RAD M26 38 B8
WGNS/IIMK WN3 14 D9
Holborn Dr CHH M8 72 E7
Holborn Gdns ROCH OL11 10 A8
Holborn Sq ROCH OL11 10 A8
Holborn St ROCH OL11 10 A8
STKP SK1 13 J5
Holbrook Av LHULT M38 52 D6
Holbrook St CMANE M1 * 7 H7
Holcombe Av GOL/RIS/CUL WA3 79 M4
TOT/BURYW BL8 38 E2
Holcombe Cl ALT WA14 107 L6
FWTH BL4 53 K7
OLDE OL4 60 D5
SLFD M6 86 D2
Holcombe Ct RAMS BL0 24 C2
Holcombe Crs FWTH BL4 53 K6
Holcombe Lee RAMS BL0 24 D1
Holcombe Old Rd
TOT/BURYW BL8 18 D7
TOT/BURYW BL8 24 C1
Holcombe Rd BOLS/LL BL3 53 J1
RUSH/FAL M14 99 H5
TOT/BURYW BL8 24 C2
Holcombe View Cl OLDE OL4 60 A2
Holden Av BOL BL1 22 B6
BURY BL9 26 B8
OLDTF/WHR M16 98 B3
RAMS BL0 18 D7
Holden Brook Cl LEIGH WN7 66 E7
Holden Clough Dr AULW OL7 75 L5
Holden Fold La ROY/SHW OL2 58 F2
Holden Lea WHTN BL5 50 B1
Holden Rd BRO M7 72 A3
LEIGH WN7 66 D7
Holden St AUL OL6 75 M8
OLDS OL8 75 J1
WHIT OL12 * 28 D2
Holden Wk WGNW/BIL/OR WN5 47 H7
Holder Av BOLS/LL BL3 37 L7
Holderness Dr ROY/SHW OL2 58 F2
Holdgate Cl HULME M15 87 H7
Holding St WGNE/HIN WN2 49 G6
Holdsworth St SWIN M27 70 A5
Holebottom AUL OL6 75 M6
Hole House Fold
MPL/ROM SK6 113 L2
Holford Av RUSH/FAL M14 98 E2
Holford Wk MILN OL16 29 G5
Holgate Dr WGNW/BIL/OR WN5 46 B7
Holgate St OLDE OL4 60 B3
Holhouse La TOT/BURYW BL8 24 C2
Holiday La OFTN SK2 113 J6
Holkar Mdw EDGW/EG BL7 22 E4
Holker Cl BRUN/LGST M13 88 A8
POY/DIS SK12 122 B8
Holkham Cl ANC M4 * 7 M3
Holland Av STLY SK15 91 K2
Holland Cl UPML OL3 45 H8
Holland Ct POY/DIS SK12 129 J1
RAD M26 38 F8
Holland Gv AUL OL6 75 L6
Holland Ri WHIT OL12 10 D3
Holland Rd BRAM/HZG SK7 121 G5
CHH M8 72 C2
HYDE SK14 91 J7
Holland St BOL BL1 22 C8
DTN/ASHW M34 90 A8
HEY OL10 41 G2
MILN OL16 21 H8
NEWH/MOS M40 88 A2
RAD M26 38 F8
SLFD M6 71 J7
WHIT OL12 10 C4
Holland St East
DTN/ASHW M34 90 A8
Holland St West
DTN/ASHW M34 89 M8
Hollies Dr MPL/ROM SK6 114 D7
Hollies La WILM/AE SK9 127 K5
The Hollies ATH M46 * 67 G1
CHD/CHDH SK8 * 110 E7
DID/WITH M20 110 C1
WGN WN1 48 A1
WGNE/HIN WN2 * 32 F7
Hollin Acre WHTN BL5 50 C4
Hollin Bank HTNM SK4 100 A5
Hollinbrook WGNNW/ST WN6 47 J2
Hollin Crs UPML OL3 61 H8
Hollin Cross La GLSP SK13 104 F4
Hollin Dr MDTN M24 41 H8
Holliney Av WYTH/NTH M22 119 H3
Holliney Rd WYTH/NTH M22 119 H3
Holling Gn MDTN M24 57 K1
Hollingwood Cl AIMK WN4 78 D1
Hollingworth Av
NEWH/MOS M40 74 C2
Hollingworth Cl STKP SK1 * 13 J6
Hollingworth Dr
MPL/ROM SK6 123 H1
Hollingworth Fold LIT OL15 * 29 M2
Hollingworth Rd LIT OL15 21 M8
MPL/ROM SK6 101 H8
Hollingworth St CHAD OL9 74 E1
Hollinhall St OLDE OL4 59 M5
Hollin Hey Rd BOL BL1 35 H1
Hollinhey Ter HYDE SK14 92 F8
Hollinhurst Dr HOR/BR BL6 34 F5
Hollinhurst Rd RAD M26 54 F2
Hollin La MDTN M24 41 J8
ROCH OL11 27 H6
WILM/AE SK9 119 H7
Hollins FWTH BL4 * 52 A4
Hollins Av HYDE SK14 102 B5
OLDE OL4 60 C4
Hollins Brook Cl BURY BL9 * 39 L7
Hollins Brook Wy BURY BL9 39 L6
Hollins Brow BURY BL9 39 J8
Hollins Cl AIMK WN4 63 G8
BURY BL9 39 L8
TYLD M29 67 K4
Hollinsclough Cl
WYTH/NTH M22 110 B7
Hollinscroft Av
HALE/TIMP WA15 109 G7
Hollins Green Rd
MPL/ROM SK6 114 C6
Hollins Gv SALE M33 96 D8
WGTN/LGST M12 99 K1
Hollins La BURY BL9 39 K7
MOSL OL5 77 G3
MPL/ROM SK6 114 C6
MPL/ROM SK6 114 F4
RAMS BL0 19 H3
Hollins Ms BURY BL9 39 M8
GLSP SK13 104 A2
Hollinsmoor Rd NM/HAY SK22 115 M5
Hollins Mt MPL/ROM SK6 114 E4
Hollins Rd OLDE OL4 60 C4
OLDS OL8 74 F2
OLDS OL8 75 J1
WGNE/HIN WN2 49 K7
Hollins St BOLE BL2 3 J7
OLDE OL4 60 C6
STLY SK15 91 J4
Hollinswood Rd BOLE BL2 3 K6
WALK M28 68 E6
Hollinwell Cl MDTN M24 41 J8
Hollinwood Av CHAD OL9 74 D2
NEWH/MOS M40 74 A2
Hollinwood La MPL/ROM SK6 123 K2
Hollinwood Rd POY/DIS SK12 123 M6
Holloway Dr WALK M28 69 M3
Hollowbrook Wy WHIT OL12 28 A2
Hollowell La HOR/BR BL6 34 A3
Hollow End RDSH SK5 100 E5
Hollowfield ROCH OL11 27 G3
Hollow Mdw RAD M26 53 M6
Hollowspell WHIT OL12 28 F1
The Hollows CHD/CHDH SK8 * 119 L3
Hollow Vale Dr RDSH SK5 100 D4
Holly Av CHD/CHDH SK8 111 G7
URM M41 95 L2
WALK M28 69 H2
Holly Bank DROY M43 89 M1
GLSP SK13 105 H4
HYDE SK14 93 G7
NEWH/MOS M40 * 73 M5
ROY/SHW OL2 43 G7
SALE M33 108 F1
Hollybank Ri DUK SK16 91 J4
Holly Bank Rd WILM/AE SK9 126 F3
Hollybank St RAD M26 54 C1
Hollybrook Dene
MPL/ROM SK6 114 B2
Hollybush Sq GOL/RIS/CUL WA3 80 B3
Hollybush St GTN M18 89 H6
Holly Cl HALE/TIMP WA15 108 D6
Holly Ct HYDE SK14 102 D2
Hollycroft Av BOLE BL2 37 H7
WYTH/NTH M22 110 A6
Hollydene WGNE/HIN WN2 * 32 E7
Holly Dene Dr HOR/BR BL6 34 E5
Holly Dr SALE M33 96 D8
Hollyedge Dr PWCH M25 71 K2
Holly Fold WHTF M45 55 J3
Holly Gra ALT WA14 116 F2
BRAM/HZG SK7 121 H1
Holly Gv BOL BL1 35 M3
CHAD OL9 8 B3
DTN/ASHW M34 101 K1
FWTH BL4 52 D4
HOR/BR BL6 34 E5
LEIGH WN7 66 B5
OLDE OL4 60 B4
SALE M33 97 G8
STLY SK15 91 H4
Holly Heath Dr WGN WN1 31 L8
Hollyhedge Av
WYTH/NTH M22 110 A7
Hollyhedge Court Rd
WYTH/NTH M22 110 B7
Hollyhedge Rd
NTHM/RTH M23 109 L7
Hollyhey Dr NTHM/RTH M23 109 L3
Hollyhouse Dr MPL/ROM SK6 101 K7
Holly House Dr URM M41 95 J2
Hollyhurst WALK M28 69 L6
Holly La OLDS OL8 74 F2
WILM/AE SK9 119 G7
Holly Mill Crs BOL BL1 22 C8
Hollymount Av OFTN SK2 112 F7
Hollymount Dr OFTN SK2 112 F7
OLDE OL4 60 B1
Hollymount Gdns OFTN SK2 113 G7
Hollymount Rd OFTN SK2 112 F7
Holly Oak Gdns HEY OL10 40 F3
Holly Rd BRAM/HZG SK7 121 G7
GOL/RIS/CUL WA3 79 M4
HTNM SK4 99 M7
MPL/ROM SK6 123 H5
POY/DIS SK12 129 J1
SWIN M27 70 A6
WGNE/HIN WN2 32 E7
WGNW/BIL/OR WN5 47 H6
Holly Rd North WILM/AE SK9 126 E6
Holly Rd South WILM/AE SK9 126 E7
Holly Royde Cl DID/WITH M20 98 D6
Holly St BOL BL1 22 C8
BURY BL9 5 J4
BURY BL9 24 F1
DROY M43 89 G2
MILN OL16 42 E2
STKP SK1 13 M5
TOT/BURYW BL8 24 C6
WGTN/LGST M12 88 B4
WHIT OL12 21 G6
Hollythorn Av CHD/CHDH SK8 120 E5
Hollyway WYTH/NTH M22 110 B4
Hollywood Rd BOL BL1 35 L2
MPL/ROM SK6 115 H4
Hollywood Wy HTNM SK4 12 E5
Holmbrook TYLD M29 67 M3
Holmbrook Wk CHH M8 72 D6
Holm Ct SLFD M6 * 86 D1
Holmcroft Rd GTN M18 100 A2
Holmdale Av BNG/LEV M19 99 H7
Holme Av TOT/BURYW BL8 24 F7
WGN WN1 47 M2
Holme Beech Gv OFTN SK2 * 112 F4
Holmebrook Dr HOR/BR BL6 34 A4
Holme Ct WGN WN1 * 47 M2
Holme Crs ROY/SHW OL2 58 F2
Holmefield SALE M33 96 E8
Holme Park Gdns WALK M28 68 D7
Holme Park Wy FAIL M35 74 E5
Holme Rd DID/WITH M20 110 C1
Holmes Cottages BOL BL1 * 35 M1
Holmes House Av
WGNS/IIMK WN3 62 F1
Holmes Rd WHIT OL12 10 B4
Holmes St BOLS/LL BL3 36 C8
CHD/CHDH SK8 111 H6
OFTN SK2 13 H8
WHIT OL12 10 B3
WHIT OL12 28 F1
Holme St HYDE SK14 102 A2
Holmeswood Cl WILM/AE SK9 127 G4
Holmeswood Rd BOLS/LL BL3 52 A2
Holme Ter WGN WN1 47 L1
Holmfield Av BKLY M9 73 J5
PWCH M25 71 M1
Holmfield Av West BKLY M9 73 J6
Holmfield Cl HTNM SK4 112 A1
Holmfield Dr CHD/CHDH SK8 120 D4
Holmfield Gn BOLS/LL BL3 51 J1
Holmfirth St BRUN/LGST M13 88 C8
Holmlea Rd DROY M43 89 H2
Holmleigh Av BKLY M9 73 H3
Holmpark Rd OP/CLY M11 89 J5
Holmsfield Cl WGNE/HIN WN2 48 D2
Holmside Gdns BNG/LEV M19 99 G8
Holmwood ALT WA14 116 C1
Holmwood Cl AIMK WN4 63 K7
Holmwood Rd DID/WITH M20 98 E7
Holroyd St MILN OL16 11 G5
OP/CLY M11 * 88 D4
Holset Dr ALT WA14 107 L7
Holst Av CHH M8 72 D6
Holstein Av WHIT OL12 20 B8
Holt Av WGNW/BIL/OR WN5 62 A8
Holtby St BKLY M9 73 H3
Holt Crs WGNW/BIL/OR WN5 62 A8
Holthouse Rd TOT/BURYW BL8 24 B7
Holt La FAIL M35 74 E5
Holt Lane Ms FAIL M35 74 D5
Holton Wy WGNS/IIMK WN3 63 H3
Holts La OLDE OL4 60 A8
WILM/AE SK9 126 D1
Holts Ter WHIT OL12 28 B2
Holt St ALT WA14 107 M5
BOLS/LL BL3 2 A8
DTN/ASHW M34 90 B4
ECC M30 84 F4
LEIGH WN7 66 B5
MILN OL16 * 29 K7
NEWH/MOS M40 73 J7
OLDE OL4 59 M4
RAMS BL0 19 G6
STKP SK1 13 K7
SWIN M27 70 C2
TYLD M29 67 K3
WGN WN1 15 M4
WGNE/HIN WN2 48 F7
WGNNW/ST WN6 47 J3
WGNS/IIMK WN3 47 K8
WGNW/BIL/OR WN5 46 A7
WHIT OL12 20 A3
Holt St West RAMS BL0 18 E7
Holtswell Cl GOL/RIS/CUL WA3 80 B3
Holt Town NEWH/MOS M40 88 B2
Holwick Rd NTHM/RTH M23 109 J3
Holwood Dr OLDTF/WHR M16 98 B4
Holy Harbour St BOL BL1 * 35 M2
Holyhurst Wk BOL BL1 * 36 B2
Holyoake Rd WALK M28 69 G2
Holyoake St DROY M43 89 M2
Holyoak St NEWH/MOS M40 73 M6
Holyrood Cl PWCH M25 55 M6
Holyrood Dr PWCH M25 55 M6
SWIN M27 69 M5
Holyrood Gv PWCH M25 55 M6
Holyrood Rd PWCH M25 55 M7
Holyrood St NEWH/MOS M40 74 A8
OLD OL1 59 K3
Holywood St RUSH/FAL M14 98 E1
Homebury Dr OP/CLY M11 * 88 E2
Home Dr MDTN M24 57 J6
Home Farm Av HYDE SK14 103 J3
Homelands Cl SALE M33 108 C2
Homelands Rd SALE M33 108 C2
Homer Dr MPL/ROM SK6 114 E4
Homerton Rd NEWH/MOS M40 73 L8
Homestead Av
RNFD/HAY WA11 * 78 B5
Homestead Cl PART M31 94 D8
Homestead Crs BNG/LEV M19 111 G1
Homestead Gdns WHIT OL12 21 H7
Homestead Rd POY/DIS SK12 123 L6
Hometel RUSH/FAL M14 98 F3
Homewood Av
WYTH/NTH M22 110 A3
Homewood Rd
WYTH/NTH M22 109 M3
Honduras St OLDE OL4 9 M5
Hondwith Cl BOLE BL2 22 E7
Honeybourne Cl TYLD M29 67 M3
Honeycombe Cottages
CHD/CHDH SK8 * 111 H7
Honey St CHH M8 72 D8
Honeysuckle Av
WGNNW/ST WN6 47 J1
Honeysuckle Cl MPL/ROM SK6 101 K7
NTHM/RTH M23 109 G3
Honeysuckle Dr STLY SK15 91 L2
Honeysuckle Wy WHIT OL12 28 A1
Honeywell La OLDS OL8 75 J1
Honeywood Cl RAMS BL0 24 D1
Honford Rd WYTH/NTH M22 109 L8
Hong Kong Av
HALE/TIMP WA15 118 C4
Honister Dr MDTN M24 57 J2
Honister Rd BKLY M9 73 J5
WGNW/BIL/OR WN5 46 E6
Honister Wy ROCH OL11 27 L8
Honiton Av HYDE SK14 102 F2
Honiton Cl CHAD OL9 58 B3
HEY OL10 40 F4
LEIGH WN7 66 A2
Honiton Dr BOLE BL2 37 K6
Honiton Gv RAD M26 38 A7
Honiton Wy ALT WA14 107 L6
Honor St BRUN/LGST M13 99 H1
Hood Cl TYLD M29 68 A3
Hood Gv LEIGH WN7 81 L1
Hood Sq OLDE OL4 60 D7
Hood St ANC M4 7 K3
Hook St WGNE/HIN WN2 48 C5
Hoole Cl CHD/CHDH SK8 111 K7
Hooley Range HTNM SK4 111 L1
Hooper St EDGY/DAV SK3 13 H5
OLDE OL4 9 M7
WGTN/LGST M12 88 A4
Hooten La LEIGH WN7 81 M1
Hooton St BOLS/LL BL3 51 M1
NEWH/MOS M40 88 B1
Hopcroft Cl BKLY M9 56 E6
Hope Av BOLE BL2 3 K7
BOLE BL2 23 H7
LHULT M38 52 E8
STRET M32 96 E1
WILM/AE SK9 127 H1
Hope Carr La LEIGH WN7 81 L2
Hope Carr Rd LEIGH WN7 81 L1
Hope Carr Wy LEIGH WN7 81 K1
Hopecourt Cl SLFD M6 70 E8
Hope Crs WGNNW/ST WN6 30 E6
Hopedale Rd RDSH SK5 100 C6
Hopefield St BOLS/LL BL3 36 A8
Hope Fold Av ATH M46 66 E2
Hopefold Dr WALK M28 69 H2
Hope Green Wy POY/DIS SK12 129 H2
Hope Hey La LHULT M38 52 C7
Hope La GOL/RIS/CUL WA3 82 B2
MCFLDN SK10 129 J3
Hopelea St DID/WITH M20 98 E5
Hope Park Cl PWCH M25 71 L1
Hope Park Rd PWCH M25 71 L1
Hope Pl ROCH OL11 * 41 M3
Hope Rd PWCH M25 71 K2
RUSH/FAL M14 88 A8
SALE M33 108 E1
Hopes Carr STKP SK1 13 K5
Hope St AIMK WN4 64 A7
AUL OL6 76 A8
BRAM/HZG SK7 121 M2
BRO M7 72 A5
CMANE M1 7 J5
DTN/ASHW M34 90 B7
DUK SK16 90 F4
GLSP SK13 105 H2
HEY OL10 41 J4
HOR/BR BL6 33 H4
HTNM SK4 12 F4
LEIGH WN7 66 C7
LHULT M38 52 D8
OLD OL1 59 L5
ORD M5 86 F3
RAMS BL0 18 E7
ROY/SHW OL2 43 L5
SWIN M27 70 D4
TYLD M29 67 L7
WGN WN1 * 14 F3
WGNE/HIN WN2 49 J1
WGNE/HIN WN2 49 J6
WGNS/IIMK WN3 48 B8
WHIT OL12 10 E2
Hope Ter DUK SK16 * 90 E4
EDGY/DAV SK3 * 13 H7
Hopkin Av OLD OL1 59 L4
Hopkins Fld ALT WA14 116 D3
Hopkinson Av DTN/ASHW M34 90 B7
Hopkinson Cl UPML OL3 61 L4
Hopkinson Rd BKLY M9 57 G7
Hopkins St HYDE SK14 91 H8
Hopkin St OLD OL1 9 K5
WGTN/LGST M12 99 K1
Hoppet La DROY M43 89 M2
Hopton Av WYTH/NTH M22 119 G1
Hopwood Av ECC M30 85 G1
HEY OL10 41 G4
Hopwood Cl BURY BL9 55 J1
GOL/RIS/CUL WA3 80 C4
Hopwood Rd MDTN M24 41 K8
Hopwood St CSLFD M3 * 6 D2
NEWH/MOS M40 73 L6
SWIN M27 70 D4
Horace Barnes Cl
RUSH/FAL M14 98 D1
Horace Gv HTNM SK4 100 B8
Horace St BOL BL1 36 A2
Horatio St GTN M18 * 89 J6
Horbury Av GTN M18 100 A1
Horbury Dr TOT/BURYW BL8 38 F2
Horeb St BOLS/LL BL3 2 A9
Horest La UPML OL3 44 E4
Horkers Nook WHTN BL5 50 A5
Horley Cl TOT/BURYW BL8 24 F5
Hornbeam Cl
HALE/TIMP WA15 109 H7
SALE M33 95 M7
Hornbeam Ct SLFD M6 86 D1
Hornbeam Crs AIMK WN4 78 E1
Hornbeam Rd BNG/LEV M19 99 L2

Hornby Av BKLY M9..............57 H7
Hornby Dr BOLS/LL BL3..........51 L3
Hornby Gv LEIGH WN7............67 G5
Hornby Rd STRET M32............86 C8
Hornby Steet WGN WN1...........47 M2
Hornby St BURY BL9..............4 F1
  CHH M8......................72 C8
  HEY OL10....................41 G3
  MDTN M24....................57 K4
  OLDS OL8.....................8 F8
Horncastle CI GOL/RIS/CUL WA3...80 C4
  TOT/BURYW BL8...............25 G7
Horncastle Rd NEWH/MOS M40.....73 L3
Hornchurch Ct HEY OL10.........41 H5
Hornchurch St HULME M15........87 H6
Horne Dr ANC M4.................7 M3
Horne Gv WGNS/IIMK WN3.........14 A9
Horne St BURY BL9..............4 E9
Hornsea CI CHAD OL9............58 C3
  TOT/BURYW BL8...............38 C2
Hornsea Rd OFTN SK2...........113 K7
Hornsea Wk OP/CLY M11 *........88 D3
Hornsey Gv WGNS/IIMK WN3.......63 G1
Horridge Av NEWLW WA12.........78 F7
Horridge Fold EDGW/EG BL7......22 B1
Horridge Fold Av WHTN BL5......51 J2
Horridge St TOT/BURYW BL8......24 E8
Horrobin Fold EDGW/EG BL7 *....22 F2
Horrobin La EDGW/EG BL7........22 F2
Horrocks Fold Av BOL BL1.......22 A6
Horrocks Rd ATH M46............67 H3
  BOLS/LL BL3.................35 K7
  LEIGH WN7...................65 K8
  LEIGH WN7...................66 B7
  RAD M26 *...................38 F8
Horsa St BOLE BL2...............3 J1
Horsedge St OLD OL1............9 K3
Horsefield Av WHIT OL12........20 A6
Horsefield CI CCHDY M21........98 B5
Horseforth La UPML OL3.........61 K8
Horseshoe La EDGW/EG BL7.......22 D4
  MDTN M24....................58 C6
  WILM/AE SK9................130 D2
Horsfield St BOLS/LL BL3.......35 K8
Horsfield Wy MPL/ROM SK6......101 J6
Horsham Av BRAM/HZG SK7.......121 L3
  WHTN BL5....................50 C6
Horsham Gv WGNE/HIN WN2........48 C2
Horsham St SLFD M6.............86 B2
Horstead Wk BNG/LEV M19........99 K2
Horton Av BOL BL1..............22 B6
Horton Rd RUSH/FAL M14.........98 D3
Horton St STKP SK1.............13 L9
  WGNW/BIL/OR WN5.............47 H3
Hortree Rd STRET M32...........97 H2
Horwood Crs DID/WITH M20.......99 G7
Hoscar Dr BNG/LEV M19..........99 H5
The Hoskers WHTN BL5...........50 A5
Hoskins Ct WGTN/LGST M12.......88 D7
Hospital Rd EDGW/EG BL7........22 D4
  SWIN M27....................70 E4
Hotel Rd MANAIR M90...........118 E5
Hotel St BOL BL1................2 E5
Hothersall Rd RDSH SK5........100 C5
Hotspur Ct RUSH/FAL M14........98 D4
Hough CI OLDS OL8..............75 K2
Hough End Av CCHDY M21.........97 M6
Houghend Crs CCHDY M21.........98 B5
Hough Fold Wy BOLE BL2.........23 G8
Hough Gn HALE/TIMP WA15......117 G7
Hough Hall Rd
  NEWH/MOS M40...............73 J4
Hough Hill Rd STLY SK15........91 L4
Hough La EDGW/EG BL7...........22 C5
  HYDE SK14...................91 J7
  MDTN M24....................42 C7
  TYLD M29....................67 M4
  WILM/AE SK9................127 H6
Hough St BOLS/LL BL3...........35 K8
  TYLD M29....................68 A4
Houghton Av OLDS OL8...........75 G2
  WGNW/BIL/OR WN5.............47 H3
Houghton CI MILN OL16..........11 L6
  NM/HAY SK22................125 J2
Houghton La SWIN M27...........70 A7
  WGNNW/ST WN6................30 C9
Houghton Rd CHH M8.............72 D3
Houghton St BOLS/LL BL3........2 C8
  BURY BL9....................4 D7
  LEIGH WN7...................66 C6
  ROY/SHW OL2.................59 H2
  SWIN M27....................71 G6
Hough Wk BRO M7................86 F1
Houghwood Gra AIMK WN4.........78 C1
Houldsworth Av ALT WA14.......108 B5
Houldsworth MI RDSH SK5 *.....100 B5
Houldsworth St CMANE M1........7 J3
  RAD M26.....................38 C7
  RDSH SK5...................100 B5
Houseley Av CHAD OL9...........74 D1
Houseman Gv WGNNW/ST WN6......47 K2
Houtmey CI WGNS/IIMK WN3.......47 K8
Houson St OLDS OL8.............9 J8
Houston Pk SALQ M50............86 C3
Hove CI TOT/BURYW BL8..........24 C3
Hove Dr RUSH/FAL M14...........99 H5
Hoveden St CHH M8..............72 C8
Hove St BOLS/LL BL3............35 M7
Hove St North BOLS/LL BL3 *....35 M7
Hovey CI CHH M8................72 C8
Hovingham St WALK M28..........11 J3
Hovis St OP/CLY M11............88 F4
Howard Av BOLS/LL BL3..........35 K8
  CHD/CHDH SK8...............120 C3
  ECC M30.....................85 C1
  FWTH BL4....................53 J5
  HTNM SK4....................99 H6
Howard CI GLSP SK13...........104 E2
  MPL/ROM SK6................113 K2
Howard Ct AUL OL6..............90 E1
  HALE/TIMP WA15.............117 J3
Howard Dr HALE/TIMP WA15......117 J3
Howard HI BURY BL9.............39 K8
Howardian CI OLDS OL8..........75 H2
Howard La DTN/ASHW M34........101 H3
Howard PI MILN OL16............10 E3
Howard Rd WYTH/NTH M22........110 A3
Howards La MOSL OL5............77 H3
  WGNW/BIL/OR WN5.............46 C5
Howard Meadow GLSP SK13.......104 E5
Howard St AULW OL7.............75 M4
  BOL BL1.....................36 C3
  CHH M8......................72 B8
  DTN/ASHW M34...............104 C3
  GLSP SK13..................104 D3
  OLDE OL4....................60 B4
  ORD M5......................86 D4
  RAD M26.....................54 C1
  ROY/SHW OL2.................43 K5
  STKP SK1....................13 J2

  STLY SK15...................77 G8
  STRET M32...................97 G2
  WGNW/BIL/OR WN5.............46 F7
  WALK M28....................10 D2
Howarth Av WALK M28............69 M5
Howarth Cross St MILN OL16.....28 C2
Howarth Dr IRL M44.............94 E3
Howarth Farm Wy WHIT OL12......28 F1
Howarth Fold EDGW/EG BL7 *.....22 A1
Howarth Sq MILN OL16...........11 H4
Howarth St FWTH BL4............53 C5
  LEIGH WN7...................66 E8
  LIT OL15....................21 M6
  OLDTF/WHR M16...............86 F6
  WHTN BL5....................50 C4
Howbridge CI WALK M28..........68 F4
Howbro Dr AULW OL7.............75 H7
How Clough CI WALK M28.........69 H2
How Clough Dr WALK M28.........69 J2
Howcroft CI BOL BL1.............2 C3
Howden CI RDSH SK5............100 B2
Howden Dr WGNS/IIMK WN3........47 M8
Howe Bridge CI IRL M46.........66 D3
Howe Dr RAMS BL0...............24 E2
Howell Cft North BOL BL1 *......2 E4
Howell Cft South BOL BL1 *......2 E5
Howells Av SALE M33............96 D7
Howe St AULW OL7...............75 H7
  BRO M7......................71 M5
Howgill Crs OLDS OL8...........75 H1
Howgill St OP/CLY M11..........89 G3
Howe Lea Dr BURY BL9...........25 J6
Howsin Av BOLE BL2.............22 E8
Howton CI WGTN/LGST M12........88 D8
Howty CI WILM/AE SK9..........127 H3
Hoxton CI MPL/ROM SK6.........101 K8
Hoy Dr URM M41.................85 C7
Hoylake CI LEIGH WN7...........81 C2
  NEWH/MOS M40...............74 A4
Hoylake Rd EDGY/DAV SK3.......111 K4
  SALE M33...................109 J2
Hoyland CI WGTN/LGST M12.......88 C6
Hoyle Av OLDS OL8..............9 C8
Hoyle's Ter MILN OL16..........29 H6
Hoyle St RAD M26...............54 E3
  WGTN/LGST M12...............7 M7
  WHIT OL12...................20 B1
Hoyle Wk BRUN/LGST M13 *.......87 L6
Hucclecote Av
  WYTH/NTH M22...............118 E2
Hucklow Av NTHM/RTH M23.......118 C2
Hudcar La BURY BL9..............5 H1
Huddart CI ORD M5..............86 E4
Huddersfield Rd MILN OL16......29 M8
  MOSL OL5....................77 H2
  OLDE OL4....................59 L5
  STLY SK15...................91 M2
  UPML OL3....................45 K8
  UPML OL3....................61 M1
Hudson Gv GOL/RIS/CUL WA3......80 B4
Hudson Rd BOLS/LL BL3..........51 L1
  HYDE SK14..................102 B5
Hudson St OLDE OL4.............74 D2
Hudsons Wk ROCH OL11...........27 L5
Hudswell CI WHTF M45...........55 H4
Hughendens Ct
  TOT/BURYW BL8...............24 C5
Hughes CI BURY BL9..............5 H3
  FAIL M35....................74 B4
Hughes St BOL BL1..............36 A2
  OP/CLY M11..................88 B4
Hughley CI ROY/SHW OL2.........43 J9
Hugh Lupus St BOL BL1..........22 D7
Hugh Oldham Dr BRO M7..........71 M5
Hugh St MILN OL16..............11 G3
Hughtrede St MILN OL16.........42 E1
Hugo St FWTH BL4...............52 E2
  NEWH/MOS M40...............73 K5
  ROCH OL11...................42 A2
Hulbert St MDTN M24............57 J6
  TOT/BURYW BL8...............38 F3
Hullet CI WGNNW/ST WN6.........30 B4
Hull Mill La UPML OL3..........45 J7
Hull Sq CSLFD M3...............6 A2
Hully St STLY SK15.............91 J2
Hulme Dr HALE/TIMP WA15.......108 F3
Hulme Gv LEIGH WN7.............65 M6
Hulme Hall CI CHD/CHDH SK8....120 C3
Hulme Hall CI CHD/CHDH SK8....120 C3
Hulme Hall Crs CHD/CHDH SK8...120 C3
Hulme Hall La NEWH/MOS M40.....73 H8
Hulme Hall Rd CHD/CHDH SK8....120 C3
  HULME M15....................6 A9
Hulme PI ORD M5 *..............86 F3
Hulme Rd BOLE BL2..............23 H6
  DTN/ASHW M34...............100 E1
  HTNM SK4...................100 E1
  LEIGH WN7...................65 M6
  RAD M26.....................53 M6
  SALE M33...................109 G1
Hulmes Rd NEWH/MOS M40.........74 B7
Hulme St AUL OL6...............76 A8
  BOL BL1......................2 F3
  HULME M15....................6 D9
  OLDS OL8....................59 H8
  ORD M5......................86 F5
  STKP SK1...................112 E5
  TOT/BURYW BL8...............4 B2
Hulton Av WALK M28.............68 E1
Hulton CI BOLS/LL BL3..........51 H1
Hulton Dr BOLS/LL BL3..........51 K1
  OLDTF/WHR M16...............87 H8
Hulton La BOLS/LL BL3..........51 K1
Hulton St DTN/ASHW M34.........90 B8
  FAIL M35....................74 A5
  ORD M5......................86 D5
Humber Dr BURY BL9.............25 J4
Humber PI WGNW/BIL/OR WN5......46 F7
Humber Rd MILN OL16............29 K6
  TYLD M29....................68 C1
Humber St CHH M8...............72 D5
  SALQ M50....................86 A3
Hume St BNG/LEV M19............99 L4
  MILN OL16...................11 H1
Humphrey Crs URM M41...........96 D2
Humphrey La URM M41............96 D2
Humphrey Pk URM M41............96 D3
Humphrey Rd OLDTF/WHR M16......86 E7
Humphrey St CHH M8.............72 C4
Huncoat Av HTNM SK4...........100 A7
Hunger Hill Av BOLS/LL BL3.....51 H2
Hunmanby Av HULME M15..........6 E9
Hunstanton Dr
  TOT/BURYW BL8...............25 G7
Hunston Rd SALE M33...........108 C1
Hunt Av AULW OL7...............75 L7
Hunter Dr RAD M26..............38 D7
Hunter Rd WGNW/BIL/OR WN5......47 H3

Hunters Cha
  WGNW/BIL/OR WN5.............62 B3
Hunters CI MPL/ROM SK6........113 J1
  WILM/AE SK9................127 K3
Hunters Ct STLY SK15...........92 A4
Hunters Gn RAMS BL0............24 C1
Hunters HI BURY BL9............39 L8
Hunters Hill La UPML OL3.......45 M6
Hunters La UPML OL3...........104 C4
  MILN OL16...................10 E3
  OLD OL1......................9 K5
Hunters Ms SALE M33............96 D8
  WILM/AE SK9................127 G5
Hunters Pool La MCFLDN SK10...131 M4
Hunterston Av ECC M30..........85 K2
Hunt Fold Dr TOT/BURYW BL8.....24 C3
Huntingdon Av CHAD OL9.........58 B2
Huntingdon Crs RDSH SK5 *.....100 F7
Huntingdon Wy BOL BL1..........36 B2
Huntington Av DID/WITH M20.....98 D5
Hunt La CHAD OL9...............58 D5
Huntley Mount Rd BURY BL9.......5 K1
Huntley Rd CHH M8..............72 B2
  EDGY/DAV SK3................12 A9
Huntley St BURY BL9............5 L2
Huntly Cha WILM/AE SK9........127 H6
Huntroyde Av BOLE BL2..........3 K1
Hunts Bank CSLFD M3............6 F2
Huntsham CI ALT WA14..........107 L6
Huntsman Dr IRL M44............94 C5
Huntspill Rd ALT WA14.........108 A4
Hunts Rd SLFD M6..............71 H8
Hunt St ATH M46................67 G1
  BKLY M9.....................73 G3
  WGN WN1.....................15 K5
Hurdlow Av BRO M7..............71 K5
Hurdlow Ms GLSP SK13..........104 A3
Hurdsfield Rd OFTN SK2........112 F8
Hurford Av GTN M18.............89 G6
Hurlbote CI WILM/AE SK9.......119 M7
Hurley Dr CHD/CHDH SK8........120 B5
Hurlston Rd BOLS/LL BL3........52 A2
Hurst Av CHD/CHDH SK8.........120 E6
  SALE M33...................107 H1
Hurstbank Av BNG/LEV M19 *.....99 G8
Hurst Bank Rd AUL OL6..........76 B8
Hurstbourne Av OP/CLY M11......88 C1
Hurst Brook CI GLSP SK13......105 J3
Hurstbrook Dr STRET M32........96 C2
Hurst CI GLSP SK13............105 J4
  WHTN BL5....................51 J5
Hurst Crs GLSP SK13...........105 H4
Hurstead Gn WHIT OL12 *........21 H8
Hurstead Rd MILN OL16..........29 J6
Hurstfield Rd WALK M28.........68 E4
Hurstfold Av BNG/LEV M19......111 L1
Hurst Green CI RAD M26.........38 C4
Hurst Gv AUL OL6...............76 B7
Hurst Hall Dr AUL OL6..........76 B7
Hursthead Rd CHD/CHDH SK8....120 D5
Hursthead Wk BRUN/LGST M13 *....7 K9
Hurst Hill Crs AUL OL6.........76 A8
Hurst La GOL/RIS/CUL WA3.......81 L6
Hurst Lea Ct WILM/AE SK9......130 D1
Hurst Lea Rd NM/HAY SK22......124 E5
Hurst Meadow MILN OL16.........42 E2
Hurst Mill La GOL/RIS/CUL WA3..81 M4
Hurst Rd GLSP SK13............105 J3
Hurst St BOLS/LL BL3...........51 M1
  BURY BL9.....................5 J6
  CHAD OL9.....................8 E5
  DUK SK16....................90 D6
  LEIGH WN7...................81 L1
  RDSH SK5...................100 B5
  ROCH OL11...................11 H9
  WALK M28....................68 E4
  WGNE/HIN WN2................48 F6
Hurstvale Av CHD/CHDH SK8.....119 K3
Hurstville Rd CCHDY M21........97 L6
Hurstway Dr BKLY M9............73 H1
Hurstwood AUL OL6..............76 C6
  BOL BL1.....................22 A7
Hurstwood CI OLDS OL8..........59 M8
Hurstwood Ct BOLS/LL BL3.......36 F8
Hurstwood Gv OFTN SK2.........113 K6
Huskisson Wy NEWLW WA12........78 E8
Hus St DROY M43................89 J4
Husteads La UPML OL3...........61 H3
Hutchins La OLDE OL4...........60 A3
Hutchinson Rd ROCH OL11........27 G3
Hutchinson St ROCH OL11........27 L5
Hutchinson Wy RAD M26..........54 D2
Hutton Av AUL OL6..............91 H2
  WALK M28....................68 C6
Hutton CI GOL/RIS/CUL WA3......80 A3
Hutton St WGN WN1..............31 K1
Huxley Av CHH M8...............72 D6
Huxley CI BRAM/HZG SK7........121 G5
Huxley Dr BRAM/HZG SK7........121 G5
Huxley PI WGNS/IIMK WN3........47 K7
Huxley St ALT WA14............108 A5
  BOL BL1.....................35 M2
  OLDE OL4....................59 M7
Huxley Ter ALT WA14 *.........116 E3
Huxton Gn BRAM/HZG SK7........121 J2
Hyacinth CI EDGY/DAV SK3......112 A7
  RNFD/HAY WA11...............78 C6
Hyacinth Wk PART M31..........106 B2
Hyatt Crs WGNNW/ST WN6.........30 F1
Hyde Bank Rd NM/HAY SK22......124 E5
Hyde CI WGNS/IIMK WN3..........47 K7
Hyde Dr WALK M28...............68 F2
Hyde Fold CI BNG/LEV M19.......99 J6
Hyde Gv BRUN/LGST M13..........87 J7
  SALE M33....................96 E8
  WALK M28....................68 F2
Hyde PI BRUN/LGST M13..........87 M7
Hyde Rd DTN/ASHW M34..........101 J1
  GTN M18.....................89 J3
  HYDE SK14..................103 J1
  MDTN M24....................58 B6
  MPL/ROM SK6................101 L2
  WALK M28....................68 F2
  WGTN/LGST M12...............7 M9
Hyde Sq MDTN M24...............57 H4
Hyde St BOLS/LL BL3 *..........51 M1
  DROY M43....................74 B1
  FWTH BL4....................53 J7
Hydon Brook Wk ROCH OL11.......27 M8
Hydra CI BRO M7................86 F1
Hydrangea CI SALE M33..........95 M7
Hyldavale Av
  CHD/CHDH SK8...............110 E6
Hylton Dr CHD/CHDH SK8........120 E4
Hypatia St BOLE BL2............3 K4
Hythe CI RUSH/FAL M14..........98 F1
Hythe Rd EDGY/DAV SK3..........12 A7
Hythe St BOLS/LL BL3 *.........35 K8
Hythe Wk CHAD OL9..............8 A7

# I

Ibsley WHIT OL12...............10 D3
Ice House CI WALK M28..........68 C1
Iceland St SLFD M6.............86 B2
Idonia St BOL BL1..............36 A1
Ilex Gv BRO M7.................72 A6
Ilford St OP/CLY M11...........88 C3
Ilfracombe Rd OFTN SK2........113 G4
Ilfracombe St NEWH/MOS M40.....74 A6
Ilkeston Dr WGNE/HIN WN2.......49 J1
Ilkley CI BOLE BL2..............3 L4
  CHAD OL9.....................8 B7
Ilkley Crs RDSH SK5...........100 B4
Ilkley Dr URM M41..............84 D8
Ilk St NEWH/MOS M40............73 K3
Illingworth Av STLY SK15.......91 M3
Illona St BRO M7...............71 K4
Ilminster OP/CLY M11...........10 C7
Imperial Dr LEIGH WN7..........67 G6
Imperial Ter SALE M33 *........96 D6
Ina Av BOL BL1.................35 J3
Ince CI DID/WITH M20...........98 E5
  HTNM SK4....................13 C1
Ince Green La WGNS/IIMK WN3....15 L7
Ince Hall Av WGNE/HIN WN2......48 C3
Ince St HTNM SK4..............112 B1
Inchcape Rd BKLY M9............56 F6
Inchfield CI ROCH OL11.........27 H4
Inchfield Rd NEWH/MOS M40......73 M4
Inchley Rd BRUN/LGST M13.......7 J9
Inchwood Ms OLDE OL4...........44 B8
Incline Rd OLDS OL8............74 E2
Independent St BOLS/LL BL3.....37 K7
Indigo St SLFD M6..............71 J7
Indus PI BRO M7................71 M8
Industrial St RAMS BL0.........18 F3
  WHTN BL5....................50 C5
Industry Rd WHIT OL12..........10 E1
Industry St CHAD OL9...........58 D8
  LIT OL15....................21 M7
  ROCH OL11...................27 H3
  WHIT OL12...................20 B2
Infant St PWCH M25.............55 M8
Infirmary St BOL BL1............2 F5
Ingersol Rd HOR/BR BL6.........34 B3
Ingham Rd ALT WA14...........108 A3
Inghams La LIT OL15............21 M7
Ingham St BURY BL9.............5 L6
  LEIGH WN7...................66 B4
  NEWH/MOS M40...............74 B8
  OLD OL1......................9 L5
Inghamwood CI BRO M7...........72 C5
Ingleby Av BKLY M9.............57 J8
Ingleby CI ROY/SHW OL2.........43 K4
  WGNNW/ST WN6................31 C2
  WHTN BL5....................50 C2
Ingleby Ct STRET M32...........97 H3
Ingleby Wy ROY/SHW OL2.........43 K4
Ingledene Av BRO M7............72 B3
Ingledene Gv BOL BL1 *.........35 K2
Ingle Dr OFTN SK2.............112 F5
Inglefield ROCH OL11...........27 H3
Inglehead CI DTN/ASHW M34.....101 K2
Ingle Rd CHD/CHDH SK8.........111 K6
Ingles Fold WALK M28...........68 C4
Inglesham CI LEIGH WN7.........81 H3
  NTHM/RTH M23...............109 L6
Ingleton Av CHH M8.............72 E3
Ingleton CI BOLE BL2...........23 C8
  CHD/CHDH SK8...............110 F6
  NEWLW WA12..................78 E3
  ROY/SHW OL2.................43 G7
Ingleton Ms TOT/BURYW BL8......24 E8
Ingleton Rd EDGY/DAV SK3.......12 C7
Inglewhite Av WGN WN1..........47 M2
Inglewhite CI BURY BL9.........39 G5
Inglewhite Crs WGN WN1 *.......47 M2
Inglewood Av WGN WN1...........15 K5
Inglewood CI AULW OL7..........75 M7
  BURY BL9.....................5 M1
  PART M31....................94 B8
Inglewood Hollow STLY SK15.....91 M4
Inglewood Rd CHAD OL9..........58 B3
Inglewood Wk
  BRUN/LGST M13 *............87 M7
Inglis St LIT OL15.............21 M6
Ingoe CI HEY OL10..............41 J1
Ingoldsby Av BRUN/LGST M13.....88 A7
Ingram Dr HTNM SK4............111 M4
Ingram St WGNE/HIN WN2.........64 D7
  WGNNW/ST WN6................14 A1
Ings Av WHIT OL12..............27 L2
Ings La WHIT OL12..............27 M3
Inkerman St HYDE SK14..........90 F8
  NEWH/MOS M40...............73 C7
  WHIT OL12...................10 E1
Ink St MILN OL16...............10 F4
Inman St BURY BL9..............4 D8
  DTN/ASHW M34...............101 J1
Innes St WGTN/LGST M12.........99 L1
Innis Av NEWH/MOS M40..........73 M4
Institute St BOL BL1............3 G5
Instow CI BRUN/LGST M13........88 A7
  CHAD OL9....................58 C3
International Ap MANAIR M90...118 D3
Intake La UPML OL3.............77 L1
Invar Rd WALK M28..............70 A3
Inverbeg Dr BOLE BL2...........37 K5
Inverlael Av BOL BL1...........35 L4
Inverness Av BKLY M9...........57 K8
Inverness Rd DUK SK16..........90 F5
Inward Dr WGNNW/ST WN6.........30 D7
Inwood Wk CHH M8...............72 F6
Inworth CI WHTN BL5............50 C6
Iona PI BOLE BL2...............36 F2
Iona Wy URM M41................85 C7
Ionian Gdns BRO M7.............71 M7
Ipswich St ROCH OL11...........10 F8
Iqbal CI WGTN/LGST M12.........88 D7
Iredale CI HYDE SK14...........92 C7
Irene Av HYDE SK14.............91 H8
Iris Av FWTH BL4...............53 J7
  FWTH BL4....................53 J7
Iris St OLDS OL8...............75 J2
  RAMS BL0....................18 E6
Irkdale St CHH M8..............72 F6
Irk Vale Dr OLD OL1............58 B3
Irlam Av ECC M30...............85 G3
Irlam Rd IRL M44...............94 E3
  SALE M33...................96 C8
Irlam Sq SLFD M6...............71 G7
Irlam St BOL BL1...............36 B1
  NEWH/MOS M40...............73 J4
Irlam Wharf Rd IRL M44.........94 D6
Irma St BOL BL1................36 C1

Ironmonger La
  WGNS/IIMK WN3...............14 F6
Iron St DTN/ASHW M34 *........101 H1
  HOR/BR BL6..................34 A1
  NEWH/MOS M40...............88 B1
Irvin Dr WYTH/NTH M22.........119 J4
Irvine Av WALK M28.............68 D6
Irvine St LEIGH WN7............66 C6
Irving CI OFTN SK2............121 J1
Irving St BOL BL1..............36 A4
  OLDS OL8....................74 E2
Irwell Av NEWH/MOS M40.........73 M6
Irwell CI WGNE/HIN WN2.........48 C4
Irwell Gv ECC M30..............85 J3
Irwell PI ECC M30..............85 J3
  ORD M5......................86 F3
  RAD M26.....................54 E2
  WGNW/BIL/OR WN5.............46 C5
Irwell Rd WGNW/BIL/OR WN5......46 C5
Irwell Sculpture Trail BRO M7..71 M6
Irwell St BURY BL9.............4 D5
  CSLFD M3.....................6 B4
  CSLFD M3....................72 B8
  RAD M26.....................54 E2
  RAMS BL0....................18 F8
Irwell Valley Wy BURY BL9......25 G3
  RAMS BL0....................18 F8
Irwin Dr WILM/AE SK9..........119 L7
Irwin Rd ALT WA14.............107 M4
Irwin St DTN/ASHW M34.........101 H1
Isaac CI ORD M5................86 D4
Isaac St BOL BL1...............35 M4
Isabella CI OLDTF/WHR M16......86 F8
Isabella Sq WGN WN1............15 K3
Isabella St WHIT OL12..........28 C2
Isabel Wk BOLS/LL BL3..........2 A9
Isaiah St OLDS OL8 *...........59 J8
Isa St RAMS BL0................18 F8
Isca St OP/CLY M11.............88 C3
Isherwood CI MPL/ROM SK6.....114 A6
Isherwood Fold EDGW/EG BL7.....17 G5
Isherwood Rd PART M31.........106 A2
Isherwood St HEY OL10..........41 H3
  LEIGH WN7...................66 B4
  ROCH OL11...................11 G8
Isis CI BRO M7.................71 K4
Islington Rd OFTN SK2.........112 F8
Islington St CSLFD M3..........6 B4
Islington Wy CSLFD M3..........6 A4
Isobel CI ECC M30..............84 E3
  OLDTF/WHR M16...............87 J8
Ivanhoe Av GOL/RIS/CUL WA3.....80 A3
Ivanhoe Ct BOLS/LL BL3.........52 F2
Ivanhoe St BOLS/LL BL3.........52 F2
  OLD OL1......................9 J1
Iveagh Ct MILN OL16............11 J7
Ivor St ROCH OL11..............11 L5
Ivy Bank CI BOL BL1............22 B7
Ivy Bank Rd BOL BL1............22 B7
Ivybridge CI BRUN/LGST M13.....88 A7
Ivy CI DROY M43................89 J1
  ROY/SHW OL2.................43 L5
Ivy Cottages WHIT OL12.........10 A1
Ivydale CI LEIGH WN7...........66 F7
Ivy Dr MDTN M24................57 J6
Ivy Farm Gdns
  GOL/RIS/CUL WA3.............81 G8
Ivygreen Dr OLDE OL4...........60 C6
Ivygreen Rd CCHDY M21..........97 J8
Ivy Gv FWTH BL4................52 E4
  FWTH BL4 *..................52 E4
  LHULT M38...................52 C8
Ivy House Rd GOL/RIS/CUL WA3...80 A3
Ivyleaf Sq BRO M7..............72 B6
Ivylea Rd BNG/LEV M19..........99 H8
Ivy Rd BOL BL1.................35 M3
  GOL/RIS/CUL WA3.............79 L4
  POY/DIS SK12...............129 J1
  TOT/BURYW BL8...............38 E2
  WHTN BL5....................50 C5
Ivy St AIMK WN4................78 E1
  BOLS/LL BL3.................35 M8
  ECC M30.....................85 G3
  NEWH/MOS M40...............73 K4
  WGN WN1.....................14 C1

# J

Jack Brady CI NTHM/RTH M23....109 H8
Jackdaw Rd TOT/BURYW BL8.......24 C2
Jack La DROY M43...............89 M2
  URM M41.....................96 B2
Jackman Av HEY OL10............41 G5
Jackroom Dr ANC M4 *...........7 L4
Jack's La WHTN BL5.............49 L5
Jackson Av DUK SK16............91 G4
Jackson CI HALE/TIMP WA15.....108 F5
  OLDS OL8.....................8 D3
Jackson Ct URM M41.............95 K1
Jackson Crs HULME M15..........6 D9
Jackson Gdns DTN/ASHW M34.....101 G2
Jackson Ms OLDE OL4............60 A3
Jacksons Edge Rd
  POY/DIS SK12...............123 K6
Jacksons La BRAM/HZG SK7......121 K4
Jacksons Rw CMANW M2...........6 E5
Jackson St AUL OL6.............75 L8
  CHD/CHDH SK8...............111 H6
  FAIL M35....................74 A6
  FWTH BL4....................53 J5
  FWTH BL4....................53 J5
  GLSP SK13...................93 M7
  GLSP SK13..................104 F5
  HYDE SK14..................102 A2
  HYDE SK14 *................103 K1
  MDTN M24....................57 J3
  MILN OL16...................11 K7
  OLDE OL4....................59 L5
  RAD M26.....................54 C2
  SALE M33....................97 G3
  STRET M32...................96 F3
  WALK M28....................52 F8
  WGNE/HIN WN2................48 D5
  WHIT OL12...................21 G6
  WHTF M45....................55 J5
Jack St BOLE BL2...............3 L1
Jack Taylor Ct WHIT OL12 *.....11 J1
Jacob Bright Ms WHIT OL12......28 C2
Jacobite CI BRO M7.............71 M7
Jacobsen Av HYDE SK14..........91 J8
James Andrew St MDTN M24 *.....57 L3
Jaffrey St LEIGH WN7...........66 B7
James Brindley Basin
  CMANE M1.....................7 L5
James Butterworth Ct
  MILN OL16...................11 J6

James Butterworth St
  MILN OL16 .... 11 K6
James Cl DUK SK16 .... 91 H4
  WGNS/IIMK WN3 .... 14 F6
James Corbett Rd SALQ M50 .... 85 M3
James Dr HYDE SK14 .... 102 B2
James Henry Av ORD M5 .... 86 E4
James Hill St LIT OL15 .... 91 M7
James Leech St STKP SK1 .... 13 H6
James Leigh St CMANE M1 .... 7 G7
Jameson St ROCH OL11 .... 41 L2
James PI WGNNW/ST WN6 .... 31 G2
  ROY/SHW OL2 .... 43 L4
James Sq WGNNW/ST WN6 .... 31 G2
James's St OLDE OL4 .... 60 A3
James St ATH M46 .... 67 H3
  BOLS/LL BL3 .... 53 L1
  BURY BL9 .... 5 J6
  DROY M43 .... 89 L2
  DTN/ASHW M34 .... 90 B4
  DTN/ASHW M34 * .... 101 K1
  DUK SK16 .... 91 H4
  EDGW/EG BL7 .... 22 A1
  EDGY/DAV SK3 .... 13 G8
  FAIL M35 .... 74 D4
  FWTH BL4 .... 53 J4
  GLSP SK13 .... 104 F4
  HEY OL10 * .... 41 G2
  HOR/BR BL6 .... 33 J1
  LIT OL15 .... 21 K7
  MPL/ROM SK6 .... 101 K7
  NEWH/MOS M40 .... 88 A1
  ORD M5 .... 6 A4
  PWCH M25 .... 55 K7
  RAD M26 .... 54 E2
  ROY/SHW OL2 .... 43 K7
  SALE M33 .... 97 G8
  TYLD M29 .... 67 J4
  WGNE/HIN WN2 .... 64 B5
  WGNS/IIMK WN3 .... 15 J7
  WHIT OL12 * .... 1 K1
  WHIT OL12 .... 20 B2
  WHTN BL5 .... 50 B2
James St North RAD M26 .... 54 E2
James St South CHAD OL9 * .... 58 D5
Jamieson Cl CHH M8 .... 72 B7
Jammy St BRO M7 .... 8 C7
Jane St CHAD OL9 .... 8 B7
  WHIT OL12 .... 10 C2
Janus Dr OLD OL1 .... 8 F1
Japan St BRO M7 .... 72 C5
Jardine Wy CHAD OL9 .... 58 C8
Jarvis St OLDE OL4 .... 9 M7
  WHIT OL12 .... 28 C3
Jasmine Av DROY M43 .... 89 M2
Jasmine Cl NTHM/RTH M23 .... 109 H3
Jasmine Ct BOLS/LL BL3 .... 52 B1
Jasmine Rd
  WGNW/BIL/OR WN5 * .... 47 G5
Jason St ANC M4 .... 87 L1
Jauncey St BOLS/LL BL3 .... 35 M7
Jayton Av DID/WITH M20 .... 110 C5
Jean Av LEIGH WN7 .... 81 H2
Jean Cl BNG/LEV M19 .... 99 K2
Jedburgh Av BOL BL1 .... 35 L4
Jefferson Wy WHIT OL12 .... 28 C1
Jeffreys Dr DUK SK16 .... 91 G4
Jeffrey St WGNE/HIN WN2 .... 48 D4
Jehlum Cl CHH M8 .... 72 E5
Jellicoe Av IRL M44 .... 94 B6
Jenkinson St HULME M15 .... 7 H9
  WGNE/HIN WN2 .... 49 G6
Jennaby Wk BOL BL1 .... 36 B2
Jennet Hey AIMK WN4 .... 63 J6
Jennet's La GOL/RIS/CUL WA3 .... 81 M3
Jennings Av ORD M5 .... 86 C4
Jennings Cl HYDE SK14 .... 91 L7
  ORD M5 .... 86 D4
Jennings St EDGY/DAV SK3 .... 12 F9
Jennison Cl WGTN/LGST M12 .... 88 E6
Jenny La BRAM/HZG SK7 .... 128 C1
Jenny Lind Cl BOLS/LL BL3 .... 52 F2
Jenny St OLDS OL8 .... 74 F2
Jepheys PI WHIT OL12 .... 28 C3
Jepheys St WHIT OL12 .... 28 C3
Jepson St OFTN SK2 .... 112 D6
Jericho Rd BURY BL9 .... 26 B8
Jermyn St WHIT OL12 .... 21 M7
Jerrold St LIT OL15 .... 21 L7
Jersey Rd RDSH SK5 .... 100 C3
Jersey St ANC M4 .... 7 K3
  AUL OL6 .... 75 L8
Jerusalem PI CMANW M2 * .... 6 E6
Jesmond Av PWCH M25 .... 71 L2
Jesmond Dr TOT/BURYW BL8 .... 24 F7
Jesmond Gv CHD/CHDH SK8 .... 120 D4
Jespersen St OLD OL1 .... 9 J4
Jessamine Av BRO M7 .... 72 A4
Jessel Cl BRUN/LGST M13 .... 87 M6
Jessica Wy LEIGH WN7 .... 65 L8
Jessie St BOLS/LL BL3 .... 35 M7
  NEWH/MOS M40 .... 73 K6
Jessop Dr MPL/ROM SK6 .... 114 D4
Jessop Forge BOLS/LL BL3 .... 53 K1
Jessop St GTN M18 .... 89 C7
Jethro St BOLE BL2 .... 3 L3
  BOLE BL2 .... 22 F8
Jetson St STN M18 .... 89 J6
Jimmy McMullen Wk
  RUSH/FAL M14 * .... 98 D1
Jinnah Cl OLDE OL4 .... 59 M7
  OP/CLY M11 .... 88 F4
J J Thomson Ms
  RUSH/FAL M14 * .... 98 F3
Joan St NEWH/MOS M40 .... 73 K5
Jobling St OP/CLY M11 .... 88 C4
Jocelyn St NEWH/MOS M40 .... 73 H6
Joddrell St CSLFD M3 .... 6 D5
Jodrell St NM/HAY SK22 .... 124 D3
Joel La HYDE SK14 .... 102 B7
Johannesburg Gdns
  NTHM/RTH M23 .... 109 J8
John Ashworth St WHIT OL12 .... 28 E3
John Atkinson Ct ORD M5 * .... 86 A2
John Av CHD/CHDH SK8 .... 111 H7
John Beeley Av OP/CLY M11 .... 89 G4
John Booth St OLDE OL4 .... 60 C7
John Brown St BOL BL1 * .... 2 C3
John Clynes Av
  NEWH/MOS M40 * .... 87 M1
John Cross St BOLS/LL BL3 .... 36 B8
John Dalton St CMANW M2 .... 6 E5
  GLSP SK13 .... 93 H7
John Foran Cl NEWH/MOS M40 .... 73 L6
John Gilbert Wy TRPK M17 .... 86 B7
John Heywood St OP/CLY M11 .... 88 F2
John Kennedy Gdn HYDE SK14 .... 103 K1
John Kennedy Rd HYDE SK14 .... 103 J1
John Knott St OLDE OL4 .... 60 C6
John Lee Fold MDTN M24 .... 57 K3
John Nash Crs HULME M15 .... 87 H6

Johnny King Cl
  NEWH/MOS M40 .... 73 G7
John Roberts Cl ROCH OL11 .... 10 D8
Johns Cl CCHDY M21 .... 97 L4
John Shepley St HYDE SK14 .... 102 B2
John Smeaton Ct CMANE M1 .... 7 L5
Johnson Av NEWLW WA12 .... 78 E7
  WGNE/HIN WN2 .... 65 J1
Johnsonbrook Rd HYDE SK14 .... 91 G7
Johnson Cl LEIGH WN7 .... 65 L8
Johnson Fold Av BOL BL1 .... 35 H2
Johnson's Sq NEWH/MOS M40 .... 73 G8
Johnson St ATH M46 .... 66 D3
  BOL BL1 .... 2 F6
  CSLFD M3 .... 6 D2
  HULME M15 .... 87 G6
  RAD M26 .... 54 E2
  SWIN M27 .... 71 G6
  TYLD M29 .... 67 J6
  WGNW/BIL/OR WN5 .... 46 G6
John PI MPL/ROM SK6 .... 113 M2
Johnston WHIT OL12 .... 10 D2
Johnston Av LIT OL15 * .... 29 J1
John St AMK WN4 .... 64 A7
  ALT WA14 .... 108 A3
  ANC M4 .... 7 H5
  BOLS/LL BL3 * .... 53 L1
  BRAM/HZG SK7 .... 121 M1
  BRO M7 .... 72 A8
  BURY BL9 .... 4 F3
  CSLFD M3 .... 6 D2
  DROY M43 .... 89 J4
  DTN/ASHW M34 * .... 90 C8
  ECC M30 .... 85 K3
  EDGW/EG BL7 .... 22 D5
  FAIL M35 .... 74 C3
  FWTH BL4 .... 53 H4
  GLSP SK13 .... 93 K7
  GOL/RIS/CUL WA3 .... 79 K4
  HEY OL10 .... 41 G2
  HYDE SK14 .... 102 A2
  IRL M44 .... 94 B7
  LEIGH WN7 .... 65 J4
  LIT OL15 .... 21 L7
  MILN OL16 .... 11 J6
  MILN OL16 .... 28 F1
  MPL/ROM SK6 .... 101 K7
  MPL/ROM SK6 .... 113 M2
  MPL/ROM SK6 .... 114 D7
  OLDS OL8 .... 9 G6
  PWCH M25 .... 56 B4
  ROY/SHW OL2 .... 43 G8
  ROY/SHW OL2 .... 43 K7
  SALE M33 .... 96 E7
  STKP SK1 .... 13 J6
  STLY SK15 .... 76 F7
  SWIN M27 .... 70 D4
  TYLD M29 .... 67 K3
  WALK M28 .... 53 G8
  WGN WN1 .... 15 J4
  WGNE/HIN WN2 .... 65 L1
  WGNW/BIL/OR WN5 * .... 47 G7
  WHIT OL12 .... 20 A3
John St East AULW OL7 .... 90 D3
John St West AULW OL7 .... 90 D3
  OP/CLY M11 * .... 88 F3
Joiner St ANC M4 .... 7 H4
  MDTN M24 .... 57 J3
John Rd SALE M33 .... 97 G8
Jolly Brows BOLE BL2 .... 37 G1
Jonas St BKLY M9 .... 73 H4
  CSLFD M3 .... 87 H1
Jonathan Fold LEIGH WN7 * .... 81 M4
Jones Sq STKP SK1 .... 13 K8
Jones St BOL BL1 .... 2 C5
  GLSP SK13 .... 93 K7
  MILN OL16 .... 11 H7
  OLD OL1 .... 9 M3
  RAD M26 .... 38 E8
  ROY/SHW OL2 .... 59 H2
  SLFD M6 .... 6 D1
Jonquil Dr WALK M28 .... 68 C2
Jopson St MDTN M24 .... 57 L3
Jordan Av ROY/SHW OL2 * .... 43 M3
Jordan St HULME M15 .... 6 D8
  HULME M15 .... 6 D8
Joseph Johnson Ms
  WYTH/NTH M22 * .... 110 B3
Joseph St ECC M30 .... 85 J2
  FAIL M35 .... 74 D4
  FWTH BL4 .... 53 H5
  LIT OL15 .... 21 M6
  MDTN M24 .... 57 J3
  MPL/ROM SK6 * .... 114 D6
  RAD M26 .... 54 E2
  WHIT OL12 .... 28 A2
Joshua La MDTN M24 .... 58 A5
Josslyn Rd ORD M5 .... 86 A1
Jo St ORD M5 .... 86 C4
Joule Cl ORD M5 .... 86 C4
Joules Ct STKP SK1 .... 13 K5
Joule St BKLY M9 .... 73 H3
Jowett St ORD M5 .... 59 M3
  OLDS OL8 .... 100 C8
Jowett's Wk AULW OL7 .... 90 D2
Jowkin La ROCH OL11 .... 27 G5
Joyce St NEWH/MOS M40 .... 73 L5
Joynson Av BRO M7 .... 72 A8
Joynson St SALE M33 .... 96 E7
Joy St RAMS BL0 .... 18 E6
  WHIT OL12 .... 28 C2
Jubilee Av DUK SK16 .... 91 H3
  RAD M26 .... 54 F3
  WGNS/IIMK WN3 .... 46 A8
Jubilee Crs RNFD/HAY WA11 .... 78 C5
Jubilee Gdns NM/HAY SK22 .... 124 E5
Jubilee Houses WALK M28 * .... 68 F1
Jubilee Rd MDTN M24 .... 57 L3
Jubilee St AULW OL7 .... 90 C3
  NM/HAY SK22 .... 124 E5
  ROY/SHW OL2 .... 43 M5
Jubilee Ter MDTN M24 .... 57 L2
Jubilee Wy BURY BL9 .... 4 E5
Judith St WHIT OL12 .... 27 M1
Judson Av CCHDY M21 .... 97 M7
Julia St CSLFD M3 .... 87 J1
  WHIT OL12 .... 10 D3
Julius St BNG/LEV M19 .... 99 H1
Junction Aly MILN OL16 .... 10 F5
Junction Rd BOLS/LL BL3 .... 35 L6
  OFTN SK2 .... 13 J8
Junction Rd West
  HOR/BR BL6 .... 35 G7
Junction St HYDE SK14 .... 90 F7
  MDTN M24 .... 57 A6
  OLDS OL8 .... 9 H8
Junction Ter WGNS/IIMK WN3 .... 15 L8

June Av HTNM SK4 .... 12 B3
  LEIGH WN7 .... 65 M6
Juniper Bank RDSH SK5 .... 100 D4
Juniper Cl BOL BL1 .... 36 B3
  OLDE OL4 .... 44 C8
  SALE M33 .... 96 D6
Juniper Dr MILN OL16 .... 29 G6
  WGNE/HIN WN2 .... 65 J1
Juno St OLD OL1 .... 9 L1
Jupiter Gv WGNS/IIMK WN3 .... 63 H2
Jura Cl DUK SK16 .... 91 C4
Jura Dr URM M41 .... 85 H7
Jura Gv HEY OL10 .... 40 E3
Jurby Av BKLY M9 .... 56 F8
Jury St CHH M8 .... 72 C8
  LEIGH WN7 .... 66 B5
Justene Cl GOL/RIS/CUL WA3 .... 79 K2
Justin Cl BRUN/LGST M13 .... 7 J9
Jutland Av ROCH OL11 .... 27 M4
Jutland Gv WHTN BL5 .... 50 B3
Jutland St CMANE M1 .... 7 K5

# K

Kale St BRUN/LGST M13 .... 7 K9
Kalima Gv BRO M7 .... 72 A9
Kane Ct GOL/RIS/CUL WA3 .... 80 D3
Kansas Av SALQ M50 .... 86 A4
Kara St SLFD M6 .... 86 B2
Karen Rd WGN WN1 .... 15 L4
Kate St RAMS BL0 .... 18 E6
Kathan Cl MILN OL16 .... 11 K5
Katherine Rd OFTN SK2 .... 112 F7
Katherine St AULW OL7 .... 90 C2
Kathleen Gv RUSH/FAL M14 .... 98 F2
Kathleen St WHIT OL12 .... 10 B3
Kay Av MPL/ROM SK6 .... 113 G1
Kay Brow HEY OL10 .... 40 F2
  RAMS BL0 .... 18 F6
Kay Cl WGN WN1 .... 15 J4
Kayfields BOLE BL2 .... 23 H8
Kay's Av STKP SK1 .... 112 E3
Kay St ATH M46 .... 67 G2
  BOL BL1 .... 2 E1
  BOL BL1 .... 2 F3
  BOLS/LL BL3 .... 53 K1
  BURY BL9 .... 5 J2
  BURY BL9 .... 24 F1
  EDGW/EG BL7 .... 16 F8
  HEY OL10 .... 40 F2
  OP/CLY M11 .... 88 C5
  ROCH OL11 .... 10 D8
  SLFD M6 .... 71 J6
  STKP SK1 .... 13 J3
  STLY SK15 .... 91 K3
Kays Wood Rd MPL/ROM SK6 .... 114 A6
Keadby Cl ECC M30 .... 85 G4
Keal Dr IRL M44 .... 83 L8
Kearsley Dr BOLS/LL BL3 .... 52 E1
Kearsley Hall Rd RAD M26 .... 53 M5
Kearsley Rd CHH M8 .... 72 D2
  RAD M26 .... 53 M4
Kearsley St ECC M30 .... 84 E2
  LEIGH WN7 .... 66 A7
  WGNNW/ST WN6 .... 14 D2
Kearsley V RAD M26 .... 53 L4
Kearton Dr ECC M30 .... 85 K3
Keary Cl GTN M18 .... 89 G6
Keaton Cl SLFD M6 .... 71 H8
Keats Av DROY M43 .... 89 K2
  DTN/ASHW M34 .... 101 K4
  WGNNW/ST WN6 .... 47 H1
  WGNS/IIMK WN3 .... 14 C9
  WGNW/BIL/OR WN5 .... 62 A3
  WHIT OL12 .... 27 K3
Keats Cl RAD M26 .... 38 B8
Keats Fold DUK SK16 .... 91 L5
Keats Ms NTHM/RTH M23 .... 108 F4
  OLD OL1 .... 59 L3
  TOT/BURYW BL8 .... 24 C7
Keats St LEIGH WN7 .... 66 A5
Keats Wy WGNE/HIN WN2 .... 65 K4
Keb La OLDS OL8 .... 75 K4
Keble Av OLDS OL8 .... 75 H1
Keble Gv LEIGH WN7 .... 65 M4
Keble St WGNE/HIN WN2 .... 48 C5
Kedleston Av RUSH/FAL M14 .... 88 B3
Kedleston Gn OFTN SK2 .... 113 G5
Keele Cl NEWH/MOS M40 .... 87 M1
Keele Wk NEWH/MOS M40 .... 87 M1
Keepers Dr WHIT OL12 .... 27 H2
The Keep BOL BL1 .... 35 H5
Keighley Av DROY M43 .... 89 K1
Keighley Cl TOT/BURYW BL8 .... 38 C2
Keighley St BOL BL1 .... 35 M2
Keilder Ms BOL BL1 .... 35 K4
Keith Dr EDGY/DAV SK3 .... 12 A9
Keith Wk NEWH/MOS M40 .... 88 A1
Kelboro Av DTN/ASHW M34 .... 90 A5
Kelbrook Ct OFTN SK2 .... 113 H7
Kelbrook Rd OP/CLY M11 .... 88 E4
Kelby Av NTHM/RTH M23 .... 109 L5
Keld Cl TOT/BURYW BL8 .... 24 A7
Kelfield Av SALE M33 .... 109 K2
Kellaton Cl WGNS/IIMK WN3 .... 15 K7
Kellbank Rd WGNS/IIMK WN3 .... 63 H1
Kellbrook Crs BRO M7 .... 71 K4
Kellet Cl WGNW/BIL/OR WN5 .... 47 G3
Kellets Rw WALK M28 * .... 53 G7
Kellett St BOL BL1 .... 22 C6
  MILN OL16 .... 11 J3
Kelling Wk HULME M15 .... 6 B9
Kells Gv WGNNW/ST WN6 .... 47 J2
Kelmarsh Cl OP/CLY M11 .... 89 C5
Kelsall Crs EDGY/DAV SK3 .... 112 A6
Kelsall Dr DROY M43 .... 89 J1
  HALE/TIMP WA15 .... 108 F6
Kelsall Rd CHD/CHDH SK8 .... 111 K7
Kelsall St CHAD OL9 .... 8 E6
  MILN OL16 .... 96 D8
  SALE M33 .... 96 D8
  WGTN/LGST M12 .... 88 C6
Kelso Cl OLDS OL8 .... 75 J3
Kelso Gv WGNE/HIN WN2 .... 49 G8
Kelson Av AULW OL7 .... 75 K7
Kelstern Av BRUN/LGST M13 .... 99 H1
Kelstern Sq BRUN/LGST M13 .... 99 H1
Kelton Cl RDSH SK5 .... 100 C7
Kelverlow St OLDE OL4 .... 59 M7
Kelvin Av MDTN M24 .... 56 E5
  SALE M33 .... 96 A3
Kelvin Cl AIMK WN4 .... 63 G8
Kelvindale Dr
  HALE/TIMP WA15 .... 108 F5
Kelvin Gv CHH M8 .... 72 D6
  WGNS/IIMK WN3 .... 63 J2
Kelvington Dr BKLY M9 .... 73 G5
Kelvin St ANC M4 .... 7 H3
  AULW OL7 .... 90 C4

Kelway Ter WGN WN1 .... 15 J1
Kemble Av NTHM/RTH M23 .... 109 M3
Kemmel Av WYTH/NTH M22 .... 110 B7
Kemp Av ROCH OL11 .... 10 B9
Kempnough Hall Rd WALK M28 .... 69 J5
Kemp Rd MPL/ROM SK6 .... 114 F4
Kempsey Ct CHAD OL9 .... 8 A3
Kempsford Cl NTHM/RTH M23 .... 109 L6
Kempster St BRO M7 .... 72 A8
Kempton Gdns BOLS/LL BL3 .... 36 B2
  DROY M43 .... 89 M2
  NEWLW WA12 .... 79 C7
Kempton Wy CHAD OL9 .... 8 C5
Kemsing Wk ORD M5 * .... 86 D2
Kendal Av AULW OL7 .... 75 J8
  DTN/ASHW M34 .... 101 K3
  HYDE SK14 .... 90 F7
  SALE M33 .... 108 F1
  URM M41 .... 84 B8
  WHIT OL12 .... 27 H2
Kendal Cl HALE/TIMP WA15 .... 109 G7
  HEY OL10 .... 41 H4
Kendal Dr BRAM/HZG SK7 .... 120 E7
  BURY BL9 .... 39 G5
  CHD/CHDH SK8 .... 110 F8
  ROY/SHW OL2 .... 44 B5
Kendal Gdns MPL/ROM SK6 .... 101 L8
Kendale AIMK WN4 .... 63 J8
  LEIGH WN7 .... 66 A7
  WALK M28 .... 69 J2
  WHTH M45 .... 55 J4
Kendall Rd CHH M8 .... 72 C1
Kendal Rd BOL BL1 .... 35 M4
  RAMS BL0 .... 24 C2
  SLFD M6 .... 70 F7
  STRET M32 .... 97 G1
  WALK M28 .... 68 D5
  WGNE/HIN WN2 .... 48 D4
  WGNE/HIN WN2 .... 49 H8
Kendal Rd West RUSH/FAL M14 .... 98 F1
Kendal St WGNNW/ST WN6 .... 14 D2
Kendon Gv DTN/ASHW M34 .... 101 H1
Kendrew Rd BOLS/LL BL3 .... 35 K8
Kendrick PI WGN WN1 .... 15 K3
Kenford Dr WGNS/IIMK WN3 .... 63 H2
Kenhall Rd LEIGH WN7 .... 66 F8
Kenilworth ROCH OL11 .... 10 D7
Kenilworth Av CHAD OL9 .... 58 B3
  CHD/WITH M20 .... 98 C7
  SWIN M27 .... 70 E1
  WHTF M45 .... 55 K6
  WILM/AE SK9 .... 127 H1
Kenilworth Cl MPL/ROM SK6 .... 114 C4
  OLDE OL4 .... 60 C8
  RAD M26 .... 38 C6
Kenilworth Dr BRAM/HZG SK7 .... 121 M4
  LEIGH WN7 .... 67 H5
  WGNE/HIN WN2 .... 49 J8
Kenilworth Gv DTN/ASHW M34 .... 89 M4
Kenilworth Rd EDGY/DAV SK3 .... 111 J3
  GOL/RIS/CUL WA3 .... 80 E5
  MILN OL16 .... 29 G8
  SALE M33 .... 96 B8
  URM M41 .... 94 F3
Kenilworth Sq BOL BL1 .... 35 L3
Kenion Rd ROCH OL11 .... 27 L6
Kenion St MILN OL16 .... 10 F5
Kenley Dr HEY OL10 .... 41 J5
Kenley Ldg BRAM/HZG SK7 * .... 120 F5
Kenley Wk CHH M8 * .... 72 F6
Kenmay Av BOLS/LL BL3 .... 35 J6
Kenmere Gv NEWH/MOS M40 .... 73 J3
Kenmor Av TOT/BURYW BL8 .... 38 D4
Kenmore Cl WHTF M45 .... 55 L4
Kenmore Dr
  HALE/TIMP WA15 .... 117 J1
Kenmore Gv AIMK WN4 .... 63 G8
  IRL M44 .... 94 A6
Kenmore Rd SALE M33 .... 107 M5
  WHTF M45 .... 55 L4
  WYTH/NTH M22 .... 109 M5
Kennard Cl BKLY M9 .... 73 J3
Kennedy Dr BOLS/LL BL3 .... 53 M1
  BURY BL9 .... 55 L2
Kennedy Rd ORD M5 .... 85 M2
  TYLD M29 .... 68 A5
Kennedy Sq HYDE SK14 * .... 103 J2
Kennedy St BOLE BL2 .... 3 M4
  CMANW M2 .... 6 F5
  OLDS OL8 .... 9 H9
Kennedy Wy
  DTN/ASHW M34 .... 101 G2
  HTNM SK4 .... 12 D3
Kennerley Rd OFTN SK2 .... 112 D7
Kennerley's La WILM/AE SK9 .... 126 E5
Kennet Cl WHTN BL5 .... 50 C3
  WILM/AE SK9 .... 127 H2
Kenneth Av LEIGH WN7 .... 66 A6
Kenneth Gv LEIGH WN7 .... 66 A6
Kenneth Sq BRO M7 .... 72 B6
Kennett Dr MPL/ROM SK6 .... 101 J8
Kennett Rd NTHM/RTH M23 .... 118 C1
Kennet Wy LEIGH WN7 .... 66 C5
Kenninghall Rd
  WYTH/NTH M22 .... 118 F1
Kennington Av
  NEWH/MOS M40 .... 73 L8
Kennington Fold BOLS/LL BL3 .... 52 A1
Kenny Cl OLDE OL4 .... 60 B7
Kensington Av AUL OL6 .... 76 B8
  CHAD OL9 .... 58 B4
  HYDE SK14 * .... 102 B3
  RAD M26 .... 38 A8
  ROY/SHW OL2 .... 42 F6
  RUSH/FAL M14 .... 98 B3
Kensington Cl MILN OL16 .... 29 K6
  TOT/BURYW BL8 .... 24 D3
Kensington Ct BOL BL1 * .... 2 B3
  HYDE SK14 .... 102 B3
  WILM/AE SK9 .... 126 E6
Kensington Dr HOR/BR BL6 .... 33 M1
  LEIGH WN7 .... 67 H5
  ORD M5 .... 86 A1
  TOT/BURYW BL8 .... 38 D4
Kensington Gdns
  HALE/TIMP WA15 .... 117 H3
  ALT WA14 .... 108 A4
Kensington Gv ALT WA14 .... 108 A4
  DTN/ASHW M34 .... 89 L8
  STLY SK15 .... 91 K4
Kensington Rd CCHDY M21 .... 97 K2
  EDGY/DAV SK3 .... 12 A9
  FAIL M35 .... 74 E4
  OLDS OL8 .... 59 G4
  WGNW/BIL/OR WN5 * .... 47 G7

Kensington St BOL BL1 .... 2 C4
  HYDE SK14 .... 102 B3
  ROCH OL11 .... 28 B8
  RUSH/FAL M14 .... 98 D1
Kenslow Av CHH M8 .... 72 C2
Kensworth Cl BOL BL1 .... 36 A3
Kensworth Dr BOL BL1 .... 36 A3
Kent Av CHAD OL9 .... 58 D6
  CHD/CHDH SK8 .... 111 M8
  DROY M43 .... 89 H3
  WGNE/HIN WN2 .... 64 D2
Kent Cl UPML OL3 .... 45 M8
  WALK M28 .... 68 D2
Kent Ct BOL BL1 .... 2 D3
Kent Dr BURY BL9 .... 5 G8
  FWTH BL4 .... 53 L6
Kentford Dr NEWH/MOS M40 .... 72 F8
Kentford Rd BOL BL1 .... 2 D1
Kentmere Av WHIT OL12 .... 28 E1
Kentmere Cl MDTN/CHDH SK8 .... 119 K1
Kentmere Dr MDTN M24 .... 57 H1
  TYLD M29 .... 67 L5
Kentmere Gv FWTH BL4 .... 52 C5
Kentmere Rd BOLE BL2 .... 37 J3
  HALE/TIMP WA15 .... 109 G6
Kentmore Cl HTNM SK4 .... 111 H2
  WGTN/LGST M12 .... 88 D5
Kenton Av GTN M18 .... 99 M1
Kenton Cl BOL BL1 .... 36 A3
  DTN/ASHW M34 .... 90 A5
Kenton Rd ROY/SHW OL2 .... 43 K5
Kenton St OLDS OL8 .... 59 L7
Kent Rd ATH M46 .... 50 F8
  DTN/ASHW M34 .... 100 D2
  EDGY/DAV SK3 .... 12 A7
  FAIL M35 .... 74 B6
  GLSP SK13 .... 105 G3
  PART M31 .... 106 B2
  TYLD M29 .... 67 J2
Kent Rd East RUSH/FAL M14 .... 98 F1
Kent Rd West RUSH/FAL M14 .... 98 F1
Kentsford Dr RAD M26 .... 54 A4
Kentstone Av BNG/LEV M19 .... 111 G1
Kent St BOL BL1 .... 2 D2
  BRO M7 .... 72 A8
  CMANW M2 * .... 6 F4
  LEIGH WN7 .... 67 G8
  OLDS OL8 .... 59 J8
  ROCH OL11 .... 10 E7
  SWIN M27 .... 70 C2
  WGN WN1 .... 15 J5
Kentucky St OLDE OL4 .... 59 M6
Kentwell Cl DUK SK16 .... 90 F5
Kenwick Dr NEWH/MOS M40 .... 74 B2
Kenwood Av BNG/LEV M19 .... 99 J4
  BRAM/HZG SK7 .... 120 F7
  CHD/CHDH SK8 .... 110 D6
  HALE/TIMP WA15 .... 117 J2
  LEIGH WN7 .... 66 F8
Kenwood Cl LEIGH WN7 .... 66 F8
  STRET M32 .... 97 G5
Kenwood La WALK M28 .... 69 J7
Kenwood Rd BOL BL1 .... 35 L3
  RDSH SK5 .... 100 B2
  STRET M32 .... 97 H3
Kenworthy Av AUL OL6 .... 76 A7
Kenworthy Cl HYDE SK14 .... 103 H2
Kenworthy Gdns UPML OL3 .... 61 L4
Kenworthy La WYTH/NTH M22 .... 110 A2
Kenworthy St MILN OL16 .... 11 L4
  STLY SK15 .... 91 K3
Kenwright St ANC M4 .... 7 H4
Kenwyn St NEWH/MOS M40 .... 73 L5
Kenyon Av DUK SK16 .... 91 H5
  OLDS OL8 .... 75 J1
  SALE M33 .... 109 H2
Kenyon Crs BURY BL9 .... 25 J6
Kenyon Fold ROCH OL11 .... 27 H7
Kenyon Gv LHULT M38 .... 52 B8
Kenyon La GOL/RIS/CUL WA3 .... 80 C6
  MDTN M24 .... 57 M4
  NEWH/MOS M40 .... 73 K4
  PWCH M25 .... 55 M8
Kenyon Rd BOLE BL2 .... 37 L7
  WGN WN1 .... 47 M2
  WGNNW/ST WN6 .... 31 G2
Kenyons La North
  RNFD/HAY WA11 .... 78 C4
Kenyon's La South
  RNFD/HAY WA11 .... 78 C4
Kenyon St AUL OL6 .... 90 C1
  BURY BL9 .... 5 L4
  DUK SK16 .... 90 E4
  GTN M18 .... 89 H6
  HEY OL10 .... 41 G2
  LEIGH WN7 .... 66 A4
  RAMS BL0 .... 18 F5
Kenyon Ter LHULT M38 .... 68 B1
Kenyon Wy LHULT M38 .... 68 C1
  TOT/BURYW BL8 .... 24 C7
Keppel Rd CCHDY M21 .... 97 L3
Keppel St AUL OL6 .... 90 F1
Kepplecove Meadow
  WALK M28 .... 68 C7
Kepwick Dr WYTH/NTH M22 .... 119 G3
Kerans Dr WHTN BL5 .... 50 B3
Kerenhappuch St RAMS BL0 .... 18 E7
Kerfoot Cl
  WYTH/NTH M22 .... 110 B4
Kerfoot St LEIGH WN7 .... 66 F8
Kermoor Av BOL BL1 .... 22 B6
Kerne Gv NTHM/RTH M23 .... 109 K3
Kerrera Dr ORD M5 * .... 86 A3
Kerridge Dr
  MPL/ROM SK6 .... 101 J8
Kerris Cl WYTH/NTH M22 .... 119 G3
Kerr St BKLY M9 .... 73 G1
Kerry Gv BOLE BL2 .... 3 K2
Kersal Av LHULT M38 .... 52 E8
  SWIN M27 .... 70 F4
Kersal Bank BRO M7 .... 71 M4
Kersal Cl PWCH M25 .... 71 M3
Kersal Crag BRO M7 .... 71 M3
Kersal Dr HALE/TIMP WA15 .... 108 F5
Kersal Hall Av BRO M7 .... 71 K4
Kersal Rd PWCH M25 .... 71 J3
Kersal Vale Rd PWCH M25 .... 71 J3
Kersal Wy BRO M7 .... 71 K4
Kerscott Rd
  NTHM/RTH M23 .... 109 H2
Kersh Av BNG/LEV M19 .... 99 L8
Kershaw Av BOLS/LL BL3 .... 37 K8
  PWCH M25 .... 71 J2
  SALE M33 .... 109 G2
Kershaw Dr CHAD OL9 .... 58 A8
Kershaw Gv
  DTN/ASHW M34 .... 89 L4
Kershaw La DTN/ASHW M34 .... 89 M4
Kershaw Rd FAIL M35 .... 74 C4

Kershaw St AULW OL7......90 C4
BOLE BL2......22 F7
BOLS/LL BL3......2 B8
BURY BL9......5 H5
DROY M43......89 J5
GLSP SK13......104 F4
HEY OL10......40 E2
ROY/SHW OL2......43 G7
ROY/SHW OL2......43 L5
TYLD M29......67 K3
WGNW/BIL/OR WN5......46 E6
WHIT OL12 *......
Kershaw St East ROY/SHW OL2......43 L5
Kershaw Wk WGTN/LGST M12......88 A4
Kershaw Wy NEWLW WA12......78 F7
Kershope Gv ORD M5......86 D4
Kersley St OLDE OL4......59 L6
Kerwin Wk OP/CLY M11 *......88 C4
Kesteven Rd BKLY M9......73 C5
Kestner Av BKLY M9......5 H5
DROY M43......89 H3
Keston Crs RDSH SK5......100 C6
Keston Rd OLD OL1......59 M3
Kestor St BOLE BL2......3 J4
Kestral Vw GLSP SK13......104 G4
Kestrel Av DTN/ASHW M34......90 A8
FWTH BL4 *......52 C5
LHULT M38......52 D7
OLDE OL4......59 M7
SWIN M27......70 E2
Kestrel Cl HYDE SK14......91 H8
MPL/ROM SK6......123 J1
PWCH M25......55 K6
Kestrel Dr AIMK WN4......63 M6
BURY BL9......5 K1
IRL M44......94 D1
Kestrel Rd TRPK M17......85 J4
Kestrel St BOL BL1......3 G3
Kestrel Wk WGTN/LGST M12......88 D6
Keswick Av AULW OL7......75 J7
CHAD OL9......58 D5
CHD/CHDH SK8......119 L4
DTN/ASHW M34......90 A8
HYDE SK14......90 F8
OLDS OL8......59 K8
URM M41......95 H3
Keswick Cl BRUN/LGST M13......88 A8
IRL M44......94 A8
MDTN M24......57 G2
STLY SK15......76 D8
Keswick Gv SLFD M6......86 C1
Keswick Pl WGNE/HIN WN2......48 D5
Keswick Rd HALE/TIMP WA15......109 M4
HTNM SK4......100 A5
MPL/ROM SK6......123 J1
STRET M32......96 F1
WALK M28......69 J2
Keswick St BOL BL1......36 C2
ROCH OL11......41 L2
Kettering Rd BNG/LEV M19......99 K3
Kettleshulme Wy
POY/DIS SK12......129 L2
Ketton Cl OP/CLY M11......89 H5
Kevin Av ROY/SHW OL2......59 H2
Kevin St BNG/LEV M19......99 L4
Kew Av HYDE SK14......102 B5
Kew Dr CHD/CHDH SK8......120 A2
URM M41......94 D8
Kew Gdns NEWH/MOS M40......73 K3
Kew Rd FAIL M35......74 D4
OLDE OL4......59 L6
ROCH OL11......42 D1
Key Ct DTN/ASHW M34......101 K4
Keymer St OP/CLY M11......88 E1
Keynsham Rd OP/CLY M11......88 E1
Keystone Cl SLFD M6......71 H8
Key West Cl OP/CLY M11......88 C3
Keyworth Wk NEWH/MOS M40......73 H8
Khartoum St OLDTF/WHR M16......87 G8
OP/CLY M11......89 G2
Kibbles Brow EDGW/EG BL7......22 E4
Kibboth Crew RAMS BL0......18 E5
Kibworth Cl WHTF M45......55 H2
Kidderminster Wy CHAD OL9......58 C3
Kidd Rd GLSP SK13......105 H6
Kid Glove Rd GOL/RIS/CUL WA3......79 J3
Kid St MDTN M24......57 J3
Kiel Cl ECC M30......84 F2
Kielder Cl AIMK WN4......63 J5
Kielder Hl MDTN M24......41 J8
Kilbride Av BOLE BL2......37 J6
Kilbuck La RNFD/HAY WA11......78 D4
Kilburn Av AIMK WN4......64 A8
BKLY M9......57 G2
Kilburn Cl CHD/CHDH SK8......119 L5
LEIGH WN7......66 A3
Kilburn Dr WGNNW/ST WN6......30 E5
Kilburn Gv WGNS/IIMK WN3......15 G1
Kilburn Rd EDGY/DAV SK3......12 D8
RAD M26......38 A8
Kilburn St OLD OL1......59 M3
Kilcoby Av SWIN M27......71 H4
Kildale Cl BOLS/LL BL3......35 L5
Kildare Crs ROCH OL11......42 D2
Kildare Rd CCHDY M21......98 A4
SWIN M27......70 B5
Kildare St FWTH BL4......52 C5
WGNE/HIN WN2......48 F7
WGNS/IIMK WN3......47 J6
Kildonan Dr BOLS/LL BL3......35 J6
Killer St RAMS BL0 *......
Killington Cl WGNS/IIMK WN3......63 L2
Killingworth Ms HOR/BR BL6 *......34 A3
Kilnerstun St BURY BL9......5 H7
Kilmaine Av BKLY M9......73 L1
Kilmaine Dr BOLS/LL BL3......35 H7
Kilmington Dr CHH M8......72 C6
Kilmory Dr BOLE BL2......37 J6
Kilmory Fold GLSP SK13......105 H1
Kiln Bank La WILM/AE SK9 *......120 A2
Kilnbrook Cl OLDE OL4......60 E8
Kiln Brow EDGW/EG BL7......22 F4
Kiln Cft MPL/ROM SK6......113 J3
Kiln Croft La WILM/AE SK9......120 A8
Kilner Cl BURY BL9......39 L8
Kilnerdeyne Ter MILN OL16......10 D6
Kilner Wk NEWH/MOS M40......72 D6
Kiln Fld EDGW/EG BL7......22 F4
Kiln Hill Cl OLD OL1......58 C2
Kiln Hill La OLD OL1......58 C2
Kilnhurst Wk BOL BL1 *......2 B3
Kiln La GLSP SK13......93 K7
MILN OL16......29 K5
Kilnside Dr BKLY M9......73 G5
Kiln St RAMS BL0 *......
Kiln Wk WHIT OL12......28 B2
Kilnwick Cl GTN M18......99 L1
The Kilphin HOR/BR BL6......34 E4
Kilrush Av ECC M30......85 G4

Kilsby Cl FWTH BL4......52 E2
HOR/BR BL6......34 F6
Kilsby Wk NEWH/MOS M40......73 G8
Kilshaw St WGNW/BIL/OR WN5......46 F7
Kilton Wk NEWH/MOS M40 *......72 F8
Kilvert Dr SALE M33......96 C7
Kilvert St TRPK M17......86 D7
Kilworth Av SALE M33......108 C1
Kilworth Dr HOR/BR BL6......35 G6
Kilworth St ROCH OL11......10 B9
Kimberley Av MPL/ROM SK6......113 J2
Kimberley Pl AIMK WN4......78 F1
Kimberley St BOL BL1......22 B7
Kimberley St BRO M7 *......72 B5
EDGY/DAV SK3......13 H9
OLDS OL8......74 F1
Kimberley Wk HULME M15......6 B9
Kimberly St WGNNW/ST WN6......14 B1
Kimbolton Cl WGTN/LGST M12......88 D5
Kinburn Rd BNG/LEV M19......111 G2
Kincardine Rd BRUN/LGST M13 *......7 J9
Kincraig Cl BOLS/LL BL3......35 H8
OP/CLY M11......88 F3
Kinder Av AUL OL6......76 D6
OLDE OL4......60 A7
Kinder Cl GLSP SK13......104 D4
Kinder Dr MPL/ROM SK6......114 D6
Kinder Fold STLY SK15......92 A6
Kinder Gv AIMK WN4......63 J6
MPL/ROM SK6......114 B2
Kinders Crs UPML OL3......61 L8
Kinders Fold LIT OL15......21 K5
Kinders La UPML OL3......61 M6
Kinders Ms UPML OL3 *......61 L7
Kinder St EDGY/DAV SK3......13 G8
STLY SK15......91 K2
Kinderton Av DID/WITH M20......98 E5
Kinder Wy MDTN M24......56 F1
Kineton Wk BRUN/LGST M13 *......87 M6
King Albert St ROY/SHW OL2......43 L5
King Charles Ct GLSP SK13......105 G5
King Edward Av GLSP SK13......105 G3
King Edward Rd HYDE SK14......102 B5
King Edward St BNG/LEV M19......99 L3
ECC M30......84 F2
ORD M5......86 E4
Kingfisher Av DTN/ASHW M34......89 M3
Kingfisher Cl WGTN/LGST M12......88 B7
Kingfisher Ct AIMK WN4......63 L6
Kingfisher Dr BURY BL9......25 L8
Kingfisher Rd OFTN SK2......113 J8
Kingfisher Wy GLSP SK13......104 C4
King George Cl AIMK WN4......78 E1
King George Rd HYDE SK14......102 B3
RNFD/HAY WA11......78 D5
Kingham Dr ANC M4 *......7 M2
Kingholm Gdns BOL BL1 *......36 A3
King La BOL BL1......44 B8
Kingmoor Av RAD M26......38 E8
King's Acre ALT WA14......116 C3
Kings Av CHD/CHDH SK8......110 D8
CHH M8......72 D4
GOL/RIS/CUL WA3......80 C5
WHTF M45......55 H2
Kingsbridge Av BOLE BL2......38 A3
HYDE SK14......102 F2
Kingsbridge Dr DUK SK16......90 E5
Kingsbridge Dr BKLY M9......72 F5
OLDS OL8 *......59 L7
Kingsbrook Rd
OLDTF/WHR M16......98 B4
Kingsbury Av BOL BL1......35 K3
Kingsbury Cl TOT/BURYW BL8......24 D6
Kingsbury Dr WILM/AE SK9......127 H4
Kingsbury Rd OP/CLY M11......88 F2
Kingscliffe St BKLY M9......73 H5
King's Ct BRAM/HZG SK7......121 H2
GTN M18......89 J6
PWCH M25......55 M7
WILM/AE SK9......126 E6
Kings Ct RDSH SK5......100 B3
Kingscourt Av BOL BL1......35 M2
Kings Crs OLDTF/WHR M16......97 L1
TYLD M29......67 H4
Kingscroft Ct WGN WN1......15 J5
Kingsdale Cl BURY BL9......39 K5
Kingsdale Rd GTN M18......89 K8
Kingsdown Dr BOL BL1......2 E1
Kingsdown Gdns BOL BL1 *......2 D4
Kingsdown Rd WGNE/HIN WN2......64 E5
WYTH/NTH M22......118 E3
Kings Dr CHD/CHDH SK8......120 C1
HTNM SK4......111 K1
MDTN M24......57 G4
MPL/ROM SK6......114 B5
Kingsfield Dr DID/WITH M20......110 F2
Kingsfield Wy TYLD M29......67 L4
Kings Fold ALT WA14......116 C3
Kingsfold Av NEWH/MOS M40 *......72 F8
Kingsford St ORD M5......86 A2
King's Gdns LEIGH WN7......66 F7
Kingsgate BOL BL1 *......2 D4
Kingsgate Rd WYTH/NTH M22......118 E3
Kings Gv STRET M32......97 J1
WHIT OL12......21 G8
Kingsheath Av OP/CLY M11......88 E1
Kingshill Ct WGNNW/ST WN6......31 J5
Kingshill Rd CCHDY M21......97 K4
Kingsholme Rd
WYTH/NTH M22......118 A4
Kingsland Cl NEWH/MOS M40......88 A1
Kingsland Rd EDGY/DAV SK3......111 K5
FWTH BL4......52 C3
ROCH OL11......41 L1
Kings La STRET M32......96 F2
Kingslea Rd DID/WITH M20......98 F7
Kingsleigh Rd HTNM SK4......99 J8
Kingsley Av BKLY M9......73 J5
BRO M7......71 K5
HTNM SK4......100 B8
STRET M32......97 J1
URM M41 *......95 L2
WGNS/IIMK WN3......63 J1
WHTF M45......55 K5
Kingsley Cl AUL OL6......76 D7
DTN/ASHW M34......101 G3
OLDE OL4......60 B5
Kingsley Dr CHD/CHDH SK8......120 C1
DTN/ASHW M34......89 M4
Kingsley Gv DTN/ASHW M34......89 M4
Kingsley Rd HALE/TIMP WA15......108 E3
MDTN M24......56 E1
OLDE OL4......59 M6
SWIN M27......70 A5
WALK M28......69 H2
WGNE/HIN WN2 *......49 J7
WYTH/NTH M22......110 A4

Kingsley St BOL BL1......36 A2
LEIGH WN7......65 M5
TOT/BURYW BL8......
King's Lynn Cl DID/WITH M20......110 E1
Kingsmead Ms BKLY M9......56 F7
Kingsmede WGN WN1......
Kingsmere Av BNG/LEV M19......99 J3
Kingsmill Av BNG/LEV M19......99 L4
Kingsmoor Flds GLSP SK13......105 G5
Kingsmoor Rd GLSP SK13......105 G2
Kingsnorth Rd URM M41......95 L1
Kingsoak Cl WGN WN1......15 H3
Kings Pk ATH M46......66 D4
King's Rd AIMK WN4......63 K7
AUL OL6......75 M8
BRAM/HZG SK7......122 A1
CCHDY M21......98 A4
CHAD OL9......74 B1
CHD/CHDH SK8......120 C1
DTN/ASHW M34......90 B3
GOL/RIS/CUL WA3......79 K5
HALE SK14......94 B6
MILN OL16......11 J9
MPL/ROM SK6......113 K1
OLDS OL8......9 K9
OLDTF/WHR M16......98 A1
PWCH M25......71 M2
ROY/SHW OL2......43 K6
SALE M33......96 C8
STRET M32......97 H2
WILM/AE SK9......
Kings St WHTN BL5......50 C3
Kings Ter STRET M32 *......97 J1
Kingston Av BOLE BL2......3 L1
CHAD OL9......58 D8
DID/WITH M20......110 E3
OLD OL1......59 L3
Kingston Cl BRO M7......72 A4
HYDE SK14......103 H2
ROY/SHW OL2......43 L5
SALE M33......108 A2
TOT/BURYW BL8......24 A5
WGNS/IIMK WN3......63 L1
Kingston Dr ROY/SHW OL2......42 F6
SALE M33......97 G2
URM M41......95 K1
Kingston Gdns HYDE SK14......101 L1
Kingston Gv BKLY M9......57 J8
Kingston Hl CHD/CHDH SK8......111 G8
Kingston Ml EDGY/DAV SK3 *......12 F5
Kingston Pl CHD/CHDH SK8......120 A2
Kingston Rd DID/WITH M20......110 E3
FAIL M35......74 C5
RAD M26......38 E6
WILM/AE SK9......119 L8
Kingston St EDGY/DAV SK3......12 F5
King St BOL BL1......2 D4
BOLE BL2......23 G7
BRO M7......72 B5
CMANW M2......6 F4
CSLFD M3......6 D2
DROY M43......89 K4
DTN/ASHW M34......90 C6
DTN/ASHW M34......101 J1
DUK SK16......90 D6
ECC M30......85 J3
EDGW/EG BL7......22 C4
FAIL M35......74 A6
FWTH BL4......53 J4
GLSP SK13......104 F4
HYDE SK14......103 K4
HYDE SK14......102 A1
LEIGH WN7......66 C8
MDTN M24......57 K3
MILN OL16......10 E4
MOSL OL5......77 G3
OLDS OL8......9 H6
RAD M26......54 E2
RAMS BL0......18 F6
SLFD M6......71 G7
STLY SK15......91 K2
UPML OL3......45 J8
WGN WN1......14 F4
WGNE/HIN WN2......48 D5
WGNE/HIN WN2......48 D5
WHIT OL12......20 B1
King St East ROCH OL11......10 E8
STKP SK1......13 J2
King St South ROCH OL11......10 D8
King St West CSLFD M3......6 E4
EDGY/DAV SK3......13 G6
HTNM SK4......12 F4
WGN WN1......14 F4
Kings Vw HTNM SK4 *......12 F3
Kingsway ALT WA14......108 A7
BNG/LEV M19......99 H5
BRAM/HZG SK7......121 H2
DID/WITH M20......110 F2
DID/WITH M20......111 G2
DUK SK16......91 H5
FWTH BL4......53 J6
MDTN M24......57 G4
MPL/ROM SK6......113 H1
STRET M32......96 F3
SWIN M27......70 F6
WALK M28......69 H2
WGN WN1......48 A2
WGNE/HIN WN2......15 M6
Kingsway Av BNG/LEV M19......99 J3
Kingsway Cl OLDS OL8......9 G9
Kingsway Crs BNG/LEV M19......99 H7
Kingsway Pk URM M41......95 G3
Kingswear Dr BOL BL1......35 M3
Kingswood Gv RDSH SK5......100 C3
Kingswood Rd ECC M30......69 L8
MDTN M24......57 J7
PWCH M25......55 J7
RUSH/FAL M14......99 H5
Kingthorpe Gdns
BOLS/LL BL3 *......36 B8
King William St ECC M30......84 D1
SALQ M50......86 D4
TYLD M29......67 K3
Kingwood Av BOL BL1......35 J4
Kingwood Crs
WGNW/BIL/OR WN5......47 G6
Kinlay Rd BOL BL1......35 J4
Kinlet Rd WGNS/IIMK WN3......46 F8
Kinloch Dr BOL BL1......35 L5
Kinloch Gdns OLDS OL8......59 K8
Kinloch St OLDS OL8......59 K8
NM/HAY SK22......124 C4
WHIT OL12......20 D2
Kinmel Av RDSH SK5......100 F8
Kinmel Wk WGTN/LGST M12......88 D7
Kinnaird Crs STKP SK1......112 E4
Kinnaird Rd DID/WITH M20......98 F7
Kinnerly Gv WALK M28......69 K3
Kinniside Cl WGNS/IIMK WN3......63 K2

Kinross Av WN4......62 F8
OFTN SK2......121 J1
Kinross Cl RAMS BL0......24 D2
Kinross Dr BOLS/LL BL3......35 J7
Kinsey Av NTHM/RTH M23......109 J5
Kinsley Dr WALK M28......68 F2
Kintbury St WGNE/HIN WN2......64 C5
Kintore Av BRAM/HZG SK7......122 B3
Kintyre Av ORD M5......86 B3
Kintyre Cl OP/CLY M11 *......88 F3
Kintyre Dr BOLS/LL BL3......35 H7
Kinver Rd NEWH/MOS M40......73 M2
Kipling Av DROY M43......89 K1
DTN/ASHW M34......101 K5
WGNS/IIMK WN3......47 K8
Kipling Cl OFTN SK2......113 J1
Kipling Gv LEIGH WN7......66 A5
Kipling Rd OLD OL1......59 L2
Kipling St BRO M7......72 A6
Kippax St RUSH/FAL M14......98 E1
Kirby Av ATH M46......50 F7
CHAD OL9......74 A1
SALE M33......108 F2
SWIN M27......70 D6
Kirby Rd LEIGH WN7......66 B7
Kiribati Wy LEIGH WN7......66 B6
Kirkbank St CHAD OL9......8 F3
Kirkbeck LEIGH WN7......81 M1
Kirkburn Vw TOT/BURYW BL8......24 B7
Kirkby Av NEWH/MOS M40......73 L5
Kirkby Cl BURY BL9......39 K5
Kirkby Dr SALE M33......109 G2
Kirkby Rd BOL BL1......35 G2
Kirkdale Av NEWH/MOS M40......74 A2
Kirkdale Dr ROY/SHW OL2......42 F7
Kirkebrok Rd BOLS/LL BL3......35 K8
Kirkfell Dr MPL/ROM SK6......123 G4
TYLD M29......67 L5
Kirkfell Wk OLD OL1......9 K1
Kirkgate Cl NEWH/MOS M40 *......7 M1
Kirkhall La BOL BL1......35 M4
LEIGH WN7......66 B6
Kirkham Av GOL/RIS/CUL WA3 *......80 B6
GTN M18......89 J6
Kirkham Cl DTN/ASHW M34......101 J1
Kirkham Rd CHD/CHDH SK8......119 L4
LEIGH WN7......81 M1
Kirkham St BOLE BL2 *......3 L1
CHAD OL9......8 F4
LHULT M38......52 D7
SALQ M50......86 B3
WGNE/HIN WN2......64 C4
Kirkhaven Sq NEWH/MOS M40......73 H8
Kirkhill Gra WHTN BL5......50 D2
Kirkhope Dr BOL BL1......36 A3
Kirkhope Wk BOL BL1 *......2 B1
Kirklands BOLE BL2......37 G2
SALE M33......108 D2
Kirklee Av CHAD OL9......58 D3
Kirklee Rd ROCH OL11......42 A2
Kirklees St TOT/BURYW BL8......24 D5
WGN WN1......15 L4
Kirkless La WGNE/HIN WN2......48 D1
Kirkless St WGNE/HIN WN2......48 D1
Kirkless Vls WGNE/HIN WN2 *......48 D2
Kirkley St HYDE SK14......102 A3
Kirkman Av ECC M30......84 F4
Kirkman Cl GTN M18......89 G8
Kirkmanshulme La GTN M18......88 E7
Kirkstall Av BURY BL9......55 J1
HEY OL10......41 G3
HYDE SK14......102 A1
LEIGH WN7......66 C8
MDTN M24......57 K3
MILN OL16......10 E4
MOSL OL5......77 G3
OLDS OL8......9 H6
RAD M26......54 E2
RAMS BL0......18 F6
SLFD M6......71 G7
STLY SK15......91 K2
UPML OL3......45 J8
WGN WN1......14 F4
Kirkstall St WGNNW/BIL/OR WN5......46 F5
Kirkstile Crs WGNS/IIMK WN3......63 K2
Kirkstile Pl SWIN M27......54 B8
Kirkstone NEWH/MOS M40 *......73 K4
Kirkstone Av WALK M28......69 J3
Kirkstone Cl OLD OL1......9 K1
Kirkstone Dr MDTN M24......57 H2
ROY/SHW OL2......42 F6
Kirkstone Rd HYDE SK14......90 F7
NEWH/MOS M40......73 M2
Kirk St GTN M18......89 G7
Kirkwall Dr BOLE BL2......3 K8
Kirkway BKLY M9......57 K8
MDTN M24......57 K6
ROCH OL11......42 C2
Kirkwood Dr NEWH/MOS M40......72 F7
Kirtley Av ECC M30......85 G1
Kirtlington Cl ROY/SHW OL2......43 K7
Kitchener St BOLS/LL BL3......52 E1
TOT/BURYW BL8......38 F3
Kitchener Wy FWTH BL4......52 C3
Kitchen St MILN OL16......11 G3
Kite Gv LEIGH WN7......66 A5
Kitepool St ECC M30 *......84 D1
Kitter St WHIT OL12......28 F1
Kitt Green Rd
WGNW/BIL/OR WN5......46 F4
Kittiwake Cl TYLD M29......67 K5
Kitt's Moss La BRAM/HZG SK7......120 F6
Kitty Wheeldon Gdns
SALE M33 *......96 D7
Kiveton Cl WALK M28......68 F2
Kiveton Dr AIMK WN4......78 E2
Kiwi St SLFD M6......86 E2
Knaresborough Cl RDSH SK5......100 B3
Knaresborough Rd
WGNE/HIN WN2......49 H8
Knarr Barn La UPML OL3......61 G1
Knarr La UPML OL3......61 H1
Knight Crs MDTN M24......57 G1
Knightley Wk NEWH/MOS M40......73 H8
Knightsbridge STKP SK1......13 J2
Knightsbridge Cl BRO M7......127 H3
WILM/AE SK9......
Knightscliffe Crs
WGNNW/ST WN6......30 B6
Knight's Cl PWCH M25......55 L7
Knightshill Crs
WGNNW/ST WN6......14 A1
Knight St AULW OL7......90 C4
BOL BL1......36 A4
DID/WITH M20......110 E2
HYDE SK14......102 A1
TOT/BURYW BL8......38 F3
Knightswood BOLS/LL BL3......51 J1
Knightswood Rd CHH M8......72 D5
Knightwake Rd NM/HAY SK22......124 C4
Kniveton Cl WGTN/LGST M12......88 D7

Kniveton Rd WGTN/LGST M12......88 C1
Knivton St HYDE SK14 *......102 C1
Knole Av POY/DIS SK12......122 D8
Knoll St BRO M7......72 A5
RAD M26......124 D4
ROCH OL11......41 L1
The Knoll MOSL OL5......76 E3
ROY/SHW OL2 *......43 M6
Knott Fold HYDE SK14......102 A4
Knott Hill La UPML OL3......45 H8
Knott La BOL BL1......35 J2
HYDE SK14......102 A4
Knott Lanes OLDS OL8......75 H4
Knotts Brow EDGW/EG BL7......17 J8
Knott St ORD M5......86 A3
Knowe Av WYTH/NTH M22......118 F3
Knowl Cl DTN/ASHW M34......100 D2
RAMS BL0......18 F8
Knowldale Wy WGTN/LGST M12......88 D7
Knowle Av AULW OL7......75 K8
Knowle Dr PWCH M25......71 K2
Knowle Pk WILM/AE SK9......127 G1
Knowle Rd MPL/ROM SK6......114 F6
Knowles Av WGNNW/ST WN6......47 J8
Knowles Edge St BOL BL1......35 M2
Knowles Pl HULME M15......6 D9
WGN WN1......15 L3
The Knowles OLDS OL8......74 E3
Knowl Hill Dr WHIT OL12......27 H2
Knowl Rd MILN OL16......29 C6
ROY/SHW OL2......43 M6
Knowls La OLDE OL4......60 C7
Knowl St OLDS OL8......74 F2
STLY SK15......91 L2
Knowl Syke St WHIT OL12......21 C5
Knowl Vw LIT OL15......29 J2
TOT/BURYW BL8......24 D6
Knowsley Av ATH M46......50 F8
GOL/RIS/CUL WA3......79 L3
OLDE OL4......86 A4
ORD M5......84 F8
URM M41......84 F8
Knowsley Crs STKP SK1......112 E4
Knowsley Dr LEIGH WN7......81 K7
OLDE OL4......60 D5
SWIN M27......70 A6
Knowsley Gra BOL BL1......35 G5
Knowsley Gn OLDE OL4......60 D5
ORD M5 *......86 A4
Knowsley Gv HOR/BR BL6......34 A3
Knowsley Rd BOL BL1......35 L2
BOLE BL2......37 M3
BRAM/HZG SK7......122 B4
STKP SK1......112 E4
WGNNW/ST WN6......47 K1
WHTF M45......55 J4
Knowsley St BOL BL1......5 D
BURY BL9......4 D7
CHH M8......72 D8
LEIGH WN7......66 A7
WHIT OL12......10 D2
Knowsley Ter OLDE OL4 *......60 D5
STKP SK1......112 E4
Knutsford Av HTNM SK4......100 A5
SALE M33......97 H8
Knutsford Rd GTN M18......88 F8
WILM/AE SK9......126 D7
Knutsford St SLFD M6......86 B2
Knutshaw Crs BOLS/LL BL3......51 G2
Knypersley Av OFTN SK2......112 F5
Krokus Sq CHAD OL9 *......58 D5
Kylemore Av BOLS/LL BL3......35 L7
Kyle Rd BRAM/HZG SK7 *......122 B3
Kynder St DTN/ASHW M34......101 J1

**L**

Labrador Quay SALQ M50......86 C5
Labtec St SWIN M27......70 E3
Laburnum Av ATH M46......67 H1
AUL OL6......75 M6
CHAD OL9......8 B1
DTN/ASHW M34......89 M3
ECC M30......84 D4
FAIL M35......74 C6
HYDE SK14......102 A4
LEIGH WN7......66 B4
ROY/SHW OL2......43 L6
STLY SK15......91 J4
SWIN M27......70 B6
TOT/BURYW BL8......24 C5
WGNS/IIMK WN3......15 M7
WHTF M45......55 J4
Laburnum Cl HALE/TIMP WA15......108 E7
Laburnum Dr WGNNW/ST WN6......31 K8
WHTF M45......55 K3
Laburnum Gv HOR/BR BL6......34 B3
PWCH M25......55 K7
TYLD M29......
Laburnum La
HALE/TIMP WA15......117 G3
MILN OL16......43 K1
Laburnum Pk BOLE BL2......22 F7
Laburnum Rd DTN/ASHW M34......100 C1
FWTH BL4......52 C4
GOL/RIS/CUL WA3......80 C4
GTN M18......89 G8
IRL M44......94 A7
MDTN M24......57 M4
OLDS OL8......74 F4
URM M41......84 D8
WALK M28......69 H2
Laburnum St AIMK WN4......78 E2
ATH M46......67 H1
BOL BL1......2 C1
SLFD M6......86 C2
Laburnum Ter ROCH OL11......28 B8
Laburnum Wy EDGY/DAV SK3......12 B6
LIT OL15......21 K7
Lacerta Ms BRO M7......86 F1
Lacey Av WILM/AE SK9......126 C3
Lacey Gv WILM/AE SK9......126 F3
Lacey St WILM/AE SK9......127 G3
Lackford Dr NEWH/MOS M40......72 F8
Lacrosse Av OLDS OL8......58 F8
Lacy Gv STRET M32......97 G3
Lacy St STKP SK1......13 J6
STRET M32......97 G3
Lacy Wk WGTN/LGST M12......88 A4
Ladbrooke Cl AUL OL6......75 M8
Ladbrooke Rd AUL OL6......75 M8
Ladcastle Rd UPML OL3......61 K3
Ladhill La UPML OL3......61 L7
Ladies La WGNE/HIN WN2......49 G6
Ladybarn Av GOL/RIS/CUL WA3......79 J5
Ladybarn Crs BRAM/HZG SK7......122 H6
RUSH/FAL M14......99 G5

Ladybarn La *RUSH/FAL* M14....99 G4
Ladybarn Rd *RUSH/FAL* M14....99 G4
Ladybower *CHD/CHDH* SK8....120 E1
Lady Bridge La *BOL* BL1....35 L5
Ladybridge Av *WALK* M28....68 F4
Ladybridge Rd *CHD/CHDH* SK8....120 E1
Ladybrook Av
 *HALE/TIMP* WA15....108 E5
Ladybrook Rd
 *BRAM/HZG* SK7....120 E3
Ladyfield St *WILM/AE* SK9....126 F5
Ladyfield Ter *WILM/AE* SK9....127 G5
Ladyhill Vw *WALK* M28....68 F4
Ladyhouse Cl *MILN* OL16....29 K8
Ladyhouse La *MILN* OL16....29 K7
Lady Kelvin Rd *ALT* WA14....107 M6
Lady La *WGNS/IIMK* WN3....47 H8
Ladypit Rd *CHF/WBR* SK23....125 H8
Lady Rd *OLDE* OL4....60 B6
Ladys Cl *POY/DIS* SK12....122 A8
Ladyshore Cl *ORD* M5....86 C5
Ladyshore Rd *BOLS/LL* BL3....53 M2
Ladysmith Av *AIMK* WN4....78 F1
 *BURY* BL9....25 K7
Ladysmith Rd *AUL* OL6....76 C7
 *DID/WITH* M20....110 F2
Ladysmith St *EDGY/DAV* SK3....13 H9
 *OLDS* OL8....74 F1
The Ladysmith *AUL* OL6....76 C7
Ladythorn Av *MPL/ROM* SK6....114 D7
Ladythorn Ct *PWCH* M25....71 K2
Ladythorn Crs *BRAM/HZG* SK7....71 H6
Ladythorne Av *PWCH* M25....71 K2
Ladythorne Dr *PWCH* M25....71 K2
Ladythorne Gv *BRAM/HZG* SK7....121 H6
Ladythorn Rd *BRAM/HZG* SK7....121 G6
Ladywell Av *LHULT* M38....52 D8
Ladywell Cl *BRAM/HZG* SK7....121 J2
Ladywell Gv *LHULT* M38....52 D7
Lagos Cl *RUSH/FAL* M14....87 K2
Laindon Rd *RUSH/FAL* M14....99 H1
Laithwaite Rd
 *WGNW/BIL/OR* WN5....47 G5
Lake Bank *LIT* OL15....29 K1
Lake Dr *MDTN* M24....57 J3
Lakeland Av *AIMK* WN4....63 M8
Lakeland Crs *BURY* BL9....39 H6
Lakeland Dr *ROY/SHW* OL2 *....42 F4
Lakelands Dr *BOLS/LL* BL3....35 J7
Lakenheath Cl *BOL* BL1....22 C6
Lakenheath Dr *BOL* BL1....22 C6
Lake Rd *DTN/ASHW* M34....90 C8
 *STLY* SK15....76 C8
 *TRPK* M17....85 M2
Lakes Dr *WGNW/BIL/OR* WN5....46 B6
Lake Side *BURY* BL9....39 J6
 *LEIGH* WN7....66 A6
 *LIT* OL15....29 K2
Lakeside *CHD/CHDH* SK8....119 L2
 *GLSP* SK13....93 K6
Lakeside Av *AULW* OL7....75 J8
 *BOLS/LL* BL3....52 D2
 *WALK* M28....53 G7
 *WGNW/BIL/OR* WN5....62 B1
Lakeside Cl *GTN* M18....89 J6
Lakeside Dr *POY/DIS* SK12....122 A7
Lakeside Gn *OFTN* SK2....112 F6
Lakeside Ri *BKLY* M9....72 D1
Lakeside Wy *BURY* BL9....4 F6
Lakes Rd *DUK* SK16....90 F4
 *MPL/ROM* SK6....114 D7
Lakes Ter *WGNE/HIN* WN2....48 D5
Lake St *BOLS/LL* BL3 *....2 E9
 *LEIGH* WN7....66 B4
 *OFTN* SK2....112 E7
Lakeswood *DUK* SK16 *....90 E4
Lake Vw *BKLY* M9....73 K2
Lakin St *NEWH/MOS* M40....73 K5
Laleham Gn *BRAM/HZG* SK7....120 F1
Lamb Cl *WGTN/LGST* M12 *....88 C7
Lamb Ct *CSLFD* M3 *....6 C3

Lancaster Cl *BOL* BL1....3 G5
 *BRAM/HZG* SK7....121 M4
 *MPL/ROM* SK6....113 K3
 *NEWLW* WA12....78 C3
Lancaster Rd *BOLS/LL* BL3....37 L8
 *BURY* BL9....25 J4
 *MPL/ROM* SK6....71 M2
Lancaster Rd *DID/WITH* M20....110 D1
 *DROY* M43....89 J1
 *DTN/ASHW* M34....101 J3
 *SLFD* M6....70 B8
 *WGNE/HIN* WN2....49 J7
 *WGNW/BIL/OR* WN5....46 F5
 *WILM/AE* SK9....127 J3
Lancaster St *CHAD* OL9....74 D1
 *MOSL* OL5....76 E3
 *RAD* M26....54 B1
 *STKP* SK1....13 L2
 *WGNS/IIMK* WN3....15 K7
Lancaster Wy *WHTN* BL5....50 K4
Lancelot Rd *WYTH/NTH* M22....119 H2
Lancelyn Dr *WILM/AE* SK9....127 H4
Lane Wood Pl
 *WGNW/BIL/OR* WN5....47 G6
Lanchester Dr *BOLS/LL* BL3....2 A8
Lanchester St
 *NEWH/MOS* M40....88 B1
Lancing Av *DID/WITH* M20....111 G1
Lancing Wk *CHAD* OL9 *....58 D6
Landau Dr *WALK* M28....68 C1
Landcross Rd
 *RUSH/FAL* M14....98 F3
Landedmans *WHTN* BL5....50 C5
Lander Gv *BKLY* M9....73 J1
Land Gate La *AIMK* WN4....63 K5
Landkey Ln *NTHM/RTH* M23....109 J2
Land La *WILM/AE* SK9....127 G6
Landor Cl *GOL/RIS/CUL* WA3....80 B4
Landos Rd
 *NEWH/MOS* M40....7 M1
Landrace Dr *WALK* M28....68 C6
Landsberg Rd *FAIL* M35....74 C4
Landseer Dr *MPL/ROM* SK6....114 C5
Landseer St *OLDE* OL4....9 L8
Lands End Rd *MDTN* M24....56 E5
Landside *LEIGH* WN7....81 J2
Landside St *WGNNW/ST* WN6....14 D3
Lane Brow *OLDE* OL4....60 E7
Lane Dr *OLDE* OL4....60 E7
Lane End *ECC* M30....85 J3
 *HEY* OL10....41 J4
Lane End *OLDE* OL4....76 D6
Lane End Rd *BNG/LEV* M19....99 G8
Lane Ends *WALK* M28....54 A1
Lanegate *HYDE* SK14....102 A4
Lane Head Av
 *GOL/RIS/CUL* WA3....80 C4
Lane Head Rd *OLDE* OL4....76 D4
Lane Meadow *ROY/SHW* OL2....43 K6
Lane North *BOLS/LL* BL3 *....35 L8
Laneside Cl *LIT* OL15....21 L6
Laneside Rd *DID/WITH* M20....110 F4
 SK22....125 H6
The Lane *BOL* BL1....35 C5
Lanfield Dr *CHH* M8....72 C5
Langdale Av *BNG/LEV* M19....99 L4
 *GOL/RIS/CUL* WA3....79 M3
 *MILN* OL16....42 F4
 *OLDS* OL8....59 G8
 *WGN* WN1....47 L2
 *WGNE/HIN* WN2....48 K4
Langdale Cl *CHD/CHDH* SK8....119 L1
 *DTN/ASHW* M34....101 H3
 *HALE/TIMP* WA15....108 B7
 *MPL/ROM* SK6....123 G4
Langdale Crs *MDTN* M24....57 J1
 *WALK* M28....69 J3
Langdale Dr *BURY* BL9....55 L1
 *MDTN* M24....57 J1
 *WALK* M28....69 J3
Langdale Gv *WGNE/HIN* WN2....64 E1
Langdale Rd *BRAM/HZG* SK7....121 J3
 *HTNM* SK4....99 M6
 *MPL/ROM* SK6....101 L7
 *PART* M31....106 B1
 *RUSH/FAL* M14....88 A8
 *SALE* M33....108 B3
 *STRET* M32 *....96 F1
 *WGNE/HIN* WN2....49 H7
 *WGNW/BIL/OR* WN5....46 E5
Langdale St *BOLS/LL* BL3....52 B1
 *FWTH* BL4....52 F5
 *LEIGH* WN7....66 B7
Langden Cl *GOL/RIS/CUL* WA3....81 G8
 *ROY/SHW* OL2....43 K4
Langdon Cl *BOL* BL1....2 B2
Langfield *GOL/RIS/CUL* WA3....80 B5
Langfield Av *OLDTF/WHR* M16....98 A1
Langfield Crs *DROY* M43 *....89 M2
Langford Dr *IRL* M44....94 D3
Langford Gdns *BOLS/LL* BL3....36 B8
Langford Rd *DID/WITH* M20....99 M8
 *HTNM* SK4....99 M8
Langford St *DTN/ASHW* M34 *....101 J1
Langham Cl *BOL* BL1....22 D6
Langham Ct *STRET* M32....85 K8
Langham Gv *HALE/TIMP* WA15....108 E4
Langham Rd *ALT* WA14....116 E2
 *HTNM* SK4....12 B4
 *OLDS* OL8....59 H8
 *SLFD* M6....86 C2
 *WGNNW/ST* WN6....31 G3
Langholm Dr *BOLE* BL2....37 J6
Langholme Cl *HULME* M15 *....6 B9
Langholm Rd *AIMK* WN4....62 F8
Langland Cl *BNG/LEV* M19....100 A2
Langland Dr *ECC* M30....84 F5
Langley Av *BRAM/HZG* SK7....121 K3
 *MDTN* M24....41 H8
 *OLDE* OL4....60 E7
 *PWCH* M25....55 L7
Langley Cl *GOL/RIS/CUL* WA3....79 M3
 *URM* M41....96 B2
 *WGNNW/ST* WN6....31 H1
Langley Ct *GLSP* SK13....93 K7
Langley Dr *BRAM/HZG* SK7....121 K3
 *WALK* M28....68 D6
 *WILM/AE* SK9....127 J1
Langley Gdns *PWCH* M25....55 L6
Langley Hall Rd *PWCH* M25....55 L6
Langley Platt La *TYLD* M29....67 C4

Langley Rd *PWCH* M25....55 K7
 *RUSH/FAL* M14....98 F3
 *SALE* M33....96 B8
 *SWIN* M27....71 J4
Langley Rd South *SLFD* M6....71 J4
Langness St *WGNE/HIN* WN2....48 F5
Lango St *OLDTF/WHR* M16....86 F8
Langport Av *WGTN/LGST* M12....88 B7
Langset Av *WGNE/HIN* WN2....49 G6
Langshaw Rd *BOLS/LL* BL3....35 M7
Langshaw St *OLDTF/WHR* M16....86 F8
 *SLFD* M6....85 M1
Langshaw Wk *BOLS/LL* BL3 *....35 M7
Langside Av *BKLY* M9....57 H8
Langside Dr *BOLS/LL* BL3....35 H8
Langstone Cl *HOR/BR* BL6....33 L1
Langston Gn *BRAM/HZG* SK7....121 J3
Langton Cl *CSLFD* M3....87 J1
Langthorne Av
 *BNG/LEV* M19....99 L4
Langthorne St
 *BNG/LEV* M19....99 L4
Langton Cl *FAIL* M35....74 E4
Langton Gn *WGNNW/ST* WN6....31 H3
Langton Pl *WGNNW/ST* WN6....31 H3
Langton St *HEY* OL10....40 F1
 *MDTN* M24....57 K4
 *SLFD* M6....86 B2
Langton Ter *ROCH* OL11....28 B8
Langtree Cl *WALK* M28....68 E5
Langtree La *WGNNW/ST* WN6....31 G1
Langworthy Av *LHULT* M38....52 E8
Langworthy Rd
 *NEWH/MOS* M40....73 K5
 *SLFD* M6....86 C1
Lanhill Dr *CHH* M8....72 F6
Lankro Wy *TRPK* M17....85 J3
Lansbury St
 *WGNW/BIL/OR* WN5....46 D6
Lansdale Gdns *BNG/LEV* M19....99 H7
Lansdale St *ECC* M30....84 D4
Lansdown Cl *CHD/CHDH* SK8....120 E5
Lansdowne Av *DTN/ASHW* M34....89 K1
 *MPL/ROM* SK6....114 A3
Lansdowne Cl *BOLE* BL2 *....36 E3
 *RAMS* BL0....18 E7
Lansdowne Ct *CHAD* OL9....8 A6
Lansdowne Dr *WALK* M28....68 F4
Lansdowne Rd *ALT* WA14....108 A6
 *ATH* M46....51 J7
 *BOLE* BL2....36 E3
 *CHAD* OL9....8 C6
 *CHH* M8....72 D4
 *ECC* M30....85 G1
 *SALE* M33....96 D6
 *URM* M41....95 H4
Lansdowne Rd North
 *URM* M41....95 H3
Lansdowne St *ROCH* OL11....27 M5
Lanstead Dr *NEWH/MOS* M40....88 B2
Lantern Pike Vw
 *NM/HAY* SK22....125 J2
Lantern Vw *NM/HAY* SK22....124 D3
Lapwing Cl *GOL/RIS/CUL* WA3....80 A4
 *ROCH* OL11....27 H5
 *STLY* SK15....76 D8
Lapwing La *DID/WITH* M20....98 D7
 *RDSH* SK5....100 F6
Larch Av *CHD/CHDH* SK8....120 C3
 *RAD* M26....54 B5
 *STRET* M32....97 G3
 *SWIN* M27....69 M6
 *WGNW/BIL/OR* WN5....47 J5
Larch Cl *FAIL* M35....74 C6
 *GOL/RIS/CUL* WA3....80 C6
 *MPL/ROM* SK6....114 B7
 *NTHM/RTH* M23....108 F4
 *POY/DIS* SK12....129 K1
 *WGNW/BIL/OR* WN5....62 A7
The Larches *MOSL* OL5....77 G3
Larch Gv *ATH* M46....50 F8
 *SWIN* M27....69 L2
Larch Rd *DTN/ASHW* M34....101 K1
 *ECC* M30....69 K8
 *LEIGH* WN7....66 B4
 *PART* M31....106 B1
 *RNFD/HAY* WA11 *....78 B5
Larch St *BURY* BL9....5 L4
 *OLDS* OL8....8 F7
Larchview Rd *MDTN* M24....57 M4
Larch Wy *GLSP* SK13....105 J4
Larchway *BRAM/HZG* SK7....120 E5
 *MILN* OL16....29 G5
 *MPL/ROM* SK6....123 H5
Larchwood *CHAD* OL9....58 B5
Larchwood Av *BKLY* M9....73 J5
Larchwood Cl *SALE* M33....95 M8
Larchwood Dr *WGN* WN1....31 L8
 *WILM/AE* SK9....127 J4
Larchwood St *BOL* BL1....36 C2
Larke Ri *DID/WITH* M20....110 C1
Larkfield Av *LHULT* M38....52 C7
 *WGN* WN1....31 L8
Larkfield Cl *AULW* OL7....75 L5
 *TOT/BURYW* BL8....24 B2
Larkfield Gv *BOLE* BL2....3 K2
Larkfield Ms *LHULT* M38....52 C7
Larkhall Ri *WYTH/NTH* M22....110 B7
Larkhill *WILM/AE* SK9....127 H4
Larkhill Cl *HALE/TIMP* WA15....108 E6
Lark Hill La *UPML* OL3....45 K8
Larkhill Pl *WHIT* OL12....28 D3
Larkhill Rd *CHD/CHDH* SK8....111 M7
Lark Hill Rd *EDGY/DAV* SK3....12 D6
 *UPML* OL3....61 L8
Larkhill Vw *CHD/CHDH* SK8....111 M7
Larkhill Wk *CHH* M8....72 E6
Larkside Av *WALK* M28....69 H1
Larkspur Cl *BOL* BL1....36 D1
Lark St *BOL* BL1....2 F3
 *FWTH* BL4 *....53 G5
 *OLD* OL1 *....60 A1
Larkswood Dr *STLY* SK15....77 H5
Larkwood Av *STLY* SK15....77 H5
Larmuth Av *CCHDY* M21....97 M6
Larne Av *EDGY/DAV* SK3....12 A1
 *STRET* M32....96 F2
Larne St *OP/CLY* M11....88 D4
Larwood Av *HTNM* SK4....12 A4
Lascar Av *ORD* M5....86 D4
Lashbrook Cl *NEWH/MOS* M40....7 K8
Lassell Fold *HYDE* SK14....91 L6
Lassell St *OP/CLY* M11 *....89 G5
Lastingham St *NEWH/MOS* M40....73 M6
Latchford St *AULW* OL7....75 L8
Latchmere Rd *RUSH/FAL* M14....98 F4

Latham Av *NEWLW* WA12....78 F8
Latham Cl *MPL/ROM* SK6....101 J7
Latham La *WGNW/BIL/OR* WN5....46 C4
Latham Rd *HOR/BR* BL6....32 F1
Latham St *BOL* BL1....36 C2
 *OP/CLY* M11....89 J5
Lathbury Rd *BKLY* M9....73 G6
Lathom Gv *SALE* M33....109 H1
Lathom Hall Av *OLDE* OL4 *....60 D5
Lathom Rd *DID/WITH* M20....99 G5
 *IRL* M44....94 C4
Lathom St *BURY* BL9....5 G1
Latimer Cl
 *WGNW/BIL/OR* WN5 *....46 C5
Latimer St *OLDE* OL4....9 M7
Latin St *MILN* OL16....10 D6
Latrigg Crs *MDTN* M24....56 F2
Latrobe St *DROY* M43....89 K4
Lauderdale Crs
 *BRUN/LGST* M13....87 M6
Launceston Cl *BRAM/HZG* SK7....121 H5
 *OLDS* OL8....59 M8
Launceston Rd *RAD* M26....38 C7
Laundry St *SLFD* M6....71 J8
Laura St *BURY* BL9....24 F2
Laureate Wy *DTN/ASHW* M34....101 K5
Laurel Av *BOLS/LL* BL3....37 H7
 *CHAD* OL9....58 A4
 *RUSH/FAL* M14....98 D2
Laurel Bank *HYDE* SK14....101 M4
 *STLY* SK15....91 L4
Laurel Bank Gdns *BKLY* M9....57 G8
Laurel Cl *BOL* BL1....2 E2
 *MILN* OL16....11 J6
Laurel Crs *WGNE/HIN* WN2....65 K1
Laurel Dr *HALE/TIMP* WA15....108 E8
 *LHULT* M38....52 D8
Laurel End La *HTNM* SK4....111 K1
Laurel Gn *DTN/ASHW* M34....101 K2
Laurel Gv *AIMK* WN4....63 L2
 *GOL/RIS/CUL* WA3....80 A4
 *LEIGH* WN7....66 B4
 *SLFD* M6....85 M2
Laurel Wk *PART* M31....106 B1
Laurel Wy *BRAM/HZG* SK7....120 E4
Laurels Dr *LIT* OL15....29 L2
The Laurels *MOSL* OL5....77 G3
 *BURY* BL9....5 K4
 *HTNM* SK4....13 G3
 *MDTN* M24....58 A4
 *OLDE* OL4....59 L8
 *TOT/BURYW* BL8....24 C6
 *WGNW/BIL/OR* WN5....47 J5
Laurence Cl *WGTN/LGST* M12....88 D6
Lauren Cl *OLDE* OL4....60 C6
Lauria Ter *BOLE* BL2....38 A3
Laurie Pl *WHIT* OL12 *....28 C3
Lausanne Rd *BRAM/HZG* SK7....121 H5
 *DID/WITH* M20....98 E5
Lavender Cl *NTHM/RTH* M23....109 H3
 *SALE* M33....95 M7
Lavender Rd *FWTH* BL4....52 D3
 *OLDE* OL4....60 B8
 *WCNNW/ST* WN6....47 J1
Lavenders Brow *STKP* SK1....13 K4
Lavender St *RAD* M26....54 A1
Lavenham Av *OP/CLY* M11....89 G3
Lavenham Cl *BRAM/HZG* SK7....122 A4
 *BURY* BL9....55 J1
Laverton Cl *BURY* BL9....40 B3
Lavington Av *CHD/CHDH* SK8....111 J4
Lavington Gv *GTN* M18....89 G8
Lavinia St *ECC* M30....84 D2
Lavister Av *BNG/LEV* M19....111 G1
Lawefield Crs *SWIN* M27....54 A7
Lawers St *CHAD* OL9....58 D4
Lawflat *WHIT* OL12....21 G7
Lawler Av *OP/CLY* M11....88 D5
Lawn Cl *OLDS* OL8....75 M1
Lawndale Cl *RAD* M26....54 E2
Lawn Dr *SALE* M33....108 B6
 *SWIN* M27....70 B5
Lawnfield *GLSP* SK13....93 H8
Lawngreen Av *CCHDY* M21....97 K5
Lawnside Ms *DID/WITH* M20....98 D7
The Lawns *ALT* WA14....116 E1
Lawn St *BOL* BL1....2 A1
Lawnswood *ROCH* OL11....27 M8
Lawnswood Dr *SWIN* M27....70 D6
 *TYLD* M29....67 M4
Lawnswood Park Rd *SWIN* M27....70 B6
Lawrence Ct *BURY* BL9....39 J8
 *EDGY/DAV* SK3....13 G5
Lawrie Av *RAMS* BL0....18 E7
Lawson Av *CHD/CHDH* SK8....110 E7
 *LEIGH* WN7....66 B3
Lawson Cl *MDTN* M24....41 K8
 *WALK* M28....69 M6
Lawson Gv *SALE* M33....96 D6
Lawson Rd *BOL* BL1....35 M2
Lawson St *BKLY* M9....72 F2
 *BOL* BL1....22 B8
Lawton Moor Rd
 *NTHM/RTH* M23....109 L3
Lawton Rd *HTNM* SK4....99 M8
Lawton Sq *OLDS* OL3 *....45 J8
Lawton St *DROY* M43....89 L2
 *OP/CLY* M11....89 G5
 *STLY* SK15....91 L3
 *WHIT* OL12 *....45 H8
Laxey Av *ATH* M46....67 G2
 *LEIGH* WN7....65 M5
Laxey St *NEWH/MOS* M40....73 L5
Laxfield Dr *URM* M41....84 A8
Laxford Gv *BOLS/LL* BL3....35 H6
Layard St *AUL* OL6....90 D1
Laycock Av *BOLE* BL2....36 E1
 *STLY* SK15....77 H8
Laycock Crs *FAIL* M35....74 C6
Laycock Dr *DUK* SK16....91 K5
Laycock Gv *FAIL* M35....74 C5
Layfield Cl *TOT/BURYW* BL8....24 C2
Layland Av *GOL/RIS/CUL* WA3....81 H8
Laystall St *CMANE* M1....7 H4
Laythe Barn Cl *MILN* OL16....29 H6
Layton Av *HYDE* SK14....101 L3

Layton Cl *STKP* SK1....13 L6
 *WGNW/BIL/OR* WN5....47 G6
Layton Dr *FWTH* BL4....53 J6
 *MPL/ROM* SK6....113 M1
Layton St *NEWH/MOS* M40....88 A2
Lazenby Crs *AIMK* WN4....78 C1
Lazonby Av *WGNE/HIN* WN2....49 J1
Leabank St *BNG/LEV* M19....99 K3
Leabrook Dr *NEWH/MOS* M40....74 A7
Leaburn Dr *BNG/LEV* M19....99 H8
Leach Cl *MILN* OL16....28 F2
Leaches Rd *RAMS* BL0....19 G4
Leach St *BOLS/LL* BL3....2 C9
 *FWTH* BL4....53 H3
 *GTN* M18....89 E7
 *MILN* OL16....11 J6
 *MILN* OL16....29 J7
 *PWCH* M25....71 K6
 *ROY/SHW* OL2....43 M6
Leach Wk *OLDE* OL4....60 B4
Leaconfield Dr *WALK* M28....69 J5
Lea Ct *FAIL* M35....74 B5
Leacroft *AIMK* WN4....63 H6
Leacroft Av *BOLE* BL2....37 J7
Leacroft Rd *CCHDY* M21....98 A7
Leadale Cl *WGNNW/ST* WN6....31 C3
Leadale Ri *OLDE* OL4 *....60 D6
Leader St *WGN* WN1....15 L4
Leader Williams Rd *IRL* M44....94 C3
Lea Dr *BKLY* M9....73 J1
Leafield *TYLD* M29....67 M3
Leafield Av *DID/WITH* M20....110 D3
 *RAD* M26....54 B1
Leafield Cl *CHD/CHDH* SK8....120 B6
 *WALK* M28....68 D6
Leafield Rd *POY/DIS* SK12....123 L6
Leaford Av *DTN/ASHW* M34....90 A8
Leaford Cl *DTN/ASHW* M34....90 A8
Leaf St *BOLE* BL2....3 L8
 *HULME* M15....87 G6
 *RDSH* SK5....100 B5
Leagate *URM* M41....96 B3
Lea Gate Cl *BOLE* BL2....23 G7
League St *MILN* OL16....11 L8
Leaholme Cl *NEWH/MOS* M40....74 A7
Leak St *OLDTF/WHR* M16....86 F6
Leal Holme Av *WGNE/HIN* WN2....48 D2
Leamington Av *BURY* BL9....25 H4
 *DID/WITH* M20....110 C1
Leamington Rd *ECC* M30....84 E1
 *RDSH* SK5....100 B5
 *URM* M41....95 L1
Leamington St *OLDE* OL4....59 M4
 *OP/CLY* M11....89 G2
 *WHIT* OL12....10 D2
Lea Mount Dr *BURY* BL9....26 A8
Leam St *AUL* OL6....76 A8
Leander Cl *BKLY* M9....73 H2
Leander Dr *ROCH* OL11....42 A3
Lea Rd *CHD/CHDH* SK8....119 K3
 *HTNM* SK4....99 L8
 *NM/HAY* SK22....125 L1
Leaside Av *OLD* OL1....58 D2
Leaside Cl *WHIT* OL12....28 A2
Leaside Dr *DID/WITH* M20....99 G7
Leaside Gv *WALK* M28....69 H1
Leaside Wy *WILM/AE* SK9....127 G6
The Leas *HALE/TIMP* WA15....117 K1
Lea St *WGN* WN1 *....14 C5
 *WGNS/IIMK* WN3....14 C5
Leaton Av *NTHM/RTH* M23....109 K6
Leavale Cl *LHULT* M38....52 C5
Lea Vw *ROY/SHW* OL2....42 F5
 *WGN* WN1....15 M2
Leaway *WGNE/HIN* WN2....15 G6
 *WHIT* OL12....21 G6
Lecester Rd *CHH* M8....72 D4
Leckenby Cl *WALK* M28....68 D6
Leconfield Dr *BKLY* M9....73 H1
Leconfield Rd *ECC* M30....69 J8
Lecturers Cl *BOLS/LL* BL3....2 A8
Ledbrooke Av *ORD* M5....86 E5
Ledburn Cl *HULME* M15 *....87 G6
Ledbury Av *URM* M41....95 M1
Ledbury Cl *MDTN* M24....57 K6
Ledbury Rd *FAIL* M35....74 B8
Ledbury St *LEIGH* WN7....66 C6
Ledge Ley *CHD/CHDH* SK8....120 B4
Ledmore Av *AIMK* WN4....78 A1
Ledsham Av *BKLY* M9....56 F7
Ledson Rd *NTHM/RTH* M23....109 J7
Ledward La *ALT* WA14....116 D2
Lee Av *ALT* WA14....107 M5
 *BOLS/LL* BL3....50 D4
Lee Bank *WHTN* BL5....50 D4
Leech Av *AUL* OL6....76 B7
Leech Brook Av
 *DTN/ASHW* M34....90 B7
Leech Brook Cl
 *DTN/ASHW* M34....90 B6
Leech St *HYDE* SK14....102 C2
 *STLY* SK15....91 K3
Lee Ct *IRL* M44....94 C3
Lee Ct *WYTH/NTH* M22 *....110 B4
Lee Crs *STRET* M32....97 H2
Lee Dale Cl
 *DTN/ASHW* M34....101 K2
Leeds Cl *BURY* BL9....55 L2
Leeds St *WGNS/IIMK* WN3....14 D5
Leefields Cl *UPML* OL3....61 L4
Lee Fold *TYLD* M29....67 M4
Lee Ga *BOLE* BL2....23 G7
Leegate Cl *HTNM* SK4....57 J8
Leegate Dr *BKLY* M9....57 J8
Leegate Gdns *HTNM* SK4....99 K8
Leegate Rd *HTNM* SK4....99 K8
Leegrange Rd *BKLY* M9....73 H3
Lee Gv *FWTH* BL4....52 C4
Lee Head *GLSP* SK13....103 M7
Lee La *EDGW/EG* BL7....16 E2
 *WGNE/HIN* WN2....64 E4
Leemans Hill St
 *TOT/BURYW* BL8....24 D7
Lee Mt *GLSP* SK13....104 C8
Lees Av *DTN/ASHW* M34....101 H2
Lees Ct *CHH* M8....60 C8
Lees Hall Crs
 *RUSH/FAL* M14....99 G4
Lees La *MCFLDN* SK10....127 M6
Lees New Rd *AUL* OL6....76 A3
 *OLDE* OL4....60 C8
Lees Park Av *DROY* M43....89 M2
Lees Rd *AUL* OL6....76 A5
 *BRAM/HZG* SK7....120 F7
 *MOSL* OL5....76 E1
 *OLDE* OL4....9 M5

**Lees St** AUL OL6 .... 75 L8
  DROY M43 .... 89 L2
  GTN M18 .... 89 H6
  MDTN M24 .... 58 A5
  MOSL OL5 * .... 76 F2
  OLDS OL8 .... 75 J4
  STLY SK15 .... 91 K2
  SWIN M27 .... 70 C3
**Lees St East** ROY/SHW OL2 .... 43 L5
**Leestone Rd**
  WYTH/NTH M22 .... 110 B6
**Lee St** ATH M46 .... 67 G2
  BURY BL9 .... 25 J4
  LIT OL15 .... 21 M6
  MDTN M24 .... 57 J1
  OLDS OL8 .... 8 F7
  STKP SK1 .... 13 J5
  UPML OL3 .... 61 L4
**Leesway** OLDE OL4 .... 60 B7
**Leesway Dr** DTN/ASHW M34 .... 101 K2
**Leeswood Av** CCHDY M21 .... 97 M6
**Lee Vale Dr** GLSP SK13 .... 104 A5
**Leewood** SWIN M27 .... 54 A8
**Left Bank** CSLFD M3 .... 6 D4
**Le Gendre St** BOLE BL2 .... 36 F3
**Legh Cl** POY/DIS SK12 .... 129 J1
**Legh Dr** DTN/ASHW M34 .... 89 L3
  MPL/ROM SK6 .... 101 L6
**Legh Rd** BRO M7 .... 72 A4
  MCFLDN SK10 .... 129 G7
  POY/DIS SK12 .... 123 J6
  SALE M33 .... 109 H1
**Legh St** AIMK WN4 .... 78 C2
  BRO M7 .... 72 B6
  ECC M30 .... 84 F3
  GOL/RIS/CUL WA3 .... 79 K4
**Legion Gv** BRO M7 .... 72 B6
**Legwood Ct** URM M41 .... 95 M3
**Leicester Av** BRO M7 * .... 72 C4
  DROY M43 .... 89 J1
  DTN/ASHW M34 .... 101 J3
  HALE/TIMP WA15 .... 108 D4
  HOR/BR BL6 .... 33 K1
  WGNE/HIN WN2 .... 49 J7
**Leicester Dr** GLSP SK13 .... 105 J5
**Leicester Rd** BRO M7 .... 72 B5
  FAIL M35 .... 74 D7
  HALE/TIMP WA15 .... 117 G2
  SALE M33 .... 96 E7
  TYLD M29 .... 67 K2
  WHTF M45 .... 55 C3
**Leicester St** AULW OL7 .... 75 L8
  OLDE OL4 .... 59 L6
  RDSH SK5 .... 100 B2
  ROCH OL11 .... 11 G9
**Leigh Ar** WGN WN1 * .... 14 F3
**Leigh Av** WGN/ROM SK6 .... 114 B6
  SWIN M27 .... 70 A7
**Leighbrook Rd** RUSH/FAL M14 .... 98 E4
**Leigh Cl** TOT/BURYW BL8 .... 24 B5
**Leigh Fold** HYDE SK14 .... 91 H7
**Leigh La** TOT/BURYW BL8 .... 38 D2
**Leigh Rd** ATH M46 .... 66 E2
  HALE/TIMP WA15 .... 117 G2
  WALK M28 .... 68 D6
  WGNE/HIN WN2 .... 49 J5
  WHTN BL5 .... 50 C5
  WILM/AE SK9 .... 126 B7
**Leigh St** FWTH BL4 .... 53 G4
  HEY OL10 .... 40 F2
  HYDE SK14 .... 102 B2
  LEIGH WN7 .... 65 M7
  MILN OL16 .... 29 J5
  TOT/BURYW BL8 .... 24 C8
  WGN WN1 .... 15 J5
  WGNE/HIN WN2 .... 49 J1
  WGNE/HIN WN2 .... 65 L3
  WHTN BL5 .... 50 B5
**Leighton Av** ATH M46 .... 66 D3
  BOL BL1 .... 35 L4
  LIT OL15 .... 21 K7
**Leighton Dr** LEIGH WN7 .... 80 E3
  MPL/ROM SK6 .... 114 A4
**Leighton Rd** OLDTF/WHR M16 .... 86 F8
**Leighton St** ATH M46 .... 66 E2
  NEWH/MOS M40 .... 73 K4
**Leinster Rd** SWIN M27 .... 70 B5
**Leinster St** FWTH BL4 .... 52 F4
**Leith Av** SALE M33 .... 96 E3
**Leith Pl** OLDS OL8 .... 75 H2
**Leith Rd** SALE M33 .... 97 H8
**Le Mans Crs** BOL BL1 .... 2 E5
**Lemnos St** OLD OL1 .... 9 L4
**Lemon St** TYLD M29 .... 67 J4
**Lena St** BOL BL1 .... 36 C2
  CMANE M1 .... 7 J5
**Len Cox Wk** ANC M4 * .... 7 J3
**Lenfield La** OLD OL1 .... 59 H3
**Leng Rd** NEWH/MOS M40 .... 74 A7
**Lenham Cl** RDSH SK5 .... 100 E6
**Lenham Gdns** BOLE BL2 .... 37 H6
**Lennox Gdns** BOLS/LL BL3 .... 35 J3
**Lennox St** AUL OL6 .... 90 F1
**Lenora St** BOLS/LL BL3 .... 35 L8
**Lenten Gv** HEY OL10 .... 41 H5
**Lentmead Dr** BKLY M9 .... 73 K3
**Lenton Gdns** WYTH/NTH M22 .... 110 B7
**Lentworth Dr** WALK M28 .... 52 F7
**Leominster Dr**
  WYTH/NTH M22 .... 119 G1
**Leominster Rd** MDTN M24 * .... 57 L6
**Leonardin Cl** ROY/SHW OL2 .... 43 J4
**Leonard St** BOLS/LL BL3 .... 52 B1
  ROCH OL11 .... 11 M3
**Leopold Av** DID/WITH M20 .... 98 D7
**Leopold St** ROCH OL11 .... 10 A5
  WGNW/BIL/OR WN5 .... 47 H5
**Lepp Crs** TOT/BURYW BL8 .... 24 F6
**Leroy Dr** BKLY M9 .... 73 G2
**Lerryn Dr** BRAM/HZG SK7 .... 120 F3
**Lesley Rd** URM M41 .... 96 D3
  CHAD OL9 .... 74 E1
**Leslie Av** BURY BL9 .... 55 J1
  CHAD OL9 .... 74 E1
**Leslie Gv** HALE/TIMP WA15 .... 108 D6
**Leslie Hough Wy** SLFD M6 .... 3 J1
**Leslie St** BOLE BL2 .... 3 J1
  RUSH/FAL M14 .... 98 E1
**Lessingham Av** WGN WN1 .... 47 L1
**Lester Rd** LHULT M38 .... 52 B7
**Lester St** STRET M32 .... 97 G2
**Letchworth Av** ROCH OL11 .... 11 G9
**Letchworth St** RUSH/FAL M14 .... 98 E1
**Letham St** OLDS OL8 .... 75 H5
**Letitia St** HOR/BR BL6 .... 33 K1
**Levedale Rd** BKLY M9 .... 57 H8
**Leven Cl** FWTH BL4 .... 53 L7
**Levengreave Cl**
  WGNE/HIN WN2 .... 65 M1
**Levenhurst Rd** CHH M8 .... 72 C5
**Levens Cl** CHD/CHDH SK8 .... 110 E8
**Levens Dr** BOLE BL2 .... 37 H3
**Levenshulme Rd** GTN M18 .... 89 G4

**Levenshulme Ter**
  BNG/LEV M19 * .... 99 K3
**Levens Pl** WGNE/HIN WN2 .... 48 D4
  WGNW/BIL/OR WN5 .... 46 F5
**Levens Rd** BRAM/HZG SK7 .... 121 L2
  SLFD M6 .... 71 L7
**Levens St** NEWH/MOS M40 .... 73 K5
  SLFD M6 .... 71 L7
**Lever Av** SWIN M27 .... 70 E2
**Lever Dr** BOLS/LL BL3 .... 2 D9
**Lever Edge La** BOLS/LL BL3 .... 51 M2
**Leverett Cl** WA14 .... 107 K7
**Lever Gv** BOLE BL2 .... 3 H8
**Lever Hall Rd** BOLE BL2 .... 37 G5
**Leverhulme Av** BOLS/LL BL3 .... 52 D1
**Lever St** BOLE BL2 .... 3 G8
  BOLS/LL BL3 .... 37 K8
  BRAM/HZG SK7 .... 121 M2
  CMANE M1 .... 7 J4
  HEY OL10 .... 41 G1
  MDTN M24 .... 57 K3
  RAD M26 .... 38 C7
  RAMS BL0 .... 18 F6
  TYLD M29 .... 67 J3
  WHTN BL5 .... 50 B1
**Lever Wk** MDTN M24 .... 57 J5
**Levington Dr** OLDS OL8 .... 75 K4
**Levi St** BOL BL1 .... 35 J3
**Lewes Av** DTN/ASHW M34 .... 101 J3
**Lewis Av** BKLY M9 .... 73 H3
  URM M41 .... 85 G7
**Lewis Cl** WGNS/IIMK WN3 .... 14 B9
**Lewis Dr** HEY OL10 .... 40 C3
**Lewisham Av**
  NEWH/MOS M40 .... 73 L8
**Lewisham Cl**
  ROY/SHW OL2 * .... 42 F6
**Lewis Rd** DROY M43 .... 89 H2
  RDSH SK5 .... 100 C3
**Lewis St** ECC M30 .... 85 G3
  HEY OL10 * .... 41 H1
  NEWH/MOS M40 .... 88 A1
  ROY/SHW OL2 .... 43 L7
**Lewtas St** ECC M30 .... 85 H3
**Lexton Av** CHH M8 .... 72 E2
**Leybourne Av**
  BNG/LEV M19 .... 99 L2
**Leybourne St** BOL BL1 .... 36 B2
**Leybrook Rd**
  WYTH/NTH M22 .... 118 E1
**Leyburn Av**
  ROY/SHW OL2 .... 43 G8
  STRET M32 .... 96 F2
  URM M41 .... 95 K3
**Leyburn Cl** WGN WN1 .... 15 M2
  WHTF M45 .... 55 H4
**Leyburn Gv** OFTN SK2 .... 112 F6
**Leyburn Rd** NEWH/MOS M40 .... 73 M2
**Leycett Dr** NTHM/RTH M23 .... 109 K3
**Ley Crs** TYLD M29 .... 67 L6
**Leycroft St** CMANE M1 .... 7 K6
**Ley Dr** HEY OL10 .... 41 H5
**Leyfield Av** MPL/ROM SK6 .... 113 M2
**Leyfield Rd** MILN OL16 .... 29 L5
**Leygate Vw** NM/HAY SK22 .... 124 D4
**Ley Hey Av** MPL/ROM SK6 .... 114 C5
**Ley Hey Rd** MPL/ROM SK6 .... 114 C5
**Leyland Av** CHD/CHDH SK8 .... 110 E6
  DID/WITH M20 .... 111 J1
  IRL M44 .... 83 L8
  WGNE/HIN WN2 .... 65 L3
**Leyland Green Rd** AIMK WN4 .... 62 F7
**Leyland Mill La** WGN WN1 .... 32 A8
**Leylands La** HYDE SK14 .... 103 H6
**Leyland St** BURY BL9 .... 39 J8
  HTNM SK4 .... 13 G4
  WGNE/HIN WN2 .... 48 F8
  WGNE/HIN WN2 .... 64 E3
**Ley La** MPL/ROM SK6 .... 114 F4
**Leys Rd** TYLD M29 .... 67 L6
**Leyton Av** NEWH/MOS M40 .... 73 L5
**Leyton Cl** FWTH BL4 .... 52 C3
**Leyton Dr** BURY BL9 .... 39 J7
**Leyton St** WHIT OL12 .... 28 C2
**Leywell Dr** OLD OL1 .... 60 A1
**Leywell Rd** BKLY M9 .... 73 J4
**Library La** CHAD OL9 .... 8 F3
**Library St** WGN WN1 .... 15 G4
  WHTN BL5 .... 50 C4
**Libra St** BOL BL1 .... 36 A2
**Lichens Crs** OLDS OL8 .... 75 K1
**Lichfield Av** AUL OL6 .... 76 A5
  BOLE BL2 .... 37 K2
  GOL/RIS/CUL WA3 .... 80 A4
  HALE/TIMP WA15 .... 117 L2
  RDSH SK5 .... 100 B5
  TYLD M29 .... 67 M5
**Lichfield Cl** FWTH BL4 .... 52 B4
  UPML OL3 .... 44 F2
**Lichfield Dr** CHAD OL9 .... 58 D3
  CHH M8 .... 72 E5
  PWCH M25 .... 71 M2
  SWIN M27 .... 70 C6
  TOT/BURYW BL8 .... 4 C1
**Lichfield Gv** AIMK WN4 .... 78 F2
**Lichfield Rd** ECC M30 .... 70 C8
  RAD M26 .... 38 A7
  URM M41 .... 85 G8
**Lichfield St** SLFD M6 .... 71 K7
  WGNW/BIL/OR WN5 .... 46 F7
**Lichfield Ter** MILN OL16 .... 28 F8
**Lichfield Wk** MPL/ROM SK6 .... 113 K3
**Lidbrook Wk** WGTN/LGST M12 .... 88 B6
**Liddington Hall Dr** RAMS BL0 .... 18 E8
**Lidgate Cl** WGNS/IIMK WN3 .... 63 G1
**Lidgett Cl** LHULT M38 .... 52 F7
**Lidiard St** CHH M8 .... 72 D3
**Liffey Av** WYTH/NTH M22 .... 119 G1
**Lifton Av** NEWH/MOS M40 .... 73 H8
**Light Alders La** POY/DIS SK12 .... 123 J5
**Lightborne Rd** SALE M33 .... 96 E5
**Lightbounds Rd** BOL BL1 .... 35 J1
**Lightbourne Av** SWIN M27 .... 70 C5
**Lightbowne Rd**
  NEWH/MOS M40 .... 73 J7
**Lightburn Av** LIT OL15 .... 21 K8
**Lightburne Av** BOL BL1 .... 35 M5
  LEIGH WN7 .... 81 H1
**Lighthorne Av** EDGY/DAV SK3 .... 111 K5
**Lighthorne Gv** EDGY/DAV SK3 .... 111 J5
**Lighthorne Rd** EDGY/DAV SK3 .... 111 J5
**Light Oaks Rd**
  GOL/RIS/CUL WA3 .... 81 M6
  SLFD M6 .... 70 E8
**Lightshaw La**
  GOL/RIS/CUL WA3 .... 64 E8
**Lightwood** WALK M28 .... 68 E4
**Lightwood Cl** FWTH BL4 .... 53 M4
**Lignum Av** CHAD OL9 .... 8 A3

**Lilac Av** AIMK WN4 .... 63 G7
  BURY BL9 .... 39 G5
  HYDE SK14 .... 102 A4
  LEIGH WN7 .... 66 B5
  MILN OL16 .... 43 K1
  SWIN M27 .... 70 D4
  WGNNW/ST WN6 .... 47 K1
**Lilac Gdns** WGNS/IIMK WN3 .... 48 D2
**Lilac Gv** CHAD OL9 .... 8 A3
  NEWH/MOS M40 .... 73 K3
  PWCH M25 .... 55 K6
  SALE M33 .... 97 H8
**Lilac La** OLDS OL8 .... 75 G2
**Lilac Rd** GOL/RIS/CUL WA3 .... 79 K3
  HALE/TIMP WA15 .... 117 J1
  ROCH OL11 .... 42 C2
**Lilac St** OFTN SK2 .... 112 C6
**Lilac View Cl** ROY/SHW OL2 .... 43 M6
**Lilac View Rd** ROY/SHW OL2 .... 43 M6
**Lila St** BKLY M9 .... 73 J5
**Lilburn Cl** RAMS BL0 .... 18 F8
**Liley St** MILN OL16 .... 11 H6
**Lilford Cl** WGTN/LGST M12 .... 88 D6
**Lilford St** ATH M46 .... 66 B8
  LEIGH WN7 .... 66 B8
**Lilian Dr** WGNNW/ST WN6 .... 47 L1
**Lilian Gv** RDSH SK5 .... 100 C4
**Lillian St** RUSH/FAL M14 .... 86 F8
**Lilly St** BOL BL1 .... 2 A2
  HYDE SK14 .... 102 C4
**Lilmore Av** NEWH/MOS M40 .... 72 F6
  NEWH/MOS M40 .... 74 A2
  ROY/SHW OL2 .... 42 F5
  URM M41 .... 95 J1
**Lily Av** FWTH BL4 .... 52 E3
**Lily Cl** EDGY/DAV SK3 .... 112 A7
**Lily Hill St** WHTF M45 .... 55 H2
**Lily La** BKLY M9 .... 73 J5
  WGNE/HIN WN2 .... 64 D4
**Lily Lanes** AUL OL6 .... 76 B4
**Lily Pl** AIMK WN4 .... 78 F2
**Lily St** AIMK WN4 .... 63 G7
  ECC M30 .... 84 E3
  MDTN M24 .... 57 M4
  MILN OL16 .... 29 J6
  OLD OL1 .... 9 G1
  ROY/SHW OL2 .... 43 J8
**Lima St** BURY BL9 .... 5 L2
**Limbert Cir** CHH M8 .... 72 F3
**Lime Av** LEIGH WN7 .... 66 B4
  NM/HAY SK22 .... 124 F3
  SWIN M27 .... 69 M6
  URM M41 .... 95 J2
  WHTF M45 .... 55 J5
**Lime Bank St** WGTN/LGST M12 .... 88 A4
**Limebrook Cl** OP/CLY M11 .... 89 H5
**Lime Cl** DUK SK16 .... 91 C6
  SLFD M6 .... 71 K4
**Lime Crs** OLDTF/WHR M16 .... 86 D1
**Lime Ct** SLFD M6 * .... 71 K4
**Lime Fld** MILN OL16 .... 29 H5
**Limefield** MDTN M24 .... 57 H5
  MOSL OL5 .... 76 E2
  WGN WN1 .... 15 H3
**Limefield Av** FWTH BL4 .... 53 C3
**Limefield Brow** BURY BL9 .... 25 J5
**Limefield Rd** BRO M7 .... 72 A3
  BURY BL9 .... 25 J5
  RAD M26 .... 54 A1
**Limefield Ter** BNG/LEV M19 .... 99 K3
**Lime Gdns** DUK SK16 .... 90 E4
  MDTN M24 .... 57 H4
**Lime Ga** OLDS OL8 .... 74 F2
**Lime Gn** OLDS OL8 .... 75 C3
**Lime Green Rd** OLDS OL8 .... 74 F2
**Lime Gv** AUL OL6 .... 75 M7
  BURY BL9 .... 25 J5
  CHD/CHDH SK8 .... 111 G6
  DTN/ASHW M34 .... 90 C8
  GOL/RIS/CUL WA3 .... 80 A6
  HALE/TIMP WA15 .... 108 E6
  HEY OL10 .... 40 F1
  LIT OL15 .... 21 K7
  OLDTF/WHR M16 .... 86 E8
  PWCH M25 .... 55 K6
  RAMS BL0 .... 19 G5
  ROY/SHW OL2 .... 43 G6
  STLY SK15 .... 91 H4
  WALK M28 .... 69 G3
  WGNE/HIN WN2 .... 65 J1
**Limehurst Av** AULW OL7 .... 75 K6
  RUSH/FAL M14 .... 98 C4
**Limehurst Ct** OLDS OL8 .... 75 C3
**Limehurst Rd** AULW OL7 .... 75 H7
**Lime Kiln La** MPL/ROM SK6 .... 114 D7
**Limekiln La** WGTN/LGST M12 .... 88 A4
**Lime La** FAIL M35 .... 74 F5
  OLDS OL8 .... 74 F3
**Lime Rd** STRET M32 .... 97 C3
**Limers Ga** WHIT OL12 .... 20 D7
**Limerston Dr**
  NEWH/MOS M40 .... 73 J7
**Limes Av** WGNNW/ST WN6 .... 31 L6
**Limesdale Cl** BOLE BL2 .... 37 L7
**Limeside Rd** OLDS OL8 .... 74 F2
**Limestead Av** CHH M8 .... 72 D4
**The Limes** GOL/RIS/CUL WA3 .... 80 A6
  GOL/RIS/CUL WA3 .... 81 G8
  MOSL OL5 .... 77 H3
  MOSL OL5 .... 77 H3
  WGNNW/ST WN6 .... 31 K6
**Lime St** ATH M46 .... 66 E2
  BOL BL1 .... 2
  DUK SK16 .... 90 E4
  ECC M30 .... 85 G3
  FWTH BL4 .... 53 H4
  MPL/ROM SK6 .... 101 H8
  NEWH/MOS M40 .... 88 A1
  OLD OL1 .... 8 D1
  ROCH OL11 .... 27 M8
  TYLD M29 .... 67 J3
  WGN WN1 .... 15 H3
**Lime Tree Cl** URM M41 .... 96 B3
**Lime Tree Gv** FAIL M35 .... 75 H5
**Limetrees Rd** MDTN M24 .... 57 J4
**Lime V** WGNS/IIMK WN3 .... 48 C3
**Limewood Meadow**
  TYLD M29 .... 67 M6
**Limley Gv** CCHDY M21 .... 97 M5
**Linacre Av** BOLS/LL BL3 .... 51 M5
**Linacre Wy** GLSP SK13 .... 105 J5
**Linbeck Gv**
  GOL/RIS/CUL WA3 .... 80 B3
**Linby St** HULME M15 .... 6 C9
**Lincoln Av** BNG/LEV M19 .... 99 L3
  BOLS/LL BL3 .... 51 L8
  CHD/CHDH SK8 .... 119 K5
  DROY M43 .... 89 K1
  DTN/ASHW M34 .... 101 J3
  GOL/RIS/CUL WA3 .... 80 A3
  STRET M32 .... 96 C1

**Lincoln Cl** AUL OL6 .... 76 A4
  LEIGH WN7 .... 80 F4
  ROCH OL11 .... 11 G7
  TYLD M29 .... 67 K2
**Lincoln Dr** AIMK WN4 .... 78 D3
  BURY BL9 .... 5 C8
  HALE/TIMP WA15 .... 108 C8
  LIT OL15 .... 29 K1
  WGNE/HIN WN2 .... 33 G1
**Lincoln Gv** BOLE BL2 .... 23 J8
  BRUN/LGST M13 .... 87 K7
  DID/WITH M20 .... 98 D8
  SALE M33 .... 97 H8
**Lincoln Leach Ct** ROCH OL11 .... 10 E8
**Lincoln Pl** WGNW/BIL/OR WN5 .... 46 F4
**Lincoln Ri** MPL/ROM SK6 .... 113 K3
**Lincoln Rd** BOL BL1 .... 35 L4
  FAIL M35 .... 74 D6
  MDTN M24 .... 57 M7
  WGNE/HIN WN2 .... 33 G1
  WILM/AE SK9 .... 127 J3
**Lincoln St** BRUN/LGST M13 .... 88 C8
  CHAD OL9 .... 8 B8
  ECC M30 .... 84 F3
  ROCH OL11 .... 11 G7
**Lincoln Wy** GLSP SK13 .... 105 J4
**Lincombe Rd** WYTH/NTH M22 .... 118 E4
**Lincroft Rd** WGNE/HIN WN2 .... 65 K1
**Linda Dr** BRAM/HZG SK7 .... 121 M3
**Lindale** HYDE SK14 .... 90 F7
**Lindale Av** BOL BL1 .... 35 F6
  BURY BL9 .... 55 K1
  CHAD OL9 .... 58 D6
  NEWH/MOS M40 .... 74 A2
  ROY/SHW OL2 .... 42 F5
  URM M41 .... 95 J1
**Lindale Cl** WALK M28 .... 68 B5
**Lindale Dr** MDTN M24 .... 57 H1
**Lindale Ri** ROY/SHW OL2 .... 44 A5
**Lindale Rd** WALK M28 .... 68 B5
**Lindbury Av** OFTN SK2 .... 112 F5
**Linden Av** AIMK WN4 .... 63 J7
  ATH M46 .... 66 E2
  BOLS/LL BL3 .... 37 K7
  DTN/ASHW M34 .... 90 A5
  HALE/TIMP WA15 .... 108 A5
  OLDE OL4 .... 60 A4
  RAMS BL0 .... 19 C6
  SALE M33 .... 96 C8
  SLFD M6 .... 71 H6
  SWIN M27 .... 70 B6
  WGNW/BIL/OR WN5 .... 46 B6
**Linden Cl** DTN/ASHW M34 .... 101 K1
  OFTN SK2 .... 113 J7
  WGTN/LGST M12 .... 88 C8
**Linden Crs** TOT/BURYW BL8 .... 24 C2
**Linden Dr** ORD M5 .... 86 B2
**Linden Gv** BRAM/HZG SK7 .... 120 F4
  LEIGH WN7 .... 66 B5
  OFTN SK2 .... 112 F5
  RUSH/FAL M14 .... 99 G4
  WGNW/BIL/OR WN5 .... 46 B6
**Linden Ms** WALK M28 .... 68 C6
**Linden Pk** BNG/LEV M19 .... 99 K4
**Linden Rd** CHD/CHDH SK8 .... 120 C1
  DID/WITH M20 .... 98 D8
  DTN/ASHW M34 .... 101 K1
  STLY SK15 .... 92 A5
  WALK M28 .... 68 C6
  WGNE/HIN WN2 .... 49 H5
**Linden St** WGNW/BIL/OR WN5 .... 46 F7
**Linden Wk** BOLE BL2 .... 22 E7
**Linden Wy** MPL/ROM SK6 .... 123 J5
**Lindenwood** CHAD OL9 .... 58 B4
**Lindeth Av** GTN M18 .... 89 C3
**Lindfield Dr** BOL BL1 .... 36 B3
**Lindfield Est North**
  WILM/AE SK9 .... 126 E6
**Lindfield Est South**
  WILM/AE SK9 .... 126 E6
**Lindfield Rd** RDSH SK5 .... 100 C3
**Lindinis Av** ORD M5 .... 86 D2
**Lindisfarne Av**
  GOL/RIS/CUL WA3 .... 80 F4
**Lindisfarne Cl** SALE M33 .... 108 E3
**Lindisfarne Dr** POY/DIS SK12 .... 121 M8
**Lindisfarne Pl** BOLE BL2 .... 36 F2
**Lindisfarne Rd** AULW OL7 .... 75 H7
**Lindley Gv** EDGY/DAV SK3 .... 112 A7
**Lindley St** BOLS/LL BL3 * .... 53 L1
  FWTH BL4 .... 53 L6
  LEIGH WN7 .... 66 B8
**Lindleywood Rd** RUSH/FAL M14 .... 99 H4
**Lindon Wy** DROY M43 .... 89 H4
**Lindop Rd** HALE/TIMP WA15 .... 117 H3
**Lindow Cl** TOT/BURYW BL8 .... 24 F6
**Lindow Ct** MPL/ROM SK6 .... 113 G1
**Lindow Fold Dr** WILM/AE SK9 .... 126 B8
**Lindow Rd** OLDTF/WHR M16 .... 97 L2
**Lindow St** LEIGH WN7 .... 81 J1
  SALE M33 .... 109 J1
**Lindrick Av** WHTF M45 .... 55 C6
**Lindrick Cl** NEWH/MOS M40 .... 73 M5
**Lindrick Ter** BOLS/LL BL3 * .... 2 A9
**Lindsay Av** BNG/LEV M19 .... 99 J3
  CHD/CHDH SK8 .... 120 D3
  SWIN M27 .... 70 B5
**Lindsay Cl** OLDE OL4 * .... 60 A2
**Lindsay Rd** BNG/LEV M19 .... 99 J3
**Lindsay St** HOR/BR BL6 .... 34 A3
  STLY SK15 .... 91 J4
**Lindsay Ter** WGNE/HIN WN2 .... 32 E7
**Lindsell Rd** ALT WA14 .... 107 M4
**Lindsgate Dr** HALE/TIMP WA15 .... 108 B6
**Lind St** NEWH/MOS M40 .... 88 A3
**Lindum Av** OLDTF/WHR M16 .... 86 F8
**Lindum St** RUSH/FAL M14 .... 98 E1
**Lindwall Cl** NTHM/RTH M23 .... 109 L2
**Linehan Cl** HTNM SK4 .... 111 G2
**Lineholme** ROY/SHW OL2 .... 58 F2
**Linen Ct** CSLFD M3 .... 6 A1
**Lines Rd** DROY M43 .... 89 L3
  IRL M44 .... 94 C4
**Linfield Cl** BOLE BL2 .... 23 G8
**Linfield St** OP/CLY M11 .... 88 E3
**Linford Av** NEWH/MOS M40 .... 73 M1
**Lingard La** MPL/ROM SK6 .... 101 L3
  WYTH/NTH M22 .... 110 A3
**Lingards La** TYLD M29 .... 67 L6
**Lingard St** LEIGH WN7 .... 66 B8
  RDSH SK5 .... 100 C3
**Lingcrest Rd** HTNM SK4 .... 99 H5
**Lingdale Rd** CHD/CHDH SK8 .... 120 D3
**Ling Dr** ATH M46 .... 67 G2
**Lingfield Av** BRAM/HZG SK7 .... 122 D3
  SALE M33 .... 107 L2
**Lingfield Cl** FWTH BL4 .... 52 F5
  TOT/BURYW BL8 .... 24 F5
**Lingfield Crs** WGNNW/ST WN6 .... 47 H1
**Lingfield Rd** OP/CLY M11 .... 88 D2
**Lingholme Dr** MDTN M24 .... 56 F7

**Lingmell Cl** BOL BL1 .... 35 J4
  MDTN M24 .... 57 C2
  URM M41 .... 96 C5
**Lingmoor Cl** MDTN M24 .... 56 F7
  WGNS/IIMK WN3 .... 63 G5
**Lingmoor Dr** TYLD M29 .... 67 L5
**Lingmoor Rd** BOL BL1 .... 35 J3
**Lingmoor Wk** HULME M15 * .... 87 G7
**Lings Wk** WYTH/NTH M22 .... 119 G3
**Link Av** URM M41 .... 96 C5
**Linkfield Dr** WALK M28 .... 68 C6
**Link La** OLDS OL8 .... 75 H2
**Link Rd** OLDE OL4 .... 60 C5
  SALE M33 .... 108 C2
**Links Av** FAIL M35 .... 74 C7
**Links Crs** PWCH M25 .... 72 B2
**Links Dr** HOR/BR BL6 .... 34 E5
**Linksfield** DTN/ASHW M34 .... 90 C7
**Linkside Av** ROY/SHW OL2 .... 43 G7
**Links Pl** AUL OL6 .... 76 B4
**Links Ri** URM M41 .... 84 D8
**Links Rd** BOLE BL2 .... 37 K1
  HEY OL10 .... 41 G4
  HOR/BR BL6 .... 34 E5
  MPL/ROM SK6 .... 114 A1
  MPL/ROM SK6 .... 114 C8
  WILM/AE SK9 .... 130 B5
**The Links** NEWH/MOS M40 .... 73 M5
**Links Vw** PWCH M25 .... 71 K3
  ROCH OL11 .... 27 L6
**Links Wy** CHAD OL9 .... 8 C3
**Linksway** CHD/CHDH SK8 .... 110 D8
  PWCH M25 .... 72 A2
  SWIN M27 .... 70 D6
**Linksway Cl** HTNM SK4 .... 99 K3
**Linksway Dr** BURY BL9 .... 39 H5
**The Link** RDSH SK5 .... 100 F6
  ROY/SHW OL2 .... 43 J3
  WILM/AE SK9 .... 127 H1
**Linkway Av** AIMK WN4 .... 64 B7
**The Linkway** HOR/BR BL6 .... 33 M4
**Linley Av** RAD M26 .... 39 H7
**Linley Cl** WGNNW/ST WN6 .... 30 F8
**Linley Dr** OLDE OL4 .... 60 A8
**Linley Gv** RAMS BL0 .... 24 D2
**Linley Rd** CHD/CHDH SK8 .... 96 E7
  SALE M33 .... 96 E7
  WGNW/BIL/OR WN5 .... 47 G7
**Linnell Dr** ROCH OL11 .... 27 H4
**Linnet Cl** DTN/ASHW M34 .... 89 M2
  OFTN SK2 .... 113 J7
  WGTN/LGST M12 .... 88 C8
**Linnet Dr** BURY BL9 .... 5 L1
  IRL M44 .... 94 D7
  LEIGH WN7 .... 66 E7
**Linnet Hl** ROCH OL11 .... 27 M6
**Linnet's Wood Ms** WALK M28 .... 69 H1
**Linney La** ROY/SHW OL2 .... 43 M5
**Linney Rd** BRAM/HZG SK7 .... 120 F2
**Linney Sq** WGN WN1 .... 15 K3
**Linn St** CHH M8 .... 72 D3
**Linslade Gdns** BOLS/LL BL3 * .... 2 C8
**Linsley St** CSLFD M3 * .... 6 D2
**Linstead Dr** CHH M8 .... 72 C6
**Linstock Wy** ATH M46 .... 66 M1
**Linthorpe Wk** BOLS/LL BL3 .... 35 L8
**Linton Av** BURY BL9 .... 25 J7
  DTN/ASHW M34 .... 100 D1
  GOL/RIS/CUL WA3 .... 79 J2
**Linton Cl** ANC M4 .... 88 A4
**Linton Rd** SALE M33 .... 96 E8
**Linton Wk** BRO M7 .... 71 M4
**Linwood Cl** WGNE/HIN WN2 .... 49 G8
**Linwood Gv** WGTN/LGST M12 .... 99 K2
**Linwood St** NEWH/MOS M40 .... 73 M6
**Lion Brow** BKLY M9 .... 73 G2
**Lion Fold La** BKLY M9 .... 73 G1
**Lion La** HOR/BR BL6 .... 32 F2
**Lions Dr** SWIN M27 .... 70 C5
**Lion St** BKLY M9 .... 73 G2
**Liptrot St** WGNW/BIL/OR WN5 .... 14 A6
**Lisbon St** ROCH OL11 .... 27 L4
**Lisburn Av** OFTN SK2 .... 113 G6
  EDGY/DAV SK3 .... 12 A7
**Lisburne Av** OFTN SK2 .... 113 G6
**Lisburne Cl** OFTN SK2 .... 113 G6
**Lisburne La** OFTN SK2 .... 112 F7
**Lisburn Rd** NEWH/MOS M40 .... 73 K4
**Liscard Av** RUSH/FAL M14 .... 98 E3
**Liscard St** ATH M46 .... 66 E1
**Lisetta Av** OLDE OL4 .... 59 L7
**Liskeard Av** ROY/SHW OL2 .... 43 K8
**Liskeard Cl** MILN OL16 .... 11 L1
**Liskeard Dr** BRAM/HZG SK7 .... 121 H5
**Lisle St** WHIT OL12 .... 11 G2
**Lismore Av** BOLS/LL BL3 .... 35 J7
  EDGY/DAV SK3 .... 12 A7
**Lismore Rd** DUK SK16 .... 91 C5
**Lismore Wy** URM M41 .... 85 C7
**Lisson Gv** HALE/TIMP WA15 .... 117 G2
**Lister Rd** MDTN M24 .... 56 E6
**Lister St** BOLS/LL BL3 .... 51 L1
**Liston St** DUK SK16 .... 91 C4
**Litcham Cl** CMANE M1 * .... 7 J8
**Litchfield Gv** WALK M28 .... 69 L5
**Litherland Av** WYTH/NTH M22 .... 119 G2
**Litherland Rd** BOLS/LL BL3 .... 52 B2
  SALE M33 .... 109 H1
**Little 66** BURY BL9 .... 39 L6
**Little Ancoats St** CMANE M1 .... 7 J3
**Little Bank St** OLDE OL4 .... 59 L6
**Littlebourne Wk** BOL BL1 * .... 36 B3
**Littlebrook Cl** CHD/CHDH SK8 .... 111 M8
  GLSP SK13 .... 93 K8
**Little Brook Rd** SALE M33 .... 107 M3
**Little Brow** EDGW/EG BL7 .... 22 D5
**Little Clegg Rd** LIT OL15 .... 29 J2
**Littledale St** WHIT OL12 .... 10 C3
**Little David St** CMANE M1 .... 7 J7
**Little Ees La** SALE M33 .... 96 C5
**Little Egerton St** STKP SK1 .... 13 G3
**Little Factory St** TYLD M29 .... 67 J3
**Littlefields** HYDE SK14 .... 92 D8
**Little Flatt** WHIT OL12 .... 10 D2
**Littlegate** WHTN BL5 .... 50 B7
**Little Gn** MDTN M24 * .... 57 L3
**Littlegreen Gdns** SLFD M6 .... 86 C1
**Little Harwood Lee** BOLE BL2 .... 37 G1
**Littlehaven Cl** WGTN/LGST M12 .... 88 C7
**Little Heath La** ALT WA14 .... 107 G7
**Little Holme St** ANC M4 .... 88 A3
**Little Holme Wk** BOLS/LL BL3 * .... 36 C8
**Little Howarth Wy** WHIT OL12 * .... 21 G8
**Little John St** CSLFD M3 .... 6 C6
**Little La** WGNS/IIMK WN3 .... 47 H8
**Little Lever St** CMANE M1 .... 7 J5
**Little London** WGN WN1 .... 14 F3
**Little Meadow Rd** ALT WA14 .... 116 D3

Little Mdw EDGW/EG BL7 *......22 C5
Little Moor Clough
  EDGW/EG BL7......22 B2
Little Moor Cottages STKP SK1..112 E4
Little Moor La OLDE OL4......59 M4
Littlemoor Rd UPML OL3......45 L8
Little Moss La SWIN M27......70 C2
Littlemoss Rd DROY M43......89 M1
Little Nelson St ANC M4 *......7 H1
Little Oak OLDE......60 B6
Little Pasture LEIGH WN7......66 A5
Little Peter St HULME M15......6 D8
Little Pitt St CMANE M1 *......7 K4
Little Quay St CSLFD M3......6 E5
Little Scotland HOR/BR BL6......32 E2
Little Stones Rd EDGW/EG BL7..22 B2
Littleton Gv WCNNW/ST WN6..31 H2
Littleton Rd BRO M7......106 B1
Little Underbank STKP SK1......13 J4
Littlewood Av BURY BL9......39 J5
Littlewood Rd WYTH/NTH M22..109 M8
Littlewood St SLFD M6......86 B2
Littondale Cl ROY/SHW OL2......43 H7
Litton Ms GLSP SK13......104 B3
Liverpool Cl RDSH SK5......100 B5
Liverpool Rd AIMK WN4......78 A2
  CSLFD M3......6 B6
  ECC M30......84 A6
  IRL M44......94 E1
  IRL M44......94 A7
  WGNE/HIN WN2......64 E1
Liverpool St RDSH SK5......100 B5
  SLFD M6......86 B2
Liverstudd Av RDSH SK5......100 C4
Livesey Av ANC M4......87 M1
  BNG/LEV M19......99 M4
  OLD OL1......59 M4
Livingston Av WYTH/NTH M22..118 D2
Livingstone Av MOSL OL5......76 E3
Livingstone St OLDE OL4......60 B7
Livsey Cl BOL BL1......2 E2
Livsey La HEY OL10......40 D2
Livsey St MILN OL16......11 C5
  WHTF M45......55 J4
Liza St LEIGH WN7......66 B4
Lizmar Ter BKLY M9......73 J4
Llanberis Rd CHD/CHDH SK8..120 A3
Llanfair Rd EDGY/DAV SK3......12 D7
Lloyd Av CHD/CHDH SK8......110 D6
Lloyd Ct LEIGH WN7 *......66 A5
Lloyd Gdns ALT WA14......116 F1
Lloyd Rd BNG/LEV M19......99 L5
Lloyd Sq WA14......108 A8
Lloyd St WA14......108 A8
  CMANW M2......6 F5
  HEY OL10......41 G3
  HTNM SK4......12 F1
  ROCH OL11......10 D9
  WHIT OL12......20 A3
Lloyd St South RUSH/FAL M14..98 D3
Lobden Crs WHIT OL12......20 B5
Lobelia Av FWTH BL4......52 D3
Lobley Cl WHIT OL12......28 E2
Local Board St
  WGNE/HIN WN2 *......48 C5
Lochawe Cl HEY OL10......40 D3
Lochinver Gv HEY OL10......40 D3
Lochmaddy Cl BRAM/HZG SK7..122 B3
Loch St WGNW/BIL/OR WN5......46 E6
Lockerbie Pl WGNS/IIMK WN3..63 H2
Locker La AIMK WN4......64 C8
Lockett Gdns CSLFD M3......6 B2
Lockett Rd AIMK WN4......63 L6
Lockett St CHH M8......72 B8
  SLFD M6......71 K7
Lockhart Cl WGTN/LGST M12..88 D7
Lockhart St MILN OL16......11 K8
Lockingate St AUL OL6......75 M6
Lock La HOR/BR BL6......34 F8
  PART M31......106 B1
Lock Rd ALT WA14......107 M6
Lockside MPL/ROM SK6......114 D6
Lockside Vw MOSL OL5......77 H1
Locksley Cl HTNM SK4......12 D2
Locks Vw WGN WN1......15 M4
Lockton Cl CMANE M1 *......7 K8
  RDSH SK5......100 B6
Lockton Ct CMANE M1......7 K8
Lockwood St WGTN/LGST M12..99 L1
Lodge Av URM M41......96 B2
Lodge Bank GLSP SK13......93 K6
  HOR/BR BL6......33 J1
Lodge Bank Rd LIT OL15......29 J1
Lodge Brow RAD M26......54 E2
Lodge Cl DUK SK16......91 H5
Lodge Ct HTNM SK4......111 J2
  SWIN M27......92 D8
Lodge Dr TYLD M29......67 L6
Lodge Farm Cl BRAM/HZG SK7..122 B2
Lodge Fold DROY M43......89 L2
Lodge Gn DUK SK16......91 H5
Lodge Gv ATH M46......67 H3
Lodge La ATH M46......67 G3
  DUK SK16......91 H4
  HYDE SK14......91 G8
  LEIGH WN7......67 H8
  NEWLW WA12......78 E3
  UPML OL3......45 L2
Lodge Mill La RAMS BL0......19 K3
Lodgepole Cl ECC M30......84 C3
Lodge Rd ATH M46......67 H3
  RAD M26......54 E2
  WGNW/BIL/OR WN5......46 B8
Lodgeside Cl DROY M43......89 L2
Lodge St AUL OL7 *......90 C8
  HYDE SK14......91 H7
  LIT OL15......21 M7
  MDTN M24......57 K3
  NEWH/MOS M40......73 M7
  RAMS BL0......18 F6
  RAMS BL0......19 H4
  WHIT OL12......21 G6
The Lodge GLSP SK13......93 K6
Lodge Vw DROY M43......89 L2
  RAMS BL0......19 K4
Loeminster Pl WGNE/HIN WN2..15 M6
Loen Crs BOL BL1......35 M1
Loganberry Av SLFD M6......86 D1
Logan St BOL BL1......22 B7
Logwood Av TOT/BURYW BL8 *..4 C2
  WGNW/BIL/OR WN5......47 H5
Logwood Pl
  WGNW/BIL/OR WN5......47 H4
Loire Dr WGNW/BIL/OR WN5......14 A5
Loisine Cl ROCH OL11......41 L1
Lokfu Gdns CHH M8......72 B7
Lomas Cl BNG/LEV M19......111 G1

Lomas St EDGY/DAV SK3......12 F8
  FAIL M35......74 D3
  MDTN M24......57 L3
Lomax's Buildings BOLE BL2 *..2 F6
Lomax St BOL BL1......36 E3
  BURY BL9......5 H3
  CMANE M1......7 L4
  RAD M26......54 D2
  WGNE/HIN WN2......64 D3
  WHIT OL12......10 F2
  WHTF M45 *......55 J7
Lombard Cl MPL/ROM SK6......101 J8
Lombard Gv RUSH/FAL M14......98 F4
Lombard St ATH M46......66 E1
  OLD OL1......9 H4
  WHIT OL12......10 B3
Lombardy Ct SLFD M6 *......86 D1
Lomond Av HALE/TIMP WA15..117 J1
  STRET M32......97 G1
Lomond Cl OFTN SK2......121 J1
Lomond Pl BOLS/LL BL3......35 H6
Lomond Rd WYTH/NTH M22..119 H2
Lomond Ter MILN OL16......28 E1
London Cl WGNW/BIL/OR WN5..47 H4
London Flds
  WGNW/BIL/OR WN5......62 B7
London Pl STKP SK1......13 J5
London Rd BRAM/HZG SK7......113 G8
  CMANE M1......7 K7
  OLD OL1......59 L3
  WILM/AE SK9......130 D3
London Rd North
  POY/DIS SK12......121 M8
London Rd South
  POY/DIS SK12......129 M2
London Sq STKP SK1......13 J5
London St BOLS/LL BL3......36 B8
  SLFD M6......71 L8
  WHTF M45......55 J5
Long Acres Dr WHIT OL12......20 B3
Longacres La WHIT OL12......20 B2
Longacres Rd
  HALE/TIMP WA15......117 L5
Longacre St CMANE M1......7 L6
Longbow Ct BRO M7 *......72 A8
Longbridge Rd TRPK M17......85 K6
Longbrook WGNNW/ST WN6..30 E6
Long Cswy ATH M46......66 F5
  FWTH BL4......53 G5
Longcliffe Wk BOL BL1 *......36 C2
Long Clough ROY/SHW OL2......58 F2
Longclough Dr GLSP SK13......104 D4
Longcrag Wk HULME M15 *......87 J7
Longcroft TYLD M29......67 H8
Longcroft Dr ALT WA14......107 L8
Longcroft Gv DTN/ASHW M34..89 L4
  NTHM/RTH M23......109 L5
Long Croft La CHD/CHDH SK8..120 B4
Longdale Cl ROY/SHW OL2......42 F8
Longdale Dr HYDE SK14......103 K1
Longden Av OLDE......60 B1
Longden Av WGTN/LGST M12..99 K2
Longden St BOL BL1......35 M4
Longden Ct BRAM/HZG SK7 *..128 A3
Longdendale Rd
  WGNNW/ST WN6......31 G4
Longfellow Av BOLS/LL BL3......51 L1
Longfellow Cl WGNS/IIMK WN3..47 K7
Longfellow Crs OLD OL1......44 A8
Longfield BURY BL9 *......25 K8
Longfield Av CHD/CHDH SK8..119 L5
  HALE/TIMP WA15......108 F1
  URM M41......95 J2
Longfield Cl HYDE SK14......91 H6
Longfield Crs OLDE OL4......59 M3
Longfield Dr URM M41......95 J2
Longfield La OLDE OL4......60 A3
Longfield Pk ROY/SHW OL2......43 K7
Longfield Rd BOLS/LL BL3......51 L2
  NTHM/RTH M23......109 J4
  ROCH OL11......27 M4
  ROY/SHW OL2......43 K6
Longford Av BOL BL1......35 M2
Longford Cl STRET M32......97 H2
Longford Pk STRET M32......97 J2
Longford Pl RUSH/FAL M14......88 E7
Longford Rd RDSH SK5......100 C3
  STRET M32......97 H1
Longford West
  BNG/LEV M19......100 A3
Longford St GTN M18......89 G6
  HEY OL10......40 F2
Long Grain Pl OFTN SK2......113 G7
Longham Cl BRAM/HZG SK7......120 B8
  OP/CLY M11......88 B3
Long Hey HALE/TIMP WA15..117 J1
Longhey Rd WYTH/NTH M22..110 A7
Long Hl ROCH OL11......28 A8
Longhirst Cl BOL BL1......35 L1
Longhope Rd WYTH/NTH M22..118 E2
Longhurst La MPL/ROM SK6..114 E5
Longhurst Rd BKLY M9......56 E8
  WGNE/HIN WN2......49 J8
Longlands Av NM/HAY SK22..102 L1
Longlands Dr HYDE SK14......102 E1
  NM/HAY SK22......124 D4
Longlands Rd NM/HAY SK22..124 D4
Long La BOLE BL2......37 G7
  BURY BL9......25 J8
  CHAD OL9......74 C1
  GLSP SK13......103 M5
  UPML OL3......61 K2
  WGNE/HIN WN2......49 K8
  WHTN BL5......49 M2
Longlevens Rd
  WYTH/NTH M22......118 E2
Longley Dr WALK M28......69 L6
Longley La WYTH/NTH M22..110 B5
Longley St OLD OL1......9 J7
  ROY/SHW OL2......43 L7
  WALK M28......69 G2
Long Marl Dr WILM/AE SK9..120 D8
Longmead Av AIMK WN4......63 M8
  BRAM/HZG SK7......121 M3
Longmeade Gdns
  WILM/AE SK9......127 G6
Longmeadow CHD/CHDH SK8..120 E5
Long Meadow EDGW/EG BL7..22 F5
  HYDE SK14......91 J6
Longmeadow Gv
  DTN/ASHW M34......101 H2
Longmeadow Pas HYDE SK14..102 A1
Long Meadow Pas
  HYDE SK14 *......102 A1
Longmead Rd SLFD M6......71 G7
Longmead Wy MDTN M24......57 K3
Longmere Av WYTH/NTH M22..118 D3
Long Millgate CSLFD M3......6 F2
Longmoor Rd GLSP SK13......104 D5
Longnor Ms GLSP SK13......104 A2

Longnor Rd BRAM/HZG SK7......122 A5
  CHD/CHDH SK8......119 M6
Longport Av DID/WITH M20......98 D5
Longridge EDGW/EG BL7......22 F5
Longridge Av STLY SK15......76 D8
Longridge Crs BOL BL1......35 J2
Longridge Dr HEY OL10......40 C2
  TOT/BURYW BL8......38 D4
Long Rw STLY SK15......77 J5
Long Rushes ROY/SHW OL2......43 J4
Longshaw Av SWIN M27......70 C3
  WGNW/BIL/OR WN5......62 B3
Longshaw Cl
  WGNW/BIL/OR WN5......62 B3
Longshaw Common
  WGNW/BIL/OR WN5......62 B3
Longshaw Dr LHULT M38......52 D8
Longshaw Old Rd
  WGNW/BIL/OR WN5......62 B3
Longshoot Cl WGN WN1......15 J2
Longsight La BOLE BL2......23 G8
  CHD/CHDH SK8......120 B7
Longsight Rd BOLE BL2......37 G1
  GTN M18......99 L1
  RAMS BL0......24 D2
Longsight St HTNM SK4......12 E3
Longson St BOL BL1......3 G1
Long St GTN M18......99 G6
  MDTN M24......57 K3
  SWIN M27......70 C5
Longton Av DID/WITH M20......98 D7
  GOL/RIS/CUL WA3......79 M4
Longton Rd BKLY M9......56 F8
  SLFD M6......71 J8
Longton St BURY BL9......39 J8
  WGNE/HIN WN2......64 E1
Longtown Gdns BOL BL1 *......36 B2
Longview Av SWIN M27......69 M3
Longwall Av WALK M28......68 F4
Longwood Av OFTN SK2......112 E6
Longwood Cl MPL/ROM SK6..114 D1
Longwood Rd TRPK M17......85 L6
  WYTH/NTH M22......119 G1
Longworth Av HOR/BR BL6......33 G3
Longworth Cl URM M41......95 G3
Longworth Clough
  EDGW/EG BL7......22 A2
Longworth La EDGW/EG BL7......22 A4
Longworth Rd BOLE BL2......3 L4
  CSLFD M3......6 D6
Lonsdale Av LEIGH WN7......81 G2
  MILN OL16......11 K9
  RDSH SK5......100 C1
  SWIN M27......70 A4
  URM M41......84 E8
Lonsdale Rd BNG/LEV M19......99 L2
  BOL BL1......35 L4
  OLDE OL4......61 L6
  RAMS BL0......24 E2
Lonsdale St NEWH/MOS M40..73 M6
  TOT/BURYW BL8......38 F2
Lonsdale Wk
  WGNNW/ST WN6......46 E4
Loom St ANC M4......7 K3
Loonies Ct STKP SK1 *......13 J6
Lord Av ATH M46......67 H3
Lord Byron Sq SALQ M50......86 C4
Lord Derby Rd HYDE SK14......102 B6
Lord La FAIL M35......74 B8
Lord Napier Dr ORD M5......86 A2
Lord North St NEWH/MOS M40..73 H8
Lord's Av ORD M5......86 A2
Lordsfields Av AULW OL7......75 L8
Lords Fold BOL BL1......35 J2
Lord Sheldon Wy AULW OL7......90 C1
Lordship Cl BKLY M9......73 J3
Lordsmead St HULME M15......6 B9
Lord's Stile La EDGW/EG BL7......22 E5
Lord St AIMK WN4......63 H4
  ANC M4......87 K1
  ATH M46......67 G3
  AUL OL6......75 L8
  BURY BL9......5 G5
  BURY BL9......39 M4
  DTN/ASHW M34......89 K8
  DUK SK16......91 J4
  FWTH BL4......53 H4
  GLSP SK13......104 F3
  HYDE SK14......93 G8
  LEIGH WN7......66 C7
  OLD OL1......9 J4
  RAD M26......54 D1
  STKP SK1......13 J6
  TYLD M29......67 J6
  WGN WN1......15 G1
  WGNE/HIN WN2......48 D5
  WGNE/HIN WN2......49 K8
  WHTN BL5......50 B3
Lordy Cl WGNNW/ST WN6......31 L5
Loretto Rd URM M41......96 C3
Lorgill Cl EDGY/DAV SK3......112 C8
Loring St NEWH/MOS M40......73 M7
Lorland Rd EDGY/DAV SK3......12 A8
Lorna Gv CHD/CHDH SK8......110 C6
Lorna Rd CHD/CHDH SK8......120 D2
Lorna Wy IRL M44......94 E4
Lorne Av ROY/SHW OL2......58 E1
Lorne Gv EDGY/DAV SK3......112 B6
  URM M41......96 B2
Lorne Rd RUSH/FAL M14......98 F4
Lorne St BOL BL1......2 E4
  BRUN/LGST M13......87 M7
  ECC M30......84 E4
  FWTH BL4......41 G3
  HEY OL10......41 G3
  MOSL OL5......75 M3
  OLDS OL8......59 H8
  WGN WN1......15 K4
  WHIT OL12......28 E1
Lorne Wy HEY OL10......40 C3
Lorraine Cl HEY OL10......41 H4
Lorraine Rd HALE/TIMP WA15..108 D7
Lorton Cl MDTN M24......56 F2
  WALK M28......68 F4
Lorton Gv BOLE BL2......37 J4
Lostock Av BNG/LEV M19......99 L2
  BRAM/HZG SK7......121 K3
  POY/DIS SK12......121 K3
  SALE M33......108 D3
  URM M41......95 L1
Lostock Cl HEY OL10......40 B5
Lostock Ct STRET M32......96 E1
Lostock Dr BURY BL9......25 J6
Lostock Hall Rd POY/DIS SK12..128 F1

Lostock Junction La
  HOR/BR BL6......34 E6
Lostock La HOR/BR BL6......34 B6
Lostock Park Dr HOR/BR BL6..34 D5
Lostock Rd ORD M5......86 B2
  POY/DIS SK12......129 G2
  URM M41......84 F8
  WHTN BL5......33 M8
Lostock St NEWH/MOS M40......88 A1
Lostock Wk WILM/AE SK9......119 M8
Lothian Av ECC M30......84 E1
Lottery Rw BOL BL1......2 F5
Lottery St EDGY/DAV SK3......12 F5
Lottie St SWIN M27......70 D4
Loughborough Cl SALE M33..108 A1
Loughfield URM M41......95 K2
Loughrigg Av ROY/SHW OL2......43 H4
Loughrigg Cl TYLD M29......67 L5
Louisa St BOL BL1......36 A2
  OP/CLY M11......89 G4
  WALK M28......53 G8
Louis Av BURY BL9......25 J8
Louise Cl WHIT OL12......28 F1
Louise Gdns WHIT OL12......28 E1
  WHTN BL5......50 B6
Louise St WHIT OL12......28 E1
Louvain St FAIL M35......74 B5
Lovalle St BOL BL1......35 M3
Lovat Rd BOLE BL2......37 J5
Love La HTNM SK4......13 G2
  RAMS BL0......24 D7
Lovell Dr HYDE SK14......91 J8
Lovers' La ATH M46......66 C2
  OLDE OL4......60 F6
Low Bank Rd AIMK WN4......63 J8
Lowbrook Av BKLY M9......73 L1
Lowcroft Crs CHAD OL9......58 C4
Low Crompton Rd
  ROY/SHW OL2......43 H6
Lowcross Rd NEWH/MOS M40..73 K6
Lowe Av ATH M46......50 F7
Lowe Gn ROY/SHW OL2......43 H7
Lower Albion St SWIN M27......69 M3
Lowerbank DTN/ASHW M34......90 C7
Lower Alma St DUK SK16......90 E3
Lowerbank St BOL BL1......35 M3
Lower Bank GLSP SK13......105 G4
Lower Bank Cl GLSP SK13......104 C1
Lower Bank St BURY BL9......5 G4
Lower Barn Rd GLSP SK13......93 H8
Lower Beechwood ROCH OL11..10 B8
Lower Bennett St HYDE SK14..90 F8
Lower Bents La MPL/ROM SK6..101 J8
Lower Birches OLDE OL4......60 C8
Lower Bridgeman St BOLE BL2..3 K7
Lower Broadacre STLY SK15......92 B6
Lowerbrook Cl HOR/BR BL6......34 A3
Lower Brook La WALK M28 *......69 K7
Lower Brook St CMANE M1......7 J6
Lower Broughton Rd BRO M7..71 M7
Lower Bury St HTNM SK4......12 E4
Lower Byrom St CSLFD M3......6 C6
Lower Carr La UPML OL3......61 L6
Lower Carrs AUL OL6......75 M8
  STKP SK1......13 K5
Lower Chatham St CMANE M1..7 G8
Lower Cliff NM/HAY SK22......124 A2
Lower Cft WHTF M45......54 F6
Lowercroft Rd TOT/BURYW BL8..38 C2
Lower Crossbank OLDE OL4......60 C4
Lower Darcy St BOLE BL2......3 L9
Lower Dingle OLD OL1......43 M8
Lower Drake Fold WHTN BL5..50 B7
Lower Edge Av OLD OL1......9 H2
Lower Falinge ROCH OL11......10 E2
Lowerfield Dr OFTN SK2......113 J7
Lowerfields OLDS OL8......59 L8
Lowerfields Ri ROY/SHW OL2..43 L4
Lower Fold DTN/ASHW M34..101 K2
  MPL/ROM SK6......114 E4
Lower Fold Av ROY/SHW OL2..43 H6
Lowerfold Cl WHIT OL12......20 A8
Lowerfold Crs WHIT OL12......20 A8
Lowerfold Dr WHIT OL12......20 A8
Lowerfold Wy WHIT OL12......20 A8
Lower Frenches Dr UPML OL3..61 K6
Lower Goodwin Cl BOLE BL2..37 H1
Lower Gn OL6......75 M8
  MDTN M24......57 J7
  WHIT OL12......27 M3
Lower Green La TYLD M29......82 F2
Lower Greenshall La
  POY/DIS SK12......124 B6
Lower Hague NM/HAY SK22..124 A4
Lower Hardman St CSLFD M3..6 C5
Lower Hey La MOSL OL5......77 H1
Lower Hillgate STKP SK1......13 K5
Lower House Dr HOR/BR BL6..34 F5
Lower House La WHIT OL12......20 F5
Lower House St OLD OL1......59 L4
Lower House Wk EDGW/EG BL7..22 D4
Lower Jowkin La ROCH OL11..27 G5
Lower Knoll Rd UPML OL3......45 M7
Lower Landedmans WHTN BL5..50 C5
Lower La MILN OL16......29 G8
Lowerlea POY/DIS SK12......123 J4
Lower Leigh Rd WHTN BL5......50 C5
Lower Lime Rd OLDS OL8......74 F5
Lower Longshoot WGN WN1..15 J3
Lower Lyndon Av
  WGNNW/ST WN6......30 D6
Lower Makinson Fold
  HOR/BR BL6......34 A3
Lower Marlands EDGW/EG BL7..22 C3
Lower Mead EDGW/EG BL7......22 C3
Lower Meadow EDGW/EG BL7..17 G6
Lower Meadow Rd
  WILM/AE SK9......120 A8
Lower Moat Cl HTNM SK4......112 B1
Lower Monton Rd ECC M30......85 H2
Lower Mosley St CMANE M1......6 E8
Lower Moss La HULME M15......6 B9
  WHTF M45......55 J4
Lower New Rw WALK M28......68 D3
Lower Ormond St CMANE M1..7 G8
Lower Park Crs POY/DIS SK12..121 K6
Lower Park Rd POY/DIS SK12..121 K6
  RUSH/FAL M14......87 M8
Lower Rawson St FWTH BL4......53 H3
Lower Rd RAMS BL0......19 G4
Lower Rock St NM/HAY SK22..124 D4
Lower St FWTH BL4......52 F5
  MILN OL16......28 D1
Lower Seedley Rd SLFD M6......86 B1
Lower Sheriff St WHIT OL12......10 C3
Lower Southfield WHTN BL5..50 B6
Lower St Stephen St
  WGNNW/ST WN6......14 C3
Lower Strines Rd
  MPL/ROM SK6......114 D7
Lower Sutherland St SWIN M27..70 B4

Lower Tenterfield ROCH OL11..27 G2
Lower Tong EDGW/EG BL7......22 C5
Lower Turf La OLDE OL4......60 E4
Lower Tweedale St ROCH OL11..10 F7
Lower Victoria St CHAD OL9......8 B5
Lower Wharf St AUL OL6......90 E2
Lower Wheat End MILN OL16..11 K3
Lower Woodhill Rd
  TOT/BURYW BL8......4 C3
Lowerwood La BURY BL9......36 E3
Lowes Rd BURY BL9......25 J6
Lowestead Rd OP/CLY M11......88 F2
The Lowes ALT WA14......116 D3
Lowestoft St RUSH/FAL M14......101 L1
Loweswater Av TYLD M29......67 K5
Loweswater Rd
  CHD/CHDH SK8......119 K1
  FWTH BL4......52 D6
  DROY M43......89 J1
Lowfield Gdns
  GOL/RIS/CUL WA3......81 M5
Lowfield Gv OFTN SK2......13 H9
Lowfield Rd EDGY/DAV SK3......13 H9
Low Gate La UPML OL3......45 K3
Low Gn ATH M46......51 J7
Low Grove La UPML OL3 *......61 H7
Low Hl WHIT OL12......28 F1
Lowhouse Cl MILN OL16......29 K5
Lowick Av BOLS/LL BL3......52 D1
Lowick Cl BRAM/HZG SK7......121 M2
Lowick Gn MPL/ROM SK6......101 J7
Lowland Gv AULW OL7......75 K6
Lowland Rd OFTN SK2......112 E8
Lowlands Cl MDTN M24......57 M8
Low Lea Rd MPL/ROM SK6......114 E6
Low Leighton Rd
  NM/HAY SK22......124 F5
Low Mdw ROY/SHW OL2......43 G6
Lowndes Cl OFTN SK2......112 E5
Lowndes La OFTN SK2......112 E5
Lowndes St BOL BL1......35 L4
Lowndes Wk
  BRUN/LGST M13 *......87 M6
Lownorth Rd WYTH/NTH M22..119 G4
Lowood Av URM M41......84 C8
Lowood St LEIGH WN7......66 A7
Lowry Ct MPL/ROM SK6......114 E4
  SWIN M27......70 C3
Lowry Gv HYDE SK14......103 J1
Lowry Houses ECC M30 *......85 H2
Lowry Wk BOL BL1......35 K4
Lowside Av BOL BL1......34 F6
  MPL/ROM SK6......101 M7
Lowside Dr OLDE OL4......59 L7
Low's Pl WHIT OL12......28 D2
Lowstern Cl EDGW/EG BL7......22 C3
The Lows OLDE OL4......59 L7
Lowther Av COL/RIS/CUL WA3..81 J8
  GTN M18......99 L1
  HALE/TIMP WA15......108 D6
  ROY/SHW OL2......42 F4
Lowther Cl PWCH M25......71 K1
Lowther Crs MDTN M24......57 H3
Lowther Dr LEIGH WN7......81 G4
Lowther Gdns URM M41......95 G1
Lowther Rd CHH M8......72 D3
  PWCH M25......71 J1
  ROCH OL11......10 A5
Lowther St BOLS/LL BL3......52 D2
Lowthorpe St RUSH/FAL M14..98 D2
Lowton Av BKLY M9......73 J5
Lowton Gdns COL/RIS/CUL WA3..79 L3
Lowton Rd COL/RIS/CUL WA3..79 L3
  SALE M33......108 A2
Lowton St RAD M26......38 D8
Low Wood Cl BRAM/HZG SK7..120 E3
Low Wood Rd DTN/ASHW M34..89 K8
Loxford Ct HULME M15......6 F9
Loxham St BOLS/LL BL3......53 G2
Loxton Crs WGNS/IIMK WN3..63 L1
Lubeck St BKLY M9......73 H4
Lucas Rd FWTH BL4......52 D4
Lucas St BURY BL9......5 L2
  OLDE OL4......59 L5
Lucas Wk OP/CLY M11......88 C4
Lucerne Cl CHAD OL9......8 C7
Lucerne Rd BRAM/HZG SK7......121 G1
Lucien Cl WGTN/LGST M12......88 B7
Luciol Cl TYLD M29......67 M3
Lucknow St ROCH OL11......10 E9
Lucy St BOL BL1......35 K3
  BRO M7......72 A7
  EDGY/DAV SK3......13 G7
  HULME......87 G6
Ludford Gv SALE M33......108 C2
Ludgate HI ANC M4......7 J1
Ludgate Rd NEWH/MOS M40..73 M8
  ROCH OL11......42 D2
Ludlow Av SWIN M27......70 D2
  WGNE/HIN WN2......49 K8
  WHTF M45......55 L6
Ludlow Dr LEIGH WN7......67 G5
Ludlow Pk OLDE OL4......60 A6
Ludlow Rd OFTN SK2......112 F4
Ludlow St WGNNW/ST WN6..30 F1
Ludovic Ter WGN WN1......31 M8
Lugano Rd BRAM/HZG SK7......121 G1
Luke Rd DROY M43......89 L3
Luke St AIMK WN4......64 A7
Lullington Rd WYTH/NTH M22..118 E3
Lulworth Av URM M41......95 J2
Lulworth CI TOT/BURYW BL8..24 F6
Lulworth Crs FAIL M35......74 E4
Lulworth Dr WGNE/HIN WN2..49 K8
Lulworth Gdns
  NTHM/RTH M23......109 J4
Lulworth Rd BOLS/LL BL3......51 K1
  ECC M30......84 F2
  MDTN M24......57 G2
Lumb Carr Av RAMS BL0......18 D5
Lumb Carr Rd RAMS BL0......18 D5
Lumb Cl BRAM/HZG SK7......121 G6
Lumber La WALK M28......69 H4
Lumb La BRAM/HZG SK7......121 G6
  DROY M43......89 M3
  DTN/ASHW M34......89 M3
Lumley Cl RUSH/FAL M14......87 L8
Lumn Hollow HYDE SK14......102 B2
Lumn Rd HYDE SK14......102 B2
Lumn's La SWIN M27......70 F2
Lumn St BURY BL9......25 J4
Lumsdale Rd STRET M32......85 K8
Lumsden St BOLS/LL BL3......2 C9
Lum St BOL BL1......3 G1

Lumwood BOL BL1 .....35 L1
Luna St ANC M4 .....7 J3
Lund Av RAD M26 .....54 E4
Lund St OLDTF/WHR M16 .....86 F6
Lundy Av CCHDY M21 .....97 M7
Lune Cl WHTF M45 .....55 K4
Lunedale Gn OFTN SK2 .....113 H6
Lune Dr WHIT M45 .....55 K4
Lune Gv HEY OL10 .....40 D1
  LEIGH WN7 .....65 M7
Lunehurst GOL/RIS/CUL WA3 .....80 B4
Lune Rd WGNE/HIN WN2 .....64 D2
Lune St OLDS OL8 .....59 H8
Lune Wy RDSH SK5 .....100 C7
Lunn Av GTN M18 .....89 J6
Luntswood Gv NEWLW WA12 .....78 D8
Lupin Av FWTH BL4 .....52 D5
Lupin Cl OLD OL1 .....60 B1
Lupin Dr RNFD/HAY WA11 .....78 C6
Lupton St CSLFD M3 * .....6 B3
  DTN/ASHW M34 .....90 C8
Lurden Wk CHAD OL9 * .....58 D8
Lurdin La WGNNW/ST WN6 .....31 L5
Lurgan Av SALE M33 .....108 F1
Lutener Av ALT WA14 .....107 M4
Luton Dr NTHM/RTH M23 .....109 K8
Luton Gv ATH M46 .....66 E1
Luton Rd RDSH SK5 .....100 C4
Luton St BOLS/LL BL3 .....36 D8
  TOT/BURYW BL8 .....38 E3
Luxhall Wk NEWH/MOS M40 .....73 L7
Luxor Gv DTN/ASHW M34 .....100 C1
Luzley Brook Rd ROY/SHW OL2 .....43 K7
Luzley Rd AUL OL6 .....76 E7
Lyceum Pas MILN OL16 .....10 E4
Lyceum Pl HULME M15 * .....7 G9
Lychgate Ct OLDE OL4 .....76 B1
Lychgate Ms HTNM SK4 * .....111 H2
Lydbrook Cl BOL BL1 * .....2 C6
Lydden Av OP/CLY M11 * .....89 J7
Lydford ROCH OL11 .....10 D7
Lydford Gdns BOLE BL2 .....37 J7
Lydford Gn WGNNW/ST WN6 .....31 J4
Lydford Rd SLFD M6 .....71 L8
Lydford Wk BRUN/LGST M13 * .....87 M6
Lydgate Av BOLE BL2 .....37 H4
Lydgate Cl DTN/ASHW M34 .....101 L3
  STLY SK15 .....77 H6
  WHTF M45 .....55 K4
Lydgate Dr OLDE OL4 .....59 M7
Lydgate Rd DROY M43 .....89 H1
  SALE M33 .....108 F2
Lydiate Cl BOLS/LL BL3 .....52 C2
Lydiat La WILM/AE SK9 .....130 D4
Lydney Av CHD/CHDH SK8 .....119 L5
Lydney Rd URM M41 .....95 C1
Lyefield Av WGN WN1 .....15 M2
Lyefield Wk MILN OL16 .....11 J4
Lyme Av WILM/AE SK9 .....126 F3
Lyme Clough Wy MDTN M24 .....41 J8
Lymefield Dr WALK M28 .....68 D5
Lymefield Gv OFTN SK2 .....112 E8
Lyme Gv ALT WA14 .....107 M8
  DROY M43 .....89 J4
  MPL/ROM SK6 .....114 C4
  MPL/ROM SK6 .....114 C7
  OFTN SK2 .....13 J8
Lyme Rd BRAM/HZG SK7 .....122 A3
  POY/DIS SK12 .....123 J5
Lymes ALT WA14 .....116 E3
Lyme St BRAM/HZG SK7 * .....121 M1
  HTNM SK4 .....111 H2
  RNFD/HAY WA11 .....78 B6
Lymewood Dr POY/DIS SK12 .....123 K6
  WILM/AE SK9 .....127 J4
Lymington Cl MDTN M24 .....57 L7
Lymington Dr NTHM/RTH M23 .....109 L4
  WALK M28 .....68 C1
Lymm St WGNE/HIN WN2 .....64 E1
Lynbridge Cl
  WGNW/BIL/OR WN5 .....46 B7
Lyncombe Cl CHD/CHDH SK8 .....120 D6
Lyndale Av RDSH SK5 .....100 C4
  SWIN M27 .....70 A6
Lyndale Dr LIT OL15 .....21 L6
Lyndene Av WALK M28 .....68 D5
Lyndene Gdns CHD/CHDH SK8 .....110 E6
Lyndene Rd WYTH/NTH M22 .....110 A7
Lyndhurst Av AUL OL6 .....75 L7
  BRAM/HZG SK7 .....121 L3
  CHAD OL9 .....58 C7
  DTN/ASHW M34 * .....101 H1
  IRL M44 .....94 C3
  MPL/ROM SK6 .....101 J8
  PWCH M25 .....72 B1
  ROCH OL11 .....42 A4
  SALE M33 .....108 C1
  URM M41 .....84 F8
Lyndhurst Cl WILM/AE SK9 .....126 B7
Lyndhurst Dr
  HALE/TIMP WA15 .....117 J2
Lyndhurst Rd DID/WITH M20 .....98 D8
  OLDS OL8 .....59 G1
  RDSH SK5 * .....100 B3
  STRET M32 .....96 E2
Lyndhurst St SLFD M6 .....86 B2
Lyndhurst Vw DUK SK16 * .....90 F3
Lyndon Av GWNNW/ST WN6 .....30 E5
Lyndon Cl OLDE OL4 .....60 E4
  TOT/BURYW BL8 .....24 D4
Lyndon Rd IRL M44 .....94 C3
Lyne Av GLSP SK13 .....104 D4
Lyne Edge Crs DUK SK16 .....91 J5
Lyne Edge Rd DUK SK16 .....91 J4
Lyne Vw HYDE SK14 .....91 K6
Lyngard Cl WILM/AE SK9 .....127 H3
Lyngate Cl STKP SK1 .....13 L5
Lyn Gv HEY OL10 .....40 D1
Lynham Dr HEY OL10 .....41 G4
Lynmouth Av DID/WITH M20 .....98 D6
  OLDS OL8 .....75 J1
  RDSH SK5 .....100 B3
  ROY/SHW OL2 .....58 F1
  URM M41 .....95 L4
Lynmouth Cl CHAD OL9 .....58 B3
  RAD M26 .....38 F8
  WGNNW/ST WN6 * .....47 K2
Lynmouth Gv PWCH M25 .....71 J1
Lynn Av SALE M33 .....96 F6
Lynndene Ct HEY OL10 * .....40 F1
Lynn Dr DROY M43 .....89 H2
Lynne Cl GLSP SK13 .....105 J4
Lynn St CHAD OL9 .....58 B8
Lynnwood Dr ROCH OL11 .....27 L4
Lynnwood Rd BNG/LEV M19 .....111 G3
Lynroyle Wy ROCH OL11 .....42 A1
Lynsted Av BOLS/LL BL3 .....52 D1
Lynstock Wy HOR/BR BL6 .....34 B6
Lynthorpe Av IRL M44 .....94 A6

Lynthorpe Rd NEWH/MOS M40 .....74 A2
Lynton Av HYDE SK14 .....102 F2
  IRL M44 .....94 B6
  OLDS OL8 .....74 F2
  ROCH OL11 .....41 L1
  SWIN M27 .....70 C3
  URM M41 .....94 F2
  WCNNW/ST WN6 .....47 K1
Lynton Cl CHAD OL9 .....58 C3
Lynton Crs WALK M28 .....69 G4
Lynton Dr BNG/LEV M19 .....99 J5
  MPL/ROM SK6 .....123 C4
  PWCH M25 .....55 M6
Lynton Gv HALE/TIMP WA15 .....108 D7
Lynton La WILM/AE SK9 .....130 D2
Lynton Lea RAD M26 .....39 G8
Lynton Ms WILM/AE SK9 .....130 D2
Lynton Park Rd
  CHD/CHDH SK8 .....120 B4
Lynton Rd BOLS/LL BL3 .....51 M2
  CCHDY M21 .....97 K3
  CHD/CHDH SK8 .....110 F7
  HTNM SK4 .....99 L1
  SWIN M27 .....70 C3
  TYLD M29 .....68 A4
  WGNE/HIN WN2 .....49 J6
Lynton St LEIGH WN7 .....66 A7
  RUSH/FAL M14 * .....98 E2
Lyntonvale Av CHD/CHDH SK8 .....110 D6
Lynway Dr DID/WITH M20 .....98 E7
Lynway Gv MDTN M24 .....57 L2
Lynwell Rd ECC M30 .....85 G2
Lynwood Av BOLS/LL BL3 .....52 E2
  ECC M30 .....85 G2
  GOL/RIS/CUL WA3 .....80 B6
  OLDTF/WHR M16 .....97 M2
Lynwood Dr OLDE OL4 .....60 D3
Lynwood Gv ATH M46 .....66 E1
  BOLE BL2 .....23 G8
  DTN/ASHW M34 .....89 M3
  HTNM SK4 .....99 M6
  SALE M33 .....96 F7
Lyon Gv WALK M28 .....69 K4
Lyon Rd ALT WA14 .....107 M5
  FWTH BL4 .....53 H7
  WGNNW/ST WN6 .....47 K2
Lyons Dr TOT/BURYW BL8 .....38 D3
Lyons Fold SALE M33 .....96 E6
Lyons Rd TRPK M17 .....85 K5
Lyon St AIMK WN4 .....63 J5
  ROY/SHW OL2 .....43 L5
  SWIN M27 .....70 B5
  WGNNW/ST WN3 .....14 E5
Lyra Pl BRO M7 .....86 F5
Lysander Cl RUSH/FAL M14 .....98 D4
Lytham Av CCHDY M21 .....97 M5
Lytham Cl AUL OL6 .....76 B6
Lytham Dr BRAM/HZG SK7 .....121 J5
  HEY OL10 .....40 F3
Lytham Rd AIMK WN4 .....63 J7
  CHD/CHDH SK8 .....119 K3
  RUSH/FAL M14 .....98 E3
  URM M41 .....94 F2
Lytham St EDGY/DAV SK3 .....112 C6
  WHIT OL12 .....28 B1
Lytherton Av IRL M44 .....94 A8
Lytton Av CHH M8 .....72 D6
Lytton Rd DROY M43 .....89 K2
Lytton St BOL BL1 .....36 A2

## M

Mabel Av BOLS/LL BL3 .....52 D1
  WALK M28 .....69 K5
Mabel Rd FAIL M35 .....74 D3
Mabel's Brow FWTH BL4 .....53 H5
Mabel St BOL BL1 .....35 M4
  NEWH/MOS M40 .....74 A7
  WGNW/BIL/OR WN5 .....47 K1
  WHIT OL12 .....28 A2
  WHTN BL5 .....50 E8
Maberry Cl WGNNW/ST WN6 .....30 A5
Mabfield Rd RUSH/FAL M14 .....98 F3
Mableden Cl CHD/CHDH SK8 .....119 M4
Mabs Ct AUL OL6 .....91 G7
Macaulay St ROCH OL11 .....41 M3
  ROY/SHW OL2 .....43 H8
Macauley Cl DUK SK16 .....91 K5
Macauley Rd WGNS/IIMK WN3 .....47 J8
Macauley Rd OLDTF/WHR M16 .....97 L2
  RDSH SK5 .....100 A3
Macclesfield Rd
  BRAM/HZG SK7 .....122 B4
  MCFLDN SK10 .....131 H5
  WILM/AE SK9 .....127 G6
  WILM/AE SK9 .....130 F4
Macdonald Av FWTH BL4 .....52 D5
  WGNS/IIMK WN3 .....63 K1
Macdonald Rd IRL M44 .....94 B5
Macdonald St OLDS OL8 .....59 J8
  WGNW/BIL/OR WN5 .....46 E6
Macefin Av CCHDY M21 .....98 A8
Macfarren St WGTN/LGST M12 .....99 K1
Mackenzie Av WGNS/IIMK WN3 .....63 K1
Mackenzie Gv BOL BL1 .....22 A8
Mackenzie Rd BRO M7 .....71 L6
Mackenzie St BOL BL1 .....22 A8
  WGTN/LGST M12 .....99 K1
Mackenzie Wk OLD OL1 * .....44 B7
Mackeson Dr AUL OL6 .....76 B8
Mackeson Rd AUL OL6 .....76 B8
Mackintosh Wy OLD OL1 .....9 J4
Macworth St HULME M15 .....87 G7
Maclaren Dr CHH M8 .....72 B3
Maclure Rd ROCH OL11 .....10 F6
Macnair Ct MPL/ROM SK6 .....114 C4
Macnair Ms MPL/ROM SK6 .....114 D8
Madams Wood Rd WALK M28 .....68 C1
Maddison Rd DROY M43 .....89 J4
Madeley Cl ALT WA14 .....117 G4
  WGNS/IIMK WN3 .....63 H1
Madeley Dr CHAD OL9 .....8 B7
Madeley Gdns BOL BL1 .....36 B2
Maden's Sq LIT OL15 .....21 M7
Maden St TYLD M29 .....67 J7
Maden Wk CHAD OL9 * .....8 B3
Madison Av CHD/CHDH SK8 .....120 C2
  DTN/ASHW M34 .....89 M4
Madison Gdns WHTN BL5 .....50 D2
Madison Pk WHTN BL5 .....50 D2
Madison St GTN M18 .....89 H6
Madras Rd EDGY/DAV SK3 .....12 D9
Maesbrook Dr TYLD M29 .....67 K4
Mafeking Av BURY BL9 .....25 K7
Mafeking Pl AIMK WN4 .....78 F1

Mafeking Rd BOLE BL2 * .....37 H5
Mafeking St OLDS OL8 .....74 F1
  OLD OL1 .....9 G2
Magdala St HEY OL10 * .....41 H4
Magdalen Dr AIMK WN4 .....63 J8
Magda Rd OFTN SK2 .....112 F7
Magenta Av IRL M44 .....94 B6
Magnolia Cl SALE M33 .....95 M1
Magnolia Dr CHH M8 * .....72 D6
Magpie Cl DROY M43 .....89 M1
Magpie La OLDE OL4 .....60 B8
Magpie Wk OP/CLY M11 * .....88 C3
Maguire Av GLSP SK13 .....93 K6
Maher Gdns HULME M15 .....87 H8
Mahood St EDGY/DAV SK3 .....12 F8
Maida St BNG/LEV M19 .....99 L2
Maiden Cl AUL OL6 .....75 K6
Maidford Cl ANC M4 * .....88 A3
  STRET M32 .....97 H2
Maidstone Av CCHDY M21 .....97 K3
Maidstone Cl LEIGH WN7 .....65 M2
Maidstone Ms CCHDY M21 .....97 K3
Maidstone Rd BNG/LEV M19 .....111 G2
Main Av BNG/LEV M19 .....99 J5
  TRPK M17 .....85 M8
Main Dr ALT WA14 .....116 A1
  OLD OL1 .....59 G3
Maine Rd RUSH/FAL M14 .....98 D2
Mainprice Cl SLFD M6 .....71 J8
Main Rd CHAD OL9 .....8 D4
  SWIN M27 .....69 H6
Main St FAIL M35 .....74 C4
  HYDE SK14 .....91 G8
  WGNE/HIN WN2 .....49 J5
  WGNW/BIL/OR WN5 .....62 B7
Mainwaring Dr WILM/AE SK9 .....127 H4
Mainwaring Ter
  NTHM/RTH M23 .....109 K2
Mainway MDTN M24 .....57 J6
Mainway East MDTN M24 .....57 M6
Mainwood Rd
  HALE/TIMP WA15 .....108 F7
Maismore Rd WYTH/NTH M22 .....118 C3
Maitland Av CCHDY M21 .....97 M8
Maitland Cl WHIT OL12 .....28 F1
Maitland St STKP SK1 .....112 E5
Maitland Wk CHAD OL9 * .....8 B3
Major St CMANE M1 * .....7 H6
  MILN OL16 .....29 J8
  RAMS BL0 .....18 E6
  WGNW/BIL/OR WN5 .....46 F6
Makants Cl ATH M46 .....51 J6
  TYLD M29 .....68 A4
Makerfield Dr NEWLW WA12 .....78 D8
Makerfield Wy WGNE/HIN WN2 .....48 E5
Makinson Ar WGN WN1 * .....14 F3
Makinson Rd HOR/BR BL6 .....34 B3
  WGNE/HIN WN2 .....49 G5
Makin St CMANE M1 * .....7 H7
Makkah Cl NEWH/MOS M40 .....73 K7
Malaga Av MANAIR M90 .....118 D5
Malakoff St STLY SK15 .....91 H4
Malbrook Wk
  BRUN/LGST M13 * .....87 M6
Malby St OLD OL1 * .....9 J3
Malcolm Av SWIN M27 .....70 D2
Malcolm Dr SWIN M27 .....70 D2
Malcolm St ROCH OL11 .....42 A1
Maiden Gv NTHM/RTH M23 .....109 K5
Maldon Cl BOLS/LL BL3 .....53 K1
  OFTN SK2 .....113 L7
  WGNE/HIN WN2 .....48 C2
Maldon Crs SWIN M27 .....70 C6
Maldon Dr ECC M30 .....70 B8
Maldon Rd WGNNW/ST WN6 .....31 J4
Maldon St ROCH OL11 .....10 F8
Maldwyn Av BOLS/LL BL3 .....51 L2
  CHH M8 .....72 D2
Maleham St BRO M7 * .....72 B6
Malgam Dr DID/WITH M20 .....110 E4
Malham Av WGNS/IIMK WN5 .....63 K2
Malham Cl LEIGH WN7 .....65 M7
  ROY/SHW OL2 .....43 C8
Malham Ct OFTN SK2 .....113 C6
Malham Dr WHTF M45 .....55 K5
Malika Pl AIMK WN4 .....63 H6
Mallard Cl DUK SK16 .....91 H5
  OFTN SK2 .....113 K7
  OLDS OL8 .....75 G2
Mallard Crs POY/DIS SK12 .....121 J8
Mallard Dr HOR/BR BL6 .....33 K1
Mallard Gn ALT WA14 .....107 L4
Mallards Reach MPL/ROM SK6 .....113 L2
Mallet Crs BOL BL1 .....35 J2
Malling Rd NTHM/RTH M23 .....109 K6
Mallison St BOL BL1 .....36 C1
Mallory Av AULW OL7 .....75 L7
Mallory Dr WILM/AE SK9 .....126 E3
Mallory Rd HYDE SK14 .....91 K8
Mallow Cft MILN OL16 .....28 F8
Mallowdale Av RUSH/FAL M14 .....98 E4
Mallowdale Cl BOL BL1 .....35 G6
Mallowdale Rd OFTN SK2 .....113 H7
Mallow St HULME M15 .....87 H6
The Mall BURY BL9 .....4 F5
  STLY SK15 .....92 B6
Mally Gdns MOSL OL5 .....77 G4
Malmesbury Rd
  CHD/CHDH SK8 .....120 D6
Malpas Av WGN WN1 .....15 J1
Malpas Cl CHD/CHDH SK8 .....111 K7
  WILM/AE SK9 .....127 J3
Malpas Dr ALT WA14 .....108 B4
Malpas St OP/CLY M11 .....88 B4
  OLD OL1 .....9 K4
  WGTN/LGST M12 .....88 D6
Malpas Wk OLDTF/WHR M16 * .....87 G7
Malrae HALE/TIMP WA15 * .....117 G3
Malsham Rd NTHM/RTH M23 .....109 J2
Malta Cl MDTN M24 .....58 A5
Malta St ANC M4 .....88 A3
  OLDE OL4 .....60 A6
Maltby Ct OLDE OL4 .....60 C7
Maltby Dr BOLS/LL BL3 .....51 M2
Maltby Rd NTHM/RTH M23 .....109 J6
Maltings La ROCH OL11 .....41 M3
Malton Av BOLS/LL BL3 .....35 K8
  CCHDY M21 .....97 L5
  GOL/RIS/CUL WA3 .....80 B5
  WHTF M45 .....55 J2
Malton Cl CHAD OL9 .....58 C3
  LEIGH WN7 .....65 M6
Malton Dr ALT WA14 .....107 L4
  BRAM/HZG SK7 .....121 M5
Malton Rd HTNM SK4 .....99 H8
Malton St OLDS OL8 .....8 F8
Malt St HULME M15 .....86 F6
Malus Ct SLFD M6 .....86 D1
Malverley Dr LEIGH WN7 .....66 F7

Malvern Av ATH M46 .....51 J7
  AUL OL6 .....75 M5
  BOL BL1 .....35 M3
  BURY BL9 .....25 J7
  CHD/CHDH SK8 .....110 C7
  DROY M43 .....89 M2
  URM M41 .....95 L2
  WGNE/HIN WN2 .....49 K8
Malvern Cl AIMK WN4 .....63 L8
  FWTH BL4 .....52 C3
  HTNM SK4 .....12 F1
  MILN OL16 .....29 K5
  PWCH M25 .....55 M7
  ROY/SHW OL2 .....43 J4
  ROY/SHW OL2 .....58 F1
  SWIN M27 .....71 G6
  WGNS/IIMK WN3 .....62 F1
Malvern Crs
  WGNS/IIMK WN3 .....48 C8
Malvern Dr ALT WA14 .....107 L7
  SWIN M27 .....71 G6
Malvern Gv DID/WITH M20 .....98 D6
  SLFD M6 .....85 M1
  WALK M28 .....69 G1
Malvern Ri GLSP SK13 .....93 K7
Malvern Rd MDTN M24 .....57 K7
Malvern Rw HULME M15 * .....86 F6
Malvern St OLDS OL8 .....8 F8
  WGNNW/ST WN6 .....30 F1
Malvern St East ROCH OL11 .....27 M5
Malvern St West ROCH OL11 .....27 M5
Malvern Ter LEIGH WN7 .....81 J1
Manby Rd GTN M18 .....88 E8
Manby Sq GTN M18 .....88 E8
Manchester Chambers
  OLD OL1 * .....9 H5
Manchester New Rd
  MDTN M24 .....57 J6
  PART M31 .....106 C1
Manchester Old Rd
  BURY BL9 .....4 D7
  MDTN M24 .....56 F5
Manchester Rd ALT WA14 .....108 A6
  AULW OL7 .....90 B3
  BOLE BL2 .....3 G8
  BOLS/LL BL3 .....52 F1
  BURY BL9 .....4 C5
  CCHDY M21 .....97 L3
  DID/WITH M20 .....111 G4
  DROY M43 .....89 H3
  DTN/ASHW M34 .....89 L5
  DTN/ASHW M34 .....101 H1
  FWTH BL4 .....53 L6
  GLSP SK13 .....93 L5
  HEY OL10 .....41 G6
  HOR/BR BL6 .....33 G2
  HTNM SK4 .....100 A7
  HYDE SK14 .....101 L1
  LEIGH WN7 .....66 F8
  MDTN M24 .....42 A5
  MOSL OL5 .....76 F5
  OLDS OL8 .....58 F8
  PART M31 .....94 D8
  RAMS BL0 .....19 H6
  RAMS BL0 .....19 H7
  ROCH OL11 .....10 A9
  ROCH OL11 .....41 M1
  ROY/SHW OL2 .....43 K7
  SWIN M27 .....54 A8
  SWIN M27 .....70 A3
  TYLD M29 .....67 K8
  TYLD M29 .....67 L3
  UPML OL3 .....61 J8
  WALK M28 .....69 C1
  WGN WN1 .....15 M4
  WGNE/HIN WN2 .....48 D5
  WHTN BL5 .....50 C7
  WILM/AE SK9 .....127 G4
Manchester Rd East
  LHULT M38 .....52 D8
Manchester Rd North
  DTN/ASHW M34 .....89 M8
Manchester Rd South
  DTN/ASHW M34 .....100 F1
Manchester Rd West
  LHULT M38 .....52 B7
Manchester St CHAD OL9 .....8 E8
  HEY OL10 .....41 G2
  OLDTF/WHR M16 .....86 F7
Manchet St ROCH OL11 .....41 L3
Mancroft Av BOLS/LL BL3 .....36 A8
Mancroft Ter BOLS/LL BL3 * .....36 A8
Mancroft Wk CMANE M1 * .....7 J8
Mancunian Rd
  DTN/ASHW M34 .....101 K4
Mancunian Wy WGTN/LGST M12 .....7 M8
Mandalay Gdns
  MPL/ROM SK6 .....114 A5
Mandarin Gn ALT WA14 .....107 L4
Mandarin Wk SLFD M6 * .....86 D1
Manderville Cl WGNS/IIMK WN3 .....63 G2
Mandeville St BNG/LEV M19 .....99 L4
Mandley Av NEWH/MOS M40 * .....74 A2
Mandley Cl BOLS/LL BL3 .....37 L7
Mandley Park Av BRO M7 .....72 B5
Mandon Cl RAD M26 .....38 B7
Manesty Cl MDTN M24 .....56 F2
Manet Cl BRO M7 .....71 L4
Mangle St CMANE M1 .....7 J4
Mango Pl SLFD M6 .....86 D2
Manifold Dr MPL/ROM SK6 .....114 A5
Manifold St SLFD M6 .....71 L7
Manilla Wk OP/CLY M11 .....88 C3
Manipur St OP/CLY M11 .....88 B4
Manley Av COL/RIS/CUL WA3 .....79 J2
  SWIN M27 .....54 C8
Manley Cl BURY BL9 .....24 F7
  LEIGH WN7 .....66 A4
Manley Crs WHTN BL5 .....50 E3
Manley Gv BRAM/HZG SK7 .....121 C6
  HYDE SK14 .....103 J1
Manley Rd CCHDY M21 .....97 M3
  OLDS OL8 .....59 H8
  OLDTF/WHR M16 .....98 B2
  ROCH OL11 .....27 M8
  SALE M33 .....108 C3
Manley St BRO M7 .....72 A6
  WGNS/IIMK WN3 .....15 K8
Manley Ter BOL BL1 * .....22 B8
Manning Av WGNNW/ST WN6 .....47 K2
Manningham Rd BOLS/LL BL3 .....35 L7
Mannington Dr BKLY M9 .....72 F6
Mannock St OLDS OL8 .....59 J8
The Manns UPML OL3 .....61 J7
Manor Av BOLS/LL BL3 .....53 M1
  GOL/RIS/CUL WA3 .....79 M4
  NEWLW WA12 .....78 C8
  OLDTF/WHR M16 .....98 A2
  SALE M33 .....96 A8
  URM M41 .....95 K3

Manor Cl CHAD OL9 .....8 C3
  CHD/CHDH SK8 .....120 E4
  DTN/ASHW M34 .....101 L3
  OLDE OL4 .....61 H7
  WILM/AE SK9 .....126 C4
Manor Ct GOL/RIS/CUL WA3 .....79 M4
  STRET M32 .....96 E3
Manor Dr CCHDY M21 .....98 A8
  ROY/SHW OL2 .....59 H1
Manor Farm Cl AULW OL7 .....75 J7
Manor Farm Ri OLDE OL4 .....60 A5
Manorfield Cl BOL BL1 .....35 K3
Manor Gdns WILM/AE SK9 .....127 H5
Manor Gate Rd BOLE BL2 .....37 K4
Manor Gv LEIGH WN7 .....81 M1
  WGNE/HIN WN2 .....32 F7
  WGNW/BIL/OR WN5 .....46 E4
Manor Hill Rd MPL/ROM SK6 .....114 C6
Manorial Dr LHULT M38 .....52 B7
Manor Ml CHAD OL9 * .....8 C2
Manor Mill Cl MILN OL16 .....29 G1
Manor Pk URM M41 .....96 A3
Manor Park Rd GLSP SK13 .....105 H3
Manor Pl WGNS/IIMK WN3 .....15 M8
Manor Rd BNG/LEV M19 .....99 L2
  CHD/CHDH SK8 .....120 E4
  DROY M43 .....89 H3
  DTN/ASHW M34 .....89 L5
  DTN/ASHW M34 .....101 H1
  HALE/TIMP WA15 .....108 B8
  HYDE SK14 .....91 J7
  MDTN M24 .....57 J6
  MPL/ROM SK6 .....101 J7
  MPL/ROM SK6 .....114 C5
  OLDE OL4 .....59 M8
  RDSH SK5 .....100 E7
  RNFD/HAY WA11 .....78 D5
  ROY/SHW OL2 .....43 G5
  SALE M33 .....96 E7
  SLFD M6 .....71 G8
  STRET M32 .....96 E3
  SWIN M27 .....67 M6
  TYLD M29 .....67 M6
  WGNE/HIN WN2 .....32 F7
  WGNNW/ST WN6 .....30 D6
  WILM/AE SK9 .....126 C4
Manor St BOL BL1 .....2 F4
  BURY BL9 .....5 H4
  DTN/ASHW M34 .....90 C5
  FWTH BL4 .....52 F5
  FWTH BL4 .....53 L7
  GLSP SK13 .....105 G3
  GOL/RIS/CUL WA3 .....79 L3
  MDTN M24 .....57 K2
  MOSL OL5 .....76 F2
  RAMS BL0 .....18 E6
  ROY/SHW OL2 .....59 K2
  WGN WN1 .....14 F4
  WGNW/BIL/OR WN5 .....47 J6
  WGTN/LGST M12 .....7 L8
Manor Vw MPL/ROM SK6 .....101 J7
Mansart Cl AIMK WN4 .....79 C1
Manse Gdns NEWLW WA12 .....79 G8
Mansell Wy HOR/BR BL6 .....34 A4
The Manse MOSL OL5 .....76 F4
Mansfield Av BKLY M9 .....57 G8
  DTN/ASHW M34 .....90 A7
  RAMS BL0 .....24 E5
Mansfield Cl AULW OL7 .....90 C3
  DTN/ASHW M34 .....90 A7
Mansfield Crs DTN/ASHW M34 .....90 A7
Mansfield Dr BKLY M9 .....57 H8
Mansfield Gra ROCH OL11 .....27 M6
Mansfield Gv BOL BL1 .....35 J3
Mansfield Rd BKLY M9 .....57 H8
  HYDE SK14 .....102 B3
  MOSL OL5 .....77 H3
  OLDS OL8 .....59 L7
  ROCH OL11 .....27 H5
  URM M41 .....95 K3
Mansfield St AULW OL7 .....90 B4
  GOL/RIS/CUL WA3 .....79 H3
Mansford Dr NEWH/MOS M40 .....73 J7
Manshaw Crs DTN/ASHW M34 .....89 M5
Manshaw Rd OP/CLY M11 .....89 K5
Mansion Av WHTF M45 .....55 H1
Manson Av HULME M15 .....6 A9
Manstead Wk
  NEWH/MOS M40 * .....88 B2
Manston Dr CHD/CHDH SK8 .....120 C2
Manswood Dr CHH M8 .....72 D5
Manthorpe Av WALK M28 .....69 G5
Mantley La UPML OL3 .....44 C5
Manton Av BKLY M9 .....73 J1
  DTN/ASHW M34 .....100 D1
Manton Cl BRO M7 .....72 C6
Manvers St RDSH SK5 .....112 B1
Manwaring St FAIL M35 .....74 B4
Maple Av ATH M46 .....50 E8
  BOL BL1 * .....35 J4
  BURY BL9 .....5 L4
  CCHDY M21 .....97 L4
  CHD/CHDH SK8 .....120 E2
  DTN/ASHW M34 .....101 H1
  DTN/ASHW M34 .....89 L3
  ECC M30 .....69 K8
  GOL/RIS/CUL WA3 .....80 C5
  HALE/TIMP WA15 .....109 H7
  HOR/BR BL6 .....34 B3
  MPL/ROM SK6 .....114 C8
  POY/DIS SK12 .....124 C6
  POY/DIS SK12 .....129 K1
  STLY SK15 .....91 J4
  STRET M32 .....97 G3
  WGNE/HIN WN2 .....65 J1
  WHTF M45 .....55 J3
Maple Cl FWTH BL4 .....52 B4
  MDTN M24 .....58 A4
  OFTN SK2 .....112 E6
  ROY/SHW OL2 .....43 J4
  SLFD M6 .....71 G6
  WGNW/BIL/OR WN5 .....62 A7
Maple Crs LEIGH WN7 .....66 B5
Maplecroft STKP SK1 .....112 F4
Maple Dr
  WGNE/HIN WN2 .....64 E5
Maplefield Dr WALK M28 .....68 B4
Maple Gv FAIL M35 .....74 B7
  NEWH/MOS M40 .....73 G5
  PWCH M25 .....55 K6
  RAMS BL0 .....19 G2
  TOT/BURYW BL8 .....24 D4
  WALK M28 .....69 G4
Maple Rd BRAM/HZG SK7 .....121 C6
  CHAD OL9 .....8 B4
  FWTH BL4 .....53 K7
  NTHM/RTH M23 .....108 F4
  PART M31 .....106 B1
  SWIN M27 .....70 B6
  WILM/AE SK9 .....130 C2

**Maple Rd West**
NTHM/RTH M23 .............................108 F4
Maple St AIMK WN4 .........................63 K6
  BOLE BL1 ....................................22 F7
  BOLS/LL BL3 ..................................2 B8
  OLDS OL8 ....................................74 F1
  ROCH OL11 ..................................10 B6
Maplewood Wk NTHM/RTH M23 .........108 H4
Maplewood Cl BKLY M9 ....................72 F2
  ROY/SHW OL2 ...............................58 F2
  URM M41 .....................................72 A5
Maplewood Dr BRO M7 .....................72 A5
Maplewood Gdns BOL BL1 * ..............36 B2
Maplewood Gv STLY SK15 .................91 M1
Maplewood Rd WILM/AE SK9 ...........127 J4
Mapley Av WYTH/NTH M22 ..............110 A4
Maplin Cl BRUN/LGST M13 .................7 L9
Maplin Dr OFTN SK2 ........................113 K6
Marble St CMANW M2 .........................7 G4
  OLD OL1 * ....................................59 L4
Marbury Av RUSH/FAL M14 ...............98 F2
Marbury Cl EDGY/DAV SK3 ...............111 K5
  URM M41 .....................................95 G1
Marbury Gv WGNNW/ST WN6 ...........31 H4
Marbury Rd RDSH SK5 .....................100 A5
  WGNE/HIN WN2 * ...........................48 A7
March Av HTNM SK4 ........................126 E3
Marcer Rd NEWH/MOS M40 ...............88 A2
March La ROY/SHW OL2 ....................44 A6
Marchbank WGNE/HIN WN2 ...............48 D3
Marchbank Dr CHD/CHDH SK8 .........110 F6
March Dr TOT/BURYW BL8 .................25 G7
Marchers Ms ECC M30 * ...................84 E3
Marchioness St GTN M18 * ...............89 J6
Marchmont Cl BRUN/LGST M13 ...........8 E4
March St MILN OL16 .........................11 H4
Marchwood Av CCHDY M21 ................98 A3
Marcliffe Dr BNG/LEV M19 ................99 M3
  ROCH OL11 ..................................27 L6
Marcliffe Gv HTNM SK4 ....................12 A3
Marcroft Pl ROCH OL11 ....................28 D8
Marcus Gv RUSH/FAL M14 .................98 F2
Marcus St BOL BL1 ..........................35 L3
Mardale Av DID/WITH M20 .................42 F4
  ROY/SHW OL2 ...............................42 F4
  SWIN M27 ....................................69 M2
  URM M41 .....................................95 J1
Mardale Cl ATH M46 .........................50 F7
  BOLE BL2 .....................................37 J3
  OLDE OL4 ....................................60 A5
  PWCH M25 ...................................55 M5
  STLY SK15 ...................................91 K1
Mardale Dr BOLE BL2 .......................37 J3
  CHD/CHDH SK8 .............................110 B8
  MDTN M24 ....................................57 H3
Mardale Rd SWIN M27 ......................70 A6
Mardyke WHIT OL12 .........................10 D3
Marfield Av CHAD OL9 ......................58 D7
Marford Av WYTH/NTH M22 ..............110 A6
Marford Crs SALE M33 .....................108 C2
Margaret Ashton Cl BKLY M9 ............73 G5
  WGNNW/ST WN6 ...........................30 F8
Margaret Av MILN OL16 ....................11 L5
Margaret Rd DROY M43 * ...................89 H2
  DTN/ASHW M34 ..............................7 M9
Margaret Sands St HULME M15 * .......87 G6
Margaret St AUL OL6 ........................90 D2
  BURY BL9 ......................................5 L4
  HEY OL10 ....................................40 E2
  OLDS OL8 ....................................74 E2
  RDSH SK5 ...................................100 B5
  ROY/SHW OL2 * .............................43 L6
  WGNE/HIN WN2 .............................49 G6
  WGNNW/ST WN6 ...........................14 C2
Margaret Ter NEWH/MOS M40 ...........73 L7
Margate Rd RDSH SK5 .....................100 C5
Margrove Cha HOR/BR BL6 ...............34 F7
Margrove Cl FAIL M35 ......................53 K8
Margrove Rd SLFD M6 ......................70 F8
Margroy Cl WHIT OL12 .......................9 L2
Marguerita Rd NEWH/MOS M40 .........74 A8
Marham Cl CCHDY M21 * ..................98 B6
  HYDE SK14 ...................................91 G6
Marian Rd RNFD/HAY WA11 ..............78 B3
Marie Cl DTN/ASHW M34 ..................101 K3
Marie St BRO M7 * ...........................72 B5
Marigold St ROCH OL11 ....................10 E9
  WGNW/BIL/OR WN5 ........................47 C5
Mariman Dr CHH M8 .........................72 D2
Marina Av DTN/ASHW M34 ..............101 K3
Marina Cl OP/CLY M11 ......................88 E1
Marina Dr MPL/ROM SK6 .................113 M5
  WGNW/BIL/OR WN5 ........................47 G2
  MPL/ROM SK6 ..............................101 H8
Marine Av PART M31 .......................106 A1
Marion Pl WGNE/HIN WN2 .................64 C4
Marion St BOLS/LL BL3 ....................52 C7
  OLDS OL8 ....................................75 J1
Maritime Cl NEWLW WA12 ................78 A2
Marjorie Cl GTN M18 ........................88 E6
Mark Av SLFD M6 ............................71 L8
Markenfield Dr ROY/SHW OL2 ...........43 J5
Market Ap AIMK WN4 * ....................63 H7
Market Pde BURY BL9 * ......................4 F5
Market Pl AUL OL6 ...........................90 E1
  BURY BL9 ......................................4 E4
  HYDE SK14 * ...............................103 K1
  LEIGH WN7 ...................................66 C7
  MDTN M24 ....................................57 K3
  OLD OL1 * ....................................9 H5
  RAMS BL0 ....................................18 E5
  STKP SK1 ....................................13 J3
  WGN WN1 ....................................14 F4
  WGNNW/ST WN6 ...........................31 H8
Market St ALT WA14 ......................108 A8
  ATH M46 ......................................66 F1
  BOL BL1 ......................................... 2 E4
  BOLS/LL BL3 .................................53 K1
  BURY BL9 ......................................4 E5
  CMANE M2 .....................................7 G4
  DROY M43 ....................................89 K4
  DTN/ASHW M34 ............................101 J1
  FWTH BL4 .....................................53 L3
  GLSP SK13 ..................................104 F4
  HEY OL10 ....................................40 D2
  HYDE SK14 ...................................92 D8
  HYDE SK14 ...................................93 G7
  HYDE SK14 ..................................102 A1
  MDTN M24 ....................................57 J3
  MOSL OL5 ....................................76 E3
  NEWLW WA12 ..............................78 A8
  NM/HAY SK22 ..............................124 D5
  OLD OL1 .......................................9 J4
  POY/DIS SK12 ..............................123 M6
  RAD M26 .....................................53 L4
  ROY/SHW OL2 ...............................43 L6
  STLY SK15 ...................................91 K2
  SWIN M27 ....................................70 D3

  TOT/BURYW BL8 .............................24 C6
  TYLD M29 .....................................67 J3
  WGN WN1 ....................................14 F4
  WGNE/HIN WN2 .............................49 G7
  WGNNW/ST WN6 ...........................31 H5
  WHIT OL12 ...................................20 A6
  WHTN BL5 ....................................50 B4
Market Wy SALE M33 * ....................96 E8
Market Wy SLFD M6 .........................86 C1
Markfield Av BRUN/LGST M13 ...........88 A7
Markham Cl WGTN/LGST M12 ...........88 B4
Markham St HYDE SK14 ...................91 G6
Markington St RUSH/FAL M14 ...........98 D1
Markland Hl BOL BL1 ........................35 H4
Markland Hill La BOL BL1 .................35 J3
Markland Hill La BOL BL1 .................35 H4
Marklands Rd TYLD M29 ...................67 K8
Markland St BOL BL1 .........................2 E6
  HYDE SK14 .................................102 B3
  RAMS BL0 ....................................18 F6
  WGN WN1 ....................................15 L5
Marks St RAD M26 ...........................54 D1
Mark St CHAD OL9 .............................8 F4
  WALK M28 ....................................68 C5
Markwood UPML OL3 * ......................45 J8
Marland Av CHD/CHDH SK8 ............120 B2
  OLDS OL8 ....................................75 K3
  ROCH OL11 ..................................27 L8
Marland Cl ROCH OL11 .....................27 L7
Marland Crs RDSH SK5 ...................100 C4
Marland Fold ROCH OL11 ..................27 L8
Marland Fold La OLDS OL8 ...............75 J3
Marland Gn ROCH OL11 ....................27 L8
Marland Hill Rd ROCH OL11 ..............27 M7
Marland Old Rd ROCH OL11 ...............27 L8
Marland St CHAD OL9 .......................74 D1
Marland Wy STRET M32 ....................97 G1
**Marlborough Av**
  CHD/CHDH SK8 ............................120 D3
  OLDTF/WHR M16 ............................97 M3
  WGNS/IIMK WN3 ...........................48 C8
  WILM/AE SK9 ...............................130 C2
Marlborough Cl AULW OL7 * ..............90 B4
  DTN/ASHW M34 ............................101 J1
  MPL/ROM SK6 ..............................114 A3
  RAMS BL0 ....................................24 F1
Marlborough Dr FAIL M35 ..................53 M8
  HTNM SK4 * ................................100 A3
**Marlborough Gdns** FWTH BL4 .........52 C4
Marlborough Rd ALT WA14 ..............116 F2
  ATH M46 ......................................51 M8
  BRO M7 .......................................72 C6
  ECC M30 .....................................70 D8
  HYDE SK14 .................................102 B4
  IRL M44 .......................................94 E1
  ROY/SHW OL2 ...............................59 H2
  SALE M33 ....................................96 E8
  STRET M32 ..................................97 G3
  URM M41 .....................................95 J2
Marlborough St AULW OL7 ................90 C3
  BOL BL1 ........................................2 B3
  HEY OL10 ....................................41 H4
  OLDE OL4 ......................................9 L7
  WHIT OL12 ...................................27 M3
**Marlborough Wy**
  RNFD/HAY WA11 ...........................78 B4
Marlbrook Dr WHTN BL5 ...................50 B7
Marlbrook Ms WHTN BL5 * ...............50 C7
Marlbrook Wk BOLS/LL BL3 ..............36 C8
Marlcroft Av HTNM SK4 * ..................12 B3
Marlcroft Cl NTHM/RTH M23 ...........109 K5
Marld Crs BOL BL1 * .........................35 J2
Marle Av MOSL OL5 .........................77 H3
Marle Cft WHTF M45 .........................54 F6
Marled Hey EDGW/EG BL7 ................17 G7
Marle Ri MOSL OL5 ...........................77 H3
Marler Rd HYDE SK14 .......................91 H8
Marley Cl HALE/TIMP WA15 .............108 C5
Marley Dr SALE M33 .........................96 D6
Marleyer Cl NEWH/MOS M40 ............73 M5
Marleyer Ri MPL/ROM SK6 ..............113 K4
Marley Rd BNG/LEV M19 ..................99 L4
  POY/DIS SK12 .............................129 J2
**Marlfield Rd**
  HALE/TIMP WA15 ..........................117 M6
  ROY/SHW OL2 ...............................43 H4
Marlfield St BKLY M9 ........................73 H5
Marl Gv WGNW/BIL/OR WN5 .............46 A8
Marlhill Cl OFTN SK2 .......................113 H7
**Marlinford Dr**
  NEWH/MOS M40 ............................73 M7
Marlor Cl DTN/ASHW M34 .................90 B8
Marlow Brow GLSP SK13 ...................93 K8
Marlow Cl BOLE BL2 .........................37 J3
  CHD/CHDH SK8 ............................120 B2
  URM M41 .....................................94 B5
Marlow Dr ALT WA14 .......................116 B2
  IRL M44 .......................................94 D1
  SWIN M27 ....................................70 B6
  WILM/AE SK9 ...............................119 L7
**Marlowe Cl**
  WGNS/IIMK WN3 ...........................47 K7
**Marlowe Dr**
  DID/WITH M20 ...............................98 E8
Marlowe Wks MPL/ROM SK6 ...........113 H2
Marlow Rd BKLY M9 .........................73 J3
Marlow St GLSP SK13 .......................93 K8
Marlwood Rd BOL BL1 ......................35 J2
Marmion Cl GOL/RIS/CUL WA3 ..........80 B3
Marmion Dr CCHDY M21 ...................97 K4
Marne Av AUL OL6 ...........................76 D7
  WGNW/BIL/OR WN5 ........................47 C2
Marne Crs ROCH OL11 ......................27 M5
Marnland Gv BOLS/LL BL3 ................35 H8
Maroon Rd WYTH/NTH M22 .............119 H5
Marple Av BOL BL1 ...........................22 D8
Marple Cl OLDS OL8 .........................75 H3
  WGNNW/ST WN6 ...........................30 D2
Marple Gv STRET M32 ......................96 F1
Marple Hall Dr MPL/ROM SK6 .........114 A6
Marple Old Rd OFTN SK2 ................113 K6
Marple Rd GLSP SK13 .....................103 K7
  OFTN SK2 ....................................113 G5
Marple St HULME M15 * ....................87 C7
Marquis Av BURY BL9 ......................25 H8
Marquis Dr CHD/CHDH SK8 .............119 M5
Marquis St BNG/LEV M19 ................100 A3
Marrick Av CHD/CHDH SK8 .............110 F7
  RAD M26 .....................................37 G3
Marriotts Ct CMANW M2 * ...................7 G4
Marron Pl CMANW M2 * ......................6 E6
Mars Av BOLS/LL BL3 .......................51 M1
Marsden Dr HALE/TIMP WA15 .........108 F6
  MILN OL16 ....................................42 F4
Marsden Rd BOL BL1 ..........................2 D4
  MPL/ROM SK6 ..............................113 M1

Marsden St BURY BL9 .........................4 F2
  CMANW M2 .....................................7 F4
  ECC M30 ......................................84 F1
  GLSP SK13 ....................................93 K8
  MDTN M24 ....................................57 M5
  WALK M28 ....................................68 C6
  WGN WN1 ....................................15 G3
  WGNS/IIMK WN3 ...........................48 B8
  WGNW/BIL/OR WN5 ........................47 J5
  WHTN BL5 ....................................50 B4
Marsett Cl WHIT OL12 ......................27 J3
Marshall Cl AUL OL6 ..........................91 G2
  .......................................................9 G1
Marshall Rd BNG/LEV M19 ...............99 K3
**Marshall Stevens Wy**
  TRPK M17 ....................................85 L7
Marshall St ANC M4 ...........................7 J2
  LEIGH WN7 ...................................66 B8
  MILN OL16 ....................................11 K5
  WGTN/LGST M12 ...........................87 M6
  OLDE OL4 * ..................................60 E7
Marsham Dr MPL/ROM SK6 .............114 D7
Marsham Rd BRAM/HZG SK7 ..........121 K3
Marshbank WHTN BL5 ......................50 B5
Marshbrook Cl WGNE/HIN WN2 ........49 K5
Marshbrook Dr BKLY M9 ..................72 F3
Marsh Brook Fold WHTN BL5 ...........49 K5
Marsh Cl EDGY/DAV SK3 ................112 A6
Marshdale Rd BOL BL1 .....................35 J4
**Marshfield Rd**
  HALE/TIMP WA15 ..........................108 F7
**Marshfield Wk**
  BRUN/LGST M13 .............................87 M6
Marsh Fold La BOL BL1 .....................35 M4
Marsh Hey Cl LHULT M38 ..................52 C6
Marsh La FWTH BL4 ..........................52 D4
  KNUT WA16 ..................................116 C8
  NM/HAY SK22 .............................124 F6
  WGN WN1 ....................................15 G3
Marsh Rd BOLS/LL BL3 ....................37 K8
  LHULT M38 ...................................52 E8
Marsh Rw WGNE/HIN WN2 ...............49 K8
Marsh St WALK M28 .........................69 J1
  WHTN BL5 ....................................50 B3
**Marshway Dr** NEWLW WA12 .........78 E8
**Marsland Av**
  HALE/TIMP WA15 ..........................108 E4
**Marsland Cl**
  DTN/ASHW M34 ............................100 F8
Marsland Green La TYLD M29 ...........67 H8
**Marsland Rd**
  HALE/TIMP WA15 ..........................108 E6
  MPL/ROM SK6 ..............................114 D5
  SALE M33 ....................................108 D1
Marslands UPML OL3 ........................61 L1
**Marsland St**
  BRAM/HZG SK7 * ..........................121 M2
  STKP SK1 .....................................13 K1
Marsland St North BRO M7 ................72 B5
Marsland St South BRO M7 ...............72 C5
Marsland Ter STKP SK1 ...................112 E4
Mars St CHAD OL9 .............................8 D4
  EDGW/EG BL7 ..............................17 H6
Marston Cl FAIL M35 ........................74 E6
  HOR/BR BL6 .................................34 C4
  WHTF M45 ....................................55 M4
Marston Dr IRL M44 ..........................94 E2
Marston Rd BRO M7 .........................72 B4
  STRET M32 ...................................97 H2
**Marston Wy South** CMANE M1 * .....6 F4
Marsworth Dr ANC M4 * ......................7 M3
Martens Rd IRL M44 ..........................94 E2
Marthall Dr SALE M33 .....................109 H2
Martham Dr OFTN SK2 .....................113 K7
Martha's Ter MILN OL16 * .................28 F1
Martha St BOLS/LL BL3 .....................36 A8
  OLD OL1 ........................................9 F3
Martin Av BOLS/LL BL3 .....................53 M1
  NEWLW WA12 ..............................78 E7
  OLDE OL4 ....................................59 M7
Martin Cl DTN/ASHW M34 ................90 C7
  OFTN SK2 ...................................113 J7
Martindale Cl ROY/SHW OL2 ............43 H7
Martindale Crs MDTN M24 ................57 C1
  WGNW/BIL/OR WN5 .......................47 H6
  WGTN/LGST M12 ...........................88 B6
Martindale Gdns BOL BL1 .................36 B2
Martin Dr IRL M44 ............................83 K8
Martingale Cl RAD M26 ....................38 D7
Martingale Wy DROY M43 .................90 A1
Martin Gv FWTH BL4 .........................53 J5
Martin La WHIT OL12 ........................27 L3
Martin Rd SWIN M27 ........................70 C2
Martinsclough HOR/BR BL6 ...............34 F6
Martins Ct WGNE/HIN WN2 ..............49 K6
**Martinscroft Rd**
  NTHM/RTH M23 ...........................109 K7
Martins Fld WHIT OL12 .....................27 J3
Martin St ATH M46 ...........................67 G1
  BURY BL9 ....................................40 A1
  DTN/ASHW M34 .............................7 M9
  EDGW/EG BL7 ..............................17 G8
  HYDE SK14 .................................102 B2
  ORD M5 .......................................86 A2
Martland Av GOL/RIS/CUL WA3 .........80 A5
  WGNW/BIL/OR WN6 .......................30 C3
Martland Crs WGNNW/ST WN6 .........47 H1
**Martland Mill La**
  WGNW/BIL/OR WN5 .......................47 C2
Martlesham Wk ANC M4 * ...................7 H3
Martlet Av POY/DIS SK12 ...............123 L6
  ROCH OL11 ..................................27 H5
Martlet Cl RUSH/FAL M14 .................98 D3
Martlew Dr ATH M46 .........................51 J8
Martock Av WYTH/NTH M22 ...........119 G1
Martock Av BOLE BL2 .........................3 L2
  DID/WITH M20 ...............................110 F2
Marton Cl GOL/RIS/CUL WA3 .............81 M8
Marton Dr ATH M46 ..........................67 H1
Marton Gra PWCH M25 .....................72 B2
Marton Gn EDGY/DAV SK3 ..............112 A6
Marton Pl SALE M33 .........................96 D8
Marton St WGN WN1 ........................14 F2
Marus Av WGNS/IIMK WN3 ...............63 J1
Marwick Cl WGTN/LGST WN6 ...........31 C2
Marwood Cl ALT WA14 ...................107 L2
  RAD M26 .....................................53 M4
Marwood Dr NTHM/RTH M23 ..........118 F3
Maryfield Ct OLDTF/WHR M16 * .........98 B4
Mary France St HULME M15 * ...........87 H4
Mary Hulton Ct WHTN BL5 ................50 C5
Maryland Av BOLE BL2 .....................37 G5
Marylebone Pl WGN WN1 .................48 A1
Marylon Dr WYTH/NTH M22 ............110 B4
Maryport Dr HALE/TIMP WA15 .........108 F6

Mary St CHD/CHDH SK8 ..................111 G6
  CSLFD M3 ......................................87 J1
  DROY M43 ....................................89 L3
  DTN/ASHW M34 * ...........................90 C8
  DUK SK16 .....................................90 E4
  FWTH BL4 .....................................53 G5
  HEY OL10 ....................................40 F2
  HYDE SK14 .................................101 M1
  MILN OL16 ....................................21 H8
  RAMS BL0 ....................................18 E7
  STKP SK1 ....................................13 L3
  TYLD M29 * ...................................67 K3
Masboro St BKLY M9 .........................72 C5
Masbury Cl BOL BL1 .........................22 B4
Masefield Av LEIGH WN7 ..................66 A5
  PWCH M25 ...................................71 J1
  RAD M26 ......................................38 B8
  WGNW/BIL/OR WN5 .......................46 D6
Masefield Cl DUK SK16 .....................91 L5
Masefield Crs DROY M43 ..................89 K3
Masefield Dr FWTH BL4 .....................52 E5
  HTNM SK4 ...................................111 K2
  WGNS/IIMK WN3 ...........................47 K7
Masefield Rd BOLS/LL BL3 ...............37 L8
  DROY M43 ....................................89 K3
  OLD OL1 ......................................59 L2
Mason Cl AIMK WN4 .........................64 A8
Mason Gdns BOLS/LL BL3 * ...............2 C7
Mason La ATH M46 ...........................67 H2
Masons Gv GLSP SK13 ......................93 K6
Mason St ANC M4 ..............................7 J2
  AULW OL7 ....................................90 C3
  BURY BL9 ......................................5 H5
  EDGW/EG BL7 * .............................22 B3
  HEY OL10 ....................................40 E2
  HOR/BR BL6 .................................33 K1
  MILN OL16 ....................................10 F5
  WGNE/HIN WN2 .............................64 E4
  WGNS/IIMK WN3 ...........................14 D5
Massey Av AUL OL6 ..........................75 M6
  FAIL M35 ......................................74 E4
Massey Cft WHIT OL12 .....................20 A5
Massey Rd HALE/TIMP WA15 ..........108 B8
  SALE M33 ....................................97 H8
Massey St BURY BL9 ..........................5 K2
  STKP SK1 .....................................13 J5
  WILM/AE SK9 ...............................130 A1
Massey Wk WYTH/NTH M22 ...........119 H3
Massie St CHD/CHDH SK8 ...............111 G6
Matham Wk HULME M15 * ...................7 G9
**Mather Av**
  DTN/ASHW M34 ............................101 J4
  ECC M30 ......................................85 H2
  GOL/RIS/CUL WA3 .........................80 B6
  PWCH M25 ...................................71 M3
  WHTF M45 ....................................55 J2
Mather Cl WHTF M45 ........................55 J5
Mather Fold Rd WALK M28 ...............68 E3
Mather La LEIGH WN7 .......................66 D8
Mather Rd BURY BL9 ........................25 J5
  ECC M30 ......................................85 H2
Mather St ATH M46 ...........................67 G1
  BOLS/LL BL3 * ................................2 F7
  FAIL M35 ......................................74 A5
  FWTH BL4 .....................................53 H4
  RAD M26 ......................................54 D7
Mather Wy SLFD M6 .........................86 D1
Matheson Dr
  WGNW/BIL/OR WN5 .......................47 G4
Matisse Wy BRO M7 .........................71 L4
Matley Cl HYDE SK14 .......................91 L7
Matley Gn RDSH SK5 ......................100 C6
Matley La STLY SK15 ........................91 M6
Matlock Av AUL OL6 ..........................76 C6
  BRO M7 .......................................71 K5
  DID/WITH M20 ...............................98 C6
  DTN/ASHW M34 ............................101 K4
  URM M41 .....................................95 L4
Matlock Cl ATH M46 ..........................67 G2
  FWTH BL4 .....................................53 H4
  SALE M33 ....................................96 F8
Matlock Dr BRAM/HZG SK7 .............122 A4
Matlock Rd CHD/CHDH SK8 .............119 C5
  RDSH SK5 ...................................100 C3
  STRET M32 ...................................96 F3
Matlock St ECC M30 ..........................84 F4
Matt Busby Cl SWIN M27 ..................70 D5
Matthew Cl GLSP SK13 .....................93 J5
  OLDS OL8 ....................................59 M8
Matthew Moss La ROCH OL11 ...........27 L8
Matthews Av FWTH BL4 ....................53 J5
Matthews La BNG/LEV M19 ..............99 L2
Matthew's St WGTN/LGST M12 .........88 C5
Mattison St MPL/ROM SK6 ..............114 D6
Mattison St OP/CLY M11 ...................89 H5
Maud St ROCH OL11 .........................41 M3
Mauldeth Cl HTNM SK4 ...................111 K1
Mauldeth Rd BNG/LEV M19 ..............99 J8
  BNG/LEV M19 ...............................99 J8
  DID/WITH M20 ...............................98 F5
  RUSH/FAL M14 .............................99 C5
Mauldeth Rd West CCHDY M21 .........98 B4
Maunby Gdns LHULT M38 ..................68 F1
Maureen Av CHH M8 .........................72 D4
Maureen St WHIT OL12 .....................10 D6
Maurice Cl DUK SK16 ........................91 H5
Maurice Dr SLFD M6 .........................71 J8
Maurice St SLFD M6 .........................71 J8
Maveen Gv OFTN SK2 .....................112 D8
Mavis Gv MILN OL16 .........................29 K6
Mavis St ROCH OL11 ........................41 M3
Mawdsley Dr CHH M8 .......................72 F4
Mawdsley St BOL BL1 .........................2 E5
Maxwell Av OFTN SK2 .....................112 F7
Maxwell St BOL BL1 ..........................22 B8
  BURY BL9 ......................................5 K3
**Max Woosnam Wk**
  RUSH/FAL M14 .............................98 D1
Mayall St MOSL OL5 ..........................76 F3
Mayall St East OLDE OL4 * ................59 M5
Mayan Av CSLFD M3 .........................86 D3
May Av CHD/CHDH SK8 ...................120 D6
  HTNM SK4 ....................................12 C3
  LEIGH WN7 ...................................66 A4
  WGNE/HIN WN2 .............................64 F5
Maybank St BOLS/LL BL3 ...................2 A9
Mayberth Av CHH M8 ........................72 D2
Maybreck Cl BOLS/LL BL3 ................35 M7
Mayburn Cl MDTN M24 .....................57 M7
Maybury Cl RAMS BL0 ......................18 E7
Maybury St GTN M18 ........................89 H6
Maycroft Av DID/WITH M20 ...............98 F7
May Dr BNG/LEV M19 .......................99 J6
Mayer St OFTN SK2 ........................112 F7
Mayes Gdns ANC M4 .........................88 A3
Mayes St ANC M4 ..............................7 H2
Mayfair HOR/BR BL6 .........................34 A1
Mayfair Av RAD M26 .........................38 A8
  SLFD M6 .......................................85 J1
  URM M41 .....................................95 J3
  WHTF M45 * ..................................55 J5

Mayfair Cl DUK SK16 .........................91 J4
  POY/DIS SK12 .............................122 F4
Mayfair Ct HALE/TIMP WA15 * .........108 E5
Mayfair Crs FAIL M35 ........................74 E4
**Mayfair Dr**
  IRL M44 .......................................94 D2
  ROY/SHW OL2 ...............................59 G2
  SALE M33 ....................................108 B2
  WGNE/HIN WN2 .............................49 G3
  WILM/AE SK9 ...............................63 J2
Mayfair Gdns ROCH OL11 .................10 A9
Mayfair Ms WILM/AE SK9 .................98 C8
Mayfair Pk CHD/CHDH SK8 * ...........98 C8
Mayfair Rd WYTH/NTH M22 .............110 B8
  WHTF M45 ....................................23 G7
**Mayfield** BOLE BL2 .........................23 J7
**Mayfield Av**
  BOLS/LL BL3 .................................52 E1
  DTN/ASHW M34 ............................101 K5
  FWTH BL4 .....................................52 F5
  OLDE OL4 ....................................60 D5
  RDSH SK5 ...................................100 C3
  SALE M33 ....................................97 H8
  STRET M32 ...................................96 E3
  WALK M28 ....................................69 M6
  WALK M28 ....................................69 M6
Mayfield Cl HALE/TIMP WA15 ..........108 E6
  RAMS BL0 ....................................24 D2
Mayfield Dr LEIGH WN7 .....................80 F4
Mayfield Gv CTN M18 ........................100 C1
  RDSH SK5 ....................................12 C3
  WILM/AE SK9 ...............................126 C7
Mayfield Houses RAD M26 * ..............54 B2
**Mayfield Rd** BRAM/HZG SK7 .........121 G8
  BRO M7 ........................................71 L3
  HALE/TIMP WA15 ..........................108 E6
  MPL/ROM SK6 ..............................114 E3
  OLD OL1 .......................................9 K1
  OLDTF/WHR M16 ............................98 B1
  RAMS BL0 ....................................18 E6
  WGNW/BIL/OR WN5 .......................46 A4
**Mayfield St** AIMK WN4 ....................78 D1
  ATH M46 ......................................66 F1
  DTN/ASHW M34 .............................90 B7
  MILN OL16 ....................................11 K1
Mayfield Ter MILN OL16 .....................28 E3
Mayflower Av ORD M5 .......................86 D4
Mayflower Cl GLSP SK13 .................105 H4
Mayford Rd BNG/LEV M19 .................99 K2
Maygate CHAD OL9 ............................8 E2
May Gv BNG/LEV M19 .......................99 L4
Mayhill Dr SLFD M6 ...........................70 D8
  WALK M28 ....................................68 A6
Mayhurst Av CCHDY M21 .................110 A1
Mayorlowe Av RDSH SK5 ................100 F8
Mayor's Rd HALE/TIMP WA15 .........108 B8
Mayor St BOL BL1 ...............................2 A6
  TOT/BURYW BL8 .............................4 A2
Mayo St WGTN/LGST M12 .................88 A4
Maypool Dr RDSH SK5 .....................100 C6
May Rd CHD/CHDH SK8 ...................120 C6
  OLDTF/WHR M16 ............................98 B1
  SWIN M27 ....................................70 E6
May St BOLE BL2 ................................3 H5
  ECC M30 ......................................69 M8
  EDGW/EG BL7 * .............................17 H6
  GOL/RIS/CUL WA3 .........................79 L2
  HEY OL10 ....................................41 H4
  LEIGH WN7 ...................................65 M7
  NEWH/MOS M40 ............................73 H7
  OLDS OL8 ....................................58 F8
  RAD M26 ......................................54 D1
Mayton St OP/CLY M11 .....................88 D4
May Tree Dr WGN WN1 .....................31 L8
Mayville Dr DID/WITH M20 .................98 E7
Maywood Av DID/WITH M20 .............110 D4
Maze St BOLS/LL BL3 .........................37 G7
McConnell Rd NEWH/MOS M40 .........73 K5
McCormack Dr WGN WN1 ..................15 J4
McCready Dr ORD M5 * .....................86 E5
McDonna St BOL BL1 ........................35 M1
McDonough Cl OLDS OL8 ..................75 K1
McEvoy St BOL BL1 ...........................35 L1
McKean Cl BOLS/LL BL3 ...................36 D8
McKie Cl OLDS OL8 ...........................75 K1
McLaren Ct CCHDY M21 ....................97 K3
McLean Dr IRL M44 ...........................94 D1
Mc Naught St MILN OL16 ...................11 J7
Meachin Av CCHDY M21 ....................98 A5
Meade Gv URM M41 ..........................95 M2
Meade Ov BRUN/LGST M13 ...............99 J2
Meade Hill Rd CHH M8 ......................72 C1
**The Meade** BOLS/LL BL3 .................52 B2
  WILM/AE SK9 ...............................126 F4
Meadfoot Av PWCH M25 ...................71 M1
Meadfoot Rd GTN M18 ......................89 G8
Meadland Gv BOL BL1 .......................22 C8
**Meadow** HALE/TIMP WA15 ...........117 K1
  SWIN M27 ....................................70 E3
Meadowbank AULW OL7 ...................75 K6
Meadow Bank CCHDY M21 ................97 K5
  GLSP SK13 ..................................104 C5
  HALE/TIMP WA15 ..........................108 D5
  HTNM SK4 ....................................12 B3
  HYDE SK14 ...................................93 G6
  MPL/ROM SK6 ..............................113 J1
**Meadowbank Gdns**
  GOL/RIS/CUL WA3 .........................81 M5
Meadowbank Rd BOLS/LL BL3 ..........51 L2
Meadow Bank Cl OLDE OL4 * .............60 D8
Meadow Bank Ct STRET M32 .............96 E3
**Meadowcroft**
  AIMK WN4 * ...................................92 C8
  RAD M26 ......................................38 C8
  WHTN BL5 ....................................50 C5
Meadowcroft La OLD OL1 ..................27 J6
  ROCH OL11 ..................................10 A9
Meadowcroft Wy LEIGH WN7 ............81 L2
Meadowfold HOR/BR BL6 ..................42 E1
  MILN OL16 ....................................42 D1
Meadowfield Cl GLSP SK13 ..............104 C1
Meadowfield Dr WALK M28 ...............68 C6
Meadow Fold UPML OL3 ....................61 M4

Meadowgate URM M41....96 A3
WALK M28....69 J4
Meadowgate Rd SLFD M6....85 M2
Meadow Head Av WHIT OL12...20 B6
Meadow La ALT WA14....106 D8
BOLE BL2....37 K5
DTN/ASHW M34....101 K5
DUK SK16....91 G4
OLDS OL8....75 H2
POY/DIS SK12....123 M6
WALK M28....69 J7
Meadow Pit La WGNE/HIN WN2...32 E4
Meadow Ri GLSP SK13....104 C5
ROY/SHW OL2....43 K3
Meadow Rd BRO M7....86 F2
MDTN M24....57 H6
URM M41....85 J4
Meadows Cl BRAM/HZG SK7...122 A1
WGNE/HIN WN2....49 G7
Meadowside BRAM/HZG SK7....120 C2
MCFLDN SK10....129 K4
MILN OL16....29 M8
POY/DIS SK12....124 C6
Meadowside Av AIMK WN4....63 K4
BOLE BL2....3 M4
IRL M44....94 D2
WALK M28....53 H8
WYTH/NTH M22....110 A8
Meadowside Cl RAD M26....38 D7
Meadowside Gv WALK M28....69 H1
Meadowside Rd
WGNE/HIN WN2....49 K8
Meadows La BOLE BL2....37 J1
Meadows Rd CHD/CHDH SK8...119 K3
CHD/CHDH SK8....120 B4
HTNM SK4....99 M6
NM/HAY SK22....125 M2
SALE M33....109 J1
Meadows St WGNNW/ST WN6....14 B2
The Meadows IRL M44....94 A6
MDTN M24....57 L6
MPL/ROM SK6....101 L8
OLDE OL4....60 D6
PWCH M25....55 L8
RAD M26....38 B7
UPML OL3....61 L5
WHIT OL12....20 A3
Meadow St HYDE SK14....102 B3
NM/HAY SK22....124 D4
OFTN SK2....112 F7
The Meadow BOL BL1....35 G5
Meadowvale Dr
WGNW/BIL/OR WN5....46 F6
Meadow Vw WHIT OL12....27 K3
Meadow Wk FWTH BL4....52 D5
LIT OL15....21 K7
Meadow Wy EDGW/EG BL7...17 G6
HALE/TIMP WA15....117 K1
HOR/BR BL6....33 H3
NEWH/MOS M40....73 M6
TOT/BURYW BL8....24 B6
WILM/AE SK9....126 C8
Meadscroft Dr WILM/AE SK9....130 C3
Meads Gv FWTH BL4....52 A4
TYLD M29....68 D6
The Meads CHAD OL9....58 D6
The Mead CCHDY M21 *....97 L5
ORD M5....86 B2
Meadway BRAM/HZG SK7....121 G7
BURY BL9....39 J6
CHAD OL9....74 B2
DUK SK16....91 H5
GOL/RIS/CUL WA3....80 A4
MPL/ROM SK6....123 H4
POY/DIS SK12....121 K7
RAMS BL0....18 F3
ROCH OL11....27 L8
SALE M33....108 B2
STLY SK15....92 B6
TYLD M29....67 J2
WGNE/HIN WN2....15 M6
Meadway Cl ALT WA14....107 M6
Meadway Dr FWTH BL4....53 L7
HOR/BR BL6....34 A4
Meadway Pl WGNW/BIL/OR WN5....47 G5
Meadway Rd OLDS OL8....75 H4
ROY/SHW OL2....43 K4
WALK M28....68 G4
The Medway HEY OL10....40 E1
Medway Wk NEWH/MOS M40....88 A1
Medway Cl WGNE/HIN WN2....49 G1
Meece St ROY/SHW OL2....59 K2
Meek St ROY/SHW OL2....59 K2
Meerbrook Rd EDGY/DAV SK3...111 K4
Mee's Sq ECC M30....84 C2
Megfield WHTN BL5....51 H2
Megna Cl CHAD OL9....8 D4
Melandra Castle Rd GLSP SK13...104 C3
Melandra Crs HYDE SK14....103 H2
Melandra Rd GLSP SK13....104 A1
Melanie Cl SK13....104 D4
Melanie Dr RDSH SK5....100 C4
Melba St OP/CLY M11....89 H4
Melbecks Wk NTHM/RTH M23...58 C5
MANAIR M90....118 C4
STRET M32....97 G2
Melbourne Cl HOR/BR BL6....33 M1
ROCH OL11....42 D2
Melbourne Gv HOR/BR BL6....33 M1

Melbourne Rd BOLS/LL BL3....35 L7
BRAM/HZG SK7....121 G6
ROCH OL11....42 E2
Melbourne St BKLY M9....73 H4
BRO M7....72 A7
CHAD OL9....8 A5
DTN/ASHW M34....101 H2
HULME M15....6 D9
RDSH SK5....100 C4
STLY SK15....91 K3
SWIN M27....70 E4
Melbourne St North AUL OL6....75 M8
Melbourne St South AUL OL6....90 F1
Melbury Av DID/WITH M20....99 G8
Melbury Dr HOR/BR BL6....34 C4
Melbury Rd CHD/CHDH SK8....120 D6
Meldon Rd BRUN/LGST M13....99 H2
Meldrum St OLDS OL8....59 J8
Melford Av NEWH/MOS M40....74 B3
Melford Dr AIMK WN4....63 K8
WGNW/BIL/OR WN5....62 A1
Melford Gv OLDE OL4....60 A6
Melford Rd BRAM/HZG SK7....122 B3
Melfort Av STRET M32....97 H3
Meliden Crs BOL BL1 *....35 L3
WYTH/NTH M22....119 G2
Melksham St ORD M5....86 E2
Mellalieu St MDTN M24....57 H3
ROY/SHW OL2....59 H2
Melland Av CCHDY M21....97 M7
Melland Rd BRUN M18....99 M1
Meller Rd BRUN/LGST M13....99 J2
Melling Av CHAD OL9....58 B8
HTNM SK4....100 B6
Melling Cl LEIGH WN7....81 J5
Melling Rd OLDE OL4....59 M6
Mellings Av
WGNW/BIL/OR WN5 *....62 B3
Melling St WGNW/BIL/OR WN5...47 H7
WGTN/LGST M12....88 D8
Melling Wy WGNS/IIMK WN3....63 G3
Mellodew Dr OLD OL1....60 A1
Mellor Brook Dr
WGNE/HIN WN2 *....64 D3
Mellor Brow HEY OL10....40 E2
WGNNW/ST WN6....31 H2
Mellor Cl AUL OL6....91 H7
Mellor Ct OFTN SK2....113 H1
Mellor Dr BURY BL9....39 G5
WALK M28....68 F3
Mellor Gv BOL BL1....35 L3
Mellor Rd AUL OL6....76 C8
CHD/CHDH SK8....120 D3
NM/HAY SK22....124 E1
Mellors Rd TRPK M17....85 L5
Mellor St DROY M43....89 J3
ECC M30....85 G3
FAIL M35....74 A5
NEWH/MOS M40....88 A1
OLDE OL4....60 B6
OLDS OL8....74 F2
PWCH M25....55 J8
RAD M26....54 E2
ROY/SHW OL2....43 A3
STRET M32....86 A8
Mellor Wy CHAD OL9....58 D8
Mellowstone Dr CCHDY M21...98 C4
Melloy Pl CHH M8....72 D8
Melmerby Cl AIMK WN4....78 C1
Melon Pl SLFD M6....86 E2
Melrose Av BOL BL1....35 K3
DID/WITH M20....110 F1
ECC M30....69 K8
EDGY/DAV SK3 *....111 J5
HEY OL10....40 F1
LEIGH WN7....66 A3
LIT OL15....21 L5
SALE M33....108 E1
TOT/BURYW BL8....38 F1
Melrose Cl WHTF M45....55 J2
Melrose Ct CHAD OL9 *....58 D8
Melrose Crs EDGY/DAV SK3....112 A8
HALE/TIMP WA15....117 K3
POY/DIS SK12....122 F7
Melrose Dr WGNS/IIMK WN3....63 G1
Melrose Gdns RAD M26....38 B7
Melrose Rd BOLS/LL BL3....53 J1
RAD M26....38 B7
Melrose St NEWH/MOS M40....73 M7
OLD OL1....59 L3
RAMS BL0....24 E2
ROCH OL11....10 A5
Melsomby Rd NTHM/RTH M23...109 K2
Meltham Av DID/WITH M20....98 D6
Meltham Cl HTNM SK4....111 H5
Meltham Pl BOLS/LL BL3 *....35 M8
Meltham Rd HTNM SK4....111 H3
Melton Av DTN/ASHW M34....100 D1
URM M41....94 F1
Melton Cl HEY OL10....40 E3
TYLD M29....67 L4
WALK M28....68 F2
Melton Dr BURY BL9....39 K7
Melton Rd CHH M8....72 B3
Melton St BKLY M9....73 J3
HEY OL10....40 E3
RAD M26....38 C6
RDSH SK5....100 C8
Melverley Rd BKLY M9....56 D7
Melverley St WGNS/IIMK WN3...14 C6
Melville Cl OP/CLY M11....89 H5
Melville Rd FWTH BL4....53 J6
STRET M32....96 F1
Melville St AUL OL6....75 L8
BOLS/LL BL3....36 D8
CSLFD M3....6 B3
OLDE OL4....60 B7
ROCH OL11....42 A3
Melvin Av WYTH/NTH M22....110 B8
Melyncourt Rd HYDE SK14 *...103 H1
Memorial Cottages SWIN M27 *...70 C1
Memorial Rd WALK M28....69 G1
Menai Gv CHD/CHDH SK8....111 K6
Menai Rd EDGY/DAV SK3....112 B6
Menai St BOLS/LL BL3 *....35 L8
Mendip Av WGNS/IIMK WN3....62 F1
WYTH/NTH M22....110 C8
Mendip Cl BOLE BL2....37 K5
CHAD OL9 *....58 D7
CHD/CHDH SK8....119 K3
HTNM SK4....13 G1
ROY/SHW OL2....58 F1
Mendip Crs TOT/BURYW BL8...38 D1
Mendip Dr BOLE BL2....37 K6
BOLE BL2....37 L6
Mendip Rd OLDS OL8....75 G1
Mendips Cl ROY/SHW OL2....43 J4
Menston Av NEWH/MOS M40...74 B3
Mentmore Rd MILN OL16....29 G5

Mentone Crs WYTH/NTH M22...110 B8
Mentone Rd HTNM SK4....111 L1
Mentor St BRUN/LGST M13....99 J2
Mercer Cl ROCH OL11....27 H4
Mercer Rd GTN M18....89 G7
HEY OL10....40 E4
Mercer St BNG/LEV M19....99 L3
DROY M43....89 L2
NEWLW WA12....79 G8
Merchants Quay
GOL/RIS/CUL WA3....80 B3
Merchants Quay SALQ M50....86 D6
Mercian Ml AUL OL6 *....90 E1
Mercian Wy EDGY/DAV SK3....12 F8
Mercia St BOLS/LL BL3....35 M7
Mercury Pk URM M41....85 J6
Mercury Wy URM M41....85 J7
Mere Av DROY M43....89 H4
LEIGH WN7....65 M8
MDTN M24....57 K6
SLFD M6....86 B2
Merebank Cl ROCH OL11....27 H4
Mere Bank Cl WALK M28....68 F1
Mere Cl BURY BL9....39 L7
DTN/ASHW M34....100 E2
SALE M33....109 J1
Mereclough Av WALK M28....69 H4
Meredew Av SWIN M27....70 B6
Meredith St BOLS/LL BL3....52 C1
RUSH/FAL M14....99 G5
Mere Dr DID/WITH M20....98 E8
SWIN M27....70 D2
Merefield Av ROCH OL11....10 C9
Merefield Cl WGNE/HIN WN2...49 G1
Merefield Rd
HALE/TIMP WA15....108 F7
Merefield St ROCH OL11....10 C9
Merefield Ter ROCH OL11 *....10 C9
Mere Fold WALK M28....68 E1
Mere Gdns BOL BL1....2 C2
Merehall Cl BOL BL1....2 C2
Merehall Dr BOL BL1....2 C2
Merehall St BOL BL1....2 C2
Mereland Av DID/WITH M20...98 F8
Mereland Cl
WGNW/BIL/OR WN5....46 B6
Mere La ROCH OL11....10 E8
Meremanor WALK M28....69 J3
Merepool Cl MPL/ROM SK6....113 M5
Mere Rd AIMK WN4....63 M8
NEWLW WA12....79 J8
Mereside Cl CHD/CHDH SK8...111 J8
Mereside Gv WALK M28....69 H1
Mere St LEIGH WN7....66 A7
ROCH OL11....10 E7
WGNW/BIL/OR WN5....14 A8
The Mere AUL OL6....76 B6
CHD/CHDH SK8....111 J8
Mere Wk BOL BL1....2 C2
Merewood Av WYTH/NTH M22...110 A6
Meriden Cl RAD M26....38 G5
Meriden Gv HOR/BR BL6....35 G6
Meridian Pl DID/WITH M20....98 D8
Merinall Cl MILN OL16....11 M5
Meriton Rd WILM/AE SK9....119 G8
Merlewood Rd RAMS BL0....19 H4
Merlewood Av BNG/LEV M19...99 M5
DTN/ASHW M34 *....89 L3
UPML OL3....61 L4
Merlewood Dr SWIN M27....69 M6
Merlin Cl LIT OL15....29 K2
OFTN SK2....113 K6
OLDS OL8....75 K4
Merlin Dr SWIN M27....70 E2
Merlin Gv BOL BL1....35 J5
Merlin Rd IRL M44....83 K8
MILN OL16....11 M5
Merlyn Av DID/WITH M20....98 F3
DTN/ASHW M34....101 H2
SALE M33....96 F7
Merrick Av WYTH/NTH M22...110 B8
Merrick St HEY OL10....41 H3
Merridale Rd NEWH/MOS M40...73 M3
The Merridale
HALE/TIMP WA15....117 J4
Merrill St ANC M4....88 A3
Merriman St OLDTF/WHR M16...87 H8
Merrion St FWTH BL4....52 F2
Merrow Wk CMANE M1....7 J8
Merrybent Cl ECC M30....113 G8
Merrybower Rd BRO M7....72 B4
Merrydale Av ECC M30....70 B8
Merryman Hall WHIT OL12 *...28 E8
Merseybank Av CCHDY M21...98 A8
Mersey Bank Rd GLSP SK13....93 J8
Mersey Cl WGNE/HIN WN2....55 L3
WHTF M45....55 L3
Mersey Crs DID/WITH M20....110 A1
Mersey Dr PART M31....94 D8
WHTF M45....55 L3
Mersey Mdw DID/WITH M20...110 C1
HTNM SK4....111 J2
SALE M33....96 E6
WGNE/HIN WN2....49 J4
WGNW/BIL/OR WN5....46 C5
Mersey Rd North FAIL M35....74 D3
Mersey Sq STKP SK1....13 H4
Mersey St DROY M43....89 H4
LEIGH WN7....65 M8
STKP SK1....13 L2
Mersey Vw URM M41 *....95 H4
Merston Dr DID/WITH M20....110 F5
Merton Av BRAM/HZG SK7....122 B4
MPL/ROM SK6....101 K8
OLDS OL8....75 G1
Merton Cl BOLS/LL BL3 *....35 M7
Merton Dr DROY M43....89 H3
Merton Gv CHAD OL9....74 A1
HALE/TIMP WA15....108 E6
TYLD M29....67 M6
Merton Rd EDGY/DAV SK3....12 A8
POY/DIS SK12....121 K8
PWCH M25....55 M7
SALE M33....96 D7
WGNS/IIMK WN3....46 E8
Merton St TOT/BURYW BL8....4 B2
Merville Av NEWH/MOS M40...73 K8
Mervyn Pl WGNS/IIMK WN3....47 K8
Mervyn Rd BRO M7....71 K6
Merwell Rd URM M41....95 H3
Merwood Av CHD/CHDH SK8...118 D5
Merwood Gv RUSH/FAL M14...88 B8
Meshaw Cl NTHM/RTH M23....109 H3
Mesnefield Rd BRO M7....71 K4
Mesne Lea Gv WALK M28 *....69 H4
Mesne Lea Rd WALK M28....69 H4
Mesnes Av WGNS/IIMK WN3...14 B9

Mesnes Park Ter WGN WN1....14 F2
Mesnes Rd WGN WN1....47 M2
Mesnes St WGN WN1....14 F3
Mesnes Ter WGN WN1....14 F3
Metcalfe Ct LHULT M38....52 C8
Metcalfe Dr MPL/ROM SK6....113 L2
Metcalf Gdns UPML OL3....61 L4
Metfield Pl BOL BL1....35 M4
Methuen St WGTN/LGST M12...99 L1
Methwold St BOLS/LL BL3 *...35 M8
The Mews BOL BL1....35 L4
CHD/CHDH SK8....110 E7
NEWH/MOS M40....88 B1
PWCH M25....71 L1
SALE M33....108 F1
WGNE/HIN WN2....49 G7
WHTF M45 *....55 G4
Mexborough St OLDE OL4....60 A4
Meyer St EDGY/DAV SK3....112 C6
Meynell Dr LEIGH WN7....81 J2
Meyrick Rd SLFD M6....86 B2
Meyrick St WGNW/BIL/OR WN5...14 A7
Miall St ROCH OL11....10 F8
Micawber Rd POY/DIS SK12...129 J3
Michael St MDTN M24....57 J4
Michael Wife La RAMS BL0....19 J2
Michigan Av SALQ M50....86 D6
Mickleby Wk NEWH/MOS M40 *...7 M1
Micklehurst Av DID/WITH M20...98 B8
Micklehurst Gn OFTN SK2....113 H7
Micklehurst Rd MOSL OL5....77 H3
Mickleton ATH M46....51 H8
Middlebourne St SLFD M6....86 B2
Middlebrook Dr HOR/BR BL6...34 F6
Middlecot Cl
WGNW/BIL/OR WN5....46 B7
Middlefield OLDS OL8....75 K4
Middle Fld ROCH OL11....27 H3
Middlefields CHD/CHDH SK8...111 L8
Middlegate NEWH/MOS M40...74 A1
Middle Ga OLDS OL8....75 G2
Middle Gn AUL OL6....75 M8
Middleham St
RUSH/FAL M14....98 D2
Middle Hl WHIT OL12....20 B4
Middle Hillgate STKP SK1....13 K5
Middlesex Dr BURY BL9....5 G3
Middlesex Rd BKLY M9....73 G2
RDSH SK5....100 F6
Middlesex Wk CHAD OL9....8 F6
Middlestone Dr BKLY M9....73 G5
Middle St WHIT OL12....20 A3
Middleton Av FAIL M35....74 C5
Middleton Dr BURY BL9....55 J1
Middleton Old Rd BKLY M9....73 G2
Middleton Rd BKLY M9....56 C7
CHAD OL9....8 B4
CHH M8....72 C2
HEY OL10....41 H4
RDSH SK5....100 C2
ROY/SHW OL2....58 E1
Middleton Wy MDTN M24....57 J4
Middle Turn EDGW/EG BL7....17 G5
Middleway OLDE OL4....60 E2
Middlewood GOL/RIS/CUL WA3...80 B4
Middlewood Dr HTNM SK4....111 K3
Middlewood Gn CHAD OL9....58 D5
Middle Wood La LIT OL15....21 G6
Middlewood Rd
MPL/ROM SK6....122 F5
POY/DIS SK12....122 F8
Middlewood St ORD M5....86 F3
Middlewood Wy
BRAM/HZG SK7....122 E4
MCFLDN SK10....129 M3
Midford Av ECC M30....84 C2
Midford Dr BOL BL1....22 B5
Midge Hall Dr ROCH OL11....27 K6
Midgley Av GTN M18....89 H6
Midgley Crs AUL OL6....76 B8
Midgley Dr MILN OL16....42 E2
Midgley St SWIN M27....70 B6
Midhurst Av NEWH/MOS M40 *...73 L8
Midhurst Cl CHD/CHDH SK8...120 B4
Midhurst St ROCH OL11....10 F9
Midland Cl LEIGH WN7....65 K9
Midland Rd BRAM/HZG SK7...121 G1
RDSH SK5....100 C2
Midland St WGTN/LGST M12...88 C3
NM/HAY SK22....124 E1
Midland Wk BRAM/HZG SK7...121 G1
Midlothian St OP/CLY M11....88 E2
Midville Rd OP/CLY M11....88 F1
Midway CHD/CHDH SK8....120 D7
Midway Dr POY/DIS SK12....129 H2
Midway St WGTN/LGST M12...99 K2
Milan St BRO M7....72 B6
Milbourne Rd BURY BL9....25 J6
Milburn Av NTHM/RTH M23...109 L2
Milburn Dr BOLE BL2....37 K4
Milbury Dr LIT OL15....29 K2
Milden Cl DID/WITH M20 *....98 F8
Mildred Av OLDE OL4....60 E7
PWCH M25....71 M2
ROY/SHW OL2....59 H2
Mildred St BRO M7....71 M7
Mile End La OFTN SK2....112 F6
Mile La TOT/BURYW BL8....38 D4
Miles La TOT/BURYW BL8....38 D4
Miles St BOL BL1....36 A2
HYDE SK14....102 C2
OLD OL1....9 L4
WGTN/LGST M12....88 D3
Milford Av OLDS OL8....74 F2
Milford Brow OLDE OL4....60 B5
Milford Crs LIT OL15....21 M6
Milford Dr BNG/LEV M19....99 M5
Milford Gv OFTN SK2....112 F5
Milford Rd BOLE BL2....23 J8
BOLS/LL BL3....52 B1
WGNE/HIN WN2....48 C3
Milford St BKLY M9....72 E1
SLFD M6....86 B3
WGNS/IIMK WN3....15 K8
WHIT OL12....28 C3
Milk St CMANW M1....7 G4
HYDE SK14....102 A2
RAMS BL0....18 E7
ROCH OL11....10 F6
TYLD M29....67 K3
WGNS/IIMK WN3....14 C7
Milkwood Gv GTN M18....89 G8
Millais St NEWH/MOS M40....73 K4
Millard St CHAD OL9....58 D5
Mill Bank RAD M26....54 E2
WGNNW/ST WN6....30 A5
Millbank Gdns BOL BL1 *....35 M3

Millbank St CMANE M1....7 L5
HEY OL10....40 E2
Millbeck Farm
WGNW/BIL/OR WN5....47 G7
Millbeck Gv BOLS/LL BL3 *....36 B5
Millbeck Rd MDTN M24....57 G2
Millbrae Gdns ROY/SHW OL2...43 G5
Millbrae Av ATH M46....51 H7
DTN/ASHW M34....101 G3
Millbrook Av ATH M46....51 H7
DTN/ASHW M34....101 G3
Millbrook Bank ROCH OL11....27 G3
Millbrook Cl GOL/RIS/CUL WA3...81 M7
ROY/SHW OL2....44 A3
Millbrook Fold BRAM/HZG SK7...122 C5
Millbrook Rd NTHM/RTH M23...109 K8
Millbrook St STKP SK1....13 J6
Mill Brow AUL OL6....75 M3
CHH M8....72 C1
HYDE SK14 *....103 K4
MPL/ROM SK6....115 G4
OLD OL1....58 D2
WALK M28....69 J6
Mill Brow Rd MPL/ROM SK6...115 H4
Mill Court Dr RAD M26....53 L4
Millcrest Cl WALK M28....68 C7
Mill Cft BOL BL1....2 B2
ROY/SHW OL2....43 M6
Millcroft Av
WGNW/BIL/OR WN5....46 A7
Mill Croft Cl WHIT OL12....26 F2
Mill Croft La UPML OL3....45 J6
Milldale Cl ATH M46....66 F1
HOR/BR BL6....34 F5
Milldale Rd LEIGH WN7....80 A4
Miller Rd OLDS OL8....75 H1
Millers Brook Cl HEY OL10 *...41 G1
Millers Cl SALE M33....109 K1
Millers Ct ORD M5....85 K2
Millersdale Ct GLSP SK13....105 J3
Miller's La ATH M46....67 G3
WGNE/HIN WN2....64 D3
Millers St ECC M30....84 F3
Millett St BURY BL9....4 C5
RAMS BL0....19 G5
Millfield Ct HALE/TIMP WA15...117 G2
Millfield Dr WALK M28....68 G6
Millfield Gv WGNE/HIN WN2....11 J7
Millfield La AIMK WN4....78 E5
Millfield Rd BOLE BL2....37 K5
Millfold WHIT OL12....20 B2
Mill Fold Gdns LIT OL15....21 L8
Mill Fold Rd MDTN M24....57 J5
Millford Av URM M41....95 H3
Mill Ga OLDS OL8....75 G1
Millgate ANC M4 *....7 G3
EDGW/EG BL7....22 A2
STKP SK1....13 K3
UPML OL3....45 J8
WGN WN1....15 H4
Millgate La DID/WITH M20....110 D3
Mill Green St WGTN/LGST M12 *...88 A4
Millhall Cl HULME M15....87 H7
Millhead Av NEWH/MOS M40...88 B2
Mill Hl BOLE BL2 *....3 H5
LHULT M38....52 B6
Mill Hill Av POY/DIS SK12....121 H6
Mill Hill Caravan Pk BOLE BL2...3 H3
Mill Hill Gv HYDE SK14....103 J2
Mill Hill Hollow POY/DIS SK12...121 M5
Mill Hill St BOLE BL2....3 H3
Millhouse Av NTHM/RTH M23...109 K8
Mill House Cl WHIT OL12....21 H8
Millhouse St RAMS BL0....19 H4
Milliner Ct OFTN SK2 *....113 G5
Millingford Av
GOL/RIS/CUL WA3....79 J2
Millingford Gv AIMK WN4....79 K2
Millington Wk HULME M15....87 G6
Mill La AUL OL6....90 E2
BRAM/HZG SK7....122 B4
CHAD OL9....58 F8
CHD/CHDH SK8....111 G6
CHD/CHDH SK8....120 D1
DTN/ASHW M34....101 L3
FAIL M35....73 M5
HALE/TIMP WA15....118 A4
LEIGH WN7....66 E8
MCFLDN SK10....128 A7
MCFLDN SK10....128 A7
MOSL OL5....76 F2
MPL/ROM SK6....101 K7
MPL/ROM SK6....113 M5
RDSH SK5....100 D5
ROY/SHW OL2....42 F8
TOT/BURYW BL8....24 E8
UPML OL3....61 G3
WGNE/HIN WN2....49 J1
WHTN BL5....50 B8
WYTH/NTH M22....110 B3
Mill Nook WHIT OL12....28 C1
Millom Av NTHM/RTH M23....109 L3
Millom Cl MILN OL16....11 L1
Millom Ct HALE/TIMP WA15 *...109 G6
Millom Dr BURY BL9....55 K2
Millom Pl CHD/CHDH SK8....119 K1
Millow St ANC M4....7 G1
Millpond Av BOLS/LL BL3....52 D1
Mill Pond Av NM/HAY SK22...124 E3
Mill Pond Cl ROY/SHW OL2....25 J4
Mill Rd BURY BL9....25 J6
WGNW/BIL/OR WN5....46 A7
Mills Farm Cl OLDS OL8....75 K3
Mills Hill Rd MDTN M24....58 A3
Mills St HEY OL10....40 E2
WHIT OL12....13 K1
Millstone Cl MPL/ROM SK6...113 K1
POY/DIS SK12....122 B7
Millstone Rd BOL BL1....35 J3
Millstream La NEWH/MOS M40...89 H1
Mill St AIMK WN4....78 F2
ALT WA14....108 B7
ATH M46....67 H3
BOL BL1....3 G4
BRAM/HZG SK7....121 H4
EDGW/EG BL7....22 C4
FAIL M35....73 M5
FWTH BL4....52 F4
GLSP SK13....105 G3
GOL/RIS/CUL WA3....79 K4
HYDE SK14....91 H7
LEIGH WN7....66 B6
MOSL OL5....76 F4
OP/CLY M11....90 D4
RAD M26....38 C8

RAMS BL0 .....18 D8
ROY/SHW OL2 .....43 G8
SLFD M6 .....71 K8
STLY SK15 .....91 M3
TOT/BURYW BL8 .....24 C4
UPML OL3 .....61 L4
WALK M28 .....68 D5
WGNE/HIN WN2 .....49 G7
WGNS/IIMK WN3 .....14 E5
WHTN BL5 .....50 C4
WILM/AE SK9 .....126 F5
Milltown GLSP SK13 .....105 G3
Milltown St RAD M26 .....54 E2
Mill View La HOR/BR BL6 .....34 B1
Millwall Cl GTN M18 .....89 G7
Millway HALE/TIMP WA15 .....117 G5
Millwell La BOL BL1 .....2 E4
Millwood Cl AIMK WN4 .....65 K7
  CHD/CHDH SK8 .....120 A4
Millwood Ct BURY BL9 .....39 J6
Millwood Ter HYDE SK14 .....101 M2
Millwright Cl NEWH/MOS M40 .....73 L2
Mill Yd BURY BL9 .....5 H3
Milne Av ALT WA14 .....107 L5
  BURY BL9 .....25 J7
Milner Rd OLDTF/WHR M16 .....87 G8
  RAD M26 .....54 B1
  SWIN M27 .....70 D4
  WHIT OL12 .....20 A4
Milnes Av LEIGH WN7 .....81 J2
Milne St CHAD OL9 .....8 A4
  CHAD OL9 .....8 C1
  CHAD OL9 .....8 C1
  OLD OL1 .....59 K2
  ROCH OL11 .....41 M2
  ROY/SHW OL2 .....43 L6
Milngate Cl MILN OL16 .....42 F1
Milnholme BOL BL1 .....35 L1
Milnrow Cl BRUN/LGST M13 .....7 K8
Milnrow Rd LIT OL15 .....29 L2
  MILN OL16 .....11 L5
  ROY/SHW OL2 .....43 L5
Milnthorpe Rd BOLE BL2 .....37 H4
Milnthorpe St SLFD M6 .....71 K7
Milnthorpe Wy
  WGTN/LGST M12 .....88 B6
Milo St BKLY M9 .....73 C1
Milsom Av BOLS/LL BL3 .....51 M1
Milton Av BOLS/LL BL3 .....37 L8
  BOLS/LL BL3 .....51 L1
  DROY M43 .....89 K3
  IRL M44 .....94 B6
  ORD M5 * .....86 A2
  STLY SK15 .....77 H8
Milton Cl DUK SK16 .....91 L1
  MPL/ROM SK6 .....114 C8
  STRET M32 .....97 H1
Milton Ct CHD/CHDH SK8 .....110 F7
  FWTH BL4 .....52 E6
Milton Crs CHD/CHDH SK8 .....110 F7
  HALE/TIMP WA15 .....108 D3
  POY/DIS SK12 .....121 M8
  SALE M33 .....96 D6
Milton Dr CHAD OL9 .....58 D6
  HALE/TIMP WA15 .....108 D3
  POY/DIS SK12 .....121 M8
  SALE M33 .....96 D6
Milton Gv OLDTF/WHR M16 .....97 M2
  SALE M33 .....96 D6
  WGN WN1 .....47 H1
  WGNW/BIL/OR WN5 .....46 D6
  WGNW/BIL/OR WN5 .....62 A3
Milton Pl SLFD M6 .....86 D1
Milton Rd BRAM/HZG SK7 .....121 G5
  DTN/ASHW M34 .....90 A3
  GOL/RIS/CUL WA3 .....80 A5
  PWCH M25 .....55 M7
  RAD M26 .....38 A8
  STRET M32 .....97 H1
  SWIN M27 .....70 A3
Milton St BRO M7 .....72 B8
  ECC M30 .....85 G2
  HYDE SK14 .....91 G8
  LEIGH WN7 .....66 B7
  MDTN M24 .....57 J3
  MILN OL16 .....11 G6
  MOSL OL5 .....76 F2
  RAMS BL0 .....18 E6
  ROY/SHW OL2 .....43 H7
Milton Vw MOSL OL5 .....77 G1
Milverton Av HYDE SK14 .....102 F2
Milverton Cl HOR/BR BL6 .....35 C7
Milverton Dr BRAM/HZG SK7 .....120 D7
Milverton Rd RUSH/FAL WA14 .....99 G3
Milverton Wk HYDE SK14 .....102 F2
Milwain Dr HTNM SK4 .....99 M6
Milwain Rd BNG/LEV M19 .....99 J4
  STRET M32 .....96 F3
Mimosa Dr SWIN M27 .....70 C2
Mincing St ANC M4 * .....7 H1
Minden Cl DID/WITH M20 .....98 F8
  TOT/BURYW BL8 .....38 E2
Minden Pde BURY BL9 .....4 F6
Minehead Av DID/WITH M20 .....98 C5
  LEIGH WN7 .....66 A2
  URM M41 .....95 L4
Minerva Rd DUK SK16 .....90 F2
  FWTH BL4 .....52 C3
Mine St HEY OL10 .....27 G8
Mine Wy RNFD/HAY WA11 .....78 C3
Minnie St BOLS/LL BL3 * .....35 L8
  WHIT OL12 .....20 B1
Minoan Gdns BRO M7 .....71 M7
Minorca Cl ROCH OL11 .....27 H4
Minorca St BOLS/LL BL3 .....36 B8
Minor St FAIL M35 .....74 D4
  OLDS OL8 .....9 H8
  ROCH OL11 .....41 K1
Minshull Cl CMANE M1 * .....7 K6
Minshull St South CMANE M1 * .....7 J6
Minstead Cl HYDE SK14 .....102 D3
Minster Cl BOLE BL2 .....36 F2
  DUK SK16 .....91 G6
Minster Dr ALT WA14 .....116 C3
  CHD/CHDH SK8 .....111 K7
  URM M41 .....95 K1
Minster Gv TYLD M29 .....67 L5
Minsterley Pde
  WYTH/NTH M22 .....118 E3
Minster Rd BKLY M9 .....73 H1
  BOLE BL2 .....36 F2
Minster Wy CHAD OL9 .....58 D3
Minstrel Cl SWIN M27 .....70 D3
  WGNE/HIN WN2 .....64 E5
Minton St NEWH/MOS M40 .....73 M4
  OLDE OL4 .....9 L8
Minto St AULW OL7 .....75 K8
Mint St RAMS BL0 .....18 F2
Mirabel St CSLFD M3 .....6 E1
Mirfield Av BKLY M9 .....57 G8
  HTNM SK4 .....12 A3
  OLDS OL8 .....59 H8
Mirfield Cl GOL/RIS/CUL WA3 .....80 A5

Mirfield Dr ECC M30 .....70 A8
  MDTN M24 .....57 J3
  URM M41 .....84 F8
Mirfield Rd BKLY M9 .....57 G8
Miriam Gv LEIGH WN7 .....66 B3
Miriam St BOLS/LL BL3 * .....35 L8
  FAIL M35 .....74 B7
Miry La WGNNW/ST WN6 .....14 A2
  WHTN BL5 .....50 B7
Mission St HEY OL10 .....40 F2
Missouri Av SALQ M50 .....86 B3
Mistletoe Gv CSLFD M3 * .....6 B1
Mitcham Av BKLY M9 .....73 K1
Mitchell Cl CHD/CHDH SK8 * .....110 C6
Mitchell Hey WHIT OL12 .....10 C4
Mitchell Rd WGNW/BIL/OR WN5 .....62 B7
Mitchells Quay FAIL M35 .....74 B5
Mitchell St AIMK WN4 .....78 F2
  ECC M30 .....85 J1
  COL/RIS/CUL WA3 .....79 K5
  LEIGH WN7 .....65 L7
  MILN OL16 .....28 F1
  NEWH/MOS M40 .....73 L7
  OLD OL1 .....8 F2
  OP/CLY M11 * .....88 C5
  TOT/BURYW BL8 .....24 F8
  WGNE/HIN WN2 .....48 D5
  WGNW/BIL/OR WN5 .....47 L3
  WHIT OL12 .....10 B3
Mitcheson Gdns SLFD M6 .....86 C1
Mitford Rd RUSH/FAL M14 .....98 F5
Mitford St STRET M32 .....96 F3
Mitre Rd BRUN/LGST M13 .....88 C8
Mitre St BOL BL1 .....2 C3
  FAIL M35 .....74 C4
Mitton Cl GOL/RIS/CUL WA3 .....81 H7
  HEY OL10 .....40 C7
  TOT/BURYW BL8 .....38 C2
Mizpah Gv TOT/BURYW BL8 .....38 E2
Mizzy Rd WHIT OL12 .....28 B3
Moadlock MPL/ROM SK6 .....101 M8
Moat Av WYTH/NTH M22 .....109 M8
Moatfield Gdns BOL BL1 .....2 A2
Moat Gdns WYTH/NTH M22 .....109 M8
Moat Hall Av ECC M30 .....84 D4
Moat House St WGNE/HIN WN2 .....48 D5
Moat Rd WYTH/NTH M22 .....109 M8
Mobberley Cl BNG/LEV M19 .....99 H8
Mobberley Rd BOLE BL2 .....37 G4
  WILM/AE SK9 .....126 A3
Mocha Pde BRO M7 .....87 G1
Modbury Cl BRAM/HZG SK7 .....121 J3
Mode Hill La WHTF M45 .....55 M4
Model Cottages
  HALE/TIMP WA15 * .....109 G8
Mode Wheel Rd South
  SALQ M50 .....86 A3
Modwen Rd ORD M5 .....86 B6
Moelfre Dr CHD/CHDH SK8 .....120 E5
Moffat Cl BOLE BL2 .....37 J6
Moggle La MCFLDN SK10 .....129 K3
Moisant St BOLS/LL BL3 .....52 A1
Mold St BOL BL1 .....36 B1
  OLD OL1 .....9 H2
Molesworth St MILN OL16 .....11 G5
Mollets Wd DTN/ASHW M34 .....90 D7
Mollington Rd WYTH/NTH M22 .....119 G4
Mollis Gv OLD OL1 .....60 B1
Molyneux Rd BNG/LEV M19 .....99 M3
  WHTN BL5 .....50 E3
Molyneux St WGN WN1 .....15 J3
  WHIT OL12 .....10 A2
Mona Av CHD/CHDH SK8 .....119 M5
  STRET M32 .....96 F1
Monaco Dr WYTH/NTH M22 .....110 A2
Monarch Cl IRL M44 .....94 B6
  ROY/SHW OL2 .....59 H2
Mona Rd CHAD OL9 .....8 A9
Monart Rd BKLY M9 .....73 H3
Mona St HYDE SK14 .....102 B2
  SLFD M6 .....71 M8
  WGNE/HIN WN2 .....14 E3
Mona Wy IRL M44 .....94 E4
Moncrieffe St BOLS/LL BL3 .....3 G7
Mond Rd IRL M44 .....83 L8
Money Ash Rd
  HALE/TIMP WA15 .....116 F1
Monfa Av OFTN SK2 .....112 D8
Monica Av CHH M8 .....72 C2
Monica Gv BNG/LEV M19 .....99 J4
Monica Ter AIMK WN4 .....78 E2
Monks Cl MILN OL16 .....29 H6
Monksdale Av URM M41 .....95 L2
Monks Hall Gv ECC M30 .....85 J2
Monks La BOLE BL2 .....37 G6
Monks' Rd GLSP SK13 .....104 B6
Monkton Av GTN M18 .....99 H1
Monkwood Dr BKLY M9 * .....73 H4
Monmouth Av BURY BL9 .....25 J5
  SALE M33 .....96 C7
Monmouth Crs AIMK WN4 .....78 F2
Monmouth Rd
  CHD/CHDH SK8 .....120 C5
Monmouth St CHAD OL9 .....8 C9
  GTN M18 .....89 H6
  MDTN M24 .....57 M4
  ROCH OL11 .....10 D7
Monroe Cl SLFD M6 .....71 H8
  WGNS/IIMK WN3 .....63 K1
Monsal Av BRO M7 .....71 K5
  OFTN SK2 .....113 G5
Monsall Cl BURY BL9 .....55 K2
Monsall Rd NEWH/MOS M40 .....73 H6
Monsall St NEWH/MOS M40 .....73 G7
  OLDS OL8 .....75 H1
Mons Av ROCH OL11 .....27 M4
Montague Rd BOLS/LL BL3 * .....51 L1
Montague Wy STLY SK15 .....91 H3
Montagu Rd OFTN SK2 .....113 G5
Montagu St MPL/ROM SK6 .....114 E2
Montana Sq OP/CLY M11 .....89 H1
Montcliffe Crs OLDTF/WHR M16 .....98 C3
Monteagle St BKLY M9 .....56 F8
Montford Ri WGNE/HIN WN2 .....48 D2
Montford St SALQ M50 .....86 C4
Montfort Cl WHTN BL5 .....50 A6
Montgomery ROCH OL11 .....10 D7
Montgomery Dr BURY BL9 .....55 L2
Montgomery Rd
  BRUN/LGST M13 .....99 J2
Montgomery St OLDS OL8 .....74 F2
  ROCH OL11 .....27 M8
Montgomery Wy RAD M26 .....37 M7
Monton Av ECC M30 .....85 H1
Montondale ECC M30 .....84 F1
Montonfields Rd ECC M30 .....84 F1
Monton Gn ECC M30 .....70 A8
Monton La ECC M30 .....85 G2
Monton Mill Gdns ECC M30 .....84 F1

Monton Rd ECC M30 .....85 G1
  RDSH SK5 .....100 F8
Monton St BOLS/LL BL3 .....52 B1
  RAD M26 .....54 C1
  RUSH/FAL M14 .....87 K8
Montpellior Rd
  WYTH/NTH M22 .....118 F2
Montreal St BNG/LEV M19 .....99 L3
  OLDS OL8 .....59 J8
Montrose Av BOLE BL2 .....3 L1
  DID/WITH M20 .....98 C7
  DUK SK16 .....90 F5
  OFTN SK2 .....121 J1
  RAMS BL0 .....24 D2
  STRET M32 .....96 E2
  WGNW/BIL/OR WN5 .....46 F5
Montrose Crs BNG/LEV M19 .....99 K5
Montrose Dr EDGW/EG BL7 .....22 F5
Montrose St ROCH OL11 .....41 M4
Montserrat Brow BOL BL1 .....34 F1
Montserrat Rd BOL BL1 .....34 F1
Monument Man WGN WN1 * .....47 M2
Monument Rd WGN WN1 .....48 A2
Monyash Ms GLSP SK13 .....104 A3
Monyash St WGNNW/ST WN6 .....30 B4
Moody St WGN RUSH/FAL M14 .....99 G2
Moon St CHAD OL9 .....8 D4
Moor Av WGNNW/ST WN6 .....30 B4
Moor Bank La MILN OL16 .....29 G8
Moorbank La MILN OL16 .....43 H1
Moorbottom Rd
  TOT/BURYW BL8 .....18 B6
Moorby Av BNG/LEV M19 .....99 H8
Moorby St OLD OL1 .....9 L3
Moorby Wk BOLS/LL BL3 * .....2 E6
Moor Cl RAD M26 .....38 B7
Moorclose St MDTN M24 .....57 M4
Moorcock Av SWIN M27 .....70 E4
Moor Crs UPML OL3 .....61 L1
Moorcroft RAMS BL0 .....19 G2
  ROCH OL11 .....42 C1
Moorcroft Dr BNG/LEV M19 .....99 J8
Moorcroft Rd NTHM/RTH M23 .....109 J3
Moorcroft St DROY M43 * .....89 K3
  OLDS OL8 .....74 F2
Moordale Av OLDE OL4 .....60 B3
Moordale St DID/WITH M20 .....98 D7
Moordown Cl CHH M8 .....72 E6
Moor Edge Rd MOSL OL5 .....77 J3
Mooredge Ter ROY/SHW OL2 .....59 H2
Moore Dr RNFD/HAY WA11 .....78 C6
Moor End WYTH/NTH M22 .....110 A4
Moor End Av BRO M7 .....71 M4
Moor End Rd MPL/ROM SK6 .....115 K7
Moore's Ct BOL BL1 .....35 M4
Moores La WGNNW/ST WN6 .....31 G2
Moore St MILN OL16 .....10 F5
  WGN WN1 .....48 A2
  WGN WN1 .....15 K1
Moorfield EDGW/EG BL7 .....17 G6
  WALK M28 .....68 C5
  WALK M28 .....69 J4
Moorfield Av DID/WITH M20 .....98 C6
  DTN/ASHW M34 .....101 K3
  LIT OL15 .....21 J5
  STLY SK15 .....92 A5
Moorfield Cha FWTH BL4 .....53 C5
Moorfield Cl IRL M44 .....94 E1
  SWIN M27 .....70 A6
Moorfield Crs
  GOL/RIS/CUL WA3 .....80 D5
Moorfield Dr HYDE SK14 .....91 H7
  WILM/AE SK9 .....126 C7
Moorfield Gv BOLE BL2 .....36 E3
  HTNM SK4 .....99 L8
  SALE M33 .....109 G1
Moorfield Hts STLY SK15 .....77 H5
  STLY SK15 .....77 K6
Moorfield Ms ROY/SHW OL2 * .....43 L5
Moorfield Pl WHIT OL12 * .....28 B3
Moorfield Rd DID/WITH M20 .....98 C6
  IRL M44 .....94 E1
  OLDS OL8 .....74 E2
  POY/DIS SK12 .....122 B8
  TOT/BURYW BL8 .....38 C5
  WILM/AE SK9 .....127 J1
Moorfield St
  DID/WITH M20 .....98 E5
  HYDE SK14 .....93 G6
  WGNE/HIN WN2 .....64 E7
Moorfield Ter HYDE SK14 .....93 G7
Moorgate BURY BL9 .....5 G3
Moorgate Av DID/WITH M20 .....98 C6
  ROCH OL11 .....27 K5
Moorgate Ct BOLE BL2 .....3 K1
Moorgate Dr STLY SK15 .....77 H6
  TYLD M29 .....67 M6
Moorgate La LIT OL15 .....21 J5
Moorgate Ms STLY SK15 * .....77 H5
Moorgate Rd RAD M26 .....38 B4
  STLY SK15 .....77 H5
Moorgate St UPML OL3 .....61 L4
Moorhead St ANC M4 .....7 K1
Moorhey Rd LHULT M38 .....52 E6
Moorhey St OLDE OL4 .....59 L6
Moor Hl ROCH OL11 .....27 J3
Moorhouse Farm
  MILN OL16 .....29 H6
Moor House Fold
  MILN OL16 .....29 H6
Moorings Cl WGN WN1 .....15 M4
Moorings Rd TRPK M17 .....85 L4
The Moorings MOSL OL5 .....77 H1
  POY/DIS SK12 .....124 A6
  WALK M28 .....69 K7
Moorland Av CHH M8 .....72 C2
  DROY M43 .....89 H3
  MILN OL16 .....29 G6
  ROCH OL11 .....27 J3
  SALE M33 .....108 F1
  UPML OL3 .....61 J1
  WHIT OL12 .....20 A6
Moorland Crs WHIT OL12 .....20 B5
Moorland Dr CHD/CHDH SK8 .....120 B4
  HOR/BR BL6 .....34 C1
  LHULT M38 .....52 B6
Moorland Rd AIMK WN4 .....64 D7
  DID/WITH M20 .....110 E1
  OFTN SK2 .....112 D8
  STLY SK15 .....77 H7
  WGNE/HIN WN2 .....49 H7
Moorlands Av LEIGH WN7 .....81 J1
  URM M41 .....95 L1
Moorlands Crs MOSL OL5 .....77 H3
Moorlands Dr MOSL OL5 .....77 H1
Moorland St ROY/SHW OL2 .....59 H2
Moorland St WHIT OL12 .....28 B3
Moorlands Vw
  BOLS/LL BL3 .....51 K2
Moorland Ter WHIT OL12 .....27 K3

Moor La BOL BL1 .....2 D5
  BRAM/HZG SK7 .....128 D3
  BRO M7 .....71 K4
  LEIGH WN7 .....66 B4
  NTHM/RTH M23 .....109 K2
  UPML OL3 .....61 M2
  URM M41 .....95 K1
  WILM/AE SK9 .....126 A7
Moor Nook SALE M33 .....109 G1
Moor Park Av ROCH OL11 .....41 L2
Moor Park Rd DID/WITH M20 .....110 F4
Moor Platt Cl HOR/BR BL6 .....34 C1
Moor Rd NTHM/RTH M23 .....109 H4
  TOT/BURYW BL8 .....18 D6
  WGNW/BIL/OR WN5 .....46 B6
Moorsholme Av
  NEWH/MOS M40 .....73 K5
Moorside HALE/TIMP WA15 * .....108 F5
  ROCH OL11 .....42 C1
  SWIN M27 .....70 A5
Moorside Av BOL BL1 .....35 K2
  BOLE BL2 .....38 A3
  DROY M43 .....89 M1
  FWTH BL4 .....52 E5
  OLDE OL4 .....44 C8
Moorside Cl GLSP SK13 .....104 E4
Moorside Crs DTN/ASHW M34 .....90 C8
Moorside La DTN/ASHW M34 .....90 C8
Moor Side La RAMS BL0 .....19 L5
Moorside Rd BRO M7 .....71 M3
  CHH M8 .....72 D3
  EDGW/EG BL7 .....17 H4
  HTNM SK4 .....111 K2
  MOSL OL5 .....77 H3
  SWIN M27 .....69 M5
  TOT/BURYW BL8 .....24 B7
  URM M41 .....95 H1
Moorside St DROY M43 .....89 L1
Moorside Vw TOT/BURYW BL8 .....24 C6
Moorside Wk
  WGNW/BIL/OR WN5 .....46 A4
Moorsley Dr BKLY M9 .....57 J8
Moor St BURY BL9 .....5 G3
  ECC M30 .....84 E3
  HEY OL10 .....40 E2
  OLD OL1 * .....59 L5
  ROY/SHW OL2 .....43 K6
  SWIN M27 .....70 A4
Moorsview RAMS BL0 .....18 G6
Moorton Av BNG/LEV M19 .....99 J5
Moorton Dr WGNE/HIN WN2 .....64 D1
Moor Wk HULME M15 .....87 J8
Moortop Cl BKLY M9 .....56 F7
Moor Top Pl HTNM SK4 .....12 A1
Moor View Cl WHIT OL12 .....27 J3
Moorville Dr SLFD M6 .....70 F7
Moorville Rd SLFD M6 .....70 F7
Moorway Dr BKLY M9 .....57 K8
Moorwood Dr OLDS OL8 .....59 M8
  SALE M33 .....108 B1
Mora Av CHAD OL9 .....8 B1
Moran Cl WILM/AE SK9 .....127 H2
Morano Dr WGNE/HIN WN2 .....64 D1
Moran Wk HULME M15 .....87 J8
Morar Dr BOLE BL2 .....37 K5
Morar Rd DUK SK16 .....91 G5
Mora St BKLY M9 .....73 J5
Moravian Cl BOLS/LL BL3 .....50 F3
Moravian Fld DROY M43 * .....89 K4
Moray Cl RAMS BL0 .....18 D8
Moray Rd CHAD OL9 .....58 D2
Morbourne Cl WGTN/LGST M12 .....88 B6
Morden Av AIMK WN4 .....78 C3
Morecambe Cl NEWH/MOS M40 .....73 L6
Morely Av OLDE OL4 .....60 B3
Moresby Cl LEIGH WN7 .....66 A7
Moresby Dr DID/WITH M20 .....110 E4
Moreton Av BRAM/HZG SK7 .....121 G7
  SALE M33 .....108 B1
  STRET M32 .....97 G2
  WHTF M45 .....55 J3
Moreton Cl DUK SK16 .....91 G6
  GOL/RIS/CUL WA3 .....79 J3
Moreton Dr LEIGH WN7 .....81 H3
  POY/DIS SK12 .....122 B8
  TOT/BURYW BL8 .....38 C5
  WILM/AE SK9 .....127 J1
Moreton La OFTN SK2 .....112 F5
Moreton St CHAD OL9 .....58 C4
Morgan Pl RDSH SK5 .....100 C8
Morgan St LIT OL15 .....21 M7
Morillon Rd IRL M44 .....83 K8
Morland Rd NM/HAY SK22 .....125 J7
  OLDTF/WHR M16 .....86 F8
Morley Av RUSH/FAL M14 .....98 D3
  SWIN M27 .....70 B6
Morley Green Rd
  WILM/AE SK9 .....126 A3
Morley Rd RAD M26 .....38 A8
Morley's La TYLD M29 .....82 D1
Morley St ATH M46 .....66 F1
  BOLS/LL BL3 .....2 B6
  BURY BL9 .....4 F8
  GLSP SK13 .....105 G4
  MILN OL16 .....11 J1
  WHTF M45 .....55 H4
Morley Wy UPML OL3 .....61 L7
Morna Wk WGTN/LGST M12 .....88 A3
Morningside Cl MILN OL16 * .....11 J6
  OP/CLY M11 .....89 J5
Morningside Dr
  DID/WITH M20 .....110 E2
Mornington Av
  CHD/CHDH SK8 .....111 G8
Mornington Crs RUSH/FAL M14 .....98 D4
Mornington Rd ATH M46 .....51 J6
  BOL BL1 .....35 L4
  CHD/CHDH SK8 .....111 G8
  ROCH OL11 .....42 C5
  SALE M33 .....97 G7
  WGNE/HIN WN2 .....49 J7
Morpeth Cl AULW OL7 .....75 H8
  WGTN/LGST M12 .....88 B7
Morpeth St SWIN M27 .....70 B6
Morrell Rd WYTH/NTH M22 .....110 D3
Morris Gn BOLS/LL BL3 .....51 K2
Morris Green La BOLS/LL BL3 .....51 M1
Morris Green St BOLS/LL BL3 * .....51 M1
Morris Gv URM M41 .....95 H4
Morrison St BOLS/LL BL3 .....51 K8
Morris St BOL BL1 .....3 G4
  DID/WITH M20 .....98 E5
  OLDE OL4 .....9 M7
  RAD M26 .....39 H7
  TYLD M29 .....67 J3
  WGN WN1 .....15 J4
  WGNE/HIN WN2 .....49 G7
Morrowfield Av CHH M8 .....72 C5
Morse Rd NEWH/MOS M40 .....73 L7

Mortar St OLDE OL4 .....59 M5
Mortfield Gdns BOL BL1 * .....2 A2
Mortfield La BOL BL1 .....2 A2
Mortimer Av BKLY M9 .....57 H8
Mortimer St OLD OL1 .....9 L2
Mortlake Cl WALK M28 .....68 C3
Mortlake Dr NEWH/MOS M40 .....73 L7
Mort La TYLD M29 .....68 B2
Morton Av WGNS/IIMK WN3 .....14 D9
Morton Cl WGNS/IIMK WN3 .....62 F2
Morton St FAIL M35 .....73 M5
  HTNM SK4 .....100 B8
  MDTN M24 .....57 K3
  RAD M26 .....54 E2
Mort St FWTH BL4 .....52 E4
  LEIGH WN7 .....66 B3
  WGNE/HIN WN2 .....49 K7
  WGNNW/ST WN6 .....14 B1
Morven Av BRAM/HZG SK7 .....122 D3
Morven Dr NTHM/RTH M23 .....109 K7
Morven Gv BOLE BL2 .....37 J5
Morville Dr WGNS/IIMK WN3 .....47 L3
Morville Rd CCHDY M21 .....98 A3
Morville St CMANE M1 * .....7 L6
Moscow Rd EDGY/DAV SK3 .....12 F9
Moscow Rd East EDGY/DAV SK3 .....12 F9
Mosedale Cl NTHM/RTH M23 .....109 H6
  TYLD M29 .....67 M6
Mosedale Rd MDTN M24 .....57 G2
Moseldene Rd OFTN SK2 .....113 G7
Moseley Rd BNG/LEV M19 .....99 J4
  CHD/CHDH SK8 .....120 B1
  RUSH/FAL M14 .....99 H4
Moseley St EDGY/DAV SK3 .....13 G7
Mosley Av BURY BL9 .....25 J7
Mosley Cl HALE/TIMP WA15 .....108 C5
Mosley Common Rd WALK M28 .....68 B8
Mosley Rd HALE/TIMP WA15 .....108 E6
  TRPK M17 .....85 M4
Mosley Rd North TRPK M17 .....85 M4
Mosley St CMANE M1 * .....6 F5
  CMANW M2 .....6 F5
  RAD M26 .....38 C8
Mossack Av WYTH/NTH M22 .....118 F3
Moss Av LEIGH WN7 .....66 E7
  MILN OL16 .....11 M6
  WGNW/BIL/OR WN5 .....62 A1
  CHH M8 .....72 D4
Moss Bank BRAM/HZG SK7 .....120 E7
  CHH M8 .....72 D4
Moss Bank Av DROY M43 .....89 M2
Moss Bank Cl BOL BL1 .....22 A8
Moss Bank Ct DROY M43 .....89 M2
Moss Bank Gv SWIN M27 .....69 M2
Moss Bank Pk BOL BL1 * .....35 J1
Moss Bank Rd SWIN M27 .....70 A2
Moss Bank Wy BOL BL1 .....35 L1
Mossbray Av BNG/LEV M19 .....99 G8
Moss Bridge Rd MILN OL16 .....11 K8
Mossbrook Dr LHULT M38 .....52 B6
Moss Brook Rd BKLY M9 .....73 H5
Moss Cl RAD M26 .....38 A7
Mossclough Ct BKLY M9 .....73 H5
Moss Colliery Rd SWIN M27 .....70 B1
Moss Croft Cl URM M41 .....95 H1
Mossdale Av BOL BL1 .....35 G5
Mossdale Rd AIMK WN4 .....63 K4
  NTHM/RTH M23 .....109 J3
  SALE M33 .....108 C3
Mossdown Rd ROY/SHW OL2 .....59 L1
Moss Dr HOR/BR BL6 .....34 C1
Moss Farm Cl MDTN M24 .....57 L6
Mossfield Cl BURY BL9 .....5 L2
  HTNM SK4 .....12 A2
Mossfield Ct BOL BL1 .....2 C2
Mossfield Dr BKLY M9 .....57 K8
Mossfield Rd FWTH BL4 .....53 J7
  FWTH BL4 .....53 J7
  HALE/TIMP WA15 .....109 G6
  SWIN M27 .....70 B2
Moss Fold TYLD M29 .....67 M5
Mossgate Rd ROY/SHW OL2 .....43 J4
Moss Grange Av
  OLDTF/WHR M16 * .....98 A1
Moss Gn PART M31 .....95 J6
Moss Gv ROY/SHW OL2 .....43 K4
  WGNNW/ST WN6 .....31 H4
Mossgrove Rd
  HALE/TIMP WA15 .....108 C6
Mosshall Cl HULME M15 .....87 J8
Moss Hall Rd BURY BL9 .....40 A4
Moss Hey Dr NTHM/RTH M23 .....109 M3
Moss Hey St ROY/SHW OL2 .....43 M6
Moss House La WALK M28 .....68 D4
Moss House Ter BKLY M9 * .....72 F3
Mossland Cl HEY OL10 .....41 G4
Mossland Gv BOLS/LL BL3 .....51 G2
Moss La AULW OL7 .....90 B2
  BOL BL1 .....35 K1
  BRAM/HZG SK7 .....120 E7
  FWTH BL4 .....53 L7
  GOL/RIS/CUL WA3 .....79 L7
  HALE/TIMP WA15 .....108 B8
  HALE/TIMP WA15 .....108 C5
  HOR/BR BL6 .....33 J2
  HYDE SK14 .....103 J4
  IRL M44 .....94 A7
  LYMM WA13 .....106 B3
  MCFLDN SK10 .....131 K2
  MDTN M24 .....57 J7
  MILN OL16 .....11 C6
  PART M31 .....106 D1
  ROY/SHW OL2 .....59 K1
  SALE M33 .....96 B8
  SALE M33 .....107 L1
  SWIN M27 .....70 A3
  TYLD M29 .....82 D3
  URM M41 .....85 H7
  WALK M28 .....69 J1
  WGNE/HIN WN2 .....30 B1
  WGNNW/ST WN6 .....30 B1
  WHTF M45 .....55 J4
  WILM/AE SK9 .....119 G6
  WILM/AE SK9 .....130 E3
Moss La East
  OLDTF/WHR M16 .....87 H8
Moss La West HULME M15 .....87 K8
  RUSH/FAL M14 .....87 K8
Moss Lea BOL BL1 .....22 A8
Mosslee Av CHH M8 .....72 C1
Mossley Rd AUL OL6 .....76 F8
  MOSL OL5 .....61 G8
Moss Meadow WHTN BL5 .....50 C1
Moss Meadow Rd SLFD M6 * .....70 F8
Mossmere Rd
  CHD/CHDH SK8 .....111 K8
Moss Mill St MILN OL16 .....11 J8
Moss Park Rd STRET M32 .....96 D2
Moss Pl BURY BL9 .....4 E9

Moss Rd SALE M33 95 L8
STRET M32 96 F1
WGNW/BIL/OR WN5 62 A1
WILM/AE SK9 130 F2
Moss Rose WILM/AE SK9 130 E2
Moss Rw BURY BL9 4 F6
Moss Shaw Wy RAD M26 38 B7
Moss Side La MILN OL16 11 M9
Moss Side Rd IRL M44 94 A6
Moss St BRO M7 72 A7
BURY BL9 4 E5
BURY BL9 25 G2
DROY M43 89 L2
FWTH BL4 53 H3
HEY OL10 40 F2
HYDE SK14 93 G7
MILN OL16 11 J6
OLDE OL4 60 B4
WGNNW/ST WN6 14 B1
WGNS/IIMK WN3 64 C1
WGNW/BIL/OR WN5 * 46 E6
Moss St West AULW OL7 * 90 C2
Moss Ter MILN OL16 11 J6
WGNW/BIL/OR WN5 46 E7
The Moss MDTN M24 57 L6
Moss Vale Crs STRET M32 85 J8
Moss Vale Rd STRET M32 96 C1
Moss View Rd BOLE BL2 37 H4
PART M31 106 D1
Mossway MDTN M24 57 J7
Moss Wy SALE M33 96 B8
Mosswood Pk DID/WITH M20 110 E4
Mosswood Rd WILM/AE SK9 127 J3
Mossylea Cl MDTN M24 57 L7
Mossy Lea Fold
WGNNW/ST WN6 30 C1
Moston Bank Av BKLY M9 73 H5
Moston La BKLY M9 73 H4
NEWH/MOS M40 73 K4
Moston La East
NEWH/MOS M40 74 B3
Moston Rd MDTN M24 58 A6
RDSH SK5 100 C5
Moston St BRO M7 72 C5
Mostyn Av BURY BL9 25 J7
CHD/CHDH SK8 120 A3
RUSH/FAL M14 99 H4
Mostyn Rd BRAM/HZG SK7 121 L3
Mostyn St DUK SK16 91 J4
Motcombe Farm Rd
CHD/CHDH SK8 119 K3
Motcombe Gv CHD/CHDH SK8 119 J1
Motcombe Rd CHD/CHDH SK8 119 J2
Motherwell Av BNG/LEV M19 99 K3
Mottershead Av BOLS/LL BL3 37 K8
Mottershead Rd
WYTH/NTH M22 109 L8
Mottram Av CCHDY M21 97 M7
Mottram Cl CHD/CHDH SK8 111 K7
Mottram Dr HALE/TIMP WA15 108 D7
WGNS/IIMK WN3 47 L7
Mottram Fold STKP SK1 13 J6
Mottram Moor HYDE SK14 92 F8
Mottram Old Rd HYDE SK14 102 D4
STLY SK15 91 M3
Mottram Rd HYDE SK14 102 C2
HYDE SK14 103 K4
SALE M33 109 H1
STLY SK15 91 M3
WILM/AE SK9 130 E3
Mottram St STKP SK1 13 J6
Mough La CHAD OL9 74 A1
Mouldsworth Av
DID/WITH M20 98 D5
HTNM SK4 100 A6
Moulton St CHH M8 72 B8
Mouncey St CMANE M1 * 7 G8
Mountain Ash WHIT OL12 27 L1
Mountain Ash Cl SALE M33 95 M7
WHIT OL12 27 L1
Mountain Gv WALK M28 52 F8
Mountain St MOSL OL5 76 F3
NEWH/MOS M40 74 A8
STKP SK1 13 M3
WALK M28 52 F8
Mount Av LIT OL15 21 L5
WHIT OL12 21 J8
Mountbatten Av DUK SK16 91 J6
Mountbatten Cl BURY BL9 55 L2
Mountbatten St GTN M18 88 F7
Mount Carmel Crs ORD M5 * 86 F5
Mount Crs WGNW/BIL/OR WN5 46 C6
Mount Dr MPL/ROM SK6 114 C7
URM M41 96 C2
Mountfield PWCH M25 55 L8
Mountfield Rd BRAM/HZG SK7 121 G7
EDGY/DAV SK3 12 D9
Mountfield Wk OP/CLY M11 88 C3
Mount Fold MDTN M24 57 K5
Mountford Av CHH M8 * 72 C2
Mount Gv CHD/CHDH SK8 110 C7
Mount La UPML OL3 61 H3
Mountmorres Cl WHTN BL5 51 J5
Mount Pleasant BOLS/LL BL3 * 3 M9
BRAM/HZG SK7 121 M1
BURY BL9 25 J1
MDTN M24 56 F4
PWCH M25 56 B4
WILM/AE SK9 126 F3
Mount Pleasant Rd
DTN/ASHW M34 101 J2
FWTH BL4 52 C4
Mount Pleasant St AUL OL6 75 M8
DTN/ASHW M34 90 C6
HOR/BR BL6 34 A3
OLDE OL4 * 59 L5
Mount Pleasant Wk RAD M26 38 D8
Mount Rd GTN M18 * 88 E7
HTNM SK4 12 D2
HYDE SK14 102 D6
MDTN M24 57 K5
PWCH M25 55 M5
Mountroyal Cl HYDE SK14 91 J7
Mount St Joseph's Rd
BOLS/LL BL3 35 L7
Mountside Cl WHIT OL12 28 C2
Mountside Crs PWCH M25 55 J8
Mount Sion Houses RAD M26 * 54 A2
Mount Sion Rd RAD M26 54 B2
Mount Skip La LHULT M38 52 D8
Mount St BOL BL1 36 B3
CMANW M2 6 F6
CSLFD M3 6 B2
ECC M30 84 F4
GLSP SK13 104 F4
HEY OL10 41 G3
HOR/BR BL6 34 A3
HYDE SK14 102 B2
LEIGH WN7 65 M8
RAMS BL0 18 E5
ROCH OL11 41 M3
ROY/SHW OL2 59 H1
SWIN M27 70 C5
WHIT OL12 10 C3
The Mount ALT WA14 108 A7
HALE/TIMP WA15 117 L4
Mount Vw WGNS/IIMK WN3 15 J9
Mount View Rd ROY/SHW OL2 44 A6
Mount Zion Rd BURY BL9 39 J7
Mousell St CHH M8 72 D8
Mouselow Cl GLSP SK13 104 C1
Mowbray Av PWCH M25 71 M2
SALE M33 108 F1
Mowbray St AULW OL7 90 C2
BOL BL1 * 35 L3
OLD OL1 9 K6
ROCH OL11 41 L1
STKP SK1 13 K6
Mow Halls La UPML OL3 61 K3
Moxley Rd CHH M8 72 B3
Moxon Wy AIMK WN4 64 A8
Moyse Av TOT/BURYW BL8 24 C7
Mozart Cl ANC M4 7 M2
Muirfield Av MPL/ROM SK6 101 K8
Muirfield Cl BOLS/LL BL3 51 J1
HEY OL10 41 G3
NEWH/MOS M40 73 M5
WILM/AE SK9 127 H4
Muirfield Dr TYLD M29 67 M5
Mulberry Av GOL/RIS/CUL WA3 80 C5
Mulberry Cl CHD/CHDH SK8 119 L5
RAD M26 54 D2
ROCH OL11 10 C8
WGNW/BIL/OR WN5 47 G6
Mulberry Ct SLFD M6 * 86 D1
Mulberry Ms HTNM SK4 13 G2
Mulberry Mount St
EDGY/DAV SK3 13 H7
Mulberry Rd SLFD M6 86 D2
Mulberry St AUL OL6 * 90 F1
CMANW M2 6 E5
Mulberry Wk DROY M43 89 H4
SALE M33 96 A6
Mule St BOLE BL2 3 H3
Mulgrave Rd WALK M28 69 K4
Mulgrave St BOLS/LL BL3 51 M2
SWIN M27 70 A3
Mullacre Rd WYTH/NTH M22 110 A6
Mull Av WGTN/LGST M12 88 B7
Mullein Cl GOL/RIS/CUL WA3 80 A4
Mulliner St BOL BL1 * 36 C3
Mullins Av NEWLW WA12 78 F7
Mullion Cl BNG/LEV M19 100 A2
Mullion Dr HALE/TIMP WA15 108 B5
Mullion Wk CHH M8 72 E6
Mulmount Cl OLDS OL8 74 F1
Mumps Rbt OLD OL1 9 M5
Munday St ANC M4 88 A3
Municipal Cl HEY OL10 * 41 G2
Munn Rd BKLY M9 56 F7
Munro Av WGNW/BIL/OR WN5 46 B6
WYTH/NTH M22 119 H2
Munster St ANC M4 * 7 G1
Muriel St BRO M7 72 A7
HEY OL10 41 H2
MILN OL16 11 K8
Murieston Rd
HALE/TIMP WA15 117 G2
Murphy Cl WGNS/IIMK WN3 14 B9
Murrayfield ROCH OL11 27 H6
Murray Rd BURY BL9 4 F5
Murray St ANC M4 7 L3
ATH M46 66 E2
BRO M7 72 A6
Musabbir Sq MILN OL16 * 11 G2
Musbury Av CHD/CHDH SK8 120 D2
Museum St CMANW M2 6 F6
Musgrave Gdns BOL BL1 35 M4
Musgrave Rd BOL BL1 35 M4
WYTH/NTH M22 118 F1
Muslin St ORD M5 86 F3
Muter Av WYTH/NTH M22 119 H2
Mutual St HEY OL10 41 H1
Mycroft Cl LEIGH WN7 66 B4
Myerscroft Cl NEWH/MOS M40 74 A4
Myrrh St BOL BL1 36 B1
Myrtle Av AIMK WN4 63 J6
LEIGH WN7 66 B5
Myrtle Bank PWCH M25 71 K3
Myrtle Cl OLDS OL8 9 H9
Myrtle Gdns BURY BL9 5 K4
Myrtle Gv DROY M43 89 M2
DTN/ASHW M34 100 C1
PWCH M25 71 L2
WGNW/BIL/OR WN5 * 62 A8
WHTF M45 55 G2
Myrtleleaf Gv ORD M5 * 86 A2
Myrtle Pl BRO M7 71 M8
Myrtle Rd MDTN M24 57 M3
PART M31 106 A2
Myrtle St BOL BL1 2 B3
EDGY/DAV SK3 12 B6
OLDTF/WHR M16 * 86 F8
OP/CLY M11 88 B4
WGN WN1 14 E4
Myrtle St North BURY BL9 5 K4
Myrtle St South BURY BL9 5 K5
My St ORD M5 86 B3
Mytham Rd BOLS/LL BL3 53 L1
Mytton Rd BOL BL1 35 L1
Mytton St HULME M15 87 H7


## N


Nabbs Fold TOT/BURYW BL8 24 C1
Nabbs Wy TOT/BURYW BL8 24 D3
Naburn Cl RDSH SK5 100 F6
Naburn Dr WGNW/BIL/OR WN5 46 B7
Naburn St BRUN/LGST M13 88 A8
Nada Rd CHH M8 72 C3
Nadine St SLFD M6 86 B1
Nadin St OLDS OL8 75 H1
Nairn Cl NEWH/MOS M40 * 88 B1
WGNNW/ST WN6 31 C3
Nailgate MILN OL16 42 F2
Nall St BNG/LEV M19 99 L5
MILN OL16 29 H6
Nameplate Cl ECC M30 84 E2
Nancy St HULME M15 87 G6
Nandywell BOLS/LL BL3 53 L1
Nangreave Rd OFTN SK2 112 E6
Nangreaves St LEIGH WN7 65 M7
Nan Nook Rd NTHM/RTH M23 109 J3
Nansen Av ECC M30 84 F1
Nansen Cl STRET M32 86 B8
Nansen Rd CHD/CHDH SK8 110 D8
Nansen St OP/CLY M11 88 B4
SLFD M6 86 B2
STRET M32 86 B8
Nansmoss La WILM/AE SK9 126 B3
Nantwich Av WHIT OL12 28 C1
Nantwich Rd RUSH/FAL M14 98 D3
Nantwich Wk BOLS/LL BL3 * 36 B8
Napier Ct HULME M15 * 86 F6
Napier Gn ORD M5 86 E5
Napier Rd CCHDY M21 97 L4
ECC M30 84 F1
HTNM SK4 111 L1
Napier St BRAM/HZG SK7 121 M1
HYDE SK14 102 B3
ROY/SHW OL2 43 L4
SWIN M27 70 A5
Napier St East OLDS OL8 8 F8
Napier St West OLDS OL8 8 D9
Naples Rd EDGY/DAV SK3 111 L6
Naples St ANC M4 7 J1
Narbonne Av ECC M30 70 D8
Narborough Cl WGNE/HIN WN2 49 H8
Narbuth Dr CHH M8 72 C5
Narrowgate Brow
ROY/SHW OL2 43 G5
Narrow La MCFLDN SK10 129 L3
The Narrows ALT WA14 107 M8
Naseby Av BKLY M9 57 J8
Naseby Pl PWCH M25 55 M7
Naseby Rd RDSH SK5 100 B4
Naseby Wk WHTF M45 55 M4
Nash Rd TRPK M17 85 H4
Nash St HULME M15 87 H6
Nasmyth Av DTN/ASHW M34 90 D8
Nasmyth Rd ECC M30 84 F4
Nasmyth St CHH M8 72 F7
HOR/BR BL6 33 M1
Nately Rd OLDTF/WHR M16 * 97 K2
Nathan Dr CSLFD M3 6 C2
RNFD/HAY WA11 78 B6
Nathans Rd WYTH/NTH M22 109 M8
National Dr ORD M5 86 D4
Naunton Av LEIGH WN7 65 M7
Naunton Rd MDTN M24 57 L5
Naval St ANC M4 7 L3
Nave Ct SLFD M6 71 J8
Navenby Av OLDTF/WHR M16 86 F8
Navenby Rd WGNS/IIMK WN3 63 K2
Navigation Cl LEIGH WN7 66 B8
Navigation Rd ALT WA14 108 A5
Naylor Av GOL/RIS/CUL WA3 79 L4
Naylorfarm Av
WGNNW/ST WN6 30 C7
Naylor St ATH M46 66 F1
NEWH/MOS M40 88 A1
OLD OL1 9 H4
Nazeby Wk CHAD OL9 8 D9
Naze Ct OLD OL1 * 9 G2
Neal Av AUL OL6 91 G1
CHD/CHDH SK8 119 J4
Neale Av UPML OL3 61 M7
Neale Rd CCHDY M21 97 K5
Near Birches Pde OLDE OL4 60 B8
Nearbrook Rd WYTH/NTH M22 109 M8
Nearcroft Rd NTHM/RTH M23 109 L5
Near Hey Cl RAD M26 54 B1
Nearmaker Av
WYTH/NTH M22 109 M8
Nearmaker Rd
WYTH/NTH M22 109 M8
Neary Wy URM M41 84 F7
Neasden Gv BOLS/LL BL3 * 35 M7
Neath Av WYTH/NTH M22 110 A5
Neath Cl POY/DIS SK12 121 M7
WHTF M45 55 M5
Neath Fold BOLS/LL BL3 52 A1
Neath St CHAD OL9 8 F5
Nebo St BOLS/LL BL3 36 A8
Nebraska St BOL BL1 * 36 B3
Neden Cl OP/CLY M11 88 E4
Needham Av CCHDY M21 97 L4
Needwood Cl NEWH/MOS M40 73 G7
Needwood Rd MPL/ROM SK6 101 M7
Neenton Sq WGTN/LGST M12 88 D5
Neild Gdns LEIGH WN7 66 B8
Neild St CMANE M1 7 K7
OLDS OL8 59 H8
Neill St BRO M7 72 B8
Neilson Cl MDTN M24 57 M5
Nell Carrs RAMS BL0 19 H5
Nellie St HEY OL10 40 E2
Nell La CCHDY M21 98 B6
Nell St BOL BL1 22 C8
Nel Pan La LEIGH WN7 65 M4
Nelson Av ECC M30 85 G1
POY/DIS SK12 129 L1
Nelson Cl POY/DIS SK12 129 L1
Nelson Dr DROY M43 89 G2
IRL M44 94 B6
WGNE/HIN WN2 48 D4
Nelson Fold SWIN M27 70 D3
Nelson Rd BKLY M9 57 G7
Nelson Sq BOL BL1 2 F5
Nelson St ATH M46 66 E1
BOLS/LL BL3 3 G9
BOLS/LL BL3 * 53 L1
BRAM/HZG SK7 113 J8
BRO M7 72 A7
BRUN/LGST M13 87 L7
BURY BL9 4 F9
DTN/ASHW M34 90 C6
ECC M30 85 G2
FWTH BL4 53 H4
HEY OL10 41 G3
HOR/BR BL6 34 A1
HYDE SK14 102 B2
LIT OL15 21 M7
MDTN M24 57 M5
MILN OL16 10 F5
NEWH/MOS M40 73 G8
OLDE OL4 * 60 B7
ORD M5 86 B3
STRET M32 97 G3
TYLD M29 67 L4
WGNE/HIN WN2 49 G6
Nelson Wy CHAD OL9 * 58 D8
Nelstrop Crs HTNM SK4 100 A6
Nelstrop Rd HTNM SK4 99 M6
Nelstrop Rd North
BNG/LEV M19 100 A4
Nene Gv WGNE/HIN WN2 49 H8
Nepaul Rd BKLY M9 73 H3
Neptune Gdns BRO M7 71 M8
Nesbit St BOLE BL2 * 36 E1
Nesfield Rd NTHM/RTH M23 109 J2
Neston Av BOL BL1 22 C7
DID/WITH M20 98 D6
SALE M33 109 H2
Neston Cl ROY/SHW OL2 44 A5
Neston Gv EDGY/DAV SK3 112 A7
Neston Rd MILN OL16 28 F8
TOT/BURYW BL8 24 C8
Neston St OP/CLY M11 89 J5
Neston Wy WILM/AE SK9 127 H1
Netherbury Cl GTN M18 99 M1
Netherby Rd WGNNW/ST WN6 47 K1
Nethercote Av
NTHM/RTH M23 109 L6
Nethercroft ROCH OL11 27 H4
Nethercroft Rd
HALE/TIMP WA15 108 F7
Netherfield Cl OLDS OL8 58 F8
Netherfield Rd BOLS/LL BL3 52 B2
Netherfields LEIGH WN7 66 A5
WILM/AE SK9 130 D4
Netherhey La ROY/SHW OL2 58 F2
Nether Hey St OLDS OL8 59 L8
Netherhouse Rd ROY/SHW OL2 43 K5
Netherland St SALQ M50 86 C3
Netherlees OLDE OL4 60 A7
Nether St HYDE SK14 102 C4
WGTN/LGST M12 * 7 L7
Netherton Rd RUSH/FAL M14 98 D3
Nethervale Dr BKLY M9 73 H5
Netherwood FAIL M35 74 E4
Netherwood Rd
WYTH/NTH M22 109 M5
Netherwood Wy WHTN BL5 50 D2
Netley Av WHIT OL12 28 C1
Netley Gv OLDS OL8 * 59 M8
Netley Rd NTHM/RTH M23 109 K8
Nettlebarn Rd WYTH/NTH M22 109 M7
Nettleford Rd CCHDY M21 98 B4
Nettleton Gv BKLY M9 73 J3
Nevada St BOL BL1 * 36 B3
Nevendon Dr NTHM/RTH M23 109 J8
Nevern Cl BOL BL1 35 J4
Nevile Rd BRO M7 71 L4
Neville Cardus Wk
RUSH/FAL M14 98 F2
Neville Cl BOL BL1 2 D3
Neville Dr IRL M44 83 K8
Neville St BRAM/HZG SK7 121 M1
CHAD OL9 8 D4
WGNE/HIN WN2 64 D1
Nevill Rd BRAM/HZG SK7 121 G2
Nevin Av CHD/CHDH SK8 120 A3
Nevin Cl BRAM/HZG SK7 121 J5
Nevin Rd NEWH/MOS M40 74 A3
Nevis Gv BOL BL1 22 A7
Nevis St ROCH OL11 42 D2
Nevy Fold Av HOR/BR BL6 34 C1
New Allen St NEWH/MOS M40 87 M1
Newall Gv LEIGH WN7 66 C5
Newall Rd NTHM/RTH M23 118 B1
Newall St CHAD OL9 74 E2
LIT OL15 21 M6
Newark Av RAD M26 37 M7
RUSH/FAL M14 98 E1
Newark Park Wy ROY/SHW OL2 42 F6
Newark Rd RDSH SK5 100 C7
SWIN M27 70 E2
WGNE/HIN WN2 48 F8
WHIT OL12 28 C1
Newark Sq WHIT OL12 28 C1
Newark St WGNNW/ST WN6 14 A1
New Bailey St CSLFD M3 6 C4
Newbank Cha CHAD OL9 58 D4
Newbank Cl MDTN M24 57 L5
UPML OL3 61 J3
New Bank St TYLD M29 * 67 K4
WGTN/LGST M12 88 B7
New Barn Av AIMK WN4 78 F1
New Barn Cl ROY/SHW OL2 43 K5
New Barn La LEIGH WN7 81 H2
ROCH OL11 10 B9
New Barns Av CCHDY M21 97 M6
New Barn St BOL BL1 35 L3
MILN OL16 11 H9
ROY/SHW OL2 43 K5
New Barton St SLFD M6 70 F7
Newbeck Cl HOR/BR BL6 34 A3
Newbeck St ANC M4 * 7 H2
New Beech Rd HTNM SK4 111 H2
New Beech St HYDE SK14 102 A1
Newberry Gv EDGY/DAV SK3 112 A7
Newbold Hall Dr MILN OL16 11 L4
Newbold Moss MILN OL16 11 K4
Newbold St MILN OL16 11 M4
TOT/BURYW BL8 38 F2
Newboult Rd CHD/CHDH SK8 111 H6
Newbourne Cl BRAM/HZG SK7 121 M1
Newbreak Cl OLDE OL4 60 A4
Newbridge Cl AIMK WN4 78 A1
Newbridge Gdns BOLE BL2 23 H8
New Bridge Gdns BURY BL9 39 H7
Newbridge La STKP SK1 13 L4
New Bridge St CSLFD M3 6 F1
Newbridge Vw MOSL OL5 * 77 G4
New Briggs Fold EDGW/EG BL7 22 B2
New Broad La MILN OL16 42 F1
Newbrook Av CCHDY M21 110 A1
Newbrook Rd ATH M46 51 J6
New Brunswick St HOR/BR BL6 33 L1
New Buildings Pl MILN OL16 10 E3
Newburn Av BKLY M9 57 J8
Newburn Cl WGNS/IIMK WN3 47 H8
Newbury Av SALE M33 95 M8
Newbury Cl CHD/CHDH SK8 120 C6
Newbury Ct
HALE/TIMP WA15 * 108 C6
Newbury Dr ECC M30 84 E1
URM M41 84 F7
Newbury Gv HEY OL10 40 F4
Newbury Rd BOLS/LL BL3 53 J1
CHD/CHDH SK8 119 L5
Newbury Wk BOL BL1 * 2 C2
CHAD OL9 8 C4
Newby Cl BURY BL9 39 K5
Newby Dr ALT WA14 * 108 A6
CHD/CHDH SK8 110 D7
MDTN M24 57 J1
SALE M33 109 G1
Newby Rd BOLE BL2 37 H3
BRAM/HZG SK7 121 M2
HTNM SK4 12 C3
Newby Sq
WGNW/BIL/OR WN5 * 46 E7
Newcastle St HULME M15 6 F9
New Chapel La HOR/BR BL6 34 C2
Newchurch OLDS OL8 75 K4
Newchurch Pl ROCH OL11 * 41 M3
New Church Rd BOL BL1 35 J2
New Church St RAD M26 54 E1
Newchurch St OP/CLY M11 88 C4
ROCH OL11 41 M3
New City Rd WALK M28 68 D4
Newcliffe Rd BKLY M9 57 J8
New Coin St ROY/SHW OL2 59 G1
Newcombe Cl OP/CLY M11 88 C3
Newcombe Dr LHULT M38 52 C6
Newcombe Rd RAMS BL0 24 D3
Newcombe St CSLFD M3 * 87 J1
New Copper Moss
HALE/TIMP WA15 108 C8
New Court Dr
EDGW/EG BL7 22 B1
Newcroft FAIL M35 74 E6
Newcroft Crs URM M41 96 C3
Newcroft Dr BKLY M9 72 F3
EDGY/DAV SK3 112 A6
URM M41 96 C3
Newcroft Rd URM M41 96 C3
New Cross St ORD M5 85 M2
SWIN M27 70 D5
Newdale Rd WGTN/LGST M12 99 L2
New Drake Gn WHTN BL5 50 B7
Newearth Rd WALK M28 68 E4
New Earth St MOSL OL5 77 G2
OLDE OL4 59 M7
New Ellesmere Ap WALK M28 52 F8
New Elm Rd CSLFD M3 6 B7
Newenden Rd WGN WN1 31 L8
New Field Cl MILN OL16 11 L3
RAD M26 54 B1
Newfield Head La MILN OL16 29 M6
Newfield Vw MILN OL16 29 K6
New Forest Rd
NTHM/RTH M23 108 F4
Newgate MILN OL16 10 E4
Newgate Av WGNNW/ST WN6 30 B4
Newgate Cottages WHTN BL5 * 51 K3
Newgate Dr LHULT M38 52 C6
Newgate Rd SALE M33 107 L3
WILM/AE SK9 126 B5
New George St
TOT/BURYW BL8 38 F1
New Hall Av BRO M7 72 A4
CHD/CHDH SK8 119 K5
Newhall Av BOLE BL2 37 L6
ECC M30 84 D5
New Hall Cl SALE M33 97 J8
Newhall Dr NTHM/RTH M23 109 K2
New Hall La BOL BL1 35 K4
New Hall Ms BOL BL1 35 G3
New Hall Pl BOL BL1 35 K4
New Hall Rd BRO M7 72 A5
BURY BL9 26 B8
SALE M33 * 109 J1
Newhall Rd RDSH SK5 100 D2
Newham Av OP/CLY M11 88 E2
Newham Dr TOT/BURYW BL8 38 E4
Newhart Gv WALK M28 68 F2
Newhaven Av LEIGH WN7 66 C4
OP/CLY M11 89 J5
Newhaven Cl CHD/CHDH SK8 120 E2
TOT/BURYW BL8 24 F5
New Herbert St SLFD M6 70 F7
Newhey Av WYTH/NTH M22 110 A7
New Hey Rd CHD/CHDH SK8 111 H7
Newhey Rd MILN OL16 29 K8
WYTH/NTH M22 110 A8
New Heys Wy BOLE BL2 23 G6
New Holder St BOL BL1 2 C5
Newholme Gdns WALK M28 68 F1
Newholme Rd DID/WITH M20 98 B7
Newhouse Cl WHIT OL12 21 G6
Newhouse Crs ROCH OL11 27 H4
Newhouse Dr WGNS/IIMK WN3 63 G3
Newhouse Rd HEY OL10 41 G4
New Houses OLDE OL4 60 F4
Newington Av CHH M8 72 C1
Newington Ct ALT WA14 116 D1
Newington Dr BOL BL1 * 2 E1
TOT/BURYW BL8 38 D4
Newington Wk BOL BL1 * 2 D1
New Islington ANC M4 7 M3
New Kings Head Yd CSLFD M3 * 6 E2
Newland Av
WGNW/BIL/OR WN5 47 G7
Newland Dr WHTN BL5 51 J5
Newland Ms GOL/RIS/CUL WA3 81 H7
Newlands FAIL M35 74 B8
Newlands Av BOLE BL2 37 J3
BRAM/HZG SK7 121 G4
CHD/CHDH SK8 120 C5
ECC M30 84 C4
IRL M44 94 C1
TYLD M29 67 K6
WHIT OL12 28 C1
WHTF M45 * 55 H3
Newlands Cl CHD/CHDH SK8 120 C5
WHIT OL12 28 C1
Newlands Dr DID/WITH M20 110 F4
GLSP SK13 93 J8
GOL/RIS/CUL WA3 79 M4
HOR/BR BL6 33 H5
PWCH M25 55 K7
SWIN M27 70 F6
WILM/AE SK9 126 C7
Newlands Rd CHD/CHDH SK8 111 H6
LEIGH WN7 81 J1
NTHM/RTH M23 109 J4
Newland St CHH M8 72 E3
New La BOLE BL2 37 G3
ECC M30 84 E2
MDTN M24 57 K3
ROY/SHW OL2 43 G8
New Lane Ct BOLE BL2 37 H2
New Lawns RDSH SK5 100 D3
Newlea Cl BOL BL1 35 M2
New Lees St AUL OL6 76 A7
New Lester Cl TYLD M29 67 L3
New Lester Wy LHULT M38 52 B8
New Ldg WGN WN1 47 M2
Newlyn Av STLY SK15 92 A1
Newlyn Cl BRAM/HZG SK7 121 M3
Newlyn Dr AIMK WN4 78 E2
MPL/ROM SK6 113 K1
SALE M33 108 F3
Newlyn St RUSH/FAL M14 98 E2
Newman Av WGNNW/ST WN6 47 K2
Newman Cl WGNE/HIN WN2 48 F6
Newman St AUL OL6 90 D1
HYDE SK14 102 B1
MILN OL16 28 F1
WGN WN1 48 B2
New Market CMANW M2 6 F4
Newmarket Cl SALE M33 107 L2
Newmarket Gv AULW OL7 75 H7
New Market La CMANW M2 6 F4
Newmarket Rd AULW OL7 75 H7
BOLS/LL BL3 53 K2
New Market St WGN WN1 14 F3
New Meadow HOR/BR BL6 34 F5
New Miles La
WGNNW/ST WN6 30 C6
New Mills Rd GLSP SK13 103 M8
NM/HAY SK22 125 K2
New Mill St LIT OL15 21 L7
New Moor La
BRAM/HZG SK7 121 M1
New Moss Rd IRL M44 94 A6
New Mount St ANC M4 * 7 H1
Newnham St BOL BL1 36 C1
New Park Rd ORD M5 86 E5
Newpark Wk CHH M8 72 D6
Newport Av RDSH SK5 100 B5
Newport Rd BOLS/LL BL3 52 D1
CCHDY M21 97 K3
DTN/ASHW M34 101 L4

Newport St BOL BL1 2 E6
FWTH BL4 53 C5
MDTN M24 57 M3
OLDS OL8 8 E8
RUSH/FAL M14 98 E1
SLFD M6 86 B2
TOT/BURYW BL8 24 D7
Newquay Av BOLE BL2 38 A3
RDSH SK5 100 B5
Newquay Dr BRAM/HZG SK7 121 H5
New Quay St CSLFD M3 6 C4
New Radcliffe St OLD OL1 9 H5
New Raven Ct BOLS/LL BL3 * 53 K1
New Ridd Ri HYDE SK14 102 A4
New Riven Ct BOLS/LL BL3 53 K1
New Rd GLSP SK13 93 J5
LIT OL15 21 J8
OLDS OL8 59 H8
RAD M26 54 E2
WGNE/HIN WN2 32 D6
New Royd Av OLDE OL4 60 C3
Newry Rd ECC M30 85 H4
Newry St BOL BL1 36 A1
Newsham Cl BOLS/LL BL3 2 A7
Newsham Rd EDGY/DAV SK3 112 B6
Newsham Wk
WGNNW/ST WN6 * 14 A1
WGTN/LGST M12 * 99 L1
Newshaw La GLSP SK13 104 C1
Newsholme St CHH M8 72 C5
New Springs BOL BL1 * 35 L1
Newstead WHIT OL12 10 D3
Newstead Av AUL OL6 75 M5
DID/WITH M20 99 G7
Newstead Cl POY/DIS SK12 121 M7
Newstead Dr BOLS/LL BL3 51 K2
Newstead Gv MPL/ROM SK6 113 J1
Newstead Rd URM M41 96 B1
WGNS/IIMK WN3 63 H1
Newstead Ter
HALE/TIMP WA15 108 C5
New St ALT WA14 107 M8
BOLS/LL BL3 2 D6
DROY M43 89 K4
ECC M30 84 F3
HYDE SK14 103 K4
LIT OL15 21 K8
MILN OL16 29 K7
NEWH/MOS M40 73 H8
NM/HAY SK22 124 E5
OLDE OL4 60 B6
RAD M26 54 E2
STLY SK15 91 K4
SWIN M27 70 D3
TOT/BURYW BL8 24 C6
UPML OL3 61 L4
WGNE/HIN WN2 64 D3
WGNW/BIL/OR WN5 46 E7
WHIT OL12 28 B2
New Tempest Rd HOR/BR BL6 34 F8
New Ter HYDE SK14 * 102 B3
New Thomas St SLFD M6 * 71 K8
Newton Av DID/WITH M20 98 D6
WGTN/LGST M12 88 C8
Newton Cl WGN WN1 48 A2
Newton Crs MDTN M24 57 G1
Newton Dr TOT/BURYW BL8 24 D3
Newton Gdns
GOL/RIS/CUL WA3 80 D4
New Tong Fld EDGW/EG BL7 22 C5
Newton Hall Rd HYDE SK14 90 F7
Newton La GOL/RIS/CUL WA3 79 J5
Newton Rd ALT WA14 108 B5
FAIL M35 74 B7
GOL/RIS/CUL WA3 80 B6
MDTN M24 56 E5
URM M41 95 M2
WGNW/BIL/OR WN5 62 C6
WILM/AE SK9 126 E3
Newton St AUL OL6 * 90 F1
BOL BL1 36 B2
BURY BL9 25 J6
CMANE M1 7 J4
DROY M43 89 M1
EDGY/DAV SK3 13 G7
FAIL M35 * 73 M6
HYDE SK14 91 G8
LEIGH WN7 66 C7
MILN OL16 11 J9
STLY SK15 * 91 J2
STRET M32 97 G3
Newton Ter BOL BL1 * 36 B2
Newton Wk BOL BL1 36 B2
Newton Wood Rd DUK SK16 90 F6
Newtown Av DTN/ASHW M34 101 J2
Newtown Cl OP/CLY M11 88 E4
SWIN M27 70 C2
Newtown St PWCH M25 55 M8
ROY/SHW OL2 43 L6
New Union St ANC M4 7 L3
New Vernon St BURY BL9 5 G1
New Viaduct St
NEWH/MOS M40 88 B2
Newville Dr DID/WITH M20 99 G7
New Vine St HULME M15 * 87 J6
New Wakefield St CMANE M1 6 F8
New Wy WHIT OL12 20 A3
New York BOLS/LL BL3 35 J8
New York St HEY OL10 40 E2
New Zealand Rd STKP SK1 13 M3
Neyland Cl BOL BL1 35 J5
Ney St AULW OL7 75 J6
Niagara St OFTN SK2 112 D6
Nicholas Cft ANC M4 7 G3
Nicholas Owen Cl OP/CLY M11 88 F4
Nicholas Rd OLDS OL8 59 H8
Nicholas St BOLE BL2 3 H3
CMANW M2 7 G5
Nicholls St SLFD M6 * 86 D1
Nicholson Rd HYDE SK14 90 F7
Nicholson Sq DUK SK16 * 90 E4
Nicholson St HTNM SK4 13 H2
OLDE OL4 60 B6
ROCH OL11 10 F8
Nichols St SLFD M6 86 E1
Nickleby Rd POY/DIS SK12 129 J1
Nicolas Rd CCHDY M21 97 K3
Nicol Mere Dr AIMK WN4 63 L7
Nicol Rd AIMK WN4 63 K7
Nield Rd DTN/ASHW M34 101 J1
Nield's Brow ALT WA14 * 116 E2
Nield St MOSL OL5 76 E2
Nields Wy MPL/ROM SK6 115 G8
Nigel Rd BKLY M9 73 J5
Nigher Moss Av MILN OL16 11 M6
Nightingale Cl WILM/AE SK9 126 F3
Nightingale Dr
DTN/ASHW M34 89 M2
Nightingale Gdns
NTHM/RTH M23 109 K3
Nightingale Rd
HOR/BR BL6 32 F1
Nile St AULW OL7 90 C4
BOLS/LL BL3 2 E8
MILN OL16 11 H3
OLD OL1 9 H3
Nile Ter BRO M7 72 A7
Nimble Nook CHAD OL9 58 D7
Nina Dr NEWH/MOS M40 73 M1
Nine Acre Dr ORD M5 86 E5
Ninehouse La BOLS/LL BL3 36 C8
Ninfield Rd NTHM/RTH M23 109 L8
Ninth Av OLDS OL8 75 G3
Nipper La WHTF M45 55 H3
Nisbet Av WYTH/NTH M22 119 G1
Niven St WGTN/LGST M12 88 A6
Nixon Rd BOLS/LL BL3 51 M1
Nixon Rd South BOLS/LL BL3 51 M1
Nixon St EDGY/DAV SK3 13 H7
FAIL M35 74 B5
ROCH OL11 41 L1
No 11 Pas DID/WITH M20 * 98 C7
Noble Meadow WHIT OL12 * 21 H8
Noble St BOLS/LL BL3 2 C8
LEIGH WN7 * 66 D7
OLDS OL8 59 J8
Noel Dr SALE M33 97 G8
Noel St BOL BL1 2 D4
Nolan St BKLY M9 73 H5
Nona St SLFD M6 86 B2
Nook Farm Av WHIT OL12 28 C1
Nook Flds BOLE BL2 37 H2
Nook La AUL OL6 76 A6
GOL/RIS/CUL WA3 79 L4
TYLD M29 83 G2
The Nook ECC M30 84 D1
URM M41 96 A3
WALK M28 69 J4
WGNNW/ST WN6 30 B5
Noon Sun Cl UPML OL3 61 K8
Noon Sun St WHIT OL12 28 C3
Norbet Wk BKLY M9 * 73 H5
Norbreck Av CCHDY M21 97 L5
CHD/CHDH SK8 111 K6
Norbreck Crs WGNNW/ST WN6 47 K2
Norbreck Gdns BOLE BL2 3 L3
Norbreck St BOLE BL2 3 J2
Norburn Rd BRUN/LGST M13 99 J2
Norbury Av MPL/ROM SK6 114 B6
OLDE OL4 60 F6
SALE M33 96 C8
SLFD M6 71 G7
WGNW/BIL/OR WN5 62 A6
Norbury Cl NEWH/MOS M40 * 73 G8
Norbury Crs BRAM/HZG SK7 121 M2
Norbury Dr MPL/ROM SK6 114 C6
Norbury Gv BOL BL1 22 C8
BRAM/HZG SK7 121 M2
SWIN M27 70 C3
Norbury Hollow Rd
BRAM/HZG SK7 122 D4
Norbury La OLDS OL8 76 A1
Norbury Ms MPL/ROM SK6 * 114 B6
Norbury St BRO M7 72 B6
LEIGH WN7 66 A7
MILN OL16 * 28 E8
STKP SK1 13 J5
Norcot Wk HULME M15 * 87 G6
Norcross Cl OFTN SK2 113 G7
Nordale Pk WHIT OL12 27 G2
Nordek Cl ROY/SHW OL2 43 G7
Nordek Dr ROY/SHW OL2 42 F7
Norden Av DID/WITH M20 98 D6
Norden Cl ROCH OL11 26 F2
Norden Ct BOLS/LL BL3 36 B8
Norden Rd ROCH OL11 27 G7
Nordens Dr CHAD OL9 58 C3
Nordens Rd CHAD OL9 58 C4
Nordens St CHAD OL9 58 D4
Norden Wy ROCH OL11 26 F2
Noreen Av PWCH M25 55 M7
Norfield Cl DUK SK16 90 F4
Norfolk Av DROY M43 89 J1
DTN/ASHW M34 100 D1
GTN M18 * 88 F8
HEY OL10 40 C2
HTNM SK4 99 M6
WHTF M45 55 K4
Norfolk Cl BOLS/LL BL3 37 L8
ROY/SHW OL2 43 J5
WGNE/HIN WN2 49 K6
Norfolk Crs FAIL M35 74 B6
Norfolk Dr FWTH BL4 53 G3
Norfolk Gdns URM M41 95 G1
Norfolk Rd ATH M46 50 F7
GTN M18 88 F8
WGNW/BIL/OR WN5 62 B3
Norfolk St CHAD OL9 58 F8
CMANW M2 6 F4
GLSP SK13 105 G3
HYDE SK14 102 A2
ROCH OL11 10 D6
SLFD M6 71 K7
WALK M28 53 G6
WGNNW/ST WN6 47 K2
WGNW/BIL/OR WN5 14 A7
Norfolk Wy ROY/SHW OL2 59 G2
Norford Wy ROCH OL11 27 H5
Norgate St DID/WITH M20 110 E1
Norlan Av DTN/ASHW M34 90 B5
Norleigh Rd
WYTH/NTH M22 110 A4
Norley Av STRET M32 97 J1
Norley Cl OLD OL1 58 E2
Norley Dr BNG/LEV M19 99 M2
SALE M33 109 H1
Norley Hall Av
WGNW/BIL/OR WN5 46 F6
Norley Rd LEIGH WN7 65 L8
WGNW/BIL/OR WN5 46 E5
Norman Av BRAM/HZG SK7 121 L1
RNFD/HAY WA11 78 D5
Normanby Cha ALT WA14 107 L8
Normanby Gv SWIN M27 70 B3
Normanby Rd WALK M28 68 F3
Normanby St BOLS/LL BL3 51 L2
RUSH/FAL M14 87 K8
SWIN M27 70 B3
WGNW/BIL/OR WN5 46 E6
Norman Cl MDTN M24 * 57 M3
Normandale Av BOL BL1 35 K3
Normandy Crs RAD M26 54 C1
Norman Gv RDSH SK5 100 B5
WGTN/LGST M12 * 88 D8
Norman Rd ALT WA14 107 M6
AUL OL6 75 M6
BRO M7 * 72 B5
HTNM SK4 111 L1
ROCH OL11 10 B7
RUSH/FAL M14 99 G2
SALE M33 96 E8
STLY SK15 91 J2
Norman Rd West BKLY M9 * 73 J5
Norman's Pl ALT WA14 108 A8
Norman St BURY BL9 5 K1
FAIL M35 74 D3
HYDE SK14 102 B2
MDTN M24 57 L3
OLD OL1 8 F3
WGTN/LGST M12 88 E7
Normanton Av SLFD M6 85 M1
Normanton Cl
WGNNW/ST WN6 31 H8
Normanton Dr BKLY M9 57 H8
Normanton Rd EDGY/DAV SK3 111 K5
Norman Weall Ct MDTN M24 * 57 K2
Normington St OLDE OL4 * 59 L5
Norreys Av URM M41 95 H1
Norreys St MILN OL16 11 G3
Norris Av HTNM SK4 12 C3
Norris Bank Ter HTNM SK4 12 C4
Norris Hill Dr HTNM SK4 12 C2
Norris Rd SALE M33 108 F2
Norris St BOLS/LL BL3 2 C8
BOLS/LL BL3 53 K1
FWTH BL4 52 F5
TYLD M29 * 67 K4
Northallerton Rd BRO M7 71 L6
Northam Cl WGNNW/ST WN6 31 G3
Northampton Rd
NEWH/MOS M40 73 H6
North Av BNG/LEV M19 99 J5
BURY BL9 39 L8
FWTH BL4 52 D4
STLY SK15 91 K1
TOT/BURYW BL8 24 C2
UPML OL3 61 M7
URM M41 85 H5
North Back Rock BURY BL9 4 F4
Northbank Gdns BNG/LEV M19 99 H6
North Blackfield La BRO M7 71 M4
Northbourne St SLFD M6 86 B2
Northbrook Av CHH M8 56 C8
North Brook Rd GLSP SK13 93 H8
North Cir WHTF M45 55 K6
North Clifden La BRO M7 72 B6
Northcliffe Rd OFTN SK2 112 F4
North Cl GLSP SK13 93 J5
Northcombe Rd
EDGY/DAV SK3 112 B7
Northcote Av WYTH/NTH M22 118 F1
Northcote Rd BRAM/HZG SK7 121 H5
North Crs NEWH/MOS M40 74 A1
OP/CLY M11 89 G1
North Cft OLDS OL8 75 L1
Northdale Rd BKLY M9 56 E7
North Dean St SWIN M27 70 D3
Northdene Dr ROCH OL11 27 J6
Northdown Av HULME M15 87 G6
MPL/ROM SK6 101 M7
North Downs Rd
CHD/CHDH SK8 120 B1
Northdowns Rd ROY/SHW OL2 43 J4
North Dr DTN/ASHW M34 89 M3
SWIN M27 70 E5
North Edge LEIGH WN7 66 E6
Northenden Rd
CHD/CHDH SK8 110 D7
SALE M33 96 F8
Northend Rd STLY SK15 91 M1
Northen Gv DID/WITH M20 98 C8
Northern Av SWIN M27 70 F1
Northern Gv BOL BL1 35 M3
Northern Service Rd
NTHM/RTH M23 * 109 J7
Northfield Av NEWH/MOS M40 74 C2
Northfield Dr WILM/AE SK9 127 H4
Northfield Rd BURY BL9 25 J6
NEWH/MOS M40 74 C2
Northfield St BOLS/LL BL3 35 M7
Northfleet Rd ECC M30 84 C4
North Florida Rd
RNFD/HAY WA11 78 B4
North Ga OLDS OL8 75 H1
Northgate WHIT OL12 20 A5
Northgate La OLD OL1 44 B8
Northgate Rd EDGY/DAV SK3 12 C6
North George St CSLFD M3 6 A2
North Gv BRUN/LGST M13 88 A7
URM M41 95 M3
WALK M28 68 F1
North Hill St CSLFD M3 6 B1
Northland Rd BKLY M9 73 K1
BOL BL1 22 C6
Northlands RAD M26 38 B7
North La TYLD M29 67 K6
WHIT OL12 10 F2
Northleach Cl TOT/BURYW BL8 38 D1
Northleigh Dr PWCH M25 * 72 A1
Northleigh Rd OLDTF/WHR M16 97 L1
North Lonsdale St STRET M32 * 97 H1
North Md CCHDY M21 97 L5
Northmoor Rd WGTN/LGST M12 88 D8
North Nook OLDE OL4 60 C4
Northolme Gdns BNG/LEV M19 99 H8
Northolt Av LEIGH WN7 66 C4
Northolt Ct OP/CLY M11 * 89 G2
Northolt Dr BOLS/LL BL3 36 C8
Northolt Fold HEY OL10 41 H5
Northolt Rd NTHM/RTH M23 109 K3
North Pde CSLFD M3 6 E4
MILN OL16 29 M8
SALE M33 109 G2
North Park Rd BRAM/HZG SK7 121 G2
North Phoebe St ORD M5 86 E4
North Pl STKP SK1 13 J4
Northridge Rd BKLY M9 57 G6
North Ri UPML OL3 61 L7
North Rd ATH M46 50 E7
DTN/ASHW M34 90 A3
GLSP SK13 104 F1
HALE/TIMP WA15 117 J4
MANAIR M90 118 E6
NM/HAY SK22 125 M1
OP/CLY M11 88 F2
PART M31 95 G8
PWCH M25 55 J7
STRET M32 85 L8
Northside Av URM M41 95 J3
North Star Dr CSLFD M3 6 B4
Northstead Av
DTN/ASHW M34 101 L2
North St AIMK WN4 64 A7
ATH M46 67 H1
AUL OL6 90 D2
CHH M8 72 D8
HEY OL10 40 E2
LEIGH WN7 66 E8
MDTN M24 57 K2
MILN OL16 11 G2
RAD M26 38 F8
RAMS BL0 18 F2
RNFD/HAY WA11 78 B6
ROY/SHW OL2 59 G1
WHIT OL12 20 A3
Northumberland Av AULW OL7 75 L8
Northumberland Cl
OLDTF/WHR M16 86 F7
Northumberland Crs
OLDTF/WHR M16 * 86 F7
Northumberland Rd
OLDTF/WHR M16 86 F8
PART M31 106 B2
RDSH SK5 100 E6
Northumberland St BRO M7 72 A5
WGN WN1 15 L1
Northumberland Wy
WYTH/NTH M22 110 B6
Northumbria St BOLS/LL BL3 35 M7
Northurst Dr CHH M8 72 C1
North Vale Rd
HALE/TIMP WA15 108 C6
North Veiw WHTF M45 55 H2
North View Cl OLDE OL4 60 F7
Northward Rd WILM/AE SK9 126 D6
North Wy BOL BL1 22 E8
North Wy DROY M43 89 K4
North Wy HYDE SK14 102 B2
RDSH SK5 100 F6
Northway WGN WN1 14 F2
Northways WGNNW/ST WN6 31 G2
Northwell St LEIGH WN7 66 B4
North Western St
BNG/LEV M19 99 K4
CMANE M1 7 L6
Northwold Cl WGNS/IIMK WN3 62 F1
Northwold Dr BKLY M9 73 L1
BOL BL1 35 H4
Northwood BOLE BL2 23 G8
Northwood Av NEWLW WA12 79 J8
Northwood Crs BOLS/LL BL3 * 35 M7
Northwood Gv SALE M33 96 E8
Norton Av DTN/ASHW M34 100 D1
SALE M33 96 A7
URM M41 85 G8
WGTN/LGST M12 99 L1
Norton Gra PWCH M25 72 A1
Norton Gv HTNM SK4 12 B4
Norton Rd WALK M28 68 B5
WHIT OL12 28 C1
Norton St BOL BL1 36 C1
BRO M7 72 B5
CMANE M1 * 7 M5
CSLFD M3 6 E2
NEWH/MOS M40 73 H8
Norview Dr DID/WITH M20 110 E5
Norville Av NEWH/MOS M40 74 A1
Norway Gv RDSH SK5 * 100 C8
Norway St BOL BL1 * 36 A2
SLFD M6 86 B2
STRET M32 97 H1
Norweb Wy LEIGH WN7 81 L1
Norwell Rd WYTH/NTH M22 110 B7
Norwich Av AIMK WN4 79 G2
CHAD OL9 58 D3
DTN/ASHW M34 101 J3
GOL/RIS/CUL WA3 80 A4
ROCH OL11 27 K5
Norwich Cl AUL OL6 76 A4
DUK SK16 91 K5
Norwich Dr TOT/BURYW BL8 4 B2
Norwich Rd STRET M32 96 C1
Norwich St ROCH OL11 11 G8
Norwick Cl BOLS/LL BL3 35 H8
Norwood PWCH M25 71 L2
Norwood Av AIMK WN4 63 J6
BRAM/HZG SK7 120 E7
BRO M7 71 L4
CHD/CHDH SK8 120 C1
DID/WITH M20 99 G8
GOL/RIS/CUL WA3 80 B5
MPL/ROM SK6 122 F5
TYLD M29 67 K6
WGNNW/ST WN6 47 K1
Norwood Cl ROY/SHW OL2 43 K4
WALK M28 69 H4
Norwood Crs ROY/SHW OL2 59 H2
Norwood Dr HALE/TIMP WA15 109 G7
SWIN M27 70 A5
Norwood Gv BOL BL1 * 35 M4
Norwood Rd CHD/CHDH SK8 110 E6
OFTN SK2 112 E8
STRET M32 97 H3
Nostell Rd AIMK WN4 63 K7
Nottingham Av RDSH SK5 100 F7
Nottingham Cl RDSH SK5 100 F6
Nottingham Dr AUL OL6 75 L5
BOL BL1 2 C1
FAIL M35 74 D7
RDSH SK5 100 F6
Nottingham Pl WGN WN1 15 L1
Nowell Rd MDTN M24 57 K1
Nudger Cl UPML OL3 61 J2
Nudger Gn UPML OL3 61 J2
Nuffield Cl BOL BL1 35 L3
Nuffield Rd WYTH/NTH M22 110 B8
Nugent Rd BOLS/LL BL3 52 B1
Nugget St OLDE OL4 * 59 L6
Nuneaton Dr
NEWH/MOS M40 88 A1
Nuneham Av
DID/WITH M20 98 F5
Nunfield Cl NEWH/MOS M40 73 L2
Nunnery Rd BOLS/LL BL3 35 L8
Nunthorpe Dr CHH M8 72 F4
Nursery Av
HALE/TIMP WA15 117 G4
Nursery Cl GLSP SK13 104 F4
OFTN SK2 113 G5
SALE M33 97 G8
Nursery Dr POY/DIS SK12 121 M8
Nursery Gdns MILN OL16 11 M3
Nursery Gv PART M31 94 C8
Nursery La EDGY/DAV SK3 111 K5
MCFLDN SK10 130 A7
WILM/AE SK9 126 D6
Nursery Rd CHD/CHDH SK8 120 B3
FAIL M35 74 D6
HTNM SK4 12 C2
PWCH M25 55 K6
URM M41 84 E8
Nursery St OLDTF/WHR M16 98 C1
SLFD M6 86 C1
Nuthatch Av WALK M28 69 G4
Nuthurst Rd
NEWH/MOS M40 73 M3
Nutsford V WGTN/LGST M12 88 D8
Nut St BOL BL1 * 36 A2
Nuttall Av BOLS/LL BL3 53 M1
HOR/BR BL6 33 K1
WHTF M45 55 J4
Nuttall Cl RAMS BL0 18 F7
Nuttall Hall Rd
RAMS BL0 19 G8
Nuttall La RAMS BL0 18 F8
Nuttall Ms WHTF M45 55 J4
Nuttall Rd RAMS BL0 19 G8
Nuttall Sq BURY BL9 39 J7
Nuttall St ATH M46 67 H1
BURY BL9 5 H6
IRL M44 94 B6
MILN OL16 11 G5
OLDS OL8 * 59 L8
OLDTF/WHR M16 86 F7
OP/CLY M11 88 D5
Nutt La PWCH M25 56 B4
Nutt St WGN WN1 15 K1


## O


Oadby Cl WGTN/LGST M12 88 D8
Oadby Pl RDSH SK5 100 C1
Oak Av BOLS/LL BL3 53 L1
CCHDY M21 97 L4
CHD/CHDH SK8 120 B2
GOL/RIS/CUL WA3 79 L4
HTNM SK4 12 A2
IRL M44 94 A7
MDTN M24 57 K5
MPL/ROM SK6 113 M2
POY/DIS SK12 124 C6
RAMS BL0 24 D2
RNFD/HAY WA11 78 B5
ROY/SHW OL2 43 G6
WGNE/HIN WN2 64 F5
WGNE/HIN WN2 65 K1
WGNNW/ST WN6 31 J4
WHTF M45 55 J5
WILM/AE SK9 126 D7
Oak Bank BKLY M9 73 G4
PWCH M25 71 J3
Oakbank WGNE/HIN WN2 64 E1
Oak Bank Av BKLY M9 73 J3
Oakbank Av CHAD OL9 58 B4
Oak Bank Cl WHTF M45 55 L4
Oakbank Dr BOL BL1 22 A6
Oakbarton HOR/BR BL6 34 F8
Oakcliffe Rd NTHM/RTH M23 109 K5
WHIT OL12 21 G8
Oak Cl HYDE SK14 92 D8
WILM/AE SK9 126 D6
Oak Coppice BOL BL1 35 K5
Oakcroft STLY SK15 92 B5
Oakcroft Wy WYTH/NTH M22 110 B6
Oakdale BOLE BL2 23 G8
Oakdale Cl WHTF M45 55 G4
Oakdale Ct UPML OL3 61 H1
Oakdale Dr CHD/CHDH SK8 119 K2
DID/WITH M20 110 F3
TYLD M29 67 M6
Oak Dene UPML OL3 61 K8
Oakdene WALK M28 69 L6
Oakdene Av CHD/CHDH SK8 119 K5
HTNM SK4 100 A7
Oakdene Crs MPL/ROM SK6 114 C5
Oakdene Gdns MPL/ROM SK6 114 C5
Oakdene Rd HALE/TIMP WA15 108 E4
MDTN M24 57 M4
MPL/ROM SK6 114 C5
Oakdene St BKLY M9 73 J4
Oak Dr BRAM/HZG SK7 120 E5
DTN/ASHW M34 89 K8
MPL/ROM SK6 114 A6
RUSH/FAL M14 99 G3
Oaken Bank Rd HEY OL10 41 J6
Oakenbottom Rd BOLE BL2 37 G6
Oaken Clough AULW OL7 75 J6
Oakenclough Cl WILM/AE SK9 127 H2
Oaken Clough Dr AULW OL7 75 J6
Oakenclough Dr BOL BL1 35 J2
Oakenden Cl AIMK WN4 63 K6
Oakengates WGNNW/ST WN6 31 J3
Oakenrod Hl ROCH OL11 27 M5
Oakenshaw Av WHIT OL12 20 A6
Oakenshaw Vw WHIT OL12 20 A6
Oaker Av DID/WITH M20 98 B8
Oakes St FWTH BL4 53 J5
The Oakes GLSP SK13 104 D5
Oakfield DUK SK16 91 H6
PWCH M25 72 A1
SALE M33 96 D7
Oakfield Av ATH M46 50 F8
CHD/CHDH SK8 111 H6
DROY M43 89 J3
GOL/RIS/CUL WA3 79 J3
OLDTF/WHR M16 97 K1
OLDTF/WHR M16 98 A1
STLY SK15 77 H6
Oakfield Cl BRAM/HZG SK7 121 G8
HOR/BR BL6 34 C2
WILM/AE SK9 130 E1
Oakfield Crs WGNE/HIN WN2 32 F7
Oakfield Dr LHULT M38 52 B7
Oakfield Gv FWTH BL4 52 F6
GTN M18 89 G8
Oakfield Rd DID/WITH M20 110 D1
EDGY/DAV SK3 112 C7
GLSP SK13 104 B1
HALE/TIMP WA15 108 B7
HYDE SK14 91 H7
POY/DIS SK12 122 B8
WILM/AE SK9 130 E2
Oakfield St CHH M8 72 D6
HALE/TIMP WA15 108 B7
Oakfield Ter ROCH OL11 27 M4
Oakfold Av AUL OL6 76 A6
Oakford Wk BOLS/LL BL3 35 M8
Oak Gates EDGW/EG BL7 22 B3
Oak Gv AUL OL6 76 A6
CHD/CHDH SK8 111 H7
ECC M30 84 E3
POY/DIS SK12 121 M8
URM M41 96 B2
Oakham Av DID/WITH M20 98 D4
Oakham Cl TOT/BURYW BL8 25 H7
Oakham Ms BRO M7 71 M3
Oakham Rd DTN/ASHW M34 * 101 K3
Oakhead LEIGH WN7 81 M1
Oak Hl LIT OL15 21 K7
Oakhill Cl BOLE BL2 37 K5
Oak Hill Cl WGN WN1 * 47 L1
Oakhill Wy CHH M8 72 C5
Oakhouse Dr CCHDY M21 97 L5
Oakhurst Cha WILM/AE SK9 130 D2
Oakhurst Dr EDGY/DAV SK3 111 L7
Oakhurst Gdns PWCH M25 55 K8
Oakhurst Gv WHTN BL5 49 M5
Oakington Av
RUSH/FAL M14 * 98 E1
Oakland Av BNG/LEV M19 99 H8
OFTN SK2 112 F6
SLFD M6 70 D8
Oakland Gv BOL BL1 * 35 K2
Oaklands BOL BL1 35 J5
Oaklands Av CHD/CHDH SK8 120 C2
MPL/ROM SK6 114 F4
Oaklands Cl WILM/AE SK9 127 J3
Oaklands Dene HYDE SK14 102 D2

Oaklands Dr *BRAM/HZG* SK7 ...... 122 A3
  *HYDE* SK14 ........................ 102 D2
  *PWCH* M25 ............................ 55 L7
  *SALE* M33 ............................... 96 D7
Oaklands Pk *OLDE* OL4 ............... 61 H7
Oaklands Rd *BRO* M7 .................. 71 K5
  *GOL/RIS/CUL* WA3 ................ 80 C5
  *RAMS* BL0 ............................... 19 G2
  *ROY/SHW* OL2 ........................ 59 H2
  *SWIN* M27 ............................... 70 A6
  *UPML* OL3 ............................... 61 J7
Oak La *WHTF* M45 ...................... 55 L4
  *WILM/AE* SK9 ........................ 126 D6
Oaklea *WGNNW/ST* WN6 ........... 30 D2
Oak Lea Av *WILM/AE* SK9 .......... 126 D7
Oaklea Rd *BRAM* M33 ................. 96 B6
Oakleigh Av *BNG/LEV* M19 ......... 99 J5
  *BOLS/LL* BL3 ......................... 52 D2
  *HALE/TIMP* WA15 ................. 108 D5
Oakleigh CI *HEY* OL10 ................. 41 H5
Oakleigh Rd *CHD/CHDH* SK8 ..... 120 A8
Oakley Av *WGNW/BIL/OR* WN5 ... 62 A6
Oakley CI *NEWH/MOS* M40 ......... 73 H7
  *RAD* M26 ................................ 54 D4
Oakley Dr *OLD* OL1 .................... 44 A8
  *WGNW/BIL/OR* WN5 ............. 47 H6
Oakley Pk *BOL* BL1 ...................... 35 J5
Oakley St *ORD* M5 ...................... 86 A3
Oakley Vls *HTNM* SK4 ................. 12 B1
The Oaklings *WGNE/HIN* WN2 .... 65 K1
Oak Ldg *BRAM/HZG* SK7 * .......... 121 H5
Oakmere Av *ECC* M30 .................. 69 M8
Oakmere CI *WYTH/NTH* M22 ..... 110 A8
Oakmere Rd *CHD/CHDH* SK8 ...... 111 J8
  *WILM/AE* SK9 ........................ 119 M7
Oak Ms *WILM/AE* SK9 ................ 127 G3
Oakmoor Dr *BRO* M7 ................... 71 K4
Oakmoor Rd *NTHM/RTH* M23 .... 109 K6
Oak Mt *DID/WITH* M20 ............... 110 E2
Oak Rd *BRO* M7 ........................... 71 M6
  *CHD/CHDH* SK8 .................... 111 H6
  *DID/WITH* M20 ...................... 98 C7
  *FAIL* M35 ............................... 74 C6
  *HALE/TIMP* WA15 ................. 117 C1
  *MCFLDN* SK10 ...................... 131 L3
  *OLDS* OL8 .............................. 74 F2
  *PART* M31 ............................. 106 A2
  *SALE* M33 .............................. 97 G8
Oaks Av *BOLE* BL2 ...................... 22 F8
  *NM/HAY* SK22 ..................... 125 M4
Oak Shaw CI *BKLY* M9 ................. 73 C2
Oakshaw Dr *WHIT* OL12 .............. 27 K3
Oaks La *BOLE* BL2 ....................... 22 E7
The Oaks *CHD/CHDH* SK8 ......... 119 J2
  *HYDE* SK14 ........................... 102 D1
Oak St *ANC* M4 ............................. 7 J3
  *ATH* M46 ................................ 66 D3
  *BRAM/HZG* SK7 ................... 121 M1
  *DTN/ASHW* M34 .................... 90 C6
  *ECC* M30 ................................ 85 G3
  *EDGY/DAV* SK3 ..................... 12 B7
  *GLSP* SK13 ........................... 104 F3
  *HEY* OL10 ............................... 40 E1
  *HYDE* SK14 ........................... 91 H8
  *LEIGH* WN7 ............................ 81 J1
  *MDTN* M24 ............................ 58 A5
  *MILN* OL16 ............................. 10 E5
  *MILN* OL16 ............................. 43 K7
  *RAMS* BL0 * ........................... 18 C3
  *ROY/SHW* OL2 ........................ 43 K6
  *SWIN* M27 ............................. 70 D3
  *TYLD* M29 ............................... 67 K3
  *WGN* WN1 .............................. 15 K4
Oak Tree CI *ATH* M46 .................. 66 D3
  *OFTN* SK2 ............................. 113 G4
Oak Tree Ct *CHD/CHDH* SK8 .... 111 H7
Oak Tree Crs *STLY* SK15 ............. 91 L4
Oak Tree Dr *DUK* SK16 ................. 91 J5
Oak Vw *OLD* OL1 ............................ 8 E1
Oakville Dr *BRO* M7 .................... 70 D8
Oakville Ter *NEWH/MOS* M40 ..... 73 H6
Oakway *DID/WITH* M20 ............... 98 A5
  *MDTN* M24 ............................ 41 J8
Oakwell Dr *BRO* M7 .................... 72 B3
  *BURY* BL9 .............................. 55 L1
Oakwell Man *BRO* M7 .................. 72 B3
Oakwood *CHAD* OL9 .................... 58 B5
  *GLSP* SK13 ........................... 104 C4
  *SALE* M33 .............................. 95 M8
Oakwood Av *AIMK* WN4 .............. 78 D2
  *CHD/CHDH* SK8 .................... 110 E7
  *DTN/ASHW* M34 ..................... 90 B5
  *NEWH/MOS* M40 .................... 74 A8
  *SWIN* M27 ............................. 54 B8
  *WALK* M28 ............................. 69 J2
  *WGNNW/ST* WN6 .................. 30 C7
  *WILM/AE* SK9 ....................... 127 G3
Oakwood CI *TOT/BURYW* BL8 .... 38 E1
Oakwood Ct *ALT* WA14 ............. 116 D4
Oakwood Dr *BOL* BL1 ................. 35 J4
  *LEIGH* WN7 ............................ 81 H3
  *SLFD* M6 ................................ 70 E7
  *WALK* M28 ............................. 69 J2
Oakwood La *ALT* WA14 .............. 116 C3
Oakwood Rd *MPL/ROM* SK6 ..... 113 M2
  *POY/DIS* SK12 * ................... 123 M6
Oakworth Cft *OLDE* OL4 .............. 44 C8
Oakworth St *BKLY* M9 ................. 72 F1
Oatlands *WILM/AE* SK9 .............. 130 E4
Oatlands Rd *WYTH/NTH* M22 ... 118 C2
Oat St *STKP* SK1 .......................... 13 L8
Oban Av *NEWH/MOS* M40 ......... 73 L8
  *OLD* OL1 ................................ 59 L3
Oban Crs *EDGY/DAV* SK3 ......... 112 A8
Oban Dr *WN4* WN4 ...................... 62 F8
  *SALE* M33 ............................. 109 H1
Oban Gv *BOL* BL1 * ...................... 22 B7
Oban St *BOL* BL1 * ...................... 36 A1
Oban Wy *WGNE/HIN* WN2 * ....... 33 G7
Oberlin St *OLDE* OL4 .................... 60 A5
  *ROCH* OL11 ............................ 10 B9
Occlestone CI *SALE* M33 ............ 109 H3
Occupiers La *BRAM/HZG* SK7 * .. 122 D3
Ocean St *ALT* WA14 .................. 107 L6
Ockendon Dr *BKLY* M9 ................. 73 H5
Octagon Ct *BOL* BL1 * .................... 2 E5
Octavia Dr *NEWH/MOS* M40 ...... 73 M8
Odell St *OP/CLY* M11 * ................ 89 G4
Odessa Av *SLFD* M6 ..................... 70 E8
Odette St *GTN* M18 ...................... 89 G3
Offerton Dr *OFTN* SK2 ............... 113 K6
Offerton Fold *OFTN* SK2 ............ 112 F5
Offerton Gn *OFTN* SK2 ............... 113 K6
Offerton La *OFTN* SK2 ............... 112 F4
Offerton Rd *BRAM/HZG* SK7 ...... 122 C1
  *OFTN* SK2 ............................. 113 K8
Offerton St *HOR/BR* BL6 ............. 33 K1
  *STKP* SK1 ............................. 112 E2
Off Grove Rd *STLY* SK15 ............. 77 G8
Off Ridge Hill La *STLY* SK15 * ..... 91 J2

Off Stamford St *STLY* SK15 * ....... 77 C8
Ogbourne Wk *BRUN/LGST* M13 .. 87 M6
Ogden CI *HEY* OL10 ...................... 40 D2
  *WHTF* M45 ............................. 55 K3
Ogden Gv *CHD/CHDH* SK8 * ..... 110 C8
Ogden La *OP/CLY* M11 ................. 89 G5
Ogden Rd *BRAM/HZG* SK7 ........ 120 F7
  *FAIL* M35 ............................... 74 B6
Ogden Sq *DUK* SK16 .................... 90 E4
Ogden St *CHAD* OL9 ...................... 8 B3
  *CHAD* OL9 ............................. 110 E1
  *HYDE* SK14 ........................... 103 L4
  *MDTN* M24 ............................ 57 K4
  *OLDE* OL4 * ............................ 60 A6
  *PWCH* M25 ............................. 55 M8
  *ROCH* OL11 ............................ 41 M2
  *SWIN* M27 .............................. 70 C5
Ogwen Dr *PWCH* M25 .................. 55 L7
Ohio Av *SALQ* M50 ...................... 86 C4
Okehampton CI *RAD* M26 ............ 37 M7
Okehampton Crs *SALE* M33 ........ 96 A7
Okell Gv *LEIGH* WN7 .................... 66 F7
Okeover Rd *BRO* M7 .................... 72 A4
Olaf St *BOLE* BL2 ............................ 3 J1
Olanyian Dr *CHH* M8 .................... 72 B7
Old Bank CI *MPL/ROM* SK6 ....... 113 K1
Old Bank La *CMANW* M1 ............... 6 F4
Old Bank Vw *OLD* OL1 ................. 43 M8
Old Barn Pl *EDGW/EG* BL7 ......... 22 D4
Old Barton Rd *ECC* M30 .............. 84 F5
Old Beechfield Gdns
  *WGNNW/ST* WN6 .................. 31 G3
Old Bent La *WHIT* OL12 ............... 20 E5
Old Birley St *HULME* M15 ........... 87 J7
Old Boston *RNFD/HAY* WA11 ..... 78 D5
Old Broadway *DID/WITH* M20 ..... 98 F7
Old Brook CI *ROY/SHW* OL2 ........ 44 A4
Old Brow *MOSL* OL5 .................... 76 F4
Old Brow La *MILN* OL16 .............. 28 F1
Old Brown Ct *MOSL* OL5 ............. 76 F4
Oldbury CI *HEY* OL10 ................... 41 G5
  *NEWH/MOS* M40 .................... 88 A1
Oldcastle Av *DID/WITH* M20 ...... 98 D5
Old Chapel St *EDGY/DAV* SK3 .... 12 D8
Old Church Ms *DUK* SK16 ........... 91 H4
Old Church St *NEWH/MOS* M40 .. 73 L6
  *OLD* OL1 * ................................ 9 K5
Old Clay Dr *WHIT* OL12 ............... 21 H8
Old Clough La *WALK* M28 ........... 69 J4
Oldcott CI *WALK* M28 .................. 68 C7
Old Court St *HYDE* SK14 ........... 102 A2
The Old Ctyd
  *WYTH/NTH* M22 * ................ 110 C7
Old Cft *OLDE* OL4 ........................ 60 D6
Old Croft Ms *STKP* SK1 .............. 112 E6
Old Crofts Bank *URM* M41 .......... 84 F8
Old Cross St *AUL* OL6 * ................ 90 F7
Old Dairy Ms *HYDE* SK14 ............ 90 F7
Old Delph Rd *ROCH* OL11 ........... 27 J3
Old Doctors St *TOT/BURYW* BL8 .. 24 C1
Old Eagley Ms *BOL* BL1 .............. 22 C6
Old Edge La *ROY/SHW* OL2 ........ 59 H2
Old Elm St *BRUN/LGST* M13 * ..... 87 M6
Oldershaw Dr *BKLY* M9 ................ 73 G6
Old Farm Crs *DROY* M43 ............. 89 J4
Old Farm Dr *OFTN* SK2 .............. 113 J6
Oldfield CI *WHTF* M45 .................. 54 C4
Oldfield Dr *HALE/TIMP* WA15 .... 108 C6
Oldfield Gv *SALE* M33 .................. 96 F7
Oldfield Ms *ALT* WA14 ............... 107 M7
Oldfield Rd *ALT* WA14 ................ 107 K7
  *ORD* M5 ................................. 86 F5
  *PWCH* M25 ............................ 55 M5
  *SALE* M33 ............................. 96 F7
Oldfield St *OP/CLY* M11 * ........... 88 E3
Old Fold *WGNW/BIL/OR* WN5 ..... 46 E6
Old Fold Rd *WGNE/HIN* WN2 ...... 33 G7
  *WHTN* BL5 ............................. 49 L5
Old Gardens St *STKP* SK1 ........... 13 K6
The Old Gdn
  *HALE/TIMP* WA15 ................. 108 E5
Oldgate Wk *HULME* M15 * ........... 87 G6
Old Gn *BOLE* BL2 ......................... 23 H7
Old Greenwood La
  *HOR/BR* BL6 .......................... 34 A3
Old Ground St *RAMS* BL0 * ......... 18 F6
Old Hall CI *GLSP* SK13 ............... 105 G2
  *TOT/BURYW* BL8 .................. 24 E5
Old Hall Clough
  *HOR/BR* BL6 .......................... 34 F5
Old Hall Crs *WILM/AE* SK9 ........ 127 J1
Old Hall Dr *AIMK* WN4 ................. 78 D2
  *GTN* M18 .............................. 89 G8
  *OFTN* SK2 ............................. 113 H6
Old Hall La *BRAM/HZG* SK7 ...... 128 C4
  *HOR/BR* BL6 .......................... 34 F3
  *HYDE* SK14 ........................... 92 D7
  *MPL/ROM* SK6 ..................... 114 F7
  *PWCH* M25 ............................ 56 C5
  *RUSH/FAL* M14 ..................... 99 G3
  *WALK* M28 ............................. 69 H5
  *WHTF* M45 ............................. 54 F6
  *WHTN* BL5 ............................. 50 B7
Old Hall Mill La *ATH* M46 ............ 66 C4
Old Hall Rd *BRO* M7 .................... 72 A4
  *CHD/CHDH* SK8 .................... 110 D6
  *NEWH/MOS* M40 ................... 73 L5
  *SALE* M33 .............................. 97 H8
  *STRET* M32 ........................... 85 K8
  *WHTF* M45 ............................. 54 F6
Old Hall Sq *GLSP* SK13 ............... 93 K7
Old Hall St *DUK* SK16 ................... 90 D5
  *FWTH* BL4 ............................. 53 H5
  *MDTN* M24 ............................ 57 K4
  *OP/CLY* M11 * ....................... 89 H5
  *WGNS/IIMK* WN3 ................... 15 L8
Old Hall St North *BOL* BL1 * .......... 2 E5
Oldham Av *STKP* SK1 .................. 112 E3
Oldham Dr *MPL/ROM* SK6 ......... 101 M3
Oldham Rd *ANC* M4 ....................... 7 K2
  *AULW* OL7 ............................. 75 K8
  *FAIL* M35 ............................... 74 C4
  *MDTN* M24 ............................ 57 M4
  *MILN* OL16 ............................. 10 F5
  *NEWH/MOS* M40 .................... 73 M6
  *OLDE* OL4 .............................. 60 D6
  *ROCH* OL11 ............................ 11 G1
  *ROCH* OL11 ............................ 42 E4
  *ROY/SHW* OL2 ........................ 59 H2
  *UPML* OL3 .............................. 44 D6
  *UPML* OL3 .............................. 61 K8
Oldhams La *BOL* BL1 ................... 22 A7
Oldham Sq *NM/HAY* SK22 * ...... 124 E5
Oldham St *CMANE* M1 ................... 7 H4
  *DROY* M43 ............................. 89 J2
  *DTN/ASHW* M34 .................... 100 A1
  *HYDE* SK14 ........................... 102 A2
  *ORD* M5 ................................... 6 A5
  *RDSH* SK5 ............................. 100 B5

Onchan Av *OLDE* OL4 .................. 59 L6
One Ash CI *WHIT* OL12 ................ 28 C2
One Oak La *WILM/AE* SK9 ......... 127 H5
Onslow Av *NEWH/MOS* M40 ...... 74 B3
Onslow CI *OLD* OL1 ....................... 9 G3
Onslow Rd *EDGY/DAV* SK3 ......... 12 C7
Onslow St *ROCH* OL11 ................. 27 M8
Onward St *HYDE* SK14 ............... 102 A2
Oozewood Rd *MDTN* M24 ........... 42 D7
Opal CI *RUSH/FAL* M14 * ............ 99 G4
Opal Gv *LEIGH* WN7 .................... 66 E8
Opal St *BNG/LEV* M19 ................. 99 L4
Openshaw Fold Rd *BURY* BL9 ..... 39 G5
Openshaw La *IRL* M44 ................. 94 B6
Openshaw Pl *FWTH* BL4 .............. 52 E4
Openshaw St *BURY* BL9 ................ 5 H6
Orama Av *SLFD* M6 ...................... 70 D8
Orama Ms *WHIT* OL12 * ............... 20 A4
Oram St *BURY* BL9 ........................ 5 H2
Orange Hill Rd *PWCH* M25 .......... 55 M7
Orange St *SLFD* M6 ...................... 86 D1
Orbital Wy *DTN/ASHW* M34 ...... 101 G1
Orchard CI *OFTN* SK2 ................ 113 C6
  *WGNW/BIL/OR* WN5 ............. 62 A1
Orchard Crs *MCFLDN* SK10 ....... 130 C6
Orchard Dr *GLSP* SK13 ............... 104 B3
  *HALE/TIMP* WA15 ................. 108 E5
  *WILM/AE* SK9 ....................... 127 J2
Orchard Gdns *BOLE* BL2 ............. 37 J1
Orchard Gn *WILM/AE* SK9 ........ 130 E3
Orchard Gv *DID/WITH* M20 ......... 98 C2
  *ROY/SHW* OL2 ........................ 43 K5
Orchard La *LEIGH* WN7 ............... 66 C5
  *POY/DIS* SK12 * ................... 121 M8
Orchard Pl *HALE/TIMP* WA15 ... 108 E5
  *POY/DIS* SK12 * ................... 121 M8
  *SALE* M33 .............................. 96 E7
Orchard Ri *HYDE* SK14 ............... 102 C4
Orchard Rd *FAIL* M35 ................... 74 C5
  *HALE/TIMP* WA15 ................. 108 B7
  *MPL/ROM* SK6 ..................... 114 C2
Orchard Rd East
  *WYTH/NTH* M22 .................. 110 A2
Orchard Rd West
  *WYTH/NTH* M22 .................. 110 A2
The Orchards
  *WGNW/BIL/OR* WN5 ............. 46 B7
Orchard St *AIMK* WN4 ................. 78 C3
  *DID/WITH* M20 ...................... 98 C7
  *HEY* OL10 ............................... 41 H5
  *HYDE* SK14 ........................... 102 B2
  *SLFD* M6 ................................ 71 K8
  *STKP* SK1 .............................. 13 K4
  *WGN* WN1 .............................. 15 H3
The Orchard *WHTN* BL5 .............. 50 B3
Orchard V *EDGY/DAV* SK3 ........ 111 M6
Orchid Av *FWTH* BL4 ................... 52 E3
Orchid CI *IRL* M44 ........................ 94 B4
  *OLD* OL1 .................................. 8 E1
Orchid Dr *BURY* BL9 ..................... 39 K5
Orchid Gdns *CHD/CHDH* SK8 .... 110 C6
Orchid St *BKLY* M9 ...................... 73 G5
Ordsall Av *LHULT* M38 ................ 52 E8
Ordsall Dr *ORD* M5 ...................... 86 E5
Ordsall La *ORD* M5 ........................ 6 A6
Oregon Av *OLD* OL1 ....................... 9 G1
Oregon CI *BRUN/LGST* M13 * ..... 87 M6
Orford Av *POY/DIS* SK12 .......... 123 M7
Orford CI *GOL/RIS/CUL* WA3 ...... 79 K5
  *MPL/ROM* SK6 ..................... 123 C5
Orford Ct *LEIGH* WN7 ................. 81 L2
Orford Rd *NEWH/MOS* M40 ........ 73 M7
  *PWCH* M25 ............................ 55 K7
Organ St *LEIGH* WN7 .................. 66 B7
  *WGNE/HIN* WN2 * ................. 16 A8
Oriel Av *OLDS* OL8 ...................... 75 H1
Oriel CI *CHAD* OL9 ........................ 8 B7
  *OFTN* SK2 ............................. 112 E6
Oriel Rd *AIMK* WN4 ...................... 63 J8
  *DID/WITH* M20 ...................... 98 D8
Oriel St *BOLS/LL* BL3 * ................ 36 A8
  *ROCH* OL11 ............................ 10 F7
Orient Rd *SLFD* M6 ...................... 70 D8
Orient St *BRO* M7 ........................ 72 C5
Oriole CI *WALK* M28 .................... 68 E5
Oriole Dr *WALK* M28 .................... 68 E4
Orion Pl *BRO* M7 * ....................... 71 M8
Orkney CI *NTHM/RTH* M23 ....... 109 K8
  *RAD* M26 ................................ 38 E8
Orkney Dr *URM* M41 .................... 85 G7
Orlanda Av *SLFD* M6 ................... 70 D8
Orlanda Dr *BRO* M7 .................... 72 C6
Orlando St *BOLE* BL2 .................... 3 G8
Orleans Wy *OLD* OL1 ................... 9 H4
Orley Wk *OLD* OL1 * ..................... 44 A8
Orme Av *MDTN* M24 .................... 57 K5
  *SLFD* M6 ................................ 70 B8
Orme CI *OP/CLY* M11 .................. 88 B3
  *URM* M41 ............................... 96 C2
Ormerod Av *ROY/SHW* OL2 ........ 59 H1
Ormerod CI *MPL/ROM* SK6 ....... 113 J3
Ormerod St *HEY* OL10 ................. 41 H3
Orme St *OLDE* OL4 ........................ 9 L8
  *STKP* SK1 * ........................... 112 E2
  *WILM/AE* SK9 ....................... 130 D3
Ormonde Av *SLFD* M6 ................. 70 E8
Ormonde Ct *AUL* OL6 .................. 75 H8
Ormond St *BOLS/LL* BL3 ............. 37 G7
  *BURY* BL9 ................................ 5 H3
Ormrod St *BOLE* BL2 ................... 22 F7
  *BOLS/LL* BL3 .......................... 2 D6
  *BURY* BL9 ................................ 5 J5
  *FWTH* BL4 ............................. 52 F4
Orsmby Av *GTN* M18 ................... 88 E3
Ormsby CI *EDGY/DAV* SK3 ........ 112 B8
  *WGNNW/ST* WN6 .................. 31 H3
Orms Gill Pl *OFTN* SK2 * ............ 113 H6
Ormsgill St *HULME* M15 .............. 87 J6
Ormside St *WGNE/HIN* WN2 ....... 65 L1
Ormskirk Av *DID/WITH* M20 ....... 98 C6
Ormskirk CI *TOT/BURYW* BL8 .... 38 C1
Ormskirk Rd *RDSH* SK5 ............. 100 C6
  *WGNW/BIL/OR* WN5 ............. 14 B6
Ormston Gv *LEIGH* WN7 ............. 66 C5
Ornatus St *BOL* BL1 ..................... 22 C7
Orphanage St *HTNM* SK4 ............ 13 H1
Orpington Dr *TOT/BURYW* BL8 .. 38 E1
Orpington Rd *BKLY* M9 ................ 73 H5
Orpington St
  *WGNW/BIL/OR* WN5 ............. 46 F6
Orrell Ar *WGN* WN1 ...................... 14 F3
Orrell Gdns
  *WGNW/BIL/OR* WN5 ............. 46 C6

Orrell Hall CI
  *WGNW/BIL/OR* WN5 ............. 46 C6
Orrell Rd *WGNW/BIL/OR* WN5 ... 46 B5
Orrell St *OP/CLY* M11 * ............... 89 G4
  *TOT/BURYW* BL8 .................... 4 E3
  *WGN* WN1 .............................. 15 J6
Orrel St *SLFD* M6 ......................... 86 B2
Orrishmere Rd *CHD/CHDH* SK8 . 120 B1
Orron St *LIT* OL15 ......................... 21 L7
Orsett CI *NEWH/MOS* M40 ......... 87 M1
Orthes Gv *HTNM* SK4 ................. 100 A1
Orton Av *HTNM/RTH* SK4 .......... 109 K3
Orton Rd *NTHM/RTH* M23 ........ 109 K3
Orton Wy *AIMK* WN4 ................... 78 C1
Orvietto Av *SLFD* M6 ................... 70 A8
Orville Dr *BNG/LEV* M19 ............. 99 J5
Orwell Av *DTN/ASHW* M34 ....... 100 D1
  *WYTH/NTH* M22 .................. 110 A6
Orwell CI *TOT/BURYW* BL8 * ....... 4 F1
  *WGNNW/ST* WN6 .................. 47 H1
  *WILM/AE* SK9 ....................... 127 H2
Orwell Rd *BOL* BL1 ...................... 35 L2
Osborne CI *TOT/BURYW* BL8 ..... 38 E4
Osborne Dr *SWIN* M27 ................ 70 F5
Osborne Gv *BOL* BL1 ................... 35 M4
  *CHD/CHDH* SK8 .................... 119 J1
  *LEIGH* WN7 ............................ 67 G6
Osborne Pl *GLSP* SK13 ................ 93 K7
  *BKLY* M9 ............................... 73 H5
  *BNG/LEV* M19 ....................... 99 J3
  *DTN/ASHW* M34 ..................... 90 C8
  *GOL/RIS/CUL* WA3 ................ 80 C5
  *HYDE* SK14 ........................... 102 B3
  *OFTN* SK2 .............................. 13 J9
  *OLDS* OL8 .............................. 85 K1
  *SLFD* M6 * .............................. 85 K1
Osborne St *CHAD* OL9 .................. 8 B3
  *HEY* OL10 ............................... 41 G3
  *MPL/ROM* SK6 ..................... 112 F1
  *NEWH/MOS* M40 .................... 72 F4
  *ROCH* OL11 ............................ 10 D9
  *ROY/SHW* OL2 ........................ 43 L6
  *SLFD* M6 ................................ 86 C1
Osborne Ter *SALE* M33 ............... 96 E8
Osbourne CI *FWTH* BL4 ............... 53 C3
  *WILM/AE* SK9 ....................... 127 H1
Osbourne St *DID/WITH* M20 ...... 110 D1
Oscar St *BOL* BL1 * ...................... 35 M2
  *NEWH/MOS* M40 .................... 73 K5
Oscott Av *LHULT* M38 .................. 52 D7
Oscroft CI *CHH* M8 ....................... 72 C2
Osmond St *OLDE* OL4 .................. 59 M5
Osmund Av *BOLE* BL2 ................. 37 G5
Osprey Av *WHTN* BL5 .................. 49 M6
Osprey CI *DUK* SK16 .................... 91 H5
  *HULME* M15 .......................... 87 H7
Osprey Dr *DROY* M43 .................. 89 M1
  *IRL* M44 ................................. 94 D7
  *WILM/AE* SK9 ....................... 127 G4
The Ospreys *WGNS/IIMK* WN3 ... 62 C1
Osprey Wk *BRUN/LGST* M13 * .... 87 M6
Ossory Rd *RUSH/FAL* M14 ......... 98 C1
Osterley Rd *BKLY* M9 ................... 73 K1
Ostlers Ga *DROY* M43 .................. 90 A2
Ostrich La *PWCH* M25 ................. 71 M1
Oswald CI *SLFD* M6 ..................... 71 K7
Oswald La *CCHDY* M21 ............... 97 L3
Oswald Rd *CCHDY* M21 .............. 97 L3
Oswald St *ANC* M4 ........................ 7 G1
  *ANC* M4 * .............................. 88 A3
  *BOLS/LL* BL3 ......................... 35 M8
  *CHAD* OL9 .............................. 8 E2
  *MILN* OL16 ............................. 11 H2
  *RDSH* SK5 ............................ 100 C1
  *ROY/SHW* OL2 ........................ 43 M4
Oswestry CI *TOT/BURYW* BL8 .... 24 B4
Otago Rd *OLDE* OL4 .................... 59 M3
Otago St *OLDE* OL4 * ................... 59 M3
Othello Dr *ECC* M30 ..................... 85 G2
Otley Av *SLFD* M6 ........................ 86 A5
Otley CI *CHAD* OL9 ........................ 8 B7
Otley Gv *EDGY/DAV* SK3 ........... 112 A8
Otmoor Wy *ROY/SHW* OL2 ......... 43 K8
Otranto Av *SLFD* M6 .................... 86 A5
Ottawa CI *NTHM/RTH* M23 ....... 109 J8
Ott CI *HULME* M15 ....................... 87 H6
Otterburn Pl *OFTN* SK2 ............. 113 C6
Otterbury CI *TOT/BURYW* BL8 ... 38 C2
Otter Dr *BURY* BL9 ...................... 39 L8
  *CHH* M8 ................................. 72 B7
Otterspool Rd *MPL/ROM* SK6 ... 113 L3
Otterwood Sq
  *WGNW/BIL/OR* WN5 ............. 46 F2
Oulder HI *ROCH* OL11 ................. 27 L5
Oulder Hill Dr *ROCH* OL11 .......... 27 L5
Oulder Mt *ROCH* OL11 * .............. 27 L5
Ouldfield CI *MILN* OL16 ............... 11 J6
Oulton Av *SALE* M33 ................... 97 H7
Oulton CI *LEIGH* WN7 .................. 66 D8
Oulton St *BOL* BL1 ....................... 22 D7
Oulton Wk *NEWH/MOS* M40 ...... 88 A2
Oundle CI *RUSH/FAL* M14 ........... 98 F1
Ouse St *SALQ* M50 ....................... 85 M3
Outram CI *MPL/ROM* SK6 * ....... 114 C8
Outram Rd *DUK* SK16 .................. 90 E6
Outram Sq *DROY* M43 * ............... 89 K4
Outrington Dr *OP/CLY* M11 ........ 88 D4
Outwood Av *SWIN* M27 ............... 54 A8
Outwood Dr *CHD/CHDH* SK8 ... 119 J4
Outwood Gv *BOL* BL1 .................. 22 B7
Outwood La *MANAIR* M90 ......... 118 E4
Outwood La West
  *MANAIR* M90 ....................... 118 D4
Outwood Rd *CHD/CHDH* SK8 ... 119 K4
  *RAD* M26 ................................ 54 D3
Oval Dr *DUK* SK16 ....................... 90 E5
The Oval *CHD/CHDH* SK8 .......... 119 K4
  *WGNNW/ST* WN6 .................. 30 C7
Oven Hill Rd *NM/HAY* SK22 * ... 125 J4
Overbeck CI *WGNNW/ST* WN6 ... 31 K8
Overbridge Rd *BRO* M7 ............... 72 B8
Overbrook Av *NEWH/MOS* M40 . 73 C7
Overbrook Dr *PWCH* M25 ............ 71 L1
Overdale *SWIN* M27 ..................... 70 D6
Overdale CI *OLD* OL1 ..................... 9 H1
Overdale Crs *URM* M41 ............... 85 K5
Overdale Dr *BOL* BL1 ................... 35 K5
  *GLSP* SK13 ........................... 104 C4
Overdale Rd *MPL/ROM* SK6 ...... 113 M5
  *POY/DIS* SK12 .................... 124 B3
  *WYTH/NTH* M22 .................. 110 A7
Overdell Dr *WHIT* OL12 ............... 27 M1
Overens St *OLDE* OL4 .................. 59 L5
Overfield Wy *WHIT* OL12 ............. 28 C2
Overgreen *BOLE* BL2 ................... 23 K5
Overhill Dr *WILM/AE* SK9 .......... 127 J5
Overhill La *WILM/AE* SK9 ......... 127 L5

Overhill Rd CHAD OL9 58 C4
Over Hill Rd NM/HAY SK22 125 J7
Overhill Rd WILM/AE SK9 127 H5
Overhill Wy WGNS/IIMK WN3 63 G1
Overlea Dr BNG/LEV M19 99 H7
Overlinks Dr SLFD M6 70 E7
Overshores Rd EDGW/EG BL7 16 D5
Overstone Dr CHH M8 72 C5
Overton Av WYTH/NTH M22 110 A7
Overton Cl RAD M26 54 E3
Overton Crs BRAM/HZG SK7 113 H8
SALE M33 108 A2
Overton Rd WYTH/NTH M22 110 A7
Overton St LEIGH WN7 66 B8
Over Town La WHIT OL12 26 D1
Overt St ROCH OL11 10 F8
Overwood Rd WYTH/NTH M22 110 A4
Owenington Gv LHULT M38 52 D7
Owens Cl CHAD OL9 58 B4
Owens Farm Dr OFTN SK2 113 H5
Owens Pk RUSH/FAL M14 * 99 G3
Owen St ECC M30 84 E3
EDGY/DAV SK3 12 F5
LEIGH WN7 * 66 A7
OLD OL1 60 B1
SLFD M6 71 K7
Owlerbarrow Rd
TOT/BURYW BL8 38 D1
Owler La CHAD OL9 74 A1
Owlwood Cl LHULT M38 68 B1
Owlwood Dr LHULT M38 68 B1
Owsten Ct HOR/BR BL6 33 J1
Oxbridge Cl SALE M33 108 A1
Oxbrow Wy WHTF M45 55 K4
Oxburgh Rd WGNS/IIMK WN3 48 C8
Oxendale Dr MDTN M24 56 F3
Oxenhurst Gn OFTN SK2 113 H7
Oxford Av DROY M43 89 J1
ROCH OL11 27 K6
SALE M33 96 A8
WHTF M45 55 K4
Oxford Cl FWTH BL4 52 C4
Oxford Ct CMANW M2 * 6 F7
OLDTF/WHR M16 * 87 G7
WGN WN1 15 J2
Oxford Dr MDTN M24 57 M2
MPL/ROM SK6 101 M8
Oxford Gv BOL BL1 2 A2
Oxford Ml AULW OL7 * 90 C4
Oxford Pl MILN OL16 11 H9
RUSH/FAL M14 87 M8
Oxford Rd ALT WA14 116 F1
ATH M46 67 H1
BOLS/LL BL3 53 J1
BRUN/LGST M13 87 L7
CMANE M1 7 G8
DUK SK16 91 G4
HOR/BR BL6 34 C4
SLFD M6 70 D8
WGNW/BIL/OR WN5 46 C5
Oxford St BOL BL1 2 E5
BURY BL9 5 H6
CHAD OL9 8 C9
CMANE M1 6 F6
ECC M30 85 H3
LEIGH WN7 66 C5
ROY/SHW OL2 43 L5
STLY SK15 77 G8
WGNE/HIN WN2 49 J5
Oxford St East AULW OL7 90 C4
Oxford St West AULW OL7 90 C4
Oxford Wy HTNM SK4 12 F1
WHIT OL12 28 B2
Ox Ga BOLE BL2 23 G7
Ox Hey Cl HOR/BR BL6 34 B4
RAMS BL0 18 F5
Ox Hey La HOR/BR BL6 34 C5
UPML OL3 45 H3
Oxlea Gv WHTN BL5 50 B5
Oxney Rd RUSH/FAL M14 87 M8
Ox St RAMS BL0 18 E7
Oxton Av WYTH/NTH M22 109 M8
Oxton St OP/CLY M11 89 J5


# P


Pacific Rd ALT WA14 107 K6
Pacific Wy SALQ M50 85 M4
Packer St BOL BL1 35 M2
MILN OL16 10 E4
Packwood Cha CHAD OL9 58 C4
Padbury Cl URM M41 95 G1
Padbury Wy BOLE BL2 37 H2
Padden Brook MPL/ROM SK6 113 L2
Paddington Av
NEWH/MOS M40 * 73 L7
Paddington Cl SLFD M6 86 D2
Paddison St SWIN M27 70 B5
Paddock Cha POY/DIS SK12 122 B6
Paddock Cl ATH M46 51 H7
Paddock La ALT WA14 106 D7
FAIL M35 74 C7
LYMM WA13 106 A5
Paddock Ri WGNNW/ST WN6 47 H1
Paddock Rd HYDE SK14 * 102 A4
The Paddocks EDGY/DAV SK3 112 D7
Paddock St WGTN/LGST M12 7 L8
The Paddock AIMK WN4 63 J6
BRAM/HZG SK7 120 F3
CHD/CHDH SK8 111 H7
HALE/TIMP WA15 108 E8
HYDE SK14 93 H7
RAMS BL0 18 E5
UPML OL3 61 J8
WALK M28 69 H5
Paderborn Ct BOL BL1 2 C6
Padfield Ga GLSP SK13 105 G5
Padfield Main Rd GLSP SK13 93 L6
Padiham Cl BURY BL9 39 G5
LEIGH WN7 66 D7
Padstow Cl HYDE SK14 103 G1
Padstow Dr BRAM/HZG SK7 121 H5
Padstow St NEWH/MOS M40 * 88 B1
Padstow Wk HYDE SK14 103 G1
Pagan St MILN OL16 10 F3
Pagefield Cl WGNNW/ST WN6 14 C2
Pagefield St WGNNW/ST WN6 14 C1
Paget St NEWH/MOS M40 73 G7
Pagnall Ct CHAD OL9 * 8 A8
Paignton Av BNG/LEV M19 99 J4
HYDE SK14 102 F2
Paignton Cl
WGNW/BIL/OR WN5 62 B4
Paignton Dr SALE M33 96 A7
Paignton Gv RDSH SK5 100 B5
Pailin Dr DROY M43 89 M2
Pailton Cl HOR/BR BL6 35 G6
Painswick Rd WYTH/NTH M22 118 D3
Paisley Pk FWTH BL4 53 G3
Paiton St BOL BL1 35 M5
Palace Ar AIMK WN4 78 E1
Palace Gdns ROY/SHW OL2 59 G2
Palace Rd AUL OL6 76 B7
SALE M33 96 D7
Palace St BOL BL1 2 E3
BURY BL9 5 J5
CHAD OL9 8 D5
Palatine Av DID/WITH M20 98 E6
Palatine Cl IRL M44 94 C3
WGNS/IIMK WN3 47 H8
Palatine Crs DID/WITH M20 98 E7
Palatine Dr BURY BL9 25 J4
Palatine Rd DID/WITH M20 110 C1
ROCH OL11 27 K4
WYTH/NTH M22 110 B2
Palatine Sq LEIGH WN7 66 A7
Palatine St BOL BL1 2 E4
DTN/ASHW M34 90 B7
MILN OL16 11 L5
RAMS BL0 18 F6
Palewood Cl WGN WN1 15 K1
Paley St BOL BL1 2 F4
Palfrey Pl WGTN/LGST M12 7 M9
Palgrave Av NEWH/MOS M40 73 G7
Palin St WGNE/HIN WN2 65 L1
Palin Wood Rd UPML OL3 45 J7
Pall Ml CMANW M2 6 F5
Palma Av HALE/TIMP WA15 118 C4
Palm Av AIMK WN4 63 G7
Palm Cl SALE M33 95 M7
Palmer Av CHD/CHDH SK8 111 J6
Palmer Cl OLDS OL8 59 J8
Palmer Gv LEIGH WN7 66 B3
Palmerston Av
OLDTF/WHR M16 98 A2
Palmerston Cl DTN/ASHW M34 100 E1
RAMS BL0 24 E1
WGNE/HIN WN2 48 F8
Palmerston Rd
DTN/ASHW M34 100 E1
OFTN SK2 121 K1
Palmerston St WGTN/LGST M12 88 A4
Palmer St BRO M7 71 M7
DUK SK16 90 E3
SALE M33 96 D8
Palm Gv CHAD OL9 8 B2
WGNW/BIL/OR WN5 47 G6
Palm St BOL BL1 36 C1
BRUN/LGST M13 99 J1
DROY M43 89 G2
OLDE OL4 59 M4
Pandora St DID/WITH M20 98 D7
Panfield Rd WYTH/NTH M22 109 M8
Pangbourne Av URM M41 96 B1
Pangbourne Cl EDGY/DAV SK3 111 M6
Pankhurst Wk RUSH/FAL M14 98 E1
Panmure St OLDS OL8 59 J8
Pansy Rd FWTH BL4 52 D4
Panton St HOR/BR BL6 34 A3
Paper Mill Rd EDGW/EG BL7 22 C5
Paprika Cl OP/CLY M11 89 G5
Parade Rd MANAIR M90 118 E5
Paradise St DTN/ASHW M34 90 C5
GLSP SK13 93 K7
RAMS BL0 18 F6
Paramel Av BOLS/LL BL3 37 L7
Parbold Av DID/WITH M20 98 D5
The Parchments NEWLW WA12 79 G8
Pargate Cha ROCH OL11 27 K4
Paris Av ORD M5 86 E5
WGNS/IIMK WN3 62 F1
Parish Vw ORD M5 86 E4
Paris St BOLS/LL BL3 35 L8
Park 66 BURY BL9 * 39 L6
Park Av ALT WA14 108 B4
BNG/LEV M19 99 J3
BOL BL1 * 22 B8
BRAM/HZG SK7 120 E7
BRO M7 72 C4
CHAD OL9 58 E3
CHD/CHDH SK8 120 B3
EDGY/DAV SK3 111 J5
FAIL M35 74 A4
GOL/RIS/CUL WA3 79 J2
HALE/TIMP WA15 117 H3
HYDE SK14 91 G8
MPL/ROM SK6 113 M2
OLDTF/WHR M16 86 F7
POY/DIS SK12 122 A8
PWCH M25 55 L8
RAD M26 39 G8
RAMS BL0 19 G6
SALE M33 96 D6
URM M41 95 M2
WGNNW/ST WN6 30 E5
WGNW/BIL/OR WN5 62 B3
WHTF M45 55 G6
WILM/AE SK9 127 G4
Park Bank ATH M46 51 J6
Park Bridge Rd AULW OL7 75 K5
Parkbrook La
WGNNW/ST WN6 30 E5
Parkbrook Rd
NTHM/RTH M23 109 L5
Park Brow Cl CCHDY M21 97 M5
Park Cl ALT WA14 108 C4
CHAD OL9 8 A1
GLSP SK13 105 G2
STLY SK15 91 J1
WHTF M45 55 J6
Park Cottages BOL BL1 * 35 M1
ROY/SHW OL2 43 J4
Park Court Ms
CHD/CHDH SK8 * 111 H8
Park Crs AUL OL6 91 H2
CHAD OL9 58 C3
GLSP SK13 104 E1
RUSH/FAL M14 98 F1
WGN WN1 14 E1
WILM/AE SK9 126 F3
Park Crs West WGN WN1 14 D2
Parkdale CHAD OL9 58 E3
TYLD M29 67 L7
Parkdale Av
DTN/ASHW M34 90 A5
GTN M18 88 F7
Parkdale Rd BOLE BL2 3 L1
Parkdene Cl BOLE BL2 23 G8
Park Dene Dr GLSP SK13 104 F2
Park Dr ECC M30 70 A8
HALE/TIMP WA15 108 D5
HALE/TIMP WA15 117 H3
HTNM SK4 12 B3
HYDE SK14 91 G8
OLDTF/WHR M16 97 M2
WILM/AE SK9 126 F3
Park Edge WHTN BL5 50 D5
Parkedge Cl LEIGH WN7 81 H1
Parkend Dr LEIGH WN7 81 G2
Parkend Rd NTHM/RTH M23 109 K7
Parker St BURY BL9 5 H5
CMANE M1 7 H5
Parkfield CHAD OL9 58 D3
DROY M43 89 K2
ECC M30 * 83 M8
ORD M5 86 A2
WGNNW/ST WN6 30 E5
Parkfield Av FWTH BL4 52 F5
MPL/ROM SK6 114 C6
OLDS OL8 74 E2
PWCH M25 72 A1
RUSH/FAL M14 98 E1
TYLD M29 67 L6
URM M41 95 L3
Parkfield Cl LEIGH WN7 66 D5
TYLD M29 67 L6
Parkfield Dr MDTN M24 57 H4
TYLD M29 68 A3
Parkfield Rd ALT WA14 107 M8
BOLS/LL BL3 52 C1
CHD/CHDH SK8 120 B3
OLDE OL4 61 H6
Parkfield Rd North
NEWH/MOS M40 74 B2
Parkfield Rd South
DID/WITH M20 98 D8
Parkfields STLY SK15 92 A1
WGNE/HIN WN2 64 E5
Parkfield St MILN OL16 42 E2
RUSH/FAL M14 98 E1
Parkgate CHAD OL9 58 E3
TOT/BURYW BL8 24 B7
Park Gate Av DID/WITH M20 98 E6
Park Gate Cl MPL/ROM SK6 101 H7
Parkgate Dr BOL BL1 22 C7
OFTN SK2 112 E8
SWIN M27 70 E5
Parkgate Rd ALT WA14 107 M4
Park Gates Av CHD/CHDH SK8 120 E3
Park Gates Dr CHD/CHDH SK8 120 E3
Park Gv BNG/LEV M19 99 K2
HTNM SK4 99 L8
RAD M26 38 C8
WALK M28 69 G4
Parkham Cl WHTN BL5 50 C6
Park Hey Dr WGNNW/ST WN6 30 B5
Park Hl PWCH M25 * 72 A2
Parkhill Av CHH M8 72 E2
Park Hill Cl NM/HAY SK22 124 E3
Park Hill Dr WHTF M45 55 H4
Park Hill Rd HALE/TIMP WA15 117 J3
Parkhills Cl BURY BL9 5 G8
Parkhills Rd BURY BL9 4 F9
Park Hill St BOL BL1 2 A3
Park House Bridge Est
SLFD M6 * 71 J5
Park House Bridge Rd SLFD M6 71 J6
Parkhouse St OP/CLY M11 88 F4
Parkhurst Av NEWH/MOS M40 74 B3
Parkin Cl DUK SK16 90 F4
Parkinson St BOLS/LL BL3 35 M7
BURY BL9 25 J7
Parkin St WGTN/LGST M12 99 K1
Parklake Av BRO M7 72 B4
Parkland Av NM/HAY SK22 124 E3
Parklands ROY/SHW OL2 42 F6
ROY/SHW OL2 44 A4
WHTF M45 55 H4
Parklands Dr SALE M33 108 A2
WGNE/HIN WN2 32 F6
Parklands Rd NTHM/RTH M23 109 J5
The Parklands HTNM SK4 100 B8
RAD M26 53 L4
Parklands Wy POY/DIS SK12 122 A8
Park La BRO M7 72 A4
DUK SK16 90 F4
HALE/TIMP WA15 117 J3
HOR/BR BL6 34 A1
LEIGH WN7 66 F8
OLDS OL8 75 J2
POY/DIS SK12 122 A8
ROY/SHW OL2 43 H7
SLFD M6 70 F7
STKP SK1 112 E4
UPML OL3 61 M7
WGNE/HIN WN2 64 E5
WGNE/HIN WN2 65 H6
WHIT OL12 10 E3
WHTF M45 55 H5
Park Lane Ct WHTF M45 * 55 G5
Park La West SWIN M27 71 G5
Parkleigh Dr NEWH/MOS M40 74 B2
Park Ldg BNG/LEV M19 99 K3
Park Lodge Cl CHD/CHDH SK8 111 H8
Park Meadow WHTN BL5 50 D4
Park Ms OLDTF/WHR M16 97 M2
Parkmount Rd BKLY M9 73 H3
Park Pde AUL OL6 90 D2
ROY/SHW OL2 43 M3
Park Pl ANC M4 87 K1
HTNM SK4 111 J2
PWCH M25 55 M7
SLFD M6 85 K1
Park Range RUSH/FAL M14 99 G1
Park Ri MPL/ROM SK6 113 M1
Park Rd ALT WA14 116 C2
BOL BL1 2 A5
BOLS/LL BL3 37 J8
BURY BL9 4 E1
CHD/CHDH SK8 110 C6
CHD/CHDH SK8 111 H6
CHD/CHDH SK8 120 E3
DTN/ASHW M34 90 A4
DTN/ASHW M34 101 H1
DUK SK16 91 G3
ECC M30 70 A8
GLSP SK13 93 L8
GOL/RIS/CUL WA3 79 J5
HALE/TIMP WA15 108 C4
HALE/TIMP WA15 117 H3
HTNM SK4 99 L7
HYDE SK14 91 G8
MDTN M24 57 J4
MPL/ROM SK6 113 M1
NM/HAY SK22 124 E5
OLDS OL8 9 J8
PART M31 106 D1
POY/DIS SK12 123 H6
PWCH M25 72 A1
RAMS BL0 24 C1
SALE M33 96 D6
SLFD M6 70 D8
STRET M32 96 F2
WALK M28 68 F3
WGNE/HIN WN2 65 H1
WGNNW/ST WN6 14 C1
WGNNW/ST WN6 31 H4
WGNW/BIL/OR WN5 46 D6
WGNW/BIL/OR WN5 62 C2
WHIT OL12 28 E3
WHTN BL5 50 C4
WHTN BL5 50 E3
WILM/AE SK9 126 D5
Park Rd North URM M41 95 M2
Park Rd South URM M41 95 M2
Park Rw BOL BL1 22 C6
HTNM SK4 111 J3
Park Seventeen WHTF M45 55 J4
Parkside MDTN M24 57 H6
WGNE/HIN WN2 49 H6
Park Side Av ROY/SHW OL2 43 M4
Parkside Av AIMK WN4 63 J4
BRO M7 72 B4
ECC M30 84 F3
FAIL M35 74 B7
WALK M28 69 G3
Parkside Cl MPL/ROM SK6 122 F4
RAD M26 39 H8
RAD M26 54 E1
Parkside Crs
WGNW/BIL/OR WN5 46 C6
Parkside La MPL/ROM SK6 114 F6
Parkside Ms WHTF M45 55 J3
Parkside Rd RUSH/FAL M14 98 C2
SALE M33 109 G1
Parkside St BOLE BL2 * 36 F3
WGTN/LGST M12 * 7 M8
Parkside Wk BRAM/HZG SK7 121 G1
BURY BL9 4 F7
Parks Nook FWTH BL4 52 F5
Park Sq AUL OL6 76 B8
OLDTF/WHR M16 97 K2
Parkstead Dr BKLY M9 73 G6
The Parks NEWLW WA12 78 E3
Parkstone Av GTN M18 89 J6
WHTF M45 55 G6
Parkstone Cl TOT/BURYW BL8 38 C2
Parkstone Dr SWIN M27 70 E6
Parkstone La WALK M28 69 J8
Parkstone Rd IRL M44 94 D1
Park St ATH M46 51 H8
AUL OL6 90 E2
BOL BL1 2 A3
BRO M7 71 M4
CSLFD M3 6 A4
CSLFD M3 87 J1
DROY M43 89 M2
DTN/ASHW M34 101 G1
FWTH BL4 53 G3
HEY OL10 41 H4
MILN OL16 10 E6
MOSL OL5 76 F4
MPL/ROM SK6 113 J1
OLDS OL8 9 H7
PWCH M25 55 M8
RAD M26 38 F8
ROY/SHW OL2 43 H8
ROY/SHW OL2 43 L6
STKP SK1 13 J3
STLY SK15 91 L3
SWIN M27 70 D5
TYLD M29 67 K3
WGNS/IIMK WN3 14 E7
Parksway BKLY M9 56 E6
PWCH M25 71 M2
SWIN M27 70 F6
Parks Yd BURY BL9 4 E4
Park Ter HEY OL10 41 G1
MOSL OL5 * 76 F4
The Park OLDE OL4 61 G7
UPML OL3 61 M7
Park Vw AIMK WN4 78 E2
BKLY M9 72 F6
CHAD OL9 58 D3
DTN/ASHW M34 * 90 A4
EDGY/DAV SK3 111 J5
FWTH BL4 53 G3
FWTH BL4 53 J5
LIT OL15 21 M6
RUSH/FAL M14 * 99 H5
STKP SK1 112 E5
WGNE/HIN WN2 64 E3
WGNW/BIL/OR WN5 * 46 E7
Park View Ct PWCH M25 * 71 L1
Park View Ri NM/HAY SK22 124 E3
Park View Rd BOLS/LL BL3 * 35 M8
PWCH M25 71 L1
Parkville Rd DID/WITH M20 98 F7
WHTF M45 55 M5
Park Wy STRET M32 85 J8
Parkway BRAM/HZG SK7 121 G2
CHAD OL9 58 D3
DTN/ASHW M34 100 F1
EDGY/DAV SK3 111 J5
LHULT M38 68 B1
NM/HAY SK22 124 E3
ROCH OL11 27 L4
WGNNW/ST WN6 30 D2
WHTN BL5 50 A7
WILM/AE SK9 126 F6
Parkway Gv LHULT M38 52 B8
Parkwood Cl
WGNS/IIMK WN3 15 L8
Parkwood Dr WHTN BL5 51 J5
Parkwood Rd
NTHM/RTH M23 109 M5
Parliament Pl BURY BL9 4 D7
Parliament St BURY BL9 4 E7
WGNS/IIMK WN3 15 J7
Parndon Dr OFTN SK2 112 F5
Parnell Av WYTH/NTH M22 110 A4
Parnell Cl TYLD M29 67 L7
Parnham Cl RAD M26 37 L7
Parrbrook Cl BURY BL9 55 K3
Parr Cl FWTH BL4 52 E4
Parrenthorn Rd PWCH M25 55 M5
Parrfield Rd WALK M28 69 K5
Parr Fold BURY BL9 55 L2
Parr Fold Av WALK M28 68 F3
Parrin La ECC M30 84 F1
Parr La BURY BL9 55 K3
Parrot St BOLS/LL BL3 2 C9
OP/CLY M11 88 F3
Parrs Mount Ms HTNM SK4 111 J2
Parr St ECC M30 85 G3
OP/CLY M11 * 89 H5
TYLD M29 67 J4
Parrs Wood Av
DID/WITH M20 110 F3
Parrs Wood La DID/WITH M20 111 G3
Parrs Wood Rd
DID/WITH M20 110 F3
Parry Md MPL/ROM SK6 101 K8
Parry Rd WGTN/LGST M12 88 D8
Parslow Av CHH M8 72 D4
Parsonage Cl BURY BL9 5 J4
ORD M5 86 F4
Parsonage Dr WALK M28 68 F2
Parsonage Gdns CSLFD M3 * 6 E4
MPL/ROM SK6 114 D8
Parsonage La CSLFD M3 * 6 E3
Parsonage Rd DID/WITH M20 98 F5
HTNM SK4 99 L8
RAD M26 * 53 M5
URM M41 95 H3
WALK M28 68 F2
Parsonage St BURY BL9 5 J4
CHH M8 72 C3
HTNM SK4 13 G3
HULME M15 87 H7
HYDE SK14 * 102 A2
Parsonage Wk MILN OL16 * 29 J5
Parsonage Wy CHD/CHDH SK8 111 K7
LEIGH WN7 66 B6
Parsons Dr MDTN M24 57 J2
Parsons Fld SLFD M6 * 71 K7
Parson's La BURY BL9 4 F3
Parson's Wk WGN WN1 14 E2
Parsons Wy BKLY M9 73 H5
Parth St BURY BL9 40 A3
Partington Ct FWTH BL4 52 F3
GLSP SK13 105 J3
Partington La SWIN M27 70 B5
Partington Pk GLSP SK13 104 F2
ROCH OL11 41 M4
Partington Pl SALE M33 96 E7
Partington St BOLS/LL BL3 51 M2
ECC M30 85 G1
FAIL M35 74 C5
HEY OL10 40 D2
NEWH/MOS M40 73 J7
OLD OL1 * 9 L5
ROCH OL11 41 L2
WALK M28 69 M4
WGNW/BIL/OR WN5 47 H4
Partridge Av NTHM/RTH M23 109 L6
Partridge Cl ROCH OL11 27 J5
Partridge Ct OFTN SK2 * 112 E8
Partridge Ri DROY M43 90 A1
Partridge Rd FAIL M35 74 F6
Partridge St STRET M32 86 C7
Partridge Wy CHAD OL9 58 A4
Part St WHTN BL5 50 B2
Parvet Av DROY M43 89 J1
Pascal St BNG/LEV M19 99 K4
Passmonds Crs ROCH OL11 27 L4
Passmonds Wy ROCH OL11 27 L4
Pass St CHAD OL9 8 E7
The Pass MILN OL16 11 H3
Paston Rd WYTH/NTH M22 110 A5
Pasture Cl AIMK WN4 63 H6
HEY OL10 40 E3
Pasturefield Cl SALE M33 109 J1
Pasture Field Rd
WYTH/NTH M22 119 H3
Pasturegreen Wy IRL M44 94 E1
Pastures La OLDE OL4 60 E4
Patch Croft Rd
WYTH/NTH M22 119 H3
Patchett St WGTN/LGST M12 88 C6
Patch La BRAM/HZG SK7 121 G7
Pateley Sq WGNNW/ST WN6 47 L2
Patey St WGTN/LGST M12 99 K1
Patience St WHIT OL12 27 M3
Patmos St RAMS BL0 19 G6
Paton Av BOLS/LL BL3 52 D1
Paton Ct BRO M7 71 M8
Paton St CMANE M1 7 J5
WHIT OL12 28 A1
Patricia Dr WALK M28 69 H2
Patricroft Rd WGNE/HIN WN2 15 M7
Patten St DID/WITH M20 98 E6
Patterdale Av AULW OL7 75 J7
URM M41 84 E8
Patterdale Cl OLD OL1 9 L1
ROCH OL11 41 L1
Patterdale Dr BURY BL9 39 H5
MDTN M24 57 H2
Patterdale Pl WGNE/HIN WN2 48 D5
Patterdale Rd AIMK WN4 63 K4
AULW OL7 75 J7
BOLE BL2 23 H8
LEIGH WN7 66 F8
MPL/ROM SK6 101 L8
PART M31 106 B1
STKP SK1 112 E6
WYTH/NTH M22 110 B4
Patterson Av CCHDY M21 97 K3
Patterson St BOLS/LL BL3 35 K8
DTN/ASHW M34 90 C8
NEWLW WA12 78 E8
WHTN BL5 49 L5
Patting Cl IRL M44 94 F1
Pattishall Cl ANC M4 88 A3
Pattison Cl WHIT OL12 27 M1
Patton Cl BURY BL9 55 L2
Paulden Av NTHM/RTH M23 109 L6
OLDE OL4 60 B3
Paulden Dr FAIL M35 74 D5
Paulette St BOL BL1 36 B2
Paulhan Rd DID/WITH M20 99 G8
Paulhan St BOLS/LL BL3 52 B1
Pauline St WGNE/HIN WN2 65 L3
Pavilion Cl WHIT OL12 28 C2
Pavilion Dr AUL OL6 76 A7
Pavilion Gdns WHTN BL5 50 B4
The Pavilions CHD/CHDH SK8 111 G8
Pavilion Wk RAD M26 38 C8
Paxford Pl WILM/AE SK9 126 E7
Paythorne Gn OFTN SK2 113 H7
Peabody St BOLS/LL BL3 36 B8
Peacefield MPL/ROM SK6 114 B7
Peace St ATH M46 67 H1
BOLS/LL BL3 2 A9
FAIL M35 * 74 D3
TYLD M29 67 J6
Peaceville Rd BNG/LEV M19 99 J3
Peach Bank MDTN M24 57 K4
Peach Gv RNFD/HAY WA11 * 78 B5
Peach Rd OLDE OL4 60 A4
Peach St PWCH M25 55 M7
Peach Tree Cl BRO M7 * 72 C6
Peach Tree Ct SLFD M6 * 86 D2
Peacock Av SLFD M6 71 H7
Peacock Cl GLSP SK13 93 H8
GTN M18 88 F6
Peacock Dr CHD/CHDH SK8 119 K6
Peacock Fold LEIGH WN7 66 A6
Peacock Gv GTN M18 89 G8
Peak Av ATH M46 50 F7
Peak Bank MPL/ROM SK6 113 K2
Peak Cl OLDE OL4 44 C8
Peakdale Av CHD/CHDH SK8 119 J3
Peakdale Rd DROY M43 89 H1
GLSP SK13 104 B1
MPL/ROM SK6 114 D8
Peaknaze Cl GLSP SK13 104 D4
SWIN M27 70 E4
Peak Rd NM/HAY SK22 124 F4
Peak St BOL BL1 36 A2
CHAD OL9 8 C7
CMANE M1 7 K5
STKP SK1 13 L4
Peak Vw GLSP SK13 93 J8
Pear Av BURY BL9 5 M3
Pear Cl MDTN M24 57 L6
Peardale Cl ECC M30 84 F4
Pearl Av BRO M7 72 B3

Pearl Mill Cl *OLDS* OL8 .................59 L8
Pearl St *BRAM/HZG* SK7 ...........113 H8
   *DTN/ASHW* M34 .....................101 H1
   *ROCH* OL11 ..................................27 M4
   *WGNNW/ST* WN6 .......................47 L1
Pearly Bank *OLD* OL1 ....................44 A8
Pearn Rd *BNG/LEV* M19 ................99 J7
Pearson Cl *MILN* OL16 ...................29 J5
   *PART* M31 ...................................106 D1
Pearson Gv *OLDE* OL4 ..................60 B6
Pearson St *BURY* BL9 .......................5 K2
   *DUK* SK16 ....................................9 H4
   *MILN* OL16 ..................................11 M2
   *RDSH* SK5 ..................................112 C1
Peart Av *MPL/ROM* SK6 ...............101 M6
Pear Tree Cl *GLSP* SK13 ................93 H8
   *MPL/ROM* SK6 ............................114 E4
   *SLFD* M6 ......................................86 D2
Pear Tree Ct *SLFD* M6 ....................86 D2
   *WGNE/HIN* WN2 ..........................32 F6
Pear Tree Dr *FWTH* BL4 .................52 D5
   *STLY* SK15 ...................................91 L2
Pear Tree Gv *TYLD* M29 .................68 B3
Pear St *DTN/ASHW* M34 ..............101 H1
Peary St *ANC* M4 ...........................87 L1
Peaslake Cl *MPL/ROM* SK6 ..........114 A2
Peatfield Av *SWIN* M27 ...................70 A2
Peatfield Wk *HULME* M15 * ............87 J7
Pebble Cl *STLY* SK15 ......................76 D8
Pebworth Cl *MDTN* M24 ..................57 J7
Peckford Dr *NEWH/MOS* M40 .......73 K7
Peckforton Cl *CHD/CHDH* SK8 .....110 D7
Peckmill Cl *WILM/AE* SK9 .............127 C2
Pedder St *BOL* BL1 .........................35 M3
Pedler Brow La *WHIT* OL12 ............21 J6
Pedley Hl *MCFLDN* SK10 ..............129 K5
Pedley Wk *BRUN/LGST* M13 ...........7 K8
Peebles Cl *AIMK* WN4 ....................62 F8
Peebles Dr *NEWH/MOS* M40 ..........74 A8
Peel Av *ALT* WA14 ........................116 F2
Peel Brow *RAMS* BL0 .....................19 G6
Peel Cir *URM* M41 ..........................85 H6
Peel Cl *ATH* M46 ............................66 E2
Peel Cross Rd *ORD* M5 ...................86 D3
Peel Dr *LHULT* M38 .........................52 C8
   *SALE* M33 ....................................97 H8
Peelgate Dr *CHD/CHDH* SK8 ........119 J2
Peel Green Rd *ECC* M30 .................84 F4
Peel Gv *WALK* M28 .........................69 H4
   *WGTN/LGST* M12 ........................88 D8
Peel Hall Av *TYLD* M29 ...................67 L3
Peel Hall Rd *RAMS* BL0 ..................24 C1
   *WYTH/NTH* M22 ........................119 H1
Peel La *CHH* M8 ..............................72 D1
   *HEY* OL10 ....................................40 E1
   *LHULT* M38 .................................52 C8
   *TYLD* M29 ...................................67 L8
Peel Moat Rd *HTNM* SK4 ...............99 L3
Peel Mt *RAMS* BL0 ..........................18 D8
   *SLFD* M6 ......................................86 E1
Peel Park Crs *LHULT* M38 ...............52 C8
Peel Rd *HALE/TIMP* WA15 ............117 G1
Peels Av *OLDE* OL4 ........................60 D5
Peel St *AUL* OL6 ..............................90 E1
   *CHAD* OL9 .....................................8 B6
   *DROY* M43 ...................................89 J4
   *DTN/ASHW* M34 ..........................90 B8
   *DUK* SK16 ....................................90 F3
   *ECC* M30 ......................................85 J2
   *FAIL* M35 .....................................74 A6
   *FWTH* BL4 ...................................53 H4
   *GLSP* SK13 ..................................93 M7
   *HEY* OL10 ....................................40 E2
   *HYDE* SK14 ................................102 C3
   *LEIGH* WN7 .................................66 B7
   *LIT* OL15 ......................................21 M7
   *OFTN* SK2 ..................................112 C6
   *RAD* M26 .....................................54 C2
   *STLY* SK15 ...................................91 J3
   *WGNE/HIN* WN2 ..........................64 D2
   *WHIT* OL12 ..................................10 C2
   *WHTN* BL5 ...................................50 B3
Peel Vw *TOT/BURYW* BL8 .............24 D6
Peel Wk *BURY* BL9 ...........................4 D1
   *BURY* BL9 ...................................25 H4
   *RAMS* BL0 ...................................24 E1
   *TOT/BURYW* BL8 ........................25 G5
   *TOT/BURYW* BL8 ........................18 C7
   *TOT/BURYW* BL8 ........................25 G6
Peel Wy *BURY* BL9 ...........................4 E4
Peelwood Av *LHULT* M38 ...............52 D8
Peelwood Gv *ATH* M46 ...................67 K2
Peers Cl *URM* M41 ..........................84 A8
Peers St *TOT/BURYW* BL8 ...............4 A5
Pegamoid St *BOLE* BL2 ...................36 E3
Pegasus Ct *ROCH* OL11 * ..............27 M6
Pegasus Sq *BRO* M7 .......................86 F1
Pegwell Dr *BRO* M7 .........................72 B7
Pekin St *AUL* OL6 ............................75 M8
Pelham Gv *WGNE/HIN* WN2 ...........49 G8
Pelham Pl *CHH* M8 ..........................72 E1
Pelham St *AULW* OL7 .....................90 B4
   *BOLS/LL* BL3 ..............................51 M1
   *OLDS* OL8 ...................................75 J2
Pellowe Rd *OLDS* OL8 ....................75 H1
Pelton Av *SWIN* M27 .......................70 A2
Pemberlei Rd *WGNE/HIN* WN2 ......49 G2
Pemberton Rd
   *WGNS/IIMK* WN3 ........................62 E3
Pemberton St *BOL* BL1 * ................22 B8
   *LHULT* M38 .................................52 E8
   *ROCH* OL11 ................................41 M2
Pemberton Wy *ROY/SHW* OL2 ......43 L4
Pembridge Fold *MDTN* M24 ............57 J8
Pembridge Rd *BKLY* M9 ..................57 J8
Pembroke Av *ECC* M30 ...................85 G2
   *SALE* M33 ....................................96 C7
Pembroke Cl *BRUN/LGST* M13 ......88 A6
Pembroke Ct *BRAM/HZG* SK7 * ...122 A2
   *WHIT* OL12 ..................................10 E1
Pembroke Dr *BURY* BL9 .................39 H5
   *OLDE* OL4 ...................................44 B8
Pembroke Rd *WGNE/HIN* WN2 .......65 M1
   *WGNW/BIL/OR* WN5 ....................47 G3
Pembroke St *BOL* BL1 ....................72 B6
   *BRO* M7 ........................................72 B6
   *LIT* OL15 ......................................21 M6
   *OLDS* OL8 * ...................................8 F7
   *SLFD* M6 ......................................86 B3
Pembry Cl *RDSH* SK5 ...................100 E7
Pembury Cl *WYTH/NTH* M22 .........118 F1
Penarth Rd *BOLS/LL* BL3 ...............35 L8
   *WYTH/NTH* M22 ........................110 A4
Penbury Rd *WGN* WN1 ...................31 L7
Pencarrow Cl *DID/WITH* M20 .......110 C1
Pencombe Cl *WGTN/LGST* M12 ....88 D4
Pencroft Wy *HULME* M15 ...............87 K7
Pendale Av *CHH* M8 ........................72 E4
Pendeen Cl *TYLD* M29 .....................67 K5
   *WYTH/NTH* M22 ........................119 G3
Pendennis *ROCH* OL11 ...................10 D7
Pendennis Av *HOR/BR* BL6 ............35 G7

Pendennis Cl *RAD* M26 ...................37 M7
Pendennis Crs *WGNE/HIN* WN2 ....65 K1
Pendle Av *HTNM* SK4 ......................12 D1
Pendle Cl *BOL* BL1 ..........................22 B6
Pendlebury Cl *PWCH* M25 ..............71 J2
Pendlebury Fold *BOLS/LL* BL3 .......51 G2
Pendlebury La *WGN* WN1 ...............31 M6
   *WGNE/HIN* WN2 ..........................32 B5
Pendlebury Rd
   *CHD/CHDH* SK8 ........................110 D6
   *SWIN* M27 ...................................70 D4
Pendlebury St *BOL* BL1 ..................36 C1
Pendle Ct *OLDE* OL4 * .....................60 A7
   *TOT/BURYW* BL8 ........................38 E1
   *WGNW/BIL/OR* WN5 ....................47 C7
Pendle Dr *BOL* BL1 ..........................36 A1
   *LEIGH* WN7 .................................66 E8
Pendlecroft Av *SWIN* M27 ..............70 F5
Pendlegreen Cl *OP/CLY* M11 ..........88 C4
Pendle Rd *ROY/SHW* OL2 ...............58 F1
Pendleton Gn *SLFD* M6 * ................86 C1
Pendleton Wy *SLFD* M6 ..................86 D1
Pendleway *SWIN* M27 ......................70 D3
Pendragon Pl *FAIL* M35 ...................74 D5
Penelope Rd *SLFD* M6 .....................71 G7
Penerley Dr *BKLY* M9 ......................73 G6
Penfield Cl *CMANE* M1 ......................7 J8
Penfold Wk *WGTN/LGST* M12 * .....88 C6
Pengwern Av *BOLS/LL* BL3 ............35 L7
Penhale Ms *BRAM/HZG* SK7 .......121 H5
Penistone Av *BKLY* M9 ...................73 K1
   *MILN* OL16 ..................................11 M7
   *SLFD* M6 ......................................85 M1
Penketh Av *GTN* M18 ......................88 E3
   *TYLD* M29 ...................................67 L6
Penketh St *WGNNW/ST* WN6 ........47 L2
Penleach Av *LEIGH* WN7 .................66 E7
Penmere Gv *SALE* M33 ..................108 B3
Penmoor Cha *BRAM/HZG* SK7 .....121 K3
Penmore Cl *ROY/SHW* OL2 ............43 M5
Pennant Dr *PWCH* M25 ...................55 K7
Pennant St *OL* OL1 ..........................59 L4
Pennell Dr *WGNS/IIMK* WN3 ..........47 J7
Pennell St *OP/CLY* M11 ...................89 G3
Penn Gn *CHD/CHDH* SK8 .............120 D3
Penn House Cl *BRAM/HZG* SK7 ...121 G5
Pennine Av *CHAD* OL9 ....................58 D7
   *WGNS/IIMK* WN3 ........................62 F1
Pennine Bridleway *WHIT* OL12 .......20 B6
Pennine Cl *BKLY* M9 ........................57 J8
   *TOT/BURYW* BL8 ........................38 D1
Pennine Ct *STLY* SK15 ....................92 A1
   *AUL* OL6 ......................................76 B8
   *MILN* OL16 ..................................29 K7
   *WHIT* OL12 ..................................21 G6
Pennine Gv *AUL* OL6 .......................76 B6
   *LEIGH* WN7 .................................65 M4
Pennine La *COL/RIS/CUL* WA3 .......79 M3
Pennine Rd *BRAM/HZG* SK7 ........121 K3
   *GLSP* SK13 ................................104 D3
   *MPL/ROM* SK6 ..........................101 M6
Pennine V *ROY/SHW* OL2 ...............43 M4
Pennine Vw *DTN/ASHW* M34 ..........90 B7
   *MOSL* OL5 ...................................77 G3
   *ROY/SHW* OL2 ............................43 H8
   *STLY* SK15 ...................................76 F7
Pennington Av *LEIGH* WN7 .............81 H1
Pennington Cl *LHULT* M38 ..............52 B8
   *WGNE/HIN* WN2 ..........................49 H3
Pennington Gdns *LEIGH* WN7 ........81 H1
Pennington Green La
   *WGNE/HIN* WN2 ..........................49 H2
Pennington La *COL/RIS/CUL* WA3 ..32 B3
   *WGNE/HIN* WN2 ..........................48 D4
Pennington Rd *BOLS/LL* BL3 ..........52 C1
   *LEIGH* WN7 .................................81 H1
Pennington St *CHAD* OL9 ...............74 E1
   *TOT/BURYW* BL8 ........................24 B8
   *WALK* M28 ...................................69 H2
   *WGNE/HIN* WN2 ..........................49 G6
   *WGTN/LGST* M12 ........................99 K2
Pennon Cl *BRO* M7 ..........................72 B6
Penn St *FWTH* BL4 ..........................52 F4
   *HEY* OL10 ....................................41 G3
   *HOR/BR* BL6 ................................33 M1
   *MILN* OL16 ..................................10 F3
   *NEWH/MOS* M40 ........................73 J4
   *OLDS* OL8 ...................................75 J2
Penny Bridge La *URM* M41 ..............95 K2
Pennygate Cl *WGNE/HIN* WN2 ......49 G6
Pennyhurst St *WGNS/IIMK* WN3 ....14 D5
Penny La *RDSH* SK5 ........................13 J1
   *RNFD/HAY* WA11 .........................78 D5
Penny Meadow *AUL* OL6 ................90 F1
Pennymoor Dr *ALT* WA14 .............107 L6
Penrhos Av *CHD/CHDH* SK8 ........110 D6
Penrhyn Av *CHD/CHDH* SK8 ........120 A3
   *MDTN* M24 ..................................57 K5
Penrhyn Crs *BRAM/HZG* SK7 ......121 L4
Penrhyn Dr *BRAM/HZG* SK7 ........121 L3
   *PWCH* M25 ..................................55 L8
Penrhyn Gv *ATH* M46 ......................50 F7
Penrhyn Rd *EDGY/DAV* SK3 ...........12 C7
Penrice Av *RAD* M26 ........................38 A7
Penrice Fold *WALK* M28 ..................68 E5
Penrith Av *AULW* OL7 ......................75 J7
   *BOL* BL1 .......................................22 F6
   *OLDS* OL8 ...................................74 F1
   *RDSH* SK5 .................................100 C3
   *SALE* M33 .................................108 F2
   *WALK* M28 ...................................69 J2
   *WHTF* M45 ...................................55 L5
Penrith Cl *PART* M31 .......................94 B8
Penrith Crs *AIMK* WN4 ....................63 L8
Penrith St *ROCH* OL11 ....................10 F9
Penrod Pl *SLFD* M6 ..........................71 L8
Penrose Cl *CHH* M8 .........................72 D6
Penrose Gdns *MDTN* M24 ..............57 L3
Penrose St *BOLE* BL2 * .....................3 L4
Penrose Wk *MDTN* M24 ..................41 J8
Penroy Av *DID/WITH* M20 ............110 A1
Penruddock Wk
   *BRUN/LGST* M13 * .......................88 C8
Penry Av *IRL* M44 ............................94 B6
Penryn Av *ROY/SHW* OL2 ...............59 J1
   *SALE* M33 .................................108 F3
Pensarn Av *WASH/FAL* M14 ............99 H4
Pensarn Gv *RDSH* SK5 ..................100 C8
Pensby Cl *SWIN* M27 .......................70 F5
Pensford Cl *BOLE* BL2 .....................23 H6
Pensford Rd *NTHM/RTH* M23 .......118 D1
Penshaw Av *WGNS/IIMK* WN3 .......63 L1
Penshurst Rd *RDSH* SK5 ...............100 E6
Penson St *WGN* WN1 .......................48 A3
Penswick Rd *WGNE/HIN* WN2 ........66 A1
Penthorpe Dr *ROY/SHW* OL2 .........59 J1
Pentland Av *NEWH/MOS* M40 ........73 M2
Pentland Cl *BRAM/HZG* SK7 ........121 K3
Pentlands Av *BRO* M7 ......................72 A6

The Pentlands *ROY/SHW* OL2 ........43 J4
Pentland Ter *BOL* BL1 * ...................36 B3
   *ECC* M30 ......................................85 C3
   *OLDE* OL4 ...................................59 M4
   *ROCH* OL11 ................................10 F8
Pentland Wy *HYDE* SK14 ................91 L6
Pentwyn Gv *NTHM/RTH* M23 .......109 L5
Penwell Fold *OLD* OL1 * ....................9 H1
Penwortham St
   *NEWH/MOS* M40 ........................73 J8
Penydarren Vw *BOLS/LL* BL3 .........52 F2
Penzance St *NEWH/MOS* M40 .......88 B7
Penzance St
   *NEWH/MOS* M40 * ......................88 B1
Peover Av *SALE* M33 .......................97 H8
Peover Rd *WILM/AE* SK9 ..............120 A7
Pepler Av *NTHM/RTH* M23 ............109 L2
Pepperhill Rd *OLDTF/WHR* M16 .....87 J8
Pepper La *WGNNW/ST* WN6 .........30 E1
Pepper Mill La *WGN* WN1 ...............15 H6
Peppermint Cl *MILN* OL16 .............29 M8
Pepperwood Dr
   *WGNS/IIMK* WN3 ........................63 H2
Pepys Pl *WGNS/IIMK* WN3 .............47 K8
Perch St *WGN* WN1 .........................15 H1
Percival Cl *CHH* M8 .........................72 C6
Percival Rd *DROY* M43 ....................89 L3
Percival Wy *NEWH/MOS* M40 ........48 F8
Percy Dr *ORD* M5 .............................86 E5
Percy St *DTN/ASHW* M34 ..............101 E5
   *BOLS/LL* BL3 * ..............................36 C2
   *BURY* BL9 .......................................5 J2
   *FWTH* BL4 ...................................53 H5
   *HULME* M15 ................................87 C6
   *MILN* OL16 ..................................11 J9
   *OLDE* OL4 ...................................59 M5
   *RAMS* BL0 ...................................18 E7
   *STKP* SK1 ......................................13 J3
   *STLY* SK15 ...................................91 L3
Peregrine Crs *DROY* M43 ................89 M1
Peregrine Dr *IRL* M44 .......................94 D1
   *LEIGH* WN7 .................................66 E7
Peregrine Rd *OFTN* SK2 ................113 K8
Peregrine St *HULME* M15 ...............87 J7
Perendale Ri *BOL* BL1 .....................22 B8
Perivale Dr *OLDS* OL8 .....................59 M5
Pernham St *OLDE* OL4 ...................59 M5
Perrin St *HYDE* SK14 .....................102 A2
Perry Av *HYDE* SK14 .......................91 K8
Perry Cl *ROCH* OL11 .......................10 E9
Perrygate Av *DID/WITH* M20 ........98 D6
Perrymead *PWCH* M25 ...................55 L6
Perryn Pl *WGNNW/ST* WN6 ...........31 J3
Perry St *HALE/TIMP* WA15 ...........108 E6
Pershore *WHIT* OL12 .......................10 E1
Pershore Rd *MDTN* M24 ..................57 K1
Perth Av *CHAD* OL9 .........................58 D8
   *WGNE/HIN* WN2 ..........................48 D2
Perth Cl *BRAM/HZG* SK7 ..............121 C2
Perth Rd *ROCH* OL11 ......................42 E2
Perth St *BOLS/LL* BL3 .....................51 M1
   *ROY/SHW* OL2 ............................43 K8
   *SWIN* M27 ...................................70 A5
Peru St *SLFD* M3 ................................6 A2
Peterborough Cl *AUL* OL6 ...............75 L6
Peterborough Dr *BOL* BL1 ................2 D1
Peterborough St *GTN* M18 ..............89 J2
Peterborough Wk *BOL* BL1 ...............2 D1
Peterhead Cl *BOL* BL1 * ....................2 B1
Peterhead Wk *ORD* M5 * .................86 D3
Peterhouse Gdns
   *MPL/ROM* SK6 ..........................101 M8
Peterloo Ct *SLFD* M6 * ....................86 B2
Peter Moss Wy *BNG/LEV* M19 ........99 M3
Petersburg Rd *EDGY/DAV* SK3 ....111 M6
Petersfield Dr *NTHM/RTH* M23 .....109 G5
Petersfield Gdns
   *GOL/RIS/CUL* WA3 .......................81 H8
Petersfield Wk *BOL* BL1 * .................2 C1
Peter St *AIMK* WN4 .........................78 F1
   *ALT* WA14 ..................................116 F1
   *BRAM/HZG* SK7 ........................121 M1
   *BURY* BL9 .......................................5 G2
   *CMANE* M1 .....................................6 F6
   *DTN/ASHW* M34 ........................101 K1
   *ECC* M30 ......................................85 G3
   *GLSP* SK13 ..................................93 K6
   *GOL/RIS/CUL* WA3 .......................79 K4
   *LEIGH* WN7 .................................66 E8
   *OLD* OL1 ........................................9 J4
   *STKP* SK1 ......................................13 L2
   *TYLD* M29 ...................................67 J3
   *WGNE/HIN* WN2 ..........................49 G7
   *WGNW/BIL/OR* WN5 ....................46 E4
   *WHTN* BL5 ...................................49 K5
Peterswood Cl
   *WYTH/NTH* M22 ........................118 C1
Peterwood Gdns *STRET* M32 ..........96 D3
Petheridge Dr
   *WYTH/NTH* M22 ........................118 D3
Petrel Av *POY/DIS* SK12 ...............121 J8
Petrel Cl *DROY* M43 .........................89 M1
   *EDGY/DAV* SK3 ........................112 A6
   *ROCH* OL11 ................................27 M8
   *TYLD* M29 ...................................67 K4
Petrie St *WHIT* OL12 ........................10 F3
Petticoat La *WGNE/HIN* WN2 .........48 E5
Petts Crs *LIT* OL15 ..........................21 M5
Petworth Av *WGNS/IIMK* WN3 ......63 G2
Petworth Cl *WYTH/NTH* M22 ........110 B7
Petworth Rd *CHAD* OL9 ....................8 A6
Pevensey Rd *SLFD* M6 .....................71 H7
Pevensey Wk *CHAD* OL9 * ...............8 A7
Peveril Av *NM/HAY* SK22 ..............124 E3
Peveril Cl *WHTF* M45 .......................55 M5
Peveril Crs *CLSP* SK13 ..................105 J4
   *CCHDY* M21 ................................97 K2
Peveril Ct *BRAM/HZG* SK7 ...........122 B4
Peveril Crs *CCHDY* M21 ..................97 K2
Peveril Gdns *POY/DIS* SK12 .........124 C6
Peveril Ms *POY/DIS* SK12 .............124 C6
Peveril Rd *ALT* WA14 .....................108 A1
   *OLD* OL1 ......................................59 M3
   *ORD* M5 .......................................86 A2
Peveril St *BOLS/LL* BL3 ...................51 L1
Peveril Ter *HYDE* SK14 ..................102 C4
Pewfist Gn *WHTN* BL5 .....................50 B6
The Pewfist Spinney
   *WHTN* BL5 ...................................50 A5
The Pewfist *WHTN* BL5 ...................50 B5
Pewsey Rd *WYTH/NTH* M22 .........119 H1
Pexwood *OLD* OL1 ...........................58 B3
Pheasant Cl *WALK* M28 ..................68 E6
Pheasant Dr *CCHDY* M21 ...............98 A5
Pheasant Ri *ALT* WA14 ..................116 F3
Phelan Cl *NEWH/MOS* M40 * .........73 H4
Phethean St *BOLE* BL2 .....................3 H4
   *FWTH* BL4 ...................................52 F3
Philip Av *DTN/ASHW* M34 ...............90 A7
Philip Cl *WGNW/BIL/OR* WN5 .........47 G7
Philip Dr *SALE* M33 .........................108 C2
Philip Howard Rd *GLSP* SK13 .......104 F3
Philips Av *FWTH* BL4 .......................53 J5
Philips Park Rd *OP/CLY* M11 ..........88 B2
   *WHTF* M45 ...................................54 F7

Philip St *BOLS/LL* BL3 * .....................2 B9
   *ECC* M30 ......................................85 C3
   *OLDE* OL4 ...................................59 M4
   *ROCH* OL11 ................................10 F8
Phillimore St *OLDE* OL4 ..................60 B7
Phillips Park Rd *WHTF* M45 .............55 J6
Phillips St *LEIGH* WN7 .....................66 B4
Phipps St *WALK* M28 .......................52 F8
Phoebe St *BOLS/LL* BL3 * ...............35 M8
   *ORD* M5 .......................................86 D4
Phoenix Cl *HEY* OL10 ......................41 J4
Phoenix St *BOL* BL1 .........................3 G5
   *BURY* BL9 .......................................4 C4
   *CMANW* M2 * ..................................7 G4
   *FWTH* BL4 ...................................53 G5
   *LIT* OL15 ......................................21 M6
   *OLD* OL1 ........................................9 J5
   *WHIT* OL12 ..................................27 M3
Phoenix Wy *HULME* M15 .................87 J7
   *RAD* M26 .....................................54 D2
   *URM* M41 .....................................85 H6
Phyllis St *MDTN* M24 .......................57 M5
   *WHIT* OL12 ..................................27 L3
Picadilly *CMANE* M1 ..........................7 J5
Piccadilly *CMANE* M1 ........................7 J5
   *STKP* SK1 ......................................13 J5
Piccadilly Plaza *CMANE* M1 * ............7 H5
Piccadilly South *CMANE* M1 ..............7 J6
Piccard Cl *ANC* M4 ............................7 L1
Pickering Cl *HALE/TIMP* WA15 .....108 F3
   *RAD* M26 .....................................53 K4
   *TOT/BURYW* BL8 ........................24 E7
   *URM* M41 .....................................95 L2
Pickering St *HULME* M15 * ..............87 H7
Pickford Av *BOLS/LL* BL3 ................53 H8
Pickford Ct *DUK* SK16 * ..................90 F4
Pickford La *DUK* SK16 ......................90 F4
Pickford Ms *DUK* SK16 * .................90 F4
Pickford's Brow *STKP* SK1 ..............13 J4
Pickford St *ANC* M4 ...........................7 K3
Pickhill La *UPML* OL3 .......................61 L4
Pickhill Ms *UPML* OL3 ......................61 L4
Pickley Gdns *LEIGH* WN7 ................66 B8
Pickmere Av *DID/WITH* M20 ...........98 E4
Pickmere Cl *DROY* M43 ...................89 L3
   *EDGY/DAV* SK3 ........................111 M6
   *SALE* M33 .................................109 J2
Pickmere Gdns
   *CHD/CHDH* SK8 ........................111 J7
Pickmere Ms *UPML* OL3 ..................61 L4
Pickmere Rd *WILM/AE* SK9 ..........119 M7
Picksley St *LEIGH* WN7 ...................66 B8
Pickthorn Cl *WGNE/HIN* WN2 ........64 E1
Pickup St *MILN* OL16 .......................11 G5
   *WGNE/HIN* WN2 ..........................48 C5
Pickwick Rd *POY/DIS* SK12 ..........129 H1
Picton Cl *CSLFD* M3 ..........................6 C2
Picton Dr *WILM/AE* SK9 ................127 C3
Picton Sq *OLDE* OL4 * ........................9 L7
Picton St *AULW* OL7 ........................75 K6
   *BRO* M7 ........................................87 C1
Picton Wk *OLDTF/WHR* M16 ...........98 C1
Piele Rd *RNFD/HAY* WA11 ..............78 B5
Pierce St *OLD* OL1 ...........................59 M3
Piercy Av *OLDE* OL4 ........................44 B3
   *FAIL* M35 * ...................................74 B5
Piethorne Cl *MILN* OL16 ..................29 M8
Pigeon St *CMANE* M1 .........................7 K4
Pigginshaw *WILM/AE* SK9 ............126 C4
Piggott St *FWTH* BL4 .......................52 F4
Pigot Pl *WGNW/BIL/OR* WN5 .........46 E6
Pike Av *ATH* M46 ..............................66 D2
   *FAIL* M35 .....................................74 F6
Pike Cl *NM/HAY* SK22 ....................125 L1
Pike Fold La *BKLY* M9 ......................72 F1
Pike Rd *BOLS/LL* BL3 .......................36 A8
Pike's La *GLSP* SK13 ......................104 E4
Pike St *ROCH* OL11 ..........................10 F9
Pike View Cl *OLDE* OL4 ...................59 L7
Pilgrim Dr *OP/CLY* M11 ...................88 C3
Pilgrims Wy
   *WGNNW/ST* WN6 ........................31 K5
Pilgrim Wy *OLD* OL1 ........................60 A1
Pilkington Dr *WHTF* M45 .................55 L2
Pilkington Rd *BKLY* M9 ....................73 G6
   *FWTH* BL4 ...................................53 J6
   *RAD* M26 .....................................38 C7
Pilkington St *BOLS/LL* BL3 ................2 D8
   *MDTN* M24 ..................................57 M3
   *RAMS* BL0 ...................................18 E7
   *WGNE/HIN* WN2 ..........................49 G6
Pilkington Wy *RAD* M26 ...................54 D2
Pilling Fld *EDGW/EG* BL7 .................22 B3
Pilling St
   *DTN/ASHW* M34 ........................101 J1
   *LEIGH* WN7 .................................66 A7
   *NEWH/MOS* M40 ........................73 J7
   *TOT/BURYW* BL8 ........................38 F1
   *WHIT* OL12 ..................................10 E2
Pilning St *BOLS/LL* BL3 ...................36 D8
Pilot St *BURY* BL9 ..............................5 G7
Pilsley Cl
   *WGNW/BIL/OR* WN5 ....................46 D3
Pilsworth Rd *BURY* BL9 ...................39 K6
   *HEY* OL10 ....................................40 C5
Pilsworth Wy *BURY* BL9 ..................39 K6
Pimblett Rd
   *RNFD/HAY* WA11 .........................78 B5
Pimblett St *CSLFD* M3 .....................87 J1
   *GOL/RIS/CUL* WA3 .......................79 K5
Pimhole Fold *BURY* BL9 ....................5 J5
Pimhole Rd *BURY* BL9 .......................5 J5
Pimlico Cl *BRO* M7 * .........................72 B6
Pimlott Gv *HYDE* SK14 .....................91 G7
   *PWCH* M25 ..................................71 H2
Pimlott Rd *BOL* BL1 ..........................36 E1
Pimmcroft Wy *SALE* M33 ..............109 J1
Pine Av *WHTF* M45 ..........................55 J5
Pine Cl *DTN/ASHW* M34 ................101 K1
   *DUK* SK16 ....................................91 J4
   *ECC* M30 ......................................70 B8
   *FWTH* BL4 ...................................52 E4
   *GOL/RIS/CUL* WA3 .......................79 M4
   *PWCH* M25 ..................................55 K6
   *ROY/SHW* OL2 ............................43 G6
   *RUSH/FAL* M14 ............................88 B3
   *SALE* M33 ....................................96 A6
   *SWIN* M27 ...................................70 A5
   *WALK* M28 ...................................69 H4
   *WHTN* BL5 ...................................50 B5
Pinehurst Rd
   *NEWH/MOS* M40 ........................73 H7
Pine Ldg *BRAM/HZG* SK7 * ..........121 H5
Pine Meadow *RAD* M26 ...................53 M6
Pine Rd *BRAM/HZG* SK7 ...............121 H4
   *DID/WITH* M20 ............................98 D8
   *DUK* SK16 ....................................91 J4
   *POY/DIS* SK12 ..........................129 K1
   *WGNW/BIL/OR* WN5 ....................47 H6
The Pines *LEIGH* WN7 ......................81 J1

Pine St *AUL* OL6 ...............................75 L8
   *BOL* BL1 .......................................36 C2
   *BURY* BL9 .......................................5 K5
   *CHAD* OL9 ...................................58 D4
   *CMANE* M1 .....................................7 G5
   *HEY* OL10 ....................................41 G2
   *HYDE* SK14 ..................................91 G7
   *LIT* OL15 ......................................21 M6
   *MDTN* M24 ..................................57 M5
   *MILN* OL16 ..................................11 J5
   *MILN* OL16 ..................................43 L1
   *MPL/ROM* SK6 ..........................101 L7
   *TYLD* M29 ...................................67 K3
Pine St North *BURY* BL9 ...................5 K3
Pine St South *BURY* BL9 ...................5 K5
Pinetop Cl *CCHDY* M21 ...................98 A5
Pine Tree Rd *OLDS* OL8 ...................75 G3
Pinetree St *GTN* M18 .......................88 F7
Pinevale *WGNNW/ST* WN6 .............31 K5
Pineway *OLDE* OL4 ..........................60 E3
Pine Vw *WGNS/IIMK* WN3 ...............62 E3
Pinewood *AIMK* WN4 .......................78 D2
   *ALT* WA14 ..................................116 C2
   *CHAD* OL9 ...................................58 B5
   *SALE* M33 ....................................96 A8
Pinewood Cl *BOL* BL1 ......................36 B2
   *DUK* SK16 ....................................90 F3
   *HTNM* SK4 .................................111 K1
   *WGNE/HIN* WN2 ..........................64 E5
Pinewood Ct *ALT* WA14 .................117 C3
   *SALE* M33 ....................................97 G7
Pinewood Crs *WGNE/HIN* WN2 ......15 M1
   *WGNW/BIL/OR* WN5 ....................46 B6
Pinewood Rd *CCHDY* M21 ..............97 K5
   *WILM/AE* SK9 .............................127 J4
The Pinewoods *MPL/ROM* SK6 ......113 H8
Pinfold *GLSP* SK13 ...........................93 H3
Pinfold Av *BKLY* M9 .........................73 K2
Pinfold Cl *HALE/TIMP* WA15 .........117 M5
   *WHTN* BL5 ...................................50 A6
Pinfold Dr *CHD/CHDH* SK8 ...........120 C3
Pinfold La *HALE/TIMP* WA15 .........118 B6
   *MPL/ROM* SK6 ..........................102 B8
   *WHTF* M45 ...................................55 H4
Pinfold St *WGNE/HIN* WN2 .............48 D5
Pinfold Vw *RAD* M26 ........................53 M6
Pingate Dr *CHD/CHDH* SK8 ..........120 C6
Pingate La *CHD/CHDH* SK8 ..........120 C6
Pingate La South
   *CHD/CHDH* SK8 ........................120 C6
Pingle La *UPML* OL3 .........................45 C7
Pingot Av *NTHM/RTH* M23 ...........109 L3
Pingot La *HYDE* SK14 .....................103 M2
Pingot Rd *NM/HAY* SK22 ...............125 C4
   *WGNW/BIL/OR* WN5 ....................62 B7
The Pingot *IRL* M44 ..........................94 E1
   *LEIGH* WN7 .................................66 A7
Pingott La *GLSP* SK13 ......................93 K7
Pink Bank La *WGTN/LGST* M12 ......88 D8
Pinnacle Dr *EDGW/EG* BL7 .............22 A2
Pinner Pl *BNG/LEV* M19 ..................99 K7
Pinners Ct *RAMS* BL0 .......................18 F5
Pinnington La *STRET* M32 * .............97 C3
Pinnington Rd *GTN* M18 ..................89 C6
Pintail Av *EDGY/DAV* SK3 ..............112 A6
Pintail Cl *WHIT* OL12 ........................27 L2
Pioneer Rd *SWIN* M27 ......................71 C2
Pioneer St *LIT* OL15 .........................21 M7
   *OP/CLY* M11 ...............................88 E1
   *ROCH* OL11 ................................11 C7
Piperhill Av *WYTH/NTH* M22 .........110 A3
Pipers Cl *ROCH* OL11 ......................27 C4
Pipers Ct *IRL* M44 ............................94 F1
The Pipers *GOL/RIS/CUL* WA3 ........80 C4
Pipewell Av *GTN* M18 ......................88 F7
Pipit Cl *DTN/ASHW* M34 ..................89 M2
Pitchcombe Rd
   *WYTH/NTH* M22 ........................118 D2
Pitcombe Cl *BOL* BL1 ......................22 A5
Pitfield Gdns *NTHM/RTH* M23 .......109 J5
Pitfield La *BOLE* BL2 ........................37 J1
Pitfield St *BOLE* BL2 ...........................3 J5
Pit La *ROY/SHW* OL2 ........................42 F4
Pitman Cl *OP/CLY* M11 ....................88 D4
Pits Farm Av *ROCH* OL11 ...............27 M5
Pitsford Rd *NEWH/MOS* M40 ..........73 H7
Pitshouse La *WHIT* OL12 * ..............27 H2
Pit St *CHAD* OL9 ..............................58 E8
   *DTN/ASHW* M34 ........................101 J1
Pitt St East *OLDE* OL4 .....................59 L7
Pixmore Av *BOL* BL1 ........................22 E8
Place Rd *ALT* WA14 ........................107 M6
Plain Pit St *HYDE* SK14 ....................90 F7
Plainsfield Cl
   *OLDTF/WHR* M16 .........................87 J8
Plainsfield St
   *OLDTF/WHR* M16 .........................87 H8
Plane Av
   *WGNW/BIL/OR* WN5 ....................47 H5
Plane Ct *SLFD* M6 * ..........................86 D2
Plane Rd *FAIL* M35 ...........................74 C7
Plane St *OLDE* OL4 ..........................59 L5
Plane Tree Cl
   *MPL/ROM* SK6 ..........................114 A7
Plane Tree Gv
   *RNFD/HAY* WA11 * ......................78 D5
Planetree Rd
   *HALE/TIMP* WA15.......................117 J2
Plane Tree Rd *PART* M31 ...............106 A1
Planet Wy *DTN/ASHW* M34 .............90 B7
Plank La *LEIGH* WN7 ........................65 K8
Plantation Av *WALK* M28 .................52 F8
Plantation Gates *WGN* WN1 .............4 E5
Plantation Rd *EDGW/EG* BL7 ..........17 J5
Plantation St *AUL* OL6 .....................91 C3
   *GTN* M18 ....................................89 H7
Plant Cl *SALE* M33 ...........................96 D7
Plant Hill Rd *BKLY* M9 ......................56 F7
Plant St *CMANE* M1 ............................7 J5
Plant Ter *BKLY* M9 * .........................57 G7
Plate St *OLD* OL1 ...............................9 K5
Plato St *CHAD* OL9 ..........................59 J8
Platt Av *AUL* OL6 ..............................75 M6
Plattbrook Cl
   *RUSH/FAL* M14 ............................98 E3
Platt Cl *MILN* OL16 ...........................29 K7
Platt Cft *LEIGH* WN7 ........................66 F6
Platt Fold Rd *LEIGH* WN7 ................66 D7
Platt Fold St *LEIGH* WN7 .................66 D7
Platt La *WGNW/BIL/OR* WN5 ..........47 K6
Platting Gv *AULW* OL7 ....................75 J7
Platting La *RUSH/FAL* M14 ..............98 E3
   *WHIT* OL12 ..................................11 J8
Platting Rd *OLDE* OL4 ......................60 F6

Platt La RUSH/FAL M14 ...........98 C3
 UPML OL3 ..........................61 J2
 WGN WN1 ...........................15 K3
 WGN WN1 ...........................31 K1
 WGNE/HIN WN2 ...................49 G7
 WHTN BL5 ...........................50 E6
Platts Dr IRL M44 ..................94 D2
Platt St CHD/CHDH SK8 ........111 H6
 DUK SK16 ...........................90 D5
 GLSP SK13 ..........................93 L7
 LEIGH WN7 .........................66 C6
 OLDE OL4 ...........................60 C6
Plattwood Wk HULME M15 * ....87 G6
Playfair St HEY OL10 .............41 H5
Playfair St BOL BL1 ...............87 L8
 RUSH/FAL M14 .....................87 L8
Pleachway HTNM SK4 ...........111 J2
Pleasance Wy NEWLW WA12 ....78 F8
Pleasant Gdns BOL BL1 ............2 C2
Pleasant Rd ECC M30 .............85 H3
Pleasant St BKLY M9 ..............73 G5
 HEY OL10 ............................26 C5
 ROCH OL11 ..........................41 M2
 TOT/BURYW BL8 ...................24 C8
Pleasant Wy CHD/CHDH SK8 ...120 E6
Pleasington Dr
 NEWH/MOS M40 ...................73 M2
 TOT/BURYW BL8 ...................38 B2
Plevna St BOLE BL2 ..................3 H4
Plodder La FWTH BL4 .............52 A4
 WHTN BL5 ...........................51 K4
Ploughbank Dr CCHDY M21 ....97 L6
Plough Cl URM M41 ................94 F3
Plough Flds WALK M28 ...........68 C7
Ploughfields WHTN BL5 .........50 B1
Plough St DUK SK16 ...............91 G4
Plover Cl GLSP SK13 .............105 H4
 ROCH OL11 ..........................27 H5
Plover Dr ALT WA14 .............107 L4
 BURY BL9 ............................25 L8
 IRL M44 ..............................83 K8
Plover Wy GOL/RIS/CUL WA3 ...80 D4
Plowden Av BOLS/LL BL3 ........51 M1
Plowden Rd WYTH/NTH M22 ...118 D2
Plowley Cl DID/WITH M20 ......110 E2
Plucksbridge Rd
 MPL/ROM SK6 .....................123 J1
Plumbley Dr OLDTF/WHR M16 ...89 H1
Plumbley St OP/CLY M11 * ......89 M5
Plumley Cl EDGY/DAV SK3 ....112 C7
Plumley Rd WILM/AE SK9 ......119 M7
Plummer Av CCHDY M21 .........97 L6
Plumpton Cl ROY/SHW OL2 .....59 H3
Plumpton Dr BURY BL9 ...........25 H6
Plumpton Rd ROCH OL11 ........42 E4
Plumpton Wk
 BRUN/LGST M13 * ..................88 C8
Plum St OLDS OL8 ....................8 E8
Plum Tree Ct SLFD M6 ...........86 D2
Plunge Rd RAMS BL0 ..............19 H1
Pluto Cl SLFD M6 * ...................7 J3
Plymouth Av BRUN/LGST M13 ...88 B7
Plymouth Cl AUL OL6 .............75 M5
Plymouth Dr BRAM/HZG SK7 ...121 H5
 FWTH BL4 ............................52 C4
Plymouth Gv BRUN/LGST M13 ...88 A8
 EDGY/DAV SK3 .....................12 A8
 RAD M26 .............................38 A7
 WGNNW/ST WN6 ...................31 K5
Plymouth Gv West
 BRUN/LGST M13 .....................88 B7
Plymouth Rd SALE M33 ...........96 A4
Plymouth St OLDS OL8 ............59 J8
Plymouth Vw BRUN/LGST M13 ...87 M6
Plymtree Cl CHH M8 ...............72 B2
Pochard Dr ALT WA14 ...........107 L5
 POY/DIS SK12 ......................121 J8
Pochin St NEWH/MOS M40 ......88 B1
Pocket Nook La
 GOL/RIS/CUL WA3 ..................80 E5
Pocket Nook Rd HOR/BR BL6 ...50 E1
Pocklington Dr
 NTHM/RTH M23 ....................109 J5
Podnor La MPL/ROM SK6 .......115 K6
Podsmead Rd WYTH/NTH M22 ...118 D2
Poet's Nook LEIGH WN7 ..........66 B8
Poise Brook Dr OFTN SK2 ......113 J7
Poise Brook Rd OFTN SK2 ......113 J7
Poise Cl BRAM/HZG SK7 ........122 C1
Poke St WGNW/BIL/OR WN5 ....46 E6
Poland St ANC M4 ...................7 L2
 DTN/ASHW M34 ....................90 B4
Polden Cl OLDS OL8 ...............75 H1
Polding St WGNS/IIMK WN3 ....48 B8
Poleacre La MPL/ROM SK6 .....115 K3
Pole Ct BURY BL9 * .................55 M7
Polefield Ap PWCH M25 .........55 L6
Polefield Cir PWCH M25 .........55 L6
Polefield Gdns PWCH M25 ......55 L6
Polefield Gra PWCH M25 ........55 L6
Polefield Gv PWCH M25 .........55 L6
Polefield Hall Rd BKLY M9 ......73 G2
 PWCH M25 ..........................55 L5
Polegate Dr LEIGH WN7 .........55 M2
Pole La BURY BL9 ..................55 M2
 FAIL M35 .............................35 M2
 WHTF M45 ...........................56 A3
Pole St BOLE BL2 * ..................3 J1
 WGNNW/ST WN6 ...................31 H3
Polesworth Cl WGTN/LGST M12 ...88 D6
Police St ALT WA14 ...............108 A7
 CMANW M2 ............................6 E4
 ECC M30 ..............................84 F2
Pollard Ct OLD OL1 * ...............9 G2
Pollards La BURY BL9 .............24 F2
Pollard Sq PART M31 .............106 D1
Pollard St ANC M4 ...................7 M5
Pollard St East ANC M4 ............7 M5
Pollen Cl SALE M33 ................96 C1
Pollen Rd ALT WA14 .............107 M6
Polletts Av RDSH SK5 ...........100 F6
Pollit Av AUL OL6 ..................75 L6
Pollitt Cft MPL/ROM SK6 .......113 J3
Pollitt St WGTN/LGST M12 * ....88 C6
Pollitts Cl ECC M30 ...............84 E2
Polonia Ct OLDS OL8 ..............74 F1
Polperro Cl ROY/SHW OL2 ......43 K8
Polruan Rd CCHDY M21 ..........97 K3
Polworth Rd BKLY M9 .............73 G6
Polygon Av BRUN/LGST M13 ....87 M6
Polygon Rd CHH M8 .................7 L9
Polygon St BRUN/LGST M13 ......7 L9
The Polygon SLFD M6 .............71 M6
 ECC M30 ..............................85 K2
Pomfret St SLFD M6 * .............70 F7
 WGTN/LGST M12 ....................88 D6
Pomona Crs ORD M5 ..............86 D5
Pomona Strd HULME M15 .......86 D7
 ORD M5 ...............................86 D7
Pomona St ROCH OL11 ...........10 F9

Ponds Cl CCHDY M21 * ..........97 L3
Pond St GOL/RIS/CUL WA3 .....80 D4
Pondwater Cl WALK M28 ........68 C1
Ponsford Av BKLY M9 ............73 K1
Ponsonby Rd STRET M32 .......97 G1
Pontefract Cl SWIN M27 ........70 E5
Pool Bank St MDTN M24 ........56 F5
Poolcroft SALE M33 ..............109 J1
Poole Cl BRAM/HZG SK7 .......120 F3
Pooley Cl MDTN M24 .............56 E3
Poolfield Cl RAD M26 ............54 D1
Pool Fold FAIL M35 ...............74 D6
Pool House Rd POY/DIS SK12 ...122 E7
Poolstock WGNS/IIMK WN3 .....14 D8
Poolstock La WGNS/IIMK WN3 ...47 K8
Pool St BOL BL1 .....................2 D4
 OLDS OL8 ............................59 J8
 WGNE/HIN WN2 ....................49 G8
 WGNS/IIMK WN3 ...................14 E8
Pool Ter BOL BL1 ..................35 K2
Poolton Rd BKLY M9 ..............56 E8
Poorfield St OLDS OL8 .............9 H8
Poplar Av AIMK WN4 .............63 G7
 ALT WA14 ..........................108 A6
 BNG/LEV M19 .......................99 L5
 BOL BL1 ..............................22 C8
 BOLE BL2 .............................22 F6
 BURY BL9 ............................34 B3
 HOR/BR BL6 .........................34 A7
 NM/HAY SK22 ......................124 F3
 OLDE OL4 ............................60 F8
 OLDS OL8 ............................75 G2
 WGNW/BIL/OR WN5 ...............47 G6
 WILM/AE SK9 ......................126 C7
Poplar Cl CHD/CHDH SK8 ......110 E7
 DTN/ASHW M34 * ..................90 C6
 EDGY/DAV SK3 ....................112 C7
Poplar Dr PWCH M25 .............71 K2
 GTN M18 .............................89 G8
 IRL M44 ..............................94 A6
 OFTN SK2 ...........................112 F8
 RAMS BL0 ............................19 G5
 SALE M33 ...........................108 L1
 URM M41 .............................96 B2
 WGNE/HIN WN2 ....................50 D2
 WHTN BL5 ...........................50 L2
Poplar Gv AUL OL6 ................75 M8
Poplar Rd BNG/LEV M19 ........99 L6
 DUK SK16 ...........................91 J5
 ECC M30 ..............................70 B4
 STRET M32 ...........................96 F4
 SWIN M27 ............................70 A1
 WALK M28 ............................69 H2
Poplars Rd STLY SK15 ............92 A1
The Poplars LEIGH WN7 .........80 F4
 MOSL OL5 ............................77 H3
Poplar St DTN/ASHW M34 ......90 C6
 FAIL M35 .............................74 A4
 GOL/RIS/CUL WA3 ..................79 L3
 HTNM SK4 ..........................111 H2
 LEIGH WN7 ..........................81 J1
 TYLD M29 ............................67 K3
Poplar Wk CHAD OL9 ..............8 A3
Poplar Wy MPL/ROM SK6 ......123 J5
Poplin Dr CSLFD M3 ................6 D1
Poppy Cl CHAD OL9 ...............58 A5
 NTHM/RTH M23 ....................109 H3
Poppyfield Vw ROCH OL11 .....27 H4
Poppythorn La PWCH M25 .....55 K7
Porchester Dr RAD M26 .........37 M7
Porchfield Sq CSLFD M3 ..........6 D6
Porlock Av DTN/ASHW M34 ....89 M4
 HYDE SK14 .........................102 F2
Porlock Cl STKP SK1 .............112 F4
 WGNE/HIN WN2 ....................64 D1
Porlock Rd NTHM/RTH M23 ...109 L6
 URM M41 .............................95 L4
Porritt Cl ROCH OL11 ............27 H6
Porritt St BURY BL9 .................5 K1
Porritt Wy RAMS BL0 ............18 F5
Portal Cl DTN/ASHW M34 ......101 L3
Porter Av NEWLW WA12 ........78 F1
Porter Dr NEWH/MOS M40 .....73 G6
Porterfield Dr TYLD M29 ........67 K4
Porter St BURY BL9 ...............25 J8
Porters Wood Cl
 WGNW/BIL/OR WN5 ...............46 E5
Portfield Cl BOL BL1 ..............35 J4
Porthleven Crs TYLD M29 ......67 M4
Porthleven Dr
 NTHM/RTH M23 ....................109 H6
Portinscale Cl TOT/BURYW BL8 ...38 F1
Portland Cl BRAM/HZG SK7 ....121 K3
 WGNE/HIN WN2 ....................64 D1
Portland Crs BRUN/LGST M13 ...88 A8
Portland Dr BRUN/LGST M14 ...99 J3
Portland Houses
 MPL/ROM SK6 * ...................114 B7
 HOR/BR BL6 .........................33 M1
Portland Pl AULW OL7 ...........90 D3
 BRUN/LGST M13 ....................99 J1
 ECC M30 ..............................85 J1
 NM/HAY SK22 ......................124 F3
 STRET M32 ...........................97 H1
 SWIN M27 ............................70 D5
 WALK M28 ............................52 F7
Portland Rd ALT WA14 .........116 F1
 BRUN/LGST M13 ....................99 J3
Portland St North AUL OL6 .....90 D1
Portland St South AUL OL6 .....90 D1
Portloe Rd CHD/CHDH SK8 ....119 K5
Portman Rd OLDTF/WHR M16 ...98 B1
Portrea Cl EDGY/DAV SK3 .....112 B7
Portree Cl ECC M30 ...............84 E2
Portrush Rd WYTH/NTH M22 ...119 G2
Portside Cl WALK M28 ...........68 E7
Portsmouth Cl BRO M7 ..........72 A7
Portsmouth St BRUN/LGST M13 ...87 L1
Port Soderick Av ORD M5 ......86 D3
Portstone Cl OLDTF/WHR M16 ...87 H7
Portstone St
 OLDTF/WHR M16 * ..................87 H7
Port St CMANE M1 ..................7 J4
 OLDS OL8 ............................59 J8
 STKP SK1 .............................13 G5
Portugal Rd PWCH M25 .........71 L2
Portugal St ANC M4 * ..............7 M1
 AULW OL7 ...........................90 C4
Portugal St East CMANE M1 .....7 L6
Portville Rd BNG/LEV M19 .....99 K3
Portway WYTH/NTH M22 ......118 D2
Portwood Pl RDSH SK5 ..........13 J2
Posnett St EDGY/DAV SK3 .....12 C6
Postal St CMANE M1 * ............7 J3
Postbridge Cl BRUN/LGST M13 ...87 M6
Post Office St ALT WA14 .......108 A7

Post St GLSP SK13 ................93 L7
Potato Whf CSLFD M3 ..............6 B7
Pot Hl AUL OL6 ....................75 M8
Pot Hill Sq AUL OL6 ..............75 M8
Potter Rd GLSP SK13 ...........104 B1
Potters La BKLY M9 ...............73 H5
Potter St BURY BL9 .................5 J2
 RAD M26 .............................39 G8
Pottery La OP/CLY M11 .........88 D4
Pottery Rd WGNS/IIMK WN3 ...14 C6
Pottery Ter WGNS/IIMK WN3 ...14 C6
Pottinger St AULW OL7 .........90 C4
Pott St SWIN M27 .................70 C2
Poulton Av BOLE BL2 .............37 H5
Poulton Dr AIMK WN4 ...........63 J8
Poulton St OP/CLY M11 .........89 H5
Poundswick La
 WYTH/NTH M22 ....................118 F1
Powder Mill Cl IRL M44 .........94 D3
Powell Av HYDE SK14 ..........102 B1
Powell St OLDTF/WHR M16 ....86 F8
 OP/CLY M11 .........................89 G2
 TOT/BURYW BL8 ...................38 C3
 WGN WN1 ............................15 G2
 WGNE/HIN WN2 ....................64 E3
Pownall Av BRAM/HZG SK7 ...121 H6
 DID/WITH M20 ......................99 M8
Pownall Rd ALT WA14 .........116 F1
 CHD/CHDH SK8 ....................120 C3
 WILM/AE SK9 ......................126 D4
Pownall St BRAM/HZG SK7 ...121 M1
 LEIGH WN7 ..........................66 D7
Powys St ATH M46 ...............67 H3
Poynings Dr WYTH/NTH M22 ...118 E3
Poynt Cha WALK M28 ............68 C1
Poynter St NEWH/MOS M40 ....73 M3
Poynton St BURY BL9 .............5 H7
 HULME M15 ..........................87 J6
Praed Rd TRPK M17 ..............85 M7
Praeton Cl ATH M46 ..............66 D5
The Precinct EDGY/DAV SK3 * ...13 G8
 LEIGH WN7 ..........................66 B5
 OFTN SK2 ...........................113 G6
Preece Cl HYDE SK14 ............91 K8
Preesall Av CHD/CHDH SK8 ...119 K4
Preesall Cl TOT/BURYW BL8 ...38 C4
Prefect Pl WGNW/BIL/OR WN5 ...46 F4
Premier Rd CHH M8 ..............72 C8
Premier St OLDTF/WHR M16 ...87 G8
Prenton Wy TOT/BURYW BL8 ...24 C7
Presall St BOLE BL2 * ..............3 L3
Presbyterian Fold
 WGNE/HIN WN2 ....................49 G6
Prescot Av ATH M46 .............51 H8
 TYLD M29 ............................67 M3
Prescot Cl BURY BL9 ...............5 H7
Prescot Rd BKLY M9 ..............73 G5
 HALE/TIMP WA15 ..................117 H2
Prescott Av GOL/RIS/CUL WA3 ...79 J2
Prescott Cl
 WGNW/BIL/OR WN5 ...............46 E4
Prescott Rd WILM/AE SK9 .....126 A8
 GOL/RIS/CUL WA3 ..................79 K3
 LEIGH WN7 ..........................66 C6
 MILN OL16 ...........................28 F2
 WALK M28 ............................68 E1
 WGNE/HIN WN2 ....................14 C4
Press St OP/CLY M11 .............89 G5
Presswood Ct SLFD M6 * ........70 F6
Prestage St OLDTF/WHR M16 ...87 G8
 WGTN/LGST M12 ....................99 L2
Prestbury Av HALE/TIMP WA15 ...108 B6
 RUSH/FAL M14 .....................98 C3
 WGNS/IIMK WN3 ...................63 H1
Prestbury Cl BURY BL9 ...........5 H7
 EDGY/DAV SK3 ....................113 G8
Prestbury Dr MPL/ROM SK6 ...113 H1
 OLD OL1 ..............................59 G3
Prestbury Rd BOL BL1 ...........22 D7
 MCFLDN SK10 ......................131 K6
 WILM/AE SK9 ......................127 J1
Preston Av ECC M30 ..............85 K1
 IRL M44 ..............................94 C5
Preston Cl ECC M30 * ............85 K1
Preston Rd BNG/LEV M19 ......99 K4
 WGNNW/ST WN6 ...................31 G1
Preston St BOLS/LL BL3 * ........36 E8
 GTN M18 .............................88 F6
 MDTN M24 ...........................57 K4
 OLDE OL4 ..............................9 L7
 WHIT OL12 ...........................27 M4
Prestt Gv WGNS/IIMK WN3 .....14 B9
Prestwich Av LEIGH WN7 .......66 E5
 OFTN SK2 ...........................112 E5
Prestwich Hills WHTF M45 .....71 K2
Prestwich Park Rd South
 PWCH M25 ...........................71 K1
Prestwich St ATH M46 ...........50 E8
Prestwood Cl BOL BL1 ...........35 M1
Prestwood Dr BOL BL1 ..........36 A3
Prestwood Rd FWTH BL4 .......52 D3
 SLFD M6 ..............................70 F8
Pretoria Rd AIMK WN4 ..........63 G8
 BOLE BL2 .............................37 H5
 OLDS OL8 ............................74 F1
Pretoria St WHIT OL12 * ........27 M3
Prettywood BURY BL9 ...........40 A2
Price St ANC M4 * ................88 A3
 BURY BL9 ..............................5 H7
 DUK SK16 ...........................90 F4
 FWTH BL4 ............................53 G3
Prichard St STRET M32 .........97 G2
Pridmouth Rd
 DID/WITH M20 ......................98 F6
Priest Av CHD/CHDH SK8 .....110 D8
Priestfields LEIGH WN7 .........66 E7
Priestley La MCFLDN SK10 ...131 M1
Priestley Rd WALK M28 .........69 M4
Priestley Wy ROY/SHW OL2 ...44 A5
Priestnall Rd HTNM SK4 ......111 J1
Priestners Wy LEIGH WN7 .....66 B6
Priest St STKP SK1 ...............13 K9
Priestwood Av OLDE OL4 ......44 C8
Primrose Av FWTH BL4 .........52 D3
 HYDE SK14 .........................102 B5
 MPL/ROM SK6 .....................114 B6
 UPML OL3 ............................61 M3
 URM M41 .............................96 A2
 WALK M28 ............................68 E2

Primrose Bank ALT WA14 .....116 E3
 OLDS OL8 ..............................9 G9
 TOT/BURYW BL8 ...................24 B5
 WALK M28 ............................68 E2
Primrose Cl BOLE BL2 ...........23 K8
 ORD M5 ...............................86 C2
Primrose Cottages ALT WA14 ...116 E3
Primrose Crs HYDE SK14 ......102 A4
Primrose Gv RNFD/HAY WA11 ...75 H5
 WGNW/BIL/OR WN5 ...............47 H5
Primrose Hl BOLE BL2 ...........23 J8
Primrose La GLSP SK13 ........104 E4
 WGNNW/ST WN6 ...................31 G2
Primrose St ANC M4 ...............7 K2
 BOL BL1 ..............................22 C8
 FWTH BL4 ............................53 H5
 LEIGH WN7 ..........................66 A7
 OLDS OL8 ..............................9 H8
 WHIT OL12 ...........................10 B3
Primrose St North TYLD M29 ...67 K3
Primrose Ter GLSP SK13 .......104 E4
Primrose Vw AIMK WN4 ........78 E2
Primrose Wk AIMK WN4 ........78 E2
Primula St BOL BL1 ...............22 C8
Prince Albert Av
 BNG/LEV M19 .......................99 K2
Prince Charlie St OLD OL1 .....59 L4
Princedom St BKLY M9 ..........73 H4
Prince Edward Av
 DTN/ASHW M34 ....................101 K2
 OLDE OL4 ............................59 M5
Prince George St OLD OL1 .....59 M3
Prince Mead Pl TRPK M17 .....85 L7
Prince Rd POY/DIS SK12 ......122 F7
Prince's Av BOLS/LL BL3 .........37 L8
 DID/WITH M20 ......................98 F8
 IRL M44 ..............................94 F1
 MPL/ROM SK6 .....................113 K1
 TYLD M29 ............................67 K6
Princes Dr ECC M30 * ............85 G1
Prince's Dr MPL/ROM SK6 ....114 B5
 SALE M33 ...........................109 G1
Princes Gdns LEIGH WN7 .......66 F7
Prince's Pk WGNNW/ST WN6 ...30 C8
Princes Rd ALT WA14 ..........108 A6
 HTNM SK4 ............................99 K8
 MPL/ROM SK6 .....................113 K1
 SALE M33 ...........................108 F1
Princess Av AIMK WN4 ..........78 E1
 ATH M46 .............................50 F7
 CHD/CHDH SK8 ....................120 C1
 DTN/ASHW M34 ....................101 H1
 FWTH BL4 ............................53 M2
 PWCH M25 ...........................71 M2
 RNFD/HAY WA11 ...................78 D5
 WHIT OL12 ...........................21 G8
Princess Cl DUK SK16 ...........91 G4
 HEY OL10 ............................41 G3
 MOSL OL5 ............................77 H4
Princess Dr MDTN M24 .........57 H4
Princess Gv FWTH BL4 .........53 C4
Princess Pde BURY BL9 ..........4 F5
 RUSH/FAL M14 .....................98 C3
Princess Pkwy
 WYTH/NTH M22 ....................109 M4
Princess Rd AIMK WN4 ..........78 E1
 CHAD OL9 ............................74 B1
 DID/WITH M20 ......................110 A1
 HOR/BR BL6 .........................34 E5
 HULME M15 ..........................87 J7
 MILN OL16 ...........................29 G5
 PWCH M25 * .........................55 M8
 ROY/SHW OL2 .......................43 K6
 RUSH/FAL M14 .....................95 L2
 URM M41 .............................95 L2
 WGNNW/ST WN6 ...................30 F8
 WILM/AE SK9 ......................126 D7
Princess St ALT WA14 .........107 M4
 AUL OL6 ..............................76 A8
 BOL BL1 ................................2 F5
 CMANW M2 ............................6 F5
 ECC M30 ..............................84 F2
 FAIL M35 .............................74 B5
 GLSP SK13 ..........................102 B2
 HYDE SK14 .............................7 D7
 OLDE OL4 ..............................9 B6
 RAD M26 .............................54 E4
 SLFD M6 ..............................71 K8
 SWIN M27 ............................70 D5
 WGNE/HIN WN2 ....................48 F7
 WGNS/IIMK WN3 ...................14 C6
 WHIT OL12 ...........................10 F1
Prince's St STKP SK1 ............13 H4
Prince St AIMK WN4 .............63 K7
 BOL BL1 ................................2 F4
 HEY OL10 ............................41 G2
 MILN OL16 ...........................11 H9
 OLD OL1 ................................9 L5
 RAMS BL0 ............................18 F6
Princes Wk BRAM/HZG SK7 ...121 J5
Princethorpe Cl HOR/BR BL6 ...35 G6
Princeton Cl SLFD M6 ...........85 M1
Prinknash Rd WYTH/NTH M22 ...118 F3
Printers Cl BNG/LEV M19 ......99 H4
Printers Dr STLY SK15 ...........77 K5
Printers Fold HYDE SK14 .......93 H7
Printers La BOL BL1 ..............23 J7
Printers Pk HYDE SK14 .........93 H7
Printer St OLD OL1 .................9 K4
 OP/CLY M11 * .......................89 G4
Printon Av BKLY M9 ..............72 E1
Printshop La ATH M46 ...........67 H1
Printworks La BNG/LEV M19 ...99 H3
Printworks Rd STLY SK15 ......91 L1
Prior St OLDS OL8 ...............59 L8
Priory Av BRO M7 ................71 M6
 CCHDY M21 ..........................97 L4
 LEIGH WN7 ..........................66 A3
Priory Cl DUK SK16 ..............91 G6
 OLDS OL8 ............................75 G1
 SALE M33 ...........................109 H1
 WGNW/BIL/OR WN5 ...............46 E7
Priory Ct RDSH SK5 .............100 B4
Priory Gv BRO M7 ................71 M6
 CHAD OL9 ............................58 D8
Priory La RDSH SK5 .............100 B4
Priory Pl BOLE BL2 ..............36 F2
Priory Rd AIMK WN4 .............63 J7
 ALT WA14 ..........................116 A4
 CHD/CHDH SK8 ....................120 A7
 SALE M33 .............................97 C2
 SWIN M27 ............................70 A1
 WILM/AE SK9 ......................126 C4
Priory St ALT WA14 ............116 A4
The Priory BRO M7 ..............71 M6
Pritchard St CMANE M1 * .......7 H7
Privet St OLDE OL4 ...............60 A3
Proctor Cl WGNW/BIL/OR WN5 ...47 H3

Proctor St TOT/BURYW BL8 ....38 F3
Prodesse Ct WGNE/HIN WN2 ...49 G6
Progress Av DTN/ASHW M34 ...90 C7
Progress St AUL OL6 ............90 D1
 BOL BL1 ..............................36 C3
 ROCH OL11 ..........................41 M3
 WGNE/HIN WN2 ....................49 G7
Promenade St HEY OL10 .......41 H2
Propps Hall Dr FAIL M35 ........73 M6
Prospect Av FWTH BL4 .........53 C5
 IRL M44 ..............................94 B6
Prospect Ct TOT/BURYW BL8 ...24 C5
Prospect Dr FAIL M35 ...........73 M5
 HALE/TIMP WA15 ..................117 H5
Prospect Hl BOLE BL2 ...........23 J8
Prospect Pl AUL OL6 .............76 A7
 FWTH BL4 ............................52 F5
 HEY OL10 ............................41 G9
Prospect Rd AUL OL6 ............76 B7
 CHAD OL9 ..............................8 C4
 DUK SK16 ...........................91 G4
 IRL M44 ..............................94 B6
 WGNNW/ST WN6 ...................31 H5
Prospect St BOL BL1 .............41 H4
 HEY OL10 ............................41 H4
 LIT OL15 .............................21 M6
 ROCH OL11 ..........................28 B8
 TYLD M29 ............................67 J3
 WGNE/HIN WN2 ....................49 G7
Prospect Ter WGNE/HIN WN2 ...4 D7
Prospect V CHD/CHDH SK8 ...119 K3
Prospect Vw SWIN M27 ........70 D5
Prosser Av ATH M46 .............66 D2
Prout St WGTN/LGST M12 .....99 K1
Provender Cl ALT WA14 .......108 A4
Providence St ANC M4 ..........88 A3
 AUL OL6 ..............................75 M8
 BOLS/LL BL3 ...........................2 F8
 DTN/ASHW M34 ....................90 C5
Provident Av BNG/LEV M19 ...99 H3
Provident St ROY/SHW OL2 * ...43 L5
Provident Wy
 HALE/TIMP WA15 ..................108 D5
Provis Rd CCHDY M21 ..........97 L5
Prubella Av DTN/ASHW M34 ...90 B7
Pryce Av WGNE/HIN WN2 ......15 M5
Pryce St BOL BL1 ...................2 B1
Pryme St HULME M15 .............6 C8
Pudding La HYDE SK14 ........102 F1
Puffin Av POY/DIS SK12 ......128 E4
Puffingate Cl STLY SK15 .......77 H5
Pulborough Cl TOT/BURYW BL8 ...24 C5
Pulford Av CCHDY M21 .........98 A8
Pulford Rd SALE M33 ..........108 F2
Pullman Cl BNG/LEV M19 ......99 L4
Pullman Dr STRET M32 .........96 F4
Pullman St ROCH OL11 .........10 F7
Pump St WGNE/HIN WN2 .......49 G7
Pump St NEWH/MOS M40 ......88 B1
Punch St BOLS/LL BL3 ...........51 G2
Punch St BOLS/LL BL3 ............2 B7
The Pungle WHTN BL5 .........50 L7
Purbeck Cl WYTH/NTH M22 ...118 E3
Purbeck Dr HOR/BR BL6 .......34 C4
 TOT/BURYW BL8 ...................24 F6
Purbeck Wy TYLD M29 .........67 K5
Purcell Cl BOL BL1 ...............36 A3
Purcell St WGTN/LGST M12 ....99 K1
Purdon St BURY BL9 .............25 J6
Purley Av NTHM/RTH M23 ...109 L3
Purple St BOL BL1 ..................2 F4
Purslow Cl WGTN/LGST M12 ...88 B3
Putney Cl OLD OL1 ..............59 H3
Pye Cl RNFD/HAY WA11 ........78 E4
Pyegrove GLSP SK13 ..........105 J3
Pyegrove Rd GLSP SK13 ......105 H3
Pyke St WGN WN1 ...............15 J1
Pymgate Dr CHD/CHDH SK8 ...119 J2
Pymgate La CHD/CHDH SK8 ...119 J2
Pym St ECC M30 .................85 G2
 HEY OL10 ............................41 G3
 NEWH/MOS M40 ...................73 J4
Pyramid Ct BRO M7 .............72 A6
Pyrus Cl ECC M30 ...............84 C4
Pytha Fold Rd DID/WITH M20 ...99 G7

## Q

The Quadrant BKLY M9 .........73 K1
 DROY M43 ............................89 J3
 MPL/ROM SK6 .....................113 K2
 STKP SK1 ...........................112 E3
Quail Dr IRL M44 .................94 D1
Quail St OLDE OL4 ...............59 M7
Quakerfields WHTN BL5 ........50 A5
Quakers Fld TOT/BURYW BL8 ...24 C5
Quakers' Pl WGNNW/ST WN6 ...31 H3
Quantock Cl HTNM SK4 .........13 C2
 WGNS/IIMK WN3 ...................62 F2
Quantock Dr OLDS OL8 .........75 J1
Quantock St
 OLDTF/WHR M16 * ..................87 H8
Quarlton Dr
 TOT/BURYW BL8 ...................23 L9
Quarmby Rd GTN M18 ..........89 J8
Quarry Bank Rd
 WILM/AE SK9 ......................126 D1
Quarry Cl GLSP SK13 ...........105 G3
Quarry Clough STLY SK15 ......92 A4
Quarry Hts STLY SK15 ...........91 J4
Quarry La UPML OL3 ............61 G3
Quarry Pl WGN WN1 .............15 L3
Quarry Pond Rd WALK M28 ...68 C1
Quarry Ri MPL/ROM SK6 ......113 L2
 STLY SK15 ...........................91 J3
Quarry Rd FWTH BL4 ...........53 K5
 MPL/ROM SK6 .....................113 L2
 NM/HAY SK22 ......................124 F5
 NM/HAY SK22 ......................125 H1
Quarry St MPL/ROM SK6 ......101 L2
 RAD M26 .............................54 E1
 RAMS BL0 ............................18 E2
 STLY SK15 ...........................91 J3
 WHIT OL12 ...........................10 D1
Quarry Wk OP/CLY M11 * ......88 C3
Quayside LEIGH WN7 ............66 B8
Quayside Cl WALK M28 .........68 E7
The Quays SALQ M50 ...........86 C5
Quay St CSLFD M3 ................6 C5
 CSLFD M3 ..............................6 D5
 HEY OL10 ............................41 H3
Quay Vw ORD M5 .................86 D4
Quebec Pl BOLS/LL BL3 .........35 M7
Quebec St BOLS/LL BL3 ..........2 E7
 CHAD OL9 ..............................8 D3
 DTN/ASHW M34 ....................90 B8
Queen Alexandra Ci ORD M5 * ...7 M6
Queen Ann Dr WALK M28 ......68 E5
Queenhill Dr HYDE SK14 .......91 J7
Queenhill Rd
 WYTH/NTH M22 ....................110 B3

Queen's Av AIMK WN4 ...... 63 L8
  ATH M46 ...... 50 F7
  EDGW/EG BL7 ...... 22 D5
  GOL/RIS/CUL WA3 ...... 81 M5
  MPL/ROM SK6 ...... 113 K1
  WHIT OL12 ...... 21 C8
Queensbrook BOL BL1 * ...... 2 A5
Queensbury Cl BOL BL1 ...... 22 A7
  WILM/AE SK9 ...... 127 H4
Queensbury Pde
  NEWH/MOS M40 * ...... 88 B7
Queens Cl HTNM SK4 ...... 111 K2
  HYDE SK14 * ...... 102 B5
  WALK M28 ...... 68 C5
Queens Ct NEWH/MOS M40 ...... 73 G7
Queens Dr CHD/CHDH SK8 ...... 120 C1
  GLSP SK13 ...... 105 J3
  GOL/RIS/CUL WA3 ...... 79 M4
  HTNM SK4 ...... 111 K2
  HYDE SK14 ...... 102 C5
  NEWLW WA12 ...... 78 F7
  PWCH M25 ...... 71 M2
  ROCH OL11 ...... 42 B1
Queensferry St
  NEWH/MOS M40 ...... 73 M6
Queens Gdns LEIGH WN7 ...... 66 F7
Queensgate BOL BL1 ...... 35 L4
  BRAM/HZG SK7 ...... 121 G2
Queensgate Dr
  ROY/SHW OL2 ...... 42 F6
Queen's Gv WGTN/LGST M12 ...... 88 D8
Queens Hall Pas WGN WN1 * ...... 14 F4
Queensmere Dr SWIN M27 ...... 70 D2
Queensmere St
Queens Pk BOL BL1 * ...... 2 A5
Queen's Park Rd HEY OL10 ...... 41 G1
Queens Pl BURY BL9 ...... 4 F2
Queen's Rd AIMK WN4 ...... 78 E1
  AUL OL6 ...... 76 A8
  BOLS/LL BL3 ...... 35 L8
  BRAM/HZG SK7 ...... 122 A1
  CHAD OL9 ...... 58 D5
  CHD/CHDH SK8 ...... 111 J8
  CHH M8 ...... 72 E7
  HALE/TIMP WA15 ...... 117 C1
  LIT OL15 ...... 21 M7
  MPL/ROM SK6 ...... 113 K1
  NEWH/MOS M40 ...... 73 G7
  OLDS OL8 ...... 9 L8
  RNFD/HAY WA11 ...... 78 D3
  SALE M33 ...... 96 C8
  URM M41 ...... 96 A3
  WILM/AE SK9 ...... 126 E6
Queenston Rd DID/WITH M20 ...... 98 F6
Queen St AUL OL6 ...... 91 G1
  BOL BL1 ...... 5 J5
  BURY BL9 ...... 5 H4
  CHD/CHDH SK8 ...... 111 H6
  CSLFD M3 ...... 6 D2
  CSLFD M3 ...... 6 E5
  DTN/ASHW M34 ...... 90 A4
  DTN/ASHW M34 ...... 90 C6
  DUK SK16 ...... 90 E3
  ECC M30 * ...... 85 J3
  FAIL M35 ...... 74 B6
  FWTH BL4 ...... 53 C4
  GLSP SK13 ...... 93 K8
  GLSP SK13 ...... 104 E4
  GOL/RIS/CUL WA3 * ...... 79 L4
  HEY OL10 ...... 41 G2
  HOR/BR BL6 ...... 33 K1
  HYDE SK14 ...... 102 B3
  LEIGH WN7 * ...... 66 D8
  LHULT M38 ...... 68 E1
  LIT OL15 ...... 21 M7
  MDTN M24 ...... 57 M4
  MOSL OL5 ...... 76 F3
  MPL/ROM SK6 ...... 114 C6
  OLD OL1 ...... 9 K5
  RAD M26 ...... 54 F2
  RAMS BL0 ...... 18 E7
  ROY/SHW OL2 ...... 43 G8
  ROY/SHW OL2 ...... 43 L6
  SLFD M6 ...... 71 G7
  STLY SK15 * ...... 91 K2
  TOT/BURYW BL8 ...... 24 D7
  WGNE/HIN WN2 ...... 49 C6
  WGNE/HIN WN2 ...... 64 D2
  WGNS/IIMK WN3 ...... 14 E5
  WGNW/BIL/OR WN5 ...... 46 E6
  WGNW/BIL/OR WN5 ...... 47 C7
  WHIT OL12 ...... 10 F2
  WHTN BL5 ...... 50 B4
Queen St West DID/WITH M20 ...... 98 E5
Queens Vw LIT OL15 ...... 29 K1
Queensway BNG/LEV M19 ...... 111 G2
  CHD/CHDH SK8 ...... 119 L4
  DUK SK16 ...... 91 J5
  FWTH BL4 ...... 53 J6
  IRL M44 ...... 94 C2
  LEIGH WN7 ...... 67 G7
  MOSL OL5 ...... 77 G5
  PART M31 ...... 94 C8
  POY/DIS SK12 ...... 129 H1
  ROCH OL11 ...... 42 A1
  SWIN M27 ...... 70 D2
  UPML OL3 ...... 61 L6
  URM M41 ...... 85 H8
  WALK M28 ...... 68 E4
  WGN WN1 ...... 47 L2
  WGNE/HIN WN2 ...... 48 D4
  WGNW/ST WN6 ...... 30 C8
Queen Victoria St ECC M30 ...... 84 F2
  ROCH OL11 ...... 42 D1
Quenby St HULME M15 ...... 87 G6
Quendon Av BRO M7 ...... 72 B8
Quickedge La OLDE OL4 ...... 60 E8
Quickedge Rd MOSL OL5 ...... 76 F2
  OLDE OL4 ...... 60 F8
Quick Rd MOSL OL5 ...... 60 F8
Quick Vw MOSL OL5 ...... 77 H1
Quill Ct IRL M44 ...... 94 B6
Quilter Gv BKLY M9 ...... 72 F2
Quinney Crs OLDTF/WHR M16 ...... 98 C1
Quinn St OP/CLY M11 ...... 88 D3
Quinton Wk BRUN/LGST M13 ...... 87 L6

**R**

Rabbit La HYDE SK14 ...... 92 D6
Raby St OLDTF/WHR M16 ...... 87 H8
  RUSH/FAL M14 ...... 87 J7
Racecourse Pk WILM/AE SK9 ...... 126 D6
Racecourse Rd WILM/AE SK9 ...... 126 C6
Racefield Rd ALT WA14 ...... 107 M8
The Race WILM/AE SK9 ...... 127 H2
Rachel St WGTN/LGST M12 ...... 7 M8
Rackhouse Rd
  NTHM/RTH M23 ...... 109 L3

Radbourne Cl WGTN/LGST M12 ...... 88 D6
Radbourne Gv BOLS/LL BL3 ...... 35 J8
Radcliffe Gv LEIGH WN7 ...... 66 C5
Radcliffe Moor Rd BOLE BL2 ...... 37 L7
Radcliffe New Rd RAD M26 ...... 54 F2
  WHIT M24 ...... 55 H3
Radcliffe Park Crs SLFD M6 ...... 70 F4
Radcliffe Park Rd SLFD M6 ...... 70 F4
Radcliffe Rd BOLE BL2 ...... 3 J5
  BOLS/LL BL3 ...... 37 H7
  BURY BL9 ...... 39 H5
  OLDE OL4 ...... 60 A2
Radcliffe St OLD OL1 ...... 9 J4
  OLDE OL4 ...... 60 D6
  ROY/SHW OL2 ...... 43 H8
Radclyffe St CHAD OL9 ...... 8 B3
  MDTN M24 ...... 57 K2
Radden Gv RAD M26 ...... 38 A8
Radford Cl STKP SK1 ...... 113 G5
Radford Dr BKLY M9 ...... 73 H4
  IRL M44 ...... 94 D1
Radford St BRO M7 ...... 71 M4
Radiant St DTN/ASHW M34 ...... 100 L1
Radium St ANC M4 ...... 7 K2
Radlet Dr HALE/TIMP WA15 ...... 108 D4
Radlett Wk BRUN/LGST M13 * ...... 87 M7
Radley Cl BOL BL1 ...... 35 K3
  SALE M33 ...... 108 A1
Radley St DROY M43 ...... 89 H4
  OLDTF/WHR M16 ...... 98 C1
Radnor Av DTN/ASHW M34 ...... 100 L1
Radnor Cl WGNE/HIN WN2 ...... 65 K1
Radnor Dr LEIGH WN7 ...... 65 M7
Radnormere Dr
  CHD/CHDH SK8 ...... 111 J8
Radnor St CHAD OL9 ...... 8 C1
  GTN M18 ...... 88 F8
  HULME M15 ...... 87 J7
  STRET M32 ...... 97 G3
Radstock Cl BOL BL1 ...... 22 B5
  RUSH/FAL M14 ...... 98 E3
Radstock Rd STRET M32 ...... 98 F3
Radway TYLD M29 ...... 67 M3
Raeburn Dr MPL/ROM SK6 ...... 114 C4
Rae St EDGY SK3 ...... 12 D6
Raglan Av SWIN M27 ...... 70 E2
  WHTF M45 ...... 55 L5
Raglan Dr ALT WA14 ...... 108 B4
  SALE M33 ...... 108 C3
  STRET M32 ...... 96 F1
Raglan Rd BOL BL1 ...... 36 A2
  HYDE SK14 ...... 101 M2
  ROCH OL11 ...... 41 M9
Raglan Wk HULME M15 * ...... 87 J6
Ragley Cl POY/DIS SK12 ...... 122 B8
Raikes La BOLS/LL BL3 ...... 36 E8
Raikes Rd BOLS/LL BL3 ...... 37 G7
Raikes Wy BOLS/LL BL3 ...... 37 G7
Railton Av OLDTF/WHR M16 ...... 98 A1
Railton Ter BKLY M9 * ...... 73 J5
Railway Ap ROCH OL11 ...... 41 M2
Railway Rd CHAD OL9 ...... 8 E7
  CHAD OL9 ...... 74 D2
  GOL/RIS/CUL WA3 * ...... 79 L4
  LEIGH WN7 ...... 66 B7
  STKP SK1 ...... 13 H6
  STRET M32 ...... 86 C7
  URM M41 ...... 96 A2
Railway St ALT WA14 ...... 108 A8
  ATH M46 ...... 50 E8
  BURY BL9 ...... 24 E2
  DUK SK16 ...... 90 E4
  FWTH BL4 ...... 53 H3
  GLSP SK13 ...... 93 K7
  GLSP SK13 ...... 104 F3
  GTN M18 ...... 88 F6
  HEY OL10 ...... 41 H3
  HTNM SK4 ...... 12 F4
  LIT OL15 ...... 21 M7
  MILN OL16 ...... 11 G6
  MILN OL16 ...... 29 M8
  RAD M26 ...... 54 D2
  RAMS BL0 ...... 18 F6
  WGNE/HIN WN2 ...... 49 H5
  WGNW/ST WN6 ...... 14 B2
Railway Ter TOT/BURYW BL8 ...... 4 A6
Railway Vw OLDE OL4 ...... 60 C6
  ROY/SHW OL2 ...... 43 M4
Raimond St BOL BL1 ...... 35 M1
Rainbow Cl CCHDY M21 ...... 97 L5
Rainbow Dr ATH M46 ...... 51 C8
Raincliff Av BRUN/LGST M13 ...... 99 J3
Raines Crest MILN OL16 ...... 29 K6
Rainford Cl DID/WITH M20 ...... 98 D4
  HALE/TIMP WA15 ...... 108 D7
Rainford Rd
  WGNW/BIL/OR WN5 ...... 62 A7
Rainford St BOLE BL2 ...... 22 F6
Rainforth St BRUN/LGST M13 ...... 99 J1
Rainham Dr CHH M8 ...... 72 D5
Rainham Wy CHAD OL9 * ...... 8 E2
  RDSH SK5 ...... 100 B3
Rainow Av DROY M43 ...... 89 H4
Rainow Dr POY/DIS SK12 ...... 129 L2
Rainow Rd EDGY/DAV SK3 ...... 111 M6
Rainshaw St BOL BL1 ...... 22 C6
  OLDE OL4 * ...... 60 A4
Rainsough Av PWCH M25 ...... 71 J3
Rainsough Brow PWCH M25 ...... 71 J3
Rainsough Cl PWCH M25 ...... 71 K3
Rainwood CHAD OL9 ...... 58 B4
Raithby Dr WGNS/IIMK WN3 ...... 63 K1
Raja Cl CHH M8 ...... 72 E5
Rake Rd ROCH OL11 ...... 27 G5
Rake La SWIN M27 ...... 70 C1
Rake St BURY BL9 ...... 25 J8
Rakewood Dr OLDE OL4 ...... 44 C8
Rakewood Rd LIT OL15 ...... 29 L1
Raleigh Cl DID/WITH M20 ...... 98 D7
  OLD OL1 ...... 9 L5
Raleigh St RDSH SK5 ...... 100 B8
  STRET M32 ...... 97 G2
Ralli Cts CSLFD M3 ...... 6 C4
Ralph Av HYDE SK14 ...... 102 B5
Ralph Green St CHAD OL9 ...... 74 F2
Ralphs La DUK SK16 ...... 90 F5
  UPML OL3 ...... 45 G2
Ralph St BOL BL1 ...... 36 A2
  OP/CLY M11 ...... 89 G3
  WHIT OL12 ...... 11 G1
Ralston Cl BRO M7 ...... 72 A4
Ralstone Av OLDS OL8 ...... 59 J8
Ramillies Av CHD/CHDH SK8 ...... 120 D3
Rampit Cl RNFD/HAY WA11 ...... 78 C5
Ramp Rd East MANAIR M90 ...... 118 E5
Ramp Rd South MANAIR M90 ...... 118 D5
Ramp Rd West MANAIR M90 ...... 118 D5
Ramsay Av FWTH BL4 ...... 53 G6
Ramsay Pl MILN OL16 ...... 11 G3
Ramsay St BOL BL1 ...... 35 M3
  MILN OL16 ...... 11 G3
Ramsay Ter MILN OL16 * ...... 11 G3

Ramsbottom La RAMS BL0 ...... 18 F5
Ramsbottom Rd HOR/BR BL6 ...... 33 L1
  TOT/BURYW BL8 ...... 23 K2
Ramsbury Dr NEWH/MOS M40 ...... 74 A2
Ramsdale Cl BRAM/HZG SK7 ...... 121 G5
Ramsdale St CHAD OL9 ...... 58 D5
Ramsden Cl GLSP SK13 ...... 104 F2
  OLD OL1 ...... 9 G4
  WGNS/IIMK WN3 ...... 14 B9
Ramsden Crs OLD OL1 * ...... 9 G4
Ramsden Fold SWIN M27 ...... 70 C2
Ramsden Rd WHIT OL12 ...... 100 A3
Ramsden St AUL OL6 ...... 75 L8
  BOLS/LL BL3 ...... 37 G7
Ramsey Av BNG/LEV M19 ...... 100 A3
Ramsey Cl AIMK WN4 ...... 78 E2
  ATH M46 ...... 67 H2
Ramsey Gv TOT/BURYW BL8 ...... 38 E2
Ramsey St CHAD OL9 ...... 8 A9
  LEIGH WN7 * ...... 66 D8
  NEWH/MOS M40 ...... 73 L5
  OLD OL1 ...... 9 G4
Ramsgate Rd NEWH/MOS M40 ...... 73 M8
  RDSH SK5 ...... 100 C5
Ramsgate St BRO M7 ...... 72 B7
Ramsgill Cl NTHM/RTH M23 ...... 109 H5
Ramsgreave Cl BURY BL9 ...... 39 G5
Ram St LHULT M38 ...... 52 C8
Ramwell Gdns BOLS/LL BL3 * ...... 2 A8
Ramwells Brow EDGW/EG BL7 ...... 22 E4
Ramwells Ct EDGW/EG BL7 * ...... 22 E4
Ramwells Ms EDGW/EG BL7 * ...... 22 E4
Ranby Av BKLY M9 ...... 73 H7
Randale Dr BURY BL9 ...... 55 K2
Randall Av WGNNW/ST WN6 ...... 30 D7
Randal St BOLS/LL BL3 ...... 35 M8
Randerson St WGTN/LGST M12 * ...... 7 L8
Randlesham St PWCH M25 ...... 55 M8
Randolph Pl EDGY/DAV SK3 ...... 13 H8
Randolph Rd FWTH BL4 ...... 53 J5
Randolph St BNG/LEV M19 ...... 99 K2
  BOLS/LL BL3 ...... 2 A6
  OLDS OL8 ...... 74 F2
Rands Clough Dr WALK M28 ...... 68 E6
Rand St OLD OL1 ...... 60 A3
Ranelagh Rd SWIN M27 ...... 70 F5
Ranelagh St OP/CLY M11 ...... 88 E2
Raneley Gv ROCH OL11 ...... 42 D2
Ranford Rd BNG/LEV M19 ...... 99 K4
Range Dr MPL/ROM SK6 ...... 101 M6
Range La UPML OL3 ...... 45 G3
Rangemore Av
  WYTH/NTH M22 * ...... 110 A4
Range Rd EDGY/DAV SK3 ...... 13 H9
  OLDTF/WHR M16 ...... 98 B1
  STLY SK15 ...... 91 L4
Range St BOLS/LL BL3 ...... 36 A8
  OP/CLY M11 ...... 89 H2
Ranicar Street WGNE/HIN WN2 * ...... 65 M11
Rankine Ter BOLS/LL BL3 * ...... 2 B8
Ranmore Av AIMK WN4 ...... 63 G8
Rannoch Rd BOLE BL2 ...... 37 J5
Ransfield Rd CCHDY M21 ...... 97 K2
Ranulph Ct SLFD M6 * ...... 71 G7
Ranworth Av HTNM SK4 ...... 111 J2
Ranworth Cl BOL BL1 ...... 22 D6
Ranworth Dr GOL/RIS/CUL WA3 ...... 80 B6
Raper St OLDE OL4 ...... 59 M4
Raphael St BOL BL1 ...... 36 A2
Rappax Rd HALE/TIMP WA15 ...... 117 J4
Raspberry La IRL M44 ...... 83 J3
Rassbottom Brow STLY SK15 * ...... 91 J2
Rassbottom St STLY SK15 ...... 91 J2
Rassey Cl WGNNW/ST WN6 ...... 31 K5
Ratcliffe Av IRL M44 ...... 94 D2
Ratcliffe St WGNE/HIN WN2 ...... 32 F6
Ratcliffe St BNG/LEV M19 ...... 99 L3
  LEIGH WN7 ...... 66 C6
  STKP SK1 ...... 13 J7
  TYLD M29 ...... 67 L3
Rathan Rd URM M41 ...... 84 F8
Rathbone St MILN OL16 ...... 11 L5
Rathbourne Av BKLY M9 ...... 73 G1
Rathen Av WGNE/HIN WN2 ...... 48 D3
Rathen Rd DID/WITH M20 ...... 98 E7
Rathmel Rd NTHM/RTH M23 ...... 108 F3
Rathmore Av NEWH/MOS M40 ...... 73 H7
Rathvale Dr WYTH/NTH M22 ...... 118 E4
Rathybank Cl BOL BL1 ...... 35 M3
Rattenbury Ct SLFD M6 ...... 70 F7
Raveden Cl BOL BL1 ...... 35 M1
Raveley Av RUSH/FAL M14 ...... 99 M1
Ravelston Dr BKLY M9 ...... 73 G6
Raven Av CHAD OL9 ...... 58 D7
Raven Cl DROY M43 ...... 89 M1
  HALE/TIMP WA15 ...... 108 E3
Ravendale Cl WHIT OL12 ...... 27 K3
Raven Dr IRL M44 ...... 94 D1
Ravenfield Gv BOL BL1 * ...... 2 B2
Ravenhead Cl RUSH/FAL M14 ...... 99 G4
Ravenhead Sq STLY SK15 ...... 77 H7
Ravenhurst Pl BOL BL1 ...... 35 G6
Raven Oak Av NTHM/RTH M23 ...... 109 G5
Ravenoak Av BNG/LEV M19 ...... 99 L4
Ravenoak Rd FAIL M35 ...... 74 D4
Ravenoak Park Rd
  CHD/CHDH SK8 ...... 120 D4
Ravenoak Rd CHD/CHDH SK8 ...... 120 D4
  OFTN SK2 ...... 112 D8
Raven Rd BOLS/LL BL3 * ...... 35 K8
Ravensbury St OP/CLY M11 ...... 88 E2
Ravenscar Crs
  WYTH/NTH M22 ...... 118 F4
Ravens Cl PWCH M25 ...... 72 B2
Ravenscraig Rd LHULT M38 ...... 52 E6
Ravensdale Gdns ECC M30 ...... 85 H1
Ravensdale St RUSH/FAL M14 ...... 98 F1
Ravens Holme BOL BL1 ...... 35 H5
Ravenside Pk CHAD OL9 ...... 58 D7
Ravenstonedale Dr
  ROY/SHW OL2 ...... 43 H7
Ravenstone Dr SALE M33 ...... 97 H7
  UPML OL3 ...... 61 M1
Raven St BURY BL9 ...... 5 G1
  ROCH OL11 ...... 27 G3
  WGTN/LGST M12 ...... 7 M7
Ravensway PWCH M25 ...... 72 A2
Ravens Wd BOL BL1 ...... 35 H5
Ravenswood Av HTNM SK4 ...... 111 K3
  WGNS/IIMK WN3 ...... 63 K2
Ravenswood Dr BKLY M9 ...... 73 H1
  BOL BL1 ...... 35 H5
  CHD/CHDH SK8 ...... 120 D4
Ravenswood Rd STRET M32 ...... 86 C7
  WILM/AE SK9 ...... 126 D8
Ravenwood CHAD OL9 ...... 58 A5

Ravenwood Dr DTN/ASHW M34 ...... 90 B6
  HALE/TIMP WA15 ...... 117 M5
Ravine Av BKLY M9 ...... 73 H5
Rawcliffe Av BOLE BL2 ...... 37 J5
Rawcliffe St RUSH/FAL M14 ...... 98 E1
Rawdon Cl BNG/LEV M19 ...... 99 J3
Rawkin Cl HULME M15 ...... 87 H7
Rawlyn Rd BOL BL1 ...... 35 J3
Rawpool Gdns
  NTHM/RTH M23 ...... 109 H5
Rawson Av FWTH BL4 ...... 53 K3
Rawson Cl LEIGH WN7 ...... 66 D4
Rawsons Rake TOT/BURYW BL8 ...... 18 D6
Rawson St FWTH BL4 ...... 53 K3
Rawsthorne Av GTN M18 ...... 100 A1
Rawsthorne St BOL BL1 ...... 36 B2
  TYLD M29 ...... 68 A4
Rawstron St WHIT OL12 ...... 20 A3
Rawthey Pl WGNE/HIN WN2 ...... 64 C2
Raycroft Av BKLY M9 ...... 73 K2
Raydale Cl GOL/RIS/CUL WA3 ...... 80 B3
Rayden Crs WHTN BL5 ...... 50 B6
Raydon Av NEWH/MOS M40 ...... 73 G7
Rayleigh Av OP/CLY M11 ...... 89 J3
Raymond Av BURY BL9 ...... 25 J7
  CHAD OL9 ...... 74 E1
Raymond Rd NTHM/RTH M23 ...... 109 L2
Raymond St SWIN M27 ...... 70 C3
Rayner La AULW OL7 ...... 90 A3
Rayners Cl STLY SK15 ...... 91 J3
Rayner St STKP SK1 ...... 112 E4
Raynham Av DID/WITH M20 ...... 110 E1
Raynham St AUL OL6 ...... 90 C1
Rayson Hill Dr BKLY M9 ...... 72 F2
Reabrook Av WGTN/LGST M12 ...... 88 C6
The Reach WALK M28 ...... 69 H2
Read Cl BURY BL9 ...... 39 C5
  ROY/SHW OL2 ...... 43 L6
Reade Av URM M41 ...... 95 H3
Reading Cl OP/CLY M11 ...... 88 F4
Reading Dr SALE M33 ...... 96 A8
Reading St SLFD M6 ...... 71 L7
Readitt Wk OP/CLY M11 ...... 88 E2
Read St HYDE SK14 ...... 101 M1
Read St West HYDE SK14 ...... 101 M1
Reaney Wk WGTN/LGST M12 ...... 88 D6
Reather Wk NEWH/MOS M40 ...... 87 M1
Rebecca St CHH M8 ...... 72 D4
Recreation Av AIMK WN4 ...... 64 A3
Recreation Dr
  WGNW/BIL/OR WN5 ...... 62 B7
Recreation Rd FAIL M35 ...... 74 D3
Rectory Av BOLE BL2 ...... 23 H7
  BOLS/LL BL3 ...... 36 B8
  PWCH M25 ...... 55 M8
Rectory Cl DTN/ASHW M34 ...... 101 K2
  GOL/RIS/CUL WA3 ...... 79 M4
  PWCH M25 ...... 55 L8
Rectory Flds STKP SK1 ...... 13 L6
Rectory Gdns PWCH M25 ...... 55 L8
  WHTN BL5 ...... 50 B8
Rectory Gn PWCH M25 ...... 55 K8
  STKP SK1 ...... 13 J5
Rectory Gv PWCH M25 ...... 71 L1
Rectory Hl BURY BL9 ...... 26 A8
Rectory La BURY BL9 ...... 26 A8
  PWCH M25 ...... 55 K8
  RAD M26 ...... 54 F1
  WGNNW/ST WN6 ...... 31 J3
Rectory Rd AIMK WN4 ...... 63 G7
  CHH M8 ...... 72 C3
Rectory St MDTN M24 ...... 57 J3
The Rectory ROY/DIS SK12 ...... 122 B6
Redacre POY/DIS SK12 ...... 122 B6
Redacre Rd GTN M18 ...... 89 H7
Red Bank ANC M4 ...... 87 K1
Red Bank Rd RAD M26 ...... 38 A8
Redbarn Cl MPL/ROM SK6 ...... 101 J8
Redbourne Dr URM M41 ...... 84 C8
Redbrick Ct AULW OL7 ...... 90 D3
Redbrook Av NEWH/MOS M40 ...... 73 H7
Redbrook Cl FWTH BL4 * ...... 53 M8
Redbrook Rd
  HALE/TIMP WA15 ...... 109 G5
  PART M31 ...... 106 D2
  WGNS/IIMK WN3 ...... 15 K7
Redbrook Wy MCFLDN SK10 ...... 129 G7
Redbrow Hollow
  MPL/ROM SK6 ...... 114 D4
Redburn Ct WGNS/IIMK WN3 ...... 14 B9
Redburn Rd NTHM/RTH M23 ...... 109 L5
Redby St OP/CLY M11 * ...... 88 F4
Redcar Av DID/WITH M20 ...... 88 E6
  URM M41 ...... 84 D8
Redcar Rd BOLS/LL BL3 ...... 53 K1
  SWIN M27 ...... 70 F5
Redcar St WHIT OL12 ...... 10 F2
Red Cedar Pk BOLE BL2 ...... 37 G7
Redclyffe Av RUSH/FAL M14 ...... 98 F1
Redclyffe Rd DID/WITH M20 ...... 98 D7
  ECC M30 ...... 85 G4
Redcot Cl BOL BL1 * ...... 35 L5
Redcote St NEWH/MOS M40 ...... 73 K4
Redcourt Av DID/WITH M20 ...... 98 E8
Redcroft Gdns BNG/LEV M19 ...... 99 H4
Redcroft Rd SALE M33 ...... 96 B6
Redcross St North WHIT OL12 ...... 10 E1
Redcross St WHIT OL12 ...... 10 E1
Reddaway Cl SLFD M6 ...... 71 K7
Reddish Cl BOLE BL2 ...... 23 H7
Reddish La GTN M18 ...... 100 B1
Reddish Rd RDSH SK5 ...... 100 C6
Reddish Vale Rd RDSH SK5 ...... 100 D5
Redesmere Cl DROY M43 ...... 89 L3
  HALE/TIMP WA15 ...... 109 G6
Redesmere Dr CHD/CHDH SK8 ...... 111 J8
  WILM/AE SK9 ...... 130 C3
Redesmere Pk URM M41 ...... 95 L4
Redesmere Rd WILM/AE SK9 ...... 119 M7
Redfearn Wd WHIT OL12 ...... 27 L2
Redfern Av SALE M33 ...... 109 H1
Redfern St ANC M4 ...... 7 G2
Redfern Wy ROCH OL11 ...... 27 C3
Redfield Cl OP/CLY M11 ...... 88 C3
Redfield Cft LEIGH WN7 ...... 66 D7
Redford Dr BRAM/HZG SK7 ...... 121 G5
Redford Rd CHH M8 ...... 56 C8
Redford St TOT/BURYW BL8 ...... 38 F7
Redgate GLSP SK13 ...... 93 K8
  HYDE SK14 ...... 102 A4
Redgate La WGTN/LGST M12 ...... 88 D7
Redgate Wy FWTH BL4 ...... 52 C7

Redgrave Pas OLDE OL4 ...... 60 A4
Redgrave Ri WGNS/IIMK WN3 ...... 63 G1
Redgrave St OLDE OL4 ...... 60 A4
Red Hall St OLDE OL4 ...... 59 M6
Redhill Dr MPL/ROM SK6 ...... 113 G1
Redhill Gv BOL BL1 ...... 2 C1
Redhill St ANC M4 ...... 7 K4
Red Hill Wy WGNW/BIL/OR WN5 * ...... 49 C6
Redhouse La ALT WA14 ...... 106 F4
Redhouse La MPL/ROM SK6 ...... 101 J8
  POY/DIS SK12 ...... 124 A6
Redington Cl WALK M28 ...... 68 D7
Redisher Cl RAMS BL0 ...... 24 C1
Redisher Cft RAMS BL0 ...... 24 C1
Redisher La TOT/BURYW BL8 ...... 24 B1
Redland Av RDSH SK5 ...... 100 C2
Redland Cl LIT OL15 ...... 21 M6
Redland Ct WGNE/HIN WN2 ...... 64 B5
Redland Crs CCHDY M21 ...... 97 L6
Red La BOLE BL2 ...... 37 G3
  POY/DIS SK12 ...... 123 K7
  WHIT OL12 ...... 28 C2
Red Lion St ANC M4 ...... 7 H3
Redmain Gv GOL/RIS/CUL WA3 ...... 80 A3
Redmans Cl ECC M30 ...... 84 E3
Redmayne Cl NEWLW WA12 ...... 78 E8
Redmere Dr BURY BL9 ...... 5 J9
Redmere Gv RUSH/FAL M14 ...... 98 F4
Redmire Ms DUK SK16 ...... 91 J5
Redmond Cl DTN/ASHW M34 ...... 90 B5
Redmoor La POY/DIS SK12 ...... 124 C8
Redmoss Rw SWIN M27 ...... 71 C4
Rednal Wk WGNS/IIMK WN3 ...... 14 D8
Redpol Av LEIGH WN7 ...... 66 E5
Redpoll Cl WALK M28 ...... 68 C5
Red Rock La RAD M26 ...... 54 A6
  ...... 32 A4
Red Rose Crs BNG/LEV M19 ...... 99 M5
Redruth St RUSH/FAL M14 ...... 98 E2
Redshank Cl NEWLW WA12 ...... 78 F8
Redshank Gv LEIGH WN7 ...... 66 D6
Redshaw Av BOLE BL2 ...... 22 F6
Redstart Cl GOL/RIS/CUL WA3 ...... 80 B4
Redstart Gv WALK M28 ...... 69 C4
Redstock Cl WHTN BL5 ...... 50 D3
Redstone Rd BNG/LEV M19 ...... 111 G1
Red St ATH M46 ...... 67 H1
Redthorn Av BNG/LEV M19 ...... 99 J5
Redthorpe Cl BOLE BL2 ...... 36 E3
Redvale Rd BRO M7 ...... 72 B6
Redvales Rd BURY BL9 ...... 38 F5
Redvers St OLD OL1 ...... 8 F3
Redwater Cl WALK M28 ...... 68 D6
Red Waters LEIGH WN7 ...... 66 D6
Redwing Rd TOT/BURYW BL8 ...... 24 C2
Redwood CHAD OL9 ...... 58 A5
  SALE M33 ...... 95 M8
Redwood Av WGNNW/ST WN6 ...... 47 J1
  WGNW/BIL/OR WN5 ...... 46 D6
Redwood Cl EDGY/DAV SK3 ...... 12 A7
  WHIT OL12 ...... 27 L1
Redwood Dr CHH M8 ...... 72 E7
  DTN/ASHW M34 ...... 90 B6
  MPL/ROM SK6 ...... 113 J1
Redwood La OLDE OL4 ...... 60 C4
Redwood Park Gv MILN OL16 ...... 29 K3
Redwood Rd UPML OL3 ...... 61 M5
Redwood St SLFD M6 ...... 71 K7
Reeceton Gdns BOL BL1 ...... 35 K5
Reedbank RAD M26 ...... 54 D4
Reed Ct OLD OL1 * ...... 9 G2
Reed Crs WGNS/IIMK WN3 ...... 14 D8
Reedham Cl BOL BL1 ...... 35 M4
Reedham Wk CHAD OL9 * ...... 58 F8
  NEWH/MOS M40 ...... 73 G8
Reed Hl MILN OL16 ...... 10 E3
Reedley Dr WALK M28 ...... 68 F4
Reedmace Cl WALK M28 ...... 69 H3
Reedsmere Bank OFTN SK2 ...... 113 G7
Reedshaw Rd BKLY M9 ...... 73 H4
Reedsmere Cl
  WGNW/BIL/OR WN5 ...... 47 J6
Reed St GTN M18 ...... 89 C6
  OLD OL1 * ...... 9 L5
Reedymoor WHTN BL5 ...... 50 B8
Reeman Cl MPL/ROM SK6 ...... 101 K8
Reepham Cl WGNS/IIMK WN3 ...... 62 F1
Reeve Cl OFTN SK2 ...... 113 J7
Reeves Rd CCHDY M21 ...... 97 G6
Reeves St LEIGH WN7 ...... 66 C6
Reeve St GOL/RIS/CUL WA3 ...... 80 A6
Reevey Av BRAM/HZG SK7 ...... 121 C2
Reform St WHIT OL12 ...... 10 E2
Reform Wk OP/CLY M11 ...... 88 E4
Regaby Gv WGNE/HIN WN2 ...... 49 K7
Regal Cl WHTF M45 ...... 55 L4
Regal Fold WHIT OL12 ...... 20 F8
Regan Av CCHDY M21 ...... 98 A1
Regan St BOL BL1 ...... 36 A1
  RAD M26 ...... 54 D3
Regatta Cl CHAD OL9 ...... 74 D1
Regatta St SLFD M6 ...... 71 K6
Regency Cl GLSP SK13 ...... 105 G3
  NEWH/MOS M40 ...... 73 M4
  OLDS OL8 ...... 59 G8
Regency Ct
  HALE/TIMP WA15 * ...... 117 K3
  ROCH OL11 ...... 27 J5
  WGN WN1 ...... 15 H3
Regency Gdns CHD/CHDH SK8 ...... 120 A4
  HYDE SK14 ...... 91 J8
Regency Ldg PWCH M25 * ...... 71 K1
Regency Pk WILM/AE SK9 ...... 126 D7
Regent Av AIMK WN4 ...... 63 G8
  LHULT M38 ...... 52 F8
  RUSH/FAL M14 ...... 98 C2
Regent Cl BRAM/HZG SK7 ...... 121 G8
  CHD/CHDH SK8 ...... 111 M8
  HEY OL10 ...... 40 E5
  WILM/AE SK9 ...... 126 D7
Regent Crs FAIL M35 ...... 74 B6
  ROY/SHW OL2 ...... 59 G2
Regent Dr DTN/ASHW M34 ...... 101 G3
  HOR/BR BL6 ...... 34 E5
  LEIGH WN7 ...... 67 G5
Regent Pl RUSH/FAL M14 ...... 87 M8
Regent Rd ALT WA14 ...... 108 A8
  HOR/BR BL6 ...... 34 E6
  OFTN SK2 ...... 112 D6
  ORD M5 ...... 86 E4
  SLFD M6 ...... 6 A1
  WGNE/HIN WN2 ...... 64 D2
Regents Dr MOSL OL5 ...... 77 G5
Regents Hl HOR/BR BL6 ...... 34 F6
Regents Pk ORD M5 ...... 86 A4
  WILM/AE SK9 ...... 126 F6
The Regents
  WILM/AE SK9 ...... 127 G4

Regent St ATH M46 67 H2
BURY BL9 4 F1
ECC M30 85 K2
GLSP SK13 105 G3
HEY OL10 40 E3
LIT OL15 21 M7
MDTN M24 57 J2
NEWH/MOS M40 74 A7
OLD OL1 9 L5
RAMS BL0 18 D8
WGNE/HIN WN2 48 F7
WHIT OL12 28 C3
Regent Wk FWTH BL4 * 53 G4
Regina Av STLY SK15 91 K2
Regina Crs LEIGH WN7 67 H6
Reginald St BOLS/LL BL3 * 51 K2
ECC M30 84 D4
OP/CLY M11 89 J5
SWIN M27 70 A3
Reid Cl DTN/ASHW M34 101 K4
Reigate Cl TOT/BURYW BL8 * 38 E3
Reigate Rd URM M41 95 H4
Reilly St HULME M15 87 J6
Reins Lee Av OLDS OL8 75 K2
Reins Lee Rd AULW OL7 75 K6
Reliance St NEWH/MOS M40 73 M6
Rembrandt Wk OLD OL1 44 A7
Rena Cl HTNM SK4 12 E1
Rendel Cl STRET M32 97 G2
Renfrew Cl WGNS/IIMK WN3 63 K1
Renfrew Dr BOLS/LL BL3 51 J1
Renfrew Rd WGNE/HIN WN2 33 G7
Rennie Cl STRET M32 97 G2
Renshaw Av ECC M30 85 G3
Renshaw Dr BURY BL9 5 M2
Renshaw St ECC M30 85 G3
Renton Rd BOLS/LL BL3 51 L1
STRET M32 97 H2
WYTH/NTH M22 110 A8
Renwick Sq AIMK WN4 78 C1
Repton Av DROY M43 89 G1
DTN/ASHW M34 100 D1
HYDE SK14 102 B1
NEWH/MOS M40 74 B3
OLDS OL8 75 G1
URM M41 95 G2
WGNS/IIMK WN3 48 C8
Repton Cl SALE M33 108 A1
Reservoir Rd EDGY/DAV SK3 12 F9
Reservoir St CSLFD M3 6 D1
MILN OL16 11 L2
SLFD M6 86 C2
WGNE/HIN WN2 48 D4
WGNE/HIN WN2 49 J1
The Residences PWCH M25 71 M1
Retford Av MILN OL16 28 E8
Retford Cl TOT/BURYW BL8 25 H7
Retford St OLDE OL4 * 59 L7
Retiro St OLD OL1 9 K5
The Retreat MPL/ROM SK6 113 L3
Reuben St HTNM SK4 100 B8
Revers St TOT/BURYW BL8 4 B3
Reveton Gn BRAM/HZG SK7 121 J2
Rexcine Wy HYDE SK14 91 K7
Reynard Rd CCHDY M21 97 L5
Reynard St HYDE SK14 * 102 A1
Reynell Rd BRUN/LGST M13 99 J2
Reyner St AUL OL6 91 H2
CMANE M1 7 G6
Reynolds Cl WHTN BL5 51 J6
Reynolds Dr GTN M18 89 G6
MPL/ROM SK6 114 E4
WHTN BL5 51 J5
Reynolds Ms WILM/AE SK9 127 J4
Reynolds Rd OLDTF/WHR M16 86 F8
Reynold St HYDE SK14 102 A2
Rhine Cl TOT/BURYW BL8 24 C5
Rhine Dr CHH M8 72 B7
Rhiwlas Dr BURY BL9 5 G8
Rhodes Av OLDE OL4 60 C7
UPML OL3 61 M3
Rhodes Bank OLD OL1 9 L6
Rhodes Crs ROCH OL11 42 C1
Rhodes Dr BURY BL9 55 K2
Rhodes Hl OLDE OL4 60 C7
Rhodes St GLSP SK13 93 L7
HYDE SK14 101 M1
NEWH/MOS M40 73 H8
OLD OL1 9 L5
OLDE OL4 60 C5
WHIT OL12 28 E1
Rhodes St North HYDE SK14 101 M1
Rhode St TOT/BURYW BL8 24 C6
Rhodeswood Dr GLSP SK13 93 K6
Rhos Av CHD/CHDH SK8 120 B3
MDTN M24 57 J3
RUSH/FAL M14 99 H4
Rhos Dr BRAM/HZG SK7 121 M3
Rhosleigh Av BOL BL1 22 B8
Rhyl Fold LEIGH WN7 * 67 H7
Rialto Gdns BRO M7 * 72 B6
Ribblesford Rd WGNS/IIMK WN3 46 F8
Ribble Av BOLE BL2 37 H5
CHAD OL9 58 C3
LIT OL15 21 K6
Ribble Dr BURY BL9 25 J4
FWTH BL4 53 L7
WALK M28 68 C6
WGNW/BIL/OR WN5 46 F5
WHTF M45 55 K3
Ribble Gv LEIGH WN7 65 M7
Ribble Rd OLDS OL8 74 F1
WGNE/HIN WN2 64 D2
WGNNW/ST WN6 30 E2
Ribblesdale Cl HEY OL10 * 41 H5
Ribblesdale Dr
NEWH/MOS M40 72 F7
Ribblesdale Rd BOLS/LL BL3 36 A8
Ribble St ROCH OL11 28 B8
Ribbleton Cl TOT/BURYW BL8 38 C5
Ribchester Dr BURY BL9 55 K1
Ribchester Gv BOLE BL2 37 H3
Riber Bank GLSP SK13 104 B3
Ribston St HULME M15 87 H6
Rice St CSLFD M3 6 C7
Richard Burch St BURY BL9 5 G2
Richard Gwyn Cl WHTN BL5 50 A7
Richards Cl DTN/ASHW M34 90 B5
Richardson Cl WHTF M45 55 G4
Richardson Rd ECC M30 85 H2
Richardson St OP/CLY M11 89 H5
STKP SK1 13 L9
Richards Rd WGNNW/ST WN6 30 E1
Richard St FAIL M35 74 C5
RAD M26 54 C1
RAMS BL0 19 H5
ROCH OL11 10 F6
STKP SK1 13 K2
WGNS/IIMK WN3 15 J7
Richbell Cl IRL M44 94 C5
Richborough Cl BRO M7 72 B7
Richelieu St BOLS/LL BL3 36 D8
Richmond Av CHAD OL9 58 D8
PWCH M25 71 M3
ROY/SHW OL2 43 G8
URM M41 96 B2
WILM/AE SK9 119 M7
Richmond Cl DUK SK16 91 G6
GLSP SK13 93 K7
GOL/RIS/CUL WA3 81 G8
MILN OL16 42 F1
MOSL OL5 77 H4
ROY/SHW OL2 43 L7
SALE M33 109 J1
STLY SK15 91 K3
TOT/BURYW BL8 24 C6
WGN WN1 31 L5
WHTF M45 55 G5
Richmond Crs MOSL OL5 77 H4
Richmond Dr LEIGH WN7 67 H5
WALK M28 69 M4
Richmond Gdns BOLS/LL BL3 52 E1
Richmond Gn ALT WA14 116 D2
BRAM/HZG SK7 * 121 H6
Richmond Gv BRUN/LGST M13 88 B8
CHD/CHDH SK8 120 B3
FWTH BL4 * 52 D3
LEIGH WN7 67 G6
Richmond Gv East
WGTN/LGST M12 88 B7
Richmond Hl
WGNW/BIL/OR WN5 46 F6
Richmond Hill Rd
CHD/CHDH SK8 110 F7
Richmond Rd AIMK WN4 63 J7
ALT WA14 108 A7
ALT WA14 116 D2
DTN/ASHW M34 * 100 D1
DUK SK16 91 G6
FAIL M35 74 D4
HTNM SK4 111 J2
MPL/ROM SK6 113 M1
RUSH/FAL M14 99 G4
TRPK M17 85 K5
WALK M28 68 B5
WGNE/HIN WN2 65 K1
Richmond St AULW OL7 75 J8
AULW OL7 90 C1
BURY BL9 4 E9
CMANE M1 7 H6
CSLFD M3 6 C1
DROY M43 * 89 M2
DTN/ASHW M34 90 B6
HOR/BR BL6 33 L1
HYDE SK14 102 B2
STLY SK15 91 L2
WGN WN1 14 E3
WGNS/IIMK WN3 47 K7
Richmond Wk CHAD OL9 8 E6
Ricroft Rd MPL/ROM SK6 114 E1
Ridding Av WYTH/NTH M22 119 G1
Ridding Cl OFTN SK2 113 G6
Riddings Ct HALE/TIMP WA15 108 D4
Riddings Rd HALE/TIMP WA15 108 D4
HALE/TIMP WA15 117 H3
Ridge Av HALE/TIMP WA15 117 L6
MPL/ROM SK6 114 D8
WGN WN1 31 L5
Ridge Cl GLSP SK13 93 H8
MPL/ROM SK6 114 B2
Ridge Crs MPL/ROM SK6 123 H1
WHTF M45 55 L4
Ridgecroft AULW OL7 75 L6
The Ridgedales OLD OL1 44 B8
Ridge End Fold MPL/ROM SK6 123 J3
Ridgefield CMANW M2 6 E5
Ridgefield St FAIL M35 74 B6
Ridgegreen WALK M28 * 68 D7
Ridge Gv WHTF M45 55 L4
Ridge Hill La STLY SK15 91 K1
Ridgemont Av HTNM SK4 12 B2
Ridgemont Cl HOR/BR BL6 34 C1
Ridge Pk BRAM/HZG SK7 120 F6
Ridge Rd MPL/ROM SK6 114 D8
Ridge Top La NM/HAY SK22 125 M2
Ridgeway BOL BL1 * 2 E4
GOL/RIS/CUL WA3 80 B5
SWIN M27 70 E3
WILM/AE SK9 127 K5
Ridgeway Gates BOL BL1 2 E4
Ridgeway Rd
HALE/TIMP WA15 108 F7
Ridgeway St NEWH/MOS M40 88 A2
The Ridgeway POY/DIS SK12 123 L5
Ridgewell Av GOL/RIS/CUL WA3 80 A4
Ridgewood Av CHAD OL9 58 B4
NEWH/MOS M40 73 H7
Ridgmont Dr HOR/BR BL6 34 C1
WALK M28 68 C6
Ridgmont Rd BRAM/HZG SK7 121 G8
Ridgway HOR/BR BL6 32 F2
The Ridgway MPL/ROM SK6 113 K3
Riding Cl SALE M33 97 J8
TYLD M29 68 A5
Riding Fold DROY M43 89 M1
Riding Fold La WALK M28 69 K7
Riding Ga BOLE BL2 23 H6
Riding Gate Ms BOLE BL2 23 H6
Riding Head La RAMS BL0 19 J4
Riding La AIMK WN4 64 B7
Ridings Ct UPML OL3 61 K5
Ridings Rd GLSP SK13 93 J7
Ridings St NEWH/MOS M40 73 J7
OP/CLY M11 88 E4
The Ridings RNFD/HAY WA11 78 A6
Riding St CSLFD M3 6 C4
Ridings Wy CHAD OL9 8 B8
Ridley Dr ALT WA14 108 B3
Ridley Gv SALE M33 109 J1
Ridley St OLDE OL4 9 M7
Ridley Wk HULME M15 * 87 J7
Ridling La HYDE SK14 102 B2
Ridsdale Av DID/WITH M20 98 D6
Ridyard St LHULT M38 52 F8
WGNE/HIN WN2 64 E1
WGNW/BIL/OR WN5 47 H5
Riefield BOL BL1 35 L1
Rifle Rd SALE M33 97 J7
Rifle St OLD OL1 9 J3
Riga Rd RUSH/FAL M14 98 F3
Riga St ANC M4 7 H2
Rigby Av HOR/BR BL6 * 32 F2
RAD M26 38 F7
Rigby Ct BOLS/LL BL3 36 C8
Rigby Gv LHULT M38 52 C8
Rigby La BOLE BL2 23 G7
Rigbys La AIMK WN4 79 G1
Rigby St AIMK WN4 78 D1
ALT WA14 116 F1
BOLS/LL BL3 36 C8
BRO M7 72 A5
GOL/RIS/CUL WA3 79 K4
WGNE/HIN WN2 49 H6
Rigel St ANC M4 7 M1
Rigton Cl WGTN/LGST M12 88 D7
Rildene Wk ROCH OL11 27 G4
Riley Cl SALE M33 107 L3
Riley Ct BOL BL1 36 C3
Riley La WGNE/HIN WN2 32 E5
Riley Sq WGN WN1 15 J3
Riley St ATH M46 66 D3
Riley Wood Cl MPL/ROM SK6 * 113 J3
Rimington Av
GOL/RIS/CUL WA3 79 M3
Rimington Fold MDTN M24 41 G8
Rimmer Cl OP/CLY M11 88 B4
Rimmington Cl BKLY M9 73 K2
Rimsdale Cl CHD/CHDH SK8 119 J1
Rimworth Dr NEWH/MOS M40 72 F8
Rindle Rd TYLD M29 82 F4
Ringcroft Gdns
NEWH/MOS M40 73 L3
Ringley Av GOL/RIS/CUL WA3 79 J3
Ringley Cha WHTF M45 55 H4
Ringley Cl WHTF M45 55 G4
Ringley Dr WHTF M45 55 G5
Ringley Gv BOL BL1 22 B7
Ringley Hey WHTF M45 55 G4
Ringley Mdw RAD M26 53 M5
Ringley Old Brow RAD M26 53 M5
Ringley Pk WHTF M45 55 G4
Ringley Rd RAD M26 53 L4
RAD M26 54 A5
RAD M26 54 E4
Ringley Rd West RAD M26 54 B4
Ringley St BKLY M9 * 73 G4
Ringlow Av SWIN M27 69 M5
Ringlow Park Rd SWIN M27 69 M6
Ring Lows La WHIT OL12 20 E8
Ringmer Dr WYTH/NTH M22 118 E3
Ringmere Ct OLD OL1 * 9 H2
Ringmore Rd BRAM/HZG SK7 121 J2
Ring-o-bells La POY/DIS SK12 123 M6
Rings Cl FAIL M35 74 C6
Ringstead Cl WILM/AE SK9 127 H3
Ringstead Dr NEWH/MOS M40 87 M1
WILM/AE SK9 127 H3
Ringstone PWCH M25 71 K1
Ringway Av LEIGH WN7 66 C4
Ringway Gv SALE M33 109 H2
Ringway Rd MANAIR M90 118 E5
WYTH/NTH M22 119 G5
Ringway Rd West
WYTH/NTH M22 118 E4
Ringwood Av BRAM/HZG SK7 121 K3
DTN/ASHW M34 89 M3
HYDE SK14 102 D3
RAD M26 54 E3
RAMS BL0 18 D8
WGTN/LGST M12 99 L2
Ringwood Wy CHAD OL9 8 C3
Rink St RUSH/FAL M14 99 G5
Ripley Av CHD/CHDH SK8 120 D7
OFTN SK2 112 E8
Ripley Cl ANC M4 * 88 A4
BRAM/HZG SK7 122 A4
Ripley Crs URM M41 84 C7
Ripley Dr LEIGH WN7 66 C6
WGNS/IIMK WN3 46 F8
Ripley St BOLE BL2 22 E8
Ripon Av BOL BL1 35 J3
GOL/RIS/CUL WA3 80 A4
WHTF M45 55 J2
Ripon Cl BOLS/LL BL3 53 J1
CHAD OL9 8 B7
HALE/TIMP WA15 117 L3
NEWLW WA12 78 F8
RAD M26 39 G7
STKP SK1 13 J7
WHTF M45 55 J2
Ripon Crs STRET M32 96 C1
Ripon Dr AIMK WN4 79 G2
BOL BL1 36 A2
Ripon Gv SALE M33 96 C6
Ripon Hall Av RAMS BL0 18 E5
Ripon Rd STRET M32 96 D1
Ripon St AUL OL6 * 90 F1
OLD OL1 8 F2
Rippenden Av CCHDY M21 97 K2
Rippingham Rd
DID/WITH M20 98 E5
Rippleton Rd WYTH/NTH M22 110 B8
Ripponden Rd OLDE OL4 60 A3
UPML OL3 45 G2
Ripponden St OLD OL1 59 M3
The Rises GLSP SK13 93 J7
The Rise OLDE OL4 60 C5
WGNNW/ST WN6 46 F1
Rishton Av BOLS/LL BL3 52 C2
Rishton La BOLS/LL BL3 52 C1
Rishworth Cl OFTN SK2 113 G7
Rishworth Dr NEWH/MOS M40 74 B4
Rishworth Ri ROY/SHW OL2 43 J3
Rising La OLDS OL8 75 H2
Risley Av BKLY M9 73 G4
Risley St OLD OL1 9 J2
Rissington Av
NTHM/RTH M23 109 L6
Rita Av RUSH/FAL M14 * 98 F3
Ritson Cl GTN M18 88 E6
Riva Rd BNG/LEV M19 111 G2
Riverbank UPML OL3 61 J3
Riverbank Dr TOT/BURYW BL8 4 C1
Riverbanks BOLS/LL BL3 3 M9
The Riverbank RAD M26 53 K4
Riverbank Wy GLSP SK13 105 J5
Riverbrook Rd ALT WA14 107 M3
Riverdale Cl WGNNW/ST WN6 47 G1
Riverdale Rd BKLY M9 72 D1
River La PART M31 94 C8
Rivermead MILN OL16 43 L1
Rivermead Av
HALE/TIMP WA15 117 L5
Rivermead Cl DTN/ASHW M34 101 K5
Rivermead Rd DTN/ASHW M34 101 L5
Rivermead Wy WHTF M45 55 K4
Riverpark Rd
NEWH/MOS M40 88 D1
River Pl HULME M15 6 D8
MILN OL16 * 29 J6
Riversdale Dr OLDS OL8 75 K3
Riversdale Rd CHD/CHDH SK8 110 F7
Riversdale Vw MPL/ROM SK6 101 K7
The Rivers Edge WHIT OL12 20 A4
Rivershill SALE M33 96 D6
Rivershill Dr HEY OL10 40 E3
Rivershill Gdns
HALE/TIMP WA15 117 L6
Riverside BOL BL1 36 C2
BRO M7 86 F1
DUK SK16 90 F2
OLD OL1 8 B3
Riverside Av IRL M44 94 D3
WGN WN1 15 J1
Riverside Cl GLSP SK13 105 G3
Riverside Ct MPL/ROM SK6 * 114 D4
Riverside Dr BURY BL9 24 E1
MILN OL16 28 F2
RAD M26 53 L4
URM M41 95 L4
Riverside Gdns SALE M33 96 D6
Riverside Rd RAD M26 39 G8
Rivers La URM M41 84 F7
Riversleigh Cl BOL BL1 35 J1
Riversmeade EDGW/EG BL7 22 F5
LEIGH WN7 66 D6
Rivers St WGNW/BIL/OR WN5 46 B6
Riverstone Br LIT OL15 21 M7
Riverstone Dr NTHM/RTH M23 109 G5
River St BOLE BL2 3 G5
HEY OL10 27 G8
HULME M15 6 E9
MILN OL16 10 F4
RAD M26 54 E1
RAMS BL0 18 F6
STKP SK1 112 E1
WGTN/LGST M12 7 M7
WILM/AE SK9 126 F4
Riverton Rd DID/WITH M20 110 E5
River Vw RDSH SK5 100 D5
River View Cl PWCH M25 71 J2
Riverview Wk BOL BL1 * 2 A6
River Wy WGN WN1 15 G4
Riviera Ct WHIT OL12 26 F2
Rivington Av GOL/RIS/CUL WA3 79 M3
SWIN M27 70 F5
WGN WN1 47 L2
WGNE/HIN WN2 64 E1
Rivington Dr ROY/SHW OL2 44 A5
TOT/BURYW BL8 38 D3
WGNE/HIN WN2 65 J3
Rivington Gv DTN/ASHW M34 89 M4
IRL M44 94 A6
Rivington Rd
HALE/TIMP WA15 117 H2
OLDE OL4 60 D5
SLFD M6 70 F8
Rivington St ATH M46 66 D2
HOR/BR BL6 33 G2
OLD OL1 9 J1
WHIT OL12 10 F1
Rivington Wk
WGTN/LGST M12 * 88 B7
Rivington Wy WGNNW/ST WN6 31 J4
Rixon St OLDE OL4 60 A3
Rixson St OLDE OL4 * 60 A3
Rix St BOL BL1 36 B2
Rixton Dr TYLD M29 67 L4
Rixtonleys Dr IRL M44 94 E4
Roach Bank Rd BURY BL9 39 M5
Roaches Ms MOSL OL5 77 G1
Roaches Wy MOSL OL5 77 H1
Roach Gn WGN WN1 15 L2
Roachill Cl ALT WA14 107 L7
Roach Pl MILN OL16 11 G3
Roach St BURY BL9 39 J8
Roach V MILN OL16 28 F2
Roachwood Cl CHAD OL9 58 B5
Roading Brook Rd BOLE BL2 37 L1
Road La WHIT OL12 20 B8
Roads Ford Av MILN OL16 29 J5
Roadside Ct GOL/RIS/CUL WA3 79 M4
Roan Wy WILM/AE SK9 130 E4
Roaring Gate La
HALE/TIMP WA15 118 A1
Robert Hall St ORD M5 86 E5
Robert Lawrence Ct
URM M41 * 95 K3
Robert Malcolm Cl
NEWH/MOS M40 73 G7
Robert Owen Gdns
WYTH/NTH M22 * 110 A4
Robert Salt Ct ALT WA14 108 B6
Robertscroft Cl
WYTH/NTH M22 109 M8
Robertshaw Av CCHDY M21 97 L6
Robertshaw St LEIGH WN7 66 B5
Robertson St RAD M26 38 D8
Roberts St ECC M30 85 G3
Robert St ATH M46 * 67 H3
BOLE BL2 * 23 H7
CSLFD M3 87 J1
DUK SK16 90 E4
FAIL M35 74 D3
HEY OL10 41 H4
HYDE SK14 101 M2
MILN OL16 10 F3
NEWH/MOS M40 73 J7
OLDS OL8 74 E2
PWCH M25 55 M8
RAMS BL0 18 F3
SALE M33 97 H8
TOT/BURYW BL8 38 F1
WGNE/HIN WN2 64 D1
Robeson Wy WYTH/NTH M22 110 C6
Robin Cft MPL/ROM SK6 113 H2
Robin Dr IRL M44 94 D1
Robin Hill Dr WGNNW/ST WN6 30 E2
Robin Hill La WGNNW/ST WN6 30 E1
Robin Hood St CHH M8 72 C4
Robinia Cl ECC M30 84 C4
Robin Park Rd
WGNW/BIL/OR WN5 14 B6
Robin Rd ALT WA14 107 M3
BURY BL9 24 E2
Robinsbay Rd WYTH/NTH M22 119 G5
Robins Cl BRAM/HZG SK7 121 G5
DROY M43 89 M1
Robin's La BRAM/HZG SK7 121 G5
Robinson La AULW OL7 90 C1
Robinson Pk STLY SK15 91 H3
Robinson St CHAD OL9 8 A7
EDGY/DAV SK3 12 F8
HYDE SK14 * 102 C1
MILN OL16 11 G4
OLDS OL8 75 J1
STLY SK15 91 J3
Robin St OLD OL1 9 G2
Robinsway ALT WA14 116 E3
Robinswood Rd
WYTH/NTH M22 118 F3
Rob La NEWLW WA12 79 H8
Robson Av URM M41 85 H5
Robson St OLD OL1 9 K6
Robson Wy
GOL/RIS/CUL WA3 80 C4
Roby Rd ECC M30 84 F4
Roby St CMANE M1 7 J5
Roby Well Wy
WGNW/BIL/OR WN5 62 A7
Roch Av HEY OL10 40 D2
Roch Bank BKLY M9 72 C1
Rochbury Cl ROCH OL11 27 J6
Roch Cl WHTF M45 55 L3
Roch Crs WHTF M45 55 L3
Rochdale La HEY OL10 41 G2
ROY/SHW OL2 43 G7
Rochdale Old Rd BURY BL9 39 M1
Rochdale Rd ANC M4 7 J2
BKLY M9 73 G5
BURY BL9 4 F4
HEY OL10 41 G2
MDTN M24 57 L1
MILN OL16 29 G5
NEWH/MOS M40 72 F8
OLD OL1 9 G3
RAMS BL0 19 K3
ROY/SHW OL2 42 F6
UPML OL3 44 E1
Rochdale Rd East HEY OL10 41 J1
Rochdale Wy MILN OL16 43 H2
Roche Gdns CHD/CHDH SK8 120 D6
Roche Rd UPML OL3 45 H7
Rochester Av BOLE BL2 37 H3
CCHDY M21 98 A6
PWCH M25 71 M2
WALK M28 68 F3
Rochester Cl AUL OL6 75 M5
DUK SK16 91 K5
GOL/RIS/CUL WA3 79 K4
Rochester Dr ALT WA14 108 B3
Rochester Gv BRAM/HZG SK7 122 A1
Rochester Rd URM M41 85 G8
Rochester Wy CHAD OL9 8 A7
Rochford Av WHTF M45 55 G5
Rochford Cl WHTF M45 55 G5
Rochford Rd ECC M30 84 C4
Roch Mills Crs ROCH OL11 27 M7
Roch Mills Gdns ROCH OL11 27 M7
Roch Pl WGNE/HIN WN2 64 C2
Roch St MILN OL16 28 E3
Roch Valley Wy ROCH OL11 27 M7
Roch Wy WHTF M45 55 L3
Rockall Wk OP/CLY M11 * 88 C3
Rock Av BOL BL1 35 M2
Rock Bank BRO M7 * 71 M6
MOSL OL5 * 76 F3
Rockbourne Cl WGNE/HIN WN2 49 G8
Rockdove Av HULME M15 6 E9
Rocket Wy CSLFD M3 6 B4
Rockfield Dr BKLY M9 * 73 H4
Rock Fold EDGW/EG BL7 * 22 C3
Rockhampton St GTN M18 89 H7
Rockhouse Cl ECC M30 85 G4
Rockingham Cl ROY/SHW OL2 43 H4
WGTN/LGST M12 88 A6
Rockingham Dr
WGNE/HIN WN2 48 F8
Rockley Gdns SLFD M6 71 L8
Rocklyn Av NEWH/MOS M40 73 M2
Rocklynes MPL/ROM SK6 113 L2
Rockmead Dr BKLY M9 73 H1
Rock Mill La NM/HAY SK22 124 D5
Rock Rd URM M41 96 C2
WALK M28 83 L2
Rock St AULW OL7 75 K7
BRO M7 72 A6
GOL/RIS/CUL WA3 79 K2
HEY OL10 41 H3
HOR/BR BL6 33 L1
HYDE SK14 102 B5
NM/HAY SK22 124 D5
OLD OL1 9 J5
OP/CLY M11 89 H5
RAD M26 54 E2
RAMS BL0 19 H5
Rock Ter EDGW/EG BL7 22 C3
MOSL OL5 77 G1
The Rock BURY BL9 4 E4
Rocky Bank Ter
WGNS/IIMK WN3 * 15 K9
Rocky La ECC M30 70 A8
Roda St BKLY M9 73 J5
Rodborough Rd
NTHM/RTH M23 118 C1
Rodeheath Cl WILM/AE SK9 127 H5
Rodenhurst Dr
NEWH/MOS M40 73 K6
Rodepool Cl WILM/AE SK9 127 H2
Rodgers Cl WHTN BL5 50 B6
Rodgers Wy WHTN BL5 50 B6
Rodmell Av NEWH/MOS M40 * 73 G7
Rodmell Cl EDGW/EG BL7 22 C5
Rodmill Ct RUSH/FAL M14 98 F3
Rodmill Dr CHD/CHDH SK8 110 D8
Rodney Ct ANC M4 7 L1
Rodney Dr MPL/ROM SK6 101 K7
Rodney St ANC M4 7 M2
ATH M46 * 66 F2
AUL OL6 76 A8
CSLFD M3 6 A4
ROCH OL11 41 L2
WGN WN1 15 G5
Roeacre St HEY OL10 41 H2
Roebuck Gdns SALE M33 * 96 D8
Roebuck La OLDE OL4 60 D1
SALE M33 96 D8
Roebuck St WGNE/HIN WN2 65 M1
Roecliffe Cl WGNS/IIMK WN3 14 E8
Roe Cross Gn HYDE SK14 92 C7
Roe Cross Rd HYDE SK14 92 C7
Roedean Gdns URM M41 95 G2
Roefield Ter WHIT OL12 27 M4
Roe Gn WALK M28 69 K4
Roe Green Av WALK M28 69 K4
Roe La OLDE OL4 60 A7
Roe St ANC M4 7 L1
WHIT OL12 27 M3
Rogate Dr NTHM/RTH M23 109 K7
Roger Cl MPL/ROM SK6 113 J3
Rogerson Cl HALE/TIMP WA15 108 F5
Rogerstead BOLS/LL BL3 * 35 M6
Roger St ANC M4 87 K1
Rogerton Cl LEIGH WN7 66 E8
Roger Wy CHD/CHDH SK8 120 C2
Rokeby Av GOL/RIS/CUL WA3 80 A3
STRET M32 97 G3
Rokeden NEWLW WA12 79 G8
Roker Av BRUN/LGST M13 99 J2
Roker Park Av DTN/ASHW M34 90 B5
Roland Rd BOLS/LL BL3 35 M7
RDSH SK5 100 C5
Rolla St CSLFD M3 6 D2
Rollesby Cl TOT/BURYW BL8 25 G7
Rolleston Av ANC M4 88 A2
Rollins La MPL/ROM SK6 114 D3
Rolls Crs HULME M15 87 H6
Rollswood Dr NEWH/MOS M40 73 K6
Romana Sq ALT WA14 108 B4
Roman Rd AIMK WN4 63 K7
FAIL M35 74 D4
HTNM SK4 13 H3
PWCH M25 71 J3
ROY/SHW OL2 59 G1
Roman St RAD M26 54 B1
Romer Av NEWH/MOS M40 * 74 B3
Rome Rd NEWH/MOS M40 7 L1
Romer St BOLE BL2 3 M5
Romford Av DTN/ASHW M34 90 B8
LEIGH WN7 66 C6

Romford Cl *OLDS* OL8................9 H9
Romford Pl *WGNE/HIN* WN2......49 H7
Romford Rd *SALE* M33...............96 B6
Romford St *WGNE/HIN* WN2........49 G7
Romiley Crs *BOLE* BL2...............37 G4
Romiley Dr *BOLE* BL2.................37 G4
Romiley Sq *WGNNW/ST* WN6......31 H4
Romiley St *SLFD* M6..................71 C7
  *STKP* SK1...........................112 E2
Romley Rd *URM* M41.................85 G8
Romney Av *ROCH* OL11..............42 B2
Romney Cha *BOL* BL1.................22 B8
Romney Rd *BOL* BL1..................35 H2
Romney St *AUL* OL6...................90 F1
  *NEWH/MOS* M40.................73 K4
  *SLFD* M6..............................71 K7
Romney Wk *CHAD* OL9................3 G8
Romney Wy *RDSH* SK5...............100 E6
  *WGN* WN1............................47 L1
Romsey *WHIT* OL12...................10 D3
Romsey Av *MDTN* M24...............57 J1
Romsey Dr
  *CHD/CHDH* SK8...................120 D6
Romsey Gv *WGNS/IIMK* WN3.......63 G3
Romsley Cl *WGTN/LGST* M12......88 D2
Romsley Dr *BOLS/LL* BL3............51 M1
Rona Cl *WGTN/LGST* M12............88 C7
Ronald Av *STLY* SK15.................91 K3
Ronaldsay Gdns *ORD* M5............86 B3
Ronald St *OLDE* OL4..................59 M5
  *OP/CLY* M11........................89 G3
  *ROCH* OL11.........................41 M5
Rondin Cl *WGTN/LGST* M12........88 B5
Rondin Rd *WGTN/LGST* M12........88 B5
Roocroft Cl *BOL* BL1...................2 B1
Roocroft Sq *HOR/BR* BL6...........32 F2
Roods La *ROCH* OL11.................26 F3
Rookery Av *AIMK* WN4...............78 E2
  *GTN* M18.............................89 J6
  *WGNNW/ST* WN6.................30 B4
Rookery Cl *STLY* SK15...............92 B5
Rookerypool Cl *WILM/AE* SK9....127 H2
The Rookery *NEWLW* WA12.........79 G8
Rooke St *ECC* M30....................84 D4
Rookfield Av *SALE* M33..............96 F7
Rookley Wk *RUSH/FAL* M14 *......98 F1
Rook St *HULME* M15..................87 H7
  *OLDE* OL4...........................9 L2
  *RAMS* BL0...........................18 F6
Rookswood Dr *ROCH* OL11.........41 L1
Rookway *MDTN* M24..................57 J5
Rookwood *OLD* OL1...................58 B3
Rookwood Av
  *NTHM/RTH* M23...................109 J5
Rookwood Hl *BRAM/HZG* SK7....121 C3
Rooley Moor Rd *WHIT* OL12........27 K1
Rooley St *WHIT* OL12................27 M3
Roosevelt Rd *FWTH* BL4.............53 J3
Rooth St *HTNM* SK4..................12 E3
Ropefield Wy *WHIT* OL12............28 B1
Rope St *WHIT* OL12...................10 E2
Rope Wk *CSLFD* M3...................6 D1
Rosa Gv *BRO* M7......................72 A6
Rosamond Dr *CSLFD* M3............6 B5
Rosamond St *BOLS/LL* BL3..........35 M8
  *HULME* M15.........................87 K6
Rosamond St West
  *HULME* M15.........................87 K6
Rosary Cl *OLDS* OL8.................75 J3
Rosary Rd *OLDS* OL8.................75 K3
Roscoe Ct *WHTN* BL5.................50 C5
Roscoe Rd *EDGY/DAV* SK3.........112 B7
  *OLD* OL1.............................9 L6
  *WN1* WN1...........................15 K5
Roscow Av *BOLE* BL2.................37 H4
Roscow Rd *FWTH* BL4................53 K6
Rose Acre *WALK* M28.................68 E5
Roseacre Cl *BOLE* BL2................3 L2
Roseacre Dr *CHD/CHDH* SK8......119 L3
Rose Av *IRL* M44......................94 C3
  *LIT* OL15............................29 J1
  *RNFD/HAY* WA11.................78 B6
  *ROCH* OL11.........................41 J7
  *WGNE/HIN* WN2..................64 E5
  *WGNNW/ST* WN6.................47 J1
Rosebank *HOR/BR* BL6..............34 F5
  *RAMS* BL0...........................19 G3
Rosebank Cl *BOLE* BL2..............37 M3
Rose Bank Cl *HYDE* SK14...........93 G7
  *WGN* WN1...........................31 L8
Rosebank Rd *NEWH/MOS* M40....73 L8
Rosebay Cl *ROY/SHW* OL2..........43 J8
Roseberry Cl *RAMS* BL0.............24 F1
Roseberry Rd *AIMK* WN4.............63 K7
Roseberry St *BOLS/LL* BL3..........35 M8
  *OLDS* OL8...........................8 F7
Rosebery St *OFTN* SK2...............113 G8
  *RUSH/FAL* M14....................98 C1
  *WHTN* BL5...........................50 C4
Rosebridge Ct *WGN* WN1 *.........15 M5
Rosebridge Wy *WGN* WN1...........15 M5
Rosebury Av *LEIGH* WN7.............66 D7
  *OLD* OL1.............................59 L3
Rosebury Gv *LEIGH* WN7.............66 E6
Rose Cottage Rd
  *DID/WITH* M20.....................98 E5
Rose Crs *IRL* M44.....................94 C3
Rosecroft Cl *EDGY/DAV* SK3......112 B8
Rosedale Av *ATH* M46................66 F1
  *BOL* BL1.............................22 B7
  *GOL/RIS/CUL* WA3...............79 M5
Rosedale Cl *OLD* OL1................59 L3
Rosedale Ct *DTN/ASHW* M34 *....101 H1
Rosedale Dr *LEIGH* WN7.............66 F7
Rosedale Rd *HTNM* SK4..............100 A7
  *RUSH/FAL* M14....................98 F6
Rosedale Wy *DUK* SK16.............90 F6
Rosefield Cl *EDGY/DAV* SK3......112 B8
Rosefield Crs *MILN* OL16............11 K5
Rosegarth Av *DID/WITH* M20.......98 A8
Rose Gv *FWTH* BL4....................53 J5
  *TOT/BURYW* BL8.................38 C7
Rosehay Av *DTN/ASHW* M34.......101 J2
Rose Hey La *FAIL* M35...............74 B8
Rose Hl *BOLE* BL2.....................3 H8
  *DTN/ASHW* M34...................101 G1
  *STLY* SK15..........................91 J4
  *UPML* OL3..........................61 K6
Rose Hill Av *NEWH/MOS* M40 *....73 L8
  *WGN/BIL/OR* WN5...............46 F6
Rose Hill Cl *EDGW/EG* BL7.........22 D5
Rosehill Cl *SLFD* M6..................86 C2
Rose Hill Rd *AUL* OL6................76 C7
Rosehill Rd *SWIN* M27...............70 C2
Rose Hill St *HEY* OL10................40 E2
Rose Hill Vw *AIMK* WN4.............63 J5
Roseland Av *DID/WITH* M20.......98 E8
Roseland Dr *PWCH* M25..............55 M6
Roselands Av *SALE* M33.............108 C2
Rose La *MPL/ROM* SK6..............114 D7
Rose Lea *BOLE* BL2....................23 H8
Rosemary Crs *WGN* WN1............48 A2
Rosemary Dr *HYDE* SK14...........102 A5
  *LIT* OL15............................21 K6
Rosemary Gv *BRO* M7................71 M7
Rosemary La *STKP* SK1..............13 L5
  *WHTN* BL5..........................51 L6
Rosemary Rd *CHAD* OL9.............58 B4
Rosemount *HYDE* SK14..............91 G7
Rose Mt *MDTN* M24...................57 J2
Rosemount Crs *HYDE* SK14.........91 G7
Roseneath *BRAM/HZG* SK7.........121 F3
Roseneath Av *BNG/LEV* M19........99 M3
Roseneath Gv *BOLS/LL* BL3.........52 A1
Roseneath Rd *BOLS/LL* BL3.........52 A1
  *URM* M41............................95 M1
Rosen Sq *CHAD* OL9..................8 A4
Rose St *BOLE* BL2.....................3 G8
  *CHAD* OL9..........................74 D1
  *MDTN* M24.........................57 M4
  *RDSH* SK5...........................112 C1
  *WGN* WN1..........................15 M5
  *WGNE/HIN* WN2..................49 G7
Rose Ter *STLY* SK15..................91 K3
Rosethorns *MDTN* M24...............41 J8
Rosevale Av *BNG/LEV* M19..........99 H1
Roseway *BRAM/HZG* SK7...........121 F4
Rosewell Cl
  *NEWH/MOS* M40..................73 G8
Rose Wd *DTN/ASHW* M34...........101 G1
  *WHTN* BL5..........................49 M6
Rosewood Av *DROY* M43............89 M1
  *HTNM* SK4..........................111 K3
  *TOT/BURYW* BL8.................26 A7
Rosewood Cl *DUK* SK16..............91 G6
  *WGNE/HIN* WN2..................64 E5
Rosewood Crs *CHAD* OL9............8 B1
Rosewood Gdns
  *CHD/CHDH* SK8...................110 C6
Rosford Av *RUSH/FAL* M14.........98 E2
Rosgill Cl *HTNM* SK4.................111 H2
Rosgill Dr *MDTN* M24................57 G3
Rosina Av *AIMK* WN4................63 J6
Rosina St *OP/CLY* M11...............89 J5
Rosley Rd *WGNS/IIMK* WN3.......63 L1
Roslin St *OP/CLY* M11................89 G2
Roslyn Av *URM* M41..................95 H4
Roslyn Rd *EDGY/DAV* SK3.........112 B7
Rossall Av *RAD* M26...................54 F4
  *STRET* M32.........................96 F1
Rossall Cl *BOLE* BL2..................3 J5
Rossall Crs *LEIGH* WN7..............81 K1
Rossall Dr *BRAM/HZG* SK7.........121 H6
Rossall Rd *BOLE* BL2.................3 J5
  *WHIT* OL12.........................28 D2
Rossall St *BOLE* BL2..................3 J5
Rossall Wy *SLFD* M6..................86 D1
Ross Av *CHAD* OL9....................74 C1
  *EDGY/DAV* SK3....................112 B7
  *WHTF* M45..........................55 J6
Ross Cl *WGNE/HIN* WN2............48 C2
  *WGNW/BIL/OR* WN5.............62 B7
Rossdale Gv *WGNNW/ST* WN6....31 K5
Ross Dr *SWIN* M27....................54 B8
Rossenclough Rd
  *WILM/AE* SK9......................127 H3
Rossendale Av *BKLY* M9.............73 J3
Rossendale Rd *ROY/SHW* OL2......44 A5
Rossendale Rd *CHD/CHDH* SK8....119 L4
Rossendale Wy *RAMS* BL0..........18 E2
  *RAW/HAS* BB4.....................18 B1
  *WHIT* OL12.........................20 A6
  *WHIT* OL12.........................20 E1
Rossett Av *HALE/TIMP* WA15......108 D4
  *WYTH/NTH* M22....................118 F3
Rossett Cl *WGNS/IIMK* WN3.......63 G2
Rossett Dr *URM* M41..................84 C3
Rosshill Wk *HULME* M15 *...........87 G6
Rossington St *NEWH/MOS* M40....74 A7
Rossini St *BOL* BL1...................2 E6
Rosslare Rd *WYTH/NTH* M22........119 G2
Ross Lave La *DTN/ASHW* M34......100 F3
Rosslyn Gv *HALE/TIMP* WA15......108 D6
Rosslyn Rd *CHD/CHDH* SK8.........119 M3
  *NEWH/MOS* M40..................73 K3
  *OLDTF/WHR* M16..................97 K2
Rossmere Av *ROCH* OL11...........27 M6
Rossmill La *HALE/TIMP* WA15.....117 L5
Ross St *OLDS* OL8.....................8 F8
Rostherne Av
  *GOL/RIS/CUL* WA3...............80 A4
  *MPL/ROM* SK6.....................123 G4
  *RUSH/FAL* M14....................98 D3
Rostherne Gdns *BOLS/LL* BL3.....35 L8
Rostherne Rd *EDGY/DAV* SK3......112 B7
  *SALE* M33...........................109 J1
  *WILM/AE* SK9......................126 C7
Rostherne St *ALT* WA14..............116 F1
  *SLFD* M6 *..........................86 B3
Rostron Av *BRO* M7...................72 B4
Rostrevor Rd *EDGY/DAV* SK3......112 B7
Rostron Av *WGTN/LGST* M12......88 D3
Rostron Rd *RAMS* BL0................18 E6
Rostron St *BNG/LEV* M19............99 L3
Rothay Cl *BOLE* BL2..................37 J3
  *WHTF* M45..........................55 M4
Rothay St *LEIGH* WN7...............66 E8
Rothbury Av *AULW* OL7..............75 H7
Rothbury Cl *TOT/BURYW* BL8......38 C2
Rothbury Ct *BOLS/LL* BL3...........51 L1
Rotherby Rd *WYTH/NTH* M22......110 B8
Rotherdale Av
  *HALE/TIMP* WA15................109 G7
Rotherhead Cl *HOR/BR* BL6.........33 J2
Rotherwood Av *STRET* M32.........97 H1
Rotherwood Rd *WILM/AE* SK9....126 B7
Rothesay Av *DUK* SK16..............90 F5
Rothesay Crs *SALE* M33.............107 M2
Rothesay Rd *BOLS/LL* BL3 *........51 L1
  *CHH* M8.............................72 B2
  *OLD* OL1.............................59 M3
Rothesay Ter *MILN* OL16............28 F8
Rothiemay Rd *URM* M41.............95 H3
Rothley Av *WYTH/NTH* M22.........110 A7
Rothman Cl *NEWH/MOS* M40......73 M6
Rothwell Crs *LHULT* M38............52 B6
Rothwell La *LHULT* M38..............52 B6
Rothwell Rd *GOL/RIS/CUL* WA3...79 M3
Rothwell St *BOLS/LL* BL3............2 D9
  *FAIL* M35...........................74 B6
  *NEWH/MOS* M40..................73 M6
  *RAMS* BL0...........................18 E6
  *ROY/SHW* OL2......................58 F1
  *WALK* M28..........................69 J1
  *WHIT* OL12.........................28 D3
Rottingdene Dr
  *WYTH/NTH* M22....................118 E3
Roughey Gdns
  *WYTH/NTH* M22....................109 M8
Rough Hey Wk *MILN* OL16..........11 J7
Rough Hill La *BURY* BL9.............26 B8
Roughlea Av *GOL/RIS/CUL* WA3...81 G8
Roughlee Av *SWIN* M27..............70 A5
Roughtown Ct *MOSL* OL5............77 G2
Roughtown Rd *MOSL* OL5...........77 G2
Round Barn *EDGW/EG* BL7 *.......16 E1
Roundcroft *MPL/ROM* SK6..........114 A1
Roundhey Av *CHD/CHDH* SK8......119 K4
Round Hey *MOSL* OL5................76 F4
Round Hill Cl *GLSP* SK13...........104 C1
Round Hill Wy *BOL* BL1..............2 F2
Roundhill Wy *OLD* OL4...............60 B3
Round House Av *WGN* WN1.........15 L1
Roundmoor Rd
  *WGNNW/ST* WN6.................31 K5
Roundthorn La *WHTN* BL5...........50 B5
Round Thorn Rd *MDTN* M24........57 L5
Roundthorn Rd
  *NTHM/RTH* M23...................109 J6
  *OLDE* OL4...........................59 M7
Roundway *BRAM/HZG* SK7.........120 F6
Round Wy *MK/HAY* SK22............124 F4
Roundwood Rd
  *WYTH/NTH* M22....................110 A5
Roundy La *MCFLDN* SK10..........129 K7
Rousdon Cl *NEWH/MOS* M40 *....73 G7
Rouse St *ROCH* OL11.................27 M8
Rovan St *GOL/RIS/CUL* WA3.......80 C5
  *HOR/BR* BL6........................34 B3
  *OLDTF/WHR* M16..................97 M1
  *SALE* M33...........................108 F2
  *URM* M41............................96 A1
  *WGNNW/ST* WN6.................47 J1
Rowan Cl *FAIL* M35...................74 C7
  *WHIT* OL12.........................27 K1
Rowan Crs *DUK* SK16................91 J5
  *CHD/CHDH* SK8...................120 E4
Rowanhill *WGN* WN1..................15 J1
Rowanlea *PWCH* M25 *..............55 M8
Rowan Pl *PWCH* M25.................71 L1
Rowans Cl *STLY* SK15................91 J5
Rowanside Dr *WILM/AE* SK9.......127 J4
Rowans St *BOL* BL1..................3 H5
The Rowans *BOL* BL1................4 A1
  *MOSL* OL5...........................77 C3
Rowanswood Dr *HYDE* SK14.......102 C3
Rowan Tree Dr *SALE* M33...........108 E3
Rowan Tree Rd *OLDS* OL8..........75 C3
Rowan Wk *GLSP* SK13...............93 H8
Rowanwood *CHAD* OL9...............58 B5
Rowany Cl *PWCH* M25................71 K2
Rowarth Av *DTN/ASHW* M34.......101 H4
Rowarth Rd *NTHM/RTH* M23.......118 B2
Rowbotham Sq *WGN* WN1..........14 F4
Rowbottom Wk *OLDS* OL8...........9 H9
Rowcon Cl *DTN/ASHW* M34.........90 B7
Rowdell Wk *NTHM/RTH* M23........118 B2
Rowden Rd *OLDE* OL4...............60 B8
Rowe Gn *DTN/ASHW* M34...........101 J2
Rowena St *BOLS/LL* BL3.............52 F2
Rowendale St *HULME* M15 *........6 E7
Rowe St *TYLD* M29 *.................67 L4
Rowfield Dr *NTHM/RTH* M23.......118 B1
Rowland Av *URM* M41................96 B1
Rowland Ct *MILN* OL16..............11 J7
Rowlands Rd *BURY* BL9.............25 H3
Rowland St *ATH* M46.................66 F1
  *MILN* OL16.........................11 K7
  *ORD* M5.............................86 D4
Rowlandsway
  *WYTH/NTH* M22....................118 F2
Rowland Wy *OLDE* OL4...............60 B5
Rowley Rd *BRAM/HZG* SK7.........122 A4
Rowley St *AUL* OL6...................76 A6
Rowood Av *CHH* M8..................72 E6
  *RDSH* SK5...........................100 C2
Rowrah Crs *MDTN* M24...............56 E3
Rowsley Av *BOL* BL1.................35 K3
  *DID/WITH* M20.....................98 B8
Rowsley Gv *RDSH* SK5...............100 B5
Rowsley Ms *GLSP* SK13.............104 B2
Rowsley Rd *ECC* M30.................84 F4
  *STRET* M32.........................96 D1
Rowsley St *OP/CLY* M11.............88 B2
  *ORD* M5.............................6 C1
Rowson Ct *SALE* M33 *..............96 C8
Rowson Dr *IRL* M44...................94 A6
Rowton Ri *WGN* WN1.................14 F4
Rowton St *BOLE* BL2.................36 E1
Roxalina St *BOLS/LL* BL3............36 B8
Roxburgh St *GTN* M18................89 G7
Roxbury Av *OLDE* OL4................60 A7
Roxby Cl *WALK* M28..................68 E1
Roxholme Wk *WYTH/NTH* M22....118 E4
Roxton Rd *HTNM* SK4................99 M6
Royal Ar *WGN* WN1...................15 G3
Royal Av *BURY* BL9...................5 J2
  *CCHDY* M21.......................97 K5
  *DROY* M43..........................89 L2
  *HEY* OL10...........................41 G3
  *URM* M41............................96 A2
Royal Court Dr *BOL* BL1 *...........2 B3
Royal Crs *CHD/CHDH* SK8..........119 L2
Royal Dr *LEIGH* WN7.................67 G6
Royal Ex *CMANW* M2 *..............6 F4
Royal Exchange Ar
  *CMANW* M2 *......................6 F4
Royal Gdns *ALT* WA14...............116 B2
Royal George St
  *STKP* SK3............................13 H7
Royal Oak Rd *NTHM/RTH* M23....109 H7
Royal Pde *OLD* OL1 *.................9 G1
Royal Rd *POY/DIS* SK12..............123 M7
Royal St *MILN* OL16..................28 F2
Royalthorn Dr
  *WYTH/NTH* M22....................109 M6
Royalthorn Rd
  *WYTH/NTH* M22....................110 A6
Royce Av *HALE/TIMP* WA15........108 B7
Royce Rd *HULME* M15................87 H6
Roydale St *NEWH/MOS* M40.......88 B1
Royden Av *BKLY* M9..................73 G2
  *IRL* M44.............................94 C4
  *WGNS/IIMK* WN3.................63 J1
Royden Crs
  *WGNW/BIL/OR* WN5.............62 B7
Royds Cl *BRUN/LGST* M13.........87 L2
Royds St *MDTN* M24..................57 L2
Royds Pl *MILN* OL16.................11 H8
Royds St *BURY* BL9...................26 A8
  *MILN* OL16.........................11 J8
  *MILN* OL16.........................29 K7
  *TOT/BURYW* BL8.................24 C5
Royds St West *MILN* OL16..........11 H9
Royd St *OLDS* OL8...................58 F8
Royland Av *BOLS/LL* BL3...........52 D1
Royle Av *GLSP* SK13.................105 G2
Royle Barn Rd *ROCH* OL11.........41 M2
Royle Cl *OFTN* SK2...................112 D7
  *OLDS* OL8...........................75 J1
Royle Green Rd
  *WYTH/NTH* M22....................110 B4
Royle Rd *ROCH* OL11................42 A1
Royle St *DTN/ASHW* M34...........90 C7
  *OFTN* SK2...........................13 K8
  *RUSH/FAL* M14....................99 G5
  *SLFD* M6 *..........................86 C3
  *WALK* M28..........................69 G2
Royley *ROY/SHW* OL2................58 F1
Royley Crs *ROY/SHW* OL2...........58 F1
Royley Rd *OLDS* OL8.................59 H8
Royon Dr *EDGY/DAV* SK3..........12 A9
Royston Av *BOLE* BL2................3 J2
  *DTN/ASHW* M34...................100 C1
  *OLDTF/WHR* M16..................98 A1
Royston Cl *GOL/RIS/CUL* WA3....80 B4
  *TOT/BURYW* BL8.................24 C3
Royston Rd *OLDTF/WHR* M16......97 L1
  *URM* M41............................96 B1
Roy St *BOLS/LL* BL3..................35 L8
  *ROY/SHW* OL2......................43 G8
Royton Av *SALE* M33.................109 H2
Rozel Sq *CSLFD* M3...................6 D6
Ruabon Crs *WGNE/HIN* WN2.......49 J8
Ruabon Rd *DID/WITH* M20..........110 F2
Rubens Cl *DID/WITH* M20..........110 F2
Ruby Gv *LEIGH* WN7.................66 B8
Ruby St *BOL* BL1......................36 C1
  *BURY* BL9...........................5 J4
  *DTN/ASHW* M34...................101 H1
  *HULME* M15.........................87 K6
Rudcroft Cl *BRUN/LGST* M13......87 L6
Rudding St *ROY/SHW* OL2...........59 K2
Ruddpark Rd
  *WYTH/NTH* M22....................118 E3
Rudd St *NEWH/MOS* M40...........73 K5
Rudford Gdns *BOLS/LL* BL3.........36 C8
Rudgwick Dr *TOT/BURYW* BL8....24 F5
Rudheath Av *DID/WITH* M20........98 D5
Rudman Dr *ORD* M5...................86 F4
Rudman St *AULW* OL7................90 D3
  *WHIT* OL12.........................28 B2
Rudolph St *BOLS/LL* BL3............52 C1
Rudston Av *NEWH/MOS* M40.......73 L2
Rudyard Av *MDTN* M24..............57 M1
  *WGNNW/ST* WN6.................31 H2
Rudyard Gv *HTNM* SK4..............100 A6
  *ROCH* OL11.........................42 C2
  *SALE* M33...........................108 D2
Rudyard Rd *SLFD* M6.................70 F7
Rudyard St *BRO* M7...................72 A6
Ruecroft Cl *WGNNW/ST* WN6......30 A4
Rufford Cl *HYDE* SK14...............102 C2
  *ROCH* OL11.........................28 A8
Rufford Cl *AUL* OL6...................75 M5
  *ROY/SHW* OL2......................43 G5
  *WHTF* M45..........................55 K2
Rufford Dr *BOLS/LL* BL3.............52 A2
  *WHTF* M45..........................55 J2
Rufford Gv *BOLS/LL* BL3.............52 A2
Rufford Pl *GTN* M18 *................89 J8
  *TYLD* M29..........................67 J8
Rufford Rd *OLDTF/WHR* M16......98 A1
Rufus St *RUSH/FAL* M14.............99 H5
  *WGNW/BIL/OR* WN5.............46 C4
Rugby Dr *SALE* M33..................108 D2
Rugby Rd *LEIGH* WN7................81 J1
  *SLFD* M6............................85 K1
  *WHIT* OL12.........................11 C1
Rugby St *CHH* M8.....................72 B8
Rugeley St *SLFD* M6..................71 L7
Ruins La *BOLE* BL2...................23 H8
Ruislip Av *NEWH/MOS* M40.........73 H7
Ruislip Cl *OLDS* OL8.................59 L8
Rumbles La *UPML* OL3...............45 J8
Rumworth Rd *HOR/BR* BL6.........34 F6
Rumworth St *BOLS/LL* BL3..........36 A8
Runcorn St *HULME* M15.............86 F5
Runger La *HALE/TIMP* WA15.......118 B4
Runhall Cl *WGTN/LGST* M12.......88 B6
Runnymeade *SWIN* M27..............70 D6
Runnymede Ct *EDGY/DAV* SK3....12 D9
Runnymede Ct *BOLS/LL* BL3........2 A7
  *ROY/SHW* OL2......................43 H8
Runshaw Av *WGNNW/ST* WN6....30 A4
Rupert St *BOLS/LL* BL3..............52 C1
  *NEWH/MOS* M40..................74 B8
  *RAD* M26............................54 E3
  *RDSH* SK5...........................100 B5
  *WGN* WN1..........................15 K5
  *WHIT* OL12.........................27 M3
Ruscombe Fold *MDTN* M24.........57 C1
Rush Acre Cl *RAD* M26..............54 B1
Rush Bank *ROY/SHW* OL2...........43 J4
Rushbrooke Av *OP/CLY* M11........88 F1
Rushbury Dr *ROY/SHW* OL2.........43 K8
Rushcroft Rd *ROY/SHW* OL2........43 J8
Rushdene *WGNS/IIMK* WN3.........47 K8
Rushden Rd *BNG/LEV* M19..........99 L2
Rushen St *OP/CLY* M11...............88 D3
The Rushes *GLSP* SK13.............93 J8
Rushey Cl *HALE/TIMP* WA15.......117 M5
Rushey Fld *EDGW/EG* BL7..........22 C4
Rushey Fold La *BOL* BL1.............36 A2
Rusheylea Cl *BOL* BL1................36 A2
Rushey Rd *WYTH/NTH* M22.........109 M7
Rushfield Dr *BRUN/LGST* M13.....99 H1
Rushfield Rd *CHD/CHDH* SK8......120 B6
Rushford Av *BNG/LEV* M19..........99 K2
Rushford St *WGTN/LGST* M12......88 D8
Rush Gv *UPML* OL3...................61 L5
Rush Hill La *UPML* OL3..............61 L5
Rush Hill Ter *UPML* OL3.............61 L5
Rushlake Gdns *ROCH* OL11.........27 H4
Rushley Av *BRO* M7..................71 L6
Rushmere *AUL* OL6...................76 B6
  *GLSP* SK13..........................105 H4
Rushmere Av *BNG/LEV* M19........99 L3
Rushmere Dr *TOT/BURYW* BL8....24 F7
Rushmere Wk *OLDTF/WHR* M16...87 G7
Rushmoor Av *AIMK* WN4.............64 B8
Rushmoor Cl *IRL* M44................94 E4
Rush Mt *ROY/SHW* OL2..............43 J3
Rushside Rd *CHD/CHDH* SK8......120 B6
Rush St *DUK* SK16....................91 J4
Rushton Av *LEIGH* WN7..............66 A4
  *NEWLW* WA12.....................78 E8
Rushton Cl *MPL/ROM* SK6 *.......114 D7
Rushton Dr *BRAM/HZG* SK7........122 A1
  *MPL/ROM* SK6.....................113 H1
  *MPL/ROM* SK6.....................114 C8
Rushton Fold *MCFLDN* SK10.......131 K7
Rushton Gv *OLDE* OL4...............60 B1
  *OP/CLY* M11........................89 H5
Rushton Rd *BOL* BL1.................35 L3
  *CHD/CHDH* SK8...................120 C6
  *EDGY/DAV* SK3....................12 B9
Rushton St *DID/WITH* M20..........110 E2
  *WALK* M28..........................69 G2
Rushway Av *BKLY* M9................73 J2
Rushwick Av *NEWH/MOS* M40....73 H4
Rushworth St *HTNM* SK4............99 H1
Rushycroft *HYDE* SK14..............92 B3
Rushyfield Crs *MPL/ROM* SK6.....114 A1
Ruskin Av *CHAD* OL9.................74 C1
  *DTN/ASHW* M34...................89 M5
  *DTN/ASHW* M34...................101 H3
  *FWTH* BL4...........................53 J5
  *NEWLW* WA12.....................78 F8
  *RUSH/FAL* M14....................87 L8
  *WGNS/IIMK* WN3.................63 J1
Ruskin Crs *PWCH* M25...............71 J1
  *WGNE/HIN* WN2..................64 E3
Ruskin Dr *SALE* M33.................95 M4
Ruskin Gdns *MPL/ROM* SK6........113 K1
Ruskin Gv *MPL/ROM* SK6...........113 K1
Ruskington Dr *BKLY* M9.............73 G5
Ruskin Rd *BOLS/LL* BL3.............37 L8
  *DROY* M43..........................89 K2
  *OLDTF/WHR* M16..................97 M1
  *PWCH* M25.........................71 H1
  *RDSH* SK5...........................100 B3
  *ROCH* OL11.........................42 B2
Ruskin St *OLD* OL1...................8 F1
  *RAD* M26............................38 F8
Rusland Ct *OFTN* SK2 *.............112 E5
Rusland Dr *BOLE* BL2................37 H2
Russeldene Rd
  *WGNS/IIMK* WN3.................63 H1
Russell Av *MPL/ROM* SK6...........123 C5
  *OLDTF/WHR* M16..................98 A2
  *SALE* M33...........................97 G7
Russell Cl *BOL* BL1...................35 M4
Russell Ct *FWTH* BL4 *..............53 H4
  *LHULT* M38.........................68 F1
Russell Dr *IRL* M44...................94 D2
Russell Gdns *HTNM* SK4.............12 B4
Russell Rd *OLDTF/WHR* M16......98 A1
  *PART* M31..........................106 D1
  *SLFD* M6............................70 E7
Russell St *ATH* M46..................66 F1
  *AUL* OL6.............................76 A8
  *BURY* BL9...........................5 G1
  *CHAD* OL9..........................8 B4
  *CHH* M8.............................72 C8
  *DUK* SK16...........................90 F2
  *ECC* M30............................85 H2
  *FWTH* BL4...........................53 G5
  *HEY* OL10...........................41 H3
  *LHULT* M38.........................68 F1
  *MOSL* OL5...........................77 G6
  *OFTN* SK2...........................112 C6
  *OLDTF/WHR* M16..................98 C1
  *PWCH* M25.........................55 M8
  *WGNE/HIN* WN2..................48 D4
  *WGNE/HIN* WN2..................65 M2
Russet Rd *BKLY* M9..................73 G3
Russet Wy *WILM/AE* SK9............130 E3
Ruth Av *NEWH/MOS* M40...........74 B3
Ruthen La *OLDTF/WHR* M16........86 E8
Rutherford Av *RUSH/FAL* M14......98 E1
Rutherford Cl *HYDE* SK14...........102 A2
Rutherford Dr *WHTN* BL5...........51 J5
Rutherglade Cl
  *NEWH/MOS* M40..................72 F6
Rutherglen Dr *BOLS/LL* BL3........35 J6
Rutherglen Wk
  *NEWH/MOS* M40..................73 H7
Ruthin Av *BKLY* M9..................56 F7
  *CHD/CHDH* SK8...................120 A2
  *MDTN* M24.........................57 K6
Ruthin Cl *OLDS* OL8.................74 E2
  *SLFD* M6............................86 A1
Ruth St *BOL* BL1......................2 C3
  *BURY* BL9...........................5 J4
  *GTN* M18............................100 A1
  *OLD* OL1.............................9 K3
  *WHIT* OL12.........................20 E3
Rutland *ROCH* OL11.................10 D7
Rutland Av *ATH* M46.................51 J7
  *DID/WITH* M20.....................98 D7
  *GOL/RIS/CUL* WA3...............80 A5
  *OLDTF/WHR* M16..................97 K1
  *SWIN* M27..........................70 C2
  *URM* M41............................96 B2
Rutland Cl *AUL* OL6..................91 G2
  *BOLS/LL* BL3.......................37 L8
  *CHAD* OL9..........................8 C9
  *CHD/CHDH* SK8...................118 E6
Rutland Crs *RDSH* SK5..............101 G2
Rutland Dr *AIMK* WN4...............63 M8
  *BRO* M7.............................71 M4
  *BURY* BL9...........................5 G1
  *FWTH* BL4 *........................52 F5
Rutland La *SALE* M33................95 K7
Rutland Rd *ALT* WA14................108 A6
  *BRAM/HZG* SK7...................122 A4
  *DROY* M43..........................89 H2
  *ECC* M30............................85 J1
  *IRL* M44.............................94 A7
  *PART* M31..........................106 B2
  *TYLD* M29..........................67 J2
  *WALK* M28..........................69 C3
  *WGNE/HIN* WN2..................49 J6
Rutland Wy *ROY/SHW* OL2.........43 M4
Rutters La *BRAM/HZG* SK7.........121 L2
Ryall Av *ORD* M5......................86 E4
Ryall Av South *ORD* M5.............86 E4
Ryan St *OP/CLY* M11.................89 L4
Rydal *BRAM/HZG* SK7...............121 L1
  *CHAD* OL9..........................58 B3
  *DROY* M43..........................89 H3
  *ECC* M30............................85 J1
  *HYDE* SK14.........................90 F7
  *MDTN* M24.........................57 J4
  *MPL/ROM* SK6.....................123 G4
  *ROY/SHW* OL2......................42 F4
  *SALE* M33...........................96 C7
  *URM* M41............................95 L5
  *WGNE/HIN* WN2..................49 H7
  *WGNW/BIL/OR* WN5.............46 C6
Rydal Cl *AIMK* WN4...................63 M8
  *BURY* BL9...........................39 H5
  *CHD/CHDH* SK8...................119 K1

DTN/ASHW M34 100 E2
HOR/BR BL6 32 F1
TYLD M29 67 K5
Rydal Ct BOL BL1 * 35 J3
Rydal Crs SWIN M27 70 C6
WALK M28 69 H3
Rydal Dr HALE/TIMP WA15 117 M4
Rydal Gv AULW OL7 75 J8
FWTH BL4 52 C5
HEY OL10 41 G4
WHTF M45 55 J4
Rydal Pl WGNE/HIN WN2 48 E4
WGNE/HIN WN2 64 E4
Rydal Rd BOL BL1 35 K4
BOLS/LL BL3 53 K1
STRET M32 97 G1
Rydal St LEIGH WN7 66 B7
Ryde Av DTN/ASHW M34 101 L4
HTNM SK4 12 A2
Ryder Av ALT WA14 108 B5
Ryder Brow GTN M18 89 G8
Ryderbrow Rd GTN M18 89 G8
Ryder Gv LEIGH WN7 81 M2
Ryder St BOL BL1 35 M2
HEY OL10 * 41 G2
NEWH/MOS M40 73 G8
Ryde St BOLS/LL BL3 * 35 K8
WGNW/BIL/OR WN5 47 H6
Rydings La WHIT OL12 20 E6
Rydings Rd WHIT OL12 20 F7
Rydley St BOLE BL2 3 J6
Ryebank Gv AUL OL6 76 A7
Ryebank Ms CCHDY M21 * 97 J3
Ryebank Rd CCHDY M21 97 J3
Rye Bank Rd OLDTF/WHR M16 97 K2
Ryeburn Av WYTH/NTH M22 118 F1
Ryeburn Dr BOLE BL2 22 E7
Ryeburne St OLDE OL4 59 M5
Ryeburn Wk URM M41 84 C8
Rye Cft WHTF M45 54 F5
Rye Croft Av SLFD M6 85 M1
Ryecroft Av GOL/RIS/CUL WA3 80 B3
HEY OL10 41 H2
TOT/BURYW BL8 24 C6
Ryecroft Cl CHAD OL9 74 C1
Ryecroft Dr WHTN BL5 50 A1
Ryecroft Gv NTHM/RTH M23 109 K5
Ryecroft La DTN/ASHW M34 90 B5
WALK M28 69 J8
Ryecroft Rd STRET M32 96 F3
Ryecroft St AULW OL7 90 C3
Ryecroft Vw DTN/ASHW M34 89 M4
Ryedale Av NEWH/MOS M40 73 G7
Ryedale Cl HTNM SK4 12 B1
Ryefield Cl HALE/TIMP WA15 108 F7
Ryefield Rd SALE M33 107 M2
Ryefields ROCH OL11 27 K6
Ryefields Dr UPML OL3 61 L3
Ryefield St BOL BL1 3 G1
Ryeford Cl WGNS/IIMK WN3 15 M8
Rye Hl WHTN BL5 * 50 C4
Ryeland Cl MILN OL16 28 E8
Ryelands WHTN BL5 50 C4
Ryelands Ct WHTN BL5 * 50 C4
Rye St HEY OL10 41 H1
Rylance St OP/CLY M11 88 B3
Rylands St GTN M18 * 89 H6
WGNNW/ST WN6 47 K2
Rylane Wk NEWH/MOS M40 73 G7
Ryley Av BOLS/LL BL3 35 L7
Ryleys La WILM/AE SK9 130 C3
Ryley St BOLS/LL BL3 * 2 A7
Rylstone Av CCHDY M21 110 A1
Ryther Gv BKLY M9 56 E7
Ryton Av GTN M18 99 M1
Ryton Cl WGNS/IIMK WN3 14 D8


## S


Sabden Brook Dr
WGNE/HIN WN2 * 64 C2
Sabden Cl BURY BL9 25 J5
HEY OL10 40 D2
NEWH/MOS M40 88 B1
Sabden Rd BOL BL1 35 H2
Sabrina St CHH M8 72 B7
Sackville Cl ROY/SHW OL2 43 K3
Sackville St AUL OL6 90 E1
BOLE BL2 * 3 M4
CMANE M1 7 H7
CSLFD M3 6 C3
ROCH OL11 41 M3
Saddleback Cl WALK M28 68 E6
Saddleback Crs
WGNW/BIL/OR WN5 46 E5
Saddleback Rd
WGNW/BIL/OR WN5 46 E5
Saddlecote WALK M28 69 K8
Saddlecote Cl CHH M8 72 E4
Saddle Gv DROY M43 90 A1
Saddle St BOLE BL2 36 E2
Saddlewood Av BNG/LEV M19 111 G2
Sadie Av STRET M32 85 K8
Sadler Ct HULME M15 87 H7
Sadler St BOLS/LL BL3 36 D8
MDTN M24 57 J3
Saffron Cl GOL/RIS/CUL WA3 80 B5
Saffron Dr OLDE OL4 60 A2
Sagars Rd WILM/AE SK9 119 L8
Sagar St CHH M8 72 C8
St Agnes Rd BRUN/LGST M13 99 J2
St Agnes St RDSH SK5 100 C1
St Aidan's Cl ROCH OL11 10 A9
WGNW/BIL/OR WN5 62 C6
St Aidan's Gv BRO M7 71 L6
St Albans Av AUL OL6 75 L6
HTNM SK4 99 M7
NEWH/MOS M40 73 L7
St Albans Cl OLDS OL8 59 J8
RNFD/HAY WA11 78 C5
St Albans Crs ALT WA14 107 M4
St Alban's St MILN OL16 10 D6
NM/HAY SK22 124 E4
St Alban's Ter CHH M8 72 C7
ROCH OL11 10 C7
St Aldates MPL/ROM SK6 113 J2
St Aldwyn's Rd DID/WITH M20 98 E7
St Ambrose Gdns SLFD M6 * 86 C2
St Ambrose Rd OLD OL1 59 M3
TYLD M29 67 K7
St Andrew's Av DROY M43 89 H3
ECC M30 85 H3
HALE/TIMP WA15 108 B5
St Andrews Cl HTNM SK4 99 L8
LIT OL15 21 J8
Saint Andrew's Cl
MPL/ROM SK6 113 L3
St Andrew's Cl RAMS BL0 18 F7
SALE M33 107 M3
St Andrews Ct BOL BL1 * 2 E5
St Andrew's Crs
WGNE/HIN WN2 49 G7
St Andrew's Dr HEY OL10 41 G3
LEIGH WN7 66 F7
WGNNW/ST WN6 47 J2
St Andrews Rd CHD/CHDH SK8 119 L3
HOR/BR BL6 34 D5
HTNM SK4 99 L8
RAD M26 38 C6
STRET M32 96 E2
St Andrew's Sq CMANE M1 7 M6
St Andrew's St CMANE M1 7 L6
St Andrew's Vw RAD M26 38 C6
St Anne's Av ATH M46 67 H3
ROY/SHW OL2 59 H1
SLFD M6 86 B1
St Anne's Ct DTN/ASHW M34 * 90 C6
SALE M33 96 F8
SLFD M6 * 71 J8
WGNNW/ST WN6 30 D7
St Anne's Crs OLDE OL4 60 F7
St Anne's Dr DTN/ASHW M34 90 D8
WGNNW/ST WN6 30 D7
St Anne's Gdns HEY OL10 41 J2
St Annes Meadow
TOT/BURYW BL8 24 C5
St Annes Rd CCHDY M21 97 L5
DTN/ASHW M34 90 C6
DTN/ASHW M34 90 D8
St Annes Sq UPML OL3 45 J8
St Annes St BURY BL9 * 25 J8
HYDE SK14 103 K4
St Anns Cl PWCH M25 71 K1
St Anns Pas CMANW M2 6 F4
St Ann's Rd BRAM/HZG SK7 121 L3
MILN OL16 11 M3
PWCH M25 71 J1
St Ann's Rd North
CHD/CHDH SK8 119 K3
St Ann's Rd South
CHD/CHDH SK8 119 L3
St Ann's Sq CHD/CHDH SK8 119 L4
CMANW M2 6 F4
St Ann's St CMANW M2 6 E4
SALE M33 109 J1
SWIN M27 70 B4
St Ann St BOL BL1 36 B3
St Anthonys Dr MOSL OL5 77 G2
St Asaphs Dr AUL OL6 75 L6
St Aubin's Rd BOLE BL2 3 J7
St Aubyn's Rd WGN WN1 * 31 M8
St Augustine's Rd
EDGY/DAV SK3 12 B7
St Augustine St BOL BL1 36 A2
NEWH/MOS M40 73 H7
St Austell Av TYLD M29 67 M4
St Austell Dr CHD/CHDH SK8 119 K4
TOT/BURYW BL8 24 C2
St Austell Rd OLDTF/WHR M16 98 B4
St Austells Dr PWCH M25 55 L7
SWIN M27 70 F6
St Barnabas's Dr LIT OL15 21 L6
St Barnabas Sq OP/CLY M11 88 E4
St Bartholomew's Dr ORD M5 86 F4
St Bartholomew St
BOLS/LL BL3 36 D8
St Bede's Av BOLS/LL BL3 51 L2
St Bees Cl CHD/CHDH SK8 119 K1
RUSH/FAL M14 87 K8
St Bees Rd BOLE BL2 36 F2
St Benedicts Av
WGTN/LGST M12 * 88 C6
St Benedict's Sq
WGTN/LGST M12 88 C6
St Bernard's Av SLFD M6 71 M7
St Boniface Rd BRO M7 71 M8
St Brannocks Rd CCHDY M21 97 M3
CHD/CHDH SK8 120 D5
St Brelades Dr BRO M7 72 C4
St Brendans Rd DID/WITH M20 98 E5
St Brendans Rd North
DID/WITH M20 98 E5
St Brides Wy OLDTF/WHR M16 87 G7
St Catherines Dr FWTH BL4 52 C4
St Catherine's Rd
DID/WITH M20 98 E5
St Chads Av MPL/ROM SK6 113 M2
St Chad's Cl MILN OL16 10 F6
St Chads Cl MILN OL16 10 F5
St Chads Crs OLDS OL8 75 G3
UPML OL3 61 M4
St Chads Gv MPL/ROM SK6 113 M2
St Chad's Rd DID/WITH M20 99 G5
St Chad's St CHH M8 * 72 D8
St Charles Cl GLSP SK13 93 J7
St Christopher Ct
WGNNW/ST WN6 * 30 F8
St Christopher's Av AUL OL6 76 B6
St Christophers Cl
DID/WITH M20 98 C6
St Christophers Dr
MPL/ROM SK6 113 K2
St Christopher's Rd AUL OL6 76 A6
St Clair Rd TOT/BURYW BL8 * 24 C1
St Clare Ter HOR/BR BL6 * 34 C4
St Clements Ct OLDS OL8 9 J8
St Clement's Dr ORD M5 86 E5
St Clements Fold URM M41 * 96 B2
St Clements Rd CCHDY M21 97 K5
WGN WN1 47 M1
St Clement's St
WGNS/IIMK WN3 48 C8
St Cuthberts Fold OLDS OL8 75 K3
St Davids Av MPL/ROM SK6 113 L2
St David's Cl AUL OL6 76 A5
St David's Crs WGNE/HIN WN2 32 E7
St David's Rd BRAM/HZG SK7 121 L3
CHD/CHDH SK8 111 K7
St Domingo Pl OLD OL1 * 9 H5
St Dominics Ms BOLS/LL BL3 51 M1
St Dominics Wy MDTN M24 57 K5
St Edmund Hall Cl RAMS BL0 18 F8
St Edmund's Rd
NEWH/MOS M40 73 H6
St Edmund St BOL BL1 2 D4
St Elisabeth's Wy RDSH SK5 100 B5
St Elizabeth's Rd
WGNE/HIN WN2 32 E7
St Elmo Av OFTN SK2 113 G5
St Elmo Pk POY/DIS SK12 122 E8
St Ethelbert's Av BOLS/LL BL3 35 L7
St Gabriel's Cl ROCH OL11 42 A3
St George's Av
HALE/TIMP WA15 108 D4
WHTN BL5 50 B6
St George's Ct ALT WA14 107 L5
BOL BL1 2 E3
HYDE SK14 * 102 A2
STRET M32 * 96 F3
TYLD M29 67 J4
St George's Crs
HALE/TIMP WA15 108 D4
SLFD M6 * 85 K1
WALK M28 69 G2
St Georges Dr HYDE SK14 102 A3
NEWH/MOS M40 73 L5
St Georges Gdns
DTN/ASHW M34 101 K3
St George's Pl ATH M46 * 50 E8
St George's Rd BOL BL1 2 B3
BURY BL9 39 M8
DROY M43 89 J1
NM/HAY SK22 124 E4
PART M31 95 G6
ROCH OL11 27 J4
RUSH/FAL M14 99 H5
STRET M32 96 E2
St Georges Sq BOL BL1 2 F3
CHAD OL9 74 B1
St George's St BOL BL1 2 E3
STLY SK15 91 K1
TYLD M29 67 J4
St George's Wy SLFD M6 71 K8
St Germain St FWTH BL4 52 F4
St Giles Dr HYDE SK14 102 C2
St Gregorys Cl FWTH BL4 52 F5
St Gregorys Rd WGTN/LGST M12 7 M8
St Helena Rd BOL BL1 2 C4
St Helens Rd BOLS/LL BL3 35 M8
GOL/RIS/CUL WA3 80 E4
LEIGH WN7 81 G3
WHTN BL5 51 K3
St Helier's Dr BRO M7 72 C4
St Heliers St BOLS/LL BL3 36 A8
St Hilarys Pk WILM/AE SK9 130 D3
St Hilda's Dr OLD OL1 8 F2
St Hilda's Rd DTN/ASHW M34 90 B6
OLDTF/WHR M16 86 F7
WYTH/NTH M22 110 A3
St Hilda's Vw DTN/ASHW M34 90 B7
St Hugh's Cl ALT WA14 108 B4
St Ignatius Wk ORD M5 * 86 E4
St Ives Av CHD/CHDH SK8 111 K6
St Ives Crs SALE M33 108 D3
St Ives Rd RUSH/FAL M14 98 E2
St James Av BOLE BL2 37 H4
TOT/BURYW BL8 38 E1
St James Cl GLSP SK13 104 F4
MILN OL16 42 F4
St James Ct HALE/TIMP WA15 108 B8
SLFD M6 * 85 L1
St James Crs WGNE/HIN WN2 65 J4
St James Dr SALE M33 108 D1
WILM/AE SK9 126 E6
St James Gv WGNS/IIMK WN3 14 E8
St James Rd HTNM SK4 99 L7
WGNW/BIL/OR WN5 46 A8
St James's Gv ALT WA14 108 C3
St James's Rd BRO M7 72 B6
St James's Sq CMANW M2 6 F5
St James's St OLD OL1 59 L5
St James's Ter HEY OL10 41 G2
St James St AUL OL6 91 G2
CMANE M1 7 G6
ECC M30 * 85 H2
FWTH BL4 52 F4
HEY OL10 40 F2
MILN OL16 29 J6
ROY/SHW OL2 43 L5
WHTN BL5 50 C7
St James' Wy CHD/CHDH SK8 120 B6
St John's Av DROY M43 89 L2
WHTN BL5 50 A1
St John's Cl BRO M7 72 A6
DUK SK16 91 H4
MPL/ROM SK6 113 L2
St Johns Ct BRO M7 * 72 A6
HOR/BR BL6 34 E8
HYDE SK14 102 C1
MILN OL16 11 J6
OLDE OL4 60 C5
RAD M26 54 E2
WGNE/HIN WN2 64 E3
WHTN BL5 50 B1
St John's Dr HYDE SK14 102 C1
MILN OL16 11 J6
St John's Gdns MOSL OL5 76 F2
St John's Rd ALT WA14 116 E1
BRAM/HZG SK7 121 K3
BRUN/LGST M13 88 C8
DTN/ASHW M34 90 C7
HOR/BR BL6 50 E1
HTNM SK4 111 H2
OLDTF/WHR M16 86 F8
WALK M28 68 C5
WGNE/HIN WN2 32 E7
WILM/AE SK9 130 B1
St John's St BRO M7 72 A6
CHAD OL9 8 D8
FWTH BL4 53 H4
RAD M26 54 E2
WGNE/HIN WN2 64 E4
St John St ATH M46 67 G1
CSLFD M3 6 D6
DUK SK16 * 91 H4
ECC M30 85 G3
HOR/BR BL6 33 L1
IRL M44 94 D2
NM/HAY SK22 125 L2
OLDE OL4 60 B6
SWIN M27 71 G6
WALK M28 52 F8
WGNW/BIL/OR WN5 46 E6
St John's Wk CHAD OL9 8 D7
EDGY/DAV SK3 * 12 B6
St Johns Wd HOR/BR BL6 34 E8
St Josephs Av WHTF M45 55 M5
St Josephs Cl ROY/SHW OL2 43 M4
St Joseph's Dr MILN OL16 28 E8
ORD M5 86 E4
St Joseph St BOL BL1 36 A2
St Katherines Dr HOR/BR BL6 32 F1
St Kilda Av FWTH BL4 53 J6
St Kildas Av DROY M43 89 J1
St Kilda's Dr BRO M7 72 C4
St Lawrence Quay SALQ M50 86 C5
St Lawrence Rd
DTN/ASHW M34 101 J1
St Leonard's Av HOR/BR BL6 34 C3
St Leonard's Ct SALE M33 96 C8
St Leonards Dr
HALE/TIMP WA15 108 C6
St Leonard's Rd HTNM SK4 100 A7
St Leonard's St MDTN M24 57 K3
St Lesmo Rd EDGY/DAV SK3 12 C8
St Luke's Av GOL/RIS/CUL WA3 80 A4
St Lukes Ct CHAD OL9 58 D5
St Luke's Dr
WGNW/BIL/OR WN5 46 A8
St Luke's Rd SLFD M6 86 A2
St Luke St ROCH OL11 10 F9
St Malo Rd WGN WN1 31 M8
St Margaret's Av BNG/LEV M19 99 J6
St Margaret's Cl ALT WA14 107 M8
BOL BL1 * 35 L4
PWCH M25 55 M6
St Margarets Gdns OLDS OL8 * 74 F1
St Margaret's Rd ALT WA14 107 M8
BOL BL1 35 L4
CHD/CHDH SK8 111 K6
NEWH/MOS M40 74 A1
PWCH M25 55 M7
St Mark's Av ALT WA14 107 K7
ROY/SHW OL2 43 K8
WGNW/BIL/OR WN5 47 J5
St Mark's Cl ROY/SHW OL2 43 K8
St Mark's Crs WALK M28 69 G3
St Mark's La BRO M7 72 C4
St Mark's Sq BURY BL9 5 G1
St Mark's St BNG/LEV M19 99 M3
BOLS/LL BL3 2 E9
MPL/ROM SK6 101 K8
St Mark St DUK SK16 90 E3
St Mark's Vw BOLS/LL BL3 * 2 E9
St Marks Wk BOLS/LL BL3 36 B8
St Martin's Av HTNM SK4 12 C3
St Martins Cl DROY M43 89 J1
HYDE SK14 * 102 C2
St Martin's Dr BRO M7 72 C4
St Martin's Rd MPL/ROM SK6 114 D6
OLDS OL8 75 K2
SALE M33 96 B6
St Martin's St ROCH OL11 41 M3
St Mary's Av BOLS/LL BL3 35 K7
DTN/ASHW M34 101 K4
St Mary's Cl ATH M46 67 H2
MILN OL16 28 E8
PWCH M25 55 K8
STKP SK1 13 L4
WGNE/HIN WN2 * 32 E7
St Mary's Ct GOL/RIS/CUL WA3 80 E3
NEWH/MOS M40 73 L4
OLD OL1 * 9 H4
St Mary's Crest UPML OL3 61 M7
St Mary's Dr CHD/CHDH SK8 * 111 J6
RDSH SK5 100 C7
UPML OL3 61 M7
St Marys Est OLD OL1 9 J4
St Mary's Ga CMANE M1 6 F3
MILN OL16 10 D3
ROY/SHW OL2 * 43 L5
UPML OL3 * 61 L4
St Mary's Hall Rd CHH M8 72 C3
St Mary's Parsonage CSLFD M3 6 E4
St Mary's Pl BURY BL9 4 D5
St Mary's Rd ALT WA14 116 D2
ECC M30 85 J2
GLSP SK13 104 F4
HYDE SK14 91 J7
NEWH/MOS M40 73 L5
NM/HAY SK22 124 D4
POY/DIS SK12 123 M7
PWCH M25 55 K8
SALE M33 96 C7
WALK M28 52 F8
WGNE/HIN WN2 32 E6
St Mary's St CSLFD M3 6 E4
HULME M15 87 H7
OLD OL1 9 J3
OLDTF/WHR M16 87 J8
St Mary's Wy LEIGH WN7 * 66 C7
OLD OL1 9 H4
STKP SK1 13 L7
St Matthew's Cl
WGNS/IIMK WN3 46 F8
St Matthews Ct STRET M32 * 96 F3
St Matthew's Dr OLD OL1 58 D2
St Matthews Gra BOL BL1 * 36 B3
St Matthew's Rd
EDGY/DAV SK3 12 F7
St Matthews Ter
EDGY/DAV SK3 * 12 F7
St Matthews Wk BOL BL1 * 36 B3
St Mawes Ct RAD M26 * 37 M7
St Michael's Av ATH M46 66 D3
BOLS/LL BL3 52 E2
BRAM/HZG SK7 121 G5
St Michaels Cl TOT/BURYW BL8 38 D4
St Michaels Ct SALE M33 96 B6
WGN WN1 15 G1
St Michaels Gdns WHTF M45 55 L3
St Michael's Rd HYDE SK14 102 C2
St Michael's Sq ANC M4 * 7 H1
St Modwen Rd STRET M32 85 J7
St Nicholas Rd
GOL/RIS/CUL WA3 80 D4
HULME M15 6 C9
St Osmund's Dr BOLE BL2 37 H5
St Osmund's Gv BOLE BL2 37 H5
St Oswalds Rd AIMK WN4 78 D2
BNG/LEV M19 99 L2
St Patrick St WGN WN1 15 K4
St Patricks Wy WGN WN1 15 J4
St Paul's Av WGNS/IIMK WN3 47 J8
St Pauls Cl STLY SK15 91 M2
St Paul's Ct RAD M26 54 D3
WALK M28 69 G2
St Paul's Hill Rd HYDE SK14 102 C2
St Paul's Rd BRO M7 71 M3
DID/WITH M20 98 F6
HTNM SK4 99 L8
WALK M28 * 69 H2
St Paul's St BURY BL9 5 J3
HYDE SK14 102 B1
RAMS BL0 * 18 F6
STKP SK1 13 M1
STLY SK15 91 M2
St Pauls Vls BURY BL9 5 J3
St Peter's Av BOL BL1 35 K2
St Peters Cl AULW OL7 90 C2
St Peters Ct STRET M32 * 97 H1
St Peter's Dr HYDE SK14 * 102 C2
St Petersgate STKP SK1 13 J4
St Peter's Rd BURY BL9 39 J6
SWIN M27 70 B5
St Peters Sq CMANE M1 * 6 F6
CMANW M2 6 F6
STKP SK1 13 H4
St Peter's St AUL OL6 90 D2
MILN OL16 11 J7
St Peter's Ter FWTH BL4 53 G5
St Peter's Wy BOL BL1 2 F3
BOLE BL2 3 H7
BOLS/LL BL3 * 36 E8
FWTH BL4 53 G2
St Philip's Av BOLS/LL BL3 36 A8
St Philip's Pl CSLFD M3 * 6 A3
St Philip's Rd GTN M18 89 G8
St Phillip's Dr ROY/SHW OL2 59 H3
St Richards Cl ATH M46 50 F8
St Saviour's Rd OFTN SK2 112 F7
Saintsbridge Rd
WYTH/NTH M22 118 E2
St Simons Cl OFTN SK2 112 F4
St Simon St CSLFD M3 6 C1
St Stephen's Av
DTN/ASHW M34 90 B4
WGN WN1 48 B2
St Stephen's Cl BOLE BL2 3 L8
BRUN/LGST M13 88 A7
TYLD M29 67 K7
St Stephens Ct BKLY M9 * 73 G5
St Stephen's Rd
WGNNW/ST WN6 30 F3
St Stephens St OLD OL1 9 L3
St Stephen St CSLFD M3 6 C3
OLD OL1 9 L3
St Stephens Vw DROY M43 89 K2
St Teresa's Rd OLDTF/WHR M16 97 K1
St Thomas Ct BURY BL9 5 J4
UPML OL3 * 45 H8
St Thomas' Pl CHH M8 72 D8
St Thomas's Cir OLDS OL8 8 F9
St Thomas's Pl STKP SK1 13 J7
St Thomas St BOL BL1 * 36 A2
WGNS/IIMK WN3 14 F6
St Thomas St North OLDS OL8 8 F8
St Thomas St South OLDS OL8 8 F9
St Vincent St ANC M4 7 M3
St Werburghs Rd CCHDY M21 97 M4
St Wilfred's Dr WHIT OL12 * 20 B8
St Wilfrid's Rd WGNNW/ST WN6 31 J4
St Wilfrids St HULME M15 87 H6
St Williams Av BOLS/LL BL3 52 B1
Salcombe Av BOLE BL2 38 A3
Salcombe Cl SALE M33 96 B7
WGN WN1 48 B2
Salcombe Gv BOLE BL2 37 J6
Salcombe Rd OFTN SK2 112 F4
OP/CLY M11 89 G4
Salcot Wk NEWH/MOS M40 * 87 M1
Sale Heys Rd SALE M33 108 C1
Sale La TYLD M29 68 A3
WALK M28 68 C4
Salem Gv OLDE OL4 60 A6
Sale Rd NTHM/RTH M23 109 K2
Salesbury Wy WGNS/IIMK WN3 63 K2
Sales's La BURY BL9 25 L2
Sale St LIT OL15 21 M6
Salford Rd WHTN BL5 51 K4
Salford St BURY BL9 25 K8
OLDE OL4 59 M7
Salik Gdns ROCH OL11 10 E8
Salisbury Av HEY OL10 40 F4
WGNE/HIN WN2 49 H6
Salisbury Crs AUL OL6 76 A5
Salisbury Dr DUK SK16 91 K5
PWCH M25 71 M2
Salisbury Rd AIMK WN4 * 63 K7
CCHDY M21 97 L3
ECC M30 70 C8
HOR/BR BL6 34 C3
OLDE OL4 59 L6
RAD M26 38 B7
RNFD/HAY WA11 78 B4
SWIN M27 70 B5
URM M41 85 G8
WHTF M45 55 J4
Salisbury St BOLS/LL BL3 2 B6
GLSP SK13 93 K7
GOL/RIS/CUL WA3 79 K4
MDTN M24 57 L3
RDSH SK5 100 C4
ROY/SHW OL2 43 J4
RUSH/FAL M14 87 K8
Salisbury Ter BOLS/LL BL3 53 M1
Salisbury Wy TYLD M29 67 L5
Salkeld Av AIMK WN4 78 C1
Salkeld St ROCH OL11 10 F9
Sallowfields
WGNW/BIL/OR WN5 46 A7
Salmon Flds ROY/SHW OL2 59 J1
Salmon St ANC M4 7 H3
WGN WN1 * 15 K1
Salmsbury Hall Cl RAMS BL0 18 E8
Salop St BOLE BL2 3 G6
SLFD M6 71 K8
Saltash Cl WYTH/NTH M22 118 F3
Saltdene Rd WYTH/NTH M22 118 E3
Saltergate BOLS/LL BL3 35 J8
Saltergate Ms ORD M5 * 86 D2
Salters Ct ATH M46 67 G1
Salterton Dr BOLS/LL BL3 51 J2
Salteye Rd ECC M30 84 D3
Saltford Av ANC M4 7 M3
Saltford Ct ANC M4 7 M3
Salthill Av HEY OL10 41 H5
Salthill Dr WYTH/NTH M22 119 G2
Salthouse Cl TOT/BURYW BL8 24 F6
Saltire Gdns BRO M7 72 B4
Saltney Av DID/WITH M20 98 C5
Saltram Cl RAD M26 37 M7
Saltram Rd WGNS/IIMK WN3 46 F8
Saltrush Rd WYTH/NTH M22 118 F2
Salts Dr LIT OL15 21 L6
Salts St ROY/SHW OL2 43 L5
Saltwood Gv BOL BL1 2 E1
Salutation St HULME M15 87 J6
Salvin Cl AIMK WN4 79 G1
Salwick Cl WGNS/IIMK WN3 47 H8
Sam Cowan Cl RUSH/FAL M14 98 D1
Samian Gdns BRO M7 71 M7
Samlesbury Cl
DID/WITH M20 110 C1
ROY/SHW OL2 43 J5
Samouth Cl NEWH/MOS M40 88 A1
Sampson Sq RUSH/FAL M14 87 K8
Sam Rd UPML OL3 45 M8
Samson St MILN OL16 11 M2
Sam Swire St HULME M15 87 H7
Samuel La ROY/SHW OL2 43 H4
Samuel Ogden St CMANE M1 7 H7
Samuel St ATH M46 67 J3
BNG/LEV M19 99 L4
BURY BL9 5 H2
FAIL M35 74 C4
HTNM SK4 112 A1
ROCH OL11 41 M2
Sanby Av GTN M18 88 F8
Sanby Rd GTN M18 88 F8
Sanctuary Cl HULME M15 87 L7
The Sanctuary HULME M15 87 H6
Sandacre Rd
NTHM/RTH M23 109 L5
Sandal St NEWH/MOS M40 88 B1
Sandalwood WHTN BL5 50 A6
Sandalwood Dr
WGNNW/ST WN6 47 J1
Sandbach Av RUSH/FAL M14 98 C4
Sandbach Rd RDSH SK5 * 100 B2
SALE M33 109 J1
Sandbank Gdns WHIT OL12 20 A2
Sand Banks BOL BL1 22 C6
Sandbed La MOSL OL5 76 F2
UPML OL3 45 K7
Sandbrook Gdns
WGNW/BIL/OR WN5 46 A7
Sandbrook Pk ROCH OL11 * 28 B8

Sandbrook Wy *DTN/ASHW* M34.....90 C7
ROCH OL11.....28 B8
Sandby Dr *MPL/ROM* SK6.....114 E4
Sanderling Cl *WHTN* BL5.....50 A6
Sanderling Dr *NEWLW* WA12.....78 F8
OFTN SK2.....113 K7
Sanderson Cl *WALK* M28.....69 L4
Sanderson's Cft *LEIGH* WN7.....66 F8
Sanderson St *BURY* BL9.....5 J3
LEIGH WN7.....66 B7
NEWH/MOS M40.....73 H7
Sanderstead Dr *BKLY* M9.....73 H1
Sandfield Cl *GOL/RIS/CUL* WA3.....80 B4
Sandfield Crs *GOL/RIS/CUL* WA3.....81 M5
Sandfield Dr *HOR/BR* BL6.....34 F6
Sandfield Rd *MILN* OL16.....11 J8
Sandfold La *BNG/LEV* M19.....99 M2
Sandford Av *GTN* M18.....89 C6
Sandford Cl *BOLE* BL2.....37 H1
Sandford Rd *SALE* M33.....109 J1
Sandford St *RAD* M26.....39 G8
RAD M26.....53 L5
Sandgate Av *OP/CLY* M11.....89 G8
WHTF M45.....55 L5
Sandgate Cl *LEIGH* WN7.....66 C6
Sandgate Dr *URM* M41.....84 F8
Sandgate Rd *CHAD* OL9.....8 A7
WHTF M45.....55 L5
Sandham St *BOLS/LL* BL3.....36 C8
Sandham Wk *BOLS/LL* BL3 *.....36 C8
Sandheys *DTN/ASHW* M34.....90 C7
Sandheys Gv *GTN* M18.....89 H8
Sandhill Cl *BOLS/LL* BL3.....36 C8
Sandhill La *GLSP* SK13.....115 K1
MPL/ROM SK6.....115 H3
Sandhill St *HYDE* SK14.....102 C1
Sandhill Wk *WYTH/NTH* M22.....118 D2
Sandhole La *ROCH* OL11.....27 H7
Sand Hole La *ROCH* OL11.....42 C3
Sand Hole Rd *FWTH* BL4.....53 L6
Sandhurst Av *DID/WITH* M20.....98 D6
Sandhurst Cl *TOT/BURYW* BL8.....38 E1
Sandhurst Ct *BOLE* BL2.....37 H6
Sandhurst Dr *BOLE* BL2.....37 H6
WILM/AE SK9.....127 G4
Sandhurst Rd *DID/WITH* M20.....110 E2
OFTN SK2.....112 E7
Sandhurst St *OLDE* OL4.....59 M8
Sandhutton Rd *BKLY* M9.....73 G3
Sandiacre *WGNNW/ST* WN6.....31 H4
Sandilands Rd
NTHM/RTH M23.....109 G4
Sandileigh Av *CHD/CHDH* SK8.....111 K6
DID/WITH M20.....98 E7
HALE/TIMP WA15.....117 H1
RDSH SK5.....100 E8
Sandileigh Dr *BOL* BL1.....36 E1
HALE/TIMP WA15.....117 H1
Sandiway *BRAM/HZG* SK7.....121 G2
GLSP SK13.....105 J5
HEY OL10.....41 H2
IRL M44.....94 D2
MPL/ROM SK6.....113 J1
Sandiway Dr *DID/WITH* M20.....110 D1
Sandiway Pl *ALT* WA14.....108 A7
Sandiway Rd *ALT* WA14.....108 A6
SALE M33.....96 C8
WILM/AE SK9.....119 M7
Sand La *MCFLDN* SK10.....130 C7
Sandling Dr *GOL/RIS/CUL* WA3.....79 K2
Sandon St *BOLS/LL* BL3.....36 A8
Sandown Cl *GOL/RIS/CUL* WA3 *.....81 J8
OLD OL1.....59 K3
WILM/AE SK9.....127 H4
Sandown Crs *BOLS/LL* BL3.....53 K2
GTN M18.....100 A1
Sandown Dr *DTN/ASHW* M34.....101 L4
HALE/TIMP WA15.....117 M6
SALE M33.....108 B1
Sandown Gdns *URM* M41.....95 K3
Sandown Rd *BOLE* BL2.....37 J1
BRAM/HZG SK7.....122 C3
BURY BL9.....55 K2
EDGY/DAV SK3.....12 A7
WGNNW/ST WN6.....47 H1
Sandown St *GTN* M18.....89 H6
Sandpiper Cl *DUK* SK16.....91 H5
FWTH BL4.....52 C5
NEWLW WA12.....78 F8
ROCH OL11.....27 J5
Sandpiper Dr *EDGY/DAV* SK3.....112 A6
Sandpiper Rd *WGNS/IIMK* WN3.....46 E8
Sandray Cl *BOLS/LL* BL3.....35 J7
Sandray Gv *ORD* M5.....86 B3
Sandridge Cl *FWTH* BL4.....53 H4
Sandridge Wk *WGTN/LGST* M12.....88 B6
Sandringham Av
DTN/ASHW M34.....90 A6
DTN/ASHW M34.....100 D1
STLY SK15.....91 K1
Sandringham Cl *ALT* WA14.....116 B3
WGNNW/BIL/OR WN5.....47 H7
Sandringham Dr *DUK* SK16.....91 J6
HTNM SK4.....111 K3
LEIGH WN7.....67 H8
MILN OL16.....29 K6
POY/DIS SK12.....129 H1
TOT/BURYW BL8.....24 D3
Sandringham Gra *PWCH* M25.....72 B1
Sandringham Rd
BRAM/HZG SK7.....122 B2
CHD/CHDH SK8.....120 C1
HOR/BR BL6.....34 A2
HYDE SK14.....102 B5
MPL/ROM SK6.....112 F1
WALK M28.....68 D6
WGNE/HIN WN2.....49 H8
Sandringham St *GTN* M18.....88 F8
Sandringham Wy
ROY/SHW OL2.....42 F6
WILM/AE SK9.....126 E6
Sands Av *CHAD* OL9.....58 B4
Sands Cl *HYDE* SK14.....103 G3
Sandsend Cl *CHH* M8.....72 B7
Sandsend Rd *URM* M41.....95 M1
Sandstone Rd *MILN* OL16.....29 J5
Sandstone Wy *CCHDY* M21.....97 H2
WGNS/IIMK WN3.....63 H2
Sand St *NEWH/MOS* M40.....72 F8
STLY SK15.....91 J2
Sandway *WGNNW/ST* WN6.....47 J2
Sandwell Dr *SALE* M33.....96 E6
Sandwich Rd *ECC* M30.....85 J1
Sandwich St *WALK* M28.....69 G2
Sandwick Crs *BOLS/LL* BL3.....2 B9
Sandwith Cl *WGNS/IIMK* WN3.....63 L2
Sandwood Av *BOLS/LL* BL3.....35 H7
Sandy Acre *MOSL* OL5.....76 F4

Sandyacre Cl *WHTN* BL5.....51 K6
Sandy Bank *ROY/SHW* OL2.....43 J4
Sandy Bank Av *HYDE* SK14.....103 G3
Sandybank Cl *GLSP* SK13.....93 H8
Sandy Bank Rd *CHH* M8.....72 C4
Sandy Bank Wk
HYDE SK14 *.....103 G3
Sandybrook Cl
TOT/BURYW BL8.....24 C6
Sandybrook Dr *BKLY* M9.....72 F2
Sandy Brow *BKLY* M9.....73 G2
Sandy Cl *BURY* BL9.....39 J8
Sandy Ct *GOL/RIS/CUL* WA3.....80 D3
Sandycroft Av *WGN* WN1.....14 F1
WYTH/NTH M22.....118 F1
Sandygate Cl *SWIN* M27.....70 B5
Sandy Gv *DUK* SK16.....91 G4
SLFD M6.....86 B1
SWIN M27.....70 C4
Sandy Haven Cl *HYDE* SK14.....103 G3
Sandyhill Rd *BKLY* M9.....72 F2
Sandyhills *BOLS/LL* BL3.....36 B8
Sandylands Dr *PWCH* M25.....71 J3
Sandy La *CCHDY* M21.....97 L4
DROY M43.....89 M1
DUK SK16.....91 G4
GLSP SK13.....103 K8
GOL/RIS/CUL WA3.....79 J4
GOL/RIS/CUL WA3.....80 D2
IRL M44.....94 D1
MDTN M24.....57 L5
MPL/ROM SK6.....113 M1
NTHM/RTH M23.....109 G5
OLDS OL8 *.....8 F7
PWCH M25.....71 K2
RDSH SK5.....112 B1
ROCH OL11.....27 M5
ROY/SHW OL2.....43 G8
SLFD M6.....86 B1
STRET M32.....96 E3
TYLD M29.....67 K8
TYLD M29.....82 E3
UPML OL3.....61 L2
WGNE/HIN WN2.....49 K6
WGNNW/BIL/OR WN5.....46 A8
WILM/AE SK9.....126 B4
Sandy Meade *PWCH* M25.....71 K1
Sandy Pk *WGNE/HIN* WN2.....49 K6
Sandywarps *IRL* M44.....94 D4
Sandy Wy *WGNE/HIN* WN2.....71 K1
Sandywell Cl *OP/CLY* M11.....89 G5
Sandywell St *OP/CLY* M11.....89 G4
Sandy Wd *SLFD* M6.....86 B1
Sangster St *ORD* M5.....86 D4
Sankey Gv *BKLY* M9.....72 E1
Sankey St *BURY* BL9.....4 C4
GOL/RIS/CUL WA3.....79 K4
Santiago St *RUSH/FAL* M14.....98 E1
Santley St *WGTN/LGST* M12.....99 K1
Santon Av *RUSH/FAL* M14.....99 H4
Santon Dr *GOL/RIS/CUL* WA3.....80 B4
Sapling Cl *SALE* M33.....108 A2
Sapling Rd *BOLS/LL* BL3.....51 M2
SWIN M27.....70 A7
Sarah Butterworth Ct
MILN OL16 *.....11 K5
Sarah Butterworth St
MILN OL16.....11 K5
Sarah St *ECC* M30.....84 E3
MDTN M24.....57 J4
OP/CLY M11.....88 C4
RAMS BL0.....19 H1
ROCH OL11 *.....10 F7
ROY/SHW OL2.....43 L7
WGNE/HIN WN2.....65 L2
Sargent Dr *OLDTF/WHR* M16.....87 H8
Sargent Rd *MPL/ROM* SK6.....113 G2
Sark Rd *CCHDY* M21.....97 K2
Sarn Av *WYTH/NTH* M22.....110 A8
Sarsfield Av *GOL/RIS/CUL* WA3.....80 A4
Sathinwood St *AIMK* WN4.....78 C2
Saturn Gv *SLFD* M6.....71 M8
Saunton Av *BOLE* BL2.....37 J2
Saunton Rd *OP/CLY* M11.....89 G4
Sautridge Cl *MDTN* M24.....42 A5
Savernake Rd *MPL/ROM* SK6.....101 M7
Savick Av *BOLE* BL2.....37 H5
Saville Rd *CHD/CHDH* SK8.....110 E6
RAD M26.....38 C5
Saville St *BOLE* BL2.....3 G5
MDTN M24.....58 A5
Saviours St *BOLS/LL* BL3 *.....35 M7
Savio Wy *MDTN* M24.....57 K5
Savoy Cl *WHTF* M45 *.....55 H3
Savoy Dr *ROY/SHW* OL2.....59 G2
Savoy St *OLDE* OL4.....59 L7
ROCH OL11.....27 M4
Sawley Av *GOL/RIS/CUL* WA3.....80 A3
LIT OL15.....21 L5
OLDE OL4.....60 A8
WGNNW/ST WN6.....47 J1
WHTF M45.....55 J2
Sawley Cl *CHD/CHDH* SK8.....120 D6
Sawley Rd *NEWH/MOS* M40.....73 G8
Sawmill Wy *LIT* OL15.....21 L8
Sawpit St *LYMM* WA13.....106 D5
Saw St *BOL* BL1.....36 B2
Sawyer Brow *HYDE* SK14.....91 J8
Sawyer Dr *AIMK* WN4.....79 G1
Sawyer St *TOT/BURYW* BL8.....24 E8
WHIT OL12.....10 E1
Saxby Av *EDGW/EG* BL7.....22 C4
Saxby St *SLFD* M6.....70 F7
Saxelby Dr *CHH* M8.....72 E6
Saxfield Dr *NTHM/RTH* M23.....109 M6
Saxon Av *CHH* M8.....72 D2
DUK SK16.....90 F4
Saxon Cl *TOT/BURYW* BL8.....38 E2
Saxon Dr *CHAD* OL9.....58 B4
DROY M43.....89 K2
DTN/ASHW M34.....90 B5
Saxonholme Rd *ROCH* OL11.....41 M5
Saxon St *DROY* M43.....89 L2
DTN/ASHW M34.....101 J1
MDTN M24.....57 L4
NEWH/MOS M40.....88 B1
OLDE OL4.....59 M5
RAD M26.....54 C1
Saxthorpe Cl *SALE* M33.....96 E6
WGNS/IIMK WN3.....63 G1
Saxthorpe Wk *WGTN/LGST* M12.....88 B2
Saxwood Cl *WHIT* OL12.....27 J3
Scafell Av *AULW* OL7.....75 J3
Scafell Cl *MPL/ROM* SK6.....123 G4
OLD OL1.....9 K1
Scafell Dr *WGNNW/BIL/OR* WN5.....46 A6
Scafell Gv *WGNE/HIN* WN2.....64 E2
Scaie St *ORD* M5.....86 E3
Scaliot Cl *NM/HAY* SK22.....124 D4
Scant Rw *HOR/BR* BL6 *.....34 F1

Scarborough St
NEWH/MOS M40.....73 K4
Scarcroft Rd *WGTN/LGST* M12.....88 D7
Scardale Av *BOL* BL1.....35 K3
Scarfield Dr *ROCH* OL11.....27 H7
Scargill Cl *RUSH/FAL* M14 *.....98 F4
Scargill Rd *BOLS/LL* BL3.....35 K8
Scarisbrick Av *DID/WITH* M20.....111 G1
Scarisbrick Rd *BNG/LEV* M19.....99 J3
Scarisbrick St *WGN* WN1.....15 C1
Scarr Av *RAD* M26.....54 F3
Scarr Dr *WHIT* OL12.....28 C2
Scarr La *ROY/SHW* OL2.....43 M5
Scarsdale Rd *RUSH/FAL* M14.....88 B4
Scarsdale St *SLFD* M6.....86 E1
Scarthwood Cl *BOLE* BL2.....23 H7
Scawfell Av *BOLE* BL2.....36 E2
Schofield Gdns *LEIGH* WN7.....81 H1
Schofield La *ATH* M46.....66 C1
Schofield Rd *DROY* M43.....89 L3
ECC M30.....84 D3
Schofield St *FAIL* M35 *.....74 C4
HEY OL10.....41 G3
LEIGH WN7.....81 H1
MILN OL16.....29 K7
OLDS OL8.....75 H1
OP/CLY M11.....88 F2
ROCH OL11.....28 D8
ROY/SHW OL2.....43 G7
Scholar Green Rd *STRET* M32.....85 K7
Scholars Dr *DID/WITH* M20.....98 D5
Scholars Wy *MDTN* M24.....57 J4
Scholefield La *WGN* WN1.....15 J3
Scholes *WGN* WN1.....15 J3
Scholes Dr *NEWH/MOS* M40.....74 B2
Scholes La *PWCH* M25.....71 M1
Scholes St *CHAD* OL9.....58 D8
FAIL M35.....74 D3
OLD OL1.....9 L5
ROCH OL11.....41 M3
SWIN M27.....70 D4
TOT/BURYW BL8.....24 D7
Scholes Wk *PWCH* M25.....71 M1
Scholey St *BOLE* BL2.....3 H9
School Av *AUL* OL6.....76 A6
STRET M32 *.....97 J1
WGN WN1.....15 K1
School Brow *BURY* BL9.....4 F3
MPL/ROM SK6.....113 K2
WALK M28.....69 J6
School Cl *POY/DIS* SK12.....129 K1
School Ct *ANC* M4.....7 L3
EDGY/DAV SK3.....112 C6
RAMS BL0.....19 G3
School Crs *STLY* SK15.....91 K1
School Dr *WGNNW/BIL/OR* WN5.....62 B7
Schoolfold La *MCFLDN* SK10.....129 L5
School Gv *DID/WITH* M20.....98 F6
PWCH M25.....71 K2
School Gv West
DID/WITH M20.....98 F6
School Hl *BOL* BL1.....2 D2
School House Flats *OLDS* OL8 *.....74 F2
School La *ALT* WA14.....107 C8
BKLY M9.....72 F2
BURY BL9.....25 H4
DID/WITH M20.....110 F1
EDGW/EG BL7.....17 G4
HTNM SK4.....99 M7
HYDE SK14.....102 B5
IRL M44.....94 A7
IRL M44.....94 C2
MCFLDN SK10.....131 J6
MILN OL16.....10 E8
MPL/ROM SK6.....102 E5
MPL/ROM SK6.....114 E1
PART M31.....95 H6
POY/DIS SK12.....129 K1
ROCH OL11.....26 A4
STLY SK15.....91 H3
WGN WN1.....15 H3
WGNE/HIN WN2.....32 B4
WGNNW/ST WN6.....31 G3
School Ms *MILN* OL16 *.....29 L8
School Rd *ECC* M30.....84 F4
FAIL M35.....74 C5
HALE/TIMP WA15.....117 H1
OLDS OL8.....74 E2
SALE M33.....96 D7
STRET M32.....96 C2
WILM/AE SK9.....119 M8
Schools Hl *CHD/CHDH* SK8.....119 M1
Schoolside Cl *CHH* M8.....72 E6
Schoolside La *MDTN* M24.....56 F5
School St *AIMK* WN4.....64 A7
ANC M4.....7 H1
ATH M46.....66 E2
BOLS/LL BL3.....53 L1
BRAM/HZG SK7.....122 A2
BURY BL9.....5 K6
ECC M30.....84 E1
EDGW/EG BL7.....22 C5
GOL/RIS/CUL WA3.....79 K4
HEY OL10.....40 F2
HOR/BR BL6.....33 H1
LEIGH WN7.....66 B4
LIT OL15.....21 J7
OLDE OL4.....60 D6
OLDS OL8.....8 F8
RAD M26.....54 C1
RAMS BL0.....18 E7
TYLD M29.....67 J4
TYLD M29.....82 E3
UPML OL3.....61 L4
WGN WN1.....15 H3
WGNE/HIN WN2.....48 C5
WHIT OL12.....10 E3
WHTN BL5.....50 B4
School Ter *GOL/RIS/CUL* WA3 *.....79 K4
School Wk *OLDTF/WHR* M16 *.....87 G7
School Wy *WGNNW/BIL/OR* WN5.....46 F6
Schuster Rd *RUSH/FAL* M14.....98 F1
Schwabe St *MDTN* M24.....56 F4
Scobell St *TOT/BURYW* BL8.....24 C7
Scoltock Wy *OLD* OL1 *.....9 J4
Score St *OP/CLY* M11.....88 D3
Scorton Av *BOLE* BL2.....37 J5
Scorton St *BOL* BL1 *.....35 M4
Scotforth Cl *HULME* M15.....6 C9
Scotland Hall Rd
NEWH/MOS M40.....73 L8
Scotland La *BURY* BL9.....25 M4
Scotland St *AUL* OL6.....90 F2
NEWH/MOS M40.....73 M7
Scot La *WGNE/HIN* WN2.....33 G6
WGNNW/BIL/OR WN5.....47 H5
Scott Av *CCHDY* M21.....97 L2
ECC M30.....84 F1
WGNE/HIN WN2.....49 H6

Scott Cl *RDSH* SK5.....100 C8
Scott Dr *HALE/TIMP* WA15.....108 C8
MPL/ROM SK6.....114 E4
Scottfield *OLDS* OL8.....9 H9
Scottfield Rd *OLDS* OL8.....9 H9
Scott Ga *DTN/ASHW* M34.....90 B5
Scott Rd *DROY* M43.....89 K3
DTN/ASHW M34.....101 H3
GOL/RIS/CUL WA3.....80 A3
PWCH M25.....71 J1
Scott St *LEIGH* WN7.....66 A7
OLDS OL8.....9 J9
RAD M26.....54 A5
TYLD M29.....67 M8
WGNNW/ST WN6.....14 D2
WHTN BL5.....50 B2
Scott Vw *LEIGH* WN7.....66 E8
Scotty Brook Crs
GLSP SK13.....105 H4
Scout Dr *NTHM/RTH* M23.....109 J3
Scout Gn *MDTN* M24.....57 K1
Scout Rd *RAMS* BL0.....19 K2
Scovell St *BRO* M7.....72 D6
Scowcroft La *ROY/SHW* OL2.....43 G8
Scowcroft St *BOLE* BL2.....3 J1
Scroggins La *PART* M31.....94 E3
Scropton St *NEWH/MOS* M40.....73 C7
Seabright Wk *OP/CLY* M11 *.....88 C3
Seabrook Crs *URM* M41.....84 E5
Seabrook Rd *NEWH/MOS* M40.....73 M8
Seacombe Av *RUSH/FAL* M14.....98 B2
Seacombe Gv *EDGY/DAV* SK3.....12 A6
Seaford Rd *BOLE* BL2.....23 H6
SLFD M6.....71 L7
Seaford Wk *CHAD* OL9 *.....8 B7
Seaforth Av *ATH* M46.....50 F8
Seaforth Rd *BOL* BL1.....22 B7
Seaham Dr *TOT/BURYW* BL8.....24 E1
Seaham St *RUSH/FAL* M14.....98 E1
Sealand Cl *SALE* M33.....109 H2
Sealand Dr *ECC* M30.....84 D3
Sealand Rd *NTHM/RTH* M23.....109 J2
Seale Av *DTN/ASHW* M34.....90 A5
Sealey Wk *NEWH/MOS* M40 *.....73 H8
Seal Rd *BRAM/HZG* SK7.....121 J5
Seaman Wy *WGNE/HIN* WN2.....48 C5
Seamon's Dr *ALT* WA14.....107 K7
Seamon's Rd *ALT* WA14.....107 K6
Searby Rd *GTN* M18.....88 D2
Searness Rd *MDTN* M24.....56 F2
Seascale Av *OP/CLY* M11.....88 E1
Seascale Crs *WGN* WN1.....47 M1
Seathwaite Cl *MDTN* M24.....57 G3
TYLD M29.....67 K5
Seathwaite Rd *FWTH* BL4.....52 C5
Seatoller Dr *MDTN* M24.....56 F3
Seatoller Pl
WGNNW/BIL/OR WN5.....46 E5
Seaton Cl *BRAM/HZG* SK7.....121 M3
Seaton Ms *AULW* OL7.....75 J4
Seaton Rd *BOL* BL1.....35 M2
Sebastian Cl *MPL/ROM* SK6.....114 E5
Sebastopol Wk *ANC* M4.....7 L3
Second Av *ATH* M46.....51 C8
BOL BL1.....35 L5
BOLS/LL BL3.....37 J8
BURY BL9.....26 A8
OLDS OL8.....74 F2
OP/CLY M11.....89 G2
POY/DIS SK12.....129 H1
STLY SK15.....77 H7
SWIN M27.....70 A7
TRPK M17.....86 A7
TYLD M29.....67 L8
WGNNW/ST WN6.....47 K2
Section St *BOL* BL1.....2 E6
Sedan Cl *ORD* M5.....86 D3
Sedburgh *SALE* M33.....108 A1
Sedbury Cl *NTHM/RTH* M23.....109 J3
Seddon Av *GTN* M18.....89 G6
RAD M26.....39 G7
Seddon Cl *ATH* M46.....66 F1
RAD M26.....38 D7
Seddon Gdns *RAD* M26.....53 K4
Seddon House Dr
WGNNW/ST WN6.....47 H1
Seddon La *RAD* M26.....53 K4
Seddon Rd *ALT* WA14.....116 D2
Seddons Av *TOT/BURYW* BL8.....38 D4
Seddon St *BNG/LEV* M19.....99 L2
BOLS/LL BL3 *.....53 L1
LHULT M38.....52 C7
RAD M26.....54 D1
WHTN BL5.....50 B2
Sedgeborough Rd
OLDTF/WHR M16.....98 B1
Sedge Cl *RDSH* SK5.....100 D4
Sedgefield Cl *ORD* M5.....86 D2
Sedgefield Dr *BOL* BL1.....35 L1
WGNNW/ST WN6.....47 H1
Sedgefield Pk *OLDE* OL4.....60 A6
Sedgefield Rd *RAD* M26.....54 C4
Sedgeford Rd *NEWH/MOS* M40.....73 G7
Sedgeford Cl *WILM/AE* SK9.....127 G3
Sedgely WGNNW/ST WN6.....31 K5
Sedgemoor Cl *CHD/CHDH* SK8.....120 D2
Sedgemoor V *BOLE* BL2.....37 J2
Sedgemoor Wy *OLD* OL1.....9 H4
Sedgley Av *MILN* OL16.....28 D8
PWCH M25.....71 M2
Sedgley Cl *MDTN* M24.....57 M5
Sedgley Dr *WHTN* BL5.....50 B7
Sedgley Park Rd *PWCH* M25.....71 M2
Sedgley Rd *CHH* M8.....72 D4
Sedgley St *MDTN* M24.....57 M5
Sedgwick Cl *ATH* M46.....67 H1
WHTN BL5.....50 B2
Sedwyn St *MILN* OL16.....15 K1
Seedfield Rd *BURY* BL9.....25 J3
Seedley Av *LHULT* M38.....52 E8
Seedley Park Rd *SLFD* M6.....86 B1
Seedley Rd *SLFD* M6.....86 B1
Seedley St *RUSH/FAL* M14.....98 E1
Seedley Ter *SLFD* M6.....86 B1
Seedley View Rd *ORD* M5.....86 B1
Seed St *BOL* BL1.....35 M5
Seel St *MOSL* OL5.....76 E3
Sefton Av *ATH* M46.....50 F7
WGNW/BIL/OR WN5.....46 A7
Sefton Cl *BRUN/LGST* M13.....87 L6
MDTN M24.....57 M4
OLD OL1.....43 M8
WGNNW/BIL/OR WN5.....46 A7
Sefton Crs *SALE* M33.....96 E6
Sefton Dr *BURY* BL9.....25 K6
SWIN M27.....70 A2
WALK M28.....69 K6
WILM/AE SK9.....127 G2
Sefton Fold Dr
WGNW/BIL/OR WN5.....62 A7

Sefton Fold Gdns
WGNW/BIL/OR WN5.....62 A7
Sefton La *HOR/BR* BL6.....34 B3
Sefton Rd *AIMK* WN4.....63 H3
BOL BL1.....35 L2
MDTN M21.....97 L3
SALE M33.....96 F7
SWIN M27.....70 G3
WGNS/IIMK WN3.....47 H8
WGNW/BIL/OR WN5.....46 A7
Sefton St *BURY* BL9.....25 J6
CHAD OL9.....74 D2
CHH M8.....72 D4
GLSP SK13.....104 F4
HEY OL10.....41 H3
LEIGH WN7.....66 C7
RAD M26.....54 F3
ROCH OL11.....10 E9
WHTF M45.....55 J5
Sefton Vw *WGNW/BIL/OR* WN5.....46 A7
Segal Cl *BRO* M7.....72 A5
Selborne Rd *CCHDY* M21.....97 L3
Selbourne Cl *WHTN* BL5.....50 D5
Selbourne St *LEIGH* WN7.....66 G3
Selby Av *CHAD* OL9.....58 C3
WHTF M45.....55 J2
Selby Cl *MILN* OL16.....29 H6
POY/DIS SK12 *.....121 H1
RAD M26.....39 G7
STRET M32.....96 C1
Selby Dr *SLFD* M6.....85 L1
URM M41.....84 C7
WGNS/IIMK WN3.....46 A6
Selby Gdns *CHD/CHDH* SK8.....120 E6
Selby Rd *MDTN* M24.....57 J1
MILN OL16.....11 J2
OP/CLY M11.....88 D4
Selby St *HTNM* SK4.....111 G1
MILN OL16.....11 J2
OP/CLY M11.....88 D4
Selham Wk *BRUN/LGST* M13 *.....7 J9
Selhurst Av *OP/CLY* M11.....88 F2
Selkirk Av *AIMK* WN4.....63 G8
OLDS OL8.....59 G8
Selkirk Dr *BKLY* M9.....73 J1
Selkirk Gv *WGNW/BIL/OR* WN5.....46 A4
Selkirk Rd *BOL* BL1.....22 A7
CHAD OL9.....58 C8
Sellars Sq *DROY* M43.....89 K4
Sellers Wy *CHAD* OL9.....74 D1
Selsey Av *EDGY/DAV* SK3.....111 J5
SALE M33.....108 C1
Selsey Dr *DID/WITH* M20.....110 F4
Selside Wk *RUSH/FAL* M14.....98 F4
Selstead Rd *WYTH/NTH* M22.....118 E3
Selston Rd *BKLY* M9.....56 F8
Selworth Av *SALE* M33.....108 A1
Selworthy Rd *OLDTF/WHR* M16.....87 H8
Selwyn Av *BKLY* M9.....73 J3
Selwyn Cl *NEWLW* WA12.....78 E7
OLDS OL8.....9 G8
Selwyn Dr *CHD/CHDH* SK8.....120 E5
Selwyn St *BOLE* BL2.....3 J1
LEIGH WN7.....66 C6
OLDS OL8.....9 G8
Senecar Cl *WGNE/HIN* WN2.....48 C2
Senior Av *RUSH/FAL* M14.....99 H4
Senior Rd *ECC* M30.....84 C4
Senior St *CSLFD* M3.....6 D1
Senior Vw *HYDE* SK14.....91 H7
Sennicar La *WGN* WN1.....31 M7
Sepal Cl *RDSH* SK5.....100 C3
Sephton St *WGNS/IIMK* WN3.....14 C5
Sepia Gv *MDTN* M24.....57 J3
Sequoia St *BKLY* M9.....73 H4
Sergeants La *WHTF* M45.....54 F5
Serin Cl *OFTN* SK2.....113 J8
Service St *EDGY/DAV* SK3.....12 B6
Sesame Gdns *IRL* M44.....94 F1
Set St *STLY* SK15.....91 J3
Sett Cl *NM/HAY* SK22.....124 D5
Sett Valley Trail *NM/HAY* SK22.....125 H2
Sevenacres *UPML* OL3.....45 J7
Seven Acres La *WHIT* OL12.....27 H2
Seven Acres Rd *WHIT* OL12.....27 H2
Seven Oaks *LEIGH* WN7.....66 C6
Sevenoaks Av *HTNM* SK4.....99 K7
URM M41.....85 G3
Sevenoaks Dr *BOLS/LL* BL3.....52 B1
SWIN M27.....70 B2
Sevenoaks Rd *CHD/CHDH* SK8.....110 E6
Sevenoaks Wk
BRUN/LGST M13 *.....87 M7
Seven Stars Rd
WGNS/IIMK WN3.....14 C5
Seven Stiles Dr *MPL/ROM* SK6.....114 B5
Seventh Av *OLDS* OL8.....9 G9
Severn Cl *ALT* WA14.....107 M6
BURY BL9.....25 J5
WGNW/BIL/OR WN5.....62 A8
Severn Dr *BRAM/HZG* SK7.....120 E6
MILN OL16.....29 K6
WGNE/HIN WN2.....65 H1
WGNW/BIL/OR WN5.....46 A7
Severn Rd *AIMK* WN4.....64 B7
CHAD OL9.....58 C4
HEY OL10.....40 D1
OLDS OL8.....74 E3
Severn St *LEIGH* WN7.....66 E8
Severn Wy *FWTH* BL4.....53 L7
RDSH SK5.....100 C3
Seville St *ROY/SHW* OL2.....43 K7
ROY/SHW OL2.....59 H2
Sewell Wy *LHULT* M38.....68 C1
Sewerby Cl *OLDTF/WHR* M16.....87 J3
Sewerby St
OLDTF/WHR M16.....87 H8
Sexa St *OP/CLY* M11.....89 G4
Sexton St *CLSP* SK13.....93 J5
HEY OL10.....40 F2
Seymour Av *OP/CLY* M11.....89 G2
Seymour Cl *OLDTF/WHR* M16.....98 B1
Seymour Dr *BOLE* BL2.....37 G1
Seymour Gv *FWTH* BL4.....52 D5
HALE/TIMP WA15.....108 D7
MILN OL16.....42 E1
MPL/ROM SK6.....114 B6
OLDTF/WHR M16.....98 B1
OFTN SK2.....112 E6
Seymour Pl *OLDTF/WHR* M16 *.....86 E7
Seymour Rd *BOL* BL1.....36 C1
CHD/CHDH SK8.....120 C4
CHH M8.....72 D3
OFTN SK2.....112 E6
Seymour Rd South
OP/CLY M11.....89 G2

Seymour St BOLE BL2 .......... 22 F6
  DTN/ASHW M34 .......... 90 A8
  GTN M18 .......... 89 G6
  HEY OL10 .......... 40 F3
  RAD M26 .......... 54 E1
Shackleton St BOL BL1 .......... 35 J2
Shackleton St ECC M30 .......... 84 F1
Shackliffe Rd NEWH/MOS M40 .......... 27 J3
Shaddock Av WHIT OL12 .......... 27 J3
Shade Av OLDE OL4 .......... 60 C7
Shadowbrook Av
  NTHM/RTH M23 .......... 109 K8
Shadowbrook Cl OLD OL1 .......... 9 H1
Shadowmoss Rd
  WYTH/NTH M22 .......... 119 G4
Shadows La MOSL OL5 .......... 61 H8
Shadwell Gv LEIGH WN7 .......... 65 M4
Shadwell St East HEY OL10 .......... 41 H1
Shadwell St West HEY OL10 .......... 41 G1
Shadworth Cl MOSL OL5 .......... 61 H8
Shady La EDGW/EG BL7 .......... 22 E6
  NTHM/RTH M23 .......... 109 G6
Shady Oak Rd OFTN SK2 .......... 113 J6
Shaftesbury Av
  CHD/CHDH SK8 .......... 120 E3
  ECC M30 .......... 84 F4
  HALE/TIMP WA15 .......... 108 E7
  HOR/BR BL6 .......... 34 C4
  LIT OL15 .......... 29 K2
Shaftesbury Dr WHIT OL12 .......... 21 H6
Shaftesbury Gdns URM M41 .......... 94 F2
Shaftesbury Rd CHH M8 .......... 72 D5
  EDGY/DAV SK3 .......... 111 K6
  SWIN M27 .......... 70 C5
Shaftsbury Dr HEY OL10 .......... 40 F4
Shaftsbury Rd
  WGNW/BIL/OR WN5 .......... 46 D4
Shaftsbury St WGNNW/ST WN6 .......... 47 J1
Shaftway Cl RNFD/HAY WA11 .......... 78 C5
Shakerley La ATH M46 .......... 51 J8
Shakerley Rd TYLD M29 .......... 67 J3
Shakespeare Av BURY BL9 .......... 39 J6
Shakespeare Crs DROY M43 .......... 89 K2
  ECC M30 .......... 85 G2
Shakespeare Dr
  CHD/CHDH SK8 .......... 111 J6
Shakespeare Rd
  WGNS/IIMK WN3 .......... 47 K8
Shakespeare Rd DROY M43 .......... 89 K2
  MPL/ROM SK6 .......... 113 H1
  OLD OL1 .......... 59 L2
  PWCH M25 .......... 71 J1
  SWIN M27 .......... 70 A4
Shakespeare Wk
  BRUN/LGST M13 .......... 87 M7
Shakleton Av BKLY M9 .......... 73 K1
Shalbourne Rd WALK M28 .......... 68 F1
Shaldon Dr NEWH/MOS M40 .......... 74 B8
Shalebrook Ct ATH M46 .......... 66 D2
Shalemere Ct ATH M46 .......... 66 D2
Shalewood Av ATH M46 .......... 66 D2
Shalfleet Cl BOLE BL2 .......... 23 H7
Shambles Sq CMANE M1 .......... 6 F3
Shandon Av WYTH/NTH M22 .......... 110 A3
Shanklin Av URM M41 .......... 95 M2
Shanklin Cl CCHDY M21 .......... 97 K3
  DTN/ASHW M34 .......... 101 L4
Shanklin Wk BOLS/LL BL3 .......... 3 M9
Shanley Ct CHAD OL9 * .......... 8 B3
Shannon Cl HEY OL10 .......... 40 D1
Shannon Rd WYTH/NTH M22 .......... 110 B8
Shap Av HALE/TIMP WA15 .......... 109 C7
Shap Dr WALK M28 .......... 69 J2
Shap Ga WGNW/BIL/OR WN5 .......... 46 E5
Sharcott Cl OLDTF/WHR M16 .......... 87 J8
Shared St WGN WN1 .......... 15 L4
Shargate Cl WILM/AE SK9 .......... 127 G3
Sharman St BOLS/LL BL3 .......... 3 J9
Sharnford Cl BOLE BL2 .......... 3 J9
Sharnford Sq WGTN/LGST M12 .......... 88 D6
Sharon Av OLDE OL4 .......... 61 G6
Sharon Cl AULW OL7 .......... 90 B3
Sharon Sq WGNE/HIN WN2 .......... 64 C4
Sharples Av BOL BL1 .......... 22 B6
Sharples Dr TOT/BURYW BL8 .......... 24 C8
Sharples Hall Dr BOL BL1 .......... 22 C6
Sharples Hall Ms BOL BL1 .......... 22 C6
Sharples Hall Fold BOL BL1 .......... 22 C7
Sharples Pk BOL BL1 .......... 22 A8
Sharples St ANC M4 .......... 7 J1
Sharp St MDTN M24 .......... 57 K4
  PWCH M25 .......... 71 J1
  TOT/BURYW BL8 .......... 24 E8
  WALK M28 .......... 69 H1
  WGNS/IIMK WN3 .......... 15 K8
Sharrington Dr
  NTHM/RTH M23 .......... 109 H6
Shaving La WALK M28 .......... 69 G3
Shaw Av HYDE SK14 .......... 102 C4
Shawbrook Av WALK M28 .......... 69 H3
Shawbrook Rd BNG/LEV M19 .......... 99 K7
Shawbury Cl HOR/BR BL6 .......... 33 G3
Shawbury Gv SALE M33 .......... 108 C2
Shawbury St MDTN M24 .......... 57 M5
Shawclough Cl WHIT OL12 .......... 28 A1
Shawclough Dr WHIT OL12 .......... 27 M1
Shawclough Ri WHIT OL12 .......... 28 A2
Shawclough Rd WHIT OL12 .......... 27 M1
Shawclough Wy WHIT OL12 .......... 43 K7
Shawcross Fold STKP SK1 .......... 13 J3
Shawcross La WYTH/NTH M22 .......... 102 C4
Shawcross St HYDE SK14 .......... 86 C3
  SLFD M6 .......... 13 K7
  STKP SK1 .......... 13 K7
Shawdene Rd WYTH/NTH M22 .......... 109 M4
Shawe Hall Av URM M41 .......... 95 K3
Shawe Hall Crs URM M41 .......... 95 K3
Shawe Rd URM M41 .......... 95 K2
Shawe Vw URM M41 .......... 95 K2
Shawfield Cl RUSH/FAL M14 .......... 98 D4
Shawfield La WHIT OL12 .......... 27 K2
Shawfield Rd GLSP SK13 .......... 104 C1
Shawford Crs NEWH/MOS M40 .......... 73 M2
Shaw Hall Av HYDE SK14 .......... 91 G7
Shaw Hall Bank Rd UPML OL3 .......... 61 J7
Shaw Hall Cl UPML OL3 .......... 61 J6
Shaw Head Dr FAIL M35 .......... 74 C6
Shaw Heath EDGY/DAV SK3 .......... 13 H7
Shawhill Wk NEWH/MOS M40 .......... 88 B2

Shaw La GLSP SK13 .......... 104 C1
  MILN OL16 .......... 29 L4
Shawlea Av BNG/LEV M19 .......... 99 H6
Shaw Moor Av STLY SK15 .......... 91 M3
Shaw Rd HTNM SK4 .......... 99 L7
  MILN OL16 .......... 42 F4
  MILN OL16 .......... 43 L1
  OLD OL1 .......... 9 L2
  ROY/SHW OL2 .......... 43 J8
Shaw Rd South EDGY/DAV SK3 .......... 13 J9
  EDGY/DAV SK3 .......... 112 B6
Shaws Fold OLDE OL4 .......... 60 E6
Shaws La UPML OL3 .......... 61 M5
Shaw's Rd ALT WA14 .......... 116 C2
Shaw St AIMK WN4 .......... 63 L7
  AUL OL6 .......... 91 G1
  BOLS/LL BL3 .......... 2 E3
  BURY BL9 .......... 5 K3
  CSLFD M3 .......... 6 F1
  FWTH BL4 .......... 52 F2
  GLSP SK13 .......... 104 F4
  HYDE SK14 .......... 92 D8
  OLD OL1 .......... 9 K4
  OLDE OL4 .......... 60 D6
  RNFD/HAY WA11 .......... 78 B6
  ROY/SHW OL2 .......... 43 H8
  UPML OL3 .......... 61 K7
  WGN WN1 .......... 15 G1
  WHIT OL12 .......... 28 E2
Sheader Dr OLDM OL5 .......... 85 M2
Sheaf Field Wk RAD M26 .......... 38 D8
Sheard Av AUL OL6 .......... 76 A6
Sheardhall Av POY/DIS SK12 .......... 124 A7
Shearer Wy SWIN M27 .......... 71 G5
Shearing Av WHIT OL12 .......... 27 J3
Shearsby Cl HULME M15 .......... 87 H6
Shearwater Av TYLD M29 .......... 67 K4
Shearwater Dr WALK M28 .......... 68 F1
  WHTN BL5 .......... 50 A6
Shearwater Gdns ECC M30 .......... 84 D4
Shearwater Rd OFTN SK2 .......... 113 J7
The Sheddings BOLS/LL BL3 .......... 36 D8
Sheed St WHIT OL12 .......... 20 B3
Sheepfoot La OLD OL1 .......... 59 G3
  PWCH M25 .......... 72 A1
Sheepfoot Wk OLD OL1 .......... 59 G3
Sheep Gap Dr WHIT OL12 .......... 24 B7
Sheep Gate Dr TOT/BURYW BL8 .......... 24 B7
Sheep Hey RAMS BL0 .......... 19 G3
Sheerness St GTN M18 .......... 89 G7
Sheffield Rd GLSP SK13 .......... 105 H3
  HYDE SK14 .......... 91 J8
Sheffield St CMANE M1 .......... 7 K6
  HTNM SK4 .......... 13 H1
Shefford Av WGTN/LGST M12 .......... 88 C4
Shefford Crs WGNS/IIMK WN3 .......... 62 F2
Sheiling Ct ALT WA14 .......... 107 M8
The Sheilings GOL/RIS/CUL WA3 .......... 35 L2
Shelbourne Av BOL BL1 .......... 35 J2
Shelburne Dr WGNE/HIN WN2 .......... 48 F8
Shelden Ms GLSP SK13 .......... 104 A3
Shelderton Cl NEWH/MOS M40 .......... 73 K5
Sheldon Av WGNNW/ST WN6 .......... 31 K4
Sheldon Cl PART M31 .......... 106 C1
Sheldon Rd AULW OL7 .......... 75 L7
Sheldon Rd BRAM/HZG SK7 .......... 122 A5
  SLFD M6 .......... 13 J2
Sheldrake Cl DUK SK16 .......... 91 H5
Sheldrake Rd ALT WA14 .......... 107 L4
Sheldwich Cl LEIGH WN7 .......... 81 J1
Shelfield La ROCH OL11 .......... 27 J3
Shelford Av GTN M18 .......... 88 E7
Shelley Av MDTN M24 .......... 57 L2
Shelley Dr WGNE/HIN WN2 .......... 64 E3
  WGNW/BIL/OR WN5 .......... 46 D6
Shelley Gv DROY M43 .......... 89 K3
  HYDE SK14 .......... 91 G8
  STLY SK15 .......... 77 H8
Shelley Ri DUK SK16 .......... 91 L5
Shelley Rd CHAD OL9 .......... 74 C1
  LHULT M38 .......... 52 D7
  OLD OL1 .......... 59 L2
  PWCH M25 .......... 71 J1
  RDSH SK5 .......... 100 A3
  SWIN M27 .......... 70 A4
Shelley St LEIGH WN7 .......... 65 M5
  NEWH/MOS M40 .......... 73 M4
Shelley Wk BOL BL1 .......... 36 A3
Shellingford Cl
  WGNNW/ST WN6 .......... 30 C6
Shelton Av SALE M33 .......... 96 A8
Shenfield Wk NEWH/MOS M40 .......... 88 A1
Shenhurst Cl WILM/AE SK9 .......... 126 C8
Shentonfield Rd
  WYTH/NTH M22 .......... 110 B6
Shenton Park Av SALE M33 .......... 107 H3
Shenton St HYDE SK14 .......... 90 F8
Shepherd Cross St BOL BL1 .......... 35 M3
Shepherds Cl HOR/BR BL6 .......... 32 F1
  TOT/BURYW BL8 .......... 24 C3
Shepherd's Dr HOR/BR BL6 .......... 34 D1
Shepherd St BKLY M9 * .......... 73 G3
  BURY BL9 .......... 5 G6
  HEY OL10 .......... 40 F2
  ROCH OL11 .......... 27 G3
  ROY/SHW OL2 .......... 43 H8
  TOT/BURYW BL8 .......... 24 C4
  WHIT OL12 * .......... 10 C1
Shepherds Wy MILN OL16 .......... 29 H7
Shepley Av BOLS/LL BL3 .......... 35 M7
Shepley Cl BRAM/HZG SK7 .......... 121 M4
  DUK SK16 .......... 91 G4
Shepley Dr BRAM/HZG SK7 .......... 121 M4
Shepley La MPL/ROM SK6 .......... 114 C8
Shepley Rd DTN/ASHW M34 .......... 90 C5
Shepley St DTN/ASHW M34 .......... 90 C5
  FAIL M35 .......... 74 D3
  GLSP SK13 .......... 105 H2
  HYDE SK14 .......... 102 B3
  OLDE OL4 .......... 60 B6

Sherbourne Dr HEY OL10 .......... 40 D1
Sherbourne Pl WGNS/IIMK WN3 .......... 35 K9
Sherbourne Rd BOL BL1 .......... 35 K3
Sherbourne St PWCH M25 * .......... 55 K8
Sherbrook Cl SALE M33 .......... 108 C1
Sherbrooke Av UPML OL3 .......... 61 M3
Sherbrooke Ri WILM/AE SK9 .......... 127 G6
Sherdley Ct CHH M8 .......... 72 D3
Sherdley Rd CHH M8 .......... 72 D3
Sherford Cl BRAM/HZG SK7 .......... 121 J2
Sheridan Av GOL/RIS/CUL WA3 .......... 80 A5
Sheridan Wy CHAD OL9 * .......... 58 B4
Sheriffs Dr TYLD M29 .......... 68 A3
Sheriff St BOLE BL2 .......... 36 E3
  MILN OL16 .......... 29 K7
  WHIT OL12 .......... 10 C3
Sheringham Dr HYDE SK14 .......... 102 D1
  SWIN M27 .......... 70 C6
  TOT/BURYW BL8 .......... 24 C7
Sheringham Pl BOLS/LL BL3 * .......... 2 A9
Sheringham Rd DID/WITH M20 .......... 99 J5
Sherlock Av RNFD/HAY WA11 .......... 78 B5
Sherlock St RUSH/FAL M14 .......... 99 G5
Sherratt St ANC M4 .......... 7 K2
Sherrington St
  WGTN/LGST M12 .......... 99 K1
Sherway Dr HALE/TIMP WA15 .......... 108 F6
Sherwell Rd BKLY M9 .......... 72 E1
Sherwin Wy ROCH OL11 .......... 42 A3
Sherwood Av AIMK WN4 * .......... 63 M8
  BRO M7 .......... 71 L5
  DROY M43 .......... 89 M2
  HTNM SK4 .......... 111 K3
  RAD M26 .......... 38 C4
  RUSH/FAL M14 .......... 98 F4
  SALE M33 .......... 96 F7
  TYLD M29 .......... 67 K6
Sherwood Cl AUL OL6 .......... 75 M5
  MPL/ROM SK6 .......... 114 C8
  ORD M5 .......... 86 A1
  TOT/BURYW BL8 .......... 24 C5
Sherwood Crs WGNE/HIN WN2 .......... 66 D2
  WGNW/BIL/OR WN5 .......... 47 G5
Sherwood Dr SWIN M27 .......... 70 E5
  WGNW/BIL/OR WN5 .......... 47 G5
Sherwood Fold GLSP SK13 .......... 104 A5
Sherwood Gv LEIGH WN7 .......... 81 L2
  WGNW/BIL/OR WN5 .......... 47 G5
Sherwood Rd DTN/ASHW M34 .......... 100 E1
  MPL/ROM SK6 .......... 101 J2
Sherwood St BOL BL1 .......... 36 C1
  OLD OL1 .......... 8 E2
  ROCH OL11 .......... 42 A2
  RUSH/FAL M14 .......... 98 F4
Sherwood Wy ROY/SHW OL2 .......... 43 K6
Shetland Av SALE M33 .......... 96 D8
Shetland Wy RAD M26 .......... 38 C7
  URM M41 .......... 85 G7
Shevington Gdns
  NTHM/RTH M23 .......... 109 L3
Shevington La
  WGNNW/ST WN6 .......... 30 D6
Shevington Moor
  WGNNW/ST WN6 .......... 30 D2
Shieldborn Dr BKLY M9 .......... 73 G5
Shield Cl OLDS OL8 .......... 9 M8
Shield Dr WALK M28 .......... 69 M4
Shiel St EDGY/DAV SK3 .......... 13 G6
Shiel St WALK M28 .......... 69 G1
Shiers Dr CHD/CHDH SK8 .......... 111 H8
Shiffnall St BOLE BL2 .......... 3 G6
Shildon Cl WGNE/HIN WN2 .......... 48 C2
Shilford Dr ANC M4 .......... 7 K1
Shillingford Rd FWTH BL4 .......... 52 F4
Shillingstone Cl BOLE BL2 .......... 37 K1
Shillingten Cl WALK M28 .......... 68 C1
Shiloh La OLDE OL4 .......... 60 D4
Shiloh Rd MPL/ROM SK6 .......... 115 M5
Shilton Gdns BOLS/LL BL3 .......... 2 E8
Shilton St RAMS BL0 .......... 18 E7
Shipgate BOL BL1 .......... 7 K9
Shipham Cl LEIGH WN7 .......... 66 A5
Shipla Cl CHAD OL9 .......... 9 G8
Ship La OLDE OL4 .......... 44 E7
Shipley Av ORD M5 .......... 85 M1
Shipley Vw URM M41 .......... 84 C7
Shipper Bottom La RAMS BL0 .......... 19 H6
Shippey St RUSH/FAL M14 .......... 99 G5
Shipston Cl TOT/BURYW BL8 .......... 38 E1
Shipton St BOL BL1 .......... 35 L3
Shirburn ROCH OL11 .......... 10 B2
Shirebrook Dr GLSP SK13 .......... 105 J4
Shiredale Cl CHD/CHDH SK8 .......... 111 L8
Shiredale Dr BKLY M9 .......... 73 G5
Shiregreen Av NEWH/MOS M40 .......... 72 F7
Shirehills PWCH M25 .......... 71 K1
Shireoak Rd DID/WITH M20 .......... 99 G5
Shires Cl WGNE/HIN WN2 .......... 49 H8
The Shires DROY M43 .......... 90 A1
Shire Wy GLSP SK13 .......... 105 H1
Shirewell Rd
  WGNW/BIL/OR WN5 .......... 46 B7
Shirley Av BRO M7 .......... 71 K5
  CHAD OL9 .......... 74 B2
  CHD/CHDH SK8 .......... 119 L6
  DTN/ASHW M34 .......... 89 M4
  DTN/ASHW M34 .......... 100 C1
  ECC M30 .......... 84 F4
  HYDE SK14 .......... 91 G7
  MPL/ROM SK6 .......... 114 B6
  STRET M32 .......... 97 J1
  SWIN M27 .......... 70 F5
Shirley Cl BRAM/HZG SK7 .......... 121 L5
Shirley Gv EDGY/DAV SK3 .......... 112 B7
Shirley Rd CHH M8 .......... 72 D5
Shirley St ROCH OL11 .......... 41 M1
Shoecroft Av DTN/ASHW M34 .......... 101 H2
Sholver Hill Cl OLD OL1 .......... 44 B8
Sholver La OLD OL1 .......... 44 A8
Shone Av WYTH/NTH M22 .......... 119 H2
Shoreditch Cl HTNM SK4 .......... 99 L1
Shorefield Cl MILN OL16 .......... 29 J5
Shorefield Mt EDGW/EG BL7 .......... 22 B4
Shore Fold LIT OL15 .......... 21 K6
Shoreham Wk CHAD OL9 * .......... 21 K6
Shore Lea LIT OL15 .......... 21 K6
Shore Mt LIT OL15 .......... 21 K6
Shore Rd LIT OL15 .......... 21 K6
Shore St MILN OL16 .......... 29 K6
  OLD OL1 .......... 9 L4
Shoreswood BOL BL1 .......... 22 A7
Shorland St SWIN M27 .......... 69 M5
Shorrocks St TOT/BURYW BL8 .......... 38 C1
Short Av DROY M43 .......... 89 J4
Shortcroft St HULME M15 .......... 6 E8
Shortland Crs BNG/LEV M19 .......... 111 C1

Shortland Pl
  WGNE/HIN WN2 .......... 65 K4
Shortlands Av BURY BL9 .......... 5 C8
Short St BRAM/HZG SK7 .......... 121 H1
  BRO M7 .......... 87 H1
  CMANE M1 .......... 7 H4
  GOL/RIS/CUL WA3 * .......... 79 C3
  HEY OL10 .......... 40 E3
  HTNM SK4 .......... 13 C1
  RNFD/HAY WA11 .......... 78 B6
  WGNE/HIN WN2 .......... 46 E6
  WGNE/HIN WN2 .......... 13 H1
Shotton Wk
  RUSH/FAL M14 * .......... 98 E1
Shrewsbury Cl
  WGNE/HIN WN2 .......... 49 J6
Shrewsbury Ct
  OLDTF/WHR M16 * .......... 87 G7
Shrewsbury Gdns
  CHD/CHDH SK8 .......... 120 E6
Shrewsbury Rd BOL BL1 .......... 35 L4
  DROY M43 .......... 89 K2
  PWCH M25 .......... 71 K1
  SALE M33 .......... 108 D2
  OLDE OL4 .......... 59 M4
  OLDTF/WHR M16 .......... 87 G7
Shrigley Cl
  WILM/AE SK9 .......... 127 H3
Shrigley Rd MCFLDN SK10 .......... 129 M8
Shropshire Av RDSH SK5 .......... 100 M8
Shropshire Dr GLSP SK13 .......... 105 J4
Shropshire Rd FAIL M35 .......... 74 D6
Shropshire Sq
  WGTN/LGST M12 * .......... 88 B6
Shrowbridge Wk
  WGTN/LGST M12 .......... 88 D6
Shudehill ANC M4 .......... 7 H2
  NM/HAY SK22 * .......... 125 M1
Shudehill Rd WALK M28 .......... 68 D3
Shurdington Rd ATH M46 .......... 51 J7
Shurmer St BOLS/LL BL3 .......... 35 M8
Shutt La UPML OL3 .......... 61 J2
Shuttle Hillock Rd
  WGNE/HIN WN2 .......... 65 J3
Shuttle St ECC M30 * .......... 85 J2
  RAD M26 .......... 54 F3
  TYLD M29 .......... 67 J3
  WGNE/HIN WN2 .......... 49 H6
Shuttleworth Cl
  OLDTF/WHR M16 .......... 98 B4
Shutts La STLY SK15 .......... 92 A4
Siam St OP/CLY M11 .......... 88 C4
Sibley Av AIMK WN4 .......... 64 A8
Sibley Rd HTNM SK4 .......... 111 L1
Sibley St GTN M18 .......... 89 G7
Sibson Rd CCHDY M21 .......... 97 K3
  SALE M33 .......... 96 D8
Sickle St CMANW M2 .......... 7 G4
  OLDE OL4 .......... 9 L8
Sidbrook St WGNE/HIN WN2 .......... 48 F7
Sidbury Rd CCHDY M21 .......... 97 K4
Sidcup Rd NTHM/RTH M23 .......... 109 J7
Siddall St HEY OL10 .......... 41 H4
  RAD M26 .......... 38 D8
  ROY/SHW OL2 .......... 43 L5
  WGTN/LGST M12 .......... 99 K2
Siddeley St LEIGH WN7 .......... 66 A7
  EDGY/DAV SK3 .......... 111 M6
Siddington Rd POY/DIS SK12 .......... 129 K2
  WILM/AE SK9 * .......... 119 M7
Siddow Common LEIGH WN7 .......... 81 K1
Side Av ALT WA14 .......... 116 E3
Sidebotham St MPL/ROM SK6 .......... 101 J8
  OLDE OL4 .......... 60 B4
  STLY SK15 .......... 91 K2
Side St OP/CLY M11 .......... 88 E3
Sidford Cl BOLS/LL BL3 .......... 37 G7
The Sidings WALK M28 .......... 69 K7
Sidlaw Cl OLDS OL8 .......... 75 J2
Sidley Av BKLY M9 .......... 57 J8
Sidley St HYDE SK14 .......... 102 C1
Sidmouth Av URM M41 .......... 95 H1
Sidmouth Dr BKLY M9 .......... 73 G2
Sidmouth Gv CHD/CHDH SK8 .......... 120 B5
  WGNS/IIMK WN3 .......... 63 H1
Sidmouth Rd SALE M33 .......... 96 A3
Sidmouth St CHAD OL9 .......... 9 M8
  DTN/ASHW M34 .......... 90 A5
Sidney Rd BKLY M9 .......... 73 G3
Sidney St BOLS/LL BL3 .......... 3 M3
  CMANE M1 .......... 7 H7
  CSLFD M3 .......... 6 E5
  CSLFD M3 * .......... 6 E5
  LEIGH WN7 .......... 66 D7
  OLD OL1 .......... 59 K3
Sidwell Wk ANC M4 * .......... 88 A3
Siebers Bank WHIT OL12 * .......... 28 A3
Siemens Rd IRL M44 .......... 94 B7
Siemens St HOR/BR BL6 .......... 33 M2
Sienna Cl IRL M44 .......... 94 B6
Signal Cl ECC M30 .......... 84 E2
Signal Dr NEWH/MOS M40 .......... 73 G6
Signet Wk CHH M8 * .......... 72 E7
Silas St AUL OL6 .......... 76 A7
Silburn Wy MDTN M24 .......... 56 F5
Silchester Dr NEWH/MOS M40 .......... 73 G6
Silchester Wy BOLE BL2 .......... 37 H3
Silcock St GOL/RIS/CUL WA3 .......... 79 K3
Silfield Cl OP/CLY M11 .......... 88 B3
Silkhey Gv WALK M28 .......... 69 G3
Silkin Cl BRUN/LGST M13 .......... 7 M9
Silkstone Cl OP/CLY M11 .......... 88 E5
Silk St ANC M4 .......... 7 J3
  CSLFD M3 .......... 6 A1
  GLSP SK13 .......... 105 H3
  LEIGH WN7 .......... 66 D7
  MDTN M24 .......... 57 J4
  NEWH/MOS M40 .......... 73 M6
  ROCH OL11 .......... 28 A4
  WHTN BL5 .......... 50 B3
Sillavan Wy CSLFD M3 .......... 6 C5
Sillitoe Dr WGNNW/ST WN6 .......... 14 C2
Silsbury Gv WGNNW/ST WN6 .......... 31 K4
Silsden Av BKLY M9 .......... 56 E7
  GOL/RIS/CUL WA3 .......... 80 A3
Silton St BKLY M9 .......... 73 J5
Silver Birch Gv AIMK WN4 .......... 63 M4
  SWIN M27 .......... 70 E6
Silver Birch Ms DUK SK16 .......... 91 K5
Silverbirch Wy FAIL M35 .......... 74 B6
Silver Cl DUK SK16 .......... 90 F5
Silvercroft St HULME M15 .......... 6 C8
Silverdale SWIN M27 .......... 70 D2

Silverdale Av CHAD OL9 .......... 58 D7
  DTN/ASHW M34 .......... 101 K2
  IRL M44 .......... 83 L8
  PWCH M25 .......... 72 B2
  WGNE/HIN WN2 .......... 48 D4
Silverdale Cl BURY BL9 .......... 5 J9
  MPL/ROM SK6 .......... 123 G4
Silverdale Ct WGN WN1 .......... 15 J4
Silverdale Dr OLDE OL4 .......... 60 C6
  WILM/AE SK9 .......... 126 E8
Silverdale Rd BOL BL1 .......... 35 M5
  CCHDY M21 .......... 97 M3
  CHD/CHDH SK8 .......... 110 E8
  FWTH BL4 .......... 52 D3
  HTNM SK4 .......... 99 M8
  NEWLW WA12 .......... 78 E8
  WGNE/HIN WN2 .......... 49 J7
  WGNW/BIL/OR WN5 .......... 46 E5
Silverdale St OP/CLY M11 .......... 89 J5
Silver Hl MILN OL16 .......... 29 H8
Silver Hill Rd HYDE SK14 .......... 102 B3
Silver Jubilee Wk ANC M4 .......... 7 J3
Silverlea Dr BKLY M9 .......... 72 F2
Silvermere AUL OL6 .......... 76 B6
Silver Spring HYDE SK14 .......... 102 C4
Silverstone Dr NEWH/MOS M40 .......... 74 A8
Silver St BURY BL9 .......... 4 F5
  CMANE M1 .......... 7 H5
  IRL M44 .......... 83 L8
  OLD OL1 .......... 9 H6
  RAMS BL0 .......... 18 F6
  WGNE/HIN WN2 .......... 64 E2
  WHIT OL12 .......... 10 B2
  WHTF M45 .......... 55 H3
Silver Ter WGN WN1 .......... 15 H4
Silverthorne Cl STLY SK15 .......... 91 K3
Silverton Cl HYDE SK14 .......... 103 H3
Silverton Gv BOL BL1 .......... 22 C8
  MDTN M24 .......... 41 G8
Silverwell La BOL BL1 .......... 2 F5
Silverwell St BOL BL1 .......... 2 F5
  NEWH/MOS M40 .......... 74 A7
Silverwell Yd BOL BL1 * .......... 2 F5
Silverwood CHAD OL9 .......... 58 B5
Silverwood Av CCHDY M21 .......... 97 L4
Silvington Wy WGNE/HIN WN2 .......... 48 D2
Simeon St ANC M4 * .......... 7 J1
Simfield Cl WGNNW/ST WN6 .......... 31 G3
Simister Dr BURY BL9 .......... 55 K2
Simister Gn PWCH M25 .......... 56 B5
Simister La MDTN M24 .......... 56 D3
  PWCH M25 .......... 56 A4
Simister Rd FAIL M35 .......... 74 C5
Simkin Wy OLDS OL8 .......... 75 K3
Simmondley Gv GLSP SK13 .......... 104 D3
Simmondley La GLSP SK13 .......... 104 D4
Simmondley New Rd
  GLSP SK13 .......... 104 D5
Simms Cl CSLFD M3 .......... 6 A3
Simonbury Cl TOT/BURYW BL8 .......... 38 C2
Simon Freeman Cl
  BNG/LEV M19 .......... 99 M6
Simon La MDTN M24 .......... 56 D2
Simons Cl GLSP SK13 .......... 104 D5
  SALE M33 .......... 108 D1
Simonsway NTHM/RTH M23 .......... 118 C3
Simpson Av SWIN M27 .......... 70 F2
Simpson Gv WALK M28 .......... 69 M4
Simpson Hill Cl HEY OL10 .......... 41 J1
Simpson Rd WALK M28 .......... 68 C6
Simpson St ANC M4 .......... 7 J1
  CHAD OL9 .......... 58 B8
  EDGY/DAV SK3 * .......... 13 H7
  HYDE SK14 .......... 101 H1
  OP/CLY M11 .......... 89 J3
  WILM/AE SK9 .......... 126 D6
Sinclair Pl WGNW/BIL/OR WN5 .......... 47 H4
Sinclair St ROCH OL11 .......... 42 A1
Sinderland La ALT WA14 .......... 106 F3
  ALT WA14 .......... 106 H3
Sinderland Rd ALT WA14 .......... 106 F3
  ALT WA14 .......... 107 L4
Sindsley Gv BOLS/LL BL3 .......... 52 B1
Sindsley Rd SWIN M27 .......... 70 A2
Singapore Av MANAIR M90 .......... 119 M8
Singleton Av BOLE BL2 .......... 37 L5
  BRO M7 .......... 71 M3
Singleton Gv WHTN BL5 .......... 50 E4
Singleton Rd BRO M7 .......... 71 M3
  HTNM SK4 .......... 99 L8
Singleton St RAD M26 .......... 38 A4
Sion St RAD M26 .......... 54 C2
Sirdar St OP/CLY M11 * .......... 89 J4
Sirius Pl BRO M7 .......... 87 G1
Sir Matt Busby Wy TRPK M17 .......... 86 C7
Sir Richard Fairey Rd
  .......... 99 K5
Sir Robert Thomas Ct
  BKLY M9 * .......... 73 G4
Siskin Cl LEIGH WN7 .......... 66 E7
Siskin Rd OFTN SK2 .......... 113 J7
Sisley Cl BRO M7 .......... 71 L4
Sisson St FAIL M35 .......... 74 B5
Sister St DROY M43 .......... 89 K4
Sitch La NM/HAY SK22 .......... 125 H1
Sittingbourne Rd WGN WN1 .......... 31 M8
Sixpools Gv WALK M28 .......... 68 F4
Sixth Av BOL BL1 .......... 35 L5
  BOLS/LL BL3 .......... 37 J8
  BURY BL9 .......... 26 A8
  OLDS OL8 .......... 74 F3
Sixth St TRPK M17 .......... 86 M7
Size House Pl LEIGH WN7 * .......... 66 D7
Size St WHIT OL12 .......... 20 B3
Skagen Ct BOL BL1 .......... 2 D1
Skaife Rd SALE M33 .......... 97 H8
Skarratt Ct WGTN/LGST M12 .......... 88 C6
Skegness Cl TOT/BURYW BL8 .......... 25 C7
Skellorn Green La
  MCFLDN SK10 .......... 129 J4
Skelton Gv BOLE BL2 .......... 37 J4
  BRUN/LGST M13 .......... 99 J2
Skelton Rd ALT WA14 .......... 108 B5
  STRET M32 .......... 97 G1
Skelwith Av BOLS/LL BL3 .......... 52 C2
Skelwith Cl URM M41 .......... 84 D8
Skerry Cl BRUN/LGST M13 .......... 7 K9
Skerton Rd OLDTF/WHR M16 .......... 86 E8
Skiddaw Cl MDTN M24 .......... 41 K2
Skiddaw Pl WGNW/BIL/OR WN5 .......... 46 F6
Skip Pl ANC M4 .......... 7 K1
Skipton Av CHAD OL9 .......... 58 C3
  NEWH/MOS M40 .......... 74 A3
  WGNE/HIN WN2 .......... 49 K8
Skipton Cl BRAM/HZG SK7 .......... 121 L4
  RDSH SK5 .......... 100 B4
  TOT/BURYW BL8 .......... 38 C2

Skipton Dr *URM* M41 .............. 84 C7
Skipton St *BOLE* BL2 .............. 3 L4
Skipton Wk *BOLE* BL2 .............. 3 L4
Skull House La
  *WCGNW/ST* WN6 .............. 30 A4
Skye Cl *HEY* OL10 .............. 40 C3
Skye Cft *MPL/ROM* SK6 .............. 114 A1
Skye Rd *URM* M41 .............. 85 G7
Slackcote La *UPML* OL3 .............. 44 F5
Slackey Brow *FWTH* BL4 .............. 53 M7
Slackey Fold
  *WCNE/HIN* WN2 .............. 65 L3
Slack Fold La *FWTH* BL4 .............. 52 M4
Slack Ga *WHIT* OL12 .............. 20 C4
Slack Gate La *UPML* OL3 .............. 45 G4
Slack Hall *OLDE* OL4 .............. 60 C4
Slack La *BOLE* BL2 .............. 23 H5
  *SWIN* M27 .............. 70 D3
  *UPML* OL3 .............. 45 G6
  *WHTN* BL5 .............. 50 C2
Slack Rd *BKLY* M9 .............. 72 F3
Slack St *HYDE* SK14 .............. 91 J8
  *MILN* OL16 .............. 10 F4
Slade Hall Rd
  *WCTN/LGST* M12 .............. 99 K2
Slade La *BNG/LEV* M19 .............. 99 J4
  *MCFLDN* SK10 .............. 131 H7
Slade Mt *BNG/LEV* M19 * .............. 99 J4
Sladen St *WHIT* OL12 .............. 10 E1
Slade St *BOLS/LL* BL3 .............. 53 K1
Slades View Cl *UPML* OL3 .............. 45 M7
Slag La *GOL/RIS/CUL* WA3 .............. 80 C2
Slaidburn Av *BOLE* BL2 .............. 37 J6
Slaidburn Cl *MILN* OL16 .............. 29 J7
  *WCNS/IIMK* WN3 .............. 63 J4
Slaidburn Crs
  *GOL/RIS/CUL* WA3 .............. 79 J2
Slaidburn Dr *TOT/BURYW* BL8 .............. 38 B1
Slaithwaite Dr *OP/CLY* M11 .............. 88 F2
Slant Cl *GLSP* SK13 .............. 105 G4
Slateacre Rd *HYDE* SK14 .............. 102 C5
Slate Av *ANC* M4 * .............. 7 M4
Slatelands Av *GLSP* SK13 .............. 104 E4
Slatelands Rd *GLSP* SK13 .............. 104 E4
Slate La *AULW* OL7 .............. 90 B4
  *DTN/ASHW* M34 .............. 89 M4
Slaterfield *BOLS/LL* BL3 .............. 2 D9
Slater La *BOL* BL1 .............. 3 C4
Slater's Nook *WHTN* BL5 .............. 50 B3
Slater St *BOL* BL1 .............. 2 D2
  *CHAD* OL9 .............. 9 G6
  *ECC* M30 .............. 84 E2
  *FAIL* M35 .............. 74 C3
  *FWTH* BL4 .............. 53 G4
Slater St North *LEIGH* WN7 .............. 66 A7
Slate Whf *HULME* M15 * .............. 6 B7
Slawson Wy *HEY* OL10 .............. 41 J1
Sleaford Cl *NEWH/MOS* M40 * .............. 87 J2
  *TOT/BURYW* BL8 .............. 25 G7
Sledbrook St
  *WCNW/BIL/OR* WN5 * .............. 46 F7
Sleddale Cl *OFTN* SK2 .............. 113 G7
Sledmere Cl *BOL* BL1 .............. 36 C2
  *OP/CLY* M11 .............. 88 D2
Sledmoor Rd *NTHM/RTH* M23 .............. 109 J3
Slimbridge Cl *BOLE* BL2 .............. 37 K3
Sloane Av *OLDE* OL4 .............. 60 B4
Sloane St *AUL* OL6 .............. 91 G1
  *BOLS/LL* BL3 .............. 2 F5
  *OP/CLY* M11 * .............. 88 D2
Smallbridge Cl *WALK* M28 .............. 68 F4
Smallbrook La *LEIGH* WN7 .............. 66 B1
Smallbrook Rd *ROY/SHW* OL2 .............. 43 M2
Smalldale Av *OLDTF/WHR* M16 .............. 98 C1
Smalley St *ROCH* OL11 .............. 41 M2
  *WCNNW/ST* WN6 .............. 31 H3
Smallfield Dr *BKLY* M9 .............. 73 G4
Smallridge Cl *NEWH/MOS* M40 .............. 88 A1
Smallshaw La *AIMK* WN4 .............. 78 D2
Smalshaw La *AUL* OL6 .............. 75 M7
Smallwood St *NEWH/MOS* M40 * .............. 73 M4
Smart St *WCTN/LGST* M12 .............. 99 K1
Smeaton Cl *STRET* M32 .............. 97 H2
Smeaton St *CHH* M8 .............. 72 C5
  *HOR/BR* BL6 * .............. 33 M2
Smedley Av *BOLS/LL* BL3 .............. 52 D1
Smedley La *CHH* M8 .............. 72 E6
Smedley Rd *CHH* M8 .............. 72 E6
Smedley St *CHH* M8 .............. 72 D6
Smethurst Hall Rd *BURY* BL9 .............. 26 C8
Smethurst La *BOLS/LL* BL3 .............. 51 L2
  *WCNW/BIL/OR* WN5 .............. 46 F7
Smethurst St *BKLY* M9 .............. 73 G3
  *HEY* OL10 .............. 40 E2
  *MDTN* M24 .............. 58 A5
  *TOT/BURYW* BL8 .............. 24 B8
  *WCNW/BIL/OR* WN5 .............. 46 F7
Smith Av *WCNW/BIL/OR* WN5 .............. 46 E4
Smith Brow *HOR/BR* BL6 .............. 32 F2
Smithfold La *WALK* M28 .............. 68 D1
Smith Hl *MILN* OL16 .............. 29 J6
Smithies Av *MDTN* M24 .............. 57 K2
Smithies St *HEY* OL10 .............. 41 H2
Smithills Croft Rd *BOL* BL1 .............. 35 L1
Smithills Dr *BOL* BL1 .............. 35 J2
Smithills Hall Cl *RAMS* BL0 .............. 18 E8
Smith La *EDGW/EG* BL7 .............. 22 C4
Smith's La *WCNE/HIN* WN2 .............. 65 K4
Smiths Lawn *WILM/AE* SK9 .............. 126 E7
Smith's Rd *BOLS/LL* BL3 .............. 53 G1
Smith St *ATH* M46 * .............. 66 F1
  *AULW* OL7 .............. 90 C3
  *BURY* BL9 .............. 5 H2
  *CHD/CHDH* SK8 * .............. 111 J6
  *DTN/ASHW* M34 .............. 101 J2
  *HEY* OL10 .............. 41 G2
  *HYDE* SK14 .............. 91 G7
  *LEIGH* WN7 .............. 66 D7
  *LIT* OL15 .............. 21 M7
  *MILN* OL16 .............. 10 F2
  *MOSL* OL5 .............. 76 E2
  *OLDE* OL4 .............. 60 B4
  *OLDTF/WHR* M16 .............. 86 F6
  *RAMS* BL0 .............. 18 E7
  *WALK* M28 .............. 69 G1
  *WCNE/HIN* WN2 .............. 49 J6
Smithwood Av *WCNE/HIN* WN2 .............. 49 J6
Smithybridge Rd *LIT* OL15 .............. 29 J1
  *MILN* OL16 .............. 21 J8
Smithy Cl *GLSP* SK13 .............. 105 G3
Smithy Cft *EDGW/EG* BL7 .............. 22 C4
Smithy Fold *WHIT* OL12 .............. 27 M3
Smithy Fold Rd *HYDE* SK14 .............. 102 B4
Smithy Glen Dr
  *WCNW/BIL/OR* WN5 .............. 46 B8
Smithy Gn *CHD/CHDH* SK8 * .............. 120 C4
  *MPL/ROM* SK6 .............. 101 L7
  *WCNE/HIN* WN2 * .............. 48 D3
Smithy Gv *AUL* OL6 .............. 75 M8
Smithy Hl *BOLS/LL* BL3 .............. 35 K8

Smithy La *ALT* WA14 .............. 116 A1
  *CSLFD* M3 * .............. 6 E4
  *HYDE* SK14 .............. 102 B3
  *MCFLDN* SK10 .............. 131 M2
  *MPL/ROM* SK6 .............. 115 J3
  *PART* M31 .............. 106 C1
  *UPML* OL3 .............. 61 L4
Smithy St *BRAM/HZG* SK7 .............. 121 M1
  *LEIGH* WN7 .............. 66 C8
  *RAMS* BL0 * .............. 18 F6
Smock La *WHN* WN4 .............. 62 F8
Smyrna St *HEY* OL10 .............. 40 F3
  *OLDE* OL4 * .............. 59 M7
  *ORD* M5 .............. 86 B3
  *RAD* M26 .............. 38 C8
Snake Pass *GLSP* SK13 .............. 105 M4
Snape St *RAD* M26 .............. 38 C7
Snell St *ANC* M4 .............. 88 A3
Snipe Av *ROCH* OL11 .............. 27 J5
Snipe Cl *POY/DIS* SK12 .............. 128 E1
Snipe Rd *OLDS* OL8 .............. 75 L2
Snipe St *BOLS/LL* BL3 .............. 2 F9
Snipe Wy *AULW* OL7 .............. 90 A3
Snowden Av *URM* M41 .............. 95 L4
  *WCNS/IIMK* WN3 .............. 47 K8
Snowden St *BOL* BL1 .............. 2 D3
  *HEY* OL10 .............. 41 H4
  *OLDS* OL8 .............. 59 J8
Snowdon Rd *ECC* M30 .............. 85 K1
Snowdon St *ROCH* OL11 .............. 42 D2
Snow Hill Rd *BOLS/LL* BL3 .............. 37 G7
Snowshill Dr *WCNS/IIMK* WN3 .............. 46 F8
Snydale Cl *WHTN* BL5 .............. 50 D2
Snydale Wy *BOLS/LL* BL3 .............. 51 G2
  *WHTN* BL5 .............. 50 F3
Soane Cl *WCNE/HIN* WN2 .............. 79 G1
Soapstone Wy *IRL* M44 .............. 94 D4
Soap St *ANC* M4 .............. 7 H3
Society St *ROY/SHW* OL2 .............. 43 L5
Sofa St *BOL* BL1 .............. 35 L3
Soham Cl *WCNE/HIN* WN2 .............. 49 H8
Soho St *BOL* BL1 .............. 2 E6
  *OLDE* OL4 .............. 60 A7
  *WCNW/BIL/OR* WN5 .............. 14 A5
Solent Av *CHH* M8 .............. 72 D2
Solent Dr *BOLS/LL* BL3 .............. 3 M8
Sole St *WGN* WN1 .............. 15 L1
Solness St *BURY* BL9 .............. 25 J6
Soloman Rd *ALT* WA14 .............. 107 M3
Solway Cl *AIMK* WN4 .............. 63 K8
  *BOLS/LL* BL3 .............. 52 A1
  *OLDS* OL8 .............. 9 H9
  *SWIN* M27 .............. 54 B8
Solway Rd *WYTH/NTH* M22 .............. 110 B4
Somerby Dr *WYTH/NTH* M22 .............. 118 C3
Somerdale Av *BOL* BL1 .............. 35 K5
Somerfield Rd *BKLY* M9 .............. 73 G3
Somerford Av *DID/WITH* M20 .............. 98 D4
Somerford Rd *RDSH* SK5 .............. 100 D2
Somersby Dr *EDGW/EG* BL7 .............. 22 C4
Somerset Av *ROY/SHW* OL2 .............. 43 J5
  *TYLD* M29 .............. 67 J1
Somerset Cl *IRL* M44 .............. 94 A6
  *RDSH* SK5 .............. 100 F8
Somerset Dr *BURY* BL9 .............. 5 C9
Somerset Gv *ROCH* OL11 .............. 27 K4
Somerset Pl *SALE* M33 .............. 96 E6
Somerset Rd *ALT* WA14 .............. 108 A6
  *ATH* M46 .............. 50 E8
  *BOL* BL1 .............. 35 L4
  *DROY* M43 .............. 89 K1
  *ECC* M30 .............. 70 D8
  *FAIL* M35 .............. 74 B6
  *WCNW/BIL/OR* WN5 .............. 46 F6
Somerset St *OLDE* OL4 .............. 59 M6
Somerton Av *SALE* M33 .............. 108 F1
  *WYTH/NTH* M22 * .............. 118 C3
Somerton Cl *WCNNW/ST* WN6 .............. 31 G3
Somerton Rd *BOLE* BL2 .............. 37 J7
Somerville Gdns
  *HALE/TIMP* WA15 .............. 108 C3
Somerville Rd *WGN* WN1 .............. 31 M8
Somerville Sq *BOL* BL1 .............. 35 L1
Somerville St *BOL* BL1 .............. 35 M1
Somerwood Wk
  *WGTN/LGST* M12 * .............. 88 C6
Sonning Dr *BOLS/LL* BL3 .............. 51 K2
Sopwith Dr *RUSH/FAL* M14 .............. 98 D3
Sorby Rd *IRL* M44 .............. 94 D5
Sorrel Bank *SLFD* M6 .............. 71 J8
Sorrel Dr *LIT* OL15 .............. 21 K6
Sorrell Bank *RDSH* SK5 .............. 100 D4
Sorrel St *HULME* M15 .............. 87 H6
Sorrel Wy *OLDE* OL4 .............. 60 B2
Sorton St *CMANE* M1 * .............. 7 H8
Sossmoss La *MCFLDN* SK10 .............. 130 A6
Soudan Rd *OFTN* SK2 .............. 112 D6
Soudan St *MDTN* M24 .............. 57 M3
Sougher's La *AIMK* WN4 .............. 63 J6
The Sound *UPML* OL3 .............. 45 J8
Souracre Fold *STLY* SK15 .............. 91 L1
South Acre La *WILM/AE* SK9 .............. 127 H1
Southall St *CSLFD* M3 .............. 87 J1
Southampton Cl *BRO* M7 .............. 72 A7
Southam St *BRO* M7 .............. 72 C5
South Av *BNG/LEV* M19 .............. 99 J5
  *FWTH* BL4 .............. 53 J7
  *HEY* OL10 .............. 40 E2
  *LEIGH* WN7 .............. 81 M1
  *SWIN* M27 .............. 70 A7
  *UPML* OL3 .............. 61 L6
  *URM* M41 .............. 85 H6
  *WHTF* M45 .............. 55 H3
South Back Rock *BURY* BL9 * .............. 4 F4
South Bank Cl *WILM/AE* SK9 * .............. 130 E4
Southbank Rd *BNG/LEV* M19 .............. 99 G7
South Bank Rd *BURY* BL9 .............. 4 F4
Southbourne Av *URM* M41 .............. 96 C2
Southbourne St *SLFD* M6 .............. 86 B3
Southbrook Av *CHH* M8 .............. 72 C1
Southbrook Cl *GLSP* SK13 .............. 93 H8
Southbrook Gv *BOLS/LL* BL3 .............. 52 C1
Southcliffe Rd *RDSH* SK5 .............. 100 C6
South Cliffe St *OP/CLY* M11 .............. 89 J5
South Cl *BURY* BL9 .............. 55 K1
  *GLSP* SK13 .............. 93 J5
  *WILM/AE* SK9 .............. 126 D6
Southcourt *LEIGH* WN7 .............. 66 E6
South Crs *NEWH/MOS* M40 .............. 74 A1
  *OP/CLY* M11 .............. 89 G2
South Cft *OLDS* OL8 .............. 75 L1
Southcross Rd *GTN* M18 .............. 100 A1
South Cross St *BURY* BL9 .............. 5 G3
  *GLSP* SK13 .............. 93 J5
  *WILM/AE* SK9 .............. 126 D6
South Croston St
  *OLDTF/WHR* M16 .............. 87 G8
Southdene Av *DID/WITH* M20 .............. 98 B4
Southdown Cl *HTNM* SK4 .............. 12 F7
  *ROCH* OL11 .............. 27 M1
Southdown Crs *BKLY* M9 .............. 73 K2
  *CHD/CHDH* SK8 .............. 120 B4
Southdown Dr *WALK* M28 .............. 68 C6

Southdowns Cl *ROY/SHW* OL2 .............. 43 J4
South Downs Dr *ALT* WA14 .............. 116 F4
South Downs Rd *ALT* WA14 .............. 116 F3
South Dr *BOLE* BL2 .............. 37 H1
  *CHDY* M21 .............. 97 L6
  *CHD/CHDH* SK8 .............. 110 D8
  *HALE/TIMP* WA15 .............. 108 D5
  *WILM/AE* SK9 .............. 126 F6
Southend Av *HULME* M15 .............. 87 G6
Southend St *BOLS/LL* BL3 .............. 51 M1
Southern Ap *SWIN* M27 .............. 70 F2
Southernby Cl
  *BRUN/LGST* M13 * .............. 88 C8
Southern Cl *BRAM/HZG* SK7 .............. 121 H1
  *DTN/ASHW* M34 .............. 101 H4
Southern Crs *BRAM/HZG* SK7 .............. 121 H3
Southern Rd *SALE* M33 .............. 96 D6
Southern's Fold
  *WCNE/HIN* WN2 .............. 48 D1
Southern St *CSLFD* M3 .............. 6 D6
  *SLFD* M6 .............. 86 B2
  *WALK* M28 .............. 53 C7
Southery Av *WCNS/IIMK* WN3 .............. 63 C1
Southey Cl *LIT* OL15 .............. 29 J2
Southfield *WCNE/HIN* WN2 .............. 64 E2
Southfield Av *BURY* BL9 .............. 25 H6
Southfield Cl *DUK* SK16 .............. 91 G6
Southfield Dr *WHTN* BL5 .............. 50 C5
Southfield Rd *RAMS* BL0 .............. 24 D2
Southfields Av *OP/CLY* M11 .............. 88 F2
Southfields Dr
  *HALE/TIMP* WA15 .............. 108 E5
Southfield St *BOLS/LL* BL3 .............. 36 E6
South Gdns *TYLD* M29 * .............. 67 K7
Southgarth Rd *SLFD* M6 .............. 86 B1
Southgate *BOLE* BL2 .............. 23 H8
  *CCHDY* M21 .............. 97 L5
  *HTNM* SK4 .............. 99 M7
  *UPML* OL3 .............. 45 J4
  *URM* M41 .............. 95 L4
Southgate Av
  *NEWH/MOS* M40 * .............. 73 K8
Southgate College Land
  *CSLFD* M3 .............. 6 E4
Southgate Rd *BURY* BL9 .............. 55 J1
  *CHAD* OL9 .............. 74 B1
Southgate St *OLD* OL1 .............. 9 K6
South Gv *BRUN/LGST* M13 * .............. 88 A7
  *SALE* M33 .............. 108 E1
  *WALK* M28 .............. 68 F2
  *WILM/AE* SK9 .............. 130 D3
Southgrove Av *BOL* BL1 .............. 35 L5
Southhey Cl *DID/WITH* M20 .............. 99 G7
South Hl *OLDE* OL4 .............. 60 C7
South Hill St *OLDE* OL4 * .............. 9 M7
  *ECC* M30 .............. 84 E2
South King St *CSLFD* M3 .............. 6 E4
South Langworthy Rd *ORD* M5 .............. 86 C3
Southlea Rd *DID/WITH* M20 .............. 99 G7
Southleigh Dr *BOLE* BL2 .............. 37 K6
Southlink *OLDE* OL4 * .............. 9 M6
South Lonsdale St *STRET* M32 .............. 97 H1
South Marlow St *GLSP* SK13 .............. 93 K8
South Md *POY/DIS* SK12 .............. 121 K7
South Meade *CCHDY* M21 .............. 97 L5
  *HALE/TIMP* WA15 .............. 108 D5
  *PWCH* M25 .............. 72 A2
South Meadway
  *MPL/ROM* SK6 .............. 123 H5
South Mesnefield Rd *BRO* M7 .............. 71 K5
Southmill St *CMANE* M2 .............. 6 E6
Southmoor Rd
  *NTHM/RTH* M23 .............. 109 H7
Southmoor Wk *BOLS/LL* BL3 * .............. 2 C9
South Oak La *WILM/AE* SK9 .............. 126 D6
Southover *WHTN* BL5 .............. 50 B6
South Pde *BRAM/HZG* SK7 .............. 121 H2
  *MILN* OL16 .............. 11 M6
South Park Dr *POY/DIS* SK12 .............. 122 A8
South Park Rd *CHD/CHDH* SK8 .............. 110 F4
Southpool Cl *BRAM/HZG* SK7 .............. 121 J2
South Pump St *CMANE* M1 * .............. 7 H6
South Radford St *BRO* M7 .............. 71 K5
South Rdg *DTN/ASHW* M34 .............. 90 C7
South Rd *ALT* WA14 .............. 116 E2
  *DID/WITH* M20 .............. 110 E2
  *STRET* M32 .............. 85 K8
  *SWIN* M27 .............. 71 G2
  *TRPK* M17 .............. 85 M8
South Rw *PWCH* M25 .............. 71 J3
South Royd St *TOT/BURYW* BL8 .............. 24 C5
Southsea St *OP/CLY* M11 .............. 89 G5
Southside *MPL/ROM* SK6 .............. 101 H6
  *WILM/AE* SK9 * .............. 118 D8
South St *ATH* M46 .............. 67 H1
  *AULW* OL7 .............. 90 B4
  *BOLS/LL* BL3 .............. 52 B1
  *MILN* OL16 .............. 11 G3
  *OLDS* OL8 .............. 74 E2
  *OP/CLY* M11 .............. 88 F5
  *RAMS* BL0 .............. 19 G6
  *WGTN/LGST* M12 .............. 88 B7
South Ter *BURY* BL9 .............. 39 G5
South Terrace Ct *MILN* OL16 .............. 11 H9
South Vale Crs
  *HALE/TIMP* WA15 .............. 108 C7
South Vw *ATH* M46 .............. 66 F1
  *MPL/ROM* SK6 .............. 101 M6
  *RDSH* SK5 .............. 100 C1
  *ROCH* OL11 .............. 27 H6
  *STLY* SK15 .............. 77 J8
South View Gdns
  *CHD/CHDH* SK8 .............. 119 L1
Southview Rd *GLSP* SK13 .............. 105 J5
South Vw Rd *MILN* OL16 .............. 29 H1
South View Rd *BOLE* BL2 .............. 3 M5
South View Ter *MILN* OL16 .............. 21 J8
Southview Wk *OLDE* OL4 .............. 60 B3
Southward Rd *RNFD/HAY* WA11 .............. 78 D5
Southwark Dr *DUK* SK16 .............. 91 G6
Southway *ALT* WA14 .............. 108 B6
  *AULW* OL7 .............. 75 K6
  *DROY* M43 .............. 89 K4
  *NEWH/MOS* M40 .............. 73 H3
South Wy *OLDS* OL8 .............. 75 H2
Southwell Cl *BOL* BL1 .............. 2 C9
  *GOL/RIS/CUL* WA3 .............. 79 M4
Southwell Ct *STRET* M32 .............. 96 F3
Southwell Gdns *AUL* OL6 .............. 75 M8
Southwell St *BKLY* M9 .............. 73 H5
Southwood *ROCH* OL11 * .............. 27 K1
Southwood Cl *BOLS/LL* BL3 .............. 52 C1
Southwood Dr *BKLY* M9 .............. 56 D7
South Woodley Gdns *RAD* M26 .............. 54 F4

Southwood Rd *OFTN* SK2 .............. 112 E8
Southworth Rd *NEWLW* WA12 .............. 79 B4
Southyard St *BNG/LEV* M19 * .............. 99 L4
Sovereign Cl
  *GOL/RIS/CUL* WA3 .............. 80 B5
Sovereign Fold Rd *LEIGH* WN7 .............. 66 B4
Sovereign Rd *WGN* WN1 .............. 15 H6
Sovereign St *SLFD* M6 .............. 71 K8
Sowerby Cl *TOT/BURYW* BL8 .............. 38 C2
Spa Cl *RDSH* SK5 .............. 100 B4
Spa Crs *LHULT* M38 .............. 52 D6
Spa Gv *LHULT* M38 .............. 52 D6
Spa La *LHULT* M38 .............. 52 D6
  *OLDE* OL4 .............. 60 A7
Spalding Dr *NTHM/RTH* M23 .............. 118 C2
Sparkford Av *NTHM/RTH* M23 .............. 109 G3
Sparkle St *CMANE* M1 .............. 7 K5
Spark Rd *NTHM/RTH* M23 .............. 109 J5
Spa Rd *ATH* M46 .............. 50 F7
  *BOL* BL1 .............. 2 B6
Sparrow Cl *RDSH* SK5 .............. 100 B2
Sparrowfield Cl *STLY* SK15 .............. 77 H5
Sparrow Hl *MILN* OL16 .............. 10 D5
Sparrow St *ROY/SHW* OL2 .............. 59 H2
Sparta Av *WALK* M28 .............. 68 F2
Sparta Wk *OP/CLY* M11 .............. 88 D4
Sparthbottoms Rd *ROCH* OL11 .............. 10 B6
Sparthfield Av *ROCH* OL11 .............. 10 C9
Sparthfield Rd *HTNM* SK4 .............. 12 E1
Sparth La *HTNM* SK4 .............. 12 E1
Sparth Rd *NEWH/MOS* M40 .............. 74 A7
Spa St *HULME* M15 .............. 87 L2
Spath Av *WILM/AE* SK9 .............. 119 M7
Spath La East *CHD/CHDH* SK8 .............. 120 D7
Spath Rd *DID/WITH* M20 .............. 110 D1
Spath Wk *CHD/CHDH* SK8 .............. 120 D7
Spawell Cl *GOL/RIS/CUL* WA3 .............. 80 B3
Spaw St *CSLFD* M3 .............. 6 C3
Speakman Av *LEIGH* WN7 .............. 66 E3
  *NEWLW* WA12 .............. 78 F7
Spear St *CMANE* M1 .............. 7 J4
Spectator St *ANC* M4 .............. 88 A2
Speedwell Cl *GLSP* SK13 .............. 93 J5
  *GOL/RIS/CUL* WA3 .............. 80 B4
Spencer Av *BOLS/LL* BL3 .............. 53 M1
  *HYDE* SK14 .............. 91 G7
  *OLDTF/WHR* M16 .............. 97 M2
  *WHTF* M45 .............. 55 H2
Spencer La *ROCH* OL11 .............. 27 H7
Spencer Rd *WGN* WN1 .............. 47 L1
Spencer Rd West
  *WCNNW/ST* WN6 .............. 47 K1
Spencer's La
  *WCNW/BIL/OR* WN5 .............. 46 A5
Spencer St *CHAD* OL9 .............. 58 E8
  *DUK* SK16 .............. 90 F4
  *ECC* M30 .............. 84 F3
  *MOSL* OL5 .............. 76 E3
  *OLD* OL1 .............. 9 M3
  *RAMS* BL0 .............. 18 E7
  *RDSH* SK5 .............. 100 C4
  *TOT/BURYW* BL8 .............. 4 B6
Spender Av *CHH* M8 .............. 72 D6
Spen Fold *LIT* OL15 .............. 21 L8
  *TOT/BURYW* BL8 .............. 38 D4
Spenleach La *TOT/BURYW* BL8 .............. 17 M8
Spenlow *LEIGH* WN7 .............. 81 M1
Spenlow Cl *POY/DIS* SK12 .............. 129 J3
Spennithorne Rd *URM* M41 .............. 95 L2
Spenser Av *DTN/ASHW* M34 .............. 101 K4
  *RAD* M26 .............. 38 B8
Spenwood Rd *LIT* OL15 .............. 21 K7
Spey Cl *ALT* WA14 .............. 107 M6
Spey Gv *UPML* OL3 .............. 61 L2
  *WGN* WN1 .............. 15 J5
  *WHTF* M45 .............. 55 H2
Speyside Cl *WHTF* M45 * .............. 55 K4
Speyside Sq *WCNS/IIMK* WN3 .............. 63 K2
Spindle Av *STLY* SK15 .............. 91 M1
Spindle Cft *FWTH* BL4 .............. 53 G6
Spindle Hillock *AIMK* WN4 .............. 63 C8
Spindlepoint Dr *WALK* M28 .............. 68 F4
The Spindles *MOSL* OL5 .............. 77 G4
Spindle Wk *WHTN* BL5 .............. 50 C5
Spindlewood Cl *STLY* SK15 .............. 92 K2
Spindlewood Rd
  *WCNS/IIMK* WN3 .............. 15 L8
Spingfield Cl *BOLS/LL* BL3 .............. 36 D8
Spiningdale *LHULT* M38 .............. 52 A6
Spinks St *OLDE* OL4 .............. 59 L7
Spinnerbottom *NM/HAY* SK22 .............. 125 H2
Spinnerette Cl *LEIGH* WN7 .............. 66 D7
Spinners Gdns *WHIT* OL12 .............. 21 G8
Spinners Gn *WHIT* OL12 .............. 28 C2
Spinners La *POY/DIS* SK12 .............. 121 L8
Spinners Ms *BOL* BL1 .............. 2 D2
Spinners Wy *OLDE* OL4 .............. 44 C8
Spinney Cl *GLSP* SK13 .............. 104 F2
  *SALE* M33 .............. 108 A1
Spinney Dr *BURY* BL9 .............. 25 J6
Spinney Gv *DTN/ASHW* M34 .............. 90 C7
Spinney Nook *BOLE* BL2 .............. 37 G2
Spinney Rd *NTHM/RTH* M23 .............. 109 L5
The Spinney *CHD/CHDH* SK8 .............. 120 A1
  *EDGW/EG* BL7 .............. 22 F2
  *OLDE* OL4 .............. 60 D4
  *URM* M41 * .............. 95 K2
  *WALK* M28 * .............. 69 M6
  *WCNW/BIL/OR* WN5 .............. 47 H7
  *WGN* WN1 .............. 14 A1
  *WHTF* M45 .............. 54 F5
Spinningfields *BOL* BL1 * .............. 2 A2
Spinningfield Wy *HEY* OL10 .............. 41 G5
Spinning Jenny Wk *ANC* M4 * .............. 7 M3
Spinning Jenny Wy *LEIGH* WN7 .............. 66 D8
Spinning Meadow *BOL* BL1 .............. 2 B2
Spinning Mdw *BOL* BL1 * .............. 2 B2
The Spinnings *BURY* BL9 * .............. 24 F1
Spion Kop *AIMK* WN4 .............. 78 E1
Spiredale Brow
  *WCNNW/ST* WN6 .............. 31 J3
Spire Hollin *GLSP* SK13 .............. 104 F1
Spires Cft *LEIGH* WN7 .............. 66 E7
Spire Wk *WGTN/LGST* M12 * .............. 88 A7
Spirewood Gdns
  *MPL/ROM* SK6 .............. 113 G2
Spodden Fold *WHIT* OL12 .............. 20 A4
Spodden St *WHIT* OL12 .............. 10 B7
Spod Rd *WHIT* OL12 .............. 27 M3
Spokeshave Wy *MILN* OL16 .............. 28 F2
Sportside Av *WALK* M28 .............. 69 G1
Sportside Cl *WALK* M28 .............. 69 H1
Sportside Gv *WALK* M28 .............. 53 G8
Sportsmans Dr *OLDS* OL8 .............. 75 K1
Sportsman St *LEIGH* WN7 .............. 66 A7
Spotland Rd *WHIT* OL12 .............. 10 B2
Spotland Tops *WHIT* OL12 .............. 27 L3
Spreadbury St *NEWH/MOS* M40 .............. 73 K6
Spring Av *HYDE* SK14 .............. 102 C4
  *WHTF* M45 .............. 55 H2
Springbank *CHAD* OL9 .............. 58 D5
  *GLSP* SK13 .............. 93 J7

Spring Bank *GLSP* SK13 * .............. 104 E4
  *STLY* SK15 .............. 91 L4
Spring Bank Av *AUL* OL6 .............. 75 L7
  *DTN/ASHW* M34 .............. 90 A3
Springbank Cl *MPL/ROM* SK6 .............. 101 M3
Springbank Gdns
  *NM/HAY* SK22 .............. 124 D4
Spring Bank La *ROCH* OL11 .............. 27 H4
  *STLY* SK15 .............. 76 F7
Springbank Pl *STKP* SK1 * .............. 13 H6
Springbank Rd *MPL/ROM* SK6 .............. 101 M3
Spring Bank Rd *NM/HAY* SK22 .............. 124 E4
Spring Bank St *OLDS* OL8 .............. 58 F8
Springbourne *WCNNW/ST* WN6 .............. 47 J2
Spring Bridge Rd
  *OLDTF/WHR* M16 .............. 98 C2
Springburn Cl *MOR/BR* BL6 .............. 34 A3
  *WALK* M28 .............. 68 D6
Spring Cl *AULW* OL7 .............. 75 K6
  *OLDE* OL4 .............. 60 A7
  *RAMS* BL0 .............. 18 E6
  *TOT/BURYW* BL8 .............. 24 B6
Spring Clough *WALK* M28 .............. 69 L7
Spring Clough Av *WALK* M28 .............. 69 L7
Spring Clough Dr *OLDS* OL8 .............. 59 M8
  *WALK* M28 .............. 69 L7
Springdale Gdns
  *DID/WITH* M20 .............. 110 D1
Springfield *GLSP* SK13 .............. 103 M6
  *RAD* M26 .............. 53 M6
  *URM* M41 .............. 95 M2
Springfield Av *BRAM/HZG* SK7 .............. 121 M1
  *CHH* M8 .............. 72 A4
  *GOL/RIS/CUL* WA3 .............. 79 J4
  *HTNM* SK4 .............. 100 B3
  *LIT* OL15 .............. 21 L5
  *MPL/ROM* SK6 .............. 114 C8
Springfield Cl *FAIL* M35 .............. 74 B4
  *GLSP* SK13 .............. 93 H8
Springfield Dr *WILM/AE* SK9 .............. 126 B7
Springfield Gdns *FWTH* BL4 .............. 53 K6
Springfield La *CSLFD* M3 .............. 6 D1
  *IRL* M44 .............. 94 C2
  *MILN* OL16 .............. 29 C1
  *ROY/SHW* OL2 .............. 42 F5
Springfield Rd *ALT* WA14 .............. 108 A3
  *ATH* M46 .............. 51 H8
  *BOL* BL1 .............. 2 A1
  *CHD/CHDH* SK8 .............. 110 E7
  *DROY* M43 .............. 89 J1
  *FWTH* BL4 .............. 53 J6
  *HOR/BR* BL6 .............. 34 A4
  *MDTN* M24 .............. 57 J2
  *RAMS* BL0 .............. 24 D2
  *SALE* M33 .............. 96 E8
  *WCNE/HIN* WN2 .............. 48 E6
  *WCNNW/ST* WN6 .............. 47 J2
Springfield St *AUL* OL6 .............. 76 B7
  *DTN/ASHW* M34 .............. 90 C6
  *HEY* OL10 .............. 40 D2
  *WGN* WN1 .............. 47 M1
Springfield Ter *NM/HAY* SK22 * .............. 125 H2
Spring Gdns *BOLE* BL2 .............. 23 J8
  *BRAM/HZG* SK7 .............. 121 M1
  *CMANW* M2 .............. 7 G4
  *GLSP* SK13 .............. 93 J7
  *HALE/TIMP* WA15 .............. 108 F7
  *HYDE* SK14 .............. 91 G8
  *MDTN* M24 .............. 57 K2
  *SLFD* M6 .............. 86 C1
  *STKP* SK1 .............. 13 M5
  *WGN* WN1 .............. 14 E4
Spring Garden St *ROY/SHW* OL2 .............. 43 G8
Spring Gv *UPML* OL3 .............. 61 L7
  *WGN* WN1 .............. 15 J5
  *WHTF* M45 .............. 55 H2
Spring Hall Ri *OLDE* OL4 .............. 44 C8
Springhead Av *DID/WITH* M20 .............. 98 D5
  *OLDE* OL4 .............. 60 C7
Springhill *ROY/SHW* OL2 .............. 43 G8
Spring La *OLDE* OL4 .............. 60 B7
  *RAD* M26 .............. 54 F4
Springlawn *BOL* BL1 .............. 35 J4
Springlawns *BOL* BL1 * .............. 35 J4
Spring Meadow *GLSP* SK13 .............. 104 A5
Spring Meadow La *UPML* OL3 .............. 61 M4
Spring Mill Wk *MILN* OL16 .............. 28 F2
Springmount *GOL/RIS/CUL* WA3 .............. 80 B5
Spring Mt *NM/HAY* SK22 .............. 124 C4
Spring Pl *WHIT* OL12 .............. 20 B2
Springpool *WCNS/IIMK* WN3 .............. 62 E2
Spring Ri *GLSP* SK13 .............. 104 D5
  *ROY/SHW* OL2 .............. 43 G3
Spring Rd *ALT* WA14 .............. 116 F2
  *POY/DIS* SK12 .............. 129 K2
  *WCNW/BIL/OR* WN5 .............. 46 B8
Springside *WALK* M28 .............. 69 H1
Springside Av *WALK* M28 .............. 69 H1
Springside Cl *WALK* M28 .............. 69 H1
Springside Gv *WALK* M28 .............. 69 H1
Springside Rd *BURY* BL9 .............. 25 H4
Springside Vw *TOT/BURYW* BL8 .............. 24 F5
Springside Wk *HULME* M15 * .............. 87 G6
Springs La *STLY* SK15 .............. 76 C8
Springs Rd *MDTN* M24 .............. 58 B6
The Springs *ALT* WA14 .............. 116 D3
  *ROCH* OL11 .............. 27 H5
Spring St *BOLS/LL* BL3 .............. 2 E9
  *BURY* BL9 .............. 5 G6
  *FWTH* BL4 .............. 53 G3
  *GLSP* SK13 .............. 104 E4
  *HYDE* SK14 .............. 92 F7
  *MOSL* OL5 .............. 76 F2
  *OLDE* OL4 .............. 59 M4
  *RAMS* BL0 .............. 18 E6
  *STLY* SK15 .............. 91 K2
  *TOT/BURYW* BL8 .............. 24 B5
  *TOT/BURYW* BL8 .............. 38 D2
  *UPML* OL3 * .............. 61 L4
  *WGN* WN1 .............. 15 J5
  *WCNS/IIMK* WN3 .............. 48 B8
  *WGTN/LGST* M12 .............. 99 K2
  *WILM/AE* SK9 .............. 126 E5
Spring Ter *CHAD* OL9 .............. 58 D5
  *MILN* OL16 .............. 43 L1
Spring Thyme Fold *LIT* OL15 .............. 21 L7
Spring V *BRAM/HZG* SK7 * .............. 122 A2
  *MDTN* M24 .............. 57 K4
  *PWCH* M25 .............. 71 K2
Springvale *AULW* OL7 .............. 75 K6
Spring Vale Dr *TOT/BURYW* BL8 .............. 24 B6
Spring Vale Rd *NM/HAY* SK22 .............. 125 M2
Spring Vale St *TOT/BURYW* BL8 .............. 24 C6
Spring Vw *BURY* BL9 .............. 5 K1
Spring Vw Rd *ROY/SHW* OL2 .............. 43 K7
Springville Av *BKLY* M9 .............. 73 J3
Springwater Av *RAMS* BL0 .............. 24 D1
Spring Water Dr *GLSP* SK13 .............. 104 B1
Springwater La *WHTF* M45 .............. 55 H1

Springwell Cl SLFD M6 * ...........86 B2
Springwell Gdns HYDE SK14......103 H5
Springwood GLSP SK13.............104 C4
  UPML OL3.........................45 H7
Springwood Av CHAD OL9...........58 B4
  SWIN M27.........................70 E6
Springwood Crs
  MPL/ROM SK6....................114 B2
Springwood Hall Rd OLDS OL8....75 K2
Springwood La MPL/ROM SK6....114 C2
Spring Wood St RAMS BL0.........18 E5
Spruce Av BURY BL9................5 L4
Spruce Cl GOL/RIS/CUL WA3......80 C5
Spruce Crs BURY BL9..............25 J5
Spruce Rd WGNNW/ST WN6........47 H1
Spruce St HULME M15.............87 H6
  MILN OL16.........................11 H5
  RAMS BL0..........................18 D8
Sprucewood CHAD OL9.............58 A4
Spurn La UPML OL3................61 L1
The Spur OLDS OL8................75 H4
Square St RAMS BL0...............18 F6
The Square DUK SK16 *...........91 J5
  HALE/TIMP WA15.................117 L4
  HTNM SK4..........................12 C1
  SWIN M27.........................70 B7
  UPML OL3.........................61 K2
  WHIT M45.........................55 H4
Squire Rd CHH M8.................72 C5
Squires La TYLD M29..............67 M4
Squirrel Dr ALT WA14...........107 H4
Squirrel's Jump WILM/AE SK9...130 E3
Stableford MOSL OL5..............76 F4
Stable Fold RAD M26..............38 D8
Stablefold Walk RAD M26.........69 K7
Stableford Av ECC M30...........69 M8
The Stables DROY M43............90 A1
  WHIT OL12.........................20 A3
Stable St CHAD OL9...............74 D2
The Stablings WILM/AE SK9.....126 E7
Stadium Wy WGNW/BIL/OR WN6...14 B4
  WGNW/BIL/OR WN5...............47 H3
Stafford Cl GLSP SK13..........105 J4
Stafford Rd ECC M30.............85 J4
  FAIL M35..........................74 D7
  SWIN M27.........................70 C4
  WALK M28.........................68 F3
Stafford St CHAD OL9............58 F8
  LEIGH WN7.........................67 G8
  NM/HAY SK22.....................124 E3
  TOT/BURYW BL8...................25 G8
  WGNE/HIN WN2....................48 F7
Stag Pasture Rd OLDS OL8........75 G3
Stainburn Rd WGNNW/ST WN6...30 A6
Stainburne Rd OFTN SK2.........112 F6
Stainburn Rd OP/CLY M11.........88 C4
Staindale OLDE OL4...............60 A6
Stainer Cl NEWLW WA12...........78 E7
Stainer St WGTN/LGST M12........99 K1
Stainforth Cl GOL/RIS/CUL WA3..81 G8
  TOT/BURYW BL8...................38 C1
Stainmoor Cl OP/CLY M11.........88 C4
Stainmore Av OFTN SK2..........113 G6
Stainmore Av AUL OL6............75 M5
Stainton Av GTN M18.............89 H8
Stainton Cl RAD M26.............38 C8
Stainton Dr MDTN M24............57 C1
Stainton Rd RAD M26.............38 B7
Staithes Rd WYTH/NTH M22......118 F4
Stakeford Dr CHH M8.............72 F4
Stakehill La MDTN M24...........42 B7
Staley Cl STLY SK15.............91 M2
Staley Hall Crs STLY SK15.......91 M1
Staley Hall Rd STLY SK15........91 M2
Staley St OLDE OL4..............59 M6
  OLDE OL4.........................60 C6
Stalham Cl NEWH/MOS M40.......88 B1
Stalmine Av CHD/CHDH SK8.....119 K4
Stalybridge Rd HYDE SK14.......92 D8
Stalyhill Dr STLY SK15..........92 B5
Stamford Av ALT WA14..........107 K6
  STLY SK15.........................91 H2
Stamford Cl STLY SK15...........91 H2
Stamford Dr FAIL M35............74 E7
  STLY SK15.........................91 H2
Stamford Gv STLY SK15...........91 J2
Stamford New Rd ALT WA14....108 A8
Stamford Park Rd
  HALE/TIMP WA15.................117 H1
Stamford Pl SALE M33............96 F8
Stamford Rd ALT WA14..........116 E2
  BRO M7............................71 L6
  BRUN/LGST M13..................99 J1
  DTN/ASHW M34...................90 A5
  MOSL OL5.........................76 F2
  OLDE OL4.........................60 C4
  PART M31.........................95 G5
  URM M41..........................95 L2
  WILM/AE SK9....................126 E3
  WILM/AE SK9....................130 D3
Stamford Sq AUL OL6.............91 G2
Stamford St ALT WA14..........108 A7
  ATH M46...........................51 H8
  HEY OL10..........................41 H3
  MILN OL16.........................11 J6
  MOSL OL5.........................76 L3
  OLDE OL4.........................60 B6
  OLDTF/WHR M16.................87 G8
  SALE M33..........................96 D6
  STLY SK15.........................77 G8
  STLY SK15.........................91 K2
  SWIN M27.........................70 D3
Stamford St Central AUL OL6....90 F1
Stamford St East AUL OL6........90 F2
Stamford St West AUL OL6.......90 E2
Stamford Wy ALT WA14..........108 A7
Stampstone St OLD OL1...........59 L5
Stanage Av BKLY M9..............57 J8
Stanbank St HTNM SK4...........100 B3
Stanbourne Dr BOL BL1...........22 C8
Stanbrook St BNG/LEV M19........99 M4
Stanbury Cl BURY BL9 *..........40 A3
Stanbury Dr DUK SK16............91 G4
Stanbury Wk
  NEWH/MOS M40 *................88 A1
Stancliffe Gv WYTHN/NTH WN2..32 F6
Stancliffe Rd WYTH/NTH M23...110 B8
Stancross Rd NTHM/RTH M23....108 F4
Stand Av WHTF M45...............55 H4
Stand Cl WHTF M45...............54 F4
Standedge Rd UPML OL3..........45 M7
Standfield Wk WALK M28.........68 D6
Standish Av
  WGNNW/BIL/OR WN5...........62 B7
Standish Gallery WGN WN1 *.....15 G3
Standishgate WGN................15 G3
Standish Rd RUSH/FAL M14.......99 G4
Standish St TYLD M29............67 K4
Standish Wood La
  WGNNW/ST WN6..................31 H5
Stand La RAD M26................54 E2

Standmoor Ct WHTF M45 *........55 G5
Standmoor Rd WHTF M45..........55 G5
Standrick Hill Ri STLY SK15....77 H5
Stand Ri RAD M26................54 E4
Standring La RAMS BL0...........18 F8
Stanford Cl RAD M26 *...........53 H5
Stanford Hall Crs RAMS BL0.....18 E4
Stanhope Av DTN/ASHW M34.....90 B7
  PWCH M25.........................55 K6
Stanhope Ct DTN/ASHW M34......90 B7
  WILM/AE SK9....................127 H4
Stanhope Ct PWCH M25...........55 K6
Stanhope Rd ALT WA14..........116 C2
  SLFD M6...........................71 H7
Stanhope St AUL OL6 *...........76 A8
  BNG/LEV M19.....................99 L3
  DTN/ASHW M34...................90 B7
  LEIGH WN7.........................66 A6
  MOSL OL5.........................76 F4
  RDSH SK5........................100 B3
  ROCH OL11.........................10 F9
Stanhope Wy FAIL M35............74 B4
Stanhorne Av CHH M8.............72 D2
Stanier Av ECC M30..............85 G1
Stanier Pl HOR/BR BL6...........33 K2
Stanier St BKLY M9..............73 H1
Stanion Gv DUK SK16.............90 F4
Stan Jolly Wk OP/CLY M11........88 F4
Stanley Av BRAM/HZG SK7.......121 M3
  HYDE SK14.........................91 H8
  MPL/ROM SK6....................114 A5
  RUSH/FAL M14...................98 F1
Stanley Av North PWCH M25......55 K6
Stanley Av South PWCH M25......55 K6
  WHTN BL5.........................50 D5
Stanley Ct BURY BL9.............5 L4
  OLDTF/WHR M16.................86 F7
Stanley Dr CHD/CHDH SK8......119 M6
  HALE/TIMP WA15.................108 D7
  LEIGH WN7.........................66 A4
  WHTF M45.........................55 J3
Stanley Gv GTN M18.............88 E8
  HOR/BR BL6......................34 A3
  HTNM SK4..........................99 L8
  URM M41..........................96 A2
  WGTN/LGST M12.................88 D8
Stanley Hall La POY/DIS SK12..123 J5
Stanley La WGNE/HIN WN2.......32 F5
Stanley Ms BOLE BL2.............37 G5
Stanley Mt BOLE BL2............108 D1
Stanley Park Wk BOLE BL2 *.....3 M4
Stanley Pl WGN WN1..............15 K3
  WHIT OL12.........................10 D2
Stanley Rd BOL BL1..............35 L3
  BRO M7............................72 B4
  CHAD OL9.........................74 F1
  CHD/CHDH SK8.................119 M6
  DTN/ASHW M34..................100 E1
  ECC M30...........................84 F3
  FWTH BL4.........................52 B4
  HTNM SK4..........................99 L8
  OLDTF/WHR M16.................86 F7
  OLDTF/WHR M16.................98 E2
  RAD M26...........................38 B6
  SWIN M27.........................70 D4
  WALK M28.........................69 C2
  WGNE/HIN WN2...................32 F6
  WGNE/HIN WN2...................64 D1
  WHTF M45.........................55 J3
Stanley St ATH M46..............66 F2
  BKLY M9............................73 H4
  CHAD OL9..........................8 B4
  CHH M8............................72 D3
  CSLFD M3..........................6 C4
  HEY OL10..........................41 G3
  NEWH/MOS M40...................73 J7
  OLDE OL4.........................60 B7
  OP/CLY M11......................89 H5
  PWCH M25.........................55 M8
  RAMS BL0..........................18 E7
  STKP SK1..........................13 L3
  STLY SK15.........................91 J3
  WGNE/HIN WN2...................14 A7
  WHIT OL12.........................10 D1
  WHTF M45.........................55 J3
Stanley St South BOLS/LL BL3...2 C6
Stanmere Ct TOT/BURYW BL8....23 L1
Stanmoor Dr WGNE/HIN WN2.....32 F7
Stanmore Av STRET M32..........96 E2
Stanmore Dr BOLS/LL BL3.........35 M7
Stannard Rd ECC M30.............84 C3
Stannybrook Cl MILN OL16.......11 K3
Stanney Cl MILN OL16............29 H7
Stanneylands Cl WILM/AE SK9..127 G2
Stanneylands Dr WILM/AE SK9..126 F2
Stanneylands Rd
  WILM/AE SK9....................119 K8
Stannybrook Rd FAIL M35........75 G8
Stanrose Cl EDGW/EG BL7........22 B3
Stansbury Pl OFTN SK2..........113 H1
Stansby Gdns WGTN/LGST M12...88 B6
Stansfield Cl BOLE BL2..........3 M4
  LEIGH WN7.........................81 M2
Stansfield Dr ROCH OL11.........27 H3
Stansfield Rd BOLE BL2..........3 J3
  FAIL M35..........................74 D3
  HYDE SK14.........................91 H8
Stansfield St CHAD OL9..........8 B8
  NEWH/MOS M40...................74 A8
  OLDE OL4.........................60 C4
  OP/CLY M11......................89 G4
Stanstead Cl WGNE/HIN WN2.....48 C2
Stanthorne Av DID/WITH M20....98 D5
Stanton Av BRO M7..............71 L6
  DID/WITH M20...................98 B8
Stanton Gdns WGNS/IIMK WN3...63 L1
Stanton Gdns HTNM SK4..........12 B4
Stanton St CHAD OL9.............74 E1
  OP/CLY M11......................88 F2
  STRET M32.........................86 A8
Stanway Av BOLS/LL BL3 *.......2 C6
Stanway Cl BOLS/LL BL3 *........2 B7
  MDTN M24..........................57 L6
Stanway Dr HALE/TIMP WA15...117 H1
Stanway Rd WHTF M45............55 J3
Stanway St BKLY M9.............73 H4
  STRET M32.........................97 G1
Stanwell Rd NEWH/MOS M40.....73 M5
  SWIN M27.........................70 A8
Stanworth Av BKLY M9...........56 D8
Stanworth Cl BOLE BL2..........37 H5
Stanyard Ct ORD M5.............86 D4
Stanycliffe La MDTN M24........57 L1
Stanyforth St GLSP SK13........93 K8
Stapleford Cl NTHM/RTH M23...109 H4
  SALE M33..........................97 H7
  TOT/BURYW BL8...................38 D2
  WHTN BL5.........................51 K6

Staplehurst Cl LEIGH WN7.......65 M2
Staplehurst Rd
  NEWH/MOS M40...................73 K8
Stapleton Av BOL BL1...........35 H4
Stapleton St SLFD M6............70 F7
  SWIN M27.........................70 D2
Starbeck Cl TOT/BURYW BL8.....38 C2
Starcliffe St BOLS/LL BL3.......53 G2
Starfield Av LIT OL15...........29 J2
Star Gv BRO M7.................72 B6
Starkey St HEY OL10............41 G1
Starkie Rd BOLE BL2.............8 K4
The Starkies BURY BL9 *........39 H5
Starkie St WALK M28............69 K4
Star La HOR/BR BL6.............33 J1
Starling Av RAD M26............90 A1
  WYTH/NTH M22...................110 B6
Starling Dr FWTH BL4............52 C5
Starmoor Dr RAD M26............38 B4
Starmount Cl BOLE BL2..........37 K6
Starring La LIT OL15............21 K7
Starring Rd LIT OL15............21 J7
Starring Wy LIT OL15............21 K7
Stash Gv NTHM/RTH M23.........109 L5
Statford Av ECC M30.............84 F4
Statham Cl DTN/ASHW M34......101 K1
Statham Fold HYDE SK14........101 K1
Statham St SLFD M6.............86 E2
Station Ap CMANE M1.............7 G7
  CMANE M1..........................7 J5
  UPML OL3.........................61 J1
Station Av WGNE/HIN WN2........65 G3
  WGNW/BIL/OR WN5...............46 A7
Station Cl HYDE SK14...........101 H3
Station Cottages TYLD M29 *....82 F5
Stationers Entry MILN OL16.....10 E4
Station La OLDE OL4.............60 E7
Station Ms OLDE OL4.............78 A1
Station Rd ALT WA14...........106 E7
  CHD/CHDH SK8...................120 D3
  CHF/WBR SK23...................124 F8
  CHH M8............................72 D3
  DID/WITH M20...................98 C4
  EDGW/EG BL7......................22 E4
  FWTH BL4.........................52 B3
  GLSP SK13.........................93 K7
  HOR/BR BL6......................33 H3
  HTNM SK4.........................111 H3
  HYDE SK14........................102 E2
  IRL M44............................94 B5
  LIT OL15...........................21 M7
  MILN OL16.........................29 J7
  MOSL OL5.........................77 G3
  MPL/ROM SK6....................101 L7
  MPL/ROM SK6....................123 L3
  NM/HAY SK22.....................125 G2
  OLDE OL4.........................60 D7
  RDSH SK5........................100 B2
  STRET M32.........................97 G1
  TOT/BURYW BL8...................70 C3
  UPML OL3.........................61 L4
  URM M41..........................96 A3
  WHIT OL12.........................20 B1
  WILM/AE SK9....................126 E5
  WILM/AE SK9....................126 F5
Station St AUL OL6..............90 E5
  BOLS/LL BL3.......................2 F7
  BRAM/HZG SK7...................121 M2
  OLDE OL4.........................60 C6
Station to Station Wk LIT OL15..29 L1
Station Vw BNG/LEV M19.........99 K3
Station Yd NM/HAY SK22........124 D6
Staton Av BOLE BL2.............3 M2
Staton St OP/CLY M11...........88 F4
Statter St BURY BL9.............39 K8
Staveleigh Ml AUL OL6 *.........90 E1
Staveley Av BOL BL1............22 B6
  STLY SK15.........................91 K1
Staveley Cl MDTN M24...........57 H3
  ROY/SHW OL2......................44 A6
Stavesacre LEIGH WN7...........81 J1
Staveton Dr BRAM/HZG SK7.....121 H1
Stavordale WHIT OL12...........10 D3
Staycott St OLDTF/WHR M16.....87 J8
Stayley Dr STLY SK15............77 G4
Stayley Rd MOSL OL5............77 G4
Stead St RAMS BL0..............18 F6
Steadway UPML OL3..............61 M7
Stedman Cl OP/CLY M11..........88 B3
Steele Gdns BOLE BL2...........37 G7
Steeles Av HYDE SK14..........102 B1
Steeple Cl CHH M8..............72 C7
Steeple Dr ORD M5.............86 D4
Steeple End Fold
  NM/HAY SK22....................125 M2
Steeple Vw ROY/SHW OL2.........43 G8
Stein Av GOL/RIS/CUL WA3......80 B4
Stelfox Av HALE/TIMP WA15....108 F5
  RUSH/FAL M14...................98 D3
Stelfox La DTN/ASHW M34 *.....90 C2
Stelfox St ECC M30.............84 E4
Stella St BKLY M9..............56 E8
Stelling St GTN M18............88 E8
Stenbury Cl RUSH/FAL M14.......98 F1
Stenner La DID/WITH M20.......110 D2
Stenner Cl TOT/BURYW BL8 *....38 D2
Stephens Av DROY M43...........89 K3
Stephenson Rd STRET M32........97 H3
Stephenson St FAIL M35.........74 D3
  HOR/BR BL6......................33 L2
  OLDE OL4.........................60 A4
  WGNE/HIN WN2...................64 E4
Stephens Rd DID/WITH M20.......98 D8
  STLY SK15.........................76 D8
Stephens St BOLE BL2...........37 H4
Stephen St South
  TOT/BURYW BL8...................38 F3
Stephen St WGNS/IIMK WN3.....47 J5
Stephen Wk STKP SK1 *.........112 E4
Steps Meadow WHIT OL12........27 L1
Steptoe Dr OLD OL1.............8 F1
Stern Av ORD M5................86 D4
Sterndale Rd EDGY/DAV SK3....112 D7
  MPL/ROM SK6....................113 L3
  WALK M28.........................68 C6
Sterratt St BOL BL1.............2 D4
Stetchworth Dr WALK M28.......68 E5
Steuber Dr IRL M44.............94 C7
Stevenson Dr OLD OL1...........44 B8

Stevenson Pl CMANE M1 *........7 J4
Stevenson Rd CMANE M27........70 B4
Stevenson Sq CMANE M1..........7 J4
  WHIT OL12.........................28 E1
Stevenson St ORD M5.............6 A4
  WALK M28.........................68 E1
Stevens St WILM/AE SK9........130 D3
Stewart Av FWTH BL4............52 E5
Stewart St WGNS/IIMK WN3.....63 J1
Stewart St AULW OL7............90 C2
  BOL BL1............................35 J6
  MILN OL16.........................43 L1
  TOT/BURYW BL8...................24 F8
Stewerton Cl GOL/RIS/CUL WA3.79 J2
Steynton Cl BOL BL1............35 J4
Stile Cl URM M41...............94 F2
Stiles Av MPL/ROM SK6.........114 B5
Stiles Cl GLSP SK13.............93 H7
Stillwater Dr OP/CLY M11........88 D2
Stilton Dr OP/CLY M11..........88 C2
Stirling Av BRAM/HZG SK7.....121 M3
  DID/WITH M20...................98 C4
  MPL/ROM SK6....................114 C2
  WGNE/HIN WN2...................48 D4
Stirling Cl EDGY/DAV SK3......111 M6
  LEIGH WN7.........................67 G7
  STLY SK15.........................91 K1
Stirling Gv WHTF M45...........55 H4
Stirling Rd BOL BL1............22 B7
  CHAD OL9.........................58 C8
  WGNE/HIN WN2...................49 J8
Stirling St CHAD OL9............8 A6
  WGN WN1..........................47 L2
Stirrup Brook Gv WALK M28.....68 C2
Stirrup Ga WALK M28............69 K7
Stitch La HTNM SK4.............12 F1
Stitch-Mi-Lane BOLE BL2........37 J2
Stiups La MILN OL16............28 F8
Stobart Av PWCH M25...........71 M2
Stockburn Dr FAIL M35..........74 E5
Stockdale Av EDGY/DAV SK3....112 C2
Stockdale Gv BOLE BL2..........37 J3
Stockdale Rd BKLY M9...........57 H8
Stockfield Mt CHAD OL9..........8 B6
Stockfield Rd CHAD OL9..........8 A5
Stock Gv MILN OL16.............29 J7
Stockholm Rd EDGY/DAV SK3....112 A6
Stockholm St OP/CLY M11........88 G4
Stockland Cl BRUN/LGST M13.....7 J9
Stock La CHAD OL9..............8 A5
Stockley Av BOLE BL2...........37 H2
Stockley Dr WGNNW/ST WN6.....30 B4
Stockley Wk HULME M15 *........87 G6
Stockport Rd AULW OL7..........90 C4
  BNG/LEV M19.....................99 K4
  BOLS/LL BL3 *....................13 G6
  CHD/CHDH SK8...................111 G6
  DTN/ASHW M34..................101 H5
  HALE/TIMP WA15.................108 C7
  HYDE SK14........................102 A5
  HYDE SK14........................103 H3
  MOSL OL5.........................76 F2
  MPL/ROM SK6....................113 L2
  MPL/ROM SK6....................113 M6
  OLDE OL4.........................60 D7
  WGTN/LGST M12.................88 B8
Stockport Rd East
  MPL/ROM SK6....................101 J8
Stockport Rd West
  MPL/ROM SK6....................112 F1
Stockport Village STKP SK1 *...13 H4
Stocks Brow GLSP SK13..........93 K5
Stocksfield Dr BKLY M9.........73 H1
  LHULT M38........................52 F7
Stocks Gdns STLY SK15..........91 M3
Stocksgate WHIT OL12...........27 L1
Stocks La STLY SK15............91 L3
Stocks Park Dr HOR/BR BL6.....34 B3
Stocks St CHH M8...............72 B2
Stocks St East CHH M8..........72 B2
The Stocks GLSP SK13...........93 K5
Stock St TOT/BURYW BL8........25 H7
Stockton Av EDGY/DAV SK3.....112 B7
Stockton Dr TOT/BURYW BL8.....24 D7
Stockton Pk OLDE OL4...........60 A6
Stockton Rd CCHDY M21.........97 H3
  FWTH BL4.........................52 C6
  WILM/AE SK9....................126 D2
Stockton St LIT OL15...........21 L7
  OLDTF/WHR M16.................87 H8
  SWIN M27.........................70 A6
Stockwell Cl WGNS/IIMK WN3....63 G1
Stoke Abbott Cl
  BRAM/HZG SK7...................121 G5
Stokesay Cl BURY BL9...........39 J7
  ROY/SHW OL2......................43 K8
Stokesay Dr BRAM/HZG SK7.....121 H1
Stokesay Rd SALE M33...........96 B7
The Stokes Ct
  GOL/RIS/CUL WA3...............80 A4
  GTN M18............................88 E7
Stokes St OP/CLY M11...........89 G3
Stoke St MILN OL16.............11 K7
Stokoe Av ALT WA14...........107 K6
Stonall Av HULME M15...........87 G6
Stoneacre HOR/BR BL6...........34 A5
Stoneacre Ct SWIN M27..........70 C5
Stoneacre Rd WYTH/NTH M22...118 E2
Stonebeck Rd NTHM/RTH M23....109 J7
Stone Breaks Rd OLDE OL4.......60 E5
Stonebridge Cl HOR/BR BL6.....34 A5
Stonechat Cl DROY M43 *........89 M1
  GOL/RIS/CUL WA3...............80 B4
  WALK M28.........................68 E4
Stone Cross La North
  GOL/RIS/CUL WA3...............79 M5
Stone Cross La South
  GOL/RIS/CUL WA3...............79 M6
Stonedelph Cl BOLE BL2.........38 A3
Stonefield TYLD M29............67 M3
Stonefield Dr CHH M8...........72 B7
Stonefield St MILN OL16........29 J7
Stonehaven BOLS/LL BL3.........51 J1
Stone Hvn WGNS/IIMK WN3.......63 G2
Stonehead St BKLY M9 *.........73 H5
Stonehewer St RAD M26.........54 C2
Stonehill Crs WHIT OL12........27 K1
Stonehill Dr WHIT OL12.........27 K1
Stone Hill La WHIT OL12........27 K1
Stonehill Rd FWTH BL4..........52 C5
Stonehouse EDGW/EG BL7........22 D4
Stonehouse Rd
  WGNNW/BIL/OR WN5...........47 G3
Stonehurst Cl WGTN/LGST M12..88 B7
Stonelands Wy OLDE OL4........60 E5

Stone Lea Wy ATH M46..........66 D2
Stoneleigh Av SALE M33........96 F8
Stoneleigh Dr RAD M26.........53 L5
Stoneleigh Rd OLDE OL4........60 D5
Stoneleigh St OLD OL1.........59 L3
Stonelow Cl HULME M15.........87 J6
Stone Md MPL/ROM SK6.........114 B1
Stone Mead Av
  HALE/TIMP WA15.................117 L5
Stonemead Cl BOLS/LL BL3......36 C5
Stonemead Dr BKLY M9..........57 G8
Stonepail Cl CHD/CHDH SK8....110 C7
Stonepail Cottages
  CHD/CHDH SK8...................110 C7
Stonepail Rd CHD/CHDH SK8...110 D7
Stone Pale WHTF M45...........55 J5
Stone Pit Cl GOL/RIS/CUL WA3..80 C5
Stone Pits RAMS BL0...........19 H1
Stone Pl RUSH/FAL M14.........98 F1
Stoneridge GLSP SK13..........93 J7
Stone Rw MPL/ROM SK6.........114 D6
Stonesby Cl OLDTF/WHR M16.....87 H8
Stonesdale Cl ROY/SHW OL2.....43 H7
Stonesteads Dr EDGW/EG BL7....22 D4
Stonesteads Wy EDGW/EG BL7....22 D4
Stone St BOLE BL2.............3 J1
  SLFD M6...........................77 G2
Stoneswood Dr UPML OL3........61 H4
Stoneswood Rd UPML OL3........61 H4
Stoney Bank RAD M26...........53 M5
Stoney Bridge La
  HALE/TIMP WA15.................108 D5
Stoneyfield STLY SK15.........76 D8
Stoneyfield Cl OLDTF/WHR M16..98 C2
Stoneygate Wk OP/CLY M11......89 G5
Stoneyhurst Cl HULME M15......87 J6
Stoneyland Dr NM/HAY SK22...124 D6
Stoney La UPML OL3............45 G5
  WILM/AE SK9....................126 D3
Stoneyroyd WHIT OL12 *........20 B2
Stoneyside Av WALK M28........53 H8
Stoneyside Gv WALK M28........69 H1
Stonie Heyes Av WHIT OL12.....28 E2
Stonyford St SALE M33.........97 G3
Stonyhurst Av BOL BL1.........22 B7
  WGNS/IIMK WN3..................15 J3
Stonyhurst Crs
  GOL/RIS/CUL WA3...............81 G7
Stopes Rd BOLS/LL BL3.........53 L1
Stopford Av LIT OL15..........21 J8
Stopford St EDGY/DAV SK3......12 F7
  OP/CLY M11......................89 H5
  WGNE/HIN WN2...................48 C5
Stopforth St WGNNW/ST WN6...14 B2
Stores Cottages OLDE OL4 *....61 M8
Stores St PWCH M25............55 M8
Store St AULW OL7.............75 K6
  CMANE M1..........................7 K6
  OFTN SK2........................112 F8
  OP/CLY M11 *....................88 E5
  RAD M26...........................39 G8
  ROCH OL11.........................27 H3
  ROY/SHW OL2......................43 H4
Storeton Cl WYTH/NTH M22.....119 G2
Stortford Dr NTHM/RTH M23....109 L2
Storth Bank GLSP SK13........104 C5
Storth Meadow Rd GLSP SK13...104 D5
Storwood Cl
  WGNW/BIL/OR WN5...............46 B3
Stothard Rd STRET M32.........96 E3
Stott Dr URM M41..............94 F3
Stottfield ROY/SHW OL2........58 E1
Stott La BOLE BL2.............36 E3
  MDTN M24..........................41 J7
  SLFD M6...........................85 L1
Stott Milne St CHAD OL9.......8 A8
Stott Rd CHAD OL9.............70 A6
  SWIN M27.........................70 A6
Stott's La NEWH/MOS M40.......74 A6
  MILN OL16.........................21 H8
  MILN OL16.........................29 J8
  WHIT OL12.........................20 C8
Stourbridge Av LHULT M38......52 D6
Stour Cl ALT WA14............107 H6
Stourport Cl MPL/ROM SK6....113 K3
Stourport St OLD OL1..........9 M1
Stour Rd TYLD M29.............67 M6
Stout St LEIGH WN7............65 M8
Stovell Av WGTN/LGST M12......99 K2
Stovell Rd NEWH/MOS M40.......73 K4
Stow Cl TOT/BURYW BL8.........25 G7
Stowe Gdns LEIGH WN7..........66 C7
Stowell Ct BOL BL1............2 B1
Stowell St BOL BL1............36 B3
  ORD M5.............................6 E8
Stowfield Cl BKLY M9..........56 E8
Stow Gdns DID/WITH M20........98 A4
Stracey St NEWH/MOS M40 *.....88 B1
Stradbroke Cl
  GOL/RIS/CUL WA3...............80 D5
  GTN M18............................88 E7
Strain Av BKLY M9.............57 G8
The Straits TYLD M29..........67 M6
Strand Av AIMK WN4............63 L8
Strand Ct STRET M32...........96 F4
The Strand AIMK WN4...........63 L8
  HOR/BR BL6......................34 A1
  ROCH OL11.........................42 C2
Strand Wy ROY/SHW OL2........59 G2
Strange Rd AIMK WN4...........78 A1
Strange St LEIGH WN7..........65 L8
Strangford St RAD M26.........38 B4
Strang St RAMS BL0............18 F6
Stranraer Rd
  WGNW/BIL/OR WN5...............46 F3
Stranton Dr WALK M28.........69 M4
Stratfield Av NTHM/RTH M23...109 J4
Stratford Av BOL BL1..........35 H4
  BURY BL9..........................25 H4
  DID/WITH M20...................98 B8
  OLDS OL8.........................75 H1
  ROCH OL11.........................10 C9
Stratford Cl FWTH BL4.........52 B5
Stratford Gdns MPL/ROM SK6...113 L2
Stratford Rd MDTN M24.........57 L7
Stratford St WGNNW/ST WN6....14 B1
Strathblane Cl DID/WITH M20...98 E5
Strathfield Dr OP/CLY M11.....88 C2
Strathmore Av STRET M32.......97 G1
  AIMK WN4.........................63 K7
  CCHDY M21........................97 L2
  DTN/ASHW M34..................101 L2
Strathmore Cl RAMS BL0........18 E5
Strathmore Rd BOLE BL2........37 H3
Stratton Rd OFTN SK2.........112 F4
  OLDTF/WHR M16.................70 C2
  SWIN M27.........................70 C2
Strawberry Bank SLFD M6 *.....86 E1
Strawberry Cl ALT WA14.......107 L5
Strawberry Hl SLFD M6.........86 E1

Strawberry Hill Rd *BOLE* BL2 .......... 3 J8
Strawberry La *MOSL* OL5 .......... 61 G8
   *WILM/AE* SK9 .......... 126 C6
Strawberry Rd *SLFD* M6 .......... 86 D1
Stray St *OP/CLY* M11 .......... 89 H4
The Stray *BOL* BL1 .......... 22 E8
Streamside Ct
   *HALE/TIMP* WA15 .......... 108 E8
Stream Ter *STKP* SK1 .......... 112 E3
Streetbridge *OLD* OL1 .......... 58 D2
Street Bridge Rd *OLD* OL1 .......... 58 D2
Street Elmfield *BOL* BL1 .......... 36 C2
Streetgate *LHULT* M38 .......... 52 D7
Streethouse La *UPML* OL3 .......... 61 J3
Street Kirklees *TOT/BURYW* BL8 .... 24 C5
Street La *MCFLDN* SK10 .......... 129 H4
   *RAD* M26 .......... 38 B4
Stretford Rd *HULME* M15 .......... 87 J6
   *OLDTF/WHR* M16 .......... 86 F7
   *URM* M41 .......... 96 A3
Stretton Rd *DID/WITH* M20 .......... 110 F1
   *GOL/RIS/CUL* WA3 * .......... 80 C4
   *SALE* M33 .......... 96 B8
   *STRET* M32 .......... 96 D1
Stretton Cl *NEWH/MOS* M40 .......... 73 C7
   *WGNW/BIL/OR* WN5 .......... 62 B7
Stretton Rd *BOLS/LL* BL3 .......... 35 L8
   *RAMS* BL0 .......... 24 D2
Striding Edge Wk *OLD* OL1 * .......... 9 L1
Strines Rd *WGNE/HIN* WN2 .......... 49 G6
Strines Rd *MPL/ROM* SK6 .......... 114 D7
Stringer Av *ECC* M30 .......... 84 E1
Stringer Cl *HYDE* SK14 .......... 103 J2
Stringer St *LEIGH* WN7 .......... 66 C7
   *STKP* SK1 .......... 13 M3
Stroma Gdns *URM* M41 .......... 84 F7
Strong St *BRO* M7 .......... 72 B8
Strongstry Rd *RAMS* BL0 .......... 18 F2
Stroud Av *ECC* M30 .......... 84 E1
Stroud Cl *MDTN* M24 .......... 57 K7
   *WGNE/HIN* WN2 .......... 48 C2
Stuart Av *IRL* M44 .......... 94 C2
   *MPL/ROM* SK6 .......... 113 M5
   *WGNE/HIN* WN2 .......... 65 L1
Stuart Cl *WGNE/HIN* WN2 .......... 64 C3
Stuart Crs *WGNW/BIL/OR* WN5 .......... 62 A7
Stuart Rd *ALT* WA14 .......... 107 L5
   *MPL/ROM* SK6 .......... 101 G6
   *STRET* M32 .......... 97 G1
Stuart St *MDTN* M24 .......... 57 M4
   *MILN* OL16 .......... 11 J7
   *OLDS* OL8 .......... 9 G9
   *OP/CLY* M11 .......... 88 D2
Stuart St East *OP/CLY* M11 .......... 88 D2
Stuart Wk *MDTN* M24 .......... 57 J5
Stubbins Cl *NTHM/RTH* M23 .......... 109 H3
Stubbins La *RAMS* BL0 .......... 18 F4
Stubbins Rd *RAMS* BL0 .......... 18 F3
Stubbins Vale Rd *RAMS* BL0 .......... 18 F3
Stubbs Cl *BRO* M7 .......... 71 L4
Stubley Gdns *LIT* OL15 .......... 21 L7
Stubley La *LIT* OL15 .......... 21 K8
Stubley Mill Rd *LIT* OL15 .......... 21 K8
Studforth Wk *HULME* M15 * .......... 87 J7
Studland Rd *WYTH/NTH* M22 .......... 119 H1
Studley Cl *ROY/SHW* OL2 .......... 43 H1
Studley Ct *TYLD* M29 .......... 67 H4
Sturton Av *WGNS/IIMK* WN3 .......... 63 H1
Styal Av *RDSH* SK5 .......... 100 C7
   *STRET* M32 .......... 96 D1
Styal Gv *CHD/CHDH* SK8 .......... 119 J1
Styal Rd *WILM/AE* SK9 .......... 126 E3
   *WYTH/NTH* M22 .......... 119 J4
Styal Vw *WILM/AE* SK9 .......... 126 F2
Styhead Dr *MDTN* M24 .......... 57 G1
Style St *ANC* M4 .......... 7 H1
Styperson Wy *POY/DIS* SK12 .......... 129 J1
Sudbrook Cl
   *GOL/RIS/CUL* WA3 * .......... 80 B4
Sudbury Cl *WGNS/IIMK* WN3 .......... 63 L2
   *HOR/BR* BL6 .......... 34 F6
Sudbury Dr *CHD/CHDH* SK8 .......... 119 L5
Sudbury Rd *BRAM/HZG* SK7 .......... 122 A4
Sudden St *ROCH* OL11 .......... 27 M8
Sudell St *ANC* M4 .......... 7 K1
Sudley Rd *ROCH* OL11 .......... 27 M7
Sudlow St *MILN* OL16 .......... 28 E2
Sudren St *TOT/BURYW* BL8 .......... 38 C1
Suffield St *MDTN* M24 .......... 57 J4
Suffolk Av *DROY* M43 .......... 89 K1
Suffolk Cl *BOLS/LL* BL3 .......... 37 L7
   *WGN* WN1 .......... 31 L4
Suffolk Dr *RDSH* SK5 .......... 100 F6
   *WILM/AE* SK9 .......... 127 G3
Suffolk Gv *LEIGH* WN7 .......... 65 M7
Suffolk Rd *ALT* WA14 .......... 107 L8
Suffolk St *CHAD* OL9 .......... 58 E8
   *ROCH* OL11 .......... 10 E6
   *SLFD* M6 .......... 71 K7
Sugar La *MCFLDN* SK10 .......... 129 K8
   *UPML* OL3 .......... 61 K2
Sugar Mill Sq *ORD* M5 * .......... 86 A2
Sugden St *AUL* OL6 .......... 91 G1
Sulby St *STRET* M32 .......... 97 G1
Sulby St *NEWH/MOS* M40 .......... 73 K4
   *RAD* M26 .......... 53 L4
Sulgrave Av *POY/DIS* SK12 .......... 122 B8
Sullivan St *WGTN/LGST* M12 .......... 99 K1
Sullivan Wy *WGN* WN1 .......... 15 J2
Sultan St *BURY* BL9 .......... 4 E9
Sulway Cl *SWIN* M27 .......... 70 D7
Sumac St *OP/CLY* M11 .......... 89 G2
Summer Av *URM* M41 .......... 96 B2
Summer Castle *MILN* OL16 .......... 10 F5
Summercroft *CHAD* OL9 .......... 74 E1
Summercroft Cl
   *GOL/RIS/CUL* WA3 .......... 79 K5
Summerdale Dr *RAMS* BL0 .......... 24 E2
Summerfield Av *DROY* M43 .......... 89 H1
Summerfield Dr *MDTN* M24 .......... 57 M2
   *TYLD* M29 .......... 67 L4
Summerfield Pl *WILM/AE* SK9 .......... 126 E6
Summerfield Rd *BOLS/LL* BL3 .......... 36 E8
   *WALK* M28 .......... 69 K5
   *WYTH/NTH* M22 .......... 118 E2
Summerfields Vw *OLDS* OL8 .......... 75 M1
Summer Hl *MOSL* OL5 * .......... 77 G2
Summerhill Vw *UPML* OL3 .......... 45 G3
Summerlea *CHD/CHDH* SK8 .......... 120 D4
Summers Av *STLY* SK15 .......... 91 M2
Summers Pl *RUSH/FAL* M14 .......... 98 F2
Summerseat Cl *OLDE* OL4 .......... 60 D5
   *ORD* M5 * .......... 86 D4
Summerseat La *RAMS* BL0 .......... 24 D2
Summershades La *OLDE* OL4 .......... 61 G6
Summershades Ri *OLDE* OL4 .......... 61 G6
Summers St *CHAD* OL9 .......... 8 C5
Summer St *MILN* OL16 .......... 11 G5
Summerville Av *BKLY* M9 .......... 73 J5
Summerville Rd *SLFD* M6 .......... 71 H7
Summit Cl *BURY* BL9 .......... 26 C8

Summit St *HEY* OL10 .......... 40 C2
Sumner Av *BOLE* BL2 .......... 38 A3
Sumner Rd *SLFD* M6 .......... 71 J2
Sumner St *ATH* M46 .......... 66 F1
   *GLSP* SK13 .......... 104 F4
   *ROY/SHW* OL2 .......... 43 L7
   *WGNE/HIN* WN2 .......... 33 G2
Sumner Wy *URM* M41 .......... 95 M2
Sunadale Cl *BOLS/LL* BL3 .......... 35 L7
Sunbank Cl *WHIT* OL12 .......... 18 E3
Sunbank La *HALE/TIMP* WA15 .......... 117 M6
Sunbury Cl *DUK* SK16 .......... 91 J4
   *WILM/AE* SK9 .......... 127 J2
Sunbury Dr *NEWH/MOS* M40 .......... 74 A8
Sunderland Av *AUL* OL6 .......... 75 M8
Sunderland Pl
   *WGNW/BIL/OR* WN5 .......... 47 G3
Sundew Pl *MDTN* M24 .......... 58 A5
Sundial Cl *HYDE* SK14 .......... 103 G1
Sundial Rd *OFTN* SK2 .......... 113 G6
Sundown Cl *NM/HAY* SK22 .......... 124 C4
Sundridge Cl *BOLS/LL* BL3 .......... 51 K1
Sunfield *MPL/ROM* SK6 .......... 113 L1
Sunfield Av *OLDE* OL4 .......... 44 B8
Sunfield Crs *ROY/SHW* OL2 .......... 59 H1
Sunfield Dr *ROY/SHW* OL2 .......... 59 J1
Sunfield Est *UPML* OL3 .......... 45 M8
Sunfield La *UPML* OL3 .......... 45 M8
Sunfield Rd *OLD* OL1 .......... 9 H2
Sunfield Wy *OLDE* OL4 .......... 60 B5
Sunflower Meadow *IRL* M44 .......... 94 E2
Sunhill Cl *MILN* OL16 .......... 42 E2
Sunk La *MDTN* M24 .......... 57 K5
Sunlaws Ct *GLSP* SK13 .......... 104 E4
Sunlaws St *GLSP* SK13 .......... 104 E3
Sunleigh Rd *WGNE/HIN* WN2 .......... 49 H6
Sunlight Rd *BOL* BL1 .......... 35 M5
Sunningdale Av *OP/CLY* M11 .......... 88 C2
   *RAD* M26 .......... 38 A7
   *SALE* M33 .......... 109 H1
   *WHTF* M45 .......... 54 F5
Sunningdale Cl *HYDE* SK14 .......... 91 J8
   *TOT/BURYW* BL8 .......... 38 D4
Sunningdale Dr
   *BRAM/HZG* SK7 .......... 121 J5
   *GLSP* SK13 .......... 105 H3
   *HEY* OL10 .......... 41 G4
   *IRL* M44 .......... 94 C1
   *PWCH* M25 .......... 55 K7
   *SLFD* M6 .......... 70 D7
Sunningdale Rd
   *CHD/CHDH* SK8 .......... 120 C5
   *DTN/ASHW* M34 .......... 101 L3
   *URM* M41 .......... 95 L3
Sunningdale Wk
   *BOLS/LL* BL3 * .......... 35 M7
Sunning Hill St *BOLS/LL* BL3 .......... 36 A8
Sunny Av *BURY* BL9 .......... 25 J7
Sunny Bank *OLDE* OL4 .......... 60 D4
   *RAD* M26 .......... 53 K4
   *WILM/AE* SK9 .......... 126 B8
Sunny Bank Av *DROY* M43 .......... 89 J3
Sunnybank Av *ECC* M30 .......... 85 J1
   *HTNM* SK4 .......... 99 J8
Sunnybank Cl *NEWLW* M12 .......... 78 F8
Sunny Bank Rd *ALT* WA14 .......... 116 E4
   *BRUN/LGST* M13 .......... 99 H1
   *BURY* BL9 .......... 55 K1
Sunnybank Rd *BOL* BL1 .......... 35 M2
   *DROY* M43 .......... 89 J3
   *TYLD* M29 .......... 67 L6
Sunny Banks *GLSP* SK13 .......... 104 E4
Sunny Bower St
   *TOT/BURYW* BL8 .......... 24 B6
Sunny Brow Rd *GTN* M18 .......... 88 F7
   *MDTN* M24 .......... 57 H4
Sunny Dr *PWCH* M25 .......... 55 J8
   *WGNW/BIL/OR* WN5 .......... 46 C6
Sunnyfield Rd *HTNM* SK4 .......... 111 J2
   *PWCH* M25 .......... 55 M5
Sunnyfields *WGNS/IIMK* WN3 .......... 62 F2
Sunny Garth *WHTN* BL5 .......... 50 B4
Sunnylea Av *BNG/LEV* M19 .......... 99 H4
Sunnymead Av *BOL* BL1 .......... 22 C8
Sunnymede V *RAMS* BL0 .......... 24 D1
Sunnyside Ct *DROY* M43 * .......... 89 J1
Sunnyside Crs *AUL* OL6 * .......... 91 G2
Sunnyside Gv *AUL* OL6 .......... 91 G2
Sunnyside La *DROY* M43 .......... 74 C8
Sunnyside Rd *AIMK* WN4 .......... 63 J6
   *BOL* BL1 .......... 35 M2
   *DROY* M43 .......... 89 K1
Sunnywood Dr
   *TOT/BURYW* BL8 .......... 24 D6
Sunnywood La
   *TOT/BURYW* BL8 .......... 24 D6
Sunset Av *WYTH/NTH* M22 .......... 110 A3
Sun St *MOSL* OL5 .......... 76 F3
   *RAMS* BL0 .......... 18 E5
Sunwell Ter *MPL/ROM* SK6 .......... 123 H1
Surbiton Rd *NEWH/MOS* M40 .......... 73 H8
Surma Cl *CHAD* OL9 .......... 8 E4
   *MILN* OL16 .......... 11 J8
Surrey Av *DROY* M43 .......... 89 J1
   *LEIGH* WN7 .......... 67 H8
   *ROY/SHW* OL2 .......... 43 J5
Surrey Cl *BOLS/LL* BL3 .......... 37 L8
Surrey Dr *BURY* BL9 .......... 5 G9
Surrey Park Cl *ROY/SHW* OL2 * .......... 43 L4
Surrey Rd *BKLY* M9 .......... 73 G2
Surrey St *AUL* OL6 .......... 76 A7
   *BKLY* M9 * .......... 72 F2
   *CHAD* OL9 .......... 8 C3
   *GLSP* SK13 .......... 104 F3
Surtees Rd *NTHM/RTH* M23 .......... 109 K2
Sussex Av *BURY* BL9 .......... 40 B3
   *DID/WITH* M20 .......... 98 B3
Sussex Cl *CHAD* OL9 .......... 8 A7
   *SWIN* M27 .......... 70 D2
   *WGN* WN1 .......... 31 J3
   *WGNE/HIN* WN2 .......... 49 K7
Sussex Dr *BURY* BL9 .......... 5 G9
   *DROY* M43 .......... 89 K1
Sussex Pl *HYDE* SK14 .......... 91 J7
Sussex Rd *EDGY/DAV* SK3 .......... 12 A7
   *PART* M31 .......... 106 B2
Sussex St *BRO* M7 .......... 87 G1
   *CMANW* M2 .......... 6 F7
   *LEIGH* WN7 .......... 67 H8
   *ROCH* OL11 .......... 10 E6
Sutcliffe Av *WGTN/LGST* M12 .......... 99 K2
Sutcliffe St *AULW* OL7 .......... 90 C3
   *BOL* BL1 .......... 36 B2
   *LIT* OL15 .......... 21 M6
   *MDTN* M24 .......... 57 M4
   *OLDS* OL8 .......... 9 H9
   *OLD* OL1 .......... 59 K1
Sutherland Cl *OLDS* OL8 .......... 75 J3
Sutherland Gv *FWTH* BL4 .......... 52 F4

Sutherland Rd *BOL* BL1 .......... 35 K4
   *HEY* OL10 .......... 40 C3
   *OLDTF/WHR* M16 .......... 97 K1
   *WGNS/IIMK* WN3 .......... 63 K1
Sutherland St *AUL* OL6 .......... 91 H1
   *ECC* M30 .......... 69 K8
   *FWTH* BL4 .......... 52 F4
   *SWIN* M27 .......... 70 B3
   *WGNE/HIN* WN2 .......... 48 F7
   *TOT/BURYW* BL8 .......... 24 C7
Suthers St *CHAD* OL9 .......... 8 C7
   *RAD* M26 .......... 54 F5
Sutton Av *GOL/RIS/CUL* WA3 .......... 81 H4
Sutton Cl *TOT/BURYW* BL8 .......... 38 E4
Sutton Dr *DROY* M43 .......... 89 K1
Sutton Dwellings *SLFD* M6 .......... 86 C1
Sutton Rd *BOLS/LL* BL3 .......... 35 J8
   *GTN* M18 .......... 99 M1
   *HTNM* SK4 .......... 111 M1
   *POY/DIS* SK12 .......... 129 L2
   *WILM/AE* SK9 .......... 130 C3
Suttons La *MPL/ROM* SK6 .......... 114 D7
Sutton Wy *GLSP* SK13 .......... 93 K7
Swaine St *EDGY/DAV* SK3 .......... 13 G5
Swailes St *OLDE* OL4 .......... 59 L6
Swainsthorpe Dr *BKLY* M9 .......... 73 H4
Swain St *WHIT* OL12 * .......... 28 B3
Swalecliff Av *NTHM/RTH* M23 .......... 109 G3
Swaledale Cl *ROY/SHW* OL2 .......... 43 H7
Swale Cl *WILM/AE* SK9 .......... 127 J2
Swale Dr *ALT* WA14 .......... 107 M6
Swallow Bank Dr *ROCH* OL11 * .......... 41 L1
Swallow Cl *STLY* SK15 .......... 77 J5
Swallow Dr *BURY* BL9 .......... 25 L8
   *IRL* M44 .......... 94 D1
   *ROCH* OL11 .......... 27 J5
Swallowfield *LEIGH* WN7 .......... 66 D7
Swallow Fold *GLSP* SK13 .......... 104 C3
Swallow House Crs
   *NM/HAY* SK22 .......... 125 L1
Swallow House La
   *NM/HAY* SK22 .......... 125 L1
Swallow La *STLY* SK15 .......... 77 J5
Swallow St *OLDS* OL8 .......... 75 G2
   *OP/CLY* M11 .......... 88 C5
   *STKP* SK1 .......... 13 K8
   *WGTN/LGST* M12 * .......... 99 M1
Swanage Av *NTHM/RTH* M23 .......... 109 H4
   *OFTN* SK2 .......... 113 G6
Swanage Cl *TOT/BURYW* BL8 .......... 24 F6
Swanage Rd *ECC* M30 .......... 84 E1
Swanbourne Gdns
   *EDGY/DAV* SK3 .......... 111 M6
Swan Cl *POY/DIS* SK12 .......... 121 K8
   *ROY/SHW* OL2 * .......... 43 L6
Swanfield Wk
   *GOL/RIS/CUL* WA3 .......... 79 J2
Swanhill Cl *GTN* M18 .......... 89 J6
Swan La *WGNE/HIN* WN2 .......... 49 L8
Swanley Av *NEWH/MOS* M40 .......... 73 H7
Swan Meadow Rd
   *WGNS/IIMK* WN3 .......... 14 E6
Swann Gv *CHD/CHDH* SK8 .......... 120 C4
Swann La *CHD/CHDH* SK8 .......... 120 D3
Swann St *WGNS/IIMK* WN3 .......... 14 D5
Swan Rd *HALE/TIMP* WA15 .......... 108 D3
   *NEWLW* M12 .......... 78 B8
   *TOT/BURYW* BL8 .......... 24 C2
Swansea St *OLDS* OL8 .......... 59 L8
Swan St *ANC* M4 .......... 7 H2
   *AUL* OL6 .......... 90 F1
   *WILM/AE* SK9 .......... 126 F5
Swarbrick Dr *PWCH* M25 .......... 71 J2
Swayfield Av *BRUN/LGST* M13 .......... 99 J1
Swaylands Dr *SALE* M33 .......... 108 E3
Sweetbriar Cl *ROY/SHW* OL2 .......... 43 L5
Sweet Briar Cl *WHIT* OL12 .......... 28 B2
Sweet Briar La *WHIT* OL12 .......... 28 B2
Sweetlove's Gv *BOL* BL1 .......... 22 B7
Sweetlove's La *BOL* BL1 .......... 22 B7
Sweetnam Dr *OP/CLY* M11 .......... 88 E2
Swettenham Rd *WILM/AE* SK9 .......... 119 M1
Swift Bank *GLSP* SK13 .......... 104 C4
Swift Cl *MPL/ROM* SK6 .......... 101 M7
   *ROCH* OL11 .......... 27 J5
Swift Rd *OLD* OL1 .......... 44 B7
Swift St *AUL* OL6 * .......... 76 A7
   *WGNW/BIL/OR* WN5 .......... 14 B6
Swinbourne Gv *DID/WITH* M20 .......... 98 F5
Swinburne Av *DROY* M43 .......... 89 K1
Swinburne Gn *RDSH* SK5 .......... 100 A3
Swinburn Gv
   *WGNW/BIL/OR* WN5 .......... 62 A3
Swinburn St *BKLY* M9 .......... 73 J3
Swindells St *HYDE* SK14 .......... 91 H7
   *OP/CLY* M11 * .......... 89 H5
Swindon Cl *GTN* M18 .......... 89 G7
Swinfield Av *CHD/CHDH* M21 .......... 97 J4
Swinford Gv *ROY/SHW* OL2 .......... 43 K7
Swinley Cha *WILM/AE* SK9 .......... 127 K3
Swinley St *WGN* WN1 .......... 47 M2
Swinley St *WGN* WN1 .......... 48 C3
Swinside *WGN* WN1 .......... 47 M2
Swinside Cl *MDTN* M24 .......... 56 F2
Swinside Rd *BOLE* BL2 .......... 37 J4
Swinstead Av *NEWH/MOS* M40 .......... 73 H7
Swinton Crs *BURY* BL9 .......... 55 K3
Swinton Gv *BRUN/LGST* M13 .......... 87 M7
Swinton Hall Rd *SWIN* M27 .......... 70 D4
Swinton Park Rd *SLFD* M6 .......... 70 F7
Swinton St *BOLE* BL2 .......... 37 H5
   *OLDE* OL4 .......... 59 M7
Swiss Hl *WILM/AE* SK9 .......... 130 E3
Swithin Rd *WYTH/NTH* M22 .......... 119 C4
Swithland Rd *ALT* WA14 * .......... 107 M3
Swythamley Ct *EDGY/DAV* SK3 .......... 111 K4
Swythamley Rd
   *EDGY/DAV* SK3 .......... 111 K4
Sybil St *LIT* OL15 .......... 21 L6
Sycamore Av *ALT* WA14 .......... 107 K7
   *CHAD* OL9 .......... 74 C1
   *DTN/ASHW* M34 .......... 101 J3
   *GOL/RIS/CUL* WA3 .......... 79 K3
   *HEY* OL10 .......... 41 H4
   *MILN* OL16 .......... 43 K1
   *OLDE* OL4 .......... 60 A4
   *RAD* M26 .......... 54 C4
   *TYLD* M29 .......... 68 A3
   *WGNE/HIN* WN2 .......... 65 J1
   *WGNW/BIL/OR* WN5 .......... 31 J8
Sycamore Cl *AUL* OL6 .......... 91 H2
   *DID/WITH* M20 * .......... 98 F5
   *DUK* SK16 .......... 91 J4
   *LIT* OL15 .......... 21 K7
   *NM/HAY* SK22 .......... 125 G4
   *WILM/AE* SK9 .......... 126 B6
Sycamore Ct *SLFD* M6 .......... 86 D1
Sycamore Crs *AUL* OL6 .......... 75 M7
Sycamore Dr *BURY* BL9 .......... 25 J6
Sycamore Gv *FAIL* M35 .......... 74 E5

Sycamore Ldg
   *BRAM/HZG* SK7 * .......... 121 H5
Sycamore Pl *WHTF* M45 .......... 55 M5
Sycamore Rd *ATH* M46 .......... 67 H1
   *ECC* M30 .......... 69 K8
   *MPL/ROM* SK6 .......... 101 K8
   *NM/HAY* SK22 .......... 125 G2
   *PART* M31 .......... 106 A1
   *TOT/BURYW* BL8 .......... 24 C7
The Sycamores *GLSP* SK13 .......... 104 C1
   *MOSL* OL5 .......... 77 H3
   *OLDE* OL4 .......... 60 C4
   *RAD* M26 .......... 53 L6
   *STLY* SK15 .......... 91 L4
Sycamore St *DTN/ASHW* M34 .......... 101 J1
   *SALE* M33 .......... 97 H8
Sycamore Wk *CHD/CHDH* SK8 .......... 111 G6
   *HOR/BR* BL6 .......... 34 B2
Sydall Cl *BRAM/HZG* SK7 .......... 120 F7
Sydall Crs *BRAM/HZG* SK7 .......... 120 F8
Sydall Gn *BRAM/HZG* SK7 .......... 120 F8
Sydall Av *CHD/CHDH* SK8 .......... 119 M4
Sydall St *HYDE* SK14 .......... 102 A3
Sydall Rd *BRAM/HZG* SK7 .......... 120 F7
Sydenham St *OLD* OL1 .......... 59 L3
Syderstone Cl *WGNE/HIN* WN2 .......... 49 H8
Sydney Av *ECC* M30 .......... 85 G2
   *LEIGH* WN7 .......... 81 G2
   *MANAIR* M90 .......... 118 C4
Sydney Barnes Cl *ROCH* OL11 .......... 41 L2
Sydney Jones Ct
   *NEWH/MOS* M40 .......... 73 M3
Sydney Rd *BRAM/HZG* SK7 .......... 121 H7
Sydney St *FAIL* M35 .......... 74 B5
   *MOSL* OL5 .......... 77 G4
   *OFTN* SK2 .......... 112 F5
   *SLFD* M6 .......... 86 B2
   *STRET* M32 .......... 97 G2
   *SWIN* M27 .......... 70 A4
   *WGNE/HIN* WN2 .......... 64 D1
Syke La *WHIT* OL12 .......... 20 D8
Syke Rd *LIT* OL15 .......... 29 M2
   *WHIT* OL12 .......... 20 D8
Sykes Av *BURY* BL9 .......... 39 L8
Sykes Cl *MILN* OL16 .......... 61 L7
Sykes Ct *MILN* OL16 .......... 11 K6
Sykes Crs *WGNS/IIMK* WN3 .......... 62 F3
Sykes Meadow *EDGY/DAV* SK3 .......... 111 M6
Sykes St *BURY* BL9 .......... 5 H2
   *MILN* OL16 * .......... 11 L6
   *MILN* OL16 .......... 29 K8
   *RDSH* SK5 .......... 100 C4
Sylvan Av *FAIL* M35 .......... 74 B7
   *HALE/TIMP* WA15 .......... 108 C4
   *SALE* M33 .......... 108 F1
   *URM* M41 .......... 96 A1
   *WILM/AE* SK9 .......... 126 D7
Sylvan Cl *MDTN* M24 .......... 57 G2
Sylvandale Av *BNG/LEV* M19 .......... 99 K3
Sylvan Gv *ALT* WA14 .......... 108 A7
Sylvan St *CHAD* OL9 .......... 8 C4
Sylvester Av *OFTN* SK2 .......... 112 E6
Sylvester Cl *HYDE* SK14 .......... 103 H1
Sylvia Gv *RDSH* SK5 .......... 100 B5
Symms St *SLFD* M6 .......... 71 L8
Symond Rd *BKLY* M9 .......... 71 L4
Symons Rd *SALE* M33 .......... 96 F7
Symons St *BRO* M7 .......... 72 B5
Syndall Av *WGTN/LGST* M12 .......... 88 A6
Syndall St *WGTN/LGST* M12 .......... 88 A6
Syresham St *WGNE/HIN* WN2 .......... 64 E2

## T

Taberner Cl *WGNW/ST* WN6 .......... 31 H3
Taberner St *WGNE/HIN* WN2 .......... 64 E2
Tabley Av *RUSH/FAL* M14 .......... 98 D2
Tabley Gdns *MPL/ROM* SK6 .......... 114 D8
Tabley Gv *BRUN/LGST* M13 .......... 99 J2
   *HALE/TIMP* WA15 .......... 108 D4
   *RDSH* SK5 .......... 100 C5
Tabley Mere Gdns
   *CHD/CHDH* SK8 .......... 120 B1
Tabley Ms *ALT* WA14 .......... 108 A7
Tabley Rd *BOLS/LL* BL3 .......... 35 J4
   *SALE* M33 * .......... 109 H2
   *WILM/AE* SK9 .......... 119 M7
Tabley St *DUK* SK16 .......... 91 H4
   *MOSL* OL5 .......... 77 G4
   *SLFD* M6 .......... 71 L7
Tabor St *MDTN* M24 .......... 57 J2
Tackler Cl *SWIN* M27 .......... 70 C5
Tadcaster Dr *NEWH/MOS* M40 .......... 73 G6
Tadman Gv *ALT* WA14 .......... 107 K6
Tadmor Cl *LHULT* M38 .......... 52 C7
Tagore Cl *BRUN/LGST* M13 .......... 88 B8
Tag Wood Vw *RAMS* BL0 .......... 18 D8
Tahir Cl *CHH* M8 .......... 72 E5
Tait Ms *HTNM* SK4 .......... 111 J2
Talavera St *BRO* M7 .......... 72 A7
Talbenny Cl *BOL* BL1 .......... 35 J4
Talbot Av *BOLS/LL* BL3 .......... 37 K8
Talbot Cl *OLDE* OL4 .......... 59 M4
Talbot Ct *BOL* BL1 .......... 22 C8
Talbot Gv *BURY* BL9 .......... 25 K6
Talbot Pl *OLDTF/WHR* M16 .......... 86 F5
Talbot Rd *ALT* WA14 .......... 116 D2
   *GLSP* SK13 .......... 104 F2
   *HYDE* SK14 .......... 91 H7
   *RUSH/FAL* M14 .......... 98 F5
   *SALE* M33 * .......... 97 H8
   *STRET* M32 .......... 86 C8
   *WILM/AE* SK9 .......... 130 G5
Talbot St *AIMK* WN4 * .......... 64 A8
   *AUL* OL6 .......... 90 D1
   *BRAM/HZG* SK7 .......... 113 G8
   *ECC* M30 .......... 85 H3
   *GLSP* SK13 .......... 104 F3
   *GOL/RIS/CUL* WA3 .......... 79 K4
   *MDTN* M24 .......... 57 K2
   *ROCH* OL11 .......... 10 E7
Talford Gv *DID/WITH* M20 .......... 98 D7
Talgarth Rd *NEWH/MOS* M40 .......... 72 F8
Talkin Dr *MDTN* M24 .......... 57 H1
Talland Wk *BRUN/LGST* M13 .......... 88 B7
Tallarn Cl *DID/WITH* M20 .......... 98 F5
Tallis St *WGTN/LGST* M12 .......... 99 K1
Tallow Wy *IRL* M44 .......... 94 D4
Tall Trees Cl *ROY/SHW* OL2 .......... 42 F8
Tall Trees Pl *OFTN* SK2 .......... 112 D5
Talmine Av *AIMK* WN4 .......... 79 G1
Talman Gv *AIMK* WN4 .......... 79 J4
Tamar Cl *HULME* M15 .......... 87 G6
Tamar Dr *NTHM/RTH* M23 .......... 109 H4
Tamarin Cl *SWIN* M27 .......... 69 M3
Tamebank *MOSL* OL5 .......... 77 G1
Tame Barn Cl *MILN* OL16 .......... 29 K6

Tame Cl *STLY* SK15 .......... 91 M1
Tame La *UPML* OL3 .......... 44 F5
Tamer Gv *LEIGH* WN7 .......... 65 M4
Tamerton Dr *CHH* M8 .......... 72 D6
Tameside Ct *DUK* SK16 * .......... 90 E5
Tame St *ANC* M4 .......... 88 A3
   *DTN/ASHW* M34 .......... 90 C5
   *DTN/ASHW* M34 .......... 90 C8
   *MOSL* OL5 .......... 77 H1
   *STLY* SK15 .......... 91 H3
   *UPML* OL3 .......... 61 L4
Tame Valley Cl *MOSL* OL5 .......... 77 H1
   *WHTF* M45 .......... 55 L5
Tamworth Av *ORD* M5 .......... 86 E4
Tamworth Av West *ORD* M5 * .......... 86 D4
Tamworth Cl *BRAM/HZG* SK7 * .......... 121 L4
   *HULME* M15 .......... 87 H5
Tamworth Dr *TOT/BURYW* BL8 .......... 24 F7
   *WGNE/HIN* WN2 .......... 48 C2
Tamworth Gn *STKP* SK1 .......... 112 E2
Tamworth St *CHAD* OL9 .......... 8 C8
   *STKP* SK1 .......... 112 E2
Tamworth Wk *ORD* M5 .......... 86 D4
Tandis Ct *SLFD* M6 * .......... 85 K1
Tandle Hill Rd *ROY/SHW* OL2 .......... 42 F6
Tandlewood Ms
   *NEWH/MOS* M40 .......... 73 M7
Tandlewood Pk *ROY/SHW* OL2 .......... 42 E6
Tanfield Dr *RAD* M26 .......... 53 L5
Tangmere Av *HEY* OL10 .......... 41 J5
Tangmere Cl *NEWH/MOS* M40 * .......... 73 M1
Tanhill Cl *OFTN* SK2 .......... 113 H6
Tanhill La *OLDS* OL8 .......... 75 K2
Tanhouse Av *TYLD* M29 .......... 68 A5
Tan House Dr *WGNS/IIMK* WN3 .......... 62 F3
Tan House La *WGNS/IIMK* WN3 .......... 62 F2
Tanhouse Rd *URM* M41 .......... 95 G1
Tanners Cft *RAMS* BL0 .......... 18 E6
Tanners Fold *OLDS* OL8 .......... 75 K2
Tanners Gn *SLFD* M6 .......... 86 C1
Tanner's La *GOL/RIS/CUL* WA3 .......... 79 L4
Tanners St *RAMS* BL0 .......... 18 E6
Tannery St *HYDE* SK14 * .......... 102 A1
Tannery Wy *ALT* WA14 .......... 108 A5
Tannock Rd *BRAM/HZG* SK7 .......... 122 B5
Tanpits Rd *BURY* BL9 .......... 4 D3
Tansey Gv *BRO* M7 .......... 72 C6
Tansley Rd *CHH* M8 .......... 72 D2
Tansley Sq *WGNW/BIL/OR* WN5 .......... 47 G7
Tanworth Wk *BOL* BL1 * .......... 35 J2
Tan Yard Brow *GTN* M18 .......... 89 H7
Tanyard Dr *HALE/TIMP* WA15 .......... 117 L6
Tanyard Gn *RDSH* SK5 .......... 100 C7
Tanyard La *HALE/TIMP* WA15 .......... 117 H7
Taper St *RAMS* BL0 .......... 18 E6
Tapley Av *POY/DIS* SK12 .......... 129 J2
Taplin Dr *GTN* M18 .......... 88 F7
Taplow Gv *CHD/CHDH* SK8 .......... 120 B2
Taplow Wk *RUSH/FAL* M14 .......... 99 H1
Tarbet Dr *BOLE* BL2 .......... 37 J6
Tarbet Rd *DUK* SK16 .......... 90 F5
Tarbolton Crs
   *HALE/TIMP* WA15 .......... 117 L1
Tariff St *CMANE* M1 .......... 7 K4
Tarleton Av *ATH* M46 .......... 50 E7
Tarleton Cl *TOT/BURYW* BL8 .......... 38 C3
Tarleton Pl *BOLS/LL* BL3 .......... 51 M1
Tarleton Wk *BRUN/LGST* M13 * .......... 87 M6
Tarnbrook Wk *HULME* M15 * .......... 87 J7
Tarn Cl *AIMK* WN4 .......... 63 L7
Tarn Dr *BURY* BL9 .......... 39 H6
Tarn Gv *WALK* M28 .......... 69 G2
Tarnrigg Cl *WGNS/IIMK* WN3 .......... 63 H1
Tarnside Cl *MILN* OL16 .......... 28 F1
   *OFTN* SK2 .......... 113 J6
Tarnside Fold *GLSP* SK13 .......... 104 D5
Tarnside Rd
   *WGNW/BIL/OR* WN5 .......... 46 B6
The Tarns *CHD/CHDH* SK8 .......... 119 K1
Tarnway *GOL/RIS/CUL* WA3 .......... 81 H4
Tarporley Av *RUSH/FAL* M14 .......... 98 D2
Tarporley Cl *EDGY/DAV* SK3 .......... 111 M7
Tarran Dr *DTN/ASHW* M34 .......... 101 L3
Tarran Pl *ALT* WA14 .......... 108 B6
Tarrant Cl *WGNS/IIMK* WN3 .......... 63 G2
Tarrington Cl *WGTN/LGST* M12 .......... 88 D7
Tartan St *OP/CLY* M11 .......... 88 E2
Tarvin Av *DID/WITH* M20 .......... 98 B3
   *HTNM* SK4 .......... 100 A5
Tarvin Cl *GOL/RIS/CUL* WA3 .......... 80 B5
Tarvin Dr *MPL/ROM* SK6 .......... 101 H8
Tarvington Cl
   *NEWH/MOS* M40 * .......... 72 F6
Tarvin Rd *CHD/CHDH* SK8 .......... 111 K8
Tarvin Wk *BOL* BL1 .......... 36 B2
Tasle Aly *CMANW* M2 .......... 6 F5
Tatchbury Rd *FAIL* M35 .......... 74 D5
Tate St *OLDS* OL8 .......... 9 J9
Tatham Cl *BRUN/LGST* M13 .......... 99 J1
Tatham St *MILN* OL16 .......... 11 C5
Tatland Dr *WYTH/NTH* M22 .......... 119 H1
Tatlock Cl *WGNW/BIL/OR* WN5 .......... 62 B7
Tattenhall Av *BOL* BL1 .......... 35 H2
Tattersall Av *BOL* BL1 .......... 35 J2
Tattersall St *CHAD* OL9 .......... 8 E7
Tatton Cl *BRAM/HZG* SK7 .......... 113 J8
   *CHD/CHDH* SK8 .......... 120 A1
Tatton Dr *AIMK* WN4 .......... 63 J8
Tatton Gdns *MPL/ROM* SK6 .......... 102 A7
Tatton Gv *DID/WITH* M20 .......... 98 E6
Tatton Mere Dr *DROY* M43 .......... 89 L3
Tattonmere Gdns
   *CHD/CHDH* SK8 .......... 111 K8
Tatton Pl *SALE* M33 .......... 96 E7
Tatton Rd *DTN/ASHW* M34 .......... 101 K3
   *SALE* M33 * .......... 96 E7
   *WILM/AE* SK9 .......... 120 A7
Tatton Rd North *HTNM* SK4 .......... 99 M7
Tatton Rd South *HTNM* SK4 .......... 99 M8
Tatton St *HULME* M15 .......... 87 G6
   *HYDE* SK14 .......... 102 B5
   *ORD* M5 .......... 86 E4
   *STKP* SK1 .......... 13 J4
   *STLY* SK15 .......... 91 K4
Taunton Av *AULW* OL7 .......... 75 K8
   *ECC* M30 .......... 84 E1
   *LEIGH* WN7 .......... 66 A2
   *RDSH* SK5 .......... 100 F7
   *URM* M41 .......... 95 L4
Taunton Brook La *AULW* OL7 .......... 75 K8
Taunton Cl *BOL* BL1 * .......... 35 M3
   *BRAM/HZG* SK7 .......... 122 C5
Taunton Dr *FWTH* BL4 .......... 52 C3
Taunton Gn *AULW* OL7 .......... 75 K8
Taunton Gv *WHTF* M45 .......... 55 K6
Taunton Hall Cl *AULW* OL7 .......... 75 J8
Taunton Lawns *AULW* OL7 * .......... 75 K8
Taunton Pl *AULW* OL7 * .......... 75 J7
Taunton Platting *AULW* OL7 * .......... 75 J6

Taunton Rd AULW OL7 75 K8
CHAD OL9 58 D3
SALE M33 96 A8
Taunton St ANC M4 88 A3
Taurus St OLDE OL4 59 M4
Tavern Court Av FAIL M35 74 D5
Tavern Rd GLSP SK13 104 B1
Tavery Cl ANC M4 * 7 M3
Tavistock Cl HYDE SK14 103 H2
Tavistock Dr CHAD OL9 58 C3
Tavistock Rd BOL BL1 2 A6
ROCH OL11 42 C1
SALE M33 96 A7
WGNE/HIN WN2 49 K8
Tavistock St ATH M46 66 E1
Tawton Av HYDE SK14 103 H2
Tay Cl OLDS OL8 9 G9
Tayfield Rd WYTH/NTH M22 118 E2
Taylor Av ROCH OL11 27 J4
Taylor Green Wy OLDE OL4 60 C5
Taylor Gv WGNE/HIN WN2 65 M1
Taylor La DTN/ASHW M34 90 A8
Taylor Rd ALT WA14 107 K7
RNFD/HAY WA11 78 C6
URM M41 85 H5
WGNE/HIN WN2 65 M1
Taylor's La BOLE BL2 37 L5
WGNS/IIMK WN3 64 C1
Taylorson St ORD M5 86 E5
Taylorson St South ORD M5 86 D6
Taylors Pl WHIT OL12 * 10 E1
Taylor's Rd STRET M32 86 B8
Taylor St BOLS/LL BL3 * 2 F6
BURY BL9 5 H2
CHAD OL9 58 D5
DROY M43 89 K3
DTN/ASHW M34 90 C8
GTN M18 88 F6
HEY OL10 40 F2
HOR/BR BL6 33 L1
HYDE SK14 93 G7
HYDE SK14 102 C1
LEIGH WN7 66 A4
MDTN M24 57 K4
OLD OL1 59 M4
OLDE OL4 60 B6
PWCH M25 55 M8
RAD M26 54 D1
ROY/SHW OL2 * 43 G7
RUSH/FAL M14 98 F1
STLY SK15 91 L3
WGNS/IIMK WN3 14 D5
WHIT OL12 20 B4
WHIT OL12 28 C3
Tayton Cl TYLD M29 67 M3
Taywood Rd BOLS/LL BL3 51 G2
Teak Dr FWTH BL4 54 A8
Teak St BURY BL9 5 K4
Teal Av POY/DIS SK12 121 J8
Tealby Av OLDTF/WHR M16 86 F8
Tealby Rd GTN M18 88 E8
Teal Cl ALT WA14 107 L4
OFTN SK2 113 J7
WGNS/IIMK WN3 46 E8
Teal Ct ROCH OL11 27 J5
Teal St BOLS/LL BL3 36 C8
Teasdale Cl CHAD OL9 74 B1
Tebbutt St ANC M4 7 K1
Tebworth Dr WGNE/HIN WN2 49 H8
Tedder Cl BURY BL9 55 L2
Tedder Dr WYTH/NTH M22 119 H5
Teddington Rd
NEWH/MOS M40 73 M3
Ted Jackson Wk OP/CLY M11 * 88 C4
Teer St ANC M4 88 A2
Teesdale Av URM M41 84 D8
Teesdale Cl OFTN SK2 113 H6
Teesdale Dr LEIGH WN7 66 F7
Tees St MILN OL16 * 11 K7
Teignmouth Av
NEWH/MOS M40 * 72 F8
Teignmouth St
NEWH/MOS M40 72 F8
Telfer Av BRUN/LGST M13 99 H2
Telfer Rd BRUN/LGST M13 99 H2
Telford Cl DTN/ASHW M34 90 B5
Telford Crs LEIGH WN7 66 A4
Telford Ms UPML OL3 61 L3
Telford Rd MPL/ROM SK6 114 D8
Telford St ATH M46 66 D2
CHH M8 72 F7
HOR/BR BL6 33 M2
Telford Wk OLDTF/WHR M16 87 G8
Telford Wy ROCH OL11 42 D2
Tellers Cl ATH M46 67 G1
Tellson Cl SLFD M6 71 G6
Tellson Crs SLFD M6 71 G6
Tell St WHIT OL12 10 B4
Temperance St BOLS/LL BL3 2 C8
HYDE SK14 103 K4
WGTN/LGST M12 7 M8
Tempest Cha HOR/BR BL6 34 E8
Tempest Ct HOR/BR BL6 * 34 F8
Tempest Rd HOR/BR BL6 34 F1
WILM/AE SK9 130 F3
Tempest St BOLS/LL BL3 35 L8
Temple Av GLSP SK13 93 M7
Temple Cl OLDE OL4 60 B4
Templecombe Dr BOL BL1 22 A6
Temple Dr BOL BL1 35 M1
SWIN M27 70 E5
Templegate Cl
WGNNW/ST WN6 31 J2
Temple Rd BOL BL1 35 M1
SALE M33 97 G8
Temple Sq CHH M8 72 D7
Temple St GLSP SK13 93 M7
HEY OL10 41 G2
MDTN M24 57 L3
OLD OL1 59 L5
Templeton Cl ALT WA14 107 L6
WHTN BL5 50 B4
Templeton Rd WGNE/HIN WN2 64 E3
Ten Acre Ct WHTF M45 * 55 G5
Ten Acre Dr WHTF M45 55 G5
Ten Acres La NEWH/MOS M40 73 K8
Tenax Rd TRPK M17 85 L5
Tenbury Cl SLFD M6 * 86 C1
Tenbury Dr AIMK WN4 63 J8
MDTN M24 57 K7
Tenby Av BOL BL1 35 K3
DID/WITH M20 98 E6
STRET M32 86 B8
Tenby Ct OLDTF/WHR M16 * 86 F6
Tenby Dr CHD/CHDH SK8 120 D3
SLFD M6 71 H7
Tenby Gv WHIT OL12 27 M3
Tenby Rd EDGY/DAV SK3 12 A8
OLDS OL8 74 E2
Tenby St WHIT OL12 27 M3
Tenement La BRAM/HZG SK7 120 F2
Tenement St WGNE/HIN WN2 64 E3
Teneriffe St BRO M7 72 A7
Ten Foot Cl GLSP SK13 104 E2
Tennis St BOL BL1 36 A2
OLDTF/WHR M16 86 E8
Tennyson Av BURY BL9 39 J6
DTN/ASHW M34 * 101 K5
DUK SK16 91 K5
LEIGH WN7 65 M4
RAD M26 38 B8
Tennyson Cl HTNM SK4 111 K3
Tennyson Dr WGN WN1 47 M1
WGNW/BIL/OR WN5 62 A3
Tennyson Gdns PWCH M25 71 J1
Tennyson Rd CHD/CHDH SK8 111 J6
DROY M43 89 K2
FWTH BL4 52 E6
MDTN M24 57 L2
RDSH SK5 100 A3
SWIN M27 70 A4
Tennyson St BOL BL1 36 B3
BRUN/LGST M13 87 M7
OLD OL1 59 M3
ROCH OL11 11 G9
Tensing Av ATH M46 50 F7
AULW OL7 75 L7
Tensing St OLDS OL8 75 J2
Tentercroft WHIT OL12 10 C4
Tenterden St BURY BL9 4 C5
Tenter Dr WGNNW/ST WN6 31 L5
Tenterhill La ROCH OL11 27 G2
Tenters St BURY BL9 4 C5
Tenth St TRPK M17 86 A6
Terence St NEWH/MOS M40 74 A7
Terminal Rd East MANAIR M90 118 D5
Terminal Rd North
MANAIR M90 118 E5
Terminal Rd South
MANAIR M90 118 D5
Tern Cl ALT WA14 107 L4
DUK SK16 91 H5
ROCH OL11 27 J5
Tern Dr POY/DIS SK12 121 K8
Ternhill Ct FWTH BL4 53 H4
Terrace St OLDE OL4 59 L5
The Terrace PWCH M25 71 L1
Terrington Cl CCHDY M21 98 B5
Tetbury Cl WGNW/BIL/OR WN5 47 G3
Tetbury Dr BOLE BL2 37 J4
Tetbury Rd WYTH/NTH M22 118 D3
Tetlow Gv ECC M30 84 F3
Tetlow La BRO M7 72 B4
Tetlow St CHAD OL9 * 8 F7
HYDE SK14 * 91 H7
MDTN M24 57 K4
NEWH/MOS M40 73 M7
Teviot St BRUN/LGST M13 88 B8
Tewkesbury Av AUL OL6 75 M5
DROY M43 89 K1
HALE/TIMP WA15 117 L1
MDTN M24 57 J1
URM M41 85 G8
Tewkesbury Cl CHD/CHDH SK8 120 D6
POY/DIS SK12 121 M8
Tewkesbury Dr PWCH M25 71 M2
Tewkesbury Rd EDGY/DAV SK3 111 L6
GOL/RIS/CUL WA3 79 L4
NEWH/MOS M40 88 B1
Texas St AUL OL6 90 F2
Textile St WGTN/LGST M12 88 D5
Textilose Rd TRPK M17 85 L7
Thackeray Cl CHH M8 72 D6
Thackeray Gv DROY M43 89 K2
Thackeray Pl WGNS/IIMK WN3 47 K7
Thackeray Rd OLD OL1 59 M3
Thames Av LEIGH WN7 81 J3
Thames Cl BURY BL9 25 J5
OP/CLY M11 88 E4
Thames Ct HULME M15 87 G6
Thames Dr WGNW/BIL/OR WN5 46 C5
Thames Rd MILN OL16 29 K6
Thames St MILN OL16 11 J7
OLD OL1 9 L3
Thanet Cl BRO M7 72 B7
Thanet Gv LEIGH WN7 66 D7
Thankerton Av DTN/ASHW M34 90 A3
Thatcher Cl ALT WA14 116 E4
Thatcher St OLDS OL8 75 K1
Thatch Leach CHAD OL9 58 C7
Thatch Leach La WHTF M45 55 K5
Thaxmead Dr NEWH/MOS M40 74 A8
Thaxted Dr OFTN SK2 113 K7
Thaxted Pl BOL BL1 35 M4
Thbeechwood La STLY SK15 76 F8
Theatre St OLD OL1 9 K5
Thekla St CHAD OL9 8 F3
Thelma St RAMS BL0 18 E6
Thelwall Av BOLE BL2 37 G4
RUSH/FAL M14 98 C4
Thelwall Cl HALE/TIMP WA15 108 B6
LEIGH WN7 65 L8
Thelwall Rd SALE M33 109 H1
Theobald Rd ALT WA14 116 F3
Theta Cl OP/CLY M11 88 E2
Thetford WHIT OL12 10 C3
Thetford Cl TOT/BURYW BL8 25 G7
WGNE/HIN WN2 49 H8
Thetford Dr CHH M8 72 E5
Thicketford Brow BOLE BL2 37 G3
Thicketford Cl BOLE BL2 36 F2
Thicketford Rd BOLE BL2 36 E3
Thicknesse Av WGNNW/ST WN6 47 J1
Thimble Cl WHIT OL12 21 H8
The Thimbles WHIT OL12 21 H8
Third Av BOL BL1 35 L5
BOLS/LL BL3 37 J8
BURY BL9 26 A8
OLDS OL8 74 F2
OP/CLY M11 88 F2
POY/DIS SK12 129 H3
STLY SK15 77 H7
SWIN M27 70 B7
TRPK M17 86 A7
TYLD M29 67 L8
WGNNW/ST WN6 47 K2
Thirlby Dr WYTH/NTH M22 118 F3
Thirlemere Rd STKP SK1 112 E3
Thirlmere Av AIMK WN4 63 M8
AULW OL7 75 J8
HOR/BR BL6 33 M2
STRET M32 96 F1
SWIN M27 70 D5
TYLD M29 67 K5
WGNE/HIN WN2 48 E5
WGNE/HIN WN2 64 E4
WGNNW/ST WN6 31 K5
WGNW/BIL/OR WN5 46 C5
Thirlmere Cl WILM/AE SK9 130 C3
Thirlmere Dr BURY BL9 * 39 H5
LHULT M38 52 D7
MDTN M24 57 H2
Thirlmere Gv FWTH BL4 52 B4
ROY/SHW OL2 43 G6
Thirlmere Rd GOL/RIS/CUL WA3 79 M3
HOR/BR BL6 32 F1
PART M31 94 B8
ROCH OL11 27 L8
URM M41 95 H1
WGNE/HIN WN2 49 H7
WGNW/BIL/OR WN5 46 F5
WHTN BL5 51 J5
WYTH/NTH M22 118 D3
Thirlmere St LEIGH WN7 66 B7
Thirlspot Cl BOL BL1 22 B6
Thirlstone Av OLDE OL4 * 44 C8
Thirsfield Dr OP/CLY M11 88 F2
Thirsk Av CHAD OL9 58 C3
SALE M33 107 M1
Thirsk Cl TOT/BURYW BL8 24 E7
Thirsk Rd BOLS/LL BL3 53 K2
Thirsk St WGTN/LGST M12 7 L8
Thistle Bank Cl BKLY M9 72 F3
Thistle Cl STLY SK15 92 B5
Thistledown Cl ECC M30 84 F4
WGNNW/ST WN6 47 K2
Thistle Gn MILN OL16 29 H5
Thistle Sq PART M31 106 B2
Thistleton Rd BOLS/LL BL3 51 J1
Thistle Wy OLDE OL4 60 A2
Thistlewood Dr WILM/AE SK9 127 H5
Thistleyfields MILN OL16 * 29 H5
Thomas Cl DTN/ASHW M34 90 D8
Thomas Dr BOLS/LL BL3 2 B9
Thomas Gibbon Cl STRET M32 * 96 F3
Thomas Henshaw Ct
ROCH OL11 27 M8
Thomas Holden St BOL BL1 2 C3
Thomas Johnson Cl ECC M30 * 84 F3
Thomas More Cl FWTH BL4 53 J6
Thomasson Cl BOL BL1 36 B3
Thomas St ANC M4 7 H3
ATH M46 67 G1
BOLS/LL BL3 2 B9
CHH M8 72 C4
FWTH BL4 53 H4
GLSP SK13 105 H3
GOL/RIS/CUL WA3 79 K4
HALE/TIMP WA15 108 B8
MILN OL16 11 G2
MPL/ROM SK6 113 K1
MPL/ROM SK6 114 E2
OFTN SK2 13 J8
OLDE OL4 60 B7
RAD M26 54 E1
ROY/SHW OL2 43 M6
ROY/SHW OL2 59 J1
STRET M32 97 G1
WGNE/HIN WN2 65 L1
WHTN BL5 * 50 B1
Thomas St West OFTN SK2 13 J8
Thomas Telford Basin
CMANE M1 7 K5
Thompson Av BOLE BL2 38 A3
WHTF M45 55 K5
Thompson Cl DTN/ASHW M34 100 E1
Thompson Ct DTN/ASHW M34 100 E1
Thompson Dr BURY BL9 5 M3
Thompson Fold STLY SK15 91 J2
Thompson La CHAD OL9 58 D8
Thompson Rd BOL BL1 35 L3
DTN/ASHW M34 100 E1
TRPK M17 85 H4
Thompson St AIMK WN4 64 A8
ANC M4 7 J2
BOLS/LL BL3 * 2 E9
CSLFD M3 * 87 H1
HOR/BR BL6 33 K1
LEIGH WN7 65 L7
NEWH/MOS M40 73 J7
WGN WN1 15 K1
WGNS/IIMK WN3 47 K8
Thomson Rd GTN M18 88 F8
Thomson St BRUN/LGST M13 87 M6
EDGY/DAV SK3 13 H7
Thoralby Cl WGTN/LGST M12 88 D7
Thorburn Rd
WGNW/BIL/OR WN5 46 F6
Thoresby Cl RAD M26 37 M7
WGNS/IIMK WN3 63 H1
Thoresway Rd BRUN/LGST M13 99 H1
WILM/AE SK9 126 D7
Thor Gv ORD M5 86 F4
Thorley Cl CHAD OL9 74 B2
Thorley Dr HALE/TIMP WA15 108 E7
URM M41 96 A2
Thorley La HALE/TIMP WA15 108 E6
HALE/TIMP WA15 118 B3
Thorley Ms BRAM/HZG SK7 121 H5
Thorley St FAIL M35 74 C4
Thornage Dr NEWH/MOS M40 72 F8
Thorn Av FAIL M35 74 C6
Thornbank BOLS/LL BL3 35 M6
Thorn Bank DROY M43 * 89 J1
Thornbank Cl HEY OL10 41 H5
Thornbeck Dr BOL BL1 35 J3
Thornbeck Rd BOL BL1 35 J3
Thornbridge Av CCHDY M21 97 L4
Thornbury ROCH OL11 10 D7
Thornbury Av
GOL/RIS/CUL WA3 80 B5
HYDE SK14 103 H1
Thornbury Cl CHD/CHDH SK8 120 E3
Thornbury Rd STRET M32 86 B8
Thornbury Wy GTN M18 88 F7
Thornbush Cl GOL/RIS/CUL WA3 80 B4
Thornbush Wy MILN OL16 11 L3
Thorncliff Av OLDS OL8 75 H1
Thorncliffe Av DUK SK16 90 F5
ROY/SHW OL2 42 F6
Thorncliffe Gv BNG/LEV M19 99 M3
Thorncliffe Pk ROY/SHW OL2 42 F6
Thorncliffe Rd BOL BL1 22 C7
GLSP SK13 104 C1
Thorn Cl HEY OL10 40 E1
Thorncombe Rd
OLDTF/WHR M16 98 B1
Thorn Ct SLFD M6 86 B2
Thorncross Cl HULME M15 86 F5
Thorndale Cl ROY/SHW OL2 43 H7
Thorndale Gv
HALE/TIMP WA15 108 D7
Thorn Dr WYTH/NTH M22 119 J4
Thorne Av URM M41 95 K1
Thorneside DTN/ASHW M34 90 C7
Thorne St FWTH BL4 52 F3
Thorneycroft LEIGH WN7 66 F7
Thorneycroft Av CCHDY M21 97 M7
Thorneycroft Rd
HALE/TIMP WA15 108 E7
Thorney Dr CHD/CHDH SK8 120 E6
Thorney Hill Cl OLDE OL4 * 9 M7
Thorneyholme Cl HOR/BR BL6 34 F6
Thorneylea WHIT OL12 20 B3
Thornfield Av AUL OL6 91 H1
Thornfield Cl GOL/RIS/CUL WA3 79 M4
Thornfield Crs LHULT M38 52 C7
Thornfield Dr SWIN M27 70 B5
Thornfield Gv CHD/CHDH SK8 120 C2
LHULT M38 52 C7
Thornfield Hey WILM/AE SK9 127 J4
Thornfield Houses
CHD/CHDH SK8 * 120 C2
Thornfield Rd BNG/LEV M19 99 H7
HTNM SK4 111 K1
TOT/BURYW BL8 24 A5
Thornfield St ORD M5 86 A3
Thorngate Rd CHH M8 72 D7
Thorn Gv CHD/CHDH SK8 120 D5
HALE/TIMP WA15 117 G1
RUSH/FAL M14 99 G4
SALE M33 96 E8
Thorngrove Av
NTHM/RTH M23 109 G5
Thorngrove Dr WILM/AE SK9 127 G6
Thorngrove Hl WILM/AE SK9 127 G6
Thorngrove Rd WILM/AE SK9 127 G6
Thornham Cl TOT/BURYW BL8 24 F6
Thornham Ct ROY/SHW OL2 42 F4
Thornham Dr BOL BL1 22 C6
Thornham La MDTN M24 42 B6
Thornham New Rd ROCH OL11 42 B4
Thornham Rd ROY/SHW OL2 43 G5
SALE M33 108 C1
Thornhill Dr WALK M28 69 H4
Thornhill Rd AIMK WN4 62 F8
DROY M43 89 L2
HTNM SK4 111 J2
RAMS BL0 24 D3
Thornholme Cl GTN M18 99 L1
Thornholme Rd MPL/ROM SK6 114 D8
Thorniley Brow ANC M4 7 G3
Thorn Lea ATH M46 67 H2
BOLE BL2 23 G8
Thornlea DROY M43 89 H3
HALE/TIMP WA15 108 C8
Thornlea Av OLDS OL8 74 F3
SWIN M27 70 A6
Thorn Lea Cl BOL BL1 35 J5
Thornlea Dr WHIT OL12 27 L2
Thornleigh Rd RUSH/FAL M14 98 E3
Thornley Av BOL BL1 35 M2
Thornley Cl OLDE OL4 60 D7
Thornley Crs MPL/ROM SK6 101 K8
OLDE OL4 60 D7
Thornley La OLDE OL4 60 D7
Thornley La North RDSH SK5 100 C1
Thornley La South RDSH SK5 100 D3
Thornley Ms BOL BL1 * 35 M2
Thornley Park Rd OLDE OL4 60 D7
Thornley Rd DTN/ASHW M34 90 D8
PWCH M25 55 M5
Thornley St HYDE SK14 102 B3
MDTN M24 57 L3
RAD M26 54 E2
Thornmere Cl SWIN M27 69 M2
Thorn Rd BRAM/HZG SK7 121 G7
OLDS OL8 75 M1
SWIN M27 70 B6
Thorns Av BOL BL1 36 A1
Thorns Cl BOL BL1 36 A1
Thorns Clough UPML OL3 45 M7
Thornsett NM/HAY SK22 124 F2
Thornsett Cl BKLY M9 * 73 H4
Thornsgreen Rd
WYTH/NTH M22 118 F4
Thorns Rd BOL BL1 36 A1
The Thorns CCHDY M21 97 L5
Thorn St BOL BL1 36 C2
BURY BL9 24 F1
WGNE/HIN WN2 49 G8
Thorns Villa Gdns WALK M28 68 D7
Thornton Av BOL BL1 35 J3
DTN/ASHW M34 89 M4
URM M41 95 K2
Thornton Cl AIMK WN4 63 J8
BOLS/LL BL3 53 M2
FWTH BL4 52 E5
LEIGH WN7 81 J3
WALK M28 68 B5
Thornton Crs PWCH M25 55 J7
Thornton Dr WILM/AE SK9 127 H1
Thornton Ga CHD/CHDH SK8 110 D6
Thornton Pl HTNM SK4 99 L8
Thornton Rd CHD/CHDH SK8 119 L3
RUSH/FAL M14 98 D2
WALK M28 68 B5
Thornton St BOLE BL2 3 H4
NEWH/MOS M40 72 F8
OLDE OL4 9 K8
ROCH OL11 10 E9
Thornton St North
NEWH/MOS M40 73 G8
Thorntree Cl BKLY M9 73 H5
Thorntree Pl WHIT OL12 10 E2
Thornvale WGNE/HIN WN2 64 F5
Thorn Vw BURY BL9 39 M1
Thornway BRAM/HZG SK7 120 E4
MPL/ROM SK6 123 H5
WALK M28 69 J6
Thornway Dr AULW OL7 90 C2
Thorn Well WHTN BL5 50 B4
Thornwood Av GTN M18 89 H8
Thornydyke Av BOL BL1 22 C7
Thorold Gv SALE M33 97 H8
Thorpe Av RAD M26 39 G7
SWIN M27 70 B3
Thorpebrook Rd
NEWH/MOS M40 73 K6
Thorpe Cl DTN/ASHW M34 90 C8
OLDE OL4 60 D4
Thorpe Gv HTNM SK4 100 A6
Thorpe Hall Gv HYDE SK14 91 J6
Thorpe La OLDE OL4 60 D4
Thorpeness Sq GTN M18 89 G6
Thorpe St BOL BL1 36 A2
GLSP SK13 105 G1
MDTN M24 56 F5
OLDTF/WHR M16 86 F8
RAMS BL0 * 18 E7
WALK M28 53 G8
Thorp Rd NEWH/MOS M40 73 K6
ROY/SHW OL2 43 G8
Thorp St ECC M30 84 E4
WHTF M45 55 H4
Thorp Vw ROY/SHW OL2 42 F7
Thorsby Av HYDE SK14 102 C1
Thorsby Cl EDGW/EG BL7 22 C4
Thorsby Rd HALE/TIMP WA15 108 B7
Thrapston Av DTN/ASHW M34 90 A3
Threadfold Wy EDGW/EG BL7 22 C5
Threaphurst La
BRAM/HZG SK7 122 E3
Threapwood Rd
WYTH/NTH M22 119 G3
Three Acre Av ROY/SHW OL2 43 K8
Three Acres La
CHD/CHDH SK8 120 A5
Three Sisters Rd AIMK WN4 63 M5
Threlkeld Cl MDTN M24 56 F3
Threlkeld Rd BOL BL1 22 A5
MDTN M24 56 F3
Thresher Cl SALE M33 109 J1
Threshfield Cl BURY BL9 25 J5
Threshfield Dr
HALE/TIMP WA15 108 F5
Throstle Bank St HYDE SK14 90 F8
Throstle Gv MPL/ROM SK6 114 B7
TOT/BURYW BL8 24 F7
Throstle Hall Ct MDTN M24 * 57 J3
Throstle Nest Av
WGNNW/ST WN6 14 B1
Throstles Cl DROY M43 89 M1
Thrum Fold WHIT OL12 20 B8
Thrum Hall La WHIT OL12 28 B1
Thrush Dr BURY BL9 5 K1
Thrush St WHIT OL12 27 M3
Thruxton Cl OLDTF/WHR M16 98 B1
Thurcaston Rd ALT WA14 * 107 M3
Thurland Rd OLDE OL4 59 M6
Thurland St CHAD OL9 58 B4
Thurlby Av BKLY M9 57 H7
Thurlby Cl AIMK WN4 64 A8
Thurlby St BRUN/LGST M13 88 A8
Thurleigh Rd DID/WITH M20 98 E8
Thurlestone Av BOLE BL2 38 A3
Thurlestone Dr
BRAM/HZG SK7 121 K2
URM M41 95 M1
Thurlestone Rd ALT WA14 107 L6
Thurloe St RUSH/FAL M14 98 F1
Thurlow GOL/RIS/CUL WA3 80 B5
Thurlow St SALQ M50 86 C4
Thurlston Crs CHH M8 72 E5
Thurlwood Av DID/WITH M20 98 D5
Thurlwood Cft WHTN BL5 50 B3
Thurnham St BOLS/LL BL3 51 M1
Thursfield St SLFD M6 71 L7
Thursford Gv HOR/BR BL6 33 G3
Thurstane St BOL BL1 35 M2
Thurstan St WGNS/IIMK WN3 48 B8
Thurston Av WGNS/IIMK WN3 63 L1
Thurston Cl BURY BL9 55 K2
Thurston Clough Rd OLDE OL4 61 G3
Thurston Gn WILM/AE SK9 130 D3
Thynne St BOLS/LL BL3 2 F8
FWTH BL4 52 F3
Tiber Av OLDS OL8 74 F3
Tib La CMANW M2 6 F5
Tib St CMANE M1 7 H4
DTN/ASHW M34 101 J2
RAMS BL0 * 18 E7
Tideswell Av NEWH/MOS M40 88 A1
WGNW/BIL/OR WN5 46 D3
Tideswell Cl CHD/CHDH SK8 119 M4
Tideswell Rd BRAM/HZG SK7 122 A4
DROY M43 89 H1
Tideway Cl BRO M7 71 J4
Tidworth Av ANC M4 7 M3
Tiflis St WHIT OL12 10 D2
Tig Fold Rd FWTH BL4 52 B4
Tilbury Gv WGNNW/ST WN6 30 A5
Tilbury St OLD OL1 9 G2
Tilby Cl URM M41 95 H2
Tildsley St BOLS/LL BL3 36 B8
Tile St BURY BL9 4 F2
Tillard Av EDGY/DAV SK3 12 B7
Tillerman Cl SWIN M27 71 G4
Tillhey Rd WYTH/NTH M22 118 F2
Tilney Av STRET M32 97 H3
Tilshead Wk BRUN/LGST M13 * 87 M6
Tilside Gv HOR/BR BL6 34 E6
Tilson Rd NTHM/RTH M23 109 J7
Tilton St OLD OL1 59 M2
Timberbottom BOLE BL2 22 F8
Timberhurst BURY BL9 40 A2
Times St MDTN M24 57 L4
Timothy Cl SLFD M6 85 L1
Timperley Cl OLDS OL8 75 K2
Timperley Fold AUL OL6 75 M6
Timperley La LEIGH WN7 81 L2
Timperley Rd AUL OL6 75 L6
Timperley St OP/CLY M11 * 88 F4
Timpson Rd NTHM/RTH M23 109 H5
Timsbury Cl BOLE BL2 37 J7
Timson St FAIL M35 74 C5
Tindall St ECC M30 84 E4
RDSH SK5 100 C1
Tindle St WALK M28 69 J1
Tinkersfield LEIGH WN7 66 A5
Tinline St BURY BL9 5 J5
Tinningham Cl OP/CLY M11 89 H5
Tinshill Cl WGTN/LGST M12 88 D7
Tinsley Cl NEWH/MOS M40 88 B2
Tinsley Gv BOLE BL2 3 K2
Tin St BOLS/LL BL3 2 D8
Tintagel Ct RAD M26 37 M7
STLY SK15 91 J2
Tintagel Rd WGNE/HIN WN2 49 K8
Tintern Av AIMK WN4 79 G1
BOLE BL2 36 E2
DID/WITH M20 98 C7
HEY OL10 26 F8
LIT OL15 21 L5
TYLD M29 67 M5
URM M41 95 K4
WHIT OL12 28 B2
WHTF M45 55 J3
Tintern Cl POY/DIS SK12 121 M7
Tintern Dr HALE/TIMP WA15 117 L2
Tintern Gv STKP SK1 112 E3
Tintern Pl HEY OL10 26 F8
Tintern Rd CHD/CHDH SK8 120 D6
MDTN M24 57 J1
Tintern St RUSH/FAL M14 98 E2
Tinwald Pl WGN WN1 15 M2
Tipperary St STLY SK15 77 H7
Tipping St ALT WA14 116 F1
WGNS/IIMK WN3 14 D8
Tipton Cl CHD/CHDH SK8 111 L8
RAD M26 38 A7
Tipton Dr NTHM/RTH M23 109 K2
Tiree Cl BRAM/HZG SK7 122 B3
Tirza Av BNG/LEV M19 99 J5
Titanian Ri OLD OL1 44 A7
Titchfield Rd OLDS OL8 59 M8
Tithe Barn Cl WHIT OL12 * 21 H8
Tithe Barn Crs BOL BL1 22 E8
Tithebarn Rd
HALE/TIMP WA15 117 L4
Tithe Barn Rd HTNM SK4 99 J8
Tithebarn St BURY BL9 4 F4
Tithe Barn St WHTN BL5 50 B3
Titherington Cl
BNG/LEV M19 * 100 A3
Titterington Av CCHDY M21 97 L2
Tiverton Av LEIGH WN7 66 A2
SALE M33 108 C1
Tiverton Cl RAD M26 38 A7
TYLD M29 67 M5

Tiverton Dr SALE M33....108 C1
WILM/AE SK9....127 H3
Tiverton Pl AULW OL7....75 K7
Tiverton Rd URM M41....85 H8
Tiverton Wk BOL BL1 *....35 M3
Tiviot Dl STKP SK1....13 J3
Tiviot Wy RDSH SK5....112 C1
Tivoli St M3....6 E5
Toad La WHIT OL12....10 D3
Tobermory Cl OP/CLY M11....89 G3
Tobermory Rd CHD/CHDH SK8....119 L2
Toddington La
WGNE/HIN WN2....32 E4
Todd St BRO M7....72 A6
BURY BL9....4 F1
CSLFD M3....7 G2
GLSP SK13....105 G4
HEY OL10....40 D2
MILN OL16....11 G5
Toft Rd GTN M18....88 C7
Toledo St OP/CLY M11....89 G3
Tolland La HALE/TIMP WA15....117 H4
Tollard Av NEWH/MOS M40....73 G7
Tollard Cl CHD/CHDH SK8....120 D5
Toll Bar St STKP SK1....13 K6
WGTN/LGST M12....88 B6
Tollemache Rd HYDE SK14....92 D7
Tollemache Rd HYDE SK14....92 D7
Tollesbury Cl NEWH/MOS M40....73 M8
Toll Gate Cl BRUN/LGST M13....88 B8
Tollgate Wy WHIT OL16....11 L3
Tollgreen Cl WGNE/HIN WN2....49 G5
Toll St RAD M26....38 A8
WGNE/HIN WN2....64 D3
Tolworth Dr CHH M8....72 E5
Tomcroft La DTN/ASHW M34....101 G2
Tom La ALT WA14....116 A6
Tomlinson Cl OLDS OL8....9 H9
Tomlinson St HOR/BR BL6....33 L1
HULME M15....87 H6
NEWH/MOS M40....73 M1
ROCH OL11....27 M8
Tomlin Sq BOLE BL2....3 M4
Tommy Browell Cl
RUSH/FAL M14....98 D1
Tommy Johnson Wk
RUSH/FAL M14....98 D1
Tommy La BOLE BL2....37 M3
Tommy Taylor Cl
NEWH/MOS M40 *....73 M7
Tom Shepley St HYDE SK14....102 B2
Tomwood Ri GLSP SK13....103 M6
Tonacliffe Rd WHIT OL12....20 A5
Tonacliffe Ter WHIT OL12....20 A5
Tonacliffe Wy WHIT OL12....20 A3
Tonbridge Cl TOT/BURYW BL8....24 F5
Tonbridge Rd BNG/LEV M19....99 L4
RDSH SK5....100 C4
Tonge Bridge Wy BOLE BL2....3 J4
Tonge Cl WHTF M45....55 L3
Tonge Fold Rd BOLE BL2....3 L5
Tonge Gn STLY SK15 *....92 B6
Tonge Hall Cl MDTN M24....57 L4
Tonge Meadow MDTN M24....57 L4
Tonge Moor Rd BOLE BL2....3 K1
Tonge End WHIT OL12....20 A2
Tonge Old Rd BOLE BL2....3 M4
Tonge Park Av BOLE BL2....36 F3
Tonge Roughs MDTN M24....58 A3
Tonge St HEY OL10....41 G2
MILN OL16 *....11 G6
WGTN/LGST M12 *....88 A1
Tongfields EDGW/EG BL7....22 C4
Tong Head Av BOL BL1....22 E8
Tong La WHIT OL12....20 A3
Tong Rd BOLS/LL BL3....37 K8
Tong St FWTH BL4....53 L7
Tonman St CSLFD M3....6 D6
Toon Crs TOT/BURYW BL8....24 F6
Tootal Dr SLFD M6....85 M1
Tootal Gv SLFD M6....85 M2
Tootal Rd ORD M5....85 M2
Toothill Rd AIMK WN4....63 L7
Topcroft Cl WYTH/NTH M22....110 B4
Topfield Rd WYTH/NTH M22....118 C1
Topgate Brow SWIN M27....71 G4
Topham St BURY BL9....5 H8
Topley St BKLY M9....72 F6
Top o' th' Brow BOLE BL2 *....23 H6
Top o' th' Gorses BOLE BL2 *....3 M8
Top o' th' Gn CHAD OL9....58 F8
Top o' th' La BOLS/LL BL3 *....37 G7
Top o' th' Meadows La
OLDE OL4....60 D3
Topping Fold Rd BURY BL9....5 M2
Toppings Gn EDGW/EG BL7....22 C5
The Toppings MPL/ROM SK6....113 K1
Topping St BOL BL1....36 B3
BURY BL9....5 G3
Topp St FWTH BL4....53 H5
Topp Wy BOL BL1....2 D3
Top Schwabe St MDTN M24....56 F7
Topside OLD OL1....59 H3
Top St MDTN M24....58 C8
OLDE OL4....60 A4
Torah St CHH M8....72 D8
Tor Av TOT/BURYW BL8....24 C3
Torbay Dr OFTN SK2....112 E5
Torbay Rd CCHDY M21....97 M4
URM M41....96 B3
Torcross Rd BKLY M9....56 E7
Tor Heg Ms TOT/BURYW BL8....24 C2
Torkington Av SWIN M27....70 C3
Torkington La BRAM/HZG SK7....122 F1
Torkington Rd BRAM/HZG SK7....122 G2
CHD/CHDH SK8....110 E7
WILM/AE SK9....130 E3
Torkington St EDGY/DAV SK3....12 E8
Torness Wk OP/CLY M11....88 E3
Toronto Av MANAIR M90....118 D5
Toronto Rd OFTN SK2....112 D6
Toronto St BOLE BL2....37 H4
Torquay Cl BRUN/LGST M13....88 A7
Torquay Dr WGNW/BIL/OR WN5....62 B4
Torquay Gv OFTN SK2....112 E8
Torra Barn Cl EDGW/EG BL7....22 B2
Torrax Cl SLFD M6....70 E6
Torre Cl MDTN M24....57 K1
Torrens St SLFD M6....71 G7
Torridon Cl WGNNW/ST WN6....31 K5
Torridon Rd BOLE BL2....37 M3
Torrin Cl EDGY/DAV SK3....112 C7
Torrington Av BKLY M9....73 K1
BOL BL1....36 B2
Torrington Dr HYDE SK14....103 G2
Torrington Rd SWIN M27....70 D3
Torrington St HEY OL10....41 H4
Torrisdale Cl BOLS/LL BL3....35 L7
Torrs Va NM/HAY SK22....124 C3
Torr Top St NM/HAY SK22....124 E4
Torvale Rd NM/HAY SK22....124 D5
Torside Cl WGNE/HIN WN2....49 G6

Torside Wy GLSP SK13....93 K7
SWIN M27....70 C2
Torver Cl WGNS/IIMK WN3....63 K2
Torver Dr BOLE BL2....37 J4
MDTN M24....57 G2
Torwood Rd CHAD OL9....58 B3
Totland Cl WGTN/LGST M12....99 K1
Totley Ms GLSP SK13....104 A3
Totnes Av BRAM/HZG SK7....121 J3
CHAD OL9....58 C3
Totnes Rd CCHDY M21....97 M4
SALE M33....96 A7
Totridge Cl OFTN SK2....113 G7
Tottenham Dr NTHM/RTH M23....109 G5
Tottington Av OLDE OL4....60 C5
Tottington La PWCH M25....55 H7
Tottington Rd BOLE BL2....23 H7
EDGW/EG BL7....23 J2
TOT/BURYW BL8....4 A1
Tottington St OP/CLY M11....88 F2
Totton Rd FAIL M35....74 C5
Touchet Hall Rd MDTN M24....42 B8
Toulston Rd WGNNW/ST WN6....47 J2
Tours Av NTHM/RTH M23....109 K2
Towcester Cl ANC M4....88 A3
Tower Buildings HOR/BR BL6 *....34 D1
Tower Ct EDGW/EG BL7....16 F8
TOT/BURYW BL8 *....24 C4
Tower Gv LEIGH WN7....67 G6
Towers Av BOLS/LL BL3....53 J3
Towers Cl POY/DIS SK12....122 B7
Tower Sq BRUN/LGST M13 *....87 M6
Towers Rd POY/DIS SK12....122 B7
Towers St OLDE OL4....60 A3
Tower St DUK SK16....91 G3
EDGW/EG BL7....16 F8
HEY OL10....40 F2
HYDE SK14....102 A3
RAD M26....39 G8
Towey Cl GTN M18....89 G6
Towncliffe Wk HULME M15 *....87 G6
Towncroft DTN/ASHW M34....90 C8
Towncroft Av MDTN M24....57 J2
Towncroft La BOL BL1....35 H4
Townend St HYDE SK14....102 B2
Townley Rd MILN OL16....29 K6
Townley St CHH M8....72 C7
MDTN M24....57 K3
OP/CLY M11 *....88 C4
Townley Ter MPL/ROM SK6 *....114 D6
Town Mdw MILN OL16....10 D5
Town Mill Brow WHIT OL12....10 D3
Townrow St HEY OL10 *....41 G1
Townscliffe La MPL/ROM SK6....114 D6
Townsend Rd SWIN M27....70 C3
Townsfield Rd WHTN BL5....50 B5
Townside Rw BURY BL9....4 F6
Townsley Gv AUL OL6....76 B7
Townson Dr LEIGH WN7....81 J3
Towns St BRLY M9....73 H4
Towton St BRLY M9....73 H4
Towyn Av ORD M5....86 D2
Toxhead Cl HOR/BR BL6....33 K1
Toxteth St OP/CLY M11....89 H5
Tracey St CHH M8....72 D3
Tracks La WGNW/BIL/OR WN5....62 A1
Traders Av URM M41....85 H5
Trafalgar Av DTN/ASHW M34....89 M5
POY/DIS SK12....129 L1
Trafalgar Gv BRO M7....72 A7
Trafalgar Pl DID/WITH M20....98 D8
Trafalgar Rd SALE M33....96 F6
SLFD M6....85 K1
WGNE/HIN WN2....14 F1
Trafalgar Sq AULW OL7....90 C3
Trafalgar St AULW OL7....90 C3
BRO M7....72 B7
MILN OL16....11 H3
OLD OL1....9 G7
Trafford Av URM M41....96 B1
Trafford Bank Rd
OLDTF/WHR M16 *....86 F7
URM M41....84 F6
Trafford Dr HALE/TIMP WA15....108 E4
LHULT M38....52 E7
Trafford Gv FWTH BL4....53 H3
STRET M32....97 G3
Trafford Park Rd TRPK M17....85 M5
Trafford Pl OLDTF/WHR M16 *....87 G6
WILM/AE SK9 *....127 H6
Trafford Rd ECC M30....85 G4
SALQ M50....85 H4
WGNE/HIN WN2....48 F7
WILM/AE SK9....126 E3
WILM/AE SK9....130 E3
Trafford St CSLFD M3....6 D7
FWTH BL4....53 G3
OLDS OL8....9 H8
ROCH OL11....10 D8
Trafford Wharf Rd TRPK M17....85 M5
Tragan Cl OFTN SK2....113 G6
Tragan Dr OFTN SK2....113 G6
Trail St SLFD M6....86 B2
Tram St OP/CLY M11....88 F5
WGNE/HIN WN2....64 D3
Tramway Rd AUL OL6....90 F1
IRL M44....94 C5
Tranby Cl WYTH/NTH M22....110 C8
Tranmere Cl GTN M18....88 E7
Tranmere Dr WILM/AE SK9....127 J2
Tranmere Rd EDGY/DAV SK3....12 A6
Transvaal St OP/CLY M11....89 G5
Travis Brow STKP SK4....12 B2
Travis St CMANE M1....7 L6
HYDE SK14....102 B2
MILN OL16....29 L8
ROY/SHW OL2....43 M5
Trawden Av BOL BL1....35 M2
Trawden Dr BURY BL9....25 H4
Trawden Gn OFTN SK2....113 G8
Traylen Wy WHIT OL12....27 K3

Traynor Cl MDTN M24....57 J3
Trecastell Cl WGN WN1....15 M2
Tredcroft St GLSP SK13....104 E4
Tredgold St HOR/BR BL6....33 M2
Tree Av DROY M43....89 K1
Tree House Av AULW OL7....75 J6
Treelands Wk ORD M5....86 E6
Treen Rd TYLD M29....67 M4
Tree Tops EDGW/EG BL7....22 F6
Treetops Av RAMS BL0....24 D1
Treetops St UPML OL3 *....61 J3
Trefoil Wy LIT OL15....21 K6
Tregaer Fold MDTN M24....57 M4
Tregaron Gv WGNE/HIN WN2....65 K1
Trenam Pl ORD M5....86 E2
Trenant Rd SLFD M6....71 G8
Trenchard Dr WYTH/NTH M22....119 H5
Trencherbone RAD M26....38 B7
Trencherfield Ml
WGNS/IIMK WN3 *....14 E6
Trengrove St WHIT OL12 *....27 M3
Trent Av CHAD OL9....58 B4
HEY OL10....40 D1
MILN OL16....29 K6
Trent Bridge Wk
OLDTF/WHR M16....97 K1
Trent Cl BRAM/HZG SK7....120 E6
RDSH SK5....100 F7
Trent Ct HULME M15 *....87 G6
Trent Dr BURY BL9....25 J4
WALK M28....68 E2
WGNE/HIN WN2....65 M1
Trent Gv LEIGH WN7....65 H8
Trentham Av FWTH BL4....52 F3
HTNM SK4....111 J1
Trentham Gv NEWH/MOS M40....73 K3
Trentham Lawns SLFD M6....71 K8
Trentham Rd OLDTF/WHR M16....97 K1
Trentham St FWTH BL4....52 F3
HULME M15....86 F5
SWIN M27 *....70 B3
Trent Rd AIMK WN4....64 B7
ROY/SHW OL2....43 K4
WGNW/BIL/OR WN5....46 F5
Trent St MILN OL16 *....11 J7
Trent Wk DROY M43....89 L4
Trent Wy FWTH BL4....52 F3
Tresco Av STRET M32....97 H3
Trescott Ms WGNNW/ST WN6....31 H4
Treswell Cl WGNE/HIN WN2....65 H2
Trevarrick Ct HOR/BR BL6....34 B2
Trevelyan Dr
WGNW/BIL/OR WN5....62 A3
Trevelyan St ECC M30....85 K2
Trevor Av BOLS/LL BL3....52 A5
Trevor Dr NEWH/MOS M40....74 B2
Trevore Dr WGN WN1....31 M3
Trevor Gv STKP SK1....13 M6
Trevor Rd ECC M30....84 E1
SWIN M27....70 B6
URM M41....95 J1
Trevor St OP/CLY M11....89 H5
ROCH OL11....41 L1
The Triangle HALE/TIMP WA15....108 E5
Tribune Av ALT WA14....107 L5
Trident Rd ECC M30....84 C5
Trillo Av BOLE BL2....3 K7
Trimdon Cl OP/CLY M11....88 E2
Trimingham Dr
TOT/BURYW BL8....25 C6
Trimley Av NEWH/MOS M40....73 C7
Trinity Av SALE M33....97 G8
Trinity Buildings MOSL OL5 *....77 C2
Trinity Cl DUK SK16....91 H4
Trinity Crs WALK M28....69 C2
Trinity Gdns AIMK WN4....63 J8
EDGY/DAV SK3....121 H1
Trinity Gn RAMS BL0....24 E2
Trinity Rd SALE M33....96 F8
Trinity St BOLS/LL BL3....2 D7
BURY BL9....4 F6
MDTN M24 *....57 J4
MPL/ROM SK6 *....114 C6
OLD OL1....9 J2
STLY SK15....91 K5
Trinity Wy CSLFD M3....6 B5
Trippier Rd ECC M30....84 C4
Tripps Ms DID/WITH M20....98 C8
Triscombe Wy OLDTF/WHR M16....98 B1
Tristam Cl BRUN/LGST M13....87 M6
Trojan Gdns BRO M7....71 M7
Troon Cl BOLS/LL BL3....51 J1
BRAM/HZG SK7....121 J5
Troon Dr CHD/CHDH SK8....119 L3
Troon Rd NTHM/RTH M23....109 H6
Trough Ga OLDS OL8....75 G2
Troutbeck Av ANC M4....7 M3
NEWLW WA12....78 B8
Troutbeck Cl TOT/BURYW BL8....23 L2
Troutbeck Dr RAMS BL0....18 F5
TYLD M29....67 K5
Troutbeck Ri
WGNW/BIL/OR WN5....46 E6
Troutbeck Rd AIMK WN4....63 M7
CHD/CHDH SK8....119 K1
HALE/TIMP WA15....109 G7
Troutbeck Wy ROCH OL11....27 L8
Trowbridge Dr
NEWH/MOS M40....73 M3
Trowbridge Rd
DTN/ASHW M34....101 K3
Trows La ROCH OL11....42 A3
Trowtree Av WGTN/LGST M12....88 B6
Troydale Dr NEWH/MOS M40....73 K6
Troy Wk ORD M5 *....86 E5
Trumpet St CMANE M1....6 E7
Truro Av AUL OL6....76 A5
RDSH SK5....100 F7
STRET M32....97 H4
Truro Cl BRAM/HZG SK7....121 H5
TOT/BURYW BL8 *....4 C2
Truro Dr SALE M33....96 A8
Truro Rd CHAD OL9....58 D3
TYLD M29....67 M4
Trust Rd GTN M18....99 H1
Tucana Av BRO M7....86 F1
Tucker's Hill Brow HOR/BR BL6....32 E3
Tudbury Wy CSLFD M3....6 B2
Tudor Av BKLY M9....73 H3
BOLS/LL BL3....35 L5
CHAD OL9....74 A1
FWTH BL4....53 J7
STLY SK15....92 A1
Tudor Cl MOSL OL5....77 M1
RDSH SK5....100 B5
Tudor Ct PWCH M25....71 M1
WHIT OL12 *....28 B1
Tudor Gn WILM/AE SK9....126 E7
Tudor Gv MDTN M24....57 G1
WGNS/IIMK WN3....63 H2

Tudor Hall St ROCH OL11....41 M2
WILM/AE SK9....127 L5
Tudor St BOLS/LL BL3 *....35 M8
MDTN M24....57 L4
OLDS OL8....8 F8
ROY/SHW OL2....43 L5
Tuffley Rd NTHM/RTH M23....109 K8
Tugford Cl OLDTF/WHR M16....98 B1
Tuley St OP/CLY M11....88 C5
Tulip Av FWTH BL4....52 D3
FWTH BL4....53 J7
Tulip Cl CHAD OL9....58 B5
EDGY/DAV SK3....112 A7
SALE M33....95 M8
Tulip Dr HALE/TIMP WA15....108 C6
WGNNW/ST WN6....47 J1
Tulip Gv WHIT OL12....28 B7
Tulip Rd PART M31....106 B2
RNFD/HAY WA11....78 C6
Tully Pl BRO M7....72 B8
Tully St BRO M7....72 B5
Tully St South BRO M7....72 B6
Tulpen Sq CHAD OL9....8 A4
Tulworth Rd POY/DIS SK12....121 M8
Tumblewood Dr
CHD/CHDH SK8....111 H8
Tunbridge Sq ORD M5....86 D2
Tunshill La MILN OL16....29 M5
Tunshill Rd NTHM/RTH M23....109 H3
Tunstall Cl BURY BL9....39 K5
Tunstall La WGNW/BIL/OR WN5....47 C7
Tunstall Rd OLDE OL4....59 M6
Tunstall St HTNM SK4....13 H2
OP/CLY M11 *....89 H5
Tunstead Av DID/WITH M20....98 C6
Tunstead La UPML OL3....61 M7
Turbary Wk MILN OL16....29 M6
Turf Cl ROY/SHW OL2....59 H1
Turf Hill Rd MILN OL16....11 K9
Turf House Cl LIT OL15....21 K5
Turfland Av ROY/SHW OL2....59 H1
Turf La CHAD OL9....74 D1
ROY/SHW OL2....59 J1
Turf Lea Rd MPL/ROM SK6....123 K3
Turf Park Rd ROY/SHW OL2....59 J1
Turf Pit La OLDE OL4....44 C8
Turf St RAD M26....54 C1
Turf Ter LIT OL15....21 L6
Turfton Rd ROY/SHW OL2....59 J1
Turks Rd RAD M26....38 A7
Turk St BOL BL1....35 M4
Turley St CHH M8....72 E6
Turnberry BOLS/LL BL3....51 J1
Turnberry Dr WILM/AE SK9....127 H4
Turnberry Rd CHD/CHDH SK8....119 L3
Turnbull Av PWCH M25....55 M5
Turnbull Rd ALT WA14....107 L4
BRUN/LGST M13....99 J2
GTN M18....100 C1
Turnbury Cl SALE M33....96 E6
Turnbury Rd WYTH/NTH M22....110 B7
Turncliff Crs MPL/ROM SK6....114 A5
Turncroft La STKP SK1....13 L4
STKP SK1....112 F4
Turncroft Wk WALK M28....68 C5
Turnditch Cl WGNNW/ST WN6....31 K3
Turnell Wy WALK M28....69 K7
Turner Av FAIL M35....74 B6
IRL M44....94 D1
WGNE/HIN WN2....65 H3
Turner Bridge Rd BOLE BL2....3 L2
Turner Dr URM M41....96 C2
Turnerford Cl EDGW/EG BL7....22 B3
Turner Gdns HYDE SK14....91 H8
Turner La AUL OL6....75 L8
HYDE SK14....91 H8
MPL/ROM SK6....101 J6
Turner Rd MPL/ROM SK6....114 C7
Turners Pl WHIT OL12....28 B1
Turner St ANC M4....7 H3
AUL OL6....75 L8
BOL BL1....3 G2
BRO M7....72 B5
DTN/ASHW M34....90 C7
GTN M18....89 G7
LEIGH WN7....66 D4
OLDE OL4....60 B4
OLDTF/WHR M16....86 F6
OP/CLY M11....88 F3
STKP SK1....13 J3
WGN WN1....15 J3
WHIT OL12....28 B3
WHTN BL5....50 B7
Turners Yd
WGNW/BIL/OR WN5 *....46 B6
Turnfield Cl MILN OL16....29 C1
Turnfield Rd CHD/CHDH SK8....119 L1
Turnhill Rd MILN OL16....42 E1
Turnill Dr AIMK WN4....78 E2
Turnlee Cl GLSP SK13....104 F5
Turnlee Dr GLSP SK13....104 F5
Turnlee Rd GLSP SK13....104 F5
Turn Moss Rd STRET M32....97 J4
Turnough Rd MILN OL16....29 J5
Turnpike Cl UPML OL3....45 M7
Turnpike Gn SLFD M6 *....86 C1
The Turnpike MPL/ROM SK6....114 A5
Turnpike Wk OP/CLY M11....88 C3
Turn Rd RAMS BL0....19 H4
Turnstone Av NEWLW WA12....78 B8
Turnstone Cl LEIGH WN7....66 D6
Turnstone Rd BOLE BL2....3 G7
OFTN SK2....113 K7
Turn St AUL OL6....76 A3
Turret Hall Dr
GOL/RIS/CUL WA3....80 A3
Turriff Gv WGNE/HIN WN2....48 D3
Turton Cl HEY OL10....40 D2
TOT/BURYW BL8....38 D4
Turton Ct BOL BL1....3 G2
Turton Hts BOLE BL2....22 E6
Turton La PWCH M25....55 J7
Turton Rd BOLE BL2....22 E6
TOT/BURYW BL8....24 B4
Turton St BOL BL1....2 F2
GOL/RIS/CUL WA3....79 K4
OP/CLY M11 *....89 K4
Turves Rd CHD/CHDH SK8....120 B3
Tuscan Rd DID/WITH M20....110 D4
Tuscany Vw BRO M7....71 L4
Tutbury St ANC M4....88 A3
Tuxford Wk NEWH/MOS M40....73 M4
Tweedale Av BKLY M9....56 C7
Tweedale St ROCH OL11....10 D7
Tweedale Wy CHAD OL9....74 C2
Tweed Cl ALT WA14....107 M6
OLDS OL8....9 H8
Tweedle Hill Rd BKLY M9....56 F8
Tweed St LEIGH WN7....66 E3

Tweenbrook Av
NTHM/RTH M23....118 C1
Tweesdale Cl WHTF M45....55 L3
Twelve Yards Rd ECC M30....84 A5
IRL M44....82 F8
Twigworth Rd
WYTH/NTH M22....118 E2
Twillbrook Dr CSLFD M3 *....6 C1
Twinegate WHIT OL12....28 B1
Twingates Cl ROY/SHW OL2....43 L7
Twining Brook Rd
CHD/CHDH SK8....120 D1
Twining Rd ECC M30....85 C4
Twinnies Rd WILM/AE SK9....126 F3
Twin St HEY OL10....41 H3
Twirl Hill Rd AUL OL6....76 B4
Twisse Rd BOLE BL2....37 J5
Twiss Green Dr
GOL/RIS/CUL WA3....81 H8
Twiss Green La
GOL/RIS/CUL WA3....81 H8
Twist Av GOL/RIS/CUL WA3....79 M4
Twist La LEIGH WN7....66 B8
Twoacre Av WYTH/NTH M22....109 M7
Two Acre Dr ROY/SHW OL2....43 J4
Two Acre La OLDE OL4....60 E2
Two Bridges Rd MILN OL16....43 L1
Two Brooks La
TOT/BURYW BL8....23 L2
Two Trees La DTN/ASHW M34....101 K3
Twyford Cl DID/WITH M20....110 C1
Tydden St OLDS OL8....75 J1
Tydeman Wk MILN OL16 *....29 K7
Tyldesley Ar WGN WN1 *....15 G3
Tyldesley Old Rd ATH M46....67 G2
Tyldesley Pas TYLD M29....67 J3
Tyldesley Rd ATH M46....67 G2
RUSH/FAL WA3....98 D1
Tyler St WILM/AE SK9....130 D3
Tymm St NEWH/MOS M40....73 M4
Tyndall Av NEWH/MOS M40....73 K3
Tyndall St OLDE OL4....59 M7
Tyne Ct WALK M28....68 B7
Tynedale Cl RDSH SK5....100 B7
Tynesbank WALK M28....68 C2
Tynesbank Cottages
WALK M28 *....68 F1
Tyne St OLDE OL4....59 M5
Tynwald St OLDE OL4....59 M5
Tyrer Av WGNS/IIMK WN3....14 A9
Tyrol Wk OP/CLY M11....88 C4
Tyrone Cl NTHM/RTH M23....109 G4
Tyrone Dr ROCH OL11....27 J7
Tyro St OLDS OL8....75 J1
Tyrrell Gv HYDE SK14....102 D3
Tyrrel Rd RDSH SK5....100 C3
Tysoe Gdns CSLFD M3....6 B2
Tyson St CHH M8....72 C4
Tytherington Dr
BNG/LEV M19....100 A3

## U

Uganda St BOLS/LL BL3....51 M2
Ukraine Rd BRO M7....71 K6
Uldale Dr MDTN M24....57 H3
Ullesthorpe WHIT OL12....10 D3
Ulleswater Cl BOLS/LL BL3....53 J1
Ulleswater St BOL BL1....36 C2
Ullswater Av AULW OL7....75 K8
ROY/SHW OL2....43 G6
WGNW/BIL/OR WN5....46 C5
WHIT OL12....27 M3
Ullswater Dr BURY BL9....39 K5
FWTH BL4....52 B5
MDTN M24....57 J1
WGNE/HIN WN2....48 E5
Ullswater Gv HEY OL10....41 G4
Ullswater Rd
GOL/RIS/CUL WA3....79 M3
STKP SK1....112 E5
TYLD M29....67 K5
URM M41....84 B8
WILM/AE SK9....119 L8
WYTH/NTH M22....118 D2
Ullswater St LEIGH WN7....66 E7
Ullswater Ter STLY SK15....76 D8
Ulster Av ROCH OL11....10 D9
Ulundi St RAD M26....54 C1
Ulverston Av CHAD OL9....58 C6
DID/WITH M20....98 C5
Ulverston Rd WGNS/IIMK WN3....63 J1
Umberton Rd WHTN BL5....51 H5
Uncouth Rd MILN OL16....29 H5
Underhill MPL/ROM SK6....113 M2
Underhill Rd OLD OL1....9 H1
Underhill Wk NEWH/MOS M40....74 E1
Under La CHAD OL9....74 E1
OLDE OL4....60 E8
Underwood WHIT OL12....10 D4
Underwood Cl GTN M18....89 J6
Underwood Rd HYDE SK14....103 G6
WILM/AE SK9....130 F3
Underwood St DUK SK16....90 E4
Underwood Wy ROY/SHW OL2....44 A4
Undsworth Ct HEY OL10 *....41 G2
Unicorn St ECC M30....84 E4
Union Ar BURY BL9....4 F4
Union Buildings BOLE BL2....2 F6
Union Ct BOLE BL2 *....36 D2
Union Rd AUL OL6....75 M8
BOLE BL2....3 H1
MPL/ROM SK6 *....114 C6
NM/HAY SK22....124 D5
WHIT OL12....21 J8
Union St ANC M4....7 K4
AUL OL6....75 L8
BURY BL9....4 F4
CHAD OL9....58 E8
EDGW/EG BL7....22 B2
GLSP SK13....104 F4
GTN M18....89 H6
HYDE SK14....102 B3
LEIGH WN7....66 C7
MDTN M24....57 K3
OLD OL1....9 J6
OLDE OL4....60 B6
RAMS BL0....18 F6
ROY/SHW OL2....43 G8
RUSH/FAL M14 *....71 K8
SLFD M6....71 K8
STKP SK1....13 G6
SWIN M27....70 B4
SWIN M27....70 D2
TYLD M29....67 M3
WGNE/HIN WN2....48 D4
WGTN/LGST M12....10 E2
WHIT OL12....20 A4

Union St West OLDS OL8 .... 9 G8
Union Ter BRO M7 * .... 72 C4
United St OLDTF/WHR M16 .... 86 B7
Unity Cl HEY OL10 .... 40 E3
Unity Crs HEY OL10 .... 40 E3
Unity Dr BRO M7 .... 72 B6
Unity St HEY OL10 .... 40 E3
Unity Wy STKP SK1 .... 13 L7
University Rd ORD M5 .... 86 E2
University Rd West ORD M5 * .... 86 E2
Unsworth Av GOL/RIS/CUL WA3 .... 80 B5
  TYLD M29 .... 67 L4
Unsworth Wy OLD OL1 .... 9 H3
Unwin St GTN M18 .... 89 G8
Upavon Rd WYTH/NTH M22 .... 119 H1
Upcast La WILM/AE SK9 .... 130 A1
Upholland Rd
  WGNW/BIL/OR WN5 .... 46 A8
Upland Dr AIMK WN4 .... 64 A8
  LHULT M38 .... 52 C6
Uplands Dr OLDS OL8 .... 59 H8
Uplands MDTN M24 .... 57 H6
Uplands Av RAD M26 .... 54 F2
Uplands Rd GLSP SK13 .... 105 G4
  HYDE SK14 .... 102 D6
  URM M41 .... 95 H4
The Uplands MOSL OL5 .... 77 G3
Upper Brook St
  BRUN/LGST M13 .... 87 L6
  STKP SK1 .... 13 K5
Upper Camp St BRO M7 .... 72 A7
Upper Chorlton Rd
  OLDTF/WHR M16 .... 97 M1
Upper Cleminson St CSLFD M3 .... 6 A3
Upper Cliff Hl ROY/SHW OL2 .... 43 M3
Upper Conran St BKLY M9 .... 73 H4
Upper Diccon St WGN WN1 .... 15 C2
Upper Downs ALT WA14 .... 116 E1
Upper George St TYLD M29 .... 67 K4
  WHIT OL12 .... 10 F1
Upper Gloucester St SLFD M6 .... 86 D1
Upper Hayes Cl MILN OL16 .... 11 L3
Upper Helena St
  NEWH/MOS M40 .... 88 B2
Upper Hibbert La
  MPL/ROM SK6 .... 114 C8
Upper Kent Rd RUSH/FAL M14 .... 99 C1
Upper Kirby St ANC M4 .... 7 M4
Upper Lees Dr WHTN BL5 .... 50 D3
Upper Lloyd St ROY/SHW OL2 .... 43 L7
  RUSH/FAL M14 .... 98 D1
Upper Md EDGW/EG BL7 .... 22 C3
Upper Medlock St HULME M15 .... 87 M8
Uppermill Dr BNG/LEV M19 .... 111 G1
Upper Monsall St
  NEWH/MOS M40 .... 73 H6
Upper Moss La HULME M15 .... 87 M6
Upper Park Rd BRO M7 .... 72 B3
  RUSH/FAL M14 .... 87 M8
Upper Passmonds Gv
  ROCH OL11 .... 27 L4
Upper St Stephen St
  WGNNW/ST WN6 .... 14 D3
Upper Stone Dr MILN OL16 .... 29 C6
Upper West Gv
  BRUN/LGST M13 .... 88 A7
Upper Wharf St ORD M5 .... 86 F3
Upper Wilton St PWCH M25 .... 55 M8
Uppingham Dr RAMS BL0 .... 18 E5
Upton ROCH OL11 .... 10 D7
Upton Av CHD/CHDH SK8 .... 120 C4
  HTNM SK4 .... 99 H8
Upton Cl COL/RIS/CUL WA3 .... 80 A4
  MDTN M24 .... 57 K7
Upton La TYLD M29 .... 67 M4
Upton Rd ATH M46 .... 51 H8
Upton Wy TOT/BURYW BL8 .... 24 C7
Upwood Rd GOL/RIS/CUL WA3 .... 80 A5
Urban Dr HALE/TIMP WA15 .... 108 B8
Urban Rd HALE/TIMP WA15 .... 108 B8
  SALE M33 .... 96 D8
Urmson St OLDS OL8 .... 75 J1
Urmston Av NEWLW WA12 .... 78 E7
Urmston La STRET M32 .... 96 D3
Urmston Pk URM M41 .... 96 A7
Urmston Rd LEIGH WN7 .... 66 A7
Urwick Rd MPL/ROM SK6 .... 113 L3
Usk Cl WHTF M45 .... 55 M5
Uttley St BOL BL1 .... 36 A2
  ROCH OL11 .... 27 M8
Uxbridge Av OP/CLY M11 .... 88 F2
Uxbridge St AUL OL6 .... 90 D1

## V

Vaal St OLDS OL8 .... 74 F1
Valance Cl WGTN/LGST M12 .... 88 D6
Valdene Cl FWTH BL4 .... 53 G5
Valdene Dr FWTH BL4 .... 53 G5
  WALK M28 .... 69 G4
Vale Av BURY BL9 .... 39 G5
  HOR/BR BL6 .... 33 K1
  HYDE SK14 .... 102 D1
  RAD M26 .... 53 M5
  SALE M33 .... 97 H7
  SWIN M27 .... 70 D3
  URM M41 .... 95 H4
Vale Cl BRAM/HZG SK7 .... 113 H8
  HTNM SK4 .... 111 J2
  MPL/ROM SK6 .... 114 C2
  WGNNW/ST WN6 .... 30 B4
Vale Coppice HOR/BR BL6 .... 33 K1
  RAMS BL0 .... 24 F1
Vale Cottages LIT OL15 .... 21 L7
Vale Crs CHD/CHDH SK8 .... 120 B2
Vale Dr CHAD OL9 .... 8 E7
  PWCH M25 .... 71 K2
Vale Edge RAD M26 .... 38 D7
Vale Head WILM/AE SK9 .... 127 H2
Vale House Dr GLSP SK13 .... 93 K7
Vale La FAIL M35 .... 74 D8
Valemount GLSP SK13 .... 93 K7
Valencia Rd BRO M7 .... 72 A6
Valentia Rd BKLY M9 .... 57 G8
Valentines Rd ATH M46 .... 66 D3
Valentine St FAIL M35 .... 74 B5
  OLDE OL4 .... 59 M6
Vale Park Wy CHH M8 .... 72 F5
Valerie Wk HULME M15 .... 6 F9
Vale Rd ALT WA14 .... 116 D3
  DROY M43 .... 89 L1
  HALE/TIMP WA15 .... 108 D7
  MDTN M24 .... 111 J3
  MPL/ROM SK6 .... 113 L4
  ROY/SHW OL2 .... 44 A6
  STLY SK15 .... 77 H6
  WGN WN1 .... 126 C4
Vale Side MOSL OL5 .... 76 F4

Vale St AULW OL7 .... 75 K6
  BOLE BL2 .... 37 K5
  EDGW/EG BL7 .... 17 G8
  HEY OL10 .... 40 E3
  MDTN M24 .... 57 L4
  OP/CLY M11 .... 88 F2
The Vale MOSL OL5 .... 76 E3
  WN6 .... 30 A4
Vale Top Av BKLY M9 .... 73 H5
Valetta Cl RUSH/FAL M14 .... 98 E4
Vale Vw ALT WA14 .... 116 E3
  WGNW/BIL/OR WN5 .... 47 C4
Valletts La BOL BL1 .... 35 M3
Valley Av TOT/BURYW BL8 .... 24 E8
Valley Cl CHD/CHDH SK8 .... 120 A1
  MOSL OL5 .... 76 E2
Valley Dr WILM/AE SK9 .... 127 G1
Valley Gv DTN/ASHW M34 .... 101 L2
Valley Ms UPML OL3 .... 61 M8
Valley Ml EDGW/EG BL7 * .... 22 C4
Valley Mill La BURY BL9 .... 5 H7
Valley New Rd ROY/SHW OL2 .... 59 H1
Valley Park Rd PWCH M25 .... 55 J7
Valley Ri ROY/SHW OL2 .... 43 K3
Valley Rd BRAM/HZG SK7 .... 121 H3
  CHD/CHDH SK8 .... 120 A1
  GLSP SK13 .... 104 C4
  HYDE SK14 .... 103 H4
  MDTN M24 .... 57 L2
  MPL/ROM SK6 .... 101 G8
  NM/HAY SK22 .... 125 M2
  ROY/SHW OL2 .... 59 H1
  URM M41 .... 84 A8
  WGNW/BIL/OR WN5 .... 47 G7
Valley Rd North ROCH OL11 .... 41 M3
Valley Rd South ROCH OL11 .... 41 M3
Valley Rd West HOR/BR BL6 .... 32 F2
Valley Sq LEIGH WN7 * .... 66 C7
Valley St BOLS/LL BL3 .... 74 F2
Valpy Gv HEY OL10 .... 36 E1
Vanbrugh Gv
  WGNW/BIL/OR WN5 .... 46 E3
Vancouver Quay SALQ M50 .... 86 C5
Vandyke Av SLFD M6 .... 85 L1
Vandyke St WHIT OL12 .... 27 J3
Vane St ECC M30 .... 84 F2
Vannes Gv HYDE SK14 .... 103 J1
Vantomme St BOL BL1 .... 22 B8
Varden St OLDE OL4 .... 59 M8
Varden Gv EDGY/DAV SK3 .... 112 A7
Varden Rd POY/DIS SK12 .... 129 J1
Vardon Dr WILM/AE SK9 .... 127 H6
Varey St GTN M18 .... 89 J7
Varley Rd BOLS/LL BL3 .... 35 K8
Varley St NEWH/MOS M40 .... 73 G8
Varna St OP/CLY M11 .... 89 C5
Vauban Dr SLFD M6 .... 85 L1
Vaudrey Dr BRAM/HZG SK7 .... 122 A1
  CHD/CHDH SK8 .... 120 C2
  HALE/TIMP WA15 .... 108 D4
Vaudrey La DTN/ASHW M34 .... 101 K2
Vaudrey Rd MPL/ROM SK6 .... 101 K3
  STLY SK15 .... 91 K3
Vaughan Av NEWH/MOS M40 .... 73 H4
  CCHDY M21 .... 98 A4
  HTNM SK4 .... 112 A1
Vaughan St ECC M30 .... 85 J2
  ROY/SHW OL2 .... 59 H1
  WGTN/LGST M12 .... 88 C5
Vauxhall Rd WGN WN1 .... 15 J4
Vauxhall St NEWH/MOS M40 .... 72 E8
Vauze Av HOR/BR BL6 .... 33 G3
Vauze House Cl HOR/BR BL6 .... 33 G3
Vavasour St MILN OL16 * .... 11 J6
Vawdrey Dr NTHM/RTH M23 .... 109 J3
Vaynor WHIT OL12 .... 10 D2
Vega St CHH M8 .... 72 B8
Vela Wk BRO M7 .... 86 F1
Velmere Av BKLY M9 .... 56 D7
Velour Cl CSLFD M3 .... 6 A1
Vendale Av SWIN M27 .... 70 A6
Venetia St NEWH/MOS M40 * .... 73 M7
Venice St BOLS/LL BL3 .... 35 M8
  CMANE M1 * .... 7 H7
Venlow Gdns CHD/CHDH SK8 .... 120 D3
Ventnor Av BNG/LEV M19 .... 99 M4
  BOL BL1 .... 36 C1
  BURY BL9 .... 55 J1
  SALE M33 .... 96 E6
Ventnor Cl DTN/ASHW M34 .... 101 L4
Ventnor Rd DID/WITH M20 .... 110 F1
  HTNM SK4 .... 12 A1
Ventnor St ROCH OL11 .... 10 E8
  SLFD M6 .... 71 L7
Ventor St BKLY M9 .... 73 G4
Ventura Cl RUSH/FAL M14 .... 98 D3
Ventura Ct NM/HAY SK22 .... 124 F3
Venture Scout Wy CHH M8 .... 72 C6
Venture Wy POY/DIS SK12 .... 129 K1
Venwood Ct PWCH M25 .... 71 J2
Venwood Rd PWCH M25 .... 71 J2
Verbena Av FWTH BL4 .... 53 G5
Verbena Cl PART M31 .... 106 C1
Verdant La ECC M30 .... 84 C4
Verdant Wy MILN OL16 .... 42 F1
Verda St WCNE/HIN WN2 .... 64 D4
Verdun Av SLFD M6 .... 85 L1
Verdun Crs ROCH OL11 .... 27 M4
Verdun Rd ECC M30 .... 69 L8
Verdure Av BOL BL1 .... 35 H4
  SALE M33 .... 108 D3
Verdure Cl FAIL M35 .... 74 E4
Vere St SALQ M50 .... 86 C5
Verity Cl DID/WITH M20 .... 98 E6
  ROY/SHW OL2 .... 59 G1
Vermont St BOL BL1 .... 2 A2
Verne Av SWIN M27 .... 70 B4
Verne Dr OLD OL1 .... 44 B7
Verney Rd ROY/SHW OL2 .... 59 H2
Vernham Wk BOLS/LL BL3 .... 85 J2
Vernon Av ECC M30 * .... 85 J2
  STKP SK1 .... 112 E2
  STRET M32 .... 97 G3
Vernon Cl CHD/CHDH SK8 .... 120 A3
  POY/DIS SK12 .... 129 J2
Vernon Dr MPL/ROM SK6 .... 113 M5
  PWCH M25 .... 71 K2
Vernon Gv SALE M33 .... 97 M3
Vernon Pk HALE/TIMP WA15 .... 108 D5
Vernon Rd BRO M7 .... 71 M3
  DROY M43 .... 89 H2
  MPL/ROM SK6 .... 113 L4
  POY/DIS SK12 .... 129 J2
  TOT/BURYW BL8 .... 24 C3
Vernon St AUL OL6 .... 75 M8
  BKLY M9 .... 73 H5
  BOL BL1 .... 2 C3
  BRAM/HZG SK7 .... 121 H4
  BRO M7 .... 72 A7
  BURY BL9 .... 4 F1

  FWTH BL4 .... 53 H4
  HYDE SK14 .... 102 D2
  LEIGH WN7 .... 66 C7
  MOSL OL5 .... 76 E3
  OLDTF/WHR M16 .... 86 F7
  OP/CLY M11 .... 88 F2
  STKP SK1 .... 13 J3
Vernon Wk BOL BL1 * .... 2 D2
Verona Dr NEWH/MOS M40 .... 73 M8
Veronica Rd DID/WITH M20 .... 110 F1
Verrill Av NTHM/RTH M23 .... 109 M3
Vesper St FAIL M35 .... 74 D4
Vesta St ANC M4 .... 7 M4
  RAMS BL0 .... 18 E6
Vestris Dr SLFD M6 .... 85 L1
Viaduct Rd ALT WA14 .... 108 A5
Viaduct St CSLFD M3 .... 6 D2
  EDGY/DAV SK3 .... 13 C5
  WGTN/LGST M12 .... 88 B4
Vicarage Av CHD/CHDH SK8 .... 120 B2
Vicarage Cl BURY BL9 .... 25 H4
  DUK SK16 .... 60 C5
  OLDE OL4 .... 60 C5
  SLFD M6 .... 86 B1
Vicarage Dr DUK SK16 .... 91 H4
  MILN OL16 .... 28 F1
Vicarage Gdns EDGY/DAV SK3 * .... 13 G7
  HYDE SK14 .... 102 B2
Vicarage Gv ECC M30 .... 85 J2
Vicarage La ALT WA14 .... 116 E3
  MDTN M24 .... 58 A5
  NM/HAY SK22 .... 125 M2
  POY/DIS SK12 .... 122 A7
  SWIN M27 .... 70 B4
Vicarage Rd AIMK WN4 .... 78 E2
  AULW OL7 .... 75 L7
  EDGY/DAV SK3 .... 112 B6
  HOR/BR BL6 .... 33 C2
  IRL M44 .... 94 D2
  SWIN M27 .... 70 B4
  URM M41 .... 84 E8
  WGNE/HIN WN2 .... 64 E3
  WGNW/BIL/OR WN5 .... 46 A8
Vicarage Rd North ROCH OL11 .... 41 M3
Vicarage Rd South ROCH OL11 .... 41 M3
Vicarage Rd West HOR/BR BL6 .... 32 F2
Vicarage Sq LEIGH WN7 * .... 66 C7
Vicarage St BOLS/LL BL3 .... 2 B8
  OLDS OL8 .... 74 F2
  RAD M26 .... 54 D1
  ROY/SHW OL2 .... 43 L5
Vicarage Vw ROCH OL11 .... 42 A3
Vicar's Dr MILN OL16 .... 10 E5
Vicar's Ga MILN OL16 .... 10 E5
Vicars Hall Gdns WALK M28 .... 68 C7
Vicars Hall La WALK M28 .... 68 C7
Vicars Rd CCHDY M21 .... 97 K4
Vicars St ECC M30 .... 85 J2
Vicker Cl SWIN M27 .... 70 C2
Vicker Gv DID/WITH M20 .... 98 C7
Vickerman St BOL BL1 .... 36 A2
Vickers Rw FWTH BL4 .... 52 E4
Vickers St BOLS/LL BL3 * .... 2 B8
  NEWH/MOS M40 .... 88 B1
Victor Av BURY BL9 .... 25 H8
Victor Cl WGNW/BIL/OR WN5 .... 47 H4
Victoria Av BKLY M9 .... 56 F7
  BNG/LEV M19 .... 99 K4
  LIT OL15 .... 21 L6
  MDTN M24 .... 57 K2
  MILN OL16 .... 11 H7
  OP/CLY M11 .... 88 F2
Victoria Av East BKLY M9 .... 57 J8
Victoria Bridge St CSLFD M3 .... 6 E3
Victoria Cl BRAM/HZG SK7 .... 120 F6
  EDGY/DAV SK3 .... 13 H8
  WALK M28 * .... 68 D6
  WGNE/HIN WN2 .... 64 D2
Victoria Ct AULW OL7 .... 90 D3
  FWTH BL4 .... 52 C2
  GLSP SK13 .... 104 F2
Victoria Crs ECC M30 .... 85 J1
  WGNNW/ST WN6 .... 31 H4
Victoria Dr SALE M33 .... 109 G1
Victoria Gdns HYDE SK14 .... 91 J8
  ROY/SHW OL2 * .... 43 L5
Victoria Gv BOL BL1 .... 35 M3
  HTNM SK4 .... 99 M7
  RUSH/FAL M14 .... 98 F1
Victoria La WHTF M45 .... 55 J5
  WHTF M45 .... 55 J5
Victoria Ldg BRO M7 * .... 71 M7
Victoria Ms BURY BL9 .... 55 L2
Victoria Pk STKP SK1 * .... 112 E4
Victoria Pl TRPK M17 .... 86 C7
Victoria Rd AIMK WN4 .... 63 G8
  ALT WA14 .... 116 F2
  BOL BL1 .... 35 G5
  DUK SK16 .... 90 F6
  ECC M30 .... 85 H1
  FWTH BL4 .... 53 K6
  HALE/TIMP WA15 .... 108 D6
  HOR/BR BL6 .... 33 G2
  IRL M44 .... 94 C3
  NEWLW WA12 .... 78 F8
  OLDTF/WHR M16 .... 98 A2
  RUSH/FAL M14 .... 98 F1
  SALE M33 .... 109 G1
  SLFD M6 .... 70 D8
  STKP SK1 .... 112 E5
  STRET M32 .... 97 G2
  URM M41 .... 95 L2
  WGNE/HIN WN2 .... 64 D3
  WILM/AE SK9 .... 126 E6
  WYTH/NTH M22 .... 110 A4
Victoria Sq ANC M4 * .... 7 K2
  BOL BL1 .... 2 E5
Victoria Station Ap CSLFD M3 .... 6 F2
Victoria St ALT WA14 .... 108 A7
  AULW OL7 .... 90 D3
  BOLE BL2 .... 37 M3
  CHAD OL9 .... 8 C4
  CSLFD M3 .... 6 F2
  DTN/ASHW M34 .... 101 H1
  DUK SK16 .... 91 G4
  FAIL M35 .... 74 A6
  FWTH BL4 .... 52 E3
  GLSP SK13 .... 104 F4
  HYDE SK14 .... 91 J8
  LEIGH WN7 .... 66 B6

  LIT OL15 .... 21 M7
  MDTN M24 .... 57 K4
  NM/HAY SK22 .... 124 D6
  OLDE OL4 .... 9 M6
  OLDE OL4 .... 60 B8
  OLDS OL8 .... 75 J4
  OP/CLY M11 .... 88 F2
  RAD M26 .... 54 D1
  RAMS BL0 .... 18 E6
  ROY/SHW OL2 .... 43 L5
  STLY SK15 .... 77 G8
  STLY SK15 .... 91 J2
  TOT/BURYW BL8 .... 4 B3
  TOT/BURYW BL8 .... 24 B5
  WALK M28 .... 68 D6
  WGNE/HIN WN2 .... 64 D2
  WGNW/BIL/OR WN5 .... 47 H6
  WHIT OL12 .... 10 E1
  WHIT OL12 .... 20 A4
  WHTN BL5 .... 50 C4
Victoria Ter ROY/SHW OL2 * .... 43 G7
  WGNE/HIN WN2 .... 65 J4
  WGTN/LGST M12 .... 88 C5
Victoria Wk CHAD OL9 .... 8 C1
Victoria Wy BRAM/HZG SK7 .... 120 F6
  LEIGH WN7 .... 66 B5
Victor Mann St OP/CLY M11 .... 89 K5
Victor St CSLFD M3 .... 6 B3
  HEY OL10 .... 41 H4
  NEWH/MOS M40 .... 72 F8
  OLDS OL8 .... 74 E3
Victory Gv DTN/ASHW M34 .... 89 M5
Victory Rd BOLS/LL BL3 .... 37 K8
  RUSH/FAL M14 .... 98 F1
Vienna Rd EDGY/DAV SK3 .... 112 A6
Vienna Rd East EDGY/DAV SK3 .... 112 A6
Viewlands Dr WILM/AE SK9 .... 127 H2
View St BOLS/LL BL3 .... 2 A9
Vigo Av BOLS/LL BL3 .... 51 L1
Vigo St HEY OL10 .... 41 H3
  OLDE OL4 .... 60 A7
  OLDE OL4 * .... 48 C2
Viking Cl OP/CLY M11 .... 88 C3
Viking St BOLS/LL BL3 .... 36 D8
  ROCH OL11 .... 27 M4
Villa Av WGNNW/ST WN6 .... 31 K8
Village Ct TRPK M17 .... 85 L6
Village Mnr UPML OL3 * .... 61 M1
Village St BRO M7 .... 71 M7
The Village URM M41 .... 95 J4
Village Vw WGNW/BIL/OR WN5 .... 62 B7
Village Wy (Ashburton
  Rd East) TRPK M17 .... 85 M6
Villa Rd OLDS OL8 .... 59 J8
Villdale Av OFTN SK2 .... 112 F5
Villiers Ct WHTF M45 * .... 55 K6
Villiers Dr OLDS OL8 .... 9 C8
Villiers St AUL OL6 .... 91 G2
  BURY BL9 .... 5 J2
  HYDE SK14 .... 102 C1
Vinca Gv BRO M7 .... 72 A6
Vincent Av CCHDY M21 .... 97 K3
  ECC M30 .... 84 C4
Vincent St BOL BL1 .... 2 A6
  BRO M7 .... 72 B5
  HYDE SK14 .... 102 C3
  MDTN M24 .... 57 K2
  MILN OL16 .... 11 H7
  OP/CLY M11 .... 88 F2
Vine Av SWIN M27 .... 70 E4
Vine Cl ROY/SHW OL2 .... 43 L5
  SALE M33 .... 95 M7
Vine Ct MILN OL16 * .... 11 J5
  STRET M32 .... 97 G3
Vine Fold NEWH/MOS M40 .... 74 C3
Vine Gv OFTN SK2 .... 112 F6
  WGNS/IIMK WN3 .... 14 F5
Vine Pl ROCH OL11 .... 10 D7
Vinery Gv DTN/ASHW M34 .... 101 H1
Vine St BRAM/HZG SK7 .... 122 A1
  BRO M7 .... 71 L4
  CHAD OL9 .... 74 E1
  ECC M30 .... 84 F3
  OP/CLY M11 .... 89 H5
  PWCH M25 .... 55 M7
  RAMS BL0 .... 18 E6
  WGN WN1 .... 15 J1
  WGNE/HIN WN2 .... 49 G6
Vineyard Cl WHIT OL12 .... 21 G5
Vineyard St OLDE OL4 .... 59 L5
Viola St OP/CLY M11 .... 89 G2
Viola St WGNNW/ST WN6 .... 31 G2
Violet Av FWTH BL4 .... 52 E4
Violet St AIMK WN4 .... 78 E2
Violet Wy MDTN M24 .... 58 A5
Virgil St OLDTF/WHR M16 .... 86 F6
Virginia Cha CHD/CHDH SK8 .... 120 B4
Virginia St NTHM/RTH M23 .... 109 M3
  ROCH OL11 * .... 28 B8
Virginia Wy
  WGNW/BIL/OR WN5 .... 46 F4
Viscount Dr CHD/CHDH SK8 .... 119 M5
  MANAIR M90 .... 118 B5
Viscount Rd
  WGNW/BIL/OR WN5 .... 47 C4
Viscount St RUSH/FAL M14 .... 98 F1
Vista Av NEWLW WA12 .... 78 D8
Vista Rd NEWLW WA12 .... 78 D8
The Vista NEWLW WA12 .... 78 D8
Vivian St ROCH OL11 .... 10 D9
Vixen Cl CCHDY M21 .... 98 B5
Voltaire Av SLFD M6 .... 85 L1
Vorlich Dr CHD/CHDH SK8 .... 58 C4
Vulcan Dr WGN WN1 .... 15 J3
Vulcan Rd WGNW/BIL/OR WN5 .... 47 G4
Vulcan St OLD OL1 .... 59 M4
Vyner Gv SALE M33 .... 96 C4

## W

Waddicor Av AUL OL6 .... 76 B6
Waddington Cl
  GOL/RIS/CUL WA3 * .... 80 C4
  TOT/BURYW BL8 .... 38 B2
Waddington Fold MILN OL16 .... 42 F2
Waddington Rd BOL BL1 .... 35 K3
Wade Bank WHTN BL5 .... 50 C4
Wadebridge Av
  NTHM/RTH M23 .... 109 G3
Wadebridge Dr
  TOT/BURYW BL8 .... 38 C2
Wadeford Cl ANC M4 .... 7 M2
Wade Hill La UPML OL3 .... 61 H4
Wade Rw UPML OL3 .... 61 L4
Wadesmill Wk BRUN/LGST M13 * .... 7 J9
Wadeson Rd BRUN/LGST M13 .... 7 K9
Wade St BOLS/LL BL3 .... 52 C1
Wade Wk OP/CLY M11 .... 88 D4
Wadham Gdns MPL/ROM SK6 .... 101 M7
Wadham Wy HALE/TIMP WA15 .... 117 H3
Wadhurst Wk BRUN/LGST M13 * .... 87 M7
Wadlow Cl CSLFD M3 * .... 6 C1
Wadsley St BOL BL1 .... 2 B5
Wadsworth Cl WILM/AE SK9 .... 127 J1
Wadsworth Dr
  WGNNW/ST WN6 .... 47 J2
Waggoners Ct SWIN M27 .... 70 C5
Waggon Rd AULW OL7 .... 75 L4
  BOLE BL2 .... 37 G4
  MOSL OL5 .... 76 F4
Wagner St BOL BL1 .... 36 A1
Wagstaffe Dr FAIL M35 .... 74 C5
Wagstaffe St MDTN M24 .... 57 K3
Wagtail Cl WALK M28 .... 69 G3
Waincliffe Av CCHDY M21 .... 98 A8
Wainfleet Cl WGNS/IIMK WN3 .... 63 H1
Waingap Crs WHIT OL12 .... 20 B5
Waingap Ri WHIT OL12 .... 20 D8
Waingap Vw WHIT OL12 .... 20 B5
Wainhouse Brow
  NM/HAY SK22 .... 125 J4
Wainman St SLFD M6 .... 71 L7
Wainscot Cl TYLD M29 .... 67 L5
Wainwright Av
  DTN/ASHW M34 .... 100 C1
  OLDE OL4 .... 13 M9
Wainwright Rd ALT WA14 .... 107 L7
Wainwright St DUK SK16 .... 91 H3
  OLDE OL4 .... 60 A7
Waithlands Rd MILN OL16 .... 11 K6
Wakefield Crs MPL/ROM SK6 .... 101 M7
  WGNNW/ST WN6 .... 31 K5
Wakefield Dr OLD OL1 .... 8 D1
  SWIN M27 .... 54 A8
Wakefield Ms EDGW/EG BL7 * .... 22 C5
Wakefield St CMANE M1 * .... 7 G7
  GOL/RIS/CUL WA3 * .... 79 K5
  OLD OL1 .... 8 D1
Wakeling Rd DTN/ASHW M34 .... 101 H4
Walcot Pl WGNS/IIMK WN3 .... 63 K2
Walcott Cl BRUN/LGST M13 .... 88 A7
Wald Av RUSH/FAL M14 .... 99 H5
Waldeck St BOL BL1 .... 35 M4
Walden Av OLDE OL4 .... 60 A7
Walden Cl RUSH/FAL M14 .... 98 D4
Walderton Av NEWH/MOS M40 .... 73 K6
Waldon Av CHD/CHDH SK8 .... 111 G7
Waldon Cl BOLS/LL BL3 .... 35 M8
  WGNE/HIN WN2 .... 49 J8
Waldorf Cl WGNS/IIMK WN3 .... 63 G2
Wales St OLD OL1 .... 59 M3
Walford St AIMK WN4 .... 78 F1
Walkdale Brow GLSP SK13 .... 104 E5
Walkden Av WGN WN1 .... 47 L2
Walkden Av East WGN WN1 .... 47 M2
Walkdene Dr WALK M28 .... 68 C1
Walkden Market Pl
  WALK M28 .... 69 G1
Walkden Rd WALK M28 .... 68 G6
Walkdens Av ATH M46 .... 66 D2
Walkden St MILN OL16 .... 10 E1
Walker Av BOLS/LL BL3 .... 52 C1
  FAIL M35 * .... 74 E6
  STLY SK15 .... 91 M2
  WHTF M45 .... 55 K6
Walkers Cl UPML OL3 .... 61 L4
Walkers Ct FWTH BL4 .... 53 C4
Walker's Cft CSLFD M3 .... 6 F2
Walker Dr LEIGH WN7 .... 66 D7
Walker's La OLDE OL4 .... 60 C6
Walker Rd AIMK WN4 .... 78 C4
Walker's Rd OLDS OL8 .... 74 F2
Walker St BOL BL1 .... 2 B6
  BURY BL9 .... 4 F3
  DTN/ASHW M34 .... 90 B8
  ECC M30 .... 69 K8
  HEY OL10 .... 40 F3
  MDTN M24 .... 56 F7
  MILN OL16 .... 11 H5
  OLDS OL8 .... 8 E7
  RAD M26 .... 54 F3
  STKP SK1 .... 13 H4
  WHTN BL5 .... 50 B4
Walkerwood Dr STLY SK15 .... 92 K2
Walkmill UPML OL3 .... 61 J3
Walk Mill Cl WHIT OL12 .... 21 H8
Walk Mill Rd NM/HAY SK22 .... 125 M1
The Walk ATH M46 .... 67 C1
  MILN OL16 .... 10 E4
The Walkway BOLS/LL BL3 .... 35 M7
Wallace Av RUSH/FAL M14 .... 99 G1
Wallace La WGN WN1 .... 15 K1
Wallasey Av RUSH/FAL M14 .... 98 D3
Wallbank Rd BRAM/HZG SK7 .... 121 J3
Wallbrook Av
  WGNW/BIL/OR WN5 .... 62 B3
Wallbrook Crs LHULT M38 .... 52 D6
Wallbrook Dr BKLY M9 .... 72 F2
The Walled Gdn SWIN M27 .... 70 A6
Waller Av RUSH/FAL M14 .... 98 F4
Walley St BOL BL1 .... 36 B1
Wallgarth St WGNS/IIMK WN3 .... 63 G2
Wallgate WGN WN1 .... 14 F5
Wallhead Rd MILN OL16 .... 29 G5
Wall Hill Rd UPML OL3 .... 61 J3
Wallingford Rd URM M41 .... 96 B1
  WILM/AE SK9 .... 119 J2
Wallis St CHAD OL9 .... 58 D8
  NEWH/MOS M40 * .... 73 M7
Wallness La SLFD M6 .... 86 F1
Wallshaw Pl OLD OL1 .... 9 M5
Wallshaw St OLD OL1 .... 9 L5
Walls St WGNE/HIN WN2 .... 65 M2
Wall St OLDS OL8 .... 9 J8
  SLFD M6 .... 86 C2
  WGNNW/ST WN6 .... 14 A1
Wall Wy GTN M18 .... 89 H8
Wallwork Cl ROCH OL11 .... 27 H3

Wallwork Rd TYLD M29 68 A6
Wallwork St OP/CLY M11 89 H4
RAD M26 38 D8
RDSH SK5 * 100 C2
Wallworth Av GTN M18 89 G7
Wally Sq BRO M7 72 B6
Walmer Dr BRAM/HZG SK7 121 J3
Walmer Rd WGNE/HIN WN2 49 K7
Walmersley Ct
MPL/ROM SK6 * 114 C6
Walmersley Old Rd BURY BL9 25 J2
Walmersley Rd BURY BL9 5 G2
NEWH/MOS M40 74 B3
Walmer St GTN M18 89 H6
RUSH/FAL M14 98 E1
Walmer St East RUSH/FAL M14 98 F1
Walmesley Dr WGNE/HIN WN2 48 E5
Walmesley Rd LEIGH WN7 66 B7
Walmesley St WGN WN1 15 H5
Walmley Gv BOLS/LL BL3 51 M1
Walmsley Av LIT OL15 29 J1
Walmsley Gv URM M41 96 A2
Walmsley St NEWLW WA12 79 G8
RDSH SK5 * 112 B1
STLY SK15 91 K4
TOT/BURYW BL8 24 E8
Walney Rd WGNS/IIMK WN3 63 G2
WYTH/NTH M22 110 A8
Walnut Av BURY BL9 5 L3
OLDE OL4 60 A4
WGN WN1 48 A2
Walnut Cl HYDE SK14 102 D2
SWIN M27 54 A8
WILM/AE SK9 127 J4
Walnut Gv LEIGH WN7 66 C4
Walnut Rd ECC M30 69 K8
PART M31 106 A1
Walnut St BOL BL1 36 C1
GTN M18 89 G6
Walnut Tree Rd EDGY/DAV SK3 111 K5
Walnut Wk STRET M32 96 F4
Walpole Av WGNS/IIMK WN3 63 J1
Walpole St MILN OL16 11 H5
Walsall St SLFD M6 71 K7
Walsden St OP/CLY M11 88 F2
Walsh Av BKLY M9 72 F2
Walshaw Brook Cl
TOT/BURYW BL8 24 C8
Walshaw Dr SWIN M27 70 C5
Walshaw La TOT/BURYW BL8 24 C8
Walshaw Rd TOT/BURYW BL8 4 A2
Walsh Cl NEWLW WA12 78 F7
Walshe St BURY BL9 4 C5
Walsh St CHAD OL9 8 B7
Walsingham Av DID/WITH M20 98 C8
MDTN M24 57 K7
Walter Scott Av WGN WN1 31 L8
Walter Scott St OLD OL1 59 L4
Walters Dr OLDS OL8 75 K1
Walters Green Crs
GOL/RIS/CUL WA3 79 K3
Walter St AIMK WN4 * 64 A8
BKLY M9 73 G4
GTN M18 89 H6
LEIGH WN7 65 L7
OLD OL1 9 K6
OLDTF/WHR M16 86 F8
PWCH M25 55 J8
RAD M26 38 C6
WALK M28 69 G2
WGNW/BIL/OR WN5 47 G6
Waltham Av GOL/RIS/CUL WA3 81 M5
WGNNW/ST WN6 47 J1
Waltham Dr CHD/CHDH SK8 120 D6
Waltham Gdns LEIGH WN7 66 F8
Waltham Rd OLDTF/WHR M16 98 B3
Waltham St OLDE OL4 59 M8
Walthew House La
WGNW/BIL/OR WN5 46 E3
Walthew La WGNE/HIN WN2 64 D2
Walton Cl MDTN M24 56 F3
Walton Ct BOLS/LL BL3 36 C8
Walton Dr BURY BL9 25 H4
MPL/ROM SK6 114 A5
Walton Hall Dr BNG/LEV M19 100 A3
Walton Houses FAIL M35 * 74 C4
Walton Pl FWTH BL4 53 H5
Walton Rd ALT WA14 107 L7
BKLY M9 57 G7
SALE M33 108 C3
Walton St ATH M46 * 51 H8
AULW OL7 75 J7
HEY OL10 41 G4
MDTN M24 * 57 K2
STKP SK1 * 13 K8
Walwyn Cl STRET M32 97 H3
Wanborough Cl LEIGH WN7 66 C5
Wandsworth Av OP/CLY M11 89 G2
Wansbeck Cl STRET M32 97 H3
Wansfell Wk ANC M4 88 A2
Wansford St RUSH/FAL M14 98 D1
Wanstead Av BKLY M9 73 K1
Wapping St BOL BL1 36 A2
Warbeck Cl RDSH SK5 100 D2
WGNE/HIN WN2 65 H1
Warbeck Rd NEWH/MOS M40 74 A2
Warbreck Cl BOLE BL2 37 J5
Warbreck Dr URM M41 95 M3
Warbreck Gv SALE M33 109 G1
Warburton Cl
HALE/TIMP WA15 117 M6
MPL/ROM SK6 113 K3
Warburton Dr
HALE/TIMP WA15 117 M6
Warburton La PART M31 106 C1
Warburton Pl ATH M46 67 G1
Warburton Rd WILM/AE SK9 119 M8
Warburton St BOL BL1 36 C2
DID/WITH M20 110 E1
ECC M30 85 H3
ORD M5 86 E6
Warburton Wy
HALE/TIMP WA15 108 F5
Warcock Rd OLDE OL4 59 M5
Wardend Cl LHULT M38 * 52 D6
Wardens Bank WHTN BL5 50 B7
Warden St NEWH/MOS M40 73 L6
Warde St HULME M15 87 H6
Ward La POY/DIS SK12 124 A8
UPML OL3 45 M8
Wardle Brook Av HYDE SK14 103 G1
Wardle Cl RAD M26 38 B7
STRET M32 97 H2
Wardle Edge WHIT OL12 28 E1
Wardle Fold WHIT OL12 21 G5
Wardle Gdns WHIT OL12 28 F1
Wardle Rd SALE M33 108 E1
WHIT OL12 21 G7
Wardle St BOLE BL2 3 K8
LIT OL15 21 L6
NEWH/MOS M40 88 B1
OLDE OL4 59 L6
Wardley Av CCHDY M21 98 B4
WALK M28 68 E2
Wardley Hall La WALK M28 69 K4
Wardley Hall Rd WALK M28 69 L3
Wardley Rd TYLD M29 68 A4
Wardley Sq TYLD M29 68 A4
Wardley St SWIN M27 70 C4
WGNW/BIL/OR WN5 46 E7
Wardlow Av
WGNW/BIL/OR WN5 46 D4
Wardlow Ms GLSP SK13 104 A3
Wardlow St BOLS/LL BL3 35 L8
Wardour St ATH M46 67 G2
Ward Rd DID/WITH M20 110 E1
DROY M43 89 L3
Wardsend Wk HULME M15 * 87 G6
Ward St BKLY M9 72 F2
CHAD OL9 8 C5
FAIL M35 74 B4
HYDE SK14 102 B2
MPL/ROM SK6 113 J1
NEWH/MOS M40 73 J4
OLD OL1 8 F2
STKP SK1 13 L8
WGNE/HIN WN2 49 G5
Ware Cl AIMK WN4 79 G1
Wareham Gv ECC M30 84 F1
Wareham St CHH M8 * 72 E3
Wareing St TYLD M29 67 J4
Wareings Yd ROCH OL11 28 D8
Wareing Wy BOLS/LL BL3 2 C6
Warford Av POY/DIS SK12 129 L2
Warford St ANC M4 72 E8
Warham St WILM/AE SK9 126 F5
The Warke WALK M28 69 J6
Warley Cl CHD/CHDH SK8 111 H6
Warley Gv DUK SK16 90 F4
Warley Rd OLDTF/WHR M16 97 K1
Warley St LIT OL15 21 M6
Warlingham Cl TOT/BURYW BL8 38 E3
Warlow Crest UPML OL3 61 K8
Warlow Dr LEIGH WN7 66 A3
UPML OL3 61 K8
Warmington Dr
WGTN/LGST M12 88 B6
Warminster Gv
WGNS/IIMK WN3 63 G2
Warmley Rd NTHM/RTH M23 109 G4
Warncliffe St
WGNW/BIL/OR WN5 47 G7
Warne Av DROY M43 89 M2
Warnford Cl NEWH/MOS M40 74 A8
Warnford St WGN WN1 47 M2
War Office Rd ROCH OL11 27 H6
Warren Av CHD/CHDH SK8 111 G7
Warren Bank BKLY M9 72 F1
Warren Bruce Rd TRPK M17 86 A6
Warren Cl ATH M46 51 H8
BRAM/HZG SK7 120 F2
DTN/ASHW M34 101 G2
POY/DIS SK12 121 K8
Warren Dr HALE/TIMP WA15 117 M5
NEWLW WA12 79 J8
SWIN M27 70 A7
Warrener St SALE M33 109 G1
Warren Hey WILM/AE SK9 127 J4
Warren La OLDS OL8 59 L8
Warren Lea MPL/ROM SK6 114 E2
POY/DIS SK12 122 A7
Warren Rd CHD/CHDH SK8 120 C2
EDGY/DAV SK3 112 B6
TRPK M17 85 L6
WALK M28 69 H1
Warren St BKLY M9 72 F2
BRO M7 72 C4
STKP SK1 13 J3
TOT/BURYW BL8 38 E3
Warre St AUL OL6 90 E1
Warrington La WGN WN1 15 H4
Warrington Rd AIMK WN4 78 E2
BKLY M9 56 F8
LEIGH WN7 81 L2
NEWLW WA12 79 K6
WGNE/HIN WN2 64 D2
WGNS/IIMK WN3 15 J8
WGNS/IIMK WN3 48 B7
Warrington St AUL OL6 90 E2
OLDE OL4 60 B7
STLY SK15 91 L3
Warsall Rd WYTH/NTH M22 110 B5
Warslow Dr SALE M33 109 H3
Warsop Av WYTH/NTH M22 110 B7
Warstead Wk
BRUN/LGST M13 * 87 M7
Warth Fold Rd RAD M26 38 F6
Warth Rd BURY BL9 38 F5
Warton Cl BRAM/HZG SK7 121 J5
TOT/BURYW BL8 38 C3
Warton Dr NTHM/RTH M23 109 K7
Warwick Av AIMK WN4 79 G2
DID/WITH M20 98 C8
DTN/ASHW M34 101 J3
SWIN M27 70 A2
WHTF M45 55 L5
Warwick Cl CHD/CHDH SK8 111 K8
DUK SK16 90 F6
GLSP SK13 105 J4
HTNM SK4 99 M8
MDTN M24 57 K7
ROY/SHW OL2 43 J5
TOT/BURYW BL8 24 D3
TOT/BURYW BL8 24 E8
WHTF M45 55 K5
Warwick Ct MDTN M24 * 57 K4
OLDTF/WHR M16 97 K1
Warwick Dr BRAM/HZG SK7 121 M4
HALE/TIMP WA15 117 G3
SALE M33 97 G8
URM M41 84 E8
WGNE/HIN WN2 49 J6
Warwick Gdns BOLS/LL BL3 51 L2
Warwick Gv DTN/ASHW M34 89 M4
Warwick Rd ATH M46 50 F7
AUL OL6 75 M7
CCHDY M21 97 L3
FAIL M35 74 C7
HALE/TIMP WA15 117 G3
HTNM SK4 12 C1
IRL M44 94 A7
MDTN M24 57 L7
MPL/ROM SK6 113 K2
OLDTF/WHR M16 86 D8
RAD M26 38 C6
STRET M32 86 C7
TYLD M29 67 K2
WALK M28 68 F3
WGNE/HIN WN2 * 32 F7
Warwick Rd South
OLDTF/WHR M16 97 K1
Warwick St ANC M4 7 J3
BOL BL1 22 B8
CHAD OL9 8 C9
HULME M15 87 H6
LEIGH WN7 82 A1
PWCH M25 55 K8
SWIN M27 70 C3
WHIT OL12 28 E2
Wasdale Av BOLE BL2 37 J3
URM M41 95 L1
Wasdale Dr CHD/CHDH SK8 119 K1
MDTN M24 57 H2
Wasdale Rd AIMK WN4 63 K4
Wasdale St ROCH OL11 41 M3
Wasdale Ter STLY SK15 76 D8
Wasdale Wk OLD OL1 9 L3
Washacre WHTN BL5 50 C5
Washacre Cl WHTN BL5 50 C5
Washbrook CHAD OL9 58 E8
Washbrook Av WALK M28 68 E3
Washbrook Dr STRET M32 96 E3
Washburn Cl WHTN BL5 50 B2
Wash Ford TOT/BURYW BL8 24 E8
Washford Dr NTHM/RTH M23 109 G4
Washington Cl CHD/CHDH SK8 120 B4
Washington Ct BURY BL9 5 G2
Washington St BOLS/LL BL3 35 M6
CHAD OL9 8 D5
Wash La BURY BL9 5 J3
BURY BL9 5 L5
LEIGH WN7 66 F7
Wash Lane Ter BURY BL9 5 L4
Wash Ter TOT/BURYW BL8 24 E7
Washway Rd SALE M33 108 B3
Washwood Cl LHULT M38 * 52 E6
Wasnidge Wk HULME M15 * 87 J7
Wasp Av ROCH OL11 42 D1
Wasp Mill Dr WHIT OL12 21 G6
Wastdale Av BURY BL9 55 K1
Wastdale Rd NTHM/RTH M23 109 J8
Waste St OLD OL1 * 9 M4
Wastwater St OLD OL1 9 L1
Watburn Rd NM/HAY SK22 124 F3
Watchgate BRAM/HZG SK7 121 L2
Watchgate Cl MDTN M24 57 G1
Waterbeck Cl WGN WN1 15 M2
Waterbridge WALK M28 69 K7
Watercroft ROCH OL11 27 G3
Waterdale Cl WALK M28 68 E7
Waterdale Dr WHTF M45 55 K4
Water Dr WGNNW/ST WN6 31 L5
Wateredge Cl LEIGH WN7 81 G1
Waterfield Cl BURY BL9 25 J5
Waterfield Wy FAIL M35 74 D6
Waterfold La BURY BL9 5 L7
Waterfoot Cottages
HYDE SK14 92 D8
Waterford Av DID/WITH M20 110 A1
MPL/ROM SK6 114 C3
Waterfront Quay SALQ M50 86 C5
Watergate DTN/ASHW M34 89 M4
Water Ga UPML OL3 61 L4
Watergate Dr WHTN BL5 51 M5
Watergate La WHTN BL5 51 M5
Water Grove Rd DUK SK16 91 J5
Waterhead OLDE OL4 60 B4
Waterhouse Cl WHIT OL12 21 G7
Waterhouse Rd GTN M18 89 H8
Waterhouse St WHIT OL12 10 E3
Waterhouse Wy RDSH SK5 100 B5
Water La DROY M43 89 H3
FWTH BL4 53 H5
HYDE SK14 93 G7
MILN OL16 29 K7
RAD M26 54 C1
RAMS BL0 19 G2
WILM/AE SK9 126 E5
Water Lane St RAD M26 54 C1
Waterloo Ct BURY BL9 4 D8
Waterloo Gdns AUL OL6 76 B7
Waterloo Pl STKP SK1 * 13 K5
Waterloo Rd AUL OL6 75 L7
BKLY M9 73 G3
BRAM/HZG SK7 121 H3
CHH M8 72 B8
MPL/ROM SK6 114 B2
POY/DIS SK12 129 L2
STKP SK1 13 K5
STLY SK15 91 K2
Waterloo St AUL OL6 76 A8
BOL BL1 2 F1
CHH M8 72 F4
CMANE M1 7 G6
OLD OL1 9 K6
TOT/BURYW BL8 4 B4
WGNNW/ST WN6 14 B1
Watermans Cl BKLY M9 73 J4
Waterman Vw MILN OL16 11 L2
Watermead SALE M33 108 D3
Watermead Cl EDGY/DAV SK3 112 B8
Watermede
WGNW/BIL/OR WN5 62 B1
Watermeetings La
MPL/ROM SK6 114 B2
Watermill Cl MILN OL16 29 G6
Water Mill Clough
ROY/SHW OL2 58 F2
Watermill Ct AULW OL7 75 K7
Watermillock Gdns BOL BL1 36 C1
Waterpark Rd BRO M7 72 B4
Waters Edge AUL OL6 76 B7
FWTH BL4 52 D2
MPL/ROM SK6 114 D4
WALK M28 69 J2
Watersedge Cl CHD/CHDH SK8 120 D1
Waters Edge Fold OLD OL1 43 M8
Watersfield Cl CHD/CHDH SK8 120 B4
Watersheddings St OLDE OL4 60 A3
Waterside GLSP SK13 93 K7
HYDE SK14 103 G2
MPL/ROM SK6 114 C8
POY/DIS SK12 124 A5
SALE M33 96 F7
TRPK M17 86 C6
UPML OL3 61 M8
Waterside Av MPL/ROM SK6 114 C7
Waterside Cl CCHDY M21 98 A8
HYDE SK14 103 G2
OLD OL1 43 M8
RAD M26 39 G8
Waterside Ct URM M41 * 95 G2
Waterside Dr WGNS/IIMK WN3 14 F7
Waterside La MILN OL16 11 K3
Waterside Rd BURY BL9 24 F2
NM/HAY SK22 124 B4
Waterside Vw DROY M43 89 H4
Watersiea ECC M30 84 F2
Watersiea Dr BOL BL1 35 J5
Watersmead Cl BOL BL1 36 C2
Watersmead St BOL BL1 36 C2
Watersmeet STRET M32 85 M8
Waters Meeting Rd BOL BL1 36 C1
Water's Nook Rd WHTN BL5 50 D4
Waterson Av NEWH/MOS M40 73 K5
Waters Reach MOSL OL5 61 H8
POY/DIS SK12 122 B8
TRPK M17 86 C6
WGN WN1 15 M4
Water Sreet RAD M26 54 D1
Water St ATH M46 67 G1
AUL OL6 90 E1
BKLY M9 73 G4
BOL BL1 2 F4
CSLFD M3 6 B7
DTN/ASHW M34 90 C5
EDGW/EG BL7 22 A2
GLSP SK13 105 H2
HYDE SK14 102 A1
MDTN M24 57 J4
MILN OL16 10 F4
NEWLW WA12 78 F8
ROY/SHW OL2 43 K8
STKP SK1 13 K1
STLY SK15 * 91 K2
WGN WN1 15 G3
Waterton Av MOSL OL5 76 E2
Waterton La MOSL OL5 76 E2
Waterview Cl MILN OL16 43 L1
Waterview Pk LEIGH WN7 66 B8
Waterworks Dr NEWLW WA12 79 J8
Waterworks Rd OLDE OL4 60 B3
UPML OL3 45 K6
Watford Av RUSH/FAL M14 98 E2
Watford Bridge Rd
NM/HAY SK22 124 F3
Watford La NM/HAY SK22 124 E2
Watford Rd NM/HAY SK22 124 E2
Watkin Av GLSP SK13 93 H8
Watkin Cl BRUN/LGST M13 87 L6
Watkins Dr PWCH M25 72 B1
Watkin St CSLFD M3 * 87 G1
HYDE SK14 91 K7
Watling St LIT OL15 21 K7
TOT/BURYW BL8 23 J2
TOT/BURYW BL8 38 C4
Watlington Cl OLD OL1 60 A1
Watson Av AIMK WN4 78 F1
GOL/RIS/CUL WA3 79 J3
Watson Gdns WHIT OL12 28 A1
Watson Rd FWTH BL4 52 C4
Watson Sq STKP SK1 13 K5
Watson St CSLFD M3 6 E7
DTN/ASHW M34 101 L1
ECC M30 84 F2
OLDE OL4 59 M4
RAD M26 38 D8
SWIN M27 70 C3
Watton Cl SWIN M27 * 70 C2
Watts St BNG/LEV M19 99 L4
CHAD OL9 8 B4
HOR/BR BL6 33 L2
OLDS OL8 75 G2
WHIT OL12 10 F2
Waugh Av FAIL M35 74 C6
Wavell Dr BURY BL9 55 K3
Wavell Rd WYTH/NTH M22 118 F2
Waveney Dr ALT WA14 107 M6
WILM/AE SK9 127 H2
Waveney Rd ROY/SHW OL2 43 K4
WYTH/NTH M22 110 B8
Waverley WHIT OL12 10 D2
Waverley Av FWTH BL4 53 J6
STRET M32 97 H1
Waverley Ct WGNS/IIMK WN3 63 G1
Waverley Crs DROY M43 89 K1
Waverley Dr CHD/CHDH SK8 120 D6
Waverley Gv LEIGH WN7 * 67 G6
Waverley Rd BKLY M9 73 J5
BOL BL1 36 B1
EDGY/DAV SK3 12 D8
GOL/RIS/CUL WA3 80 A3
HYDE SK14 102 A4
MDTN M24 57 K1
SALE M33 96 F6
SWIN M27 70 F5
WALK M28 68 E3
WGNE/HIN WN2 48 F7
Waverley Rd West BKLY M9 73 J6
Waverley St OLD OL1 59 L4
ROCH OL11 41 M3
Waverton Av HTNM SK4 100 A5
Waverton Rd RUSH/FAL M14 98 D3
Wavertree Av ATH M46 50 E8
Wavertree Rd BKLY M9 56 F8
Wayfarer Dr TYLD M29 67 K4
Wayfarers Wy SWIN M27 70 B5
Wayfaring WHTN BL5 50 C2
Wayland Rd GTN M18 100 A1
Wayland Rd South GTN M18 100 A1
Wayne Cl DROY M43 74 F8
Wayne St OP/CLY M11 89 H4
Wayoh Cft EDGW/EG BL7 17 G6
Wayside Dr POY/DIS SK12 121 L8
Wayside Gdns BRAM/HZG SK7 122 C2
Wayside Gv WALK M28 53 H8
Weald Cl BRUN/LGST M13 87 M6
Wealdstone Gv BOLE BL2 * 36 E2
Weardale Rd BKLY M9 56 E7
Wearhead Cl GOL/RIS/CUL WA3 79 K5
Wearish La WHTN BL5 49 M6
Weaste Av LHULT M38 52 E8
Weaste Dr ORD M5 86 A1
Weaste La ORD M5 86 A1
Weaste Rd ORD M5 86 A3
Weatherall St North BRO M7 72 C5
Weatherley Cl OLDS OL8 75 J3
Weatherley Dr MPL/ROM SK6 114 A6
Weaver Av WALK M28 68 D2
Weaver Cl ALT WA14 116 E3
Weaver Ct HULME M15 * 87 G6
Weaver Dr BURY BL9 25 J4
Weaver Gv LEIGH WN7 65 M8
Weaverham Cl BRUN/LGST M13 99 J1
Weavers Ct BOLS/LL BL3 2 D8
MDTN M24 57 J3
Weavers Gn FWTH BL4 53 G5
Weavers La BRAM/HZG SK7 120 F6
Weavers Rd MDTN M24 57 J3
Webb Gv HYDE SK14 103 H3
Webb La STKP SK1 13 M5
Webb St HOR/BR BL6 33 M2
TOT/BURYW BL8 4 B3
Webdale Dr NEWH/MOS M40 73 K5
Weber Dr BOLS/LL BL3 * 2 B9
Webster Gv PWCH M25 71 J2
Webster's St WGNE/HIN WN2 64 D2
Webster St BOLS/LL BL3 3 J9
MOSL OL5 76 F2
OLDS OL8 9 J8
Wedgewood Dr
WGNNW/ST WN6 47 G1
Wedgewood St
NEWH/MOS M40 73 J8
Wedgwood Rd SWIN M27 70 F2
Wedhurst St OLDE OL4 59 M5
Wedneshough HYDE SK14 92 F7
Weedall Av ORD M5 86 D6
Weedon Av NEWLW WA12 78 E7
Weedon St MILN OL16 11 J3
Weeton Av BOLE BL2 37 J5
Weighbridge Ct IRL M44 94 E1
Weir Rd MILN OL16 29 H5
Weir St FAIL M35 74 B5
Welbeck Av CHAD OL9 74 A1
LIT OL15 21 L6
URM M41 96 B1
Welbeck Cl MILN OL16 29 H6
WHTF M45 55 J2
Welbeck Gv BRO M7 72 B5
Welbeck Rd AIMK WN4 63 L7
BOL BL1 35 K4
ECC M30 70 B8
HYDE SK14 102 C2
MILN OL16 28 E8
RDSH SK5 100 C4
WALK M28 69 L6
WGNS/IIMK WN3 63 J1
Welbeck St GTN M18 89 G6
Welbeck St South AUL OL6 90 D2
Welburn Av WYTH/NTH M22 119 G1
Welburn St ROCH OL11 10 F8
Welbury Rd NTHM/RTH M23 109 J3
Welby St BRUN/LGST M13 88 A8
Welch Hill St LEIGH WN7 66 B8
Welch Rd HYDE SK14 91 J8
Welcomb Cl MPL/ROM SK6 101 J8
Welcomb St OP/CLY M11 88 E5
Welcome Pde OLDS OL8 75 M1
Welcroft St STKP SK1 13 K6
Weldon Av BOLS/LL BL3 51 K2
Weldon Crs EDGY/DAV SK3 112 B8
Weldon Dr BKLY M9 57 G7
Weldon Gv WGN WN1 48 B2
Weldon Rd ALT WA14 107 M6
Weld Rd DID/WITH M20 99 G5
Welford Av GOL/RIS/CUL WA3 79 M5
Welford Cl WILM/AE SK9 127 J4
Welford Gn RDSH SK5 100 C7
Welford Rd CHH M8 56 C8
Welford St SLFD M6 71 L8
Welkin Rd MPL/ROM SK6 112 F1
Wellacre Av URM M41 95 G2
Welland Av HEY OL10 40 C1
Welland Cl HULME M15 * 87 G6
Welland Ct HULME M15 87 G6
Welland Rd AIMK WN4 64 B7
ROY/SHW OL2 43 K4
WILM/AE SK9 127 H2
Welland St OP/CLY M11 89 G4
RDSH SK5 100 C3
The Welland WHTN BL5 50 B4
Wellbank PWCH M25 * 71 J1
STLY SK15 91 M4
Wellbank Av AUL OL6 76 B6
Wellbank Cl BOLS/LL BL3 53 L1
OLDS OL8 59 K8
Wellbank St TOT/BURYW BL8 24 C6
Wellbank Vw WHIT OL12 27 J3
Wellbrooke Cl AIMK WN4 78 F1
Wellbrow Ter WHIT OL12 28 A3
Wellens Wy MDTN M24 56 F5
Weller Av CCHDY M21 98 A5
POY/DIS SK12 129 H2
Weller Cl POY/DIS SK12 129 H2
Wellesbourne Dr
NTHM/RTH M23 109 J5
Wellesley Av GTN M18 89 G6
Wellesley Cl NEWLW WA12 78 E7
WGNW/BIL/OR WN5 47 H4
Wellfield Cl BURY BL9 39 H6
Wellfield La HALE/TIMP WA15 108 F8
Wellfield Pl ROCH OL11 * 11 G9
Wellfield Rd BOLS/LL BL3 35 M7
CHH M8 72 D4
GOL/RIS/CUL WA3 81 H8
NTHM/RTH M23 109 K5
OFTN SK2 112 F6
WGNE/HIN WN2 49 K8
WGNNW/ST WN6 31 J8
Wellfield St ROCH OL11 11 G9
Well Ga GLSP SK13 105 H2
Wellgate Av BNG/LEV M19 99 L4
Wellgreen Cl HALE/TIMP WA15 117 L1
Well Green Ldg
HALE/TIMP WA15 * 117 L1
Well Gv WHTF M45 55 H1
Wellham Rd WGNS/IIMK WN3 63 L1
Wellhead Cl HULME M15 87 J7
Wellhouse Dr NEWH/MOS M40 73 M1
Well-i-hole Rd UPML OL3 61 J8
Welling Rd NEWH/MOS M40 74 B4
Welling St BOLE BL2 3 J1
Wellington Av OLDTF/WHR M16 98 A2
Wellington Cl SALE M33 96 F6
Wellington Clough AULW OL7 75 J6
Wellington Ct OLDS OL8 * 59 G8
Wellington Crs
OLDTF/WHR M16 97 M1
Wellington Dr TYLD M29 68 B4
Wellington Gv HULME M15 87 G6
OFTN SK2 13 J9
WGNS/IIMK WN3 15 J9
Wellington Ms EDGW/EG BL7 17 G8
Wellington Pl ALT WA14 116 F1
MILN OL16 11 H3
Wellington Rd ATH M46 51 J7
AUL OL6 90 E1
BRAM/HZG SK7 122 D4
BURY BL9 4 F7
CHH M8 72 E4
ECC M30 85 H2
EDGW/EG BL7 17 G8
HALE/TIMP WA15 108 C6
OLDS OL8 58 F8
OLDTF/WHR M16 98 B2
RUSH/FAL M14 98 F5
SWIN M27 70 C4
UPML OL3 61 K6
Wellington Rd North
BNG/LEV M19 99 L5
HTNM SK4 12 F2
Wellington Rd South OFTN SK2 13 J8
Wellington Sq TOT/BURYW BL8 38 E3
Wellington St AUL OL6 90 E2
BOLS/LL BL3 2 B6
BRAM/HZG SK7 122 B1
CHAD OL9 8 A3
CSLFD M3 6 B2
DTN/ASHW M34 90 C6
FAIL M35 * 74 D3
FWTH BL4 53 G4
GTN M18 89 G7
HYDE SK14 101 M1
LIT OL15 21 M7
MILN OL16 29 K6
OLD OL1 9 K6
RAD M26 38 F8
STKP SK1 13 J5
STRET M32 96 F3

**TOT/BURYW** BL8 * ....4 B6
**WGN** WN1 ....15 J4
**WHIT** OL12 ....10 F1
**WHTN** BL5 ....50 B2
**Wellington St East** *BRO* M7 ....72 A5
**Wellington St West** *BRO* M7 ....72 A6
**Wellington Ter** *ORD* M5 ....86 A2
**Wellington Vls** *TOT/BURYW* BL8 * ....2 C6
**Well i' th' La** *ROCH* OL11 ....11 H9
**Well La** *WHTF* M45 ....55 J2
**Well Md** *MPL/ROM* SK6 ....113 H1
**Wellmead Cl** *CHH* M8 ....72 C7
**Well Meadow** *HYDE* SK14 ....91 G8
**Well Meadow La** *UPML* OL3 ....61 M4
**Well Rd** *LEIGH* WN7 ....66 A3
**Wells Av** *CHAD* OL9 ....7 H5
*PWCH* M25 ....71 M2
**Wells Dr** *DUK* SK16 ....90 F6
*DROY* M43 ....89 J4
*MDTN* M24 ....56 F5
*TYLD* M29 ....67 L5
**Wells Ct** *DUK* SK16 ....90 F6
*HTNM* SK4 ....111 H2
*WGNE/HIN* WN2 ....48 C2
**Wells Pl** *WGN* WN1 ....15 L3
**Wells Rd** *OLD* OL1 ....44 B7
**Wells St** *BURY* BL9 ....4 D7
**Wellstock La** *LHULT* M38 ....52 C6
**Well St** *BOL* BL1 ....2 F4
*BOLE* BL2 ....3 M3
*HEY* OL10 ....41 H5
*NM/HAY* SK22 ....124 D4
*ROCH* OL11 ....11 H9
*TYLD* M29 ....67 K4
**Well St West** *RAMS* BL0 ....18 E7
**Wellwood Dr** *NEWH/MOS* M40 * ....73 H7
**Wellyhole St** *OLDE* OL4 ....60 A6
**Welman Wy** *HALE/TIMP* WA15 ....108 C8
**Welney Rd** *OLDTF/WHR* M16 ....97 L1
**Welshpool Cl** *NTHM/RTH* M23 ....109 L2
**Welsh Rw** *MCFLDN* SK10 ....130 D6
**Weltdown Gdns** *ROY/SHW* OL2 ....43 J4
**Welton Av** *DID/WITH* M20 ....110 F2
**Welton Cl** *LEIGH* WN7 ....66 F7
*WILM/AE* SK9 ....126 C8
**Welton Dr** *WILM/AE* SK9 ....126 C8
**Welton Gv** *WILM/AE* SK9 ....126 C8
**Welwyn Cl** *URM* M41 ....84 F7
**Welwyn Dr** *SLFD* M6 ....70 D7
**Welwyn Wk** *NEWH/MOS* M40 ....88 A2
**Wembley Cl** *EDGY/DAV* SK3 ....112 A7
**Wembley Gv** *RUSH/FAL* M14 ....98 F4
**Wembley Rd** *GTN* M18 * ....99 M1
**Wembury Rd** *BKLY* M9 ....73 H5
**Wembury St North** *BKLY* M9 ....73 H4
**Wemsley Gv** *BOLE* BL2 ....36 E3
**Wem St** *CHAD* OL9 ....58 D8
**Wemyss Av** *RDSH* SK5 ....100 C3
**Wendlebury Cl** *LEIGH* WN7 ....66 F7
**Wendlebury Gn** *ROY/SHW* OL2 ....43 K7
**Wendon Rd** *NTHM/RTH* M23 ....109 L7
**Wendover Dr** *BOLS/LL* BL3 ....35 H7
**Wendover Rd** *NTHM/RTH* M23 ....109 L8
*URM* M41 ....95 M3
**Wenfield Dr** *BKLY* M9 ....73 K1
**Wenlock Av** *AULW* OL7 ....75 L1
**Wenlock Cl** *OFTN* SK2 ....113 K6
**Wenlock Gv** *WGNE/HIN* WN2 ....49 G8
**Wenlock Rd** *LEIGH* WN7 ....81 H2
*SALE* M33 ....108 D2
*WGNE/HIN* WN2 * ....49 G8
**Wenlock St** *SWIN* M27 ....70 A4
**Wenlock Wy** *WGTN/LGST* M12 ....88 D6
**Wenning Cl** *WHTF* M45 ....55 M3
**Wensleydale Av**
*CHD/CHDH* SK8 ....110 F6
**Wensleydale Cl** *BURY* BL9 ....55 K1
*NTHM/RTH* M23 ....118 B1
*ROY/SHW* OL2 ....42 F7
**Wensleydale Rd** *LEIGH* WN7 ....66 F7
**Wensley Dr** *BRAM/HZG* SK7 ....121 M5
*DID/WITH* M20 ....98 E7
**Wensley Rd** *BRO* M7 ....71 K3
*CHD/CHDH* SK8 ....110 F6
*GOL/RIS/CUL* WA3 ....80 B5
*RDSH* SK5 ....100 C3
**Wensley Wy** *MILN* OL16 ....11 L6
**Wentbridge Rd** *BOL* BL1 ....2 A3
**Wentworth Av** *FWTH* BL4 ....52 F5
*GTN* M18 ....89 H7
*HALE/TIMP* WA15 ....108 D6
*HEY* OL10 ....41 G4
*IRL* M44 * ....94 D1
*SLFD* M6 ....85 M1
*TOT/BURYW* BL8 ....24 E8
*WHTF* M45 ....55 H4
**Wentworth Cl** *MDTN* M24 ....57 H4
*MPL/ROM* SK6 ....114 C4
*RAD* M26 ....38 A8
**Wentworth Dr** *BRAM/HZG* SK7 ....121 J5
*SALE* M33 ....96 C7
**Wentworth Rd** *AIMK* WN4 ....63 J3
*ECC* M30 ....70 C8
*RDSH* SK5 ....100 C3
*SWIN* M27 ....70 A6
**Wenworth Av** *URM* M41 ....95 L3
**Werneth Av** *HYDE* SK14 ....102 C4
*RUSH/FAL* M14 ....98 E2
**Werneth Cl** *BRAM/HZG* SK7 * ....113 H8
*DTN/ASHW* M34 ....101 J2
**Werneth Crs** *OLDS* OL8 ....58 F8
**Werneth Hall Rd** *OLDS* OL8 ....8 E9
**Werneth Hollow**
*MPL/ROM* SK6 ....101 L6
**Werneth Low Rd** *HYDE* SK14 ....102 B7
**Werneth Ri** *HYDE* SK14 ....102 C5
**Werneth Rd** *GLSP* SK13 ....102 C2
*HYDE* SK14 ....102 C5
*MPL/ROM* SK6 ....101 M7
**Werneth St** *DTN/ASHW* M34 ....90 C7
*STKP* SK1 ....112 E1
**Wescoe Cl** *WGNNW/ST* WN5 ....46 B7
**Wesley Av** *RNFD/HAY* WA11 ....78 B5
**Wesley Cl** *WHIT* OL12 ....108 C2
*WHTN* BL5 ....50 B2
**Wesley Ct** *WALK* M28 * ....53 G8
**Wesley Dr** *AUL* OL6 ....76 A6
*WHTN* BL5 ....50 B2
**Wesley Gn** *ORD* M5 ....86 E4
**Wesley Ms** *BOLE* BL2 * ....3 J3
**Wesley Sq** *URM* M41 ....95 K2
**The Wesleys** *FWTH* BL4 ....67 H1
**Wesley St** *ATH* M46 ....67 H1
*BOLS/LL* BL3 ....2 C9
*BRAM/HZG* SK7 ....122 A1
*ECC* M30 ....84 D7
*EDGW/EG* BL7 ....22 D4

*FAIL* M35 ....74 D3
*FWTH* BL4 ....53 H5
*GLSP* SK13 ....93 K7
*GLSP* SK13 ....105 H2
*HEY* OL10 ....40 F2
*MILN* OL16 ....29 H6
*OP/CLY* M11 ....88 D4
*ROY/SHW* OL2 ....59 H1
*STKP* SK1 ....13 K5
*STRET* M32 ....97 H1
*SWIN* M27 ....70 C4
*TOT/BURYW* BL8 ....24 B5
*WGNW/BIL/OR* WN5 ....47 G8
*WHIT* OL12 * ....28 E1
*WHTN* BL5 ....50 B2
**Wessenden Bank East**
*OFTN* SK2 ....113 G7
**Wessenden Bank West**
*OFTN* SK2 ....113 G7
**Wessex Cl** *WGN* WN1 ....31 L3
**Wessex Park** *ROY/SHW* OL2 ....43 L4
**Wessex Rd** *WGNW/BIL/OR* WN5 ....47 G3
**Wessington Ms** *GLSP* SK13 ....104 B2
**Westage Gdns**
*NTHM/RTH* M23 ....109 K5
**West Ashton St** *SALO* M50 ....86 C4
**West Av** *ALT* WA14 ....107 K7
*BNG/LEV* M19 ....99 J5
*CHD/CHDH* SK8 ....119 L3
*FWTH* BL4 ....52 E4
*GOL/RIS/CUL* WA3 ....79 L3
*GTN* M18 * ....89 H7
*LEIGH* WN7 ....81 J3
*NEWH/MOS* M40 ....74 A3
*STLY* SK15 ....91 K2
*WALK* M28 ....68 F1
*WHTF* M45 ....55 H1
**West Bank** *OP/CLY* M11 ....89 K5
**Westbank** *DID/WITH* M20 ....99 H1
*HOR/BR* BL6 ....35 G6
**West Bank St** *ATH* M46 ....67 H3
*ORD* M5 ....86 F4
**Westbourne Av** *BOLS/LL* BL3 ....52 D1
*LEIGH* WN7 ....66 C5
*SWIN* M27 ....54 A7
*WHTF* M45 ....55 G3
**Westbourne Dr** *WILM/AE* SK9 ....127 H4
*DID/WITH* M20 ....98 D6
*RDSH* SK5 ....100 C4
*SALE* M33 ....96 D8
**Westbourne Pk** *URM* M41 ....96 A1
**Westbourne Range** *GTN* M18 ....100 D3
**Westbourne Rd**
*DTN/ASHW* M34 ....101 H2
*ECC* M30 ....69 L8
*RUSH/FAL* M14 ....99 G4
*URM* M41 ....96 A2
**Westbourne St** *CHAD* OL9 ....8 C5
**Westbridge Ms** *WGN* WN1 ....15 G5
**West Bridgewater St**
*LEIGH* WN7 ....66 C8
**Westbrook Cl** *BOLE* BL2 * ....3 G7
*ROCH* OL11 ....42 A4
**Westbrook Ct** *BOLE* BL2 * ....3 H7
**Westbrook Rd** *SWIN* M27 ....70 B5
*TRPK* M17 ....85 M5
**Westbrook Sq** *WGTN/LGST* M12 ....88 D6
**Westbrook St** *BOLE* BL2 * ....3 H7
**Westbury Av** *SALE* M33 ....107 H3
*WGNS/IIMK* WN3 ....63 G2
**Westbury Cl** *TOT/BURYW* BL8 ....38 D3
*WHTN* BL5 ....50 D3
**Westbury Dr** *CHH* M8 * ....72 D3
*HYDE* SK14 ....90 F7
**Westbury St** *AUL* OL6 ....90 F7
**Westbury Wy** *ROY/SHW* OL2 ....59 G2
**Westby Cl** *BRAM/HZG* SK7 ....121 J5
**Westby Gv** *BOLE* BL2 ....3 K3
**West Canteen Rd** *TRPK* M17 ....85 M8
**West Central Dr** *SWIN* M27 ....70 E5
**West Charles St** *ORD* M5 ....86 E3
**West Church St** *HEY* OL10 ....40 F2
**Westcliffe Rd** *BOL* BL1 ....22 C6
**West Cl** *ATH* M46 ....67 H3
**Westcombe Dr**
*TOT/BURYW* BL8 ....24 F8
**Westcott Av** *DID/WITH* M20 ....98 D6
**Westcott Cl** *BOLE* BL2 ....23 H7
**Westcott Dr** *WGNS/IIMK* WN3 ....46 F8
**Westcott Gv** *ROY/SHW* OL2 ....43 K7
**Westcourt Rd** *BOLS/LL* BL3 ....52 A1
*SALE* M33 ....96 D7
**Westcraig Av** *NEWH/MOS* M40 ....73 M1
**West Craven St** *ORD* M5 ....86 E5
**West Crs** *MDTN* M24 ....57 J5
**Westcroft** *WGNE/HIN* WN2 ....64 E2
**Westcroft Rd** *DID/WITH* M20 ....99 G8
**West Crown Av** *ORD* M5 ....86 E4
**Westdale Gdns** *BNG/LEV* M19 ....99 K7
**Westdean Crs** *BNG/LEV* M19 ....99 J7
**Dean St** *ORD* M5 ....86 F3
**West Downs Rd**
*CHD/CHDH* SK8 ....120 B1
**West Dr** *BURY* BL9 ....25 H7
*CHD/CHDH* SK8 ....110 D8
*DROY* M43 ....89 J3
*GLSP* SK13 ....93 H6
*SLFD* M6 ....71 H4
*SWIN* M27 ....70 E5
**West Duke St** *ORD* M5 ....6 A5
**West Egerton St** *ORD* M5 ....86 E3
**West End Av** *CHD/CHDH* SK8 ....110 D6
**West End St** *CHAD* OL9 ....8 F5
**Westend St** *FWTH* BL4 ....52 E4
**Westerdale** *OLDE* OL4 ....59 M6
**Westerdale Dr** *BOLS/LL* BL3 ....35 K7
*ROY/SHW* OL2 ....42 F7
**Westerham Av** *ORD* M5 ....86 D3
**Westerham Cl** *TOT/BURYW* BL8 ....24 E5
**Wester Hill Rd** *OLDS* OL8 ....75 K3
**Westerling Wy**
*OLDTF/WHR* M16 ....98 B1
**Western Access** *TRPK* M17 * ....85 J4
**Western Cir** *BNG/LEV* M19 ....99 J6
**Western Rd** *URM* M41 ....95 H3
**Western St** *GTN* M18 ....89 H6
*SLFD* M6 ....86 B1
**Westerton Ct** *BOLS/LL* BL3 * ....2 A8
**Westfield** *SLFD* M6 ....71 H8
**Westfield Av** *AIMK* WN4 ....57 K6
**Westfield Cl** *ROCH* OL11 ....27 J3
**Westfield Dr** *MPL/ROM* SK6 ....101 M4
**Westfield Gv** *DTN/ASHW* M34 ....90 B7
*WGN* WN1 ....47 L1
**Westfield Rd** *BOLS/LL* BL3 ....51 L2
*CCHDY* M21 ....97 L3

*CHD/CHDH* SK8 ....120 B4
*DROY* M43 ....89 H2
**Westfields** *HALE/TIMP* WA15 ....117 H4
**Westfield St** *BRO* M7 ....72 A3
*CHAD* ....8 C2
**Westgate** *HALE/TIMP* WA15 ....117 G2
*SALE* M33 ....96 D8
*URM* M41 ....95 L3
*WILM/AE* SK9 ....126 E7
**Westgate Av** *BKLY* M9 ....72 F2
*BOL* BL1 ....35 M5
*BURY* BL9 ....4 D7
*RAMS* BL0 ....24 C2
**Westgate Dr** *SWIN* M27 ....70 C6
*TYLD* M29 ....67 M6
*WGNW/BIL/OR* WN5 ....46 A7
**Westgate Rd** *SLFD* M6 ....70 E8
**West Gn** *MDTN* M24 ....56 E5
**West Gv** *BRUN/LGST* M13 ....88 A7
*MOSL* OL5 ....76 F4
*SALE* M33 ....108 E1
*STLY* SK15 ....91 J2
**West Hope St** *ORD* M5 ....86 E3
**Westhulme Av** *OLD* OL1 ....8 E1
**Westhulme St** *OLD* OL1 ....8 E1
**Westhulme Wy** *OLD* OL1 ....58 F3
**Westinghouse Cl**
*WGNNW/ST* WN6 ....14 C4
**Westinghouse Rd** *TRPK* M17 ....85 M7
**West King St** *CSLFD* M3 ....6 C2
**Westlake St** *OP/CLY* M11 * ....89 K5
**Westland Av** *BOL* BL1 ....35 K3
*FWTH* BL4 ....52 F6
*STKP* SK1 ....112 E3
**Westland Dr** *BKLY* M9 ....57 G8
**Westlands** *WHTF* M45 ....55 J6
**The Westlands** *SWIN* M27 ....70 E6
**West Lea** *DTN/ASHW* M34 ....101 K1
**Westlea Dr** *GTN* M18 ....100 A1
**Westleigh Dr** *PWCH* M25 ....55 M8
**Westleigh La** *LEIGH* WN7 ....66 A2
**Westleigh St** *BKLY* M9 ....73 H3
**West Malling Cl** *HEY* OL10 ....41 J5
**Westmarsh Cl** *BOL* BL1 ....2 D1
**West Marwood St** *BRO* M7 ....72 B6
**Westmead** *WGNNW/ST* WN6 ....31 H4
**Westmead Dr**
*HALE/TIMP* WA15 ....108 E5
**West Meade** *BOLS/LL* BL3 ....52 B2
*CCHDY* M21 ....97 K5
*PWCH* M25 ....72 A2
*SWIN* M27 ....70 B6
**Westmeade Rd** *WALK* M28 ....53 G4
**West Meadow** *RDSH* SK5 ....100 D3
**Westmere Dr** *BKLY* M9 ....72 F6
**Westminster Cl** *ROY/SHW* OL2 ....43 L4
**Westminster Av** *AUL* OL6 ....74 A5
*FWTH* BL4 ....52 A4
*OLDTF/WHR* M16 ....97 M2
*RAD* M26 ....38 A4
*RDSH* SK5 ....100 B5
*ROY/SHW* OL2 ....43 L4
*WHTF* M45 ....55 J4
**Westminster Dr**
*CHD/CHDH* SK8 ....120 D6
*LEIGH* WN7 ....67 H6
*RNFD/HAY* WA11 ....78 C5
*WILM/AE* SK9 ....126 D8
**Westminster Rd** *BOL* BL1 ....35 H1
*ECC* M30 ....85 H1
*FAIL* M35 ....74 E4
*HALE/TIMP* WA15 ....117 J1
*URM* M41 ....96 B1
*WALK* M28 ....69 G2
**Westminster St** *BNG/LEV* M19 * ....99 J4
*BURY* BL9 ....4 E7
*FWTH* BL4 ....52 C4
*OLD* OL1 ....59 L4
*ROCH* OL11 ....10 A9
*SWIN* M27 ....70 A3
*WGNW/BIL/OR* WN5 ....47 J6
**Westminster Wy** *DUK* SK16 ....90 F6
**Westmoorland St** *WGN* WN1 ....15 K2
**Westmoreland Cl** *ALT* WA14 ....116 C4
*BURY* BL9 ....39 H6
**Westmorland Av** *AULW* OL7 ....75 L8
*DUK* SK16 ....91 H4
**Westmorland Dr** *RDSH* SK5 ....100 E6
*WHIT* OL12 ....21 H6
**Westmorland Rd**
*DID/WITH* M20 ....110 D2
*ECC* M30 ....70 D7
*PART* M31 ....106 B2
*SALE* M33 ....108 F2
*TYLD* M29 ....67 K2
*URM* M41 ....95 M3
**West Mosley St** *CMANW* M2 ....7 G5
**West Mt** *WGN* WN1 ....48 A2
*WGNW/BIL/OR* WN5 ....46 C7
**Westmount Cl**
*NEWH/MOS* M40 ....72 F6
**West Oak Pl** *CHD/CHDH* SK8 * ....120 B3
**Weston Av** *MILN* OL16 ....28 E8
*NEWH/MOS* M40 ....74 B3
*SWIN* M27 ....54 C8
*URM* M41 ....95 M8
**Westonby Ct** *AIMK* WN4 ....79 G1
**Weston Dr** *CHD/CHDH* SK8 ....111 M8
*DTN/ASHW* M34 ....101 K1
**Weston Gv** *HTNM* SK4 ....99 M6
*WYTH/NTH* M22 ....110 B4
**Weston Pk** *WGNNW/ST* WN6 ....47 L1
**Weston Rd** *IRL* M44 ....94 D2
**Weston St** *ATH* M46 ....51 H8
*BOLS/LL* BL3 ....36 C8
*MILN* OL16 ....29 H6
*NEWH/MOS* M40 * ....88 A2
*OLDE* OL4 ....59 M8
*STKP* SK1 ....100 D8
**Westover** *MPL/ROM* SK6 ....113 K4
**Westover Rd** *URM* M41 ....95 M1
**Westover St** *SWIN* M27 ....70 B3
**West Pk** *HYDE* SK14 ....102 B5
**West Park Rd** *DTN/ASHW* M34 ....101 J2
*POY/DIS* SK12 ....121 J8
**West Park St** *BRAM/HZG* SK7 ....122 C2
*STKP* SK1 ....112 E2
**West Park St** *ORD* M5 ....86 E5

**West Pl** *BNG/LEV* M19 * ....99 J5
**Westray Crs** *ORD* M5 * ....86 B3
**Westray Rd** *BRUN/LGST* M13 ....99 H2
**Westrees** *LEIGH* WN7 ....66 D5
**Westridge Cha** *ROY/SHW* OL2 ....43 G7
**West Rd** *ALT* WA14 ....116 E2
*PWCH* M25 ....55 J7
*STRET* M32 ....85 K8
**West Rw** *PWCH* M25 ....71 J3
**West Starkey St** *HEY* OL10 ....40 F1
**West St** *AUL* OL6 ....90 E1
*BOL* BL1 ....35 M5
*CHAD* OL9 ....8 E6
*DUK* SK16 ....90 E3
*EDGY/DAV* SK3 ....13 H6
*FAIL* M35 ....74 B5
*FWTH* BL4 ....53 H3
*GLSP* SK13 ....93 J6
*HYDE* SK14 * ....91 G7
*LIT* OL15 ....21 M7
*MDTN* M24 ....57 K2
*MILN* OL16 ....11 G2
*MILN* OL16 ....29 C5
*OLD* OL1 ....9 H5
*OLDE* OL4 ....60 B7
*OP/CLY* M11 ....88 E2
*RAMS* BL0 ....18 E7
*STLY* SK15 ....91 J2
*WGNE/HIN* WN2 ....48 D4
*WGN* WN1 ....14 D2
*WILM/AE* SK9 ....130 D3
**West Towers Ms**
*MPL/ROM* SK6 ....114 D8
**West Towers St** *SLFD* M6 ....86 C3
**West V** *RAD* M26 ....38 D7
**West Vale Rd**
*HALE/TIMP* WA15 ....108 C7
**West Vw** *RAMS* BL0 ....18 F2
*WILM/AE* SK9 ....126 C5
**West View Av** *WHTF* M45 ....55 G3
**West View Rd** *WYTH/NTH* M22 ....110 B4
**Westville Gdns** *BNG/LEV* M19 ....99 H7
**West Wk** *EDGW/EG* BL7 ....22 K2
**Westward Ho** *MILN* OL16 ....29 H6
**Westward Rd** *WILM/AE* SK9 ....126 D6
**Westway** *BKLY* M9 ....56 D6
**West Wy** *BOL* BL1 ....36 E1
**West Wy** *LHULT* M38 ....52 D7
**Westway** *OLDE* OL4 ....60 B7
*ROY/SHW* OL2 ....43 L6
**Westwell Gv** *LEIGH* WN7 ....66 A4
**Westwell St** *LEIGH* WN7 ....66 B4
**Westwood Av** *BRO* M7 ....72 A4
*HALE/TIMP* WA15 ....108 C5
*HYDE* SK14 ....102 E1
*NEWH/MOS* M40 ....74 B3
*URM* M41 ....96 C3
*WALK* M28 ....68 D2
**Westwood Cl** *FWTH* BL4 ....53 G4
**Westwood Crs** *ECC* M30 ....69 L8
**Westwood Dr** *CHAD* OL9 ....8 C5
*SALE* M33 ....108 E2
*SWIN* M27 ....70 B3
**Westwood La** *WGNS/IIMK* WN3 ....15 J9
**Westwood Pk** *WGNS/IIMK* WN3 ....15 G8
**Westwood Rd** *BOL* BL1 ....35 M4
*CHD/CHDH* SK8 ....119 K4
*OFTN* SK2 ....112 E8
*STRET* M32 ....96 E2
*WGNS/IIMK* WN3 ....14 F7
**Westwood Ter** *RUSH/FAL* M14 ....87 J8
**Westwood Wy** *OLD* OL1 * ....9 K9
**West Works Rd** *TRPK* M17 ....85 M8
**Wetworth Cl** *BOL* BL1 ....2 B1
**Wet Gate La** *LYMM* WA13 ....106 A8
**Wetheral Cl** *WGNE/HIN* WN2 ....65 M1
**Wetheral Dr** *BOLS/LL* BL3 ....52 B1
**Wetherall St** *BNG/LEV* M19 ....99 L3
**Wetherby Cl** *NEWLW* WA12 ....78 F7
**Wetherby Dr** *BRAM/HZG* SK7 ....122 C2
*ROY/SHW* OL2 ....42 F7
**Wetherby St** *OP/CLY* M11 ....89 H5
**Wexham Gdns** *WGNE/HIN* WN2 ....64 D1
**Weybourne Av** *BKLY* M9 ....73 K2
**Weybourne Dr** *MPL/ROM* SK6 ....101 J8
*WGNS/IIMK* WN3 ....63 H1
**Weybourne Gv** *BOLE* BL2 ....22 E8
**Weybridge Dr** *ANC* M4 ....7 M3
**Weybrook Rd** *BNG/LEV* M19 ....99 M5
**Weycroft Cl** *BOLE* BL2 ....37 K6
**Weygates Dr**
*HALE/TIMP* WA15 ....117 L6
**Weyhill Rd** *NTHM/RTH* M23 ....109 H8
**Weylands Gv** *SLFD* M6 ....70 E7
**Weymouth Dr** *WGNE/HIN* WN2 ....49 G8
**Weymouth Rd** *AUL* OL6 ....76 B6
*ECC* M30 ....84 E1
**Weymouth St** *BOL* BL1 ....36 B2
**Weythorne Dr** *BOL* BL1 ....22 C8
*BURY* BL9 ....26 C7
**Whalley Av** *BNG/LEV* M19 ....99 L3
*BOL* BL1 ....35 J1
*CCHDY* M21 ....97 M5
*GOL/RIS/CUL* WA3 ....81 M5
*LIT* OL15 ....21 L6
*OLDTF/WHR* M16 ....97 M1
*SALE* M33 ....96 B1
*URM* M41 ....96 B1
**Whalley Cl** *HALE/TIMP* WA15 ....108 C4
*MILN* OL16 * ....29 H6
*WGNS/IIMK* WN3 ....63 K1
*WHTF* M45 ....55 J3
**Whalley Dr** *TOT/BURYW* BL8 ....38 C2
**Whalley Gdns** *WHIT* OL12 ....27 L3
**Whalley Gv** *AUL* OL6 ....75 M5
*LEIGH* WN7 ....66 A3
*OLDTF/WHR* M16 ....98 A3
**Whalley Rd** *HALE/TIMP* WA15 ....117 J2
*HEY* OL10 ....40 D2
*MDTN* M24 ....57 J1
*OFTN* SK2 ....112 F5
*OLDTF/WHR* M16 ....98 A1
*RAMS* BL0 ....19 H3
*WHIT* OL12 ....21 L3
*WHTF* M45 ....55 J3
**Whalley St** *NEWH/MOS* M40 ....40 D2
**Wham Bar Dr** *HEY* OL10 ....40 D2
**Wham Bottom La** *WHIT* OL12 ....20 B8
**Wham La** *UPML* OL3 ....45 G3
**Wham St** *HEY* OL10 ....40 D2
**Wharf Cl** *CMANE* M1 ....7 K1
**Wharfedale** *WHTN* BL5 ....51 J7
**Wharfedale Av**
*NEWH/MOS* M40 ....73 M3
**Wharfedale Rd** *RDSH* SK5 ....100 B4
**Wharf End** *TRPK* M17 ....86 D6
**Wharf Rd** *ALT* WA14 ....108 A5
*SALE* M33 ....96 C7

**Wharfside Av** *ECC* M30 ....85 G4
**Wharf St** *CHAD* OL9 ....74 E1
*DUK* SK16 ....90 F3
*HTNM* SK4 ....13 H1
**Wharmby Rd** *RNFD/HAY* WA11 ....78 B6
**Wharmton Ri** *MOSL* OL5 ....61 G6
**Wharmton Vw** *MOSL* OL5 ....77 H1
*UPML* OL3 ....61 K6
**Wharncliffe Cl** *GLSP* SK13 ....93 H8
**Wharncliffe St**
*WGNE/HIN* WN2 ....49 G7
**Wharton Av** *CCHDY* M21 ....98 A5
**Wharton Hall Cl** *TYLD* M29 ....67 L3
**Wharton La** *LHULT* M38 ....52 B7
**Wharton Ldg** *ECC* M30 ....85 H1
**Wheat Cl** *BRUN/LGST* M13 ....87 M7
**Wheat Cft** *EDGY/DAV* SK3 ....112 C7
**Wheatcroft** *GLSP* SK13 ....93 H8
**Wheaters St** *BRO* M7 * ....71 M8
**Wheaters Ter** *BRO* M7 ....72 A8
**Wheatfield** *STLY* SK15 ....92 B5
**Wheatfield Cl** *BURY* BL9 ....25 J3
*MPL/ROM* SK6 ....101 K8
**Wheatfield Crs** *ROY/SHW* OL2 ....58 F1
**Wheatfield St** *BOLE* BL2 ....3 J8
**Wheathill St** *MILN* OL16 ....28 D8
**Wheatlea Rd** *WGNS/IIMK* WN3 ....63 J5
**Wheatley Av** *NEWLW* WA12 ....78 F7
**Wheatley Rd** *SWIN* M27 ....70 A2
**Wheatley Wk** *WGTN/LGST* M12 ....88 C6
**Wheatsheaf Wk**
*WGNNW/ST* WN6 ....31 L3
**Wheeldale** *OLDE* OL4 ....60 A6
**Wheeldale Cl** *BOL* BL1 ....36 B2
**Wheelock Cl** *WILM/AE* SK9 ....127 H5
**Wheelton Cl** *TOT/BURYW* BL8 ....38 D3
**Wheelwright Cl** *MPL/ROM* SK6 ....114 C4
*ROCH* OL11 * ....27 L8
**Wheelwright Dr** *MILN* OL16 ....28 F1
**Whelan Av** *BURY* BL9 ....39 H5
**Whelan Cl** *BURY* BL9 ....39 H5
**Wheler St** *OP/CLY* M11 ....89 G4
**Whelley** *WGN* WN1 ....48 B2
**Whernside Av** *AUL* OL6 ....75 M5
*NEWH/MOS* M40 ....73 K3
**Wherside Cl** *HTNM* SK4 ....13 H2
**Whetmorhurst Rd**
*MPL/ROM* SK6 ....115 H8
**Whetstone Hill Cl** *OLD* OL1 ....59 M2
**Whetstone Hill La** *OLD* OL1 ....59 M3
**Whetstone Hill Rd** *OLD* OL1 ....59 L2
**Whewell Av** *RAD* M26 ....39 G5
**Whickham Cl** *RUSH/FAL* M14 ....98 E1
**Whiley St** *BRUN/LGST* M13 ....88 C3
**Whimberry Cl** *ORD* M5 ....86 F5
**Whimberry Dr** *STLY* SK15 ....77 G7
**Whimberry Wy** *DID/WITH* M20 ....99 G6
**Whimbrel Rd** *OFTN* SK2 ....113 K7
*TYLD* M29 ....67 M5
**Whinberry Dr** *STLY* SK15 ....77 H8
**Whinberry Rd** *ALT* WA14 ....107 L5
**Whinberry Wy** *OLDE* OL4 ....44 B8
**Whinchat Av** *NEWLW* WA12 ....78 F6
**Whinchat Cl** *GOL/RIS/CUL* WA3 ....80 B5
*OFTN* SK2 ....113 K8
**Whinfell Dr** *MDTN* M24 ....56 E3
**Whinfield Cl** *WGNNW/ST* WN6 ....14 C4
**Whins Av** *FWTH* BL4 ....52 B4
**Whins Crest** *HOR/BR* BL6 ....34 F5
**Whinslee Dr** *HOR/BR* BL6 ....34 F5
**Whinstone Wy** *OLD* OL1 ....58 B3
**Whipp St** *HEY* OL10 ....40 E1
**Whirley Cl** *HTNM* SK4 ....100 A7
**Whistlecroft Ct**
*WGNS/IIMK* WN3 ....15 M8
**Whistley St** *WGNE/HIN* WN2 ....64 E1
**Whiston Dr** *BOLE* BL2 ....3 L7
**Whiston Rd** *CHH* M8 ....72 E4
**Whitaker St** *MDTN* M24 ....57 J4
**Whitbeam Gv** *WGNE/HIN* WN2 ....65 H2
**Whitbrook Wy** *MDTN* M24 ....41 M7
**Whitburn Av** *BRUN/LGST* M13 ....99 H3
**Whitburn Cl** *AIMK* WN4 ....63 G8
*BOLS/LL* BL3 ....35 H5
**Whitburn Dr** *TOT/BURYW* BL8 ....24 F7
**Whitburn Rd** *NTHM/RTH* M23 ....109 H8
**Whitby Av** *HEY* OL10 ....40 F1
*OLDTF/WHR* M16 ....98 A2
*RUSH/FAL* M14 ....99 H4
*SLFD* M6 ....71 G4
*WGNS/IIMK* WN3 ....46 B1
**Whitby Cl** *CHD/CHDH* SK8 ....110 F6
*POY/DIS* SK12 ....121 L8
*TOT/BURYW* BL8 ....38 C2
**Whitby Rd** *OLDS* OL8 ....75 M1
*RUSH/FAL* M14 ....99 G4
**Whitby St** *MDTN* M24 ....57 M3
*ROCH* OL11 ....11 G8
**Whitchurch Dr**
*OLDTF/WHR* M16 ....87 G7
**Whitchurch Gdns** *BOL* BL1 ....36 B2
**Whitchurch Rd** *DID/WITH* M20 ....98 C5
**Whitchurch St** *BRO* M7 ....87 H1
**Whiteacre** *WGNNW/ST* WN6 ....30 D2
**Whiteacre Rd** *AUL* OL6 ....76 A4
**Whiteacres** *SWIN* M27 ....69 M5
**White Bank Av** *RDSH* SK5 ....100 F6
**White Bank Rd** *OLDS* OL8 ....75 G4
**Whitebarn Rd** *WILM/AE* SK9 ....130 G4
**Whitebeam Cl**
*HALE/TIMP* WA15 ....109 M1
*MILN* OL16 ....43 H1
*SLFD* M6 ....86 D1
**Whitebeam Ct** *SLFD* M6 ....86 D1
**Whitebeam Wk** *WHTN* BL5 ....50 C2
**White Birk Cl** *TOT/BURYW* BL8 ....24 C2
**White Brook La** *UPML* OL3 ....61 M4
**Whitebrook Rd** *RUSH/FAL* M14 ....98 E3
**Whitecar Av** *NEWH/MOS* M40 ....74 B3
**White Carr La** *BURY* BL9 ....25 L3
**Whitecarr La**
*HALE/TIMP* WA15 ....117 M1
**Whitechapel Cl** *BOLE* BL2 ....37 H5
**Whitechapel St**
*DID/WITH* M20 ....110 E1
**White City Wy**
*OLDTF/WHR* M16 ....86 F7
**Whitecliff Cl** *RUSH/FAL* M14 ....98 F1
**Whitecroft Av**
*GOL/RIS/CUL* WA3 ....80 B3
*ROY/SHW* OL2 ....44 A5
**Whitecroft Dr** *TOT/BURYW* BL8 ....38 C2
**Whitecroft Gdns** *BNG/LEV* M19 ....99 H8
**Whitecroft Rd** *BOL* BL1 ....35 K3
*MPL/ROM* SK6 ....123 L4
*WGNS/IIMK* WN3 ....63 K2
**Whitecroft St** *OLD* OL1 ....59 M3
**Whitefield** *HTNM* SK4 ....112 A4
**Whitefield Av** *ROCH* OL11 ....27 J4
**Whitefield Rd** *BURY* BL9 ....39 H8
*MPL/ROM* SK6 ....101 H8
*SALE* M33 ....96 C7

Whitegate BOLS/LL BL3 50 F2
LIT OL15 21 J8
Whitegate Av CHAD OL9 58 C8
Whitegate Cl NEWH/MOS M40 74 B3
Whitegate Dr BOL BL1 22 C7
ORD M5 86 A1
SWIN M27 70 E2
Whitegate La CHAD OL9 58 D8
Whitegate Pk URM M41 95 H2
Whitegate Rd CHAD OL9 74 A1
Whitegates Cl
HALE/TIMP WA15 108 E7
Whitegates La OLDE OL4 60 E2
Whitegates Rd CHD/CHDH SK8 111 G7
MDTN M24 41 M8
Whitehall Av WGNNW/ST WN6 30 B4
Whitehall Cl WILM/AE SK9 126 E7
Whitehall La BOL BL1 22 A6
HOR/BR BL6 33 G1
OLDE OL4 44 C8
Whitehall Rd DID/WITH M20 110 F1
SALE M33 108 E2
Whitehall St OLD OL1 9 K3
WGNS/IIMK WN3 15 K8
WHIT OL12 10 E1
White Hart Meadow
MDTN M24 57 K2
White Hart St HYDE SK14 91 G8
Whitehaven Gdns
DID/WITH M20 110 D2
Whitehaven Rd
BRAM/HZG SK7 120 E7
Whitehead Crs RAD M26 53 L5
TOT/BURYW BL8 24 F7
Whitehead Rd CCHDY M21 97 J4
SWIN M27 70 E2
Whitehead St DTN/ASHW M34 90 C5
MILN OL16 * 29 H6
ROY/SHW OL2 43 J4
WALK M28 53 G8
White Hill Cl WHIT OL12 20 B8
Whitehill Dr NEWH/MOS M40 73 K5
Whitehill St HTNM SK4 100 B8
Whitehill St West HTNM SK4 100 A8
Whiteholme Av CCHDY M21 98 A8
White Horse Gdns SWIN M27 * 69 M6
White Horse Gv WHTN BL5 50 D2
White Horse Mdw MILN OL16 * 42 F2
Whitehouse Av OLDE OL4 59 M7
White House Av PWCH M25 72 B1
White House Cl HEY OL10 41 G5
Whitehouse Dr
HALE/TIMP WA15 117 K4
NTHM/RTH M23 109 K7
Whitehouse La ALT WA14 107 G5
Whitehurst Rd HTNM SK4 99 J8
Whitekirk Cl BRUN/LGST M13 87 L6
White Lady Cl WALK M28 68 C1
Whitelake Av URM M41 95 J1
Whitelake Vw URM M41 95 H1
Whiteland Av BOLS/LL BL3 35 L7
Whitelands DUK SK16 90 F2
Whitelands Rd AUL OL6 90 F2
Whitelea Dr EDGY/DAV SK3 112 A7
White Lee Cft ATH M46 66 E1
Whitelees Rd LIT OL15 21 L7
Whitelegge St TOT/BURYW BL8 24 E8
Whiteley Dr MDTN M24 57 M5
Whiteley Pl ALT WA14 108 A6
Whiteley St CHAD OL9 58 E8
OP/CLY M11 88 E2
White Lion Brow BOL BL1 2 C5
White Lodge Dr AIMK WN4 64 B8
Whitelow Rd BURY BL9 19 H7
CCHDY M21 97 K4
HTNM SK4 111 K1
Whitemoss WHIT OL12 * 27 L2
White Moss Av CCHDY M21 97 M4
White Moss Rd BKLY M9 73 H1
Whitemoss Rd East BKLY M9 57 J8
Whiteoak Cl MPL/ROM SK6 114 B5
Whiteoak Rd RUSH/FAL M14 98 F4
Whiteoak Vw BOLS/LL BL3 37 G7
White Rd NM/HAY SK22 124 E3
Whites Cft SWIN M27 70 C4
Whiteside Av WGNE/HIN WN2 49 G5
WGNNW/ST WN6 14 B1
Whiteside Cl ORD M5 86 A2
Whiteside Fold WHIT OL12 27 K3
Whitesmead Cl POY/DIS SK12 123 M7
Whitestone Cl HOR/BR BL6 35 G6
Whitestone Wk
BRUN/LGST M13 * 88 A7
White St HULME M15 87 G6
LEIGH WN7 66 F8
SLFD M6 86 B3
TOT/BURYW BL8 38 F3
WGNW/BIL/OR WN5 46 E6
White Swallows Rd SWIN M27 70 D6
Whitethorn Av BNG/LEV M19 99 K5
OLDTF/WHR M16 98 A1
Whitethorn Cl MPL/ROM SK6 114 B5
Whitewater Dr BRO M7 71 J5
Whiteway St BKLY M9 73 H5
Whitewell Cl BURY BL9 39 G5
MILN OL16 11 L2
Whitewillow Cl FAIL M35 74 D6
Whitewood Cl AIMK WN4 63 K6
Whitfield Av GLSP SK13 104 F5
Whitfield Crs MILN OL16 43 L1
Whitfield Cross GLSP SK13 105 G5
Whitfield Dr MILN OL16 29 H7
Whitfield Pk GLSP SK13 104 F5
Whitfield Ri ROY/SHW OL2 43 K3
Whitfield St CSLFD M3 87 K1
LEIGH WN7 66 F8
Whiting Gv BOLS/LL BL3 35 H6
Whitinlea Cl WGNE/HIN WN2 65 M1
Whitland Av BOL BL1 35 J4
Whitland Dr OLDS OL8 74 E2
Whit La SLFD M6 71 K7
Whitle Bank Rd NM/HAY SK22 124 D2
Whitledge Gn AIMK WN4 63 K7
Whitledge Rd AIMK WN4 63 K7
Whitle Rd NM/HAY SK22 124 E3
Whitley Crs WGN WN1 31 L8
WGNE/HIN WN2 64 E5
Whitley Gdns
HALE/TIMP WA15 108 F5
Whitley Pl HALE/TIMP WA15 108 E5
Whitley Rd HTNM SK4 111 L1
NEWH/MOS M40 72 F8
SKEL WN8 46 A2
Whitley St BOLS/LL BL3 53 G2
Whitley Wk GLSP SK13 104 C4
Whitlow Av ALT WA14 107 L4
GOL/RIS/CUL WA3 79 J3
Whitman St BKLY M9 73 J4
Whitmore Rd RUSH/FAL M14 98 E3
Whitnall Cl OLDTF/WHR M16 98 B1
Whitnall St HYDE SK14 * 91 G7
Whitsand Rd WYTH/NTH M22 110 B7
Whitsbury Av GTN M18 100 A1
WGNE/HIN WN2 49 G8
Whitstable Cl CHAD OL9 8 B7
Whitstable Rd
NEWH/MOS M40 * 73 M3
Whitsters Hollow BOL BL1 35 L1
Whitsundale WHTN BL5 50 C2
Whittaker Dr LIT OL15 29 J2
Whittaker La PWCH M25 55 M8
ROCH OL11 27 G3
Whittaker St AUL OL6 76 A7
CHAD OL9 8 B3
NEWH/MOS M40 73 K4
RAD M26 38 E8
ROCH OL11 * 27 H3
WGTN/LGST M12 88 A4
Whittingham Dr RAMS BL0 18 F8
Whittingham Gv OLD OL1 * 8 F2
Whittington St AULW OL7 90 D3
Whittlebrook Gv HEY OL10 41 H5
Whittle Ct WGNS/IIMK WN3 63 H2
Whittle Dr ROY/SHW OL2 44 A4
WALK M28 53 G7
Whittle Gv BOL BL1 35 L3
WALK M28 69 H1
Whittle Hl EDGW/EG BL7 22 B1
Whittle La HEY OL10 40 D7
Whittles Av DTN/ASHW M34 101 K2
Whittle's Cft CMANE M1 * 7 K5
Whittle St ANC M4 * 7 J3
LIT OL15 21 K7
SWIN M27 70 B5
TOT/BURYW BL8 4 A2
WALK M28 69 H1
Whitwell Cl WGNNW/ST WN6 31 G2
Whitwell Wy GTN M18 88 F7
Whitworth Cl AUL OL6 75 M8
Whitworth La RUSH/FAL M14 99 G3
Whitworth Rake WHIT OL12 20 B4
Whitworth Rd WHIT OL12 28 C2
Whitworth Sq WHIT OL12 20 B4
Whitworth St CMANE M1 7 J6
HOR/BR BL6 33 M2
MILN OL16 * 28 F2
MILN OL16 29 J6
OP/CLY M11 88 E5
Whitworth St East OP/CLY M11 88 F5
Whitworth St West CMANE M1 6 F7
Whixhall Av WGTN/LGST M12 88 B6
Whoolden St FWTH BL4 52 F3
Whowell Fold BOL BL1 35 M1
Whowell St BOLS/LL BL3 2 C7
Wibbersley Pk URM M41 * 95 J2
Wichbrook Rd WALK M28 68 C1
Wicheaves Crs WALK M28 68 C1
The Wicheries WALK M28 68 C1
Wicken Bank HEY OL10 41 H5
Wickenby Dr SALE M33 96 D8
Wicken St OFTN SK2 112 F5
Wickentree Holt WHIT OL12 27 K2
Wickentree La FAIL M35 74 D3
Wicker La HALE/TIMP WA15 117 K4
Wicket Gv SWIN M27 54 B8
Wickliffe Pl ROCH OL11 10 E6
Wickliffe St BOL BL1 2 D3
Wicklow Av EDGY/DAV SK3 12 A8
Wicklow Dr WYTH/NTH M22 119 G2
Wicklow Gv OLDS OL8 75 H1
Widcombe Dr BOLE BL2 37 J7
Widdop St CHAD OL9 8 E5
Widdow's St LEIGH WN7 66 E8
Widdrington Rd WGN WN1 48 A2
Widecombe Cl URM M41 * 84 E8
Widgeon Cl POY/DIS SK12 121 K8
RUSH/FAL M14 98 E4
Widgeon Rd ALT WA14 107 L5
Widnes St OP/CLY M11 * 88 F5
Wiend WGN WN1 15 G4
Wigan Investment Centre
WGNS/IIMK WN3 14 E7
Wigan La WGN WN1 15 G1
Wigan Lower Rd
WGNNW/ST WN6 30 F8
Wigan Pier WGNS/IIMK WN3 * 14 D6
Wigan Rd AIMK WN4 78 E1
ATH M46 66 C2
BOLS/LL BL3 51 H1
GOL/RIS/CUL WA3 79 L1
LEIGH WN7 65 M5
WGNE/HIN WN2 48 D1
WGNNW/ST WN6 30 E7
WGNW/BIL/OR WN5 62 C5
WHTN BL5 49 K5
Wigan Sq WGN WN1 * 14 F3
Wigan St WGNE/HIN WN2 64 D2
Wiggins Wk RUSH/FAL M14 * 98 F1
Wightman Av NEWLW WA12 78 F7
Wigley St WGTN/LGST M12 88 B5
Wigmore Rd CHH M8 72 E5
Wigmore St AUL OL6 76 A8
Wigsby Av NEWH/MOS M40 73 M3
Wigshaw Cl LEIGH WN7 81 J3
Wigwam Cl POY/DIS SK12 121 L8
Wike St TOT/BURYW BL8 4 B3
Wilbraham Rd CCHDY M21 97 L4
OLDTF/WHR M16 98 B3
RUSH/FAL M14 98 E3
WALK M28 69 G1
Wilbraham St LEIGH WN7 65 M7
WHTN BL5 50 B4
Wilburn St ORD M5 6 A6
Wilby Av BOLS/LL BL3 37 K7
Wilby Cl TOT/BURYW BL8 * 25 G7
Wilby St CHH M8 72 E6
Wilcock Cl OLDTF/WHR M16 87 H8
Wilcock Rd RNFD/HAY WA11 78 D4
Wilcock St WGNS/IIMK WN3 14 D5
Wilcott Dr SALE M33 96 B7
WILM/AE SK9 126 D8
Wilcott Rd CHD/CHDH SK8 110 D7
Wild Arum Cl
GOL/RIS/CUL WA3 80 B4
Wildbank Cha STLY SK15 92 B5
Wildbrook Cl LHULT M38 68 B1
Wildbrook Crs OLDS OL8 75 K1
Wildbrook Gv LHULT M38 68 B1
Wildbrook Rd LHULT M38 52 B8
Wildbrook Ter OLDS OL8 * 75 K1
Wild Clough HYDE SK14 102 C3
Wildcroft Av NEWH/MOS M40 73 K3
Wilders Moor Cl WALK M28 68 F4
Wilderswood Cl DID/WITH M20 98 F7
Wilde St DTN/ASHW M34 101 J1
Wildhouse La LIT OL15 29 J3
Wilding St WGNS/IIMK WN3 15 K8
Wildman La FWTH BL4 52 C4
Wildmoor Av OLDE OL4 60 B8
Wild Moor Wood Cl STLY SK15 77 G7
Wilds Pas LEIGH WN7 66 C8
Wilds Pl RAMS BL0 * 18 E7
Wild St BRAM/HZG SK7 * 121 M2
DUK SK16 91 G4
HEY OL10 41 H2
MPL/ROM SK6 113 J2
OLD OL1 9 M4
OLDE OL4 60 B6
RAD M26 39 G8
ROY/SHW OL2 43 M6
Wildwood Cl OFTN SK2 112 D7
RAMS BL0 18 D8
Wilford Av SALE M33 108 D2
Wilfred Dr BURY BL9 5 K1
Wilfred Rd ECC M30 84 D4
WALK M28 69 G2
Wilfred St BRO M7 72 B8
EDGW/EG BL7 * 22 D5
NEWH/MOS M40 73 K4
WGNW/BIL/OR WN5 47 J5
Wilfrid's Pl WGNNW/ST WN6 31 H3
Wilfrid St SWIN M27 70 C4
Wilkesley Av WGNNW/ST WN6 31 G4
Wilkes St OLD OL1 60 A1
Wilkin Cft CHD/CHDH SK8 120 A4
Wilkins La WILM/AE SK9 119 G7
Wilkinson Av BOLS/LL BL3 37 K8
Wilkinson Rd BOL BL1 22 A7
HTNM SK4 13 G2
Wilkinson St AUL OL6 90 D1
HTNM SK4 13 G2
LEIGH WN7 66 B7
MDTN M24 57 J4
SALE M33 97 G8
Wilks Av WYTH/NTH M22 119 H2
Willand Cl BOLE BL2 37 K6
Willand Dr BOLE BL2 37 K7
Willan Rd BKLY M9 56 F8
ECC M30 85 H2
Willard Av WGNW/BIL/OR WN5 62 A1
Willard St BRAM/HZG SK7 * 121 M1
Willaston Cl CCHDY M21 97 K5
Willbutts La ROCH OL11 27 M4
Willdale Cl OP/CLY M11 88 D2
Willdor Gv EDGY/DAV SK3 111 L6
Willenhall Rd NTHM/RTH M23 109 M2
Willerby Rd BRO M7 72 B7
Willesden Av BRUN/LGST M13 99 H1
Will Griffith Wk OP/CLY M11 88 B4
William Chadwick Cl
NEWH/MOS M40 87 M1
William Cl URM M41 95 M3
William Greenwood Cl
HEY OL10 40 F2
William Henry St ROCH OL11 28 D8
William Jessop Ct CMANE M1 7 L5
William Kay Cl OLDTF/WHR M16 87 H8
William Lister Cl
NEWH/MOS M40 * 74 A8
Williams Av NEWLW WA12 78 F7
Williams Crs CHAD OL9 74 C1
Williamson Av MPL/ROM SK6 101 K8
RAD M26 38 C6
Williamson La DROY M43 89 L4
Williamson St ANC M4 87 L1
AUL OL6 90 E2
RDSH SK5 100 B5
Williams Rd GTN M18 88 F7
NEWH/MOS M40 73 L5
Williams St BOLS/LL BL3 53 L1
GTN M18 88 F8
William St AULW OL7 90 D3
CSLFD M3 6 C3
DID/WITH M20 110 E1
FAIL M35 74 D3
HOR/BR BL6 33 K1
LEIGH WN7 66 D7
LIT OL15 21 L7
MDTN M24 57 L4
MILN OL16 21 H8
RAD M26 38 E8
RAMS BL0 18 F3
ROCH OL11 10 E7
STKP SK1 112 E5
WGNE/HIN WN2 49 H7
WGNS/IIMK WN3 15 J8
WGTN/LGST M12 88 A4
WHIT OL12 20 A3
Willingdon Cl TOT/BURYW BL8 24 F5
Willingdon Dr PWCH M25 55 L7
Willis Rd EDGY/DAV SK3 112 B6
Willis St BOLS/LL BL3 35 M8
Willock St BRO M7 72 B6
Willoughby Av DID/WITH M20 98 F8
Willoughby Cl SALE M33 96 D7
Willow Av CHD/CHDH SK8 120 B2
MDTN M24 57 M5
NEWLW WA12 79 G8
RDSH SK5 100 C8
TYLD M29 67 K6
URM M41 96 B2
Willow Bank CHD/CHDH SK8 120 C6
OLDE OL4 60 B4
RUSH/FAL M14 98 F4
Willowbank RAD M26 54 D4
Willowbank Av BOLE BL2 3 K7
Willow Bank Cl OFTN SK2 113 G5
Willowbrook Av
NEWH/MOS M40 73 K5
Willowbrook Dr
WGNNW/ST WN6 30 E5
Willow Cl BOLS/LL BL3 35 L8
BURY BL9 55 L2
DUK SK16 91 J5
POY/DIS SK12 129 J1
Willow Ct MPL/ROM SK6 114 C7
SALE M33 97 H7
Willow Crs LEIGH WN7 66 B4
Willowcroft Av
WGNE/HIN WN2 49 J1
Willowdale Av CHD/CHDH SK8 119 K2
Willowdene Cl EDGW/EG BL7 22 C4
NEWH/MOS M40 72 F7
Willow Dr BURY BL9 55 L2
SALE M33 108 B2
WGNE/HIN WN2 65 J1
WILM/AE SK9 127 H1
Willowfield Gv AIMK WN4 78 D2
Willowfield Rd OLDE OL4 60 A2
Willow Fold DROY M43 89 L4
Willow Gv AIMK WN4 64 B7
CHAD OL9 8 B3
DTN/ASHW M34 101 H1
GOL/RIS/CUL WA3 79 K3
GTN M18 * 89 H8
MPL/ROM SK6 114 C7
Willow Hey EDGW/EG BL7 22 F6
Willow Hill Rd CHH M8 72 D3
Willow Lawn CHD/CHDH SK8 * 120 C2
Willow Ldg WGNE/HIN WN2 64 E3
Willowmead Wy WHIT OL12 27 K2
Willowmoss Cl WALK M28 69 H3
Willow Ri LIT OL15 29 J1
Willow Rd ECC M30 69 K8
MPL/ROM SK6 123 H5
NEWLW WA12 79 H8
PART M31 106 B2
PWCH M25 55 K6
RNFD/HAY WA11 78 B5
UPML OL3 61 M5
WGNNW/ST WN6 31 J8
Willows Dr FAIL M35 74 C8
Willows End STLY SK15 92 A1
Willows La BOLS/LL BL3 35 M8
MILN OL16 29 H5
Willows Rd ORD M5 * 86 A2
The Willows BOLS/LL BL3 37 K7
CCHDY M21 97 K5
MOSL OL5 77 H3
PART M31 106 C1
Willow St ATH M46 50 F8
BURY BL9 5 L4
CHH M8 72 B8
HEY OL10 41 G2
OLD OL1 9 M4
OP/CLY M11 88 D3
SWIN M27 70 A7
WALK M28 69 M5
Willow Tree Cl WGN WN1 31 L8
Willow Tree Ms
CHD/CHDH SK8 119 K3
Willow Tree Rd ALT WA14 116 F2
Willow Wy BRAM/HZG SK7 120 E5
DID/WITH M20 110 F1
Willow Wood Cl AUL OL6 91 H1
Wilma Av BKLY M9 56 F8
Wilmans Wk GLSP SK13 93 K6
Wilmcote Cl HOR/BR BL6 35 G6
Wilmcote Rd NEWH/MOS M40 72 F8
Wilmington Rd STRET M32 * 96 E2
Wilmot Dr GOL/RIS/CUL WA3 79 J5
Wilmot St BOL BL1 35 M1
Wilmott St HULME M15 6 F9
Wilmslow Av BOL BL1 22 B7
Wilmslow Old Rd
HALE/TIMP WA15 118 B6
MCFLDN SK10 131 K1
Wilmslow Park Rd
WILM/AE SK9 127 H5
Wilmslow Rd BRAM/HZG SK7 127 M3
CHD/CHDH SK8 111 G8
DID/WITH M20 98 E8
HALE/TIMP WA15 118 B7
MCFLDN SK10 127 L8
MCFLDN SK10 128 A6
RUSH/FAL M14 87 M8
WILM/AE SK9 119 M7
WILM/AE SK9 130 D2
Wilmur Av BRO M7 72 B6
WHTF M45 55 K5
Wilpshire Av WGTN/LGST M12 99 L1
Wilsford Cl GOL/RIS/CUL WA3 79 L3
Wilsham Rd
WGNW/BIL/OR WN5 46 B7
Wilshaw Gv AULW OL7 75 L6
Wilshaw La AULW OL7 75 K7
Wilson Av HEY OL10 40 D2
SWIN M27 70 E3
WGNNW/ST WN6 47 L2
Wilson Crs AUL OL6 76 B8
Wilson Fold Av HOR/BR BL6 34 C3
Wilson Rd BKLY M9 73 G3
HTNM SK4 99 L8
Wilsons Pk NEWH/MOS M40 * 73 H7
Wilson St BOLS/LL BL3 * 2 E6
BRUN/LGST M13 87 M6
BURY BL9 5 H6
FWTH BL4 53 H4
HYDE SK14 102 B2
OLDS OL8 59 H8
OP/CLY M11 88 D4
RAD M26 38 C8
STRET M32 86 B8
UPML OL3 61 K7
WHIT OL12 10 E2
Wilson Wy OLD OL1 9 J4
Wilsthorpe Cl BNG/LEV M19 99 M6
Wilton Av CHD/CHDH SK8 119 L5
OLDTF/WHR M16 97 K1
PWCH M25 72 A2
SWIN M27 70 F5
WGNE/HIN WN2 48 C2
Wilton Ct GTN M18 89 K8
Wilton Crs WILM/AE SK9 130 C2
Wilton Dr BURY BL9 39 K7
HALE/TIMP WA15 117 L4
Wilton Gdns RAD M26 38 F7
Wilton Gv DTN/ASHW M34 89 K8
HEY OL10 41 G3
Wilton La GOL/RIS/CUL WA3 80 D7
Wilton Paddock
DTN/ASHW M34 89 K8
Wilton Pl CSLFD M3 6 A3
Wilton Rd BOL BL1 22 B7
CCHDY M21 97 L4
CHH M8 72 D2
SLFD M6 70 E8
WGNNW/ST WN6 30 D6
Wilton St AIMK WN4 63 J6
BOL BL1 36 C1
CHAD OL9 74 E1
DTN/ASHW M34 90 B8
HEY OL10 40 F2
MDTN M24 56 E5
PWCH M25 55 M8
RDSH SK5 100 C2
WGN WN1 15 H6
WHTF M45 55 J5
Wilton Ter WHIT OL12 10 C2
Wiltshire Av RDSH SK5 100 F8
Wiltshire Cl BURY BL9 5 H8
Wiltshire Dr GLSP SK13 105 J4
Wiltshire Pl
WGNW/BIL/OR WN5 46 F6
Wiltshire Rd CHAD OL9 8 B9
FAIL M35 74 C6
PART M31 106 B2
Wiltshire St BRO M7 72 B6
Wimberry Cl UPML OL3 61 L7
Wimberry Hill Rd WHTN BL5 50 A1
Wimbledon Dr EDGY/DAV SK3 111 M6
ROCH OL11 10 B9
Wimbledon Rd FAIL M35 74 E4
Wimborne Av URM M41 85 G8
Wimborne Cl CHD/CHDH SK8 111 M8
HOR/BR BL6 34 C3
Wimborne Rd
WGNW/BIL/OR WN5 46 D4
Wimbourne Av CHAD OL9 58 D3
Wimpole St AUL OL6 90 F1
OLD OL1 9 L2
Wimpory St OP/CLY M11 89 G5
Winbolt St OFTN SK2 112 F8
Winby St ROCH OL11 11 H9
Wincanton Av NTHM/RTH M23 109 G4
Wincanton Dr BOL BL1 22 A5
Wincanton Pk OLDE OL4 60 A6
Wince Cl MDTN M24 57 M6
Wincham Cl HULME M15 87 G6
Wincham Rd SALE M33 108 B2
Winchcombe Cl LEIGH WN7 81 H3
Winchester Av AIMK WN4 78 D1
AUL OL6 76 A5
CHAD OL9 58 C3
DTN/ASHW M34 101 J3
HEY OL10 40 F4
PWCH M25 71 M2
TYLD M29 67 M5
Winchester Cl ROCH OL11 27 J5
TOT/BURYW BL8 24 F5
WGNW/BIL/OR WN5 46 C5
WILM/AE SK9 126 C7
Winchester Dr HTNM SK4 12 B2
SALE M33 96 A8
Winchester Gv
WGNS/IIMK WN3 15 J8
Winchester Pk DID/WITH M20 110 C1
Winchester Rd DUK SK16 91 K5
ECC M30 70 D8
HALE/TIMP WA15 117 L3
RAD M26 38 A7
RNFD/HAY WA11 78 B3
SLFD M6 70 F8
URM M41 96 A1
WGNW/BIL/OR WN5 62 A3
Winchester Wy BOLE BL2 37 G3
Wincle Av POY/DIS SK12 129 K2
Wincombe St RUSH/FAL M14 98 E2
Windale WALK M28 68 E1
Windcroft Cl OP/CLY M11 88 C4
Winder Dr ANC M4 7 M4
Windermere Av ATH M46 51 G7
BOLS/LL BL3 37 K8
DTN/ASHW M34 100 D2
SALE M33 109 G1
SWIN M27 70 D5
Windermere Cl OP/CLY M11 88 D4
PWCH M25 55 H7
STRET M32 96 F1
Windermere Crs AULW OL7 * 75 J8
Windermere Dr BURY BL9 39 H5
RAMS BL0 18 F5
WILM/AE SK9 130 C3
Windermere Gv LEIGH WN7 66 B7
Windermere Rd DUK SK16 90 F4
FWTH BL4 52 B5
HYDE SK14 90 F7
LEIGH WN7 66 B7
MDTN M24 56 F2
MPL/ROM SK6 122 F3
ROY/SHW OL2 43 G6
STKP SK1 112 E5
STLY SK15 91 K1
URM M41 * 95 M3
WGNE/HIN WN2 48 D5
WGNE/HIN WN2 49 H7
WGNE/HIN WN2 64 E4
WGNW/BIL/OR WN5 46 C4
WILM/AE SK9 119 L8
Windermere St BOL BL1 36 C1
WGN WN1 15 K2
Winder St BOL BL1 2 E2
Winders Wy SLFD M6 71 L8
Windfields Cl CHD/CHDH SK8 120 D1
Wind Gate Ri STLY SK15 77 G8
Windham St MILN OL16 28 F1
Windle Av CHH M8 72 C1
Windle Ct OFTN SK2 113 H7
Windlehurst Dr WALK M28 68 E5
Windlehurst Old Rd
MPL/ROM SK6 123 H2
Windlehurst Rd MPL/ROM SK6 122 F4
Windleshaw St
WGNS/IIMK WN3 15 K8
Windley St BOLE BL2 3 H2
Windmill Av ORD M5 86 E5
Windmill Cl DTN/ASHW M34 100 E2
WGN WN1 15 J3
Windmill Ct MILN OL16 11 J6
Windmill La DTN/ASHW M34 100 D2
TYLD M29 67 J8
Windmill Rd SALE M33 109 J1
WALK M28 52 F7
Windmill St CMANW M2 6 E6
MILN OL16 11 J6
Windover Cl WHTN BL5 51 K5
Windover St BOLS/LL BL3 35 K8
Windrush Av RAMS BL0 24 D2
Windrush Dr BKLY M9 73 G5
WHTN BL5 50 C3
The Windrush WHIT OL12 20 A8
Windsor Av BOLS/LL BL3 53 K1
CHAD OL9 58 D8
CHD/CHDH SK8 110 C7
FAIL M35 74 E4
HEY OL10 40 E2
HTNM SK4 111 K1
IRL M44 94 E1
LHULT M38 52 E7
SALE M33 96 E6
SWIN M27 70 D2
TYLD M29 67 K6
URM M41 95 J2
WHTF M45 55 K5
WILM/AE SK9 126 D6
Windsor Cl POY/DIS SK12 121 M8
TOT/BURYW BL8 24 D3
Windsor Crs PWCH M25 72 B1
WGNE/HIN WN2 33 G7
Windsor Dr ALT WA14 108 C4
ALT WA14 116 B3
AULW OL7 75 J8
DTN/ASHW M34 90 A3
DUK SK16 91 J5
HOR/BR BL6 34 B2
MPL/ROM SK6 114 B7
RNFD/HAY WA11 78 D5
STLY SK15 91 K1
TOT/BURYW BL8 38 E4
Windsor Gv AUL OL6 75 M5
BOL BL1 35 M3
CHD/CHDH SK8 120 B4
MPL/ROM SK6 114 B2
RAD M26 53 L5
WGNE/HIN WN2 65 L1
Windsor Rd AIMK WN4 78 E2
BKLY M9 73 H5
BNG/LEV M19 99 J3
BRAM/HZG SK7 122 B2
DROY M43 89 G2
DTN/ASHW M34 100 D1
EDGW/EG BL7 22 D5
GOL/RIS/CUL WA3 79 M4
HYDE SK14 102 A5
LEIGH WN7 67 H6
MPL/ROM SK6 112 F1
NEWH/MOS M40 74 B8
OLDS OL8 8 E8
PWCH M25 72 B1
WGNW/BIL/OR WN5 62 C7

Windsor St ATH M46 67 H2
FAIL M35 74 D5
GTN M18 88 F8
NEWH/MOS M40 74 B8
OFTN SK2 112 D6
OLD OL1 59 K3
ORD M5 86 E3
ROCH OL11 11 G9
WGN WN1 15 J2
Windsor Ter MILN OL16 11 M4
MILN OL16 29 H6
Windybank BKLY M9 56 F7
Windy Bank Av
GOL/RIS/CUL WA3 80 B4
Windy Harbour La
EDGW/EG BL7 22 E4
Windyhill Dr BOLS/LL BL3 51 K1
Winfell Dr NEWH/MOS M40 88 A1
Winfield Av DID/WITH M20 99 G7
Winfield Dr GTN M18 89 G6
Winfield Gv MPL/ROM SK6 114 E3
Winfield St HYDE SK14 102 C2
Winford St BKLY M9 73 H4
Wingate Av TOT/BURYW BL8 38 E2
Wingate Dr DID/WITH M20 110 F2
HALE/TIMP WA15 108 E7
WHTF M45 55 H3
Wingate Rd HTNM SK4 99 M8
LHULT M38 52 E8
Wingates Gv WHTN BL5 50 A1
Wingates La WHTN BL5 34 B8
Wingates Rd WGN WN1 31 M7
Wingates Sq WHTN BL5 50 B1
Wingate St ROCH OL11 27 G3
Wingfield Av WILM/AE SK9 126 C6
Wingfield Cl WGNNW/ST WN6 31 K8
Wingfield Dr SWIN M27 70 D6
WILM/AE SK9 126 C6
Wingfield Gv GLSP SK13 105 J5
Wingfield St STRET M32 86 A8
Wings Gv HEY OL10 41 G5
Winhill Rd NM/HAY SK22 124 E3
Winifred Av BURY BL9 26 C8
Winifred Rd DID/WITH M20 110 E1
FWTH BL4 52 D3
NEWH/MOS M40 73 L5
OFTN SK2 112 D7
URM M41 95 M1
Winifred St ECC M30 84 E3
HYDE SK14 102 B5
RAMS BL0 18 E7
WGNS/IIMK WN3 15 K8
WHIT OL12 27 L3
Winmarith Dr
HALE/TIMP WA15 117 M5
Winmarleigh Cl
TOT/BURYW BL8 38 C3
Winmarleigh Gdns LEIGH WN7 81 H1
Winnard St GOL/RIS/CUL WA3 79 L2
Winnats Cl GLSP SK13 105 J4
Winnie St NEWH/MOS M40 73 K4
Winning Hill Cl GTN M18 89 G8
Winnington Gn OFTN SK2 113 G7
Winnington Rd MPL/ROM SK6 114 C4
Winnipeg Quay SALQ M50 86 C5
The Winnows DTN/ASHW M34 101 G1
Winscar Rd WGNE/HIN WN2 49 G6
Winscombe Dr
NEWH/MOS M40 72 F8
Winser St CMANE M1 7 G7
Winsfield Rd BRAM/HZG SK7 121 M4
Winsford Cl RNFD/HAY WA11 78 C5
Winsford Dr ROCH OL11 27 J7
Winsford Gv BOLS/LL BL3 35 K7
Winsford Rd RUSH/FAL M14 98 D3
Winskill Rd IRL M44 94 D4
Winslade Cl BRAM/HZG SK7 121 J2
OLDE OL4 60 A3
Winslade Ms FWTH BL4 53 G3
Winsley Rd NTHM/RTH M23 109 J2
Winslow Av HYDE SK14 102 B2
Winslow Pl BNG/LEV M19 99 J6
Winslow Rd BOLS/LL BL3 50 F2
Winslow St OP/CLY M11 88 D4
Winsmoor Dr WGNE/HIN WN2 49 H8
Winstanley Pl WGNS/IIMK WN3 15 K9
Winstanley Rd AIMK WN4 62 E5
NEWH/MOS M40 88 A1
SALE M33 96 F7
WGNE/HIN WN2 64 C4
WGNW/BIL/OR WN5 62 C1
Winstanley St
WGNW/BIL/OR WN5 14 A7
Winster Av BRO M7 71 L6
DID/WITH M20 98 B8
STRET M32 96 D1
Winster Cl BOLE BL2 37 J3
WHTF M45 55 L4
Winster Dr BOLE BL2 37 H3
MDTN M24 57 H2
Winster Gv OFTN SK2 112 D6
Winster Rd ECC M30 84 E4
Winston Av BOLS/LL BL3 53 M1
ROCH OL11 27 H6
Winston Cl MPL/ROM SK6 114 A5
RAD M26 38 B7
Winston Rd BKLY M9 73 J3
SALE M33 96 C7
Winswell Cl OP/CLY M11 88 E2
Winterbottom Gv HYDE SK14 103 J2
Winterbottom St CHAD OL9 8 F5
Winterburn Av BOLE BL2 22 E6
CCHDY M21 97 M8
Winterburn Gn OFTN SK2 113 H7
Winterdyne St BKLY M9 73 H5
Winterfield Dr BOLS/LL BL3 51 K1
Winterford Av BRUN/LGST M13 88 A7
Winterford Rd BRO M7 72 C5
MOSL OL5 77 H3
Winter Hey La HOR/BR BL6 33 L1
Winter Hill Vw EDGW/EG BL7 22 A1
Wintermans Rd CCHDY M21 98 A6
Winterslow Av
NTHM/RTH M23 109 G3
Winter St BOL BL1 36 A1
Winterton Cl WHTN BL5 50 D3
Winterton Rd RDSH SK5 100 D3
Winthrop Av NEWH/MOS M40 73 G8
Winton Av DTN/ASHW M34 90 A5
NEWH/MOS M40 74 A3
WGNW/BIL/OR WN5 47 G7
Winton Cl BRAM/HZG SK7 120 F3
Winton Gn HOR/BR BL6 34 C4
Winton Gv BOLS/LL BL3 35 H8
Winton Rd ALT WA14 116 E2
GOL/RIS/CUL WA3 80 B7
SLFD M6 71 G6
Winton St AUL OL6 90 E1
LIT OL15 21 M7
STLY SK15 91 L3
Winward St BOLS/LL BL3 * 35 K8
LEIGH WN7 65 L7
WHTN BL5 50 B3
Winwood Dr MDTN M24 57 L2
Winwood Rd DID/WITH M20 110 F4
Wirksmoor Rd NM/HAY SK22 124 D5
Wirral Cl SWIN M27 * 70 D2
Wirral Crs EDGY/DAV SK3 111 K4
Wirral Dr WGNS/IIMK WN3 62 F2
Wisbech Dr NTHM/RTH M23 109 J3
Wisbeck Rd BOLE BL2 3 M3
Wiseley St OP/CLY M11 88 B4
Wiseman Ter PWCH M25 55 M8
Wishaw Sq CCHDY M21 98 B6
Wisley Cl RDSH SK5 100 C4
Wistaria Rd GTN M18 89 G7
Witham Av WYTH/NTH M22 110 B7
Witham Cl HEY OL10 40 D1
WGNNW/ST WN6 31 G3
Witham St AUL OL6 76 B8
Withenfield Rd
NTHM/RTH M23 109 J4
Withens Gn OFTN SK2 113 H6
Withington Av
GOL/RIS/CUL WA3 81 K8
Withington Cl ATH M46 50 E8
Withington Dr TYLD M29 67 M5
Withington Gra
WGNE/HIN WN2 48 E2
Withington Gn MDTN M24 41 K8
Withington La WGNE/HIN WN2 48 E2
Withington Rd CCHDY M21 98 A4
OLDTF/WHR M16 98 A1
Withington St HEY OL10 * 41 H4
Withinlea Cl WHTN BL5 50 D2
Withinlee Rd MCFLDN SK10 131 M6
Withins Av RAD M26 38 F7
Withins Cl BOLE BL2 37 H4
Withins Dr BOLE BL2 37 H4
Withins Gv BOLE BL2 37 H4
Withins Hall Rd FAIL M35 74 E6
Withins La BOLE BL2 37 H4
RAD M26 38 F7
Withins Rd OLDS OL8 74 E2
RNFD/HAY WA11 78 B4
Withins St RAD M26 38 F8
Withnell Cl WGNNW/ST WN6 14 A1
Withnell Dr TOT/BURYW BL8 38 D3
Withnell Rd BNG/LEV M19 111 G1
Withycombe Pl SLFD M6 71 K7
Withy Gv ANC M4 7 G3
Withypool Dr OFTN SK2 112 F7
Withy Tree Gv
DTN/ASHW M34 * 101 K2
Witley Dr SALE M33 96 A6
Witley Rd MILN OL16 11 K6
Wittenbury Rd HTNM SK4 12 A2
Witterage Cl WGTN/LGST M12 * 88 C6
Witton Weavers Wy DWN BB3 16 A4
EDGW/EG BL7 16 D6
EDGW/EG BL7 17 H7
EDGW/EG BL7 23 G1
Woburn Abbey UPML OL3 * 61 K3
Woburn Av BOLE BL2 36 F1
LEIGH WN7 66 A3
Woburn Cl MILN OL16 11 H6
RNFD/HAY WA11 78 C5
Woburn Dr BURY BL9 39 J7
HALE/TIMP WA15 117 K2
Woburn Rd OLDTF/WHR M16 97 K2
Woburn St OLDTF/WHR M16 98 C1
Wodens Av ORD M5 86 F5
Woden St ORD M5 86 F5
Woking Back Gdns BOL BL1 36 B3
Woking Rd CHD/CHDH SK8 120 C6
Woking Ter BOL BL1 * 36 B3
Wolfenden St BOL BL1 36 B2
Wolfenden Ter BOL BL1 * 36 B2
Wolford Dr TYLD M29 67 M3
Wolfreton Crs SWIN M27 70 D1
Wolfson Sq AIMK WN4 63 J8
Wolmer St AIMK WN4 63 K8
Wolseley Pl DID/WITH M20 98 E7
Wolseley Rd SALE M33 96 E6
Wolseley St MILN OL16 29 L8
TOT/BURYW BL8 38 E3
Wolsey Cl AIMK WN4 63 K7
Wolsey Dr ALT WA14 116 C3
Wolsey St HEY OL10 40 F3
RAD M26 54 D1
Wolstenholme Av BURY BL9 25 J6
Wolstenholme Coalpit La
WHIT OL12 26 E2
Wolstenholme La WHIT OL12 26 F2
Wolstenvale Cl MDTN M24 57 L3
Wolver Cl LHULT M38 * 52 D6
Wolverton Av OLDS OL8 75 G1
Wolverton Dr WILM/AE SK9 127 G3
Wolvesey ROCH OL11 * 10 D7
Wolveton St OP/CLY M11 88 C5
Woodacre OLDTF/WHR M16 98 B3
Woodacres Ct WILM/AE SK9 126 D6
Woodall Cl SALE M33 97 G8
Woodark Cl OLDE OL4 60 C7
Woodbank BOLE BL2 37 G2
Woodbank Av MPL/ROM SK6 113 H1
STKP SK1 112 E4
Woodbank Ct URM M41 * 95 L1
Woodbank Dr TOT/BURYW BL8 24 F8
Wood Bank Rd LIT OL15 29 K1
Woodbine Av IRL M44 94 A8
Woodbine Crs OFTN SK2 13 K9
Woodbine Rd BOLS/LL BL3 51 M1
Woodbine St MILN OL16 11 H8
Woodbine St East MILN OL16 11 J8
Woodbourne Rd HTNM SK4 99 M6
NM/HAY SK22 124 C7
SALE M33 108 D2
Woodbray Av BNG/LEV M19 99 H7
Woodbridge Av
DTN/ASHW M34 90 A5
Woodbridge Gdns WHIT OL12 27 M2
Woodbridge Gv
NTHM/RTH M23 109 K3
Woodbridge Rd URM M41 95 G1
Woodbrook Av OLDE OL4 60 E5
Woodbrook Dr
WGNS/IIMK WN3 47 G8
Wood Brook La OLDE OL4 60 E5
Wood Brook Rd OLDE OL4 60 E5
Woodbrook Rd WILM/AE SK9 130 E3
Woodburn Dr BOL BL1 35 L1
Woodburn Rd WYTH/NTH M22 110 A4
Woodbury Crs DUK SK16 * 90 E5
Woodbury Rd EDGY/DAV SK3 12 A9
Woodchurch WGN WN1 15 M1
Woodchurch Wk CHAD OL9 * 8 A7
Woodcock Cl DROY M43 89 M1
ROCH OL11 27 J5
Woodcock Dr WGNE/HIN WN2 64 E2
Woodcock Gv GLSP SK13 105 J3
Woodcock Rd GLSP SK13 105 K3
Woodcock Sq WGN WN1 * 14 F3
Woodcote Av BRAM/HZG SK7 120 E3
Woodcote Rd ALT WA14 108 A3
PART M31 95 K8
SALE M33 107 K1
Woodcote Vw WILM/AE SK9 127 K3
Wood Cottage Cl WALK M28 68 C1
Woodcott Bank BOL BL1 22 A8
Woodcourt WGNS/IIMK WN3 14 E8
Wood Crs OLDE OL4 60 B4
Woodcroft OFTN SK2 113 G6
WGNNW/ST WN6 30 B6
Woodcroft Av BNG/LEV M19 99 H8
Wooddagger Cl
WGNE/HIN WN2 49 J7
Woodeaton Cl ROY/SHW OL2 43 K8
Wooded Cl BURY BL9 25 J7
Woodedge AIMK WN4 78 D1
Wood Edge Cl BOLS/LL BL3 * 52 F1
Wood End BRAM/HZG SK7 120 F2
Woodend ROY/SHW OL2 43 M3
Woodend Dr STLY SK15 92 A6
Woodend La HYDE SK14 101 M3
STLY SK15 92 A5
WHIT OL12 21 H6
Woodend Rd EDGY/DAV SK3 112 C8
WYTH/NTH M22 110 A8
Woodend St OLD OL1 9 H1
OLDE OL4 60 C7
Woodfield WYTH/NTH M22 118 F1
Woodfield Av HYDE SK14 102 A4
MPL/ROM SK6 101 K8
WHIT OL12 * 28 B2
Woodfield Cl GLSP SK13 93 J7
OLDS OL8 58 F8
Woodfield Ct OFTN SK2 * 112 D8
Woodfield Crs AIMK WN4 78 D2
MPL/ROM SK6 113 J2
Woodfield Dr WALK M28 68 E6
Woodfield Gv ECC M30 84 F3
FWTH BL4 52 F6
SALE M33 96 D6
Woodfield Ms HYDE SK14 * 102 A4
Woodfield Rd ALT WA14 107 M6
CHD/CHDH SK8 120 D5
CHH M8 72 D3
MDTN M24 57 H6
SLFD M6 71 G8
Woodfield St BOLS/LL BL3 52 D1
WGNE/HIN WN2 48 D1
Wood Fold EDGW/EG BL7 22 F6
Woodfold Av BNG/LEV M19 99 K2
Woodfold Rd FAIL M35 74 D4
Woodford Av DTN/ASHW M34 90 D8
ECC M30 84 E2
GOL/RIS/CUL WA3 80 A5
ROY/SHW OL2 44 A5
Woodford Dr SWIN M27 70 B2
Woodford Gdns
DID/WITH M20 110 D2
Woodford Gv BOLS/LL BL3 35 M8
Woodford La MCFLDN SK10 128 A6
Woodford Rd BRAM/HZG SK7 121 G7
POY/DIS SK12 121 K7
WILM/AE SK9 127 M4
Woodford St WGNE/HIN WN2 49 H6
WGNW/BIL/OR WN5 46 E6
Wood Gdns NM/HAY SK22 125 L1
Woodgarth LEIGH WN7 * 65 M7
Woodgarth Av
NEWH/MOS M40 74 A7
Woodgarth Dr SWIN M27 70 B6
Woodgarth La WALK M28 69 J7
Woodgate Av BURY BL9 26 A8
ROCH OL11 27 K6
Woodgate Cl MPL/ROM SK6 113 J1
Woodgate Dr PWCH M25 55 M6
Woodgate Hill Rd BURY BL9 5 M2
BURY BL9 26 A8
Woodgate Rd OLDTF/WHR M16 98 B3
Woodgate St BOLS/LL BL3 52 D1
Woodgrange Cl SLFD M6 86 B2
Woodgreen Cl WGNE/HIN WN2 49 G8
Woodgreen Dr RAD M26 54 D4
Wood Gv DTN/ASHW M34 90 C8
MPL/ROM SK6 101 K7
WHTF M45 55 H1
Woodhall Av DID/WITH M20 98 D5
WHTF M45 55 G6
Woodhall Cl BOLE BL2 36 F1
BRAM/HZG SK7 128 B1
TOT/BURYW BL8 * 25 G7
Woodhall Crs RDSH SK5 100 D8
Woodhall Rd RDSH SK5 100 D8
Woodhall St FAIL M35 74 C4
Woodhalt Rd CHH M8 72 D4
Woodham Rd NTHM/RTH M23 109 J3
Woodham Wk BOLS/LL BL3 2 A8
Woodhead Cl OLDE OL4 60 B5
RAMS BL0 18 F8
Woodhead Dr
HALE/TIMP WA15 117 H3
Woodhead Gv WGNS/IIMK WN3 63 L2
Woodhead Rd GLSP SK13 93 L5
GLSP SK13 105 G1
HALE/TIMP WA15 117 H3
Woodhead St OLDTF/WHR M16 87 H8
Wood Hey Cl RAD M26 54 A1
Wood Hey Gv
DTN/ASHW M34 * 101 K2
WHIT OL12 20 D8
Woodhey Rd RAMS BL0 24 D1
Woodheys HTNM SK4 111 J1
Woodheys Cottages
MPL/ROM SK6 * 103 H8
Woodheys Dr SALE M33 108 A3
Woodheys Rd LIT OL15 29 K2
Woodhill Cl MDTN M24 57 J2
WGTN/LGST M12 88 E8
Woodhill Dr PWCH M25 71 L2
Woodhill Fold TOT/BURYW BL8 4 C2
Woodhill Gv PWCH M25 71 L1
Woodhill Rd TOT/BURYW BL8 4 C1
Woodhill St TOT/BURYW BL8 4 B1
Woodhill V TOT/BURYW BL8 4 B2
Woodhouse Dr
WGNNW/ST WN6 47 H1
Woodhouse Knowl UPML OL3 45 H8
Woodhouse La ALT WA14 106 F8
SALE M33 107 M2
WGNNW/ST WN6 14 B1
WHIT OL12 27 G1
WYTH/NTH M22 110 A7
WYTH/NTH M22 118 F5
Woodhouse La East
HALE/TIMP WA15 108 E3
Woodhouse Rd ROY/SHW OL2 43 M4
URM M41 84 C8
WYTH/NTH M22 118 F4
Woodhouse St ATH M46 67 G2
GTN M18 89 H7
Woodhurst Dr WGNNW/ST WN6 31 G3
Wooding Cl PART M31 94 D8
Woodlake Av CCHDY M21 97 M8
Woodland Av BOLS/LL BL3 52 E2
BRAM/HZG SK7 122 A3
GTN M18 89 H8
WGNE/HIN WN2 65 K1
Woodland Crs PWCH M25 71 L2
Woodland Dr AIMK WN4 63 L7
WGNNW/ST WN6 31 H2
Woodland Gv EDGW/EG BL7 22 A2
WGN WN1 48 A2
Woodland Pk ROY/SHW OL2 42 E6
Woodland Rd BNG/LEV M19 99 K4
GTN M18 89 H8
HEY OL10 41 H2
TYLD M29 67 L5
WHIT OL12 27 M2
Woodlands FAIL M35 74 B8
URM M41 95 M1
Woodlands Av CHD/CHDH SK8 120 C2
ECC M30 84 C4
IRL M44 94 D1
LEIGH WN7 81 J1
MPL/ROM SK6 101 K7
ROCH OL11 27 K5
STRET M32 97 G2
URM M41 94 F2
WALK M28 69 M6
WGNS/IIMK WN3 15 M8
WHTF M45 55 H3
Woodlands Cl CHD/CHDH SK8 120 C4
GLSP SK13 93 J6
HYDE SK14 103 J3
STLY SK15 92 A5
WALK M28 69 H5
Woodlands Dr ATH M46 51 J7
MPL/ROM SK6 101 L7
OFTN SK2 112 F4
SALE M33 108 F3
WGNNW/ST WN6 30 C8
Woodlands Gv HYDE SK14 103 J3
TOT/BURYW BL8 38 E1
Woodlands La
HALE/TIMP WA15 108 B7
Woodlands Pk NEWLW WA12 78 F6
Woodlands Park Rd OFTN SK2 113 G4
Woodlands Pkwy
HALE/TIMP WA15 108 B7
Woodlands Rd ALT WA14 108 B7
AUL OL6 76 B6
CHH M8 72 D4
HTNM SK4 111 G2
MILN OL16 29 H7
NM/HAY SK22 * 124 C4
OLDTF/WHR M16 98 B3
POY/DIS SK12 123 J6
RAMS BL0 19 G2
SALE M33 96 F8
STLY SK15 92 A5
WALK M28 69 J5
WILM/AE SK9 126 C3
WILM/AE SK9 127 J1
Woodlands St CHH M8 72 C4
The Woodlands DROY M43 * 89 H1
HEY OL10 41 H4
HOR/BR BL6 34 F4
TOT/BURYW BL8 25 G7
WGN WN1 48 A1
Woodland St HEY OL10 41 G2
WGTN/LGST M12 88 E7
WHIT OL12 28 D2
Woodlands Vw MILN OL16 11 L3
Woodland Vw EDGW/EG BL7 22 E4
HYDE SK14 102 C1
Woodland Wy MDTN M24 57 J6
Wood La AULW OL7 75 L7
HALE/TIMP WA15 108 D7
MDTN M24 57 L5
MPL/ROM SK6 114 A7
NM/HAY SK22 125 M2
PART M31 106 A1
RAMS BL0 19 G2
Wood La North MCFLDN SK10 129 M4
Wood La South MCFLDN SK10 129 M4
Wood La West MCFLDN SK10 129 K4
Woodlark Cl CSLFD M3 * 6 B4
Woodlawn Ct
OLDTF/WHR M16 97 M1
Woodlea CHAD OL9 58 A5
WALK M28 69 H4
Woodlea Av BNG/LEV M19 99 H7
Woodlea Cha SWIN M27 54 A7
Woodlea Rd GLSP SK13 104 E5
Woodleigh Ct
TOT/BURYW BL8 24 E7
Woodleigh Dr DROY M43 74 F8
Woodleigh Rd OLDE OL4 60 D5
Woodleigh St BKLY M9 73 J3
Woodley Av RAD M26 54 E3
Woodley Cl OFTN SK2 113 G5
Woodley Gv LEIGH WN7 66 A7
Woodley St BURY BL9 4 F9
Woodman Dr BURY BL9 25 H6
Woodman St STKP SK1 13 H3
Woodmeadow Ct MOSL OL5 76 F2
Woodmere Dr BKLY M9 73 H1
Wood Mt HALE/TIMP WA15 108 E7
Woodmount Cl MPL/ROM SK6 114 B2
Woodnewton Cl GTN M18 88 F8
Woodnook Rd
WGNNW/ST WN6 30 B4
Woodpark Cl OLDS OL8 75 K1
Woodpecker Pl WALK M28 * 69 G4
Woodridge Dr BOLE BL2 36 E3
Wood Rd HALE/TIMP WA15 108 D3
OLDTF/WHR M16 97 M1
Wood Road La BURY BL9 24 F4
Wood Rd North
OLDTF/WHR M16 97 M1
Woodrow Wk WGTN/LGST M12 88 C6
Woodrow Wy IRL M44 94 C4
Woodroyd Cl BRAM/HZG SK7 120 F3
Woodroyd Dr BURY BL9 5 M2
Woodruffe Gdns
MPL/ROM SK6 113 K4
Woodrush Rd WGNNW/ST WN6 47 G1
Woods Ct BOL BL1 2 F4
Woodseats La GLSP SK13 103 K5
Woodseaves Cl IRL M44 94 E3
Woodsend Cir URM M41 95 G1
Woodsend Crescent Rd
URM M41 95 G2
Woodsend Rd URM M41 84 A8
Woodsend Rd South URM M41 95 H3
Woods Gv CHD/CHDH SK8 120 D5
Woodshaw Gv WALK M28 68 F4
Woodside HTNM SK4 111 J3
MILN OL16 29 M7
ROY/SHW OL2 44 A4
Woodside Av AIMK WN4 63 K4
BNG/LEV M19 99 J7
WALK M28 69 J2
Woodside Cl OLDE OL4 60 B6
Woodside Dr HYDE SK14 102 B3
MPL/ROM SK6 123 G5
RAMS BL0 18 D7
SLFD M6 85 M1
Woodside La POY/DIS SK12 122 A8
Woodside Pl BOLE BL2 * 3 M8
Woodside Rd OLDTF/WHR M16 97 L2
RNFD/HAY WA11 78 B5
Woodside Sq BOLE BL2 3 M8
Woodside St NM/HAY SK22 124 D6
STLY SK15 77 H6
Woodside Vw ATH M46 51 H7
Wood's La AIMK WN4 63 M8
CHD/CHDH SK8 120 D5
UPML OL3 61 K3
Woods Lea BOL BL1 35 J5
Woodsley Rd BOL BL1 35 J2
Woodsmoor La EDGY/DAV SK3 112 D8
Woodsmoor Rd SWIN M27 70 A5
Wood Sorrel Wy
GOL/RIS/CUL WA3 80 B4
Wood Sq DROY M43 89 K4
UPML OL3 61 L6
Woods Rd IRL M44 94 C4
WGNE/HIN WN2 32 F8
Wood's St WGNS/IIMK WN3 14 E6
The Woods ALT WA14 108 B6
OLDE OL4 60 E6
ROCH OL11 27 M8
Woodstock Av CHD/CHDH SK8 120 C5
RDSH SK5 100 C7
Woodstock Cl HEY OL10 41 H2
LEIGH WN7 81 H3
Woodstock Crs MPL/ROM SK6 101 L7
Woodstock Dr BOL BL1 35 K3
SWIN M27 70 D6
TOT/BURYW BL8 24 A5
WALK M28 69 K6
Woodstock Gn RDSH SK5 100 D7
Woodstock Rd ALT WA14 107 M4
MPL/ROM SK6 101 K7
NEWH/MOS M40 73 M3
OLDTF/WHR M16 97 L1
Woodstock St OLDE OL4 9 K8
WHIT OL12 27 M3
Wood St ALT WA14 108 A8
ATH M46 50 E8
AUL OL6 90 E2
BOL BL1 2 F5
CHD/CHDH SK8 111 G6
CSLFD M3 6 D3
CSLFD M3 6 D5
DTN/ASHW M34 90 C8
DUK SK16 90 F6
EDGY/DAV SK3 12 E6
GLSP SK13 104 F4
GOL/RIS/CUL WA3 79 L4
HOR/BR BL6 33 M1
HYDE SK14 93 G7
HYDE SK14 102 B2
LIT OL15 21 M7
MDTN M24 57 G2
MDTN M24 57 J3
MILN OL16 11 G6
MILN OL16 29 M8
NM/HAY SK22 124 D5
OLD OL1 59 L4
OP/CLY M11 88 E5
RAD M26 54 B4
RAMS BL0 18 E7
ROY/SHW OL2 43 H5
STLY SK15 91 J2
TOT/BURYW BL8 38 F1
TYLD M29 67 L4
WGNE/HIN WN2 65 L1
WGNS/IIMK WN3 15 G6
WGNW/BIL/OR WN5 14 A6
WHTN BL5 50 B4
Wood Ter BOLE BL2 38 A3
Woodthorpe Ct PWCH M25 72 A2
Woodthorpe Dr
CHD/CHDH SK8 120 C2
Woodthorpe Gra PWCH M25 72 A2
Woodtop Av ROCH OL11 27 J7
Wood Top Cl OFTN SK2 113 H5
Woodvale ALT WA14 116 E2
MDTN M24 41 K8
Woodvale Av ATH M46 50 E7
BOLS/LL BL3 52 A2
WGNE/HIN WN2 49 J1
Woodvale Dr BOLS/LL BL3 52 A2
GOL/RIS/CUL WA3 80 B3
Woodvale Gdns BOLS/LL BL3 52 A2
Woodvale Gv BOLS/LL BL3 52 A2
Woodvale Rd RAD M26 54 E3
Woodvale Wk OP/CLY M11 * 88 C3
Wood Vw HEY OL10 26 F8
WGNNW/ST WN6 30 D7
WYTH/NTH M22 110 A3
Woodview Av BNG/LEV M19 99 J7
Woodville Dr MPL/ROM SK6 114 B8
SALE M33 96 D7
STLY SK15 92 A1
Woodville Gv RDSH SK5 100 C6
Woodville Rd ALT WA14 107 M8
SALE M33 96 D7
WGNS/IIMK WN3 48 C8
Woodville Ter NEWH/MOS M40 73 J3
Woodward Cl BURY BL9 25 J7
Woodward Ct ANC M4 7 M3
Woodward Pl ANC M4 7 M3
Woodward Rd PWCH M25 71 J2
Woodwards Rd WHTN BL5 50 B6
Woodward St ANC M4 7 M3
Woodwise La NTHM/RTH M23 109 H3
Woodyates St
WGNW/BIL/OR WN5 14 A8
Woolden St ECC M30 84 E1
WGNW/BIL/OR WN5 47 J6
Wooler Gv WGNE/HIN WN2 65 G2
Woollacot St OLD OL1 * 9 K6
Woollam Pl CSLFD M3 6 B6
Woolley Av POY/DIS SK12 129 H2
Woolley Bridge Rd GLSP SK13 93 G8
Woolley Cl HYDE SK14 93 G8
Woolley La HYDE SK14 92 F8
Woolley Mill La GLSP SK13 93 G6
Woolley St CHH M8 72 C8
Woolmore Av OLD OL1 9 H1
Woolpack Gn SLFD M6 * 86 C1
Wool Rd UPML OL3 61 L2
Woolston Dr TYLD M29 67 M4
Woolston Rd RNFD/HAY WA11 78 A6
Woolton Cl AIMK WN4 63 J7
Wootton St HYDE SK14 91 G8
Worcester Av DTN/ASHW M34 101 K3
GOL/RIS/CUL WA3 * 79 L4
RDSH SK5 100 F8
WGNE/HIN WN2 49 J6
Worcester Cl AUL OL6 76 A4
BURY BL9 5 H9
MPL/ROM SK6 113 K3
Worcester Gv GLSP SK13 105 J4

Worcester Rd *BOLS/LL* BL3....53 J1
 *CHD/CHDH* SK8.....111 H6
 *MDTN* M24....57 J7
 *SALE* M33....108 A1
 *SLFD* M6....70 F8
 *SWIN* M27....70 A2
Worcester St *BOL* BL1 *....36 B3
 *BRO* M7....72 B6
 *CHAD* OL9....8 B8
 *ROCH* OL11....8 B8
 *TOT/BURYW* BL8....25 G8
Wordsworth Av *ATH* M46....51 G7
 *BURY* BL9 *....39 J6
 *CHH* M8....72 D6
 *DROY* M43....89 J2
 *FWTH* BL4....52 E5
 *LEIGH* WN7....66 A5
 *RAD* M26....54 B1
 *WGN* WN1....47 M1
 *WGNW/BIL/OR* WN5....46 C6
 *WGNW/BIL/OR* WN5....62 A3
Wordsworth Cl *DUK* SK16....91 K5
Wordsworth Crs *AULW* OL7....75 H7
 *LIT* OL15....29 J2
Wordsworth Gdns
 *PWCH* M25....71 J1
Wordsworth Rd
 *DTN/ASHW* M34....101 K5
 *LHULT* M38....52 D7
 *MDTN* M24....57 J8
 *OLD* OL1....59 L3
 *OLDTF/WHR* M16....97 L1
 *RDSH* SK5....100 A3
 *SWIN* M27....70 A3
Wordsworth St *BOL* BL1 *....36 A2
Wordsworth Wy *ROCH* OL11....27 H6
Workesleigh St
 *NEWH/MOS* M40....73 M7
Works *RAD* M26 *....38 D8
World Wy *MANAIR* M90....118 D4
Worrall St *EDGY/DAV* SK3....13 G8
 *NEWH/MOS* M40....73 K6
 *ORD* M5....85 J5
 *WHIT* OL12....28 A2
Worsbrough Av *WALK* M28....68 F2
Worsefold St
 *NEWH/MOS* M40 *....73 K4
Worseley Av *NEWH/MOS* M40....73 J3
Worsel St *BOLS/LL* BL3....35 M8
Worsley Av *WALK* M28....68 D2
Worsley Brow *WALK* M28....69 H6
Worsley Cl
 *WGNW/BIL/OR* WN5 *....46 E7
Worsley Ct *WALK* M28....69 G1
Worsley Crs *OFTN* SK2....112 E5
Worsley Gn
 *WGNW/BIL/OR* WN5....46 E7
Worsley Gv *BNG/LEV* M19....99 K3
 *WALK* M28....68 D2
Worsley Mesnes Dr
 *WCNS/IIMK* WN3....47 K8
Worsley Pl *ROY/SHW* OL2....43 K6
Worsley Rd *BOLS/LL* BL3....35 K8
 *ECC* M30....84 E2
 *FWTH* BL4....53 G6
 *SWIN* M27....70 A6
 *WALK* M28....69 K7
Worsley Rd North *WALK* M28....53 L7
Worsley St *BOLS/LL* BL3 *....2 D9
 *CSLFD* M3....6 D4
 *CSLFD* M3....6 D7
 *GOL/RIS/CUL* WA3....79 K4
 *HULME* M15....6 A6
 *MILN* OL16....11 J6
 *OLDS* OL8....9 J8
 *SWIN* M27....70 C2
 *SWIN* M27....70 D5
 *TOT/BURYW* BL8....24 B5
 *WGNW/BIL/OR* WN5....46 E7
Worsley Ter *WGN* WN1....15 G2
Worston Av *BOL* BL1....35 J2
Worth Ct *POY/DIS* SK12....129 H2
Worthenbury Wk
 *BRUN/LGST* M13....99 H1
Worthing Cl *OFTN* SK2....113 C6
Worthing Gv *ATH* M46....51 H5
Worthing St *RUSH/FAL* M14....98 E2
Worthington Av *HEY* OL10....41 H5
 *PART* M31....106 C1
Worthington Cl *HYDE* SK14 *....103 H2
Worthington Dr *BRO* M7....72 A3

Worthington Rd
 *DTN/ASHW* M34....101 L3
 *SALE* M33....97 H8
Worthington St *AULW* OL7....75 K7
 *BOLS/LL* BL3....51 M1
 *NEWH/MOS* M40....73 M4
 *STLY* SK15....91 J3
 *WGNE/HIN* WN2....49 G6
Worthington Wy
 *DTN/ASHW* M34....90 B8
 *WGNS/IIMK* WN3....63 H2
Worths La *DTN/ASHW* M34....101 K5
Wortley Av *SLFD* M6....85 M1
Wortley Gv *NEWH/MOS* M40....73 L2
Wotton Dr *AIMK* WN4....79 L1
Wragby Cl *TOT/BURYW* BL8....25 G7
Wrath Cl *BOLE* BL2....22 E7
Wraxhall Crs *LEIGH* WN7....66 A5
Wray Cl *WYTH/NTH* M22....118 F1
Wray Gdns *BNG/LEV* M19....99 M4
Wray Pl *MILN* OL16....11 L7
Wray St *WGN* WN1....15 L4
Wrekin Av *NTHM/RTH* M23....118 C1
Wren Av *SWIN* M27....70 E1
Wrenbury Av *DID/WITH* M20....98 C5
Wrenbury Cl
 *WGNW/BIL/OR* WN5....46 E7
Wrenbury Crs *EDGY/DAV* SK3....111 M7
Wrenbury Dr *BOL* BL1....22 C6
 *CHD/CHDH* SK8....111 H6
 *MILN* OL16....28 F8
Wren Cl *DTN/ASHW* M34....89 M2
 *FWTH* BL4....52 C4
 *OFTN* SK2....113 J7
 *WGNW/BIL/OR* WN5....46 E3
Wren Dr *BURY* BL9....25 L8
 *IRL* M44....83 K8
Wren Gdns *MDTN* M24....57 J3
Wren Gn *MILN* OL16....11 K6
Wren Nest Cl *GLSP* SK13....104 E4
Wren Nest Rd *GLSP* SK13....104 E3
Wren Nest Ter *GLSP* SK13....104 E3
Wren's Nest Rd *ROY/SHW* OL2....43 M4
Wren St *OLDE* OL4....59 M6
Wrenswood Dr *WALK* M28....68 F4
Wren Wy *OP/CLY* M11....88 B4
Wrexham Cl *OLDS* OL8....74 E2
Wrigglesworth Cl
 *TOT/BURYW* BL8....38 C1
Wrightington St *WGN* WN1....14 F1
Wright Robinson Cl
 *OP/CLY* M11....88 B4
Wrights Bank North *OFTN* SK2....113 H7
Wrights Bank South *OFTN* SK2....113 G7
Wright St *AIMK* WN4....63 J6
 *AUL* OL6....76 A3
 *CHAD* OL9....8 A4
 *DTN/ASHW* M34....90 B4
 *FAIL* M35....74 C4
 *OLD* OL1....9 L3
 *OLDTF/WHR* M16....97 M3
 *RAD* M26....54 C1
 *WGN* WN1....15 K2
 *WGNE/HIN* WN2....64 D1
 *WGNE/HIN* WN2....64 E5
Wrigley Crs *FAIL* M35....74 C5
Wrigley Fold *MDTN* M24....40 F8
Wrigley Head *FAIL* M35....74 C4
Wrigley Head Crs *FAIL* M35 *....74 C4
Wrigley La *MCFLDN* SK10....131 L8
Wrigley Pl *LIT* OL15 *....29 J1
Wrigley Rd *RNFD/HAY* WA11....78 B6
Wrigley St *AUL* OL6....75 L8
 *OLDE* OL4....59 L5
 *OLDE* OL4....60 C6
 *OLDE* OL4....60 C6
Wrington Cl *LEIGH* WN7....66 A4
Wroe St *CSLFD* M3....6 A4
 *OLDE* OL4....60 C6
 *SWIN* M27....70 C1
Wroe Ter *SWIN* M27 *....70 C1
Wrotham Cl *ORD* M5....86 D3
Wroxham Av *DTN/ASHW* M34....100 D1
 *URM* M41....95 L1
Wroxham Cl *TOT/BURYW* BL8 *....25 G7
Wroxham Rd *BKLY* M9....72 F1
Wuerdle Cl *MILN* OL16....29 H1
Wuerdle Farm Wy *MILN* OL16....21 J8
Wuerdle Pl *MILN* OL16....21 J8
Wuerdle St *MILN* OL16....21 J8
Wyatt Av *ORD* M5 *....86 F5

Wyatt Gv *AIMK* WN4....79 G1
Wyatt St *DUK* SK16....90 F4
 *HTNM* SK4....13 G5
Wybersley Rd *MPL/ROM* SK6....123 J3
Wychbury St *ORD* M5....86 B2
Wychelm Rd *PART* M31....106 C1
Wycherley Rd *WHIT* OL12....27 L2
Wych Fold *HYDE* SK14....102 B5
Wych La *MCFLDN* SK10....129 G5
Wych St *AUL* OL6 *....90 E2
Wychwood *ALT* WA14....116 D3
Wychwood Cl *MDTN* M24....57 L5
Wycliffe Av *WILM/AE* SK9....126 E6
Wycliffe Rd *ENF/HAY* WA11....78 B5
 *URM* M41....95 M2
Wycliffe St *ECC* M30....84 F2
 *HTNM* SK4....12 F3
Wycombe Av *GTN* M18....89 H6
Wycombe Cl *URM* M41....84 F7
Wycombe Dr *TYLD* M29....67 L5
Wye Av *FAIL* M35 *....74 C5
Wyecroft Cl *MPL/ROM* SK6....101 L2
Wye St *OLDS* OL8....8 F8
Wykeham Av *WGNS/IIMK* WN3....15 M8
Wykeham Gv *WHIT* OL12....27 L3
Wykeham Ms *BOL* BL1....35 K5
Wyke Pk *OLDE* OL4....60 A6
Wylam Wk *WGTN/LGST* M12....99 L1
The Wylde *BURY* BL9....4 E4
Wynard Av *WGN* WN1....15 J2
Wynchgate Rd
 *BRAM/HZG* SK7....122 C1
Wyndale Dr *FAIL* M35....74 C7
Wyndale Rd *OLDS* OL8....75 J1
Wyndcliff Dr *URM* M41....95 H3
Wyndham Av *BOLS/LL* BL3....51 K2
 *SWIN* M27....70 C2
Wyndham Cl *BRAM/HZG* SK7....121 G5
Wyne Cl *BRAM/HZG* SK7....122 C1
Wyngate Rd *CHD/CHDH* SK8....120 B3
 *HALE/TIMP* WA15....117 H4
Wynne Av *SWIN* M27....70 C1
Wynne Cl *DTN/ASHW* M34....101 J3
 *OP/CLY* M11....88 C4
Wynne Gv *DTN/ASHW* M34....101 J3
Wynne St *BOL* BL1....36 B2
 *LHULT* M38....52 D8
 *SLFD* M6....71 L8
 *TYLD* M29....67 J3
Wynnstay Gv *RUSH/FAL* M14....98 F4
Wynnstay Rd *SALE* M33....96 E7
Wynton Cl *LEIGH* WN7....81 H2
Wynyard Cl *SALE* M33....109 G2
Wynyard Rd *WYTH/NTH* M22....118 E1
Wyre Av *WGNE/HIN* WN2....64 D2
Wyre Dr *WALK* M28....68 E5
Wyresdale Rd *BOL* BL1....35 M4
Wyre St *CMANE* M1....7 K7
 *MOSL* OL5....76 E3
Wyrevale Gv *AIMK* WN4....78 F1
Wythall Av *LHULT* M38....52 E6
Wythburn Av *BOL* BL1....35 K3
 *CHH* M8....72 F6
 *URM* M41....95 L1
Wythburn Rd *MDTN* M24....57 H1
 *STKP* SK1....112 E5
Wythburn St *ORD* M5....86 B2
Wythenshawe Pk
 *NTHM/RTH* M23 *....109 K4
Wythenshawe Rd
 *NTHM/RTH* M23....109 H4
 *SALE* M33....97 H8
Wythens Rd *CHD/CHDH* SK8....119 K4
Wythop Gdns *ORD* M5....86 D3
Wyvern Av *HTNM* SK4....100 D7
Wyverne Rd *CCHDY* M21....98 A4
Wyville Dr *BKLY* M9....56 E6
 *SLFD* M6....85 C1
 *SWIN* M27....70 B6

Yale Rd *GTN* M18....88 E7
Yarburgh St *OLDTF/WHR* M16....98 B1
Yardley Av *STRET* M32....96 D3

Yardley Cl *STRET* M32....96 D2
Yarmouth Dr *NTHM/RTH* M23....109 L3
Yarn Cft *TYLD* M29....67 L4
Yarnton Cl *ROY/SHW* OL2....43 K7
Yarrow Cl *ROCH* OL11....10 E9
Yarrow Pl *BOL* BL1....2 B1
Yarrow St *WGNE/HIN* WN2....48 F8
Yarwell *WHIT* OL12....10 D2
Yarwood Av *NTHM/RTH* M23....109 J5
Yarwood Cl *HEY* OL10....41 H1
Yarwoodheath La *ALT* WA14....116 A4
Yarwood St *ALT* WA14....116 F1
 *BURY* BL9....5 H4
Yasmin Gdns *OLD* OL1....8 F2
Yates Dr *WALK* M28....68 D1
Yates Gv *WGNNW/ST* WN6....31 J8
Yates Rd *NM/HAY* SK22....124 E5
Yates St *BOLE* BL2....3 H1
 *LEIGH* WN7....66 B5
 *MDTN* M24....56 F5
 *OLD* OL1....9 M2
 *STKP* SK1....112 E1
 *WGNS/IIMK* WN3....14 C5
Yates Ter *TOT/BURYW* BL8....25 H7
Yattendon Av
 *NTHM/RTH* M23....109 G4
Yeadon Rd *GTN* M18....100 A1
Yea Fold *LIT* OL15....29 H1
Yealand Av *HTNM* SK4....12 L1
Yealand Cl *ROCH* OL11....27 L5
Yealand Gv *WGNE/HIN* WN2....49 K7
Yeardsley Cl *BRAM/HZG* SK7....121 G1
Yeb Fold *NEWH/MOS* M40 *....73 L3
Yellow Brook Cl
 *WGNE/HIN* WN2....32 F7
Yellow Lodge Dr *WHTN* BL5....50 E3
Yeoford Dr *ALT* WA14....107 L6
Yeoman Cl *BRAM/HZG* SK7 *....121 M1
Yeoman's Cl *MILN* OL16....29 J5
Yeoman Wk *OP/CLY* M11....88 C3
Yeovil St *OLDTF/WHR* M16....98 C1
Yewbarrow Cl *TYLD* M29....67 L5
Yewbarrow Rd *OLD* OL1....9 L2
Yew Cl *BOLS/LL* BL3....35 L8
Yew Crs *OLDE* OL4....60 A4
Yewdale *SWIN* M27....70 E2
 *WGNNW/ST* WN6....30 E6
Yewdale Crs *WGN* WN1....47 L2
Yewdale Dr *FAIL* M35....74 E4
 *MDTN* M24....57 H3
Yewdale Gdns *BOLE* BL2....37 J2
Yew Dale Gdns *ROCH* OL11....27 L8
Yewdale Rd *AIMK* WN4....63 K5
 *STKP* SK1....112 E6
Yew Gv *WGNNW/ST* WN6....47 J1
Yewlands Av *BKLY* M9....57 G7
Yew St *BRO* M7....71 M6
 *BURY* BL9....5 M2
 *DTN/ASHW* M34....90 C7
 *HEY* OL10....40 E2
 *HTNM* SK4....12 B6
 *HULME* M15....87 H7
Yewtree Av *ATH* M46....51 J7
Yew Tree Av *BNG/LEV* M19....99 K3
 *BRAM/HZG* SK7....122 D4
 *NEWLW* WA12....78 D8
 *RUSH/FAL* M14....98 D1
 *WYTH/NTH* M22....110 A3
Yew Tree Cl *AULW* OL7....75 K6
 *MPL/ROM* SK6....114 D7
 *WILM/AE* SK9....127 H5
Yew Tree Crs *RUSH/FAL* M14....98 E3
Yew Tree Dr *HOR/BR* BL6....34 E6
 *MDTN* M24....58 A5
 *MPL/ROM* SK6....113 G1
 *PWCH* M25....55 J8
 *SALE* M33....97 H8
 *URM* M41....84 C3
 *WYTH/NTH* M22....110 A3
Yew Tree Gv *CHD/CHDH* SK8....119 J1
 *POY/DIS* SK12....129 K1
 *WYTH/NTH* M22....110 A3
Yew Tree Park Rd
 *CHD/CHDH* SK8....120 D6
Yew Tree Rd *DTN/ASHW* M34....101 H3
 *EDGY/DAV* SK3....121 H1
 *MCFLDN* SK10....129 M3

Yew Tree Wy
 *GOL/RIS/CUL* WA3....79 L5
 *RUSH/FAL* M14....98 E3
York Cl *BOLS/LL* BL3....53 K1
 *OLDS* OL8....59 G8
 *OLDTF/WHR* M16....97 M2
 *PWCH* M25....72 A2
 *ROCH* OL11....27 K6
 *SALE* M33....96 E7
 *SWIN* M27....70 A2
 *TYLD* M29....67 J2
York Chambers *WGN* WN1 *....14 F4
York Cl *CHD/CHDH* SK8....111 H6
York Crs *WILM/AE* SK9....127 H5
Yorkdale Rd *OLDE* OL4....60 A5
York Dr *ALT* WA14....116 F3
 *BRAM/HZG* SK7....122 C2
 *MANAIR* M90....118 B5
 *RAMS* BL0....16 D2
York Pl *AULW* OL7....90 D2
York Rd *AIMK* WN4....78 F2
 *ALT* WA14....116 E3
 *CCHDY* M21....97 L4
 *CHAD* OL9....58 C4
 *DROY* M43....89 J1
 *DTN/ASHW* M34....90 D8
 *HTNM* SK4....99 L7
 *HYDE* SK14....102 B4
 *IRL* M44....94 A7
 *SALE* M33....96 D7
 *WGNE/HIN* WN2....49 J7
York Rd East *MDTN* M24....57 M7
York Rd South *AIMK* WN4....78 F2
York Rd West *MDTN* M24....57 M7
Yorkshire Rd *PART* M31....106 B2
Yorkshire St *AULW* OL7....75 L8
 *CSLFD* M3....6 D3
 *MILN* OL16....10 F3
 *OLD* OL1....9 K5
 *WHIT* OL12....11 H2
Yorkshire Wy *GLSP* SK13....105 J4
York St *ATH* M46....67 G1
 *AULW* OL7....90 B4
 *BNG/LEV* M19....99 K4
 *BURY* BL9....5 H4
 *CHAD* OL9....9 G6
 *CMANE* M1....7 H9
 *CMANE* M1....7 J9
 *CMANW* M2....7 G4
 *DID/WITH* M20....110 E1
 *EDGY/DAV* SK3....13 G6
 *FWTH* BL4....53 H4
 *GLSP* SK13....105 L3
 *GOL/RIS/CUL* WA3....79 K3
 *HALE/TIMP* WA15....117 G1
 *HEY* OL10....41 G2
 *LEIGH* WN7....67 G8
 *MILN* OL16....11 K7
 *RAD* M26....39 H7
 *WGNS/IIMK* WN3....14 D5
 *WHTF* M45....55 J4
York Ter *GLSP* SK13....104 F4
 *SALE* M33 *....96 D6
Youd St *LEIGH* WN7....66 B7
Youlgreave Crs *GLSP* SK13....104 A3
Young St *CSLFD* M3....6 D5
 *FWTH* BL4....53 H4
 *LEIGH* WN7....67 H8
 *RAMS* BL0....16 E6
Yulan Dr *SALE* M33....95 M8
Yule St *EDGY/DAV* SK3....12 E6
Yvonne Cl *AIMK* WN4....64 A7

**Z**

Zama St *RAMS* BL0 *....18 C4
Zealand St *OLDE* OL4....59 M4
Zedburgh *WHIT* OL12....10 D2
Zeta St *BKLY* M9....73 J5
Zetland Av *BOLS/LL* BL3....51 L2
Zetland Av North *BOLS/LL* BL3....51 L2
Zetland Rd *CCHDY* M21....97 L4
Zetland St *DUK* SK16....91 G5
Zinnia Dr *IRL* M44....94 B4
Zion Ter *WHIT* OL12....28 C3
Zulu St *BOLE* BL2....3 K4
Zurich Gdns *BRAM/HZG* SK7....121 G1
Zyburn Ct *SLFD* M6 *....85 K1

## Index - featured places

AA Office
 *CHD/CHDH* SK8....111 H6
Abbey College Manchester
 *CMANW* M2....6 F5
Abbey Hey Primary School
 *GTN* M18....89 H7
Abbey Lakes Sports Centre
 *WGNW/BIL/OR* WN5....46 A5
Abbey Tutorial College
 *CMANE* M1....7 G4
Abbotsford
 Preparatory School
 *URM* M41....95 K2
Abbott Primary School
 *NEWH/MOS* M40....87 M1
Abingdon Primary School
 *RDSH* SK5....100 C5
Abraham Guest High School
 *WGNW/BIL/OR* WN5....46 D6
Abraham Moss High School
 *CHH* M8....72 E4
Abram Bryn Gates
 Primary School
 *WGNE/HIN* WN2....64 C5
Abram CE Primary School
 *WGNE/HIN* WN2....64 E3
Acacias CP School
 *BNG/LEV* M19....99 J5
Acorn Business Centre
 *LEIGH* WN7....66 E8
Acorn Business Park
 *EDGY/DAV* SK3....12 F5
Acorns School
 *MPL/ROM* SK6....114 C7
Acre Hall Primary School
 *URM* M41....95 J2
Adlington Industrial Estate
 *MCFLDN* SK10....129 G3
Adlington Primary School
 *MCFLDN* SK10....129 L1
Adswood Clinic
 *EDGY/DAV* SK3....112 B7
Adswood Industrial Estate
 *EDGY/DAV* SK3....112 A7

Adswood Primary School
 *EDGY/DAV* SK3....112 A7
Adult Learning Centre
 *RUSH/FAL* M14....87 K8
Agecroft Crematorium
 *SWIN* M27....71 J4
Air & Space Museum
 *CSLFD* M3....6 D6
Al-Afifah High School for Girls
 *OLDTF/WHR* M16....86 F8
Albany Trading Estate
 *CCHDY* M21....97 L3
Albert Close Trading Estate
 *WHTF* M45....55 K4
Albion Drive Clinic
 *DROY* M43....89 K1
The Albion High School
 *BRO* M7....72 A7
Albion Trading Estate
 *AUL* OL6....91 G1
 *SLFD* M6....71 K8
Alder Community
 High School
 *HYDE* SK14....103 G2
Alderley Edge CC
 *WILM/AE* SK9....130 E3
Alderley Edge Golf Club
 *WILM/AE* SK9....130 B1
Alderley Edge Hotel
 *WILM/AE* SK9....130 E4
Alderley Edge Primary School
 *WILM/AE* SK9....130 C2
Alderley Edge School for Girls
 *WILM/AE* SK9....130 D2
Alderman Kay Special School
 *MDTN* M24....57 K1
Alder Park CP School
 *ECC* M30....69 L8
Aldwyn CP School
 *DTN/ASHW* M34....89 M3
Alexander House Health Centre
 *WGNE/HIN* WN2....64 E1
Alexandra Business Centre
 *UPML* OL3....61 L5

The Alexandra Hospital
 *CHD/CHDH* SK8....111 G6
Alexandra Industrial Estate
 *DTN/ASHW* M34....90 D8
Alexandra Park Junior School
 *EDGY/DAV* SK3....12 D9
 *OLDS* OL8....59 K8
Alexandra Retail Park
 *OLDE* OL4....9 K7
Alice Ingham RC Primary School
 *MILN* OL16....28 F2
Al-jamiyah-islamiyah-darul-Uloom
 Islamic College
 *EDGW/EG* BL7....22 D4
Alkrington Clinic Centre
 *MDTN* M24....57 K7
Alkrington Moss Primary School
 *MDTN* M24....57 L7
Alkrington Primary School
 *MDTN* M24....57 K6
All Hallows RC High School
 *ORD* M5....86 A1
Alliance Francaise
 *CMANE* M1....7 G7
Alliston House Medical Centre
 *URM* M41....96 A2
All Saints Catholic College
 *DUK* SK16....91 G5
All Saints Catholic Primary
 School
 *GLSP* SK13....105 G2
All Saints CE Primary School
 *FWTH* BL4....53 G3
 *HTNM* SK4....100 A8
 *MPL/ROM* SK6....114 D7
 *NEWH/MOS* M40....73 M7
 *WHIT* OL12....28 D3
 *WHTF* M45....55 K2
All Saints Primary School
 *GTN* M18....88 E6
All Saints RC Primary School
 *GOL/RIS/CUL* WA3....79 L4
All Souls CE Primary School
 *HEY* OL10....41 J1

All Souls RC Primary School
 *ORD* M5....86 A3
Alma Industrial Estate
 *WHIT* OL12....11 G1
Alma Lodge Hotel
 *OFTN* SK2....112 D6
Alma Park Primary School
 *BNG/LEV* M19....99 K4
Alpha Court Industrial Estate
 *DTN/ASHW* M34....100 F1
Alt Primary School
 *OLDS* OL8....76 A1
Altrincham CE Primary School
 *ALT* WA14....107 M7
Altrincham College of Arts
 *HALE/TIMP* WA15....108 D8
Altrincham Crematorium
 *ALT* WA14....107 G4
Altrincham FC
 *HALE/TIMP* WA15....117 K1
Altrincham General Hospital
 *ALT* WA14....107 M8
Altrincham Golf Club
 *HALE/TIMP* WA15....108 C7
Altrincham Grammar School
 for Boys *ALT* WA14....116 F2
Altrincham Grammar School
 for Girls *ALT* WA14....116 E1
Altrincham Ice Rink
 *ALT* WA14....108 A6
Altrincham Industrial Centre
 *ALT* WA14....107 K6
Altrincham (Kersal) RFC
 *HALE/TIMP* WA15....108 F5
Altrincham Leisure Centre
 *HALE/TIMP* WA15....108 B7
Altrincham Preparatory
 School *ALT* WA14....116 E2
Altrincham Priory Hospital
 *HALE/TIMP* WA15....117 J4
Altrincham Retail Park
 *ALT* WA14....107 M5
Alvanley Industrial Estate
 *MPL/ROM* SK6....101 J8

All Souls RC Primary School
Amalgamated Sports Club
 *POY/DIS* SK12....123 K6
Amberhurst Hotel
 *SALE* M33....96 D8
AMC Cinema
 *CSLFD* M3....6 E7
AMF Bowling
 *WGNS/IIMK* WN3....14 E5
Ancoats Hospital
 *ANC* M4....7 M4
Angel Trading Estate
 *ANC* M4....7 H1
Angouleme Way Retail Park
 *BURY* BL9....5 G5
Ann Street Health Centre
 *DTN/ASHW* M34....101 H1
Anson Medical Centre
 *RUSH/FAL* M14....88 A8
Aquinas College
 *OFTN* SK2....112 E6
Arcades Shopping Centre
 *AUL* OL6....90 E1
Arcadia Sports Centre
 *BNG/LEV* M19....99 K3
Arden Business Centre
 *MPL/ROM* SK6....101 H6
Arden Primary School
 *MPL/ROM* SK6....113 G1
Arlies Primary School
 *STLY* SK15....76 D7
Armitage CE Primary School
 *WGTN/LGST* M12....88 B6
Arndale Shopping Centre
 *STRET* M32....96 F3
Arrow Trading Estate
 *DTN/ASHW* M34....90 A7
Arts & Craft College
 *BURY* BL9....4 E5
Art Theatre
 *NM/HAY* SK22....124 D5
Arundale Primary School
 *HYDE* SK14....103 H1
Ashbury Meadow Primary
 School *OP/CLY* M11....88 C4

Ashdene Independant
  Pre School *WILM/AE* SK9 .......... 126  D7
Ashfield Valley Primary School
  *ROCH* OL11 ................................ 28  B3
Ashgate Specialist Primary
  Support School
  *WYTH/NTH* M22 ....................... 110  C8
Ash Lea School
  *ECC* M30 ..................................... 85  H1
Ashton Grange Industrial Estate
  *AIMK* WN4 ................................... 63  L6
Ashton-in-Makerfield Golf Club
  *AIMK* WN4 ................................... 78  B2
Ashton Leisure Centre
  *AIMK* WN4 ................................... 63  K8
Ashton Medical Centre
  *AIMK* WN4 ................................... 63  K7
Ashton on Mersey School
  *SALE* M33 ................................... 96  C8
Ashton Retail Park
  *AUL* OL6 ..................................... 90  E1
Ashton Swimming Pool
  *AUL* OL6 ..................................... 90  E1
Ashton Town AFC
  *AIMK* WN4 ................................... 64  A8
Ashton-under-Lyne Golf Club
  *AUL* OL6 ..................................... 76  B5
Ashton-under-Lyne RFC
  *AUL* OL6 ..................................... 75  L5
Ashton-under-Lyne Sixth Form
  College *AUL* OL6 ........................ 76  A4
Ashton United FC
  *AUL* OL6 ..................................... 76  A4
Ashton upon Mersey Cricket
  & Tennis Club
  *SALE* M33 ................................... 96  C8
Ashton upon Mersey Golf Club
  *SALE* M33 ................................... 96  B5
Aspinal Primary School
  *GTN* M18 ................................... 100  B1
Aspull Church Primary School
  *WGNE/HIN* WN2 ......................... 33  H8
Aspull Clinic
  *WGNE/HIN* WN2 ......................... 32  F7
Astley Bridge CC
  *BOL* BL1 ..................................... 22  A8
Astra Business Park
  *TRPK* M17 ................................... 85  J4
Astra Industrial Centre
  *ROCH* OL11 ................................. 41  M1
Atherton Industrial Centre
  *ATH* M46 ..................................... 51  M4
Atherton Public Baths
  *ATH* M46 ..................................... 66  F1
Atlantic Business Centre
  *ALT* WA14 ................................. 107  M5
Atlas Trading Estate
  *RDSH* SK5 ................................. 100  B5
Audenshaw Primary School
  *DTN/ASHW* M34 .......................... 89  M1
Audenshaw School
  *DTN/ASHW* M34 .......................... 90  B1
Austerlands CC
  *OLDE* OL4 ................................... 60  D4
Avenue Medical Centre
  *BKLY* M9 ..................................... 57  H7
Aviation Viewing Park
  *HALE/TIMP* WA15 ..................... 118  C1
Avicenna Grammar School
  *DID/WITH* M20 ............................ 98  C4
Avondale Health Centre
  *BOL* BL1 ..................................... 35  M3
Avondale High School
  *EDGY/DAV* SK3 ........................... 12  C8
Avondale Industrial Estate
  *EDGY/DAV* SK3 ........................... 12  B7
Avondale Recreation Centre
  *EDGY/DAV* SK3 ........................... 12  B8
Avro Golf Club
  *BRAM/HZG* SK7 ......................... 128  C4
Bag Lane Industrial Estate
  *ATH* M46 ..................................... 50  F8
Baguley Hall Primary School
  *NTHM/RTH* M23 ......................... 109  K6
Baillie Street Health Centre
  *MILN* OL16 ................................... 10  F3
Balderstone Technology College
  *ROCH* OL11 ................................. 42  D1
Bamford Business Park
  *RDSH* SK5 ................................. 100  B7
Bamford Primary School
  *ROCH* OL11 ................................. 27  H6
Band on the Wall
  *ANC* M4 ....................................... 7  L2
Bankfield Trading Estate
  *HTNM* SK4 ................................. 100  B8
Bank Meadow Primary School
  *WGTN/LGST* M12 ......................... 88  A4
Banks Lane Infant School
  *STKP* SK1 ................................. 112  E4
Bare Trees J & I School
  *CHAD* OL9 ..................................... 8  A2
Baring Street Industrial Estate
  *CMANE* M1 ................................... 7  L7
Barlow Hall Primary School
  *CCHDY* M21 ................................. 97  M7
Barlow Medical Centre
  *DID/WITH* M20 ........................... 110  D1
The Barlow RC High School
  *DID/WITH* M20 ........................... 110  F2
Barrack Hill Primary School
  *MPL/ROM* SK6 ........................... 113  K2
Barrington Medical Centre
  *ALT* WA14 ................................. 108  A6
Barton Business Park
  *ECC* M30 ..................................... 84  F3
Barton Clough Primary School
  *STRET* M32 ................................. 85  J8
Barton Moss Community
  Primary School
  *ECC* M30 ..................................... 84  C3
Bayley Industrial Estate
  *STLY* SK15 ................................... 91  J3
BBC North
  *CMANE* M1 ................................... 7  H8
Bealey Community Hospital
  *RAD* M26 ..................................... 39  G8
Bealey Industrial Estate
  *RAD* M26 ..................................... 39  G7
Beal Vale Primary School
  *ROY/SHW* OL2 ............................. 43  L5
Beaumont Hospital
  *HOR/BR* BL6 ................................. 34  E4
Beaumont Primary School
  *BOLS/LL* BL3 ............................... 35  H7
Beaver Road Primary School
  *DID/WITH* M20 ........................... 110  E1
Bedford Hall Methodist
  Primary School
  *LEIGH* WN7 ................................... 81  L1
Bedford High School
  *LEIGH* WN7 ................................... 67  G8

Beech Hill Primary School
  *WGNNW/ST* WN6 ......................... 47  K1
Beech House School
  *ROCH* OL11 ................................. 10  C7
Beech Street Primary School
  *ECC* M30 ..................................... 84  E3
Bee Fold Medical Centre
  *ATH* M46 ..................................... 66  E2
Bee Hive Industrial Estate
  *HOR/BR* BL6 ............................... 34  B5
Beetham Tower
  *CSLFD* M3 ..................................... 6  D7
Beever Primary School
  *OLD* OL1 ....................................... 9  L3
Beis Rochel Girls School
  *CHH* M8 ....................................... 72  C3
The Beis Yaakov Jewish High
  School *BRO* M7 ........................... 71  M4
Bel-Air Hotel
  *WGN* WN1 ................................... 31  M8
Belfield Community Primary
  School *MILN* OL16 ....................... 11  L2
Belfield Trading Estate
  *MILN* OL16 ................................... 29  G3
Belford College
  *OLDS* OL8 ................................... 58  F8
Belfry House Hotel
  *WILM/AE* SK9 ............................. 119  M6
Belle Green Industrial Estate
  *WGNE/HIN* WN2 ......................... 48  D4
Belle Vue Regional Hockey
  Centre
  *WGTN/LGST* M12 ......................... 88  D8
Benchill Primary School
  *WYTH/NTH* M22 ......................... 109  M6
Bentfield Industrial Units
  *CHAD* OL9 ..................................... 8  A9
Bentinck Street Industrial Estate
  *HULME* M15 ................................... 6  A9
Best Western Cresta Court Hotel
  *ALT* WA14 ................................. 108  A7
Best Western Hotel
  Smokies Park
  *OLDS* OL8 ..................................... 75  J4
Bickershaw CE Primary School
  *BNG/LEV* M19 ............................. 65  J4
Billinge Chapel End
  Parish Council
  *WGNW/BIL/OR* WN5 ..................... 62  B7
Billinge Chapel End Primary
  School *WGNW/BIL/OR* WN5 ........ 62  B8
Billinge Clinic
  *WGNW/BIL/OR* WN5 ..................... 62  A8
Billinge Hospital
  *WGNW/BIL/OR* WN5 ..................... 62  A2
Birches Health Centre
  *PWCH* M25 ................................... 55  M6
Birchfields Primary School
  *RUSH/FAL* M14 ........................... 99  H3
Birch Industrial Estate
  *HEY* OL10 ..................................... 40  D6
Birchinley Manor Showground
  *MILN* OL16 ................................... 29  J4
Birchley St Marys RC Primary
  School
  *WGNW/BIL/OR* WN5 ..................... 62  A8
Birch Vale Industrial Estate
  *NM/HAY* SK22 ........................... 125  J2
Birtenshaw Hall School
  *EDGW/EG* BL7 ............................. 22  E6
Birtle View Special School
  *HEY* OL10 ..................................... 40  E2
Bishop Bilsborrow Memorial RC
  Primary School
  *OLDTF/WHR* M16 ......................... 98  C2
Bishop Bridgeman CE Primary
  School *BOLS/LL* BL3 ................... 36  B8
B & J Leisure Centre
  *WILM/AE* SK9 ............................. 126  E5
Blackbrook Trading Estate
  *BNG/LEV* M19 ............................. 99  L4
Blackley Cemetery
  *BKLY* M9 ..................................... 56  D8
Blackley Crematorium
  *BKLY* M9 ..................................... 56  D8
Blackley Golf Club
  *BKLY* M9 ..................................... 57  L8
Blackrod Church School
  *HOR/BR* BL6 ................................. 32  F2
Blackrod Primary School
  *HOR/BR* BL6 ................................. 33  H4
Blackshaw Lane CP School
  *ROY/SHW* OL2 ............................. 43  K8
Blackshaw Primary School
  *BOL* BL1 ..................................... 37  K6
Blessed Thomas Holford RC
  School
  *HALE/TIMP* WA15 ..................... 108  B8
Blue Chip Business Park
  *ALT* WA14 ................................. 107  L5
Blue Coat CE School
  *OLD* OL1 ....................................... 9  K4
Bnos Yisroel Schools
  *BRO* M7 ....................................... 72  B5
Boarshaw Industrial Estate
  *MDTN* M24 ................................... 57  L4
Boarshurst Business Park
  *UPML* OL3 ..................................... 61  L6
Bodmin Road Clinic
  *SALE* M33 ..................................... 96  A7
Boggart Hole Clough Track
  *BKLY* M9 ..................................... 73  J2
Boilholt Country Park Hotel
  *TOT/BURYW* BL8 ......................... 24  D8
Bollin CP School
  *ALT* WA14 ................................. 116  D3
Bolshaw Primary School
  *CHD/CHDH* SK8 ......................... 119  K5
Bolton Business Centre
  *BOLE* BL2 ..................................... 3  G8
Bolton CC
  *BOLS/LL* BL3 ............................... 52  D2
Bolton Community College
  *BOLE* BL2 ..................................... 3  G7
Bolton Gates Retail Park
  *BOL* BL1 ....................................... 2  F2
Bolton Golf Club
  *HOR/BR* BL6 ................................. 34  D4
Bolton Institute
  *BOLS/LL* BL3 ................................. 2  C7
Bolton Little Theatre
  *BOL* BL1 ....................................... 2  C5
Bolton Muslim Girls School
  *BOLS/LL* BL3 ............................... 36  A8
Bolton Old Links Golf Club
  *BOL* BL1 ..................................... 35  G1
Bolton Open Golf Club
  *BOLE* BL2 ..................................... 37  G1
Bolton Parish CE Primary School
  *BOLE* BL2 ..................................... 3  J4

Bolton Road Industrial Estate
  *WHTN* BL5 ................................... 50  C3
Bolton Rugby Union FC
  *RDSH* SK5 ..................................... 2  A2
Bolton Running Track
  *HOR/BR* BL6 ................................. 33  M5
Bolton School (Beech House,
  Infant Department)
  *BOL* BL1 ..................................... 35  L5
Bolton School (Girls Division)
  *BOL* BL1 ..................................... 35  L5
Bolton School
  (Junior Boys Division)
  *BOL* BL1 ..................................... 35  M5
Bolton School
  (Senior Boys Division)
  *BOL* BL1 ..................................... 35  M5
Bolton Sports Arena
  *HOR/BR* BL6 ................................. 33  M5
Bolton Trophy & Sports Centre
  *BOLE* BL2 ..................................... 3  L4
Bolton Wanderers FC
  (Reebok Stadium)
  *HOR/BR* BL6 ................................. 34  A5
Bond Street Industrial Estate
  *WGTN/LGST* M12 ......................... 7  L7
Bonholt Industrial Estate
  *TOT/BURYW* BL8 ......................... 24  D8
Booth Hall Hospital School
  *BKLY* M9 ..................................... 73  J1
Booth House Trading Estate
  *CHAD* OL9 ..................................... 8  D7
Boothstown Methodist Primary
  School *WALK* M28 ....................... 68  C6
The Borchardt Medical Centre
  *DID/WITH* M20 ............................. 98  C6
Bormore Industrial Centre
  *TOT/BURYW* BL8 ......................... 38  E1
Borron Road Industrial Estate
  *NEWLW* WA12 ............................. 78  F8
Boundary Industrial Estate
  *BOLE* BL2 ..................................... 37  K5
Boundary Trading Estate
  *IRL* M44 ....................................... 83  M8
Bowdon CE Primary School
  *ALT* WA14 ................................. 116  E3
Bowdon CC
  *ALT* WA14 ................................. 116  E3
Bowdon Preparatory School
  for Girls *ALT* WA14 ................... 116  E2
Bowdon RUFC
  *HALE/TIMP* WA15 ..................... 108  F8
Bowdon Vale CC
  *ALT* WA14 ................................. 116  E4
Bowker Bank Industrial Park
  *CHH* M8 ....................................... 72  E2
Bowker Vale Primary School
  *CHH* M8 ....................................... 56  C8
Bowness Primary School
  *BOLS/LL* BL3 ............................... 53  J1
Brabyns Recreation Centre
  *MPL/ROM* SK6 ........................... 114  D5
Brabyns School
  *MPL/ROM* SK6 ........................... 114  D5
Brackley Municipal Golf Club
  *LHULT* M38 ................................... 52  B6
Bradley Fold Trading Estate
  *BOLE* BL2 ..................................... 37  M6
Bradley Green Primary School
  *HYDE* SK14 ................................... 91  J6
Bradley Hall Trading Estate
  *WGNNW/ST* WN6 ......................... 31  K2
Bradshaw CC
  *BOLE* BL2 ..................................... 22  F7
Bradshaw Hall J & I School
  *CHD/CHDH* SK8 ......................... 120  A3
Bradshaw Trading Estate
  *MDTN* M24 ................................... 58  A7
Bramall Hall & Park
  *BRAM/HZG* SK7 ......................... 121  G3
Bramall Park Golf Club
  *CHD/CHDH* SK8 ......................... 120  E3
Bramall Park Lawn Tennis Club
  *BRAM/HZG* SK7 ......................... 120  F2
Bramall Park Tennis Club
  *BRAM/HZG* SK7 ......................... 120  F4
Bramhall Golf Club
  *BRAM/HZG* SK7 ......................... 121  H6
Bramhall Health Centre
  *BRAM/HZG* SK7 ......................... 121  G6
Bramhall High School
  *BRAM/HZG* SK7 ......................... 121  H4
Bramhall Moor
  Industrial Estate
  *BRAM/HZG* SK7 ......................... 121  K2
Bramhall Park Medical Centre
  *BRAM/HZG* SK7 ......................... 121  G2
Bramhall Village Shopping
  Centre *BRAM/HZG* SK7 .............. 120  F6
Brandwood Primary School
  *BOLS/LL* BL3 ............................... 35  M8
Branwood Preparatory School
  *ECC* M30 ..................................... 85  H1
Bredbury Clinic
  *MPL/ROM* SK6 ........................... 101  J8
Bredbury Green Primary
  School *MPL/ROM* SK6 ............... 113  J3
Bredbury Hall Hotel
  & Country Club
  *MPL/ROM* SK6 ........................... 113  G2
Breeze Hill Comprehensive
  School *OLDE* OL4 ......................... 60  A7
Breightmet FC
  *BOLE* BL2 ..................................... 37  J5
Breightmet Golf Club
  *BOLE* BL2 ..................................... 37  K3
Breightmet Industrial Estate
  *BOLE* BL2 ..................................... 37  J5
Brentnall Primary School
  *BRO* M7 ....................................... 72  A5
Brentwood Special School
  *ALT* WA14 ................................. 108  B5
Bridge College
  *OFTN* SK2 ................................. 113  G4
Bridge Hall Primary School
  *EDGY/DAV* SK3 ......................... 112  A6
Bridge House Medical Centre
  *CHD/CHDH* SK8 ......................... 120  D1
Bridge Mills Business Park
  *SLFD* M6 ..................................... 71  J7
Bridgeside Business Centre
  *MPL/ROM* SK6 ........................... 101  G6
Bridge Trading Estate
  *TOT/BURYW* BL8 ......................... 4  B4
Bridgewater Concert Hall
  *CMANE* M1 ................................... 6  F7
Bridgewater Primary School
  *LHULT* M38 ................................... 52  F8
Bridgewater School
  *WALK* M28 ................................... 69  K6
Brighton Road Industrial Estate
  *HTNM* SK4 ................................... 12  B4

Brimrod Primary School
  *ROCH* OL11 ................................. 10  A9
Brindale Primary School
  *RDSH* SK5 ................................. 100  F8
Brindle Heath Industrial Estate
  *SLFD* M6 ..................................... 71  J3
Brindle House Community
  Mental Health Centre
  *HYDE* SK14 ................................. 102  E1
Brinksway Trading Estate
  *HTNM* SK4 ................................... 12  D6
Brinnington Health Centre
  *RDSH* SK5 ................................. 100  F7
Briscoe Lane Primary School
  *NEWH/MOS* M40 ......................... 73  L7
Britannia Bridge Primary School
  *WGNS/IIMK* WN3 ......................... 15  K7
Britannia Business Park
  *BOLE* BL2 ..................................... 36  E2
Britannia Mill Industrial Estate
  *HEY* OL10 ..................................... 40  E2
Broadbent Fold Primary School
  *DUK* SK16 ..................................... 91  K5
Broadbottom Primary School
  *HYDE* SK14 ................................. 103  J4
Broadfield Industrial Estate
  *HEY* OL10 ..................................... 40  E3
Broadfield Primary School
  *MILN* OL16 ................................... 10  E5
  *OLDS* OL8 ..................................... 59  J8
Broadheath Industrial Estate
  *ALT* WA14 ................................. 107  M4
Broadhurst Primary School
  *NEWH/MOS* M40 ......................... 73  M5
Broad Oak Business Park
  *TRPK* M17 ..................................... 85  J5
Broad Oak High School
  *BURY* BL9 ..................................... 5  M4
Broadoak High School
  *PART* M31 ................................. 106  B2
Broadoak Primary School
  *AUL* OL6 ..................................... 75  M7
  *SWIN* M27 ................................... 69  M6
Broad Oak Business Park
  *DID/WITH* M20 ........................... 110  E4
Broadoak Sports Centre
  *AUL* OL6 ..................................... 75  M6
Broadstone Hall Primary School
  *HTNM* SK4 ................................. 100  A6
Broadwalk Primary School
  *SLFD* M6 ..................................... 86  D1
Broadway Business Park
  *CHAD* OL9 ..................................... 58  A8
Broadway Industrial Estate
  *HYDE* SK14 ................................... 90  E7
  *ORD* M5 ..................................... 86  D4
Brookburn Primary School
  *CCHDY* M21 ................................. 97  K5
Brookdale Golf Club
  *FAIL* M35 ..................................... 74  E7
Brookfield Business Park
  *CHD/CHDH* SK8 ......................... 111  J7
Brookfield High School
  *WGNE/HIN* WN2 ......................... 49  H8
Brookfield Industrial Estate
  *GLSP* SK13 ................................. 104  B1
Brookhead Junior School
  *CHD/CHDH* SK8 ......................... 111  J7
Brooklands Primary School
  *SALE* M33 ................................. 108  D2
Brook Mill Medical Centre
  *LEIGH* WN7 ................................... 66  D7
Brooks Bar Medical Centre
  *OLDTF/WHR* M16 ......................... 87  G8
Brookside Business Park
  *MDTN* M24 ................................... 58  A6
Brookside Primary School
  *MPL/ROM* SK6 ........................... 113  G6
Brookway High School
  & Sports College
  *NTHM/RTH* M23 ......................... 109  H4
Broomwood CP School
  *HALE/TIMP* WA15 ..................... 109  G7
Broughton Baths
  *BRO* M7 ....................................... 72  A6
Broughton CC
  *BRO* M7 ....................................... 71  M6
Broughton Jewish Cassel-Fox
  Primary School
  *BRO* M7 ....................................... 72  A4
Brownhill Countryside Centre
  *UPML* OL3 ..................................... 61  K3
Brownhill Special School
  *WHIT* OL12 ................................... 10  D1
Brownlow Business Centre
  *BOL* BL1 ..................................... 36  A3
Brownlow Fold Community
  Learning Centre
  *BOL* BL1 ..................................... 36  A3
Brownlow Fold Primary School
  *BOL* BL1 ..................................... 36  A3
Brunswick Health Centre
  *BRUN/LGST* M13 ......................... 87  L6
Bruntwood Primary School
  *CHD/CHDH* SK8 ......................... 120  A2
Buckley Road Industrial Estate
  *WHIT* OL12 ................................... 28  E2
Buckley School of Dance
  *WGNNW/ST* WN6 ......................... 47  K1
Buckstones Primary School
  *ROY/SHW* OL2 ............................. 44  A4
Buckton Vale Primary School
  *STLY* SK15 ................................... 77  J5
Buile Hill High School
  *SLFD* M6 ..................................... 71  G8
Bullough Moor Primary School
  *HEY* OL10 ..................................... 40  D2
Burgess Primary School
  *BKLY* M9 ..................................... 73  H5
Burnage High School For Boys
  *BNG/LEV* M19 ............................. 99  J7
Burnage Rugby Club
  *HTNM* SK4 ................................. 111  H3
Burnden Industrial Estate
  *BOLS/LL* BL3 ............................... 36  E8
Burnley Brow Community
  School *CHAD* OL9 ......................... 8  C1
Burrs Country Park
  *TOT/BURYW* BL8 ......................... 25  G6
Bury Antheneum
  *BURY* BL9 ..................................... 4  E5
Bury Business Centre
  *BURY* BL9 ..................................... 5  J1
Bury Catholic
  Preparatory School
  *BURY* BL9 ..................................... 4  D8
Bury CE High School
  *BURY* BL9 ..................................... 4  C8
Bury Cemetery
  *BURY* BL9 ..................................... 39  G3
Bury College
  *BURY* BL9 ..................................... 4  E6

Bury County Court
  *BURY* BL9 ..................................... 4  C5
Bury FC (Gigg Lane)
  *BURY* BL9 ..................................... 39  J5
Bury Golf Club
  *BURY* BL9 ..................................... 39  J8
Bury Grammar School (Boys)
  *BURY* BL9 ..................................... 4  C5
Bury Industrial Estate
  *BOLE* BL2 ..................................... 37  J4
Bury Market
  *BURY* BL9 ..................................... 4  F5
Bury Sports Club
  *BURY* BL9 ..................................... 4  D9
Bury & Whitefield Jewish
  Primary School
  *BURY* BL9 ..................................... 55  L1
Business & Arts Centre
  *HTNM* SK4 ................................. 100  A5
Butterstile Primary School
  *PWCH* M25 ................................... 71  K2
Button Lane School
  *NTHM/RTH* M23 ......................... 109  J2
Byrchall High School
  *NEWLW* WA12 ............................. 78  E3
Byron Street Infant & Nursery
  Community School
  *ROY/SHW* OL2 ............................. 43  H8
Cadishead Primary School
  *IRL* M44 ....................................... 94  A6
Cadishead Recreation Centre
  *IRL* M44 ....................................... 94  A7
Caius House School
  *URM* M41 ..................................... 95  M3
Caldershaw Primary School
  *WHIT* OL12 ................................... 27  J3
Camberwell Park School
  *BKLY* M9 ..................................... 56  F8
Cambrian Business Park
  *BOLS/LL* BL3 ................................. 2  C9
Cambridge Industrial Estate
  *BRO* M7 ....................................... 72  B8
Campanile Hotel
  *ORD* M5 ....................................... 6  A7
Cams Lane Primary School
  *RAD* M26 ..................................... 54  C1
Canalside Industrial Estate
  *MILN* OL16 ................................... 11  G3
Cannon Street Health Centre
  *BOLS/LL* BL3 ................................. 2  B8
Canon Burrows CE Primary
  School *AULW* OL7 ....................... 75  J7
Canon Johnson CE Primary
  School *AULW* OL7 ....................... 75  L8
Canon Sharples Primary School
  *WGN* WN1 ................................... 48  B2
Canon Slade School
  *BOLE* BL2 ..................................... 22  E8
Cansfield High School
  *AIMK* WN4 ................................... 63  K8
Capital Business Centre
  *BRAM/HZG* SK7 ......................... 120  F6
Cardinal Langley RC
  High School
  *MDTN* M24 ................................... 41  M8
Cariocca Business Park
  *NEWH/MOS* M40 ......................... 88  B1
  *WGTN/LGST* M12 ......................... 88  A6
Carlton Industrial Centre
  *BOLE* BL2 ..................................... 3  G6
Carrbrook Industrial Estate
  *STLY* SK15 ................................... 77  K6
Carrington Business Park
  *PART* M31 ................................... 95  M1
Castlebrook High School
  *BURY* BL9 ..................................... 55  M1
Castlefield Gallery
  *CSLFD* M3 ..................................... 6  D7
Castle Hawk Golf Club
  *ROCH* OL11 ................................. 41  K3
Castle Hill Primary School
  *BOLE* BL2 ..................................... 36  E2
Castle Hill St Philips CE Primary
  School *WGNE/HIN* WN2 ............... 49  J6
Castle Hill School
  *RDSH* SK5 ................................. 100  F6
Castle Leisure Centre
  *BURY* BL9 ..................................... 4  D4
Castle Park Industrial Estate
  *OLD* OL1 ..................................... 59  L5
Castleton Primary School
  *ROCH* OL11 ................................. 42  A2
Castleton Swimming Pool
  *ROCH* OL11 ................................. 41  M1
Cathedral Gardens
  *ANC* M4 ....................................... 6  F2
Cavendish Industrial Estate
  *AUL* OL6 ..................................... 90  D1
Cavendish Road Primary School
  *DID/WITH* M20 ............................. 98  D7
Central Art Gallery
  *AUL* OL6 ..................................... 90  E2
Central Industrial Estate
  *BOLS/LL* BL3 ................................. 2  E9
  *MDTN* M24 ................................... 57  K4
Central Leisure Centre
  *MILN* OL16 ................................... 11  G4
Central Primary School
  *DTN/ASHW* M34 ......................... 101  H1
Central Retail Park
  *ANC* M4 ....................................... 7  L4
Century Mill Industrial Estate
  *FWTH* BL4 ................................... 52  E4
CE School of the Resurrection
  *OP/CLY* M11 ................................. 88  C3
Chadderton AFC
  ........................................................ 8  A3
Chadderton Cemetery
  *CHAD* OL9 ..................................... 58  D4
Chadderton Hall Junior School
  *CHAD* OL9 ..................................... 58  D2
Chadderton Industrial Estate
  *MDTN* M24 ................................... 57  M7
Chadderton Sports Centre &
  Public Baths
  *CHAD* OL9 ..................................... 8  B4
Chadderton Town Health Centre
  *CHAD* OL9 ..................................... 8  A4
Chadkirk Industrial Estate
  *MPL/ROM* SK6 ........................... 113  L4
Chanters Industrial Estate
  *ATH* M46 ..................................... 67  J2
Chantlers Primary School
  *TOT/BURYW* BL8 ......................... 38  D2
Chapelfield Primary School
  *RAD* M26 ..................................... 54  F3
Chapel Medical Centre
  *IRL* M44 ....................................... 94  D2
Chapel Street Primary School
  *BNG/LEV* M19 ............................. 99  L3
Charleston Industrial Estate
  *AULW* OL7 ................................... 75  L7

Charlestown Health Centre
*BKLY* M9 ... 73 K2
Charlestown Primary School
*BKLY* M9 ... 73 L1
*SLFD* M6 ... 71 L8
Charlesworth School
*GLSP* SK13 ... 103 M6
Cheadle Catholic Primary School *CHD/CHDH* SK8 ... 120 A2
Cheadle CC
*CHD/CHDH* SK8 ... 110 F7
Cheadle Golf Club
*CHD/CHDH* SK8 ... 111 H8
Cheadle Heath Clinic
*EDGY/DAV* SK3 ... 111 K4
Cheadle Heath Primary School *EDGY/DAV* SK3 ... 111 K5
Cheadle Heath Sports Centre *CHD/CHDH* SK8 ... 111 K6
Cheadle Hulme High School *CHD/CHDH* SK8 ... 120 D5
Cheadle Hulme Medical Centre *CHD/CHDH* SK8 ... 120 C4
Cheadle Hulme Recreation Centre *CHD/CHDH* SK8 ... 120 D5
Cheadle Hulme School
*CHD/CHDH* SK8 ... 120 C4
Cheadle & Marple Sixth Form College *CHD/CHDH* SK8 ... 120 A1
Cheadle Primary School
*CHD/CHDH* SK8 ... 111 C6
Cheadle Royal Business Park *CHD/CHDH* SK8 ... 119 L1
Cheadle Royal Hospital
*CHD/CHDH* SK8 ... 119 L2
Cheadle Royal Shopping Centre *CHD/CHDH* SK8 ... 119 M2
Cheadle Swimming & Recreation Centre *CHD/CHDH* SK8 ... 111 H8
Cheadle Town FC
*CHD/CHDH* SK8 ... 111 H7
Cheetham CE Community School *BRO* M7 ... 72 C5
Cheetham Hill CC
*CHH* M8 ... 72 B3
Cheetwood Community & Sports Centre *BRO* M7 ... 72 C6
Cheetwood Primary School
*CHH* M8 ... 72 B8
Cherry Manor Primary School *SALE* M33 ... 107 M2
Cherry Tree Hospital
*OFTN* SK2 ... 112 F7
Cherry Tree Primary School *FWTH* BL4 ... 52 B4
Chesham Industrial Estate *BURY* BL9 ... 25 K8
Chesham Primary School
*BURY* BL9 ... 25 K6
Chester Court Hotel
*STRET* M32 ... 86 C8
Chethams Library & Music School *CSLFD* M3 ... 6 F2
Chichester Business Centre *MILN* OL16 ... 11 H5
Child Health Clinic
*MDTN* M24 ... 57 J3
Chinese Medical Centre
*CSLFD* M3 ... 6 D6
Chorley New Road Primary School *HOR/BR* BL6 ... 33 M2
Chorlton CE Primary School *CCHDY* M21 ... 97 K4
Chorlton-cum-Hardy CC
*CCHDY* M21 ... 97 L6
Chorlton-cum-Hardy Golf Club *CCHDY* M21 ... 97 M7
Chorlton High School
*CCHDY* M21 ... 97 M5
Chorlton Leisure Centre *CCHDY* M21 ... 97 L3
Chorlton Park Primary School *CCHDY* M21 ... 97 M5
Chorlton Shopping Centre *CCHDY* M21 ... 97 K3
Chorlton Water Park
*CCHDY* M21 ... 97 M8
Chowbent Primary School
*ATH* M46 ... 67 H1
Christchurch Ainsworth CE Primary School *BOL* BL2 ... 37 M3
Christ Church CE Primary School *CHAD* OL9 ... 58 D6
*UPML* OL3 ... 45 G2
Christchurch CE Primary School *ECC* M30 ... 84 F2
*TOT/BURYW* BL8 ... 24 C8
Christ Church Pennington CE Primary School *LEIGH* WN7 ... 66 C8
Christie Hospital & Holt Radium Institute *DID/WITH* M20 ... 98 E6
Christie Street Industrial Estate *STKP* SK1 ... 13 L8
Christs Church CE Primary School *BOLE* BL2 ... 37 J2
Christ the King RC Primary School *NEWH/MOS* M40 ... 73 M7
*WALK* M28 ... 69 H2
Christ the King School
*SALE* M33 ... 108 C1
Church Road Primary School *BOL* BL1 ... 35 K2
Church Street Industrial Estate *MDTN* M24 ... 57 K2
Cineworld
*BOL* BL1 ... 36 D1
*DID/WITH* M20 ... 111 G3
*STKP* SK1 ... 13 H6
*WGNW/BIL/OR* WN5 ... 47 H4
City Centre Campus
*CSLFD* M3 ... 6 C4
City College Manchester
*CHH* M8 ... 72 E4
*DID/WITH* M20 ... 98 C8
*NTHM/RTH* M23 ... 109 M3
*NTHM/RTH* M23 ... 109 J4
*NTHM/RTH* M23 ... 109 L4
City Course Trading Estate *OP/CLY* M11 ... 88 D5
City Court Trading Estate *ANC* M4 ... 7 L2
City Park Business Village *OLDTF/WHR* M16 ... 86 E7
Claremont Primary School *RUSH/FAL* M14 ... 98 D1
Clarendon Cottage School *ECC* M30 ... 85 J1

Clarendon CP School
*BOLS/LL* BL3 ... 2 D9
Clarendon Fields Primary School *DUK* SK16 ... 90 E4
Clarendon Industrial Estate *HYDE* SK14 ... 102 B1
Clarendon Road Primary School *ECC* M30 ... 85 J1
Clarendon Square Shopping Centre *HYDE* SK14 ... 102 A2
Clarke Industrial Estate
*STRET* M32 ... 85 K8
Clarksfield Primary School *OLDE* OL4 ... 59 M6
Claypool Primary School
*HOR/BR* BL6 ... 34 B3
Clayton Health Centre
*OP/CLY* M11 ... 88 E2
Clayton Industrial Estate *OP/CLY* M11 ... 89 G5
Cleavley Athletics Track
*ECC* M30 ... 84 D1
Cleggs Lane Industrial Site *LHULT* M38 ... 52 E6
Clevelands Preparatory School *BOL* BL1 ... 35 K5
Clifton Country Park
*SWIN* M27 ... 54 B7
Clifton Industrial Estate
*SWIN* M27 ... 70 F1
Clifton Primary School
*SWIN* M27 ... 70 C1
Cloughside School
*PWCH* M25 ... 55 J7
Cloverlea Primary School *HALE/TIMP* WA15 ... 108 E7
The Club Theatre
*ALT* WA14 ... 116 F1
Cobden Mill Industrial Estate *FWTH* BL4 ... 52 E3
Coldhurst Community Centre *OLD* OL1 ... 9 G3
Coldhurst Industrial Estate *OLD* OL1 ... 9 H3
Coliseum Theatre
*OLD* OL1 ... 9 L5
College Street Health Centre *LEIGH* WN7 ... 66 D7
Collegiate Medical Centre
*CHH* M8 ... 72 D5
Collier Brook Industrial Estate *ATH* M46 ... 66 F1
Comfort Inn
*WGTN/LGST* M12 ... 88 D6
Commonwealth House
*MANAIR* M90 ... 118 D4
Community Hall
*STLY* SK15 ... 91 K2
Comtech Business Park
*WHTN* BL5 ... 50 B1
Concord Business Park
*WYTH/NTH* M22 ... 119 G3
Constellation Trading Estate *RAD* M26 ... 38 C6
Co-operative College
*ANC* M4 ... 7 G2
Co-operative Museum
*WHIT* OL12 ... 10 D3
Copley High School
*STLY* SK15 ... 92 A2
Copper Beeches School
*SALE* M33 ... 96 C8
Coppice Industrial Estate *OLDS* OL8 ... 8 E8
Coppice J & I School
*OLDS* OL8 ... 59 H8
Copthorne Hotel
*SALQ* M50 ... 86 D6
Cornbrook Estate
*HULME* M15 ... 6 A8
Cornerhouse Cinema
*CMANE* M1 ... 7 G5
Cornishway Industrial Estate *WYTH/NTH* M22 ... 118 F4
Cornwall Street Industrial Estate *OP/CLY* M11 ... 89 G5
Corpus Christi RC Primary School *OLDE* OL4 ... 58 E8
Corpus Christi with St Anne RC Primary School *ANC* M4 ... 88 A1
Corrie Primary School
*DTN/ASHW* M34 ... 101 J3
Counthill School
*OLDE* OL4 ... 60 A2
County End Business Centre *OLDE* OL4 ... 60 C5
Covenant Christian School *HTNM* SK4 ... 99 M8
Crab Lane Primary School
*BKLY* M9 ... 56 E8
Cravenwood Primary School *CHH* M8 ... 72 C4
Crescent Community High School for Girls *RUSH/FAL* M14 ... 99 G1
The Cricketer Sports Club *WGNS/IIMK* WN3 ... 14 D8
Cricket Street Business Centre *WGNW/ST* WN6 ... 14 C4
Croft Industrial Estate
*BURY* BL9 ... 39 K7
Cromer Industrial Estate
*MDTN* M24 ... 57 L3
Cromford Business Park
*OLD* OL1 ... 59 L4
Crompton CC
*ROY/SHW* OL2 ... 43 L4
Crompton Fold Primary School *BOLE* BL2 ... 37 H5
Crompton Health Centre
*ROY/SHW* OL2 ... 43 L6
Crompton House CE School *ROY/SHW* OL2 ... 43 J5
Crompton Place Shopping Centre *BOL* BL1 ... 2 E5
Crompton Primary School
*ROY/SHW* OL2 ... 43 M6
Crompton & Royton Golf Club *ROY/SHW* OL2 ... 43 J7
Crompton Swimming Pool *ROY/SHW* OL2 ... 43 L6
Cromwell High School
*DUK* SK16 ... 91 H6
Cromwell House Community Mental Health Centre *ECC* M30 ... 85 G2
Cromwell Special School *RDSH* SK5 ... 100 C2
Cronshaw Industrial Estate *ROCH* OL11 ... 11 G7
Crosland Industrial Estate *MPL/ROM* SK6 ... 101 H8

Crossacres Primary School *WYTH/NTH* M22 ... 110 C8
Crossgates Primary School *MILN* OL16 ... 29 K5
Crosslee Primary School
*BKLY* M9 ... 57 K8
Crowcroft Park Primary School *WGTN/LGST* M12 ... 99 K1
Crown Business Centre
*FAIL* M35 ... 74 C4
Crown Industrial Estate
*ALT* WA14 ... 108 B5
*ANC* M4 ... 7 L2
Crown Royal Industrial Park *STKP* SK1 ... 13 K6
Crumpsall Lane Primary School *CHH* M8 ... 72 D3
Cuba Industrial Estate
*RAMS* BL0 ... 18 F4
Culcheth Hall School
*ALT* WA14 ... 116 E1
Curzon Ashton FC
*AULW* OL7 ... 90 C2
Curzon Cinema
*URM* M41 ... 95 L1
Cutgate Shopping Precinct *OLDE* OL4 ... 27 L3
Dagenham Road Industrial Estate *RUSH/FAL* M14 ... 98 F1
Daisy Nook Country Park
*OLDS* OL8 ... 75 H5
Dale Grove Primary School (Bankside) *HYDE* SK14 ... 102 C3
Dale Grove Special School *AULW* OL7 ... 75 K7
The Dale Primary School
*MPL/ROM* SK6 ... 114 A5
Dale Street Industrial Estate *RAD* M26 ... 54 D2
Dancehouse Theatre & Northern Ballet School *CMANE* M1 ... 7 G8
Dane Bank Primary School
*RDSH* SK5 ... 100 D2
Dane Road Industrial Estate *SALE* M33 ... 96 F7
Darnhill CP School
*HEY* OL10 ... 40 C3
Darul Uloom Al Arabiya Al Islamia *TOT/BURYW* BL8 ... 18 D8
Davaar Medical Centre
*DUK* SK16 ... 90 F4
Davenport Golf Club
*POY/DIS* SK12 ... 122 D8
David Cuthbert Business Centre *OP/CLY* M11 ... 88 F5
David Lloyd Fitness Centre *BOL* BL1 ... 2 A3
David Medical Centre
*CCHDY* M21 ... 97 M6
Davyhulme J & I School
*URM* M41 ... 96 A1
Davyhulme Park Golf Club *URM* M41 ... 84 C8
Deakins Business Park
*EDGW/EG* BL7 ... 22 A2
Deane Golf Club
*BOLS/LL* BL3 ... 35 K7
Deane Leisure Centre
*BOLS/LL* BL3 ... 35 J8
Deanery CE High School
*WGN* WN1 ... 14 E3
Dean Lane Medical Centre *BRAM/HZG* SK7 ... 121 M4
Dean Row Community Junior School *WILM/AE* SK9 ... 127 J3
The Deans CP School
*SWIN* M27 ... 70 B4
Deans Road Industrial Estate *SWIN* M27 ... 70 A4
Deanway Trading Estate
*WILM/AE* SK9 ... 127 H1
Deeplish Primary School
*ROCH* OL11 ... 10 F8
Delamere School
*URM* M41 ... 95 G2
Delph Clinic
*UPML* OL3 ... 45 H8
Delph & Dobcross CC
*UPML* OL3 ... 45 J8
Delph Primary School
*UPML* OL3 ... 45 H7
Delta Business Park
*DTN/ASHW* M34 ... 90 B5
Denton Cemetery
*DTN/ASHW* M34 ... 101 J4
Denton Cricket & Sports Club *DTN/ASHW* M34 ... 90 B7
Denton Golf Club
*DTN/ASHW* M34 ... 89 L8
Denton St Lawrence CC
*DTN/ASHW* M34 ... 101 J2
Denton West End Primary School *DTN/ASHW* M34 ... 100 D1
Department of Clinical Psychology *ROY/SHW* OL2 ... 59 H2
Derby High School
*BURY* BL9 ... 4 C9
Derby Shopping Centre
*BOLS/LL* BL3 ... 2 A8
Derwent Street Trading Estate *ORD* M5 ... 86 F5
The Designer Outlet
*SALQ* M50 ... 86 C5
De Vere Mottram Hall Golf Club *MCFLDN* SK10 ... 128 A8
De Vere Mottram Hall Hotel *MCFLDN* SK10 ... 128 B8
De Vere Whites Hotel
*HOR/BR* BL6 ... 34 A5
Devonshire Road Primary School *BOL* BL1 ... 35 K4
Devonshire Street Industrial Estate *WGTN/LGST* M12 ... 88 A6
Dial Park Primary School
*OFTN* SK2 ... 113 H6
Diamond Lodge
*GTN* M18 ... 88 E7
Didsbury CC
*DID/WITH* M20 ... 110 F3
Didsbury CE Primary School *DID/WITH* M20 ... 110 E1
Didsbury Golf Club
*WYTH/NTH* M22 ... 110 C3
Didsbury Medical Centre
*DID/WITH* M20 ... 98 D8
Didsbury Road Primary School *HTNM* SK4 ... 111 J2
Didsbury School
*DID/WITH* M20 ... 98 E8

Diggle School
*UPML* OL3 ... 45 M7
Dinting CE Primary School *GLSP* SK13 ... 104 D3
Dinting Lane Industrial Estate *GLSP* SK13 ... 104 D3
Dinting Lodge Industrial Estate *GLSP* SK13 ... 104 C1
Dinting Vale Business Park *GLSP* SK13 ... 104 B2
Disley Golf Club
*POY/DIS* SK12 ... 123 L5
Disley Primary School
*POY/DIS* SK12 ... 123 M6
Dobson Park Industrial Estate *WGNE/HIN* WN2 ... 48 D6
Dodd Lane Industrial Estate *WHTN* BL5 ... 33 L8
Doffcocker Lodge Nature Reserve *BOL* BL1 ... 35 H3
Douglas Valley Business Park *WGN* WN1 ... 31 M7
Downing Street Industrial Estate *WGTN/LGST* M12 ... 7 K8
Dowry Park Industrial Estate *OLDE* OL4 ... 60 B5
Dowson Primary School
*HYDE* SK14 ... 102 B4
Droylsden AFC
*DROY* M43 ... 89 K3
Droylsden High School for Girls *DROY* M43 ... 89 H4
Droylsden Sports Centre
*DROY* M43 ... 89 H2
Droylsden Swimming Pool *DROY* M43 ... 89 K4
Ducie Athletics Ground Running Track *WGTN/LGST* M12 ... 88 E8
Ducie High School
*RUSH/FAL* M14 ... 87 K3
Ducie Sports Centre
*HULME* M15 ... 87 L8
Duke of Norfolk CE Primary School *GLSP* SK13 ... 105 G3
Dukesgate Primary School *LHULT* M38 ... 52 D7
Dukinfield Crematorium
*DUK* SK16 ... 91 G3
Dukinfield Golf Club
*DUK* SK16 ... 91 K5
Dukinfield Joint Cemetery *DUK* SK16 ... 91 G3
Dunham Forest Golf & Country Club *ALT* WA14 ... 107 J8
Dunscar Golf Club
*EDGW/EG* BL7 ... 22 A4
Dunscar Industrial Estate *EDGW/EG* BL7 ... 22 B5
Dunstan Medical Centre
*BOLE* BL2 ... 3 L4
Durnford Medical Centre
*MDTN* M24 ... 57 J3
Eagley Infant School
*EDGW/EG* BL7 ... 22 C4
Eagley Junior School
*EDGW/EG* BL7 ... 22 E4
East Crompton St Georges CE Primary School *ROY/SHW* OL2 ... 43 M5
East Crompton St James CE Primary School *ROY/SHW* OL2 ... 43 L5
East Lancashire Railway
*BURY* BL9 ... 5 J7
*BURY* BL9 ... 25 G4
*BURY* BL9 ... 40 B4
*RAMS* BL0 ... 18 F7
East Ward Primary School
*BURY* BL9 ... 5 L4
Eaton Place Business Centre *SALE* M33 ... 96 D8
Eccles Crematorium
*ECC* M30 ... 84 C4
Eccles Health Centre
*ECC* M30 ... 85 J2
Eccles Recreation Centre *ECC* M30 ... 85 J3
Eccles Town Hall
*ECC* M30 ... 85 H3
Edenfield CC
*RAMS* BL0 ... 19 H1
Edge Fold Industrial Estate *FWTH* BL4 ... 51 M3
Edgworth CC
*EDGW/EG* BL7 ... 17 H6
Egerton CC
*EDGW/EG* BL7 ... 22 A1
Egerton & Dunscar Health Centre *EDGW/EG* BL7 ... 22 C4
Egerton High School
*URM* M41 ... 85 H8
Egerton House Hotel
*EDGW/EG* BL7 ... 22 B2
Egerton Park Arts College *DTN/ASHW* M34 ... 90 B7
Egerton Park Community High School *DTN/ASHW* M34 ... 90 A8
Egerton Primary School
*EDGW/EG* BL7 ... 22 A1
Elk Mill Central Retail Park *OLD* OL1 ... 58 E1
Ellenbrook Primary School *WALK* M28 ... 68 E5
Ellesmere Bowling & Tennis Club *WALK* M28 ... 69 G3
Ellesmere Golf Club
*WALK* M28 ... 68 F1
Ellesmere Retail Park
*WALK* M28 ... 68 F1
Ellesmere Shopping Centre *LHULT* M38 ... 68 F1
Elmridge Primary School *HALE/TIMP* WA15 ... 117 L4
Elms Bank Community High School *WHTF* M45 ... 55 J1
Elms Medical Centre
*WHTF* M45 ... 55 H3
Elm Wood Primary School *MDTN* M24 ... 57 M4
Elsinore Business Centre *OLDTF/WHR* M16 ... 86 D8
The Elton High School
*TOT/BURYW* BL8 ... 38 D1
Elton Primary School
*TOT/BURYW* BL8 ... 38 F1
Emmanuel Christian School *WHIT* OL12 ... 28 B3
Emmanuel Holcombe Primary School *TOT/BURYW* BL8 ... 18 D6

Empress Business Centre *OLDTF/WHR* M16 ... 86 F6
Empress Industrial Estate *WGNE/HIN* WN2 ... 15 M5
English Martyrs RC Primary School *URM* M41 ... 95 M2
Ensor Trading Estate
*NM/HAY* SK22 ... 124 F6
Enterprise Trading Estate *GTN* M18 ... 89 H6
*TRPK* M17 ... 85 K4
Esplanade Arts & Heritage Centre *ROCH* OL11 ... 10 D5
Estcourt Preparatory School *OLDS* OL8 ... 59 G8
Etchells Primary School
*CHD/CHDH* SK8 ... 119 L3
Etherow Country Park *MPL/ROM* SK6 ... 115 G1
Etherow Industrial Estate *HYDE* SK14 ... 93 G8
Eton Hill Industrial Estate *RAD* M26 ... 38 F7
Etrop Grange Hotel
*MANAIR* M90 ... 118 D3
Etz Chaim School
*CHH* M8 ... 72 B2
Europa Business Park
*EDGY/DAV* SK3 ... 111 L6
Europa Trading Estate
*RAD* M26 ... 53 L5
Ewing School
*DID/WITH* M20 ... 98 D7
Express by Holiday Inn
*SALQ* M50 ... 86 C5
Express Trading Estate
*FWTH* BL4 ... 53 G6
The Eye Clinic
*CMANW* M2 ... 6 F5
Fahay Industrial Estate
*NEWH/MOS* M40 ... 88 B2
Failsworth Health Centre *FAIL* M35 ... 74 B5
Failsworth Industrial Estate *FAIL* M35 ... 73 M6
Failsworth Shopping Centre *FAIL* M35 ... 74 C4
Fairfield Community Primary School *BURY* BL9 ... 40 A1
Fairfield General Hospital *BURY* BL9 ... 26 B8
Fairfield Golf & Sailing Club *DTN/ASHW* M34 ... 89 L5
Fairfield High School for Girls *DROY* M43 ... 89 J4
Fairfield Road Primary School *DROY* M43 ... 89 J4
Fairhill Industrial Estate *IRL* M44 ... 94 C5
Fairview Medical Centre
*URM* M41 ... 95 L2
Fairway Primary School
*OFTN* SK2 ... 113 H5
Fairways Lodge
*PWCH* M25 ... 71 L3
Falcon Business Centre
*CHAD* OL9 ... 8 C2
Falinge Park High School *WHIT* OL12 ... 10 B1
Fall Birch Hospital Lodge *HOR/BR* BL6 ... 34 D3
Fallowfield Medical Centre *RUSH/FAL* M14 ... 99 G4
Fallowfield Shopping Centre *RUSH/FAL* M14 ... 99 H3
Farjo Medical Centre
*CMANE* M1 ... 7 H5
Farnworth Cemetery
*FWTH* BL4 ... 53 H4
Farnworth Leisure Centre *FWTH* BL4 ... 53 G4
Farnworth Little Theatre *FWTH* BL4 ... 53 G4
Farnworth Park Industrial Estate *FWTH* BL4 ... 53 G3
Farnworth Social Circle CC *FWTH* BL4 ... 52 F5
Farrowdale House School *ROY/SHW* OL2 ... 43 L6
Fiddlers Lane Primary School *IRL* M44 ... 94 E1
Fieldhouse CC
*ROCH* OL11 ... 27 H6
Fieldhouse Industrial Estate *WHIT* OL12 ... 28 C2
Firbank Primary School
*ROY/SHW* OL2 ... 43 G5
Firgrove Business Park
*MILN* OL16 ... 29 G4
Firs CP School
*SALE* M33 ... 96 A8
Firsdale Industrial Estate *LEIGH* WN7 ... 65 M6
Fir Tree Primary School
*RDSH* SK5 ... 100 B2
Firwood Industrial Estate *BOLE* BL2 ... 36 F2
Firwood Manor Preparatory School *CHAD* OL9 ... 8 A1
Firwood Special School
*BOLE* BL2 ... 36 F2
Fishbrook Industrial Estate *FWTH* BL4 ... 53 J5
Fishwicks Industrial Estate *RNFD/HAY* WA11 ... 78 C4
Fitton Hill Shopping Precinct *OLDS* OL8 ... 75 J1
Five Fold Industrial Park *CHAD* OL9 ... 8 F6
Flixton CC
*URM* M41 ... 95 H1
Flixton FC
*URM* M41 ... 95 G1
Flixton Girls High School *URM* M41 ... 95 K2
Flixton Golf Club
*URM* M41 ... 95 K4
Flixton Health Clinic
*URM* M41 ... 95 G2
Flixton J & I School
*URM* M41 ... 95 J2
Flowery Field Primary School *HYDE* SK14 ... 91 G8
Forest Gate Community Primary School *PART* M31 ... 106 A1
Forest Park School
*SALE* M33 ... 96 D8
Forest School
*HALE/TIMP* WA15 ... 108 L3
Forge Industrial Estate
*OLDE* OL4 ... 59 L5

Forum Leisure Centre
WYTH/NTH M22 .......... 118 E1
Fourways Trading Estate
TRPK M17 .......... 85 K6
Fowler Industrial Estate
HOR/BR BL6 .......... 33 M2
Foyer & Coops Business Centre
WGN WN1 .......... 14 E4
Fred Longworth High School
TYLD M29 .......... 67 H3
Freehold Community Primary
School CHAD OL9 .......... 8 C8
Freetown Business Park
BURY BL9 .......... 5 H1
The Friars Primary School
CSLFD M3 .......... 6 B1
Friezland Primary School
OLDE OL4 .......... 61 H1
Fulshaw CE Primary School
WILM/AE SK9 .......... 126 D6
Furness Vale Business centre
CHF/WBR SK23 .......... 124 F8
Furrow Community School
MDTN M24 .......... 56 F1
Galleon Leisure Centre
DID/WITH M20 .......... 110 F4
The Galleries Shopping Centre
WGN WN1 .......... 14 E4
Gallery of Costume
RUSH/FAL M14 .......... 98 C3
Gallery Oldham, Library
& Lifelong Learning Centre
OLD OL1 .......... 9 K6
Gamesley Community Primary
School GLSP SK13 .......... 104 B2
Garrett Hall Primary School
TYLD M29 .......... 68 A5
Garrick Playhouse
ALT WA14 .......... 108 A6
Garrick Theatre
EDGY/DAV SK3 .......... 13 H5
Garswood Primary School
AIMK WN4 .......... 62 E7
Garswood United FC
AIMK WN4 .......... 62 E7
Gaskell Primary School
BOL BL1 .......... 2 E1
The Gates Primary School
WHTN BL5 .......... 50 C4
The Gates Shopping Centre
BOL BL1 .......... 2 E4
Gateway Industrial Estate
CMANE M1 .......... 7 K5
Gathurst Golf Club
WGNNW/ST WN6 .......... 30 C7
Gatley Golf Club
CHD/CHDH SK8 .......... 119 K1
Gatley Health Centre
CHD/CHDH SK8 .......... 110 D6
Gatley Primary School
CHD/CHDH SK8 .......... 110 D7
Gee Cross Holy Trinity CE
Primary School
HYDE SK14 .......... 102 C4
Gee Cross Social & Sports Club
HYDE SK14 .......... 102 B4
Gelder Wood Country Park
ROCH OL11 .......... 26 B2
George H Carnall Leisure Centre
URM M41 .......... 85 H4
George Tomlinson School
FWTH BL4 .......... 53 H6
Georgian Health Centre
OLD OL1 .......... 9 K5
Gidlow Cemetery
WGNNW/ST WN6 .......... 31 K7
Gilded Hollins Primary School
LEIGH WN7 .......... 80 F3
Gilnow Mill Industrial Estate
BOL BL1 .......... 35 M6
Gilnow Primary School
BOL BL1 .......... 35 M6
Glazebury CE Primary School
GOL/RIS/CUL WA3 .......... 81 M1
Glebe House School
MILN OL16 .......... 10 D6
Glen Trading Estate
OLDE OL4 .......... 60 A6
Globe Industrial Estate
RAD M26 .......... 54 E1
Globe Lane Industrial Estate
DUK SK16 .......... 90 E6
Globe Lane Primary School
DUK SK16 .......... 90 E6
Glodwick Health Centre
OLDE OL4 .......... 59 L6
Glodwick Infant School
OLDE OL4 .......... 59 L7
Glossopdale Community College
GLSP SK13 .......... 93 J8
GLSP SK13 .......... 104 F2
Glossop & District Golf Club
GLSP SK13 .......... 105 K4
Glossop RUFC
GLSP SK13 .......... 104 B5
Glossop Victorian
Swimming Pool
GLSP SK13 .......... 104 F2
Gloucester House Medical
Centre
URM M41 .......... 96 A2
GMB National College
OLDTF/WHR M16 .......... 97 M2
Godfrey Ermen Memorial CE
Primary School
ECC M30 .......... 84 F4
Godley CP School
HYDE SK14 .......... 102 C1
Golborne Clinic
GOL/RIS/CUL WA3 .......... 79 L3
Golborne CP School
GOL/RIS/CUL WA3 .......... 79 K4
Golborne High School
GOL/RIS/CUL WA3 .......... 79 M3
Golden Tulip Hotel
TRPK M17 .......... 86 C6
Gorrells Industrial Estate
ROCH OL11 .......... 42 D4
Gorsefield Primary School
RAD M26 .......... 38 D8
Gorse Hall Primary School
STLY SK15 .......... 91 J3
Gorse Hill Health Centre
STRET M32 .......... 97 H1
Gorse Hill Infant School
STRET M32 .......... 86 H2
Gorsey Bank Primary School
WILM/AE SK9 .......... 126 D6
Gorton Brook First School
WGTN/LGST M12 .......... 88 D4
Gorton Industrial Estate
GTN M18 .......... 88 F6

Gorton Medical Centre
GTN M18 .......... 89 G7
Gorton Mount Primary School
GTN M18 .......... 99 L1
Gorton Retail Market
GTN M18 .......... 89 G7
Goshen Sports Centre
BURY BL9 .......... 39 K6
Goyt Valley Industrial Estate
CHF/WBR SK23 .......... 124 F8
Grafton House Preparatory
School OL6 .......... 90 E2
Granada Studios
CSLFD M3 .......... 6 C5
Grand Arcade Shopping Centre
WGN WN1 .......... 15 G3
Grange Primary School
WILM/AE SK9 .......... 119 L8
Grange School
CHAD OL9 .......... 8 C4
RUSH/FAL M14 .......... 99 G1
Grange Valley Primary School
RNFD/HAY WA11 .......... 78 A7
Grasmere Street Health Centre
LEIGH WN7 .......... 66 B6
Grasscroft Independent School
OLDE OL4 .......... 60 F7
Greater Manchester
Police Headquarters
OLDTF/WHR M16 .......... 86 D7
Great Lever & Farnworth
Golf Club FWTH BL4 .......... 52 A3
Great Moor Clinic
OFTN SK2 .......... 112 F7
Great Moor Infant School
OFTN SK2 .......... 112 E7
Great Northern Shopping &
Leisure Centre
CSLFD M3 .......... 6 E6
Greave Primary School
MPL/ROM SK6 .......... 101 M8
Greenacres Primary School
OLDE OL4 .......... 59 M5
Greenbank Industrial Estate
WGNE/HIN WN2 .......... 65 K1
Greenbank School
CHD/CHDH SK8 .......... 120 B3
Greenbrow Infant School
NTHM/RTH M23 .......... 118 B1
Greencourts Business Park
WYTH/NTH M22 .......... 119 J5
Green Eind Junior School
BNG/LEV M19 .......... 99 H7
Greenfield CC
UPML OL3 .......... 61 L7
Greenfield Primary School
HYDE SK14 .......... 102 B3
UPML OL3 .......... 61 L6
Green Fold Special School
FWTH BL4 .......... 52 C4
Greengate Industrial Estate
MDTN M24 .......... 57 M7
Green Hall Primary School
ATH M46 .......... 51 J8
Greenheys Business Centre
HULME M15 .......... 87 K7
Greenhill Primary School
OLDE OL4 .......... 9 K8
TOT/BURYW BL8 .......... 38 C3
Green Lane Industrial Estate
HTNM SK4 .......... 12 D3
Greenmount CC
TOT/BURYW BL8 .......... 24 C3
Greenmount Primary School
TOT/BURYW BL8 .......... 24 B2
Green Room Theatre
CMANE M1 .......... 6 F7
Greenside Primary School
DROY M43 .......... 89 J2
Greenside Trading Centre
DROY M43 .......... 89 K3
Greenwood Business Centre
ORD M5 .......... 86 D3
Greenwood Primary School
ECC M30 .......... 70 B8
Greswell Primary School
DTN/ASHW M34 .......... 101 H2
Greyhound & Speedway Stadium
GTN M18 .......... 88 E7
Greyland Medical Centre
PWCH M25 .......... 55 L6
Griffin Business Centre
SLFD M6 .......... 71 M7
Grosvenor Business Park
MPL/ROM SK6 .......... 101 J6
Grosvenor Industrial Estate
AULW OL7 .......... 90 D3
Grosvenor Road Primary School
SWIN M27 .......... 70 E6
Guardian Angels RC
Primary School
TOT/BURYW BL8 .......... 38 E1
Guide Bridge Industrial Estate
AULW OL7 .......... 90 B4
Guide Bridge Theatre
DTN/ASHW M34 .......... 90 B4
Guide Bridge Trading Estate
DTN/ASHW M34 .......... 90 B4
Guinness Road Trading Estate
TRPK M17 .......... 85 J4
Hadfield Clinic
GLSP SK13 .......... 93 K7
Hadfield Industrial Estate
GLSP SK13 .......... 93 J6
Hadfield Infant School
GLSP SK13 .......... 93 J8
Hadfield St Charles RC
Primary School
GLSP SK13 .......... 93 H7
Hague Bar Primary School
NM/HAY SK22 .......... 124 A4
Haigh Hall Country Park
WGNE/HIN WN2 .......... 32 C6
Haigh Hall Golf Complex
WGNE/HIN WN2 .......... 32 C6
Hale Barns CC
HALE/TIMP WA15 .......... 118 A4
Hale Golf Club
HALE/TIMP WA15 .......... 117 J5
Hale Preparatory School
HALE/TIMP WA15 .......... 117 G1
Halfpenny Bridge Industrial
Estate
MILN OL16 .......... 11 G6
Hallgate Bus Station
WGN WN1 .......... 14 F3
Hall i' th' Wood Museum
BOL BL1 .......... 22 D8
Halliwell Industrial Estate
BOL BL1 .......... 36 A1
Hamer CP School
MILN OL16 .......... 28 E2

Hampson Street Trading Estate
ORD M5 .......... 6 A5
Handforth Dean
Shopping Centre
WILM/AE SK9 .......... 120 A8
Handforth Health Centre
WILM/AE SK9 .......... 127 H1
Hanover Business Park
ALT WA14 .......... 107 L5
Harcourt Industrial Centre
WALK M28 .......... 53 G7
Hardman Fold Special School
FAIL M35 .......... 74 A5
Hardy Mill Primary School
BOLE BL2 .......... 23 J8
Hare Hill (NT)
MCFLDN SK10 .......... 131 K6
Harper Green School
FWTH BL4 .......... 52 E3
Harp Industrial Estate
ROCH OL11 .......... 42 A2
Harp Trading Estate
TRPK M17 .......... 85 K4
Harpurhey Business Centre
BKLY M9 .......... 73 G3
Harpurhey Health Centre
BKLY M9 .......... 73 G4
Harpur Mount Primary School
BKLY M9 .......... 73 G4
Harrop Fold School
WALK M28 .......... 68 E1
Harrytown Catholic High School
MPL/ROM SK6 .......... 113 K2
Hart Common Golf Club
WHTN BL5 .......... 49 L5
Hartford Industrial Estate
CHAD OL9 .......... 8 D7
Hartshead High School
AUL OL6 .......... 76 B5
Harwood Golf Club (Bolton)
BOLE BL2 .......... 23 K8
Harwood Health Centre
BOLE BL2 .......... 23 G7
Harwood Meadows Primary
School BOLE BL2 .......... 37 J1
Harwood Park Primary School
HEY OL10 .......... 41 G3
Haslam Park Primary School
BOLS/LL BL3 .......... 35 L7
Haslemere Industrial Estate
AIMK WN4 .......... 63 K4
Hathershaw Technology College
OLDS OL8 .......... 75 J2
Hattersley Health Clinic
HYDE SK14 .......... 103 H2
Hattersley Industrial Estate
HYDE SK14 .......... 103 H3
Haveley Hey Primary School
WYTH/NTH M22 .......... 109 M8
Hawkins Clinic
MILN OL16 .......... 10 F5
Hawkley Brook Trading Estate
WGNS/IIMK WN3 .......... 63 H2
Hawkley Hall High School
WGNS/IIMK WN3 .......... 63 L1
Hawksley Industrial Estate
DTN/ASHW M34 .......... 74 F1
Hawthorns Special School
DTN/ASHW M34 .......... 90 A7
Haydock CC
RNFD/HAY WA11 .......... 78 A5
Haydock English Martyrs Catholic
Primary School
RNFD/HAY WA11 .......... 78 A5
Haydock Lane Industrial Estate
RNFD/HAY WA11 .......... 78 B4
Haydock Medical Centre
RNFD/HAY WA11 .......... 78 A6
Haydock Park Golf Club
NEWLW WA12 .......... 79 J7
Haydock Park Racecourse
AIMK WN4 .......... 78 F3
Hayfield Primary School
WALK M28 .......... 125 L1
Hayward School
BOLS/LL BL3 .......... 51 M2
Hayward Sports Centre
BOLS/LL BL3 .......... 51 M2
Hazeldene Medical Centre
NEWH/MOS M40 .......... 74 B3
Hazel Grove Clinic
BRAM/HZG SK7 .......... 122 A1
Hazel Grove Golf Club
BRAM/HZG SK7 .......... 122 D3
Hazel Grove High School
BRAM/HZG SK7 .......... 121 L3
Hazel Grove Pools
& Fitness Centre
BRAM/HZG SK7 .......... 121 J3
Hazel Grove Primary School
BRAM/HZG SK7 .......... 122 A1
Hazel Grove Recreation Centre
BRAM/HZG SK7 .......... 121 L4
Hazlehurst Community
Primary School
RAMS BL0 .......... 18 D8
Heald Green Medical Centre
CHD/CHDH SK8 .......... 119 K4
Heald Place Primary School
RUSH/FAL M14 .......... 98 E1
Healey Primary School
WHIT OL12 .......... 28 B1
The Health Centre
ALT WA14 .......... 108 A7
Heap Bridge Primary School
BURY BL9 .......... 40 A3
Heathfield Primary School
BOLS/LL BL3 .......... 51 K2
Heaton CC
BOL BL1 .......... 35 K2
Heaton Cemetery
BOL BL1 .......... 35 L6
Heaton Medical Centre
BOL BL1 .......... 35 J3
Heaton Moor Golf Club
HTNM SK4 .......... 99 K7
Heaton Moor Medical Centre
HTNM SK4 .......... 99 L7
Heaton Moor Rugby Union FC
HTNM SK4 .......... 12 B1
Heaton Norris Health Centre
HTNM SK4 .......... 12 F1
Heaton Park
PWCH M25 .......... 56 B7
Heaton Park Golf Centre
PWCH M25 .......... 56 B6
Heaton Park Primary School
WHTF M45 .......... 55 L6
Heaton Special School
HTNM SK4 .......... 99 L7
Helen O'Grady Drama Academy
ALT WA14 .......... 107 M8

Hempshaw Business Centre
STKP SK1 .......... 112 E5
Henshaw Society for the Blind
OLDTF/WHR M16 .......... 86 D8
Hertford Industrial Estate
AULW OL7 .......... 90 D3
Hesketh Fletcher CE High School
ATH M46 .......... 66 F2
Hewitt Business Park
WGNW/BIL/OR WN5 .......... 46 B3
Heybrook Primary School
WHIT OL12 .......... 11 H1
Heyes Lane Infant School
HALE/TIMP WA15 .......... 108 E4
The Heys Primary School
AUL OL6 .......... 91 G1
Hey-with-Zion Primary School
OLDE OL4 .......... 60 D5
Heywood Cemetery
HEY OL10 .......... 27 J8
Heywood Community High
School BURY BL9 .......... 40 B3
Heywood Industrial Park
HEY OL10 .......... 40 D1
Heywood Sports Complex
HEY OL10 .......... 40 E1
Higginshaw Sports Club
OLD OL1 .......... 9 J1
Highbank Trading Estate
OP/CLY M11 .......... 89 G5
Highbarn Junior School
ROY/SHW OL2 .......... 43 H7
High Birch Special School
ROCH OL11 .......... 27 L7
Higher Broughton Health Centre
BRO M7 .......... 72 B6
Higher Failsworth
Primary School
FAIL M35 .......... 74 D4
Higher Folds Primary School
LEIGH WN7 .......... 67 G5
Higher Lane Primary School
WHTF M45 .......... 55 H4
Higher Openshaw Community
School OP/CLY M11 .......... 89 G4
Highfield Cemetery
MPL/ROM SK6 .......... 113 J7
Highfield CC
WGNS/IIMK WN3 .......... 46 F8
Highfield Hospital
ROCH OL11 .......... 10 B8
Highfield Primary School
FWTH BL4 .......... 52 D4
URM M41 .......... 96 C2
Highfield St Matthews
CE Primary School
WGNS/IIMK WN3 .......... 46 F8
High Lane Medical Centre
MPL/ROM SK6 .......... 123 G5
High Lane Primary School
MPL/ROM SK6 .......... 123 G4
High Lawn Primary School
BOL BL1 .......... 22 B6
Highlea Secondary School
WALK M28 .......... 68 C4
Hillcrest Grammar School
EDGY/DAV SK3 .......... 112 C6
Hillgate Business Centre
STKP SK1 .......... 13 K7
Hill Top Community Primary
School ROCH OL11 .......... 42 D8
Hill Top Community Special
School OLDE OL4 .......... 44 D8
Hilton Lane Primary School
WALK M28 .......... 68 D1
Hindley All Saints CE Primary
School WGNE/HIN WN2 .......... 49 H7
Hindley Business Centre
WGNE/HIN WN2 .......... 49 G7
Hindley Green Primary School
WGNE/HIN WN2 .......... 65 L2
Hindley Hall Golf Club
WGNE/HIN WN2 .......... 49 G4
Hindley High School - Arts
College WGNE/HIN WN2 .......... 49 J7
Hindley Leisure Centre
WGNE/HIN WN2 .......... 49 J7
Hindley Primary School
WGNE/HIN WN2 .......... 49 G7
Hindsford CE Primary School
ATH M46 .......... 67 H3
HM Prison
CHH M8 .......... 72 C8
WGNE/HIN WN2 .......... 65 H2
Hodge Clough Infant School
OLD OL1 .......... 60 A1
Hodge Clough Junior School
OLD OL1 .......... 60 A1
Holcombe Brook Primary School
RAMS BL0 .......... 24 D2
Holcombe Brook Sports Club
RAMS BL0 .......... 24 D1
Holden Clough Primary School
AUL OL6 .......... 76 A5
Holden Road Trading Estate
LEIGH WN7 .......... 66 D7
Holiday Inn
BOL BL1 .......... 2 E5
NEWH/MOS M40 .......... 73 J4
Hollingworth High School
MILN OL16 .......... 29 K6
Hollingworth Lake Activity
Centre LIT OL15 .......... 29 K2
Hollingworth Lake Country Park
LIT OL15 .......... 29 M2
Hollingworth Primary School
HYDE SK14 .......... 92 F7
Hollin Primary School
MDTN M24 .......... 57 K1
Hollins Grundy Primary School
BURY BL9 .......... 39 K7
Hollins Industrial Park
GLSP SK13 .......... 93 L7
Hollinwood Business Centre
FAIL M35 .......... 74 E4
Hollinwood Cemetery
OLDS OL8 .......... 74 F3
Hollinwood CC
OLDS OL8 .......... 74 F4
Holly Bank Industrial Estate
HALE/TIMP WA15 .......... 54 C1
Holly Mount RC Primary School
TOT/BURYW BL8 .......... 24 A3
Hollywood Bowl
HOR/BR BL6 .......... 34 A4
NEWH/MOS M40 .......... 74 A3
Holt Town Industrial Estate
NEWH/MOS M40 .......... 88 B2
Holy Cross & All Saints RC
Primary School ECC M30 .......... 85 G4
Holy Cross College
BURY BL9 .......... 4 E8

Holy Family Catholic Primary
School SALE M33 .......... 97 H8
Holy Family RC Primary School
OLDS OL8 .......... 75 G4
WGNE/HIN WN2 .......... 64 D3
Holy Family RC School
WALK M28 .......... 68 B5
Holy Family VA RC Primary
School ROCH OL11 .......... 42 D2
Holy Infant RC Primary School
BOL BL1 .......... 22 B8
Holy Name RC Primary School
HULME M15 .......... 87 K7
Holy Rosary RC Primary School
OLDS OL8 .......... 75 J2
Holy Trinity CE Dobcross
Primary School
UPML OL3 .......... 61 J2
Holy Trinity CE Primary School
AUL OL6 .......... 90 D1
BKLY M9 .......... 73 H4
BURY BL9 .......... 4 F6
Hong Sing Chinese
Medical Centre
BRAM/HZG SK7 .......... 122 A1
Hooley Bridge Industrial Estate
HEY OL10 .......... 26 F8
Hope High School
SLFD M6 .......... 70 F8
Hope Hospital
SLFD M6 .......... 85 L2
Hope Special School
WGNS/IIMK WN3 .......... 63 J2
Hopwood Hall College
MDTN M24 .......... 41 L7
WHIT OL12 .......... 10 D4
Hopwood Medical Centre
HEY OL10 .......... 41 H3
Hopwood Primary School
HEY OL10 .......... 41 H4
Horton Mill Primary School
OLDE OL4 .......... 59 K6
Horwich Business Park
HOR/BR BL6 .......... 33 L2
Horwich Golf Club
HOR/BR BL6 .......... 34 A2
Horwich Leisure Centre
HOR/BR BL6 .......... 33 M1
Hotel Ibis
CMANE M1 .......... 7 G6
CMANE M1 .......... 7 H8
Hotel Rossetti
CMANE M1 .......... 7 J5
Houldsworth Golf Club
RDSH SK5 .......... 100 B4
Houldsworth Medical Centre
RDSH SK5 .......... 100 C5
Howe Bridge Crematorium
ATH M46 .......... 66 C3
Howe Bridge Sports Centre
ATH M46 .......... 66 E3
Hubert House Jewish Boys
School
BRO M7 .......... 72 A4
Hulme Adult Education Centre
HULME M15 .......... 87 H6
Hulme Arch
HULME M15 .......... 87 J6
The Hulme Court Preparatory
School OLDS OL8 .......... 59 G8
The Hulme Grammar School
for Boys
OLDS OL8 .......... 59 G8
Hulme Hall Grammar School
CHD/CHDH SK8 .......... 120 C3
Hulton Hospital
BOLS/LL BL3 .......... 51 K1
Hurstfield Industrial Estate
RDSH SK5 .......... 100 B6
Hursthead Junior School
CHD/CHDH SK8 .......... 120 E6
Hurst Knoll CE Primary School
AUL OL6 .......... 75 M8
Hurst Mills Industrial Estate
GLSP SK13 .......... 105 K3
Hyde Clarendon Sixth Form
College HYDE SK14 .......... 91 G8
Hyde CC
HYDE SK14 .......... 102 C6
Hyde Leisure Pool
HYDE SK14 .......... 102 B2
Hyde Technology School
HYDE SK14 .......... 90 F8
Hyde United FC
HYDE SK14 .......... 102 C2
IKEA Store Manchester
AUL OL6 .......... 90 D1
IMAX Cinema
ANC M4 .......... 7 G3
IMEX Business Park
BRUN/LGST M13 .......... 99 J1
Imperial War Museum North
TRPK M17 .......... 86 B5
Ince CE Primary School
WGNE/HIN WN2 .......... 48 D5
Ince Clinic & Community Centre
WGNE/HIN WN2 .......... 48 D5
Indoor Tennis Centre
OP/CLY M11 .......... 88 C2
Innes Special School
WHIT OL12 .......... 27 M3
Innkeeper's Lodge
GOL/RIS/CUL WA3 .......... 80 B6
HTNM SK4 .......... 99 M7
OLD OL1 .......... 58 E2
WILM/AE SK9 .......... 130 D1
Inscape House School
CHD/CHDH SK8 .......... 119 M1
Inscape House Special School
WALK M28 .......... 69 H3
The Instructor College
STKP SK1 .......... 13 J5
International Convention Centre
CSLFD M3 .......... 6 E6
International Swimming Pool
WGN WN1 .......... 15 G5
Iranian School of Manchester
WGTN/LGST M12 .......... 99 L1
Irlam & Cadishead Community
High School IRL M44 .......... 94 B5
Irlam CP School
IRL M44 .......... 94 B4
Irlam Endowed Primary School
IRL M44 .......... 94 D2
Irlam Industrial Estate
IRL M44 .......... 94 B5
Irlam Swimming Pool
IRL M44 .......... 94 D3
James Brindley Primary School
WALK M28 .......... 68 F3
The Jeff Joseph Sale Moor
Technology College
SALE M33 .......... 109 G2

Jewish Museum
*CHH* M8 .......... 72 D8
Jewish Senior Boys School
*BRO* M7 .......... 72 A5
John Rylands Library
*CSLFD* M3 .......... 6 E5
Johnson Fold Community
Primary School
*BOL* BL1 .......... 35 J1
John Street Medical Centre
*GOL/RIS/CUL* WA3 .......... 79 K4
Joseph Adamson Industrial
Estate *HYDE* SK14 .......... 101 M2
Joseph Rayner Independent
School *AULW* OL7 .......... 75 K5
Jumbles Country Park
*BOLE* BL2 .......... 23 G3
Jurys Inn
*CMANE* M1 .......... 6 E7
Kaskenmoor School
*OLDS* OL8 .......... 74 E3
Kassim Darwish Grammar
School for Boys
*OLDTF/WHR* M16 .......... 98 B3
Kayley Industrial Estate
*AULW* OL7 .......... 90 C1
Kearsley West Primary School
*FWTH* BL4 .......... 53 H5
Kenmore Medical Centre
*WILM/AE* SK9 .......... 126 E6
Kentmere Primary School
*WHIT* OL12 .......... 28 E1
Kenyon Business Park
*BOLS/LL* BL3 .......... 2 D8
Kershaw Business Centre
*BOLS/LL* BL3 .......... 2 B8
Kiely Business Park
*BURY* BL9 .......... 5 H1
Kilhey Court Hotel
*WGN* WN1 .......... 31 M2
King David Junior
& High School
*CHH* M8 .......... 72 C3
Kingfisher Community Special
School *CHAD* OL9 .......... 58 C7
The King of Kings School
*ANC* M4 .......... 7 H1
Kingsdown High School
*WGNW/BIL/OR* WN5 .......... 46 F5
Kingshill School
*TYLD* M29 .......... 67 J4
Kings Road Primary School
*OLDTF/WHR* M16 .......... 97 K1
King Street Remedial Clinic
*DUK* SK16 .......... 90 E3
Kingsway CP School
*CHD/CHDH* SK8 .......... 110 F8
Kingsway Retail Park
*MILN* OL16 .......... 29 G5
Kingsway School
*CHD/CHDH* SK8 .......... 110 F7
Kingsway Secondary School
*CHD/CHDH* SK8 .......... 110 F7
Kingsway West Business Park
*MILN* OL16 .......... 11 K8
Kirkfield Hotel
*NEWLW* WA12 .......... 79 H8
Kirkless Industrial Estate
*WGNE/HIN* WN2 .......... 48 D2
Knoll Street Industrial Park
*BRO* M7 .......... 72 A5
Knowsley Junior School
*OLDE* OL4 .......... 60 D5
Kratos Industrial Estate
*URM* M41 .......... 85 J7
Lacey Green Primary School
*WILM/AE* SK9 .......... 126 E3
Lady Barn House School
*CHD/CHDH* SK8 .......... 119 M1
Ladybarn Primary School
*DID/WITH* M20 .......... 99 G6
Ladybridge High School
*BOLS/LL* BL3 .......... 35 J8
Ladybridge Primary School
*BOLS/LL* BL3 .......... 35 J7
*CHD/CHDH* SK8 .......... 111 L7
Ladybrook Primary School
*BRAM/HZG* SK7 .......... 121 H5
Ladysmith Shopping Centre
*AUL* OL6 .......... 90 E1
Ladywell Hospital Lodge
*SALQ* M50 .......... 85 K2
Ladywood School
*BOLS/LL* BL3 .......... 37 L8
Lamberhead Green Community
Primary School
*WGNW/BIL/OR* WN5 .......... 46 D5
Lamberhead Industrial Estate
*WGNW/BIL/OR* WN5 .......... 46 E7
Lancashire CCC (Old Trafford)
*STRET* M32 .......... 97 J1
Lancasterian School
*DID/WITH* M20 .......... 98 B7
Lance Burn Health Centre
*SLFD* M6 .......... 86 D2
Landgate Industrial Estate
*AIMK* WN4 .......... 63 K4
The Landgate School
*AIMK* WN4 .......... 63 K5
Lane End Primary School
*CHD/CHDH* SK8 .......... 120 E2
Langley Primary School
*MDTN* M24 .......... 57 H1
Langworthy Clinic
*SLFD* M6 .......... 86 C2
Langworthy Road Primary
School *SLFD* M6 .......... 86 C1
La Pergola Hotel
*UPML* OL3 .......... 44 E1
Lark Hill Primary School
*EDGY/DAV* SK3 .......... 12 D6
*SLFD* M6 .......... 86 C2
Last Drop Village Hotel
*EDGW/EG* BL7 .......... 22 D3
The Last Drop Village
*EDGW/EG* BL7 .......... 22 D3
Lavenham Business Centre
*CHAD* OL9 .......... 8 D7
Law Courts
*BOL* BL1 .......... 2 D5
Lawn Cemetery
*ALT* WA14 .......... 107 G4
Lawnhurst Trading Estate
*CHD/CHDH* SK8 .......... 111 J4
Leigh Business Park
*LEIGH* WN7 .......... 81 L1
Leigh CC
*LEIGH* WN7 .......... 81 H2
Leigh CE Infant School
*LEIGH* WN7 .......... 66 C7
Leigh CE Junior School
*LEIGH* WN7 .......... 66 C7

Leigh Central Primary School
*LEIGH* WN7 .......... 66 C7
Leigh Centurions RLFC
*LEIGH* WN7 .......... 66 B6
Leigh County Court
*LEIGH* WN7 .......... 66 C7
Leigh FC
*LEIGH* WN7 .......... 66 B6
Leigh Golf Club
*GOL/RIS/CUL* WA3 .......... 81 G8
Leigh Infant & Primary School
*HYDE* SK14 .......... 102 B2
Leigh Infirmary
*LEIGH* WN7 .......... 66 C6
Leigh Rangers ARLFC
*LEIGH* WN7 .......... 67 G8
Leigh RUFC
*LEIGH* WN7 .......... 81 H3
Leigh Street Primary School
*HYDE* SK14 .......... 102 B2
Lemon Park Industrial Estate
*HEY* OL10 .......... 41 H3
Levenshulme Baths
*BNG/LEV* M19 .......... 99 L3
Levenshulme Health Centre
*BNG/LEV* M19 .......... 99 L3
Levenshulme High School
*BNG/LEV* M19 .......... 99 K5
Levenshulme Trading Estate
*BNG/LEV* M19 .......... 99 M2
Lever Edge Primary School
*BOLS/LL* BL3 .......... 52 A2
Leverhulme Park Athletics
Stadium *BOLS/LL* BL3 .......... 37 G6
Lever Park School
*HOR/BR* BL6 .......... 35 M1
Light Oaks Junior School
*SLFD* M6 .......... 70 E8
Lily Lane J & I School
*NEWH/MOS* M40 .......... 73 K4
Limehurst Primary School
*OLDS* OL8 .......... 75 G4
Limeside Primary School
*OLDS* OL8 .......... 74 F3
The Limes School
*OLDE* OL4 .......... 75 K8
Lime Tree Primary School
*SALE* M33 .......... 109 H1
Linden Road Primary School
*DTN/ASHW* M34 .......... 101 K1
Lindow Primary School
*WILM/AE* SK9 .......... 130 A1
Linguard Business Park
*MILN* OL16 .......... 11 G5
Linkway Industrial Estate
*MDTN* M24 .......... 57 L1
Linnyshaw Industrial Estate
*FWTH* BL4 .......... 53 H6
Littleborough CC
*LIT* OL15 .......... 21 M6
Littleborough Primary School
*LIT* OL15 .......... 21 M5
Little Heaton VC CE Primary
School *MDTN* M24 .......... 56 F5
Little Hulton Skills Centre
*WALK* M28 .......... 52 D8
Little Lever School Specialist
Language College
*BOLS/LL* BL3 .......... 53 H1
Littlemoor Primary School
*OLDE* OL4 .......... 59 M4
Littlemoss Business Park
*DROY* M43 .......... 89 M4
Littlemoss High School
*DROY* M43 .......... 74 F8
Little Theatre
*TYLD* M29 .......... 67 J4
Livingstone Primary School
*MOSL* OL5 .......... 76 D4
L & M Business Park
*ALT* WA14 .......... 107 L6
Lobden Golf Club
*WHIT* OL12 .......... 20 C5
Local Studies Library
*OLD* OL1 .......... 9 K6
Lockett Business Park
*AIMK* WN4 .......... 63 M7
Lockside Medical Centre
*STLY* SK15 .......... 91 L2
Longdendale Community
Language College
*HYDE* SK14 .......... 92 F7
Longdendale Recreation Centre
*HYDE* SK14 .......... 103 J1
Longford Park Special School
*STRET* M32 .......... 97 J2
Longford Trading Estate
*STRET* M32 .......... 97 G1
Longshoot Health Centre
*WGN* WN1 .......... 15 J2
Longsight CC
*WGTN/LGST* M12 .......... 99 K1
Longsight Health Centre
*WGTN/LGST* M12 .......... 88 C8
Longsight Industrial Estate
*WGTN/LGST* M12 .......... 88 C8
Lords College
*BOLE* BL2 .......... 3 G7
Loreto Grammar School
*ALT* WA14 .......... 107 M7
Lostock College
*STRET* M32 .......... 96 D1
Lostock Hall Primary School
*POY/DIS* SK12 .......... 128 F1
Lostock Industrial Estate
*HOR/BR* BL6 .......... 34 B5
Lostock Primary School
*HOR/BR* BL6 .......... 34 F6
Lower Broughton Health Centre
*BRO* M7 .......... 72 A8
Lowercroft Primary School
*TOT/BURYW* BL8 .......... 38 B2
Lower Kersal Primary School
*BRO* M7 .......... 71 L6
Lower Park Primary School
*POY/DIS* SK12 .......... 121 J1
Lowerplace Primary School
*MILN* OL16 .......... 28 E8
Lowes Park Golf Club
*BURY* BL9 .......... 25 K6
Low Hall Community Primary
School *WGNE/HIN* WN2 .......... 64 D1
The Lowry Hotel
*CSLFD* M3 .......... 6 D3
The Lowry
*MDTN* M17 .......... 86 B5
Lowton Business Park
*GOL/RIS/CUL* WA3 .......... 80 D4
Lowton Community Sports
College *GOL/RIS/CUL* WA3 .......... 80 E4
Lowton J & I School
*GOL/RIS/CUL* WA3 .......... 80 D5

Lowton St Marys CE Primary
School *GOL/RIS/CUL* WA3 .......... 80 E4
Lowton West Primary School
*GOL/RIS/CUL* WA3 .......... 79 M4
Ludworth Primary School
*MPL/ROM* SK6 .......... 114 D4
Lum Head Primary School
*CHD/CHDH* SK8 .......... 119 K1
The Lyceum Musical Theatre
*OLD* OL1 .......... 9 J6
Lyme Community Primary
School *NEWLW* WA12 .......... 78 C8
Lyndhurst Primary School
*DUK* SK16 .......... 90 F2
*OLDS* OL8 .......... 75 G1
Lyntown Trading Estate
*ECC* M30 .......... 85 G2
Lyon Industrial Estate
*ALT* WA14 .......... 107 L5
Lyon Road Industrial Estate
*FWTH* BL4 .......... 53 H7
Mabs Cross Primary School
*WGN* WN1 .......... 15 H1
Macdonald Norton Grange Hotel
*ROCH* OL11 .......... 41 M5
Macdonald Road Medical Centre
*IRL* M44 .......... 94 B4
Mackenzie Industrial Estate
*CHD/CHDH* SK8 .......... 111 L6
Magda House Medical Centre
*OFTN* SK2 .......... 113 C8
Malbern Industrial Estate
*DTN/ASHW* M34 .......... 89 M8
The Mall Shopping Centre
*ECC* M30 .......... 85 J2
Malmaison Hotel
*CMANE* M1 .......... 7 J5
Mancentral Trading Estate
*ORD* M5 .......... 6 B4
Manchester Academy
*RUSH/FAL* M14 .......... 87 K8
Manchester Airport Hotel
*MANAIR* M90 .......... 118 E5
Manchester Airport World
Freight Terminal
*MANAIR* M90 .......... 118 C6
Manchester Aquatics Centre
*BRUN/LGST* M13 .......... 7 J9
Manchester Arndale Shopping
Centre *CMANE* M1 .......... 7 G3
Manchester Art Gallery
*CMANE* M1 .......... 7 G5
Manchester (Barton) Airfield
*ECC* M30 .......... 84 B5
Manchester Business Park
*MANAIR* M90 .......... 118 E4
Manchester Business School
*HULME* M15 .......... 87 K6
Manchester Cathedral
*CSLFD* M3 .......... 6 F2
Manchester Cathedral
Visitor Centre
*CSLFD* M3 .......... 6 F3
Manchester Central
*CSLFD* M3 .......... 6 D6
Manchester Central Library
*CMANW* M2 .......... 6 F6
Manchester Centre for the Deaf
*BRUN/LGST* M13 .......... 87 L6
Manchester Centre for Vision
*BRUN/LGST* M13 .......... 87 L7
Manchester City FC (City of
Manchester Stadium)
*OP/CLY* M11 .......... 88 C3
Manchester City Museum & Tour
*OP/CLY* M11 .......... 88 C2
Manchester College of Arts
& Technology
*CSLFD* M3 .......... 6 C5
*WGTN/LGST* M12 .......... 88 A5
*CMANE* M1 .......... 7 G4
*OP/CLY* M11 .......... 88 E5
Manchester Conference Centre
& Hotel *CMANE* M1 .......... 7 J7
The Manchester Crematorium
*CCHDY* M21 .......... 97 M6
Manchester Golf Club
*MDTN* M24 .......... 41 M6
Manchester Grammar School
*BRUN/LGST* M13 .......... 99 H2
Manchester High School for Girls
*RUSH/FAL* M14 .......... 98 F3
Manchester Industrial Centre
*CSLFD* M3 .......... 6 B6
Manchester International Airport
*MANAIR* M90 .......... 118 D7
Manchester Islamic High School
for Girls *CCHDY* M21 .......... 97 K4
Manchester Junior Girls School
*BRO* M7 .......... 72 A3
Manchester Mesivta High School
*PWCH* M25 .......... 71 L1
Manchester Mesivta School
*PWCH* M25 .......... 71 L1
Manchester Metropolitan
University
*BRUN/LGST* M13 .......... 87 M8
*CMANE* M1 .......... 7 G8
*CMANE* M1 .......... 7 H6
*DID/WITH* M20 .......... 110 C1
*DID/WITH* M20 .......... 110 E2
*HULME* M15 .......... 87 K6
*OLDTF/WHR* M16 .......... 98 C2
*RUSH/FAL* M14 .......... 98 F1
Manchester Metropolitan
University Institute of
Education Didsbury
*DID/WITH* M20 .......... 110 E2
Manchester Museum
*BRUN/LGST* M13 .......... 87 L6
Manchester Road Primary
School *DROY* M43 .......... 89 H3
Manchester Royal Infirmary
*BRUN/LGST* M13 .......... 87 M7
Manchester RUFC
*CHD/CHDH* SK8 .......... 120 C6
MEN Arena
*CSLFD* M3 .......... 6 F1
Manchester School of
Management *BRUN/LGST* M13 .......... 87 K6
Manchester Southern Cemetery
*CCHDY* M21 .......... 98 A6
Manchester United FC
(Old Trafford)
*OLDTF/WHR* M16 .......... 86 C7
Manchester United Museum &
Tour Centre
*TRPK* M17 .......... 86 B7
Manchester University
*BRUN/LGST* M13 .......... 87 M1
Manchester Victoria & Albert
Hotel *CSLFD* M3 .......... 6 B5
Manchester Youth Theatre
*HULME* M15 .......... 87 J7

Mandelay Health Centre
*BOL* BL1 .......... 22 B6
Manley Park Junior School
*OLDTF/WHR* M16 .......... 97 M2
Manley Park Primary School
*OLDTF/WHR* M16 .......... 97 M2
Manor Golf Club
*FWTH* BL4 .......... 53 L8
Manor Green Primary School
*DTN/ASHW* M34 .......... 101 K4
Manor High School
*SALE* M33 .......... 95 M7
Manor House Surgery
*GLSP* SK13 .......... 105 G3
Manway Business Park
*ALT* WA14 .......... 108 B5
The Maples Medical Centre
*NTHM/RTH* M23 .......... 109 J8
Marcliffe Industrial Estate
*BRAM/HZG* SK7 .......... 122 B3
Marjory Lees Health Centre
*OLD* OL1 .......... 9 K4
Marketgate Shopping Centre
*WGN* WN1 .......... 14 F3
Market Place Shopping Centre
*BOL* BL1 .......... 2 E4
Market Street Athletics Track
*BURY* BL9 .......... 4 F7
Market Street Medical Centre
*WGNE/HIN* WN2 .......... 49 G6
Markland Hill Primary School
*BOL* BL1 .......... 35 J4
Marland Hill Primary School
*ROCH* OL11 .......... 27 M7
Marland Park Golf Club
*ROCH* OL11 .......... 27 K7
Marlborough Road Primary
School *BRO* M7 .......... 72 C6
Marple Clinic
*MPL/ROM* SK6 .......... 114 C6
Marple Golf Club
*MPL/ROM* SK6 .......... 123 G1
Marple Hall School
*MPL/ROM* SK6 .......... 113 M5
Marriott Hotel
*HALE/TIMP* WA15 .......... 118 A5
Marriott Worsley Park Hotel &
Country Club
*WALK* M28 .......... 69 H5
Marsh Green CP School
*WGNW/BIL/OR* WN5 .......... 47 G4
Marsh Green Health Centre
*WGNW/BIL/OR* WN5 .......... 47 G3
Marsh Lane Trading Estate
*NM/HAY* SK22 .......... 124 F5
Marsland Street Industrial
Centre *BRAM/HZG* SK7 .......... 121 M2
Marston Bentley Industrial
Estate *WGNE/HIN* WN2 .......... 48 C3
Martland Mill Business Park
*WGNW/BIL/OR* WN5 .......... 47 G2
Martland Mill Industrial Estate
*WGNW/BIL/OR* WN5 .......... 47 F2
Marus Bridge Health Centre
*WGNS/IIMK* WN3 .......... 63 J2
Marus Bridge Primary School
*WGNS/IIMK* WN3 .......... 63 H2
Masefield Primary School
*BOLS/LL* BL3 .......... 37 L8
Mason Street Industrial Estate
*WGNS/IIMK* WN3 .......... 14 D5
Maternity & Child Welfare Clinic
*WGNE/HIN* WN2 .......... 48 F7
Mather Street Primary School
*FAIL* M35 .......... 74 A4
Matthew Moss High School
*HEY* OL10 .......... 27 K8
Mauldeth Medical Centre
*DID/WITH* M20 .......... 99 G5
Mauldeth Road Primary School
*RUSH/FAL* M14 .......... 99 H5
Mayfield Industrial Park
*IRL* M44 .......... 94 F1
Mayfield Primary School
*OLD* OL1 .......... 59 L4
Mayflower Brewery
*WGN* WN1 .......... 15 G2
Maypole Farm Estate
*PART* M31 .......... 95 G6
Maypole Industrial Estate
*WGNE/HIN* WN2 .......... 64 F5
Meade Hill School
*CHH* M8 .......... 56 F8
Meadowbank Primary School
*ATH* M46 .......... 50 F8
*CHD/CHDH* SK8 .......... 111 J7
Meadow Industrial Estate
*FAIL* M35 .......... 74 A6
*STKP* SK1 .......... 13 K1
The Meadows School
*BKLY* M9 .......... 57 J8
Meadway Health Centre
*SALE* M33 .......... 108 C3
Meanwood Primary School
*WHIT* OL12 .......... 27 M3
Mechinoh School
*BRO* M7 .......... 72 B3
Medlock Infant School
*BRUN/LGST* M13 .......... 7 K9
Medlock Leisure Centre
*DROY* M43 .......... 89 L1
Medlock Primary School
*BRUN/LGST* M13 .......... 7 L9
Medlock Valley Community
School *OLDS* OL8 .......... 75 K1
Megabowl
*BURY* BL9 .......... 39 L6
*OLDTF/WHR* M16 .......... 86 D7
Melland High School
*CTN* M18 .......... 100 A3
Mellor Primary School
*MPL/ROM* SK6 .......... 115 H6
Mellor Sports Club
*MPL/ROM* SK6 .......... 115 G6
Mellor & Townscliffe Golf Club
*MPL/ROM* SK6 .......... 115 G6
Mental Health Centre
*BOLE* BL2 .......... 37 J3
Mere Oaks School
*WGN* WN1 .......... 31 L1
Mereside Educational Trust
*SALE* M33 .......... 109 G1
Meridian Clinic
*BURY* BL9 .......... 4 D5
Mersey Drive Primary School
*BURY* BL9 .......... 55 M2
Mersey Road Industrial Estate
*FAIL* M35 .......... 74 E3
Mersey Trading Estate
*HTNM* SK4 .......... 111 J3

Mersey Vale Primary School
*HTNM* SK4 .......... 111 K3
Merseyway Centre
*STKP* SK1 .......... 13 H5
Mesne Lea Primary School
*WALK* M28 .......... 69 H3
Methodist Cemetery
*BOLE* BL2 .......... 23 H8
Metro Cinema
*AUL* OL6 .......... 90 E2
Micklehurst All Saints Primary
School *MOSL* OL5 .......... 77 H5
Micklehurst CC
*MOSL* OL5 .......... 77 H5
Middlebrook Retail & Leisure Park
*HOR/BR* BL6 .......... 34 A4
Middleton Cemetery
*MDTN* M24 .......... 57 M2
Middleton Crematorium
*MDTN* M24 .......... 57 M2
Middleton CC
*MDTN* M24 .......... 57 J2
Middleton Parish Church School
*MDTN* M24 .......... 57 J2
Middleton Public Baths
*MDTN* M24 .......... 57 K4
Middleton Shopping Centre
*MDTN* M24 .......... 57 J4
Middleton Technology School
*MDTN* M24 .......... 57 L4
Midland Hotel
*CMANW* M2 .......... 6 F6
Miles Platting Pool
*NEWH/MOS* M40 .......... 88 A1
Milking Green Industrial Estate
*OLDE* OL4 .......... 60 B7
Mill 5 Belgrave Industrial Estate
*OLDS* OL8 .......... 75 K1
Millbrook Business Centre
*NTHM/RTH* M23 .......... 109 H6
Millbrook Industrial Estate
*NTHM/RTH* M23 .......... 109 H6
Millbrook Primary School
*STLY* SK15 .......... 77 H7
Mill Gate Shopping Centre
*BURY* BL9 .......... 4 E5
Millingford Industrial Estate
*GOL/RIS/CUL* WA3 .......... 79 L4
Mills Hill Primary School
*CHAD* OL9 .......... 58 B4
Mill Street Industrial Estate
*BOL* BL1 .......... 3 G4
Millwood Primary Special School
*BURY* BL9 .......... 39 J6
Milnrow CC
*MILN* OL16 .......... 29 J7
Milnrow CE Aided Primary
School *MILN* OL16 .......... 29 J6
Milnrow Health Centre
*MILN* OL16 .......... 29 J7
Milo Industrial Park
*DROY* M43 .......... 89 L2
Milton St Johns CE Primary
School *MOSL* OL5 .......... 76 F2
Minden Medical Centre
*BURY* BL9 .......... 5 G4
Moat House School
*HTNM* SK4 .......... 112 A1
Monde Trading Estate
*TRPK* M17 .......... 85 K6
Montague Business Park
*OLDTF/WHR* M16 .......... 86 D8
Monton Bowling Club
*ECC* M30 .......... 70 B8
Monton CC
*ECC* M30 .......... 70 B8
Monton Green Primary School
*ECC* M30 .......... 70 B8
Monton House Hotel
*ECC* M30 .......... 85 G1
Monton Medical Centre
*ECC* M30 .......... 69 M8
Montrose School
*WGNW/BIL/OR* WN5 .......... 47 G5
Moor Allerton School
*DID/WITH* M20 .......... 98 C8
Moorfield Community Primary
School
*IRL* M44 .......... 94 D1
Moorfield Primary School
*BRAM/HZG* SK7 .......... 121 L3
Moorgate Primary School
*BOLE* BL2 .......... 3 K2
Moorgate Retail Park
*BURY* BL9 .......... 5 G3
Moorhouse Primary School
*MILN* OL16 .......... 29 H6
Moorlands Junior School
*SALE* M33 .......... 97 H7
Moor Lane Bus Station
*BOL* BL1 .......... 2 D5
Moorside High School
*SWIN* M27 .......... 70 A5
Moorside Leisure Centre
*SWIN* M27 .......... 70 A5
Moorside Primary School
*DROY* M43 .......... 89 L3
*SWIN* M27 .......... 70 A5
Moravian College
*DROY* M43 .......... 89 K4
Mornington High School
*WGNE/HIN* WN2 .......... 49 J7
Morris Green Business Park
*BOLS/LL* BL3 .......... 35 M8
Moses Gate Country Park
*FWTH* BL4 .......... 53 H2
Moses Park Country Park
*BOLS/LL* BL3 .......... 37 G8
Moss Field Community Primary
School *HEY* OL10 .......... 40 F1
Mossfield CP School
*SWIN* M27 .......... 70 C3
Moss Hey Primary School
*BRAM/HZG* SK7 .......... 120 E7
Moss Industrial Estate
*GOL/RIS/CUL* WA3 .......... 80 L3
*MILN* OL16 .......... 11 K8
Moss Lane Industrial Estate
*ROY/SHW* OL2 .......... 59 K1
Mossley AFC
*MOSL* OL5 .......... 76 F3
Mossley Health Centre
*MOSL* OL5 .......... 76 F3
Mossley Hollins High School
*MOSL* OL5 .......... 77 H3
Moss Park J & I School
*STRET* M32 .......... 96 F3
Moss Side Health Centre
*RUSH/FAL* M14 .......... 87 K4
Moss Side Leisure Centre
*HULME* M15 .......... 87 J4

Moss View Primary School
*PART* M31 .......... 106 D1
Moston Fields Primary School
*NEWH/MOS* M40 .......... 73 K3
Moston Indoor Market
*NEWH/MOS* M40 .......... 73 J4
Moston Lane Primary School
*BKLY* M9 .......... 73 H4
Mottram CE Primary School
*HYDE* SK14 .......... 103 K1
Mottram St Andrew
Primary School
*MCFLDN* SK10 .......... 131 L2
Mount Carmel RC Junior School
*BKLY* M9 .......... 73 G2
Mount Carmel RC Primary School
*BKLY* M9 .......... 73 G3
Mountheath Industrial Park
*PWCH* M25 .......... 71 L3
Mount Pleasant Business Centre
*OLDE* OL4 .......... 59 L6
Mount St Joseph Business &
Enterprise College
*BOLS/LL* BL3 .......... 52 C2
The Museum of Science &
Industry in Manchester
*CSLFD* M3 .......... 6 B6
Museum of the Manchester
Regiment *AUL* OL6 .......... 90 E1
Museum of Trade Union History
*CMANE* M1 .......... 7 G6
Museum of Transport
*CHH* M8 .......... 72 D6
The Music School
*CHH* M8 .......... 72 D4
Mytham Primary School
*BOLS/LL* BL3 .......... 53 L1
Nasmyth Business Centre
*ECC* M30 .......... 84 F2
National Cycling Centre
(Velodrome)
*OP/CLY* M11 .......... 88 D2
National Industrial Estate
*AULW* OL7 .......... 90 C1
National Squash Centre
*OP/CLY* M11 .......... 88 D2
National Trading Estate
*BRAM/HZG* SK7 .......... 121 L1
Natural History Museum
*CHAD* OL9 .......... 8 D9
Navigation Primary School
*ALT* WA14 .......... 108 A6
Navigation Trading Estate
*NEWH/MOS* M40 .......... 73 K7
Nelson Business Centre
*DTN/ASHW* M34 .......... 90 C8
Nether Alderley Mill
*MCFLDN* SK10 .......... 130 D7
Nether Alderley Primary School
*MCFLDN* SK10 .......... 130 D6
Neville Street Industrial Estate
*CHAD* OL9 .......... 8 C5
Nevill Road Infant School
*BRAM/HZG* SK7 .......... 121 G2
Newall Green High School
*NTHM/RTH* M23 .......... 109 J8
Newall Green Primary School
*NTHM/RTH* M23 .......... 109 L8
New Ardwick Sports Centre
*WGTN/LGST* M12 .......... 88 A4
New Bridge School
*OLDS* OL8 .......... 74 E4
Newbridge Special School
*OLDS* OL8 .......... 75 L2
Newbrook School
*DID/WITH* M20 .......... 98 B7
Newby Road Industrial Estate
*BRAM/HZG* SK7 .......... 121 M2
New Croft Community
High School
*SLFD* M6 .......... 86 C1
New Harvest Learning Centre
*CSLFD* M3 .......... 6 B3
Newhaven Business Park
*ECC* M30 .......... 85 H3
Newhey Community Primary
School
*MILN* OL16 .......... 29 K8
New Kingsway Health Centre
*BNG/LEV* M19 .......... 99 G8
Newlands Medical Centre
*BOL* BL1 .......... 35 K5
New Mills FC
*NM/HAY* SK22 .......... 124 F4
New Mills Golf Club
*NM/HAY* SK22 .......... 124 C3
New Mills Leisure Centre &
Swimming Pool
*NM/HAY* SK22 .......... 124 E4
New Mills Primary School
*NM/HAY* SK22 .......... 124 D4
New Mills School & Sixth Form
Centre *NM/HAY* SK22 .......... 124 E4
New Moston Primary School
*NEWH/MOS* M40 .......... 74 D2
New Museum
*OLD* OL1 .......... 9 H3
New North Manchester Golf Club
*MDTN* M24 .......... 57 G4
New Springs Holy Family RC
Primary School
*WGNE/HIN* WN2 .......... 48 D2
Newton Bank Preparatory
School *NEWLW* WA12 .......... 79 H8
Newton Business Park
*HYDE* SK14 .......... 91 K7
Newton Health Clinic
*NEWLW* WA12 .......... 78 E8
Newton-le-Willows Community
High School
*NEWLW* WA12 .......... 79 G1
Newton-le-Willows High School
*NEWLW* WA12 .......... 79 G7
Newton-le-Willows Sports Club
*NEWLW* WA12 .......... 78 F8
Newton Moor Industrial Estate
*HYDE* SK14 .......... 91 H7
Newton Street Police Museum
*CMANE* M1 .......... 7 J4
Newton Westpark Primary School
*LEIGH* WN7 .......... 65 M4
Newtown Primary School
*NM/HAY* SK22 .......... 124 D6
Nicholas Varley Community
School
*NEWH/MOS* M40 .......... 73 H8
Nicholls Sixth Form Centre
*WGTN/LGST* M12 .......... 88 A4
Nicol Mere School
*AIMK* WN4 .......... 63 K7
Norbury Hall Primary School
*BRAM/HZG* SK7 .......... 122 A3

Norden Community Primary
School *WHIT* OL12 .......... 27 J2
Norden CC
*WHIT* OL12 .......... 27 H2
Norley Hall CC
*WGNW/BIL/OR* WN5 .......... 46 E6
Norris Bank Medical Centre
*HTNM* SK4 .......... 12 C4
Norris Bank Primary School
*HTNM* SK4 .......... 12 B1
Nortex Business Centre
*BOL* BL1 .......... 35 M4
Northbank Industrial Park
*IRL* M44 .......... 94 B6
North Cestrian Grammar School
*ALT* WA14 .......... 107 M7
North Chadderton School
*CHAD* OL9 .......... 58 D2
North Cheshire Jewish Primary
School
*CHD/CHDH* SK8 .......... 119 K2
Northenden Golf Club
*WYTH/NTH* M22 .......... 110 B2
Northenden Primary School
*WYTH/NTH* M22 .......... 110 A3
Northern A & O Medical Centre
*BURY* BL9 .......... 4 F4
Northern Cemetery
*SWIN* M27 .......... 71 J5
Northern Moor Clinic
*NTHM/RTH* M23 .......... 109 J3
North Grecian Street Primary
School *BRO* M7 .......... 71 M6
North Heaton Primary School
*HTNM* SK4 .......... 99 M6
North Manchester General
Hospital *CHH* M8 .......... 72 F3
North Manchester High School
for Boys *BKLY* M9 .......... 73 L1
North Manchester High School
for Girls *NEWH/MOS* M40 .......... 73 K2
North Quarry Business Park
*WGNNW/ST* WN6 .......... 30 A3
North Quays Business Park
*ALT* WA14 .......... 108 B3
North Reddish Health Centre
*RDSH* SK5 .......... 100 B3
North Reddish J & I School
*RDSH* SK5 .......... 100 C3
North Trafford College
*STRET* M32 .......... 86 C8
North Walkden Primary School
*WALK* M28 .......... 52 F7
Novotel
*CMANE* M1 .......... 6 F6
*WALK* M28 .......... 69 H7
Nugent House School
*WGNW/BIL/OR* WN5 .......... 62 A8
Oakdale Special School
*DUK* SK16 .......... 91 G6
Oakenclough Primary School
*WILM/AE* SK9 .......... 127 H3
Oakfield Primary School
*HYDE* SK14 .......... 91 H7
Oakfield Trading Estate
*HALE/TIMP* WA15 .......... 108 B7
Oakgrove School
*CHD/CHDH* SK8 .......... 119 L5
Oakhill Trading Estate
*WALK* M28 .......... 52 E7
Oaklands Infant School
*WILM/AE* SK9 .......... 127 J3
Oakleigh Medical Centre
*CHH* M8 .......... 72 E3
The Oaks Business Park
*NTHM/RTH* M23 .......... 109 G5
Oaks Primary School
*BOL* BL1 .......... 22 C6
Oakwood High School
*CCHDY* M21 .......... 97 L7
*SLFD* M6 .......... 70 F7
Octagon Theatre
*BOL* BL1 .......... 2 E5
Odeon Cinema
*ROCH* OL11 .......... 28 B8
Offerton Green Clinic
*OFTN* SK2 .......... 113 J7
Offerton Health Centre
*OFTN* SK2 .......... 112 E4
Offerton High School
*OFTN* SK2 .......... 113 H5
Offerton Industrial Estate
*STKP* SK1 .......... 112 E5
Old Boston Trading Estate
*RNFD/HAY* WA11 .......... 78 D4
Oldfield Brow Primary School
*ALT* WA14 .......... 107 J7
Old Hall Clinic
*CHD/CHDH* SK8 .......... 110 E6
Old Hall Drive Primary School
*GTN* M18 .......... 89 G8
Old Hall Primary School
*TOT/BURYW* BL8 .......... 24 E5
Oldham Athletic FC
(Boundary Park)
*ROY/SHW* OL2 .......... 59 G2
Oldham Broadway Business Park
*CHAD* OL9 .......... 58 B4
Oldham Business Centre
*OLD* OL1 .......... 9 H7
Oldham Central Industrial Park
*OLD* OL1 .......... 9 M3
Oldham Central Trading Park
*OLD* OL1 .......... 9 M2
Oldham College
*CHAD* OL9 .......... 8 F5
Oldham County Court
*OLD* OL1 .......... 9 G4
Oldham Crematorium
*OLDS* OL8 .......... 74 F3
Oldham CC
*OLD* OL1 .......... 59 M3
Oldham Golf Club
*OLDE* OL4 .......... 60 C8
Oldham RUFC
*OLDS* OL8 .......... 75 J4
Oldham Sixth Form College
*OLDS* OL8 .......... 9 G7
Oldham Sports Centre
*OLD* OL1 .......... 9 J5
Oldham West Business Centre
*CHAD* OL9 .......... 8 B5
Old Mill Hotel
*RAMS* BL0 .......... 18 E5
Old Moat J & I School
*DID/WITH* M20 .......... 98 B3
Old Rectory Hotel
*DTN/ASHW* M34 .......... 101 K5
Old Trafford Community
School *OLDTF/WHR* M16 .......... 86 F6
Oldwood Primary School
*WYTH/NTH* M22 .......... 118 D2

Olympia Trading Estate
*HULME* M15 .......... 6 D8
Olympic House
*MANAIR* M90 .......... 118 E5
Open University
*CCHDY* M21 .......... 97 L3
Opera House
*CSLFD* M3 .......... 6 D5
The Operating Theatre
*STRET* M32 .......... 97 H1
Orchard House Day Hospital
*ROY/SHW* OL2 .......... 43 H8
Orchard Industrial Estate
*SLFD* M6 .......... 71 K8
Orchard Trading Estate
*SLFD* M6 .......... 71 J7
Ordsall Hall Museum
*ORD* M5 .......... 86 E6
Ordsall Health Centre
*ORD* M5 .......... 86 E4
Ordsall Recreation Centre
*ORD* M5 .......... 86 D5
Oriel Bank High School
*OFTN* SK2 .......... 112 C7
Oriental Arch
*CMANE* M1 .......... 7 G5
Orion Business Park
*EDGY/DAV* SK3 .......... 111 M7
Orion Trading Estate
*TRPK* M17 .......... 85 K4
Orrell Clinic
*WGNW/BIL/OR* WN5 .......... 46 B5
Orrell Holgate Primary School
*WGNW/BIL/OR* WN5 .......... 46 B7
Orrell Newfold Community
Primary School
*WGNW/BIL/OR* WN5 .......... 46 A8
Orrell RUFC
*WGNW/BIL/OR* WN5 .......... 46 B7
Orrell Water Park
*WGNW/BIL/OR* WN5 .......... 46 B8
Orrismere Primary School
*CHD/CHDH* SK8 .......... 120 C1
Osborne Trading Estate
*CHAD* OL9 .......... 8 D3
Oswald Road Primary School
*CCHDY* M21 .......... 97 K3
Oulder Hill Community School
Language College
*ROCH* OL11 .......... 27 L5
Our Lady Immaculate Catholic
Primary School
*AIMK* WN4 .......... 63 G6
Our Lady of Grace RC Primary
School *PWCH* M25 .......... 55 K6
Our Lady of Lourdes Catholic
Primary School
*PART* M31 .......... 106 B1
Our Lady of Lourdes RC Primary
School *FWTH* BL4 .......... 52 D4
*TOT/BURYW* BL8 .......... 24 F6
Our Lady of Mount Carmel RC
Primary School
*AUL* OL6 .......... 76 A8
Our Lady of the Rosary RC
Primary School
*LEIGH* WN7 .......... 65 L7
*URM* M41 .......... 84 F8
Our Lady RC Primary School
*WGNE/HIN* WN2 .......... 32 F7
Our Lady & St Anselms RC
Primary School
*WHIT* OL12 .......... 20 B2
Our Lady & St Pauls RC Primary
School *HEY* OL10 .......... 40 B2
Our Ladys Catholic
Primary School
*EDGY/DAV* SK3 .......... 13 G7
Our Lady's RC High School
*BKLY* M9 .......... 57 G6
Our Ladys RC High School
*ROY/SHW* OL2 .......... 59 G3
Our Ladys RC Primary School
*OLDE* OL4 .......... 60 B1
*OLDTF/WHR* M16 .......... 98 A1
Our Lady & the Lancashire
Martyrs RC Primary School
*WALK* M28 .......... 68 D1
Outwood Primary School
*CHD/CHDH* SK8 .......... 119 L5
Overdale Crematorium
*BOL* BL1 .......... 35 K6
Overdale School
*MPL/ROM* SK6 .......... 113 J3
Owl Business Centre
*OLDE* OL4 .......... 60 A6
Oxford Grove Primary School
*BOL* BL1 .......... 35 M3
OYY Lubavitch Girls School
*BRO* M7 .......... 72 A3
Padfield Primary School
*GLSP* SK13 .......... 93 L7
Pagefield Industrial Estate
*WGNNW/ST* WN6 .......... 14 A2
Palace Cinema
*STLY* SK15 .......... 91 K2
The Palace Hotel
*CMANE* M1 .......... 7 G7
Palace Theatre
*CMANE* M1 .......... 7 G7
Palm Business Centre
*CHAD* OL9 .......... 8 A5
Paragon Business Park
*HOR/BR* BL6 .......... 34 B4
Paragon Industrial Estate
*LIT* OL15 .......... 29 J1
Parish Church CE Junior School
*OLD* OL1 .......... 9 J3
Park Business Centre
*WGNE/HIN* WN2 .......... 49 G5
Parker International Estate
*DUK* SK16 .......... 90 E5
Parkfield Industrial Estate
*MDTN* M24 .......... 57 H4
Parkfield Primary School
*MDTN* M24 .......... 57 H3
Park Industrial Estate
*AIMK* WN4 .......... 78 B1
Parklands High School
*WYTH/NTH* M22 .......... 118 E1
Park Mill Industrial Estate
*MOSL* OL5 .......... 61 G8
Park Parade Industrial Estate
*AUL* OL6 .......... 90 D2
Park Road CP School
*SALE* M33 .......... 96 D6
Park Road Primary School
*ALT* WA14 .......... 108 B4
Park School
*NTHM/RTH* M23 .......... 109 J4
Parkside Industrial Estate
*ROY/SHW* OL2 .......... 43 H8

Parkview Centre
*OLDS* OL8 .......... 9 K8
Parkway Business Centre
*OLDTF/WHR* M16 .......... 98 C3
Parkway Four Industrial Estate
*TRPK* M17 .......... 85 K5
Parkway Trading Estate
*STRET* M32 .......... 85 K7
Parochial CE Primary School
*AUL* OL6 .......... 90 F1
*WHTN* BL5 .......... 50 B4
Parrenthorn High School
*PWCH* M25 .......... 55 M6
Parrs Wood Technology College
*DID/WITH* M20 .......... 111 G3
Parsonage Retail Park
*LEIGH* WN7 .......... 66 B6
Partington CP School
*PART* M31 .......... 106 C1
Partington Health Centre
*PART* M31 .......... 106 C1
Partington Shopping Centre
*PART* M31 .......... 106 C1
Partington Sports Centre
*PART* M31 .......... 106 C2
Peacefield Primary School
*MPL/ROM* SK6 .......... 114 D7
Peacock CP School
*GTN* M18 .......... 88 F6
Peacock Primary School
*HULME* M15 .......... 6 C9
Pearlbrook Industrial Estate
*HOR/BR* BL6 .......... 33 L1
Pear New Mill Industrial Estate
*MPL/ROM* SK6 .......... 112 F2
Peel Brow Primary School
*RAMS* BL0 .......... 19 G6
The Peel Centre
*STKP* SK1 .......... 13 L3
Peel Hall CP School
*LHULT* M38 .......... 68 C1
Peel Hall Primary School
*WYTH/NTH* M22 .......... 119 H1
Peel Health Centre
*BURY* BL9 .......... 4 F6
Peel Moat Recreation Centre
*HTNM* SK4 .......... 99 L7
Peerglow Industrial Estate
*ALT* WA14 .......... 108 B4
Pemberton Business Centre
*WGNW/BIL/OR* WN5 .......... 46 F6
Pemberton Clinic
*WGNW/BIL/OR* WN5 .......... 47 G6
Pendleton College
*SLFD* M6 .......... 85 M1
Pendleton Medical Centre
*SLFD* M6 .......... 86 D2
Pennant Industrial Estate
*OLDE* OL4 .......... 59 L4
Pennine Business Park
*HEY* OL10 .......... 40 E4
Pennington Flash Country Park
*LEIGH* WN7 .......... 80 F1
Pennington Golf Club
*LEIGH* WN7 .......... 80 F1
Pepper Mill Business Park
*WGN* WN1 .......... 15 H5
Peterloo Medical Centre
*MDTN* M24 .......... 57 H4
Philips High School
*WHTF* M45 .......... 55 H4
Phoenix Industrial Estate
*FAIL* M35 .......... 74 D4
Phoenix Medical Centre
*STKP* SK1 .......... 13 K7
Phoenix Park Industrial Estate
*HEY* OL10 .......... 41 J4
Piccadilly Trading Estate
*CMANE* M1 .......... 7 M6
Pictor Special School
*SALE* M33 .......... 96 C8
Pike Fold Primary School
*BRAM/HZG* M9 .......... 72 F1
Pikes Lane Primary School
*BOLS/LL* BL3 .......... 2 A7
Pilot Industrial Estate
*BOLS/LL* BL3 .......... 36 E8
Pilsworth Industrial Estate
*BURY* BL9 .......... 39 L6
Pinfold J & I School
*HYDE* SK14 .......... 103 H1
Pinnacle Business Centre
*HTNM* SK4 .......... 13 H1
Pioneer Industrial Estate
*WGNW/BIL/OR* WN5 .......... 47 G7
Piper Hill School
*NTHM/RTH* M23 .......... 109 J4
Plantation Industrial Estate
*AUL* OL6 .......... 90 F2
Plant Hill High School
*BKLY* M9 .......... 56 F8
Plasman Industrial Centre
*BNG/LEV* M19 .......... 99 K3
Platt Bridge Clinic
*WGNE/HIN* WN2 .......... 64 D2
Players Theatre
*UPML* OL3 .......... 45 H8
Playhouse Theatre
*OLD* OL1 .......... 86 D2
Plodder Lane Primary School
*FWTH* BL4 .......... 52 E3
Plymouth Court Business Centre
*BRUN/LGST* M13 .......... 87 M7
Plymouth Grove Primary School
*BRUN/LGST* M13 .......... 88 B7
The Point Retail Park
*MILN* OL16 .......... 11 G4
Poland Industrial Estate
*ANC* M4 .......... 7 L2
Portland Basin Museum
*AULW* OL7 .......... 90 D3
Portland Industrial Estate
*RAMS* BL0 .......... 25 K8
Portwood Trading Estate
*STKP* SK1 .......... 13 M2
Potters House School
*BURY* BL9 .......... 25 J6
Pownall Green Primary School
*BRAM/HZG* SK7 .......... 121 G5
Pownall Hall School
*WILM/AE* SK9 .......... 126 D4
Poynton Clinic
*POY/DIS* SK12 .......... 122 A8
Poynton High School &
Performing Arts College
*POY/DIS* SK12 .......... 129 K2
Poynton Leisure Centre
*POY/DIS* SK12 .......... 129 K2
Poynton Sports Club
*POY/DIS* SK12 .......... 122 A8
Premier Travel Inn
*AIMK* WN4 .......... 78 E2

*ALT* WA14 .......... 108 B3
*ALT* WA14 .......... 108 A6
*CCHDY* M21 .......... 98 A7
*CHAD* OL9 .......... 74 B2
*CHD/CHDH* SK8 .......... 119 L2
*CHH* M8 .......... 56 C8
*CMANE* M1 .......... 6 F6
*DTN/ASHW* M34 .......... 100 F1
*GOL/RIS/CUL* WA3 .......... 79 L5
*HOR/BR* BL6 .......... 34 C4
*HULME* M15 .......... 6 E9
*HYDE* SK14 .......... 103 H1
*MDTN* M24 .......... 56 E5
*MILN* OL16 .......... 29 K8
*OFTN* SK2 .......... 112 D2
*PWCH* M25 .......... 55 K7
*SALE* M33 .......... 96 A6
*SALQ* M50 .......... 86 D5
*STKP* SK1 .......... 13 K4
*SWIN* M27 .......... 70 B6
*SWIN* M27 .......... 70 F5
*TRPK* M17 .......... 85 G6
*WGNNW/ST* WN6 .......... 30 E3
*WGNS/IIMK* WN3 .......... 63 J3
*WGNW/BIL/OR* WN5 .......... 46 C5
*WILM/AE* SK9 .......... 127 H1
*WILM/AE* SK9 .......... 126 C5
*WILM/AE* SK9 .......... 130 D4
*WYTH/NTH* M22 .......... 119 J4
Premier Travel Inn
(Manchester Trafford Centre)
*URM* M41 .......... 85 G5
Prestolee Primary School
*RAD* M26 .......... 53 L4
Prestwich Arts College
*PWCH* M25 .......... 55 L7
Prestwich Golf Club
*PWCH* M25 .......... 71 K3
Prestwich Health Centre
*PWCH* M25 .......... 55 K7
Prestwich Hospital
*PWCH* M25 .......... 55 J6
Prestwich Industrial Estate
*ATH* M46 .......... 50 E8
Prestwich Preparatory School
*PWCH* M25 .......... 55 M7
Priestnall School
*HTNM* SK4 .......... 111 J1
Prince of Wales Business Park
*OLD* OL1 .......... 59 M4
Princess on Portland
*CMANE* M1 .......... 7 G6
The Printworks Leisure Complex
*ANC* M4 .......... 7 G2
Priorsleigh Medical Centre
*POY/DIS* SK12 .......... 122 A8
Propps Hall Primary School
*FAIL* M35 .......... 74 B6
Prospect House Medical Centre
*WGNW/BIL/OR* WN5 .......... 46 D6
Prospect Industrial Estate
*WGNE/HIN* WN2 .......... 49 G7
Prospect Vale Primary School
*CHD/CHDH* SK8 .......... 119 K3
Pump House People's History
Museum
*CSLFD* M3 .......... 6 C4
The Quadrangle Business Centre
*WGNE/HIN* WN2 .......... 49 L8
Quality Hotel
*WGN* WN1 .......... 15 H3
Quality Hotel (Altrincham)
*ALT* WA14 .......... 116 F2
Quarry Bank Mill & Styal
Estate (NT) *WILM/AE* SK9 .......... 126 C2
Queen Elizabeth Hall
*OLD* OL1 .......... 9 H5
Queen Elizabeths School
*MDTN* M24 .......... 41 J8
Queensbridge Primary School
*FWTH* BL4 .......... 52 F4
Queensgate Primary School
*BRAM/HZG* SK7 .......... 121 G8
Queens Road Primary School
*CHD/CHDH* SK8 .......... 120 C1
Rack House Primary School
*NTHM/RTH* M23 .......... 109 K3
Radcliffe Borough AFC
*RAD* M26 .......... 38 B8
Radcliffe CC
*RAD* M26 .......... 38 B8
Radcliffe Hall CE Methodist
Primary School
*RAD* M26 .......... 38 F8
Radcliffe Hall CE Primary School
*RAD* M26 .......... 38 B8
Radcliffe Riverside School
*RAD* M26 .......... 54 C1
Radcliffe Tower (Remains of)
*RAD* M26 .......... 38 G1
Radclyffe Athletics Centre
*CHAD* OL9 .......... 58 C5
Radclyffe Primary School
*ORD* M5 .......... 86 D5
The Radclyffe School (Lower)
*CHAD* OL9 .......... 58 C6
The Radclyffe School (Upper)
*CHAD* OL9 .......... 58 C5
Radisson SAS Hotel
*MANAIR* M90 .......... 118 D5
Raikes Lane Industrial Estate
*BOLS/LL* BL3 .......... 36 E8
Railway Street Industrial Estate
*GTN* M18 .......... 88 F6
Ralph Williams Clinic
*WHIT* OL12 .......... 28 F1
Ramada Hotel
*HOR/BR* BL6 .......... 33 K5
Ramillies Hall School
*CHD/CHDH* SK8 .......... 120 E2
Ramsbottom Cemetery
*RAMS* BL0 .......... 18 D8
Ramsbottom Cottage Hospital
*RAMS* BL0 .......... 18 F7
Ramsbottom Health Centre
*RAMS* BL0 .......... 18 E6
Ramsbottom Swimming Pool
*RAMS* BL0 .......... 18 F5
Rassbottom Industrial Estate
*STLY* SK15 .......... 91 J2
Ravensbury Community School
*OP/CLY* M11 .......... 88 D2
Ravensfield Industrial Estate
*DUK* SK16 .......... 90 D3
Ravenside Retail Park
*BOLE* BL2 .......... 2 F4
Rectory CE Primary School
*AIMK* WN4 .......... 63 G7
Reddish Vale Golf Club
*RDSH* SK5 .......... 100 D6
Reddish Vale Technology College
*RDSH* SK5 .......... 100 C5

Red Lane Community School
*BOLE* BL2 ............... 37  J3
Red Rose Retail Centre
*ORD* M5 ............... 86  E3
Reebok Museum
*HOR/BR* BL6 ............... 34  A4
Regal Industrial Estate
*WGTN/LGST* M12 ............... 88  C5
Regent Cinema
*MPL/ROM* SK6 ............... 114  A4
Regent Park Golf Course
*HOR/BR* BL6 ............... 34  E5
Regent Trading Estate
*ORD* M5 ............... 6  A4
The Regimental Museum of the
Lancashire Fusiliers
*TOT/BURYW* BL8 ............... 38  E3
Reliance Trading Estate
*NEWH/MOS* M40 ............... 73  M5
Renaissance Hotel
*CSLFD* M3 ............... 6  A4
Ribble Drive Primary School
*WHTF* M45 ............... 55  K3
Richmond Medical Centre
*AUL* OL6 ............... 90  F1
Richmond Park Athletics
Stadium *AULW* OL7 ............... 75  H8
Richmond Park School
*WGTN/LGST* M12 ............... 88  B7
Richmond Primary School
*CHAD* OL9 ............... 8  F6
The Ridge College
*MPL/ROM* SK6 ............... 114  B7
Ridge Danyers College
*CHD/CHDH* SK8 ............... 120  A1
Ridgmont Cemetery
*HOR/BR* BL6 ............... 34  A1
Ringway Golf Club
*HALE/TIMP* WA15 ............... 117  L3
Ringway Primary School
*WYTH/NTH* M22 ............... 118  F4
Ringway Trading Estate
*WYTH/NTH* M22 ............... 119  G4
Riverside Business Park
*WILM/AE* SK9 ............... 126  F5
R L Hughes Primary School
*AIMK* WN4 ............... 78  D1
Roaches Industrial Estate
*MOSL* OL5 ............... 61  H8
Robin Park Arena
*WGNW/BIL/OR* WN5 ............... 14  A3
Robin Park Sports Centre
*WGNW/BIL/OR* WN5 ............... 47  J4
Rochdale AFC
(Spotland Stadium)
*ROCH* OL11 ............... 27  M4
Rochdale Cemetery
*ROCH* OL11 ............... 27  L5
Rochdale Crematorium
*ROCH* OL11 ............... 27  L5
Rochdale Cricket, Lacrosse &
Squash Club
*ROCH* OL11 ............... 10  A4
Rochdale Curtain Theatre
*ROCH* OL11 ............... 10  D7
Rochdale Golf Club
*ROCH* OL11 ............... 27  K4
Rochdale Healthcare
*WHIT* OL12 ............... 21  H7
Rochdale Industrial Centre
*ROCH* OL11 ............... 10  A6
Rochdale Infirmary
*WHIT* OL12 ............... 10  E1
Rodney House School
*BNG/LEV* M19 ............... 99  J4
Roe Cross Industrial Park
*HYDE* SK14 ............... 92  D7
Roker Industrial Estate
*OLD* OL1 ............... 59  L4
Rolls Crescent Primary School
*HULME* M15 ............... 87  H7
Roman Fort
*CSLFD* M3 ............... 6  C7
Romiley Golf Club
*MPL/ROM* SK6 ............... 114  A1
Romiley Health Centre
*MPL/ROM* SK6 ............... 113  M2
Romiley Primary School
*MPL/ROM* SK6 ............... 114  A2
Roscow Fold Primary School
*BOLE* BL2 ............... 37  H4
Rose Bridge High School
*WGN* WN1 ............... 15  M3
Rosedale Shopping Centre
*NEWH/MOS* M40 ............... 73  M7
Rosehill Methodist Community
Primary School
*AUL* OL6 ............... 76  C6
Rosehill Methodist Community
School *AUL* OL6 ............... 76  C7
Rose Hill Primary School
*MPL/ROM* SK6 ............... 114  B6
Ross Business Centre
*WGNW/BIL/OR* WN5 ............... 47  G7
Rossendale School
*RAMS* BL0 ............... 19  J5
Roundthorn Industrial Estate
*NTHM/RTH* M23 ............... 109  H6
Roundthorn Primary School
*OLDE* OL4 ............... 59  M7
Roundwood School
*WYTH/NTH* M22 ............... 109  M5
Roxy Cinema
*OLDS* OL8 ............... 74  D3
Royal Albert Edward Infirmary
*WGN* WN1 ............... 47  M2
Royal Bolton Hospital
*FWTH* BL4 ............... 52  C3
Royal Exchange Clinic
*CMANW* M2 ............... 6  F4
Royal Exchange Shopping
Centre
*CMANE* M1 ............... 6  F3
*MILN* OL16 ............... 10  D4
Royal Exchange Theatre
*CSLFD* M3 ............... 6  F4
Royal Manchester Childrens
Hospital *SWIN* M27 ............... 70  E5
Royal Northern College of Music
*HULME* M15 ............... 87  K6
Royal Oak Industrial Estate
*STKP* SK1 ............... 13  K7
Royal Oak Primary School
*NTHM/RTH* M23 ............... 109  K5
Royal Oldham Hospital
*OLD* OL1 ............... 8  F1
Royal Pennine Trading Estate
*ROCH* OL11 ............... 41  L1
Royce Trading Estate
*TRPK* M17 ............... 85  J5
Royle Pennine Trading Estate
*ROCH* OL11 ............... 42  A1

Royton & Crompton School
*ROY/SHW* OL2 ............... 43  K8
Royton Medical Centre
*ROY/SHW* OL2 ............... 43  G8
Royton Public Baths
*ROY/SHW* OL2 ............... 43  H8
Rugby Road Industrial Estate
*WHIT* OL12 ............... 11  G1
Rumworth School
*BOLS/LL* BL3 ............... 35  J7
Rushcroft Primary School
*ROY/SHW* OL2 ............... 43  L4
Russell Scott Primary School
*DTN/ASHW* M34 ............... 90  D8
Rycroft Park Sports Club
*CHD/CHDH* SK8 ............... 120  B3
Rydings Special School
*WHIT* OL12 ............... 20  F8
Ryecroft Business Park
*AULW* OL7 ............... 90  C3
The Ryleys School
*WILM/AE* SK9 ............... 130  C3
Sacred Heart Catholic Primary
School *WGNE/HIN* WN2 ............... 65  L1
Sacred Heart RC Infant School
*GTN* M18 ............... 88  F8
Sacred Heart RC Junior School
*GTN* M18 ............... 88  F8
Sacred Heart RC Primary
School *ATH* M46 ............... 67  H3
*LEIGH* WN7 ............... 66  B7
*MILN* OL16 ............... 11  L6
*NTHM/RTH* M23 ............... 109  J6
*OLD* OL1 ............... 59  M2
*WCNNW/ST* WN6 ............... 47  J2
*WHTN* BL5 ............... 50  C3
Saddleworth Business Centre
*UPML* OL3 ............... 45  J8
Saddleworth Golf Club
*UPML* OL3 ............... 61  K4
Saddleworth Museum &
Art Gallery
*UPML* OL3 ............... 61  K4
Saddleworth Preparatory School
*OLDE* OL4 ............... 60  F4
Saddleworth School
*UPML* OL3 ............... 61  L3
Saddleworth Swimming Pool
*UPML* OL3 ............... 61  L5
St Aelreds RC Technology College
*NEWLW* WA12 ............... 79  G8
St Agnes CE Primary School
*BRUN/LGST* M13 ............... 99  J1
*OLDE* OL4 ............... 60  D7
St Aidan & Oswalds RC Primary
School *ROY/SHW* OL2 ............... 59  G1
St Aidans Catholic Primary
School
*NTHM/RTH* M23 ............... 109  L3
St Aidans CE Primary School
*WGNW/BIL/OR* WN5 ............... 62  B7
St Aidans RC Primary School
*WGNS/IIMK* WN3 ............... 63  G1
St Alphonsus RC Primary School
*OLDTF/WHR* M16 ............... 86  F7
St Ambrose Barlow RC High
School & Salford College
*SWIN* M27 ............... 70  C5
St Ambrose Barlow RC Primary
School *TYLD* M29 ............... 67  K7
St Ambrose College
*HALE/TIMP* WA15 ............... 117  K5
St Ambrose RC Primary School
*CCHDY* M21 ............... 98  A8
*EDGY/DAV* SK3 ............... 112  A7
St Andrews CE Junior School
*GLSP* SK13 ............... 93  J8
St Andrews CE Primary School
*BNG/LEV* M19 ............... 99  L4
*RAD* M26 ............... 38  B6
*RAMS* BL0 ............... 18  C6
*WALK* M28 ............... 68  D7
*WCNNW/ST* WN6 ............... 47  J2
*WHTN* BL5 ............... 51  K4
St Andrew's CE Primary School
*WHIT* OL12 ............... 21  J8
St Andrews CE School
*ECC* M30 ............... 85  H3
St Andrews Medical Centre
*ECC* M30 ............... 85  H2
St Andrews Methodist Primary
School *WALK* M28 ............... 68  E1
St Annes CE Lydgate Primary
School *OLDE* OL4 ............... 60  F6
St Annes CE Primary School
*ROY/SHW* OL2 ............... 59  H1
*SALE* M33 ............... 96  F8
*WCNNW/ST* WN6 ............... 47  G1
St Annes Ear Nose & Throat
Hospital *ALT* WA14 ............... 116  E1
St Annes Primary School
*DTN/ASHW* M34 ............... 90  D8
St Annes RC High School
*HTNM* SK4 ............... 100  A4
St Annes RC Primary School
*CHH* M8 ............... 72  D4
*DTN/ASHW* M34 ............... 89  K5
*OLDE* OL4 ............... 59  M5
St Anns RC Primary School
*STRET* M32 ............... 97  G2
St Anthonys RC Primary School
*WYTH/NTH* M22 ............... 118  F3
St Antonys Catholic College
*STRET* M32 ............... 96  C2
St Augustine of Canterbury RC
School *OLDS* OL8 ............... 75  G1
St Augustines CE Primary School
*NEWH/MOS* M40 ............... 73  H7
*SWIN* M27 ............... 70  E4
St Barnabas CE Primary School
*OP/CLY* M11 ............... 88  E4
St Bartholomews CE Primary
School *WHIT* OL12 ............... 20  A4
St Bede CE Primary School
*BOLS/LL* BL3 ............... 51  M2
St Bede's Preparatory School
*OLDTF/WHR* M16 ............... 98  B1
St Benedicts Catholic Primary
School *WGNE/HIN* WN2 ............... 48  F6
St Benedict's Catholic Primary
School *WILM/AE* SK9 ............... 127  J1
St Bernadettes Catholic Primary
School *WCNNW/ST* WN6 ............... 30  D6
St Bernadettes RC Primary
School *RDSH* SK5 ............... 100  E8
St Bernard RC Primary School
*WHTF* M45 ............... 55  J2
St Bernard's RC Primary School
*BOLS/LL* BL3 ............... 35  H7
St Bernard's RC Primary School
*BNG/LEV* M19 ............... 99  J6
St Boniface RC Primary School
*BRO* M7 ............... 71  M6

St Brendan RC Primary School
*BOLE* BL2 ............... 23  H7
St Brigids RC Primary School
*OP/CLY* M11 ............... 88  D3
St Catharines CE Primary School
*WGN* WN1 ............... 15  K4
St Catherines CE Primary School
*HOR/BR* BL6 ............... 33  L1
St Catherines Preparatory
School
*MPL/ROM* SK6 ............... 114  E5
St Catherines RC Primary
School *DID/WITH* M20 ............... 110  F1
*GOL/RIS/CUL* WA3 ............... 80  B4
St Chads CE Primary School
*UPML* OL3 ............... 61  M3
St Chads RC Primary School
*CHH* M8 ............... 72  D7
St Charles RC Primary School
*SWIN* M27 ............... 70  A4
St Christophers RC Primary
School
*AUL* OL6 ............... 76  B6
*MPL/ROM* SK6 ............... 113  K2
St Chrysostoms CE Primary
School
*BRUN/LGST* M13 ............... 87  M7
St Clares RC Primary School
*BKLY* M9 ............... 56  F7
St Clement (Egerton) CE Primary
School
*ORD* M5 ............... 86  E4
St Clement's CE Primary School
*OP/CLY* M11 ............... 89  H5
St Columbas RC Primary School
*BOLE* BL2 ............... 22  F8
St Cuthberts RC High School
*MILN* OL16 ............... 42  E3
St Cuthberts RC Primary School
*DID/WITH* M20 ............... 98  F7
*WGNW/BIL/OR* WN5 ............... 47  G6
St Damians RC High School
*AUL* OL6 ............... 76  B5
St Davids CE Primary School
*WGNE/HIN* WN2 ............... 32  E5
St Dunstans RC Primary School
*NEWH/MOS* M40 ............... 73  K4
St Edmund Arrowsmith Catholic
High School
*AIMK* WN4 ............... 78  D2
St Edmunds RC Primary School
*LHULT* M38 ............... 52  E8
*NEWH/MOS* M40 ............... 73  H6
St Edwards CE Primary School
*ROCH* OL11 ............... 41  L2
St Edwards RC Primary School
*OLDE* OL4 ............... 60  B5
*RUSH/FAL* M14 ............... 98  E2
St Elisabeths CE Primary School
*RDSH* SK5 ............... 100  B4
St Elizabeth RC Primary School
*WYTH/NTH* M22 ............... 119  G2
St Ethelbert RC Primary School
*BOLS/LL* BL3 ............... 35  L7
St Gabriels CE Primary School
*MDTN* M24 ............... 57  M5
St Gabriels Medical Centre
*PWCH* M25 ............... 72  A2
St Gabriels RC High School
*TOT/BURYW* BL8 ............... 4  B6
St Gabriels RC Primary School
*LEIGH* WN7 ............... 67  H5
*ROCH* OL11 ............... 42  A3
St Georges Central CE Primary
School *TYLD* M29 ............... 67  K3
St Georges CE Primary School
*ATH* M46 ............... 50  E3
*HYDE* SK14 ............... 102  A3
*MOSL* OL5 ............... 76  E3
*NM/HAY* SK22 ............... 124  C4
*OFTN* SK2 ............... 112  C6
*WHTN* BL5 ............... 50  A5
St Georges Craft Centre
*BOL* BL1 ............... 2  E3
St Georges RC High School
*WALK* M28 ............... 68  F2
St Gilberts RC Primary School
*ECC* M30 ............... 84  D2
St Gregory RC Primary School
*FWTH* BL4 ............... 53  H4
St Helens Community College
*NEWLW* WA12 ............... 78  E8
St Herberts RC Primary School
*CHAD* OL9 ............... 58  D5
St Hilarys School
*WILM/AE* SK9 ............... 130  D3
St Hildas CE Primary School
*OLD* OL1 ............... 9  G3
*PWCH* M25 ............... 55  M8
St Hugh of Lincoln RC Primary
School *STRET* M32 ............... 96  C1
St Hughs Catholic Primary
School *HALE/TIMP* WA15 ............... 108  C5
St Hughs CE Primary School
*OLDE* OL4 ............... 76  A1
St James Catholic High School
*CHD/CHDH* SK8 ............... 120  B5
St James Catholic Primary
School *HYDE* SK14 ............... 103  G2
*WGNW/BIL/OR* WN5 ............... 46  A8
St James CE Primary School
*AUL* OL6 ............... 90  F1
*FWTH* BL4 ............... 52  E5
*GTN* M18 ............... 89  G6
*RUSH/FAL* M14 ............... 99  G2
*WGNS/IIMK* WN3 ............... 14  A9
*WHIT* OL12 ............... 21  G6
St James CE School
*GLSP* SK13 ............... 104  E4
St James (Daisy Hill) CE Primary
School *WHTN* BL5 ............... 50  C7
St James Primary School
*RNFD/HAY* WA11 ............... 78  B6
St James School
*HTNM* SK4 ............... 13  G1
St James's RC School
*SLFD* M6 ............... 86  C1
St John Bosco RC Primary School
*BKLY* M9 ............... 57  J8
St John CE Primary School
*FWTH* BL4 ............... 53  H4
St John Fisher Catholic High
School *WCNNW/ST* WN6 ............... 47  J1
St John Fisher RC Primary
School *DTN/ASHW* M34 ............... 101  L3
*MDTN* M24 ............... 57  L1
St John Fisher & St Thomas
More RC Primary School
*WYTH/NTH* M22 ............... 110  A8

St John RC Primary School
*MILN* OL16 ............... 10  F6
St John Rigby College
*WGNW/BIL/OR* WN5 ............... 46  C2
St Johns Cathedral
*CSLFD* M3 ............... 6  A3
St Johns CE Infant School
*FAIL* M35 ............... 74  C4
*LEIGH* WN7 ............... 66  C6
St Johns CE Junior School
*FAIL* M35 ............... 74  D5
St Johns CE Primary School
*BRUN/LGST* M13 ............... 88  B8
*HTNM* SK4 ............... 111  H2
*MDTN* M24 ............... 42  B6
*RAD* M26 ............... 54  D3
*SLFD* M6 ............... 70  F6
*STLY* SK15 ............... 91  H4
*WGNE/HIN* WN2 ............... 65  L1
*WGNW/BIL/OR* WN5 ............... 46  E6
St Johns Industrial Estate
*OLDE* OL4 ............... 60  B6
St Johns Medical Centre
*ALT* WA14 ............... 116  E1
St Johns Mosley Common CE
Primary School
*WALK* M28 ............... 68  C4
St Johns RC Primary School
*CCHDY* M21 ............... 97  K3
St Johns with St Marks CE
Primary School
*BURY* BL9 ............... 25  H8
St John the Evangelist RC
Primary School
*EDGW/EG* BL7 ............... 22  C5
St John Vianney School
*HTNM* SK4 ............... 12  A3
St John Vianney Upper School
*OLDTF/WHR* M16 ............... 97  L2
St Josephs & St Bedes RC Primary
School *BURY* BL9 ............... 25  L8
St Josephs Catholic Primary
School
*WGNNW/ST* WN6 ............... 30  C1
St Josephs RC High School
*HEY* OL10 ............... 40  F4
St Josephs RC Infant School
*RDSH* SK5 ............... 100  B4
St Josephs RC Junior School
*RDSH* SK5 ............... 100  B4
St Josephs RC Primary School
*BOL* BL1 ............... 35  M2
*BRUN/LGST* M13 ............... 88  B8
*HEY* OL10 ............... 40  F3
*LEIGH* WN7 ............... 66  D8
*LHULT* M38 ............... 52  D7
*MOSL* OL5 ............... 76  F3
*ORD* M5 ............... 86  E4
*RAMS* BL0 ............... 18  C6
*ROY/SHW* OL2 ............... 43  K7
*SALE* M33 ............... 96  E8
*STKP* SK1 ............... 13  J4
St Josephs RC School
*HOR/BR* BL6 ............... 34  B3
St Josephs the Worker RC
Primary School
*IRL* M44 ............... 94  D1
St Judes Catholic
Primary School
*WCNS/IIMK* WN3 ............... 47  J7
St Judes CE Primary School
*ANC* M4 ............... 7  L3
St Kentigerns RC Primary School
*RUSH/FAL* M14 ............... 98  D3
St Lukes CE Primary School
*BRUN/LGST* M13 ............... 88  B7
*BURY* BL9 ............... 4  F9
*CHAD* OL9 ............... 58  D5
*GLSP* SK13 ............... 104  F5
*GOL/RIS/CUL* WA3 ............... 80  F3
*HEY* OL10 ............... 41  G1
St Lukes RC Primary School
*SLFD* M6 ............... 70  F7
St Lukes with All Saints CE
Primary School
*ORD* M5 ............... 86  A3
St Malachys RC Primary School
*NEWH/MOS* M40 ............... 72  F7
St Margaret Marys RC Primary
School *NEWH/MOS* M40 ............... 74  A1
St Margarets CE Primary School
*HEY* OL10 ............... 40  D3
*OLDS* OL8 ............... 74  F2
*OLDTF/WHR* M16 ............... 98  A2
*PWCH* M25 ............... 56  A3
St Margarets RC Primary School
*GLSP* SK13 ............... 104  A4
St Margaret Ward RC Primary
School *SALE* M33 ............... 107  M2
St Maries RC Primary School
*BURY* BL9 ............... 4  F6
*WCNNW/ST* WN6 ............... 31  H7
St Marks CE Primary School
*MPL/ROM* SK6 ............... 101  K8
*NEWH/MOS* M40 ............... 88  A1
*WALK* M28 ............... 69  J6
*WGNW/BIL/OR* WN5 ............... 47  J5
St Marks RC Primary School
*SWIN* M27 ............... 70  D2
St Martins CE Primary School
*OLDS* OL8 ............... 75  L2
St Martins School
*SALE* M33 ............... 96  B7
St Mary CE Primary School
*BOLS/LL* BL3 ............... 35  J8
St Mary RC Primary School
*HOR/BR* BL6 ............... 34  A2
St Mary's Catholic Cemetery
*WALK* M28 ............... 69  L4
St Marys Catholic Junior School
*NEWLW* WA12 ............... 78  E8
St Marys Catholic School
*NEWLW* WA12 ............... 78  F8
St Marys CE J & I School
*WCNS/IIMK* WN3 ............... 48  C3
St Marys CE Primary School
*DROY* M43 ............... 89  K3
*NEWH/MOS* M40 ............... 73  M3
*OLDTF/WHR* M16 ............... 87  H8
*PWCH* M25 ............... 55  K7
*RDSH* SK5 ............... 100  D6
*ROCH* OL11 ............... 28  D8
*ROY/SHW* OL2 ............... 43  J4
*TOT/BURYW* BL8 ............... 23  L2
*UPML* OL3 ............... 61  M8
St Mary's CE Primary School
*SALE* M33 ............... 96  C3
St Mary's Hospital
*BRUN/LGST* M13 ............... 87  M8
St Marys Medical Centre
*OLD* OL1 ............... 9  K5

St Marys RC High School
*TYLD* M29 ............... 67  K8
St Marys RC Primary School
*BNG/LEV* M19 ............... 99  K4
*DTN/ASHW* M34 ............... 101  H3
*DUK* SK16 ............... 91  H6
*FAIL* M35 ............... 74  B4
*GLSP* SK13 ............... 105  G4
*HTNM* SK4 ............... 13  H3
*LEIGH* WN7 ............... 57  H2
*MPL/ROM* SK6 ............... 114  D5
*NM/HAY* SK22 ............... 124  D4
*RAD* M26 ............... 38  D8
*SWIN* M27 ............... 70  C4
St Mary's RC Primary School
*ECC* M30 ............... 85  K3
*LIT* OL15 ............... 21  L6
St Marys & St Johns RC Primary
School *WGN* WN1 ............... 15  L7
St Matthew CE Primary School
*BOL* BL1 ............... 2  D1
*BOL* BL1 ............... 36  B3
*BOLS/LL* BL3 ............... 53  K1
St Matthews CE Infant School
*OLD* OL1 ............... 58  C2
St Matthews CE Primary School
*EDGY/DAV* SK3 ............... 13  G7
*STRET* M32 ............... 96  F4
St Matthews RC High School
*NEWH/MOS* M40 ............... 73  M2
St Maxentius CE Primary School
*BOLE* BL2 ............... 23  G7
St Michael CE Primary School
*BOLS/LL* BL3 ............... 52  E1
St Michaels CE Aided Primary
School *URM* M41 ............... 95  J3
St Michaels CE Primary Howe
Bridge School
*ATH* M46 ............... 66  E2
St Michaels CE Primary School
*HEY* OL10 ............... 26  F8
*MDTN* M24 ............... 57  K7
St Michaels RC Primary School
*WHTF* M45 ............... 55  L3
St Monicas RC High School
*PWCH* M25 ............... 71  M1
St Monicas RC Primary School
*URM* M41 ............... 95  G3
St Nathaniels CE Primary School
*WGNE/HIN* WN2 ............... 64  E1
St Osmunds & St Andrews
Primary School
*BOLE* BL2 ............... 37  G5
St Oswalds RC J & I School
*AIMK* WN4 ............... 78  E1
St Patrick's Catholic High School
*ECC* M30 ............... 84  E2
St Patricks RC Primary School
*ANC* M4 ............... 87  M1
*CHAD* OL9 ............... 8  F7
*WGN* WN1 ............... 15  J4
St Patricks VA RC Primary School
*LEIGH* WN7 ............... 28  D3
St Paul CE Primary School
*BOL* BL1 ............... 36  C1
St Pauls Catholic High School
*NTHM/RTH* M23 ............... 109  L8
St Pauls Catholic Primary School
*POY/DIS* SK12 ............... 129  J2
St Paul's Cemetery
*BOL* BL1 ............... 35  M2
St Pauls CE Primary School
*BRO* M7 ............... 71  L4
*BURY* BL9 ............... 5  K1
*DID/WITH* M20 ............... 98  E6
*ORD* M5 ............... 86  E3
*RDSH* SK5 ............... 100  E8
*ROY/SHW* OL2 ............... 58  F1
*STLY* SK15 ............... 91  H2
*WALK* M28 ............... 69  H2
*WGNS/IIMK* WN3 ............... 63  J1
St Pauls Peel CE Primary School
*LHULT* M38 ............... 52  C7
St Pauls RC Primary School
*HYDE* SK14 ............... 91  J8
St Pauls Trading Estate
*STLY* SK15 ............... 91  M2
St Peter CE Primary School
*FWTH* BL4 ............... 53  G5
St Peter & St John Primary School
*CSLFD* M3 ............... 6  B2
St Peter & St Paul Primary
School *BOLS/LL* BL3 ............... 2  A7
St Peters Catholic High School
*WGNW/BIL/OR* WN5 ............... 46  C5
St Peters Catholic Primary
School *BRAM/HZG* SK7 ............... 121  M3
*NTHM/RTH* M23 ............... 118  C1
*STLY* SK15 ............... 91  L3
St Peters CE Infant School
*LEIGH* WN7 ............... 65  M7
St Peters CE Junior School
*LEIGH* WN7 ............... 65  M7
St Peters CE Primary School
*AIMK* WN4 ............... 63  J6
*AULW* OL7 ............... 90  D3
*BURY* BL9 ............... 39  F5
*SWIN* M27 ............... 70  B4
*WGNE/HIN* WN2 ............... 48  F7
St Peter's CE Primary School
*NEWLW* WA12 ............... 79  G8
St Peters RC High School Upper
School *DROY* M43 ............... 89  H4
St Peter's RC Primary School
*MDTN* M24 ............... 57  K5
St Peters VC CE Primary School
*MILN* OL16 ............... 11  K9
St Philip Howard Catholic School
*GLSP* SK13 ............... 104  E3
St Philips Catholic Primary School
*OFTN* SK2 ............... 113  H6
St Philips CE Primary School
*ATH* M46 ............... 66  H1
*HULME* M15 ............... 87  H7
St Philips RC Primary School
*PWCH* M25 ............... 71  M3
St Philips School
*CSLFD* M3 ............... 6  A4
St Raphaels Catholic Primary School
*STLY* SK15 ............... 77  H7
St Richards RC Primary School
*WGTN/LGST* M12 ............... 99  L1
St Saviour Primary School Ringley
*RAD* M26 ............... 53  M5
St Sebastians RC Primary School
*SLFD* M6 ............... 71  K7
St Simons Catholic
Primary School
*BRAM/HZG* SK7 ............... 122  A1
St Stephen & All Martyrs
CE Primary School
*BOLE* BL2 ............... 3  L7

St Stephens & All Martyrs Infant
School *OLD* OL1 .......... 9 K3
St Stephens CE Primary School
*DTN/ASHW* M34 .......... 90 B4
*FWTH* BL4 .......... 53 K6
*OFTN* SK2 .......... 113 J3
*TOT/BURYW* BL8 .......... 38 E3
*TYLD* M29 .......... 67 L6
St Stephens RC School
*DROY* M43 .......... 89 K2
St Teresa RC Primary School
*BOLS/LL* BL3 .......... 53 K1
St Teresas RC Primary School
*IRL* M44 .......... 94 B4
*OLDTF/WHR* M16 .......... 97 K1
St Thomas Aquinas
RC High School
*CCHDY* M21 .......... 97 M5
St Thomas CE Primary School
*AIMK* WN4 .......... 78 F1
*BOL* BL1 .......... 36 A2
*BURY* BL9 .......... 5 K6
*GOL/RIS/CUL* WA3 .......... 79 L3
*HTNM* SK4 .......... 99 M6
*LEIGH* WN7 .......... 66 E8
*MILN* OL16 .......... 29 J1
*OLDS* OL8 .......... 9 G8
*STKP* SK1 .......... 13 K6
*WHTN* BL5 .......... 50 E3
St Thomas Leesfield CE Primary
School *OLDE* OL4 .......... 60 B7
St Thomas Mooreside CE (VA)
Primary School
*OLD* OL1 .......... 44 B8
St Thomas More Catholic High
School
*WGNW/BIL/OR* WN5 .......... 14 A6
St Thomas More RC College
*DTN/ASHW* M34 .......... 101 J2
St Thomas More
RC Primary School
*MDTN* M24 .......... 57 K7
St Thomas of Canterbury RC
Primary School
*BOL* BL1 .......... 35 K4
*BRO* M7 .......... 72 B6
St Thomas Primary School
*CHH* M8 .......... 72 F4
St Thomas's Hospital
*EDGY/DAV* SK3 .......... 13 H8
St Vincent RC Infant School
*HALE/TIMP* WA15 .......... 108 B7
St Vincents RC Primary School
*WHIT* OL12 .......... 27 K3
St Wilfrids Catholic Primary
School *AIMK* WN4 .......... 64 A8
St Wilfrids CE Primary School
*NEWH/MOS* M40 .......... 74 A7
*WGNNW/ST* WN6 .......... 31 J3
*WYTH/NTH* M22 .......... 110 B4
St Wilfrids RC Primary School
*HULME* M15 .......... 87 H6
St William RC Primary School
*BOLS/LL* BL3 .......... 52 B1
St Williams RC Primary School
*WGNE/HIN* WN2 .......... 48 C5
St Willibrords RC Primary School
*OP/CLY* M11 .......... 88 C7
St Winifreds RC Primary School
*HTNM* SK4 .......... 111 K2
SS Simon & Jude CE Primary
School *BOLS/LL* BL3 .......... 52 C1
Sale CC
*SALE* M33 .......... 97 G7
Sale Golf Club
*SALE* M33 .......... 97 J7
Sale Grammar School
*SALE* M33 .......... 108 F1
Sale Leisure Centre
*SALE* M33 .......... 96 F1
Sale Water Park
*SALE* M33 .......... 97 H6
Salford City Academy
*ECC* M30 .......... 84 C3
Salford City Reds RLFC
(The Willows) *ORD* M5 .......... 86 A2
Salford College
*ECC* M30 .......... 84 D2
*SALQ* M50 .......... 86 D5
*SLFD* M6 .......... 71 L8
*SWIN* M27 .......... 69 M2
*WALK* M28 .......... 69 G3
Salford County Court
*ORD* M5 .......... 86 D3
Salford Medical Centre
*SLFD* M6 .......... 86 B2
Salford Museum & Art Gallery
*ORD* M5 .......... 86 F2
Salford Shopping City
*SLFD* M6 .......... 86 D1
Salford University Business Park
*SLFD* M6 .......... 71 L8
Samuel Laycock Special School
*AUL* OL6 .......... 91 G1
Sandbrook Community Primary
School *ROCH* OL11 .......... 42 B1
Sandilands Primary School
*NTHM/RTH* M23 .......... 108 F4
Saviour CE Primary School
*NEWH/MOS* M40 .......... 72 F4
Savoy Cinema
*HTNM* SK4 .......... 111 K1
Saxon Hall Leisure Centre
*MILN* OL16 .......... 11 L3
Scholes Shopping Precinct
*WGN* WN1 .......... 15 J3
School Street Industrial Estate
*BRAM/HZG* SK7 .......... 122 A2
Scot Lane End CE
Primary School
*HOR/BR* BL6 .......... 33 H4
Scot Lane Industrial Estate
*HOR/BR* BL6 .......... 33 H6
Seaford Industrial Estate
*SLFD* M6 .......... 71 L8
Sedgley Park Community
Primary School
*PWCH* M25 .......... 71 H1
Sedgley Park RUFC
*WHTF* M45 .......... 55 G6
Sedgley Park Trading Estate
*PWCH* M25 .......... 71 L3
Seedley Primary School
*SLFD* M6 .......... 86 B2
Sett Valley Medical Centre
*NM/HAY* SK22 .......... 124 D3
Seven Brooks Medical Centre
*ATH* M46 .......... 67 G4
Severnside Trading Estate
*TRPK* M17 .......... 85 L7
Seymour Park Primary School
*OLDTF/WHR* M16 .......... 86 E8

Seymour Road Primary School
*OP/CLY* M11 .......... 89 G3
Shakerley CE Primary School
*TYLD* M29 .......... 67 K2
Shandon Clinic (Europe)
*HULME* M15 .......... 87 K7
Sharples Primary School
*BOL* BL1 .......... 22 D7
Shawclough Community
Primary School
*WHIT* OL12 .......... 28 B1
Shawclough Trading Estate
*WHIT* OL12 .......... 28 A1
Shawgrove School
*DID/WITH* M20 .......... 98 C6
Shaw Heath Health Centre
*EDGY/DAV* SK3 .......... 13 H8
Shay Lane Medical Centre
*HALE/TIMP* WA15 .......... 117 L3
Shepherd Cross Industrial Estate
*BOL* BL1 .......... 35 M2
Shepley North Industrial Estate
*DTN/ASHW* M34 .......... 90 D5
Shepley South Industrial Estate
*DTN/ASHW* M34 .......... 90 D6
Sherborne Trading Estate
*CHH* M8 .......... 72 C7
Sherwood Business Park
*ROCH* OL11 .......... 42 A2
Shevington Community Primary
School
*WGNNW/ST* WN6 .......... 30 C6
Shevington High School
*WGNNW/ST* WN6 .......... 30 E5
Shevington Vale Primary School
*WGNNW/ST* WN6 .......... 30 B4
Shire Hill Hospital
*GLSP* SK13 .......... 105 H1
Shiv Lodge Medical Centre
*BRUN/LGST* M13 .......... 99 J3
The Shopping Centre
*CHD/CHDH* SK8 .......... 120 C2
Showcase Cinemas Belle Vue
*GTN* M18 .......... 88 E7
Siddal Moor Sports College
*HEY* OL10 .......... 41 G5
Simmondley Primary School
*GLSP* SK13 .......... 104 D4
Skylink Walkway
*MANAIR* M90 .......... 118 C5
Slough Industrial Estate
*ORD* M5 .......... 86 F4
Smallbridge Health Centre
*WHIT* OL12 .......... 28 F1
Smallbridge Industrial Park
*MILN* OL16 .......... 28 F2
Smedleylane Junior School
*CHH* M8 .......... 72 E6
Smithills School
*BOL* BL1 .......... 35 L1
Smithy Bridge Primary School
*LIT* OL15 .......... 29 J1
The Smithy Surgery
*HYDE* SK14 .......... 93 G7
Snipe Retail Park
*AULW* OL7 .......... 90 A4
South Chadderton School
*CHAD* OL9 .......... 74 C2
Southern Cross School
*CCHDY* M21 .......... 97 M7
South Failsworth Primary
School *FAIL* M35 .......... 74 B4
Southfield Industrial Estate
*TRPK* M17 .......... 85 M7
Southgate Industrial Estate
*HEY* OL10 .......... 41 J3
South Lancashire Industrial
Estate *AIMK* WN4 .......... 63 L6
Southlink Business Park
*OLDE* OL4 .......... 9 M6
South Manchester High School
*WYTH/NTH* M22 .......... 118 F1
Southmoor Business Park
*NTHM/RTH* M23 .......... 109 H5
Southmoor Industrial Estate
*NTHM/RTH* M23 .......... 109 H5
South Oldham Business Park
*CHAD* OL9 .......... 8 D2
South Reddish Medical Centre
*RDSH* SK5 .......... 100 C8
Southside Industrial Park
*ATH* M46 .......... 50 E8
South Trafford College
*ALT* WA14 .......... 108 A4
South West Manchester CC
*CCHDY* M21 .......... 97 M3
Sovereign Business Park
*WGN* WN1 .......... 15 J6
Spa Road Industrial Estate
*BOL* BL1 .......... 2 B5
Spindle Point Primary School
*FWTH* BL4 .......... 53 L7
The Spindles Shopping Centre
*OLD* OL1 .......... 9 H6
Spinning Gate Shopping Centre
*LEIGH* WN7 .......... 66 C7
Sport City
*OP/CLY* M11 .......... 88 C2
Sports Injury Centre
*MDTN* M24 .......... 57 K5
Spotland Bridge Industrial Centre
*ROCH* OL11 .......... 27 M4
Spotland Primary School
*WHIT* OL12 .......... 10 B2
Springbank Industrial Estate
*WGNE/HIN* WN2 .......... 64 E1
Spring Brook School
*CHAD* OL9 .......... 58 C5
Springfield Business Centre
*CSLFD* M3 .......... 6 E1
Springfield Hotel
*MPL/ROM* SK6 .......... 114 C5
Springfield House
Medical Centre *OLD* OL1 .......... 59 M4
Springfield Industrial Estate
*FAIL* M35 .......... 74 B4
Springfield Primary School
*SALE* M33 .......... 96 E8
Springhead Community Infant
& First School
*OLDE* OL4 .......... 60 C6
Springhill High School
*MILN* OL16 .......... 11 L9
Springside CP School
*BURY* BL9 .......... 25 H5
Spring View CC
*WGNE/HIN* WN2 .......... 64 D1
Springwood Primary School
*MPL/ROM* SK6 .......... 114 B1
*SWIN* M27 .......... 70 D5
Spurley Hey High School
*BNG/LEV* M19 .......... 99 L2

Stag Industrial Estate
*ALT* WA14 .......... 107 L6
Stakehill Industrial Estate
*MDTN* M24 .......... 42 A8
Stalybridge Celtic AFC
*STLY* SK15 .......... 91 M4
Stalybridge CC
*DUK* SK16 .......... 91 H4
Stalybridge Millbrook CC
*STLY* SK15 .......... 77 G8
Stalybridge St Pauls CC
*DUK* SK16 .......... 91 J5
Stalyhill Infant School
*STLY* SK15 .......... 92 B5
Stalyhill Junior School
*STLY* SK15 .......... 92 A5
Staly Industrial Estate
*STLY* SK15 .......... 91 L2
Stamford Golf Club
*STLY* SK15 .......... 77 H5
Stamford High School
*AUL* OL6 .......... 76 B8
Stamford Park Junior School
*HALE/TIMP* WA15 .......... 117 G1
Standish Golf Club
*WGNNW/ST* WN6 .......... 31 H4
Standish Community High
School
*WGNNW/ST* WN6 .......... 30 F2
Standish Court Golf Club
*WGNNW/ST* WN6 .......... 31 J3
Standish CC
*WGNNW/ST* WN6 .......... 31 H4
Stanley Green Industrial Estate
*CHD/CHDH* SK8 .......... 120 A6
*WILM/AE* SK9 .......... 120 A8
Stanley Green Retail Park
*CHD/CHDH* SK8 .......... 120 B6
Stanley Grove Primary School
*WGTN/LGST* M12 .......... 88 C8
Stanley Road Primary School
*CHAD* OL9 .......... 58 E8
Stanneylands Hotel
*WILM/AE* SK9 .......... 126 F2
Star Industrial Estate
*OLDS* OL8 .......... 9 J8
Station Approach Business
Estate *ROCH* OL11 .......... 10 E7
Staveleigh Medical Centre
*STLY* SK15 .......... 91 K2
Stella Maris School
*HTNM* SK4 .......... 111 H2
Stepping Hill Hospital
*OFTN* SK2 .......... 112 E8
Stirling Industrial Estate
*HOR/BR* BL6 .......... 33 M2
Stockport Air Raid Shelter
*STKP* SK1 .......... 13 H4
Stockport Art Gallery
*EDGY/DAV* SK3 .......... 13 H6
Stockport Bus Station
*HTNM* SK4 .......... 13 G5
Stockport CC
*HTNM* SK4 .......... 112 C6
Stockport College
*HTNM* SK4 .......... 99 L6
Stockport College of Further
& Higher Education
*EDGY/DAV* SK3 .......... 13 H7
Stockport County Court
*STKP* SK1 .......... 13 H5
Stockport County FC & Sale
Sharks RUFC (Edgeley Park)
*EDGY/DAV* SK3 .......... 13 G8
Stockport Crematorium
*OFTN* SK2 .......... 13 M9
Stockport Golf Club
*OFTN* SK2 .......... 113 L7
Stockport Grammar School
*OFTN* SK2 .......... 112 E7
Stockport Mega Bowl
*STKP* SK1 .......... 13 H6
Stockport RUFC
*BRAM/HZG* SK7 .......... 121 H4
Stockport School
*OFTN* SK2 .......... 112 E7
Stockport Trading Estate
*HTNM* SK4 .......... 12 A6
Stone Cross Business Park
*GOL/RIS/CUL* WA3 .......... 79 L5
Stone Hill Industrial Estate
*FWTH* BL4 .......... 52 F5
Stoneleigh Primary School
*OLD* OL1 .......... 59 L2
The Strand Medical Centre
*ROCH* OL11 .......... 42 C2
Stretford Grammar School
*STRET* M32 .......... 97 H3
Stretford High School Community
Language College
*STRET* M32 .......... 86 B8
Stretford Leisure Centre
*STRET* M32 .......... 86 C8
Stretford Memorial Hospital
*OLDTF/WHR* M16 .......... 97 L1
Stubbins Primary School
*RAMS* BL0 .......... 19 G3
Styal Country Park (NT)
*WILM/AE* SK9 .......... 126 C1
Styal Golf Club
*WILM/AE* SK9 .......... 119 J7
Styal Primary School
*WILM/AE* SK9 .......... 119 G8
Sudden Health Centre
*ROCH* OL11 .......... 27 M8
Sudell Street Trading Estate
*ANC* M4 .......... 7 K1
Sugden Sports Centre
*CMANE* M1 .......... 7 G7
Summersales Industrial Estate
*WGNS/IIMK* WN3 .......... 46 E8
Summerseat Methodist Primary
School *BURY* BL9 .......... 25 G2
Summerville Primary School
*SLFD* M6 .......... 71 G7
Sunning Hill Primary School
*BOLS/LL* BL3 .......... 36 A8
Sunnybank Clinic
*BURY* BL9 .......... 55 K1
Sunny Bank Primary School
*BURY* BL9 .......... 55 K1
Sunset Business Centre
*FWTH* BL4 .......... 53 M7
Swan Meadow Industrial Estate
*WGNS/IIMK* WN3 .......... 14 D7
Swinton Cemetery
*SWIN* M27 .......... 70 B2
The Swinton County High
School
*SWIN* M27 .......... 70 B3
Swinton Industrial Estate
*SWIN* M27 .......... 70 D4

Swinton Leisure Centre
*SWIN* M27 .......... 70 C4
Swinton Park Golf Club
*SWIN* M27 .......... 70 D6
Talmud Torah Chinuch Norim
School
*BRO* M7 .......... 72 A5
Tameside Business Development
Centre *DTN/ASHW* M34 .......... 101 G1
Tameside Business Park
*DUK* SK16 .......... 90 E5
Tameside College
*AUL* OL6 .......... 91 G1
*HYDE* SK14 .......... 102 A5
Tameside County Court
*AUL* OL6 .......... 90 F2
Tameside General Hospital
*STLY* SK15 .......... 76 D8
Tame Valley Primary School
*RDSH* SK5 .......... 100 F5
Tandle Hill Country Park
*ROY/SHW* OL2 .......... 42 D6
Tanfield Special School
*WGNE/HIN* WN2 .......... 49 J3
Tashbar School
*BRO* M7 .......... 72 B3
Tavistock Industrial Estate
*OP/CLY* M11 .......... 89 G6
Taylors Sports Club
*ECC* M30 .......... 85 H3
Temple Primary School
*CHH* M8 .......... 72 E6
Ten Acres Sports Complex
*NEWH/MOS* M40 .......... 73 K7
Thames Industrial Estate
*WGTN/LGST* M12 .......... 88 A5
Thames Trading Centre
*IRL* M44 .......... 94 C5
Thistle Hotel
*CMANE* M1 .......... 7 H5
*RNFD/HAY* WA11 .......... 78 E4
*WILM/AE* SK9 .......... 119 M7
Thomasson Memorial Special
School *BOL* BL1 .......... 35 L5
Thorn Grove Primary School
*CHD/CHDH* SK8 .......... 120 C6
Thornham CC
*MDTN* M24 .......... 42 A5
Thornham St James CE Primary
School *ROY/SHW* OL2 .......... 43 G4
Thornleigh Salesian College
*BOL* BL1 .......... 22 A8
Thornsett Primary School
*NM/HAY* SK22 .......... 125 G1
Thornsett Trading Estate
*NM/HAY* SK22 .......... 125 G2
Thorp Primary School
*ROY/SHW* OL2 .......... 42 F7
Three Sisters Racing Circuit
*AIMK* WN4 .......... 63 M5
Times Retail Park
*HEY* OL10 .......... 40 F2
Timperley Health Centre
*HALE/TIMP* WA15 .......... 108 D5
Tintwistle CE Primary School
*GLSP* SK13 .......... 93 K5
Tithe Barn Primary School
*HTNM* SK4 .......... 111 K1
Tonacliffe Primary School
*WHIT* OL12 .......... 20 A6
Tonge Bridge Industrial Estate
*BOLE* BL2 .......... 3 J3
Tonge CC
*BOLE* BL2 .......... 36 F1
Tonge Fold Health Centre
*BOLE* BL2 .......... 3 L5
Tonge Moor Health Centre
*BOLE* BL2 .......... 36 F3
Tonge Moor Primary School
*BOLE* BL2 .......... 3 L1
Tootal Drive CP School
*ORD* M5 .......... 85 M2
Top o' th' Brow Primary School
*BOLE* BL2 .......... 37 H2
Torkington Primary School
*BRAM/HZG* SK7 .......... 122 C2
Tottington Health Centre
*TOT/BURYW* BL8 .......... 24 B5
Tottington High School
*TOT/BURYW* BL8 .......... 24 C6
Tottington Primary School
*TOT/BURYW* BL8 .......... 24 C7
Towers Business Park
*DID/WITH* M20 .......... 110 E3
Townfield Industrial Estate
*OLDE* OL4 .......... 59 L5
Towngate Business Centre
*LHULT* M38 .......... 52 B7
Town Hall & Albert Halls
*BOL* BL1 .......... 2 E5
Town Square Shopping Centre
*OLD* OL1 .......... 9 J5
Trafalgar Business Park
*CHH* M8 .......... 72 B8
Trafford Athletics Track
*CCHDY* M21 .......... 97 J3
Trafford Centre
*TRPK* M17 .......... 85 G6
Trafford Centre
Leisure Complex
*TRPK* M17 .......... 84 E6
Trafford FC
*URM* M41 .......... 95 K3
Trafford General Hospital
*URM* M41 .......... 95 K1
Trafford Healthcare
*SALE* M33 .......... 109 G1
Trafford Retail Park
*URM* M41 .......... 84 F7
Trafford Water Sports Centre
*SALE* M33 .......... 97 H6
Trans Pennine Trading Estate
*ROCH* OL11 .......... 42 A1
Travelodge
*ANC* M4 .......... 7 J3
*BURY* BL9 .......... 39 L5
*CHAD* OL9 .......... 58 B8
*CSLFD* M3 .......... 6 E3
*DID/WITH* M20 .......... 111 G3
*HEY* OL10 .......... 40 E8
*MCFLDN* SK10 .......... 129 K6
*RNFD/HAY* WA11 .......... 78 B5
Trent Industrial Estate
*ROY/SHW* OL2 .......... 43 G2
The Triangle
*ANC* M4 .......... 6 F3
Trinity CE High School
*HULME* M15 .......... 87 K6
Trinity Retail Park
*BOLE* BL2 .......... 3 H7
Trinity School
*STLY* SK15 .......... 91 J3

Tudor Industrial Estate
*DUK* SK16 .......... 90 D6
Tulip Inn Hotel
*URM* M41 .......... 84 F6
Tulketh Street Industrial Estate
*BKLY* M9 .......... 73 J4
Tunshill Golf Club
*MILN* OL16 .......... 29 M6
Turton & Edgworth CE/Methodist
Primary School
*EDGW/EG* BL7 .......... 17 H7
Turton Golf Club
*EDGW/EG* BL7 .......... 22 D2
Turton High School
*EDGW/EG* BL7 .......... 22 E5
Turton Leisure Centre
*EDGW/EG* BL7 .......... 22 D2
Turton Tower
*EDGW/EG* BL7 .......... 22 F1
Tweed Street Industrial Estate
*LEIGH* WN7 .......... 66 E8
Twelve Apostles RC
Primary School
*LEIGH* WN7 .......... 66 A4
Twine Valley Country Park
& Fishery
*RAMS* BL0 .......... 19 K4
Twiss Green Primary School
*GOL/RIS/CUL* WA3 .......... 81 H8
Two Porches School
*ATH* M46 .......... 67 G1
Two Porches Special School
*ATH* M46 .......... 50 F8
Two Trees High School
*DTN/ASHW* M34 .......... 101 L3
Tyldesley Cemetery
*TYLD* M29 .......... 68 A4
Tyldesley Primary School
*TYLD* M29 .......... 67 L5
Tyldesley Swimming Pool
*ATH* M46 .......... 67 H3
Tyntesfield CP School
*SALE* M33 .......... 108 B3
UCI Cinema
*TRPK* M17 .......... 85 G6
Union Mill Industrial Estate
*MOSL* OL5 .......... 77 G1
United Trading Estate
*OLDTF/WHR* M16 .......... 86 C7
University College Salford
*CSLFD* M3 .......... 6 A2
University Dental Hospital
of Manchester
*HULME* M15 .......... 87 K6
University of Bolton
*BOLS/LL* BL3 .......... 2 C7
University of Bolton Chadwick
Campus *BOLE* BL2 .......... 3 J6
University of Manchester
*ANC* M4 .......... 7 K7
*BRUN/LGST* M13 .......... 87 K7
*CMANE* M1 .......... 7 K5
*CMANE* M1 .......... 7 J7
*ECC* M30 .......... 84 A6
*HULME* M15 .......... 87 L7
*RUSH/FAL* M14 .......... 98 F1
*RUSH/FAL* M14 .......... 99 G3
University of Manchester Institute
of Science & Technology
*CMANE* M1 .......... 7 J9
University of Salford
*ECC* M30 .......... 85 H2
*ORD* M5 .......... 86 F2
*SLFD* M6 .......... 71 L8
*SLFD* M6 .......... 86 E1
Unsworth Medical Centre
*WGTN/LGST* M12 ..........
*BURY* BL9 .......... 55 M1
Unsworth Primary School
*BURY* BL9 .......... 55 K2
Urbis
*CSLFD* M3 .......... 6 F2
Urmston Grammar School
*URM* M41 .......... 95 M1
Urmston J & I School
*URM* M41 .......... 95 L2
Urmston Leisure Centre
*URM* M41 .......... 95 L2
Urmston Town FC
*URM* M41 .......... 95 J3
Vaishali Medical Centre
*CCHDY* M21 .......... 97 L3
Vale Park Industrial Estate
*CHH* M8 .......... 72 F5
The Valley Community School
*BOL* BL1 .......... 36 C2
The Valley Leisure Centre
*BOL* BL1 .......... 36 D1
Valley Special School
*BRAM/HZG* SK7 .......... 120 E7
Varley Street Clinic
*NEWH/MOS* M40 .......... 73 G8
Varna Street Primary School
*OP/CLY* M11 .......... 89 G6
Vaughan Street
Industrial Estate
*WGTN/LGST* M12 .......... 88 C5
Vauxhall Industrial Estate
*RDSH* SK5 .......... 100 C8
*RDSH* SK5 .......... 100 B6
Vernon Industrial Estate
*STKP* SK1 .......... 13 K3
*STKP* SK1 .......... 13 M2
The Vernon Infant School
*POY/DIS* SK12 .......... 129 J1
The Vernon Junior School
*POY/DIS* SK12 .......... 129 J1
Vernon Park Museum
*STKP* SK1 .......... 112 E2
Vernon Park Primary School
*STKP* SK1 .......... 13 L4
Vernon Road Medical Centre
*TOT/BURYW* BL8 .......... 24 D3
Victoria Avenue Primary School
*BKLY* M9 .......... 57 G7
Victoria Industrial Estate
*ANC* M4 .......... 88 A3
*LEIGH* WN7 .......... 66 B6
Victoria Medical Centre
*URM* M41 .......... 96 A2
Victoria Park Infant School
*STRET* M32 .......... 97 G2
Victoria Park Junior School
*STRET* M32 .......... 97 G2
Victoria Trading Estate
*CHAD* OL9 .......... 74 E1
*WCNS/IIMK* WN3 .......... 14 D5
Victory Trading Estate
*BOLS/LL* BL3 .......... 3 G9
The Village Hotel & Leisure Club
*HYDE* SK14 .......... 90 F6
Village Medical Centre
*LIT* OL15 .......... 21 M7

VIP Centre Industrial Estate
*OLD* OL1 .................... 59  M3
Vue Cinema
*BURY* BL9 .................... 39  L6
*HOR/BR* BL6 .................... 34  A4
*SALQ* M50 .................... 86  C5
Wadsworth Industrial Park
*BOLS/LL* BL3 .................... 36  B8
Walkden High School
*WALK* M28 .................... 69  H2
Walmersley Golf Club
*BURY* BL9 .................... 25  L4
Walmsley CE Primary School
*EDGW/EG* BL7 .................... 22  B3
Walshaw Sports Club
*TOT/BURYW* BL8 .................... 24  C7
Walton Park Leisure Centre
*SALE* M33 .................... 108  D2
Wardle High School
*WHIT* OL12 .................... 21  H7
Wardley CE Primary School
*SWIN* M27 .................... 70  B2
Wardley Industrial Estate
*WALK* M28 .................... 69  M3
Warren Wood Primary School
*OFTN* SK2 .................... 113  K7
Warrington Road Industrial
Estate
*WGNS/IIMK* WN3 .................... 47  H7
Warth Park Industrial Estate
*BURY* BL9 .................... 38  F5
Washacre Primary School
*WHTN* BL5 .................... 50  C5
Washway Road Medical Centre
*SALE* M33 .................... 96  D8
Waterfold Business Park
*BURY* BL9 .................... 5  L6
The Watergate Clinic
*MILN* OL16 .................... 10  F4
Waterloo Industrial Park
*BOL* BL1 .................... 3  G2
*STKP* SK1 .................... 13  K5
Waterloo Primary School
*AULW* OL7 .................... 75  J7
The Water Place
*BOL* BL1 .................... 2  E6
Waters Edge Business Park
*ORD* M5 .................... 86  E6
Watersheddings Primary School
*OLD* OL1 .................... 59  M3
Waterside Business Park
*GLSP* SK13 .................... 93  J6
The Waterside Hotel
*CHD/CHDH* SK8 .................... 111  G8
Waterside Industrial Park
*BOLS/LL* BL3 .................... 52  F1
Waterside Trading Estate
*LEIGH* WN7 .................... 66  E8
Watersports Centre
*SALQ* M50 .................... 86  C5
Watford Bridge Industrial
Estate *NM/HAY* SK22 .................... 124  E3
Waybridge Industrial Estate
*SALQ* M50 .................... 86  A4
Weaste Trading Estate
*ORD* M5 .................... 86  A2
Welfare Clinic
*MDTN* M24 .................... 57  G2
Welkin Road Industrial Estate
*STKP* SK1 .................... 112  E1
Wellacre Technology College
*URM* M41 .................... 95  G2
Wellfield Infant School
*SALE* M33 .................... 96  C6
Wellfield Junior School
*SALE* M33 .................... 96  C6
Wellfield Medical Centre
*CHH* M8 .................... 72  C4
Well Green Primary School
*HALE/TIMP* WA15 .................... 117  K2
Wellington Road Industrial
Estate *AUL* OL6 .................... 90  D1

Wellington School
*HALE/TIMP* WA15 .................... 108  C6
Wentworth High School
*ECC* M30 .................... 70  C8
Werneth Cricket Bowling &
Tennis Club
*OLDS* OL8 .................... 9  G9
Werneth Golf Club
*OLDS* OL8 .................... 75  H3
Werneth J & I School
*OLDS* OL8 .................... 59  G8
Werneth Low Country Park
*HYDE* SK14 .................... 102  E5
Werneth Low Golf Club
*HYDE* SK14 .................... 102  E6
Werneth School
*MPL/ROM* SK6 .................... 113  J2
Wesley Methodist Primary
School
*RAD* M26 .................... 38  B7
Westbrook Trading Estate
*TRPK* M17 .................... 86  A5
Westbury Street Industrial
Estate *HYDE* SK14 .................... 90  F7
West Croft Industrial Estate
*MDTN* M24 .................... 56  F5
West End Medical Centre
*AULW* OL7 .................... 90  C3
West End Primary School
*AULW* OL7 .................... 90  C2
West End Trading Estate
*SWIN* M27 .................... 70  C3
Westernlea Clinic
*DTN/ASHW* M34 .................... 90  B7
Westfield Community School
*WGNW/BIL/OR* WN5 .................... 46  F6
*WGNW/BIL/OR* WN5 .................... 47  H5
West Gorton Medical Centre
*WGTN/LGST* M12 .................... 88  C6
West Hill School
*STLY* SK15 .................... 91  J2
Westhoughton CC
*WHTN* BL5 .................... 50  B4
Westhoughton Clinic
*WHTN* BL5 .................... 50  B4
Westhoughton Golf Club
*WHTN* BL5 .................... 50  A3
Westhoughton High School &
Specialist Technology College
*WHTN* BL5 .................... 50  C3
Westhoughton Industrial Estate
*WHTN* BL5 .................... 50  B2
Westhoughton Primary School
*WHTN* BL5 .................... 50  C3
Westinghouse Industrial Estate
*TRPK* M17 .................... 86  A7
Westleigh CC
*LEIGH* WN7 .................... 66  A7
West Leigh House School
*LEIGH* WN7 .................... 65  M7
Westleigh Methodist Primary
School
*LEIGH* WN7 .................... 66  A3
Westleigh St Pauls CE Primary
School
*LEIGH* WN7 .................... 66  B4
Westmorland Primary School
*RDSH* SK5 .................... 100  F6
West One Retail Park
*SALQ* M50 .................... 85  K3
Westpoint Medical Centre
*BNG/LEV* M19 .................... 99  J3
Westwood Business Centre
*CHAD* OL9 .................... 8  E6
Westwood Cemetery
*WGNS/IIMK* WN3 .................... 15  H9
Westwood Industrial Estate
*CHAD* OL9 .................... 8  D5
Westwood Park Primary School
*ECC* M30 .................... 84  E1
Westwood Primary School
*CHAD* OL9 .................... 8  E5

Westwood Trading Estate
*MPL/ROM* SK6 .................... 114  A7
Whalley Range FC
*CCHDY* M21 .................... 98  A3
Whalley Range High School
*OLDTF/WHR* M16 .................... 98  C4
Wharfside Business Centre
*TRPK* M17 .................... 86  C6
Wharton Primary School
*LHULT* M38 .................... 52  B6
Wheatfield Industrial Estate
*ROY/SHW* OL2 .................... 59  G1
Wheatlea Industrial Estate
*WGNS/IIMK* WN3 .................... 63  J2
Wheatsheaf Industrial Estate
*SWIN* M27 .................... 70  E3
Wheatsheaf Shopping Centre
*MILN* OL16 .................... 10  F3
Whelley Hospital
*WGN* WN1 .................... 48  B2
White City Retail Park
*OLDTF/WHR* M16 .................... 86  D7
Whitefield Community
Primary School
*WHTF* M45 .................... 55  K4
Whitefield Golf Club
*WHTF* M45 .................... 55  H5
Whitefield Medical Centre
*WHTF* M45 .................... 55  H4
Whitegate End Primary School
*CHAD* OL9 .................... 74  B1
Whitehill Industrial Estate
*HTNM* SK4 .................... 100  B7
Whitehill Primary School
*HTNM* SK4 .................... 100  B8
White Swan Industrial Estate
*OLD* OL1 .................... 59  M4
Whitley Road Medical Centre
*NEWH/MOS* M40 .................... 72  F8
Whittaker Moss Primary School
*ROCH* OL11 .................... 27  G3
The Whitworth Art Gallery
*HULME* M15 .................... 87  L8
Whitworth Community High
School *WHIT* OL12 .................... 20  A4
Whitworth Football & CC
*WHIT* OL12 .................... 20  A3
Whitworth Park School
*RUSH/FAL* M14 .................... 87  K8
Whitworth Swimming Pool
*WHIT* OL12 .................... 20  B2
The Wiend Centre
*WGN* WN1 .................... 15  G4
Wigan Athletic FC
& Wigan Warriors RLFC
(The JJB Stadium)
*WGNW/BIL/OR* WN5 .................... 14  A3
Wigan Borough Cemetery
*WGNS/IIMK* WN3 .................... 48  A7
Wigan Crematorium
*WGNS/IIMK* WN3 .................... 48  A8
Wigan Golf Club
*WGN* WN1 .................... 32  A2
Wigan & Leigh College
*LEIGH* WN7 .................... 66  B7
*WGN* WN1 .................... 14  E2
*WGNNW/ST* WN6 .................... 47  L2
Wigan & Leigh College &
Community Sixth Form
College *LEIGH* WN7 .................... 81  H1
Wigan Little Theatre
*WGN* WN1 .................... 15  H3
Wigan Magistrates Court
*WGN* WN1 .................... 15  H5
Wigan Pier
*WGNS/IIMK* WN3 .................... 14  D6
Wigan RUFC
*WGN* WN1 .................... 32  A7
Wilbraham Primary School
*RUSH/FAL* M14 .................... 98  D3
Wild Bank Community School
*STLY* SK15 .................... 92  A2

Willan Industrial Estate
*ORD* M5 .................... 86  C3
William Andrews Swimming
Baths *DUK* SK16 .................... 91  G5
William Hulmes Preparatory
School *OLDTF/WHR* M16 .................... 98  C3
William Wroe Municipal Golf
Course *URM* M41 .................... 95  K2
Willow Bank Hotel
*RUSH/FAL* M14 .................... 98  F4
Willow Grove Cemetery
*RDSH* SK5 .................... 100  D7
Willow Grove School
*AIMK* WN4 .................... 64  B7
The Willows Primary School
*HALE/TIMP* WA15 .................... 108  C6
*WYTH/NTH* M22 .................... 118  E2
Wilmslow Albion FC
*WILM/AE* SK9 .................... 126  E1
Wilmslow Grange Community
Primary School
*WILM/AE* SK9 .................... 119  M7
Wilmslow Health Centre
*WILM/AE* SK9 .................... 126  E6
Wilmslow High School
*WILM/AE* SK9 .................... 126  F6
Wilmslow Leisure Centre
*WILM/AE* SK9 .................... 126  F6
Wilmslow Preparatory School
*WILM/AE* SK9 .................... 126  F5
Wilmslow RFC
*WILM/AE* SK9 .................... 126  D3
Wilmslow Road Medical Centre
*RUSH/FAL* M14 .................... 98  F1
*WILM/AE* SK9 .................... 119  M8
Wind in the Willows Hotel
*GLSP* SK13 .................... 105  J4
Windlehurst School
*MPL/ROM* SK6 .................... 123  H2
Windmill Lane
Industrial Estate
*DTN/ASHW* M34 .................... 100  F2
Wingates Industrial Estate
*WHTN* BL5 .................... 50  A1
Winstanley College
*WGNW/BIL/OR* WN5 .................... 62  B1
Winstanley Medical Centre
*WGNS/IIMK* WN3 .................... 63  G1
Winstanley Primary School
*WGNS/IIMK* WN3 .................... 62  F2
Withington Bowling Club
*RUSH/FAL* M14 .................... 98  F5
Withington Girls School
*RUSH/FAL* M14 .................... 98  E4
Withington Golf Club
*DID/WITH* M20 .................... 110  C2
Withington Hospital
*DID/WITH* M20 .................... 98  F5
Withington Swimming Baths
*DID/WITH* M20 .................... 98  E6
Withins High School
*BOLE* BL2 .................... 37  H2
Wolfenden Primary School
*BOL* BL1 .................... 36  B2
Woodbank CC
*TOT/BURYW* BL8 .................... 25  G8
Woodbank Park Athletics Track
*OFTN* SK2 .................... 112  F3
Woodbank Primary School
*TOT/BURYW* BL8 .................... 25  G8
Woodend Mills Industrial Estate
*OLDE* OL4 .................... 60  C7
Woodfield Primary School
*WGN* WN1 .................... 31  M8
Woodfields Retail Park
*BURY* BL9 .................... 4  E3
Wood Fold Primary School
*WGNNW/ST* WN6 .................... 31  G4
Woodford Aerodrome
*BRAM/HZG* SK7 .................... 128  D3
Woodford CC
*BRAM/HZG* SK7 .................... 128  C2

Woodhey High School
*RAMS* BL0 .................... 24  D1
Woodheys Primary School
*SALE* M33 .................... 108  B2
Woodhouse Primary School
*URM* M41 .................... 84  D8
Woodhouses Voluntary
Controlled Primary School
*FAIL* M35 .................... 74  F6
Woodlands Hospital
*WALK* M28 .................... 52  C8
Woodlands Industrial Estate
*NEWLW* WA12 .................... 78  F6
Woodley Health Centre
*MPL/ROM* SK6 .................... 101  K7
Woodley Primary School
*MPL/ROM* SK6 .................... 101  L7
Woodley Sports Centre
*MPL/ROM* SK6 .................... 101  K6
Woodsend Primary School
*URM* M41 .................... 94  F1
Woods Hospital
*TYLD* M29 .................... 52  C8
Woolfold Industrial Estate
*TOT/BURYW* BL8 .................... 24  E8
Woolworths Sports Club
*ECC* M30 .................... 41  M1
Worsley Business Park
*WGN* WN1 .................... 68  C4
Worsley Golf Club
*WALK* M28 .................... 69  M8
Worsley Mesnes Primary School
*WGNS/IIMK* WN3 .................... 47  K8
Worsley Road Industrial Estate
*FWTH* BL4 .................... 52  F6
Worsley Trading Estate
*LHULT* M38 .................... 52  B7
Worthington Lakes Business
Park *WGN* WN1 .................... 31  M4
Worthington Primary School
*SALE* M33 .................... 97  J8
Worth Primary School
*POY/DIS* SK12 .................... 129  K1
Wrightington School
*WGNNW/ST* WN6 .................... 30  B3
Wrightington Hotel & Country
Club *WGNNW/ST* WN6 .................... 30  C1
Wright Robinson Sports College
*GTN* M18 .................... 89  J6
The Wycliffe Hotel
*EDGY/DAV* SK3 .................... 12  C8
Wythenshawe Hall Country Park
*NTHM/RTH* M23 .................... 109  L4
Wythenshawe Hospital
*NTHM/RTH* M23 .................... 109  J8
Wythenshawe Park Track
*NTHM/RTH* M23 .................... 109  K4
Xaverian Sixth Form College
*RUSH/FAL* M14 .................... 98  F1
Yeargate Industrial Estate
*BURY* BL9 .................... 40  A2
Yeshivah Ohr Torah School
*BRO* M7 .................... 72  A4
Yesoiday Hatorah School
*PWCH* M25 .................... 71  L2
Yew Tree Community School
*CHAD* OL9 .................... 58  C8
Yew Tree Primary Community
School *DUK* SK16 .................... 91  G5
Yew Tree Trading Estate
*RNFD/HAY* WA11 .................... 78  A4
YMCA Leisure Centre
*CSLFD* M3 .................... 6  C6

## Acknowledgements

Schools address data provided by Education Direct

Petrol station information supplied by Johnsons

Manchester transport information provided by GMPTE © 2007

Garden centre information provided by:

Garden Centre Association   Britains best garden centres

Wyevale Garden Centres

The statement on the front cover of this atlas is sourced, selected and quoted
from a reader comment and feedback form received in 2004